KEY TO MAP PAGES

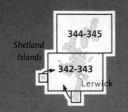

Key to Regions

South West England
South East England
London
Wales
West Midlands
East Midlands
East of England
North West England
Yorkshire
North East England
Scotland

Key to this map

236-237 — Road maps

Birmingham — Urban area maps

• Oxford — City / Town centre plans

Seasonal symbols

Spring
Summer
Autumn
Winter
Rainy day

For a full list of tourist symbols please refer to page 142

City & town centre plans

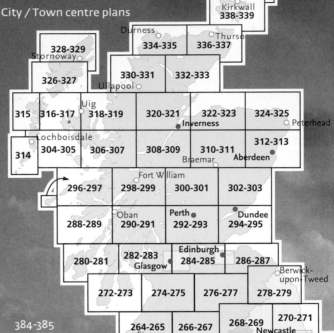

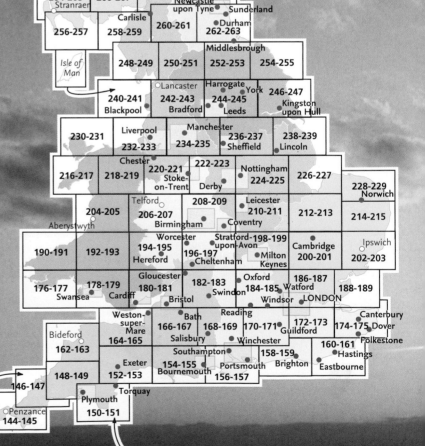

Urban area maps

DISCOVER BRITAIN

Britain is a beguiling group of islands, packed with mountains, moors, rivers, lakes and forests, brimming over with plants and wildlife, and enclosed by miles and miles of beautiful coastline.

This Touring Atlas and Guide identifies, locates and describes many of the best places to visit within Britain and gently reminds us that getting out and about is not exclusively a summer activity.

Britain is open 24 hours a day and 365 days a year and this book can be the inspiration for travel, entertainment and adventures whatever the season.

Gairloch sunset

CONTENTS

Sarsen Stones
In the dry valleys these boulders litter the landscape; they are the famous 'Sarsen' stones, used by stone age man to build Avebury stone circle and other prehistoric monuments.

Avebury stone

Discover Britain by region   23-131

The country is split into the following regions within which you will find information for over 1300 places to visit. If you know the name of the attraction you are looking for, use the index to find its details. Each description has a map reference for you to locate it and wherever applicable a phone number and website. Where appropriate there are also symbols to advise if an attraction is suited to a rainy day and if it is especially appealing during a particular season.

Symbols

❀ Spring
❅ Summer
❀ Autumn
❄ Winter
✿ Rainy day

For a full list of tourist symbols please refer to page 142.

★ **Portmeirion Village**   `217 E4`

This unique, if eccentric 'village' was created during the mid 20th century by the architect Clough Williams-Ellis in a flamboyant, Mediterranean style on his privately-owned peninsula on the beautiful Tremadoc Bay.

☎ 01766 770000   www.portmeirion-village.com

All attractions are referenced to the largest scale mapping.

Within the attraction descriptions there are 200 'Outstanding' features which are highlighted yellow.

Any description with an empty symbol ☐ can be found as a place or area name on the map.

Portmeirion Village

Route planning mapping   132-141

As well as helping you plan your journey, this mapping also shows the location of 200 'Outstanding' tourist features.

Route planning map

Key to map symbols   142-143

Road mapping   144-345

Over 1300 tourist features are highlighted on detailed road mapping.

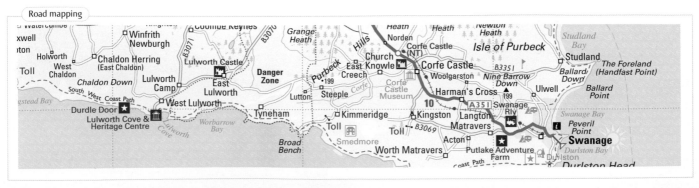

Road mapping

Urban area maps

These maps help you navigate through the suburbs of Britain's major cities.

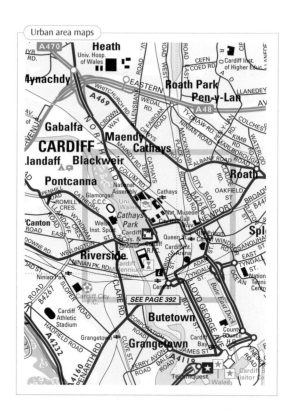

Central city maps

Six of Britain's busiest city centres are mapped in great detail to enable you to find your destination with ease.

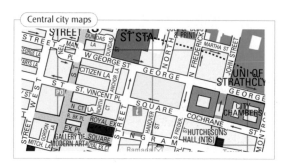

Town and city plans

Layouts of Britain's diverse towns and cities provide an overview of each location and a brief guide aids exploration.

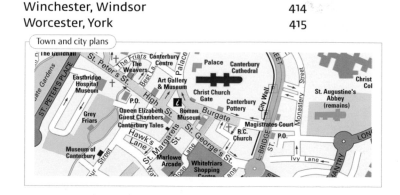

Credits

Wast Water

The rich tapestry of Britain's landscape looks permanent and immovable; in fact it is constantly changing and what we see today is just a tiny moment in time. Mountains the size of the Himalayas, vast lava flows, tropical seas, huge ice sheets and animals the size of several London buses have come and gone over the millennia and the legacy of these can be seen in the current landscape. Here in Britain, the earth is quieter now, the changes less dramatic than at times in the past, but they are still going on in the form of weathering and gradual changes in sea level, and every now and again a small tremor is a reminder of the stresses at work beneath the surface.

Since the very end of the last Ice Age, a mere 10,000 years ago, the flora and fauna we know today managed to gain a foothold and have developed over the years. Britain's landscape diversity has led to a wide variety of habitats, from the rocky and sometimes barren Scottish Highlands to the lush wooded valleys of southern England. Man, naturally adaptable, has left many marks on the face of the land, some ephemeral, but some extend back into the mists of time.

The next few pages give a brief insight into the 'hows' and 'whys' of Britain's landscape; its formation, natural history and the changes wrought by the hand of man. Look differently at the view. Take time to appreciate the beauty.

UNDERSTANDING THE LANDSCAPE

GUIDE TO GEOLOGY

SEDIMENTARY ROCKS (S)

Formed from sediments, of various sizes, deposited and slowly compacted into solid rock.

There are two types:

Transported sediments are bits of existing rocks which fall down hillsides, eventually being washed into streams. They are worn down further by rolling along the stream bed, eventually being carried into lakes or the sea, where the largest and heaviest are dropped first (they can also be blown there or deposited by ice). As further debris accumulates on top of them, they are compacted into solid rock, the size of the original particles defining the type of eventual 'sedimentary rock'. Conglomerates form from pebbles, and mudstones from the tiniest particles.

Non-transported sediments in Britain, are limestone and chalk. These are formed from the shells and skeletons of sea creatures and corals. As the creatures die, they sink to the floor, eventually being compressed into rock.

Welsh Gold (3)

Very basically, volcanic activity in Wales caused gold in solution to be forced into fissures created in earlier, solidified magma (called Greenstone). Gold was deposited along with quartz in veins.

Welsh Gold

IGNEOUS ROCKS (I)

Igneous means 'fire-formed'. These rocks were made from molten material forcing its way up into the Earth's crust.
Intrusive: The molten rock that didn't quite break through to the surface but cooled in a mass below it, formed the 'intrusive' igneous rocks such as granite and gabbro, often later exposed by erosion at the surface. **Extrusive:** Molten rock that poured out onto the land formed the 'extrusive' volcanic rocks such as basalt.

60 million years ago the Atlantic Ocean was born, caused by sea floor spreading when Greenland moved away from Scotland. This resulted in igneous activity all along the west coast of Scotland.

● Volcanic   ✕ Intrusive

ROCK AGES

The time period during which a rock was formed is given a name in geology. These names have not been used in the text for the sake of simplicity but as an example, a sedimentary rock formed 300 million years ago would be called a 'Carboniferous sedimentary rock', however, if it had been formed 100 million years ago, it would be a 'Cretaceous sedimentary rock' and so on. Refer to any geology book for the full table.

SEDIMENTARY ROCKS	
⬜ Unconsolidated Sands & Shell Banks	⬛ Sandstone
⬜ Clay	⬛ Greywacke and Slate (metamorphic)
⬜ Chalk	⬜ Mixed Hard Sediments including sandstone, shale, mudstone, greywacke, slate and limestone
⬜ Limestone	
IGNEOUS ROCKS	METAMORPHIC ROCKS
⬛ Igneous (Extrusive/intrusive)	⬜ Gneiss, Schist, Quartzite etc

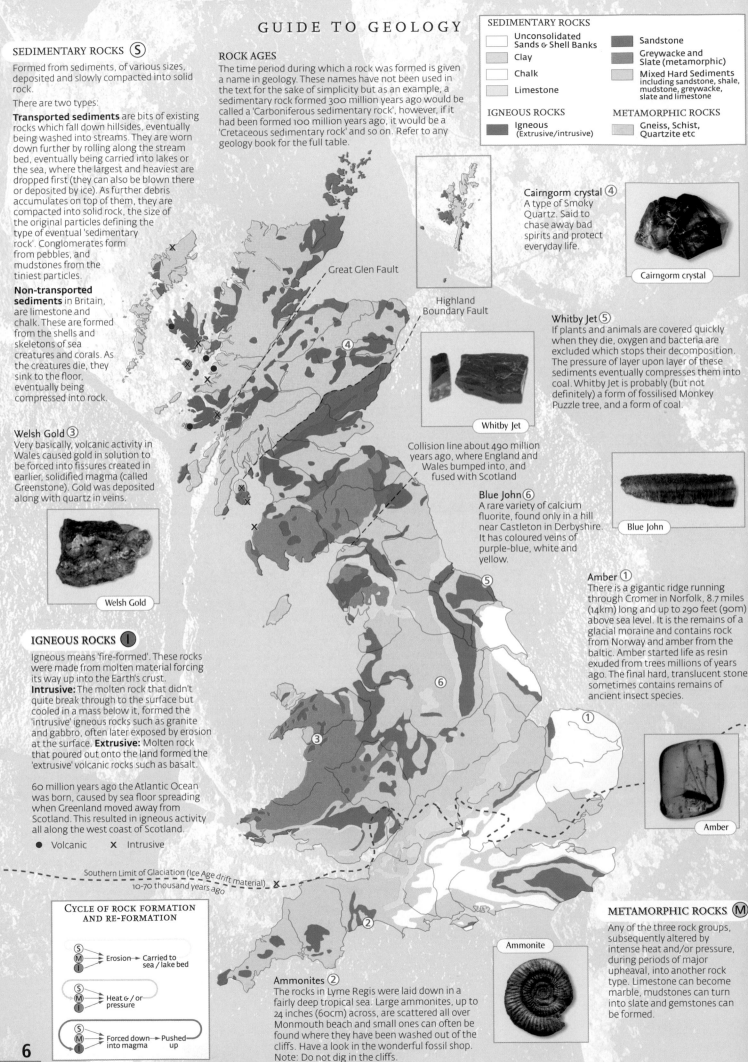

Great Glen Fault

Highland Boundary Fault

Collision line about 490 million years ago, where England and Wales bumped into, and fused with Scotland

Cairngorm crystal (4)
A type of Smoky Quartz. Said to chase away bad spirits and protect everyday life.

Cairngorm crystal

Whitby Jet (5)
If plants and animals are covered quickly when they die, oxygen and bacteria are excluded which stops their decomposition. The pressure of layer upon layer of these sediments eventually compresses them into coal. Whitby Jet is probably (but not definitely) a form of fossilised Monkey Puzzle tree, and a form of coal.

Whitby Jet

Blue John (6)
A rare variety of calcium fluorite, found only in a hill near Castleton in Derbyshire. It has coloured veins of purple-blue, white and yellow.

Blue John

Amber (1)
There is a gigantic ridge running through Cromer in Norfolk, 8.7 miles (14km) long and up to 290 feet (90m) above sea level. It is the remains of a glacial moraine and contains rock from Norway and amber from the baltic. Amber started life as resin exuded from trees millions of years ago. The final hard, translucent stone sometimes contains remains of ancient insect species.

Amber

CYCLE OF ROCK FORMATION AND RE-FORMATION

S / M / I → Erosion → Carried to sea / lake bed

S / M / I → Heat & / or pressure

S / M / I → Forced down into magma → Pushed up

Southern Limit of Glaciation (Ice Age drift material) 10-70 thousand years ago ✕

Ammonites (2)
The rocks in Lyme Regis were laid down in a fairly deep tropical sea. Large ammonites, up to 24 inches (60cm) across, are scattered all over Monmouth beach and small ones can often be found where they have been washed out of the cliffs. Have a look in the wonderful fossil shop. Note: Do not dig in the cliffs.

Ammonite

METAMORPHIC ROCKS (M)
Any of the three rock groups, subsequently altered by intense heat and/or pressure, during periods of major upheaval, into another rock type. Limestone can become marble, mudstones can turn into slate and gemstones can be formed.

UNDERSTANDING THE LANDSCAPE

GUIDE TO THE PROTECTED AREAS OF BRITAIN

PROTECTED AREAS

Areas of England, Wales and Scotland are recognised as being Nationally or even Internationally important for the habitats and flora and fauna they support. Certain areas of the countryside have therefore been given designations affording them some protection against inappropriate development and destruction.

NATIONAL PARKS

Landscapes managed to conserve and enhance the wildlife, natural beauty and cultural heritage of an area, and to inform and involve the public in this process. Most of the land is privately owned, with the various National Park Authorities working with the owners to conserve these special areas.
For more information see: www.anpa.gov.uk

GEOLOGICAL SITES

In England, there are 1200 'Geological Sites'. These have been chosen by English Nature to represent key places to understand the geology of England.
For more information see:
www.english-nature.org.uk

AREAS OF OUTSTANDING NATURAL BEAUTY (AONB)

There are over 40 'Areas of Outstanding Natural Beauty' in England and Wales. In Scotland there are around 40 'National Scenic Areas' (NSA). The principle is to conserve the natural beauty of these areas.
For more information see:
www.aonb.org.uk and www.snh.org.uk

NATIONAL NATURE RESERVES (NNR)

There are well over 200 National Nature Reserves in England, and around 73 in Scotland. Many are designated as 'Spotlight' reserves and are the best places to appreciate some of the most important examples of habitats and wildlife in the country. Although these areas have been set up primarily to protect the flora and fauna, the public are encouraged to visit them and observe wildlife, taking care not to disturb their environment. There are also Local Nature Reserves, and Marine Nature Reserves.
For further information see:
www.english-nature.org.uk and
www.snh.org.uk

Key to symbols

- National Parks
- Areas of Outstanding Natural Beauty (AONB) and National Scenic Areas (NSA)
- Heritage coast
- ② Places mentioned in pages 8 - 14

The New Forest and South Downs are currently being considered for designation as National Parks.

RAMSAR SITES

Wetlands of International Importance (particularly waterfowl habitat).

OTHER PROTECTED SITES

There are also: RSPB Nature Reserves, Special Areas of Conservation (SAC) (non-bird), Special Protection Areas (SPA) (wild birds), Wildlife Trust reserves, Wildfowl and Wetland centres, World Heritage sites and Biosphere reserves.

ENVIRONMENTALLY SENSITIVE AREAS (ESA)

In England and Wales, over 25 areas have been chosen where farmers are offered incentives to farm in a sustainable and environmentally friendly way.

For more information see:
www.defra.gov.uk

SITES OF SPECIAL SCIENTIFIC INTEREST (SSSI)

Often sites of rare habitat (such as lowland heath or raised bogs), or endangered and fragile flora, fauna or geology. There are over 5,000 sites in England and Wales and around 1,450 in Scotland. For further information see:
www.english-nature.org.uk and
www.snh.org.uk

HERITAGE COAST

Around the coast of Britain, there are informally designated stretches of coastline, managed to control inappropriate development that would detract from their natural beauty. So far, there are in the region of 46 along the coasts of England and Wales and many under consideration in Scotland. Here they are called 'Preferred Conservation Zones' - (PCZ) For further information see:
www.countryside.gov.uk and www.ccw.gov.uk and www.snh.org.uk

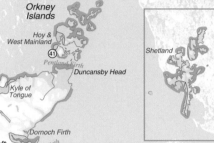

Map labels:

Orkney Islands, Hoy & West Mainland, Shetland, Cape Wrath, North-West Sutherland, Kyle of Tongue, Duncansby Head, Pentland Firth, Lewis, Assynt-Coigach, Dornoch Firth, St. Kilda, South Lewis, Harris & North Uist, 39, Harris, Trotternish, Wester Ross, North Uist, Skye, Glen Strathfarrar, Loch Ness, 34, Cairngorms, 36, Dee, Grampian Mts, 38, South Uist Machair, South Uist, Cuillin Hills, Kintail, Small Isles, Rum, Morar, Moidart & Ardnamurchan, Ben Nevis, 1344, Loch Rannoch & Glen Lyon, Loch Tummel, Deeside & Lochnagar, Barra, Coll, Loch na keal, Isle of Mull, Loch Shiel, 33, River Tay (Dunkeld), NORTH SEA, Tiree, Mull, 37, Lynn of Lorn, Loch Tay, Ochil Hills, Toy, Scarba, Lunga & the Garvellachs, Knapdale, Loch Lomond and the Trossachs, 35, Forth, Firth of Forth, ATLANTIC OCEAN, Jura, 40, Kyles of Bute, Glasgow, 32, Edinburgh, Holy Island (Lindisfarne), Islay, North Arran, Upper Tweedale, 23, Arran, Ayr, Southern Uplands, Eildon & Leaderfoot, Cheviot Hills, Northumberland Coast, Firth of Clyde, Nith Estuary, 21, Northumberland, Newcastle upon Tyne, East Stewartry Coast, Tyne, North Pennines, 19, Fleet Valley, Solway Coast, 22, Tees, North York Moors, Solway Firth, Lake District, 18, Scafell Pike, 977, 17, Nidderdale, Howardian Hills, Isle of Man, 9, Yorkshire Dales, 16, Arnside & Silverdale, Forest of Bowland, Leeds, Humber, Spurn Head, IRISH SEA, Morecambe Bay, Ribble, Lincolnshire Wolds, Anglesey, 31, Liverpool, Manchester, Mersey, Peak District, 10, Caernarfon Bay, Snowdon 1085, 26, Clwydian Range, Trent, The Wash, Norfolk Coast, Lleyn, 24, Snowdonia, Dee, Cambrian Mountains, Cannock Chase, Severn, 1, The Broads, Cardigan Bay, 25, Shropshire Hills, Birmingham, 2, The Fens, Suffolk Coast & Heaths, Malvern Hills, Avon, Wye Valley, Dedham Vale, 27, 14, Teifi, Brecon Beacons, 28, Wye, Cotswolds, 4, Chilterns, 11, Chelmer, St David's Head, Pembrokeshire Coast, 29, Cardiff, Bristol, 5, Salisbury Plain, North Wessex Downs, LONDON, Thames, Isle of Sheppey, Kent Downs, 30, Gower, 3, Mendip Hills, Surrey Hills, North Downs, Bristol Channel, Lundy, North Devon, Exmoor, Quantock Hills, 7, Cranbourne Chase & West Wiltshire Downs, East Hampshire, South Downs, High Weald, 13, Dungeness, New Forest, Southampton, Chichester Harbour, Sussex Downs, Beachy Head, Blackdown Hills, East Devon, Dorset, S. Hants Coast, 6, Isle of Wight, Tamar Valley, Dartmoor, 15, Lyme Bay, Bill of Portland, Bodmin Moor, 8, Plymouth, South Devon, Start Point, English Channel, Cornwall, Land's End, Isles of Scilly, Lizard Point, CELTIC SEA

UNDERSTANDING THE LANDSCAPE

EAST ANGLIA

Grimes Graves ②
Hundreds of saucer shaped hollows on the surface are evidence of Neolithic flint mining. Around 2300 BC, early man excavated flint and made axes with which to chop down trees and cultivate the land. The poor soils were soon spent, so the people moved on. An early example of 'slash and burn'.

Map ref. 213 G4

Grimes Graves

Norfolk Broads

Photo: Mike Page

① Norfolk Broads
This peaceful landscape of meandering waterways looks timeless. In fact, the retreating glaciers left a huge reed swamp over East Anglia, which gradually became woodland. By the early middle ages several inundations by the sea had left a patchwork of marsh, fen, woodland and swamp, the latter covering what is now the Broads. Centuries of vegetation had grown and died, creating thick layers of peat. After the Norman conquest, Norwich was developing quickly and needed fuel; peat was perfect and over the next 350 years this valuable resource was dug out by hand, until Mother Nature caused the sea level to rise once more, flooding the peat workings to create the tranquil waterways of the Broads.

Map ref. 229 E4

Flint is:
Liquid silica, fused with limestone or other sediments. This forms a hard, brittle, fine-grained rock and can be found as nodules within limestones and shales.

Flint building detail

Flint wall
Flint was used as a building material where little else was available.

CHALK DOWNS

Marlborough Downs
The smooth rounded Marlborough Hills are typical of a chalk landscape. They are divided by 'dry' valleys, probably formed when water in the chalk was frozen and glacial surface streams eroded the rock. Sometimes, steep scarps have formed, demonstrating the varying hardness of the chalk layers. Most of the downlands are waterless due to the very porous nature of chalk and spring lines are common where the water meets the impermeable clays beneath. Lower down the slopes the soil is richer, here you will find woodlands, meadows and orchards.

Marlborough Downs ③

Map ref. 182 D5

Chalk is:
The purest and whitest form of limestone. It contains a large proportion of tiny plates called Coccoliths. Chalk is very porous and relatively soft, forming rounded ridges. Water seeps down and accumulates as large underground reservoirs.

Avebury – standing stone

Map ref. 168 C1

③ Sarsen Stones
The chalk layers were overlaid with sandstone, most of which has weathered away. However, in places, the sandstone was cemented together with silica to form hard blocks. In the dry valleys these boulders litter the landscape; they are the famous 'Sarsen' stones, used by stone age man to build Avebury Ring and other prehistoric monuments.

COTSWOLDS

Cotswolds
The rolling Cotswold Hills are the result of an event that took place 180 million years ago. A bulge formed under the North Sea and as a consequence, a shallow warm sea formed over an area from Somerset to The Midlands. In the Cotswolds, Oolites (see 'Limestone is:' below for description) settled on the bottom forming the characteristic limestone of the area. This sedimentary rock has been gently folded and eroded into the hills and valleys we see today. Sheep have always been the mainstay of this rural landscape; the Saxon meaning of 'Cotswolds' actually means 'Hills of the Sheepfolds'.

Lower Slaughter – Roof tiles

④ Roof tiles
Harder blocks of limestone were quarried underground, and then left on the surface. The action of frost shattered them into thin sheets, which were used for roof tiles.

Map ref. 197 D5

Limestone is:
Bits of shells and sea creatures, which fall to the bottom in areas of shallow warm water, eventually compressing into rock. 'Oolitic' Limestone is a special type and comprises tiny round pellets formed by the particles being rolled around on the watery bed first, building up layers of calcium, then being cemented together. Stand on the Cotswold Hills and you're on what was once the bed of a tropical sea or lake.

Cotswold Water Park

Map ref. 182 C3

⑤ Cotswold Water Park
A beautiful area of over 114 lakes and ponds form the water park, the result of gravel extraction dating from the 1920s. Cotswold Oolitic Limestone underlies the park, covered in a layer of clay. On top of this, repeated glaciations dumped up to eight metres of sand and gravel. The high water table soon causes the newly dug gravel pits to fill with water. As it filters up through the limestone it becomes crystal clear, pure and alkaline; ideal for wildlife and water sports. The Thames starts just to the west of the area, water flowing into it through the lakes.

FIELDS

Ancient Field Systems

Ever since man first picked up a seed and planted it in the earth, there have been fields of a sort. In the Bronze Age, low banks of stone in narrow parallel lines with short cross divisions ran for miles across Dartmoor; the Dartmoor 'reaves'. Fields of the Iron Age were nothing more than small pastures separated by large stony banks, clustered around a settlement. The Romans probably had fields in the Fens and the Anglo-Saxons invented large 'open' field systems. The commonest patterns we see in the fields today are post-Norman Conquest; rows of 'humped' strips, around 11 yards (10m) wide, formed by the method of ploughing used; this was the 'ridge and furrow' field system which reached its peak in the mid 1300s. It is most typically found in The Midlands, North-East England and Central Scotland, and is distinguished by having no formal divisions of hedges or walls. Hedges used to enclose fields are a relatively modern invention.

Fields - Ridge & Furrow

Hedges were gradually planted between the 13th and 17th centuries. Then between the early 1700s and mid 1800s, the infamous 'Enclosure Acts' replaced Medieval ridge and furrow fields with new areas bounded by hedges. Similar reorganisation produced straight stone walls in Scotland. With mechanisation and the internal combustion engine, came bigger agricultural machinery which resulted in the removal of many hedgerows from the mid 20th century.

Portable, woven wooden hurdles were used to enclose stock before permanent settlements came into being.

Between 1750 and 1850 Oliver Rackham estimated that over 200,000 miles (320,000km) of hedges were planted.

HEDGEROWS

Ancient Hedgerows

Medieval England was full of hedges but not often around 'fields'. There are hedges described in the Anglo-Saxon 'perambulations', as boundary markers. So how do you know if you are looking at an ancient hedge? Look for clues: if a hedgerow crosses rows of wide ridge and furrow it's probably post-1700; if it follows a parish boundary it could be Saxon. If it has woodland flora underneath, it was possibly part of a woodland edge, and if it is on top of an earth bank, again it could be ancient. There is no exact science to tell the age of a hedge, although some can be identified on old maps. A rough estimation can be made by counting the number of species of shrubs and trees in any 90 foot (27.5m) length and multiplying it by 100 to give the number of years. For example, if a 90 foot (27.5m) stretch contains several Dog Rose, some Hawthorn and Elder, then three multiplied by 100 will give an age of 300 years. This only works south of Derbyshire and has many other pitfalls but it is fun and might amuse the children for a while.

The New Agricultural Landscape

Farming is entering a new age. There have always been farmers helping wildlife but now they are being encouraged to do so as the emphasis is shifting from intensive production to environmentally friendly schemes. In arable areas you may well see a large, bushy hedgerow with a permanent 6½ foot (2m) wide strip of tussocky grass next to it. This is a 'Field Margin' left unploughed and unsprayed to provide habitat for over-wintering wildlife. Next to this there might well be a wide strip of temporarily uncropped ground, this is 'Set Aside' land, again good for wildlife. In some areas, the first few metres of the crop might look rather weedy, this area is a 'Conservation Headland' and has been left free from herbicides to encourage some of our rare arable flowers to flourish. Don't be surprised to see wooden boxes put up for owls, bats, birds and even dormice.

Field margin

PREHISTORY

Glastonbury Tor

Map ref. 166 C4

(7)

Glastonbury Tor

Hard sandstone caps the Tor, protecting the softer layers of limestones and clays underneath from erosion. However, the terracing on its slopes is still a cause for controversy. Are they the result of natural differential erosion of the rock layers, medieval strip farming for grain or vines, or a Neolithic maze pattern carved into the hill to form a ritual pathway to the top?

(6) **Maiden Castle**
This chalk hilltop was inhabited from the late Stone Age through to Roman times. The original village can no longer be seen on the surface.

Maiden Castle

Map ref. 154 C4

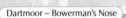
Dartmoor – Bowerman's Nose

(8)

Dartmoor

280 million years ago, a mass of molten rock was pushed up underneath the sedimentary rocks covering Dartmoor, during a period of intense folding. The magma cooled slowly deep within the Earth, forming granite, which was exposed by weathering millions of years later. Around the edges, the intense heat and pressure metamorphosed surrounding material into slate and produced deposits of tin and copper ores. The impermeable granite supports a large mire and bog; the source of many Devon rivers and local legends. Above this mire the bare rock has been shaped into dramatic tors by wind, water and ice. These rocky landmarks have names like 'Bowerman's Nose'.

Map ref. 152 A4

Grimspound

Beneath Hookney Tor you can make out a walled enclosure of about 4 acres (1.6 ha). It dates from the Bronze Age and contains circles of granite boulders or 'hut circles'. The wall was probably once topped with a wooden palisade.

WOODLAND

Ancient woodland

When the ice retreated and the climate started to get warmer, about 10,000 years ago, plants began to colonise the land. By the time the sea level rose to cut Britain off from mainland Europe, around 6,000 years ago, thirty or so types of trees and shrubs had established themselves here; these we call our 'native' species. Since that time, many other species have arrived, most deliberately introduced by man. Some of these reproduce quite happily and are called 'naturalised' species; others are still classed as 'exotic'. Of the original 'wildwood' nothing now remains, and most of our woodlands are a complex mix of old and new, natural and planted. There are pockets of 'Ancient Semi-Natural Woodland', the most precious of which are those descended from woodlands known to have been in existence from at least AD1600, having been managed in some way by man. It is difficult to date a woodland, but ancient woodland will probably have a large, wide ditch and bank or large stone wall exactly following a sinuous woodland edge. Other signs include 'indicator' species such as Herb Paris.

Management of deciduous woodland

In the past, a woodland 'stayed if it paid'; this is how many have survived. Where trees were **coppiced**, the stem was cut off at ground level to produce multiple stems for fencing and charcoal, some trees were left to develop into tall 'standards' between the coppice, and then felled for timber. This cycle allows light into the woodland, allowing flowers and shrubs to flourish, so that butterflies, dormice and birds are encouraged. Trees in some woods were **pollarded**; the same as coppicing but the stem is cut off above the browsing line so that animals could graze underneath but not eat the new wood shoots. Today, these methods are being reintroduced; new markets are opening up for woodland products with environmental schemes helping to fund them.

Coppiced Woodland

Pollarded tree

(9)

Veteran trees

Britain has many very old individual trees, unlike the rest of Europe. They are sometimes mentioned as boundary markers in the Anglo Saxon perambulations and support precious wildlife, such as the endangered Stag Beetle. In a veteran tree, the growth rate has slowed, but this does not mean it is dying. Some veterans are even hollow but still perfectly healthy. There is a register of over 126,000 ancient and rare trees growing in the British Isles today. Have a look at the Tortworth Chestnut in Gloucestershire, The Silver Fir at Strone, Argyll or the Holker Hall Great Lime, Cumbria.

Veteran tree

Stag Beetle

Holker Hall Great Lime

Map ref. 249 E5

(10) Sherwood Forest

Not an area of dense forest but open heathland with pockets of woodland. A 'forest' was simply an unfenced area where someone powerful could keep deer.

Map ref. 224 B1

Native pine woodland

Caledonian Pines are a subspecies unique to Scotland and form several ancient semi-natural woodlands there. Their management has to be entirely different to that for deciduous woodland, as they do not coppice. To allow natural regeneration, the main requirement is for deer, stock and rabbit proof fencing. Occasionally, it might be necessary to clear the ground in some way, as the trees are natural colonisers of disturbed ground. Otherwise, they can be left to themselves. These precious woods are a vital habitat for many of Scotland's endangered species.

Upper Loch Torridon – Caledonian Pines

Map ref. 319 E4

Hatfield Forest

(11) Hatfield Forest

A rare example of a Royal Forest as it was in Medieval England. It includes areas of coppice and old pollards.

Map ref. 187 E1

BRITAIN'S COASTLINE

Britain's coastline

Britain has approximately 12,100 miles (19,500km) of coastline, including all the islands, and one of the most extreme tidal ranges in the world. (In spring, the tidal range at Chepstow can be 40 feet (12.2m)). This, along with constant pounding from the Atlantic and North Sea and scouring by wind, rain and the ice age, has left a coastline of great diversity and character.

(12) Mortehoe coastline

Map ref. 163 E1

Winchelsea Beach

Map ref. 161 E2

(13)

Pembrokeshire Coastal Path

Pembrokeshire – Sand dunes

(14) *Map ref. 191 D4*

Charmouth

(15) *Map ref.153 G3*

YORKSHIRE DALES

Ingleborough

Yorkshire Dales & Hills
Sandwiches of shales, hard sandstones and limestones topped with Millstone Grit overlie almost horizontal layers of very old limestone. Differential erosion of these layers gives the characteristic 'stepped' appearance of the hills of Pen-y-Ghent and Ingleborough. Evidence of glaciation is everywhere, many valleys show the classic 'U' shape and around Ribblehead is an amazing landscape of rounded hummocks, 'drumlins'; material dumped and moulded by glaciers. Villages tend to be restricted to the valleys, with their rivers and walled fields. The slopes and moors are mostly grazed by sheep, arable farming never having been very successful here. The whole area has a feeling of timelessness and peace. Sit back and listen to the song of the skylark.

Limestone pavement
Rainwater seeps into the natural vertical cracks (joint planes) of this rock, gradually dissolving it and widening the joints (grykes) leaving large blocks (clints) between them; hence 'limestone pavements' are formed. Good examples can be seen around Ingleborough and Malham. The grykes can be several feet wide and deep and harbour some rare native alpine plants.

Limestone pavement

Malham Cove

Gaping Ghyll
(16)
Map ref. 243 E1

Water runs off the moors and tops, over the harder layers, then disappears underground through the porous limestone rock into 'swallow holes'. Gaping Ghyll is such a hole, 350 feet (91.5m) deep with the highest known waterfall in England.

Malham Cove
A river once cascaded into the valley from the top of the cliff, but it has long since found a way through the porous rock further upstream and now appears at the base.

(17)
Austwick – Norber Stones

Norber stones
Sandstone blocks were carried here by glaciers and abandoned on the limestone plateau when the ice melted. Limestone erodes more quickly than sandstone; the result is a bizarre landscape of dark, hard sandstone boulders perched precariously on small pedestals of white limestone.

LAKE DISTRICT

Lake District
A landscape full of variety, from precipitous, craggy fells to gently wooded valleys and lakes. The underlying geology is complex but basically volcanic, changed by heaving, folding, heat, pressure and glaciation. In places the mountains are the remains of lavas and ashes metamorphosed to varying degrees; the softer ones and overlying sedimentary rocks having been eroded away. The main volcanic area is in the centre, with the high craggy peaks of Sca Fell, Helvellyn and the Langdale Pikes. Underneath these volcanic rocks lies a large mass of granite, pushed up in the distant past, and exposed by erosion in areas such as Ennerdale and Shap. In the north, Skiddaw is made from the oldest rocks of the Lake District, originally fine sedimentary material, altered by heat and pressure into the 'Skiddaw Slates', then eroded into smooth but steep mountains. The lakes themselves owe their existence to the glaciers. The ice over-deepened the valleys, which slowly filled with water, giving the final touch to this beautiful landscape.

Lake District – Wast Water

NORTH PENNINES

(19) **Great Whin Sill, North Pennines**
Under the sedimentary rocks is an almost horizontal layer of dolerite, an igneous rock forced up and between the beds of sandstone. In places, millions of years of erosion by weather and ice have exposed it at the surface. This is the Great Whin Sill, which, on average, is 100 feet (30.5m) thick. It extends for 100 miles (160km) from Upper Teesdale to the Northumberland coast. On the Pennine escarpment and in Teesdale, the outcrops of dolerite appear as craggy, dark, vertical columns of rock; High Cup Nick and Cronkley Fell are good examples. Where the hot molten rock came into contact with surrounding limestone, the latter changed into a coarse grained marble called 'sugar limestone', which is home to many rare Teesdale plants.

North Pennines

Hadrian's Wall
(21)

Hadrian's Wall
The Romans took advantage of the northern escarpment of the hard Great Whin Sill, using it as a base on which to build Hadrian's Wall.

Hadrian's Wall

Teesdale – High Force

High Force waterfall
The River Tees tumbles over the exposed hard dolerite, gradually quarrying away the softer rock beneath. Eventually, the overhang becomes too heavy and crashes down. Over time therefore, the waterfall is slowly retreating upstream.

Map ref. 261 E5

(22)

Lindisfarne – Holy Island

(23)

Farne Islands
The pounding action of the North Sea waves wore away the sandstone protecting the dolerite here on the coast. The hard igneous rocks were left as isolated, craggy islands in the sea.

Map ref. 279 F2

Mardale – Blea Tarn

(18) **Map ref. 248 C2**

(20)

Blea Tarn
Blea Tarn was formed in the hollow left by a small glacier.

Map ref. 249 D2

11

Wales

A land of spectacular and varied scenery, resulting from a highly complex geological past and several inundations by the sea. The coastline has everything from wide sandy bays to spectacular cliffs. Inland, there are mountain peaks, rolling hills, valleys and lakes.

(31) Great Orme
Once an island of hard limestone; sand and alluvial deposits built up to join it to the mainland. Llandudno sits on these deposits.

Gwaun Valley
Formed by meltwater flowing beneath a glacier under extreme pressure, this beautiful sheltered wooded valley is a valuable habitat with SSSI (Site of Special Scientific Interest) status.

(29) Gwaun Valley

Map ref. 190 D4

Strumble Head
Another volcanic area but of a different sort. Here the lava erupted under the sea and cooled very quickly into typically rounded 'pillow' shapes. This happened several times before the sea level fell leaving these strange shapes exposed on the headland.

Cambrian Mountains (25)

(24) Sarn Badrig
A shallow subtidal reef, (one of several) which extends for about 15 miles (24km) from Mochras Island into Cardigan Bay. It was formed from the detritus of a glacial terminal moraine when sea levels were much lower and this was dry land; some of it can still be seen at a very low tide and you can walk out along it (check tide tables). Legends of a 'lost land' are associated with it.

(27) Pillow Lava

Snowdonia

(26) Snowdon
Snowdon is actually made up of volcanic material which erupted on the floor of an ancient sea. It was later uplifted to become dry land, and this is why you will find fossilised shells on the top.

Map ref. 217 F2

Central Wales

Smooth, flat-topped hills characterise this area, although the uniformity of the plateau is somewhat of a mystery. The rocks consist of much folded and faulted sandstones, mudstones and slates, so why are the tops flat? One theory suggests that having been inundated by the sea several times after the folding process, the peaks were eroded flat by strong currents carrying sand and stones.

Map ref. 217 F2 (26)

Llanberis Pass

Llanberis Pass
A classic glaciated valley, carved from volcanic rocks. Along it, older mudstones have been turned into high quality slate by heat and pressure. These are famous for their ability to cleave into thin, strong sheets, as a result, vast slate quarries scar the landscape.

Brecon Beacons

(28) Brecon Beacons
These mountains have been carved from a massive block of Old Red Sandstone, glaciers having scooped out the northern slopes.

Map ref. 193 G1

Teifi Valley
Today, the river Teifi between Llechryd and Cardigan has an uneven bed of slate debris. This is due to 19th century slate extraction in the gorge. Tons of slate waste was dumped in the river, almost choking it. Eventually, the waste had to be disposed of on Rosehill Marsh, as large boats could no longer travel upriver. This slate debris now forms one of the many habitats in the Welsh Wildlife Centre. It is thought that the original Teifi followed a more westerly course but during the last ice age, material dumped around the Welsh coast by the glacier that formed over Ireland, blocked it, forcing the river to carve a new, deeper gorge.

Cenarth – River Teifi

Gower
A quiet and lovely peninsula, the whole area has been designated as an 'Area of outstanding Natural Beauty' (AONB). The high ridge of Cefn Bryn, which runs across the middle of the plateau, is made of hard Old Red Sandstone, uplifted and folded. The Rhossili Downs are made from the same rock and give rise to the spectacular 200 foot (61m) high cliffs of Rhossili Bay. The southern part is tough limestone, forming cliffs with beautiful bays where the sea has exploited weaknesses in the rock.

Map ref. 178 A4

Gower – Rhossili Beach

Edinburgh Castle

Map ref. 397 E1

(32)

The Royal Mile

Map ref. 397 E2

(32)

Edinburgh Castle and the Royal Mile

Somewhere around 380 million years ago, the volcano underneath what is now Edinburgh Castle stopped pouring out lava. It cooled into a basalt 'plug'. Time passed, the surrounding sedimentary rocks were slowly worn away. Then less than two million years ago, ice sheets moved past the remains of the volcano, plucking off the rest of the softer rock and dumping it in a long tail to the east of the plug. On this ridge was built the 'Royal Mile'. To the north of the tail, the glacier carved out a gorge now occupied by Princess Street gardens and to the south, a similar hollow is the location for Grassmarket.

Rannoch Moor

Robert Louis Stevenson picked out this landscape for his novel 'Kidnapped'. Some call it desolate: blanket bog formed on impermeable rock, treacherous to cross on foot. The underlying rock is granite, usually associated with mountains, so why is the moor flat? It was once a granite mountain, but the rock is coarse and crumbles. Erosion plus several passes of ice have plucked and scraped the surface flat, leaving the surrounding mountains (which are made of even harder metamorphic rocks) resembling an amphitheatre. It is a true wilderness, one of the few left in Britain.

(33)

Rannoch Moor

Map ref. 299 F4

Loch Lomond

If you look at the pattern of Scottish Lochs to the north of Loch Lomond, you will see that they form a radial pattern. The loch was bulldozed out only ten and a half thousand years ago by a glacier, which was based somewhere in the centre of this pattern. The ice followed the line of a major crack in the land called the 'Highland Boundary Fault' plucking out the already loose rocks along the fault line and gouging out a trough with the rocks it carried. When the ice melted, the empty chasm filled with water. Today, the sea is kept at bay by debris dumped at the side of the ancient glacier. To the south of the Loch, the line of the fault can be seen clearly, running along the islands and Conic Hill.

Loch Ness

Loch Ness lies in the Great Glen Fault, the dividing line that runs from Fort William to Inverness. In the distant past, the land to the north of this fault moved south-west, then back again, the total displacement being around 80 miles (130km). Along this classic 'wrench' fault, travelled ice, plucking out the rock debris to such a depth that the Loch holds around three times the volume of water as Loch Lomond, although its surface area is much less. Significant earth tremors associated with continuing movement of the Great Glen Fault, normally occur three times a century; the last one was in 1901!

(36)

Loch Ness

Map ref. 309 E2

(35)

Loch Lomond

Map ref. 283 E1

Gneiss is:

When subjected to heat and pressure, sandy shales become gneiss. This type of rock has distinctive bands of light and dark minerals.

Suilven

Sutherland boasts some of the most spectacular and ancient, if not highest, mountain landscape in Scotland. Suilven is a monolith of almost horizontally banded hard Torridonian sandstone in a flat expanse of ancient Lewisian gneiss, itself around 2,900 million years old. Roughly 4.5 miles (7km) of sediments from the rivers of Greenland (to which Scotland was joined) were laid on top of the already eroded Lewisian gneiss about 900 million years ago, when the whole area was basking in the sun at around 15 degrees north. Earth movements and sea level changes eventually allowed the area to become dry land and millions of years of erosion have subsequently left the 'hard cores' of the sedimentary layers standing proud.

Suilven

Map ref. 331 D3

(34)

13

Staffa – Fingal's Cave

37

Staffa, Fingal's Cave

Off the west coast of Mull, the tiny island of Staffa exhibits some of the most amazing geological scenery in the world. For centuries man thought the regular basalt columns of 'Fingal's Cave' could not possibly be natural. Sixty million years ago, Greenland and North America were torn away from Scotland by the birth of the Atlantic Ocean, and lava poured out along this tear. The top slaggy crust on Staffa is the result of lots of bubbles, holes and minerals in the lava. The central part cooled to produce columns which have a polygonal structure. The base cooled more slowly, producing a denser texture and solid base.

Regular Basalt columns

Map ref. 288 C1

The Atlantic Ocean is named after the giant Atlas, who held up the sky on his shoulders. His father was the Titan Iapetus - after which the Iapetus Ocean was named.

When they were first uplifted, around 400 million years ago, the Caledonian Mountains were taller than the Himalayas are now.

Map ref. 326 C3

Isle of Jura – Raised Beach

40

Scotland has 790 islands but only about 1/6th are inhabited.

40

Taransay – Machair

Isle of Jura – Isolated sea eroded arch

Isle of Jura

Another phenomenon of the west coast can be seen on the western beaches of Jura. When the land was covered in ice, sea level fell (as it was locked in solid form). When it melted, not only did sea level rise once more, but so did the land, having been physically pushed down by the weight of ice. The land mass is still rising today; this is called 'isostatic uplift'. To further complicate matters, the whole of Britain is tilting down in the southeast and up in the northwest. As a consequence, the beaches formed at the end of the glaciation have been raised in stages, forming 'raised beaches'.

39 ## Taransay, Machair

The Outer Hebrides face the full force of the Atlantic. This position, combined with the geology, has produced a unique landscape called 'Machair'. The beach is mainly wave pounded shells and sand, blown inland onto the low-lying marshes to produce a rich, alkaline soil. Easily damaged, modern farming techniques would destroy it, so it is treated gently and as a consequence, the grassland contains many rare flowers.

Rackwick Bay

Once a continuous plateau of sandstone, the sea level rose after the last ice age and created this archipelago of over 70 individual islands, collectively known as the Orkney Islands. Around 500 million years ago, a huge igneous mass pushed up under the sea from the depths of the Earth. Over the years, this was covered by layers and layers of sediments, the youngest of which were eroded away during periods of uplift and glaciation. On Hoy, the banding in the cliffs shows strata of tough, pebbly sandstones, unique in the Orkneys. Rackwick Bay is an excellent example, with massive sea-smoothed boulders up to 10 feet (3m) across littering the beach.

The longest river in Scotland is the River Tay at 120 miles (193km).

Cairngorms & Loch Morlich

Orkney Islands – Rackwick Bay

38 ## Cairngorms

Until 420 million years ago, Scotland and England were on different continents, separated by the Iapetus Ocean. Both were in the southern hemisphere and moving north (Scotland much more slowly). At the Tropic of Capricorn, they collided, fusing into one landmass in a seamless join roughly along the line of Hadrian's Wall. Over millions of years, the force of the collision buckled the surface rocks, forming the Central Highlands. Deep below, granite was pushing its way up underneath the folding mountains, forming the infant Cairngorms. The rose-coloured granite, deeply buried for so long, is now exposed at the surface.

Map ref. 310 B4

Map ref. 338 B3

UNDERSTANDING NATURAL HISTORY

The following habitats are home to many species of the flora and fauna found in Britain today.

DECIDUOUS WOODLAND

Use Collins Gems, Wild Guides and Nature Guides for good general information. Field Guides for detail or Complete British Wildlife for everything you need in one book.

Common Dormouse

👁 Look for gnawed hazelnuts, smooth on the inside, teeth marks on surface. Has fluffy tail and ginger colour. Purrs and snores.

(Muscardinus avellanarius)

Royal Society for the Protection of Birds
www.rspb.org.uk

Ramsons
(Allium ursinum)
Smells of garlic.

Hazlenut

— Radial teeth marks
— Smooth inner surface

Tree creeper

👁 Climbs up tree trunks, often in a spiral pattern. Has a long, thin, downcurved bill.

(Certhia familiaris)

Great Spotted Woodpecker

👁 Drums on tree trunks in spring. Distinctive black and white markings. The male has a red nape. Likes large mature trees with holes for nesting.

(Dendrocopos major)

Badger

👁 Extensive system of large holes with freshly dug earth outside. Distinctive footprints (front and back different).

(Meles meles)

Tawny Owl

👁 Small owl the size of a pigeon. Likes large trees with nesting holes. Call is "Hoo hoo hoo hoooo". Pellets under trees will contain bones of small mammals.

(Strix aluco)

Blue tit

👁 Particularly likes oak trees which provide it with hundreds of caterpillars for babies in spring. Often hangs upside down on the ends of branches to reach food.

(Parus caeruleus)

Ragged robin
(Lychnis flos-cuculi)

Silver-washed fritillary

👁 Silver sheen on underside of hind wings. Likes Bramble flowers. Caterpillars feed exclusively on violets.

(Argynnis paphia)

Wood anemone
(Anemone nemorosa)
In the sun, will raise their heads and open petals.

Herb paris
(Paris quadrifolia)
Indicator of old woodland.

MOUNTAIN

Ptarmigan

👁 Turns white in winter. Summer colouring of grey brown and black makes it difficult to see. Call is a croaking noise.

(Lagopus mutus)

Don't be surprised to see wallabies hopping about in the Peak District, wild boar roaming Kent woodlands or even black panthers in the Forest of Dean.

Crowberry
(Empetrum nigrum)
Winter food for moorland and mountain birds.

Golden eagle

👁 Second largest bird in the UK. Tends not to like forests, preferring open areas.

(Aquila chrysaetos)

Mountain hare

👁 Black tipped ears. Often turns white in winter. Small tracks going directly up slopes, doesn't zig-zag.

(Lepus timidus)

Mountain avens
(Dryas octopetela)

HEDGEROWS

Natural History Museum
www.nhm.ac.uk

Wren

👁 Tiny bird with tail held almost vertically. Loud ringing song and loud, persistent 'tik tik tik' when alarmed.

(Troglodytes troglodytes)

Bird song varies according to geographical region.

Common shrew

👁 High pitched 'twitters' coming from the grass, especially in March/April.

(Sorex araneus)

Toothwort
(Lathraea squamaria)
Parasitic plant, especially on hazel.

The pygmy shrew is Britain's smallest mammal. It weighs less than a 10p coin and must eat this weight of food every day to survive.

Holly blue

👁 Flies higher than other blues. Found near Holly in spring and Ivy in late summer.

(Celastrina argiolus)

Lords-and-Ladies
(Arum maculatum)

Pignut
(Conopodium majus)
Pigs love the roots, hence the name.

Glow worm

👁 Green glow at night from the wingless female. Snails are a large part of the larvae's diet and the snails preferred are found in chalk and limestone areas.

(Lampyris noctiluca)

Song thrush

👁 Dark brown spots underneath. Repeats phrases when singing. Uses a stone to smash open snail shells.

(Turdus philomelos)

Symbols
Status (fauna) - This has been generalised to give an indication of sensitivity and rarity. Where this cannot be definitely established, no symbol is given.
For more information, see www.jncc.gov.uk

🔴 Not endangered   🟡 Of concern   🔴 Endangered   👁 Identification clues   🌙 Nocturnal z^z Hibernates

Soil (flora) - Symbols are only shown for plants that will only grow in specific conditions.

⚫ Acid (peaty) soil   ⚪ Alkaline (chalky) soil   💧 Damp soil   💧 Dry soil

GRASSLAND

Eyebright
(*Euphrasia officinalis*)
Pretty but parasitic plant.

Common blue

👁 Males are bright blue. Likes Fleabane. Usually seen in groups. Rests head down on stems.

(*Polyommatus icarus*)

The Mammal Society
www.abdn.ac.uk

Harebell
(*Campanula rotundifolia*)
Called Bluebells in Scotland.

Wild parsnip
(*Pastinaca sativa*)

Cowslip
(*Primula veris*)
Food plant of Duke of Burgundy Fritillary caterpillar.

Lapwing

👁 Black crest. Call 'kee-ee-wit'. Breeds on farmland, usually in short spring sown crops and pasture.

(*Vanellus vanellus*)

Orange tip

👁 Only males have orange tips. Prefers damp areas.

(*Anthocharis cardamines*)

Stoat

👁 Larger than a weasel with black tip on tail. In the north, some will turn white in winter. Tend to run along boundaries such as hedges, don't like to be in the open.

(*Mustela erminia*)

Quaking grass
(*Briza media*)
Makes a lovely rattling sound in the wind.

Common field grasshopper

👁 Listen for 6 to 10 half-second chirps, evenly spread over 12 seconds.

(*Chorthippus brunneus*)

The stoat has a black tip to its tail. The weasel, with no 't' in its name, doesn't.

Cuckoo flower
(Lady's smock)
(*Cardamine pratensis*)
Flowers when the cuckoo calls.

Cinnabar moth

👁 Caterpillars eat Ragwort, which makes them poisonous.

(*Tyria jacobaeae*)

LOWLAND HEATH

Adder

z^z

👁 Black or brown zig-zag marking down back – but colours and pattern can vary. Poisonous but not usually deadly. Basks in sun.

(*Vipera berus*)

Stonechat

👁 Male has black head, red chest, white on side of neck. Song sounds like pebbles being knocked together 'wee tak tak'.

(*Saxicola torquata*)

Common cudweed
(*Filago vulgaris*)
Once given to cows as medicine.

Hobby

👁 Under parts have dark streaks. Has a white neck. Wings are swept back in flight. Takes prey on the wing. Migrates in winter.

(*Falco subbuteo*)

MOORLAND & BOG

Bell heather
(*Erica cinerea*)

Gorse
(*Ulex europaeus*)

Heath spotted orchid
(*Dactylorhiza maculata*)

Clouded Buff Moth

👁 Day flying in June/July. Males have one reddish spot on each yellow forewing.

(*Diacrisia sannio*)

Exmoor pony

👁 Usually dark brown, with a broad face and back and short legs.

(*Equus caballus*)

Bog asphodel
(*Narthecium ossifragum*)

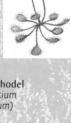

Merlin

👁 Smallest bird of prey. Long, square-ended tail.

(*Falco columbarius*)

Red deer

👁 Russet coloured coat with no white spots on adults. Largest of the British deer with branching antlers which are shed in late winter.

(*Cervus elaphus*)

Round leaved sundew
(*Drosera rotundifolia*)
Carnivorous plant. 'Dew' is really 'glue'.

Mountain ringlet

👁 Usually found above 1600 feet (500m). Likes to feed on Tormentil flowers.

(*Erebia epiphron*)

Cranberry
(*Vaccinium oxycoccus*)

Golden plover

👁 The male is gold and brown above, black underneath with a white dividing line in summer. Typically stands still, feeds, runs a bit, stops, feeds and so on.

(*Pluvialis apricaria*)

URBAN

Hedgehog

An adult hedgehog has around 5000 spines.

◉ The only spiny British mammal. Listen for noisy grunting sounds at dusk in spring. Often hibernates in piles of wood meant for bonfires, check before lighting.

(Erinaceus europaeus)

Habitat
The place where a species lives. The species shown here often move from one habitat to another for different parts of their life cycle. For example toads can breed in ponds, forage in long vegetation and hibernate in stone walls.

Mason bee

◉ Little piles of mortar at the base of walls are a clue to the nest of this solitary bee.

(Osmia rufa)

Butterfly Bush
(Buddleia davidii)
Garden escapee. Loved by butterflies and bees.

House cricket
◉ Native of warmer climes, found in warm buildings. Sometimes mistaken for a cockroach. It has a lovely song.

(Acheta domesticus)

House martin

◉ White rump and a forked tail. Mud nest below house eaves. Summer migrant. Attractive, twittering song.

(Delichon urbica)

The tiny pipistrelle bat can eat up to 3000 insects in one night.

Rosebay willowherb
(Epilobium angustifolium)
Also called 'fireweed' as it grows where fire has been.

Peacock butterfly

◉ The 'eyespots' on this butterfly supposedly confuse birds and deter other predators. Loves Buddleia.

(Inachis io)

Fox
◉ Reddish brown, tail bushier in winter. Footprints fall in one line. Mainly seen at dawn and dusk.

(Vulpes vulpes)

The Bat Conservation Trust
www.bats.org.uk

CONIFEROUS WOODLAND

Crested tit

◉ Distinctive black and white crest. Often hangs upside down on thin branches looking for seeds and insects.

(Parus cristatus)

A flock of goldfinches is called a 'charm'.

Yellow birds nest
(Monotropa hypopitys)
No green parts.

Wild cat
● ☾ (mainly) ◉ Looks like a large tabby with a thicker, blunt tail. Needs areas of varied habitat. Solitary and shy. Only found in Scotland.

(Felis sylvestris)

Injured creatures
If you find an injured creature, phone the RSPCA 0870 55 55 999 or SSPCA (Scotland) 0870 73 77 722

Pinewood mushroom
(Agaricus silvaticus)

Giant wood wasp

◉ HARMLESS! Flies May to August.

(Urocerus gigas)

Capercaillie
◉ Very large woodland bird. Males are black. Needs ground flora of short berrying shrubs. Confined to a few native Scottish pinewoods.

(Tetrao urogallus)

Ling
(Calluna vulgaris)

Pine marten
◉ Dark brown/reddish coat with orange/yellow throat/chest. Might be seen chasing red squirrels in trees.

☾ (mainly)

(Martes martes)

Biodiversity
The number of different species on Earth.

Red squirrel
◉ Thick bushy tail, large ear tufts in winter. Usually orange to red/chestnut fur. Nests high in trees using twigs and a lining of moss and grass.

(Sciurus vulgaris)

ARABLE FARMLAND

Yellowhammer
◉ Yellow with black streaks and red/orange rump. Song 'a little bit of bread and no cheese'. Likes open areas with bushy hedgerows.

(Emberiza citrinella)

Ivy-leaved speedwell
(Veronica hederifolia)

Common poppy
(Papaver rhoeas)
One plant can produce up to 500 flowers.

Harvest mouse

◉ Makes nest of woven shredded grass (still attached to the stalk) within the stalks of grasses and reeds.

(Micromys minutus)

Skylark
◉ Males ascend and sing a beautiful warbling song in spring and summer. Has a small crest. Prefers open areas with low hedges and no trees.

(Alauda arvensis)

Field forget-me-not
(Myosotis arvensis)

Brown hare

◉ Long black tipped ears. Rests in a scrape in the ground (doesn't burrow). Boxing hares are a male and a female.

(Lepus europaeus)

Grey Partridge

◉ Plump bird with orange face. Look particularly along hedgerows where there is a wide grassy margin.

(Perdix perdix)

Wild pansy
(Viola tricolor)

The common dormouse can spend up to 3/4 of its life asleep.

Barn owl
◉ White heart shaped face and pure white underneath. Completely silent in flight. Call is a loud shriek. Owl pellets on ground will contain bones of small mammals.

(Tyto alba)

Common fleabane
(Pulicaria dysenterica)
Once burnt to get rid of fleas.

FEN & MARSH

Swallowtail

👁 Likes thistles and ragged robin. Caterpillars only feed on milk parsley. Only in East Anglia.

(Papilio machaon)

Raft spider

👁 Britain's largest spider. Female's body can be almost an inch (22mm) long. Sits at boggy pool edges with legs on water.

(Dolomedes fimbriatus)

Yellow wagtail

👁 Tail has white edges which it wags up and down. Black legs. Runs a lot. Summer visitor.

(Motacilla flava)

Marsh Harrier

👁 Long tail. Wings held in a 'V' shape. Spring courtship involves aerial acrobatics.

(Circus aeruginosus)

Devil's-bit scabious
(Succisa pratensis)

Butterfly Conservation
www.butterfly-conservation.org

Marsh fritillary

👁 Sheen to underside of wings. Likes devil's-bit scabious the caterpillars spinning a fine web in its leaves.

(Euphydryas aurinia)

Redshank

👁 Long red legs and orange base to bill. Male yodels in flight "tu-udle".

(Tringa totanus)

The 'exploding' bombardier beetle has not been seen in Britain since 1928.

STILL WATER & REEDBEDS

Pintail

👁 Male has long pointed tail feathers, brown head with white foreneck.

(Anas acuta)

Marsh marigold
(Caltha palustris)

Water vole

👁 Rat-sized but longer fur, blunt nose and tiny ears. Creates a 'lawn' of shorter grass around banks. Shiny black droppings. 'Ratty' of 'Wind in the Willows' fame.

(Arvicola terrestris)

Emperor dragonfly

👁 Largest wingspan of any British dragonfly. Dark line runs full length of back. Male sky blue, female greenish.

(Anax imperator)

RIVERS & STREAMS

Atlantic Salmon

👁 Best seen when travelling upstream to spawn, jumps out of the water to traverse waterfalls.

(Salmo salar)

Banded demoiselle

👁 Male has distinctive 'thumbprint' on wings and a wingspan of 2.5 inches (60mm).

(Calopteryx splendens)

Reed bunting

👁 Male in summer has black head and throat with distinctive white stripe between the two. Tail feathers are white and deeply forked.

(Emberiza schoeniclus)

Common reed
(Phragmites australis)
Stems used for thatching.

Common newt

👁 Only seen in ponds in spring when breeding. At this time, male has an undulating crest with spotted flanks. The underside is often bright orange with spots.

(Triturus vulgaris)

Watercress
(Nasturtium officinale)
Don't eat - may have liver fluke eggs on.

Kingfisher

👁 Brilliant colouring. Makes tunnel in river bank. Often perches on branch over water.

(Alcedo atthis)

Bittern

👁 Rare. Try RSPB reserves in spring, where there are reedbeds. May hear its booming call, almost like a foghorn.

(Botaurus stellaris)

A toad can live for 40 years.

Yellow water lily
(Nuphar lutea)
Pods shaped like brandy bottles.

Common toad

👁 Dry warty skin. Prefers to walk rather than hop. Only seen in ponds in spring when breeding. Lays long strings of spawn rather than clumps.

(Bufo bufo)

Water crowfoot
(Ranunculus aquatilis)

Daubenton's bat

👁 Flies very low over water to catch prey. If you have a bat detector, listen at 35-85kHz.

(Myotis daubentonii)

Otter

👁 Brown fur, large whiskers and white chest. Can be 36 inches (90cm) long. Five-toed, webbed feet.

(Lutra lutra)

Spraint (Otter poo). Black, full of tiny fish bones.

English Nature
www.english-nature.org.uk

General advice
Do not disturb wildlife or damage their habitats.

Great crested grebe

👁 Black crest. Courtship display facing each other and moving heads quickly from side to side, usually with a bill full of water plants. Strange grating bark call.

(Podiceps cristatus)

SEA CLIFFS & BEACH

Sanderling
- Runs backwards and forwards with the waves. Winter visitor and passage migrant in autumn and spring.

(Calidris alba)

Puffin

- Unmistakable markings. Prefers high sea cliffs and offshore islands. Occasionally nest in old rabbit burrows.

(Fratercula arctica)

Green shore crab
- Usually greenish but can have considerable patterning. Up to 2.5 inches (60mm) long. Tolerant of low salinity so can be found far up in estuaries.

(Carcinus maenas)

Thrift
(Armeria maritima)

Common lizard

- Black stripe along back. Basks in sun in spring. Can shed its tail if caught, then grow a new one.

(Lacerta vivipara)

Yellow horned poppy
(Glaucium flavum)
Pods can grow up to 30cm long.

SAND DUNES

Sea holly
(Eryngium maritimum)

Green tiger beetle

- Green with two creamy yellow spots, one on each wing case. 0.625 inch (16mm) long.

(Cicindela campestris)

Sea gooseberry
- Lights run along body. Gets trapped in rock pools.

(Pleurobrachia pileus)

Sandwich Tern
- Black cap with short crest and long black bill with yellow tip. Call is a rasping "kirrick". Summer visitor.

(Sterna sandvicensis)

Common milkwort
(Polygala vulgaris)
Was once thought to increase milk production in cows.

Common brittlestar

- Five thin spiny arms around a disc of about 0.75 inches (20mm). Has five jaws.

(Ophiothrix fragilis)

Sea campion
(Silene maritima)

Fulmar

- Yellow/blue bill. Skims waves with stiff wings. If disturbed when nesting they spit a greenish oil.

(Fulmarus glacialis)

ESTUARY & SALT MARSH

Curlew

- Long down curved bill. Distinctive, haunting call, 'cooor-li'.

(Numenius arquata)

Common sea lavender
(Limonium vulgare)

Sea aster
(Aster tripolium)

Golden samphire
(Inula crithmoides)

Oystercatcher

- Long orange bill, long pink legs. Black and white plumage. Eats cockles.

(Haematopus ostralegus)

Gem anemone
- Rock pools. Up to 3 inches (80mm) tall. Up to 48 green 'tentacles'.

(Bunodactis verrucosa)

Chough

- Looks like a crow but has red bill and legs. Only on west coasts.

(Pyrrhocorax pyrrhocorax)

Sheep's-bit scabious
(Jasione montana)
Often eaten by sheep.

Sea wormwood
(Artemisia maritima)
Aromatic leaves.

Sheduck
- Large red bill with bump on the top. Chestnut/orange band around chest in the breeding season.

(Tadorna tadorna)

Research has shown that some birds dream the song they are going to sing in the morning.

COASTAL WATERS

Thornback Ray
- Diamond-shaped flat fish with spines along its long tail. Egg cases found on the beach called 'Mermaid's purses'.

(Raja clavata) Egg case

Grey seal

- Flat head and 'Roman' nose, unlike round head of Common seal. Also longer than Common. Pups born on shore late summer and autumn.

(Halichoerus grypus)

Bottle nosed dolphin
- Very social, usually in groups. Has short 'snout'. Worth going on a boat trip to see, will often swim in front or at the side of the boat.

(Tursiops truncatus)

19

REGENERATING THE LANDSCAPE

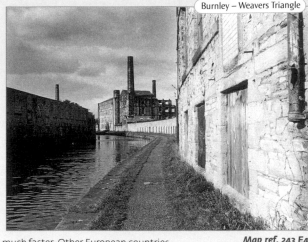
Burnley – Weavers Triangle

TRANSPORT

Canals

Canal building in Britain goes back thousands of years - short stretches were excavated to link rivers. Car Dyke, which stretched 56 miles (89km) across the Fens, was built by the Romans and can still be seen today. However, canals as we know them came into being because of the Industrial Revolution. Before the mid 1700s, goods were transported slowly and in small

Shropshire Union Canal

quantities by horse and cart on poor roads, or by sea, at great expense. With the discovery that coke could be used to smelt iron ore, huge quantities of coal were needed for this and associated industries. The first canal to be built was commissioned by the 3rd Earl of Bridgewater to transport coal from his mines to Manchester. The Bridgewater Canal opened in 1761 and was a huge success; 30 tons could be carried in a single load. By the 1830s there were over 4000 miles (7000km) of canals. However, the developing railways sounded the death knell for canal haulage. Even when wages were cut so far that boatmen had to house their families on board, railways were still more profitable and much faster. Other European countries had modernised and widened their canals, so that loads of 2,000 tons could be carried, but investment for canals here was not forthcoming. Many were abandoned and by the 1960s their numbers had halved. Luckily, at about this time, working people were taking more holidays and had more disposable income; the 'boating holiday' era had begun. Today, many miles have been restored, their narrow width making them almost unique in Europe and an historical treasure. Towpaths are being upgraded for cycling, walking and fibre-optic cableways. There is even a small revival for goods haulage due to congestion on the roads. Full circle, we might say.

Map ref. 243 E4

Brampton Valley Way

Railways

The world's first steam locomotive was built by Richard Trevithick in 1803. After that, several engineers built steam engines and in 1830 the Liverpool to Manchester line became the world's first main line railway to carry passengers and freight on a double track line of metal rails, using steam locomotives built by George and Robert Stephenson. Over the next 20 years, over 6000 miles (9650 km) of public railways were built in Britain. When World War I broke out in 1914, there were 20,053 miles (32,265km) of track and 23,000 locomotives. However, their heyday was over and by the 1960s, for various organisational and political reasons, the railways were in financial trouble and the inevitable hatchet fell. Over 2,000 stations were closed and railway lines were ripped up. It has taken many years but the value of these disused tracks is at last being realised. Many footpaths and cycleways are being created enabling us to enjoy the flora and fauna along these corridors, which escaped the chemical persecution of their arable and pastoral cousins; without the railways, we might have lost many of them.

Tyseley – railway track

Map ref. 210 C4

ENERGY

Coal

It was coal that fired the Industrial Revolution. Wherever coal could be transported, industry would spring up. Iron foundries, glass works, potteries and brickworks. However, as with any finite resource, supply eventually became a problem and cheaper foreign coal made it uneconomic to dig the deeper pits needed to access our own. Worries about global warming prompted the 1992 Earth Summit in Rio de Janeiro, where the search for alternative energy supplies started in earnest.

Rhondda Valley – colliery

Map ref. 179 F3

Short Rotation Coppice (SRC)

Look for fields of 'shrubs' or unfamiliar tall grasses; 'biofuels' grown to be burnt in pollution free, high-tech converters, producing heat, or power, or both. Around 100 acres (40ha) of 'short rotation willow coppice' (willow cut every two or three years), could keep a village of about 50 houses warm *ad infinitum*. This growing system is excellent for wildlife, soaks up pollutants and is resistant to most pests and diseases. Classed as 'carbon neutral' it only releases carbon taken up by the plant during its short growing cycle.

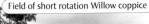
Field of short rotation Willow coppice

Wind farms

Evidence of alternative energy sources are appearing all over the landscape of Britain. Wind farms are probably the best known, taking pure energy from the air. They already supply enough power for around 400,000 households.

Llywernog – wind farm

Map ref. 204 D4

Other

In the future we may see solar panels lining motorways to power lights and signs, barrages in estuaries collecting energy from the tides and small, privately owned water mills capturing the energy of streams once more, this time to drive turbines instead of grinding stones. You may even fill your car with methane from landfill sites.

TEXTILES

Map ref. 234 C1

Until the mid 1700s, spinning and weaving was a domestic industry, but various inventions speeded up the process. In 1771, Richard Arkwright established the world's first successful water-powered cotton spinning mill at Cromford in Derbyshire, and became known as the 'father of the factory system'. Cotton production became centred in Lancashire and the west of Scotland, wool in West Yorkshire and south-west England, silk and linen in northern England. In 1912, cotton manufacture peaked at 8 billion yards (7.25 billion metres). All was well until World War I. It was no longer possible to export cloth, so countries such as Japan set up their own factories and never looked back. Between the two world wars, 800 mills closed. Although there was a slight revival in the 1950s, by the 1980s textile production in the north-west had all but ceased. Hundreds of mills lay derelict and many were pulled down. Today, the potential of the remaining fine buildings has been recognised; several are now World Heritage Sites. At Saltaire, West Yorkshire, the old mill buildings house galleries, a restaurant, antiques and other ventures. New Lanark on the banks of the Clyde has been restored to a working community and is a huge tourist attraction. Other less famous mills have found new uses - Ebley Mill in Stroud, Gloucestershire has been given a new lease of life as the District Council building.

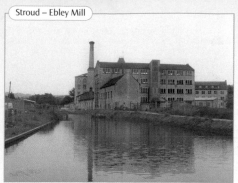
Stroud – Ebley Mill
Map ref. 182 A2

Rochdale – derelict mill

SHIPBUILDING

Britain has always been a seafaring nation and with the developments in sail and the invention of the compass. Ships were built for trade and exploration from as early as the 14th century. During the 18th century, the Navigation Acts (requiring all British trade to be carried by British ships), and the growth of the British Empire stimulated shipbuilding further; by the 19th century the British shipbuilding industry was the largest in the world. Eventually iron replaced wood and steam replaced sail. In 1914, the tonnage from British shipyards was more than the rest of the world put together; employment reached around 300,000. However, for various economic reasons, shipbuilding here started to decline. In the 1970s South Korea moved into shipbuilding, assisted by the World Bank, this was the final straw. British construction methods were outdated and none of the 'rescue packages' instigated by the government worked. 1977 saw nationalisation of the industry; 1983 saw privatisation. Warship yards survived but those producing merchant shipping all but disappeared. All is not doom and gloom however. British shipyards still produce around 27 ships a year (although we have the capacity to produce twice that number) and Britain is a world leader in ship repairs, building warships and small specialist ships, marine equipment manufacture and ship conversions. Derelict dockyards, like those at Hartlepool, have been revived with the building of a huge new marina and some of the old buildings house new industries and tourist attractions. A similar story is told of Cardiff Docks, hit in particular by the decline in the coal and steel industries, the whole area has seen a remarkable regeneration (the second largest in Europe) with a visitor centre and various tourist attractions. Many new media and IT based industries have been attracted to the revamped and new business parks.

Cardiff Bay
Map ref. 180 A5

Cranes in disused docks

FORESTRY

Scotland – block conifer plantation

Trees are a significant part of the landscape, they give it character. They can be used for screening unsightly developments, as sound barriers, for stabilising banks and spoil heaps, but mostly we see them as woodlands. After World War II, the government instigated mass planting of conifers to ensure reserves for the future. At that time, issues of wildlife and aesthetics were unheard of. Blocks and lines of conifers were planted in mostly upland areas all over the country; Kielder Forest is a prime example. Those forests are now reaching maturity but instead of chopping them all down and replanting in the same way, different methods are being used, to enhance conservation and amenity value. Landscaping and conservation now work hand in hand with commercial timber production. Trees are being removed in groups over a longer time scale so that stream sides are cleared or archaeological features enhanced, hill contours are followed and biodiversity increased. Some upland moorland is being allowed to revert to woodland (its natural state) by fencing out livestock. Within the woodlands themselves, rides are widened to let more light in, benefiting flora and fauna. This also helps access for forestry equipment, as the ground is drier.

Open ride in modern woodland

Glades and rides within a woodland provide a microclimate for wildlife - and somewhere to stack timber. When planting today, valuable habitats such as lowland heath are left alone, straight lines are avoided, trees are planted to blend in with the surrounding landscape character and contours of the land and a mix of broadleaved and coniferous trees are used. This has led to forests being areas for recreation as well as timber production, for example there are sculpture trails in the Forest of Dean. The new National Forest is being planted in the English midlands, it covers three counties and 200 square miles (518 sq km). The aim is to make one third of the area woodland (commercial and conservation), incorporating learning and recreational facilities. Over four million trees have been planted to date.

Forest of Dean – Sculpture Trail
Map ref. 181 F1

MYTHS AND LEGENDS

Dunvegan Castle

GIANTS

Where did giant tales come from? One story says they were descendents of Ham, the 'bad' son of Noah. Another, that they were the result of a union between the banished daughters of a King of Greece and demon spirits. In practice, people probably believed that the easiest explanation for monuments such as Stonehenge was that huge giants must have built them.

Callanish giants ⑨

Thirteen giant people were reputedly turned to stone when they refused to let St Kieran build a church here or be baptised by him. The Gaelic name for Callanish is "na Fir Bhreign", meaning 'the false men'.

Callanish Stones

SAINTS

Many legends surround the making of Saints, often involving birds and animals or miraculous events.

St. Brynach ⑦

St. Brynach journeyed to Nevern, where an angel appeared and told him to look for a white sow. The sow showed him where to build a church and this he did. In the churchyard stands a Celtic cross. On the seventh day of April, the Saint's day, a cuckoo is said to perch here and sing for the first time in the year.

Nevern churchyard

Cuckoo

In order to be allowed to live in this world and the Land of Eternal Youth, the cuckoo had to promise never to build a nest in either world and so never bring up or know her own children.

Cuckoo

LOST LANDS

The legend of Cantre'r Gwaelod and others relating to submerged lands could stem from actual inundations by the sea, when Neolithic man was around to witness them.

Severn Bore

WATER

Water, the giver of life, has always been associated with spirits and deities. Holy wells are often places previously used for pagan worship.

Sabrina ①

The river Severn is, according to legend, inhabited by an ancient British river spirit 'Sabrina'. One story relates that when the Roman army attempted to cross the river and attack the British leader Caractacus, and the Druids, the priests called on Sabrina and she drove the bore up the river, drowning the whole Roman army.

Fairy Flag of Dunvegan ⑥

Still kept in Dunvegan Castle is a fragile scrap of cloth. Legend says it is part of a flag given to a previous chief by his fairy wife. When unfurled, it gives victory to the MacLeod Clan in battle, makes their marriages fruitful and magically charms the herrings in the loch into the nets.

FAIRIES

Stories of folk existing in 'another dimension' to our own occur all over the world. In Britain they are best known as 'fairies'. They can be good (like the 'Brownies' who will do your housework for you), seem to be friendly towards farmers wives and always pay for anything they take. They can be spiteful, taking human babies and putting strange 'changelings' in their place. Mostly, they are seen as mischievous. The origins of these tales in Scotland seem to relate to the ancient Pictish people and in England and Wales, perhaps to the Bronze Age people, superseded by Iron Age (fairies are said to have a deep loathing of iron).

St. Winifred's Well ⑤

This well appeared on the spot where Winifred's head fell after being cut off by an unwelcome suitor called Caradog, son of a local chieftan. St. Bueno, her uncle, laid her head next to her neck, where it miraculously rejoined. Caradog was swallowed by the earth and Winifred lived out her days as a nun.

St. Winifred's Well

The Sockburn Worm

The Sockburn Worm ⑧

A venomous serpent was said to lurk in the river Tees, poisoning it and causing death and disease. A knight donned armour covered in spikes and wrestled the serpent, so that it coiled itself around him and ripped itself apart.

Cowslip

St. Peter was said to have dropped the keys to Heaven and the first Cowslip sprang up from where they fell.

Cowslip

Cantre'r Gwaelod ④

There was a land in Cardigan Bay, rich and fertile with 16 cities, protected from the sea by great sea walls. One night, the guardian of the sluice gates, Seithennin, got drunk and forgot to close the gates. The sea swept in, drowning everybody except a few survivors who escaped onto Snowdon (see Sarn Badrig, Understanding the Landscape).

Cerne Abbas giant ②

A Danish giant was terrorising the people of Dorset. One day, he ate too many sheep and became sleepy, so he lay down. While he slept, the villagers crept up on him and cut off his head. As a warning to other giants, they carved his outline into the chalk.

Cerne Abbas giant

MOVING CHURCHES

In an attempt to Christianise pagan sites of worship, many churches were built on them, sometimes in what seemed like strange places, outside of a village. There are many legends to explain these locations, often involving the devil or the building stones themselves moving.

Dunsfold church ③

According to legend, this church is half a mile from the village because the stones to build it kept moving to this site when they were left overnight.

Dunsfold church

Map labels: Stornoway ⑨, Dunvegan ⑥, Inverness, Dundee, Glasgow, Edinburgh, Newcastle upon Tyne, Carlisle, Middlesbrough ⑧, Isle of Man, Blackpool, Bradford, Leeds, Kingston upon Hull, Manchester, Liverpool, Sheffield, Chester, ⑤, Porthmadog, Stoke-on-Trent, Nottingham, Norwich, ④, Wolverhampton, Leicester, Birmingham, Ipswich, Cardigan ⑦, Gloucester ①, Oxford, LONDON, Swansea, Bristol, Cardiff, Guildford ③, Brighton, Portsmouth, Dorchester ② , Plymouth

SOUTH WEST ENGLAND

The long, tapering finger of land that forms the far south west is favoured with a temperate climate and endowed with soft, timeless beauty. The pretty coastline, sometimes rugged, other times gentle, and the green, upland expanses of Dartmoor, Exmoor and the Cotswolds, together with an abundance of charming chocolate-box villages, all merit exploration. Echoes of bygone times lie scattered through the region, adding a hint of legend and mysticism in contrast to today's more up-to-the-minute attractions.

Mevagissey Harbour

SOUTH WEST ENGLAND

A La Ronde (NT)
152 D4

A remarkable 16-sided house built in the late 18th century on the instructions of two cousins, Jane and Mary Parminter, on their return from a Grand Tour of Europe. Many items on show were collected by the ladies during their tour and amongst the more unusual features of internal decoration are a feather frieze and a gallery encrusted by shells.

☎ 01395 265514   www.nationaltrust.org.uk

Abbotsbury Swannery & Sub-Tropical Gardens
154 B4

A sheltered coastal location behind Chesil Beach provides a distinctive microclimate which has allowed this 20 acre (8ha) woodland garden to flourish. There are magnificent spring displays of camellias, magnolias and rhododendrons, exotic species such as bamboos, palms and bananas, and themed areas like the Mediterranean, Himalayan and New Zealand gardens.

Down on the shore, in the lee of Chesil Beach, there has been a swannery for over 600 years, established by Benedictine monks in the 14th century. Up to 1000 swans may be in residence at any one time, and between late May and late June it is possible to walk amongst the swans and observe newborn cygnets close up.

☎ 01305 871387 (Gardens)   www.abbotsbury-tourism.co.uk
☎ 01305 871858 (Swannery)

Alice in Wonderland Family Park
347 C2

A 7 acre (2.5ha) theme park based on the books of Lewis Carroll, the focal point being one of Europe's largest hedge mazes with over 5000 bushes trained to form shapes of characters from the Alice books. Other attractions include rides, particularly for younger children, indoor and outdoor play areas and a theatre giving short shows based on the Alice characters.

☎ 01202 483444   www.aliceinwonderlandpark.co.uk

American Museum
167 E1

An early 19th century manor house which, since the late 1950s, has been home to a museum illustrating American history, culture and way of life. 18 rooms have been decorated and furnished to depict the evolution of American homes and their fashions from the 17th to 19th centuries and there are also collections of quilts and textiles, Folk Art and Native American Art. The attractive grounds contain a re-created piece of George Washington's garden at Mount Vernon.

☎ 01225 460503   www.americanmuseum.org

Antony House (NT)
150 A2

On the Lynher River estuary, north-west of Torpoint, this fine example of an 18th century manor house contains collections of paintings, textiles and furniture. The grounds, landscaped by Humphrey Repton, contain the National Collection of Hemerocallis.

☎ 01752 812191

Avebury Ring

Arlington Court (NT)
163 G1

An early 19th century house on the site of two previous buildings. The 3000 acre (1200ha) estate was home to the Chichester family for over 500 years, and the house contains many of the diverse and exotic acquisitions of the last owner, Miss Rosalie Chichester. There are extensive formal and informal gardens, delightful woodland walks, a small carriage museum and a bat cave where a large colony of lesser horseshoe bats can be observed by closed-circuit television.

☎ 01271 850296   www.nationaltrust.org.uk

Ashton Court Estate
352 A3

A magnificent estate of 850 acres (340ha) designed by Humphrey Repton and comprising woods and parkland, red and fallow deer herds, and outstanding views over Bristol and beyond. A diversity of natural habitats makes this an important wildlife site, of great interest to naturalists, while for the more physically active there are mountain bike, orienteering and horse riding trails, and golf courses. The site is also host to a range of events, notably the Bristol International Balloon Festival held every year in August.

The 19th century mansion houses a visitor centre and café but is not otherwise open to the public.

☎ 0117 963 9174   www.bristol-city.gov.uk

At-Bristol
391 C1

Three separate attractions housed in a new complex close to the waterfront in the centre of Bristol, providing a fascinating range of educational entertainment.

'Wildwalk' is a stroll through plant and animal evolution using displays and interactive exhibits.

'Explore' is an imaginative, interactive science exhibition divided into four themes related to the brain, engineering and technology, global communications, and the Curiosity Zone which explores the oddities of the physical environment.

The IMAX theatre is a four-storey high screen with surround sound, making the viewer feel part of the action. A range of short films can be seen each day, with the emphasis on science and wildlife.

☎ 0845 345 1235   www.at-bristol.org.uk

Athelhampton
155 D3

A splendid 15th century manor house with impressive Grade I gardens. The central feature of the house is the Great Hall, built in 1493 by Sir Robert Martyn, a former Lord Mayor of London.

The 20 acre (8ha) garden was designed by Inigo Thomas in the late 19th century and, in addition to the world famous topiary pyramids, there are eight walled gardens inspired by the Renaissance, fountains, pavilions and a 16th century dovecote.

☎ 01305 848363   www.athelhampton.co.uk

Auk Walk
147 E1

A clifftop walk near Trevalga which, between April and July, overlooks the nesting sites of puffins, guillemots and razorbills.

Avebury Ring & Alexander Keiller Museum (NT)
168 C1

Around 4500 years old, this is possibly the largest stone circle in Europe, the surviving sarsen stones being enclosed by a substantial earthwork almost 1 mile (1.6km) in circumference. Within this there were two smaller stone circles, though little remains of the more northerly.

Information about Avebury Ring can be found in the Alexander Keiller Museum (for which there is a charge), named after the former owner of the site who endeavoured to restore the area following the plunder and removal of stones which took place, particularly in medieval times. The museum gives an excellent overview of the site, explains the known history and displays artefacts uncovered during archaeological excavations.

☎ 01672 539250   www.nationaltrust.org.uk
www.english-heritage.org.uk

Babbacombe Model Village
151 F1

An ingenious miniature English landscape set in 4 acres (1.5ha) of beautiful gardens with over 400 models built on a scale of 1:12. Originally intended to represent the archetypal English village and its rural surroundings, the project has expanded to incorporate a comprehensive range of buildings, with particular emphasis on domestic architecture. The setting is enhanced by the many attractive water features flowing through the gardens, and is particularly enchanting in summer when illuminated at dusk.

☎ 01803 315315   www.babbacombemodelvillage.co.uk

Babbacombe Model Village

Barrington Court (NT)
153 G1

A lovely Elizabethan manor house owned by the National Trust but let as showrooms for antique furniture. The gardens, influenced by Gertrude Jekyll, are a notable feature, consisting of a series of walled, themed 'rooms' such as the White Garden, Lily Garden and Kitchen Garden.

☎ 01460 241938   www.nationaltrust.org.uk

Bath
167 E1

The only hot springs in the country are the source of Bath's name and of its importance as a fashionable resort and tourist attraction. This in turn generated the wealth which enabled the construction of the wonderful Georgian buildings which have helped to give Bath its World Heritage Site status.

Even before the Romans arrived and built the amazing baths complex, the hot springs were a site of veneration for local Celtic tribes. However, following the Romans' departure, interest was lost in the springs and it was not until the early 18th century that it attained its position as the epitome of fashionable society. This was due largely to the efforts of Richard 'Beau' Nash, who transformed Bath from provincial town to unrivalled centre of fashion. Sea bathing eventually superseded spas as the fashionable cure, but Bath was left with a splendid architectural heritage with masterpieces such as the Circus, Royal Crescent, Assembly Rooms and Pulteney Bridge.

www.visitbath.co.uk

24

✝ Bath Abbey `388 E2`

Built between 1499 – 1616, this is one of England's last great medieval churches, known by the Elizabethans as the 'Lantern of the West' because of the abundance of stained glass. The most impressive example is the great East Window, illustrating 56 scenes from the life of Christ.

Externally, the most remarkable feature is the west front, carved angels commemorating a dream of the founder, Bishop Oliver King. A small but informative museum in the vaults traces the abbey's history.

☎ 01225 422462

❋ Batsford Arboretum `197 D4`

Overlooking the Evenlode Valley, at 55 acres (22 ha) this is one of the largest collections of trees and shrubs in the country with over 1500 species. The park dates back to the 17th century when the original gardens were more formal than those seen today. This transition took place in two stages – towards the end of the 19th century by Algernon Freeman-Mitford who created the wild garden, and after World War II when the wild garden had fallen into neglect and the 2nd Lord Dulverton set about creating the arboretum. Some of the features of the original wild garden are still present – the Japanese Rest House and Buddha, Rockeries and the Hermits Cave.

☎ 01386 701441   www.batsarb.co.uk

❋ Bennetts Water Garden `154 C4`

An 8 acre (3ha) area of landscaped lakes, formerly clay pits from the local brickworks. With 150 varieties of waterlily flowering in summer, this is one of the best displays in the country, and there are connections with Monet's Garden at Giverny. There is also a small museum devoted to local village life and the history of the site.

☎ 01305 785150   www.waterlily.co.uk

🏰 ❋ Berkeley Castle & Gardens `181 F3`

Completed in 1153 by Lord Maurice de Berkeley for Henry II in order to guard the Severn Estuary, the layout of the castle has changed little since the end of the 14th century. It is England's oldest inhabited castle and is still home to the Berkeley family after 25 generations. The cell where King Edward II was held captive for 18 months before his murder in 1327 can be seen, as can the 30ft (9m) deep dungeon. The extensive grounds feature a butterfly house, lily pond and the bowling alley where Elizabeth I played bowls with her courtiers.

☎ 01453 810332   www.berkeley-castle.com

Bath – Royal Crescent

Batsford Arboretum

🏛 Berry Pomeroy Castle `151 E1`

With a reputation as one of the most haunted castles in England, this decidedly atmospheric ruin is splendidly located on a crag above a wooded valley. The oldest part is thought to date from the 14th century, but the main building, a large mansion, was built between 1548 – 1613 and was subsequently abandoned later in the 17th century.

☎ 01803 866618   www.english-heritage.org.uk

❋ Bicton Park Gardens `153 D4`

Delightful gardens and parkland covering 63 acres (25ha) featuring an amazing 19th century domed Palm House, arguably one of the world's most beautiful garden buildings. Other highlights include the Italian Garden and Pinetum. For the less horticulturally inclined, there is a rural life museum, a 1.5 mile (2.5km) narrow-gauge railway and adventure playground.

☎ 01395 568465   www.bictongardens.co.uk

⭐ Big Sheep, The `163 E3`

Innovative attraction combining traditional sheep-related activities such as shearing, lambing, feeding and sheepdog trials, with more unusual enterprises such as Ewetopia, an adventure play area, sheep racing, complete with knitted jockeys, and duck trials.

☎ 01237 478800   www.thebigsheep.co.uk

⭐ Birdland `197 D5`

Birdland opened in 1957 and moved to its present 7 acre (3ha) natural setting in 1989. There are over 500 birds with more than 50 aviaries for parrots, hornbills and toucans, amongst many other species. The River Windrush winds through the park creating a natural habitat for flamingos, pelicans and storks. The penguins are always popular, especially at feeding time.

☎ 01451 820480   www.birdland.co.uk

🏛 Blaise Castle House Museum `352 A1`

A late 18th century castle folly in beautiful grounds designed by Humphrey Repton. The museum has a fine social history collection including an excellent range of domestic equipment, a Victorian toy room including model trains, period costumes and paintings.

☎ 0117 903 9818   www.bristol-city.gov.uk

🚂 Bodmin & Wenford Railway `147 E3`

Operating from Bodmin General station, this is

Cornwall's only standard-gauge steam railway. It consists of two lines, one interchanging with the main line at Bodmin Parkway. Most trains are steam-hauled over 6.5 miles (10km) of track.

☎ 0845 125 9678   www.bodminandwenfordrailway.co.uk

☐ Bodmin Moor `147 F2`

A large expanse of granite moorland dotted with tors in the north and many Bronze Age and Neolithic sites, particularly in the south. Brown Willy, Cornwall's highest point at 1377ft (420m), is located here in the bleaker northern part of the moor. Daphne du Maurier's famous novel 'Jamaica Inn' is set on the moor around Altarnun and Bolventor.

❋ Bowood House & Gardens `167 G1`

Built in the early 18th century, but partly demolished in 1955, Bowood is an elegant Georgian mansion. Its most notable features are Robert Adam's magnificent library, the laboratory where Joseph Priestley discovered oxygen, the Orangery, now a picture gallery, and the Sculpture Gallery. The 2000 acre (800ha) grounds, however, are arguably Bowood's chief attraction. Landscaped by Lancelot 'Capability' Brown, complete with elegant parkland, Cascade Waterfall, Hermit's Cave and a Doric temple by the tranquil lake, they make a splendid backdrop to the house. For six weeks in spring the magnificent rhododendron gardens are open, with thousands of flowering bulbs elsewhere in the grounds. For children there is an excellent adventure playground and soft play area.

☎ 01249 812102   www.bowood.org

🏠 Bradley Manor `152 B5`

A small 15th century manor house in a tranquil setting of woodland and open fields. The Great Hall is a particularly interesting feature.

☎ 01626 354513   www.nationaltrust.org.uk

⭐ Brewers Quay `154 C5`

A converted harbourside brewery housing a range of shops, activities and attractions.

'The Timewalk' depicts 600 years of Weymouth's history as seen through the eyes of the brewery cat and her predecessors. 'Brewery Days' looks at the area's brewing heritage through interactive displays and audiovisual presentations. 'Discovery' is a hands-on science centre with over 60 interactive items.

☎ 01305 777622   www.brewers-quay.co.uk

🏛 Bristol City Museum & Art Gallery `352 B2`

One of the largest museums in the south west, housed in an impressive Edwardian Baroque building. There are detailed displays relating to local geology, archaeology and natural history, interesting temporary exhibitions and some unusual art exhibits.

☎ 0117 922 3571   www.bristol-city.gov.uk

🏛 Bristol Industrial Museum `391 C1`

Located in the Floating Harbour in a converted goods transit shed, the museum is home to a wide range of exhibits relating to Bristol's industrial heritage. The port's history is told through models, paintings and memorabilia, and there are exhibitions on the printing and packaging industry, and Bristol's part in the infamous slave trade triangle.

☎ 0117 925 1470   www.bristol-city.gov.uk

SOUTH WEST ENGLAND

Bristol Zoo
352 B2

For a generation brought up on safari parks, Bristol Zoo might seem a rather modest establishment, but there is plenty to see. It comprises a 12 acre (5ha) site with delightful gardens providing a colourful backdrop to over 300 fascinating species with a particular emphasis on conservation of wildlife and its natural habitats. There are zoo trails and a good adventure playground for children.

☎ 0117 973 8951   www.bristolzoo.org.uk

British Empire & Commonwealth Museum
391 C3

A fascinating museum detailing the history of the British Empire and subsequent development of the Commonwealth, from the voyage of John Cabot in 1497 to the present day. There are 20 themed galleries devoted to exploration, trade and conquest, illustrated by a wide selection of artefacts, costumes, photographs and film clips, with an imaginative variety of interactive exhibits.

☎ 0117 925 4980   www.empiremuseum.co.uk

Brownsea Island
155 G4

Located in the sheltered waters of Poole harbour, this 500 acre (200ha) island boasts a wide range of natural habitats such as saline lagoon, heathland and freshwater lakes. This haven for wildlife is home to such rarities as red squirrels, glow worms, water voles, dragonflies and over 20 species of butterfly. There are hides to observe both breeding colonies and migrant birds, and a boardwalk through reed beds passes near the heronry.

Historically, the island is chiefly famous as the site of Lord Baden-Powell's first camp in 1907 which led to the formation of the Scout movement.

Access is by pedestrian ferry from the mainland, and away from the reserve there are woodland walks with delightful views.

☎ 01202 707744   www.nationaltrust.org.uk

Buckfast Abbey
150 D1

This was originally founded in 1018, but was abandoned after the Dissolution of the Monasteries until 1882 when Benedictine monks took over the site and rebuilt the abbey in a traditional Anglo-Norman style with some particularly striking stained glass work. There is an informative exhibition on the site and shops selling a variety of produce from Benedictine monasteries across Europe. Physic, Sensory and Lavender gardens have been re-created in the grounds.

☎ 01364 645500   www.buckfast.org.uk

Buckland Abbey (NT)
150 A1

Originally a 13th century monastery overlooking the Tavy valley, this was subsequently converted to a family home, initially owned by the sea-faring Grenville family. In 1581 the property was bought by Sir Francis Drake and it remained in his family until 1942. Features include the fine, oak-panelled Great Hall, exhibitions on Drake's achievements and adventures, Elizabethan gardens and craft workshops.

☎ 01822 853607   www.nationaltrust.org.uk

Cadhay
153 D3

An attractive Tudor manor house approached through an avenue of lime trees. The fine 15th century timbered roof of a previous dwelling has been incorporated into the Great Hall.

☎ 01404 812432   www.eastdevon.net

Caen Hill Locks
168 A1

An impressive flight of 29 locks on the Kennet and Avon Canal at Devizes, raising the water level 240ft (73m) in 2.5 miles (4km)

Canonteign Falls
152 B4

Located in a natural hillside gorge landscaped 160 years ago, this claims to be England's highest waterfall at almost 220ft (66m). After being neglected for years, the site has been restored to reveal striking rock formations, lakes and waterfalls. Additional features include a Victorian fern garden, wetland nature reserve, children's play areas and adventure playground.

☎ 01647 252434   www.canonteignfalls.com

Carnewas & Bedruthan Steps
146 C3

Spectacular coastal scenery of cliffs and rocky beach. Access to the beach is via a stairway from the clifftop at Carnewas, where a National Trust shop is housed in a former mine office. The Steps are a series of rock stacks along the beach, produced as a consequence of marine erosion.

☎ 01637 860563   www.nationaltrust.org.uk

Castle Drogo (NT)
152 A3

Contrary to appearances, this is an early 20th century building designed by Sir Edwin Lutyens and built in an outstanding position above the Teign valley. Constructed of specially quarried granite, the foundations were cut into the hillside, and in some rooms the exposed rock can be seen. Overall, it presents a striking combination of medieval style with modern comfort.

Outside, established formal gardens provide a colourful setting in spring and summer, and there are lovely woodland walks, some providing magnificent views over the Teign valley.

☎ 01647 433306   www.nationaltrust.org.uk

Chambercombe Manor
163 F1

Located in a tranquil valley, Chambercombe was mentioned in the Domesday Book, though the present house dates from the 12th century. Eight rooms are on display, with period furniture from Elizabethan to Victorian times. Very atmospheric, and rumoured to be haunted.

☎ 01271 862624   www.chambercombemanor.co.uk

Cheddar Gorge & Caves
166 B2

Cheddar Gorge is the most dramatic natural feature of the Mendip area, a mile (1.6km) long chasm with cliffs, almost vertical in places, around 400ft (120m) high. A drive through the gorge, for which access is free, is a breathtaking experience, more so when taken out of season as, not surprisingly, this is a popular attraction and can be crowded in summer. For walkers, there is a 3 mile (5km) clifftop circular walk which provides fine views, and which can be accessed by Jacob's Ladder, 274 steps up the side of the gorge.

The lower end of the gorge in Cheddar village has succumbed to commercial tourist pressure, but the caves offer visitors the chance to see some amazing stalactite and stalagmite formations in the dramatic Gough's Cave. Cox's Cave nearby is smaller, with narrow passages and some striking coloured formations. There is also an exhibition on the life of cave-dwelling man, based on remains discovered in the caves dating from Palaeolithic times.

☎ 01934 742343   www.cheddarcaves.co.uk

Chedworth Roman Villa (NT)
182 C1

Discovered in 1864 and now owned by the National Trust, the Villa sits at the head of a small valley overlooking the River Colne. It would have been one of the grandest houses in the Cotswolds at the time it was built, with evidence of 32 rooms, and there are still substantial remains including two Roman baths and some extremely well-preserved mosaic flooring. There are audiovisual demonstrations and a museum within the grounds.

☎ 01242 890256   www.nationaltrust.org.uk

Chesil Beach

Chesil Beach
154 B4

An 18 mile (29km) shingle ridge running from Burton Bradstock to Portland, effectively tying the island to the mainland. South of Abbotsbury the ridge is detached from the coast, enclosing The Fleet, a brackish lagoon and setting for J. Meade Faulkner's definitive smuggling story 'Moonfleet'.

An interesting feature of the beach is the increase in size of its component flint and quartzite stones, from pea size in the west to fist size at Portland, where the ridge can be up to 45ft (14m) high. This is a popular site with sea anglers, but powerful offshore currents, probably a factor in the feature's formation, make it very dangerous for bathers.

Chettle House
155 F1

A delightful Queen Anne manor house providing an excellent example of English Baroque architecture. Complemented by 5 acres (2ha) of attractive gardens. Limited opening.

☎ 01258 830858

Christchurch Priory
347 D3

Considered to be the longest parish church in Britain at over 300ft (90m), this splendid medieval monastic building is noted for its exceptional interior carvings. Access to the tower, via 120 steps up a spiral staircase, is sometimes available for a small charge, and is worth it for the splendid views.

☎ 01202 485804   www.christchurchpriory.org

Chysauster Ancient Village
144 B3

A late Iron Age courtyard village believed to have been inhabited at least up until the Roman occupation. The settlement consisted of eight or more oval stone houses, each surrounding a courtyard, and a stone wall enclosed the whole complex. Within the houses some rooms were for human occupation, others for animals or food storage.

☎ 01831 757934   www.english-heritage.org.uk

Cleeve Abbey
164 D3

A late 12th/early 13th century Cistercian abbey particularly noted for its well preserved cloisters, considered amongst the finest in England. Other distinctive features include the remarkable timber roof in the refectory and medieval wall paintings.

☎ 01984 640377   www.english-heritage.org.uk

Cleeve Common
196 B5

Cleeve Common is the high spot of the Cotswold Hills, rising to 1083ft (330 m) above sea level, with, on a clear day, far-reaching views across to the Malvern Hills and the Brecon Beacons in South Wales. The Common is protected by the Wildlife and Countryside Act and is a Site of Special Scientific Interest. The area was cleared of forest over 10,000 years ago and has been used for livestock grazing ever since. Rock climbing is popular on Cleeve Cloud and the public golf course is a test on the exposed hilltop.

☎ 01242 522878   www.cleevecommon.freeserve.co.uk

Clevedon Court (NT)
180 D5

Surviving virtually intact from its construction in 1320, the house incorporates parts of older buildings including a 12th century tower and 13th century hall. The contents include fine collections of glass, Eltonware and furniture, and there are sketches by William Makepeace Thackeray who wrote much of 'Vanity Fair' here. There are attractive terraced gardens giving good sea views.

☎ 01275 872257   www.nationaltrust.org.uk

Clouds Hill (NT)
155 E3

A tiny, rather isolated cottage which formed a retreat for T.E. Lawrence (Lawrence of Arabia) following his desert achievements. The four rooms on display contain memorabilia and an exhibition on his life. Open only part of each week.

☎ 01929 405616   www.nationaltrust.org.uk

Clovelly
162 D3

Cars are prohibited from this unique village where a steep cobbled street lined with delightful, flower-covered, whitewashed houses runs down to a tiny harbour. As the streets are too steep for motor transport, donkeys were formerly used for conveying heavy loads and, although now superseded by hauled sledges, are still on hand for children's rides in summer.

The harbour and distinctive quay are the most memorable features and, although fishing is no longer of major importance, it is still a feature of village life. This, together with sympathetic management, ensures the village retains its character whilst proving a popular attraction.

☎ 01237 431781   www.clovelly.co.uk

Coleridge Cottage (NT)
165 E3

For three years from 1797, this was home to the poet Samuel Taylor Coleridge where he wrote, amongst other works, 'The Rime of the Ancient Mariner'. Part of the cottage containing his memorabilia is open to the public.

☎ 01278 732662   www.nationaltrust.org.uk

Coleton Fishacre (NT)
151 F2

Built in the Arts and Crafts style of the late 19th century for the D'Oyly Carte family, this house is distinguished for its internal decoration influenced by the Art Deco movement.

The garden is particularly noted for its range of tender and exotic plants which thrive in the sheltered, moist environment. The terrace gardens are delightful with their range of colour and diversity in summer, whilst woodland pathways through the less formal stream-fed valley lead to coastal walks with panoramic views.

☎ 01803 752466   www.nationaltrust.org.uk

Combe Martin Wildlife & Dinosaur Park
163 G1

A 25 acre (10ha) parkland, ideal for children, with a range of animals and birds including falconry displays, butterfly house, otter pool, sea lions, snow leopards, wolves and a large meerkat enclosure. The dinosaur museum houses not only fossils but also models animated by computer technology, the star being a full-size Tyrannosaurus Rex. There are also botanical gardens containing subtropical plants, and a range of indoor activities.

☎ 01271 882486   www.dinosaur-park.com

Compton Acres
347 B3

The attractive 10 acre (4ha) gardens were devised around 1920 by Thomas Simpson who wanted to create a series of separate garden 'rooms', each illustrating a specific national garden style. National styles include Japanese, Egyptian, Italian, Indian, Canadian, Spanish and Scottish, each with appropriate plants and statuary. The result is a series of delightful gardens in a location giving stunning views over Poole Harbour and surrounding hills.

☎ 01202 700778   www.comptonacres.co.uk

Compton Castle (NT)
151 E1

Built between the 14th and 16th centuries, this fortified manor house has been the Gilbert family home almost continuously for the last 600 years. The original buildings, dating from 1350 and fortified in Henry VIII's reign, have remained unaltered since.

☎ 01803 875740   www.nationaltrust.org.uk

Cookworthy Museum
150 D3

Opened in 1971, this fascinating museum, housed in the Old Grammar School, displays items associated with rural life and social history in the Kingsbridge area, particularly in the 19th and early 20th centuries.

☎ 01548 853235   www.devonmuseums.net

Corfe Castle (NT)
155 F4

A hilltop ruin which dominates the surrounding countryside. Built by the Normans in the late 11th century to replace an earlier Saxon structure which had been the site of the murder of King Edward the Martyr in AD978, the castle controlled the route through the Purbeck Hills. It was used as a prison, and subsequently as a treasury and hunting lodge by King John in the early 12th century, whilst Henry III added further walls, towers and gatehouses.

The last owners were the Bankes family, Lady Mary Bankes holding the castle against Parliamentary attack for a long period during the Civil War. The steep hillside and thick walls made the castle almost impregnable, and it required the treachery of one of the besieged officers for it to be taken.

Subsequently, the destruction of the castle was ordered, and it is a credit to the soundness of the original construction that it took several months to reduce it to the ruin that can be seen today. The rubble was not wasted; much of it was used to build Corfe Castle village.

☎ 01929 481294   www.nationaltrust.org.uk

Cornish Cyder Farm, The
146 B4

Guided tours round probably the largest Cornish cider maker in Cornwall. The farm also produces liqueurs and other fruit products. Admission to the farm is free.

☎ 01872 573356   www.thecornishcyderfarm.co.uk

Cornish Engines (NT)
145 D2

Local engineer Richard Trevithick developed the high pressure steam system which originally powered these two impressive beam engines. Their purpose was to operate the winding gear to transport men and ore through the mineshafts and to pump out water from depths of around 1800ft (550m). The Industrial Discovery Centre on the same site provides an absorbing perspective on Cornwall's industrial heritage.

☎ 01209 315027

Cornish Seal Sanctuary
145 E4

On the Helford Estuary, just east of Gweek. One of Europe's leading marine animal rescue centres, comprising a hospital and rehabilitation pools, and caring for around 50 abandoned or injured seals and otters. Feeding demonstrations take place throughout the day.

☎ 01326 221361

Cotehele (NT)
150 A1

On the River Tamar just west of Calstock. Originally a medieval manor house, improved and enlarged by Sir Richard Edgcumbe and his son between 1490 and 1520. Subsequent alterations have not substantially affected their work, making this one of the least altered medieval houses in the country. The gardens provide all year round colour and are crossed by a network of woodland and riverside walks.

☎ 01579 351346

Cotswold Farm Park
196 D5

The park has a wide variety of animals including rare breeds, pets and working animals such as oxen and sheepdogs. The tractor school gives 3 to 12 year olds the chance to learn to drive battery and pedal powered tractors, and the Touch Barn enables visitors to get close to the smaller animals. There are daily and seasonal demonstrations such as milking, lambing and shearing.

☎ 01451 850307   www.cotswoldfarmpark.co.uk

Corfe Castle

Cotswold Hills
182 A3

The Cotswolds, an Area of Outstanding Natural Beauty, run for 60 miles (96km) from Bath north eastwards to the Warwickshire border and eastwards towards Oxford. The hills are not particularly high – the high point of 1083ft (330m) is on Cleeve Common near Cheltenham – but the landscape is rich and varied, from rolling hills to steep sided valleys. The picturesque towns and villages are frequently busy, especially in the north, but there are many quiet and peaceful areas to be found. The 100 mile (160km) Cotswold Way winds its way from Chipping Campden in the north, southwards to Bath. Passing such places of interest as Hailes Abbey, Woodchester Mansion, the Tyndale Monument and the Stone Age long barrows of Belas Knap and Hetty Pegler's Tump, the walk is always interesting and takes in some of the country's finest countryside. The belt of limestone that stretches across central England gives the Cotswolds much of their character in the buildings and drystone walls that help to blend the towns and villages seamlessly with the open countryside.

☎ 01242 522878   www.cotswoldsaonb.com

Cotswold village – Bibury

Cotswold Water Park
182 C3

With 133 lakes formed as the result of gravel extraction and covering over 2000 acres (809ha), this is considered Britain's largest water park. The lakes provide a variety of associated watersports including angling, sailing, canoeing, water-skiing and windsurfing, but there are also land-based activities on offer. There are several nature reserves with public access within the country park areas, the bird life being of special interest. Opportunities abound for walking, cycling and adventure activities, and a bathing beach is open in summer. Access is free, but there is a charge for activities.

☎ 01285 862962   www.waterpark.org

Crealy Adventure Park
152 D3

A good day out for families with children, having activities suitable for all ages and interests. These include adventure playgrounds, farm animals, a variety of rides and lakeside walks.

☎ 01395 233200   www.crealy.co.uk

Dartington Crystal
151 D1

Guided tours of the factory enable visitors to learn about glass production, from the initial stage of blowing the molten glass through to the finishing process of completed items. A visitor centre traces the history of glass production and holds live demonstrations of glass-making skills, whilst the activity centre provides hands-on family entertainment. There is a large factory shop on site.

☎ 01805 626242   www.dartington.co.uk

Dartmoor
149 F2

A National Park, perhaps the last untouched wilderness of southern England, this is an extensive, bare upland area of granite with clusters of rocky summits or tors of between 1000-2000ft (300-600m). Scenery ranges from almost featureless tracts of open moorland in the north, to the wooded valleys of the Teign and Dart in the south.

The more remote areas of high moorland have a rather forbidding reputation, enhanced in part by its use as an atmospheric setting for Sir Arthur Conan Doyle's story 'The Hound of the Baskervilles'. In good weather the area is outstanding walking country, with a mixture of old rail tracks (a legacy of former mineral extraction) and ancient footpaths. Possibly due to a more favourable past climate, there are around 2000 prehistoric sites on the moor, the Bronze Age village of Grimspound being perhaps the best example, and the area is considered one of the most significant locations for Bronze Age relics in Europe. The more wooded and hospitable moorland fringes are home to the many fast flowing streams tumbling down from the uplands, particularly attractive spots being Lydford Gorge and Becky Falls.

Dartmouth Castle
151 E2

The first to be designed with specific respect to artillery use, this 15th century castle has a superb location on the narrow entrance to the Dart estuary. A contributor to the coastal defence system over the last 500 years, the building is still in good repair. Informative displays recount the castle's history.

☎ 01803 833588   www.english-heritage.org.uk

Dean Heritage Centre
181 F1

Set around a restored corn mill and millpond, the centre looks at various aspects of the Forest of Dean – geology, hunting, crafts, the industrial heritage including iron and coal mining.

☎ 01594 822170   www.deanheritagemuseum.com

Dinosaur Museum
154 C3

Devoted entirely to dinosaurs and their world, this museum has a range of imaginative and interactive exhibits. It is possible to handle some of the actual fossil bones and life-size reconstructions, and there is a wealth of factual information for visitors. There is a well-stocked shop.

☎ 01305 269880   www.dinosaur-museum.co.uk

Dobwalls Family Adventure Park
147 G3

A theme park based on the miniature railway hobby of John Southern, a local farmer. Around 10 steam and diesel trains based on the American style railroads travel along 2 miles (3km) of track. Additional attractions include an impressive adventure playground, children's driving school and wildlife art gallery.

☎ 01579 320325

Dunster Castle & Gardens (NT)
164 C3

Dating from at least Norman, and possibly Saxon times, the castle has a magnificent site on a wooded hill above the village of Dunster. The chief medieval relic is the 13th century gatehouse, while the main building, dating from 1617, was substantially remodelled for domestic use in Victorian times.

The 28 acre (11ha) gardens are equally interesting with unusual and subtropical plants, including the National Collection of Arbutus (strawberry trees), probably England's oldest lemon tree, camellias, magnolias and a fine display of spring bulbs. There are extensive views across Exmoor, the Quantock Hills and the Bristol Channel.

☎ 01643 821314   www.nationaltrust.org.uk

Dartmoor

Dunster Watermill
164 C3

There was mention of a mill on this site in the Domesday Book, but the current building dates from the 18th century and has been restored. Visitors can watch the milling process and there is a collection of old-fashioned agricultural machinery, and a tearoom.

☎ 01643 821759   www.nationaltrust.org.uk

Durdle Door
155 E4

This is a natural sea arch composed of Portland limestone formed where marine erosion has exploited an area of weakness in the rock. A short but energetic and breathtaking hike of just over 1 mile (1.6km) west along the cliffs from Lulworth Cove brings the walker to this fascinating feature. Cheats can park at the nearby holiday park for a small fee and stroll to the coast.

Dyrham Park (NT)
181 G5

Impressive and little altered late 17th century house set in 268 acres (105ha) of deer park, built for William Blathwayt, a minister in William III's government. It contains some fine furnishings, paintings and a collection of Delftware, popular at the time in deference to the king's Dutch origins. Park and ride access is arranged to preserve the original setting.

☎ 0117 937 2501   www.nationaltrust.org.uk

East Lambrook Manor
154 A1

Delightful Grade I cottage style garden created in the mid 20th century by Margery Fish and portrayed in her popular book 'We Made a Garden'. Established with the conservation of endangered species in mind, the garden was neglected in the 1970s but has since been sympathetically restored to provide a wealth of colour and scent, including the National Collection of Geraniums. The house is not open to the public, but the 17th century malthouse is used for art exhibitions.

☎ 01460 240328   www.eastlambrook.com

East Somerset Railway | 167 D3

Also known as the Strawberry Line, steam trains run along the 2.5 mile (4km) track which includes a 1 in 56 gradient, one of the steepest for an English preserved railway. It was founded by the wildlife artist David Shepherd and the station complex includes an art gallery, as well as an engine shed and workshops. It is advisable to phone in advance for train times.

☎ 01749 880417   www.eastsomersetrailway.org

Eden Project | 147 E4

This has been described as 'the world's largest greenhouse' but that is a gross oversimplification of the botanical diversity contained within.

Opened in 2001 and still undergoing further development, the Eden Project was devised by Tim Smit (who also redeveloped the Lost Gardens of Heligan). Its purpose is to illustrate how the human race depends on plants, and aims to provide levels of interest appropriate to all ages and scientific abilities.

The site was originally a vast clay pit 200ft (60m) deep and 35 acres (14ha) in area. It comprises two biomes constructed from transparent hexagonal plastic on a galvanized steel tubing framework. Each of these has its own controlled environment designed to replicate conditions in one of the world's major climatic regions. Outside can be found plants from temperate climates such as the prairies, Himalayas and western Europe. Displays in each area show how man interacts with these environments and the uses to which the plants are put.

A deservedly popular attraction, which at peak times may be closed to prevent overcrowding.

☎ 01726 811911   www.edenproject.com

Eden Project

Edmondsham House | 155 G1

Delightful Tudor manor house with later Georgian additions set in an attractive 6 acre (2ha) garden with lovely spring bulbs, unusual trees and an organic walled garden. There is also an interesting octagonal Victorian dairy and the remains of a medieval cock fighting pit. Limited opening.

☎ 01725 517207

Escot | 153 D3

220 acres (88ha) of parkland designed by Lancelot 'Capability' Brown and containing a wide range of animals and related activities including falconry displays, bear enclosures, otters, an extensive collection of tropical and freshwater fish, maze and wetland conservation area. There are also children's activities and pleasant walks through the colourful gardens and parkland. Access to the aquatic centre and wetlands area is free.

☎ 01404 822188   www.escot-devon.co.uk

Exeter Cathedral | 398 B2

Miraculously escaping major structural damage during the World War II bombing of Exeter, the cathedral and its close provide an historic retreat amidst the post-war rebuilding of the city centre. Evidence of Christian worship on this site dates from the 5th century, but the oldest features of the current building are the twin Norman towers dating from the early 12th century. Much of the cathedral was rebuilt during the late 13th and 14th centuries, building materials being local stone from Beer and Purbeck limestone, and this provides perhaps England's finest example of Decorated Gothic architecture. Other notable aspects are the 14th century minstrels' gallery, the bishop's throne which dates from 1312 and is one of the finest examples of wood carving surviving from this period, the elaborate choir stalls with 13th century misericords and the 500 year old astronomical clock. Of more recent interest are the Exeter Rondels, delightfully embroidered cushions on the north and south walls of the nave depicting, in around 14 million stitches, scenes of local and national history.

☎ 01392 255573   www.exeter-cathedral.org.uk

Exmoor | 164 A3

Unlike the other moorlands of the south-west peninsula, Exmoor is composed of sandstone rather than granite, a feature reflected in its scenery which is less bleak than its neighbours. Acidic soils give rise to a typical high moorland flora of heathers interspersed with bilberry, though on the fringes are pleasant wooded river valleys which provide a greater diversity of wildlife than the upland plateau.

There are many attractive places to visit, including the area around Oare and Badgworthy Water (setting for the novel 'Lorna Doone'), Tarr Steps, and the little towns of Dulverton, Dunster, Porlock and Washford. Dunkery Beacon, the highest point at 1703ft (519m), provides views as far as the Brecon Beacons to the north and the Mendips to the east. The moor ends abruptly at the coast with a series of headlands and cliffs, the latter being amongst the highest in England. Minehead is the chief coastal resort, but Watchet, Blue Anchor and Porlock Weir are well worth a visit. Over 600 miles (960km) of foot and bridlepath cross the moor, making it a popular area for walking and riding.

Farleigh Hungerford Castle | 167 E2

Extensive ruins of a 14th century castle built by Sir Thomas Hungerford. The chapel has undergone major conservation work and contains particularly fine wall paintings, stained glass and tombs of the Hungerford family.

☎ 01225 754026   www.english-heritage.org.uk

Finch Foundry (NT) | 149 G1

Opened in 1814, this water-powered forge produced hand tools for the agricultural and mining industries until 1960. Regular demonstrations show the three waterwheels driving the massive tilt hammers and grindstone.

☎ 01837 840046   www.nationaltrust.org.uk

Flambards Village Theme Park | 145 D4

A theme park combining historical re-creations with the more characteristic adventure rides such as roller coaster and log flume.

The Victorian Village comprises shops and houses furnished and equipped with original items, while 'Britain in the Blitz' is an authentic representation of a street blitzed in World War II.

☎ 01326 573404

Fleet Air Arm Museum | 166 C5

A museum dedicated to the history of maritime aviation and in particular the Royal Naval Air Service. There are around 40 historic aircraft on display, together with a range of exhibits – a particular highlight is the Carrier Hall which contains a representation of a 1970s aircraft carrier. The Restoration Hangar has a viewing window for visitors to observe ongoing projects. For younger visitors there is an adventure playground and a flight simulator.

☎ 01935 840565   www.fleetairarm.com

Forde Abbey | 153 G2

In a superb location on the banks of the River Axe, this former Cistercian monastery, founded in 1140, became a private home in 1649. The beautifully furnished rooms have splendid plaster ceilings, and a particular treasure is the set of Mortlake Tapestries of designs originally drawn for the Sistine Chapel.

The 30 acre (12ha) gardens are considered amongst the best in England, with borders displaying vivid colour, an impressive rockery, wonderful bog garden with drifts of Asiatic primulas and a background of sweeping lawns and mature specimen trees.

☎ 01460 221900   www.fordeabbey.co.uk

Forest of Dean

Forest of Dean | 181 F1

Lying between the Rivers Wye and Severn, this former royal hunting forest has the largest area of 150 year old oak trees in Britain. Ponds, streams, an arboretum and nature reserve make this an area where peace and tranquility can be enjoyed along with a rich cultural and industrial heritage which can be investigated through several themed trails. Speech House is now a hotel and conference centre but was built in 1676 as a hunting lodge for Charles II. It later becoming a meeting place for the locals and is still a focal point for the entire forest. Amongst the diverse flora and fauna are rare birds, wild boar and even an occasional polecat. There is ample opportunity for outdoor pursuits – canoeing, caving, climbing, cycling and horse riding or just a leisurely stroll around one of the many lakes and ponds.

☎ 01594 812388   www.forestofdean.gov.uk

SOUTH WEST ENGLAND

⭐ Geevor Tin Mine `144 A3`

A working tin mine until 1990, this is one of the largest mining history sites in the country. The mine's surface buildings have been restored and visitors can look round the processing plants where the ore was crushed. A highlight is an underground tour of an adit, or horizontal passage, which gives the merest hint of the former working conditions. A small museum has a model of the site plan and describes the method of tin production.

☎ 01736 788662   www.geevor.com

✝ Glastonbury Abbey `166 B4`

Magnificent ruins of an historic abbey whose foundation by Saxon kings in the 7th century probably predates the town. The repeated target of Viking attacks in the 8th and 9th centuries, the abbey's fortunes were revitalised by St Dunstan's appointment as abbot in AD940, and the building was considerably enlarged. A devastating fire in 1184, and the subsequent need for rebuilding funds, led to the Arthurian legend when the monks fortuitously 'discovered' the bodies of Arthur and Guinevere buried in the graveyard.

The abbey did not survive the Dissolution of the Monasteries, but the remains, together with an interpretation area, clearly indicate its wealth and importance in medieval times. The Glastonbury Thorn, legendary off-shoot of Joseph of Arimathea's staff, still grows in the grounds.

☎ 01458 832267   www.glastonburyabbey.com

⭐ Glastonbury Tor `166 C4`

This solitary mound of Triassic rock rises 518ft (158m) above the southern edge of the Somerset Levels in an area subject to tidal inundations as recently as the early 17th century. The tor was settled in Neolithic times with a lake village at its base. The summit tower has been re-opened after structural repairs and the tor can be reached by a park and ride bus from the abbey, for which there is a small charge.

Goonhilly Satellite Earth Station

✱ Glendurgan (NT) `145 E4`

Located at the mouth of the Helford Estuary, this splendid 40 acre (16ha) valley garden was created in 1820. It contains many fine specimen trees, including a poplar which grew 79ft (24m) in 14 years, and an interesting laurel maze. In spring there is an outstanding display of magnolias, camellias and wild flowers.

☎ 01326 862090   www.nationaltrust.org.uk

✝ Gloucester Cathedral `399 B2`

Christian worship has taken place on this site since AD679 though the present building was started in 1089 and consecrated in 1100. King Henry III was crowned here, the only monarch to have been crowned outside Westminster since the Norman conquest. The 14th century fan vaulted cloisters are amongst the earliest and finest in the world. There are frequent exhibitions and guided tours to the top of the tower (for which there is a charge), reached by climbing 269 steps.

☎ 01452 528095   www.gloucestercathedral.org.uk

🚂 Gloucestershire & Warwickshire Railway `196 C5`

Originally part of the Great Western main line from Cheltenham to Birmingham which closed in 1960, this steam and diesel railway passes through picturesque Cotswold scenery during a 20 mile (32km) round trip from Toddington to Cheltenham Racecourse. There is a static display of locomotives and rolling stock at Toddington station.

☎ 01242 621405   www.gwsr.plc.uk

🏠 Godolphin House `144 C3`

Dating from around 1475, this delightful Tudor/Stuart mansion was for generations home to the Godolphin family whose fortune was founded on tin. The house contains some fine 16th and 17th century English oak furniture and paintings, and there are interesting formal medieval gardens and a wagon collection in the Elizabethan stables.

☎ 01736 763194   www.godolphinhouse.com

☐ Golden Cap `154 A3`

This sea cliff, the highest on the south coast at 626ft (191m), is named and formed from a sandstone outcrop weathered to a golden brown. There are spectacular views from the summit, particularly the panorama from Start Point in the west to Portland in the east.

www.nationaltrust.org.uk

⭐ Goonhilly Satellite Earth Station `145 E4`

Located on the barren uplands of the Lizard peninsula, this is one of the world's largest satellite communications centres, with a site comprising more than 60 satellite dishes. The main dish, measuring 108ft (33m), has listed building status. The station deals with huge numbers of television broadcasts, international telephone calls and e-mails via satellite equipment and fibre optic cables.

The informative visitor centre is host to a range of activities including its interactive exhibition area with high speed internet access and virtual imaging. A guided tour of the site, which is a National Nature Reserve, is also available.

☎ 0800 679593   www.goonhilly.bt.com

🏠 Great Chalfield Manor (NT) `167 F1`

Built in the late 15th century and sensitively restored in Edwardian times, this delightful moated manor house has beautiful oriel windows and the original Great Hall, complete with minstrels' gallery.

☎ 01225 782239   www.nationaltrust.org.uk

✝ Hailes Abbey (NT) `196 C4`

This Cistercian abbey was founded in 1246 and in 1270 was gifted a phial containing what was said to be the blood of Christ. After the 1539 Dissolution, parts of the site survived as a mansion house but fell into disuse in the 18th century. Excavation of the heavily overgrown site took place in the late 19th century. Little is left of the buildings apart from the remains of the cloister arches.

☎ 01242 602398   www.nationaltrust.org.uk

⭐ Hardy Monument `154 C4`

Standing 770ft (240m) above sea level on the highest point of Black Down Hill, this 70ft (21m) monument was erected in memory of Thomas Masterman Hardy, captain of the *Victory* at the Battle of Trafalgar. 121 stone steps lead to the top from where there are magnificent views.

🏠 Hardy's Cottage `154 D3`

A small cob and thatch cottage with delightful garden, birthplace of the novelist Thomas Hardy in 1840 and built by his great grandfather. Two of Hardy's books were written here and set in the local area.

☎ 01305 262366   www.nationaltrust.org.uk

☐ Hartland Quay `162 C3`

An isolated hamlet at the end of a toll road (charge in summer only), dwarfed by dramatic cliffs whose contorted structure provides evidence of former massive earth movements. Reduced now to a few cottages and tourist facilities, including a museum depicting the area's history, Hartland Quay was once a thriving little port supplying this remote area. Walks on the surrounding cliffs provide breathtaking views of this austere coastline.

www.elmscott.freeservers.com

⭐ Hay Tor Granite Tramway `152 A5`

A relic of the former granite quarrying industry, these tracks, constructed of the stone they were built to carry, run from the flanks of Hay Tor to Stover Canal some 10 miles (16km) away.

✱ Hestercombe `165 F5`

Three centuries of garden history are contained in this 50 acre (20ha) Grade I garden.

The Georgian landscape garden, designed in the late 1750s by Coplestone Warre Bampfylde whose family owned the estate from 1391 – 1872, comprises lakes, pleasant woodland walks and temples set in 40 acres (16ha). The Victorian garden was created for Viscount Portman in the late 19th century, and in summer the formal bedding provides an exuberance of colour. However, Hestercombe is best known for its Edwardian garden, designed by Sir Edwin Lutyens and planted by Gertrude Jekyll in what is considered to be their finest collaboration.

☎ 01823 413923   www.hestercombegardens.com

Hestercombe

✱ Hidcote Manor Gardens (NT) `197 D3`

The Hidcote estate was bought by a wealthy American widow in 1907. The garden was created by her son, Lawrence Johnston, who took a keen interest in gardening which grew to a point where his designs were to have influences on many other gardens, for example Sissinghurst. The garden is arranged as a series of outdoor 'rooms', creating many different moods as a journey through the garden is taken. The garden is now in the ownership of the National Trust.

☎ 01386 438333

Hidcote Manor Gardens

⭐ Holnicote Estate (NT) `164 C3`

Given to the National Trust in 1944 by Sir Richard Acland, the estate consists of more than 12,000 acres (5042ha) of varied scenery, ranging from moors and woodlands, to cliffs and beaches. It includes the high points of Exmoor at Dunkery and Selworthy Beacons, with their sensational views, and a 5 mile (8km) stretch of coastline. The village of Selworthy, one of the prettiest on the moor, was built by the Acland family for their estate workers.

☎ 01643 862452   www.nationaltrust.org.uk

🏠 Horton Court (NT) `181 G4`

The remains of a 12th century rectory, probably the oldest in England, consisting of a Norman hall and a particularly good example of an ambulatory.

☎ 0117 937 2501   www.nationaltrust.org.uk

❄ Iford Manor `167 E2`

Delightful Grade I early 20th century garden in a hillside setting by the River Frome, formerly owned by the architect and landscape gardener Harold Peto. It was designed in an Italianate style, complete with terraces, colonnade, cloisters, statuary and fountains, but there is also a lovely meadow of naturalised bulbs, notably martagon lilies. There are magnificent views of the local countryside.

☎ 01225 863146   www.ifordmanor.co.uk

⬜ Jurassic Coast `153`

This stretch of East Devon and Dorset coastline, between Exmouth in the west and Studland in the east, has been designated a World Heritage Site. Its outstanding geological and palaeontological locations, coupled with stunning and varied coastal scenery, make a visit almost compulsory to appreciate this fine example of the natural landscape.

www.jurassiccoast.com

⭐ Kennack Sands `145 E5`

Two sheltered, sandy beaches, considered amongst the cleanest in Britain, located in an Area of Outstanding Natural Beauty.

🏠 ❄ Killerton (NT) `152 C2`

A hillside garden of around 20 acres (8ha) landscaped by John Veitch. The garden is particularly lovely in spring, although attractive

throughout the year. The 18th century house contains period furniture and is home to a significant costume collection which changes annually. The extensive surrounding parkland provides delightful walks.

☎ 01392 881345   www.nationaltrust.org.uk

🏠 Kingston Lacy (NT) `155 F2`

Designed in the 17th century for the Bankes family following the slighting of Corfe Castle, and later restyled by Sir Charles Barry, this mansion is home to a wealth of treasures. These include paintings by Titian, Rubens and Raphael, an impressive marble staircase from Italy and a striking Spanish room decorated in gilded leather.

The formal garden is surrounded by 250 acres (100ha) of wooded parkland with waymarked walks, or there are longer walks along ancient trackways that can be taken through the 8795 acre (3520ha) estate.

☎ 01202 883402   www.nationaltrust.org.uk

❄ Kingston Maurward Park `154 C3`

Gardens and parkland of 35 acres (14ha) surrounding a delightful Georgian mansion which is now an agricultural college. The restored Edwardian Garden is divided into a series of outdoor 'rooms' and there is an attractive rose garden, colourful herbaceous borders and drifts of spring bulbs, while the National Collections of Penstemons and Salvias are also kept here. A small farm park provides interest for children.

☎ 01305 215000   www.kmc.ac.uk

🏠 ❄ Knightshayes Court (NT) `152 C1`

Designed by William Burges, this elaborate Victorian Gothic house features ornate interior decoration including painted ceilings and a minstrels' gallery.

The 50 acre (20ha) gardens, amongst the finest in the county, are of interest throughout the year and contain both formal and informal plantings.

☎ 01884 254665   www.nationaltrust.org.uk

❄ Knoll Gardens `347 B1`

A garden of 6 acres (2.5ha) with interesting water features and over 6000 well-labelled plants from around the world in colourful themed gardens. It includes the National Collection of Mahonias and a developing retail nursery.

☎ 01202 873931   www.knollgardens.co.uk

✝ Lacock Abbey (NT) `168 A1`

Founded in 1232, but converted to a country house around 1540 following the Dissolution of the Monasteries. The cloisters, chapter house, sacristy and monastic rooms have been preserved, while an octagonal tower was built in the Tudor period, and further work in the 18th century included a fine Gothic entrance hall. The grounds have lovely displays of spring flowers, a Victorian woodland garden and restored botanic garden. A converted 16th century barn houses the Fox Talbot Museum of Photography, which commemorates the work of the pioneering photographer who lived here.

☎ 01249 730277   www.nationaltrust.org.uk

⭐ Land's End `144 A4`

Traditionally considered the south west extremity of the British mainland, this is a granite headland with spectacular cliff scenery. Although commercialisation with a theme park is considered by some to have spoiled the area, a short walk along the cliffs provides an escape from the crowds to a more natural environment.

🏠 ❄ Lanhydrock (NT) `147 E3`

This imposing residence originally dates from the 17th century but was largely rebuilt following a devastating fire in 1881. 50 rooms are open to the public, including state rooms and nurseries, sculleries and kitchens, containing state-of-the-art Victorian furniture and equipment, and the house provides a fascinating insight into the 'Upstairs, Downstairs' way of life. However, the centrepiece is the impressive 96ft (30m) Long Gallery, chief relic of the 17th century building, with its splendid plasterwork ceiling depicting scenes from the Old Testament.

The 900 acre (364ha) estate, extending down to the banks of the River Fowey, includes both formal and woodland areas as well as parkland, and contains some exceptional specimen trees from a collection started in the early 17th century. Magnificent spring displays of magnolias, camellias and rhododendrons give way in summer to colourful herbaceous borders and annual bedding in the formal garden.

☎ 01208 265950   www.nationaltrust.org.uk

Lanhydrock

🚂 Lappa Valley Railway `146 C4`

This 15 inch (38cm) narrow-gauge railway was originally a mineral line running between Newquay and East Wheal Rose. A short section, passing through a scenic valley, has been restored. The surrounding parkland includes woodland walks and play areas.

☎ 01872 510317   www.lappavalley.co.uk

🏰 Launceston Castle `148 D2`

Located in a commanding position above the town where it formerly controlled the main route into Cornwall, this is now a medieval castle ruin built on the motte of the original Norman stronghold.

🚂 Launceston Steam Railway `147 G1`

This narrow-gauge steam railway links Launceston with the little village of New Mills, a distance of 2.5 miles (4km). The carriages are hauled by Victorian steam locomotives through scenic countryside and there are a range of walks that can be taken from both stations. The railway workshops in Launceston are open to visitors.

☎ 01566 775665

⬜ Lizard Peninsula `145 E4`

The coastal scenery of the Lizard peninsula is a striking combination of headlands, coves, cliffs and stacks cut out of the distinctive red and green serpentine rock which is typical of this area. Particularly attractive are Mullion Cove, Kynance Cove and Cadgwith village, while more dramatic locations include the west coast cliffs and the collapsed cavern which forms the Devil's Frying Pan. The peninsula culminates in Lizard Point, a headland forming the southerly tip of the British mainland.

Longleat House — 167 F3

A magnificent Elizabethan mansion set in 900 acres (360ha) of rolling park landscaped by Lancelot 'Capability' Brown.

The house, built for Sir John Thynne, and still belonging to his descendants, was completed in 1580. Inside, it has been sumptuously decorated with gilded, painted Italianate ceilings designed by John Dibblee Crace in the 1870s and 1880s. Furniture ranges from 16th century English pieces to splendid French work of the 17th and 18th centuries, together with some unusual Italian examples. Many other treasures have been accumulated by the family over the centuries, including a fine collection of paintings by English, Dutch and Italian masters, 16th and 17th century Flemish tapestries and 40,000 books housed in seven libraries.

The grounds, bordered by woodland, include formal gardens, plantings of rhododendrons and a handsome lake.

☎ 01985 844400   www.longleat.co.uk

(Longleat House)

Longleat Safari Park — 167 F3

Set in the magnificent grounds of Longleat House, the Park was opened in 1966, the first of its kind in the country. Since then, an amazing range of attractions has been added, though lions, tigers, elephants, giraffes and many other animals can still be seen in the drive-through Safari Park. The grounds boast several mazes and labyrinths, including arguably the world's largest yew hedge maze, further animal attractions, a permanent Dr Who exhibition, narrow-gauge railway, boat trips, simulator rides and children's play areas. A passport ticket is available for the attractions package.

☎ 01985 844400   www.longleat.co.uk

Lost Gardens of Heligan — 145 G2

This is one of Europe's largest garden restoration projects. Originally developed by the Tremayne family in the late 18th century, the 57 acres (23ha) of gardens gradually descended into an apparent wilderness when the house was taken over as a military hospital in World War I, and most of the workforce of 22 gardeners enlisted. Little was done to remedy the situation until the early 1990s, when the structure of the original magnificent garden was uncovered, largely at the instigation of Tim Smit who inspired the Eden Project.

The estate, including gardens and parkland, totals about 200 acres (80ha), with palm trees, tree ferns and bamboos giving it a subtropical atmosphere. Extensive flower and vegetable gardens are now back in production. Visitors can bear witness to the estate's return to productivity by sampling the results in the garden's restaurant.

☎ 01726 845100   www.heligan.com

Lulworth Castle — 155 E4

A 17th century hunting lodge badly damaged by fire in 1929 and subsequently restored. Features include a reconstructed kitchen, dairy, cellar and laundry. The adjacent Roman Catholic chapel was the first to be built after the Reformation, its design reflecting George III's stipulation that its identity should be disguised before he gave permission.

☎ 01929 400352   www.lulworth.com

Lulworth Cove & Heritage Centre — 155 E4

An accident of geology, where the sea has breached resistant coastal limestone rocks to erode the softer clay and sand deposits inland, has led to the development of this striking, circular cove. Elsewhere in the area exposed rocks bear witness to massive earth movements millions of years ago, a particularly memorable example being at Stair Hole just west of the cove's mouth.

The focal point of the Heritage Centre is a rock display tracing the geological history of the area. A video shows how the power of the sea has directly influenced the development of this amazing natural scenery.

☎ 01929 400587   www.lulworth.com

★ Lundy Island — 162 B1

A granite island, 3 miles (5km) north to south and 0.5 miles (1km) east to west, located at the entrance to the Bristol Channel 11 miles (17km) north-north-west of Hartland Point. Noted particularly for its scenery and wildlife, most of the island has been designated a Site of Special Scientific Interest, while the surrounding sea area is currently England's only Marine Nature Reserve.

The island rises to a height of 400ft (120m), the exposed west coast having the more dramatic scenery, whilst exposure to salt spray ensures a maritime flora including thrift and sea campion. Trees are restricted to the more sheltered east coast which is home to the Lundy Cabbage, found only on the island. 35 different breeding species of bird nest here, notably the puffin; Lundy means 'puffin island' in Norse. The surrounding coastal waters are home to sea anemones, sponges and corals, some brightly coloured, and also to seals and basking sharks. Access is by the *Oldenburg*, the island's own boat which sails from Bideford three times a week in summer and twice weekly in winter.

☎ 01271 863636   www.lundyisland.co.uk

(Lost Gardens of Heligan)

★ Lydford Gorge (NT) — 149 E2

Dramatic and awe-inspiring gorge carved into slate from the Upper Devonian period, a less durable rock than the granite traditionally associated with Dartmoor. The force of the water carried along rocks and boulders which have carved out sizeable potholes in the river bed, the most striking of these being the Devil's Cauldron which forms a breathtaking whirlpool.

The gorge is 1.5 miles (2.5km) long, up to 200ft (70m) deep and includes the 100ft (35m) White Lady Waterfall. A circular walk descends through woodland to the White Lady then follows a delightful route through the gorge itself and is particularly attractive in Autumn. In places the path can be narrow and slippery.

☎ 01822 820320   www.nationaltrust.org.uk

Lydiard Mansion — 182 C4

A beautifully restored Georgian mansion now under council ownership, former home of the Bolingbroke family and still containing their furniture and paintings. The surrounding parkland with its lawns, lakes and woodland offers pleasant walks, and there are children's play areas. Access to the grounds is free.

☎ 01793 770401   www.swindon.gov.uk

(Lynton & Lynmouth Cliff Railway)

Lynton & Lynmouth Cliff Railway — 164 A3

Funded by Sir George Newnes (the wealthy London publisher of 'Tit Bits' and 'The Strand') and completed in 1890, the cliff railway is a magnificent example of Victorian engineering and ingenuity. At the time, it greatly enhanced the tourist potential of this picturesque area, by giving visitors easy access from Lynmouth, where the boats docked, to Lynton, at the top of the 500ft (152m) cliff.

Open to the public at specific times; a trip on this 'green' listed monument is a must.

Lytes Cary Manor (NT) — 166 C5

Delightful manor house, with 14th century chapel, dating mainly from the 15th century when the Great Hall was built, but extended in the 16th century. The house was restored in the 20th century and furnished in period style, while the garden was also replanted in a series of 'rooms' with topiary and colourful, well-stocked herbaceous borders.

☎ 01458 224471   www.nationaltrust.org.uk

Lydford Gorge

🏛 Maiden Castle   154 C4

The name deriving from the Celtic 'Mai Dun', or Great Hill, this is one of the largest Iron Age hillforts in Europe, first developed in Stone Age times around 3000BC. Bronze Age burials have been discovered in one area, but the site was increased to its current size of 47 acres (19ha) in the Iron Age, around 450 – 300BC. Around AD43 the fort was taken by the Romans. The foundations of a Roman temple built in the 4th century can still be seen. The fort was later abandoned, but even today remains a hugely impressive site.

www.english-heritage.org.uk

❇ Mapperton   154 B3

A delightful terraced garden around a 17th century manor house (limited opening). The upper garden is Italianate, with topiary and formal borders, and steps leading down to fish ponds.

☎ 01308 862645   www.mapperton.com

❇ Marwood Hill   163 F2

A privately owned, colourful 20 acre (8ha) garden including three small lakes. The extensive collection of plants comprises, amongst others, alpines, clematis, camellias, rhododendrons and fine tree species such as eucalyptus.

☎ 01271 342528

☐ Mendips   166 B2

A ridge of Carboniferous limestone stretching some 25-30 miles (40-48km) roughly between Weston-super-Mare and Shepton Mallet. Although the landscape consists mainly of rounded summits, with a high point of 1068ft (325m) at Black Down, the hills rise quite sharply from the surrounding lowlands, particularly in the north west, and provide extensive views across Exmoor, the Bristol Channel, Somerset and Wiltshire.

The most dramatic scenery can be seen in the famous Cheddar Gorge, a mile (1.6km) long ravine exposing steep cliffs (see page 26). A smaller, unspoilt version can be found at Ebbor Gorge near Wookey Hole. Evidence of prehistoric settlement is common in the area, with Neolithic, Bronze Age and Iron Age remains. From Roman times until the 19th century, lead mining was important, and abandoned mine workings can still be seen on the plateau.

❇ Milton Lodge   166 C3

Attractive Grade II terraced gardens on a hillside overlooking Wells, providing magnificent views of the cathedral. Highlights include naturalised spring bulbs, a variety of climbers, old fashioned and shrub roses and a 7 acre (3ha) arboretum.

☎ 01749 672168

★ Minack Theatre   144 A4

The location on the granite cliffs above Porthcurno beach gives this open-air theatre a spectacular and atmospheric setting. A 17-week summer season includes a wide range of productions which are cancelled only in extreme weather conditions. The visitor centre explains the theatre's history and evolution.

☎ 01736 810181   www.minack.com

❇ Minterne   🌳 154 C2

Formality has not been a consideration in these 20 acres (8ha) of lovely gardens landscaped in the 18th century. A chain of small lakes and streams provides a home for moisture-loving and water plants, whilst major collections of rhododendrons, cherries and acers provide magnificent spring colour and splendid autumn foliage.

☎ 01300 341370

🐘 Monkey World   155 E4

A spacious rescue and rehabilitation centre for primates, set in a delightful area of Dorset heath and woodland. The unspoilt 65 acre (26ha) site is home to more than 150 animals of 15 different species, including over 50 chimpanzees, probably the largest group outside Africa.

☎ 0800 456600   www.monkeyworld.co.uk
☎ 01929 462537

🌲 Moors Valley Country Park   156 A2

A 750 acre (300ha) park providing a range of leisure and recreational facilities in a pleasant countryside setting of lakes and woodland. Attractions include an adventure playground, steam railway, golf course, cycle hire and high ropes course. There is an extensive network of foot and cycle paths, and nature trails.

☎ 01425 470721   www.moors-valley.co.uk

🏛 Morwellham Quay Museum   149 E3

Important since the 12th century as the nearest river port to Tavistock, Morwellham became particularly significant following the discovery of rich copper veins in the locality in the 1840s. The mines closed in the late 19th century and Morwellham was abandoned until 1970 when work was started on an open-air museum. This museum has carefully and accurately re-created the port and associated industrial and domestic buildings to provide a fascinating insight into the life of what was once one of Europe's major copper ports.

☎ 01822 832766   www.morwellham-quay.co.uk

🏠 Mount Edgcumbe   ♻ 346 A3

Superbly located on a hill overlooking Plymouth Sound, this was the family home of the Edgcumbes, built in the 16th century to replace the residence at Cotehele. Following bomb damage in World War II the house was restored by Adrian Gilbert Scott and is furnished with the family's possessions, including Regency furniture, paintings and 16th century tapestries.

☎ 01752 822236   www.gardensincornwall.co.uk

🌳 Mount Edgcumbe Country Park   346 A3

The grounds of Mount Edgcumbe House were developed in the late 18th century to create Cornwall's first landscaped park. The site covers 865 acres (346ha), and as well as the parkland there is a formal area comprising English, French and Italian gardens with the addition of two new gardens to celebrate the family's past links with Australia and America. The park also holds the National Collection of Camellias. There are attractive pathways through the grounds with fine sea views.

☎ 01752 822236   www.gardensincornwall.co.uk

🏛 Museum of Costume   ♻ 388 D1

A sumptuous display, arguably one of the best in the world, of more than 150 figures in original costumes and accessories, from the 16th century to the present day. Housed in the grandly decorated Assembly Rooms (to which entry is free), there is an excellent audio guide to the museum.

☎ 01225 428126   www.museumofcostume.co.uk

★ National Marine Aquarium   ♻ 407 C3

Displayed on three floors, the visitor is taken through a range of reconstructed habitats, from the start of a moorland stream through estuarine and coastal environments to the ocean depths. An engrossing array of aquatic species can be seen, from the bizarre to the beautiful, and there are displays, talks and presentations providing information on the species themselves and the environments, sometimes threatened, that they inhabit.

A new venture has been the sinking of the ex-Royal Navy frigate, *HMS Scylla*, in Whitsand Bay to form an offshore reef. The aim is to study its colonisation by marine life and this can be viewed via underwater camera technology from the aquarium.

This is an exceptionally well-thought-out attraction designed to inform the public about marine habitats.

☎ 01752 600301   www.national-aquarium.co.uk

National Marine Aquarium

National Maritime Museum Cornwall
145 F3

In a striking building which dominates the quayside, this museum is devoted to the sea, boats and their importance in people's lives, with particular emphasis on Cornwall.

☎ 01326 313388   www.nmmc.co.uk

National Maritime Museum

National Waterways Museum
399 B1

200 years of Britain's waterway heritage is exhibited over 3 floors of this historic listed warehouse built in 1873. There are many interesting displays, as well as trips along the canal. The entrance to the museum is in the form of a replica lock chamber complete with dripping water.

☎ 01452 318200   www.nwm.org.uk

Newark Park (NT)
181 G3

A Tudor hunting lodge originally built in around 1550 which was converted into a castellated house by James Wyatt at the end of the 18th century. Limited opening from April to October, but also open weekends in February for an impressive display of snowdrops.

☎ 01453 842644   www.nationaltrust.org.uk

Newquay Zoo
146 C3

The chance to see a wide range of exotic species, housed where possible in natural enclosures. Traditional zoo activities such as feeding displays and children's farm are combined with a special emphasis on wildlife conservation and the associated breeding programme for endangered species.

☎ 01637 873342   www.newquayzoo.co.uk

No. 1 Royal Crescent
167 E1

The first to be built in Royal Crescent in 1768, this imposing Palladian town house has been meticulously restored complete with authentic furnishings and pictures.

☎ 01225 428126   www.bath-preservation-trust.org.uk

Owlpen Manor
182 A3

Bought by the Mander family in 1974, since when the 16th century manor house and estate have been revived and restored. The formal gardens comprise seven hanging terraces dating back to the 16th and 17th centuries and the estate has walks through beech and bluebell woods. The house contains wall paintings, family portraits and Cotswold arts and crafts. There is also a resident ghost, Queen Margaret of Anjou, wife of Henry VI, who stayed here prior to his defeat at Tewkesbury.

☎ 01453 860261   www.owlpen.com

Paignton & Dartmouth Steam Railway
151 E2

A delightful 7 mile (11km) trip from Paignton to Kingswear which gives breathtaking views of Lyme Bay and the Devon coast before passing through woodland along the Dart estuary. It is possible to turn this into a day excursion by taking the passenger ferry from Kingswear to Dartmouth followed by a river trip to Totnes and bus back to Paignton. A 'Round Robin' ticket is available for this.

☎ 01803 555872   www.paignton-steamrailway.co.uk

Paignton Zoo
151 E2

Set in 75 acres (30ha) of attractive surroundings with the emphasis on natural habitats and endangered species conservation, this well organised zoo is home to over 1300 animals and birds. A range of feeding activities and other events takes place every day and in addition there is a miniature railway, playground and animal education centre.

☎ 01803 697500   www.paigntonzoo.org.uk

Painswick Rococo Garden
182 A1

Restoration of the heavily overgrown garden in the 1980s was inspired by a painting by local artist Thomas Robins which showed the 6 acre (2.5ha) site in its original 18th century layout. February sees a spectacular display of snowdrops.

☎ 01452 813204   www.rococogarden.co.uk

Pencarrow
147 E2

A grand, family-owned Georgian mansion with splendid collections of furniture, porcelain and pictures. The 50 acre (20ha) grounds comprise fine formal and woodland gardens with waymarked walks and over 700 varieties of rhododendron giving a spectacular display in spring. The woodland contains a large number of Monkey Puzzle trees – the name is said to have originated here after a guest scraped his hand on one and commented: 'It would puzzle a monkey.'

☎ 01208 841369   www.pencarrow.co.uk

Pendennis Castle
145 F3

This formed part of the coastal defences set up by Henry VIII in response to the threat of war from France and Spain following his divorce from Catherine of Aragon. Occupying a superb site on a headland overlooking the entrance to Carrick Roads, the castle consists of a round tower and gate surrounded by a lower curtain wall. A further outer defence was added by Elizabeth I, but the castle was only attacked during the Civil War when it was besieged by Parliamentarians for five months. A Discovery Centre incorporates interactive displays on the castle's history.

☎ 01326 316594   www.english-heritage.org.uk

Plymouth Dome
407 C2

A visitor centre using multimedia technology to trace the city's history and maritime connections, with breathtaking views of Plymouth Sound from the observation galleries.

☎ 01752 603300   www.plymouthdome.info

Porthcurno Sands
144 A4

A beautiful stretch of clean, silvery sand makes this amongst the best of Cornwall's beaches. Exhilarating walks along the coastal path to the east lead to Treryn Dinas, one of the most spectacular of the Cornish headlands, crowned by the precarious Logan Stone.

Portland Castle
154 C5

A well preserved example of Henry VIII's coastal fortresses overlooking Portland Harbour. Although not seeing action until the 17th century, when it was seized by both Parliamentarians and Royalists, the castle has always had a significant role in coastal defence, being a seaplane station in World War I and heavily involved in D-Day preparations in World War II.

☎ 01305 820539   www.english-heritage.org.uk

Powderham Castle
152 C4

Home to the Courtenay family since 1390, the castle lies in a beautiful setting in a 4000 acre (1600ha) estate on the River Exe estuary. The state rooms are richly decorated and furnished and the marble hall is also of interest, containing a 13ft (4.5m) long case clock.

The grounds provide a variety of activities, including woodland walks, working blacksmith and wheelwright, and children's secret garden.

☎ 01626 890243   www.powderham.co.uk

Prinknash Abbey & Park
182 A1

Around 30 monks live at the abbey which was not completed until 1972. The abbey buildings extend to over 300 acres (120ha) and include the workshops and the old abbey of St Peter's Grange. The surrounding Bird and Deer Park has a children's castle, a Tudor wendy house, aviaries, ponds and lakes, and an abundance of deer, geese, cranes and peacocks.

☎ 01452 812066   www.prinknash-bird-and-deerpark.com

Prior Park (NT)
167 E1

A magnificent location on a hillside to the south of Bath provides the 18th century mansion of Prior Park with splendid panoramic views of the city and surrounding countryside. The delightful landscape garden was created by local businessman Ralph Allen, with input from the poet Alexander Pope and Lancelot 'Capability' Brown. The house is now a school and not open to the public. There is no parking, but a frequent bus service runs from the city centre.

☎ 01225 833422   www.nationaltrust.org.uk

Putlake Adventure Farm
155 F5

An unpretentious farm attraction particularly suitable for younger children, hosting a whole range of activities.

☎ 01929 422917   www.putlakefarm.co.uk

Quince Honey Farm
164 A5

One of the largest honey farms in Britain, with over 1500 hives spread across Devon and Exmoor. In the exhibition area honey bees can be observed at close range, nesting in a variety of man-made and natural habitats as well as in state-of-the-art observation hives.

A wide range of honey-based products is available at the centre's shop.

☎ 01769 572401   www.quincehoney.co.uk

Red Lodge
391 B1

Elizabethan house dating from 1590, substantially modernised around 1730 and now furnished to represent both periods. The highlight is the Great Oak Room with its magnificent oak panels and splendid carved stone chimneypiece.

☎ 0117 921 1360   www.bristol-city.gov.uk

Ridgeway, The

This ancient trackway, formerly used by drovers, traders and occasionally invaders, has been in use for at least 5000 years. There is much evidence of prehistoric occupation in the surrounding area in

the form of burial mounds and hill forts, and there is a particularly memorable stretch taking in Wayland's Smithy, Uffington Castle and the adjacent White Horse. The track runs from Overton Hill near Avebury along the north edge of the Marlborough and Berkshire Downs, crosses the Thames at Goring and continues along the west edge of the Chiltern Hills to Ivinghoe Beacon. The plant life is of special interest as, in some areas, the characteristic, and increasingly rare chalk grassland can still be seen. The bird and insect life is also worthy of note.

★ Roche Chapel   147 D3

Remains of a 14th century chapel perched on a rocky outcrop on the site of what is thought to be an early Christian hermit's cell.

🏛 Roman Baths & Pump Room   388 E2

One of the outstanding Roman sites in Britain, founded in the first century AD for pilgrims visiting the sacred hot springs of the temple to Sulis Minerva. After the Romans left, the site fell into disrepair although the town continued to grow, but by the early 17th century the springs were again attracting interest. A visit in 1702 by Queen Anne further encouraged this interest and by 1720 the town was becoming a highly fashionable spa. Further development in the 19th century led to the uncovering and preservation of the Roman site.

As far back as 10,000 years ago the hot springs had generated human attention as a source of healing. The magnificent Roman complex used lead pipes to conduct the water to a series of bathing rooms which have now been excavated and can be visited, together with the temple remains, hypocausts and cold plunges, aided by an audio guide.

The elegant Pump Room (free entry) was the headquarters of fashionable 18th century society and the visitor can emulate this by taking the waters, or less adventurously, morning coffee or afternoon tea.

☎ 01225 477785   www.romanbaths.co.uk

Roman Baths & Pump Room – Bath

✿ Rosemoor   163 F4

A regional centre for the Royal Horticultural Society (RHS), second only to the gardens at Wisley in importance. Originally 8 acres (3ha), the garden was given to the RHS and a further 32 acres (13ha) was added. The surrounding woodland has been purchased to provide an attractive natural backdrop.

Many rare and interesting plants flourish here, and the woodland garden is considered to be particularly lovely. Other areas of interest include the Rose Garden with 2000 roses in around 200 varieties, stream and bog gardens, colour theme gardens and a kitchen garden.

☎ 01805 624067   www.rhs.org.uk

🏛 Russell-Cotes Art Gallery & Museum   389 F2

This museum houses a combination of the exotic and eclectic in a rather extravagant Italianate villa, built as a testament to the worldly success of Sir Merton Russell-Cotes, who gave it to the town of Bournemouth in 1922, complete with artworks and a notable collection of late 19th century furniture.

☎ 01202 451858   www.russell-cotes.bournemouth.gov.uk

★ S.S. Great Britain   352 B3

Built in Bristol by Isambard Kingdom Brunel in 1843, this is the world's first (and only surviving) ocean-going, iron hulled steam ship driven by a screw propellor. Designed as a passenger vessel for the North Atlantic crossing, she subsequently carried 15,000 migrants to Australia, 40,000 troops to the Crimea, and coal to California, but ended up abandoned in the Falkland Islands. In 1970 she was returned to Bristol, to the same dry dock where she was built. The dockside museum tells the history of this remarkable ship.

☎ 0117 926 0680   www.ss-great-britain.com

✝ St Just in Roseland   145 F3

Although architecturally the church is not of special interest, it has an enchanting waterside setting and a steeply sloping graveyard described by John Betjeman as 'Perhaps the most beautiful churchyard on Earth' with its profusion of palms and subtropical shrubs.

🏰 St Mawes Castle   145 F3

Located on a headland on the east side of the Carrick Roads, this castle was built to defend against a possible French and Spanish invasion following Henry VIII's divorce from Catherine of Aragon and is an excellent example of Tudor military architecture. Captured by Parliamentarians in 1646, with far less trouble than its neighbour Pendennis, it was not re-fortified until the early 20th century, when it formed part of the coastal defences for World Wars I and II.

☎ 01326 270526   www.english-heritage.org.uk

🏰 St Michael's Mount (NT)   144 C3

Dramatic granite island accessible on foot via a causeway at low tide and by ferry at other times. Although generally accepted as a place of spiritual significance, the original settlement on the island may have been a late Iron Age port. The 5th century saw the start of the mount's importance as a place of pilgrimage, when legend has it that a group of fishermen had a vision of St Michael. A Benedictine monastery was founded on the summit in 1135, and following the Dissolution of the Monasteries by Henry VIII the ruins of the building were incorporated into a castle.

The steep slopes of the mount are clothed in subtropical vegetation, and a unique maritime garden of some 20 acres (8ha) has been developed on terraces. The 200ft (60m) ascent to the castle via the cobbled Pilgrims' Steps is quite steep in places, but is well worth it for the spectacular views. The castle itself contains displays of weaponry and other militaria, period furniture, paintings and miniatures.

☎ 01736 710507   www.nationaltrust.org.uk

Salisbury Cathedral

✝ Salisbury Cathedral   408 F2

At Salisbury, one of the world's most celebrated spires soars above an Early English masterpiece of a cathedral, the whole comprising a singularly beautiful medieval building which inspired the famous painting by John Constable. Raised between 1220 – 1258, and with the spire added between 1285 – 1315, this comparatively rapid construction led to a remarkable conformity of style, characterised by slender Purbeck marble pillars, narrow pointed arches and high vaulting.

Inside, the cathedral is relatively austere following a sprucing up by James Wyatt in the 18th century. Treasures include one of the world's oldest working clocks dating from the 14th century, and the largest cloisters in England lead to the beautiful octagonal chapter house which contains one of the four surviving original versions of Magna Carta, considered the best preserved.

The exceptional spire, at 404ft (123m) the tallest in Britain, rests on foundations only 6ft (2m) deep. Guided tours take visitors 332 steps up the tower to the base of the spire and give splendid views over the city.

The cathedral is set in a delightful, large Close which itself contains some memorable buildings, many dating from the 18th century.

☎ 01722 555120   www.salisburycathedral.org.uk

🏠 Saltram House (NT)   346 B2

A former Tudor house redeveloped as a splendid Georgian mansion set in a landscaped park overlooking the Plym estuary. Many of the original contents remain and there are significant pieces by Chippendale and Wedgwood as well as several portraits by Sir Joshua Reynolds, who lived locally. There is some notable work by Robert Adam, and a magnificent 18th century Axminster carpet. There is also an interesting period kitchen, formal gardens and woodland walks.

☎ 01752 333500   www.nationaltrust.org.uk

🏠 Sherborne Castle   154 C1

A splendid Tudor mansion built by Sir Walter Raleigh in 1594 and subsequently extended in the 17th and 18th centuries by the Digby family who have owned it since 1617. The state rooms show a range of decorative styles from the 16th to 19th centuries and there are excellent collections of furniture and fine arts.

The grounds are considered to be amongst the finest to be created by Lancelot 'Capability' Brown, with a 50 acre (20ha) lake and magnificent specimen trees. The 20 acre (8ha) garden has delightful drifts of spring bulbs, colourful summer borders and striking autumn colour. Within the grounds are the remnants of a Norman castle destroyed in the Civil War.

☎ 01935 813182   www.sherbornecastle.com

🏛 Silbury Hill `168 B1`

Constructed around 2500BC, probably using some of the chalk rubble excavated from Avebury, this is thought to be the highest man-made mound in Europe at 130ft (40m). It is estimated that it would have taken 1000 men 10 years to build. No archaeological excavations have ever discovered anything of significance in the mound and its purpose has never been satisfactorily explained.

Unfortunately, continuous wear and tear by people climbing the mound has meant that access is now prohibited.

🦆 Slimbridge Wildfowl & Wetlands Trust `181 G2`

Originated in 1946 by Sir Peter Scott, Slimbridge is the centre of the Wildfowl and Wetlands Trust (WWT) and has become one of the most important wildfowl and wetland conservation centres in the world. 800 acres (320ha) contain species from all over the world, including the rare Hawaiian Goose (Ne Ne) which has been returned to its native habitat because of the success of the breeding project at Slimbridge. The informative visitor centre gives an insight into the birds that make Slimbridge their home, including the largest collection of ducks, geese and swans in the world. There are also sculpture trails, an art gallery and events throughout the year. Winter sees thousands of wild geese feeding in the Severn Estuary which can be viewed from the observation tower.

☎ 01453 890333   www.wwt.org.uk

Slimbridge Wildfowl & Wetlands Trust

🏛 ❋ Snowshill Manor (NT) `196 C4`

In 1919 Charles Wade bought the ruined manor with its 14 acres (5.5ha) of land which he set about restoring using traditional skills. The renovated manor was used as a storage area for the enormous variety of artefacts collected from all over the world. Wade actually lived in the small cottage in the grounds. The tranquil organic gardens give lovely views across the surrounding Cotswold countryside.

☎ 01386 852410   www.nationaltrust.org.uk

🚂 South Devon Railway `151 D1`

This scenic steam railway winds its way along 7 miles (10.5km) of the Dart valley between Buckfastleigh and Totnes on a former Great Western Railway branch line. On site at Buckfastleigh there is a small museum and the chance to see the restoration of some of the rolling stock. There are also model railway exhibits, a children's play area and riverside walks.

☎ 01364 643338   www.southdevonrailway.org

❋ Stapehill Abbey Crafts & Garden `347 B1`

A 19th century Cistercian abbey, now used for a variety of craft workshops. The attractive 30 acre (12ha) gardens are home to many rare and unusual species and include a striking Japanese Garden.

The Countryside Museum has exhibits on social and agricultural history and an assortment of village shops, and Home Farm has a selection of farm animals to be viewed.

☎ 01202 861686

🏛 STEAM Museum of the Great Western Railway `412 A1`

A fascinating museum on the restored site of the former Swindon Railway Works, as much concerned with the lives of the thousands of employees and passengers of the Great Western Railway (GWR) as with the locomotives themselves. Hands-on exhibits and ingenious displays trace the history of the GWR and give an insight into the skills and dedication of the railway workers in every aspect of the enterprise, from Isambard Kingdom Brunel's initial inspiration onwards.

☎ 01793 466646   www.steam-museum.org.uk

★ Stembridge Tower Mill (NT) `166 B4`

Located in a prominent position overlooking the Somerset Levels, this is the last remaining thatched windmill in England. It was built in 1822 and remained in operation until 1910.

☎ 01458 250818   www.nationaltrust.org.uk

✝ Stoke sub Hamdon Priory (NT) `154 A1`

A group of buildings, the remains of a chantry built for a provost and four chaplains in the 14th century by the Beauchamp family. The complex consists of a Great Hall, the only part open to the public, private rooms and a range of outbuildings.

☎ 01985 843600   www.nationaltrust.org.uk

🏛 Stonehenge `168 C3`

An awe-inspiring prehistoric monument constructed in stages between about 5000 and 3000 years ago, now designated a World Heritage Site. The original purpose is uncertain, but suggestions include an astronomical observatory, temple or other sacred site.

Stonehenge was originally a simple bank and ditch excavated by tools made of antler, wood and bone. Some centuries later an inner stone circle was added, though not completed, using bluestones from the Prescelly Mountains in Pembrokeshire. Subsequent modification led to the central altar stone being surrounded by an inner horseshoe of rearranged bluestones and an outer sarsen horseshoe. The final, and major building phase around 1500BC brought massive sarsen stones of up to 50 tons (56 tonnes) from the Marlborough Downs 20 miles (32km) away. These were erected and capped by stone lintels to make a continuous outer ring. The central axis aligns with the point of sunrise on Midsummer Day, giving credence, without supporting evidence, to the idea of Stonehenge as an astronomical calendar.

Today, Stonehenge is effectively an impressive ruin, stones having fallen or been used in the past as a surreptitious resource for other local building projects. Visitors cannot generally walk among the stones, but the site is very atmospheric and views of the stones, particularly near dawn or dusk, are breathtaking.

☎ 01980 624715   www.english-heritage.org.uk

🏰 ❋ Stourhead (NT) `167 E4`

Unlike most estates, where the house takes pride of place, here the 2600 acres (1052ha) of grounds are by far the superior draw, providing an exceptional example of the English landscape garden.

The house, built in 1721 by Colen Campbell for the banker Henry Hoare, is an elegant example of Palladian architecture and contains some good early Chippendale furniture and choice paintings.

Henry Hoare's son, also Henry, designed the garden after returning from a Grand Tour in 1741, his purpose being to emulate scenes from paintings by Poussin and other European landscape artists. The centrepiece, a magnificent lake, was formed by damming the River Stour. The rhododendrons, for which the garden is famed in spring, were a later addition.

King Alfred's Tower, the 150ft (46m) red brick folly at the far end of the estate, provides magnificent views across the grounds and surrounding countryside (open summer afternoons only).

☎ 01747 841152   www.nationaltrust.org.uk

★ Stuart Line Cruises `152 D4`

A family run firm based in Exmouth offering a variety of cruises either in the sheltered Exe estuary or along the coast to Sidmouth, Teignmouth or Torbay. A great opportunity to view the unique south Devon coastal scenery from the sea.

☎ 01395 222144   www.stuartlinecruises.co.uk

🦌 Studland Heath (NT) `155 G4`

This National Nature Reserve on the Isle of Purbeck covers around 1500 acres (631ha) and supports a variety of habitats including heathland, bog and sand dunes. A central feature is the Little Sea, an acidic freshwater lake around which are four hides to observe wintering wildfowl. Another significant area to the west of the reserve is Godlingston Heath, a large tract of lowland heath with populations of all six British species of reptile and the rare Dartford Warbler. Wading birds can be seen on coastal sites and the area is notable for its insect population, particularly dragonflies and butterflies. Footpaths, nature trails, birdwatching hides and leaflets provide access and information for the visitor. There is a parking charge.

☎ 01929 450259   www.nationaltrust.org.uk

🏰 ❋ Sudeley Castle `196 C5`

Once owned by Ethelred the Unready, and more famously home to Katherine Parr, the sixth wife of Henry VIII, Sudeley was a victim of Cromwell's destruction and lay derelict for over 200 years until the ambitious restoration project was started in 1837. There are themed exhibitions, impressive furniture and paintings from such artists as Rubens, Van Dyck and Turner. Ten distinct gardens covering 14 acres (5.5ha) surround the castle and feature a ruined 15th century Tithe Barn. The tomb of Katherine Parr lies in the 15th century St Mary's Church.

☎ 01242 602308   www.sudeleycastle.co.uk

Stonehenge

Swanage Railway 155 G5

A 6 mile (10km) stretch of standard-gauge steam railway running between Swanage and Norden on a trip lasting 25 minutes. The route passes through lovely countryside, including the spectacular ruins of Corfe Castle. A variety of special events takes place throughout the year.

☎ 01929 425800   www.swanagerailway.co.uk

Tank Museum 155 E4

With exhibits ranging from 'Little Willie', the first tank ever built in 1915, to the British Army's most recent 'Challenger 2', this museum contains one of the world's most impressive collections of armoured fighting vehicles. In school holidays, 'Tanks in Action!' displays take place.

☎ 01929 405096   www.tankmuseum.co.uk

Tate St Ives 144 C2

In a splendid location above Porthmeor beach, this art gallery displays work by modern British artists in both permanent and temporary exhibitions. The building itself is quite distinctive and has received several awards for its architecture.

☎ 01736 796226   www.tate.org.uk

Tintagel Castle 148 A2

A dramatic clifftop location gives this extensive, ruined medieval castle spectacular views along the north Cornish coast. Situated on a promontory approached via a narrow neck of land, such an excellent defensive site is likely to have been in use from much earlier times, and Iron Age, Celtic and Roman occupations have been suggested. This lengthy history of occupancy, coupled with the windswept, romantic atmosphere, has helped enhance the idea of Tintagel as the legendary castle of King Arthur.

☎ 01840 770328   www.english-heritage.org.uk

Tintagel Old Post Office 147 E1

Delightful 14th century manor house in the village centre, one room of which was used as a post office in the 19th century.

☎ 01840 770024   www.nationaltrust.org.uk

Tintinhull House (NT) 154 B1

Lovely, colourful formal garden of 1.5 acres (0.5 ha) developed around a 17th century manor house by Phyllis Reiss between 1933 – 61. The planting scheme, influenced by the style of Hidcote, is divided into seven 'rooms', each with its own theme but integrating sympathetically with the others. The house is not open to the public.

☎ 01935 822545   www.nationaltrust.org.uk

Tiverton Castle 152 C1

Although Norman in origin, only the tower and gatehouse remain; the remainder has been much altered, depicting a range of architectural styles. There are attractive gardens and an especially good collection of Civil War arms and armour. Limited opening outside July and August.

☎ 01884 253200   www.tivertoncastle.com

Tiverton Museum 152 C1

A mid 19th century school houses what is probably the largest social history collection in the south west.

☎ 01884 256295   www.tivertonmuseum.org.uk

Torre Abbey 412 E1

Founded in 1196, but partly destroyed during the Dissolution of the Monasteries in 1539, only fragments of the original buildings remain, including the medieval barn and gatehouse. It was converted to a country house and then substantially remodelled in the 19th century and now belongs to the local council, serving in part as a museum and art gallery. There are collections of silver, glass, maritime paintings, Pre-Raphaelite and 20th century art and a room devoted to Agatha Christie memorabilia. Access is free to the grounds which include palm and cactus houses.

☎ 01803 293593   www.torre-abbey.org.uk

Trebah Garden 145 E4

A subtropical garden of 25 acres (10ha) developed in a steep, wooded ravine which conjures up a jungle atmosphere. It is particularly noted for its tree ferns and palms, blue and white hydrangeas and 100 year old rhododendrons. The gardens descend over 200ft (60m) to a private beach on the Helford River estuary.

☎ 01326 250448   www.trebah-gardens.co.uk

Trelissick (NT) 145 F3

A lovely woodland park of around 370 acres (148ha) with magnificent views across the Fal estuary. As with many Cornish coastal gardens, tender and exotic plants flourish, but Trelissick is especially noted for its magnolias, camellias and hydrangeas. The house is not open to the public.

☎ 01872 862090   www.nationaltrust.org.uk

Trengwainton (NT) 144 B3

A garden of interest throughout the year, but especially in spring and early summer, with splendid displays of magnolias, camellias and rhododendrons. Many of the plants found here were brought back from Frank Kingdom Ward's plant hunting expedition in the 1920s. A series of walled gardens contain unusual species particularly suited to the mild climate, and the stream garden in particular is a feast of colour with its primulas, lysichitums and lilies. Superb coastal views can be seen from the restored terrace over Mounts Bay and the Lizard.

☎ 01736 363148   www.nationaltrust.org.uk

Trerice (NT) 146 C4

An attractive Elizabethan manor house considered to be something of an architectural gem with its detailed plaster ceilings, splendid fireplaces and distinctive gabling following the Dutch style. Furnishings include a range of oak and walnut furniture, unusual clocks, embroideries and paintings. The pleasant grounds are planted with an eye for colour and foliage, and the former stables house a small museum tracing the development and history of the lawnmower.

☎ 01637 875404   www.nationaltrust.org.uk

Tresco Abbey Gardens 146 A1

From acacias to agaves, and palms to proteas, these marvellous subtropical gardens, located on the site of a former abbey founded in AD964, contain an amazing variety of plants. The garden was developed between 1843 – 72 by Augustus Smith, who enhanced the naturally mild climate by building tall windbreaks to shelter the site from the worst of the weather.

The site also incorporates the Valhalla Museum of ships' figureheads.

☎ 01720 424105   www.tresco.co.uk

Trewithen 146 D5

Outstanding woodland garden created by George Johnstone in the first half of the 20th century.

Covering around 30 acres (12ha), the gardens are particularly famous for their splendid collections of magnolias, camellias and rhododendrons. The attractive, early Georgian house is open to the public for a limited period in summer.

☎ 01726 883647   www.trewithengardens.co.uk

Truro Cathedral 146 C5

The first cathedral in Britain to be consecrated since the Reformation, this beautiful neogothic building was designed by John Loughborough Pearson and completed in 1910. It was built on the site of St Mary's Parish Church (consecrated in 1259), and part of the old building was incorporated into the new cathedral which has a commanding central location in the city. The Victorian stained glass windows are considered amongst the finest in the world, and other notable features include the Father Willis organ and an excellent collection of Victorian embroidery.

☎ 01872 276782   www.trurocathedral.org.uk

Tyntesfield (NT) 181 E5

A splendid Victorian house built in the Gothic Revival style, with lots of towers and turrets. The interior has been little altered, and there is an extensive collection of Victorian decorative arts plus a range of domestic offices and a family chapel. The unspoilt 500 acre (200ha) estate comprises parkland, lovely formal gardens with superb views from the terrace, and a delightful kitchen garden. This is a recent acquisition by the National Trust, and is undergoing extensive renovation. Admission is by pre-booked guided tour. It will be some years before the house is fully open. Access is by a park and ride service from Nailsea.

☎ 0870 458 4500   www.nationaltrust.org.uk

Ugbrooke 152 B5

Home to the Clifford family for the past 300 years, this former Tudor mansion was substantially rebuilt by Robert Adam in 1750, the chapel and library wing being particularly characteristic of Adam's style. The house fell into some disrepair in the mid 20th century but has been handsomely and meticulously restored and contains fine displays of furniture, paintings, embroideries and a rare military collection.

The parkland was landscaped by Lancelot 'Capability' Brown and contains many fine specimen trees, while the formal gardens include a box parterre, Spanish garden and lakeside walks.

☎ 01626 852179

Watermouth Castle 163 F1

Built in 1825, this castellated mansion is now a popular family destination with a great range of attractions including mechanical music demonstrations, a maze, cider making and dairy exhibits, and a wide selection of children's rides and play activities.

☎ 01271 863879   www.watermouthcastle.com

Watersmeet House (NT) 164 A3

Former fishing lodge built in 1832 in a beautiful wooded valley at the confluence of Hoar Oak Water and the East Lyn River. It now houses a National Trust information centre and shop, serving as a focus for the many delightful walks in the area.

☎ 01271 850887   www.nationaltrust.org.uk

✠ Wells Cathedral   166 C3

Dominating the centre of Wells, England's smallest city, this has been the site of a religious building since the 8th century. The present cathedral was founded in 1180, but was built in phases over the following 400 years, thus incorporating several different architectural styles. However, the original Saxon font was retained and is still used for baptisms.

The splendid west front, one of the most outstanding façades in the country, was completed in 1250 and accommodates nearly 300 pieces of statuary. Within the magnificent Gothic interior are unusual scissor-shaped arches, constructed as additional support when the combined weight of tower and spire proved too much for the lower stage of the tower. The upper tower and spire were subsequently destroyed by fire and not rebuilt; the lower tower was rebuilt to a height of 182ft (55m), the highest in the county.

Other highlights include the 14th century clock, amongst the oldest in the world, mid 20th century colourful embroideries in the choir, medieval stained glass, and probably the longest medieval library building (168ft, 51m) in England, containing documents which date from the 10th century.

☎ 01749 674483

(Wells Cathedral)

⋔ West Kennet Long Barrow   168 C1

Possibly England's finest burial mound, this Neolithic chambered tomb was the site of around 50 burials. Measuring 343ft (105m) by 76ft (23m), the mound's entrance is protected by massive sarsen stones and it is possible to walk into the stone burial chamber a short way into the mound.

www.english-heritage.org.uk

🚂 West Somerset Railway   165 E4

At 20 miles (32km), this is one of the longest stretches of preserved steam railway in Britain. It runs along the north Somerset coast from Minehead to Watchet, then continues inland via several small stations to Bishop's Lydeard. The original line continued to Taunton, and there is a bus link for those wishing to complete the journey.

☎ 01643 704996   www.west-somerset-railway.co.uk

✺ Westbury Court (NT)   181 G1

This water garden originated between 1696 and 1705 and was the National Trust's first garden restoration. It is the earliest Dutch water garden remaining in the country and has been planted with species dating back to before 1700. A restored pavilion sits at the head of a long canal bordered by yew hedges, and in the grounds are a walled garden and a Holm oak, said to be the oldest in the country.

☎ 01452 760461   www.nationaltrust.org.uk

★ Westbury White Horse   167 F2

The chalk downs of central Wiltshire are ideal for these massive hill carvings which are not, as generally assumed, particularly ancient. The Westbury horse is considered the oldest in the county and is perhaps the best sited. It is thought to date from the late 17th century, replacing an earlier one, possibly of Saxon origin. Above the horse is a large Iron Age fort with excellent views.

www.wiltshirewhitehorses.org.uk

✺ Westonbirt – The   182 A3
     National Arboretum

The Arboretum is now in the care of the Forestry Commission but originates from 1829 when Robert Holford decided to extend his father's estate at Westonbirt. There are 18,000 trees and shrubs from all over the world, many of them rare or endangered, and some of which date back to the original planting, making this one of the finest tree collections in the world. Covering 600 acres (240 ha), it is not only the trees that make Westonbirt special but also the wild flowers, fungi, birds and animals that can be enjoyed along 17 miles (27km) of paths and trails. The displays of rhododendrons, azaleas, magnolias and the wild flowers in the Silk Wood are at their best in May, while autumn sees a spectacular change of colour throughout the gardens. The International Festival of Gardens takes place from June to September.

☎ 01666 880220

🏛 Wheal Martyn   147 E4

A fascinating look at the history of the china clay industry on a 26 acre (10ha) site dating from the 1870s and restored in the 1970s. Some areas of the site are still in active production and can be seen from a viewing platform. The visitor centre has displays and exhibits on both the raw materials and finished products of the industry and a trail takes the visitor round the old clay works. The site also contains a nature trail and adventure play area.

☎ 01726 850362   www.wheal-martyn.com

🏰 ✺ Wilton House   168 B4

Following the Dissolution of the Monasteries, the Benedictine site and land at Wilton were granted by Henry VIII to William Herbert, who incorporated the abbey ruins into a Tudor mansion. After a fire in 1647, Inigo Jones and John Webb redesigned and rebuilt the house in the Palladian style. The chief features of this rebuilding are the state rooms, particularly the Single and Double Cube rooms, so-called because of their precise dimensions, and renowned for their outstanding painted ceilings and elaborate plasterwork. The Double Cube room, arguably the foremost surviving example of a 17th century state room in England, was designed for the exhibition of family portraits by Van Dyck, and these can still be seen in their original setting. Elsewhere in the house there are paintings by Reynolds, Rembrandt, Brueghel, Rubens and Poussin, amongst others, making a collection which is considered one of the finest in Europe.

The 21 acre (8.5ha) grounds, bounded by the Rivers Nadder and Wylye, contain both formal gardens and landscaped parkland. Fine specimen trees can be seen on the woodland walks and there are architectural features such as the well-known Palladian Bridge. Other additions include the Millennium Water Feature and, for younger visitors, an adventure playground.

☎ 01722 746729   www.wiltonhouse.com

🏚 Woodchester Mansion   182 A2

A highly unusual place to visit, the mansion was abandoned before completion in 1870 and is in virtually the same state now. Much of the impressive craftsmanship of the time can be seen, something that would not have been possible if the mansion had been finished. Endangered lesser and greater horseshoe bats live in the roof spaces which can be observed by closed-circuit cameras. The mansion is open at weekends during the summer months.

☎ 01453 750455   www.woodchestermansion.org.uk

(Westonbirt – The National Arboretum)

🏯 Woodlands Leisure Park   151 E2

One of the biggest indoor activity complexes in the country, including the three-floor Ice Palace, specifically designed for the under sevens. Outdoors comprises 60 acres (24ha) of rides and activities in a wooded valley.

☎ 01803 712598   www.woodlandspark.com

★ Wookey Hole Caves   166 C3
     & Papermill

Spectacular caves carved out where underground streams have percolated through carboniferous limestone, gradually dissolving the rock over millions of years. Later precipitation of this dissolved limestone has resulted in striking formations of stalactites and stalagmites, some of which resemble human figures, most notably the Witch of Wookey. The dramatic nature of the caves is emphasised by skilful lighting.

Excavations have demonstrated that the caves were inhabited as long as 30,000 years ago, and tools have been discovered together with bones from species such as woolly rhinoceros, cave lions, mammoths and hyenas. Occupation is thought to have continued until Roman times.

The emerging underground River Axe at Wookey Hole has, in the past, been harnessed to provide water power, initially for woollen mills and subsequently for paper making. Visitors can see this traditional paper making process at the restored paper mill.

☎ 01749 672243   www.wookey.co.uk

01389 713 713

Head office

With Compliments

(Yahoo)   lochs and glens

LOCH AWE HOTEL, LOCHAWE VILLAGE, ARGYLL PA33 1AQ
Telephone 01838 200 261   Fax 01838 200 379

SOUTH EAST ENGLAND

This appealing corner of England is alive with attractive market towns, quaint villages, historical stately homes, beautiful gardens and huge, strategically sited castles. Here, the wooded Weald and the green sward of the South Downs lead down to the Channel coast with its small traditional harbours and large bustling shipping ports. From Europe this is often the gateway to England, giving visitors the opportunity to acquaint themselves with the foibles and idiosyncrasies of Britain in one of its most pleasant and verdant regions.

Bodiam Castle

Alfriston Clergy House (NT)   160 A3

A thatched, half-timbered 14th century Wealden Hall House with a pretty cottage garden. It was the first historic building acquired by the National Trust in 1896, purchased for a nominal £10. The house is oak framed and infilled with wattle and daub. One of the beams has a carving of an oak leaf which some believe gave rise to the adoption of the National Trust's famous logo.

☎ 01323 870001   www.nationaltrust.org.uk

Amberley Museum   158 C2

This 36 acre (14.5ha) open-air museum, occupying a former chalk quarry, is dedicated to south east England's industrial past, also featuring various craftspeople demonstrating their skills. Visitors can travel around the site by vintage bus and narrow-gauge railway.

☎ 01798 831370   www.amberleymuseum.co.uk

Arundel Castle   158 C3

Situated on a hill with views over the River Arun and out to sea, this castle is an impressive sight, dominating the nearby town with its towers and battlements. The castle began life at the end of the 11th century with the building of the motte. The gatehouse dates from 1070, but most of the rest is 19th century.

Arundel Castle is the ancestral home of the Dukes of Norfolk, who have played an important role in English history, the third duke being the uncle of both Anne Boleyn and Catherine Howard, wives of Henry VIII.

Within the castle there are fine collections of paintings by Van Dyck, Gainsborough, as well as 16th century furniture, tapestries, clocks and armour. The magnificent grounds include a Victorian kitchen and flower gardens. The Fitzalan Chapel is worth a visit.

☎ 01903 882173   www.arundelcastle.org

Arundel Castle

Ascott (NT)   199 D5

This was formerly a half-timbered 17th century farmhouse but was much altered and enlarged when it came into the ownership of the de Rothschild family in 1876. The outstanding art collection contains paintings by Gainsborough, Rubens, Hogarth and some of the Dutch masters, whilst there is also some notable Chinese porcelain and Chippendale furniture. Outside the grounds extend to some 260 acres (104ha) with fine specimen trees, herbaceous borders, a Dutch garden and an unusual topiary sundial.

☎ 01296 688242   www.nationaltrust.org.uk

Ashdown House (NT)   183 E4

Built in the 1660s in an isolated location high up on the Berkshire Downs, this is an unusual Dutch style house constructed from local dressed chalk blocks. It was probably designed by William Winde who spent his formative years in Holland with Royalist exiles, and who may well have been influenced by the French architect Francois Mansart who built a strikingly similar chateau in Normandy.

Public access is restricted to the hall, the impressive staircase and the cupola leading on to the roof, from where there are wonderful views. There are attractive woodland walks on the estate.

☎ 01793 762209   www.nationaltrust.org.uk

Ashmolean Museum   406 B2

Claiming to be Britain's first museum, the Ashmolean opened in 1683, displaying a collection of natural history specimens assembled by the Tradescant family. Although chiefly famed for their horticultural expertise, the Tradescants were wide-ranging and idiosyncratic collectors, their acquisitions including not only natural history items but, amongst many others, a picture made from feathers, the Passion of Christ carved on a plum stone and a hat band of snake bones. The collection was transferred to the ownership of Elias Ashmole who presented it to Oxford University. In the late 19th century, it was rehoused in the magnificent neoclassical building which is its present home. It was subsequently merged with the university's art collection.

☎ 01865 278000   www.ashmol.ox.ac.uk

Basildon Park (NT)   184 B5

Handsome late 18th century Palladian mansion with impressive classical façade, built of Bath stone and salvaged from neglect in the mid 20th century. The richly decorated interior contains some fine plasterwork, the Shell Room, with its unusual collection of sea shells, and a striking Octagon Room. Waymarked walks can be taken through the 400 acres (160ha) of attractive parkland and there are small but colourful formal gardens.

☎ 0118 984 3040   www.nationaltrust.org.uk

Bateman's (NT)   160 B1

This attractive 17th century stone-built house was home to Rudyard Kipling from 1902 to 1936, with many of the rooms kept as Kipling left them. The delightful gardens contain a water mill.

☎ 01435 882302   www.nationaltrust.org.uk

Battle Abbey   160 C2

Partially ruined abbey on the site of the Battle of Hastings, traditionally said to have been founded by William the Conqueror in 1070 to atone for the terrible loss of life incurred during the conquest of England. The gatehouse, built circa 1338, is the best preserved part of the abbey. Supposedly, the altar was located on the very spot where Harold II died.

☎ 01424 773792   www.english-heritage.org.uk

Bayham Abbey   173 F5

Now an impressive ruin, located in a pretty wooded valley, Bayham Abbey was founded around the turn of the 12th century, and built from local golden sandstone. During the 18th century the site was landscaped to create the effect of a 'romantic' ruin.

☎ 01892 890381

Beachy Head   160 A4

Forming an abrupt termination of the South Downs, the 535ft (163m) high chalk cliffs at Beachy Head are an awe-inspiring sight, dwarfing the lighthouse on the rocks below. Spectacular panoramic views are on offer.

Beale Park   184 B5

Gilbert Beale had a passion for birds, to the extent that his favourite peahen would accompany him round the estate in his Rolls Royce. Now, nearly 50 years later, this superb collection of birds has grown considerably and the park has an impressive record with rare species, both with breeding and returning them to the wild.

The site, on the banks of the River Thames, covers around 400 acres (160ha) of parkland and ancient watermeadow, and boasts a remarkable array of aviaries. There are also rare breeds of farm animals, adventure play areas, a deer park, meerkat enclosure, maze and narrow-gauge railway. Boat trips can be taken on the river, and special events take place in school holidays.

☎ 0118 984 5172   www.bealepark.co.uk

Beaulieu Abbey   348 A4

The name 'Beaulieu' is thought to derive from the Saxon 'beo ley' or bee meadow, subsequently interpreted as 'beau lieu' or beautiful place by the Norman scribes of the Domesday Book. The Cistercian abbey was founded here by King John in 1204 and built with stone brought in from the Isle of Wight and Caen in Normandy. The estate of 10,000 acres (4000ha) was a wealthy one and consequently a magnificent abbey was built. This was subsequently ruined during the Dissolution of the Monasteries, the monks' refectory being converted to form the parish church. The cloister is the best preserved part of the abbey, while the Domus, or lay brothers' dwelling, remained entire and now houses an excellent exhibition on life in the medieval abbey. The remaining stone was removed to build coastal defences at Southsea Castle.

☎ 01590 614604   www.beaulieu.co.uk

Beaulieu Palace House   348 A4

Following the Dissolution of the Monasteries, Beaulieu Abbey estate was sold to the Earl of Southampton, an ancestor of the current owner, Lord Montagu. The Palace House was built in the 19th century around the abbey gatehouse, producing a curious combination of 14th century Gothic, as seen in the fan vaulted ceilings, and Baronial style Victorian architecture. Inside can be seen family portraits and other treasures of the Montagu family.

☎ 01590 614604   www.beaulieu.co.uk

Bedgebury National Pinetum   173 G5

Covering 320 acres (129.5ha) in an attractive landscaped valley setting, the pinetum has over 6000 trees including vulnerable and endangered species. The pinetum was first established as the National Conifer Collection in 1925.

☎ 01580 211044   www.bedgeburypinetum.org.uk

Bekonscot Model Village   185 E3

This is a 1930s re-creation of Britain in miniature. A pleasantly landscaped site of more than 40,000sq ft (3716sq m) boasts scaled down models of villages, farms, churches, castles, and even a zoo and a racecourse, together with a working coal mine, fishing port and steam fair. There is also a model railway with 7000ft (2100m) of track.

☎ 01494 672919   www.bekonscot.com

⭐ Bembridge Windmill (NT)   157 F4

Built around 1700 and in use until 1913, this is the only surviving windmill on the Isle of Wight. It contains a complete set of restored wooden machinery, most of it original.

☎ 01983 873945   www.nationaltrust.org.uk

🏛 Bentley Wildfowl & Motor Museum   159 G2

The Bentley estate is centred on a Palladian style mansion containing some fine furnishings and paintings. Surrounding the house are formal gardens using yew hedging to create 'outside rooms', and a large waterfowl collection including ducks, geese, swans and flamingos in an attractive natural setting of trees, lakes and ponds. The motor museum has over 100 exhibits including veteran, vintage and classic cars, and motorcycles.

☎ 01825 840573   www.bentley.org.uk

🐘 Birdworld   ☀ 170 D3

Sufficient birds of all shapes, sizes, colours and habits for even the most demanding of ornithologists, displayed in 26 acres (10ha) of carefully designed grounds. There is an established breeding programme, particularly with the Humboldt penguins, making the peak of the breeding season in May and June a good time to visit, but there is plenty to see at other times, including Underwater World with aquarium and alligator swamp.

☎ 01420 22140   www.birdworld.co.uk

🏛 Bishop's Palace   157 E1

The impressive ruins of the medieval seat of the Bishops of Winchester, set in wooded grounds. The palace was built in 1136 by Henry de Blois, brother of King Stephen, and was subsequently enlarged in the 14th century by William of Wykeham before being reduced to its present state by Parliamentary forces in 1644. The remains of the Great Hall can be seen, together with the three-storey tower. The ground floor of the Dower House has been restored as a 19th century farmhouse.

☎ 01489 892460   www.english-heritage.org.uk

🏯 Blackgang Chine   157 D5

Originally developed in the 1840s as a scenic garden for Victorian tourists, this clifftop site of around 40 acres (16ha) has gradually evolved into a family leisure park.

The park endeavours to provide a mix of entertainment and education, the former catered for by a variety of attractions such as the water chute, roller coaster, gentler rides for younger children and nursery rhyme scenes. More informative displays can be seen in the maritime museum on the restored quayside and at the replica Victorian saw mill, complete with working engines.

☎ 01983 730330   www.blackgangchine.com

🏰 ❄ Blenheim Palace   ☁ 183 G1

A stunning example of English Baroque architecture, Blenheim Palace was built for John Churchill, 1st Duke of Marlborough, following his victory at the Battle of Blenheim.

The palace was designed by Sir John Vanbrugh and built between 1705 – 22. The building itself covers 14 acres (5.5ha), whilst the grounds, landscaped by Lancelot 'Capability' Brown in the 1760s, extend to over 2000 acres (800ha).

Internally, the palace is sumptuously and elaborately decorated and furnished; there are gold leaf ceilings by Nicholas Hawksmoor, marble and stone carvings by Grinling Gibbons, frescoes by Louis Laguerre and portraits by Reynolds, Romney and Van Dyck. The ceiling of the Great Hall, 67ft (20m) high, has a painting depicting Marlborough's victory at Blenheim and the Long Library, a particularly impressive 183ft (56m), has a magnificent stucco ceiling.

The palace was also the birthplace of Sir Winston Churchill. Five rooms, including his birth room, are devoted to the Churchill Exhibition, with memorabilia tracing his life and work.

The grounds were originally designed by Henry Wise, Queen Anne's gardener, but now only the walled garden remains, and much of the later work, including the splendid lake, was by Lancelot 'Capability' Brown, while the Italian Garden and Water Terraces were designed by Achille Duchene in the early 20th century. The parkland provides hours of pleasant walking, and there is also a maze, adventure playground and butterfly house.

☎ 01993 811091   www.blenheimpalace.com

🏛 Bletchley Park Museum   ☁ 353 C3

A Victorian mansion, formerly Britain's World War II code breaking headquarters, now housing a fascinating museum devoted to cryptography and computing. During the war, around 12,000 people worked here, their greatest success was to crack the German Enigma code. Guided tours are included in the entry fee.

☎ 01908 640404   www.bletchley park.org.uk

🚂 Bluebell Railway   ☁ 159 F1

The Bluebell Railway, named after the profusion of bluebells seen beside the line in spring, is the only all-steam, standard-gauge, preserved railway in the country. It extends for 9 miles (14.5km) from Sheffield Park in the south, via Horsted Keynes, to Kingscote in the north.

British Railways closed the line in March 1958 as a cost cutting exercise; two years later 4 miles (6.5km) to the north of Sheffield Park were reopened by a group of enthusiasts. Since then, a further 5 miles (8km) have been added. There are plans to extend the track as far as East Grinstead where it will connect with the main line.

The railway's headquarters and locomotive department are situated at Sheffield Park station where an impressive selection of engines can be found. Some older locos date from the 1870s, with the newest built as late as the 1950s. There is also a museum of small exhibits, a model railway, a shop, a restaurant and a real ale bar at this station. The restoration and maintenance of carriages and wagons takes place at Horsted Keynes where work in progress can be seen from a viewing gallery.

☎ 01825 720800   www.bluebell-railway.co.uk

⭐ Bocketts Farm Park   171 G2

This is a working farm with a variety of farm animals and crops, set in scenic downland countryside. Features include tractor rides, children's play areas, pig races, plus seasonal events such as lambing and harvesting.

☎ 01372 363764   www.bockettsfarm.co.uk

Bodiam Castle

🏰 Bodiam Castle (NT)   160 C1

Everyone's favourite; a picture book castle with massive sandstone walls and towers rising from a broad moat, spiral staircases, battlement walks and hidey-holes to explore. Today, only a small part of the interior survives.

Bodiam was built in the late 14th century by Sir Edward Dalyngrigge, who had amassed considerable wealth in the wars against France, as a defensive stronghold protecting the Rother Valley from the French. It was intended to be a comfortable home as well as a defensible castle and symbolized the movement from traditional castle to comfortable manor house.

The castle was left partially ruined after attack in 1645 during the Civil War. Repairs to the building commenced in the 19th century, and during the early 20th century the castle was sympathetically restored by its then owner Lord Curzon who bequeathed it to the National Trust in 1926.

In addition to the castle, visitor attractions include a museum containing objects found during the restoration by Lord Curzon, plus a restaurant.

☎ 01580 830436   www.nationaltrust.org.uk

❄ Borde Hill   159 F1

A large, mainly informal garden, created at the turn of the 19th century, set in 200 acres (80ha) of Grade II* parkland. The formal gardens, situated by

Blenheim Palace

the house (not open to the public) include walled, rose and herbaceous gardens; and restored Victorian greenhouses. Many of the rare trees and shrubs were introduced from the Himalayas as seed by plant hunters. Seasonal interest includes rhododrendrons and magnolias in the spring, roses and herbaceous plants in the summer, and impressive autumn colours.

☎ 01444 450326   www.bordehill.co.uk

Box Hill Country Park (NT)   171 G2

One of the best known summits of the North Downs; an area of natural beauty comprising woodland, with abundant box trees, and chalk downland with impressive views to the south. Near the summit there is an information centre, shop and a fort dating from the 1890s.

☎ 01306 885502   www.nationaltrust.org.uk

Breamore   156 A1

A red brick Elizabethan manor house, constructed in the characteristic E-shape of the period, set in beautiful parkland in the Avon valley. It is still a family home, and contains fine collections of furniture, porcelain and tapestries, whilst the wood-panelled Great Hall displays 16th and 17th century portraits. A carriage museum in a converted stable block contains the last operational stage coach in England, and there is an informative countryside museum in the old farmyard. An adventure playground and maze provide additional entertainment for children.

☎ 01725 512468   www.breamorehouse.com

Broadlands   169 E5

Originally a 16th century house, remodelled in the 18th century to create a handsome Palladian mansion, Broadlands is beautifully set in sweeping lawns bordered by the River Test and in grounds landscaped by Lancelot 'Capability' Brown.

A particular feature of the house is the magnificent Saloon with its white and gold plaster ceiling. Many of the fine furnishings, paintings and sculptures were originally acquired by the family of Lord Palmerston, noted Victorian prime minister whose birthplace this was and whose life is remembered in an exhibition here. A more recent resident was Lord Mountbatten of Burma, and an interesting and informative exhibition on his life and times has been staged by his grandson, Lord Romsey, the present owner.

Open from mid June to late August.

☎ 01794 505010   www.broadlands.net

Brooklands Museum   171 F1

This motoring and aviation museum is situated on the site of the world's first motor racing circuit. Not only is it steeped in motor racing history, but it was also the site of the first powered flight by a Briton in a British aeroplane in 1908. Today the museum contains over 30 aircraft and part of the steeply banked, original racing circuit.

☎ 01932 857381   www.brooklandsmuseum.com

Broughton Castle   197 G4

A medieval manor house built around 1300 and set on an island surrounded by a 3 acre (1ha) moat. Much of the original building remains, but it was greatly enlarged in the late 16th century, adding splendid decorative plasterwork, panelling and fireplaces. The castle was a secret meeting place for Parliamentarians during the Civil War, and at one stage it was besieged and captured by Royalists. There is an interesting display of arms and armour from this period in the Great Hall.

The grounds contain colourful herbaceous borders, roses, climbers and a formal walled garden. Not open every day; it is advisable to telephone in advance.

☎ 01295 276070   www.broughtoncastle.demon.co.uk

Buckinghamshire County Museum   184 D1

An interesting collection which uses interactive displays to recount the cultural, social and natural history of the county. Exhibits include information on woodlands, farming, fossils, Celts and Romans, and there is also a programme of temporary exhibitions and an art gallery.

The museum building is also home to the Roald Dahl Children's Gallery, a hands-on exhibition where characters from Roald Dahl's books bring to life aspects of history, natural history, science and technology. Entry is by timed ticket. There is a charge for the Dahl Gallery but the museum is free.

☎ 01296 331441   www.visitbuckinghamshire.org

Buckinghamshire Railway Centre   184 C1

This is a working steam museum boasting one of the biggest collections of locomotives, wagons and carriages in the country. As well as the opportunity to ride on steam-hauled trains, there is a good-sized miniature railway and the chance to see restoration work in progress.

☎ 01296 655450   www.bucksrailcentre.org.uk

Buckler's Hard Maritime Museum   348 A4

Buckler's Hard is a delightful, unspoilt 18th century village located on the Beaulieu River. Proximity to timber from the New Forest and a depth of water sufficient to launch substantial warships combined to create a shipbuilding industry here during the 18th century. Two rows of terraced Georgian cottages housed the workforce, and some have been reconstructed to depict the lives of the workers and their families. The Maritime Museum traces the story of this local industry. River trips are available in the summer.

☎ 01590 616203   www.bucklershard.co.uk

Burnham Beeches   185 E4

A splendid Chilterns beech wood of around 574 acres (232ha) which has been a protected public open space since 1880. The woods are home to a diversity of wildlife, including rare plants, insects and fungi, and are known for their striking autumn colour.

Buscot Park (NT)   183 E3

An 18th century Palladian mansion with a remarkable collection of paintings and furniture belonging to the Faringdon Collection Trust. Paintings include works by Rembrandt, Rubens, Murillo and Reynolds, some particularly notable Pre-Raphaelite pieces and contemporary items, and there is furniture designed by Thomas Hope and Robert Adam.

The landscaped park features an Italianate water garden created by Harold Peto in the early 20th century.

☎ 08453 453387   www.buscot-park.com
☎ 01367 240786

Canterbury Cathedral   392 B2

The cathedral was founded in AD597 by St Augustine, a missionary from Rome, and has been the centre of the English church ever since. Today, the impressive cathedral, along with nearby St Martin's Church and St Augustine's Abbey, is a World Heritage Site.

The architectural styles of the cathedral range from Norman to Perpendicular. The large crypt is the oldest part of the present building and dates from the 11th century. Rebuilt after a fire, the 12th century Quire features beautiful stained glass windows depicting miracles and stories associated with Thomas Becket. Famously murdered here in 1170, he is one of the cathedral's most notable archbishops. Two years later he was made a saint. As a result of his martyrdom the cathedral became one of the world's most important centres of pilgrimage.

The magnificent nave, comprising tall columns and vaulted arches, was built in the 14th century and took 28 years to complete. Visitors can see medieval tombs within the cathedral including those of King Henry IV and Edward, the Black Prince.

To get the most out of a visit to this remarkable building, guided and audio tours are available.

☎ 01227 762862   www.canterbury-cathedral.org

Canterbury Cathedral

Canterbury Tales, The   392 B2

A series of superb reconstructions of medieval streets and Thomas Becket's shrine set inside the historic St Margaret's Church. It tells of Chaucer's famous characters on their journey from the Tabard Inn in London to Canterbury Cathedral, bringing them all very much to life.

☎ 01227 479227   www.canterburytales.org.uk

Carisbrooke Castle & Museum   157 D4

Such an obvious defensive site almost demanded the construction of a castle, and there is evidence that people complied, certainly from Saxon times and probably before. The present castle dates from around 1100, and still retains the typical motte and bailey outline, but was considerably enlarged in the late medieval period. Following the Armada in 1588 it was further fortified, and the wellhouse and its tread wheel were added so that water could be drawn more easily from the 161ft (49m) well in the event of siege.

Carisbrooke's chief claim to fame is as the place of imprisonment of Charles I prior to his trial and execution.

The museum is housed in the Great Hall of the Constable's Lodgings and contains memorabilia on Charles I, as well as general information on the Isle of Wight's history.

☎ 01983 522107   www.english-heritage.org.uk

Chartwell (NT)   173 D3

The family home of Winston Churchill for over 40 years, he purchased it in 1924 because he fell in love with the impressive views over the Weald. The large brick built house is still full of many of his personal possessions. Churchill also left his mark on the attractive gardens, creating lakes, garden walls and rockeries.

☎ 01732 868381   www.nationaltrust.org.uk

🏛 Chastleton House (NT)   197 E5

One of the most outstanding Jacobean properties in England, Chastleton has been continuously occupied by one family since its construction in the early 17th century. Particular treasures include elaborate plasterwork, Florentine tapestries and delightful glassware. Entry is by timed ticket and it is advisable to book in advance.

☎ 01608 674355   www.nationaltrust.org.uk

★ Chatham Historic Dockyard   173 G2
& World Naval Base

The history of the dockyards extends back over 400 years. Nelson's famous flagship the *Victory* was built here in 1765. Today, on an 80 acre (32.5ha) site, visitors can see vessels including a World War II destroyer *H.M.S. Cavalier*, the modern submarine *Ocelot*, and *H.M.S. Gannet* which is the last surviving Victorian navy sloop. The site also contains a museum and an exhibition on the Royal National Lifeboat Institution.

☎ 01634 823807   www.chdt.org.uk

🏛 Chenies Manor House   185 F3

Queen Elizabeth slept in this 15th century manor house on several occasions, and the building still contains reminders of this period in its furniture and tapestries. Additionally, there is an interesting collection of antique dolls, while the restored 16th century pavilion in the grounds houses various exhibitions.

The delightful gardens are well known for their tulip display, and there are themed areas including a Tudor sunken garden, white garden, herbaceous borders, physic garden and kitchen garden.

☎ 01494 762888   www.visitbuckinghamshire.org

🏛 Chichester District Museum   158 A3

Local history museum housed in an 18th century corn store. Includes artefacts excavated from around Chichester.

☎ 01243 784683   www.chichester.gov.uk/museum/

🏛 Chiltern Open Air Museum   185 F3

Over 30 historic buildings have been constructed on this attractive 45 acre (18ha) park and woodland site. Most of the buildings were rescued from destruction and have been carefully dismantled and moved from their original locations to create this museum. The diverse display includes re-creations of a Victorian farmyard, complete with animals, a 1940s fully furnished 'prefab' and an Iron Age enclosure. There is even an Edwardian Public Convenience.

There are also demonstrations of traditional skills and information on the methods and materials used to make the buildings. There are plenty of hands-on activities and, throughout the year, there are various special events.

☎ 01494 871117   www.coam.org.uk

☐ Chilterns   184 C4

The chalk downland which makes up the Chilterns extends from Luton in the north-east and runs south-west through Buckinghamshire and Oxfordshire to the southern edge at the River Thames. The open nature of the countryside, dotted with beech hangers and attractive villages, makes this delightful walking country, and part of the Ridgeway, a prehistoric track, runs through the area. Splendid views can be seen from vantage points such as Coombe Hill, with a height of 853ft (260m), Ivinghoe Beacon, and the windmill above Turville village.

🏛 ✿ Clandon Park (NT)   171 F2

Impressive Palladian mansion built circa 1731 for the 2nd Lord Onslow. Notable for its imposing two-storey marble entrance hall with magnificent Italian plasterwork ceiling. The house contains the Gubbay collection of furniture and porcelain, along with tapestries and the Ivo Forde Meissen collection of Italian comedy figures. The gardens, designed by Lancelot 'Capability' Brown in 1781, include a grotto, Maori house and parterre.

☎ 01483 222482   www.nationaltrust.org.uk

✿ Claremont Landscape   171 G1
Garden (NT)

One of the earliest examples surviving today of a 'landscape' garden. Dating from circa 1715, many of the great names in landscape gardening played a part including Charles Bridgeman, Sir John Vanbrugh, William Kent and Lancelot 'Capability' Brown. Extending to 49 acres (20ha) the garden includes a lake, impressive grass amphitheatre and grotto.

☎ 01372 467806   www.nationaltrust.org.uk

🏛 ✿ Claydon (NT)   198 C5

A charming, mainly 18th century house belonging to the Verney family until the mid 20th century. The unassuming exterior hides a wealth of extravagance in interior decoration. This was carved in the rococo style by Luke Lightfoot and the house contains some of the most remarkable decorative carving in the country, seen at its most outstanding in the Chinese Room. The saloon, library and stairwell boast some beautiful plasterwork, whilst the stairs are decorated with mahogany, ebony and ivory parquetry.

Florence Nightingale was a frequent visitor after her sister's marriage to Sir Henry Verney, and there is a display of memorabilia relating to her life and work.

☎ 01296 730349   www.nationaltrust.org.uk

Chiltern Open Air Museum

🏛 ✿ Cliveden (NT)   185 E4

A splendid 400 acre (160ha) estate in a magnificent location 200ft (60m) above the River Thames. The impressive house, designed by Sir Charles Barry and former home to the Astor family, is now an hotel with limited public access (telephone for opening times), but the principal attractions are the gardens and views. Planting has been designed to give colour and interest throughout the year.

☎ 01628 605069   www.nationaltrust.org.uk

🏛 Cobham Hall   173 F2

Large, attractive red brick mansion dating from 1584, set in 150 acres (61ha) of parkland landscaped by Humphrey Repton. The interior features a notable hall by James Wyatt in the Gothic style and a granite staircase dating from 1602. The house is currently an independent school and opening times are therefore restricted to the Easter and summer holidays.

☎ 01474 824319

★ Coombe Hill   185 D2

At 853ft (260m), this is one of the highest points on the Chiltern Hills, with magnificent views over the surrounding countryside. The monument on the summit is dedicated to the men of Buckinghamshire who were killed during the Boer War.

🐾 Cotswold Wildlife Park   183 E2

Set in 140 acres (56ha) of attractive gardens and parkland surrounding a 19th century mansion, the Wildlife Park is home to a wide range of animals. As well as the usual large animal attractions there are also endangered species such as the giant tortoise, red panda, and Asiatic lion.

There is a children's farmyard with domestic animals and a good adventure playground. A regular programme of events and talks takes place, particularly in summer.

☎ 01993 823006   www.cotswoldwildlifepark.co.uk

🏛 Cowper & Newton Museum   199 D2

Orchard Side, one of a pair of Georgian houses which now make up the museum, was the former home of the poet and hymn-writer William Cowper. Visitors can see his manuscripts and memorabilia, together with some belonging to his friend, the local curate John Newton who composed 'Amazing Grace'. There are also local history displays and an interesting textile exhibition.

☎ 01234 711516   www.mkheritage.co.uk

🏛 Danebury Ring   169 E4

An Iron Age hill fort, dating from about 500BC, with substantial defensive earthworks enclosing a 13 acre (5ha) site. Its name comes from 'dun', meaning hill, and 'bury', meaning fort.

The earliest evidence for occupation is Neolithic artefacts but the hill fort itself was not built until around 475BC and was abandoned around 100BC.

The site has been extensively excavated to reveal evidence for 75 roundhouses and many more rectangular storage buildings, and many of the finds can be seen at the Museum of the Iron Age in Andover. The isolated site has magnificent views over the surrounding downland.

www.hants.gov.uk

🏰 Deal Castle   175 F3

Coastal defensive fort built in 1539 during the reign of Henry VIII to protect England from France and Spain. Constructed in the shape of a Tudor Rose, the walls were deliberately built low and rounded to avoid enemy fire from the sea. Visitors can explore the underground passages and see the 53 gunports.

☎ 01304 372762   www.english-heritage.org.uk

★ Denbies Wine Estate   171 G2

Extending to 265 acres (107ha) on the slopes of the North Downs, this is the largest vineyard in Britain. Visitors can tour the working winery, experience guided wine tasting, and take the vineyard train up to the North Downs Way where there are excellent views.

☎ 01306 876616   www.denbiesvineyard.co.uk

Denmans
158 B3

Richly and artistically planted, Denmans extends to approximately 4 acres (1.5ha) and is owned by garden writer and designer John Brookes. Highlights include an attractive walled garden and a glass area for the more tender species.

☎ 01243 542808   www.denmans-garden.co.uk

Dickens House Museum
175 F2

The museum commemorates Charles Dickens' association with Broadstairs. It is said that Mary Pearson Strong, who once lived here, was the inspiration for the character of Betsey Trotwood, in Dickens' famous book 'David Copperfield'. Memorabilia and personal items such as the author's own letters are on display.

☎ 01843 861232   www.dickenshouse.co.uk

Dorney Court
185 E5

A timber-framed, brick infilled 15th century building with a magnificent great hall and gallery, considered to be one of the finest examples of a Tudor manor house in England. Home to the Palmer family for over four centuries, the house contains many family portraits, fine furniture and heirlooms. The pleasant gardens have a particular claim to fame – here was grown the first pineapple to be cultivated in England. Opening is limited so it is advisable to telephone in advance.

☎ 01628 604638   www.dorneycourt.co.uk

Dover Castle
395 E2

Well preserved Norman castle, on the site of a Roman fortress which in turn occupied that of an Iron Age Fort. Situated 375 feet (114m) above sea level, the castle has played a key role in the defence of the realm: William the Conqueror saw its importance and strengthened the castle shortly after the Battle of Hastings. However, much of the castle as we see it today dates from the reign of Henry II when the impressive four-storey keep, the distinctive inner bailey and part of the outer walls were built, creating a concentric fortress. Just prior to the death of King John the castle was damaged by a French siege and his son, Henry III, was quick to carry out strengthening work completing the outer bailey. The castle maintained its defensive role right up to and including World War II, when the tunnels under the castle became the headquarters from which the evacuation of Dunkirk was directed. Exhibitions and displays highlight key events in the castle's chequered and well documented history. A walk along the battlements gives the visitor a commanding view over the harbour.

☎ 01304 201628   www.english-heritage.org.uk

Dover Castle

Druidstone Park
174 D2

In 12 acres (5ha) of attractive gardens and woodland, visitors can see a variety of animals including owls, deer, wallabies and various wildfowl. The open-air art park features sculptures in a variety of media, some by well-known artists. Children can also explore the farmyard with its pigs, llamas, donkeys and ponies.

☎ 01227 765168   www.druidstone.net/

Drusillas Park
160 A3

Ideal for children, this small zoo primarily features the smaller species of animal housed in naturalistic environments. Over 100 species can be seen, such as meerkats, monkeys and penguins. There is also a walk-through bat enclosure and a wide range of play and hands-on activities.

☎ 01323 874100   www.drusillas.co.uk

Eastbourne Pier
397 B3

Built in the 1870s, this 1000 ft (305m) long pier was designed by Eugenius Birch, using an ingenious method whereby the legs that support the pier sit on special cups allowing it to move from side to side in bad weather. Attractions include a restored Victorian Camera Obscura, bars, restaurant, café, amusement arcades and night club.

☎ 01323 410466   www.eastbournepier.com

Emmetts (NT)
173 D3

Bequeathed to the National Trust in 1965, this mainly informal hillside garden dates from 1860 - 70. In about 1900, it was extended to 5 acres (2ha). Emmetts is particularly attractive in the spring with a profusion of daffodils and, later on, bluebells.

☎ 01732 751509   www.nationaltrust.org.uk

Exbury Gardens
348 A4

A magnificent 250 acre (100ha) woodland garden set on the east side of the Beaulieu River. It is particularly famed for its rhododendron collection, started in the 1920s by the banker Lionel de Rothschild, who imported more than 1000 varieties and bred from these to produce 400 more, providing sensational colour from April to June. There are also good collections of magnolias and camellias, while the daffodil meadow, rock garden, rose garden and herbaceous borders greatly extend the garden's period of interest. Pleasant walks can be taken in the woodlands, and a 12.5 inch (30cm) narrow-gauge railway runs through part of the grounds.

☎ 023 8089 9422   www.exbury.co.uk

Finkley Down Farm Park
169 E3

A great variety of farm animals, domestic pets and poultry can be seen on this working farm. Adventure playground and informative countryside museum.

☎ 01264 324141   www.finkleydownfarm.co.uk

Firle Place
159 G3

A Tudor house remodelled in the 18th century, in an attractive setting at the foot of the South Downs. It has been home to the Gage family for over 500 years and houses collections of Old Master paintings such as Reynolds and Gainsborough, fine furniture and porcelain.

☎ 01273 858335   www.firleplace.co.uk

Fishbourne Roman Palace
158 A3

Discovered in 1960, the remains of the north wing of this 1st century palace are enclosed by a modern building. The largest collection of in-situ Roman mosaics in Britain can be seen, along with remains of a bath suite, courtyards, corridors and hypocausts. A museum displays artefacts from excavations on and around the site and there is a Roman garden that has been replanted to its original plan.

☎ 01243 785859   www.sussexpast.co.uk

Fisher's Farm Park
171 F5

Family attraction with farmyard animals including ducks, sheep, goats, shire horses and Shetland ponies. There are also adventure play areas which include a 25ft (7.5m) climbing wall, merry-go-round and trampolines.

☎ 01403 700063   www.fishersfarmpark.co.uk

Fort Brockhurst
157 F2

A 19th century fort, one of several in the area built for the protection of Portsmouth. It has remained essentially unaltered, particular features being the moated keep, parade ground and gun ramps. Opening is limited so it is advisable to telephone in advance.

☎ 023 9258 1059   www.english-heritage.org.uk

Fort Victoria Country Park
156 C4

The remains of Fort Victoria, which was built to protect the western entry to the Solent, now house a variety of attractions. These include a fascinating aquarium concentrating on local marine life, one of the largest model railway layouts in the country, a marine heritage exhibition and planetarium. The surrounding 50 acres (20ha) of grounds provide woodland and seashore walks. There is a cost for attractions but entry to the park is free.

☎ 01983 823893   www.fortvictoria.co.uk

Godstone Farm
172 C3

This popular farm park features indoor and outdoor play areas as well as farm animals, chipmunks and llamas.

☎ 01883 742546   www.godstonefarm.co.uk

Great Coxwell Barn (NT)
183 E3

A substantial medieval barn built in the 13th century as part of a Cistercian cell under the control of Beaulieu Abbey. It is constructed chiefly from Cotswold stone, with the original doors still in place on the east and west walls. Internally the roof is supported by the original oak posts and trusses, though most of the rafters have been replaced.

☎ 01793 762209   www.nationaltrust.org.uk

Great Dixter
160 D1

A beautiful Tudor house built circa 1460 and restored in 1910 by Edwin Lutyens. It has one of the largest timber framed halls in the country and is home to gardening writer Christopher Lloyd. The 5 acre (2ha) garden, also designed by Lutyens, has been developed by Lloyd, producing a combination of historical design and contemporary and adventurous planting. The garden contains clipped topiary, wild meadow flowers, mixed borders including the famous 'long border' which is some 200ft (60m) long, ponds, walls, stone steps and paths.

☎ 01797 252878   www.greatdixter.co.uk

Great Tew
197 F5

This could be described as a quintessential English village, with terraces of Cotswold stone cottages, most built in the 1630s for Lord Falkland's estate workers. The cottages are a mixture of thatched and stone-roofed, and a pub and village green complete the picture.

Grey's Court (NT)
184 C4

An unusual 14th century house, rebuilt in the 16th century and subsequently modified but still retaining one of the original towers. A distinctive feature is the Tudor wheelhouse where donkeys turned the wheel which brought water up from a 200ft (61m) well.

The 8 acre (3ha) gardens are a particularly attractive aspect, set among the ruins of the 14th century building. Telephone in advance to check for opening times.

☎ 01494 755564   www.nationaltrust.org.uk

Groombridge Place Gardens
173 E5

The walled, formal gardens were designed in the 17th century by John Evelyn and are set against a delightful moated manor house (not open to the public) of the same age. The grounds extend to 200 acres (80ha) and feature herbaceous borders, pools, woodland and rose garden. There is also the 'enchanted forest' to explore.

☎ 01892 863999   www.groombridge.co.uk

H.M.S. Victory
407 D1

Now lying in dry dock, the *Victory* is the oldest commissioned warship in the world and the flagship of the Second Sea Lord, though she is of course best known as Lord Nelson's flagship at the Battle of Trafalgar in 1805. Commissioned in 1778, her excellent sailing qualities caused several admirals to choose her as their flagship, and although her active career ended in 1812 it was agreed that she should be preserved as a memorial to Nelson and this distinguished period of the Royal Navy's history. Tours are not available from July to the end of school summer holidays due to pressure of numbers, but guides are on hand to answer visitors' questions.

☎ 023 9272 2562   www.hms-victory.com

H.M.S. Warrior
407 E1

Launched in 1860, *H.M.S. Warrior* was the world's first iron-hulled, armoured battleship and was then considered the most formidable ever seen. She was powered both by sail and steam, and has now been restored to her original launch condition. Visitors are able to explore the four large decks which illustrate life in the Victorian navy.

☎ 023 9272 2562   www.hmswarrior.org

Hammerwood Park
172 D5

This neoclassical house was built in 1792 by Benjamin Latrobe who was later responsible for the Capitol, and the porticos of the White House in Washington D.C. It was converted into flats after World War II and owned by the pop group Led Zeppelin in the 1970s. It gradually fell into disrepair until rescued in 1982 by the present owners who give guided tours and tell of the continuing process of restoration.

☎ 01342 850594   www.hammerwoodpark.com

Haslemere Educational Museum
171 E4

This family museum was founded in 1888 and opened to the public in 1895. Permanent galleries include: geology, natural history and human history. There are interactive displays, interesting collections and even a real Egyptian mummy.

☎ 01428 642112   www.haslemeremuseum.co.uk

Hastings Castle (Ruins)
400 F2

Originally built by William the Conqueror in 1066 as a wooden fort on an earth motte, it was rebuilt in stone in 1070 as the first permanent Norman castle in the country. It is now a ruin commanding panoramic views of Hastings. Visitors to the castle can see an audiovisual show 'The 1066 Story' about the Battle of Hastings and the history of the castle.

☎ 01424 781111

Hatchlands (NT)
171 F2

An 18th century brick built mansion set in a 430 acre (174ha) park designed by Humphrey Repton. The interior contains early examples of work by Robert Adam as well as a fine collection of keyboard instruments once owned, or played by famous composers including J.C. Bach, Beethoven, Chopin, Mozart and Purcell.

☎ 01483 222482   www.nationaltrust.org.uk

Herstmonceux Castle
160 B2

Beautiful parkland, woodland and well kept Elizabethan gardens extending to 550 acres (220ha) are centred on a brick built 15th century moated castle (not open to the public). There is a children's woodland play area and nature trail. The estate is also the site of the Observatory Science Centre, former home of the Royal Greenwich Observatory (separate entry fee).

☎ 01323 833816   www.herstmonceux-castle.com

Hever Castle
173 D4

This romantic, double-moated, 13th century castle was the childhood home of Anne Boleyn, and later owned by Anne of Cleves. The castle contains prayer books inscribed and signed by Anne Boleyn. There are also Tudor portraits, furniture, tapestries and a collection of miniature houses with period decoration and furnishings.

The spectacular gardens were constructed between 1904 and 1908. Features include a 35 acre (14ha) lake, Italian gardens with statuary and sculptures, a 360ft (110m) herbaceous border and herb garden. There are two mazes: a traditional yew hedge maze and an unusual water maze.

☎ 01732 865224   www.hevercastle.co.uk

High Beeches
172 B5

20 acres (8ha) of Grade II* listed woodland, water and wild flower garden dating from the early 20th century. It contains a varied and extensive collection of plants and is particularly colourful in spring and autumn.

☎ 01444 400589   www.highbeeches.com

Highclere Castle
169 F2

This former Georgian mansion, set in magnificent parkland landscaped by Lancelot 'Capability' Brown, was extravagantly refurbished both internally and externally by Sir Charles Barry in the 1840s. The lavishly decorated rooms embrace a variety of styles including Gothic, Moorish and rococo, which somehow combine to form a splendid example of High Victorian architecture.

The castle is the ancestral home of the Earls of Carnarvon, and there is an exhibition of Egyptian artefacts brought back by the 5th Earl following the Tutankhamen excavations in the 1920s.

The 7th Earl was the Queen's racing manager, and there is an exhibition on horse racing history.

Opening times are limited.

☎ 01635 253210   www.highclerecastle.co.uk

Hinton Ampner (NT)
169 G5

Considered to be one of the great gardens of the 20th century, designed on the basis of a Victorian garden by Ralph Dutton, the 8th Lord Sherborne.

The house stands on a ridge with magnificent views over downland scenery. The terraced gardens are a transformation of a Victorian remnant into a masterpiece of formal and informal plantings using predominantly pastel shades. Only open on certain days of the week in summer.

☎ 01962 771305   www.nationaltrust.org.uk

Hop Farm Country Park
173 F4

Once a working hop farm, this large group of Victorian oast houses forms the setting for this family attraction. Amongst the entertainments are shire horse displays, an animal farm, children's play areas, a military vehicle display as well as a visit to the 'Hop Story' museum.

☎ 01622 872068   www.thehopfarm.co.uk

Horton Park Farm
171 G1

Situated within the Horton Country Park, this popular attraction features a wide range of farm animals to feed and cuddle. There are also rare breeds, an adventure playground, indoor play area, a maze and tractor rides.

☎ 01372 743984   www.hortonpark.co.uk

Howletts Wild Animal Park
175 D3

Founded by the late John Aspinall, this wild animal park is set in mature parkland and has the largest breeding colony of gorillas in captivity. It is notable for encouraging bonding between the keepers and their animals as Aspinall believed that this improved the emotional wellbeing of the animals and has led to successful breeding programmes. Other animals include the largest herd of African elephants in the UK, tigers, leopards, deer and rare monkeys.

☎ 01303 264647   www.howletts.net

Hughenden Manor (NT)
185 D3

The home of former prime minister, Benjamin Disraeli, from 1847 – 71, and extensively restyled during this period by the Victorian Gothic architect E.B. Lamb. The interior has been left much as Disraeli would remember it, with his books, furniture, pictures and other memorabilia of his life. The 5 acre (2ha) gardens were designed by Disraeli's wife, Mary Anne. There are colourful herbaceous borders and formal annual bedding, woodland walks and an orchard with old varieties of apples and pears. Limited opening so it is advisable to telephone in advance.

☎ 01494 755573   www.nationaltrust.org.uk

Ightham Mote (NT)
173 E3

A very attractive moated manor house dating from 1330 surrounded by a lovely garden with lakes and woodland. The interior of the house has a rich history, with the Great Hall dating from the 1340s, a 14th century crypt, a Tudor chapel and a Jacobean fireplace.

☎ 01732 810378   www.nationaltrust.org.uk

Isle of Wight Pearl
156 D4

An extensive collection of all types of pearl jewellery. Visitors can learn how pearls are cultivated, see a replica of the world's largest pearl and learn how the jewellery is made.

☎ 01983 740352   www.isle-of-wight-pearl.com

Isle of Wight Zoo
157 F4

Specialising in big cats, the zoo is home to around 20 tigers, many actually born here, and there is plenty of opportunity to observe the animals and learn more about them and their conservation. Other big cats are represented: lions, leopards, jaguars and panthers, and there is also a fascinating lemur enclosure, snakes, insects and a good display of tarantulas. There is a regular programme of informative talks about the animals.

☎ 01983 403833   www.isleofwightzoo.com

Jane Austen's House   170 C4

An unpretentious 17th century red brick house where Jane Austen lived from 1809 – 17 and where she wrote or revised her six famous novels. The house is furnished in period style and contains many items associated with the author and her family, including letters and papers, furniture and first editions of the novels.

☎ 01420 83262   www.janeaustenmuseum.org.uk

Kent & East Sussex Railway   160 D1

Preserved steam and diesel engines run along this attractive standard-gauge line which runs for 10.5 miles (17km) from Tenterden to Bodiam (a short distance from the medieval castle). The line was built as the first light railway in Britain. At Tenterden, the headquarters, there is a museum plus the carriage and wagon workshop.

☎ 01580 765155   www.kesr.org.uk

Knole (NT)   173 E3

This enormous Tudor mansion, made of Kentish ragstone and set in a 1000 acre (405ha) deer park with 26 acre (10.5ha) landscaped grounds, was built in the mid 15th century for the Archbishop of Canterbury, Thomas Bourchier. It later passed to Henry VIII and then in 1603 it was gifted by Elizabeth I to her cousin Thomas Sackville, 1st Earl of Dorset. Extensive alterations and additions were made by the 1st Earl up to 1608 which transformed the house dramatically, particularly the interior. Today the house is notable for its 365 rooms – one for each day of the year, 52 staircases – one for each week of the year, and its 7 courtyards – one for each day of the week.

Knole contains an impressive collection of 17th century furniture started by the 1st Earl and continued by his descendents, most notably the 6th Earl who was Lord Chamberlain to William III. Later, the 3rd Duke, great-grandson of the 6th Earl, continued the collection by adding many valuable paintings.

☎ 01732 462100   www.nationaltrust.org.uk

Knole

Lamb House (NT)   161 E1

This brick fronted house, set in a one acre (0.5ha) walled garden in the centre of Rye, was built by James Lamb in 1723, the year he became mayor of Rye. George I stayed here in 1726 and acted as godfather to Lamb's son. The American novelist Henry James lived at Lamb House from 1898 to 1916 and the house is primarily devoted to mementoes of his time here.

☎ 01372 453401   www.nationaltrust.org.uk

Leeds Castle & Gardens   174 A3

Set on two islands in the middle of a large artificial lake, this beautiful castle was constructed in the 12th century as an impregnable stronghold, the barbican being built during the reign of Edward I. Six of the medieval queens of England have occupied the castle including Eleanor and Margaret, the wives of Edward I. Converted into a royal palace by Henry VIII, it has been restored and now contains a magnificent collection of medieval furnishings, French and English furniture and fabrics, tapestries and paintings by Degas, Pissarro, and Vuillard. Inside are also the Queen's Gallery, Banqueting Hall and Chapel. There are 500 acres (202ha) of parkland and gardens to explore, within which are an aviary, a maze and a grotto. The Woodland Garden provides a display of narcissi and daffodils in spring.

☎ 01622 765400   www.leeds-castle.com

Leeds Castle

Legoland   185 E5

Every small child's dream come true, Legoland is aimed at the 4-12 age group, with a mixture of incredible models, toned down theme park rides and special activities.

Particular highlights include the Rat Trap, an intricate arrangement of slides, climbing nets and walkways, The Dragon roller coaster, the water chute at Pirate Falls, and for the younger children, Duplo Land. The Mindstorms workshops will appeal more to older children, with the chance to construct robots, while visitors of all ages should appreciate Miniland, where 50 million Lego bricks have been used to re-create miniature versions of Europe's capital cities.

☎ 08705 040404   www.legoland.co.uk

Leonardslee Gardens   159 E1

This spectacular 240 acre (97ha) woodland garden is a riot of colour in May and June when the rhododendrons and azaleas are in flower. Located in a valley with seven lakes (originally used in iron smelting to provide power) this garden was acquired in 1889 by Sir Edmund Loder who set about an ambitious planting programme. Other attractions include an alpine house, bonsai exhibition, Victorian motor car collection and a herd of semi-wild wallabies that were first introduced over 100 years ago.

☎ 01403 891212   www.leonardslee.com

Lewes Castle   159 G2

This ruined castle dates from around 1069 and is unusual in having two mottes. The shell keep dates from the early 12th century and two semi-octagonal towers were built in the 13th century along with a range of buildings inside the shell wall. The impressive barbican, one of the best preserved castle barbicans in England, was added in the 14th century. There are magnificent views from the towers of the town of Lewes and the surrounding countryside.

☎ 01273 486290   www.sussexpast.co.uk

Living Rainforest   184 A5

This unique rainforest conservation project, with its thousands of weird, wonderful and, in some cases, endangered species, has been constructed under 20,000sq ft (1836sq m) of glass deep in rural Berkshire. There are two distinct regions represented, Amazonia and Lowland Tropical, each with its characteristic climate and flora. Of particular note is the splendid collection of orchids and the 8ft (2.5m) lily pads on view between June and October.

☎ 01635 202444   www.livingrainforest.org

Look Out Discovery Park   171 D1

Very much a hands-on attraction, this interactive science and nature exhibition will have a particular appeal to children. Themed zones look at topics such as light and colour, body and perception, and woodland and wildlife.

The centre is set in 2600 acres (1040ha) of Crown Estate woodland and there are plenty of nature trails and walks, and a 70ft (22m) tower providing views over the surrounding countryside. The Coral Reef swimming pool with its Wild West Rapids is also across the way.

☎ 01344 354400   www.bracknellforest.gov.uk

Loseley House   171 E3

Beautiful Elizabethan mansion set in the 1400 acre (566ha) Loseley Park. The house, dating from 1562, was built with stone from the ruins of Waverley Abbey and contains many fine works of art and panelling from Henry VIII's Nonsuch Palace. The estate comprises a formal 2.5 acre (1ha) walled garden (which is subdivided into five themed components), managed woodland and agricultural land. The well known Loseley ice cream and other dairy products are produced from the estate's herd of Jersey cows.

☎ 01483 304440   www.loseleypark.com

Legoland

Lullingstone Castle   173 E2

Situated in the lovely Darenth valley, this historic family mansion, first built in the late 15th century, was extensively altered during the reign of Queen Anne who was a frequent visitor to Lullingstone. The Tudor gatehouse was one of the earliest in England to be built entirely of bricks. There are fine state rooms, the impressive Great Hall, the grand staircase and library. Outside is the church of St Botolph containing a fine Tudor rood screen.

☎ 01322 862114

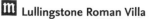

Lullingstone Roman Villa · 173 E2

Discovered in 1939, the site has been preserved within a modern building. The villa is thought to have been built during the 1st and 2nd centuries, although much of what can be seen today dates from the 4th century and includes well preserved floor mosaics, frescoes and a bathing complex. There is also the remains of one of the earliest Christian chapels.

☎ 01322 863467   www.english-heritage.org.uk

Mapledurham House & Mill · 184 B5

An attractive H-shaped red brick house built in the late 16th century and set in pleasant parkland on the banks of the River Thames. Within the house are fine plasterwork ceilings and an impressive oak staircase, while a private family chapel designed in 'Strawberry Hill' Gothic with original elaborate plasterwork was added in 1797. There are literary connections with Alexander Pope, John Galsworthy and Kenneth Grahame.

An interesting feature in the grounds is a 15th century water mill restored to full working order and producing flour and bran.

Opening mainly restricted to weekends in the summer season.

☎ 0118 972 3350   www.mapledurham.co.uk

Marwell Zoo · 169 G5

A well designed and carefully laid out zoo specialising in the conservation of endangered species but also with plenty of established favourites. Animals are housed in large, open enclosures and can be viewed via special walkways or road and rail trains. For children there is the Encounters Village where animals can be handled. There are regular special events during school holidays.

☎ 01962 777407   www.marwell.org.uk

Mary Rose · 407 D1

Built around 1510, the Mary Rose was quite innovative for her time in that she could fire a broadside using heavy cannon. Prior to this, ships engaged at close quarters for hand-to-hand fighting.

A favourite ship of Henry VIII, the Mary Rose sank in 1545; the king was watching from Southsea Castle as he took part in a skirmish with the French. She was not seen again above water until 1982 and is now on display in the Ship Hall.

A short walk away, the Mary Rose Museum displays over 1200 artefacts retrieved from the wreck and surrounding sea bed. In addition there is information on how the wreck was raised.

☎ 023 9272 2562   www.maryrose.org

Michelham Priory · 160 A3

Sitting on an island surrounded by the longest water-filled medieval moat in England, the building dates from 1229. Originally an Augustinian Priory until the Dissolution in 1537, it then became a country house. Exhibits include furniture, tapestries and artefacts. The gardens are in a variety of historic and contemporary styles and include a physic garden, cloister garden and orchard. There is also a working water mill.

☎ 01323 844224   www.sussexpast.co.uk

Mid Hants Railway · 170 B4

Delightful steam railway nicknamed 'The Watercress Line' as it was formerly used to transport fresh watercress to market. Ten miles

(16km) of track have been restored between Alresford and Alton, passing through lovely countryside – including watercress beds. The stations are restored to give a pre-war atmosphere and there is a visitor centre at Alresford. A programme of special events runs throughout the year.

☎ 01962 733810   www.watercressline.co.uk

Milton's Cottage · 185 E3

Timber-framed 16th century cottage where the poet John Milton brought his family in 1665 to escape the Great Plague in London. Here he completed 'Paradise Lost' and commenced 'Paradise Regained'. The building houses first editions and other memorabilia, and has delightful cottage gardens.

☎ 01494 572313   www.miltonscottage.org

Modern Art Oxford · 406 C2

This was established in 1965 and is arguably one of the foremost displays of contemporary art outside London, with exhibits from around the world including works by Ed Ruscha, Yoko Ono, Louise Bourgeois, Tracey Emin, David Goldblatt and Marina Abramovic. Work on display encompasses a variety of art forms; painting, sculpture, photography, design, film, video and architecture. Housed in a refurbished Victorian brewery, the museum also has a wide ranging programme of regular talks, events and children's workshops.

☎ 01865 722733   www.modernartoxford.co.uk

Monk's House (NT) · 159 G3

Small country home of novelist Virginia Woolf and her husband Leonard, purchased by them in 1919. The rooms contain mementoes of the life and times of the famous 'Bloomsbury Group' of which they were key players. Extracts of Virginia's diaries and a display of her photographs can be seen in the garden room where she used to write.

☎ 01372 453401   www.nationaltrust.org.uk

Mottisfont Abbey Gardens (NT) · 169 E5

The 12th century priory at the centre of this 20,000 acre (800ha) estate became a private house after the Dissolution of the Monasteries. However, the site's chief claim to fame, its walled rose garden designed by Graham Stuart Thomas, was only created in 1972, and is home to the National Collection of Old Fashioned Roses. Although these only have a short flowering period in June, elsewhere the gardens have been planted for interest throughout the season. The 'font' or spring, from which the place name is derived, is in the grounds.

☎ 01794 340757   www.nationaltrust.org.uk

Museum of Canterbury · 392 B1

Part of the museum is housed in what was once a hospital for poor priests dating from the 13th century. There are a wide range of exhibits, including archaeological finds and historical collections dating from pre-Roman to the present day.

☎ 01227 452747   www.canterbury-museums.co.uk

Museum of Oxford · 406 B2

Housed in the historic Town Hall, this museum traces the history of Oxford and the university. There is a particularly fine medieval collection, fascinating reconstructed interiors of city buildings from the 16th century onwards, paintings, furniture and many other items connected with the city and university.

☎ 01865 815559   www.oxford.co.uk

National Motor Museum · 348 A4

In 1952 Lord Montagu of Beaulieu inherited five historic vehicles and started the museum as a tribute to his father who had been a pioneer of motoring in Britain. The initially small display proved so popular that, in 1972, a purpose-built museum was developed in the park surrounding Lord Montagu's home at Beaulieu. This now houses over 250 historically important vehicles, a magnificent collection of motoring memorabilia including film, books, photographs and permanent displays. Highlights of the collection include some of the world's oldest cars such as Fiats and Renaults, record breakers such as Golden Arrow and Bluebird, a motorsport gallery celebrating Grand Prix racing and rallying, and a James Bond experience with cars and boats from the films. Visitors can travel round the grounds by monorail or open-topped replica 1912 London bus.

☎ 01590 612345   www.beaulieu.co.uk

Needles Pleasure Park

Needles Pleasure Park · 156 C4

A spectacular chairlift ride provides unique views of the striking coloured sands of the Alum Bay cliffs and across to The Needles and lighthouse. There are also boat trips, children's rides and games, tours round the Isle of Wight Sweet Factory and glass blowing demonstrations at Alum Bay Glass.

A short walk along the cliffs is a 19th century fort, Needles Old Battery. As well as an exhibition on the site's history, a 200ft (60m) tunnel leads to a viewpoint with unrivalled views across to the Needles, three distinctive jagged, eroded remnants of the former chalk cliffs.

☎ 0870 458 0022   www.theneedles.co.uk

New Forest · 156 B1

Contrary to expectation, much of this 150 square mile (388sq km) Area of Outstanding Natural Beauty is not actually still forested; rather it is a mixture of woodland and heath, poor sandy soils giving little incentive for cultivation. The Forest was designated a royal hunting preserve by William the Conqueror in 1079 and, at this time, punishment for trespass included mutilation and even death; now around 8 million people visit the area each year.

Although close to large centres of population, once away from the main roads there is a distinct feeling of having 'got away from it all'. The Forest itself is relatively sparsely settled, with only Lyndhurst and Brockenhurst of any significant size. However, the high visitor numbers in recent years have called for practical measures, such as the 40mph (64kph) speed limit throughout the Forest, to protect the environment, the wildlife, the ponies and other grazing animals.

The harsh penalties meted out in the 11th century were later rescinded and the local owner-occupiers, or Commoners, were granted certain rights, such as the freedom to graze livestock or more obscurely, turbary (peat cutting). These rights are administered by the Verderers, and the Verderers Court, which is held every two months, is considered to be the oldest court of law in England. The distinctive Forest landscape, with its free-grazing ponies, cattle and sheep, is a consequence of these ancient laws.

The remoter parts of the Forest, particularly the wetland areas, are home to some of Britain's rarest plant, animal and insect species, whilst the open heathland is of particular interest to birdlovers. The scenery, although not dramatic in terms of relief, makes for pleasant walking and cycling country.

New Forest

🏛 New Forest Museum & Information Centre   156 C2

The place to visit for all the background information on the Forest and its inhabitants. There are interactive displays on the area's geology, and specific exhibits on wildlife, history and culture. The famous New Forest Embroidery is on display and there is a regular programme of temporary exhibitions.

☎ 023 8028 2269   www.newforestmuseum.org

❀ Nymans (NT)   159 E1

This beautiful 30 acre (12ha) garden set on the side of a sheltered valley was created by three generations of the Messel family dating from 1890. The garden originally surrounded a 14th century manor house which was largely destroyed by fire in 1947, and the ruins give an atmospheric backdrop to the planting. The garden is designed as a series of 'rooms' with hedges, walls and trees providing shelter for rare and exotic plants.

☎ 01444 400321   www.nationaltrust.org.uk

🏰 Osborne House   157 E3

This was the rural retreat for Queen Victoria and her family, away from the pressures of ceremonial life. The house was designed by Prince Albert with technical input from Thomas Cubitt. The Prince was an admirer of Italian art and architecture and his design was based on the style of an Italian villa, complete with towers and terraces. As a widow, Victoria was a frequent visitor until her death in 1901, and many of the apartments have been preserved with little change since then, in keeping with her wishes.

The interior design of Osborne House is equally lavish. The Grand Corridor is lined by marble sculptures, and there are portraits and frescoes which underline the family's links with Europe and the Empire. Particularly sumptuous is the Durbar

Room, built in the early 1890s to celebrate the Queen's role as Empress of India.

Within the grounds, 'Swiss Cottage', the royal equivalent of a Wendy House, was built with Prince Albert's intention of providing his children with the basics of housekeeping and cookery. There is also the ultimate boys' toy, Victoria Fort, which the royal princes helped to construct.

The pleasant gardens were laid out by Prince Albert in Italianate terraces, with beautiful views across the Solent, and there is a restored walled garden.

☎ 01983 200022   www.english-heritage.org.uk

❀ Owl House, The   173 F5

This 16th century timber-framed house (not open to the public) was purchased by Lady Dufferin in 1952. The gardens, extending to 16 acres (6.5ha), were created during her time here and include expansive lawns, woodland walks and sunken water gardens.

☎ 01892 890230   www.owlhouse.com

☐ Oxford   406

Originally an important Saxon town, thanks to its strategic position where the Rivers Thames and Cherwell meet, the key date in Oxford's development as a major university town was 1167 when all Anglo-Norman students were expelled from the Sorbonne and selected Oxford as a suitable alternative. The first three colleges, Balliol, Merton and University, were built in the 13th century and others followed slowly over time so that now the university has around 15,000 students and 39 colleges. The city centre is dominated by the attractive college buildings, many of which are open to the public. Of particular interest are Christ Church, with its splendid Great Hall, Magdalen, with its riverside gardens, and Merton. Some of the colleges charge admission and access may be limited in term time. Other impressive buildings are the Bodleian Library, Ashmolean Museum and Sheldonian Theatre, an early design by Sir Christopher Wren. The city's cathedral, the smallest in England, is in Christ Church College, where it doubles as the college chapel. Famous literary, scientific and theological associations abound, and the museums contain major historical, natural history and scientific collections. Oxford is essentially a medieval city, and is best visited by public transport. The centre is compact and there is an excellent park and ride system.

www.visitoxford.org

🏛 Oxford Story   406 B2

A time car ride through the history of Oxford University in carriages designed as desks. The associated audiovisual presentation provides information both on the development of the university and the many influential people who have passed through its doors.

☎ 01865 790055   www.oxfordstory.co.uk

Osborne House

🏛 Oxfordshire Museum, The   183 G1

Located in a fine town house in Woodstock, this illuminating museum has plenty of information on the social history of the county, permanent displays tracing the story of the inhabitants, landscapes, buildings and industries from earliest times to the present day. There is also a special gallery for children and a purpose-built gallery for temporary exhibits.

☎ 01993 811456   www.oxfordshire.gov.uk

★ Palace Pier   390 F3

Opened on 20th May 1899, this 1722ft (525m) long pier (Grade II* listed) features filigree ironwork arches and some of the original kiosks. Over the years, these basic attractions have been joined by a huge array of modern-day amusements such as a funfair, arcades, night club, bars and restaurants.

☎ 01273 609361   www.brightonpier.co.uk

Oxford – Radcliffe Camera

🏯 Paradise Park   159 G3

This varied attraction, set in colourful themed gardens, is ideal for children. It focuses on the local area's history and includes life-size moving dinosaurs, a model village featuring Sussex landmarks, a collection of fossils, crazy golf and a miniature railway.

☎ 01273 512123   www.paradisepark.co.uk

🏰 ❀ Parham House   158 C2

This 'E' shaped Elizabethan house, built in 1577 with later additions, has panelled rooms hung with portraits and 17th century furniture, some of which is still covered with the original needlework. Parham is surrounded by extensive grounds including a deer park and an attractive 11 acre (4.5ha) garden featuring a brick and turf maze and a 4 acre (1.5ha) walled garden, the flowers from which are used to adorn the house.

☎ 01903 744888   www.parhaminsussex.co.uk

🏯 Paulton's Park   156 C1

A leisure park of 140 acres (56ha) particularly suitable for families, with over 50 rides and activities, including a log flume and roller coaster. In addition there is a good collection of exotic birds and wildfowl in aviaries and ponds, a 19th century working waterwheel, 10 acre (4ha) lake and Romany Museum providing insight into traditional gipsy life.

☎ 023 8081 4455   www.paultonspark.co.uk

Penshurst Place
173 E4

Built of local sandstone, this impressive castellated manor house dates from the 14th century and has been occupied by the Sidney family since 1552. The house is notable for its outstanding medieval Barons Hall built in 1341 with its 60ft (18m) high chestnut-beamed roof. The State Rooms contain a collection of paintings from the 15th to 17th centuries, furniture, tapestries and armour. The vast 10 acre (4ha) walled garden, created between 1570 and 1666, is formed into a series of garden rooms divided by a mile of yew hedging. The variety of planting gives all year round interest. Also of interest is the deer park and toy museum.

☎ 01892 870307   www.penshurstplace.com

Petworth House (NT)
171 E5

Situated on the edge of a 700 acre (283ha) landscaped deer park and adjacent to the town of Petworth, this magnificent 17th century mansion was built around an older manor house owned by the Earls of Northumberland. The park, landscaped in the mid 18th century, is considered to be one of Lancelot 'Capability' Brown's finest and is home to Europe's largest herd of fallow deer.

The house contains the National Trust's largest and finest collection of pictures, the foundations of which were laid by Charles Seymour, 6th Duke of Somerset, when he acquired the house in 1690 on his marriage to the Earl of Northumberland's daughter. On the Duke's death the house passed by marriage to the Wyndham family. Charles Wyndham, the 2nd Earl of Egremont, added to the existing collection of Italian, French and Dutch Old Masters and acquired ancient sculpture from Rome and Greece. The 3rd Earl of Egremont continued the tradition. He collected contemporary British paintings. Interestingly, he was a patron of Turner, providing a studio for him at Petworth and many of Turner's paintings can be seen in the house. The 3rd Earl also acquired work from Gainsborough and Reynolds.

Following alterations to the house in the 1870s only two of the original 17th century interiors remain: a baroque chapel and a marble hall with black and white checked floor.

☎ 01798 343929   www.nationaltrust.org.uk

Petworth House

Pevensey Castle
160 B3

Dating from Roman times, and occupied by the Normans in 1066, the castle's location as a possible invasion point led to several sieges during its history. It eventually became uninhabited by the 16th century and fell into ruin. A gun emplacement was built there during the Spanish Armada and the castle was again used during World War II. Pillboxes from that time can still be seen. There are towers, battlements and dungeons to explore.

☎ 01323 762604   www.english-heritage.org.uk

Pitt Rivers Museum
406 A2

A unique collection of objects from all over the world, with something of interest for everyone.

The museum was founded in 1884 when Lt-Gen Pitt-Rivers, a prominent figure in the world of anthropology and archaeology, donated his collection of over 18,000 items to Oxford University. This collection has now been considerably enlarged to comprise over half a million objects, displayed according to function.

☎ 01865 270927   www.prm.ox.ac.uk

Polesden Lacey (NT)
171 G2

Attractive Regency house in a beautiful setting on the North Downs. It was the home for many years of society hostess, Mrs Ronald Greville, who was a friend of Edward VII. It contains sumptuous interiors and is especially renowned for its paintings. The future George VI and Queen Elizabeth spent part of their honeymoon here in 1923. The gardens have lovely views and extend to 30 acres (12ha), including lawns, walled garden and herbaceous borders.

☎ 01372 452048   www.nationaltrust.org.uk

Port Lympne Wild Animal Park
174 D5

The park was created in 1973 when John Aspinall bought the Port Lympne estate. It comprises a 350 acre (140ha) reserve where the animals can roam in relatively unconstrained conditions. Aspinall supported an ethos of bonding between keepers and animals that has resulted in successful breeding programmes. At the park visitors can see a large group of black rhinos, Asian elephants, tigers and lions, amongst others. Also open to the public is the house, built during World War I, with its 15 acre (6ha) formal garden.

☎ 01303 264647   www.howletts.net

Portchester Castle
349 E3

One of England's oldest fortifications, Portchester was originally built in the 3rd century AD by the Romans as part of a chain of fortresses known as the Saxon Shore forts, built in response to Saxon raids. The massive walls, 20ft (6m) high and 10ft (3m) thick, are amongst the finest surviving examples of this period in northern Europe. Subsequently occupied almost continuously until the 19th century, the site was initially a walled settlement with an impressive Norman keep, part of which still stands, then respectively a castle, royal palace, military hospital and a gaol for French prisoners during the Napoleonic Wars.

☎ 023 9237 8291   www.english-heritage.org.uk

Portsmouth Cathedral
407 F1

Formerly the parish church of Portsmouth, cathedral status was granted in 1927 when the diocese of Portsmouth was created. The original building dates from the 12th century, and the transept and sanctuary still remain, combined with a 17th century nave and tower, rebuilt following Civil War damage. A cupola was added in 1703 and the modern nave and aisles in the mid 20th century, producing an unusual fusion of style with a central tower. Internally, there are several interesting features including the Navy Aisle, with its maritime connections, the remains of a 13th century wall painting, a fine 16th century Florentine majolica plaque and a 20th century bronze statue of John the Baptist.

☎ 023 9282 3300   www.portsmouthcathedral.org.uk

Portsmouth Historic Dockyard
407 E1

The development of the dockyard at Portsmouth was initiated by Richard I in the 1190s and evolved over succeeding centuries. It became the construction centre for Henry VIII's fleet and received Royal Dockyard status in 1670 when Charles II founded the Royal Navy. By 1800 the navy had nearly 700 ships and the dockyard was considered the largest industrial complex in the world. Apart from a blip at the end of the Napoleonic Wars, expansion was almost continuous throughout the 19th century. In the 20th century the dockyard was vital to Britain's successes in both World Wars, but since then has been in decline due to defence cuts and streamlining of the armed services. The Naval Base remains the premier home port for the Royal Navy, but the title of Royal Dockyard has gone.

The historic Georgian part of the dockyard is now open to the public and this provides a unique opportunity to experience 500 years of the Royal Navy's history, from the remains of the 16th century ship *Mary Rose*, to Action Stations, which uses interactive technology to illustrate the role of the modern navy. In between, a visit to *H.M.S. Victory* reveals the privations suffered by sailors in Nelson's fleet, the scrupulously restored *H.M.S. Warrior* displays a state of the art mid-19th century warship, the Royal Naval Museum gives a detailed history of the service from the 18th century onwards, while Warships by Water harbour tours give a glimpse of the modern operational fleet.

☎ 023 9272 2562   www.flagship.org

H.M.S. Victory – Portsmouth Historic Dockyard

Pulborough Brooks RSPB Nature Reserve
158 C2

Created in 1989, this 420 acre (170ha) reserve primarily consists of an area of wet grassy meadows which flood in winter. Thousands of water birds such as swans, ducks, geese and wading birds visit the site, especially as winter migrants. There is a visitor centre housed in a converted barn and a 2 mile (3.2km) circular trail.

☎ 01798 875851   www.rspb.org.uk

Quebec House (NT)
173 D3

General James Wolfe, who led the British to victory over the French in the Battle of Quebec in 1759, lived here as a boy. Named after the battle, this gabled red brick house dating from the 16th century, contains an exhibition paying tribute to his life and the victory that made his name.

☎ 01732 868381   www.nationaltrust.org.uk

Richborough Castle | 175 F2

Now a ruin, this fort is thought to date from the Roman invasion in AD43 and, with Watling Street starting at its east gate, became their main entry point into Britain en route to London. Today, flint walls rising to 25ft (7.5m) high can be seen and the foundations of a triumphal arch that was originally over 80ft (24m) high. There is a museum containing artefacts found on site and an exhibition on Roman life.

☎ 01304 612013   www.english-heritage.org.uk

River & Rowing Museum | 184 C4

A museum dedicated to rowing and the River Thames, and to Henley, the town where they are inextricably linked.

There are three themed galleries – the Rowing Gallery, the Thames Gallery and the Henley Gallery.

An additional walk-through attraction, particularly aimed at children, re-creates the characters and settings of Kenneth Grahame's 'Wind in the Willows'.

☎ 01491 415600   www.rrm.co.uk

Robin Hill Country Park | 157 E4

The 88 acres (35ha) of this country park combine nature trails and woodland walks with theme park rides and adventure playgrounds.

☎ 01983 527352   www.robin-hill.com

Rockbourne Roman Villa | 156 A1

Discovered in 1942 by a farmer digging out a ferret, this extensive villa was occupied from the 2nd century AD until the end of Roman rule in Britain in the 5th century AD. Although much of the area has been excavated, part has been backfilled for protection since the site is not under cover. However, the outlines are marked out, and mosaic floors and underfloor heating systems can be viewed. A museum displays artefacts found on the site, including pottery, jewellery and a large hoard of coins.

☎ 01725 518541   www.hants.gov.uk

Romney Marsh | 174 C5

This fertile, flat landscape (once under the sea) was reclaimed from marshland in medieval times, and is protected from flooding by a shingle bank. Running along the landward side of the marsh is the 23 mile (37km) long Royal Military Canal, which was built during the Napoleonic wars. The Marsh, as well as being home to the longwool Romney sheep, is also rich in flora and fauna, and is a favourite spot for birdwatchers.

Romney, Hythe & Dymchurch Railway | 174 D5

Originally opened in July 1927 to transport the public, this 15 inch narrow-gauge railway now covers a distance of 13.5 miles (22km) from the Cinque Port of Hythe to Dungeness. The line travels through the seaside resort of Dymchurch, and also New Romney where there is a Toy and Model Railway museum.

☎ 01797 362353   www.rhdr.org.uk

Rousham House | 197 G5

An unspoilt 17th century house, later extended and remodelled by William Kent in the style of a Gothic Tudor mansion. However, the original staircase and some 17th century panelling still remain, together with Kent's painted parlour containing some of his furniture and painted ceiling.

The landscape garden at Rousham, started by the royal gardener Charles Bridgeman, was further developed and elaborated on by Kent. It remains almost as he left it, with many 18th century water features and temples still in existence. There is also an attractive walled garden with colourful herbaceous border, parterre and pigeon house.

The house opens two days a week in summer, but the garden is open all year. No children under 15.

☎ 01869 347110   www.rousham.org

Rousham House

Royal Navy Submarine Museum | 349 E4

A fascinating museum tracing the history and explaining the principles of submarine technology and warfare. Visitors can see *Holland I*, the Royal Navy's first submarine, recovered from the sea bed almost 70 years after sinking on her way to the breakers yard and now fully restored. This can be compared to *H.M.S. Alliance*, preserved fully equipped from when she ended service in 1973 and now in dry dock.

☎ 023 9252 9217   www.rnsubmus.co.uk

Royal Pavilion | 390 F2

With its 'Hindu Style' domes and minarets, this Regency Palace is one of the most distinctive and unusual buildings in Britain. Originally a farmhouse, it was transformed for the notoriously profligate Prince Regent (later George IV). In 1787 Henry Holland was commissioned to enlarge the property; further alterations and additions were made by John Nash between 1815 and 1822 . The result was the extravagant Indian and Chinese influenced palace that we see today. The Pavilion has undergone a substantial programme to restore it to its former glory, and stands in restored Regency gardens which have been replanted to Nash's original 1820s design.

The lavish interior features impressive and unusual rooms; notably the Entrance Hall with its Chinese motif wall decorations and the 162ft (49m) Long Gallery, also with a distinctly Chinese décor. The Banqueting Room is stunning with a 45ft (14m) high painted ceiling, with the huge one ton crystal chandelier suspended from a carved dragon. In 1820, the King's Apartments were finally finished, coinciding with George IV's accession and today contain much of the original furniture. After the death of George IV in 1830, the palace was used by William IV and then Queen Victoria who sold it on to the town council in 1850.

☎ 01273 290900   www.royalpavilion.org.uk

Royal Victoria Country Park | 348 B3

Located on the site of a former military hospital, the park covers over 100 acres (40ha) of landscaped grounds, woodlands, marsh and beach, and there are nature trails, walks, a narrow-gauge railway and, in summer, a programme of events. A Sensory Garden has also been developed here, designed for scent, sound, colour and

texture. The only remaining feature of the hospital is the chapel, which houses a museum of the hospital's history.

☎ 023 8045 5157   www.hants.gov.uk

Rycote Chapel | 184 B2

A 15th century chapel retaining the original furniture, with outstanding carved and painted woodwork, two roofed pews and a musicians' gallery.

☎ 023 9258 1059   www.english-heritage.org.uk

St Mary's House | 159 D3

Originally built as a pilgrims' inn, this timber-framed house dates from 1470. Features of the house include an Elizabethan staircase, Gothic fireplaces along with 16th century marquetry and furniture. The gardens have unusual animal topiary, herbaceous borders and a rose garden.

☎ 01903 816205

Sandham Memorial Chapel (NT) | 169 F1

A red brick chapel built in the 1920s as a memorial to Lieutenant H.W. Sandham, who died following the Macedonia campaign. Inside, the chapel walls are lined with a dramatic series of murals by Stanley Spencer who had been an orderly on the campaign.

☎ 01635 278394   www.nationaltrust.org.uk

Royal Pavilion – Brighton

Savill Garden | 185 E5

Beautiful 35 acre (14ha) garden set within Windsor Great Park comprising woodland, a formal rose garden and herbaceous borders. Named after Eric Savill (deputy surveyor of Windsor Park and Woods) who began work on it for George V in 1932. The garden has a magnificent display of rhododendrons and azaleas giving it superb colour in the spring, although it is worth a visit at any time of year.

☎ 01753 847518   www.savillgarden.co.uk

Scotney Castle Garden (NT) | 173 F5

Surrounding the ruins of a 14th century moated castle are picturesque 19th century gardens created by Edward Hussey. The rich planting includes rhododendrons and azaleas giving superb spring colour, plus many Japanese maples, tulip trees and liquidambars which give a splendid display in autumn.

☎ 01892 891081   www.nationaltrust.org.uk

Sea Life Centre | 390 F3

Aquarium in a Victorian building with superb ocean tunnel display where visitors can 'walk' through the ocean amongst sharks, rays and giant turtles. There is also a giant Pacific octopus and touch tanks where visitors can hold crabs and feed rays.

☎ 01273 604234   www.sealifeeurope.com

Seven Sisters Country Park　160 A4

The country park lies within an Area of Outstanding Natural Beauty and is a designated Site of Special Scientific Interest. It was established in 1971 and encompasses 700 acres (283ha) either side of the River Cuckmere. The site comprises a wide range of habitats including the beautiful chalk downland with its unique flora and fauna, wetland, coastal and marine environments. The park takes its name from the famous Seven Sisters white cliffs formed where the chalk of the South Downs meets the sea.

There are a number of 18th century flint barns within the park, one of those in Exceat has been converted into a visitor centre. As well as enjoying the area on foot, visitors can also hire bicycles and canoes.

☎ 01323 870280　　　www.sevensisters.org.uk

Seven Sisters Country Park

Sheffield Park (NT)　159 G1

With their wide range of rare and unusual trees and shrubs, these beautiful gardens have the character of a landscaped arboretum. They were created for the first Earl of Sheffield in the late 18th century by Lancelot 'Capability' Brown and Humphrey Repton, and extend to 120 acres (48.5ha). In 1909 the estate was acquired by Arthur G. Soames who, over the next 25 years, was responsible for refining the overall design and introduced much of the varied and exotic planting we see today.

Four large lakes form the centrepiece of the garden. Waterfalls and a 25ft (7.5m) cascade connect the lakes together and are spanned by attractive ornamental bridges. In the spring there are magnificent displays of bluebells and daffodils, then later on, rhododendrons and azaleas make an impressive splash of vibrant colour. In summer, red, white and pink water lily flowers add colour to the lakes.

☎ 01825 790231　　　www.nationaltrust.org.uk

Sir Harold Hillier Gardens & Arboretum　169 E5

A unique collection of shrubs and trees which is one of the largest of its kind in the world. The gardens were established by Sir Harold Hillier in 1953, and extend to over 180 acres (70ha). The collection comprises over 42,000 plants from the world's temperate regions, grown in themed gardens which are designed so that there is colour and interest throughout the year. The Visitor and Education Pavilion describes the purpose and background history of the gardens.

☎ 01794 368787　　　www.hilliergardens.org.uk

Sissinghurst Castle (NT)　174 A5

These world famous gardens created in the 1930s by writer and poet Vita Sackville-West and her husband, diplomat and writer Sir Harold Nicolson, were first opened to the public in 1938. He was the designer who liked formality and clean lines, and she was the romantic plantswoman who liked profusion and surprise; two gifted people whose talents blended perfectly. Much of the garden's charm is due to the backdrop provided by the Elizabethan buildings, the focal point of which is a four-storey red brick tower, to one side of which is a moat.

The garden extends to 6 acres (2.5ha) and is comprised of a series of 10 'outdoor rooms' divided by hedges of rose, hornbeam and yew, as well as walls. This stunning garden has had an important influence on garden design and planting in the late 20th century.

☎ 01580 710700　　　www.nationaltrust.org.uk

Smallhythe Place (NT)　174 A5

Early 16th century half-timbered farmhouse, once home to Victorian actress Dame Ellen Terry who lived here from 1899 until her death in 1928. The house contains various mementoes from Terry and her theatrical contemporaries, including a letter from Oscar Wilde.

☎ 01580 762334　　　www.nationaltrust.org.uk

Southampton Maritime Museum　409 F2

Housed in a 14th century warehouse with impressive timber roof, built for the wool trade, the museum recounts the story of the Port of Southampton. There are models of the great passenger liners, a panoramic layout of the docks, and interactive exhibits showing how the ships and docks function.

☎ 023 8022 3941　　　www.southampton.gov.uk

Southsea Castle & Museum　157 F3

Built in 1544 as part of Henry VIII's coastal defences, and said to have been designed by the king himself. Its initial purpose was to protect the large fleet of warships based in Portsmouth Harbour, including the flagship Mary Rose which sank in front of the castle in 1545.

The building remained an active military base until 1960. During the preceding 400 years it was captured by Parliamentarians in 1642, suffered major damage from an explosion in 1759, was renovated and enlarged in the early 19th century and used as a military prison in Victorian times.

☎ 023 9282 7261　　　www.southseacastle.co.uk

Spitfire & Hurricane Memorial, R.A.F. Manston　175 F2

The permanent home of two original examples of World War II fighter aircraft along with associated memorabilia. Visitors can see a prototype of the 'Dambusters' bouncing bomb plus a display telling the story of combat over Kent during the war.

☎ 01843 821940　　　www.spitfire-museum.com

Sissinghurst Castle

Squerryes Court　172 D3

An attractive brick-built 17th century manor house, home to the Warde family since 1731. The interior of the house contains tapestries dating from 1720, 17th century paintings, as well as furniture and porcelain. The 20 acre (8ha) garden includes a lake, herbaceous borders, and a formal garden which has been restored using the original plans.

☎ 01959 562345　　　www.squerryes.co.uk

Standen (NT)　172 C5

Built between 1892 and 1894, the house was designed by Philip Webb, a lifelong friend and colleague of William Morris, and is a fine showpiece of the Arts and Crafts movement. It contains furniture, tapestries and paintings of the period, along with Morris textiles and wallpapers. There are lovely views from the beautiful 10 acre (4ha) hillside garden.

☎ 01342 323029　　　www.nationaltrust.org.uk

Staunton Country Park　157 G1

Extending to over 1000 acres (400ha), this was created by Sir George Staunton in the early 18th century as a Regency Pleasure Garden, and is now one of the few remaining Regency parks in the country. Sir George was a noted botanist and authority on China, and the park was inspired by his travels in the Far East.

The tropical glasshouses, rebuilt to Sir George's original designs, contain unusual plants from rainforest environments. There is also a yew maze, puzzle garden, play area, ornamental lake and range of unusual follies.

☎ 023 9245 3405　　　www.hants.gov.uk

Stoneacre (NT)　173 G3

An attractive half-timbered house dating from 1480 and restored in the 1920s. It features a Great Hall spanned by impressive timberwork. Outside is a 20th century cottage garden.

☎ 01622 862157　　　www.nationaltrust.org.uk

Stonor Park　184 C4

The red brick Tudor façade disguises a building dating originally from the 12th century and extended in the 14th century, set in a lovely wooded valley on the slopes of the Chilterns. Internally, the rooms are decorated in 18th century Gothic style and there are some interesting paintings and Mortlake tapestries. There is also an exhibition on the life and work of St Edmund Campion, who sought refuge here at the time of the Reformation.

The attractive hillside gardens have displays of daffodils, narcissi, irises and roses, and there are good views over the surrounding deer park.

☎ 01491 638587　　　www.stonor.com

Stowe School　198 B4

One of the finest Georgian landscape gardens (NT) in the country, covering 350 acres (140ha) of parkland, valleys, views, lakes and rivers, laid out between 1713 – 25. There are over 30 temples dotted around the grounds, designed by well-known architects of the day such as William Kent and Sir John Vanbrugh, and many of these have been restored. The Temple family, who owned Stowe at this time, were fortunate to have the successive services of three of the great landscape gardeners of the time, Charles Bridgeman, William Kent and Lancelot 'Capability' Brown.

The magnificent house at the centre of the park is

now a public school, with access limited mainly to school holidays, but the park is open on a more regular basis.

☎ 01280 822850 (Garden)   www.nationaltrust.org.uk
☎ 01280 818282 (House)   www.stowe.co.uk

🏛 Tangmere Military Aviation Museum   158 B3

Tangmere, one of Britain's earliest airfields, was operational between 1917 – 1970, and the museum, which started in 1982, traces the history of flight-based warfare, emphasising Tangmere's links with the Royal Air Force and Battle of Britain.

☎ 01243 775223   www.tangmere-museum.org.uk

❋ Thorpe Park   171 F1

This popular theme park covers over 500 acres (200ha) and is located on the site of former gravel pits which have been landscaped into a series of lakes. This watery location has been used to set the main theme of the park, that of water rides.

The park is divided into a number of areas. These include, amongst others, 'Ranger Country', 'Lost City', 'Neptune's Kingdom', 'Canada Creek' and 'Octopus Garden'. Elsewhere in the park is Nemesis Inferno, a feet-free roller coaster – a real 'white knuckle' experience.

In addition to all the rides there is also a traditional 1930s farm where children can stroke the sheep, pigs and cows.

☎ 01932 562633   www.thorpepark.co.uk

Thorpe Park

🏰 Tonbridge Castle (Ruins)   173 E4

Remains of a Norman motte and bailey castle set in 14 acres (5.5ha) of grounds. Within the impressive 13th century gatehouse visitors can experience castle life through interactive displays and an audio tour.

☎ 01732 770929   www.tonbridgecastle.org

🏛 Tunbridge Wells Museum & Art Gallery   173 E5

Museum of local and natural history, plus an art gallery, which has frequently changing art and craft exhibitions.

☎ 01892 554171   www.tunbridgewells.gov.uk/museum

🏰 Uffington Castle & White Horse (NT)   183 E4

Belying its name, Uffington Castle has no connection with medieval fortifications but is an imposing Iron Age hill fort covering 8 acres (3ha) close to the Ridgeway, an ancient track.

The White Horse, cut into the chalk of the hillside to the east of the castle, is 374ft (114m) long and

rather stylised in appearance. Tests indicate a Bronze Age origin, and the figure is thought to represent Epona, a horse goddess, though it will come as no surprise that many legends have developed around this feature.

www.english-heritage.org.uk

🏠 Uppark (NT)   157 G1

A late 17th century house in an attractive setting high on the South Downs. The estate, extending to 50 acres (20ha), was designed by Humphrey Repton. The interior is Georgian and includes paintings, furniture, textiles and ceramics, and an 18th century dolls' house with its original contents. The servants' quarters can also been seen.

☎ 01730 825857   www.nationaltrust.org.uk

❋ Valley Gardens   171 E1

These beautiful gardens with their impressive displays of rhododendrons, azaleas, magnolias, camellias and carpeting of daffodils cover an area of 200 acres (80ha) within Windsor Great Park. As well as the amazing spring colour, they are very attractive in the autumn.

☎ 01753 847518   www.crownestate.co.uk

❋ Ventnor Botanic Gardens   157 E5

One of the youngest botanical gardens in the country, started in 1970 on the site of a former hospital. The potential of the location, with its mild climate, was recognised by the late Sir Harold Hillier, the famous plantsman, and the 22 acre (9ha) garden was designed and planted with help from his nurseries, tender plants flourishing in the sheltered environment. Unfortunately a combination of harsh winters and stormy weather in the 1980s destroyed a large number of species, and the replacements have only recently become established.

☎ 01983 855397   www.botanic.co.uk

🏠 ❋ Vyne, The (NT)   170 B2

A splendid red brick Tudor mansion built for Henry VIII's Lord Chamberlain, Lord Sandys. Subsequent modifications in the 17th century include the first classical portico of its kind in the country, and there were some further 18th century alterations. Notable features include the Long Gallery, a sweeping Palladian staircase, and the Tudor chapel. The garden has some good herbaceous border displays, and the estate consists of a further 500 acres (200ha) of park and woodland, providing attractive walks.

☎ 01256 881337   www.nationaltrust.org.uk

🏠 ❋ Waddesdon Manor (NT)   184 C1

The external appearance of this late Victorian building owes more to the style of a 16th century French chateau than a conventional English country house. It was built for Baron Ferdinand de Rothschild, its primary purpose being to display his splendid collection of French decorative arts. There are also paintings by Gainsborough, Reynolds, Romney, and Dutch and Flemish masters. The wine cellars contain a collection of over 15,000 bottles, some dating back to 1868.

The late 19th century formal gardens surrounding the house are amongst the finest Victorian gardens in Britain, and include a magnificent, colourful parterre, carpet bedding, rose garden, specimen trees, fountains and an extensive collection of French, Dutch and Italian statuary. The centrepiece is the ornate, cast iron rococo aviary which has an interesting collection of exotic birds.

☎ 01296 653226   www.waddesdon.org.uk

❋ Wakehurst Place (NT)   172 C5

The setting of Wakehurst Place is superb, with fine views across the Sussex Weald. The gardens, which comprise a mixture of walled gardens, woodland, water gardens and lakes, a Himalayan glade, plus more formal planting, surround a 16th century sandstone mansion (not owned by the Trust) and extend to 170 acres (70ha). Much of the impressive collection of trees and shrubs were originally planted by Gerald Loder, 1st Lord Wakehurst, between 1903 and 1936 and then by Sir Henry Price who bequeathed the garden to the National Trust in 1963. Two years later the Royal Botanic Gardens leased the gardens from the Trust to complement their work at Kew.

The wide variety of native and exotic trees give rise to impressive autumn colours when the maples, American beech and larch come into their own. In spring the woodland floors are scattered with bluebells, and later on, rhododendrons create a superb sight.

Wakehurst Place is also home to the Millennium Seed Bank, an ambitious project to safeguard over 24,000 plant species from around the world. An exhibition allows visitors to see the ongoing seed preservation and research in progress.

☎ 01444 894066   www.nationaltrust.org.uk

🏰 ❋ Walmer Castle & Garden   175 F4

Tudor castle built 1539 – 40 as a coastal artillery fortress for Henry VIII. In 1708 the castle became the residence of the Lords Warden of the Cinque Ports, some of the most famous encumbents being the Duke of Wellington, Sir Winston Churchill and the Queen Mother. Visitors can enjoy the attractive gardens and see the room where Wellington died.

☎ 01304 364288   www.english-heritage.org.uk

❋ Waterperry   184 B2

An 80 year old garden with a fine collection of alpines, herbaceous plants, shrubs and trees.

The herbaceous borders are a particularly attractive feature, carefully planted to ensure that colour is continuous from May through to October. There are also delightful formal rose gardens, raised beds of alpines, a knot garden and riverside walks.

A fascinating collection of agricultural and horticultural tools is housed in an 18th century granary in the grounds.

☎ 01844 339226   www.waterperrygardens.co.uk

🏛 Weald & Downland Open Air Museum   158 A2

Almost 50 historic buildings dating from the 13th to the 19th century have been rebuilt on this attractive 50 acre (20ha) parkland site in the lovely South Downs countryside. The buildings were rescued from destruction and have been carefully dismantled and moved from their original locations to create this museum. The site illustrates traditional rural life in an inspiring way.

☎ 01243 811363   www.wealddown.co.uk

🏕 Wellington Country Park   170 C1

A good range of activities in this 350 acres (140ha) of woodland, parkland and lakes. For younger children there is an adventure playground, small breeds farm and miniature railway, while other options include fishing on the lake, nature trails, and camping and caravanning facilities. There are events taking place throughout the year.

☎ 0118 932 6444   www.wellington-country-park.co.uk

Wakehurst Place

🏛 West Berkshire Museum 169 F1

Two of Newbury's most historic buildings, the 17th century Cloth Hall and 18th century Granary, are now home to an absorbing museum of local history. There are specific galleries devoted to the Kennet and Avon Canal, traditional local industries, costume and local history. The Civil War is also a major theme, two battles of the period having taken place locally. There is a programme of special exhibitions.

☎ 01635 30511   www.westberks.gov.uk

❃ West Dean Gardens 158 A2

In an attractive setting at the foot of the South Downs, this 35 acre (14ha) garden contains specimen trees, herbaceous planting and a Victorian walled kitchen garden with 16 restored glasshouses and frames. A notable feature of the garden is a 300ft (100m) pergola by Harold Peto dating from 1911. Over recent years extensive planting of bulbs has taken place resulting in spectacular spring displays. The garden holds two National Collections, that of the Tulip Tree and Horse Chestnut.

☎ 01243 818210   www.westdean.org.uk/site/gardens/

🏠 ❃ West Wycombe Park (NT) 184 D3

Extravagant 18th century Italianate mansion with the external appearance of a classical temple. Inspired by Grand Tours, there are splendid painted ceilings, and furniture, paintings and sculpture dating from the mid 18th century ownership of Sir Francis Dashwood, who founded the notorious Hell Fire Club. Club members were drawn from the upper echelons of society, and local mythology had them indulging in Satanic rites, though reality was probably wine, women and a spot of free thinking. Sir Francis also created the beautiful rococo landscape garden in the 300 acres (150ha) of parkland surrounding the house.

An unusual addition to the grounds are the Hell Fire Caves. Again the inspiration of Sir Francis, the existing caves were greatly extended in the 1750s by a remarkable feat of engineering. Although providing a suitably atmospheric meeting place for the Hell Fire Club, Sir Francis's motives were partly altruistic in that the work provided employment for local villagers following a series of failed harvests. The caves are privately owned and there is an additional entry fee.

☎ 01494 533739   www.nationaltrust.org.uk

✝ Winchester Cathedral 414 B2

One of the great cathedrals of England, and perhaps one of the best examples of Gothic Perpendicular architecture to be found.

The original minster was built by King Cenwalh of Wessex in AD643 and was the royal Saxon cathedral, burial place of kings. The foundations can still be seen adjacent to the West Door but this building was replaced by Bishop Walkelin, the first Norman bishop, who laid the foundations of the present cathedral in 1079, building materials including stone from the Isle of Wight and local timber. The cathedral was completed within 14 years, but over the following centuries underwent much modification, particularly between 1350 – 1450 when the original Romanesque nave was transformed to the English Gothic style, mainly due to the efforts of Bishop William of Wykeham. The nave measures 556ft (170m), making Winchester the longest medieval church in Europe. The whole building is an ecclesiastical and architectural treasure house.

Within the cathedral is a statue to William Walker, a deep sea diver who could be said to have single-handedly saved the cathedral from collapse at the beginning of the 20th century. He spent five years working underwater in complete darkness replacing the decaying timber of the ancient foundations.

☎ 01962 857200   www.winchester-cathedral.org.uk

🏰 Windsor Castle 414 D3

Strategically placed above the River Thames and a day's march from London, William the Conqueror selected Windsor as the site for a fort to protect the western approach to the capital. Since then it has become the largest and oldest occupied castle in the world.

William's original building was a wooden motte and bailey fort constructed in 1079, Henry II replacing this with stone outer walls and a round tower in 1165. In the succeeding centuries monarchs have enlarged and modified the castle, militarily if necessary, or decoratively in more peaceful times, and the building today occupies a site of 12 acres (5ha).

The magnificent State Rooms contain outstanding pictures from the Royal Collection including works by Holbein, Rembrandt and Canaletto, fine furniture, painted ceilings and carvings by Grinling Gibbons. These rooms are used for ceremonial and state occasions and may be closed when the Queen is in residence. In the winter months the richly decorated Semi State Rooms can also be viewed. The Drawings Gallery houses changing exhibitions of material drawn from the Royal Library and other treasures.

Within the precincts is St George's Chapel, built in the late 15th century and one of Britain's finest examples of Gothic architecture. It contains the tombs of 10 monarchs and the great battle sword of Edward III hangs on one of the walls.

Outside the castle, one of the best known of British ceremonies, the Changing of the Guard, takes place throughout the year. It is advisable to telephone in advance to check days and times.

It is important to note that this is a working palace, and that some areas may be closed off at short notice.

☎ 01753 869898   www.the-royal-collection.org.uk

❃ Wisley R.H.S. Gardens 171 F2

Home to the Royal Horticultural Society since its donation by Sir Thomas Hanbury in 1903, this garden was first established by George Wilson in 1878, a scientist and keen gardener, with the aim of growing difficult plants successfully.

The gardens extend to 204 acres (97ha) along the banks of the River Wey and are of interest to both keen horticulturalists and those who are just after a visual treat. Visitors can wander amongst the model gardens which give ideas that can be easily applied at home. The gardens also feature glasshouses, sweeping lawns, 420ft (128m) long herbaceous borders, an impressive rock garden and the Jubilee arboretum.

In front of the half-timbered Tudor-style building, which is used as a laboratory and offices, is a formal canal which is an impressive sight when the water lilies are in flower. The gardens look spectacular all through the year; in spring the Alpine meadow is stunning, with its carpet of yellow daffodils, the rose gardens and herbaceous borders are a riot of colour in the summer, the large number of trees provide autumn colour and in winter the heated glasshouses come into their own with their colourful exotics.

☎ 01483 224234   www.rhs.org.uk/gardens/wisley/

★ Witley Common Information Centre (NT) 171 E3

Located on Witley Common, an area of lowland heath and woodland with a wide variety of plant and animal life, this purpose-built education and information centre houses a countryside exhibition explaining the area's importance and management.

☎ 01428 683207   www.nationaltrust.org.uk

🏛 Worthing Museum & Art Gallery 158 D3

The museum has an emphasis on local history and is housed in an Edwardian building. It contains collections of ceramics, toys, textiles, geology, a variety of temporary exhibitions and a sculpture garden.

☎ 01903 239999 ext 1140   www.worthing.gov.uk/leisure/
☎ 01903 221150 (Saturdays)   museumartgallery/

🏰 Yarmouth Castle 156 C4

Completed in 1547, this was the final castle to be built in Henry VIII's coastal defence system, following a French invasion of the Isle of Wight in 1545. It is of a fairly simple design, consisting of a basic square with no central tower. Bounded by the sea to the north and east, the south and west walls were protected by a moat, filled in at the end of the 17th century. Around 1600 a large gun battery was built in the north part of the courtyard, while domestic buildings filled the south side. The gun platform now provides splendid views across the harbour and Solent.

☎ 01983 760678   www.english-heritage.org.uk

Wisley R.H.S. Gardens

LONDON

England's multi-cultural capital vibrates with round-the-clock reminders of its long and prestigious history. 'Old Father Thames' washes through a panorama of imposing buildings old and new, offering tastes of English tradition, cultural opportunities, avant-garde events and shopping galore. London is the definitive twenty-four hour city where the leisure facilities, entertainment, sporting venues and diversity of events are amongst the best in the world.

Houses of Parliament

🏛 Bank of England Museum   356 B3

An interesting insight into the role of finance, from the foundation of the bank in 1694 by Royal Charter to the high-tech world of modern banking. Besides displays of gold and banknotes, there is also a Roman mosaic floor (uncovered during rebuilding work in the 1930s) plus a variety of interactive displays.

☎ 020 7601 5491   www.bankofengland.co.uk/museum

🏛 Britain At War   356 B3

A re-creation of what life was like for the ordinary people of London during the Blitz. There are realistic reconstructions, including an underground air-raid shelter, an Anderson shelter and a BBC studio. Through the use of sights, sounds and special effects, visitors can get a real feel for the atmosphere of war-torn London.

☎ 020 7403 3171   www.britainatwar.co.uk

🏛 British Museum   376 J3

This is the oldest public museum in the world and was founded in 1753 when Sir Hans Sloane bequeathed his considerable collection of artefacts, along with his library and herbarium, to the nation in return for paying his heirs £20,000. George II and the Parliament of the time, led by the Speaker, Arthur Onslow, were persuaded to accept the gift and a public lottery was held to raise the necessary funds. The next year Montagu House was acquired in order to house the collection which has since increased to over six million objects. Over the years the building has had to expand to accommodate this huge collection, and the bulk of the neoclassical building which visitors see today, including the impressive south front, dates from 1852.

The museum houses the world's greatest collection of antiquities including the national collections of archaeology and ethnography, with treasures from all over the globe. Highlights include the Rosetta Stone, the Elgin Marbles and the Sutton Hoo treasure. There are also Egyptian mummies, which include not only humans but cats, baboons and even crocodiles, and the 2000 year old peat-preserved Lindow Man. The exhibits are so rich and varied that to attempt to see them all in a single visit would be impossible.

☎ 020 7323 8299   www.thebritishmuseum.ac.uk

British Museum

🏛 Buckingham Palace   376 D11

Built in 1705, and originally called Buckingham House, it was purchased by George III for his wife Queen Charlotte in 1761. Over the years it has been remodelled and extended a number of times, firstly by George IV with the assistance of his architect John Nash. A new suite of rooms was added and the north and south wings were rebuilt, with the Marble Arch as a centrepiece to the courtyard. The arch was later removed and now stands near the north east corner of Hyde Park. Queen Victoria made further alterations and additions, most notably the East Front which was designed by architect Edward Blore in 1847. Due to the deterioration of the stone, this was subsequently refaced in 1913 creating the familiar façade that we see today. Soon after Queen Victoria's accession in 1837, it became the monarch's official London residence.

The palace is open during August and September with visitors able to see 19 of the state rooms. These include the Throne Room, the Blue Drawing Room, the impressive White Drawing Room and the 150ft (46m) Picture Gallery. The huge Ballroom can also be seen; at 122ft (37m) long and 60ft (18m) wide, it is used for State banquets and can accommodate 150 guests. Treasures that can be seen within the palace include paintings by artists such as Rembrandt and superb examples of English and French furniture.

☎ 020 7766 7300   www.royal.gov.uk/output/page555.asp

Buckingham Palace

🏛 Cabinet War Rooms   376 H10

An intriguing underground suite of rooms used by Winston Churchill and his war cabinet as a meeting, planning and information centre during World War II. On display are the soundproofed Cabinet War Room, a Map Room, the original hot-line and scrambler used by Churchill when communicating with President Roosevelt, Churchill's private quarters and the desk from which he made some of his famous wartime broadcasts.

☎ 020 7930 6961   www.iwm.org.uk/cabinet/

▦ Chessington World of Adventures   171 G1

This popular attraction, covering 65 acres (27ha), combines the original zoo with a modern theme park. The zoo has a wide range of animals including a family group of West Lowland gorillas, sea lions, penguins and a variety of big cats such as lions, tigers and leopards. A gentle monorail allows visitors to travel over the animal enclosures for a superb bird's-eye view.

The theme park is divided into a number of areas and has all the usual thrill rides, along with those more suitable for younger children. 'The Forbidden Kingdom' has the white-knuckle ride Rameses' Revenge which revolves riders through a full 360° and blasts them with water; 'Transylvania' features The Vampire, Britain's first hanging roller coaster which also swings riders from side to side; 'Toytown' is ideal for the little ones as they can wear themselves out on Toadie's Crazy Cars and Berry Bouncers; 'Mystic East' features Dragon Falls, a traditional log flume, which has the usual plunge at the end, and Samurai where riders are spun round – not for those with delicate stomachs! Visitors can also enjoy 'Beanoland', where foam-filled balls can be catapulted, and 'Pirates Cove' where the Black Buccaneer pirate ship rocks riders from side to side. The sheer variety of attractions means that there is something for everyone.

☎ 01372 729 560   www.chessington.co.uk

🏠 Chiswick House   355 C4

This fine 18th century domed villa, designed by Lord Burlington in 1728, was modelled on Palladio's Villa Rotonda at Vicenza. The William Kent interiors, particularly the reception rooms which include a domed saloon and velvet room, are sumptuous. Many have painted ceilings and gilded decorations, and feature period furnishings. Kent, alongside royal gardener Charles Bridgeman, was also responsible for the design of the gardens where he continued the Italianate theme with Doric columns, statues and obelisks, plus a cascade.

☎ 020 8995 0508   www.english-heritage.org.uk

★ Covent Garden   377 K6

Once the site of the famous fruit and flower market, this area is now a fashionable pedestrianised piazza. The arcades are lined with small specialist shops and there are plenty of places to eat and drink. The atmosphere is lively, with street entertainers a real highlight. The Jubilee Hall plays host to a variety of markets, including antiques, arts and crafts. Surrounding the piazza, visitors can also see St Paul's church, built by Inigo Jones and completed in 1633, London's Transport Museum, the Theatre Museum and the Royal Opera House.

★ Cutty Sark   357 C4

This famous tea clipper, built in 1869, was the fastest in the tea race from China and subsequently, when used in the Australian wool trade, she consistently set new speed records. Visitors can explore the ship and see where the sailors ate, slept and worked, and there is also an impressive collection of carved figureheads to be seen.

☎ 020 8858 3445   www.cuttysark.co.uk

🏛 Dulwich Picture Gallery   357 B5

Much of the collection was put together by French art dealer Noël Desenfans and Sir Francis Bourgeois between 1790 and 1795, for the king of Poland. Due to the king's abdication they took over responsibility for the collection and it was left in Sir Francis's will to Dulwich College in 1811, with the stipulation that the paintings should go on public display. A purpose built gallery designed by Sir John Soane houses the pictures, which include works by Claude, Cuyp, Rembrandt, Rubens, Van Dyck, Gainsborough and Canaletto.

☎ 020 8693 5254   www.dulwichpicturegallery.org.uk

🏠 Eltham Palace   186 D5

A 1930s mansion constructed around a Great Hall, built for Edward IV in the 1470s. The house was commissioned by Stephen Courtauld, millionaire patron of the arts, and his wife Virginia. It had all the latest electrical gadgets including a centralised vacuum cleaner and sound system. The interior exhibits superb examples of Art Deco styling, for example, the dining room has black and silver doors, an aluminium ceiling and maple walls. The bathroom features onyx and gold mosaic. The gardens extend to 19 acres (7.5ha) and include a moat, rose garden and pergola.

☎ 020 8294 2548   www.english-heritage.org.uk

Fenton House (NT)   354 D2

A late 17th century house containing collections of fine porcelain, early keyboard instruments and Georgian furniture. Outside is a walled garden with roses, orchard and a kitchen garden.

☎ 020 7435 3471   www.nationaltrust.org.uk

Geffrye Museum   356 B3

The museum is housed in several 18th century almshouses, with attractive gardens. Through a series of period rooms, the changing style of domestic interiors and furniture of the English middle classes from 1600 to the present day are shown.

☎ 020 7739 9893   www.geffrye-museum.org.uk

Greenwich – Old Royal Observatory

Greenwich   357 C4

Situated on the River Thames and a designated World Heritage Site, Greenwich is of international significance. It has a long and interesting history with strong royal and maritime links. Greenwich Park, which affords superb views, is the oldest royal park in London. The 17th century Royal Naval College, designed by Sir Christopher Wren, is built on the site of the Royal Palace of Greenwich. As the primary royal residence from the 15th to 17th centuries, it was the birthplace of Henry VIII and Elizabeth I. Alongside the river are the *Cutty Sark*, the fastest tea clipper of her time, and *Gipsy Moth IV*, on which Sir Francis Chichester was the first person to circumnavigate the globe single-handedly in 1967. The National Maritime Museum, which includes the Palladian style Queen's House designed by Inigo Jones, can also be visited.

The Old Royal Observatory, built by Wren in 1675, is the home of Greenwich Mean Time and the world's Prime Meridian – Longitude 0˚, where the eastern and western hemispheres meet. The brass meridian line can be seen set into the ground, and you can stand with a foot in each hemisphere. The building contains a collection of time keeping, astronomical

and navigational objects. Also of interest are the 19th century Ranger's House and St Alfege Church.

☎ 0870 608 2000   www.greenwichwhs.org.uk

★ H.M.S. Belfast   356 B3

Launched in 1938, this was the Royal Navy's largest cruiser of World War II. It participated in the sinking of the German battle cruiser *Scharnhorst* in 1943 and remained in Navy service until 1965. Most of the ship can be visited, including the engine room, boiler room and the bridge. There are displays depicting life on board during the war.

☎ 020 7940 6300   www.iwm.org.uk/belfast

Ham House (NT)   186 A5

An outstanding 17th century house, built in 1610 and enlarged in the 1670s, containing an impressive collection of paintings, furniture and textiles. The formal 17th century gardens have been restored to their original form.

☎ 020 8940 1950   www.nationaltrust.org.uk

Hampton Court Palace & Garden   355 A6

Located on the banks of the River Thames, this impressive building, covering approximately 6 acres (2.5ha), was originally built by Cardinal Thomas Wolsey, and dates from the early 16th century. He presented it to Henry VIII in 1528 to try and regain favour after he failed to annul the king's marriage to Catherine of Aragon. After becoming a royal palace, it was rebuilt and extended a number of times. Henry was responsible for the construction of the magnificent hammerbeamed hall and the vast kitchens. In the 1690s William and Mary commissioned Sir Christopher Wren to rebuild the palace, but due to a lack of time and money much of the Tudor palace survived. The two differing architectural styles can be seen clearly today. At this time the interior was decorated by some of the best artists and craftsmen of the day – Tijou, Grinling Gibbons, Laguerre and Verrio.

Visitors can enjoy the magnificent state apartments which contain furniture, tapestries and paintings from the Royal Collection. Other attractions include a rare 'real tennis' court on which Henry VIII once played. The grounds include 60 acres (25ha) of beautiful gardens. There is a 1 mile (1.6km) - long canal, extensive radiating avenues of limes and clipped yews, an orangery, and the famous maze. The privy garden, an attractive parterre, to the south of the palace, dates from William and Mary's reign and, after many years of neglect, was restored to its former glory during the 1990s.

☎ 0870 752 7777   www.hrp.org.uk

Houses of Parliament

Horniman Museum   357 B5

An eccentric and eclectic international collection of arts, crafts and artefacts housed in a purpose-built museum set in 16 acre (6ha) grounds. Originally collected by tea merchant and world traveller Frederick J Horniman, the exhibits cover a remarkable range, from torture devices, Egyptian mummy cases and masks, musical instruments to an enormous stuffed walrus. An ideal family attraction.

☎ 020 8699 1872   www.horniman.ac.uk

Houses of Parliament   377 K11

Also known as the Palace of Westminster and home to the main seat of Government. The original palace was built in the first half of the 11th century by Edward the Confessor and remained the main residence of the monarch until the first half of the 16th century when it moved to Whitehall. The Lords, however, continued to meet at Westminster. In 1834 the building was badly damaged by fire and all but the crypt, Jewel Tower and Westminster Hall survived. The hall, which is 240ft (73m) by 60ft (18m) has a magnificent hammerbeam oak roof. Most of the present building was constructed in Gothic Revival style between 1840 and 1888 by Charles Barry and Augustus Pugin and contains 1100 rooms, 100 staircases and over 2 miles (3km) of passages.

Situated on the River Thames, the building is an impressive sight with its two towers, one at each end. The Victoria Tower on the south west corner, on which the Union Jack flies when parliament is sitting, rises to a height of 336ft (102m). St Stephens clock tower (commonly known as Big Ben), to the north, is 316ft (96m) high and is famous the world over. It has four clock faces, each 23ft (7m) in diameter and contains the 13 ton bell, 'Big Ben', cast in 1858.

The Houses of Parliament are worth a visit, just to see the exterior, but visitors can also take a guided tour of the palace during the summer recess and see the impressive interiors.

☎ 020 7219 4272   www.parliament.uk

Imperial War Museum   377 P13

The museum has displays covering warfare from World War I to the present day and majors on Britain and the Commonwealth. Natural light from the domed atrium illuminates an impressive collection of tanks and weapons including a V2 rocket and also a Spitfire. Not only does it include conventional hardware of war but also interesting exhibits relating to war's impact on the population at large. For example there are displays on rationing, morale-boosting, censorship and there is also an exhibition on the Holocaust. The arts associated with wartime can also be seen, such as photographs, letters, paintings and poetry, and there are also old newsreels and period music.

☎ 020 7416 5320   www.iwm.org.uk

Kensington Palace 354 D3

Built by Sir Christopher Wren and bought by William III in 1689. Queen Victoria was born here in 1819 and on her 70th birthday the State Apartments were opened to the public. It was home to Diana, Princess of Wales, and is currently the residence of several members of the Royal Family. The Royal Ceremonial Dress Collection, dating from the 18th century, is on display, including some of Diana's dresses.

☎ 0870 751 5170   www.hrp.org.uk

Kenwood House 354 D2

This impressive neoclassical mansion, adjacent to Hampstead Heath, was remodelled by Robert Adam between 1764 and 1773. The house contains an outstanding collection of paintings with works by Turner, Gainsborough, Rembrandt, Vermeer, Van Dyck and Reynolds. The landscaped grounds, laid out by Humphrey Repton, are often the venue for lakeside open air concerts in the summer.

☎ 020 8348 1286   www.english-heritage.org.uk

★ London Aquarium 377 L10

Located in the cellars of County Hall (previously home to the now defunct Greater London Council) on the banks of the River Thames, this is one of the largest aquaria in Europe. At the centre of the aquarium there are two huge tanks extending over two floors, one displaying the sealife of the Pacific and one of the Atlantic. Visitors can see large 6ft (2m) long sharks, conger eels, stingrays and also the daily feeding of the fish by divers. Elsewhere there are slightly smaller tanks with themed areas displaying varying aquatic habitats, such as coral reefs and tropical rivers with piranha fish. There is a display of unusual and beautiful sea horses and also touch tanks where children are encouraged to touch the rays, crabs and starfish.

☎ 020 7967 8000   www.londonaquarium.co.uk

London Aquarium

★ London Dungeon 356 B3

In the vaults under London Bridge Station, this horror museum houses a gruesomely realistic exhibition of sacrifices, tortures, plagues, murders and executions. It is not recommended for the nervous or squeamish as the reconstructions and atmosphere of the place make for quite a scary experience.

☎ 020 7403 7221   www.dungeons.co.uk

★ London Eye 377 L10

Opened in 2000 as part of the millennium celebrations, at 450ft (135m) this observation wheel is the world's highest. It has become one of London's most recognisable landmarks comprising 32 capsules, each holding up to 25 people. The slow, gentle ride takes 30 minutes and gives visitors plenty of time to take in the splendid views.

Conceived and designed by architects David Marks and Julia Barfield, it is positioned in a prime location on the south bank of the River Thames and overlooks many of London's famous and impressive landmarks such as the Houses of Parliament, Westminster Abbey, St Paul's Cathedral and Buckingham Palace. On a clear day views of up to 25 miles (40km) can be seen.

To get the most from the experience it is worthwhile studying a map and the photoguide to help pick out key landmarks. These can be purchased at the London Eye shop.

☎ 0870 500 0600   www.londoneye.com

London Eye

London Zoo 356 A3

Founded in 1828, this was the world's first scientific zoo. In many ways the zoo was pioneering; in 1849 it introduced a reptile house – the first in the world, then the first public aquarium and the first insect house were built in 1853 and 1881 respectively.

Covering an area of 36 acres (14.5ha), it houses over 650 species of animals and participates in breeding programmes for over 140 of them. Visitors can follow a recommended route to ensure that they do not miss anything; this is marked by use of green footprints on the ground.

All the usual zoo animals, and more, are present, such as lions, apes, elephants and a variety of birdlife. Ever popular, the giraffes live in style within a neoclassical residence designed by Decimus Burton. Within the same hoofed animal area, extravagantly marked okapi, tapir and bongoes can be found. The children's zoo is in a farmyard setting and contains domesticated animals from around the world. These include camels, llamas and reindeer, as well as the more familiar sheep, cows, pigs, hens and ducks. Other attractions include the huge walk-through aviary, designed by Lord Snowdon, and Moonlight World, where nocturnal creatures can be seen. The Millennium Conservation Centre, with its advanced low-energy design, houses the Web of Life Exhibition; this is well worth a visit. Biodiversity is the focus, the extraordinary range of life on earth is explored, showing adaptation to different environments.

☎ 020 7722 3333   www.londonzoo.co.uk

London Zoo - Rhino Iguana

🏛 London's Transport Museum 377 K6

Telling the story of the world's largest urban passenger transport system, the museum contains gleamingly preserved survivors from the first cabs to trolleybuses and modern day tube trains. There are lots of hands-on exhibits where visitors can try out the controls. The museum, which was opened in 1980, is housed in the attractive old Covent Garden flower market building.

☎ 020 7379 6344   www.ltmuseum.co.uk

Lord's Cricket Ground & Museum 354 D3

The ground at Lord's is the headquarters of English cricket and the official home of the Marylebone Cricket Club (MCC). Guided tours are available, and include visits to the grounds, the futuristic-looking media centre, the players' dressing room, and, when not in use, the Long Room with its portraits of famous cricketers. The tour also includes a visit to the world's oldest sporting museum, the MCC Museum, where, among other exhibits, the famous Ashes urn is on show.

☎ 020 7616 8656   www.lords.org

★ Madame Tussaud's & the Planetarium 376 A1

This famous waxwork collection started out as a small touring exhibition in 1802, brought from France by Madame Tussaud. Over the years the collection has grown and diversified enormously, and in recent years topical interactive activities have been introduced. Today, visitors can see amazingly life-like and life-sized waxwork figures of villains and heroes, politicians and royalty, popstars and film stars, from the past and present; mingle with sporting and media stars, sing and dance with celebrities and learn football tips from England team members.

'The Chamber of Horrors' is probably the best known and most notorious part of the exhibition: Dr Crippen stares out from behind bars; grim and bloodthirsty punishments and a reconstruction of Jack the Ripper's London, with its eerie atmosphere,

Madame Tussaud's

can be seen. In the 'Grand Hall', many world leaders and royalty, from past and present, are gathered together. 'Premiere Night' brings together stars of the silver screen from 1914 to the present day. To finish, a ride on the 'Spirit of London' is a must, where visitors travel on small black cabs through London's turbulent history.

The Planetarium is next door and can also be visited on the same ticket. There are interactive exhibits and scale models as well as a fascinating show that takes visitors on a voyage of discovery into the solar system and beyond. Both educational and entertaining, it gives a great feel for the vastness and beauty of the universe.

☎ 0870 400 3000   www.madame-tussauds.co.uk

★ Monument, The   356 B3

Designed by Sir Christopher Wren and his colleague Dr Robert Hook, it was built between 1671 and 1677 to commemorate the Great Fire of London and to celebrate the subsequent rebuilding of the city. Made from Portland stone and standing 202ft (61.5m) tall, it is the tallest free-standing stone column in the world. Its height is significant as it is exactly 202ft away from the site of the baker's shop in Pudding Lane where the fire started in 1666. It has a spiralled, cantilevered staircase with 311 steps. The climb is worthwhile as the view from the top is superb.

☎ 020 7626 2717

⌂ ✿ Morden Hall Park (NT)   355 D6

The parkland, with the River Wandle flowing through it, extends to over 125 acres (50ha) and was once a deer park. It comprises meadows, wetlands and a superb rose garden planted in a random design with over 2000 plants. Other attractions include independently-run craft workshops, a city farm and garden centre.

☎ 020 8545 6850   www.nationaltrust.org.uk

🏛 Museum in Docklands   356 C3

Located in a converted Georgian warehouse on West India Quay, the museum traces the history of London's docks and river from Roman times, through its heyday, its post-war decline, and on to its recent regeneration. There are 12 galleries over five floors, and the exhibits include artefacts, paintings and photographs, accompanied by interactive displays.

☎ 0870 444 3856   www.museumindocklands.org.uk

🏛 Museum of Childhood   356 B3

Housing the children's section of the Victoria and Albert Museum, this museum contains an impressive collection of toys and childhood artefacts, the national collection of children's costume, plus a gallery telling the story of childhood in London's East End.

☎ 020 8980 2415   www.museumofchildhood.org.uk

⌂ Museum of Garden History   377 L13

The museum is housed in the former church of St Mary-at-Lambeth in whose churchyard are the graves of the two John Tradescants, father and son, who were royal gardeners during the reigns of Charles I and II. The museum tells the story of gardening through the ages. Part of the churchyard has been laid out as a garden in the style characteristic of the Tradescants' time, including a replica of a 17th century knot garden, along with some of the well-known plants they brought back from their travels, such as the Tulip Tree.

☎ 020 7401 8865   www.cix.co.uk/~museumgh

🏛 Museum of London   377 S3

Over 2000 years of London's history are on display, divided into seven permanent and well laid out galleries. These range from the Iron Age 'London before London', through Roman, Tudor and Stuart times, to 'World City' (1789 to 1914) when London became the world's first metropolis. Exhibits include over 1.1 million objects and there are attractive reconstructions of streets and interiors. The River Thames is shown to have a key role in the development and life of the city through the ages.

☎ 0870 444 3852   www.museumoflondon.org.uk

🏛 National Army Museum   355 D4

Tells the story of the British Army over the last 500 years, from Agincourt to the present day. It chronicles all the major British campaigns and has a large 400 sq ft (37 sq m) model of the battle of Waterloo, containing over 70,000 model soldiers. Other exhibits include the skeleton of Napoleon's horse, a reproduction of a World War I trench and a lamp used by Florence Nightingale.

☎ 020 7730 0717   www.national-army-museum.ac.uk

🏛 National Gallery   376 H7

In a commanding position on the north side of Trafalgar Square, the gallery is where the nation's major collection of historical paintings is housed. Founded in 1824, the collection has grown over the years, often due to the generosity of wealthy benefactors, and now numbers over 2300 Western European paintings, mostly dating from 1260 to 1900.

The gallery is divided into four wings. The Sainsbury Wing, opened in 1990, contains some of the earlier Renaissance paintings, including those by Van Eyck, Botticelli, Leonardo da Vinci and Raphael; the West Wing takes us from 1500 to 1600 with works by, amongst others, Titian, Holbein and Michelangelo. In the North Wing, works by Rubens, Van Dyck, Rembrandt and Vermeer are on show, taking us from 1600 to 1700; and finally the East Wing exhibits paintings dating from 1700 to 1900 and features works by Gainsborough, Constable, Monet, Cezanne and Van Gogh. To do justice to the collection it is best not to try and see everything in one visit.

☎ 020 7747 2885   www.nationalgallery.org.uk

🏛 National Maritime Museum   357 C4

Housed in architecturally important buildings including The Queen's House by Inigo Jones, the museum tells the story of Britain and the sea; its

navy, merchants and explorers. A nautical enthusiast's paradise, there are some 20 galleries with exhibits including models of ships, clocks and watches, contemporary and historic paintings, carved figureheads, weapons and fine silver collections. There are also plenty of hands-on activities.

☎ 020 8858 4422   www.nmm.ac.uk

National Portrait Gallery

🏛 National Portrait Gallery   376 H7

Founded in 1856 by historian Philip Stanhope as a gallery of original portraits to commemorate British history. Today, visitors can see over 1000 works which are arranged chronologically within the gallery, from medieval times to the present day. The focus of the collection is the subjects of the paintings rather than the painters themselves. The full portrait collection, the largest in the world, contains over 10,000 pictures in a variety of media: oils, watercolours, sculptures, caricatures, miniatures, photographs and also silhouettes. Paintings of kings, queens, politicians, musicians, artists and poets, ranging from the likes of Shakespeare to Madonna are on display. In addition to the permanent galleries there is a varied programme of temporary exhibitions throughout the year.

The well stocked shop and rooftop restaurant offering excellent views of London are worth a visit.

☎ 020 7306 0055   www.npg.org.uk

National Gallery

🏛 Natural History Museum   ⌖ `355 D4`

In 1856 Professor Richard Owen, the Superintendent of the Natural History section of the British Museum, campaigned for more space to display the exhibits. A site in South Kensington was purchased and a new, purpose-built museum was constructed, opening to the public in 1881. Lavishly decorated with plants and animals, the resulting 4 acre (1.5ha) museum building is a masterpiece. The main entrance consists of a dramatic series of recessed arches on decorated columns leading to the imposing Central Hall, which contains a huge 85ft (26m) skeleton of a dinosaur – Diplodocus.

The collection is vast and varied, covering all aspects of the natural world, both as traditional exhibits and interactive displays. The Darwin Centre allows visitors to take a look behind the scenes and see scientists working on the collection. A real favourite, especially with the children, is the Dinosaur Exhibition, where there is an animatronic Tyrannosaurus Rex, skeletons and plenty of touch screens. The Earth Galleries, entered through a giant globe, feature displays on the origins of the universe and there is an earthquake simulator where visitors can experience this phenomenon. Other exhibits worth a visit are the huge, life-sized model of a blue whale and the creepy crawlies. The museum is enormously enjoyable as well as educational and there really is too much to see in one visit.

☎ 020 7942 5000   www.nhm.ac.uk

Natural History Museum

🏛 Osterley Park & House (NT)   `355 A4`

Set in extensive parkland, the original Tudor mansion was transformed in the 18th century into a neoclassical villa by Robert Adam. Considered by many to be some of his finest work, it features superb plasterwork, carpets and furniture.

☎ 020 8232 5050   www.nationaltrust.org.uk

🏛 Royal Academy of Arts   ⌖ `376 E7`

Founded in 1768, the Royal Academy holds major temporary public exhibitions throughout the year. Sir Joshua Reynolds – who was the first president – Gainsborough, Turner and Constable all studied and have exhibited here. Located in Burlington House, a superb early 18th century mansion, one of the few surviving in the West End, the academy is probably most famous for its inspirational

annual Summer Exhibition, which displays thousands of works by living artists for view and sale. In addition to the wide range of temporary exhibitions, a suite of rooms, restored to their former 18th century grandeur, houses highlights from the permanent collection. Entry to this is free. The full collection comprises mainly British art from the last 200 years and includes at least one work by all past and present members of the academy.

☎ 020 7300 8000   www.royalacademy.org.uk

🏛 Royal Air Force Museum   ⌖ `354 C1`

Located on the former airfield at RAF Hendon, and opened in 1972, the museum, housed in five huge buildings, contains a collection of over 100 full-sized aircraft, along with artefacts and other memorabilia. 'Milestones of Flight' covers the history of flight, from the earliest attempts to modern day supersonic jet fighters. For younger visitors the Aeronauts Gallery has plenty of interactive exhibits where they can test their piloting skills.

☎ 020 8205 2266   www.rafmuseum.org.uk

✿ Royal Botanic Gardens, Kew   `355 B4`

This superb 300 acre (121.5ha) botanic garden was founded by Princess Augusta (mother of George III) in 1759, and in July 2003 it was afforded World Heritage Site status. Kew's reputation as the foremost botanical institution in the world was originally developed by its first two directors, Sir William Hooker (appointed in 1841) and his son Sir Joseph (who succeeded his father in 1865).

The gardens have one of the largest and most diverse collections of plant species in the world; over 60,000 species of plant are displayed in both formal and informal settings, and in the many greenhouses, which themselves cover an area of 4 acres (1.5ha). Within the grounds are the Queen's Garden, which has been laid out in 17th century style, the grass garden and the herbaceous garden. The lake, aquatic garden and ten-storey pagoda were designed by Sir William Chambers in 1760. Major features of Kew are the magnificent curved glass Palm House (built in 1848) and the Temperate House (completed in 1868), designed by Decimus Burton and Richard Turner. In more recent years the Princess of Wales Conservatory was constructed and has a variety of climatic areas, from the humid tropics through to desert conditions. There is plenty of interest to keep everyone happy, both botanical experts and those just wanting to absorb the beauty of the grounds.

☎ 020 8332 5655   www.rbgkew.org.uk

Royal Botanic Gardens, Kew

🏛 Royal Mews, Buckingham Palace   `376 D12`

Built in 1825 to a design by John Nash, the Mews give an insight into the work of the Royal Household department that provides transport for the Royal Family, both horse-drawn and motor. The Royal Mews are home, for most of the year, to 30 or so horses used in official and ceremonial duties. Visitors can also see the remarkable state carriages, most notably the Gold State Coach made in 1761 and the Irish State Coach bought by Queen Victoria in 1852 and used for the state opening of parliament.

☎ 020 7766 7302   www.royal.gov.uk/output/page556.asp

✝ St Martin-in-the Fields Church   ⌖ `376 J7`

Overlooking Trafalgar Square, this church was designed by James Gibbs and was consecrated in 1726. With its attractive spire and portico, its design has been much copied throughout the world, especially in the United States. Among the notable events to have taken place here are the christening of Charles II in 1630 and the burials of Nell Gwynne, William Hogarth, Sir Joshua Reynolds and Thomas Chippendale.

The church hosts lunchtime and evening concerts and has a brass rubbing centre. It also has a long history of work with the homeless.

☎ 020 7766 1100   www.stmartin-in-the-fields.org

St Paul's Cathedral

✝ St Paul's Cathedral   ⌖ `377 S5`

Designed by Sir Christopher Wren, the current St Paul's rises to a height of 365ft (111m) and is the fifth cathedral to stand on the site. It was built between 1675 and 1710, the previous cathedral having been destroyed during the Great Fire of London. Its design was revolutionary and Wren encountered opposition from the Dean and Chapter who wanted a more traditional church. Fortunately, Wren's vision and determination won through, resulting in the masterpiece of design and engineering that we see today; the magnificent dome providing one of the best known London landmarks.

After St Peter's in Rome, St Paul's dome is the second largest in the world and has three viewing galleries. The Whispering Gallery runs around the interior and has unusual acoustics – a whisper against its walls is audible on the opposite side. Encircling the outside at 173ft (53.5m) is the Stone Gallery, and at 280ft (85.5m) is the Golden Gallery which runs around the highest point of the dome, from which the views across the city are superb. To reach here, visitors need to climb 530 steps.

The enormous scale and grandeur of the interior is breathtaking, with massive arches and lofty ceilings. The decoration is extravagant, richly gilded throughout and with brightly coloured mosaics in the Quire, which were originally planned by Wren, but not installed until 1891 – 1904. The interior also features carving by Grinling Gibbons, decorative metal work by Jean Tijou, sculpture by Henry Moore and the magnificent organ, which has been played by both Handel and Mendelssohn. Among the cathedral's 300 memorials is one to the Duke of Wellington whose body lies in the crypt, alongside the tombs of Admiral Nelson and Sir Christopher Wren.

☎ 020 7236 4128   www.stpauls.co.uk

🏛 Science Museum   ♻ 355 D4

Opened in 1857, on land purchased with the profits from the Great Exhibition of 1851, the museum comprises over 40 galleries spread over seven floors. The huge collection, with over 10,000 items on show, focuses on science and scientific advances over the last 300 years, not only from Britain but also from around the world. The exhibits range from steam power, where visitors can see Stephenson's *Rocket*, to space exploration with the surprisingly small *Apollo 10* command module on display. There are a diverse range of galleries, with topics spanning computing, printing, nuclear power, flight, marine engineering and food, seen in a social as well as purely scientific light. The Wellcome Wing concentrates on contemporary science, medicine and technology and has an IMAX 3D cinema (for which there is a charge). Throughout the museum there are a vast number of interactive and hands-on displays, which really help to illustrate scientific principles, not only for the children, but for the adults too.

☎ 0870 870 4868   www.sciencemuseum.org.uk

Science Museum – Space Auditorium

🏛 Shakespeare's Globe Theatre   377 S7

The current Globe Theatre, officially opened in 1997, is a careful reconstruction of the original, which was built nearby in 1599, and for which Shakespeare wrote some of his greatest plays. The reconstruction was the dream of American actor-director Sam Wanamaker, who, sadly, never lived to see its completion. In its construction, techniques and materials as close to the original as possible have been used. It is open to the elements in the centre and has a thatched roof; as a consequence, when it rains, the 'groundlings' (the audience standing in front of the stage) get wet, just as they did in Shakespeare's day. During performances, which take place between May and September, the whole atmosphere is designed to be just as it was 500 years ago; there is no hi-tech lighting or wizardry and the crowd is encouraged to participate by shouting, cheering and jeering.

In a space beneath the theatre is the UnderGlobe where there is an exhibition of Shakespeare's life and times, with displays on the original as well as the current Globe. The exhibition includes a range of live demonstrations and interactive displays. There are also interesting tours of the whole site when there are no plays in progress.

☎ 020 7902 1500   www.shakespeares-globe.org

🏛 Somerset House   ♻ 377 L6

The building, dating from the 1770s, now houses three major art collections (for which there is a charge). The Courtauld Gallery features a collection of paintings by artists such as Michelangelo, Monet and Van Gogh. The Gilbert Collection contains mainly decorative arts including jewel-encrusted gold snuffboxes. The Hermitage Rooms provide a splendid setting for varied exhibitions often featuring collections loaned from the State Hermitage Museum in St Petersburg. Areas on free public view include the Nelson Staircase, the Seamen's Waiting Hall and the King's Barge House with multimedia presentations telling the building's story. Outside a central courtyard features an impressive 55 jet fountain which is converted to an ice rink during the winter.

☎ 020 7845 4600   www.somerset-house.org.uk

🏛 ❈ Syon House   355 B4

This 16th century house, standing in 40 acre (16ha) grounds landscaped by Lancelot 'Capability' Brown, has been home to the Dukes of Northumberland since 1594. Catherine Howard, Henry VIII's fifth wife, was imprisoned here before her execution in 1542 and Lady Jane Grey began her 9-day reign here after Edward VI's death. Robert Adam made many alterations from 1762 – 1769, creating imaginative and elegant interiors – the variety of each room is exceptional.

☎ 020 8560 0881   www.syonpark.co.uk

🏛 Tate Britain   357 A4

Overlooking the River Thames, the gallery dates from 1897 and was built on the site of the Millbank Penitentiary, a former prison, to house the collection of 19th century art given to the nation by the sugar magnate, Sir Henry Tate. The permanent collection has grown enormously over the years, and today the gallery holds the largest collection of British art in the world, with works dating from 1500 to the present day. Temporary shows include the controversial Turner Prize Exhibition.

Visitors can see work by artists such as

Tate Britain

Gainsborough, Stubbs, Blake, Constable, Bacon, Hirst, Hockney and Hepworth. The adjoining Clore Gallery houses the Turner bequest, comprising thousands of paintings and studies, left to the nation by Turner on condition that they remained together.

☎ 020 7887 8000   www.tate.org.uk/britain

🏛 Tate Modern   ♻ 377 R8

The gallery, situated on the south bank of the River Thames opposite St Paul's Cathedral, was opened in May 2000 and features international modern art from 1900 to the present day. It is housed in the vast, former Bankside Power Station, designed by Sir Giles Gilbert Scott (designer of the red telephone box) in 1947. The sheer scale of the building creates a superb setting in which to exhibit. The vast hall, once occupied by the power station turbines, allows huge works of art to be displayed.

The permanent exhibits are arranged thematically into four main areas: Still life/Object/Real Life; Nude/Action/Body; History/Memory/Society; and Landscape/Matter/Environment. Works by Picasso, Matisse, Dali, Warhol, Monet and Bacon, amongst many others, can be seen. Throughout the year there are also a series of temporary exhibitions including three major loan exhibitions.

☎ 020 7887 8000   www.tate.org.uk/modern

Tate Modern

LONDON

🏛 Thames Barrier Visitor Centre 357 D4

The visitor centre has multimedia presentations, models and displays describing the construction and operation of this movable flood barrier, which, at 1700ft (520m) long, is the world's largest. It was officially opened in 1984.

☎ 020 8305 4188

🏛 Theatre Museum 377 K6

Located in specially converted premises in Covent Garden, this museum is dedicated to artefacts associated with the performing arts, ranging from theatre to puppetry. The collection includes over a million theatre programmes and playbills (not all on display).

☎ 020 7943 4700   www.theatremuseum.vam.ac.uk

🏛 Tower Bridge Experience 356 B3

Tower Bridge has been a distinctive London landmark since 1894. Its fascinating history and the story of how it was built is told in the Tower Bridge Experience through the use of interactive displays. Visitors can see the engine rooms and climb up to the 140ft (42.5m) high walkways from which there are superb views of London.

☎ 020 7403 3761   www.towerbridge.org.uk

🏛 Tower of London 356 B3

Dating back to the 11th century, the Tower has been part of London's history for over 900 years. During this time it has had many roles, serving as a royal palace, an arsenal, royal mint, jewel house, royal menagerie (the ravens are now the only survivors) and, most notoriously, as a jail and place of execution. There are many different things for the visitor to see, either independently, or with the help of the distinctively dressed Yeoman warders (Beefeaters), who are happy to combine their traditional ceremonial role with that of tourist guide.

The oldest part is the massive rectangular 90ft (27.5m) high White Tower. Originally built as a fortress and residence providing accommodation for the king, today visitors can see a wide range of arms and armour. The Bloody Tower is associated with the deaths of the two princes in 1483. Sir Walter Raleigh was also imprisoned here for 13 years. The scaffold site on Tower Green is where seven famous prisoners were executed including Anne Boleyn, Catherine Howard and Lady Jane

Tower of London

Grey, their bodies being buried in the adjacent Chapel of St Peter ad Vincula. Prisoners often entered the Tower from the Thames through Traitor's Gate. Be sure not to miss the Crown Jewels, a glittering and well laid out array which mainly date from the Restoration in 1660, when Charles II ascended the throne. Also worth a visit is the Medieval Palace which comprises a series of rooms shown as they may have looked during the reign of Edward I. All in all, there is a vast range of things to see, with Britain's rich and turbulent royal history evident at every turn.

☎ 020 7709 0765   www.tower-of-london.org.uk

Victoria & Albert Museum

🏛 Victoria & Albert Museum 355 D4

Established in 1852 with profits from the Great Exhibition, and originally called the Museum of Manufactures, then the South Kensington Museum, it was finally renamed the V&A in 1899. This national museum of art and design has exhibits from all over the world, spanning over 2000 years. It is vast and labyrinthine, with four floors and over 145 galleries covering an area of 10 acres (4ha).

The collection is immense and wide-ranging with over 4 million objects as diverse as the carved oak Great Bed of Ware, made in 1590, which measures 12ft (3.6m) square, and the tiny Indian miniature paintings. Other exhibits include Oriental ceramics, Chippendale and Art Nouveau furniture, Italian Renaissance sculpture, and a significant collection of paintings by John Constable. The museum also contains Indian film posters, photographs and around 500,000 watercolours, engravings and etchings. The British Galleries are a popular destination with exhibits dating from the 16th to 20th centuries, encompassing works by famous designers such as William Morris, Charles Rennie Mackintosh and Robert Adam.

With 7 miles (11km) of galleries to explore it is impossible to see everything in one visit.

☎ 020 7942 2000   www.vam.ac.uk

✝ Westminster Abbey 376 J12

Steeped in history, the abbey is the coronation church of all the crowned sovereigns since William the Conqueror, whose coronation took place in the original Norman building in 1066. Very little of the Norman structure remains; most of the magnificent Gothic building seen today was built

by Henry III between 1245 and his death in 1272. After his death, progress was slow and the nave, which at 102ft (31m) is the highest in England, was not completed until 1517. The famous west towers, which rise to a height of 225ft (69m) were a much later addition and were completed in 1745.

Both architecturally and historically, the abbey is an absolute feast with an impressive array of tombs and memorials to some of Britain's most important figures. Within the chapel of St Edward the Confessor is his great shrine along with the tombs of Henry III, Edward I, Edward III, Richard II and Henry V. Nearby is the Coronation Chair, upon which all England's monarchs (except Edward V and Edward VIII) have been crowned since 1308. Henry VII's Chapel is magnificent, with an intricately detailed fan vaulted ceiling. It is the final resting place of Henry VII, Mary I and Elizabeth I. Within the nave can be seen the tomb of the unknown warrior whose body was laid here as a memorial to the thousands who died in World War I. The octagonal Chapter House, which between 1253 and 1547 was one of the regular meeting places of Parliament, still contains its original coloured tile floor and medieval wall paintings. Visitors can also see the Cloisters and the museum which is situated in the Norman undercroft.

☎ 020 7222 5152   www.westminster-abbey.org

Westminster Abbey

✝ Westminster Cathedral 376 E13

Completed in 1903, this is the principal Roman Catholic church in England. The neo-Byzantine style, with its distinctive red brickwork and horizontal white stone stripes, is eyecatching. The spacious interior has the broadest nave in England and is richly decorated with multicoloured mosaics and marble.

☎ 020 7798 9055   www.westminstercathedral.org.uk

WEST MIDLANDS

Famous as the traditional 'Black Country', for so long the powerhouse of British manufacturing and forever associated with the famous makes of motor vehicles that it designed and built. Yet, outside of this cluster of throbbing industrial towns and cities, with their lively culture and retail attractions, the surrounding counties seem to have deliberately distanced themselves from this influence. Here quaint historic charm and rural calm appear to continue unchallenged.

Acton Scott Working Farm Museum 207 D4

This museum re-creates the working practices of early 20th century farming. The land is worked using horses and machinery in use at the time and there are traditional demonstrations of the skills of the blacksmith, carpenter, wheelwright and farrier along with butter making, milking by hand, lambing, shearing and cider making. Amongst the wide variety of animals are Tamworth pigs, Longhorn cattle and Shropshire sheep.

☎ 01694 781306

Alton Towers Leisure Park 222 B3

A family day out, or maybe two days as there is so much to fit into one day. Set around the historic 19th century Gothic mansion and its landscaped gardens which date back to 1860, the theme park features exotically named rides such as Nemesis, Oblivion, the Flume and Spinball Whizzer. The famous Corkscrew is situated in UG Land which has a prehistoric theme and features virtual reality games. There are themed areas for younger children such as Cred Street, Old MacDonald's Farmyard and Adventure Land. Unfortunately it is necessary to queue for most of the rides though some have a time slot booking system. There is disabled access to most of the rides though some enforce height restrictions for safety reasons.

☎ 08705 204060   www.alton-towers.co.uk

Ancient High House 221 G5

Built in 1595 by John Dorrington, this Tudor building is the largest timber-framed town house in England. King Charles and his nephew Prince Rupert stayed here in 1642 at the beginning of the Civil War and, when overrun by the Parliamentarians the following year, it became a prison for Royalist prisoners. Extensive renovations by the Borough Council has enabled the building to be opened to the public, and exhibits of period furniture, wallpapers and costumes can be enjoyed. It is also home to the Staffordshire Yeomanry Museum.

☎ 01785 619131

Anne Hathaway's Cottage 197 D2

The pre-marital home of the wife of William Shakespeare, and of her descendants until the late 19th century. It is a Tudor 12-roomed thatched farmhouse, parts of which date back to the 15th century. Recent additions to the lovely garden are the Shakespeare Tree Garden, which has many of the trees mentioned in his plays, and a maze, the design of which dates from the Elizabethan era.

☎ 01789 292100

Arbury Hall 209 F4

The original house is Elizabethan but it was transformed in the 18th century into one of the finest examples of Gothic Revival architecture in the country. Home to the Newdegate family since the 16th century, many of the superb rooms are open to the public. There are superb vaulted ceilings and displays of art, glass, porcelain and antique furniture. The house is surrounded by fine land-scaped gardens with lakes and woodland walks.

☎ 024 7638 2804

Ash End House Children's Farm 359 F1

A small, family run farm where the visitor can get close to the animals, many of which are under cover in case of bad weather. There is wheelchair access throughout the farm.

☎ 0121 329 3240   www.ashendhouse.fsnet.co.uk

Alton Towers Leisure Park

www.visitheartofengland.com

Attingham Park (NT) 207 E1

A late 18th century mansion with magnificent interiors, built originally for the 1st Earl of Berwick, now owned by the National Trust. Guided tours are available which give an insight into life up and downstairs, as the kitchens and servants quarters are open to the public. The picture gallery was designed by John Nash who constructed the curved ceiling out of iron and glass. Surrounding the house are mature gardens, deer park, woodland and riverside walks, and in the walled garden is a children's adventure playground.

☎ 01743 708162   www.nationaltrust.org.uk

Avoncroft Museum of Historic Buildings 196 B1

An unusual museum which has over 25 historical buildings from the last 700 years, painstakingly dismantled and rebuilt on a site of 25 acres (10ha). Originally the aim was to rescue and restore only timber-framed buildings, but such has been the success of the venture that all manner of buildings are now on show, including a 1946 prefab, a working windmill, church and gaol.

☎ 01527 831363   www.avoncroft.org.uk

Baddesley Clinton (NT) 209 D5

This moated house sits in grounds of 120 acres (48ha) and has been largely unchanged for almost 400 years. The original building dates from the 15th century and stayed in the family of its owner, the Under Treasurer of England, John Broome, until it was acquired by the National Trust in 1981. The house has three priest's holes which were installed in the late 16th century by Henry Ferrers, a staunch Roman Catholic. The gardens include ponds and lakeside walks, a walled garden and nature trail.

☎ 01564 783294   www.nationaltrust.org.uk

Baggeridge Country Park 358 A1

This was largely developed by the District Council after the closure of the mineworks in 1968. It is the northern part of the park that was once one of the largest and most modern coal mines in the world. Trees have been planted to augment those that have developed naturally since the closure of the mine, and meadows have been created which now include a visitor centre and caravan park. The southern part of the park features ponds and

streams, and was designed by Lancelot 'Capability' Brown for the Earl of Dudley.

☎ 01902 882605

Benthall Hall (NT) 207 F2

A 16th century sandstone house which was given a more Gothic look in the 18th century. The magnificent interior has fine oak panelling and a carved oak staircase, while the plasterwork is equally stunning. The 3 acre (1.2ha) grounds include a restored plantsman's garden as well as a rock garden, rose garden and terraces. There is also a 17th century Restoration church which holds services on alternate Sundays.

☎ 01952 882159   www.nationaltrust.org.uk

Berrington Hall (NT) 195 E1

This elegant house was designed and built in the late 18th century by Henry Holland while the parkland was designed by his father-in-law, Lancelot 'Capability' Brown. The main feature is a 14 acre (5.6ha) lake, which has sweeping views down the valley to the Brecon Beacons. The exterior sandstone walls from which the house is built give it a severe first impression, but the interior is delicate with beautifully detailed ceilings and a spectacular staircase hall.

☎ 01568 615721   www.nationaltrust.org.uk

Biddulph Grange Garden (NT) 221 F2

These 15 acre (9ha) gardens were the conception of James Bateman in the mid 19th century in order to display his wide ranging and extensive plant collection from all over the world – a common practice for Victorian gardens. The gardens are laid out as a series of smaller themed gardens, including Egyptian and Chinese gardens, pinetum and rock garden, all connected by pathways, steps and tunnels (making access difficult for wheelchairs and pushchairs). The gardens fell into disuse during World War I when the Grange was used as a hospital, and since its acquisition by the National Trust has been, and continues to be, extensively restored. There is a quiz and trail for children.

☎ 01782 517999   www.nationaltrust.org.uk

Birmingham Botanical Gardens 378 C14

Founded in 1832, these 15 acres (6ha) of beautiful gardens have a variety of interest including exotic flora, play areas and aviaries. Many different types of habitat are on display – an alpine yard, winter garden, wetlands, pinetum and cottage garden to name but a few.

There are four glasshouses with themes of tropical, subtropical, Mediterranean and arid. It is also home to the National Bonsai Collection.

☎ 0121 454 1860 www.birminghambotanicalgardens.org.uk

Biddulph Grange Garden

Black Country Living Museum
358 B2

A faithful reproduction of a village dating from the turn of the 20th century is the centrepiece of this museum which focuses on the industrial heritage of the West Midlands. There are even caverns and an underground coal mine. Guides in period costume are on hand to demonstrate traditional skills – there is a forge, foundry, colliery, cobbler – and there is plenty to occupy the children. Most of the museum is set outdoors but there is also an interactive exhibition hall, gift shop and tearoom.

☎ 0121 557 9643   www.bclm.co.uk

Bredon Tithe Barn (NT)
196 B4

This 14th century Tithe Barn is built of local Cotswold stone and was lovingly restored after a fire in 1980. It is around 140ft (44m) in length with an aisled interior giving it a distinctly ecclesiastical feel. It also features a remarkable stone chimney cowling.

☎ 01684 855300   www.nationaltrust.org.uk

Buildwas Abbey
207 F2

Founded by the Savignacs in 1135 and merged with the Cistercian Order soon after, the abbey changed little until the Dissolution and is unusual in that the cloister is situated north of the main church. Parts of the original tiled floor of the Chapter House still exist and, apart from the roof, the building is still virtually intact. Research has uncovered evidence of water channels and fishponds, most probably used as a source of food by the monks.

☎ 01952 433274   www.english-heritage.org.uk

Burford House Gardens
195 E1

7 acres (3ha) of beautiful gardens on the banks of the River Teme, originally designed by John Treasure in 1952 to complement the Georgian Burford House. Home to the National Clematis Collection, of which there are over 300 varieties, there is also a clematis maze. Wisteria Burford cascades down the rear wall of the house and is a beautiful sight when it flowers in May. The house has a contemporary art gallery which is open during the summer months and there is a garden centre, gift shop and licensed café.

☎ 01584 810777   www.burford.co.uk

Cadbury World
359 D4

A visitor centre devoted entirely to chocolate and designed to be of particular interest to children, but with plenty to interest all. Learn the process of chocolate manufacture, experience imaginative rides through a world of chocolate. There are also television adverts from the last 40 years and a 1930s sweet shop. It is advisable to book tickets in advance, especially during the summer holidays.

☎ 0121 451 4159   www.cadburyworld.co.uk

Cannock Chase Country Park
208 B1

One of the largest country parks in Britain, covering 4000 acres (1600ha) which lies within one of the smallest Areas of Outstanding Natural Beauty, Cannock Chase. There are many designated Sites of Special Scientific Interest and the visitor centre is the starting point for many of the well-signposted walks running through the park.

☎ 01543 876741

Cannon Hill Park
359 D3

One of the most popular parks in Birmingham, with a variety of landscapes including flowerbeds, lakes, a wild flower meadow and woodland, which is part of a conservation area. There are plenty of facilities – canoeing, tennis courts, bowling and

Black Country Living Museum

putting greens and a tearoom which is housed inside the Midland Arts Centre.

☎ 0121 442 4226

Carding Mill Valley & Long Mynd (NT)
206 D3

Stretching across an area 10 miles (16km) long and 2 to 4 miles (3.5 to 6.5km) wide south of Shrewsbury, the Long Mynd holds much of interest, including several prehistoric barrows and earthworks, and is ideal walking country. Carding Mill Valley is a steep-sided valley offering a good, though strenuous route onto the ridge. There is a National Trust information centre and tearoom next to the car park.

☎ 01694 723068   www.nationaltrust.org.uk

Charlecote Park (NT)
197 E2

A 16th century house visited by both Queen Victoria and Elizabeth I – the entrance porch still has the coat of arms of Elizabeth I to commemorate her stay of two nights in 1572. All of the rooms are luxuriously furnished, the dining room and library having particularly exquisite ceilings in the Elizabethan Revival style. The formal gardens open out onto 250 acres (100ha) of parkland designed by Lancelot 'Capability' Brown where, allegedly, Shakespeare was once caught poaching deer.

☎ 01789 470277   www.nationaltrust.org.uk

Commandery, The
415 C2

An historic timber-framed building which was the headquarters of Charles II during the Civil War, though its origins date back much further than that, possibly to the 11th century. Most of the current building dates from the 15th century and has undergone many changes to reflect the style of the period.

☎ 01905 361821   www.worcestercitymuseums.org.uk

Coors Visitor Centre
222 D5

Formerly the Bass Museum, the Coors Visitor Centre tells the story of the long and distinguished history of brewing in Burton and also in Britain in general. There is a visitor centre, frequently changing exhibitions and a computerised journey around Burton in 1881 which will be of interest to children, as will the magnificent shire horses.

☎ 0845 600 0598   www.coorsvisitorcentre.co.uk

Coughton Court (NT)
196 C1

The house has been in the Throckmorton family since 1409 and has remained relatively unchanged since the Tudor gatehouse was built in 1530. There are exhibits relating to Mary, Queen of Scots, including the chemise she was wearing when she was executed, and also a Gunpowder Plot exhibition – at the time the house was rented out to one of the plotters, Sir Everard Digby. The grounds include one of the country's finest walled gardens and also a lake, riverside walk, bog garden and orchard.

☎ 01789 400777   www.coughtoncourt.co.uk

Coventry Cathedral
394 E2

The old Cathedral was famously bombed in November 1940 during the devastation of Coventry and the remains have been incorporated into the new Cathedral which was consecrated in 1962. A new chapel was added to celebrate the millennium, and the visitor centre has many displays showing the history of the Cathedral and the city of Coventry.

☎ 01203 227597   www.coventrycathedral.org.uk

Coventry Transport Museum
394 D2

The largest collection of British vehicles in the world, at the birthplace of the British motor industry. The collection includes cars, vans, trucks, bicycles and motorbikes from the present day back to 1896 when the first factory was established. Famous marques such as Daimler, Maudslay, Triumph, Jaguar, Riley and Humber are represented.

☎ 024 7683 2425   www.transport-museum.com

Croft Castle (NT)
194 D1

This impressive country manor house has fine Georgian interiors and furniture while the curtain wall and round towers at each corner date from the 14th and 15th centuries. Apart from a break of 177 years in the 18th and 19th centuries, the Croft family have lived on this site since the Norman conquest though the castle is now maintained by the National Trust. The grounds include an avenue of 350 year old Spanish chestnuts, and adjacent to the castle are the remains of the earthworks of the original fort.

☎ 01568 781246   www.nationaltrust.org.uk

Dorothy Clive Garden, The 221 E4

Set amongst lovely hilly countryside, the garden has a variety of landscapes in its 8 acres (3ha) – woodland, alpine, a water garden and summer borders. The garden has been extended into an old quarry which is now the rhododendron garden, shaded with trees and also featuring a waterfall.

☎ 01630 647237   www.dorothyclivegarden.co.uk

Drayton Manor Park 209 D2

A 250 acre (96ha) theme park with such evocatively named rides as Pandemonium, Excalibur and Apocalypse. Gentler rides can be taken in Splash Canyon, or on Excalibur where fire-breathing dragons are encountered on a journey through medieval England. Height restrictions are enforced for safety on some rides. As well as the rides there is a zoo covering 15 acres (6ha) with over 100 species, a rare breeds farm, exotic animal reserves and a museum showing the history of Drayton Manor.

☎ 08708 725252   www.draytonmanor.co.uk

Dudley Zoo & Castle 358 B2

A magnificent location for a zoo, being set in the grounds of the ruins of Dudley Castle – the route through the zoo has cleverly been designed to take in the old castle walls. The 40 acres (16ha) is home to more than 200 species, many endangered. There is a visitor centre which also concentrates on the archaeological excavations which have been carried out locally.

☎ 01384 215313   www.dudleyzoo.co.uk

Dudmaston (NT) 207 G4

This 17th century house has exhibits of the flower paintings of Francis Derby dating from the same time, as well as modern and botanical art. The grounds include rock, rose and bog gardens and are especially impressive in the spring with collections of rhododendrons and azaleas. There are also woodland and lakeside walks in the 300 acre (120ha) parkland.

☎ 01746 780866   www.nationaltrust.org.uk

Eastnor Castle 195 G4

Built by the 1st Earl Somers in 1820, and extensively restored after 1949, the castle is still privately owned by his descendants – the Hervey-Bathurst family. Much of the original work of the interior, designed by Robert Smirke, is still in evidence, particularly in the Staircase Hall, Dining Room and Red Hall, which has a magnificent collection of armour moved here in 1989 from the Great Hall. The grounds are magnificent, comprising an arboretum, lake and deer park in which there are mazes and nature trails.

☎ 01531 633160   www.eastnorcastle.com

Fleece Inn, The (NT) 196 C3

Owned by the National Trust, this half-timbered, medieval house has been used as an inn since 1848. It has remained largely unchanged since then, but was originally in use as a farmhouse and animal shelter.

☎ 01386 831173   www.nationaltrust.org.uk

Goodrich Castle 195 E5

Guarding an ancient crossing point of the River Wye, this well-preserved 12th century ruin is constructed out of the red sandstone on which it sits. Despite seeing action during the Civil War, much of the castle is complete, including the three-storey keep as well as archways, pillars and passageways, giving a good idea of the castle as it was. There are outstanding views across the Wye Valley and the surrounding countryside.

☎ 01600 890538   www.english-heritage.org.uk

Greyfriars, The (NT) 415 C2

Built in 1480 by Thomas Greene, this timber-framed merchant's house was added to in the 17th and 18th centuries, and was rescued from demolition during World War II. None of the original 15th century furnishings survive but there is Georgian wallpaper and 16th and 17th century tapestries and furniture. The large double doors open out to a cobbled passageway and a small walled garden.

☎ 01905 23571   www.nationaltrust.org.uk

Hagley Hall 358 A4

The home of Lord and Lady Cobham was originally built between 1756 and 1760 by the 1st Lord of Lyttelton at a cost of £25,000, twice the original estimate. In 1925 a fire destroyed parts of the house, including the library and some of the extensive art collection, though it was subsequently restored to its former glory. There is fine plasterwork by Francesco Vassali, Chippendale furniture, and family portraits amongst the art collection which includes works by Van Dyck, Reynolds and Lely. The Hall is surrounded by a 350 acre (135ha) deer park.

☎ 01562 882408   www.hagleyhall.info

Hall's Croft 410 F2

Once the home of John Hall, a physician, who married Shakespeare's eldest daughter, Susanna, in 1607. The hall and parlour are the oldest parts of this timber-framed house, which dates from the early seventeenth century, and is furnished as it would have been at the time. The grounds include a herb garden containing herbs that Hall would have used in his practice.

☎ 01789 204016   www.shakespeare.org.uk

Hanbury Hall (NT) 196 B1

A William and Mary style country house built in 1701 which features splendid painted ceilings and an impressive staircase. There is a collection of porcelain on display as well as exhibitions on the family and local history. The grounds include a 20 acre (8ha) garden which is surrounded by parkland covering 400 acres (160ha). Amongst the many interesting features are an orangery, mushroom house, ice house and an 18th century bowling green.

☎ 01527 821214   www.nationaltrust.org.uk

Harvard House 197 E2

This impressive timber-framed building was built in 1596 by Thomas Rogers and has remained unchanged since then. His grandson, John Harvard, emigrated to America in 1647 and died only a year later. It was a bequest in his will that helped to establish Harvard University in Cambridge, Massachusetts. The Museum of British Pewter is housed within the building.

☎ 01789 204507   www.shakespeare.org.uk

Drayton Manor Park – Pandemonium Ride

Harvington Hall
208 A5

The largest number of priest's holes in Britain are to be found in this Elizabethan manor house which was originally built in 1580 and is now owned by the Roman Catholic Archdiocese of Birmingham. Many of the original wall paintings still adorn the walls, having been discovered beneath a layer of whitewash in 1936. Large numbers of birds are attracted by the moat and the two lakes in the gardens, which also include a Georgian chapel and a malt house.

☎ 01562 777846   www.harvingtonhall.com

Hatton Country World
197 E1

Comprises two separate attractions – Hatton Shopping Village and Hatton Farm Village. The shopping village comprises arts and craft shops, alongside antique outlets and larger retailers, set amongst converted Victorian farm buildings.

The Farm Village is set in open countryside and has plenty for children – sheep racing, a guinea pig village, play areas, a maze along with demonstrations and exhibitions of farm craft. There is a charge to pay for entry.

☎ 01926 843411   www.hattonworld.com

Haughmond Abbey
207 E1

Once part of a thriving and prosperous community, this ruined Augustinian Abbey is now in the care of English Heritage. The medieval beamed ceiling in the Chapter House is impressive, as is its 12th century entrance. Work on the surrounding fields has revealed that the abbey ruins were incorporated into the grounds of the now demolished 18th century Sundome House.

☎ 01743 709661   www.english-heritage.org.uk

Hawkstone Park
220 C5

Restored after years of neglect, this 18th century parkland covers an area in excess of 100 acres (40ha) and is now a Grade 1 listed landscape. Intricate archways, a ruined medieval castle, winding pathways, tunnels, passageways and an underground grotto give the visitor a fascinating, though at times strenuous, 3 to 4 hour round trip of the grounds.

☎ 01939 200611   www.hawkstone.co.uk

Hereford Cathedral
401 B2

Standing on the banks of the River Wye, much of the original 12th century cathedral still survives today although extensive restoraton took place in the 18th and 19th centuries. It is probably most famous for the Chained Library and Mappa Mundi exhibitions housed in the New Library building. Mappa Mundi dates from around 1300 and is the most complete and largest medieval world map still in existence. There is also an interactive exhibition which makes use of both original artefacts and the latest computer technology. Entry to the Cathedral is free but there is a charge for the exhibitions.

☎ 01432 359880   www.herefordcathedral.org

Hergest Croft Gardens
194 B2

The estate dates back to 1267 but this garden of wooded valleys and glades, flower beds and open grassland was created in 1912 when the estate was bought by the Banks family. There are over 4000 shrubs and trees in four distinct areas of the garden covering over 50 acres (20ha) – the Kitchen Garden, Park Wood, the Azalea Garden and the Edwardian House which has an old rockery and croquet lawn.

☎ 01544 230160   www.hergest.co.uk

Hodnet Hall Gardens
220 D5

60 acres (24ha) of magnificent gardens in the ownership of the Heber-Parcy family. The design has changed over hundreds of years to match the three different sites of the homes of the family and their ancestors. There is a variety of shrubs and plants designed to give colour to the gardens throughout the summer, as well as woodland walks and a chain of ornamental pools. The 17th century tearoom is well worth a visit.

☎ 01630 685786

Ironbridge Gorge
207 F2

The Iron Bridge, the first bridge in the world to be constructed completely of iron, is the focal point of the 'Valley of Invention' which was at the centre of the industrial revolution in Britain. Now a World Heritage Site, ten museums tell the story of the industrial revolution and the part this area played in it. The Blists Hill Victorian Town is an open-air re-creation of a late 19th century working community where even old money can be bought at the bank and used in the local shops and pubs. On some Saturdays there are re-enactments of a Victorian wedding ceremony. The Museum of the Gorge looks at the effects of the revolution on the beautiful gorge itself, and the Broseley Pipeworks, which closed in 1957, is presented as if it were still a working factory. There is also a Museum of Iron, China Museum and Tile Museum, as well as the Bridge and Tollhouse where there is an exhibition and souvenir shop. A passport ticket can be bought to give access to all ten museums and, as they cover an area of around 6 square miles (15 sq km), a shuttle bus runs between them at weekends and on bank holidays.

☎ 01952 884391   www.ironbridge.co.uk

Kenilworth Castle
360 A3

An impressive 11th century ruined castle which has been radically altered and extended since then. John Dudley acquired the castle in the 16th century but was executed for his part in the plot to place Lady Jane Grey on the throne. His son, Robert Dudley, created formal gardens where he entertained Queen Elizabeth I on several occasions. Now in the care of English Heritage, some of the 12th century buildings in the inner courtyard survive, as does the Tudor gatehouse.

☎ 01926 852078   www.english-heritage.org.uk

Letocetum Roman Baths & Museum (NT)
208 D2

The remains of a Roman bathhouse and an inn have been excavated at this site which was an overnight halt on Watling Street, the main road from London to North Wales. A museum exhibits many of the artefacts that have been discovered on the site and gives the historical background to the site.

☎ 01543 480768   www.nationaltrust.org.uk

Lichfield Cathedral
208 D1

Situated in a peaceful close surrounded by half-timbered buildings, this Gothic cathedral dates from the 14th century. With three spires, known as the 'Ladies of the Vale', it is unique amongst medieval cathedrals. The Lichfield Gospels, an 8th century manuscript, is on display in the Chapter House, which dates from 1249 and is one of the most beautiful parts of the cathedral. There is a visitor centre and a licensed restaurant situated in an elegant 18th century house next to the cathedral.

☎ 01543 306240

Little Malvern Court
195 G3

Home to the Berington family since the Dissolution of the Monasteries in 1539 and comprising the 14th century Prior's Hall and the Victorian Manor House. The interior features paintings by the family along with many examples from Europe, and there is a fine collection of 18th and 19th century needlework. Lovely views can be taken from the gardens covering 10 acres (4ha) which once belonged to the 12th century priory that stood on the site.

☎ 01684 892988

Ludlow
207 E5

A 12th century market town, with 500 listed buildings, which retains its original grid-like layout. Amongst the listed buildings are the 17th century Feathers Hotel, the Broadgate, which is the only surviving gate from the old city walls, and the medieval Reader's House with its three-storey Jacobean porch. The Church of St Lawrence has the grandeur of a cathedral and shows, in one of its stained glass windows, the life of St Lawrence, Ludlow's patron saint. The geology of the area and the town's local history are the main themes of the museum in the Assembly Rooms.

☎ 01584 875053   www.ludlow.org.uk

Ironbridge Gorge

www.visittheartofengland.com

Ludlow Castle
207 E5

Built in the late 11th century to repel Welsh marauders, the castle has much that is original, including the keep, chapel and some of the doorways. It became a royal palace under Edward IV, and home of the Council of the Marches, responsible for the government of Wales and the borders. There are many exhibitions, displays and events throughout the year.

☎ 01584 873355   www.ludlowcastle.com

Malvern Hills
195 G3

Stretching for 9 miles (15km) with a high point of 1380ft (425m) at Worcestershire Beacon, the Malvern Hills divide the counties of Herefordshire and Worcestershire. Easily accessible either from the towns on the flanks of the hills or from the numerous car parks that are dotted around the entire length. This is a designated Area of Outstanding Natural Beauty which can be extremely busy in good weather though quieter spots can be found even during the busiest periods.

☎ 01684 560616   www.malvernhillsaonb.org.uk

Mary Arden's House
197 D2

Glebe Farm is the home of William Shakespeare's mother, Mary Arden – for years it was thought that the adjacent timber-framed Palmer's Farm was her home but it has only recently been discovered not to be so.

The Shakespeare Countryside Museum is housed in the outbuildings which include a dovecote, smithy, cider press and workshop containing a variety of Elizabethan farm implements. There are frequent displays of falconry.

☎ 01789 204016   www.shakespeare.org.uk

National Sea Life Centre
378 G8

Set in the rejuvenated canalside area of Birmingham, one of the many highlights is the completely transparent tunnel giving the impression that the visitor is completely surrounded by all manner of sea creatures, including sharks and rays. Conservation is an important part of the centre's activities and is part of the SOS (Save Our Seas) scheme which works with many worldwide conservation groups. The seahorse breeding and conservation centre allows visitors to see work normally carried on behind the scenes.

☎ 0121 643 6777   www.sealifeeurope.com

Packwood House (NT)
209 D5

This 16th century house was extensively restored between the two World Wars by Graham Baron Ash and donated to the National Trust in 1941. It played host to Henry Ireton, Cromwell's general, before the Battle of Edgehill in 1642, and also to Charles II after his defeat at Worcester in 1651. There is a large number of sundials and clocks adorning the walls while the impressive gardens include yew trees with a theme of the 'Sermon on the Mount'.

☎ 01564 783294   www.nationaltrust.org.uk

Potteries Museum & Art Gallery
410 A2

A local history museum examining all aspects of the area, from the world famous pottery industry through to community, wildlife and geology. The centrepiece of the wartime section of the museum is a Spitfire designed by Reginald Mitchell who was educated in Hanley and served his apprenticeship in Fenton before going on to design the Spitfire. He died in 1937 before he saw it enter full service.

☎ 01782 232323

RAF Museum
207 G2

Formerly the Aerospace Museum, the RAF Museum has a collection of over 70 aircraft from Britain, Germany, Argentina, America and Japan. There are also air force vehicles, missiles and engines, and ever-changing exhibitions. The aircraft are mainly housed in three hangars with themes of transport and training, warplanes, research and development. The restoration work which is ongoing at the museum can be observed from the viewing gallery, and the annual air show is always popular.

☎ 01902 376200   www.rafmuseum.org.uk

Ragley Hall
196 C2

The family home of the Marquess and Marchioness of Hertford, this magnificent Palladian house was built in 1680 and stands in grounds of over 400 acres (160ha) designed by Lancelot 'Capability' Brown. The Great Hall has superb baroque plasterwork by James Gibbs and included in the fine art collection is the mural 'The Temptation' by Graham Rust. The grounds include woodland walks, a maze, adventure playground and rose garden.

☎ 01789 762090   www.ragleyhall.com

Ryton Organic Gardens
360 C3

10 acres (4ha) of totally organic gardens covering all aspects of organic gardening – composting, pest control, flower, fruit and vegetable production amongst many others. A natural area includes trees, wild flower meadow and lake. The Paradise Garden is dedicated to the late Geoff Hamilton, the popular presenter of 'Gardeners' World'. It is also home to the headquarters of the Henry Doubleday Research Association which promotes organic gardening and farming.

☎ 024 7630 3517   www.hdra.org.uk

Severn Valley Railway
207 G3

This standard-gauge steam railway runs for a distance of 16 miles (26km) from Bridgnorth to Kidderminster and passes through beautiful Severn Valley countryside, including a trip across a 200ft (60m) single span bridge. The station at Bewdley has a model railway and workshops where restoration work on one of the largest collections of locomotives and rolling stock in the country can be viewed.

☎ 01299 403816   www.svr.co.uk

Shakespeare's Birthplace
410 D2

A half-timbered house bought by the Bard's father, John Shakespeare, in the mid 16th century, a few years before Shakespeare's birth in 1564, and which remained in the family until 1806. 16th and 17th century furniture adorn the interior and, of particular interest, are the signatures of famous visitors engraved into a window in the Birth Room. The visitor centre has a multitude of original exhibits and displays, and there is a lovely traditional English garden.

☎ 01789 204016   www.shakespeare.org.uk

Shugborough Estate (NT)
222 A5

This Georgian mansion is the ancestral home of Lord Lichfield and has exhibitions of period silver, furniture, paintings and china. Amongst the many events throughout the summer are craft, weaving and gardening weekends and also a fully working water mill where milling demonstrations take place. The 900 acres (360ha) of gardens and parkland include a yew tree which is thought to be the widest tree in the country.

☎ 01889 881 388   www.nationaltrust.org.uk

Spetchley Park
196 A2

Surrounding the 19th century mansion (not open to the public) these gardens have been owned by the Berkeley family since 1605. Formal clipped hedges, fountain gardens, herbaceous borders and winding paths offer so much of interest in this 30 acre (19ha) garden (not open to the public on Saturdays). The 110 acre (70ha) Deer Park is not open during June.

☎ 01453 810303   www.spetchleygardens.co.uk

Stafford Castle
221 G5

There is plenty to see and do at this 900 year old castle originally built by William the Conqueror but largely destroyed during the Civil War. The visitor centre has displays of finds made in archaeological excavations. Historical re-enactments and Shakespeare theatrical productions are a feature of the summer months, for which there is an admission charge. There is also a herb garden which was originally planted for medicinal purposes.

☎ 01785 257698

Stokesay Castle
206 D4

This 13th century fortified manor house, now in the care of English Heritage, is one of England's finest and is set in beautiful countryside amongst the Shropshire Hills, not far from the Welsh border. Many parts of the castle are original, including the Great Hall in which the roof timbers are soot blackened from the open hearth. The solar chamber has a magnificent Jacobean fireplace and the delightful 17th century gatehouse is probably more ornamental than strategic.

☎ 01588 672544   www.english-heritage.org.uk

Symonds Yat
181 E1

A large loop in the River Wye has Symonds Yat Rock at its narrowest point. This impressive wooded gorge is a nesting place for the rare peregrine falcon which can be observed from the RSPB information area at the top of the rock during the summer months. A steep descent from the large car park, for which there is a charge, leads to Symonds Yat East where there is a popular inn and café, while an unusual hand pulled ferry crosses the Wye to Symonds Yat West, where there is a visitor and heritage centre.

☎ 01600 713899

Tamworth Castle
209 E2

A Norman motte and bailey castle dating from the 12th century, with numerous additions since then, including the medieval Banqueting Hall. 15 rooms are open to the public with displays from throughout the castle's history. There are many events including ghost vigils and tours in search of the many ghosts allegedly seen in the castle. There are also frequent Shakespearian plays. Beneath the castle are the pleasure grounds with floral terraces, play areas, tennis courts, crazy golf and a café.

☎ 01827 709629   www.tamworthcastle.freeserve.co.uk

Thinktank
379 Q7

One of the largest millennium projects, with a wide range of different things to do and see for all the family. Science and nature are brought to life by displays, many of which are interactive, in ten different galleries. Local history is featured, as is nature, medicine, a vision of the future and the oldest working steam engine in the world, designed by James Watt.

☎ 0121 202 2222   www.thinktank.ac

Warwick Castle

Tutbury Castle — 222 D5

This 11th century castle has played host to many royal guests including giving safe harbour to Charles I and his nephew Prince Rupert during the Civil War. Because of this, Cromwell ordered the castle to be dismantled though it was rebuilt in 1662. Mary, Queen of Scots was imprisoned here and, of all the places she was imprisoned, it is said that she had a special loathing for Tutbury. There is also a secret staircase, privy garden and herbery.

☎ 01283 812129 — www.tutburycastle.com

Upton House (NT) — 197 F3

This 17th century house has wonderful collections of 18th century furniture, tapestries, art and porcelain. The house was bought by Walter Samuel, the Chairman of Shell, in 1927. He carried out extensive modifications to both interior and exterior and gave the house and his collections to the National Trust in 1948. This included his splendid art collection of works by El Greco, Canaletto, Stubbs and Hogarth. There are 31 acres (12.5ha) of terraced garden containing herbaceous borders, fruit and vegetable gardens.

☎ 01295 670266 — www.nationaltrust.org.uk

Viroconium Roman Town — 207 E2

With a population of over 6000, Viroconium (Wroxeter) was once the fourth largest city in Roman Britain. The remains are extensive and include city walls and the fully excavated public baths. Beneath these are timber buildings dating from the early part of the first century when a garrison was stationed here before it was moved to Chester and Viroconium became an important trading centre. A visitor centre explains the history of the town as well as exhibiting many of the artefacts discovered on the site.

☎ 01743 761330

Warwick Castle — 197 E1

Set on the banks of the River Avon, this is one of the finest examples of 14th century fortifications in Britain. Real-life characters help to bring the castle to life and life-sized waxworks add detail to many of the displays, which include an accurate re-creation of the visit of the Prince of Wales, later to become Edward VII, in 1898. The macabre dungeon and torture chamber are reached down a narrow flight of stairs – the writings of a Royalist held during the Civil War can still be seen on the wall. The Great Hall is amongst the luxuriously decorated state rooms which has Oliver Cromwell's death mask on display and also paintings by masters such as Van Dyck and Rubens.

The grounds were designed by Lancelot 'Capability' Brown and include walks along the Avon, an 18th century conservatory and Victorian Rose Garden. There is also a restored mill and engine house which was used to produce the electricity of the household at the turn of the 20th century. There are many events throughout the year including fireworks concerts, medieval festivals and birds of prey displays. A good day out for all the family.

☎ 0870 442 2000 — www.warwick-castle.co.uk

Wedgwood Story Visitor Centre — 364 C3

Wedgwood Pottery was founded in 1759 by Josiah Wedgwood and his legacy can be seen during a tour of the state-of-the-art factory that includes hands-on demonstrations. Film and interactive displays are used to tell the story of the company and exhibits from all periods of its history are on display. The shop sells exclusive designs as well as seconds and discontinued lines.

☎ 01782 282986 — www.thewedgwoodstory.com

West Midland Safari Park — 208 A5

A 4 mile (6km) drive through the 150 acre (94ha) park gives access to all manner of exotic animals including elephants, lions, tigers, rhinoceros, bison, llama, antelope. Home to the country's only pride of white lion, of which there are only around 70 remaining worldwide, and white tigers, of which there are only around 150. There are also shows planned out at different times of the day – sea lion shows and hippo feeding, and chances to get close to animals such as snakes and crocodiles.

☎ 01299 400700 — www.wmsp.co.uk

Weston Park — 208 A2

Mentioned in the 11th century Domesday Book, though the present house was built in 1671. There are nine elegant rooms, including a library with over 3000 books, and the magnificent dining room which has a large collection of art by Van Dyck. The expansive grounds, designed by Lancelot 'Capability' Brown, are formal around the house and include a restored terrace garden as well as parkland including lakes, pools and the deer park. There is plenty for children with a miniature railway, animal centre and adventure playground.

☎ 01952 852100 — www.weston-park.com

Wightwick Manor (NT) — 208 A3

Built by the Mander family at the end of the 19th century to designs influenced by the Arts and Crafts movement, and decorated with original William Morris materials, Kempe glass and Pre-Raphaelite art. Descendants of the family still live in part of the manor. The 17 acre (7ha) garden is a delight with topiaries, terraces and ponds.

☎ 01902 761108 — www.nationaltrust.org.uk

Wilderhope Manor (NT) — 207 E3

On the edge of Wenlock Edge stands this Elizabethan manor house. It is now in use as a youth hostel and, as such, it is largely unfurnished which allows the skill of the craftsmen who created the oak spiral staircase, timber-framed walls and plaster ceilings to be appreciated to its full extent. Limited opening.

☎ 01694 771363

Worcester Art Gallery & Museum — 415 A2

In an historic Victorian building which also houses the city library, this local museum focuses on the history, geology and natural history of the area. A fully stocked 19th century chemist shop is amongst the exhibits of interest, as is the section of the museum devoted to the Worcestershire Regiment and Yeoman Cavalry. The art gallery has frequently changing contemporary art exhibitions from local and national artists.

☎ 01905 25371 — www.worcestercitymuseums.org.uk

Worcester Cathedral — 415 C2

The Cathedral stands on the site of an ancient Saxon monastery which was largely destroyed in 1041. Rebuilding started in 1064 and, after a series of problems including a fire and collapse of the tower, was all but complete by the time of its dedication in 1218. Time took its toll on the cathedral and it was not until the Victorians undertook a massive restoration programme that it took on the form that we see today. The richly decorated tombs of Prince Arthur and King John can be found near the High Altar.

☎ 01905 28854 — www.cofe-worcester.org.uk/cathedral

Wyre Forest — 207 G5

Once a popular hunting ground with an area of 4200 acres (1680ha) but which used to cover most of the West Midlands. Forest clearance for agriculture started during Neolithic times and continued through to the 16th century when the demand for both timber products and also charcoal was at its height. The visitor centre is south-west of Bewdley at Callow Hill and is the starting point for many trails. It also has a restaurant, gift shop and information on all aspects of the forest.

☎ 01299 266944 — www.wyreforest.net

EAST MIDLANDS

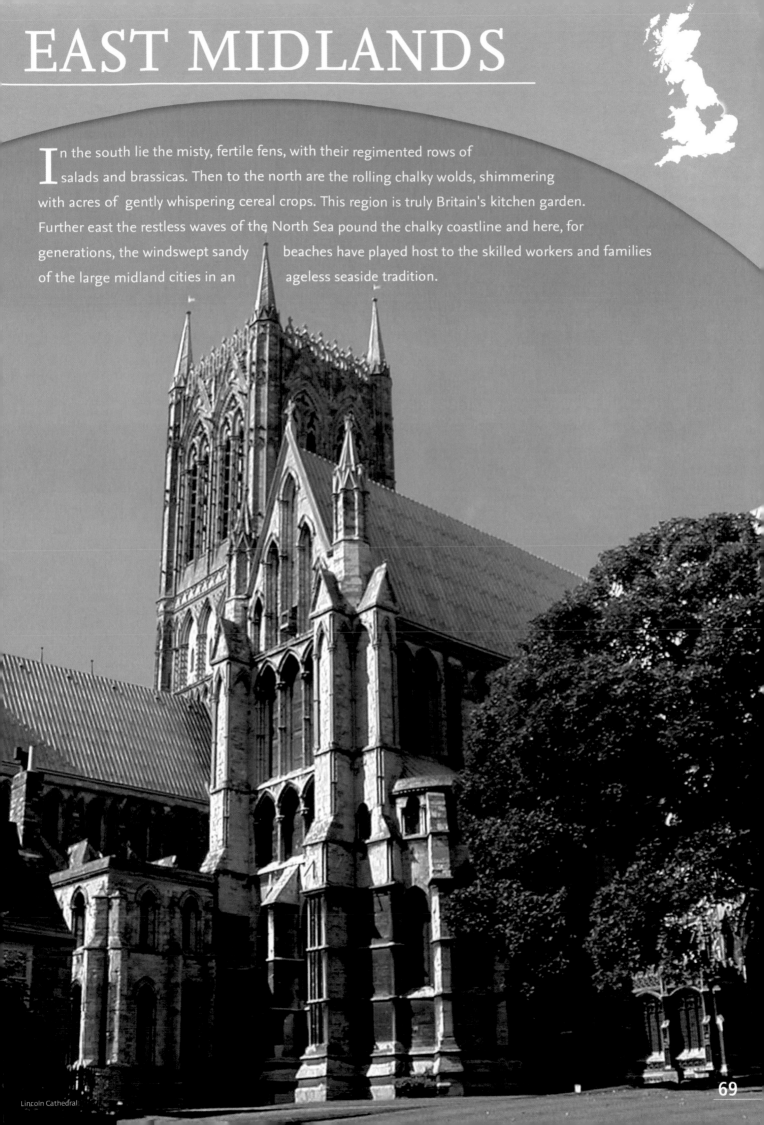

In the south lie the misty, fertile fens, with their regimented rows of salads and brassicas. Then to the north are the rolling chalky wolds, shimmering with acres of gently whispering cereal crops. This region is truly Britain's kitchen garden. Further east the restless waves of the North Sea pound the chalky coastline and here, for generations, the windswept sandy beaches have played host to the skilled workers and families of the large midland cities in an ageless seaside tradition.

Lincoln Cathedral

🏛 Althorp House `198 B1`

Since 1508, Althorp House has been home to the Spencer family. The classically-styled house in its typically English parkland was thrust into the limelight by the tragic death in 1997 of Diana, Princess of Wales, herself a member of the family. She now rests in peace on an island in the centre of the lake. Although there is no public access to the island, there is an excellent exhibition about Diana housed in the former stable block. Audiovisual displays relate to her life and work, with poignant memorabilia such as school reports and her beautiful wedding dress. Diana's involvement with various charities is well known and the Diana, Princess of Wales Memorial Fund, set up to continue this work, gets a high profile; all proceeds from the entrance fees go to this fund.

The house itself contains many treasures, which can be viewed by the public. In particular, there is an exceptional collection of portraits by artists such as Gainsborough, Van Dyck and Rubens.

Open July to September only.

☎ 0870 167 9000   www.althorp.com

Althorp House

⬡ American Adventure Theme Park `362 C1`

Right on the edge of the glorious Derbyshire Peak District and set around a 32 acre (13ha) lake (once an opencast mine), this exciting theme park includes the tallest Skycoaster in Europe, a 200ft (61m) high face-first, free-fall, white-knuckle experience. Try the Motion Master, which synchronises a seat with what is happening in an action packed film. Then there is Nightmare Niagara, a triple drop log flume, and The Missile, a roller coaster with six completely circular loops. Tiny tots and the faint-hearted are also catered for, and the management promise that with over 100 rides, there will be 'no unacceptably long queues'.

☎ 0845 330 2929   www.americanadventure.co.uk

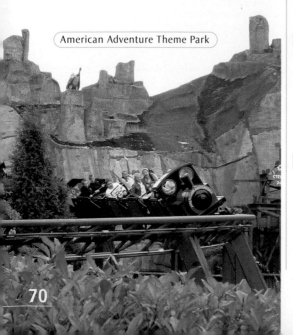
American Adventure Theme Park

✿ Barnsdale Gardens `211 E1`

Built over several years by gardener Geoff Hamilton, all the 35-plus model gardens from the various TV series can be seen here. Plant nursery and excellent coffee shop.

☎ 01572 813200   www.barnsdalegardens.co.uk

★ Battle of Britain Memorial Flight Visitor Centre `226 A2`

Exhibition and guided tours of the maintenance hangar containing the Memorial Flight aircraft, including an Avro Lancaster, Chipmunks, Dakota, Hurricanes and Spitfires.

☎ 01526 344041   www.lincolnshire.gov.uk

🌲 Beacon Hill Country Park `361 A1`

Part of Charnwood Forest, and now included as part of the new National Forest, the network of paths running through the 335 acres (135ha) of grassland, mixed woodland and heath, make the park ideal for walking and picnics. Beacon Hill itself (at 802ft (245m) the second highest point in Leicestershire) was once home to Bronze Age people and remains of their Hill Fort can still be seen. It now sports a toposcope, pointing out interesting features in the surrounding landscape.

☎ 01509 890048   www.leics.gov.uk

🏛 ✿ Belton House (NT) `225 E4`

Built in the Restoration style for Sir John Brownlow in the late 1600s, this sumptuous country house is well worth a visit for the wealth of elaborate woodcarving and plasterwork, not to mention the fine furniture, silverware and tapestries. A magnificent Orangery graces the formal gardens and the substantial landscaped parkland includes a lake; perfect for a leisurely stroll. If the children get bored, head for the Adventure Playground and Wildlife Discovery Centre. The Stables Restaurant also includes a children's menu.

☎ 01476 566116   www.nationaltrust.org.uk

🏰 Belvoir Castle `224 D4`

For 1000 years Belvoir has been home to the Dukes of Rutland. Meaning 'beautiful view', the name is actually pronounced 'beaver' and the view is right across the glorious Vale of Belvoir. The present castle was built in the early 1800s after a fire destroyed the previous one, and it contains many fine paintings and sculptures along with French furniture, tapestries and porcelain. There is also a fascinating museum dedicated to the history of the Queens Royal Lancers. Outside, the sloping lawns lead to the terraced formal gardens and the secluded Duchess' Spring Gardens.

☎ 01476 871000   www.belvoircastle.com

🌲 Bestwood Lodge Country Park `363 E1`

Just four miles (6km) north of Nottingham, this 650 acre (263ha) park was once part of the ancient Sherwood Forest. 20 miles (32km) of footpaths now wind through a remarkable range of habitats, from reedbeds to woodland and heath. Over 150 species of birds inhabit the park.

☎ 0115 927 3674   www.nottinghamshire.gov.uk

🏰 Bolsover Castle `236 B5`

Looking like a 'proper' castle, this 'Little Castle' is really a 17th century mansion house built to represent the romantic ideal of chivalry and elegance. Walking around, an imaginative audiovisual presentation re-creates the atmosphere of the time. The huge Riding House, originally built by William Cavendish to train horses

in the art of manege, has been converted into a Discovery Centre and the restored garden boasts a fountain with 23 new statues. There is a visitor centre, café, and picnics are allowed in the grounds.

☎ 01246 822844   www.english-heritage.org.uk

Boughton House

🏛 ✿ Boughton House `211 E4`

The 'English Versailles', so called because of the French-style changes made to the original 1500s Tudor monastic building. Home to the Dukes of Buccleuch, the interior is richly furnished and the ceilings are decorated with delightful mythical scenes. The Buccleuch collection of fine art is world renowned, including works by Van Dyck and Caracci. There is a superb armoury and ceremonial coach, and the grounds house a tearoom, play area and walled garden with plant centre. House open August only. Grounds open May to August.

☎ 01536 515731   www.boughtonhouse.org.uk

🌲 Bradgate Park `361 A2`

Leicestershire's largest country park is famous for its large deer herd and Lady Jane Grey (queen of England for nine days). The ruins of Bradgate house, her birthplace, lie amongst the granite outcrops. However, the chapel has survived and houses a small museum. The tower folly 'Old John' stands on the ridge and is a famous local landmark. Excellent for walking.

☎ 0116 236 2713   www.leics.gov.uk

🏛 Buxton Museum & Art Gallery `235 E5`

Follow the time line of the Peak District through seven rooms of geology, archaeology and history. Exhibitions feature work by local artists.

☎ 01298 24658   www.derbyshire.gov.uk

🏛 Calke Abbey (NT) `223 E5`

An interesting example of a baroque country house captured in its state of decline. The last baronet died here in 1924 and left splendidly decorated rooms, where the family had lived, along with deserted, run-down areas, abandoned due to lack of servants. Little restoration work has been done, in order to preserve the remarkable social history it portrays. There is an extensive natural history collection, wonderful parkland, café and shop, and a walled garden with Auricula theatre.

☎ 01332 863822   www.nationaltrust.org.uk

🏛 ✿ Canons Ashby `198 A2`

The house takes its name from an Augustinian Priory, the church surviving on a hilltop in the grounds. Home to the Dryden family since it was built in the mid 1500s, it has remained virtually the same since 1710. The Jacobean plasterwork is exceptional and the Elizabethan wall paintings have been superbly restored. The formal gardens have been brought back to their 18th century glory.

☎ 01327 861900   www.nationaltrust.org.uk

⭐ Carsington Water 223 D1

This 741 acre (300ha) reservoir was originally designed to collect water at times of high rainfall and release it back into the River Derwent in times of drought. It has also proved to be an excellent centre for water sports, fishing, walking, cycling and picnicking. The extensive modern visitor centre has an interactive display explaining how the reservoir was constructed, as well as shops, restaurant and a café. Half a million trees and shrubs were planted to landscape the area and provide habitat for wildlife and there are two hides from which to observe the many birds in the Wildlife Centre. The Watersports Centre will hire out canoes, dinghies and windsurfers, and provide instruction on how to use them, or you can take your own craft. A network of waymarked footpaths and bridleways allow for walking, horse riding and cycling (bikes can be hired). For younger children, there is a large adventure playground and families can cook their own food in the designated barbeque areas. Facilities for the less able are particularly good.

Carsington Water

🏛 ❇ Chatsworth House 235 G5

In the heart of the Derbyshire Peak District stands one of Britain's best loved stately homes, the residence of the Duke and Duchess of Devonshire. The magnificent house has over 25 beautifully decorated and furnished rooms, containing some of the finest treasures to be found in a private collection.

There are over 100 miles (161km) of walks through the 1000 acres (405ha) of Lancelot 'Capability' Brown designed parkland, which includes a lovely 100 acre (41ha) garden and the famous gravity fed waterworks, which power spectacular fountains and a waterfall cascading down a long flight of stone steps. Chatsworth has never rested on its laurels; the estate has been developed to provide a first-class adventure playground, with 'commando' style rope walks down to safe water and sand play areas for tiny tots. A working farmyard allows children to get really close to the animals and a 28-seat trailer provides tours of the woods and parkland. The maze is a challenge, and for shopaholics there is a farm shop selling Estate and local produce as well as one selling everything from furniture to porcelain. There are brass band concerts on a Sunday and events throughout the year. Truly a top-class family day out.

☎ 01246 565300   www.chatsworth-house.co.uk

Chatsworth House

🏛 Church Farm Museum 227 D1

Just outside Skegness town centre is a restored farmyard, showing life as it was in rural Lincolnshire around the turn of the 20th century. Besides the farmhouse, there is a 'mud and stud' thatched cottage and various farm buildings, all with period exhibitions. Outside, the orchard has old apple tree varieties and a herd of Lincolnshire Longwool sheep graze the paddock. There are always things going on, such as baking and threshing, and refreshments are available.

☎ 01754 766658   www.lincolnshire.gov.uk

🦅 Clumber Country Park (NT) 236 D5

Lovely country park of over 3800 acres (1537ha) with heath, woods and farmland. There is a serpentine lake and an avenue of lime trees (reputedly the longest in Europe) as well as a superb chapel in the Gothic Revival style, temples, a classical bridge and a walled kitchen garden with magnificent glasshouses. Excellent for walking and cycling (bikes can be hired) with refreshments in the stable block.

☎ 01909 476592   www.nationaltrust.org.uk

❇ Coton Manor Wildlife Garden 210 B5

Ten acre (4ha) garden with a wide range of interesting and unusual plants. Five acre (2ha) bluebell wood, which is a real picture in spring, as well as an orchard and wild flower meadow. Plant nursery and excellent tearoom.

☎ 01604 740219   www.cotonmanor.co.uk

⭐ Denby Pottery 223 E3

Get messy and have a go at making a plate or a frog. Daily tours, excellent factory shop, cookery demonstrations, museum, garden, Dartington Crystal and gift shops, restaurant and children's play area.

☎ 01773 740799   www.denbyvisitorcentre.co.uk

🏛 Derby Industrial Museum 395 A2

The site of the world's oldest factory (the silk mills, built in the early 1700s) is appropriately the location for this museum. It tells the story of Derby's industrial heritage; mining, pottery, foundry work, railway engineering and a major exhibition of Rolls Royce aero-engines form the backbone of the museum. There are regularly changing displays and events.

☎ 01332 255308   www.derby.gov.uk

🏠 Doddington Hall 237 F5

This beautiful Elizabethan mansion, gatehouse and family church were completed in 1600 and the exterior has remained unchanged. However, the interior is a surprise, having been completely redecorated and furnished in the Georgian style in the mid-1700s. The wonderful array of textiles, paintings and artefacts collected since give it a very 'lived in' air.

Outside, the lovely gardens occupy 6 acres (2.4ha), most of which are walled, with formal topiary and herbaceous planting. There is also a wild garden and intriguing turf maze. Refreshments are served in the Gatehouse.

☎ 01522 694308   www.doddingtonhall.com

🏛 Donington Grand Prix Collection 223 F5

Five halls contain the world's largest collection of Grand Prix cars (over 130), from the oldest to the newest. Also helmets, veteran and vintage cars and much more. Gift shop selling models, videos, books and other merchandise.

☎ 01332 811027   www.doningtoncollection.com

▫ Dove Dale 222 C2

The River Dove flows along a limestone gorge, giving its name to the area of Dovedale, arguably the most beautiful of the Derbyshire Dales. The river itself is excellent for trout fishing and has been immortalised by Isaac Walton in his book 'The Compleat Angler'. Classified as an Area of Outstanding Natural Beauty, the valley runs for over two miles (3.2km) and there are beautiful walks both along it and in the surrounding hills, which are the remains of ancient coral reefs.

Dove Dale

EAST MIDLANDS

🏞 Elvaston Castle Country Park `362 B3`

The first country park in Britain, Elvaston includes 200 acres (81ha) of grounds containing formal gardens, woodland, nature trails, an ornamental lake and estate museum. Refreshments and shop.

☎ 01332 571342 www.derbyshire.gov.uk

🏛 Eyam Museum `235 G5`

The rat weather vane gives a clue to the theme of this museum; the 1665 outbreak of the Bubonic Plague. The story of this community is told from its beginnings in prehistory, through the tragedy of the plague (the villagers isolated themselves so as not to spread the disease), to its recovery and regrowth through the Industrial Revolution and beyond.

☎ 01433 631371 www.eyammuseum.demon.co.uk

★ Fantasy Island `227 D1`

Rides are classified as 'Extreme Thrill' (with names such as 'Absolutely Insane' and 'The Beast') and 'Family Fun' (Europe's largest ferris wheel, for example, and a train ride through the world of the Jellikins for the little ones). Most of the rides are inside and with over 15 places to eat, a huge market and over 30 shops in the Mall, the weather is largely irrelevant.

☎ 01754 874668 www.fantasyisland.co.uk

Foxton Locks

★ Foxton Locks `210 C4`

Located on the Grand Union Canal, Foxton Locks were built to solve the problem of raising boats the 75ft (22.5m) between Market Harborough and the hill summit a few miles north. Ten locks were constructed between 1810 and 1814 to form the 'Foxton Staircase' and it takes 45 minutes and 25,000 gallons (113,650l) of water for one boat to negotiate all ten; the water passing into side ponds, where it is stored. At the start of the 20th century, in order to speed up the passage of boats in an attempt to compete with the railways, the famous 'Inclined Plane' was built. Considered one of the 'Seven Wonders of the Waterways', the structure was designed by Gordon Cale Thomas and built by Gwynne of London. It consisted of two tanks, each filled with water, large enough to carry two narrow boats or a barge. A 25 horsepower engine enabled the tanks to travel up and down the slope in 12 minutes, also saving many thousands of gallons of water. However, due to lack of improvements on the rest of the canal and the success of the railways, the Inclined Plane lift was uneconomic and only operated for about ten years before being abandoned and eventually sold for scrap in 1928. The museum on the site tells the story and shows the plans for rebuilding it.

The towpaths and surrounding area are lovely for walks and there is a pub and café at the locks.

☎ 01162 792657 www.fipt.org.uk

🏰 Gainsborough Old Hall `237 F4`

Over 500 years old, this timber framed medieval manor house has a superb Great Hall, medieval kitchen and interesting furniture. Audio tours available.

☎ 01427 612669 www.english-heritage.org.uk

🦙 Gibraltar Point `227 D2`

An internationally important National Nature Reserve, this 1000 acre (430ha) site contains many constantly changing coastal habitats, namely sand dunes, saltmarsh, freshwater marsh, sandbanks and mudbanks. Stretching from Skegness to the Wash, this is a haven for overwintering and breeding birds, and footpaths and hides have been constructed to enable visitors to observe but not disturb them.

☎ 01754 762677 www.lincstrust.org.uk

🚂 Great Central Railway `361 B3`

Britain's only main line double track steam railway offers rides from Loughborough to Leicester stations. Dine in style, drive an engine, enjoy a 'themed' ride (such as a 'who dunnit') or try a Santa Special. Museum, engine sheds and shop at the Loughborough end.

☎ 01509 230726 www.gcrailway.co.uk

🏰 Grimsthorpe Castle `225 F5`

Dating from the 13th century, this castle with its impressive baroque frontage has an interesting collection of tapestries, paintings and fine furniture, including thrones from the House of Lords. Surrounded by 3000 acres (1213ha) of parkland, there is a family cycle trail, a Woodland Adventure Playground, a tour with the Park Ranger (who will point out the wealth of wildlife), a shop and a café.

☎ 01778 591205 www.grimsthorpe.co.uk

🏰 Gunby Hall (NT) `226 C1`

Lovely red brick 18th century house with fine oak panelling and period furnishings. Nine acres (3.6ha) of beautiful gardens with traditional flowers, fruit and vegetables.

☎ 01909 486411 www.nationaltrust.org.uk

🏰 ❋ Haddon Hall `222 D1`

Parts of the hall date back to 1170, when the illegitimate son of William the Conqueror held it. However, it was not until 200 years later that the building was completed. Remarkably well preserved, it has featured in many period dramas and films.

Home of the Manners family since 1567, areas of interest include the Medieval Banqueting Hall, with Minstrels Gallery, the Great Chamber, which has many fine tapestries, and the Long Gallery, of early 17th century lineage, where the Elizabethan gentry and their ladies could take gentle walking exercise in inclement weather.

The beautiful gardens were brought back from a derelict state by the 9th Duchess of Rutland, who created a romantic garden with herbaceous borders and terraced rose gardens. The 17th century stable block houses a licensed restaurant and there is a gift shop.

☎ 01629 812855 www.haddonhall.co.uk

Haddon Hall

🏛 Harborough Museum `210 C4`

The history of this planned medieval market town (many medieval yards still exist) is told through displays in this museum. The story of Market Harborough's famous corset making industry is explained with old photographs and models, including a steam former used to shape the corsets. There is a reconstruction of a bootmaker's workshop, many photographs and texts from the town as it was, and archaeological finds, including artefacts from the nearby Drayton Roman Villa and Naseby battlefield.

☎ 01858 821085 www.leics.gov.uk

🏰 ❋ Hardwick Hall (NT) `223 F1`

Designed by Robert Smythson for the wealthy Bess of Hardwick, no expense was spared to build this magnificent example of Elizabethan grandeur. Imposing symmetrical towers and acres of glittering glass windows give a stunning first impression. Hardwick Hall displays the National Trust's most important collection of textiles in the country, including the Gideon Tapestries, which hang in the Long Gallery and cover the 167ft (50m) long wall. Other items of interest include period furniture, portraits and armour.

Before living here, Bess lived in Hardwick 'Old' Hall (now managed by English Heritage), the remains of which can be seen on the hilltop next to the 'New' Hall. It was the wealth accumulated from her four husbands that enabled her to move!

Outside, a herb garden, orchard and formal flower beds are enclosed by courtyards, and surrounding this is a country park containing rare breeds of sheep and cattle. There is also a stonemasons centre, which can be visited.

☎ 01246 850430 www.nationaltrust.org.uk

Hardwick Hall

★ Heights of Abraham
`223 E2`

The journey of discovery starts with a spectacular ride in a cable car over the River Derwent and Matlock Bath village, to the summit. At the top there is an old lead mine, the Great Rutland Cavern Nestus Mine, and the Great Masson Cavern to explore, the latter including a film presentation on how it was formed. Climb the Prospect Tower for magnificent views. There are two adventure playgrounds, woodland walks, the 'Who, Why, What' story of the Estate, excellent gift shops, and refreshments in The Terrace café, Woodlanders restaurant and the Tavern.

☎ 01629 582365   www.heights-of-abraham.co.uk

Heights of Abraham

⌂ Kedleston Hall (NT)
`362 A2`

A mansion in the neoclassical style with a remarkable array of Robert Adam interiors. The state rooms still have their original furniture, and an amazing display of Indian artefacts (collected by Lord Curzon, Viceroy of India in the early 1900s) can be seen in the Eastern Museum. The mansion is surrounded by parkland, which includes a restored 18th century garden. There is a shop and restaurant.

☎ 01332 842191   www.nationaltrust.org.uk

⌂ Lincoln Castle
`403 B2`

Built in 1068, this impressive and massive early Norman castle on its hilltop houses one of the four surviving copies of the Magna Carta, sealed by King John in 1215. There are still many original features to see, and a walk along the walls outside provides superb views across the surrounding countryside.

☎ 01522 511068   www.lincolnshire.gov.uk

✝ Lincoln Cathedral
`403 B2`

Sharing the central hill with Lincoln Castle, this magnificent cathedral is one of the finest medieval buildings in Europe. Originally built in 1072 from local limestone, it was consecrated in 1092 and has been a place of worship ever since. It was damaged by fire in 1141 and an earthquake in 1185 caused considerable collapse. Rebuilt by the Bishop of Lincoln (St Hugh), he incorporated huge flying buttresses on the outside so that fewer supporting structures were needed on the inside. This allowed large windows to be installed and gave the inside an open and airy feel. In 1237 the central tower collapsed, which was not replaced for several years. By 1549 there were three towers, each with a spire; the central one blew down and the others were eventually removed, being considered unsafe!

The cathedral library contains many important manuscripts, including one written by the Venerable Bede in the late tenth century. The medieval library often exhibits books and manuscripts and there are guided roof and floor tours daily (except Sundays).

☎ 01522 544544   www.lincolncathedral.com

🏠 Lyddington Bede House
`211 D3`

Originally built as a wing of a medieval palace, owned by the Bishops of Lincoln, it was seized by the Crown in 1547 and given to Lord Burghley. He converted it into small rooms, almshouses, for the poor, with the condition that they learn a craft and attend church. Audio tour of the rooms.

☎ 01572 822438   www.english-heritage.org.uk

🏠 Lyveden New Bield (NT)
`211 E4`

Designed in the shape of a cross, Sir Thomas Tresham built (but did not complete) this Elizabethan 'Lodge' to show his religious convictions. It has remained almost unchanged since 1605. The layout of the water garden is also original, containing terraces and fascinating spiral mounds.

☎ 01832 205358   www.nationaltrust.org.uk

★ Mam Tor
`235 F4`

Known locally as 'shivering mountain', the summit of Mam Tor stands high above Hope and Edale. Popular with walkers, several well-maintained paths reach the top and along its ridgeway, where there are impressive views. Traces of an Iron Age fort can be found on the summit.

🏠 ❁ Melbourne Hall & Gardens
`223 E5`

Two Prime Ministers and Lady Caroline Lamb (the mistress of Lord Byron) have lived here. Originally built in the 12th century, most of the building was demolished and rebuilt in the 17th century. It now contains a fine collection of furniture and paintings and is the home of Lord and Lady Kerr. The formal gardens are beautifully laid out in the French style, with delightful fountains and an intriguing yew tunnel. House open in August only.

☎ 01332 862502

🏛 Melton Carnegie Museum
`210 C1`

Through displays of local archaeology, art, industry and rural pursuits, the museum tells the story of the market town of Melton Mowbray and the surrounding area.

☎ 01664 569946   www.leics.gov.uk

🏛 Museum of Lincolnshire Life
`403 A1`

Two centuries of social history are explored in this museum, which occupies the old barracks of the Loyal North Lincoln Militia; interactive displays tell the story of the Regiment. The fascinating history of local crafts is told and there are impressive collections representing agricultural and industrial heritage.

☎ 01522 528448   www.lincolnshire.gov.uk

🏛 National Space Centre
`361 B3`

Follow the brown signs with the rocket logo to this amazing centre covering all aspects of space research. For the over 5s, the Space Theatre shows amazing films about different worlds, how the universe was born and the edge of the known universe; under 5s can be treated to a 'Sunshine Show'. There are lots of buttons to push on hands-on displays in the five galleries. The first gallery looks at astronauts, the second is about our exploration of the universe to date, the third investigates our own solar system and the fourth examines how the huge advances in technology, due to space research, affect our lives on Earth. The final gallery takes a peek into the possible future. The silver 135ft (41m) rocket-shaped building contains a glass lift, which enables observation of the huge Blue Streak and Thor Able rockets. A truly inspiring and exciting day out.

☎ 0116 261 0261   www.nssc.co.uk

🏛 National Tramway Museum
`223 E2`

Set in a restored period village, including shops, cafés, a pub and a museum (which holds the largest national collection of electric trams). One ticket allows all day rides up and down the street on trams from all over the world. A workshop enables observation of 'work in progress' on trams being restored.

☎ 0870 758 7267   www.tramway.co.uk

Lincoln Cathedral

EAST MIDLANDS

✝ Newstead Abbey
223 G2

A 'must see' for Byron devotees, Newstead houses mementoes of one of England's most notorious poets. Originally built as an Augustinian priory, it was converted into a country house by the Byron family in the mid 1500s. Although much of the Abbey is now a ruin, there are beautifully furnished period rooms – although look out for the 'White Lady' ghost!

The walled garden, lake and exquisite Japanese gardens are set within the 300 acre (121.5ha) estate.

☎ 01623 793557　　www.newsteadabbey.org.uk

⏣ Nine Ladies Stone Circle
222 D1

On Stanton Moor, a circle of nine evenly-spaced stones stand in a 33ft (10m) diameter circle in a large, open woodland glade. The tallest stone stands at 2.3ft (0.7m) and there is one outlier, the King Stone. An atmospheric reminder of the mysterious past.

☎ 01629 816200　　www.english-heritage.org.uk

🏛 Northampton Central Museum
198 C1

Fascinating museum concentrating on Northampton's boot and shoe industry. The collection of footwear is one of the largest in the world, featuring every aspect of shoe design and manufacture. There are also impressive displays of oriental and British ceramics, and Italian paintings.

In another section of the museum, the history of the county of Northamptonshire is explained with exhibits from the surrounding area.

☎ 01604 838111　　www.northampton.gov.uk

🏛 Nottingham Castle Museum & Art Gallery
405 F1

The original Nottingham Castle was built in the early 1100s but was completely demolished in 1651. A new one was built on the same site by the Duke of Newcastle, which was gutted by fire in 1831. The shell was restored in 1878 to house a museum, which now displays a superb collection of fine art, ceramics, metalwork and glass. With children in mind, there are hands-on exhibitions and the 'Look Out' playground includes watch towers and a medieval barn. Tours of the city caves are available from the museum, and there is a café and shop.

☎ 0115 915 3700　　www.nottinghamcity.gov.uk

⛫ Oakham Castle
211 D2

The superb Great Hall remains from the original 12th century castle. It contains fine sculptures and an amazing collection of horseshoes, mounted on the walls, the oldest of which probably dates from 1470. The custom was that every visiting peer of the realm had to give a horseshoe to the Lord of the Manor on his or her first visit. HRH The Princess Royal gave one of the latest in 1999.

☎ 01572 758440　　www.rutnet.co.uk

★ Peak Cavern
235 F4

This huge cavern has the largest natural cave mouth in Britain. A complete village once existed here, making ropes for the local lead mining industry. The guided tour passes various awe inspiring features, including the Great Cave which measures 150ft (45m) by 90ft (27m).

☎ 01433 620285　　www.peakcavern.co.uk

☐ Peak District
235 F3

Essentially separated into the rugged sandstone Dark Peak and gentler limestone White Peak areas,

Peak District – Monsal Head

the Peak District is very much a product of man, through farming, mining and quarrying. It has been inhabited since the end of the last Ice Age.

The first National Park, the Peak District displays an amazing variety of habitats on its uplands and in its sheltered Dales, making it very pleasant walking country. The villages are picturesque and welcoming. Look out for the floral art of 'Well Dressing' in many villages, a custom largely confined to this area, and try the famous 'Bakewell Puddings' (not tarts) in the town of Bakewell. Visit the many caverns (with a guide) or relax in one of the many teashops or traditional pubs.

☎ 01629 816200　　www.peakdistrict.org

⏣ Peveril Castle
235 F4

Built in the 11th century to guard the King's Manor, this castle, on its high vantage point, offers superb views across the Peak District of Derbyshire.

☎ 01433 620613　　www.english-heritage.org.uk

🏛 Pickfords House Museum
395 B1

The former home of Joseph Pickford (architect), this Grade 1 listed Georgian town house is furnished in period style; even down to the housekeeper's cupboard. It shows vividly how an ordinary professional gentleman and his servants would have lived at the time. There are also displays of toys and toy theatres, textiles and costumes. Outside, the garden has been re-created in the style of the period.

☎ 01332 255363　　www.derby.gov.uk

★ Poole's Cavern
235 E5

The subterranean Wye Brook has dissolved the limestone rock here over millennia to form this magnificent cavern. Neolithic man sheltered here, Celts and Romans worshipped here, a robber called Poole is said to have hidden here in the 15th century, and people have visited it to marvel at its wonders since the 1600s. There are some fantastic formations fashioned from the slowly dripping limestone rich water; stalactites, stalagmites, rimstone pools, flowstones and curtain features, some of which have been coloured by minerals leaching out from the hills above. The entrance was once quite restricted, so in the late 1800s, the owner used dynamite to enlarge it (destroying some large features in the process). In this era, the cavern held a bandstand, museum and monkey house and was illuminated by large candelabra.

Luckily, the caves are now appreciated solely for their natural beauty and today's guides will not threaten abandonment at the end of the passage without further pay!

Research has shown that the cave system stretches for around one and a half miles (2.4km) beyond the boulder rubble at the current end. The visitor centre at the entrance has information on the so far unseen caves, tells the history of the cavern and has an exhibition of artefacts found in it.

☎ 01298 26978　　www.poolescavern.co.uk

⊞ Renishaw Hall & Gardens
236 B5

The grounds of Renishaw Hall contain lakeside walks, a sculpture trail, yuccary, a host of traditional and exotic plants and a café. The stable houses art galleries and a museum, which includes an exhibition of clothing from the last 150 years. Guided tours available.

☎ 01246 432310　　www.sitwell.co.uk

🏛 Rutland County Museum
211 D2

The rural history of England's smallest county is told in a building originally designed as an indoor riding school for the Rutland Fencible Cavalry. Further buildings house galleries, local crafts, a café and shop.

☎ 01572 758440　　www.rutnet.co.uk

Poole's Cavern

Sherwood Forest Country Park | 224 B1

Natural sandy heathland and ancient oaks have produced a fascinating ecosystem, represented in this 450 acre (182ha) country park, part of the former Royal Hunting Forest. The famous hollow 'Major Oak', where the legendary Robin Hood supposedly hid, can be found here and there are many waymarked woodland trails to explore. The excellent visitor centre illustrates the legends and natural history of the Forest, with displays and videos; it also houses two shops and a café.

☎ 01623 824490   www.nottinghamshiretourism.co.uk

Sherwood Pines Forest Park | 224 B1

With over 2960 acres (1200ha) of heath and woodland, this is an excellent area for safe cycling (cycles can be hired), walking, horse riding and picnics. For young children, there is an adventure playground.

☎ 01623 822447   www.forestry.gov.uk

Shipley Country Park | 362 C1

This 600 acre (243ha) country park includes woodlands, lakes and two large, flat, open areas popular for kite flying. There are many walks and cycle tracks, a sculpture trail, bird hide, adventure playground, visitor centre, shop, picnic site and coffee shop.

☎ 01773 719961   www.derby.gov.uk

Snibston Discovery Park | 209 G1

This former 100 acre (40.5ha) colliery site has been transformed into a unique museum and discovery centre for science and technology. Ride on the colliery railway and have a go on over 90 experiments to discover the wonders of science. Ex-miners give guided tours of the old colliery and, by contrast, the Science Alive gallery is full of state of the art interactive games illustrating scientific principles in fun ways. There is a separate gallery for under 8s and under 5s. Good restaurant and excellent access for the less able.

☎ 01530 278444   www.leics.gov.uk

Speedwell Cavern | 235 F4

This is a former lead mine incorporating several naturally formed chambers and an amazing underground canal. 105 steps lead down to the waterway, where a boat will take visitors on a guided tour of this atmospheric 200 year old mine. At the end is an awesome, massive cavern, with a 65.5ft (20m) waterfall. The roof disappears into blackness, too high to be seen and the water is so deep it was believed to be bottomless.

☎ 01433 620512   www.speedwellcavern.co.uk

Springfields Outlet Shopping Village & Festival Gardens | 226 A5

25 acres (10ha) of beautiful plants to delight gardeners and florists alike. Bulbs plus trees, shrubs, herbaceous plants, a semi-tropical greenhouse and display gardens. For shopaholics, there is a factory outlet shopping village.

☎ 01775 724843

Stainsby Mill | 236 A5

On the Hardwick Estate is a water-powered mill. Producing flour as far back as the 13th century, the machinery was replaced in the mid 1800s. Now restored, flour is ground regularly and can be purchased here.

☎ 01246 850430   www.nationaltrust.org.uk

Stanford Hall | 210 A5

Lovely 17th century house in grounds alongside the River Avon. Beautifully furnished with a fine collection of Tudor and Stuart paintings and a magnificent library. The former stables house a motorcycle museum with racing and vintage machines, and there is a full scale replica of the early 'Hawk' flying machine. The grounds include a rose garden, nature trail and, of course, tearooms.

☎ 01788 860250   www.stanfordhall.co.uk

Stoke Bruerne Waterways Museum | 198 C2

A former cornmill in the lovely village of Stoke Bruerne was chosen to house this fascinating museum, which recalls 200 years of the inland waterways. The busy Grand Union Canal is immediately outside, with boat trips available along it. Refreshments can be found in the village.

☎ 01604 862229   www.thewaterwaystrust.org

Sudbury Hall (NT) | 222 C4

Richly decorated late 17th century house with a very elaborate Great Staircase. Interesting mythological decorative paintings, Grinling Gibbons woodcarvings and magnificent plasterwork. Shop, tearoom and picnic site.

☎ 01283 585337   www.nationaltrust.org.uk

Sudbury Hall Museum (NT) | 222 C4

The National Trust Museum of Childhood is housed in a service wing of the main Hall. Everything about children from the 1700s to the present day. Toys and games along with a re-created Victorian schoolroom and examples of child employment. There is a treasure hunt to play and, at Christmas, tea with Santa.

☎ 01283 585337   www.nationaltrust.org.uk

Sulgrave Manor | 198 A3

Beautiful Tudor House where George Washington's ancestors lived. Guided tours are given around the furnished rooms, gardens and George Washington Exhibition. Café and shop.

☎ 01295 760205   www.stratford.co.uk

Tales of Robin Hood | 405 E1

Travel back to Sherwood Forest in the time of Robin Hood. Experience the sights, sounds and smells of the age from a guided carriage. Opportunities to try archery and brass rubbing or listen to a storyteller. Falconry demonstrations at weekends.

☎ 0115 948 3284   www.robinhood.uk.com

Tattershall Castle (NT) | 226 A2

Imposing and impressive 15th century tower, one of the first to be built of red brick. Fortified and moated, it was restored in the early 1900s and has four storeys of huge rooms with massive Gothic fireplaces, stained glass windows and brick vaulting.

☎ 01526 342543   www.nationaltrust.org.uk

Treak Cliff Cavern | 235 F4

One of the first 'Blue John' mines, where the beautifully coloured mineral was extracted. Amazing stalactites and stalagmites can be seen on the guided tour.

☎ 01433 620571   www.bluejohnstone.com

Twycross Zoo | 209 F2

Twycross covers 40 acres (16ha) of countryside and is famous for its collection of primates. These include man's closest relative, the bonobo, along with the smallest pygmy marmosets, through orang-utans, chimpanzees, gibbons and mountain gorillas. Baby animals are always arriving and are a popular attraction, as is feeding time in the sealion pen. Other animals include lions, giraffes, flamingos, the rare Mhorr gazelle, penguins, seals, snakes, crocodiles and elephants, to name but a few. For younger children there is 'Pets Corner' and an adventure playground. Three quarters of the 1000-plus animals here are classified as endangered and one of the main functions of the zoo is as a captive breeding centre to help in their conservation; information on this and other aspects of the zoo are available through the various exhibitions and information boards.

☎ 01827 880250   www.twycrosszoo.com

Twycross Zoo – Lion Cub

Wicksteed Park | 211 D5

Opened in the 1920s, Wicksteed was one of the first big amusement parks; it still has a less 'frantic' air than some others. The large boating lake, gardens, pitch and putt and quite magical miniature railway are a welcome breath of quieter days, whereas the roller coaster, twin pirate ship and twin-seat racing cars cater for those seeking thrills. There is a huge, free playground for younger children and plenty of places to shop and eat. A very pleasant day out catering for all.

☎ 01536 512475   www.wicksteedpark.co.uk

Woolsthorpe Manor (NT) | 225 E5

Birthplace and home of Sir Isaac Newton, this small, 17th century manor house contains a 'Young Newton' exhibition and an early edition of his 'Principia' work. In the barn is a Science Discovery Centre and café, and a descendant of the apple tree, under which Newton is said to have discovered the principles of gravity, grows in the orchard.

☎ 01476 860338   www.nationaltrust.org.uk

Ye Olde Pork Pie Shoppe | 210 C1

Still made to the original recipe, pork pies have been baked by Dickinson & Morris in this shop since 1851. Next door they have opened a sausage shop, and both shops offer demonstrations.

☎ 01664 562341   www.porkpie.co.uk

EAST OF ENGLAND

Wide, pastel-hued skies, reedy flat fens, secluded nature reserves, river estuaries and delightful coastal towns characterise this area. East of Norwich, the interconnecting waterways of the Broads offer a unique area for leisure and recreation. Few hills rise to interrupt the distant views of cathedral cities and timeless villages, with their rich historic stories. This is the home of artists and musicians and also one much favoured by boatlovers, birdwatchers, equestrians and antiquarians.

Wicken Fen National Nature Reserve

Alby Crafts & Gardens
`228 D2`

Working craft centre in converted brick and flint farm buildings surrounded by 4 acres (1.5ha) of attractive gardens.

☎ 01263 761590   www.albycrafts.co.uk

Aldenham Reservoir Country Park
`186 A3`

Comprising 175 acres (70ha) of woodland and parkland with a 65 acre (26ha) reservoir. There are plenty of things to do and see including fishing, sailing, a rare breeds farm, children's adventure play area, nature trails and a re-creation of Winnie the Pooh's 100 Aker Wood. There is a charge for parking.

☎ 020 8953 9602   www.hertsdirect.org/aldenham

Anglesey Abbey (NT)
`200 D1`

This attractive Jacobean house was built on the site of an earlier Augustinian priory. Much of what visitors see today is the legacy of Huttleston Broughton, 1st Lord Fairhaven, who bought the house in 1926 and, over the next thirty years, accumulated a large collection of paintings, books, furniture, tapestries and clocks. He also landscaped the superb gardens which extend to 98 acres (40ha), and comprise both formal and informal designs. The lawns and avenues of trees combine with more structured planting to provide colour all year round and are enhanced by Lord Fairhaven's fine collection of statuary. Within the grounds is Lode Mill, an 18th century working water mill.

☎ 01223 810080   www.nationaltrust.org.uk

— Audley End —

Audley End
`200 D4`

This magnificent Jacobean mansion was built between 1603 and 1614 by Thomas Howard, the 1st Earl of Suffolk, on the site of a former abbey. At the time, it was the largest house in England. In 1668, it briefly became a royal palace when it was purchased by Charles II for £50,000, for his use when visiting the races at Newmarket. Between 1708 and 1753 a large part of the house was demolished; the building we see today is just a small part of the original.

In the 1760s much of the interior was remodelled by Robert Adam and, today, visitors can see over thirty rooms containing attractive period furnishings. Adam's work can also be seen in the extensive grounds where he created ornamental garden buildings to enhance the superb landscape park laid out by Lancelot 'Capability' Brown in 1762. There are fine Victorian gardens featuring a parterre, originally laid out in 1830 and re-created in 1993, a rose garden, as well as a walled garden of approximately 10 acres (4ha) within which is an impressive 170ft (52m) long vine house.

☎ 01799 522399   www.english-heritage.org.uk

Banham Zoo
`214 B3`

Opened in 1968 and set in 35 acres (14ha) of beautiful parkland and gardens, this attractive zoo features over 1000 animals, including big cats, reptiles, penguins and kangaroos. Visitors can tour the site on the Safari Roadtrain, which gives an excellent overview of the animals.

☎ 01953 887771   www.banhamzoo.co.uk

Bedford Museum
`199 F3`

Housed in the former Higgins & Sons Brewery, the collection of this local museum focuses on Bedfordshire's social and natural history, geology and archaeology.

☎ 01234 353323   www.bedfordmuseum.org

Beth Chatto Gardens, The
`202 B5`

In 1960 Beth and Andrew Chatto took 4 acres (1.5ha) of inhospitable wasteland and decided to create a garden. It seemed like an impossible task, with its sunbaked, sandy slopes and boggy areas, but the colourful gardens visitors can see today are a testament to their horticultural skill. On the site are four main areas: the scree, gravel, woodland and water gardens, each with their own gardening challenges.

☎ 01206 822007   www.bethchatto.co.uk

Blickling Hall (NT)
`228 C3`

An impressive sight, Blickling Hall is an early 17th century Jacobean mansion built mainly of red brick and limestone. Highlights within the house include the spectacular 125ft (38m) Long Gallery with its superb plaster ceiling, a library, an oak staircase and fine collections of paintings, furniture and tapestries. The parkland surrounding the house was landscaped in the 18th century and includes an artificial lake and 600 acres (243ha) of woodland. Unusually, within the grounds there is a burial pyramid.

☎ 01263 738030   www.nationaltrust.org.uk

Bourne Mill (NT)
`202 B5`

Originally built as a fishing lodge in 1591, this Grade I listed building, with attractive 'Dutch' gables, was converted to a mill in the 19th century. It has a 4 acre (1.5ha) mill pond and much of the machinery, including the waterwheel, is in working order.

☎ 01206 572422   www.nationaltrust.org.uk

Bressingham Steam Museum & Gardens
`214 B3`

Created by horticulturalist Alan Bloom, visitors can see main line locomotives, traction engines and an elaborate Victorian steam roundabout against a lovely backdrop of colourful landscaped gardens. Not to be missed are rides on the working narrow gauge railways that run for more than 5 miles (8km) around the gardens, lake and woods. For garden lovers, the 6 acre (2.5ha) Dell Garden, featuring 47 island beds of perennials, provides a superb show of colour in the summer. There is also a 'Dad's Army' exhibition.

☎ 01379 686900   www.bressingham.co.uk

Burghley House
`211 F2`

This superb Tudor mansion was built between 1565 and 1587 by William Cecil (later Lord Burghley), who was Elizabeth I's Lord Treasurer and principal advisor. It is set in a 300 acre (120ha) deer park landscaped in 1756 by Lancelot 'Capability' Brown. Externally, the mansion remains virtually unchanged and is considered by many to be one of the finest examples of late Elizabethan architecture. The interior was extensively remodelled in the late 17th century and contains the work of Antonio Verrio, Grinling Gibbons and Louis Laguerre. The beautiful interiors are a marvellous showcase for the house's impressive collection of art, which was amassed largely by the 5th and 9th Earls of Exeter (Lord Burghley's descendants) who were both avid collectors.

☎ 01780 752451   www.burghley.co.uk

Cambridge
`200 C2`

Situated on the banks of the River Cam, Cambridge is a combination of narrow medieval streets and magnificent buildings. Flanking the river are The Backs, a picturesque mixture of lawns, formal gardens and open spaces.

The fairly compact city centre is dominated architecturally by the historic University, the hi-tech industries that have developed in recent years tending to be confined to the outskirts. There are 31 colleges, rich both historically and architecturally. The first college, Peterhouse, was founded in 1284 by the Bishop of Ely. Queens' College is notable for its unusual wooden Mathematical Bridge – built originally without the use of nails. Perhaps the most famous of the colleges is the 15th century King's College whose chapel has an outstanding fan vaulted ceiling and exceptional stained glass windows. Other colleges include Magdalene College, where the fellows still dine by candlelight, and the most recent, Robinson College, which was founded in 1974 by a local millionaire. Many of the good and great studied at the University – luminaries include Sir Isaac Newton, Samuel Pepys, Archbishop Thomas Cranmer, Oliver Cromwell, William Wordsworth and, more recently, the likes of Stephen Hawking and the 'Pythons' John Cleese, Eric Idle and Graham Chapman. Guided walks around the city and colleges leave from the Tourist Information Centre daily throughout the year and, especially if time is short, they are a good way to get a feel for what there is to see.

Cambridge also offers a fine range of museums to visit: the Fitzwilliam Museum has an eclectic collection of art and artefacts, the Sedgwick Museum of Geology has a lovely gem collection, and the Cambridge University's Museum of Zoology has a fascinating collection of animals; visitors can see a giant ground sloth, now extinct, that was collected in Victorian times.

☎ 0906 586 2526 (60p/min)   www.visitcambridge.org

— Cambridge – The Bridge of Sighs —

EAST OF ENGLAND

 Cambridge American Military Cemetery & Memorial `200 B2`

A beautiful and moving tribute to the American servicemen and women who lost their lives in World War II. The peaceful site, with over 3800 headstones, extends to 30.5 acres (12ha) and is framed on two sides by woodland. There is a memorial building made of Portland stone within which the museum room contains a superb 30ft by 18ft (9m x 5.5m) map: 'The Mastery of the Atlantic – The Great Air Assault'.

☎ 01954 210350　　　www.abmc.gov

Cambridge University Botanic Gardens `391 F2`

This attractive 40 acre (16ha) garden was founded by Professor John Stevens Henslow (who was Charles Darwin's teacher) in 1831. It was opened to the public in 1846 and today contains thousands of plant species in lovely landscaped settings, including nine National Collections.

☎ 01223 336265　　　www.botanic.cam.ac.uk

Castle House (Sir Alfred Munnings Art Museum) `202 B4`

From 1919 to 1959 Castle House was home to Sir Alfred Munnings, artist and past president of the Royal Academy, famous for his equestrian paintings. The house, a mixture of Tudor and Georgian architecture, and surrounded by 40 acres (16ha) of land, is presented much as it was when Munnings lived in it and includes his furniture and many of his paintings.

☎ 01206 322127　　　www.siralfredmunnings.co.uk

Cecil Higgins Art Gallery `199 F3`

Originally home to the Higgins family, who were wealthy Bedford brewers, this Victorian mansion is furnished as it would have been in the late 19th century. An adjoining gallery was added in 1976, which has changing exhibitions of paintings, prints and drawings. Artists include Gainsborough, Constable, Turner, Rembrandt and Picasso. Also on display are collections of silver, glass, ceramics and the Thomas Lester lace collection.

☎ 01234 211222　　　www.cecilhigginsartgallery.org

Clacton Pier `189 E1`

The pier, which dates from 1871, was a catalyst for the development of Clacton as a seaside resort. Originally it was a landing pier, but soon became popular with day-trippers from London and for promenading. The first pier was quite a humble affair; only 160 yards (146m) long and 4 yards (3.5m) wide. The pier now covers an area of 6.5 acres (2.5ha) and is packed with fairground rides, a Seaquarium and all the usual pubs, restaurants and side stalls.

☎ 01255 421115　　　www.clactonpier.co.uk

Colchester Castle Museum `202 A5`

Housed in the largest Norman keep in Britain, the museum has a wide range of exhibits spanning 2000 years of British History. There is a superb display on the siege of Colchester during the English Civil War, and various Roman relics. Visitors can also take a tour of the Roman vaults which still lie under the present castle – it was built on the foundations of the Roman Temple of Claudius.

☎ 01206 282 939　　　www.colchestermuseums.org.uk

Colchester Zoo `202 A5`

This superb zoo, which has over 200 rare and endangered species, is set in 60 acres (24ha) of

Colchester Zoo – White Tiger

attractive parkland. The enclosures have been designed to replicate the natural environments of the animals as closely as possible. The rich animal life of Africa has several enclosures including the 'Kingdom of the Wild', which houses many of the grazing animals of the African savannah such as zebras, ostriches, pygmy hippos and white rhinos. 'Elephant Kingdom' features the zoo's breeding herd of African elephants, and 'Chimp World' is always popular. 'Playa Patagonia' is well worth seeing; an impressive 26 yard (24m) long tunnel allows visitors to view sea lions swimming above their heads. The zoo is also home to one of the best large cat collections in Europe, including the rare white tiger.

Daily displays allow visitors to get closer to the animals; the penguin parade is always a favourite and visitors even get a chance to feed the elephants and giraffes.

☎ 01206 331292　　　www.colchester-zoo.com

Cressing Temple Barns `201 F5`

There are two timber-framed barns on the site: the Barley Barn built in the early 13th century and the Wheat Barn built in the mid to late 13th century. Both barns have been rebuilt over the years but some of the original constructions remain. Also to be seen are a blacksmith's shop, a bakehouse and a reconstructed Tudor garden.

☎ 01376 584903

Cromwell Museum `212 A5`

Following the execution of Charles I in 1649, Oliver Cromwell came to power and ruled the country until his death in 1658. This museum, situated in the old Huntingdon Grammar School where he was a pupil, houses memorabilia and possessions relating to his life.

☎ 01480 375830　　　edweb.camcnty.gov.uk/cromwell

Denny Abbey & Farmland Museum `200 C1`

Originally founded in 1159, this Benedictine abbey features superb Norman interiors and displays telling the story of the abbey through the centuries. Over the years it has housed the

Knights Templars and the Poor Clares (nuns of the Franciscan order), eventually becoming a farmhouse.

The Farmland Museum looks at the rural history of the local area and farming over the years. Attractions include a village shop, a traditional farmer's cottage and a 17th century stone barn.

☎ 01223 860988　　　www.dennyfarmlandmuseum.org.uk

Docwra's Manor Gardens `200 B3`

An attractive series of enclosed gardens, designed to display differing characteristics. The gardens are divided by walls, hedging and farm buildings surrounding a Queen Anne farmhouse.

☎ 01763 261473

Dunstable Downs (NT) `199 F5`

This popular location for kite-flying comprises 510 acres (206ha) of beautiful chalk grassland and farmland with superb views over the Vale of Aylesbury. There are circular walks, a picnic area and a countryside centre with interpretive displays and a shop.

☎ 01582 608489　　　www.nationaltrust.org.uk

Dunwich Heath (NT) `203 F1`

A beautiful area of lowland heath on the Suffolk coast. The terrain, which covers 215 acres (87ha), includes large tracts of purple heather, as well as gorse, woodland, sandy cliffs and a mile (1.6km) long sandy beach. The heath is rich in insect and birdlife and is home to the now rare ant-lion and nightjar. An information centre is housed in converted coastguard cottages.

☎ 01728 648501　　　www.nationaltrust.org.uk

East Anglia Transport Museum `215 F2`

A reconstructed 1930s style street and attractive woodland area are the perfect setting for visitors to enjoy a trip on beautifully preserved vehicles from the first half of the 20th century. These include trams, buses, trolleybuses, cars, steamrollers and a variety of other light commercial vehicles.

☎ 01502 518459　　　www.eatm.org.uk

Easton Farm Park   203 D2

Set in 35 acres (14ha) of lovely countryside, this farm park has lots of things for children to see and do. There are plenty of farm animals including Suffolk Punch horses, goats, sheep, rabbits, hens and cows. Children can also ride the Shetland ponies and will be fascinated by watching chicks hatch in the Chick Nursery and by Mildred, a wooden cow who moos and can also be milked. There is also an adventure play area, and the River Deben provides lovely river walks.

☎ 01728 746475   www.eastonfarmpark.co.uk

Elton Hall   211 F3

Dating from Tudor times, this romantic house is a combination of medieval, Gothic and classical architectural styles and has been home to the Proby family for over 350 years. The house has superb furniture, porcelain and some outstanding paintings by Constable, Gainsborough and Reynolds. The Library has over 12,000 books including Henry VIII's prayer book, complete with his writing. The beautiful gardens are especially good in the summer; the herbaceous borders are a riot of colour and the rose garden, which includes highly scented old fashioned roses, is stunning. There is also a sunken garden, a knot garden and a Gothic orangery, as well as an arboretum.

☎ 01832 280468

Ely Cathedral   212 D5

This magnificent cathedral dates from the late 11th century and was originally built as a monastic church, gaining cathedral status in 1109. It still retains several monastic outbuildings. After the Dissolution it continued to exist as a cathedral except for a brief period in the 17th century when Oliver Cromwell used it as a stable for his cavalry horses. The architecture is unusual with a 248ft (75.5m) long Norman nave and a remarkable 14th century Octagon Tower.

☎ 01353 667735   www.cathedral.ely.anglican.org

Epping Forest   186 D3

This 6000 acre (1800ha) remnant of a vast medieval forest has large tracts that are recognised as Sites of Special Scientific Interest. It is part open space, part woodland and has been owned by the Corporation of London since 1878. There are some lovely walks including part of the long distance footpath, the Forest Way. In Tudor times the forest was used for hunting, and Elizabeth I's timber-framed hunting lodge can still be seen. An information centre has interesting displays on the forest.

☎ 020 8532 0188

Fairhaven Gardens   229 E4

Delightful woodland and water garden covering an area of 180 acres (73ha) which includes South Walsham Inner Broad. There are 3 miles (5km) of lovely walks, and boat trips are available on the broad at an extra cost. There are superb displays of primroses and candelabra primulas in the spring, and marvellous autumn colours afforded by the numerous mature trees.

☎ 01603 270449   www.norfolkbroads.com/fairhaven

Fairlands Valley Park   200 A5

The park extends to 120 acres (48.5ha) and includes an 11 acre (4.5ha) lake where watersports are available. It is also home to a variety of wildlife.

☎ 01438 353241   www.stevenage-leisure.co.uk/fairlands

Felbrigg Hall (NT)   228 C2

This magnificent 17th century house is set in an estate of over 1700 acres (690ha). The house contains superb 18th century furniture and paintings collected by William Windham II (who inherited the house in 1749) when on his Grand Tour. The parkland has lovely waymarked walks taking visitors past some very ancient trees. There is also a 500 acre (200ha) wood and a walled garden which includes a combination of decorative planting and a traditional kitchen garden.

☎ 01263 837444   www.nationaltrust.org.uk

Fitzwilliam Museum   391 F2

The museum owes its foundation to the bequest of Richard, the 7th Viscount Fitzwilliam of Merrion in 1816, who left his collection along with funds to house them, to the University of Cambridge. The current collection, which has grown considerably over the years, is superb, including paintings by Titian, Rubens, Canaletto, Gainsborough, Monet and Picasso, antiquities from Ancient Egypt, Rome, China and Greece, medieval manuscripts, sculpture, furniture, coins and medals.

☎ 01223 332900   www.fitzmuseum.cam.ac.uk

Flag Fen Bronze Age Centre   212 A3

Flag Fen is one of the most important Bronze Age sites in Europe. Visitors can see 3000 year old timber that was once part of a wooden structure that crossed a shallow lake, and is contained within a purpose built preservation hall. Reconstructed Iron Age and Bronze Age round houses can be seen and, within the visitor centre, there is a museum containing artefacts found on the site. During the summer archaeologists can often be seen at work.

☎ 01733 313414   www.flagfen.com

Flatford Mill & Bridge Cottage (NT)   202 B4

The 18th century mill, made famous by landscape artist John Constable (1776 – 1837) and once owned by his father, is itself not open to the public but there are organised walks (at a charge) during the summer months pointing out the locations illustrated in his work. Just upstream from the mill is the 16th century thatched Bridge Cottage which features a Constable exhibition.

☎ 01206 298260   www.nationaltrust.org.uk

Framlingham Castle   203 D1

This 12th century castle, surrounded by grass-covered earthworks, has crenellated towers topped with Tudor chimneys linked by impressive 43ft (13m) high curtain walls. The wall walk along the top is open to visitors and commands excellent views. Within the walls, the visitor centre now occupies what was once a poor house dating from 1729. This is one of a number of uses the castle has been put to over the years; it has also served its time as a prison and a school.

☎ 01728 724189   www.english-heritage.org.uk

Fritton Lake Countryworld   229 F5

Many activities are available, all centred around a 150 acre (61ha) lake. Attractions include a children's farm, heavy horse stables, formal Victorian gardens, falconry centre, adventure playground, 9 hole golf course and 18 hole putting green, a miniature railway, fishing and boating on the lake, cycle trails and lovely woodland walks.

☎ 0871 2224244   www.frittonlake.co.uk

Gainsborough's House   201 G3

This 16th century townhouse, with 18th century brick façade, is the birthplace of the artist Thomas Gainsborough (1727 - 88). The house contains a large collection of his paintings, drawings and prints along with 18th century furniture and objects. There is also a changing programme of contemporary exhibitions throughout the year.

☎ 01787 372958   www.gainsborough.org

Grafham Water   199 G1

This large water park, extending to 1500 acres (600ha), has a variety of activities including sailing, fishing, cycling, and a nature reserve with trails and hides. There is a charge for car parking.

☎ 01480 812154

Grime's Graves   213 G4

These fascinating Neolithic flint mines date from 4000 to 5000 years ago. Visitors can descend 30ft (10m) by ladder into one of the shafts and see the radiating galleries where ancient man worked the high quality flint with antler picks.

☎ 01842 810656   www.english-heritage.org.uk

Hamerton Zoo Park   211 G5

Established as a wildlife conservation sanctuary in 1990 and set in 15 acres (6ha) of parkland, the zoo specialises in rare, endangered and unusual animals with species totalling over 100. Animals that can be seen include wolves, porcupines, snakes, giant millipedes and African land snails, as well as monkeys, sloths and an array of colourful birds.

☎ 01832 293362   www.hamertonzoopark.com

Harrold-Odell Country Park   199 E2

This attractive 144 acre (58ha) park, situated beside the River Great Ouse, with its lakes, water meadows, woodland and nature reserve, is a haven for wildlife. It is worth taking binoculars as the site attracts large numbers of wildfowl, especially in winter. There is a hide, and an information centre with café.

☎ 01234 720016   www.ivelvalley.co.uk

Hatfield Forest (NT)   187 E1

There are some delightful walks and nature trails around this rare surviving example of a medieval royal hunting forest. Extending to over 1000 acres (400ha) of ancient woodland and pasture, it supports a wide variety of flora and fauna including 400 year old pollarded oaks and hornbeams, fallow deer, and, in the summer, cattle can be seen grazing. There are also two ornamental lakes and a grotto called the Shell House, both dating from the 18th century.

☎ 01279 874040   www.nationaltrust.org.uk

Hatfield House   186 B2

This superb Jacobean house, set in 4000 acres (1600ha) of parkland, was built in 1611 by Robert Cecil, 1st Earl of Salisbury, who was Chief Minister to James I. It has remained in the Cecil family ever since. The luxurious interior exhibits superb examples of Jacobean craftsmanship, such as the magnificent carved oak staircase and long gallery. There are also impressive paintings by Reynolds, Hilliard and Mytens, an armoury and fine 16th, 17th and 18th century furniture and tapestries.

The house was built on the site of an earlier 15th century palace which was home to Elizabeth I for much of her childhood. Most of the old Tudor red bricked palace was destroyed to build the new house but one wing, including the great banqueting hall, where Elizabeth held her first Council of State on her accession in 1558, still survives in the grounds of the current mansion.

The beautiful 42 acre (17ha) gardens situated adjacent to the house were originally laid out by John Tradescant the Elder, who was employed by the 1st Earl. Tradescant was a great plant hunter and he brought huge quantities of plants from Europe. Over the years the layout of the gardens has changed many times, most notably in the 18th century when the fashion for landscape gardening resulted in much of the earlier Jacobean formality being swept away. Today, the gardens are totally organic and have been restored to display much of their varied history, with a knot garden, lime walk, privy garden with yew hedges and a wilderness garden.

☎ 01707 287010   www.hatfield-house.co.uk

Hatfield House – Long Gallery

★ Henry Moore Foundation   186 D1

Seventy acre (28ha) estate, gifted to the foundation by Henry Moore, with sculpture gardens and fields. There is an ever changing display of his work. Visits by appointment only.

☎ 01279 843333   www.henry-moore-fdn.co.uk

🏛 ❁ Holkham Hall   227 G3

This impressive Palladian mansion was built on the site of an earlier manor house between 1734 and 1764 for the 1st Earl of Leicester, Thomas Coke, and is based on designs by William Kent. During his Grand Tour of Europe the 1st Earl had amassed a vast collection of valuable art and artefacts and he wanted a suitably grand house in which to display them. The resulting mansion, built of sand-coloured local brick, with its pedimented portico, square corner towers and side wings, has been little altered over the years, but unfortunately the 1st Earl never saw the finished building as he died in 1759, five years before it was completed.

The interior of the house is superb, the pink marble and alabaster entrance hall, designed by the 1st Earl in collaboration with Lord Burlington, being particularly impressive. Stairs from the hall lead to the elaborate state rooms on the first floor with their superb collections of statuary, furniture, tapestries and splendid paintings by Gainsborough, Van Dyck, Rubens, Claude Lorraine and Poussin.

The 3000 acre (120ha) landscaped grounds surrounding the house were set out by Lancelot 'Capability' Brown and include a mile-long lake and thousands of trees. Today the park is home to a large herd of fallow deer and the lake has many

species of wildfowl. There is no charge to enter the grounds and there are lovely walks around the lake and, in the summer, boat trips.

Other attractions include the Holkham Bygones Collection, the nursery garden, the Holkham Pottery and a history of farming exhibition.

☎ 01328 710227   www.holkham.co.uk

★ Horsey Windpump (NT)   229 F3

Restored five-storey windpump built in 1912. From the top there are marvellous views across Horsey Mere.

☎ 01493 393904   www.nationaltrust.org.uk

🏛 Houghton Hall   227 F5

This superb Palladian house, surrounded by 350 acres (142ha) of parkland and gardens, was built between 1722 and 1735 for Britain's first Prime Minister, Sir Robert Walpole. Designed by James Gibbs, and later refined by Colen Campbell, the whole house was built to impress; the main block features magnificent corner towers topped by domes, and is connected to service blocks by curved colonnades.

The extravagant interiors were designed and furnished by William Kent and include the highly ornamented Stone Hall, which features a bust of Sir Robert and lavish ornamentation and sculptures by Rysbrack. The Great Staircase is made of carved mahogany and rises to the full height of the house. The rooms are a magnificent showcase for the impressive collection of pictures, sculptures, china and tapestries. Visitors can also see the huge Model Soldier Collection, amassed during the lifetime of the 6th Marquess of Cholmondeley, the current owner's father.

The beautiful grounds include extensive parkland, home to a large herd of white fallow deer, and a 5 acre (2ha) walled garden which is divided into areas devoted to fruit and vegetables, a 400ft (120m) long herbaceous border, a formal rose garden with over 150 varieties, glass houses and a croquet lawn.

☎ 01485 528569   www.houghtonhall.com

Holkham Hall – Marble Hall

★ Houghton Mill (NT)   212 A5

Set in a picturesque spot on an island in the Great Ouse, this weather-boarded working water mill dates from the 18th century. There are milling demonstrations on Sunday afternoons (water levels permitting), working models, interactive displays, an art gallery and lovely riverside walks.

☎ 01480 301494   www.nationaltrust.org.uk

❁ Hyde Hall   187 G3

A lovely 24 acre (9.75ha) hilltop garden acquired by the Royal Horticultural Society in 1993. There is year round colour: highlights include lovely herbaceous borders, ornamental ponds, a large collection of roses, the National Collection of Viburnum and the acclaimed Dry Garden.

☎ 01245 400256   www.rhs.org.uk

Houghton Hall

🏛 ❁ Ickworth (NT)   201 G1

This unusual house dates from 1795 and was built to display the collection of art accumulated by Frederick Hervey, Bishop of Derry and later 4th Earl of Bristol, during his Grand Tour. The Italianate house is dominated by a massive oval 98ft (30m) high rotunda, with curved corridors leading to two wings. Many of the descendants of the 4th Earl were also great collectors and today the house has a superb array of paintings, including works by Gainsborough, Titian and Velàzquez. The Hall is set in a 1800 acre (73ha) Lancelot 'Capability' Brown landscaped park which features some magnificent ancient specimen trees. There are lovely gardens laid out in formal Italianate style dating from the 19th century, situated to the south of the house.

☎ 01284 735270   www.nationaltrust.org.uk

🏛 Imperial War Museum (Duxford)   200 C3

Built during World War I, the aerodrome at Duxford was one of the earliest RAF stations in the country and saw action during World War II. It is now home to one of the world's largest collections of preserved civil and military aircraft and is Europe's premier aviation museum. The 7 acres (2.8ha) of exhibition space include some two hundred planes. A free road train runs at regular intervals to take visitors around the site.

Original World War I hangars contrast with the award-winning American Air Museum building designed by Lord Foster. Housed within this superb modern structure is an impressive collection of American combat aircraft.

In the Land Warfare Hall is a huge collection of tanks, military vehicles and artillery. Other hangars contain naval helicopters and midget submarines, a Battle of Britain exhibition and a British aircraft collection.

Duxford is one of the largest centres for aircraft restoration in the world and visitors can view the work in progress. Most weekends during the summer there is an opportunity to experience a flight over Duxford in a 1930s passenger bi-plane and several air shows take place during the year.

☎ 01223 835000   www.iwm.org.uk/duxford

Imperial War Museum

Kentwell Hall   201 G3

This beautiful red brick moated Tudor mansion, dating from the mid 16th century, is approached by a three-quarter mile (1.2km) long lime-tree avenue. The interior of the house was remodelled in 1825 and contains a large collection of 16th century artefacts. On selected weekends visitors can enjoy re-creations of everyday Tudor life. In the courtyard there is a superb brickwork maze in the shape of a Tudor rose, and the grounds contain clipped yews, a fine walled garden with original 17th century layout, and a rare breeds animal farm.

☎ 01787 310207   www.kentwellhall.co.uk

Knebworth House   200 A5

Home to the Lytton family since 1490, the original red brick Tudor manor house underwent extensive remodelling in the 19th century. This resulted in the rather eccentric Gothic appearance we see today with its extravagant façade of turrets, domes and gargoyles.

Within the house visitors can see the superb Jacobean Banqueting Hall with early 17th century oak screen and minstrels' gallery, the Victorian-Gothic state drawing room and the armoury.

The house is situated within 250 acre (101ha) grounds which include a deer park and lovely woodland areas. There are 25 acres (10ha) of gardens designed by Sir Edwin Lutyens who married Lady Emily Lytton, sister of the 2nd Earl of Lytton, in 1897. Features of the garden include an attractive formal rose garden, twin pleached lime avenues, herbaceous borders and a maze. Other attractions include a giant children's adventure playground, a three-quarter mile (1.2km) miniature railway and a dinosaur trail with 72 life-size fibreglass dinosaurs. Knebworth is also famous for its rock concerts and as a film location.

☎ 01438 812661   www.knebworthhouse.com

Lavenham Guildhall (NT)   202 A3

This early 16th century timber-framed building overlooks Lavenham's market place and was built by one of the Guilds who regulated the local wool trade. Over the years it has been used for many different purposes: prison, town hall, workhouse and for housing evacuees during World War II. Inside there are exhibitions on the medieval woollen cloth trade, local history, farming, industry and a replica of the Guildhall at the time it was built.

☎ 01787 247646   www.nationaltrust.org.uk

Layer Marney Tower   188 C1

This 16th century Tudor gatehouse is the tallest in Britain at some 80ft (24m) tall. It was originally planned as a large palace by Henry, 1st Lord Marney, Henry VIII's keeper of the Privy Seal, but he died in 1523, followed two years later by his son, leaving no male heirs and an unfinished building.

The gatehouse has superb Italianate terracotta decoration and fine brickwork, and is set in formal gardens. There are exhibitions within the tower including a model of the palace as it may have looked had it been completed. Other attractions include a rare breeds farm and a medieval barn.

☎ 01206 330784   www.layermarneytower.co.uk

Leighton Buzzard Light Railway   199 E5

Originally built in 1919 to connect the many sand quarries in the area, this 2ft (610mm) narrow-gauge railway now runs for 3 miles (4.8km) giving a 70-minute round trip. It houses one of the largest collections of steam and diesel narrow-gauge locomotives in the United Kingdom.

☎ 01525 373888   www.buzzrail.co.uk

Linton Zoo   201 D3

Set in 16 acres (6.5ha) of gardens, a visit to this zoo provides an enjoyable day out. There is a focus on conservation, education and breeding programmes, with the animals being housed in enclosures resembling their natural habitats as closely as possible. Big cats, giant tortoises and tarantula spiders are among the animals to be seen.

☎ 01223 891308   www.lintonzoo.com

Knebworth House

Lodge RSPB Nature Reserve, The   199 G3

The gardens surrounding this 19th century Tudor-style house (the house is the RSPB's UK headquarters and is not open to the public) are run by organic methods and include formal gardens, a wildlife area, herbaceous border and large

specimen trees. There is also a nature reserve which is a mixture of sandy heath and woodland. When the bluebells are in flower in the spring, the woods are a lovely sight. In the reserve there are over 3 miles (5km) of paths to explore and a variety of birds such as woodpeckers, warblers, woodlarks and hobby may be seen.

☎ 01767 680541   www.rspb.org.uk/reserves/guide/t/thelodge/index.asp

Mangapps Railway Museum   188 C3

A standard-gauge working museum giving a three-quarter mile (1.2km) ride through pleasant countryside. Restored stations and signal boxes from various sites around East Anglia can be seen, as well as 10 locomotives and over 80 carriages and wagons. There are also impressive collections of railway signalling equipment and railway relics.

☎ 01621 784898   www.mangapps.co.uk

Melford Hall (NT)   201 G3

Queen Elizabeth I was entertained in this red brick Tudor mansion in 1578. The exterior has changed little since then and is notable for its six octagonal towers with pepper-pot roofs and tall chimneys.

The interior features a panelled banqueting hall, Regency library, an 18th century drawing room and a display of watercolours by Beatrix Potter. Outside is an attractive garden with lawns and trees.

☎ 01787 880286   www.nationaltrust.org.uk

Mole Hall Wildlife Park   201 D4

Twenty acres (8ha) of gardens and grounds surrounding a moated manor house (closed to the public). A variety of animals can be seen including otters, chimps, deer, owls and wildfowl. There is also a tropical butterfly pavilion, pets corner and a water maze.

☎ 01799 540400   www.molehall.com

Mountfitchet Castle   200 D5

A Norman castle destroyed in 1215 with only fragments of masonry remaining. In the early 1980s an earth and timber castle was constructed along with a village of thatched buildings, including a smithy, a brew house and a dovecote, where visitors can learn about life in Norman England. The scene is completed with animals such as chickens and sheep wandering about.

☎ 01279 813237   www.mountfitchetcastle.com

Muckleburgh Collection, The   228 C1

Set on the site of an anti-aircraft artillery range from World War II, the museum, located in the old NAAFI building, has Britain's largest working military collection, with over 120 vehicles including 16 working tanks and 3000 other exhibits. On Sundays visitors can usually see a tank in action and take a ride on a US armoured personnel carrier, the Gama Goat.

☎ 01263 588210   www.muckleburgh.co.uk

Museum of East Anglian Life   202 B2

This 70 acre (28ha) open-air museum has a variety of historic buildings including the 13th century Abbot's Hall tithe barn. Many of the other buildings have been moved from their original settings and reconstructed on the site, such as the attractive working Alton Water Mill, Edgar's Farmhouse and Eastridge Windpump. There are also various rare breed farm animals to see including Suffolk Punch horses, Suffolk sheep and Red Poll Cattle, as well as working steam engines.

☎ 01449 612229   www.eastanglianlife.org.uk

🏛 National Horseracing Museum   `201 E1`

The museum is full of interest even to the novice, with displays on horses and courses, famous jockeys and trainers. There are trophies, portraits and paintings as well as films of classic races.

☎ 01638 667331   www.nhrm.co.uk

🚂 Nene Valley Railway   `211 G3`

A standard-gauge 7.5 mile (12km) railway which runs between Yarwell and Peterborough. It is home to a fine collection of steam locomotives, both British and continental, as well as rolling stock. There is also a small museum and, for children, Thomas the Tank Engine has his own little branch line.

☎ 01780 784444   www.nvr.org.uk

⭐ Norfolk Broads   `229 E4`

Made up of rivers, lakes and fens, this nationally important wetland provides a unique, but delicate environment for a wide range of wildlife. Three principal rivers: the Thurne, Yare and Waveney, flow through the area, occasionally opening out into wide lakes called 'broads'. These were created by peat cutting dating back to about the 9th century. In the 13th to 14th centuries the sea level rose, flooding the peat pits.

This rare wetland habitat is a haven for a wide range of flora and fauna, including some endangered insects such as the beautiful Swallowtail butterfly and the Norfolk Hawker dragonfly which are unique to the area. The tranquil waterways are alive with ducks, swans, coots, moorhens, herons, kingfishers and the exotic-looking Great Crested Grebe who can be seen carrying their humbug-striped young on their backs in the spring. There are over 190 miles (300km) of footpaths, and bicycles can be hired to explore the peaceful country lanes, but, without a doubt, the best way to get around is by boat. Take a leisurely journey along the 125 miles (200km) of navigable lock-free waterways and Broads, and the stress of civilisation feels like it is a million miles away.

☎ 01603 610734   www.broads-authority.gov.uk

Norfolk Broads

🏛 Norwich Castle Museum & Art Gallery   `405 B2`

The museum and art gallery is housed within a magnificent Norman keep, originally part of a royal palace, situated on a mound overlooking the city. Visitors can see collections of fine art, natural history, archaeology, silverware and ceramics. In addition to the permanent displays there are also regular temporary exhibitions.

☎ 01603 493625   www.museums.norfolk.gov.uk

✝ Norwich Cathedral   `405 B2`

Founded in the 11th century, with many later changes and additions, the present cathedral has a tall elegant spire, and, at 315ft (96m), it is second only in height to Salisbury. The 180ft (55m) square monastic cloisters, which feature intricate fan vaulting, date from the 14th and 15th centuries and are the largest in England. The cathedral is also notable for the large number of attractive, brightly painted, roof bosses in the nave and cloisters.

☎ 01603 218321   www.cathedral.org.uk

🏰 Orford Castle   `203 F3`

This unusual 90ft (27m) high multi-sided keep was built in the mid to late 12th century by Henry II and was once part of a larger castle. Spiral stairs lead to a maze of rooms. A climb to the top is rewarded by views over the surrounding countryside.

☎ 01394 450472   www.english-heritage.org.uk

🦙 Orford Ness   `203 F3`

This is the largest vegetated shingle spit in Europe. It was taken over by the military in 1913 and was a secret test site until the mid-1980s. It is now a National Nature Reserve and its variety of habitats, including mudflat, shingle, salt marsh and brackish lagoons, make it an important site for flora and fauna, in particular breeding and overwintering birds. Access is by ferry and visitors can follow a fascinating 5.5 mile (8.8km) route, that can be walked in total or in part.

☎ 01394 450900   www.nationaltrust.org.uk

🏠✺ Oxburgh Hall (NT)   `213 F2`

This magnificent red brick moated manor house was built by the Bedingfeld family and dates from 1482. It has an unusual appearance with its ornate stepped gables and tall, twisted chimney stacks. Although remodelled extensively during the mid 19th century, the Gatehouse, with its octagonal turrets rising to 80ft (24m), remains relatively unaltered. Within the hall can be seen finely carved oak furniture, some original Victorian wallpapers and fine textiles, including needlework by Mary, Queen of Scots and Bess of Hardwick. Outside there are walled and kitchen gardens, a Victorian French parterre and woodland walks.

☎ 01366 328258   www.nationaltrust.org.uk

🐘 Paradise Wildlife Park   `186 C2`

Ideal for children with a variety of animals including pandas, large cats, tapirs, meerkats, camels and zebra, as well as the more familiar farmyard animals. There is also a funfair, amusements, crazy golf and a woodland railway.

☎ 01992 470490   www.pwpark.com

🏠 Paycocke's (NT)   `201 G5`

Dating from around 1500, this timber-framed house was built for cloth merchant John Paycocke as a wedding present for his son Thomas. It contains fine wood panelling and carving as well

as a display of Coggeshall lace. Outside there is an attractive cottage garden leading to a small river.

☎ 01376 561305   www.nationaltrust.org.uk

🏠✺ Peckover House & Garden (NT)   `212 C2`

This Georgian brick-built town house dates from about 1722 and has some fine rococo decoration in plaster and wood. It is the former home of Quaker banker Jonathon Peckover. Within the house there is a restored Victorian library and collections of decorative and applied art. The house sits within a lovely 2 acre (0.8ha) walled Victorian garden with mature trees, croquet lawn, herbaceous borders and an orangery.

☎ 01945 583463   www.nationaltrust.org.uk

✝ Peterborough Cathedral   `211 G3`

This magnificent Norman cathedral dates from 1118 and has a dramatic 13th century west front with three enormous arches. The interior is equally impressive with a rare 13th century painted wooden nave ceiling and exquisite fan vaulting in the retro-choir dating from about 1500. The cathedral is the burial place of Henry VIII's first wife, Catherine of Aragon.

☎ 01733 343342   www.peterborough-cathedral.org.uk

🏛 Peterborough Museum & Art Gallery   `211 G3`

This impressive town house dating from 1816 became the home of the museum and art gallery in the 1930s. It has displays of local history and archaeology including many Roman relics. There are also bone models and straw marquetry made by Napoleonic prisoners of war.

The art collection contains works dating from the 1600s to the present day including paintings by Van Huysum, Sickert and Turner.

☎ 01733 343329   www.peterboroughheritage.org.uk

🎡 Pleasure Beach   `229 G5`

Set on the seafront at Great Yarmouth, this amusement park has all the familiar rides, such as roller coasters, dodgems and carousels. All ages are catered for, with the thrill factor ranging from extreme white knuckle to gentle children's merry-go-rounds. Rides can be paid for individually by tokens, or wristbands can be purchased.

☎ 01493 844585   www.pleasure-beach.co.uk

✝ St Albans Cathedral   `186 A2`

The cathedral, which dates from the 11th century, has had numerous additions over the years including the opening of a new Chapter House in 1982. It has a long low appearance, extending 550 ft (168m) east to west with a squat sturdy looking tower. The Norman part of the building was begun in 1077 using Roman bricks and tiles salvaged from the ruins of the nearby Roman town of Verulamium. These can be seen today in the walls of the tower.

The cathedral is well known as a site of national pilgrimage as it contains the shrine of St Alban, the first British Christian martyr, who was executed on this site in AD209. Also to be seen are medieval wall paintings and decorated ceilings.

☎ 01727 860780   www.stalbanscathedral.org.uk

🏠 St George's Guildhall (NT)   `227 E5`

Constructed between 1410 and 1420, this is the largest surviving English medieval guildhall. The impressive Great Hall, situated on the upper floor, with its original open timber roof, is 101ft by 29ft

(30m x 8m). Other 15th century features which survive intact are the five large buttresses supporting the north wall. The building has now been converted into an arts centre and is generally closed on performance days.

☎ 01553 765565 www.nationaltrust.org.uk

Sandringham House 227 E5

The current house dates from 1870 and was built for the Prince of Wales (later Edward VII) in Neo-Elizabethan style from red brick with pale stone dressings. It has been passed down through the generations as a private royal residence and is used by the present Queen as her country retreat. The main ground floor rooms, which are still used regularly by the royal family, can be seen. Many objects collected by Queen Alexandra and Queen Mary are on show, and in the Ballroom there is an exhibition of the Duke of Edinburgh's collection of wildlife art. Outside in the coach and stable block there is a museum displaying many family possessions as well as some of the gifts given to the royal family over the years.

The house sits in beautiful 60 acre (24ha) gardens with lakes, glades and an abundance of trees. The acid soil allows the growth of stunning rhododendrons and azaleas, making it particularly attractive in the spring. There is also a 600 acre (243ha) country park, which is free, and which has some lovely woodland and heath areas with nature trails and a visitor centre.

☎ 01553 772675 www.sandringhamestate.co.uk

Shaw's Corner (NT) 186 A1

This red brick Edwardian house was the home of the Irish playwright George Bernard Shaw from 1902 until his death in 1950. The rooms are still set out as he left them, with his personal effects providing a fascinating insight into his life. The 3.5 acre (1.4ha) richly planted gardens have lovely views over the local countryside and contain the revolving hut where Shaw used to write.

☎ 01438 820307 www.nationaltrust.org.uk

Shepreth Wildlife Park 200 B3

Situated in a lovely countryside setting with three lakes, the centre started out as a wildlife sanctuary, and one of the park's aims is to raise money for its rescued and unwanted animals and its hospital. There are plenty of animals to see: terrapins live in Combat Lake, whilst meerkats and squirrel monkeys live on Combat Island. Mountain lions, tigers and lynx can be seen in the Big Cat House, and Waterworld and Bug City provide a home to insects and invertebrates. Just as popular are the horses, goats, ducks and geese which can be hand fed.

☎ 09066 800031 (25p/min) www.sheprethwildlifepark.co.uk

Shrine of Our Lady of Walsingham 228 A2

This has been a centre for pilgrimage since 1061, when Richeldis de Faverches, a local noblewoman, had a vision in which she was told by the Virgin Mary to build a replica of the Holy House in Nazareth. Today, a 20th century red brick church sits on the site of the shrine.

☎ 01328 820239 www.walsingham.org.uk

Somerleyton Hall & Gardens 215 F2

This extravagant Victorian mansion was built between 1844 and 1851 for the railway entrepreneur Sir Morton Peto. No expense was spared; lavish carving is evident throughout, both in wood and stone, there are sumptuous state rooms and an impressive entrance hall. The clock on the stable block is of particular interest as it was originally designed by Vulliamy for the Houses of Parliament. The superb gardens extend to 12 acres (4.8ha) and include a yew hedge maze planted in 1846, a walled garden and glasshouses by Sir Joseph Paxton (designer of the Crystal Palace).

☎ 0871 2224244 www.somerleyton.co.uk

Sandringham House

Southend Pier 188 B4

The present iron pier first opened in 1889 and was extended to its current length in 1929. At 2360 yards (2158m) it is the longest pleasure pier in the world. A train service runs the length of the pier. At the shore end is a museum (admission charge) with exhibits giving an insight into the pier's history. At the pier head sea fishing is popular; there are also pleasure boat trips, a lifeboat station and information centre to visit.

☎ 01702 215620 www.southendpier.co.uk

Standalone Farm 200 A4

This 170 acre (68ha) model farm provides visitors with an opportunity to learn about rural life and farming. There are daily milking demonstrations, exhibits of farm machinery and natural history. Animals that can be seen include sheep, cows, donkeys, shire horses, rabbits and guinea pigs. There is also an arboretum containing 35 species of newly planted trees.

☎ 01462 686775 www.letchworthgardencity.net/standalone

Suffolk Wildlife Park 215 G3

Set in 80 acres (32ha) of coastal parkland, visitors can see a wide variety of mainly African animals, including big cats, giraffes, zebras, white rhinos, buffalo and snakes. There is a safari road train to take visitors around the site.

☎ 01502 740291 www.suffolkwildlifepark.co.uk

Swiss Garden 199 G3

Created in the early 19th century by Lord Ongley, this is a lovely 10 acre (4ha) example of a Swiss picturesque garden centred around a pretty thatched cottage. There are walks and vistas, a grotto, networks of ponds and islands with ironwork bridges, some fine conifers, shrubs and woodland glades.

☎ 01767 626236

Thetford Forest Park 213 F3

This working forest is the largest lowland pine forest in Britain. The varied habitat, which also includes broadleaf woodland and areas of heathland, supports a rich variety of wildlife; there is a chance of seeing crossbills and nightjars and red deer might even be spotted.

Scattered around the forest there are a number of picnic sites where visitors can relax and explore, and at its heart is the High Lodge Forest Centre which provides a variety of activities. Bikes are available for hire and there are a number of cycle trails: gentle ones suitable for families and a black route for the more experienced and adventurous riders. For those aged 10 and over there is an exciting rope course in the tree tops high above the forest floor and an adventure playground suitable for the smaller children. Other attractions include a large maze and a giant sculpture trail which includes a huge red squirrel. There is also a shop and restaurant.

☎ 01842 810271 www.forestry.gov.uk

Tilbury Fort 187 F5

Situated in a strategic position on the north bank of the River Thames, this late 17th century fort was designed to withstand heavy artillery fire; low lying, with double moats and brick-fronted earth embankments. There are exhibitions showing how the fort protected London from seaborne attack. Nearby, Elizabeth I gave a speech rallying her forces on the eve of their battle against the Spanish Armada.

☎ 01375 858489 www.english-heritage.org.uk

Titchwell Marsh 227 F3

This wetland nature reserve on the Norfolk coast, with reed bed and shallow lagoon habitats, is managed especially for birds by the RSPB. It is an important site for breeding avocets and, in the summer, marsh harriers can be seen. The cold weather sees the arrival of migrant and overwintering birds in the lagoons including large numbers of ducks and geese. There are three easily accessible hides for the use of visitors.

☎ 01485 210779 www.rspb.org.uk/reserve/guide/t/titchwell/

Verulamium Museum 186 A2

This museum contains re-creations of Roman scenes, showing everyday Roman life. There are also displays of interesting local finds including wall paintings, jewellery and some superb mosaics. During excavations nearby in 1989, a coffin and the remains of a Roman man were found. The museum has called him 'Postumus' and a video tells the fascinating story of the associated excavation and conservation work.

☎ 01727 751810 www.stalbansmuseums.org.uk/verulamium_museum.htm

Thetford Forest Park

Verulamium Roman Town
186 A2

At the height of the Roman occupation, Verulamium, now St Albans, was the third largest town in Britain. Set within a park are sections of the boundary wall, hypocaust and the remains of a theatre built about AD140. This is the only known example in Britain of a Roman theatre with a stage, rather than an amphitheatre. The remains of some of the Roman buildings were used in the construction of St Albans Cathedral.

☎ 01754 768837   www.verulamium.co.uk

Waltham Abbey
186 C2

It is said that King Harold II left from here to face William of Normandy at the Battle of Hastings in 1066, his body being returned to the abbey for burial. Outside the present abbey church are two inscribed stones marking the spot where King Harold's body is believed to lie. Following the Dissolution, the abbey was partly demolished and the remains that can be seen today include a late 14th century gatehouse that was once part of the cloisters, and part of the Norman abbey nave which was incorporated into the present Waltham Abbey Church. Within the nave can be seen striking spiral and zig-zag patterned columns and a superb painted ceiling.

☎ 01992 767897   www.english-heritage.org.uk
www.walthamabbeychurch.co.uk

West Stow Country Park
213 F5

Set on the southern edge of the Breckland in the Lark Valley, this 125 acre (50ha) country park comprises heath, lake and woodland. Nature trails and bird hides enable visitors to enjoy the wide variety of flora and fauna that thrive in the park as a result of this habitat diversity.

An added attraction within the park is a reconstruction of an Anglo-Saxon village, built using original tools and techniques. This is located on the site of an original settlement and finds from the site are displayed in an interpretation centre.

☎ 01284 728718   www.stedmunds.co.uk/west_stow.html

Whipsnade Wild Animal Park
185 F1

Opened to the public in 1931, this is now one of Europe's largest wildlife conservation parks. It is set in nearly 600 acres (242ha) with over 3000 animals including hippos, rhinos, giraffe, vultures, cheetahs, bison, bears, tigers and much, much more. Visitors can travel around the large site using the free safari tour bus or on the narrow-gauge Great Whipsnade Railway. There is an impressive 17 acre (6.8ha) elephant paddock, the Splashzone where visitors can see the sea lions being fed, a children's farm and adventure playground, and a discovery centre where there is almost everything from seahorses to giant centipedes.

☎ 01582 872171   www.whipsnade.co.uk

Wicken Fen National Nature Reserve (NT)
212 D5

A haven for wildlife, and almost the last remnant of the extensive fen landscape that once covered eastern England. There are numerous paths enabling visitors to explore this fascinating area, as well as several hides, a restored Fenman's cottage and the last working windpump in the fens. The William Thorpe Visitor Centre has displays telling the story of the fen and its wildlife.

☎ 01353 720274   www.nationaltrust.org.uk

Wimpole Hall (NT)
200 B2

This magnificent 18th century house, the largest in Cambridgeshire, has a striking domed yellow drawing room by Sir John Soane and a library and chapel by James Gibbs; the chapel features a trompe l'oeil painting by Sir James Thornhill.

The landscaped grounds, with lakes and Gothic folly, are equally impressive: they extend to 360 acres (145ha) and were landscaped by the foremost practitioners of the time, namely Charles Bridgeman, Lancelot 'Capability' Brown and Humphrey Repton. The formal gardens around the house include parterres, a rose garden and a walled vegetable garden. The estate was purchased by Rudyard Kipling's daughter, Elsie Bambridge, who left it to the National Trust in 1976.

☎ 01223 207257   www.nationaltrust.org.uk
www.wimpole.org

Wimpole Home Farm (NT)
200 B3

This 'model' farm, built in 1794 by Sir John Soane, an agricultural and farming enthusiast, features thatched farm buildings and the Great Barn which is now home to a museum of farming methods and equipment. A variety of animals including many rare breeds of cattle, sheep, pigs and poultry can be seen, as well as a Victorian dairy.

☎ 01223 207257   www.nationaltrust.org.uk
www.wimpole.org

Woburn Abbey
199 E4

Woburn has been home to the Earls and Dukes of Bedford for nearly 400 years. The current Palladian style mansion, built on the site of a 12th century Cistercian monastery, is set in a 3000 acre (1200ha) deer park. In the 17th century the 4th Earl built a new wing on the site of the old abbey church. This contains an intriguing grotto with elaborately carved stonework resembling stalactites and seaweed, as well as 18th century furniture carved in the shape of sea shells with dolphins supporting the seats and table tops. The 4th Duke commissioned the west wing in 1747 which includes the grand series of state rooms.

Within the house there are over 250 paintings dating from as early as the 16th century, including works by Van Dyck, Gainsborough, Reynolds and Velázquez. The Venetian Room has 21 views of Venice by Canaletto, commissioned by the 4th Duke during his Grand Tour. There is also some excellent 18th century furniture, silver pieces by renowned Huguenot silversmiths, and some superb porcelain, including the Sèvres dinner service presented to the 4th Duchess by Louis XV in 1763.

The grounds were landscaped by Humphrey Repton at the beginning of the 19th century and are home to ten species of deer, including the rare Père David Chinese deer. Repton's Red Book, showing his plans for the grounds, can be seen in the Library. There is a hornbeam maze, masses of rhododendrons and a lake.

Within the estate is the famous Safari Park where visitors can enjoy seeing the animals wandering freely (additional charge).

☎ 01525 290666   www.woburnabbey.co.uk

Wood Green Animal Shelter
200 A1

The shelter at Godmanchester is one of three, the first of which was founded in Wood Green, London in 1924. At 50 acres (20ha), this is the largest and welcomes visitors who are interested in rehousing or learning about the animals, or who just want to look around. In addition to the animals there are charity, gift and pet accessory shops, water gardens, a wind turbine and a playground.

☎ 08701 904090   www.woodgreen.org.uk

Woodbridge Tide Mill
203 D3

A restored, Grade I listed working tide mill driven by the water held in a pond that is filled twice daily by the incoming tide. There are demonstrations at low tide.

☎ 01473 626618   www.tidemill.org.uk

Woodside Farm
185 F1

There are hundreds of animals to see here: monkeys, llamas, flamingos and giant tortoises, as well as the usual farm animals, all within a 7 acre (2.8ha) site. Children are encouraged to help feed and handle the animals. Other attractions include an adventure play area and an 18 hole crazy golf course.

☎ 01582 841044   www.woodsidefarm.co.uk

Wrest Park
199 F4

The magnificent gardens, which extend to some 90 acres (36ha), were originally laid out in the early 18th century, and are the main attraction here. There are woodland walks, avenues, a canal, a formal parterre, marble fountains, an orangery and a fine pavilion by Thomas Archer. The 19th century house, built in the style of an 18th century French chateau, has a few ornately plastered rooms open to visitors.

☎ 01525 860152   www.english-heritage.org.uk

Wroxham Barns
229 E3

Traditional and contemporary craftsmen and women can be seen at work in this rural craft centre located in 18th century restored farm buildings. There is also a children's farm in a farmyard setting and a funfair.

☎ 01603 783762   www.wroxham-barns.co.uk

Woburn Safari Park – Marmosets

YORKSHIRE

This vast historic area encompasses all that is best within Britain. From the south the huge, bustling conurbations gradually surrender to the individual barren moors intermingled with the beautiful dales. Then, north east, over the mighty A1(M), passing through dozens of picturesque towns and villages, are the wild, scenic moors and forests of North Yorkshire. These end abruptly at the east coast where the traditional seaside resorts with their faded gentility still provide the quintessential English holiday experience.

View from hillside, Yorkshire

YORKSHIRE

1853 Gallery
`244 A4`

The 1853 Gallery is housed in a Grade II listed textile mill that was built in 1853. Featured within its three art galleries are hundreds of works by Bradford-born artist David Hockney. The gallery exhibits his lithographs, etchings, home made prints, photo collages and oil paintings, along with his early drawings. Displays of historical old mill items and objets d'art can also be viewed amongst the pictures.

☎ 01274 531163   www.saltsmill.org.uk

★ Aysgarth Falls & National Park Centre
`251 F4`

The River Ure forms this magnificent triple flight of waterfalls as it descends over limestone rock ledges through Wensleydale. The Upper Fall featured in the film 'Robin Hood, Prince of Thieves'. Enjoy a riverside walk linking the Upper, Middle and Lower Falls, for stunning views and scenery, and discover how the Aysgarth Falls were created, by visiting the Aysgarth Falls National Park Centre.

☎ 01969 663424

Bagshaw Museum
`371 E3`

Step back in time at Bagshaw Museum, housed within this enchanting Gothic mansion, complete with imposing copper tower. As well as admiring the interior Gothic décor, find out about the social and local history of Batley and what it was like to live in the area in the 19th century. Additionally, gain a fascinating insight into Ancient Egyptian life, view the Oriental decorative arts and encounter the enchanting world of the tropical rainforest.

☎ 01924 326155

Bempton Cliffs
`255 E5`

The chalk cliffs from Flamborough Head to Bempton provide a sanctuary for over 200,000 nesting birds. An RSPB reserve, this is the largest seabird colony in England. From the specially provided viewing areas, puffins, gannets, kittiwakes, guillemots, razorbills, fulmars and herring gulls can be seen. Most rewarding if visited during the breeding season between April and August.

☎ 01262 851179   www.rspb.co.uk

Beningbrough Hall (NT)
`245 E2`

This grand Georgian mansion was built in 1716. It now houses numerous 18th century treasures, including over 100 portraits loaned from the National Portrait Gallery. Its impressive Baroque interior boasts outstanding woodcarving and plasterwork, an unusual central corridor spanning the entire length of the house, and a fully equipped Victorian laundry. Outside is a wonderful walled garden, interesting wood sculptures, potting shed, wilderness play area and 7 acres (3ha) of parkland to be enjoyed.

☎ 01904 470666   www.nationaltrust.org.uk

Bolling Hall
`370 C2`

Much of this splendid period house dates back to the 1600s and was once home to the Bolling family. The Hall displays a variety of period furnishings and oak furniture, together with stained-glass windows depicting Coats of Arms in the central hall. The house also contains a medieval tower to the 18th century wing.

☎ 01274 723057

Bolton Abbey Estate
`243 G2`

Belonging to the Duke and Duchess of Devonshire since the 1750s, this Yorkshire country estate encompasses 30,000 acres (12,200ha) of parkland beside the River Wharfe. Central to the estate, and near to the village of Bolton Abbey, is the 12th century Bolton Priory. Explore the medieval buildings and enjoy some of the 80 miles (130km) of moorland, woodland and riverside paths, including Strid Wood, the largest remaining acidic woodland in Yorkshire.

☎ 01756 718009   www.boltonabbey.com

Bolton Castle
`251 F3`

Bolton Castle is an enormous 14th century fortress, with walls 9ft (3m) thick and towers rising 100ft (30m). In 1568, Mary, Queen of Scots, was imprisoned within its walls and Royalists were besieged here during the Civil War. Within the castle, tableaux portray life here during the 15th century. Outside, there is a medieval garden and walled herb garden, together with a vineyard, rose gardens, a maze and an orchard.

☎ 01969 623981   www.boltoncastle.co.uk

Bradford Industrial Museum
`371 D1`

Originally a 19th century spinning mill, this museum depicts industrial life as it was back then. The complex is complete with the mill owner's house, back-to-back cottages, working shire horses, stables, and mill machinery.

☎ 01274 435900

Bramham Park
`244 D3`

This French-inspired garden was created in the early 18th century. Its water gardens, cascades and geometric avenues, designed by Robert Benson, First Lord Bingley, remain virtually unaltered since their formation. There are 66 acres (27ha) of impressive vistas, long pathways lined with tall beech hedges leading to surprising views, temples, ornamental ponds, cascades, and a fine rose garden. The fine Queen Anne house is open to the public by appointment only.

☎ 01937 846000   www.bramhampark.co.uk

Brontë Parsonage Museum
`243 G4`

Formerly home to the famous Brontë family, this Parsonage has been carefully preserved into a museum. On show are eleven rooms furnished as they were in the mid 1850s, including the dining room, the kitchen, Mr Brontë's study, Charlotte's room and the children's study. Throughout are displays of the siblings' books and manuscripts, letters to friends and their personal possessions.

☎ 01535 642323   www.bronte.info

Burton Constable Hall
`247 D4`

On show inside this stately Elizabethan mansion are 30 wonderfully preserved rooms in 18th and 19th century fashion. They are styled with fine furniture, paintings and sculptures. There is a 'Cabinet of Curiosities' containing an intriguing collection of fossils, natural history and scientific instruments and a library containing 5000 books. Within the stable block is a riding centre, and there are 200 acres (80ha) of parkland, landscaped by Lancelot 'Capability' Brown.

☎ 01964 562400   www.burtonconstable.com

Cannon Hall Country Park
`235 G2`

Meander around over 70 acres (30ha) of parkland and formal gardens, first landscaped in the 1760s. The historic walled garden contains over 40 varieties of pear trees, first grown in the 18th century, along with peaches and nectarines. In one of the greenhouses is the Cannon Hall vine, grown from a seed brought back from the continent in 1802. The Hall contains a museum displaying fine paintings, glassware, pottery, furniture and a collection of military items set in period rooms.

☎ 01226 790270

Captain Cook Memorial Museum
`254 C1`

From 1746, James Cook lodged in the attic of this 17th century harbourside house, whilst an apprentice to Captain John Walker. In commemoration of the great explorer, the museum recounts Cook's Whitby years and his later achievements. There are models, maps and manuscripts, letters, ship plans, original paintings and drawings, as well as artefacts from his voyages.

☎ 01947 601900   www.cookmuseumwhitby.co.uk

Castle Howard
`253 G5`

A magnificent stately home, built in 1699 by the architect Sir John Vanbrugh. Castle Howard, with its famous dome, can be found in the Howardian Hills, between Malton and Thirsk. The castle continues to be home to the Howard family, where they have resided since it was built. Inside are exceptional collections of art, including paintings by Canaletto, Holbein, Gainsborough and Reynolds, and furniture by Chippendale and Sheraton. There are also impressive antique sculptures and a splendid collection of porcelain and china. Furthermore, costumed characters take on the role of historic personalities to re-enact life as it used to be in this stately home.

More can be seen outside, in over 1000 acres (400ha) of gardens and parklands. There are also exceptional temples, lead statues and monuments, lakes, waterways and fountains. All of which makes a trip to Castle Howard a wonderful day out.

☎ 01653 648333   www.castlehoward.co.uk

Castle Howard

🏛 Colour Museum 　390 B1

Interactive galleries look at the history, development and technology aspects of colour. The perceptions, use and effects of light and colour, as well as the progress of dying techniques and textile printing, can all be explored.

☎ 01274 390955

⭐ Dalby Forest Drive 　254 B4

Dalby Forest Drive extends for 9 scenic miles (15km) across hills, through valleys, past lakes and over streams. Stop along the way to enjoy one of the many walks to access stunning views and scenery. Encounter the northern edge of the plateau and dales, ancient earthworks created before the Dark Ages, Jurassic rock formations, ravines and the valley lake. Much of the extensive woodlands comprise spruces and pines, although along the valleys there are oak, ash and alder trees, some of which are descendants of the ancient forest. In addition to the diverse plant life and outstanding landscape, wildlife, such as roe deer, crossbills and nightjars, can also be found in abundance.

The visitor centre is located 1 mile (1.5km) along the drive from the Thornton Dale entrance. Here, information about Dalby, together with maps and booklets relating to the various trails, can be obtained.

☎ 01751 472771　www.forestry.gov.uk/dalbyforest

❀ Duncombe Park 　253 F4

Duncombe Park provides a classic example of an 18th century landscaped garden, surrounding a Baroque mansion, now home to Lord and Lady Feversham. There are 35 acres (15ha) of fine terraces, lawns, trees, temples and a scented 'secret garden'. Wonderful views extend over the valley and distant moors. Beyond the gardens are over 400 acres (160ha) of parkland. Half is now a National Nature Reserve with enjoyable waymarked walks.

The house, containing 18th century portraits and period furniture, can be accessed by guided tour only.

☎ 01439 770213　www.duncombepark.com

(Eden Camp)

🏛 Eden Camp 　253 G5

Wartime Britain is magnificently brought to life at this award winning museum. Constructed within a former prisoner of war camp, the huts re-enact life during World War II. The sights, sounds and smells of everyday life during the war can be truly experienced.

Each hut conveys a different aspect of the war, including the rise of the Nazi Party, the outbreak of war, rationing, evacuees, propaganda, women at war, the Blitz, animals at war, the munitions factories, the rescue services and much more.

Additional huts depict military and political events of World War II from a worldwide perspective, including scenes such as the Dambusters and The Great Escape. Another covers conflicts experienced by British forces since 1945 and yet another looks at World War I, incorporating a re-created trench.

The Eden Camp music hall is of particular interest to children, where puppets, representing some of the great entertainers of the time, perform well-known wartime songs. There is also an assault course, a number of military vehicles and a large collection of artillery.

☎ 01653 697777　www.edencamp.co.uk

🦋 Elsham Hall Country & Wildlife Park 　238 A1

In the grounds of Elsham Hall is a unique venture, a combination of wildlife, arts and crafts. There is a theatre, craft centre, exhibition gallery, carp feeding jetty, butterfly garden walkway, adventure playground, arboretum, falconry centre and much more.

☎ 01652 688698　www.elshamhall.co.uk

🏛 Eureka! Museum for Children 　370 B3

This is an interactive museum, designed especially for children aged 3-12 years. Over 400 hands-on exhibits can be explored, touched, listened to and smelt, based around 4 main themes: Me and My Body; Invent, Create, Communicate; Living and Working Together; and Our Global Garden. Everything has been developed to inspire.

☎ 01422 330069　www.eureka.org.uk

🎡 Flamingo Land Theme Park 　253 G4

Set in 375 acres (152ha), this theme park is packed full of fun for all the family. Eight white-knuckle roller coasters and six other thrilling rides are key attractions. Ride on Wall's Magnum Force, Europe's only triple looping coaster, Cliff Hanger, Europe's tallest tower ride, or Terroriser, The Bullet, Corkscrew and Top Gun.

Another attraction is the large zoo with over 1000 animals, from around the world, including Siberian tigers, meerkats, Humboldt penguins, exotic birds and the UK's largest flock of pink flamingos. There is a water ride that travels through the Lost Kingdom – a themed area that incorporates part of the zoo, past the hippos, rhinos and giraffes. There are plenty of rides for younger children and a children's zoo. A number of family shows, too, are performed throughout the day.

☎ 01653 668287　www.flamingoland.co.uk

✠ Fountains Abbey & Studley Royal Water Garden (NT) 　244 B1

This amazing 800 acres (325ha) World Heritage Site, situated in the valley of the River Skell, shelters the ruins of over 10 historic buildings. One of these ruins is the imposing remains of a 12th century Cistercian Abbey, with its 15th century tower rising 170ft (52m). There is also an Elizabethan mansion, with two rooms open for viewing and a Victorian church, with fine stained-glass windows and ornate interior. Three floors of the 12th century monastic water mill, once used to produce flour for the monks, can be explored, too.

The wonderful landscaped gardens contain an 18th century water garden, ornamental lakes with temples, statues and cascades, all of which can be enjoyed and admired. Additionally, hundreds of red, sika and fallow deer roam in the medieval deer park.

☎ 01969 640382　www.fountainsabbey.org.uk

(Flamingo Land Theme Park)

🏰 ❀ Harewood House 　244 C3

Renowned for its wonderful architecture and interiors by Robert Adam, this exceptional stately home belongs to the Earl of Harewood. Collections include exquisite Chippendale furniture, fine porcelain, and 18th century and Italian renaissance works of art. There are also royal photographs and memorabilia, from the 1930s to 1960s, when HRH Princess Mary lived here.

The impressive grounds, landscaped by Lancelot 'Capability' Brown, include lakeside and woodland walks. Alternatively, take a boat trip across the lake.

A visit to the Bird Garden is a must, with over 100 rare and exotic birds from around the world, including threatened species from Africa, America and Australia. There is also an excellent adventure playground.

☎ 0113 218 1010　www.harewood.org

❀ Harlow Carr 　244 B2

These botanical gardens, owned by the Royal Horticultural Society, cover 68 acres (30ha) in which the suitability of growing plants in the northern climate is assessed. Of particular interest are the scented garden, the streamside garden, flower and vegetable trial gardens, the rock garden, herbs and ornamental grasses, to name just a few. There is also an arboretum, model village and plant centre.

☎ 01423 565418　www.rhs.org.uk

(Fountains Abbey)

Helmsley Castle (Ruins) `253 F4`

The dramatic ruins of Helmsley Castle include the 12th century keep and Tudor mansion. Two deep ditches cut down into the solid rock around the castle to form impressive earthworks.

☎ 01439 770442

Huddersfield Narrow Canal & Standedge Experience `235 E2`

The Huddersfield Narrow Canal, which runs for 23 miles (40km), is split in two by Standedge Tunnel. At 3.25 miles (5km) long and 645ft (200m) above sea level, it is Britain's highest, longest and deepest canal tunnel. The Standedge Visitor Centre, with its interactive exhibition and guided boat trip through part of the tunnel, provides a remarkable account of how it was engineered in the 18th century.

☎ 01484 844298   www.standedge.co.uk

Jorvik `415 E2`

Viking history is re-created using the well-preserved remains discovered on the site on which the museum now stands. Journey back over 1000 years to AD975 and experience the Viking way of life through the reconstructed streets, complete with sights, sounds and smells. Visitors travel in 'time-capsule' viewing cars to be taken past and through two-storey dwellings and over backyards and rooftops. From the archaeological finds, the houses and shops are laid out exactly as they were, and even the faces of the people on exhibition have been reconstructed from actual Viking skulls.

Also on display are over 800 items found during the archaeological dig, including a wonderfully preserved 8th century Anglo Saxon helmet. Special exhibitions throughout the year feature hands-on activities, artefacts and new academic research based around themes such as seafaring, craft skills, bones and warfare.

☎ 01904 543403   www.jorvik-viking-centre.co.uk

Jorvik

Jorvik Glass `245 G1`

Located within the splendid grounds of Castle Howard, Jorvik Glass Centre provides workshop demonstrations of glass-blowing. A variety of glassware is available in the gift shop.

☎ 01653 648555

Kirklees Light Railway `235 G1`

Take a 50 minute return trip on this steam train, admiring the beautiful scenery whilst travelling through two of the South Pennine valleys. This fifteen inch gauge railway runs 4 miles (6km) from Clayton West and into the longest tunnel on this gauge of line. There is also a visitor centre, children's play area, and steam models on display.

☎ 01484 865727

Kirkstall Abbey `244 B4`

Situated on the River Aire in attractive parkland, Kirkstall Abbey is one of the UK's best preserved Cistercian monasteries. The Abbey was built between 1152 and 1182 and much of it has survived up to eaves level including the church, part of the 16th century tower, the transept, cloisters and the Chapter House.

☎ 0113 230 5492   www.kirkstall.org.uk/abbey

Leeds City Art Gallery & Museum `384 J5`

This excellent art gallery displays a variety of fine art collections from the 19th and 20th centuries. Find outstanding English watercolours, traditional prints, Pre-Raphaelite paintings and Henry Moore sculptures, along with contemporary works. Entry is free.

☎ 0113 247 8248   www.leeds.gov.uk/artgallery

Lightwater Valley Park

Lightwater Valley Park `252 B5`

Thrills, excitement and pleasurable family entertainment can all be found at this fun-packed theme park, set in 175 acres (7ha) of parkland. For the adventurous, there are several white-knuckle rides, including the Ultimate Beast, Europe's longest coaster at 1.5 miles (2.5km), and the Sewer Rat built 40ft (12m) underground. There is also the Black Widow's Web giant ferris wheel, the Beaver Rapids log flume and the Wave giant swing boat. Younger children, too, are well catered for, with specially designed mini amusements, including the Ladybird roller coaster and Spinning Teacups.

Recover at a gentler pace with a number of more leisurely attractions. Tour the park on the Lightwater Express steam train or enjoy the boating lake. Additional amusements include go-karting and a children's farm.

☎ 0870 458 0040   www.lightwatervalley.co.uk

Lotherton Hall `245 D4`

An Edwardian country home, formerly owned by the Gascoigne family. On display are fine collections of pottery, paintings, sculpture, furniture, jewellery, ceramics, silver, oriental art and British costume. The surrounding grounds and parkland boast a re-created Edwardian garden, a medieval deer park and a 12th century chapel. The Bird Garden houses over 200 species, many of which are rare and endangered, including flamingos, snowy owls and hornbills.

☎ 0113 281 3259   www.leeds.gov.uk/lothertonhall

Magna Centre `365 B1`

This Science Adventure Centre is set in a splendidly converted former steelworks. Inside are hands-on, interactive experiences based around the four main elements used to make steel. The Fire Pavilion examines the advantages of fire and its explosive possibilities, while the Air Pavilion is in an airship structure, hovering above the floor. Be prepared to get wet in the Water Pavilion, by shooting water cannons, launching a water-powered rocket or creating a hot geyser. In the Earth zone, manoeuvre a JCB or explode a rock face.

☎ 01709 720002   www.visitmagna.co.uk

Malham Cove `243 E1`

This huge, curved rock face, rising up around 260ft (80m), is formed of natural limestone. The top of the cove provides an excellent example of limestone pavement, pitted with deep cracks and crevices as a result of the weathering of such terrain.

Manor House `244 A3`

This Elizabethan manor house is built on the site of a former Roman fort. The museum recounts Ilkley's local history with exhibits from Roman through to Victorian times, when the area became a spa town. In the gallery are displays of works from local artists and craftspeople.

☎ 01943 600066

Merchant Adventurers Hall `415 E2`

Built in the mid 14th century, this Guildhall is York's largest timber-framed building and is believed to be one of the finest medieval halls in Europe. In addition to the Great Hall, where merchants conducted their business, there is the Undercroft, or hospital, and the Chapel. On display are fine collections of furniture, portraits, silver and jewellery, together with information about the lives of the merchants during medieval times.

☎ 01904 654818   www.theyorkcompany.co.uk

Middleton Railway `244 C5`

Of great historical importance, this is the oldest working railway in the world, having been established by an Act of Parliament in 1758. It was also the first to succeed commercially with steam locomotives in 1812, as well as being the first standard gauge railway to be operated by volunteers in 1960. View the collection of industrial steam and diesel engines or travel on the railway for a family day out at Middleton Park, with woodland, nature trails, picnic area and lake.

☎ 0113 271 0320   www.middletonrailway.org.uk

National Museum of Photography, Film & TV

National Railway Museum

🏛 Millennium Galleries & Winter Gardens

409 B3

Housed within a modern and stylish complex are four galleries, showcasing visual arts, crafts and design by contemporary designers and past masters. The Metalwork Gallery exhibits decorative metalwork and silverware, and recounts the history of the city's metalworking trade. John Ruskin's collection of paintings, manuscripts, papers, books and architectural plastering are also on display and there are special collections from places including the Victoria and Albert Museum and the Tate. Adjacent are the Winter Gardens, in a stunning temperate glasshouse, containing 2500 plants and 150 different species.

Admission into the galleries and Winter Gardens is free; charges apply for the special exhibitions.

☎ 0114 278 2600

✠ Mount Grace Priory (NT)

252 D3

Built in the late 14th century, these ruins are better preserved than any of the other ten Carthusian monasteries in England. The Carthusian monks lived a hermit's life in small two-storey cells with a garden. One of these has been reconstructed to replicate how the monks lived and worked. In spring, the grounds are awash with daffodils, making it a particularly attractive place to visit. Adjacent is a 17th century manor house, built on the site of the monastery guesthouse, housing an exhibition and arts and crafts.

☎ 01609 883494   www.nationaltrust.org.uk

🏛 National Museum of Photography, Film & TV

390 C2

The museum's interactive galleries provide a fascinating insight into the world of photography, film and television, both past and present. Among over three million items on display are the world's first negative, the earliest television footage, and Louis Le Prince's 1888 film of Leeds Bridge, regarded as the first example of moving pictures. Explore the history of popular photography and discover the digital age of computers, special effects and virtual reality. Learn how television cameras work, discover how animation is created, read the news, see the cameras used on 'James Bond' films, or find the toys from 'Play School'.

Alongside these galleries is the five-storeys-high IMAX screen, which regularly features 3D and other films, as well as two other conventional cinemas, which show films from around the world.

The permanent galleries are free to visit, whilst there are admission charges for the cinemas and some special exhibitions.

☎ 0870 701 0200   www.nmpft.org.uk

🏛 National Railway Museum

415 E1

Over 200 years of railway history is celebrated in style, providing a terrific family day out – for free. Complete with sounds and smells, the atmosphere of steam and rail travel is wonderfully re-created. A splendid collection of locomotives can be found on display in the Great Hall, recounting the story of the railway from Rocket to Eurostar. Inspect the Mallard, the world's fastest steam locomotive, explore Queen Victoria's luxurious royal carriage and examine the Japanese Bullet Train, in conjunction with a short video presentation. There are millions of railway artefacts, too, including models, silver and crockery, nameplates, clocks and watches, tickets, photographs, workshop tools, posters, engineering drawings, and even a lock of Robert Stephenson's hair.

The Working Railway demonstrates how signals work, the technology behind them and their development over time. Children will enjoy the Interactive Learning Centre where hands-on exhibits explain the workings of trains and the railway. Engineers and craftspeople can be watched in the Works Wing while they carry out conservation work, and children can also build their own model train here.

Rides on the miniature railway are available most weekends and school holidays, and on the steam train during school holidays.

☎ 01904 6212621   www.nrm.org.uk
☎ 01904 686286 (24hr info line)

🌳 Normanby Hall Country Park & Farming Museum

237 G1

A mansion built in the Regency style, with a rural museum, Victorian walled garden, beautiful grounds with woodland, deer park and nature trails. For children there is an adventure playground and miniature railway. Tearoom and plant nursery.

☎ 01724 720588   www.northlincs.gov.uk

⭐ North Bay Miniature Railway

254 D4

Two trains operate on this miniature railway, which runs from Peasholm Gap in North Bay. Each train can carry up to 100 people, travelling almost a mile (1.6km), complete with a tunnel, bridges, signals, stations and gradient boards all reproduced to scale.

☎ 01723 373333

☐ North York Moors

253 F2

The vast, heather-clad moorlands, breathtaking open landscape, extensive woodlands and serenity are what make the North York Moors National Park special. Extending east of the A19, from the A170 in the south to the A171 in the north, the Moors are bounded on the eastern side by ragged cliffs and untouched coastline, overlooking the North Sea. There are over 1400 miles (2253km) of paths and tracks to follow, including the Cleveland Way National Trail.

A journey through Dalby Forest, or a steam train trip on the North Yorkshire Moors Railway, provides a wonderful way to explore the stunning and varied countryside. The area's historic heritage includes magnificent ruined abbeys, besieged castles, period buildings and gardens, and informative museums. Rievaulx Abbey, Whitby Abbey, Captain Cook Memorial Museum, Duncombe Park and Mount Grace Priory all warrant a visit. The coastal fishing villages and ancient towns of Whitby and Scarborough are popular places, whilst Robin Hood's Bay offers fossil hunting.

Many television and film makers have valued the area, having featured some of the unspoilt villages and stations of the North York Moors in 'Heartbeat', 'Harry Potter and the Philosopher's Stone', 'Brideshead Revisited', 'Poirot' and 'Sherlock Holmes', to name just a few.

www.moors.uk.net

North Yorkshire Moors Railway

🚂 North Yorkshire Moors Railway

254 B4

Travel on a steam train across the North Yorkshire Moors National Park on one of the earliest and most historic lines in the North of England. Stretching 18 miles (29km) from Pickering to Grosmont, the journey passes through beautiful countryside, charming villages and authentically restored stations. George Stephenson originally built the railway line, which includes one of the steepest rail gradients in the country between Goathland and Grosmont.

The railway and its stations have regularly featured in a variety of television programmes and films, including 'Heartbeat', 'Harry Potter and the Philosopher's Stone', 'Brideshead Revisited', 'Poirot', 'Sherlock Holmes' and 'All Creatures Great and Small'. Stop off along the way to enjoy the attractions and pleasant walks in the area. The Locomotive Shop and engine sheds can be accessed at Grosmont.

☎ 01751 472508   www.northyorkshiremoorsrailway.com
☎ 01751 473535 (Talking Timetable)

North York Moors – Goathland

YORKSHIRE

⛫ Pleasure Island Theme Park 238 D2

Six white-knuckle terror rides, lots of family rides, fun rides for the little ones, and superb classic rides on restored machines, including a 1920s 'Flying Chair' and a 1905 Carousel. Entertainment galore and lots of places to eat.

☎ 01472 211511   www.pleasure-island.co.uk

🏞 Pugneys Country Park 371 F4

One of the two lakes in this country park caters for non-powered watersports, including fishing, canoeing, windsurfing and sailing. Equipment is available for hire if required. The other smaller lake is a nature reserve with two bird hides.

☎ 01924 302360

🏰 Richmond Castle 252 A2

High on the cliffs above the River Swale stands the imposing Richmond Castle. Built by William the Conqueror to control the north, some of its original 11th century walls remain. The rectangular keep, rising 100ft (30m) with walls 11ft thick (3.5m), was built in the 12th century and remains almost intact. There is also an exhibition centre displaying some of the artefacts excavated from the site, where the castle's history can be explored.

☎ 01748 822493   www.english-heritage.org.uk

Rievaulx Abbey

✝ Rievaulx Abbey 253 E4

Set amongst the wooded hills of Rye Dale are the majestic ruins of this once powerful Cistercian monastery. Founded in 1132, this impressive abbey was built unconventionally, being hampered by the terrain, with its central aisle laid north to south, rather than the usual east to west direction.

The nave dates from 1135, whilst the towering presbytery, which is virtually intact, was rebuilt in the 13th century. Several outbuildings can also be identified, some standing to a good height. The monks' refectory is clearly evident with its wonderful arched lancet windows, along with the spectacular remains of the 13th century choir.

There is a visitor centre and a fascinating museum with interactive exhibits exploring the site's history.

☎ 01439 798228   www.english-heritage.org.uk

🏰 ❁ Ripley Castle 244 B1

Home to the Ingilby family since the early 1300s, discover 700 years of political, military, religious and social history. Most of the current building dates from the 16th century, including the three-storey, fortified tower complete with a priest's

secret hiding hole. On display are fine paintings, furniture, books and china, and the tower houses a collection of Royalist armour. The delightful gardens include a walled garden, which contains the National Hyacinth Collection, the kitchen garden, with rare vegetables, and the hot houses are filled with tropical plants. There is also a deer park and lakeside walks.

☎ 01423 770152   www.ripleycastle.co.uk

🏛 Royal Armouries Museum 385 N9

Housing a fascinating collection of arms and armour, the museum covers 3000 years of history with over 8000 exhibits. The five galleries spectacularly explore the themes of war, tournaments, hunting, self-defence and oriental warfare. Complementing the exhibits are many interactive touch-screen demonstrations, enjoyable films, costumed demonstrations and dramatised interpretations. More fun can be discovered outside, weather permitting, including jousting, falconry and horsemanship. The craft of gun making and leather working can also be observed, along with the falcons, hunting dogs and other animals in the Menagerie. Entrance for the main museum collection is free; charges apply for special themed events such as the shooting galleries.

☎ 0113 220 1999   www.armouries.org.uk

🏛 Scarborough Art Gallery 👁 254 D4

Displayed within this Italianate villa are fine art collections by local artists and by those who painted in Scarborough, such as Grimshaw, H.B. Carter and Lord Leighton. The paintings feature Scarborough's wonderful seascapes and views. The gallery is particularly appealing to a family audience. There are hands-on displays, pictures and paintings depicting Scarborough's history from fishing village to popular seaside resort. Children can also dress up in costumes and masks as one of the characters from the paintings.

☎ 01723 374753

🏰 Scarborough Castle 255 D4

Towering above the town and harbour, Scarborough Castle stands on a headland 300ft (91m) above sea level. The castle was built in the 12th century and has endured numerous Civil War sieges and bombardment during World War I. Explore the remains of the imposing, three-storey keep, built in the 12th century, medieval chapels, the curtain walls, and 13th century barbican. The site also provides evidence of earlier Iron Age settlements and remains of a Roman signal station.

☎ 01723 372451   www.english-heritage.org.uk

🏰 ❁ Sewerby Hall & Gardens 247 E1

Sewerby Hall is set in 50 acres (20ha) of parkland with fabulous coastal views over Bridlington Bay. This stylish Georgian house contains the East Yorkshire Museum featuring local history, archaeology, photography, and contemporary arts and crafts. One of the rooms is dedicated to the record-breaking aviator, Amy Johnson, displaying her souvenirs and mementoes. The gardens offer woodland walks, a delightful Old English Garden, pleasure gardens, children's zoo, adventure playground, 19th century Orangery, pitch and putt golf and putting green.

☎ 01262 673769   www.sewerby-hall.co.uk

🏰 ❁ Shandy Hall 253 E5

This authentically restored house belonged to the amusing parson, Laurence Sterne. It is where he completed his two novels, 'Tristram Shandy' and 'A

Sentimental Journey', in the 1760s. Two acres (1ha) of lovely gardens surround the house, complete with old fashioned roses and unusual cottage garden plants. The shop sells Sterne's books and unusual plants.

☎ 01347 868465

🏰 ❁ Shibden Hall 370 B3

Shibden Hall is an impressive, half-timbered manor house, dating back to 1420. Different rooms portray varying styles of architecture and furnishings associated with a particular era. Explore the 15th century kitchen, the 17th century dining room or the 16th century housebody. Its 17th century barn houses a folk museum with a notable collection of horse-drawn vehicles, while its reconstructed workshops display 19th century craft tools. The surrounding 90 acres (36ha) of parkland provide woodland walks, miniature railway, boating lake and play area.

☎ 01422 352246

🏰 Skipton Castle 243 F2

A wonderfully preserved, fully roofed, medieval castle, having survived a three-year siege during the Civil War. Inspect the banqueting hall, the kitchen, bedchamber and privy, climb to the top of the Watch Tower and back down to the dungeons below. Furthermore, unwind in the Chapel Terrace overlooking the town and surrounding woodland, or in the cobbled Tudor courtyard complete with a yew tree planted in the 17th century.

☎ 01756 792442   www.skiptoncastle.co.uk

★ Spurn Head 239 E1

Spurn Head, curling at the mouth of the Humber Estuary, marks the southernmost point of the Yorkshire Coast. The sandy peninsula extends for about 3.5 miles (5.5km) with a rough track passable by cars almost to its end (best to check the tide times). A rather uninhabited place, but its mudflats and saltmarsh attract thousands of birds and migrating species, including rare varieties such as yellow-browed warblers and wrynecks.

🏰 Temple Newsam 244 C4

Displayed within their original room settings in this wonderful Tudor-Jacobean mansion are extensive collections of fine paintings, furniture, silver, porcelain and Leeds pottery. Amongst the furniture collection are some excellent Chippendale masterpieces. The surrounding parkland, and gardens designed by Lancelot 'Capability' Brown, extend 2 sq miles (518ha) and incorporate a woodland garden, an Italian garden and a walled garden. Additionally, there is a Rare Breeds Centre, with over 400 animals.

☎ 0113 264 7321   www.leeds.gov.uk/templenewsam

❁ Thorp Perrow Arboretum 252 B4

The 85 acres (35ha) of woodland contain one of the largest and finest collections of trees and shrubs in the north of England. There are four national collections of ash, lime, walnut and laburnum, as well as oaks, ornamental cherries, willows and hazels. The arboretum is attractive throughout the year with thousands of daffodils in spring, tree blossom, bluebells and wild flowers in summer, and spectacular colours in autumn. Enjoy woodland walks, tree trails, nature trails, children's trail, lake and 16th century Spring Wood. The falconry centre provides demonstrations and hands-on experience of birds of prey.

☎ 01677 425323   www.thorpperrow.com

✺ Tropical World
`244 C4`

This attraction houses the largest tropical plant collection outside Kew Gardens. The Amazon rainforest, the African and American deserts and the North Sea waters are all captivatingly re-created. Discover over 30 varieties of butterflies, along with nocturnal owl monkeys, Egyptian fruit bats and bush babies, tropical fish and birds, terrapins and reptiles, all living amongst the tropical environments.

☎ 0113 266 1850

✝ Wakefield Cathedral
`244 C5`

First built in the 14th century and much restored in the 19th century, Wakefield Cathedral boasts the tallest spire in Yorkshire. Inside, it also features a 17th century font, 15th century masonry and carvings, and excellent Victorian stained-glass windows by Kempe.

☎ 01924 373923   www.wakefield-cathedral.org.uk

Whitby Abbey

✝ Whitby Abbey
`254 C1`

High on the cliff above the harbour stand the dramatic ruins of Whitby Abbey. Founded by Abbess St Hilda in AD657, the abbey was destroyed by the Vikings and rebuilt by the Normans in the 13th century. Amongst the ruins is the Benedictine Church, dating from the 13th and 14th centuries, complete with an impressive three-tiered choir and north transept. The abbey's 2000 year history is interactively re-created with computer-generated images, audiovisual displays and activities in the visitor centre, housed in the remains of a 17th century house. There are also displays of archaeological artefacts from the site and a restored 17th century stone garden.

This is a wonderful place to visit and has been an inspirational site for many, from saints to writers, including Bram Stoker, author of 'Dracula'.

☎ 01904 603568   www.english-heritage.org.uk

★ White Scar Cave
`250 C5`

The guided tour of White Scar Cave, one of the longest and most spectacular natural caves in Britain, covers 1 mile (1.6km) and takes about 80 minutes. Underground streams, waterfalls, stalactites, stalagmites, and other natural limestone formations can all be seen. There is also a massive cavern formed during the Ice Age containing thousands of stalactites and several prehistoric mud pools.

☎ 01524 241244   www.whitescarcave.co.uk

☐ York
`415`

The city of York is rich in history, splendour and variety. The Romans, who founded the city in AD71, the Vikings, the Normans, and the Georgians have all left their mark. The medieval walls, which include remnants of the Roman fortress walls, still surround the city, within which are narrow medieval streets and alleyways, including the infamous 'Shambles'. Visit the many museums that recount the site's changing times and display various archaeological finds, including York Castle Museum, Jorvik Viking Centre, the Yorkshire Museum and the more chilling York Dungeon.

York Minster is England's largest medieval Gothic church and the Merchants Adventurers' Hall is evidence of York's prospering times, during the Middle Ages, as a trading city operating under Guilds. With the Victorian Age came an economic revival for York through the railways, and the National Railway Museum celebrates over 200 years of railway history.

There are also interesting shops, wonderful parks and gardens, river and bus trips, bars, cafés and guided walks, including an evening 'Ghost Walk'.

www.york-tourism.co.uk

🏛 York Castle Museum
`415 E2`

Over 400 years of social history are revealed within the walls of what was once the city's old prison. The museum displays a remarkable collection of over 100,000 everyday items including period costumes, jewellery, arms, armour and toys. Encounter prison life 200 years ago by peering into cells, one of which housed the notorious highwayman, Dick Turpin, and read the graffiti still on the walls. The re-created cobbled streets, lined with replica shops, and reconstructed living rooms, provide a fascinating insight into how the Victorians lived.

☎ 01904 687687   www.yorkcastlemuseum.org.uk

★ York Dungeon
`415 E2`

Encounter the more gruesome side of York's history to discover the chilling aspects of superstition, torture, death and pain experienced over the last 2000 years. Tour round York's 14th century plague-ridden streets, meet Guy Fawkes as he is tortured to unveil the gunpowder plot and its conspirators, hear the infamous highwayman, Dick Turpin, recount his tales before being hanged. Then there are the Witchcraft trials, the ferocious Viking invaders, and the local woman crushed to death by stones – all have a story to tell.

☎ 01904 632599   www.thedungeons.com

✝ York Minster
`415 E2`

York Minster is a stunning medieval Gothic cathedral and the largest in northern Europe. Building began in the 13th century, but it took until the 15th century to be completed. The numerous, beautiful stained-glass windows are a key feature. Admire the Norman stained-glass windows in the nave, the Five Sisters Window in the north transept containing 100,000 pieces of glass, and the Great East Window with 27 panels. The Chapter House reveals fine carvings and the north transept is styled with polished stone columns.

In the Undercroft, Treasury and Crypt there is a museum that relates the cathedral's varied history over the last 2000 years. A climb to the top of the central tower is well worth the effort for magnificent views.

☎ 01904 557216   www.yorkminster.org

☐ Yorkshire Dales
`250 D4`

Outstanding beauty, spectacular natural landscapes, diverse habitats and a tranquil environment can all be used to describe the Yorkshire Dales, 1700 sq miles (4400 sq km) of which make up the Yorkshire Dales National Park.

The dramatic limestone and gritstone landscape, particularly in the southern dales (including Malhamdale and Airedale), provides stunning scenery with the rocky limestone cliffs and pavements, dramatic waterfalls and many caves. Bolton Abbey, White Scar Cave and Malham Cove are popular attractions, while the towering Three Peaks (Pen-y-Ghent, Ingleborough and Whernside) provide fabulous viewpoints.

Less rugged countryside and valleys depict the more northern and eastern dales, with wild flower and hay meadows, heather topped moors, woodland and picturesque villages. There are also many castles, abbeys, museums and gardens to explore including Constable Burton Hall, Bolton Castle, Thorp Perrow Arboretum, Fountains Abbey, and Aysgarth Falls.

The Pennine Way, Dales Way footpath, Coast to Coast Walk and the Settle to Carlisle Railway all pass through the Dales. The area, with its striking surroundings and picturesque rural villages, has also provided the backdrop to many television programmes and films, including 'Emmerdale', 'Robin Hood: Prince of Thieves', 'All Creatures Great and Small' and 'Calendar Girls'.

www.yorkshiredales.org.uk

Yorkshire Dales – Conistone

🏛 Yorkshire Museum
`415 D1`

Packed full of archaeological, Roman, Viking, Anglo-Saxon and medieval finds, the museum reveals a host of historic treasures. Amongst the collections are ancient fossils, medieval jewellery, including the spectacular Middleham Jewel, fine pottery and decorative arts. Outside, 10 acres (4ha) of botanical gardens can be explored, where there are also some interesting buildings including the ruins of the Benedictine St Mary's Abbey, a 14th century hospitium, a preserved section of a Roman fortress and a working observatory.

☎ 01904 687687   www.yorkshiremuseum.org.uk

★ Yorkshire Sculpture Park
`235 G1`

Artistically arranged within 500 acres (202ha) of pleasant 18th century landscaped parkland are major modern and contemporary sculptures. Exhibits from well-known names include those by Henry Moore, Elizabeth Frink and Barbara Hepworth. There are also two indoor galleries, a regularly changing programme of exhibitions and a visitor centre.

☎ 01924 830302   www.ysp.co.uk

NORTH WEST ENGLAND

Today the dark industrial images of the past are consigned to history and the busy urban sprawl of Manchester and Liverpool offer some of the very best in city design and culture. But nowhere in the country is the stark contrast between urban and rural life more apparent than in this region. Just a short distance up the M6 is the misty, dreamy Lake District, England's most popular national park. Here sixteen major lakes and England's highest mountains are packed into an area approximately thirty miles long and thirty miles across.

Jetty on Derwent Water

Abbot Hall Art Gallery & Museum of Lakeland Life   249 G3

Within the Georgian house of Abbot Hall there is a fine collection of British art from the 18th century onwards, including works by Ruskin, Constable and Romney. Exhibitions of national interest are held here and sculpture, arts, crafts and 18th century objets d'art also feature.

The Museum of Lakeland Life illustrates 250 years of Cumbrian history and has re-created period rooms, workshops and shops. There are personal effects and exhibits relating to 'Swallows and Amazons' author Arthur Ransome, and collections of Victoriana and costume.

☎ 01539 722464   www.abbothall.org.uk
www.lakelandmuseum.org.uk

Acorn Bank (NT)   260 C5

A walled garden with a large collection of culinary herbs, medicinal plants, shrubs, roses, herbaceous borders and orchards of old English fruit trees. A path through the ancient oak woodland leads to a restored water mill on Crowdundle Beck. Lovely displays of daffodils and wood anemones in spring.

☎ 017683 61893   www.nationaltrust.org.uk

Adlington Hall   234 D4

Originally built as a hunting lodge in 1040 by the Legh family, the present structure incorporates parts of the original building as well as Tudor, Elizabethan and more modern additions. The Hall is home to the largest 17th century organ in the country. The gardens were landscaped in the 18th century in the style of Lancelot 'Capability' Brown and now also include a maze and rose garden. Only open on selected days during the summer.

☎ 01625 820875   www.adlingtonhall.com

Adrian Sankey Glass Makers   249 E2

Visitors may view unique contemporary glass being made by craftspeople using the traditional methods of glass-blowing and hand finishing.

☎ 015394 33039   www.glassmakers.co.uk

Aira Force (NT)   260 A5

70ft (21m) waterfall set amongst woodland on the west side of Ullswater, spanned by a small arched stone bridge.

www.nationaltrust.org.uk

Anderton Boat Lift   234 A5

The boat lift is the only one of its kind in the UK, and when it was built in 1875 it was the first anywhere in the world. Boats enter one of two counterbalanced water-filled tanks which then pass each other mostly by the process of gravity. The rise is 50ft (15m) between two sections of the Trent and Mersey Canal. A visitor centre explains the processes fully and there are trips up and down the lift on a specially built glass-bottomed boat.

☎ 01606 786777   www.andertonboatlift.co.uk

Aquarium of the Lakes   249 E4

An award winning aquarium with more than 30 habitat exhibits of the creatures living in and around the streams, rivers and lakes of the Lake District. These include otters, ducks, trout, eels, pike, perch, and also the giant crabs, sharks and rays of Morecambe Bay. Imaginatively themed to follow the journey of a Lakeland river from its source to the sea, with interactive displays and a cinema presentation of life above and below the surface of Lake Windermere.

☎ 015395 30153   www.aquariumofthelakes.co.uk

Arley Hall   234 A4

The hall is set in superb gardens which are considered by many to be among the best in Europe. There are fine double herbaceous borders, two walled gardens, a shrub rose garden and yew topiary. The present day hall dates from between 1832 and 1845, although parts of the original Tudor building remain. The hall has fine wood panelling, plasterwork, porcelain and a wonderful library.

☎ 01565 777353   www.arleyhallandgardens.com

Astley Hall Museum & Gardens   233 G1

Dating back to Elizabethan times, this country house has textile, art, glassware and ceramic collections and a unique display of furniture. The house is set in extensive woodland and gardens.

☎ 01257 515555   www.astleyhall.co.uk

Beacon Fell Country Park   242 B3

The Fell lies within the Forest of Bowland Area of Outstanding Natural Beauty and the majority of its 185 acres (75ha) are covered by coniferous forest. There are panoramic views from the top of Beacon Fell where a triangulation pillar marks the site of the original warning beacon. A number of walks and cycle paths are clearly marked and a visitor centre is open during the summer.

☎ 01995 640557   www.lancashire.gov.uk/environment/
countryside/sites/beaconf.asp

Beatles Story   380 D10

Charting the history of the rise to fame of the four boys from Liverpool. There is a replica of The Cavern Club, a walk-through Yellow Submarine, and displays of Beatles memorabilia.

☎ 0151 709 1963   www.beatlesstory.com

Beeston Castle (Ruins)   220 C2

There are stunning views to be seen from this 13th century ruined castle which stands tall on sandstone crags overlooking the Cheshire Plains – it is well worth the steep climb to the top. The Castle of the Rock exhibition outlines the history of the site, from prehistoric times to the Civil War when the castle was eventually destroyed by the Parliamentarians in 1646.

☎ 01829 260464   www.english-heritage.org.uk

Birdoswald (Banna)   260 C1

In a commanding position overlooking the River Irthing, this well-preserved Roman fort was one of 16 along Hadrian's Wall. Parts of the walls and gateways remain and the fort is linked to Harrow's Scar Milecastle by an impressive section of the Wall. Excavations have revealed a basilica and granaries, and the site has an interactive visitor centre and self-guided trail. Birdoswald continued to be used after the Roman departure up until the 17th century and a farmhouse dating to that period remains.

☎ 016977 47602   www.birdoswaldromanfort.org.uk

Blackpool Piers   241 G4

Blackpool has three piers, each with its own style of entertainment. The North Pier is the oldest, built in 1863 and now a listed building, and is the quietest of the piers with the more genteel attractions. Central Pier is great for the children with a traditional funfair including a Big Wheel which gives superb views along the coastline. The South Pier is the place for adrenaline junkies to head to with various opportunities to jump, be thrown, tossed or swung out over the sea. Entrance to all the piers is free although there is a charge for amusements.

☎ 01253 343097   www.blackpoollive.com

Blackpool Pleasure Beach   241 G4

There are over 140 rides and attractions at this hugely popular amusement park on Blackpool's Promenade, founded in 1896. As well as a large selection of modern white-knuckle rides like The Big One, Europe's tallest (235ft, 72m) and fastest (85mph) roller coaster, and the Avalanche, based on a bobsleigh run, there are a selection of much older wooden roller coasters; the Big Dipper dates from 1923 and the twin track Grand National (two cars racing against each other on parallel tracks) from 1935. Valhalla is a truly spectacular ride in the dark with fire and lots of water. For younger children there is Beaver Creek, a theme park within a theme park, with its own selection of rides and amusements. There are a number of musical and dance shows performed daily and there are over 50 places to eat and drink as well as all the usual gift shops and traditional seaside entertainments. The rides vary in price, usually based on their 'scare' value, and tickets can be bought individually, in books or the cheaper option of a wristband if a whole day's visit is planned.

☎ 0870 444 5566   www.bpbltd.com

Blackpool Tower

Blackpool Tower   389 C1

The tower was opened in 1894 as the town's very own version of the Eiffel Tower in Paris, and was originally to be called the Blackpool Eiffel Tower. Just 30 years later it was considered for demolition as the steel used in its construction had become corroded, but instead, over a period of three years, the entire structure was replaced and the tower is now one of the town's most well-known attractions. It stands 518ft (158m) tall and is a spot of elegance on Blackpool's crowded seafront. An all-inclusive entry fee gives access to the Tower Circus, the Ballroom, the Aquarium, Jungle Jim's adventure playground and, of course, a trip to the top of the tower. There has been a circus here, between the legs of the tower, since the early days although the shows are now always entirely animal free. The Edwardian Ballroom is home to a mighty Wurlitzer organ on which Latin and old-time dance music is played. Visitors can take to the dance floor themselves or simply participate in high tea whilst others twirl past them. At the top of the tower the Walk of Faith is not for the faint-hearted, as a glass floor allows visitors the chance to look straight down onto the promenade far below.

☎ 01253 622242   www.blackpooltower.co.uk

NORTH WEST ENGLAND

Blackpool Zoo
241 G4

This 32 acre (13ha) zoo has a collection of over 400 animals including gorillas, lions, tigers and elephants. Gorilla Mountain allows visitors to get up close to the inhabitants and the Swimulator gives the opportunity for visitors to experience the thrill of riding with dolphins without getting wet! There are also keeper talks, animal feeding times, a miniature railway and a Children's Zoo where young children can feed and stroke many domestic animals.

☎ 01253 830830   www.blackpoolzoo.org.uk

Blackwell The Arts & Crafts House
249 F3

In a beautiful position overlooking Lake Windermere, Blackwell was designed by M.H. Baillie Scott between 1897 and 1900 as a holiday home for a wealthy Manchester brewer. It is a wonderful example of the architecture of the Arts and Crafts Movement. Much of the original interior decoration, including stained glass and carved panelling, remains intact and is complemented with furniture, paintings, arts and crafts. Changing exhibitions of historic and contemporary applied arts and crafts are held in upstairs galleries.

☎ 015394 46139   www.blackwell.org.uk

Blue Planet Aquarium
233 F5

Britain's largest aquarium attraction has two floors of exhibits, interactive displays and, for those with diving experience, a chance to swim with sharks. There is sealife on display from all over the world in imaginative displays which re-create varying water environments. Krakatoa has deadly species from the Indo-Pacific swimming amongst submerged temples and statues. The Underwater Safari conveys visitors through the longest (233ft, 71m) underwater viewing tunnel in the world where they are surrounded by sharks and other temperate fish from around the world, as well as 16,000 tons of water! Piranhas, stingrays and electric eels can be seen in the Amazonia display, and children can get their hands on starfish, rays, urchins and sea anemones in the touch pools. The knowledgeable staff are on hand to answer questions and give talks throughout the day. There is a large Caribbean-themed restaurant and a gift shop.

☎ 0151 357 8800   www.blueplanetaquarium.com

Bolton Museum, Art Gallery & Aquarium
234 B2

A good local museum with displays on Egyptology, natural and local history, geology and archaeology. The art gallery has some fine 20th century sculpture and there is a small aquarium with some rare fish species.

☎ 01204 332211   www.boltonmuseums.org.uk

Blue Planet Aquarium

Brantwood
249 E3

Standing on the east side of Coniston Water, with fine views of the lake and mountains beyond, Brantwood was the home of thinker, writer and artist John Ruskin from 1872 – 1900. Originally built in 1797, some rooms are much as Ruskin left them, and contain his art collection, own paintings, furniture, books and personal items. Extensive woodland and themed gardens created by Ruskin surround the house.

☎ 015394 41396   www.brantwood.org.uk

Bridgemere Garden World
221 E3

This huge garden nursery reputedly grows more plants, in more varieties, than anywhere else in Britain, and has over 5000 species on site at any time. 7 acres (3ha) of the nursery have been developed into a series of gardens designed to inspire customers. Many of the gardens are reconstructions of Chelsea Flower Show gold medal winners and range in style from country cottage to modern day patio gardens.

☎ 01270 520381   www.bridgemere.co.uk

Brookside Garden Centre & Miniature Railway
234 D4

This half-mile (1km) circuit makes its way around the garden with authentic signals, signal box and a replica of a West Country station. There are five locomotives in all, three steam and two diesel. The addition of a high level bridge and 65ft (20m) tunnel add to the interest. Passengers sit astride the train in the open and therefore the running of the train is weather dependent.

☎ 01625 872919   www.brookside-miniature-railway.co.uk

Camelot Theme Park
233 G1

The five magical lands at this Arthurian themed park are filled with rides, shows and other attractions which means that there is something here for all the family. The scariest rides are to be found in Land of the Brave, with the spinning roller coaster Whirlwind a popular attraction. King's Realm is filled with rides for all the family and for smaller members there is Merlin's Playland. Young children will also love Squire Bumpkin's Friendly Farm where there are plenty of animals to pat and stroke. Finally, Knight's Valley is the land of the shows – the half-hour jousting tournament is well worth a look.

☎ 01257 453044   www.camelotthemepark.co.uk

Carlisle Castle
393 B2

An imposing Norman fortress with a fascinating and eventful history due in no small part to its proximity to the English and Scottish border. Mary, Queen of Scots was imprisoned here in 1568 after her abdication from the Scottish throne, and the castle also featured in the Wars of the Roses and the Jacobite Rising.

The impressive 12th century keep still stands, as does the inner gatehouse with portcullis known as the Captain's Tower. 'Licking stones' found in a room used as a dungeon are grim testimony to the conditions of those imprisoned here. The King's Own Royal Border Regiment Museum is located within the castle.

☎ 01228 591922   www.english-heritage.org.uk

Carlisle Cathedral
393 B2

Originally founded in 1122, the cathedral today is notable for the large east window which contains some 14th century stained glass, the choir with distinctive 14th century barrel-vaulted blue starry ceiling, a 16th century carved Flemish altarpiece (Brougham Triptych) and medieval carving and paintings. Cathedral and diocesan silver is displayed in the Treasury.

☎ 01228 548151   www.carlislecathedral.org.uk

Cartmel Priory
249 E5

This fine Augustinian priory church, founded in 1188, reflects many periods of ecclesiastical architecture and is still in use today. It contains notable stained glass and carved choir stalls. Also remaining is the original priory gatehouse (National Trust) which is used as the Cartmel Heritage Centre.

☎ 015395 36874   www.nationaltrust.org.uk

Castlerigg Stone Circle
259 F4

Megalithic circle of 38 stones in a beautiful setting surrounded by Lakeland fells. Dating from about 3000 years ago, the circle is 100ft (30m) in diameter and encloses a smaller rectangle of ten stones. The site is thought to have been used as a tribal gathering place, although the precise use is unknown.

www.english-heritage.org.uk

Chester – Eastgate Clock

Chester
394

Chester has a rich history that covers nearly 2000 years. In AD79 the Romans built their largest known fortress here, named Deva after the river Dee. The Dewa Roman Experience and the Grosvenor Museum both have good insights into life in Chester during Roman times. There are various relics of Roman structures scattered around the town, including a partially excavated amphitheatre which would once have held 7000 spectators. Chester has the most complete city walls of anywhere in Britain and it is possible to walk the whole way around, a distance of about 2 miles (3km), although in a number of places the walls are not much higher than the current street height. The centre of Chester has a Tudor look to it with lots of black and white architecture. The four main streets are lined with the Rows, two-storey open galleried half-timbered arcades, some of which are thought to be 700 years old. The most picturesque of these are along Eastgate Street which is also home to the Eastgate Clock, erected to celebrate Queen Victoria's Diamond Jubilee. It is reputedly the most photographed timepiece after Big Ben. Alongside the River Dee are the Groves, a great place for riverside walks, and there are lovely views from one of the many boat trips.

✝ Chester Cathedral ⟲ `394 B2`

There has been Christian worship on the site of the cathedral since the 10th century, when a Benedictine monastery dedicated to St Werburgh was founded. During the 13th century work began on a new church on the site, built in the Gothic style. It was constructed around the original Norman church which was then taken down from the inside. Parts of this Norman building are still in evidence, for example in the refectory which now houses the cafeteria. The Gothic style church took around 250 years to complete and this long history of worship has led to all architectural styles being represented in the building. In 1541, following the dissolution of the monasteries, the church was dedicated as the Cathedral Church of Christ and the Blessed Virgin Mary. Over many years the church became neglected until, in the late 19th century, Sir George Gilbert Scott masterminded a major restoration project. Of particular note are the intricate medieval carvings above the choir stalls featuring dragons, angels and monsters. It was here that Handel first rehearsed 'The Messiah' and a copy of his annotated score is on display. Digital audio tours are available using hands-free equipment. Admission charges have now been introduced.

☎ 01244 324756   www.chestercathedral.org.uk

Chester Cathedral

🐘 Chester Zoo `233 F5`

Without doubt one of the best zoos in Europe, with a well-respected history of conservation work, Chester Zoo is the largest garden zoo in Britain, covering over 110 acres (50ha). Over 7000 animals can be seen, from around 500 different species, at least half of which are rare or endangered and many of which are part of successful breeding programmes. When the zoo was founded by George Mottershead in 1934 he wanted it to be a zoo without bars and he achieved this by creating large enclosures with natural barriers. The 11 miles (17km) of footpath wind their way around the award winning gardens and, if this

seems too much to do on foot, hop on the Zoofari overhead railway or the waterbus. The Monkey Islands exhibit is home to the largest colony of chimpanzees in the country and the Twilight Zone bat cave has free-flying bats. There are over 60 species of mammals from tiny harvest mice to the giant Asian elephants, as well as reptiles, birds, fish and amphibians. A series of short, fun and informative talks take place at various enclosures throughout the day and there is a full programme of feeding sessions. Refreshments are readily available and there is a gift shop.

☎ 01244 380280   www.chesterzoo.org.uk

Chester Zoo

✳ Cholmondeley Castle Gardens `220 C2`

Romantically landscaped gardens, pretty in any season, are set in the grounds of the Gothic style Cholmondeley Castle (not open to the public). The parkland has an ancient private chapel, rare breeds of animals, including llamas, and lakeside and woodland walks.

☎ 01829 720838

🏰 Dalton Castle (NT) `248 C4`

A rectangular 14th century tower which houses a local history exhibition.

☎ 01524 701178   www.nationaltrust.org.uk

🏛 Dock Museum ⟲ `241 E1`

The museum illustrates Barrow's history from the earliest times with particular emphasis on the 19th century industrial development through iron and steel, then shipbuilding and engineering. There is a collection of ships' models and computer access to the Vickers Photographic Archive of the workings of the Barrow Shipyard. There are also displays of archaeology, geology, natural history, and an art gallery. The museum is in a modern building over a Victorian dry dock.

☎ 01229 894444   www.dockmuseum.org.uk

🏛 Dove Cottage `249 E2`

Home of the poet William Wordsworth from 1799 – 1808, where he wrote much of his greatest poetry. Home, too, of his sister Dorothy, his wife Mary (whom he married in 1802) and three eldest children. Originally built in the 17th century as an inn, the small two-storey house has oak panelling and Westmoreland slate floors, and is little changed from Wordsworth's day. It also has a delightful cottage garden and orchard.

The adjoining Wordsworth Museum illustrates the life of the poet and his circle with rare books, personal memorabilia, portraits, paintings of Grasmere, and a unique collection of original manuscripts (including a selection of Wordsworth's poems and Dorothy Wordsworth's 'Grasmere Journals').

☎ 015394 35544   www.wordsworthlakes.co.uk

🏛 Dunham Massey Hall, Park & Gardens (NT) `368 B4`

An early Georgian manor house that was extensively remodelled in the early 20th century, resulting in sumptuous Edwardian interiors. Over 30 rooms are open to the public, including the refurbished kitchen, laundry and servants' quarters. Of particular note is the 18th century walnut furniture, the silver collection of the 2nd Earl of Warrington, and some fine paintings. The house is set in 250 acres (101ha) of wooded deer park with formal avenues of trees, an orangery and a working 17th century mill.

☎ 0161 941 1025   www.nationaltrust.org.uk

🏛 Ellesmere Port Boat Museum `233 F5`

The canal basin and historic dock where the Shropshire Union Canal meets the River Mersey is home to what claims to be the world's largest collection of traditional canal craft. The museum owns over 5000 items, ranging from large boats to canal company buttons, although not all are on display. Indoors there are exhibits of industrial heritage, waterways objects, working steam machinery and a series of dock workers' cottages re-creating scenes from domestic life between the 1840s and 1950s. Most of the boats on display can be stepped onto to give an insight into life aboard a small narrowboat. There are daily canal boat cruises with live commentary around this once busy port, now redeveloped with craft workshops.

☎ 0151 355 5017   www.boatmuseum.org.uk

⛲ Fell Foot Park (NT) ❀ `249 E4`

Restored 18 acre (8ha) Victorian park on the south shore of Windermere with trails, picnic sites and rowing boats for hire. Well suited to families with children. Lovely displays of daffodils in spring, followed by rhododendrons.

☎ 01539 531273   www.nationaltrust.org.uk

🐿 Formby Red Squirrel Reserve (NT) `233 D1`

The reserve at Formby is an unspoilt stretch of coastline with miles of walks through pine woods and sand dunes. It is one of the only places left in this country where it is possible to see red squirrels. There is a charge for car parking.

☎ 01704 878591   www.nationaltrust.org.uk

✝ Furness Abbey `248 D5`

The extensive red sandstone ruins of this medieval abbey are found in a peaceful setting in a wooded valley. Founded in 1123 by Stephen, later King of England, Furness became one of the richest Cistercian abbeys in England. The visitor centre has some interesting stone carvings from the abbey and an exhibition about the life of the monks.

☎ 01229 823420   www.english-heritage.org.uk

🏛 Gawthorpe Hall (NT) `243 E4`

Gawthorpe was the home of the Shuttleworth family and there is a fine display of needlework, lace and costume collected by the last family member to live here. Built in 1600, this imposing house was restored in the middle of the 19th century, creating the opulent interiors on display today. There are a number of society portraits, on loan from the National Portrait Gallery, hanging in the long gallery. In summer, there are pleasant walks in the riverside grounds.

☎ 01282 771084   www.nationaltrust.org.uk

Grizedale Forest Park · 249 E3

This extensive area of mixed woodland between Coniston Water and Windermere is a centre for recreational activities, including walking and cycling, with picnic areas and around 100 sculptures set within the forest. The visitor centre has a forest exhibition and keeps guide maps for all the waymarked trails. Bike hire is available and there is a high-ropes aerial adventure course.

☎ 01229 860010 · www.grizedaleforestpark.co.uk

H.M. Customs & Excise National Museum · 380 D9

The museum, located on the ground floor of the Merseyside Maritime Museum, tells the exciting story of the continual battle between smugglers and duty men from 1700 to the present day. See displays of some of the strange seizures made by customs, such as a guitar made from turtle, and learn about the techniques used to combat current day smugglers.

☎ 0151 478 4499 · www.customsandexcisemuseum.org.uk

(caption) Holker Hall

Hare Hill (NT) · 234 C5

This garden is particularly impressive in spring when the rhododendrons and azaleas are in flower. At the heart of the woodland garden is a walled garden with a pergola and wire sculptures.

☎ 01625 584412 · www.nationaltrust.org.uk

Harris Museum & Art Gallery · 242 B5

Large collections of British paintings, ceramics, glass and costume are displayed in this impressive Greek revival building. The history of the town is brought to life in the Story of Preston Gallery and there is a lively series of contemporary art and social history exhibitions.

☎ 01772 258248 · www.visitpreston.com/whats_on/museums/harris/htm

Heaton Hall · 369 D1

Heaton Hall is a fine neoclassical country house set in 650 acres (263ha) of public parkland. Many of the building's original features have been retained, such as the ornate scrolling plasterwork, the classically inspired paintings and the unusual Pompeiian Cupola room. The principal rooms in the house have been restored and furnished to reflect life here as it was in the late 18th and early 19th centuries.

☎ 0161 773 1231 · www.manchestergalleries.org.uk

High Cup Nick · 260 D5

A dramatic curved rocky basalt cliff at the head of a well-defined V-shaped valley in the North Pennines – an inspiring panorama for the determined walker.

Hill Top (NT) · 249 E3

This 17th century farmhouse owned by Beatrix Potter remains virtually unchanged, with furniture and china ornaments just as she left them. Beatrix Potter bought Hill Top in 1905 from the proceeds of the sale of her first books, which included 'The Tale of Peter Rabbit'. Although she did not live here all the time, the house was her inspiration and appears in the pictures and stories in many of her later books. Usually very busy in summer when entrance numbers are controlled.

☎ 015394 36239 · www.nationaltrust.org.uk

Holker Hall · 249 E5

The Cavendish family stately home originally dates from the 17th century but has many later additions and alterations. The pink sandstone Victorian west wing, open to the public, was rebuilt in Elizabethan style after a fire in 1871. The interior is richly furnished and decorated with ornate plaster ceilings, linenfold panelling, silk wall hangings, marble fire surrounds and a carved oak staircase. Paintings grace the walls and there is a collection of Wedgwood Jasper Ware.

Holker Hall is surrounded by a deer park and 25 acres (10ha) of award-winning formal and woodland gardens, with ornamental ponds and fountains and also a wild flower meadow. Rhododendrons, magnolias and azaleas are spectacular in spring and there is a National Collection of Styracaceae. The Great Holker Lime, probably planted in the early 17th century, has an enormous fluted trunk measuring 26ft (8m) across.

The Lakeland Motor Museum, housed in the former stables, has an extensive collection of transport and motoring memorabilia, and includes a display illustrating the record-breaking speed exploits of the Campbell family. There is a full size replica of Bluebird. A number of special events are held at Holker including an annual garden festival.

☎ 015395 58328 · www.holker-hall.co.uk

Hutton-in-the-Forest · 260 A4

Home of Lord Inglewood's family since 1605, this 17th century house is built around a medieval pele tower. Altered in the 18th and 19th centuries, Hutton-in-the-Forest now reflects a wide variety of architectural and decorative styles but retains its classical façade. The house contains fine furnishings, paintings and ceramics while the grounds include a walled garden dating from 1730, topiary terraces and a woodland walk.

☎ 017684 84449 · www.hutton-in-the-forest.co.uk

Jodrell Bank Observatory & Arboretum · 234 B5

Jodrell Bank is a leading radioastronomy facility and the huge attraction is the 200ft (76m) Lovell Radio telescope, the second largest in the world. An observational footpath allows visitors to get up close to the telescope and view it from all angles. There is a small exhibition about the work of the observatory, and a state-of-the-art visitor centre is under construction. The 35 acre (14ha) arboretum has over 2000 species of tree and shrub and there are a number of nature trails to help explore this colourful area.

☎ 01477 57133 · www.jb.man.ac.uk

Knowsley Safari Park · 367 D1

When the park opened in 1971 it was the first to have drive-through animal enclosures. There are now 5 miles (8km) of roads to drive, which allow visitors to view the wild animals, including lions, elephants, giraffes and buffalo, in natural settings. There is a bypass route for those too wary to take their cars into the baboon enclosure, where the animals can be viewed from a safe distance. The entrance fee also includes admission to Lake Farm, a children's farm, the Reptile House, the information centre and a chance to view the sealion show. There is a small amusement park, for which an additional charge is made.

☎ 0151 430 9009 · www.knowsley.com/safari

Lady Lever Art Gallery · 366 A3

Set in the garden village created by William Hesketh Lever for the workers at his soap factory, this gallery was founded in 1922 and dedicated to his wife. It has a superb collection of Victorian paintings including Turner and the pre-Raphaelite Rossetti, a large collection of Wedgwood, and a host of memorabilia relating to Lord Leverhulme's fascination with Napoleon.

☎ 0151 478 4136 · www.ladyleverartgallery.org.uk

Lake District · 248 D2

An inspiration to writers and painters, and a mecca for walkers and climbers, the Lake District is one of the most beautiful parts of Britain. It was glacial action that led to the development of the distinctive landscape of rounded mountain summits with ribbon lakes. The area is designated as a National Park, covering 885 square miles (2292 sq km) and containing over 1800 miles (2897 km) of footpaths. It encompasses England's longest and deepest lakes – Windermere and Wast Water respectively – and England's highest mountain, Scafell Pike.

The variety of scenery is breathtaking. Each of the lakes has an individual character and the mountains are broken up by crags, ridges, tarns and streams. Sheep farming has long been the agricultural heritage of the area and the fells are sheep cropped and dotted with small farms and dry stone walls. Picturesque villages and vibrant market towns complete the picture.

With unprecedented access to the countryside, walking and climbing are the most popular leisure activities but there are countless opportunities and facilities for cycling, boating, angling and other outdoor pursuits. Museums, heritage centres, historic houses and gardens, family attractions and the many literary associations of the area, most notably with Wordsworth, are also a draw to visitors. The Lake District can be very busy in the summer, Windermere in particular being a hive of activity, but the National Park and other organisations work hard to maintain the balance between preserving the unique natural beauty of the area and catering for the many visitors.

Lake District Visitor Centre at Brockhole · 249 E2

Interactive exhibitions and special events are designed to give visitors of all ages an insight into the Lake District National Park and how the unique landscape is cared for. The centre is housed in a late 19th country house set within 30 acres (12ha) of landscaped gardens on the shores of Windermere.

Visitors are encouraged to enjoy the grounds and there are lakeside walks, an adventure playground and cruises on the lake.

☎ 015394 46601   www.lake-district.gov.uk

Lakeside & Haverthwaite Railway 249 E4

Three and a half miles (6km) of track with steep gradients running through the scenic Leven Valley from Haverthwaite to Lakeside at the south end of Windermere. Both steam and diesel locomotives are in service with a daily timetable operating between April and October.

☎ 01539 31594

Lancaster City Museum 242 A1

Based in a grand Georgian former town hall built in 1873, this museum illustrates the city's history, from Neolithic times to the present day.

☎ 01524 64637   www.lancaster.gov.uk/council/museums

Leighton Hall 249 F5

This neogothic mansion is home to the furniture-making Gillow family, and is set in 1550 acres (627ha) of landscaped parkland. The hall has early and rare examples of Gillow furniture, fine paintings, a 19th century walled garden, and a small collection of birds of prey which fly daily. The hall is open to the public from May to September.

☎ 01524 734474   www.leightonhall.co.uk

Levens Hall 249 F4

An imposing grey stone Elizabethan mansion built round a large square medieval pele tower which has been lived in by the Bagot family for centuries and is still a family home. The house has fine ceiling plasterwork, oak panelling, carved oak chimney pieces, embossed leather wall coverings and notably contains a collection of Jacobean furniture and some early English patchwork.

It is for the yew topiary gardens, however, that Levens is world-renowned. The gardens were designed around 1694 by a Frenchman, Guillaume Beaumont, who had previously laid out the gardens at Hampton Court. Beaumont's original design at Levens remains unchanged today. A huge number and variety of shapes have been clipped out of the common and golden yew and there are also impressive box and beech hedges. Each year it takes from August to December for all the hedges to be clipped. The hedging provides a wonderful backdrop to seasonal bedding and herbaceous borders. Levens also has parkland with a herd of fallow deer, and a working steam engine collection.

☎ 015395 60321   www.levenshall.co.uk

Levens Hall – Topiary Gardens

Little Moreton Hall (NT) 221 F2

Arguably Britain's finest timber-framed manor house, which has an exterior virtually unchanged since it was built in 1580. The interior is unfurnished but the wainscotted long gallery, cobbled courtyard and 17th century knot garden are well worth a look.

☎ 01260 272018   www.nationaltrust.org.uk

Liverpool Cathedral 380 J11

Nothing about this cathedral has been done on a small scale. It is the largest Anglican cathedral in Europe and the fifth largest cathedral in the world. It has the largest working organ with over 9700 pipes, the highest and heaviest church bells, and the highest Gothic arches ever built. This neogothic structure looks much older than it really is – it was only completed in 1978, 74 years after it was designed by Giles Gilbert Scott. It is well worth a climb up the tower, two consecutive lifts followed by 108 steps, as there are panoramic views over Liverpool and towards the Welsh Hills. Part of the way up the tower is the Elizabeth Hoare Embroidery Gallery where there is a sumptuous display of Victorian and Edwardian ecclesiastical embroidery. The gallery also gives fine views over the interior of the cathedral from some 100ft (30m) above the floor level. Although entrance to the cathedral is free, visitors are requested to make a donation towards the running costs of this beautiful building. There is a charge for climbing the tower, and for viewing the embroidery display.

☎ 0151 702 7217   www.liverpoolcathedral.org.uk

Liverpool Museum 380 G5

This museum has hugely varied collections of exhibits covering just about every imaginable topic – from Egyptian tombs, to the night sky, via the Amazonian rainforests. There are fascinating exhibits on dinosaurs, the natural and physical sciences, an award winning hands-on Natural History exhibition, a Space and Time gallery. The Planetarium (there is a small fee) has half-hour shows including the solar system, space exploration and stunning images from the Hubble telescope. Besides the permanent displays, there is an ever-changing programme of special events and attractions.

☎ 0151 478 4399   www.liverpoolmuseum.org.uk

Lowry, The 368 C2

This shimmering building of metal and glass at the redeveloped Salford Quays houses the largest public collection of works by L.S. Lowry. There are some 350 paintings and drawings on display, including many of his well-known industrial scenes with their stylised matchstick men, as well as his lesser-known mountain and seascapes. There are changing exhibitions, combining works from the collection with those borrowed from other institutions, and private collections as well as paintings, sculptures and photographs by other local artists. ArtWorks is an interactive exhibition designed to encourage the creativity of visitors. There are also two theatres which offer a variety of performances including ballet, drama, opera and comedy. On a warm day it is possible to sit on the quayside with refreshments from one of the cafés or bars.

☎ 0161 876 2000   www.thelowry.com
☎ 0870 787 5780

The Lowry

Lyme Park (NT) 235 D4

This country estate covers nearly 1400 acres (567ha) of wild moorland and parkland which are home to red and fallow deer. The property at its centre combines Elizabethan, Georgian and Regency architecture, together with an Italianate interior. The state rooms have Mortlake tapestries, Grinling Gibbons wood carvings and a fine collection of English clocks. Back outside, the hall is surrounded by 17 acres (7ha) of Victorian gardens boasting a flowering sunken garden, Jekyll-style herbaceous borders and a reflection lake. The house featured as Pemberley in the BBC's adaptation of Jane Austen's 'Pride and Prejudice'.

☎ 01663 762023   www.nationaltrust.org.uk

Manchester Art Gallery 383 K7

There are over 2000 items on display in this city centre gallery. The collection is particularly known for its 19th century British paintings and includes works by some of the great pre-Raphaelites. There is also an exceptional collection of decorative art and craft work, from ancient Greek pottery to contemporary furniture. The Manchester Gallery houses work from local

Lake District – Tarn Hows

artists, including Lowry, and the Interactive Gallery aims to open children's minds to art. Audio tours of the collection are available.

☎ 0161 235 8888　　www.manchestergalleries.org.uk

🦙 Martin Mere　233 F1

This Wildfowl and Wetland Trust site teems with wild geese, swans, ducks and flamingos, and is a year-round attraction. In the landscaped waterfowl gardens it is possible to feed some of the world's rarest and most endangered species of bird by hand. The visitor centre is excellent and explains the need for conserving the wetlands as well as hosting exhibitions and special events.

☎ 01704 895181　　www.wwt.org.uk

★ Mersey Ferries　380 B8

One of the best ways to see Liverpool's landmark Liver building is from the equally famous Mersey Ferry. As well as the regular commuter ferry for Birkenhead and Wallasey, there is a 50-minute river explorer cruise which incorporates a lively commentary on the history of Liverpool and Europe's oldest ferry.

☎ 0151 330 1444　　www.merseyferries.co.uk

🏛 Merseyside Maritime Museum　380 D9

This huge museum in Liverpool's Albert Dock is the second largest of its kind in the country and tells the story of one of the world's greatest ports. There are a number of fascinating exhibitions including one that explores the role of Liverpool in the transatlantic slave trade and another, the Emigrant Gallery, that allows the visitor to share in the experiences of those who left Liverpool for the New World. There are numerous objects associated with nautical archaeology, maritime paintings, ships' models, and galleries about the Titanic and the Lusitania. During the summer it may be possible to board one of the preserved ships in the dock outside.

☎ 0151 478 4499　　www.merseysidemaritime
museum.org.uk

🏚 Mirehouse　259 F4

In a wonderful setting near to Bassenthwaite Lake and beneath Skiddaw, this 17th century house is still used as a family home. Wordsworth, Tennyson, Carlyle and Southey all visited Mirehouse and some of their letters are on display, together with a collection of Francis Bacon manuscripts. In front of the house is a wild flower meadow, there are adventure playgrounds in the woods, an orchard with regional fruit varieties, a bee garden and lakeside walk. The house has limited opening but the grounds are open daily from April to October.

☎ 017687 72287　　www.mirehouse.com

🏰 ✿ Muncaster Castle　248 C3

Situated in a remote part of Cumbria, Muncaster is a 19th century castle incorporating parts of earlier buildings including the medieval pele tower. It has been in the same family since the 13th century and is said to be haunted. The elegant rooms, including the Great Hall and Octagonal Library, display a great number of treasures collected over the centuries.

There are 77 acres (31ha) of gardens and woodland to explore with walks overlooking Eskdale. In late spring there are carpets of bluebells and many species of rhododendrons in flower. An Owl Centre in the grounds has owls, buzzards, kestrels and red kites, and is the headquarters of the World Owl Trust. The centre has flying displays and video footage from cameras placed in nesting boxes.

☎ 01229 717614　　www.muncaster.co.uk

🏛 Museum of Liverpool Life　380 C9

This museum celebrates Liverpool's people, their culture, achievements and contribution to life in this country over the last century. A varied range of displays looks at all aspects of Liverpool life. The City Soldiers gallery tells the story of the King's Regiment, the River Room concentrates on life around the Mersey, and the Mersey Culture section looks at popular music, home-grown soap operas, football and the Grand National.

☎ 0151 478 4080　　www.museumofliverpoollife.org.uk

🏛 Museum of Science & Industry　382 F8

An impressive museum that provides enough entertainment for a whole day out. It is based in the buildings of the world's oldest passenger railway station. George Stephenson's Rocket arrived here in 1830 on its inaugural journey from Liverpool. There are 13 galleries in all; there is a reconstruction of a Victorian sewer with all the appropriate smells, a Power Hall which has huge working engines and locomotives, and a hands-on science centre called Xperiment, all of which help to bring the industrial and scientific past to life. The newest gallery looks at the contribution that Manchester scientists past and present have made to the modern world, as well as featuring some recent developments such as odourless socks!

☎ 0161 832 2244　　www.msim.org.uk

Ness Botanic Gardens

❋ Ness Botanic Gardens　233 E5

Ness Botanic Gardens were founded by the Liverpool cotton merchant Arthur Kilpin Bulley in 1898. Bulley was interested in introducing new plant species from abroad, and in particular he believed that Himalayan and Chinese mountain plants would grow well in this country. When Bulley died the garden was gifted to the University of Liverpool who has since maintained and developed the gardens with an emphasis on research, conservation and education. There are now 62 acres (25ha) of gardens, greenhouses and experimental grounds, with an extensive collection of specimen trees and shrubs which include many rhododendrons and azaleas. There are also renowned rock, rose, heather and water gardens. The gardens have a number of interest trails, a visitor centre, gift shop, tearoom and children's play areas.

☎ 0151 353 0123　　www.nessgardens.org.uk

Quarry Bank Mill & Styal Estate

★ Nether Alderley Mill (NT)　234 C5

This restored 15th century water mill has working Victorian machinery and is powered by overshot (the water flows over the wheel rather than under it) tandem wheels. Flour grinding demonstrations occasionally take place, water supplies permitting.

☎ 01625 584412　　www.nationaltrust.org.uk

🏠 Ordsall Hall　369 D2

A fine black and white half-timbered manor house in the incongruous surroundings of Salford city centre. There is a fully restored and furnished Great Hall, a bedroom and Tudor kitchen to be explored, as well as a chance of spotting The White Lady, Ordsall Hall's ghost. Closed on Saturdays.

☎ 0161 872 0251　　www.salford.gov.uk/ordsallhall

🎡 Pleasureland Amusement Park　233 E1

Originally opened in 1920 with just a helter skelter and a roller coaster, Pleasureland has now expanded to have over 100 rides and attractions. There are a few big white-knuckle rides such as the Traumatizer, a suspended coaster, and Space Shot which launches riders 120ft (37m) into the air, as well as more traditional roller coasters, a log-flume and ghost train. There is also an area with rides especially for young children. Admission to the park is free although the rides themselves are not. Visitors can purchase a wristband which will give unlimited rides all day.

☎ 08702 200204　　www.pleasureland.uk.com

★ Quarry Bank Mill & Styal Estate (NT)　234 C4

Situated in 384 acres (155ha) of the beautiful countryside of Styal Country Estate, this museum is a fantastic place to learn about the social and industrial history of this country. Quarry Bank Mill is a fully preserved and working example of a Georgian cotton mill powered by the largest working water wheel in Europe. Cotton is still spun and woven here and is available for sale in the shop. Inside the mill there are hands-on displays, demonstrations from hand spinning to large-scale factory weaving, and an 1840s steam-powered beam engine which is worked daily. The Apprentice House was built in 1790 to house pauper children who worked at the mill. The conditions in which these children lived and worked is now brought to life with the aid of enthusiastic guides in period costume who engage visitors in conversation and discussion. Visitors are encouraged to ask questions, test the straw filled beds, touch all the objects in the house and pump water from the well in the yard. Styal village was a tiny hamlet before the mill arrived but by 1840 it was a thriving village with most of its inhabitants working at the mill. It claims to be the least altered factory colony in this country with well-preserved workers' cottages, chapel, school and shop, and the whole village has an idyllic rural atmosphere. The estate land around the village and mill has some wonderful riverside and woodland walks.

☎ 01625 527468   www.quarrybankmill.org.uk

Railway Age, The   `221 E2`

A wide range of electric, steam and miniature locomotives, a model railway and an impressive collection of signalling equipment.

☎ 01270 212130   www.therailwayage.co.uk

Ravenglass & Eskdale Railway   `248 B3`

A narrow-gauge railway running 7 miles (11km) from the coast at Ravenglass to Dalegarth Station near Boot in Eskdale, with a journey time of around 40 minutes. Small steam locomotives pull passengers through spectacular scenery with the Scafell range of mountains in view for much of the time. There is a choice of open and covered carriages, and the service is often used by walkers and cyclists to get into the heart of Lakeland. 'La'al Ratty', the water vole mascot for the railway, keeps children amused, sometimes acting as guard, train driver or stationmaster. The railway was first opened in 1875 to transport iron ore, and at Ravenglass Station there are displays of memorabilia and photographs illustrating the line's history.

☎ 01229 717171   www.ravenglass-railway.co.uk

Ravenglass & Eskdale Railway

⭐ Rheged – the Village in the Hill   `260 A5`

A vast purpose-built family attraction named after Cumbria's Celtic Kingdom of Rheged and designed to blend in with the landscape. It is built into a disused limestone quarry and has a grass covered roof, the largest in Europe. Although the building covers 85,000 square feet (719 sq m) on five different levels, the glass atriums and windows provide ample light and spectacular views. A stream runs through the building and there are small lakes outside.

Apart from the unique construction, the main draw is a giant cinema screen the size of six double-decker buses. Spectacular epic films are shown each day including features on Cumbrian

myths and legends, the Lakeland landscape, the underwater world, and the ascent of Everest.

Rheged is also home to the National Mountaineering Exhibition which celebrates Britain's mountaineering heritage. Exhibits include clothing, equipment, photographs and film. Additionally, there is a children's indoor play area, local food, craft and gift shops, restaurant, art exhibitions and a full programme of special events. Free car parking and entry to the building.

☎ 01768 868000   www.rheged.com

Ribchester Roman Fort & Museum   `242 C4`

This museum is built on the site of a Roman fort occupied from AD78 and is dedicated to the history of Bremetenacum Veteranorum, the Roman name for Ribchester. There are some interactive exhibits, Roman replicas like the Ribchester Parade Helmet, and collections of weaponry, jewellery, coins and pottery. The external remains of the Roman granary can also be seen by visitors.

☎ 01254 878261   www.ribchestermuseum.org

Rydal Mount   `249 E2`

Little has changed at Rydal Mount since William Wordsworth lived here with his family from 1813 until his death in 1850. The house was originally a 16th century farm cottage but was made much larger in the 18th century. Furnished as it would have been in Wordsworth's day, the house has some of his poetry, personal possessions and family portraits on display.

The extensive picturesque terraced gardens were designed by Wordsworth and there are wonderful views of Rydal Water, Windermere and the surrounding fells. Rydal Mount was beloved by all Wordsworth's family and was a source of inspiration to the poet.

☎ 015394 33002   www.wordsworthlakes.co.uk

Salford Museum & Art Gallery   `382 B4`

Lark Hill Place is a re-created Victorian shopping street with original shop fronts and authentic period rooms. LifeTimes focuses on real people and events to tell the story of Salford over the last 200 years. The Victorian Gallery has a permanent collection of paintings and sculpture, and hosts temporary exhibitions of work by local and national artists.

☎ 0161 736 2649   www.salford.gov.uk/leisure/museums/salfordmuseum.htm

Salt Museum   `234 A5`

Cheshire has been a large producer of salt for over 2000 years. It is the only place in Britain where it is still produced on a large scale, and this interesting museum at Northwich explains the vital importance of salt to human life, as well as describing the production process.

☎ 01606 41331   www.saltmuseum.org.uk

⭐ Silk Museum & Paradise Mill   `234 D5`

Macclesfield was one of Britain's main silk spinning and weaving centres during the late 18th and early 19th centuries. Paradise Mill is now an award winning museum where knowledgeable guides, many of them former silk workers, take visitors around the restored jacquard handlooms and demonstrate the intricate processes involved in silk work. The Silk Museum, housed in what was once the Macclesfield School of Art, has displays on the properties of silk, the textile industry and the social history of the area.

☎ 01625 612045   www.silk-macclesfield.org

Sizergh Castle & Gardens (NT)   `249 F4`

Originally built in the 14th century by the Strickland family, who still live here, the massive fortified tower developed into a manor house with the addition of a Great Hall in the 15th century and two long wings during the Elizabethan period. There are some remarkable oak-panelled rooms, most notably the bedroom known as the Inlaid Chamber, and fine Elizabethan carved wooden chimneypieces. The house contents include period oak furniture, family portraits, china and Jacobite relics.

Sizergh has an impressive limestone rock garden with a large collection of hardy ferns, a Dutch garden with flowering cherries and a rose garden underplanted with bulbs. Specimen trees and shrubs provide wonderful autumn colour. Extensive walks with views of the Lakeland fells and Morecambe Bay are to be enjoyed in the 1600 acre (638ha) estate.

☎ 015395 60070   www.nationaltrust.org.uk

South Lakes Wild Animal Park   `248 D5`

Opened in 1994, this is now a major conservation zoo park. Animals from many parts of the world are kept in mixed groups in natural surroundings, and others are free to roam the park. Among around 100 species of animals are kangaroos, bears, rhinos, giraffes, antelope, lemurs, cheetahs, lions, primates and rare Amur and Sumatran tigers. Animal hands-on sessions are held with the zoo keepers providing a wealth of information. Feeding sessions include the spectacle of the tigers climbing tall poles for their meat, a device designed to exercise their muscles. A miniature railway operates in summer.

The park takes part in coordinated breeding programmes and works to conserve natural habitats all over the world to save endangered species. It is also home of the Sumatran Tiger Trust which works in Sumatra to protect the remaining wild tigers.

☎ 01229 466086   www.wildanimalpark.co.uk

South Tynedale Railway   `260 D3`

This is England's highest narrow-gauge railway. Restored steam and diesel locomotives run for over two miles (3km) from the station at Alston through the beautiful South Tyne valley to Kirkhaugh in the North Pennines. The return journey takes 50 minutes but passengers may spend time at Kirkhaugh and return on a later train.

☎ 01434 381696   www.strps.org.uk

Stagshaw Garden (NT)   `249 E2`

A hillside woodland garden overlooking Windermere with rhododendrons, azaleas and camellias. A beck runs through the garden with several small waterfalls. Open April to June only, at other times by appointment

☎ 015394 46027   www.nationaltrust.org.uk

Stapeley Water Gardens & Palms Tropical Oasis   `221 D2`

Stapeley is the country's largest and best regarded water garden centre, with hundreds of water plants displayed, and for sale, in pools. The water lilies are particularly impressive between June and September. The Palms Tropical Oasis, for which there is a fee, has palm trees, parrots, reptiles, monkeys and creepy-crawlies in heated glasshouses.

☎ 01270 623868   www.stapeleywatergardens.com

Tabley House   234 B5

This is the only 18th century Palladian house in the north west. The son of the original owner was the first patron of British art and built up quite a collection of paintings, including works by Turner and Reynolds, many of which are still on display in the locations they were originally intended for. The house is also home to a collection of fine furniture, including pieces by Gillow and Chippendale.

☎ 01565 750151   www.tableyhouse.co.uk

Tate Liverpool   380 C9

Home to the national collection of modern art in the north of England, Tate Liverpool has four floors of contemporary art. There are exhibitions of art from the Tate Collection and special exhibitions of work from other public and private collections, including some from overseas. There are free talks and guided tours daily. There is a charge for some special exhibitions.

☎ 0151 702 7400   www.tate.org.uk

Tatton Park (NT)   234 B4

This is one of the most complete historic estates open to visitors, and there is plenty here to occupy for a whole day. There are two historic houses, 1000 acres (400ha) of parkland containing some magnificent gardens, and a working farm. The opulent mansion was built at the end of the 18th century and gives a wonderful glimpse into how the original owners, the Egerton family, lived. The state and family rooms still contain many of the original furnishings, contents and paintings, including two Canalettos. The fully restored servants' quarters are a stark contrast. The second house is the Tudor Old Hall – downstairs paints a realistic picture of medieval life, whilst upstairs the rooms are styled as they would have been in the early 1600s. The final room of the tour is a re-creation of an estate worker's cottage from 1958. The gardens, perhaps the best feature of the estate, are extensive and incorporate many different styles. There is a walled garden, a beech maze, a fernery, an Italianate garden and one of the finest examples of a Japanese garden in Europe. Home Farm is always popular with children, especially when the piglets are just being born, and the adjacent fields have sheep, cattle and chickens. The farm works as it did during the 1930s, with vintage farm implements and rare breeds of animal. All of this is set in open parkland where herds of fallow deer roam freely.

☎ 01625 534400   www.tattonpark.org.uk

Tegg's Nose Country Park   234 D5

Tegg's Nose is a distinctive hill with open heather moorland, meadows and woodland. A series of well-marked footpaths take visitors to some tremendous views over the Cheshire countryside towards North Wales. There is an excellent visitor centre.

☎ 01625 914279   www.cheshire.gov.uk/countryside/
                               outandabout/teggs_nose_country_park

Tullie House   393 B2

With collections of archaeology, history, wildlife, geology and fine and decorative arts, this modern museum has many hands-on and audiovisual exhibits, and provides interest and entertainment for all ages. The troubled history of the Borders area, from prehistory through to medieval times and beyond, is illustrated with the use of sight, sound and smell in the 'Border Galleries'. The growth of Carlisle as a main railway centre is featured and there are changing contemporary art exhibitions. Tullie House, the Jacobean House

which gave the museum its name, stands within the grounds.

☎ 01228 534781   www.tulliehouse.co.uk

★ Ullswater Steamers   259 G5

Three traditional Victorian vessels cruise the eight miles (13km) of Ullswater all year round. Steamer services started on the lake in 1859 and a passenger service has continued ever since, although the ships are now oil powered. Ullswater is unspoilt, and from the lake there are dramatic views of Helvellyn, England's second highest mountain. Passengers may travel between any of the piers at Glenridding, Howtown and Pooley Bridge or buy a round trip ticket.

☎ 017684 82229   www.ullswater-steamers.co.uk

★ Walker, The   380 G5

This gallery houses one of the country's finest collections of artwork outside London. There is European art from the 14th century right up to the present day, including works by Rembrandt, Poussin and Degas. The speciality of this gallery however is British art, including a major collection of Victorian paintings and pre-Raphaelite work. 20th century art is represented by Cezanne, Monet, Lucien Freud and David Hockney, whilst two temporary exhibition galleries show contemporary work.

☎ 0151 478 4199   www.thewalker.org.uk

✳ Walton Hall Gardens   367 F3

A heritage centre in the gardens tells the story of the Walton Estate, of Lewis Carroll and his connections with Walton Hall (not open to the public) and the local natural history. There are ornamental gardens, spacious lawns, picnic areas, a children's zoo and woodland trails, as well as a number of waymarked trails from the gardens leading out into the surrounding countryside.

☎ 01925 601617   www.warrington.gov.uk/
                               entertainment/parks/walton

★ Whinlatter Forest   259 E4

An upland forest park with waymarked trails through the forest, routes to the top of the surrounding fells, a permanent orienteering course, adventure playground and picnic areas. The first trees were planted here in 1919 and the Forestry Commission Visitor Centre at the top of Whinlatter Pass has displays about the forest. From May to September there are CCTV pictures at the visitor centre of osprey chicks being reared in

local nests. Viewpoints throughout the park afford spectacular vistas of the Lake District and across to Scotland.

☎ 017689 78469   www.whinlatterforestpark.co.uk

★ Whitworth Art Gallery   369 D2

The Whitworth is home to a collection of British watercolours, including paintings by Turner, modern art and sculpture, and the largest collection of textiles and wallpapers outside of the Victoria and Albert Museum in London. The works are grouped and displayed in themes which change once or twice a year.

☎ 0161 275 7450   www.whitworth.man.ac.uk

★ Windermere Lake Cruises 249 E3

Traditional and modern launches carry over a million passengers each year between Waterhead (Ambleside), Bowness and Lakeside on Windermere. The oldest boat in the fleet is *The Tern*, a railway steamer built in 1891. Daily services operate all year and circular cruises of the lake, the longest in England, or shorter sightseeing trips are available. Traditional rowing boats and self-drive motor boats may also be hired.

☎ 015395 31188   www.windermere-lakecruises.co.uk

Windermere Steamboat Museum   249 F3

A fascinating collection of historic steam and motor boats moored in a covered wet dock, with launch trips if the weather is fair. Among the vintage boats is the steam launch *Dolly*, reputedly the oldest mechanically powered boat in the world, built around 1850 and restored to her former glory after spending 67 years on the bed of Ullswater. Among other attractions at the museum are model boats and a model boats pond, 'Swallows and Amazons' exhibition, Beatrix Potter's rowing boat, and displays about how Windermere has been used for transport since Roman times.

☎ 015394 45565   www.steamboat.co.uk

★ World of Beatrix Potter Attraction   249 F3

The 'Tales of Beatrix Potter' are brought to life in an amazingly detailed re-creation of the scenes inhabited by her characters using sounds, music, lighting effects and even smells. Of great appeal to children and all lovers of Beatrix Potter's books.

☎ 015394 88444   www.hop-skip-jump.com

Tatton Park

NORTH EAST ENGLAND

The evocative ruin of Hadrian's Wall stretches like a ribbon across this remotely beautiful border country. Yet, in stark contrast to the armed conflicts of the past the industrial revolution brought a different type of struggle to the area. Coal, steel, railways and shipbuilding helped create dozens of 'boom' settlements. Over the years these have mellowed into towns and cities of real character bustling with residents who are genuinely proud of their heritage and unrivalled in their hospitality.

Hadrian's Wall

🏰 ✿ Alnwick Castle & Garden 　279 F5

Just to the north of Alnwick town centre and rising impressively above the River Aln, the castle has been home to the Percys, ancestral family of the Duke of Northumberland, since 1309. It is the second largest lived-in castle in England (after Windsor).

The exterior view of this austere and striking medieval fortress, with its life-size stone figures standing guard on the battlements, is in stark contrast to the sumptuous state rooms furnished in Italian Renaissance style. Adam ceilings and fireplaces are the legacy of restoration by the first Duke of Northumberland in the 18th century and there are fine paintings and porcelain.

The Regimental Museum of the Northumberland Fusiliers is housed in the Abbots Tower. Archaeological exhibits, the Percy coach, dungeon, gun terrace and landscaped grounds by Capability Brown are among other attractions. Often used as a film location, scenes from the 'Harry Potter' films have been filmed at the castle.

The Alnwick Garden (separate charge) is a project underway to transform the former 18th century sloping walled garden into a modern, innovative garden and notably features The Grand Cascade.

☎ 01665 511350　　　www.alnwickcastle.com
　　　　　　　　　　www.alnwickgarden.co.uk

Alnwick Castle & Gardens

🏛 Arbeia Roman Fort & Museum 　372 D1

In a commanding position at the mouth of the River Tyne, the Roman stone fort of Arbeia was the supply base for Hadrian's Wall. Reconstructed buildings, including the impressive West Gate, and a varied display of archaeological finds from weapons to jewellery, present a picture of life on the northern frontier of Roman Britain. Archaeologists may be seen at work on excavations and children will enjoy Time Quest, for which there is a charge, an opportunity to find out what it is like to be an archaeologist.

☎ 0191 456 1369

🏰 Auckland Castle 　262 B4

The official residence of the Bishop of Durham, dating back over 800 years, with state rooms and the magnificent 12th century St Peter's Chapel. Limited opening. Unusual 18th century Deer House in adjoining parkland.

☎ 01388 601627　　　www.auckland-castle.co.uk

🏛 BALTIC The Centre for Contemporary Art 　404 F3

Opened in 2002, the Baltic is housed in the former grain warehouse of a 1950s flour mill. It is a vast and imposing building close to the Tyne Bridge on the south bank of the river. There is no permanent collection but a changing programme of exhibitions displayed in five galleries with facilities to cater for all art media. Envisaged as an 'Art Factory', there are artists' studios and work is created through commissions and by the work of artists-in-residence. The centre has a rooftop restaurant with excellent views of Tyneside.

☎ 0191 478 1810　　　www.balticmill.com

BALTIC The Centre for Contemporary Art

🏰 Bamburgh Castle 　279 F3

Formidable Norman castle dominating the seaside village of Bamburgh, much restored in the 18th and 19th centuries but still retaining the original large square keep. The castle is stunningly situated on a rocky outcrop above a long white sandy beach with views seawards of the Farne Islands and Holy Island.

Bamburgh withstood many sieges but fell into disrepair after sustaining severe damage during the Wars of the Roses in 1464. The first Lord Armstrong, inventor, engineer and industrialist, carried out major restoration and refurbishment in the 19th century, and Bamburgh is still the home of the Armstrong family today.

Paintings, furniture, tapestries, china and glassware are displayed in the fine King's Hall and Cross Hall. The old laundry building houses an

Aviation Artefact Museum with many parts from crashed World War II aircraft, while the Armstrong Museum portrays the life of the first Lord Armstrong through his work as an engineer. There is an impressive collection of armour and a dungeon.

☎ 01668 214515　　　www.bamburghcastle.com

🏛 Beamish, North of England Open Air Museum 　262 B2

Celebrating the industrial, rural and social heritage of the north-east, Beamish shows how people lived and worked in the 1800s and early 1900s. A town, colliery village and railway station have been re-created with many authentic buildings being dismantled elsewhere and brought to the site. Staff in period costume are a wealth of information.

Visitors may go shopping in the town shops, and there is also a bank, dentist and newspaper office in the main street. Guided tours of the drift mine take visitors underground. The colliery village includes tiny pit cottages, a chapel and a school where playing with traditional toys in the playground is a popular activity. Cheese is made on a working farm, nearby is a manor house and, by way of contrast, there is a Victorian fairground.

Trams link the various areas, and replica buses and horse-drawn vehicles provide other means of transport. Covering over 300 acres (120ha), Beamish provides a full day out for all the family. Winner of both British and European Museum of the Year awards.

☎ 0191 370 4000　　　www.beamish.org.uk

🏛 Bede's World 　372 C2

Dedicated to the 8th century monk, the Venerable Bede, who chronicled the ecclesiastical history of the time, this is an absorbing day out for all the family. Bede's World incorporates the monastic site of St Paul's, a museum, an Anglo-Saxon demonstration farm and herb garden. Many fascinating archaeological finds are displayed in the interactive exhibition which explores early medieval life and Christian heritage.

☎ 0191 489 2106　　　www.bedesworld.co.uk

🏰 ✿ Belsay Hall, Castle & Gardens 　270 C4

30 acres (12ha) of picturesque landscaped gardens surround 19th century neo-classical Belsay Hall and a ruined Jacobean manor house with 14th century tower house. All were owned by the Middleton family for 600 years. Notable for a quarry garden, rhododendrons and many exotic species of plants. A winter garden ensures Belsay is worth a visit in any season.

☎ 01661 881636　　　www.english-heritage.org.uk

Bamburgh Castle

Beamish, North of England Open Air Museum

✞ Brinkburn Priory
270 D2

The Augustinian priory of Brinkburn, founded around 1135, is set amongst woodland beside the River Coquet. On a fine day the priory grounds are a lovely place for a picnic. Restored in the 19th century, the church of the original monastery survives intact and contains some striking wooden contemporary sculptures by Fenwick Lawson. Venue for the Brinkburn Music Summer Festival. Standing nearby is a Gothic style manor house.

☎ 01665 570628　　www.english-heritage.org.uk

🏛 Captain Cook Birthplace Museum
253 E1

Learn about the life of Captain James Cook and his voyages of exploration in this interesting hands-on museum that will appeal to adults and children alike. Located in the landscaped grounds of Stewart Park, close to where Cook was born.

☎ 01642 311211

🏠 ✳ Cragside (NT)
270 C1

Aptly named, the Victorian home of the first Lord Armstrong is built on a crag surrounded by rock gardens. Contains many original contents and fascinating gadgets invented by Armstrong. In the 1880s Cragside enjoyed central heating, hot and cold running water and, most remarkably, was lit by hydro-electricity using the man-made lakes in the grounds. Well-known for rhododendrons in late spring, the extensive and varied landscaped woodland estate can be explored by car or on foot.

☎ 01669 620333　　www.nationaltrust.org.uk

🏰 Dunstanburgh Castle (NT)
279 G4

Extensive and dramatic ruins of a 14th century castle on headland cliffs. Reached by coastal footpath from Craster or Embleton.

☎ 01665 576231　　www.english-heritage.org.uk/
www.nationaltrust.org.uk

Durham Cathedral

✞ Durham Cathedral
396 E2

Dominating the Durham city skyline, this awe-inspiring cathedral, with three massive towers, stands high above and in an almost complete loop of the River Wear. The present cathedral was largely built between 1093 and 1133 and is considered to be the greatest piece of Romanesque architecture in Britain. The nave, however, has pointed arches which makes it unique for this period.

The cathedral contains the tomb of Cuthbert, 7th century Bishop of Lindisfarne, and of the Venerable Bede who wrote about the life of St Cuthbert. Exhibitions tell the story of the cathedral and how it was built and 'The Treasures' in the 13th century undercroft displays St Cuthbert's cross and fragments of his coffin. The medieval Monk's Dormitory has a wonderful hammer-beam oak roof and houses part of the cathedral library. Visitors may climb the 325 steps of the tower.

Together with Durham Castle (built 1072), which is now part of the university, the cathedral is designated a World Heritage Site.

☎ 0191 386 4266　　www.durhamcathedral.co.uk

🏠 George Stephenson's Birthplace (NT)
262 A1

A small 18th century stone tenement where railway engineer George Stephenson was born in 1781. Typical of those built for mining families at that time, with whole families living in just one room, it is furnished as it may have been in Stephenson's day.

☎ 01661 843276　　www.nationaltrust.org.uk

Hadrian's Wall
261 G1

The wall is a well preserved and impressive Roman frontier fortification, built between AD122-128 on the orders of Emperor Hadrian at the height of the Roman Empire. It extends 73 miles (118km) from Bowness-on-Solway to Wallsend. No doubt intended as a symbol of Roman power, it was used to control trade and the movement of people in the region. It is now a designated World Heritage Site.

The original height of the wall was around 15ft (5m) and was bounded on the north by a defensive ditch and on the south by a ditch between turf ramparts. It included turret watch towers, milecastles and forts. The wall is all the more dramatic for much of it being built on ridges and crags and set amidst beautiful countryside. Numerous car parks on the B6318 give walkers access to the paths alongside the wall.

At the east end of the wall is Segedunum, the remains of a fort once holding a garrison of 600 soldiers, and now an award-winning museum. It includes a reconstructed section of wall and Roman baths, while nearby is 88yds (80m) of original wall.

www.hadrians-wall.org   www.english-heritage.org.uk

Hamsterley Forest
261 G5

A beautiful area of mixed woodland between Weardale and Teesdale, extending over 5000 acres (2000ha) with waymarked walks, horse riding trails and cycle routes. The Visitor Centre is the starting point of a 4 mile (6.5km) forest drive (toll charge).

☎ 01434 220242

Hancock Museum
404 D2

A small natural history museum with a wealth of exhibits, live animals and interactive displays showing how the planet and the animal and plant kingdoms evolved. A great place for children to visit, the Hancock also features the 'Land of the Pharaohs' gallery with two Egyptian mummies and a varied programme of touring exhibitions.

☎ 0191 222 6765

Hartlepool Historic Ships
263 E4

The lively Historic Quay is a reproduction of an 18th century seaport complete with shops, houses and a quayside littered with barrels, carts, anchors and ropes. Exhibitions in the quayside buildings give visitors a taste of seafaring at the time of Nelson, and there is an interactive children's maritime adventure centre. Staff in period costume add to the atmosphere.

Afloat in the dock is the restored *HMS Trincomalee*, a frigate built in 1817 by the East India Dock Company at Bombay (separate entry fee). Moored outside the nearby Museum of Hartlepool (free) is the paddle steamer *PSS Wingfield*, a former Humber ferry.

☎ 01429 860077

High Force
261 E5

Spectacular 70ft (21m) waterfall, said to be England's largest, in upper Teesdale. Reached by a pretty woodland walk.

Holy Island
279 F2

Holy Island is accessible by a causeway passable at low tide and is set within the Lindisfarne National Nature Reserve. Founded in the 7th century by St Aidan, the monastery at Lindisfarne became an important centre of Christian learning and the beautiful illuminated Lindisfarne Gospels were written here.

The ruined 12th century Benedictine priory has a rainbow arch still standing over the nave, and the museum contains notable Anglo-Saxon carvings and illustrates how the monks lived.

With stones taken from the priory, the formidable looking Lindisfarne Castle was built in the 16th century to protect the island from the Scots. Converted into a private home in 1903 by architect Edwin Lutyens, the castle contains a fine collection of early 17th century oak furniture and has a small walled garden designed by Gertrude Jekyll. Also on the island is a Heritage Centre and St Aidan's Winery, where Lindisfarne Mead is made. Entry to the island is free but there are charges for the attractions.

☎ Priory: 01289 389200   www.english-heritage.org.uk
☎ Castle: 01289 389244   www.nationaltrust.org.uk
☎ Heritage Centre: 01289 389044   www.lindisfarne-heritage-centre.org

Housesteads (Vercovicium) (NT)
261 D1

The best-preserved Roman fort in Britain, Housesteads was one of sixteen bases along Hadrian's Wall. Built around AD124 to house 800 infantry soldiers, it was in use until the end of the Roman occupation of Britain in the early 5th century. The fort contains the headquarters building, commander's house, barracks, hospital, latrines and granaries. There is a site museum.

☎ 01434 344363   www.english-heritage.org.uk
www.nationaltrust.org.uk

Howick Hall Gardens
279 G5

This was once the home of British Prime Minister Earl Grey, for whom the tea was blended to suit the water at Howick. Surrounding the 18th century house (not open) there are terraces, herbaceous borders and notably a woodland garden planted with rhododendrons, azaleas, camellias and magnolias. Lovely displays of snowdrops in February are followed by other spring bulbs. From the garden a path leads to a sandy cove at Howick Haven.

☎ 01665 577285   www.howickgarden.org.uk

Hadrian's Wall, Housesteads

Kielder Forest — 269 E2

In the remotest part of the Northumberland National Park, close to the Scottish border, Kielder Forest covers an area of 153,000 acres (62,000ha) with mainly Sitka spruce. There is estimated to be 150 million trees in the forest. Timber production is ongoing and an increasing diversity of trees is being planted. The forest is home to deer, red squirrels and many birds of prey, and surrounds Kielder Water, the largest man-made lake in Europe. Ideal for walking, cycling, boating and fishing, the area has three visitor centres and numerous tourist facilities. Sculpture trails and public art are also among the attractions in the Kielder area.

☎ 01434 220643   www.kielder.org

Laing Art Gallery — 404 E2

Internationally renowned watercolours hang in a dedicated gallery and the extensive collection of oil paintings include works by John Martin, Joshua Reynolds, Thomas Gainsborough, Holman Hunt, Burne Jones and a growing number of contemporary paintings. With the emphasis on locally produced decorative art, the Laing also has collections of silver, glass and ceramics. 'Art on Tyneside' illustrates the history of the region's art and craft traditions and there is a gallery specifically aimed at young children.

☎ 0191 232 7734

Life Science Centre — 404 F1

Interactive and entertaining educational centre which illustrates some of the mysteries of life. In innovative ways, such as a motion simulator ride and a sound and light show in a theatre modelled as a brain, the centre takes a look at evolution, the basics of DNA, what all living things have in common and what goes on in the human mind. Housed in a striking modern building next to Newcastle main line rail station.

☎ 0191 243 8223   www.lifesciencecentre.org.uk

National Glass Centre — 411 A3

An innovative metal and glass building on the north bank of the River Wear, dedicated to the use of glass in the fields of design and technology, and as contemporary art. Exhibitions and interactive galleries look at the centuries-old tradition of glassmaking in Sunderland, and illustrate the many and surprising ways in which glass is used today. Visitors may walk along the glass roof and watch students from the University of Sunderland in the glass factory. Master craftspeople also give regular demonstrations of glassmaking.

☎ 0191 515 5555   www.nationalglasscentre.com

Ormesby Hall (NT) — 253 E1

Set in an attractive garden, this 18th century Palladian mansion has some notable interior plasterwork and carved wood decoration. There is an impressive stable block still in use and a restored Victorian laundry and kitchen with scullery and game larder. Also of interest is a model railway exhibition.

☎ 01642 324188   www.nationaltrust.org.uk

Queen Elizabeth II Country Park — 271 E3

Once the site of one of the largest colliery spoil heaps in Europe, this landscaped country park features maturing woodland, a 40 acre (16ha) lake and a variety of wildlife. Ideal for picnics and walks. A cycle path runs around the lake where canoeing, windsurfing and fishing are popular. The Woodhorn Colliery Museum, on the edge of the park, is housed in former colliery buildings, and a narrow gauge railway runs for 0.6 miles (1km) linking the museum to the lakeside.

☎ 01670 856968

Raby Castle — 262 A5

An impressive medieval castle set in a 200 acre (80ha) deer park, Raby was built by the Nevills and has been home to Lord Barnard's family for over 350 years. The interior chambers provide many historical insights and range from the Barons' Hall, where 700 knights gathered to plot the 'Rising of the North', to the medieval kitchen which was used until 1954. Many of the rooms date from the 18th and 19th centuries and contain works of art and fine furniture. Visitors can also enjoy the grounds which include a large walled garden, rose garden and old yew hedges.

☎ 01833 660202   www.rabycastle.com

Seaton Delaval Hall — 271 F4

A splendid Palladian mansion designed by Sir John Vanbrugh in 1718, after he had already completed Blenheim Palace and Castle Howard. The central turreted block has a grand portico and is flanked by two substantial wings which creates a vast forecourt. A fine parterre, pond and fountain created in the 20th century complements the house and there are impressive stables in the east wing. Limited opening.

☎ 0191 237 1493

Shipley Art Gallery — 372 A2

An arts and crafts museum with a renowned collection of contemporary furniture, textiles, metalwork, ceramics, glass and jewellery. By way of contrast, there are some old masters paintings and an exhibition illustrating the history of Gateshead.

☎ 0191 477 1495

South Shields Museum & Art Gallery — 372 D1

This museum brings to life the 20th century social history of South Tyneside and illustrates the dramatic changes which have taken place during that time. Also features the story of popular novelist Catherine Cookson who was born locally in 1906 and whose writing reflects the life and times of the area. Alongside the museum's art collection, the interactive art gallery gives visitors the opportunity to explore the techniques and materials used by artists.

☎ 0191 456 8740

Teesdale Hay Meadows, Forest-in-Teesdale — 261 E5

The rich grasslands of the North Pennines provide a wonderful display in summer when the hay meadows are awash with a striking variety and abundance of tall grasses. Additionally, a vast assortment of wild flowers, including wood anemone, frog orchid, adder's tongue fern and ragged robin will be found blossoming amongst the grasses. The area also attracts nesting farmland birds such as redshank, skylark and meadow pipit.

Vindolanda (Chesterholm) Roman Fort — 261 D1

The remains of a Roman fort (AD127) and surrounding civilian settlement about 2 miles (3km) south of Hadrian's Wall. There are ongoing excavations and archaeologists have revealed a succession of forts on the site. The well-preserved artefacts in the museum include armour, boots, shoes, jewellery and coins. Among the most significant finds have been letters and documents written in ink on wood; photographs of these tablets are on display. A section of Hadrian's Wall has been reconstructed in timber and stone to its original height and there are full-scale replicas of a Roman temple, shop, house and a Northumbrian croft.

☎ 01434 344277   www.vindolanda.com

Wallington (NT) — 270 C3

Built in 1688, Wallington was for generations home to the Blackett and Trevelyan families. The house contains fine rococo plasterwork and the central hall is decorated in Pre-Raphaelite style with pictures reflecting Northumbrian history. There are paintings and porcelain as well as a collection of dolls' houses. The extensive grounds include a beautiful walled garden and Edwardian conservatory, woodland and a path along the banks of the River Wansbeck.

☎ 01670 773600   www.nationaltrust.org.uk

Warkworth Castle — 271 E1

Standing on a hill above the River Coquet, the well-preserved ruins dominate the town of Warkworth. The castle was once home to the powerful Percy family and was the setting for several scenes in Shakespeare's 'Henry IV'. Dating mainly from the 12th to the 14th centuries, the remains include a magnificent eight-towered keep, chapel, great hall and decorated lion tower. Special events for visitors are regularly staged here.

☎ 01665 711423   www.english-heritage.org.uk

Wildfowl & Wetlands Trust Washington — 372 C3

Many species of waterbirds can be enjoyed in any season in this area of ponds and woodland. It provides a stopping place and wintering habitat for migratory birds after their flight across the North Sea. Large numbers of curlew and redshank roost here and there is a breeding colony of heron. The site is easily accessible with well laid out paths. It has hides and an excellent visitor centre.

☎ 0191 416 5454

Yeavering Bell — 278 D4

This hill at the edge of the Cheviots is crowned by the largest Iron Age hillfort in Northumbria covering 14 acres (6ha) with a stone rampart enclosing much of the summit. A steep path leads to the top, from where there are spectacular views over the surrounding landscape.

WALES

Dwelling in the "Land of Song", the Welsh nation treasures a proud culture based on Europe's oldest language which is still very much alive today. Three sides of the predominantly rural principality are fringed with beckoning shorelines. Sparkling water tumbles down the rugged mountainsides into beautiful lakes which act as mirrors for the stunning scenery and ever changing sky. Experience the grandeur and wildness of three national parks with all their varied natural glory and absorb the Welsh history glimpsed in her castles, crafts and Celtic heritage.

Llynnau Mymbyr and Snowdon

Aberconwy House (NT) · 231 F5

A 14th century merchant's house within the town of Conwy containing furnished rooms and an audiovisual presentation. Displays depict scenes of daily life from nearly six centuries.

☎ 01492 592246 · www.nationaltrust.org.uk

Aberdulais Falls (NT) · 350 D1

Natural waterfalls in the Vale of Neath provide the energy for a fascinating industrial site with a unique hydroelectric scheme. Over four centuries, a waterwheel provided the power for the production of copper and tin goods. Today the Turbine House contains an interactive computer, fish pass, display panels and an observation window with good views of the falls.

☎ 01639 636674 · www.nationaltrust.org.uk

Aberglasney Gardens · 192 B5

Restored in recent years to reveal Jacobean origins, the 10 acres (4ha) of colourful gardens lie in a valley east of Carmarthen. Known as 'The Garden Lost in Time', the area features pools, a yew tunnel, walled gardens, an ancient cloister garden and woodland, as well as collections of rare plants.

☎ 01558 668998 · www.aberglasney.org.uk

Abergwesyn Pass · 193 E2

A scenic, remote 14 mile (22km) drive crosses the Cambrian Mountains following an old drovers' route. The lower forests give way to high, deserted moorland providing a taste of wild Wales.

Afan Argoed Country Park · 179 E3

Deep in the Afan valley, inland from Port Talbot, the Forest Park covers 25 tranquil square miles (10 ha) with trails for walking and cycling, orienteering, picnic areas, camping, pony trekking and educational visits. The visitor centre features the history and wildlife of the area, including historical remains from early settlements and the South Wales Miners' Museum created by ex-colliers. Charge for car parking in summer.

☎ 01639 850564 · www.neath-porttalbot.gov.uk

Anglesey Sea Zoo · 217 D1

A varied collection of local marine life is housed in Wales' largest marine aquarium, on the shores of the Menai Strait. The Sea Zoo has a walk-through shipwreck, lobster hatchery and discovery pools, as well as a shark pool and fish forest. Tropical displays are also included and conservation is an important aspect of the work of the zoo. Outside is an adventure playground, boating lake and seasonal crab fishing.

☎ 01248 430411 · www.angleseyseazoo.co.uk

Barry Island Pleasure Park · 165 E1

Occupying a promontory south of Cardiff, the Park has over 50 rides and attractions including the popular Log Flume, Viper Rollercoaster, Sea Ray Pirate Ship and Galloping Horses. The Park is surrounded by shops and catering facilities.

☎ 01446 732844 · www.barryisland.com

Beaumaris Castle · 231 E5

The castle sits in the town of Beaumaris, on the shores of the Menai Strait, and offers fine views across to the mountains of Snowdonia. This was the last and largest of King Edward's edifices, erected to establish his authority over the Welsh. Beaumaris Castle was started in 1295 and, although never fully completed, it remains remarkably intact and is a designated UNESCO World Heritage Site.

Here is an impressive example of military architecture, having an outer moat and perfectly symmetrical double concentric walls within. The fortified dock has moorings for ships of considerable size. The high walls, gatehouses and strong towers were intended as stout defences, but the castle never came under attack. The inner buildings accommodated a Great Hall, luxurious rooms, kitchens, stables and a chapel. Visitors can also explore the fascinating interior passageways found inside the walls of the inner ward.

☎ 01248 810361 · www.cadw.wales.gov.uk

Big Pit Mining Museum

Big Pit Mining Museum · 180 B2

Overlooking a traditional mining valley at Blaenavon, Big Pit had been a working coal mine for over 200 years until its closure in 1980. The present tour guides are all former miners. On the surface are colliery workings, reconstructed buildings and the old pit-head baths to explore, but the main attraction is the 300ft (90m) descent in the pit cage; hard hat and lamp are provided. The hour-long guided tour recalls life at the coal face and leads through underground roadways, air doors and stables to the shafts and coal faces. Warm clothing and appropriate footwear are advised and restrictions apply to young children going underground. The whole experience merits two to three hours and catering is supplied by the original miners' canteen. Education packs are available and special events are arranged throughout the season.

☎ 01495 790311 · www.nmgw.ac.uk/bigpit

Bodnant Gardens (NT) · 231 G5

Renowned for the dazzling springtime and early summer blooms, these 80 acres (32.5ha) of magnificent gardens overlook the river Conwy and distant Snowdonia. An array of colours is provided, especially by the collections of rhododendrons, camellias and magnolias and a vibrant laburnum arch. The garden has been developed over its hundred year history by generations of the Aberconway family and includes a succession of terraces featuring a water lily pond, roses, a croquet lawn, a canal and magnolias. A woodland valley garden, known as The Dell, provides an attractive contrast to the formal plantings of the Italianate terraces.

At the end of the formal garden sits the Pin Mill, an early 18th century lodge which became a pin factory, then a tannery, before being transported from the west of England to its present site.

The botanical collections nurtured at Bodnant are world famous, but beauties also abound which require little knowledge of plants. The gardens are planted on a hillside and run right down to the river.

☎ 01492 650460 · www.nationaltrust.org.uk

Bodnant Gardens

Brecon Beacons · 193 G5

Four distinct upland ranges lie within the beautiful national park which extends over 520 sq m (837 sq km) in the heart of southern Wales. The picturesque landscape is characterised not only by gentle, grassy hillsides and light woodlands, but also by steep craggy mountains. Central are the prominent Beacons themselves, rising to 2906ft (886m) at the summit of Pen-y-Fan. In the west are the rolling hills of Fforest Fawr with their deep valleys and ancient hunting forest and also the solitary, wild Black Mountain. The range known as the Black Mountains lies at the eastern edge of the park towards the English border. The most southerly region offers a landscape of caves and waterfalls amongst the limestone pavements.

Prehistoric sites have been identified within the park and later structures follow the progress of history through the ambitious days of castle building after the Norman conquest.

Within its five visitor centres, the park authorities promote a large variety of attractions for all ages, including museums, theatres and family activity

Beaumaris Castle

WALES

centres. In the open air are a wealth of opportunities for walking, cycling, horse-riding, caving, gliding, watersports, golf and fishing. Expert tuition is available for trying new skills and there are facilities for hiring and purchasing appropriate equipment.

☎ 01874 624437   www.breconbeacons.org

Brecon Beacons

⭐ Brecon Beacons Visitor Centre   `193 F5`

At an altitude of 1100ft (335m), amidst the grandeur of the Brecon Beacon mountains, the purpose-built centre houses resource material, souvenirs, a model and displays of the area, as well as a café. The centre is surrounded by open hillside, giving wide views across the valley to the distinctive summit of Pen y Fan, the highest peak in South Wales. Informative staff and printed guides describe local points of interest and suggest a fine variety of walks, graded from easy to moderate.

☎ 01874 623366   www.breconbeacons.org

🚂 Brecon Mountain Railway   `179 G1`

This narrow-gauge railway, starting at Pant Station just north of Merthyr Tydfil, follows a scenic 3.5 mile (5km) track into the Brecon Beacon mountains. The all-weather observation coaches are hauled by a vintage steam locomotive; the return journey takes just over an hour. Panoramic views abound from the end station where there are many opportunities for walks and a picnic site. Special events are organised at certain times of year and the train can be hired for parties.

☎ 01685 722988   www.breconmountainrailway.co.uk

☐ Cadair Idris   `204 C1`

Steeped in Celtic legends, the beautiful 11 mile (17km) ridge of Cadair Idris, on the southern flank of the Snowdonia National Park, comprises five peaks, with the highest point, Penygadair, at almost 3000ft (900m). A variety of tracks, varying in difficulty, lead to the ridge, and all give breathtaking views of the surrounding countryside and the distant coast.

🏛 Caerleon Roman Fortress, Baths & Amphitheatre   `351 D1`

North of Newport stand the substantial remains of a Roman fortress, including the baths, barrack blocks, fortress wall and 5000-seater amphitheatre, together with an imaginative Roman legionary museum. This is the site of the significant 50 acre (20ha) Roman fortress of Isca, encompassing a complete town dating from AD75, with much still on view. The museum shows how the Romans lived and fought, with interactive displays and special events suitable for all ages, sufficient for several hours' visit.

☎ 01633 423134   www.nmgw.ac.uk

Caerphilly Castle

🏰 Caernarfon Castle   `217 D1`

Built on a promontory projecting out into the Menai Strait, this UNESCO World Heritage Site castle dominates the town of Caernarfon and has

Caernarfon Castle

survived in fine condition. Construction was started by Edward I in 1283 as part of his ring of castles intended to control Welsh uprisings, and it was planned as a royal residence and seat of government. The building was completed by Edward II in 1322. Massive walls run between the 11 great polygonal towers, topped by battlemented wall walks, giving the castle formidable defences. Also incorporated into the scheme were drawbridges, heavy doors and six portcullises. Each of the towers is different and one included a water gate enabling supplies to be brought by sea.

The Queen's Tower houses the regimental museum of the Royal Welch Fusiliers. An audiovisual presentation explains the history and customs associated with the castle. Continuing a tradition established by Edward I, the castle is the venue for the investiture of the Prince of Wales, as was the scene in 1969 when Prince Charles was presented to the people here.

☎ 01286 677617   www.cadw.wales.gov.uk

🏰 Caerphilly Castle   `351 A1`

Right in the town centre, Caerphilly is the largest castle in Wales, but was never a royal residence. It was built by Red Gilbert de Clare to defend the territory of Henry III against Welsh Prince Llywelyn the Last. The medieval fortress, started in 1268, occupies a strategically important 30 acre (12ha) site, having a complex design of massive gatehouses, water defences and stout concentric walls. The most unusual feature of the castle is one of the towers which leans outwards at an angle ten degrees from vertical – the result of subsidence.

An extensive water system provided the first point of defence around the castle, followed by a rectangular enclosure with robust outer and inner walls. The latter contain two great gatehouses and the remains of the hall. In the heart of the castle are the living areas, together with kitchens, a chapel and domestic quarters.

Over the past 200 years the complex has undergone much restoration. Visitors can watch an audiovisual display and see replica siege engines in the visitor centre.

☎ 029 2088 3143   www.cadw.wales.gov.uk

🏰 Cardiff Castle & Museum   `392 E2`

The castle is situated in the heart of the city and was commissioned in Victorian times by the 3rd

Marquess of Bute in an elaborate neogothic style. Highly decorative, fantasy adornments abound, particularly in the clock tower, fountains and lavish interiors. The Welsh Regiment Museum is situated within the castle grounds.

☎ 029 2087 8100   www.cardiffcastle.com

🏰 Carew Castle   `176 D2`

The substantial ruins of Carew Castle stand on river meadows between the village and an ancient tidal mill. The castle was built between the 13th and 16th centuries and was the site of the Great Tournament of 1507. Firstly a Norman stronghold, then an elegant royal Elizabethan residence, it displays many fine architectural features. A circular walk links the castle, mill, causeway, millpond, 11th century Celtic cross and medieval bridge.

☎ 01646 651782   www.carewcastle.com

🏰 Carreg Cennen Castle   `178 C1`

These old ruins, high on a crag near Trapp in the Black Mountains, were rebuilt in the 13th and 19th centuries. Visitors can explore prehistoric caves, battlements and vaulted passageways, and enjoy the outlook from the grassy hilltop.

☎ 01558 822291   www.cadw.wales.gov.uk

🏰 Castell Dinas Bran (Ruins)   `219 F3`

Both a hillfort and medieval castle, the ruins stand high above Llangollen. It is reputedly the final hiding place of the Holy Grail, a treasured Christian relic. Access is by public footpath taking some 20 minutes each way.

☎ 01938 553670

⭐ Celtica   `204 D3`

This multimedia presentation focusing on the Celts is housed in Y Plas, a 17th century mansion just outside Machynlleth. The lively experience provides information on the heritage and culture of the Celts by way of an hour-long audio tour through eight themed galleries. Topics range from culture and beliefs to life as a tribe member, and are located within areas described, for example, as the Vortex, the Foundry, the Roundhouse and The Forest.

☎ 01654 702702   www.celticawales.com

⭐ Centre For Alternative Technology   `205 D2`

Situated in the hills north of Machynlleth, the Centre for Alternative Technology has been operating for over 25 years by a charity raising awareness of environmental concerns in daily living. The gardens and visitor centre provide information on renewable energy, environmental building, energy efficiency and organic cultivation in a captivating and educational way. Seven acres (3ha) of the site are on public display and can be accessed in summer by a water-balanced cliff railway. Attractions and resources are suitable for all ages.

☎ 01654 702400   www.cat.org.uk

🏛 Ceredigion Museum   `204 B4`

A restored Edwardian theatre is home to this museum of local history from the Stone Age to modern times. Displays include items of archaeology, folk life, agriculture, crafts, industry and art.

☎ 01970 633088   www.ceredigion.gov.uk

🏰 Chepstow Castle   `181 E3`

Strategically set overlooking a Wye Valley gorge, Chepstow was one of the first stone castles to be built in Britain. Construction was commenced in 1068 as a stronghold for the Norman conquest of south-east Wales and is unusual in having no early timber base. Over successive centuries the defences were enlarged and in the 12th century the impressive edifice was divided into four separate, connecting sections. Towering over the present-day entrance is the gatehouse containing a prison in one of its round towers. Further additions included a second hall, tower, gatehouse and comfortable living quarters with well-equipped kitchens and storerooms.

The castle came under siege twice during the Civil War and now visitors can see exhibitions on the history of its construction. Life-sized models of the medieval lords who occupied the castle, and a dramatic Civil War battle scene illustrate the changing role of Chepstow Castle through the Middle Ages. Outdoor evening theatre is often performed here in summer.

☎ 01291 624065   www.cadw.wales.gov.uk

Chepstow Castle

🏛 Chepstow Museum   `181 E3`

An elegant town house has been transformed into a museum describing the town's colourful history in imaginative settings. Displays and artistic interpretations show the development of Chepstow as a fortified stronghold and busy port.

☎ 01291 625981   www.chepstow.co.uk

🏰 Chirk Castle (NT)   `219 F4`

The castle, to the west of Chirk, still has the original 14th century high walls and drum towers and has been continuously occupied for over 400 years. The state rooms contain fine items of furniture, tapestries and portraits. The formal gardens adjoining the castle contain superb yews, roses and climbing plants, whilst further away lie a hawk house, rock garden and shrub garden with pool. Parkland surrounds the estate and particularly noteworthy are the wrought iron entrance gates.

☎ 01691 777701   www.nationaltrust.org.uk

❀ Colby Woodland Garden (NT)   `177 E2`

The garden is set in 8 acres (3ha) of beautiful woodland in a sheltered valley leading to the south Pembrokeshire coast at Amroth. The colourful bluebells, rhododendrons and azaleas are at their best in late spring, but at other times plants also feature around a themed sculpture trail, a walled kitchen garden and a Gothic-style gazebo.

☎ 01834 811885   www.nationaltrust.org.uk

🏰 Conwy Castle   `231 F5`

Occupying an imposing location over the river in the centre of Conwy town, the castle is one of the most important examples of military architecture in Europe. It was built for Edward I in 1283-9 by 1500 craftsmen, with supplies brought in by sea. Eight huge drum towers with pinnacled battlements dominate the two wards of the castle. The large outer ward was accessed from the town, whereas the inner ward, with the royal apartments, was approached only by water. The Middle Gate connected the two sections. The building remains in an excellent state of preservation, despite having suffered attacks during the Civil War and later.

An exhibition portrays Edward I and his campaign of castle building. The panoramic views from the top of the turrets stretch to the distant mountains and out across the sea, but the castle itself is best viewed from the far side of the estuary.

☎ 01492 592358   www.cadw.wales.gov.uk

🏞 Cosmeston Country Park   `165 E1`

Old quarries just west of Cardiff have been transformed into a 200 acre (81ha) landscaped park, featuring two lakes with watersports, facilities for children, orienteering courses, a forest school, bridleways, a sculpture trail and a maths trail. Woodland, grassland and wetlands support conservation areas. Within the park lies a 14th century reconstructed medieval village which hosts special events throughout the year and which can be toured on payment of an entrance charge.

☎ 029 2070 1678   www.valeofglamorgan.gov.uk

🏰 Criccieth Castle   `217 E4`

Overlooking Tremadog Bay, the ruins include the inner wall, impressive gatehouse and original wall walk dating from the 13th century. A cartoon video shows the story of Gerald of Wales and other Welsh princes.

☎ 01766 52227   www.cadw.wales.gov.uk

Conwy Castle

🏰 Denbigh Castle   219 D1

The ruins of this Norman fortification overlook Denbigh town. It retains a large gatehouse, three towers, a steep barbican and an ancient, weathered statue, probably of Edward I.

☎ 01745 813385   www.cadw.wales.gov.uk

Erddig

🐾 Dinefwr Park (NT)   192 C5

Pleasant walks cross this wooded parkland just outside Llandeilo. Deer have been a feature of the estate for over one thousand years and Lancelot 'Capability' Brown designed the landscape around a medieval castle and Newton House.

☎ 01558 823902   www.nationaltrust.org.uk

⭐ Dolaucothi Gold Mine (NT)   192 C3

At Pumsaint, in deepest Wales, the Romans discovered gold deposits in the river Cothi and evidence remains of their sophisticated and ingenious tunnels, aqueducts and caverns. A second gold rush followed in the late nineteenth century and now visitors, equipped with miners' lamps and helmets, can tour the workings, hear the history and try gold panning for themselves. Waymarked paths lead through the surrounding wooded hillsides.

☎ 01558 825146   www.nationaltrust.org.uk

⭐ Elan Valley Visitor Centre   192 F1

Four artificial lakes were created in the valley in the early 20th century to provide water for Birmingham. The Visitor Centre is approached from Rhayader and contains an exhibition and interactive resources on the history and nature of the area, renowned for its birdlife. Walks lead around the reservoirs in the peaceful Cambrian mountains, giving good vantage points of the dams and drowned valleys. The area is particularly attractive in autumn.

☎ 01597 810880   www.elanvalley.org.uk

⭐ Electric Mountain   217 E1

A fascinating view inside the Dinorwig hydroelectric station near Llanberis includes interactive exhibitions and art galleries. Visitors can book an underground minibus tour deep inside the mountain to see the enormous turbines in action. The natural science theatre offers a presentation on the natural history of the Snowdonia area.

☎ 01286 870636   www.electricmountain.co.uk

🏛 ✴ Erddig (NT)   220 A3

Dating from the 18th century, this impressive estate near Wrexham was the home of the Yorke family, whose generosity towards their staff can be appreciated by viewing the large house. The grand 'upstairs' state rooms boast fine collections of furniture and original artefacts, whilst 'below stairs' the servants' quarters give fascinating glimpses into the lives of the workers. An extensive range of outbuildings are also of considerable interest and include a display of vintage vehicles in the stable yard. There is much to attract all ages, and regular event days are planned throughout the season, including horse-drawn carriage rides.

Walks lead through the garden areas into a large park with woodland. The gardens feature an array of speciality fruit trees, the national collection of ivies, a Victorian parterre and yew walks.

As most rooms have no electric lighting, it is advisable to visit on bright days to fully appreciate the pictures and textiles.

☎ 01978 315151   www.nationaltrust.org.uk

Ffestiniog Railway

🚂 Ffestiniog Railway   217 F3

The 13.5 mile (20km) narrow-gauge railway links Blaenau Ffestiniog with the harbour at Porthmadog. Now it is a quaint passenger ride, but it was first opened in 1836 as a means of carrying slate from the quarries. The high demand for slate brought steam power to the line, which is one of its main attractions. Interesting feats of engineering can be observed on the journey, including the Cob, a substantial embankment across the river estuary, and, higher up near Tanygrisiau, the only spiral on a public railway in Britain.

Not only is the railway, with its original rolling stock, appealing to enthusiasts, but the location amidst the glorious scenery of Snowdonia makes the route highly popular with all visitors. It is possible to leave the train at a number of stations en route and the situation of Tan-y-Bwlch station makes it an ideal starting point for beautiful walks. Blaenau Ffestiniog station is now linked with the standard gauge line from Llandudno Junction. Shops can be found at three of the stations, with

displays and stocks of railway memorabilia and souvenirs. The railway runs to a set timetable and offers special 'Guest Driving' days.

☎ 01766 516024   www.festrail.co.uk

🏛 Glynn Vivian Art Gallery & Museum   411 E2

The gallery contains examples of fine art, decorative and applied art, costume, textiles and archives. Of special interest is the collection of porcelain and Swansea china, in addition to the contributions from contemporary Welsh artists.

☎ 01792 516900   www.swansea.gov.uk

⬜ Gower   178 A4

The peninsula of Gower, west of Swansea, is 15 miles (24km) long and about 6 miles (10km) wide with many historical features. Gower is also an Area of Outstanding Natural Beauty thanks to both its coastal and inland environments. The shoreline follows cliffs, dunes, beaches, marshes and river estuaries, whilst the interior comprises pleasant hills, valleys, woods, heaths, caves and commons. Gower Heritage Centre at Parkmill contains a crafts and rural life museum based around a working medieval water mill.

www.swansea.gov.uk

⭐ Great Aberystwyth Camera Obscura   204 B4

High on Constitution Hill at the north end of town, and accessed by a cliff railway, this is the world's biggest Camera Obscura. The huge 14 inch (35cm) lens focuses on over 1000 square miles (400 ha) of land and seascape, all reflected onto a circular screen in the viewing gallery below.

☎ 01970 617642   www.cardiganshirecoastandcountry.com

🌳 Great Orme Country Park   231 F4

The imposing headland to the west of Llandudno is 2 miles (3km) long and can be accessed by footpaths, road, bus, Victorian Tramway or cabin lift. Of interest are the geology, rich wildlife, archaeology and landscape of the peninsula, in addition to a visitor centre, gardens, a copper mine, and leisure facilities such as a ski slope and a programme of events on land and water.

☎ 01492 874151   www.conwy.gov.uk

🏰 Harlech Castle   217 E4

This rugged castle was built on the rocks above Cardigan Bay, once lapped by waves, but now overlooking sand dunes where the sea has retreated. Construction began during Edward I's second campaign in Wales from 1283, and its protected position, walls and artillery platforms made the castle stoutly defensible. It was taken by Owain Glyndwr in the siege of 1404, in the last great uprising of the Welsh against the occupying English, and was held by him for four years.

The castle is concentric, with strong outer walls. The inner walls contained the main living quarters, and the imposing twin-towered gatehouse, with its residential apartments, is one of the main features of the castle. The massive eastern façade, the guardroom and the castle's wide round towers, designed to intimidate attackers, are all impressive. The entrance is at the position of a second drawbridge which

Harlech Castle

used to lower onto towers, of which only the foundations remain. The mighty structure commands superb views out to sea and to the mountains of Snowdonia.

☎ 01766 780552   www.cadw.wales.gov.uk

Kidwelly Castle   178 A2

The substantial and well preserved remains of Kidwelly Castle, south of Carmarthen, are set within the site of an earlier earth and timber ringwork. The massive, concentric castle was started in the mid 13th century and developed impressively over three centuries, eventually becoming a judicial court. The entrance is guarded by a large gatehouse and visitors can climb the round towers, walk on the extensive walls and explore the dungeons.

☎ 01554 890104   www.cadw.wales.gov.uk

Lamphey Palace   176 D2

Just east of Pembroke, the ruins of this medieval bishop's palace remain an impressive sight, surrounded by fishponds, orchards and parkland. Of particular note are the shell of the Great Hall and the chapel.

☎ 01646 672224   www.pembroke-wales.uk.com

Llanberis Lake Railway   217 E1

This scenic narrow-gauge railway skirts Lake Padarn, near Llanberis, with great views of Snowdon. Steam locomotives haul the tourist carriages and the return trip of 5 miles (8km) takes about an hour, including stops.

☎ 01286 870549   www.lake-railway.freeserve.co.uk

Llanerchaeron (NT)   192 A2

This little-changed 1790s gentleman's estate comprises a carefully restored, Nash-designed house with outbuildings, now operating as an organic farm. Produce is on sale and walks lead through the wooded valleys.

☎ 01558 825147   www.nationaltrust.org.uk

Llansteffan Castle (ruins)   177 G1

The castle ruins sit on a steep ridge overlooking Carmarthen Bay and are witness to its expansion since its Norman origins. Visible now are two baileys surrounded by thick walls and a Tudor gatehouse.

☎ 01267 241756   www.cadw.wales.gov.uk

Llanthony Priory (ruins)   194 B5

Hidden in a remote valley in the Black Mountains, the substantial ruins of this ancient Cistercian priory form a striking picture against the green surrounding hillsides. The priory was built in the 12th century and includes examples of both Gothic and Norman architecture. The monastic foundation was soon abandoned and the buildings fell into disuse. However, today there is a small inn and hotel built into the part of the priory where the abbot would once have lived.

☎ 029 2082 6185   www.cadw.wales.gov.uk

Llechwedd Slate Caverns   218 A3

Tours of the massive slate caverns in Blaenau Ffestiniog include underground rides, sound and light shows, and a hard hat walk bringing to life the days of the Victorian miners. The Deep Mine tour descends steeply by railway car and the Miners' Tramway focuses on the historical details of the industry. On the surface stands the original Llechwedd village with facilities for visitors.

☎ 01766 830306   www.llechwedd-slate-caverns.co.uk

Manorbier Castle   177 D3

Accessed by a delightful narrow lane, Manorbier Castle overlooks a sandy bay in south Pembrokeshire. Once a Norman stronghold, today's structure dates from the 12th century and is in remarkably good condition. The castle has many interesting features, including a baronial hall, stout gatehouse, state apartments, gardens and a chapel. The family of the current owners have lived here for over 300 years and it was the birthplace, in 1146, of Giraldus Cambrensis who wrote extensively of his travels around Wales.

☎ 01834 871394

Museum of Welsh Life   180 A5

A fascinating open-air museum covering 100 acres (40ha) near Cardiff illustrates the rich heritage of Wales, showing lifestyles, buildings and traditions through five hundred years of folk history. Original buildings have been transported here from many parts of Wales and painstakingly reconstructed, including craftsmen's workshops, a school, cottages, shops, a mill, farmhouse and a chapel. Demonstrations of many crafts enliven a visit and hands-on opportunities are available for visitors to try their skills. Produce from the farm, mill and other sources on the site are often on sale.

The museum is situated in the grounds of the impressive St Fagans castle which is also open, as are the surrounding gardens. Purpose-built, large indoor galleries house exhibits of costume, daily life and farming implements. Traditional festivals, music and dance events are staged regularly throughout the year. To do justice to the whole enterprise, which has no entrance charge, and to allow time to explore the extensive grounds, at least a half day visit is recommended.

☎ 029 2057 3500   www.nmgw.ac.uk

National Botanic Garden of Wales   178 B1

The Millennium showpiece Garden of Wales lies in the Tywi Valley, upstream from Carmarthen in a peaceful 18th century park of 568 acres (230ha). With the aim of raising awareness of the natural and manmade world, it focuses on conservation, horticulture, science, the arts, leisure and education.

The centrepiece of the garden is the impressive Great Glasshouse, designed by Norman Foster to hold 1000 panes and containing plants from the world over in their natural climates. Outside, the landscape has been built with a deep ravine, rock terraces, waterfalls and lakes to display a multitude of different plantings. Separate sections include a genetic garden and a physic garden. Visitors are encouraged to enjoy the sights, taste the country, experience the sounds, and smell the seasonal scents.

The Gallery in the Garden has a changing schedule of exhibitions on themes such as arts and science, botanical illustration, photography, traditional and contemporary art. Educational programmes are geared to all ages using state-of-the-art technology, and the Garden has become an internationally renowned centre for botanical science.

☎ 01558 668768   www.gardenofwales.org.uk

National Museum & Gallery   392 E2

Found in the heart of Cardiff, this lively museum covers the fascinating 4600 million year history of Wales up to the present day. It is well known for its art treasures, particularly the fine collection of French Impressionist works, but also covers science and natural history through interactive hands-on exhibits. Special events are staged for families, and temporary exhibitions merit further enquiry.

☎ 029 2039 7951   www.nmgw.ac.uk

National Showcaves Centre for Wales   178 B1

An awesome series of natural caves under the Brecon Beacons at Dan-yr-Ogof offers a variety of attractions suitable for the whole family. Self-guided tours lead through the skilfully illuminated chambers of the huge Cathedral showcave and the Bronze Age Bone cave, accompanied by commentaries. It is advisable to wear warm clothing and stout shoes. Other areas are devoted to an Iron Age farm, dinosaur park, museum, shire horse centre and farmyard.

☎ 01639 730801   www.showcaves.co.uk

National Woollen Museum   191 G4

A former, busy woollen mill in northern Carmarthenshire has been transformed into a

National Botanic Garden of Wales

WALES

museum on the history of the industry. Working exhibitions demonstrate the technical process of 19th century production from the fleece to the fabric. Within the grounds are craft workshops and also Melin Teifi, a fully working mill.

☎ 01559 370929 — www.nmgw.ac.uk

🦌 Newborough Warren — 216 D1

This long stretch of dunes to the south-west of Anglesey is part of a nature reserve, giving distant views to Snowdonia. Natural life abounds and footpaths also give access to a pine forest.

🎡 Oakwood Leisure Park — 177 D1

Well signposted in south Pembrokeshire, Oakwood is a major theme park with some of the fastest, tallest and wettest rides in the country. Children are catered for with age-appropriate attractions, including the KidzWorld play area. In summer holidays the park stays open until 10pm for a spectacular fireworks and waterscreen light show.

☎ 01834 891373 — www.oakwood-leisure.com

🏰 Oystermouth Castle (ruins) — 350 A3

Although ruined, Oystermouth Castle, on its mound at the west of Swansea Bay, is well preserved. Of note are its late 13th century decorated windows, gatehouse, chapel and Great Hall.

☎ 01792 368732 — www.cadw.wales.gov.uk

🌲 Pembrey Country Park — 178 A2

A 500 acre (202ha) wooded park, Pembrey lies on a sandy stretch of coast south of Carmarthen. The 8 mile (13 km) long Cefn Sidan beach is noted for its swimming and fishing. Other facilities provided (some with entrance charges) are crazy golf, dry ski slope, forest walks, nature trails, horse riding and a small railway.

☎ 01554 833913 — www.carmarthenshire.gov.uk

🏰 Pembroke Castle — 176 C2

Its defensive situation above the river in Pembroke enhances the grandeur of this largely intact castle. The birthplace of Henry VII, the first Tudor king, it has a remarkable history dating back 800 years. The stronghold survived ferocious attacks during the Civil War, but still much remains, including the enormous 80ft (24m) high round keep, thick ramparts, a gatehouse, barbican, Great Hall and dungeon tower. There is an interpretive centre, brass rubbing and special living history days in summer.

☎ 01646 681510 — www.pembrokeshirecoast.org

◻ Pembrokeshire Coast National Park — 176 B3

Britain's only truly coastal national park covers 240 sq m (620 sq km) of spectacular landscape around Wales' south-western shore. It is renowned for its beautiful scenery, prolific variety of wildlife and historic significance.

The 200 mile (320km) coastal path can be strenuous in parts, but many stretches provide gentler walks. Nowhere in the park is further than 10 miles (16km) distant from the sea. The landscape ranges from steep cliffs to expansive beaches, wooded slopes and inland hills, all supporting special habitats for many rare and endangered plants, birds and animals. Grey seals, porpoises and dolphins may be glimpsed off shore, and some of the maritime islands are home to huge, protected colonies of seabirds. Inland areas are also worth exploring to discover rare plants and insects in the woodlands, heath and marsh areas.

Signs of human activity across the centuries are found in the shape of tombs, burial cairns, castles, crosses, cottages, quarries and quays. The many Iron Age forts, Norman castles and monuments are reminders of the people who lived here over the centuries and of the area's place in history.

☎ 01437 764636 — www.pembrokeshirecoast.org

Pembrokeshire Coast

🏰 Penhow Castle — 180 D3

This is reputedly Wales' oldest lived-in castle, spanning 860 years. Once the home of medieval knights, it is now the ancestral home of the Seymour family. Tours lead from the drawbridge through the historic periods, visiting the battlements, Norman keep and bedchamber, Great Hall with a minstrels' gallery, the Victorian housekeeper's room and kitchens. The entrance fee includes a choice of themed audio tours, such as musical, domestic history, cooks, young adventurer or, in the evening, a candlelight tour.

☎ 01633 400800 — www.penhowcastle.com

✝ Penmon Priory (ruins) — 231 E4

The ruins of the 12th century priory lie at the eastern edge of Anglesey, alongside the old St Seiriol's Well, church and ancient dovecot. The rocky coastline provides views of the Puffin Island seabird colonies.

🏰 Penrhyn Castle (NT) — 231 E5

This imposing 19th century castle outside Bangor was built in Norman style and contains remarkably luxurious furnishings, artworks and decor. The kitchen and service rooms have been restored to their 1894 state, ready prepared for a banquet for the Prince of Wales. Outbuildings house a railway museum and a doll museum. The 45 acres (18ha) of grounds include a walled garden, special plant collections and parkland overlooking the Menai Strait.

☎ 01248 371337 — www.nationaltrust.org.uk

⭐ Pistyll Rhaeadr — 219 D4

The highest waterfall in England and Wales cascades down 240ft (74m) and is known as the 'Hidden Pearl of Wales', located in the heart of the principality. It is a spectacular sight, especially after rainfall.

☎ 01691 780392 — www.pistyllrhaeadr.co.uk

❋ Plantasia — 411 E3

This giant hothouse garden pyramid is found in Swansea's Parc Tawe and houses rare and exotic plants from around the world. Butterflies, insects, reptiles, fish, monkeys and birds also inhabit the three climate zones, providing visitors with a colourful and authentic atmosphere.

☎ 01792 474555 — www.swansea.gov.uk

🏛❋ Plas Newydd, Llangollen — 219 F3

Renowned as the home of the two 'Ladies of Llangollen' from 1780 to 1831, Plas Newydd is an impressive Gothic black and white house. It is noted not only as the Regency home of the independent, eccentric spinsters, but also for its interior furnishings and fittings and newly-restored, peaceful gardens.

☎ 01824 708250 — www.denbighshire.gov.uk
www.llangollen.com/plas/html

🏛❋ Plas Newydd, Anglesey (NT) — 217 E1

Splendidly set on the Anglesey coast of the Menai Strait, this 18th century stately mansion, enjoying spectacular views to Snowdonia, was the former home of the Marquess of Anglesey. The house combines classical and Gothic architecture and featured inside are paintings by Rex Whistler, including his largest work. The cavalry museum in the servants' quarters commemorates the Battle of Waterloo and displays various campaign relics.

Expansive gardens offer informal walks among fine collections of flowering trees and shrubs, with many exotic plants thriving in the mild climate. In addition to the spring garden, there is a summer terrace, Australasian arboretum, a formal Italianate garden, a woodland area and an

Plas Newydd

adventure play trail. The rhododendron garden, situated some way from the house, is only open from April to early June during flowering time. Autumn, too, brings its own seasonal colours to the grounds.

A marine walk leads along the shore, and historical boat trips are available from the jetty in good weather.

☎ 01248 715272   www.nationaltrust.org.uk

🏠 ❀ Plas-yn-Rhiw (NT)   `216 B5`

Originating in the 16th century, this small manor house is situated towards the end of the Lleyn Peninsula, affording breathtaking sea views. Once fallen into disrepair, the attractive house has been restored and 50 acres (20ha) of gardens reclaimed, reaching down to the shoreline. The house contains much of the original furniture and utensils. Subtropical shrubs, box hedges and grass paths divide the ornamental gardens; a stream and waterfall cascade down to the sea, and snowdrop woods provide a backdrop to the house.

☎ 01758 780219   www.nationaltrust.org.uk

Portmeirion Village

⭐ Portmeirion Village   `217 E4`

This unique, if eccentric 'village' was created during the mid 20th century by the architect Clough Williams-Ellis in a flamboyant, Mediterranean style on his privately-owned peninsula on the beautiful Tremadog Bay. The 175 acres (70 ha) were transformed from a neglected wilderness into a fantasy of pastel-washed cottages, classical towers and lodges, piazzas and archways, façades and fountains, stairways and shops, grottoes and colonnades. Restaurants and hotels form an integral part of the village, as do a range of shops, including the popular Portmeirion Pottery. Here Noel Coward wrote 'Blithe Spirit', and it has been the haunt of many artists, writers and composers of world renown; the village is also well known as the location for the TV series 'The Prisoner'.

The surrounding gardens benefit from the warm influence of the Gulf Stream, enabling many subtropical plants to flourish, in addition to substantial groves of rhododendrons, azaleas and hydrangeas, and a variety of impressive evergreen trees. The woodlands enclose two lakes and reach down to sandy areas of beach and an elegant quayside. Portmeirion has a charm of its own which can only be fully experienced by allowing generous time for a visit.

☎ 01766 770000   www.portmeirion-village.com

Powis Castle & Garden

🏠 ❀ Powis Castle & Garden (NT)   `206 B2`

Both the house and gardens of this property near Welshpool are of particular interest. The medieval castle was built on a prominent rock by Welsh princes, and over the course of later centuries was endowed with fine collections of artwork and furniture by the Herbert and Clive families. Of special note are the Clive Museum with beautiful treasures from India, and the 19th century state coach and livery in the coach house.

The castle overlooks 55 acres (22ha) of world-famous terraced gardens designed in Italian and French styles with sumptuous plantings, statues, an orangery and an aviary. Rare and tender plants are sheltered by large yew hedging; the terrace walls and herbaceous beds exude colour, and containers display imaginative arrangements of plantings. In the lower gardens can be found pyramidal apple trees, a vine tunnel and roses. An informal area of woodland was laid out in the 18th century on the ridge opposite the formal gardens and specimen trees are planted on the grassland slopes.

☎ 01938 551944   www.nationaltrust.org.uk

🏰 Raglan Castle   `180 D2`

Situated in central Monmouthshire, Raglan Castle is a fine example of a medieval fortress palace. Building commenced in 1435 and it developed more as a luxurious Tudor residence than a military base, although it was subjected to siege during the Civil War and was greatly damaged by Cromwell's troops. Raglan was further ransacked after the Restoration and by the 19th century had become very much a ruin. The oldest remaining structure is known as the Yellow Tower of Gwent, named after the colour of the stone from which it

was built. The tower was surrounded by more walls and a moat. Later additions included the Pitched Stone Court, the Great Gatehouse and Fountain Court, the rather grand living quarters. The Great Hall is positioned between two courtyards and dates mainly from Elizabethan times.

Today's ruins give an insight into the lavish way of life of its former occupants, and hints of a French influence in elements of the architecture. The changing history of the castle is explained by displays in the closet tower and two rooms of the gatehouse.

☎ 01291 690228   www.cadw.wales.gov.uk

🏰 Rhuddlan Castle & Twt Hill   `232 B5`

Just south of Rhyl stand the stone remains of Edward I's 13th century stronghold. Today the most prominent structures are the gatehouse, walls and towers, as well as the decorative fireplaces of the drawing room. The grounds contain formal gardens, woodlands and ponds. Limited opening in summer only.

☎ 01745 590777   www.cadw.wales.gov.uk

✝ 🏛 St David's Cathedral & Bishop's Palace   `190 A5`

Situated in the heart of the charming, small city of St David's, the Cathedral has been a dominant presence since the 12th century. It was built in Norman transitional style and has undergone many transformations under successive bishops. The nearby ruins of the Bishop's Palace date from the 14th century. Many notable features adorn the cathedral, and the surrounding gardens are an additional attraction. There is a bookshop and guided tours; an annual classical music festival takes place in late spring.

☎ 01437 720517   www.stdavidscathedral.org.uk

⭐ St David's Head   `190 A5`

A dramatically beautiful coastline within easy walking distance from Whitesands also provides access to a ruined ancient fort. Offshore lie the islands known as The Bishops and Clerks, best viewed by boat.

🏛 Segontium Roman Museum   `217 D1`

The museum depicts the significant Roman occupation of the area, dating back to AD77. Excavated finds from the nearby Roman fort are displayed, plus records of this remote Roman regiment.

☎ 01286 675625   www.nmgw.ac.uk

Raglan Castle

WALES

Snowdon Mountain Railway `217 E2`

Starting from Llanberis, the dramatic 4.5 mile (7km) ride to the summit of Snowdon on this Victorian rack and pinion railway takes two and a half hours return and ascends 3200ft (980m).The narrow-gauge line affords breathtaking views of Snowdonia and beyond, traversing woodlands, a viaduct and then the open mountainside with an average gradient of 1 in 8. Three of the four coal-fired steam locomotives date from the late 19th century. The trip allows half an hour at the summit station.

☎ 0870 458 0033   www.snowdonrailway.co.uk

Snowdonia National Park `217 F1`

Named after the highest mountain in Wales, the national park covers 827 sq m (2142 sq km) in the counties of Gwynedd and Conwy. It is primarily a wild area of great natural beauty – a landscape of majestic mountains, lush valleys and glittering lakes, surrounded by unspoilt coastlines. The rivers of Snowdonia tumble down the mountains as rushing streams, and arrive at the sea in wide estuaries, providing, along their way, ideal habitats for a huge diversity of plants and wildlife. The area holds much appeal for the naturalist, the mountaineer, the rambler, the artist and the water lover, as well as to those who simply appreciate its stunning scenery.

The Park's study centre is located at Plas Tan y Bwlch near Maentwrog and a Welcome Centre is situated in Betws-y-Coed at one of the park gateways. The main industry of Snowdonia is still hill farming, but tourism is also a major contributor to the economy. Walking and climbing are the most popular pursuits for visitors who have over 2000 miles (3400km) of delightful footpaths to explore. The great majority of the local population regard Welsh as their first language and signs of Welsh history and culture abound, from castles to cottages and from song to sheepdog trials.

☎ 01766 770274   www.snowdonia-npa.gov.uk

South Stack Cliffs `230 A4`

Bird watching and lighthouse viewing make the journey to this far tip of Holy Island well worthwhile. The spectacularly located lighthouse sits on a rocky promontory, but it is accessible only on foot via a steep descent of over 400 steps. Spring and early summer are the best times to observe the multitude of seabirds, including shearwaters, skuas, guillemots, razorbills and puffins, wheeling around the dramatic cliffsides. The visitor centre contains exhibitions on the bird life and the natural environment, plus the history of the lighthouse.

☎ 01407 762181

Strata Florida Abbey `193 D1`

Cistercian monks built the abbey in the 12th century on the banks of the river Teifi in mid Wales, but only the ruined church and cloister survive from this once-important centre of learning.

☎ 02920 500200   www.cadw.wales.gov.uk

Swallow Falls `218 A2`

The Welsh name Rhaeadr Ewynnol (foamy rapids) aptly describes these rushing torrents above Betws-y-Coed. A pedestrian walkway overlooks the wild river, as it carries the waters of Snowdonia towards the sea. A spectacular sight, especially after rain.

Talyllyn Railway `204 C2`

The historic, narrow-gauge Talyllyn steam railway dates from 1865 and runs 7 miles (11.5km) from Tywyn on the west coast, inland to Nant Gwernol. The authentically restored rolling stock chugs through beautiful wooded countryside, with stops en route to admire dramatic waterfalls, particularly from Dolgoch station. The round trip takes just over two hours, but there are also opportunities to explore extensive forest walks in the unspoilt Fathew Valley. For real enthusiasts, Footplate Experience Courses and special events can be arranged.

☎ 01654 710472   www.talyllyn.co.uk

Techniquest `180 A5`

Located in the Cardiff Bay redevelopment area, this educational and fun discovery centre is suitable for the whole family. Techniquest aims to promote understanding and appreciation of science. On offer are 160 stimulating hands-on exhibits, puzzles and challenges in the shape of a Planetarium, a laboratory, a discovery room, a hi-tech science theatre and other enjoyable and accessible environments. Facilities are also available for groups and school tours. Allow at least two hours for a visit.

☎ 029 2047 5475   www.techniquest.org

Tintern Abbey (Ruin) `181 E3`

Once a favoured site for artists and poets including William Wordsworth, the graceful ruins of the 13th century Cistercian Abbey overlook the beautiful Wye valley north of Chepstow. Much of the Abbey is preserved and it offers a fascinating glimpse into the life and times of the medieval monks.

☎ 01291 689251   www.tintern.org.uk

Tredegar House `351 C2`

For more than five centuries this imposing mansion near Newport was home to the powerful Morgan family. Some 30 rooms are open to the public and the interior is furnished sumptuously with original pieces. Costumed guides lead tours describing life 'upstairs' and 'below stairs'. Outside are 90 acres (37ha) of landscaped gardens and parkland with lakes, carriage rides and craft workshops.

☎ 01633 815880   www.newport.gov.uk

Tretower Castle & Court `194 A5`

The stone keep of this castle in the Brecon Beacons was built as a fortification in the 13th century. The nearby Court was added in the following century to serve as a comfortable residence. Various stages in the development of both buildings can be seen, including the detailed

craftsmanship of the Court. The re-created 15th century garden is at its best in early summer.

☎ 01874 730279   www.cadw.wales.gov.uk

Tudor Merchant's House (NT) `177 E3`

A late 15th century prosperous merchant's house near Tenby harbour has been furnished to depict lifestyles from Tudor days onwards. Interesting features include original frescoes, a Flemish chimney and small herb garden.

☎ 01834 842279   www.nationaltrust.org.uk

Tŷ Mawr Wybrnant (NT) `218 A2`

Tucked away in a beautiful, peaceful valley, this small stone house holds a special significance in the history of the Welsh language. Here in the 16th century the entire Bible was first translated into Welsh by Bishop William Morgan. Restoration work has returned the house to its probable original state and it now contains a display of Welsh bibles and related exhibits.

☎ 01690 760213   www.nationaltrust.org.uk

Upton Gardens `176 D2`

Overlooking the waters of Milford Haven, the landscaped gardens cover 35 acres (14ha) and offer secluded, inclined woodland walks. The main planting contains over 250 species of trees and shrubs, including some exotic varieties.

☎ 01646 651782   www.pembrokeshirecoast.org.uk

Vale of Rheidol Railway `204 C5`

Starting from Aberystwyth main line station, this narrow-gauge steam train climbs steeply upwards along a spectacular 12 mile (19km) track and requires 3 hours for the round trip (allowing an hour at the beauty spot of Devil's Bridge). The original engines and carriages, built in 1902 to transport passengers and lead, are still in use. Highlights of the trip are three historic bridges at the summit spanning the Devil's Punchbowl whirlpool. Walks abound amid the rugged, wooded landscape.

☎ 01970 625819   www.rheidolrailway.co.uk

Welsh Slate Museum `217 E2`

The vast, old Dinorwig slate quarry in the Padarn Country Park near Llanberis has been transformed into an imaginative museum of the bygone industry. Exhibitions, demonstrations, multimedia presentations, restored buildings, children's activities and tours bring to life the work of the quarrymen. The museum offers a fascinating, free day out for the whole family.

☎ 01286 870630   www.nmgw.ac.uk

Snowdonia

SCOTLAND

From the grassy hills of the Borders to the desolate Cuillin Ridge of Skye, the landscape of Scotland is breathtaking in its variety. Lonely glens, sparkling lochs and ever-changing skies give the land a challenging character, which is reflected in the qualities of the Scottish people. Tough and self-reliant, they have produced some of Britain's finest soldiers, its boldest explorers and most astute industrialists.

Kilchurn Castle, Loch Awe

SCOTLAND

Abbot House
285 F1

This restored 15th century house was originally the residence of the Abbot of Dunfermline. It is steeped in history and even survived the great fire of 1624. Exhibits and audiovisual displays trace Scotland's story from Pictish to modern times and recount details about King Robert the Bruce, St Margaret and other figures who played a role in the history of Scotland's most ancient capital.

☎ 01383 733266 www.abbothouse.co.uk

Abbotsford House
277 G2

Sir Walter Scott, the novelist, bought a farmhouse here in 1811, replacing it with a castellated and turreted mansion in the Scottish Baronial style and naming it Abbotsford in memory of the Melrose Abbey monks who forded the River Tweed here. He gleaned architectural ideas from many sources, including Melrose Abbey, Linlithgow Palace and Rosslyn Chapel. Internally the house is little altered and visitors can see the author's personal possessions, 9000 volume library and eclectic collection of historic relics such as a lock of Bonnie Prince Charlie's hair and Mary, Queen of Scots' crucifix. The armoury bristles with historic weapons and the entrance hall is festooned with the skulls of elk and wild cattle.

☎ 01896 752043

Aberdeen Art Gallery
388 B2

An elegant building opened in 1885 that houses one of the finest art collections in the UK. It includes 18th century portraits, paintings by many well known Impressionists and important works by modern British artists such as Nash, Nicholson and Bacon. The gallery also has a collection of Aberdeen silver and other arts and crafts.

☎ 01224 523700 www.aagm.co.uk

Aberdour Castle
285 F1

Overlooking the harbour is a 13th century fortified residence. There are also the ruins of the 14th century keep along with other buildings built and extended in later centuries. One of these is still roofed and contains a gallery on the first floor, complete with painted ceiling, illustrating how it was furnished in 1650. There is also a restored walled garden with a fine circular dovecot and terraced garden.

☎ 01383 860519 www.historic-scotland.gov.uk

Angus Folk Museum (NTS)
302 B5

The museum is within Kirkwynd Cottages, a row of six reconstructed early 18th century cottages with stone-slabbed roofs. The interiors display one of the finest folk collections of domestic relics in Scotland. There is also an agricultural collection in the farm steading opposite, including a restored 19th century horse-drawn hearse, providing an insight into rural livelihoods over the last 200 years.

☎ 01307 840288 www.nts.org.uk

Antonine Wall
284 C2

This Roman fortification stretched 38 miles (61km) from Bo'ness on the Forth to Old Kilpatrick on the Clyde. Built circa AD142 – 3, it consisted of a turf rampart on stone foundation behind a ditch 12ft (3.7m) deep and 40ft (12m) wide. Forts were positioned approximately every 2 miles (3km) and linked by a cobbled road. It was probably abandoned around AD163. Remains are best preserved in the Falkirk/Bonnybridge area.

☎ 0131 668 8800 www.historic-scotland.gov.uk

Aonach Mòr Mountain Gondola & Nevis Range Ski Centre
299 D2

Britain's only mountain gondolas take passengers up Aonach Mòr, beside Ben Nevis, to 2150ft (655m). Enjoy spectacular views of the Highlands and Islands and walks through forest tracks. The gondola also provides access to Britain's largest downhill mountain bike track. During the winter season, the Nevis Range provides Scotland's highest winter ski and snowboard area, with ski school and ski hire. There is a mountain restaurant, bar and shop at 2150ft (655m).

☎ 01397 705825 www.nevisrange.co.uk

Arbroath Abbey
303 E5

The substantial ruins of a Tironesian monastery founded by William the Lion in 1178. The Abbey is most notably associated with the signing of the Declaration of Arbroath in 1320, which asserted Scotland's independence from England. There is also a herb garden, exhibits about life in the Abbey and the Declaration, and a visitor centre.

☎ 01241 878756 www.historic-scotland.gov.uk

Ardkinglas Woodland Garden
291 D3

Overlooking Loch Fyne is one of the finest collections of conifers in Britain. Within the woodland garden is one of Europe's mightiest conifers, a 250 year old silver fir with a girth of 31ft (9.6m), and one of Britain's tallest trees, a grand fir over 200ft (61m) tall. There is also a spectacular display of rhododendrons and a gazebo containing a 'scriptorium' themed around a collection of literary quotes.

☎ 01499 600261 www.ardkinglas.com

Arduaine Gardens (NTS)
289 G4

A 20 acre (8ha) garden on a promontory with fine views overlooking Loch Melfort. Noted particularly for rhododendrons, azaleas, magnolias and other interesting trees and shrubs, which flourish in the warm sheltered climate created by the North Atlantic Drift.

☎ 01852 200366 www.nts.org.uk

Auchindrain Township Open Air Museum
290 C4

Auchindrain is an original West Highland township of great antiquity and the only communal tenancy township in Scotland to have survived on its centuries-old site. The conserved township buildings are furnished and equipped as they would have been at the end of the 19th century and provide a fascinating glimpse of Highland life.

☎ 01499 500235 www.auchindrainmuseum.org.uk

Bachelors' Club (NTS)
274 C3

A 17th century thatched house with period furnishings where Robert Burns and his friends formed a debating club in 1780. Burns also attended dancing classes and was initiated as a Freemason here.

☎ 01292 541940 www.nts.org.uk

Balmacara Estate & Lochalsh Woodland Garden (NTS)
307 E2

Traditional crofting is still carried out on this beautiful Highland estate. There are wonderful views of Skye and Applecross, and the woodland garden provides sheltered lochside walks among pines, ferns, fuchsias, hydrangeas and rhododendrons. Amongst the villages on the estate is Plockton, an outstanding conservation area and location for the television series 'Hamish

Macbeth'. A small visitor centre is located at Balmacara Square. Charges apply for the garden.

☎ 01599 566325 www.nts.org.uk

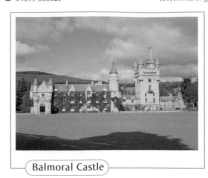

Balmoral Castle

Balmoral Castle
311 E5

Situated on the south side of the River Dee, Balmoral has been the Highland holiday home of the Royal Family since 1852. The present castle was designed by Aberdeen City architect William Smith under the keen eye of Queen Victoria's husband, Prince Albert, who considered the castle they previously leased on the site too small. The pale colour of the granite stone used in the building is quite distinctive and was quarried from nearby Glen Gelder.

The only part of the castle open to the public is the ballroom which has items from within the castle on display; paintings, porcelain and the Balmoral Tartans and Tweeds collection. In the stables there are carriages on view, while in the carriage hall there is a display of commemorative china and an exhibition about the Balmoral Estate.

Three acres (1ha) of formal gardens include a conservatory and Victorian glasshouses, kitchen garden and water garden, and there are waymarked walks along the river and through the woods. Guided ranger walks, land rover safaris and pony trekking are also available. Balmoral is only open to the public between April and July.

☎ 013397 42534 www.balmoralcastle.com

Bannockburn 1314
292 D5

This is the site of the famous battle in 1314 when Robert the Bruce, King of Scots, defeated the English Army of Edward II. The Heritage Centre stages a colourful exhibition, with life-size figures of Bruce and William Wallace, heraldic flags and an audiovisual presentation on the Battle of Bannockburn.

☎ 01786 812664 www.nts.org.uk

Barry Mill (NTS)
294 D1

A working 19th century meal mill. There are full demonstrations on weekend afternoons, and displays outline the history of the mill.

☎ 01241 856761 www.nts.org.uk

Baxters Highland Village
323 F3

The story of Baxters, the Scottish food company, began in 1868 when George Baxter opened a small grocery store in Fochabers. At the Highland Village there is a presentation of the Baxters story, cookery demonstrations and the re-creation of George Baxter's original shop.

☎ 01343 820393 www.baxters.com/village

Bealach na Ba
319 D5

Scotland's highest road, between Loch Kishorn and Applecross, provides a spectacular drive, climbing to the summit at 2056ft (625m). Bealach na Ba translates to 'Pass of the Cattle', denoting its original purpose. The challenging drive is well rewarded and there are parking areas to enjoy the fabulous views. Beyond the summit, the road descends to Applecross, a peaceful fishing village.

Beecraigs Country Park
285 D2

Nestled high in the Bathgate Hills, Beecraigs covers an area of 915 acres (370ha) and offers a wide range of leisure and recreational pursuits. There are various walks and trails as well as a well-stocked fishery, a deer farm which sells its own venison, and the opportunity to participate in archery, orienteering, abseiling and skiing. There is a charge for some of these activities.

☎ 01506 844516   www.beecraigs.com

Ben Lawers National Nature Reserve (NTS)
292 B1

Located north-east of Killin is Perthshire's highest mountain, Ben Lawers, rising 3984ft (1214m). It is noted for its rich variety of mountain plants and bird population, including raven, ring-ouzel, ptarmigan, dipper and curlew. There is a nature trail and ranger-guided walks in summer.

☎ 01567 820397   www.nts.org.uk

Ben Nevis
299 D2

At 4406ft (1344m), this is Britain's highest mountain and is popular for both rock climbing and hill walking. Ben Nevis is best seen from the north approach to Fort William, or from the Gairlochy Road, across the Caledonian Canal. At the top are the ruins of the Mountain Top Observatory, where Victorian scientists collected data, whatever the weather.

To the south, the Water of Nevis plummets through a steep wooded gorge. Glen Nevis offers wonderful gorge walks and the visitor centre provides information on the fascinating history, geology, flora and fauna of Ben Nevis and Glen Nevis. There are ranger guided walks during June, July and August.

Ben Nevis

Blackhouse
329 E3

A traditional Hebridean thatched and chimneyless house dating from the 1870s with byre, attached barn and stackyard. It is fully furnished and a peat fire burns in the hearth. Opposite is a furnished 1920s crofthouse, or whitehouse, which replaced the blackhouse dwellings. The visitor centre provides informative displays.

☎ 01851 710395   www.historic-scotland.gov.uk

Blackness Castle
285 E1

A 15th century stronghold, once one of the most important fortresses in Scotland and one of four castles the Articles of Union left fortified. Shaped like a ship with three sides surrounded by water, it has served as a royal castle, a state prison in Covenanting times and a powder magazine in the 1870s. More recently, it has been a film location for the BBC production of 'Hamlet'. Visitors can explore inside, walk the walls and climb the central tower.

www.historic-scotland.gov.uk

Blacksmith's Shop
268 B5

Built around 1712, this became a world famous centre for runaway marriages when Scottish law permitted marriage at 16 without parental consent, while English law did not. Gretna Green was the closest place to the border for eloping couples and an exhibition traces the history of these runaway weddings which took place in the Blacksmith's Shop, the nearest building to the stagecoach stop.

☎ 01461 338441   www.gretnagreen.com

Blair Castle
301 D3

This white turreted baronial castle, set within magnificent grounds, was the traditional seat of the Dukes and Earls of Atholl. The oldest part, Cumming's Tower, dates back to 1269. Over 30 rooms convey more than 700 years of history. Discover fine collections of furniture, portraits, lace, china, costumes, arms, armour, Jacobite relics and Masonic regalia. Explore the deer park, restored 18th century walled garden, woodland, riverside and mountain walks.

☎ 01796 481207   www.blair-castle.co.uk

Bonawe Iron Furnace
290 C1

The restored remains of this charcoal-fuelled furnace, once used for iron smelting, is the most complete example of its type. Established in 1753, it functioned until 1876. Displays illustrate the iron-making process. Open from end of April to September only.

☎ 01866 822432   www.historic-scotland.gov.uk

Bo'ness & Kinneil Railway
285 D1

Savour the nostalgia of the railway age and travel by steam train from Bo'ness to visit Birkhill Fireclay Mine. The scenic 7 mile (11km) round trip passes via the south shore of the Firth of Forth, through woodlands, and crosses the Antonine Wall. Regular timetable during the summer, plus special events.

☎ 01506 822298   www.srps.org.uk

Bothwell Castle
375 E3

Regarded as the finest 13th century stronghold in the country, Bothwell Castle was much fought over by the Scots and English during the Wars of Independence. Substantial ruins of this red sandstone castle remain today in a picturesque setting alongside the River Clyde.

☎ 01698 816894   www.historic-scotland.gov.uk

Bowhill House
277 F3

A splendid Georgian mansion in impressive woodland setting, containing a remarkable collection of French furniture designed by Andre Boulle, paintings by Canaletto, Gainsborough, Reynolds and Van Dyck, tapestries and fine porcelain. There are some interesting historical exhibits including letters from Queen Victoria and proof copies of Sir Walter Scott's books.

There are walks and an adventure playground in the grounds. The house is only open in July; check in advance for opening times of grounds.

☎ 01750 22204

Branklyn Gardens (NTS)
293 G2

Started in 1922 on the site of a former orchard, Branklyn is an outstanding 2 acre (0.8ha) garden with rhododendrons, alpines, herbaceous and peat garden plants. These are predominantly from China, Tibet, Bhutan and the Himalayas, and include the blue Himalayan poppy.

☎ 01738 625535   www.nts.org.uk

Britannia
373 C1

Launched in 1953 onto the Clyde, the Royal Yacht served the Queen and royal family for state visits, diplomatic functions and royal holidays for 44 years. Today Britannia is moored in Leith Docks alongside the Ocean Terminal shopping centre. The tour begins in the visitor centre where the history of the yacht and its royal connections are explained. Five decks of the ship are then open for exploration including the bridge, admiral's quarters, the officers' mess, the state rooms, the engine room and some of the living quarters used privately by the Queen and Prince Philip.

☎ 0131 555 5566   www.royalyachtbritannia.co.uk

Britannia

British Golf Museum
294 C3

Touch screen and audiovisual displays, together with a fascinating collection of memorabilia, trace the history of golf from the Middle Ages through to the present day.

☎ 01334 460046   www.britishgolfmuseum.co.uk

Brodick Castle (NTS)
273 F2

An imposing, originally 13th century red sandstone castle on a site occupied initially by Irish and later by Vikings. Extended in the 17th and 19th centuries, the pleasant interior belies the somewhat forbidding exterior.

Brodick's greatest treasures are its gardens; the woodland garden, started in 1923, is home to one of Europe's finest rhododendron collections, magnificent in spring, whilst the walled garden contains tender and exotic plants encouraged by the mild climate.

Set at the foot of Goat Fell, the estate provides scenic trails, abundant wildlife and an adventure playground.

☎ 01770 302202   www.nts.org.uk

Brodie Castle (NTS)
322 B4

The oldest parts of Brodie Castle are 16th century, although the Brodie family owned land here as early as the 12th century. The well-furnished castle interior contains fine French furniture, porcelain, and a major art collection of modern British and French paintings. There are some impressive ornate plasterwork ceilings, a large library and fully equipped Victorian kitchen.

SCOTLAND

The grounds are famous for the spring display of daffodils, many of them specialist varieties, and there are woodland walks and a four acre (2ha) pond with wildlife observation hides. The park also contains a notable carved Pictish stone.

☎ 01309 641371 www.nts.org.uk

🏠❋ Broughton House (NTS) — 266 A5

Delightful 18th century town house, home between 1901 – 33 to the artist Edward Hornel, who helped establish an artists' colony in Kirkcudbright. Some of his paintings hang in the gallery here, later ones influenced by visits to Japan.

The 2 acre (1ha) garden consists of distinct compartments including Hornel's Japanese-style garden. Check in advance for opening times.

☎ 01577 330437 www.nts.org.uk

⭐ Burg (NTS) — 288 D2

Covering an area of 1405 acres (569ha), this is a spectacular and remote part of Mull. The high, volcanic cliffs are known as 'The Wilderness', denoting the area's wild terrain. MacCulloch's Fossil Tree, engulfed by lava 50 million years ago, can be reached by a steep iron ladder down to the beach at low tide. There is no vehicular access to Berg; it is reached by a 6 mile (10km) walk from Kilfinichen Bay.

www.nts.org.uk

⭐ Burns National Heritage Park — 274 B4

Set up in 1995, this embraces several sites in the Alloway area closely connected with Robert Burns, considered Scotland's national poet.

The whitewashed Burns Cottage is the poet's birthplace, a small, dark, gloomy building giving a good impression of impoverished 18th century rural existence. Adjacent is the Museum, tracing Burns' life and displaying his manuscripts and memorabilia. A short distance away is the modern Tam O' Shanter Experience with entertaining audiovisual presentations on the poet's life and a re-enactment of his famous poem, 'Tam O' Shanter'. The ruined Alloway Kirk across the road is the burial place of Burns' father and one of the settings for 'Tam O' Shanter', as is the nearby stone arch Brig O' Doon. The neoclassical Burns Monument, decorated with characters from the poems, has pleasant, well-tended gardens.

☎ 01292 443700 www.burnsheritagepark.com

Burns National Heritage Park

🏛 Burrell Collection — 374 B3

This award winning purpose-built museum houses a magnificent collection gifted to the city of Glasgow in 1944 By Sir William Burrell, a shipping magnate, and his wife, Constance. Visitors can see ancient artworks from China, Egypt, Greece and Rome including Egyptian alabaster and Chinese jade. There are remarkable collections of tapestries, oriental rugs, medieval metalwork, stained glass and paintings by Manet, Degas and Rembrandt, as well as modern sculpture including works by Rodin and Epstein. A number of rooms from Burrell's home, the 16th century Hutton Castle, have been perfectly re-created. The building itself is light and airy and its woodland setting within Pollok Country Park ensures all the objects on display are shown at their very best. Free guided tours are available and there is a good tearoom and restaurant on the lower floor.

☎ 0141 287 2550 www.glasgowmuseums.com

🏰 Caerlaverock Castle — 267 E4

A splendid moated, triangular 13th century castle, with a substantial keep gatehouse at the northern apex, entered by a footbridge. Its impregnable appearance is reinforced by the desolate surroundings of the Solway coast, though the castle was captured on several occasions. Capture invariably resulted in damage, and the castle is consequently a mixture of building styles, both externally and internally. It was finally abandoned in 1640 when it was wrecked by the Covenanters.

☎ 01387 770244 www.historic-scotland.gov.uk

🦢 Caerlaverock Wildfowl & Wetlands Trust — 267 E4

A splendid 1350 acres (546ha) of protected saltmarsh and mudflat bordering the Solway Firth. Well designed observation towers and hides provide visitors with exceptional views of migratory wildfowl, notably the Barnacle Geese of Svalbard, most of whom overwinter here. There is still plenty of bird life in summer, and there are nature trails through the meadows and knowledgeable to staff to answer the inevitable questions.

☎ 01387 770200 www.wwt.org.uk

⭐ Cairn Gorm Mountain — 310 B4

This granite mountain mass of rounded summits includes some of Scotland's highest peaks. It is a popular area for hill walkers, climbers and skiers. The Cairngorms are Britain's only example of Arctic tundra vegetation and the area provides a habitat for populations of red deer, mountain hare, snow buntings and ptarmigans. Cairn Gorm summit, at 4086ft (1245m), provides fantastic views of the lochs, forests and surrounding mountains.

www.cairngormmountain.com

🦢 Cairngorms National Park — 310 B5

The Cairngorms National Park stretches 1400 sq miles (3800 sq km), making it Britain's largest national park area. Aviemore is the commercial centre for the area. In winter, the village is a mecca for skiers and snowboarders and in summer there are facilities for pony trekking, mountain biking, fishing, sailing, windsurfing and canoeing. Whilst the peaks are popular with climbers, there are also forest and river treks to follow, as well as walks around and through the villages, including Newtonmore and Boat of Garten.

The funicular railway, Scotland's only mountain railway, takes visitors on a spectacular and comfortable journey to Ptarmigan Station on Cairn Gorm, 490ft (150m) below the summit. The Ski

Centre can be found 9 miles (14km) south-east of Aviemore. Other attractions include the Cairngorm Reindeer Centre and Cairngorm Sled-dog Adventure Centre.

☎ 01479 861261 www.cairngorms.co.uk

Burrell Collection

🌲 Calderglen Country Park — 284 A4

The park covers an area of 440 acres (180ha) and is made up of grassland, wooded gorge and several fine waterfalls. There are over 8 miles (13km) of nature trails through the woods and alongside the River Calder. The visitor centre has information about the park. There is also an ornamental garden, children's zoo, play area, shop and café.

☎ 01355 236644

🚂 Caledonian Railway — 303 E4

From the unique Victorian terminus at Brechin, board a steam train and journey back in time as you travel the falling grade to Bridge of Dun, where the Royal Trains used to stop. From here, enjoy a scenic walk along the River South Esk and visit the bird sanctuary, Montrose Basin. Back at Brechin, there is a static display of model trains. Steam hauled trains run at weekends from the end of May to beginning of September.

☎ 01356 622992 www.caledonianrailway.co.uk

🏛 Callanish Standing Stones — 328 D4

A unique cruciform setting of megaliths, second in importance only to Stonehenge, which were erected about 3000BC. An avenue of 19 monoliths leads north from a circle of 13 stones, with rows of more stones fanning out to the south, east and west. Inside the circle is a small, chambered tomb. There is a visitor centre, including an audiovisual presentation about the stones (for which there is a small charge).

☎ 01851 621422 www.historic-scotland.gov.uk

🏛 Callendar House — 284 C2

Callendar House encapsulates 600 years of Scotland's history, from medieval times to the 20th century. Great historical visitors of the house include Mary, Queen of Scots, Cromwell and Bonnie Prince Charlie. Permanent attractions include displays on the story of Callendar House, and on the Falkirk area during the great social revolution of 1750 – 1850.

☎ 01324 503770 www.falkirkmuseums.demon.co.uk

🏰 Cardoness Castle — 265 G5

An excellent example of a fortified tower house, this late 15th century stronghold is now a well preserved ruin. The four-storey building still retains the original staircase, vaulted basement and elaborate fireplaces, and has views over the Water of Fleet to Fleet Bay.

☎ 01557 814427 www.historic-scotland.gov.uk

Carlyle's Birthplace (NTS) · 267 F3

Thomas Carlyle, the author, historian and social reformer, was born in 1795 in the unpretentious, whitewashed Arched House built by his father and uncle. It is now a tiny museum featuring his personal memorabilia. True to his roots, Carlyle refused burial in Westminster Abbey and his grave can be found in the churchyard behind the cottage.

☎ 01576 300666   www.nts.org.uk

Castle Campbell · 293 E5

Once known as Castle Gloom, the castle is set high on a promontory above Dollar Glen. Built towards the end of the 15th century by the 1st Earl of Argyll, it was burned by Cromwell in the 1650s. The original tower, however, is well preserved along with its courtyard and Great Hall. The 60 acres (24ha) of woodland in the glen make an attractive walk to the castle.

☎ 01259 742408   www.historic-scotland.gov.uk

Castle Fraser (NTS) · 312 C3

A magnificent castle completed in 1636 and one of the most sophisticated Scottish buildings of the period. It has a notable Great Hall with tall windows and a high ceiling, striking in its simplicity. Castle Fraser also contains a wealth of historic portraits, curtains, carpets and bedhangings. There is a formal walled garden in the grounds.

☎ 01330 833463   www.nts.org.uk

Castle Menzies · 300 D4

This imposing 16th century castle presents a fine example of the transition between a Z-plan clan stronghold and a later mansion house. Seat of the clan chiefs for over 400 years, Castle Menzies was involved in a number of historic occurrences, which are recounted in the museum.

☎ 01887 820982

Castle of Mey · 337 E1

Originally the seat of the earls of Caithness, 16th century Mey Castle became the Scottish summer holiday retreat of Her late Majesty Queen Elizabeth, The Queen Mother, between 1952 and 2002. It was built to a Z-plan, characteristic of its era, with towers and corbelled turrets. The Great Wall of Mey, standing 12ft (3.7m) high, protects the attractive walled garden from the strong winds and salt spray.

☎ 01847 851473   www.castleofmey.org.uk

Cawdor Castle · 322 A4

Cawdor Castle is the name romantically associated with Shakespeare's Macbeth, and dates originally from the 14th century. The medieval tower and drawbridge are still intact and generations of art lovers and scholars are responsible for the eclectic collection of paintings, books, tapestries and porcelain found in the castle. There are three beautiful gardens, five nature trails, a nine-hole golf course, putting green, and gift shop.

☎ 01667 404615   www.cawdorcastle.com

Corrieshalloch Gorge (NTS) · 320 A2

Here is one of the finest examples of a box canyon in Britain, forming a spectacular 200ft (61m) deep, mile-long (1.6km) gorge. A viewing platform stretched across the gorge looks up towards the magnificent Falls of Measach.

☎ 01445 781200   www.nts.org.uk

Craigievar Castle (NTS) · 312 A4

Completed in 1626, Craigievar is an excellent example of Scottish baronial architecture although it was built for a merchant, William Forbes. It is like the castles of fairytales with the seven storeys topped with turrets, gables and corbels. The interior has original ornate plasterwork ceilings and a fine collection of 17th and 18th century furniture. The grounds have woodland walks.

☎ 013398 83635

Craigmillar Castle · 373 C2

The oldest part of the castle is the L-shaped tower built in the early 1400s which was later surrounded by an embattled double curtain wall. By the end of the 16th century it was a comfortable residence and today, partially ruined, the castle still retains a strong sense of the mighty fortress it once was. Mary, Queen of Scots, has close links with the castle. She fled here following the murder of Rizzio, and the murder of her second husband was plotted here.

☎ 0131 661 4445   www.historic-scotland.gov.uk

Crathes Castle (NTS) · 312 C5

An impressive 16th century tower house with remarkable original painted ceilings and a collection of Scottish furniture and family portraits. It was the home of the Burnett family for more than 350 years until it was given to the National Trust in 1951. The walled garden, originally the kitchen garden, was divided in the 20th century into eight separate themed gardens with many herbaceous plants. Several waymarked trails lead through the mixed woodland of the Crathes Estate.

☎ 01330 844525   www.nts.org.uk

Crichton Castle · 286 A3

A large castle built around a medieval tower house to create an elegant interior courtyard. The arcaded range erected by the Earl of Bothwell between 1581 and 1591 has a façade of faceted stonework in an Italian Renaissance style.

☎ 01875 320017

Crossraguel Abbey · 274 A5

The substantial remains of a 13th century Cluniac monastery founded by the Earl of Carrick. The chapter house and gatehouse are amongst the best preserved and visitors can view the abbey precincts and surroundings from the top of the latter. The abbey was abandoned during the Reformation in the late 16th century.

☎ 01655 883113   www.historic-scotland.gov.uk

Cruachan Power Station Visitor Centre · 290 C2

A guided tour takes visitors 0.5 miles (1km) inside Ben Cruachan to a huge cavern to see a reversible pumped storage scheme where water power is converted into electricity. The visitor centre houses touch screen and computer video technology to explain how electricity is produced.

☎ 01866 822618   www.visitcruachan.co.uk

Cuillin Hills · 306 A2

The Cuillin Hills form a major sight on the Isle of Skye, their jagged summits of volcanic rock and granite evident from most parts of the island. Several peaks reach over 3000ft (914m), suitable for only the experienced climber. The mountains, however, can still be enjoyed on many walks, particularly from Elgol, Sligachan and the Glenbrittle road near Carbost.

Cuillin Hills

Culloden (NTS) · 321 G5

Site of the fierce battle on 16 April 1746, when the Hanoverian Army defeated the forces of Bonnie Prince Charlie, thereby ending the Jacobite uprising. Turf and stone dykes have been reconstructed on their original spot. The Graves of the Clans, the Well of the Dead, the Memorial Cairn, the Cumberland Stone and the Field of the English can also be seen. The visitor centre houses a Jacobite exhibition.

☎ 01463 790607   www.nts.org.uk

Culross Palace (NTS) · 285 D1

Built in 1597–1611 for local entrepreneur Sir George Bruce, the palace features its original decorative interiors and period 17th and 18th century furnishings. The restored 17th century garden contains rare herbs and perennials of the period. Elsewhere in Culross village, discover the remains of a Cistercian Abbey founded in 1217, the eastern part of which forms the present parish church. The Town House provides an exhibition of the area's history.

☎ 01383 880359   www.nts.org.uk

Culzean Castle (NTS) · 274 A4

A dramatic clifftop location and splendid design by Robert Adam in the late 18th century makes Culzean (pronounced Cullane) one of the most impressive of Scotland's stately homes. Replacing the original 15th century structure, the exterior, with arrow slits and battlements, evokes the medieval period, but the elegant interior exemplifies the classical designs favoured by Adam. The spectacular Oval Staircase is considered one of his finest achievements, while the sumptuous Circular Saloon makes a striking contrast to the surrounding natural scenery.

The 565 acre (233ha) estate, now a country park, provides woodland, clifftop and seashore walks, deer park, aviary and swan pond. The 30 acre (12ha) gardens include a large, colourful walled garden.

☎ 01655 884455   www.nts.org.uk

★ Dallas Dhu Distillery   322 C4

A picturesque small distillery established in 1899. Although no longer in production, Dallas Dhu is maintained in working order to enable visitors to take a close look at every part of the traditional distilling process and see exactly how whisky is made.

☎ 01309 676548   www.historic-scotland.gov.uk

🏛 David Livingstone Centre (NTS)   375 E4

Scotland's famous explorer and missionary was born here in 1813. He spent his childhood in a one-room tenement, which remains much as it was in Livingstone's day. The rest of the tenement block now houses a museum on the life of the great explorer, with many of his personal belongings on display.

☎ 01698 823140   www.nts.org.uk

🏰 Dean Castle   274 C2

A splendid collection of restored buildings comprising a 14th century fortified keep with a 15th century palace, dungeon, battlements, banqueting hall, kitchens and minstrels' gallery. The museum contains a significant collection of arms and armour, medieval musical instruments, tapestries and some Robert Burns manuscripts. Entry to the castle is by guided tour only.

The surrounding 200 acre (80ha) country park provides a variety of attractions including formal gardens, nature trails and a ranger service offering guided walks. There is a varied programme of events in summer.

☎ 01563 522702   www.deancastle.com

🏛 Dean Gallery   373 B1

This impressive neoclassical building was originally an orphanage but now houses a huge collection of work by the distinguished Scottish sculptor Eduardo Paolozzi. The gallery is also home to the Dada and Surrealist collections from the Gallery of Modern Art across the road.

☎ 0131 624 6200   www.natgalscot.ac.uk

★ Deep Sea World   285 F1

Enjoy a spectacular diver's eye view of the marine environment by travelling along a moving walkway through a long transparent viewing tunnel. Come face to face with sand tiger sharks and watch divers hand feed them. Touch the live exhibits in the large rock pools. Visit the stunning Amazonian Experience, which features ferocious piranhas, poisonous golden dart frogs, electrifying eels and the deadly stonefish.

☎ 01383 411880   www.deepseaworld.co.uk

🏰 ✿ Dirleton Castle & Gardens   286 C1

The oldest part of this romantic castle dates from the 13th century and, although the castle was destroyed in 1650, there are still large parts of the original masonry in evidence. The gardens dating from the 16th century are well worth a look.

☎ 01620 850330   www.historic-scotland.gov.uk

★ Discovery Point & R.R.S. Discovery   396 C2

Centred on the Royal Research Ship *Discovery*, Captain Scott's famous polar exploration ship, this visitor centre vividly re-creates her historic voyages. Spectacular exhibits, interactive displays and special effects bring to life the story of the ship and a short dramatic film re-enacts the Antarctic expedition and its rescue.

Combine a visit with nearby Verdant Works, a restored 19th century jute works surrounding a cobbled courtyard.

☎ 01382 201245   www.rrsdiscovery.com

R.R.S. *Discovery*

✝ Dornoch Cathedral   332 C5

This small, well maintained cathedral was founded in 1224 by Gilbert, Archdeacon of Moray and Bishop of Caithness. Partially destroyed by fire in 1570 and restored in 1835 – 37, and again in 1924, the fine 13th century stonework is still visible. There are 27 magnificent stained glass windows and impressive woodwork.

☎ 01862 810357

🏰 Drum Castle (NTS)   312 C4

The 13th century tower of Drum is one of the three oldest tower houses in Scotland. Jacobean and Victorian extensions made the house into a fine mansion and it contains notable portraits and furniture, much from the 18th century. Drum was the home of the Irvine family for more than 650 years and a room displays family memorabilia. The extensive grounds include a collection of historic roses established by the National Trust in 1991, an arboretum and the ancient oak woodland of the 'Old Wood of Drum'.

☎ 01330 811204   www.drum-castle.org.uk
     www.nts.org.uk

🏭 Drumlanrig Castle   266 C1

A sweeping drive through a wooded avenue leads to an imposing late 17th century castle built of local pink sandstone. Originally a 15th century castle, it was converted, complete with turrets, towers and cupolas, for the 1st Duke of Queensberry. The state rooms have splendid oak panelling, Louis XIV furniture and paintings by Holbein, Murillo, Rembrandt and Brueghel.

The 40 acres (16ha) of formal and informal gardens are being restored according to the original plans, and new rhododendron areas are being created using seed collected from the wild. The adjacent Drumlanrig Country Park has waymarked trails, wildlife including red squirrels and otters, and some magnificent specimen trees. There is a visitor centre and a ranger service offers a programme of guided walks.

☎ 01848 330248   www.buccleuch.com

✿ Drummond Castle Gardens   293 D3

This is one of Scotland's largest formal gardens with magnificent early Victorian parterre, fountains, terracing and topiary. It is laid out in the form of a St Andrew's cross, centred around a multi-faceted 17th century sundial, carved by John Milne, master mason to Charles I.

☎ 01764 681257   www.drummondcastlegardens.co.uk

Drummond Castle Gardens

🌳 Drumpellier Country Park   375 E2

The park covers an area of 500 acres (202ha) of open grassland, mixed woodland, lowland heath and two natural lochs, one of which is a Site of Special Scientific Interest. A diverse range of wildlife can be seen by visitors and a network of paths makes all areas of the park accessible. There is a visitor centre and café, a road train, play area, and boat hire and fishing on the lochs.

☎ 01236 422257   www.northlan.gov.uk/leisure+
     and+tourism

✝ Dryburgh Abbey   277 G2

Founded in the 12th century in a delightful location on the banks of the River Tweed, the pink sandstone abbey remains demonstrate several architectural styles as the buildings were frequently assailed by the English, until 1545 when they were abandoned. Even so, Dryburgh is the most complete of the Border abbeys, the barrel vaulted chapter house being particularly impressive. Sir Walter Scott is buried here, as is Field Marshal Earl Haig, the World War I leader.

☎ 01835 822381   www.historic-scotland.gov.uk

🏰 Duart Castle   289 G1

This is one of Scotland's oldest inhabited castles and home to the 28th Chief of Clan Maclean. The keep, built in 1360, adjoins the original courtyard. Used as a garrison for Government troops after the 1745 Rising, it then fell into ruin but was restored by Sir Fitzroy Maclean in 1911.

☎ 01680 812309   www.duartcastle.com

🏠 Duff House   324 B3

Designed by William Adam for the first Earl of Fife in 1735, Duff House is one of the best examples of Georgian baroque architecture in Britain, and houses paintings, furniture and tapestries from the collections of the National Galleries of Scotland.

Duff House is surrounded by parkland and there are woodland walks by the River Deveron. The grounds are free and open all year.

☎ 01261 818181   www.duffhouse.org.uk

★ Duncansby Head   337 F1

Duncansby Head is located at the north-eastern edge of the Scottish mainland, beyond John o' Groats. Its lighthouse commands a fine view of Orkney, the Pentland Skerries and the east coast headlands.

Slightly to the south are the Duncansby Stacks, three huge stone needles in the sea, along with the sandstone cliffs, severed with deep crevices (geos), one of which is bridged by a natural rocky arch.

🏛 Dundee Contemporary Arts 396 C1

Centre for contemporary art and film with five floors containing two galleries, cinema, print studio, craft shop, visual research centre and activity room. Admission to the galleries and exhibitions is free, with a charge for the cinema.

☎ 01382 606220   www.dca.org.uk

✝ Dunfermline Abbey & Palace 285 E1

The remains of the great Benedictine abbey founded by Queen Margaret in the 11th century. The foundations of her church are under the present 12th century Romanesque style nave. Robert the Bruce is buried in the choir, now the site of the present parish church. Of the monastic buildings, the ruins of the refectory, pend and guesthouse remain.

☎ 01383 739026   www.historic-scotland.gov.uk

🏰 Dunnottar Castle 303 G1

A spectacular ruin 160ft (48.5m) above the North Sea, recognisable to many film buffs as the setting of Franco Zeffirelli's film 'Hamlet' which starred Mel Gibson. Situated on a flat-topped promontory with sheer cliffs on three sides, and linked to the mainland by a narrow neck of land, Dunnottar's dramatic defensive position ensured a rich and colourful history.

Between the 9th and 17th centuries the castle was fought over many times and for over three hundred years was held by the Keiths, who were Earls Marischal of Scotland, the most powerful family in Scotland. In 1297 William Wallace attacked the English garrison and burnt the wooden castle here, and Mary, Queen of Scots was a visitor in 1562 and 1564. Most famously, in 1652 the Scottish crown jewels, the Honours of Scotland, were hidden here safely for eight months during a siege by Cromwell's army.

Today several buildings from different periods remain, including the 14th century tower house. Access is by means of a steep path and steps.

☎ 01569 762173   www.dunechtestates.co.uk

🎌 ✺ Dunrobin Castle 333 D4

Overlooking the sea and set within magnificent formal gardens, Dunrobin Castle has belonged to the Earls and Dukes of Sutherland for centuries. It was originally a square keep, built in the 13th

Dunrobin Castle

century by Robert, Earl of Sutherland, after whom it was named Dun Robin. Its turreted, chateau-style appearance resulted after extensive modifications by Sir Charles Barry during the 1840s, after he had completed the new Houses of Parliament. As Scotland's most northerly great house, the castle is also its largest, with 189 rooms, and its oldest continuously-inhabited home.

Period rooms display fine paintings, furniture, family memorabilia and even a steam-powered fire engine.

The sheltered gardens, with their formal parterres, were first laid in 1850 and were inspired by those of Versailles. There are falconry demonstrations and a Victorian museum includes an exceptional collection of Pictish stones.

☎ 01408 633177

✳ Duthie Park & David Welch Winter Gardens 313 E4

This popular 50 acre (20ha) park with boating lake and Winter Gardens was first laid out in the late 19th century. It is just a short walk from Aberdeen city centre, next to the River Dee. The world-renowned David Welch Winter Gardens, renamed in recognition of the work of a former Aberdeen Parks Director, covers two acres (1ha) and is one of the largest covered gardens in Europe.

★ Eas a' Chual Aluinn 331 E2

This is Britain's tallest waterfall, dropping 658ft (200m) at the head of Loch Glencoul. Seals and the occasional elusive otter may be seen on the loch.

🏛 Easdale Island Folk Museum 289 G3

The Island of Easdale was once the centre of the slate industry. This museum, set amongst former quarriers' cottages, provides a fascinating account of industrial and domestic life on the island during the 18th and 19th centuries.

☎ 01852 300370   www.slate.org.uk

◻ Edinburgh 285 G2

Edinburgh is a superb city for visitors and with most of the interesting features so close together it is great for exploring on foot. The city grew up around the castle and it still dominates the skyline today. The Royal Mile, consisting of mostly medieval buildings, runs east from the castle to the

Edinburgh – Princes Street

Palace of Holyroodhouse, through the heart of the Old Town. Numerous narrow street and alleys lead off it, many with fascinating architecture to explore. The New Town is immediately to the north, separated only by the beautiful Princes Street Gardens. In stark contrast to the Old Town, it is full of spacious terraces and crescents that are some of the finest examples of Georgian town planning in Europe. The Water of Leith walkway takes visitors to the unspoilt Dean Village. To the east of the main city centre is Holyrood Park, a 650 acre (263ha) oasis of peace with hills, crags, moorlands, marshes and lochs. Arthur's Seat, within the park, is the core of an extinct volcano (822ft, 251m high) and it is worth a walk to the top for superb views over the entire city and the Firth of Forth. Each August the city really comes to life as, over a period of three weeks, the Festival takes place. It is a combination of theatre, dance, music and comedy with performances at all hours of the day and night.

Dunnottar Castle

SCOTLAND

Edinburgh Castle　397 E1

The castle rises from an extinct volcanic outcrop and dominates the city that has grown up around it. There has been some kind of fortress up on the hill since the 7th century although the oldest part of the present castle, St Margaret's Chapel, was built during the 12th century. In its early years the castle was a royal residence but has assumed an increasingly military role over time, and today still houses an important garrison for the Scottish regiments. The Scottish crown jewels are on display alongside the Stone of Destiny. In the castle vaults, once used as cells for military prisoners, is Mons Meg cannon, a 15th century siege gun which could fire a 500 pound stone a distance of 2 miles (3km). The Royal Apartments inside the palace have been sensitively restored to their 16th century splendour and the chamber where Mary, Queen of Scots gave birth to James VI (James I of England) are especially worth a look. Each day at one o'clock a gun is fired from the castle, originally for the benefit of ships in the Firth of Forth, a tradition that has continued unbroken since the 17th century. Knowledgeable guides lead frequent tours of the castle although it is also possible to wander freely. Each August the grounds play host to the Military Tattoo with massed bands, pipes, drums and display teams from around the world.

☎ 0131 225 9846　　www.historic-scotland.gov.uk

Edinburgh Castle

Edinburgh Zoo　373 A2

Established in 1913 by the Royal Zoological Society of Scotland, and set in 80 acres (32ha) of beautiful parkland on the side of Corstorphine Hill. The zoo has over 1000 animals, many of them rare or threatened in the wild, ranging in size from the tiny blue poison arrow frogs to the giant white rhinos. The zoo is best known for its penguins, which swim in the world's largest penguin pool and participate in the Penguin Parade, to the delight of children of all ages.

☎ 0131 314 0300　　www.edinburghzoo.org.uk

Edinburgh Zoo

Edzell Castle & Garden　303 D3

The castle is a late medieval, red stoned tower house incorporated into a 16th century courtyard mansion. There is a splendid walled garden, laid out by Sir David Lindsay in 1604. Its walls incorporate a wonderful display of heraldic and symbolic sculptures, alternating with recesses filled with flowers and bird's nests. At its far corners, find a well preserved, two-storey summerhouse and the remains of a bathhouse.

☎ 01356 648631　　www.historic-scotland.gov.uk

Eilean Donan Castle　307 E2

Situated on an islet in Loch Duich, this picturesque and inhabited castle dates back to 1214. It passed into the hands of the Mackenzies of Kintail, who became the Earls of Seaforth, was garrisoned by Spanish Jacobite troops in 1715 and blown up by the English. During the 20th century, the castle was fully restored.

☎ 01599 555202　　www.eileandonancastle.com

Elgin Cathedral (Ruins)　323 E3

The magnificent and substantial ruin of the 13th century cathedral known as the 'Lantern of the North' and regarded by many as the most beautiful in Scotland. Interesting features include the 15th century octagonal chapter house with vaulted ceiling and a Pictish cross-slab in the choir. Spectacular views of the cathedral and surrounding area are possible from a platform at the top of one of the massive towers.

☎ 01343 547171　　www.historic-scotland.gov.uk

Elgin Museum　323 E3

Internationally renowned for its fossils and Pictish stones, the museum houses unique collections of natural history, geology, archaeology, art, ethnography and the social history of the Moray area.

☎ 01343 543675　　www.elginmuseum.org.uk

Fair Isle　342 A5

Situated between Orkney and Shetland, Fair Isle is one of Britain's most isolated inhabited islands. Most famous for the intricately patterned knitwear which bears its name, this craft continues today. It is important, too, for its birdlife and there are many opportunities for ornithological studies, including the Bird Observatory. The island's archaeology provides much interest and traditional crofting is also still in evidence.

www.fairisle.org.uk
www.nts.org.uk

Falkirk Wheel　284 C1

A spectacular wheel reconnects the Union Canal up 82ft (25m) to the Forth and Clyde Canal. Weighing 1300 tonnes (2205 pounds), it is equivalent in height to a nine-storey block of flats and is the world's only rotating boat lift. The visitor centre provides information about the construction of the wheel and the restoration of the canal.

☎ 01324 619888　　www.thefalkirkwheel.co.uk

Falkland Palace (NTS)　294 A4

Built in the 1500s, Falkland Palace formed the country residence of the Stewart Kings and Queens. Restored period rooms on view include the Chapel Royal, the King's Bedchamber and the Queen's Room. The fine gardens contain the original royal tennis court, built in 1539 and the oldest still in use in Britain today.

☎ 01337 857397　　www.nts.org.uk

Falls of Clyde Wildlife Reserve & Visitor Centre　284 C5

The reserve covers almost 150 acres (59ha) of ancient woodland along both sides of the gorge alongside the River Clyde. The Clyde flows over four waterfalls within the reserve, the largest of which, Corra Linn, features an 84ft (26m) drop. The reserve, run by the Scottish Wildlife Trust, has recorded sightings of over 100 species of bird and in spring and summer it is possible to catch sight of breeding peregrine falcons. The visitor centre, housed in the old Dye House at New Lanark, has information on all the wildlife that make the reserve their home.

☎ 01555 665262　　www.swt.org.uk

Fife Folk Museum　294 B3

The local museum is housed in a 17th century tollbooth and 18th century weavers' cottages overlooking the Ceres Burn. The collection illustrates the social, economic and cultural history of rural Fife.

☎ 01334 828180　　www.fifefolkmuseum.co.uk

Finlaystone House Gardens　283 E2

140 acres (57ha) of woodland, waterfalls and gardens surround the 14th century Finlaystone House (not open to the public). The family-run estate overlooks the River Clyde and there are spectacular views across the Firth. The extensive gardens were originally laid out in 1900 and are considered to be among the finest in Scotland. The whole estate can be explored via a number of trails leading to picnic sites and adventure play areas. There is also a visitor centre.

☎ 01475 540505　　www.finlaystone.co.uk

Floors Castle　278 B3

Thought to be Scotland's largest inhabited castle, this magnificent, castellated Georgian mansion was designed by William Adam although the more flamboyant turrets and cupolas were added in Victorian times. The public apartments display an outstanding collection of 17th and 18th century French furniture, together with magnificent Brussels tapestries, paintings by Matisse and Augustus John, and European and Chinese porcelain.

The herbaceous borders in the walled garden are splendidly colourful in summer, while the extensive parkland which overlooks the River Tweed offers a range of woodland walks.

☎ 01573 223333　　www.floorscastle.com

Floors Castle

Fort George
`321 G4`

A vast site of one of the most outstanding artillery fortifications in Europe, having been planned in 1747 as a base for George II's army and completed in 1769. It continues to serve as a barracks and remains virtually unaltered. There is much to see, including the Queen's Own Highlanders Regimental Museum.

☎ 01667 462777   www.historic-scotland.gov.uk

Fyvie Castle (NTS)
`312 C1`

Adorned with turrets, gables and towers, Fyvie is one of the finest examples of Scottish baronial architecture. The five towers were reputedly built by, and named after, each of the families who owned the castle in succession – Preston, Meldrum, Seton, Gordon and Leith. The oldest part dates from the 13th century and there are ghosts and legends associated with the castle. The interior has some original 17th century plaster ceilings, an impressive decorated wheel staircase and collections of portraits, arms and armour, and 17th century tapestries. In the landscaped parkland visitors can enjoy a variety of scenic lochside walks. Traditional Scottish fruits and vegetables are grown in the old walled garden.

☎ 01651 891266   www.nts.org.uk

Gallery of Modern Art
`387 M7`

Opened in 1996 and housed in an elegant neo-classical city centre building, this popular gallery shows contemporary artwork by British artists. There is also a wide range of temporary exhibitions and a programme of events including music, drama and dance.

☎ 0141 229 1996   www.glasgowmuseums.com

Georgian House (NTS)
`397 E1`

The north side of Charlotte Square has been referred to as Robert Adam's masterpiece and is perhaps the finest example of neoclassical architecture in the country. The Georgian House at number 7 has had three floors elegantly restored to reflect the way the house would have looked during its ownership by the Lamont Family who bought the house in 1796.

☎ 0131 226 3318   www.nts.org.uk

Gladstone Court Museum
`276 B2`

A reconstructed Victorian street which brings to life small town life as it was during the second half of the 19th century. The town of Biggar has more museums per head of population than anywhere else in Scotland – others are Greenhill Covenanters' House, the Gasworks Museum, the Puppet Theatre and Moat Park Heritage Centre.

☎ 01899 221573   www.biggar-net.co.uk/museums

Gladstones Land (NTS)
`397 E2`

A superb example of a 17th century tenement house, this six-storey mansion has been wonderfully restored to indicate what life was like here in the 1600s. Particularly impressive are the decorated ceilings and wall friezes of the Painted Chamber.

☎ 0131 226 5856   www.nts.org.uk

Glamis Castle
`302 B5`

Originally a 14th century, three-storey keep, the present turreted castle was modified in the 17th century. One of the oldest parts is Duncan's Hall, legendary setting for Shakespeare's 'Macbeth'. Family home to the Earls of Strathmore, it was the late Queen Mother's childhood home and birthplace of Princess Margaret. On display are fine collections of china, paintings, tapestries and furniture.

☎ 01307 840394   www.glamis-castle.co.uk

Glasgow Botanic Garden
`374 B2`

Since 1842 these gardens have been a tranquil oasis in Glasgow's bustling West End. The gardens have long been known for their glasshouses and the largest is the huge Kibble Palace erected in 1873 and home to tree ferns from Australia and New Zealand, and plants from Africa, the Far East and the Americas. Other specialist plant collections include cacti, orchids and begonias.

☎ 0141 334 2422

Glasgow School of Art
`386 J5`

The work of Charles Rennie Mackintosh (1868 – 1928) has become synonymous with Glasgow. He blends organic forms with linear and geometric designs to create fabulous architecture, furniture and art work. Mackintosh was a student at the Glasgow School of Art before winning a competition to design a new building to house the school. Built between 1897 and 1907, the building is today considered to be his finest example of work and is the earliest example of a complete art nouveau building in the country. The only way to see the interior of the building is on a student-led guided tour.

☎ 0141 353 4526   www.gsa.ac.uk

Glasgow Science Centre
`386 A8`

A stunning titanium-clad building alongside the Clyde. The site is made up of three attractions – the IMAX theatre, the three-storey Science Mall and the Glasgow Tower. The IMAX has a cinema screen larger than a five-a-side football pitch and shows 2D and 3D films. The Science Mall has hundreds of hands-on exhibits, workshops and a planetarium. The Glasgow Tower, which at 328ft (100m) is the highest free-standing structure in Scotland and the only 360 degree rotating structure in the world, has information on past and future developments in Glasgow as well as superb views from the top. Tickets can be purchased for single attractions or there is a double ticket allowing entrance to two attractions.

☎ 0141 420 5000   www.gsc.org.uk

Glencoe
`298 D4`

This is a highly dramatic and historic glen. It has been the scene of numerous feudal clashes, particularly between the MacDonald and Campbell clans, and is probably best known for the 1692 massacre of part of the MacDonald clan by soldiers of King William. In fact, its name translates as 'Valley of Weeping'.

Its steep-sided mountains offer superb walking and climbing. Geologically, they also provide an example of a collapsed volcano. Red deer, wildcats, golden eagles and rare arctic plants can be seen among the breathtaking peaks and spectacular waterfalls. There are many walks, some more challenging than others.

☎ 01854 811307   www.nts.org.uk

Glencoe Visitor Centre (NTS)
`298 D4`

The visitor centre buildings have been laid out as a 'clachan' or small settlement and have fascinating interactive displays and exhibits about the history, geology and conservation of the area. A video recording recounts the massacre of part of the MacDonald clan by soldiers of King William in 1692. The Glencoe Lookout Station shows web cam images and the 'Living on the Edge' exhibition includes information about the history of mountaineering.

☎ 01855 811307   www.nts.org.uk

Glenfiddich Distillery
`323 F5`

Situated close to the river Fiddich, the distillery produces the only Highland single malt whisky that is distilled, aged and bottled at the same site. Glenfiddich is the world's biggest selling single malt and visitors can tour the distillery where production first started on Christmas Day 1887. Although the tour is free, there is a charge for a much longer connoisseur's tour and tasting.

☎ 01340 820373   www.glenfiddich.com

Glenfinnan Monument (NTS)
`298 B1`

Set amid superb Highland scenery at the head of Loch Shiel, Glenfinnan monument was erected in 1815 in tribute to the clansmen who died for the Jacobite cause. It is sited where Bonnie Prince Charlie raised his standard in 1745. The information centre recounts the Prince's campaign with displays and an audiovisual programme. Nearby is the Glenfinnan Viaduct, a spectacular railway viaduct with 21 arches, built in 1901.

☎ 01397 722250   www.nts.org.uk

Glenluce Abbey (NTS)
`264 C5`

Founded in 1192, the Cistercian monks' diligence in draining the surrounding marshes to create productive land ensured the abbey's survival. The chapter house, built around 1500, has endured almost intact with unusual decorative carvings and a ribbed vault ceiling providing splendid acoustics. More prosaic, but equally interesting are the well preserved clay drains and waterpipes laid by the monks. A small museum displays artefacts relating to the abbey, which was finally abandoned in 1560.

☎ 01581 300541   www.historic-scotland.gov.uk

Glencoe

Glenturret Distillery
`293 D2`

Whisky is still produced in the traditional manner at Scotland's oldest Highland malt distillery (established in 1775). Set in a picturesque location, enjoy free tasting as well as the Famous Grouse Experience in the interactive visitor centre.

☎ 01764 656565   www.glenturret.com

SCOTLAND

🏛 Gordon Highlanders Regimental Museum
313 E4

Striking exhibits from a unique collection, recalling 200 years of service of the regiment which largely recruited soldiers from north east Scotland. The medal display includes 12 Victoria crosses. Interactive screens and an audiovisual theatre serve to dramatise the history of this famous regiment which was amalgamated to form The Highlanders (Seaforth, Gordons and Camerons) in 1994.

☎ 01224 311200   www.gordonhighlanders.com

🏛 Grampian Transport Museum
312 A3

An extensive collection of historic road vehicles, many of them rare and unusual, which illustrates the history of road travel and transport in north-east Scotland. Among the items is the Craigievar Express, a steam powered tricycle built in 1895. With working exhibits, video presentations and the opportunity to climb aboard many vehicles, including a snow plough, it is a lively museum with lots to do.

☎ 019755 62292   www.gtm.org.uk

🏰 Greenhill Covenanters' House
276 B2

A 17th century farmhouse, rescued from 10 miles down the road and rebuilt here piece by piece. The museum returns the visitor to troubled times when James VI, Charles I and II, and James VII tried to rule against the wishes of the majority of the population and the Kirk of Scotland. The tale is simply, but comprehensively, told through the life of Lady Greenhill, the then owner of the farmhouse.

☎ 01899 221752   www.biggar-net.co.uk/museums

★ Grey Mare's Tail (NTS)
276 C4

Spectacular 200ft (61m) waterfall tumbling from the corrie containing Loch Skene down a rocky gorge into Moffat Water. Reached by a path that is precipitous in places.

☎ 01556 502575   www.nts.org.uk

🌳 Haddo House (NTS) & Country Park
313 D1

Haddo House is an elegant Georgian mansion designed by William Adam in 1732 for the 2nd Earl of Aberdeen, while much of the splendid interior decoration is Adam Revival style dating from the 1880s. Haddo has a beautiful library and contains some fine furniture and an extensive art collection. The formal garden includes terracing with rose beds.

Adjacent is Haddo Country Park, open all year, with waymarked trails, 3 miles (5km) of surfaced paths and wildlife hides.

☎ 01651 851440   www.nts.org.uk

🏰 Hermitage Castle
268 C2

A vast, eerie ruin of a forbidding fortress in a bleak moorland setting, dating from the 14th and 15th centuries and consisting of four towers and connecting walls. The imposing medieval exterior is deceptive as certain features resulted from a Victorian restoration, and inside the structure is little more than a ruin.

☎ 01387 376222   www.historic-scotland.gov.uk

★ Hermitage, The (NTS)
301 E5

Interesting walks in mixed woodland, containing one of Britain's tallest Douglas fir trees. The focus is a delightful 18th century folly, Ossian's Hall, set above a wooded gorge of the River Braan.

☎ 01796 473233   www.nts.org.uk

🏛 Highland Folk Museum
309 G4

An open-air museum, partly housed in an 18th century shooting lodge, illustrating the social history of people in the Highlands. There is another site at Newtonmore.

☎ 01540 661307   www.higlandfolk.com

🐘 Highland Wildlife Park
310 A4

Discover Scottish wildlife, from native species to creatures long extinct, in 180 acres (73ha) of parkland. Encounter enormous bison, ancient breeds of sheep and one of the world's rarest mammals, the Przewalski's Horse, by driving through the main reserve (staff will drive those without a car). Special themed events are held at weekends.

☎ 01540 651270   www.highlandwildlifepark.org

🏰 Hill House (NTS)
283 D1

Charles Rennie Mackintosh designed this house for the publisher Walter Blackie in 1904. A masterpiece of domestic architecture synthesizing traditional Scottish style with avant-garde innovation, this extraordinary building still looks modern today. Mackintosh, with his wife Margaret, also designed the interiors and most of the furniture.

☎ 01436 67900   www.nts.org.uk

🏰✿ Hill of Tarvit Mansion House & Garden (NTS)
294 B3

Sir Robert Lorimer designed this fine Edwardian house to provide a setting for his important collection of French, Chippendale style and vernacular furniture. Superb paintings, Flemish tapestries and Chinese porcelain and bronzes adorn the interiors. Lorimer also designed the formal gardens.

☎ 01334 653127   www.nts.org.uk

Hopetoun House

🏰✿ Hopetoun House
285 E2

Set in 100 acres (40ha) of magnificent parkland on the shores of the Firth of Forth, this house is one of Scotland's finest stately homes. It is the work of William Bruce, the architect who designed Holyroodhouse, and was later extended by William Adam. The magnificent state rooms feature the original 18th century furniture, remarkable paintings including works by Gainsborough, Raeburn and Canaletto, rococo ceilings, 17th century Aubusson tapestries, Meissen porcelain and some spectacular chandeliers in the Ballroom. The extensive parkland has woodland and riverside walks, a deer park and a walled garden.

☎ 0131 331 2451   www.hopetounhouse.com

🏰 House of Dun (NTS)
303 E4

Overlooking the Montrose Basin is this beautiful Georgian house, designed in 1730 by William Adam and containing superb contemporary plasterwork.

Home during the 19th century to Lady Augusta Kennedy-Erskine, daughter of William IV, many of her belongings remain, as well as her wool work and embroidery.

☎ 01674 810264   www.nts.org.uk

🏰 House of the Binns (NTS)
285 E2

Built between 1612 and 1630 by Thomas Dalyell, the house reflects the change in style of Scottish homes during the 17th century, from fortified stronghold to spacious mansion. Four of the main rooms have elaborate plasterwork ceilings and there is some fine furniture dating mostly from the late 18th and early 19th centuries. Outside there are woodland walks to a panoramic viewpoint over the Firth of Forth. The house is only open from June to September.

☎ 01506 834225   www.nts.org.uk

★ Hugh Miller's Cottage (NTS)
321 G3

The famous stonemason, geologist, writer and church reformer, Hugh Miller (1802 – 56), was born in this furnished thatched cottage, built around 1698. His life and work can be explored through exhibits of his belongings, including his fine fossil collection, his writings and video footage.

☎ 01381 600245   www.nts.org.uk

🏰 Huntingtower Castle
293 F2

Known as Ruthven Castle until 1600, Huntingtower Castle is a 15th century castellated mansion. A 17th century range links its two fine and complete towers. A key feature is the outstanding painted ceiling. Noteworthy historic events include a visit by Mary, Queen of Scots, the capture of King James the VI, and the birth of the Jacobite commander, Lord George Murray.

☎ 01738 627231   www.historic-scotland.gov.uk

★ Hutchesons' Hall (NTS)
387 N7

Built between 1802 and 1805, this elegant building replaced a 17th century hospice, and statues of George and Thomas Hutcheson, taken from the original building, have been incorporated into the frontage. A major rebuild in 1876 heightened the hall and made the way for an impressive staircase. The hall now houses a National Trust for Scotland shop and visitor centre and an exhibition entitled Glasgow Style displaying works by young Glasgow designers.

☎ 0141 552 8391   www.nts.org.uk

🏰 Inveraray Castle
290 C4

The Duke of Argyll's family, the senior branch of the Campbell Clan, moved here in the early 15th century. The present building, in the style of a castle, was erected between 1745 and 1790, replacing a previous fortified keep. Explore the grand staterooms, and some of the former bedrooms, and view the famous collections of armour, French tapestries, paintings, and fine Scottish and European furniture. The Clan Room contains a genealogical display. Gardens are open by appointment only.

☎ 01499 302203   www.inveraray-castle.com

★ Inveraray Jail
290 C4

This award winning attraction re-creates prison life in the 1800s. There are fascinating exhibitions, such as 'Torture, Death and Damnation', where the crank machine, whipping table and hammocks can all be tested first-hand, along with the sounds and smells of everyday life locked in the cells.

☎ 01499 302381   www.inverarayjail.co.uk

Inverewe Gardens (NTS)
`319 E1`

A world-famous garden created from a once barren peninsula on the shore of Loch Ewe by Victorian gardener Osgood Mackenzie. Exotic plants from many countries flourish here in the mild climate created by the warm currents of the North Atlantic Drift. Find Himalayan rhododendrons, Tasmanian eucalypts, and other subtropical plants from New Zealand, Chile and South Africa.

Much of the garden's structure is original, with work having been started in 1863 and continued by Mackenzie's daughter, until she handed over the estate to the Trust. There is also a visitor centre and access to the wider estate.

☎ 01445 781200   www.nts.org.uk

Iona (NTS)
`288 B2`

St Columba began to spread the gospel here in AD563, from where Christianity spread throughout Scotland and beyond. Explore the abbey, home to the Iona Community, with a beautiful interior and carvings, the 13th century priory, the oldest cemetery in Scotland, containing the graves of many kings and chiefs, the restored St Oran's Chapel, and the 10th century St Martin's Cross. There are also superb long sandy beaches, turquoise seas and unrivalled views.

☎ 01631 570000 (National Trust Office)   www.nts.org.uk

Italian Chapel
`339 D2`

Italian prisoners of war, whilst constructing the Churchill Barriers in World War II, transformed two corrugated iron Nissen huts into this ornate chapel. Its beautiful interior is the result of their ingenuity and craftsmanship. The painting of Madonna and Child is by Domenico Chioccetti.

☎ 01865 781279

J.M. Barrie's Birthplace & Camera Obscura (NTS)
`302 B4`

J.M. Barrie, creator of 'Peter Pan', was born in this two-storey weaver's cottage in 1860. The upper floors have been furnished to reflect the era and an exhibition about Barrie's literary and theatrical work is housed next door. Camera Obscura, found within the cricket pavilion on Kirrie Hill, was presented to Kirriemuir by the author.

☎ 01575 572646   www.nts.org.uk

Jarlshof Prehistoric & Norse Settlement
`343 G5`

A complex of ancient settlements within 3 acres (1.2ha) can be found on this extraordinarily important site. The oldest is a Bronze Age village of oval stone huts. Above this is an Iron Age broch and wheelhouses, and even higher still is an entire Viking settlement. A house, built around 1600, sits on the crest of the mount. Displays in the visitor centre explain Iron Age life and the history of the site.

☎ 01950 460112   www.historic-scotland.gov.uk

Inveraray Jail

Inverewe Gardens

Jedburgh Abbey
`278 A5`

Dominating the skyline in Jedburgh's centre, this red sandstone abbey was founded by David I in the 12th century, probably on the site of a 9th century church. The remarkably complete abbey church is mostly Romanesque and early Gothic in design, with a fine rose window and richly carved Norman doorway. Cloister remnants have been uncovered and artefacts found are on display at the visitor centre, together with an excellent exhibition on life in the monastery.

Jedburgh suffered various assaults during border warfare and was abandoned in 1560, though the church was used for another three centuries.

☎ 01835 863925   www.historic-scotland.gov.uk

Kelburn Castle & Country Centre
`282 D4`

Family home of the Earls of Glasgow, comprising a Norman keep within a 16th century castle with later additions, all surrounded by spectacular natural scenery. Activities include assault and adventure courses, horse riding, soft play and, for the less energetic, pets corner, delightful gardens and woodland walks through the Secret Forest. Ranger service and special weekend events.

☎ 01475 568685   www.kelburncountrycentre.com

Kellie Castle (NTS)
`294 D4`

The oldest part of Kellie Castle dates from 1360, but most of the present building was completed around 1606. It was sympathetically restored by the Lorimer family, who lived here in the 1870s. Inside, there are splendid painted ceilings and panelling, as well as excellent furniture designed by Sir Robert Lorimer. The extensive grounds include a lovely organic Victorian walled garden.

☎ 01333 720271   www.nts.org.uk

Kelso Abbey
`278 B3`

The largest of the Border abbeys founded by David I in 1128, Kelso was a fine example of Romanesque architecture. Little now remains of this once wealthy and powerful establishment; English raids in the first half of the 16th century focused on the abbey and destruction was completed in 1545 when 100 defenders were slaughtered. All that remains is part of the north-west transept, tower and a fragment of the nave.

☎ 0131 668 8800   www.historic-scotland.gov.uk

Kilchurn Castle
`290 D2`

A substantial ruin based on a square tower built by Colin Campbell of Glenorchy, circa 1550. It was much enlarged in 1693 by Ian, Earl of Breadalbane, whose arms are over the gateway with those of his wife. The castle incorporates the first purpose-built barracks in Scotland and commands spectacular views down Loch Awe. Open during summer only.

☎ 0131 668 8800   www.historic-scotland.gov.uk

Kildalton Church & Crosses
`280 C5`

The Old Church at Kildalton is the site of the finest intact High Cross in Scotland. Carved in the late 8th century, the Celtic cross stands 9ft (2.7m) high. There are also several other fine carved gravestones in the churchyard.

☎ 0131 668 8800   www.historic-scotland.gov.uk

Killiecrankie
`301 E3`

Just north of Pitlochry is the site of the battle of Killiecrankie in 1689, won by the Highland Jacobites under Bonnie Dundee. On the edge of the wooded gorge is the Pass of Killiecrankie Visitor Centre, which relates the fierce encounter. From here, a path leads to 'Soldiers Leap', where a fleeing government soldier made a spectacular jump over the River Garry during the battle.

☎ 01796 473233   www.nts.org.uk

Kilmartin House Museum
`290 A5`

Within a six-mile (10km) radius of Kilmartin Valley, over 350 ancient monuments can be found, including 150 that are prehistoric. This award-winning archaeological museum examines the relationship between Scotland's richest prehistoric landscape and its people. Artefacts from ancient monuments, reconstructions and interactive audiovisual displays make a fascinating exhibition.

☎ 01546 510278   www.kilmartin.org

Kintail Estate & Morvich (NTS)
`307 G3`

This west Highland estate is home to the Falls of Glomach, an impressive 370ft (113m) high waterfall, and the Five Sisters of Kintail, four of which are over 3000ft (915m). The site of the Battle of Glen Shiel, which took place in 1719, is also within this area, 5 miles (8km) from Morvich. The best access to the mountains is from the Countryside Centre at Morvich.

☎ 01599 511231   www.nts.org.uk

Kirkcaldy Museum & Art Gallery
`294 A5`

Located in the attractive War Memorial Gardens, the gallery contains fine and decorative arts of local and national importance. There is an outstanding collection of 18th to 20th century Scottish paintings, and probably the largest public collection of works by William McTaggart and the Scottish colourist, S.J. Peploe, outside the National Galleries of Scotland.

☎ 01592 412860

SCOTLAND

Lennoxlove
286 C2

Lennoxlove House is the seat of the Duke of Hamilton and there are fine collections of furniture and family portraits belonging to the Hamilton family. The earliest part of the house, the rectangular keep, was built well before 1400 and there have been extensions and additions during every century since. The various owners of the house have associations with the Stewarts and there are a number of mementoes belonging to Mary, Queen of Scots, including her death mask.

☎ 01620 823720   www.lennoxlove.org

Lighthouse, The
387 L8

Scotland's Centre for Architecture, Design and the City is the long-term legacy of Glasgow being the UK City of Architecture and Design in 1999. This Charles Rennie Mackintosh-designed building, once owned by the Herald newspaper, has a distinctive tower at one corner which gives it the name the Lighthouse. It houses the Mackintosh Interpretation Centre which features plans, photos and models of his work, and there are great views over the city skyline from the top of the tower.

☎ 0141 221 6362   www.thelighthouse.co.uk

Linlithgow Palace
285 E2

The ruin of a great 15th century Palace on the edge of Linlithgow Loch which is associated with many of Scotland's best known historical figures; James V and Mary, Queen of Scots, were both born here. The palace was damaged by fire in 1746 and it has been a roofless ruin ever since. The chapel is worth a look and the galleried Great Hall is magnificent. The quadrangle courtyard has a richly-carved 16th century fountain.

☎ 01506 842896   www.historic-scotland.gov.uk

Linn of Tummel (NTS)
301 E3

Follow a riverside nature trail, from Garry Bridge, through mixed woodland to the meeting place of the Rivers Garry and Tummel. The Linn of Tummel, which translates as 'pool of the tumbling stream', comprises a series of rocky rapids in a beautiful setting.

☎ 01796 473233   www.nts.org.uk

Loch an Eilein Visitor Centre & Forest Trail
310 A4

An island in Loch an Eilein harbours the remains of a 15th century castle. An ancient pine forest surrounds the loch, with some species dating back to the era of Bonnie Prince Charlie. There is a waymarked forest trail and a visitor centre.

Loch Lomond & The Trossachs National Park
291 F4

In 2002, Loch Lomond and the Trossachs were inaugurated as Scotland's first National Park. The park stretches from Arrochar to Callander, west to east, and from Balloch to Crianlarich, south to north. It is an area of contrasts, depicted by the lochs, wooded hills and lowlands in the south to the rugged and dramatic Highland mountains in the north. Ben Lomond towers over Loch Lomond, Britain's largest expanse of fresh water, and visitors can enjoy the wild glens and unspoilt lochs of the Trossachs. The Breadalbane area boasts numerous mountains over 3000ft (915m), including Ben More, Ben Lui, Ben Challum and Ben Vorlich, whilst the Argyll Forest in the west is overlooked by the Arrochar Alps and bounded by sea lochs.

Loch Lomond Shores visitor centre in Balloch provides the main gateway into the National Park.

☎ 01389 722600   www.lochlomond-trossachs.org

Loch Ness Monster Exhibition Centre
309 E2

The story of Loch Ness, the monster and other mysteries of the area are presented in a wide-screen cinema. Find out about the sightings of 'Nessie' and the various search expeditions, view the account of John Cobb's world water speed record attempt in 1953 on Loch Ness and hear about the 18th century mysterious 'footprints'.

☎ 01456 450342   www.lochness-centre.com

Lochore Meadows Country Park
293 G5

Green and pleasant countryside reclaimed from coal mining wasteland in the 1960s, set around a large lake. Find a variety of activities within the 1200 acres (486ha), including golf, fishing, sailing, windsurfing, walking and horse riding. There is also a nature reserve with a bird-watching hide and ancient historical remains, such as Lochore Castle. Admission to the park is free, with charges for the activities.

☎ 01592 414300   www.lochore-meadows.co.uk

Logan Botanic Garden
256 A2

The exceptionally mild climate, courtesy of the Gulf Stream, makes this one of Scotland's most exotic gardens, allowing a colourful array of tender plants to thrive. Many specimens are of wild origin, particularly representing the temperate regions of the Southern Hemisphere. The peat garden comprises a delightful collection of meconopsis, primulas, trilliums and dwarf rhododendrons. The walled garden has spring interest with magnolis, camellias, rhododendrons and a splendid collection of half-hardy perennials for summer colour. The woodland garden boasts mature eucalyptus and unusual, colourful southern hemisphere shrubs. Recent introductions are a result of plant hunting trips to Chile. There is also a Discovery Centre informing visitors of the work of the National Botanic Gardens of Scotland.

☎ 01776 860231   www.rbge.org.uk

Maes Howe
340 B5

This chambered cairn is the finest megalithic (Neolithic) tomb in the British Isles. It consists of a large mound 115ft (35m) in diameter covering a stone-built passage and a large burial chamber with cells in the walls. Vikings and Norse crusaders carved the runic inscriptions in the walls. Admission, shop and tearoom are at the nearby 19th century Tormiston Mill.

☎ 01856 761606   www.historic-scotland.gov.uk

Manderston
287 F4

Manderston could well be described as a celebration of opulence; a relatively modest 18th century house transformed by architect James Kinross into an extravagant, neoclassical Edwardian mansion.

Luxurious rooms boast intricate plasterwork, silk and velvet wall hangings, panelling and fine furniture. Marble abounds, from inlaid floors to the magnificent, probably unique staircase with its silver-plated balustrade. For contrast, the 'below stairs' element is also on view, together with a large collection of Blue John pieces and a biscuit tin museum.

Similarly, no expense was spared on the 56 acre (22ha) grounds. There are four splendid formal Edwardian terraces overlooking a lake and informal woodland gardens, while the walled gardens combine colourful plantings with fountains and statuary.

☎ 01361 883450   www.manderston.co.uk

McManus Galleries
396 B2

Contained within this Victorian Gothic building, designed by Sir George Gilbert Scott, are some remarkable collections of national importance. The galleries feature local history, costume, natural history, archaeology, decorative arts and a superb Scottish Victorian art collection. Do not miss the magnificent Albert Hall with its fine stained glass window and vaulted roof.

☎ 01382 432350   www.dundeecity.gov.uk/mcmanus

Meigle Sculptured Stones
302 A5

This is one of the most notable collections of Dark Age sculpture in Western Europe. There are 26 carved stones, the largest over 8ft (2m) tall.

☎ 01828 640612   www.historic-scotland.gov.uk

Loch Lomond

Mellerstain

🏛 Mellerstain 278 A3

A superb Georgian mansion representing some of the best architectural work of William Adam, who began the building in 1725, and his son, Robert, who completed it some 50 years later, giving a wonderful opportunity to compare their styles. The Robert Adam interior decoration is an outstanding feature of Mellerstain, the exquisite ceilings preserved in the original colours being particularly remarkable. Interior decoration is matched by the furnishings; pieces by Chippendale, Hepplewhite and Sheraton, and paintings by Van Dyck, Gainsborough and Aikman.

The gardens are formal, comprising Italianate terraces with magnificent views of the Cheviot Hills whilst the grounds, designed by William Adam in the style of Lancelot 'Capability' Brown, make a splendid backdrop to the house.

☎ 01573 410225   www.mellerstain.com

✝ Melrose Abbey 277 G2

A Cistercian abbey founded in 1136 by David I, noted for its elegant and elaborate masonry. Largely demolished by the English in 1385, it was rebuilt in the Gothic style but was finally destroyed in 1545. It is considered the most beautiful of the great Border abbeys, delicately carved stonework giving an intimation of its former splendour. The outer shell of the abbey church is still extant, with its magnificent east window.

An embalmed heart, thought to be that of Robert the Bruce, was found here. On his express wish it was taken for burial in the Holy Land, but the courier was killed in Spain and the heart returned to Scotland.

☎ 01896 822562   www.historic-scotland.gov.uk

🏛 Mount Stuart 282 C4

A spectacular Victorian Gothic house, Mount Stuart is the ancestral home of the Marquess of Bute. Its splendid interiors and architecture include a mix of astrological designs, stained glass and marble. In the 300 acres (121ha) of grounds and gardens there is a mature Victorian pinetum, arboretum and exotic gardens.

☎ 01700 503877   www.mountstuart.com

🏛 Mousa Broch 343 D5

This is the finest surviving Iron Age broch tower, standing over 40ft (12m) high. The stairs can be climbed to the parapet.

☎ 01466 793191   www.historic-scotland.gov.uk

🏛 Museum of Childhood 397 E3

Devoted to the history of childhood, this is an enchanting, colourful and extremely noisy place! Children love this museum for the sheer quantity of dolls, trains, models, games and books from all over the world, and adults love it for its nostalgia factor.

☎ 0131 529 4142   www.cac.org.uk

🏛 Museum of Flight 286 C2

There are around 50 complete aircraft, 80 engines and 5000 items of aircraft related equipment on display at Scotland's national aviation museum. The planes range from the oldest, the Hawk glider of 1896, to modern passenger airlines, supersonic jet fighters and Concorde. There are special exhibitions on space flight, early aviation and air traffic control. An annual airshow gives visitors the chance to see many planes in flight.

☎ 01620 880308   www.nms.ac.uk/flight

🏛 Museum of Scotland 397 E2

Scotland's national museum is housed in a striking, modern sandstone building completed in 1998. The museum traces the history and achievements of Scotland and its people, from the country's geological beginnings right up to the present day. The lower floors cover the period up to about 1700 with displays of rocks and fossils, Roman, Pictish and Gaelic artefacts. Two floors are devoted to Industry and Empire and tell of how the Scots pioneered many aspects of heavy engineering. The top floor covers the 20th century and is based around items that Scottish people thought best represented their country, which has resulted in displays on Irn-Bru and football strips, amongst others. There are free themed tours at regular intervals throughout the day and audio guides are available.

☎ 0131 247 4422   www.nms.ac.uk

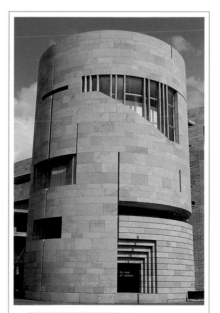

Museum of Scotland

🏛 Museum of Scottish Lead Mining 275 G4

Set in Wanlockhead, Scotland's highest village in the dramatic Lowther Hills, the museum traces 300 years of local lead mining history. A walk-through exhibition in the excellent visitor centre explains mining and extraction processes, and there is a good display of local minerals, including galena, chalcopyrite and sphalerite. A village trail includes a guided tour round Lochgell Lead Mine, together with restored miners' cottages.

☎ 01659 74387   www.leadminingmuseum.co.uk

🏛 National Gallery of Scotland 397 E2

This fine Greek temple style building was designed by William Henry Playfair and opened to the public in 1859. It houses Scotland's greatest collections of European paintings and sculpture from the Renaissance to post-impressionist periods. There are works by Raphael, Titian, El Greco, Turner, Degas and Van Gogh as well as a superb collection of Scottish art featuring important works by Wilkie, Raeburn and Ramsay.

☎ 0131 624 6200   www.natgalscot.ac.uk

★ National Wallace Monument 292 D5

The National Wallace Monument takes visitors back 700 years to the days of Scotland's first struggle for independence. The story of William Wallace, freedom fighter and national hero, is told along with events that shaped this period of history. Climb the 246 steps to the top of the 220ft (67m) high tower for superb views.

☎ 01786 472140   www.stirling.co.uk/attractions/wallace.htm

🏰 Neidpath Castle 276 D2

A rare example of a 14th century castle converted to a 17th century tower house, in a spectacular setting above the River Tweed. Massive walls, some 12ft (3.5m) thick in places, withstood Civil War bombardment longer than any other castle in the area, while inside is a pit prison cut out of the rock. The Great Hall hosts an exhibition of beautiful batik wall hangings depicting the life of Mary, Queen of Scots. Check in advance for opening times.

☎ 01721 720333

★ New Lanark World Heritage Site 284 C5

New Lanark is a superb example of a restored industrial village with plenty to keep a family busy for most of the day. Founded in 1785 by David Dale and Richard Arkwright as a centre for cotton spinning, the elegant sandstone buildings sit alongside the River Clyde in a remarkable rural setting. Dale's son-in-law, Robert Owen, took over the management of the site in 1798 and his belief in looking out for the welfare of his workers led to him setting up a cooperative store, a nursery to allow mothers with young children to work, adult education facilities, decent housing and a social centre for the community of 2500 people. Owen's 'social experiment' was viewed with scorn by all of his competitors but his beliefs soon proved fruitful and the business was greatly improved. The Institute for the Formation of Character now houses the award winning visitor centre and the Millennium Experience, an innovative ride which explains Owen's aspirations and ideas for a better future. Visitors can also look around the village store, Owen's house and mill workers' cottages. A passport ticket gives access to all of these attractions.

☎ 01555 661345   www.newlanark.org

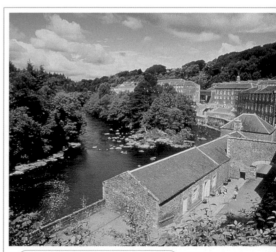

New Lanark World Heritage Site

SCOTLAND

North West Highlands – Suilven

North West Highlands [320 A5]

The North West Highlands provides a stunning and dramatic landscape of rugged mountains, hidden glens, moorlands, pine forests, secluded sandy beaches and sea lochs.

In Torridon, find mountain peaks towering over 3000ft (914m), whilst Ullapool is a thriving fishing village. Other remote villages along the north-west coast include Lochinver and Kinlochbervie. In Poolewe, find Inverewe Gardens, formed from a once barren peninsula on the shore of Loch Ewe, where exotic plants flourish in the warm climate created by the North Atlantic Drift. Alternatively, drive on Scotland's highest road, Bealach na Ba, climbing to the summit at 2056ft (625m) for spectacular views.

There are many natural features to look out for, too. Eas a' Chual Aluinn is Britain's tallest waterfall, and Corrieshalloch Gorge is one of Britain's finest examples of a box canyon. From here, a viewing platform stretched across the gorge looks up towards the magnificent Falls of Measach. Smoo Cave, in Durness, is an impressive limestone cave which has formed at the head of a narrow coastal inlet. The wild surroundings are also home to a variety of wildlife including red deer, eagles, otters and seals.

⭐ Old Man of Hoy [338 A2]

Standing off the magnificent cliffs of north-west Hoy is this prominent, isolated sea stack. Comprised of red sandstone, it stands at 450ft (137m) high. The Old Man of Hoy can also be seen from the Scrabster to Stromness ferry.

⭐ Our Dynamic Earth [397 E3]

This is a great family attraction based in a tented futuristic looking dome. Ten themed areas make use of dramatic special effects, stunning imagery and state-of-the-art interactive displays to take the visitor on a journey of discovery from the very beginning of time to our unknown future. Visitors begin their journey in the time machine elevator which takes them back to the creation of the universe before moving through a series of galleries that explain how the earth and continents were formed, how life has developed on earth and all about the seas and oceans.

☎ 0131 550 7800   www.dynamicearth.co.uk

🏛 Paisley Museum & Art Galleries [374 A3]

The Paisley Pattern is a well-known fabric design of swirling teardrops or pine cones. Paisley Museum has the world's largest collection of Paisley shawls, as well as the looms on which these intricately patterned garments were created. There is also a nationally important collection of ceramics and many fine 19th century Scottish paintings.

☎ 0141 889 3151   www.renfrewshire.gov.uk

🏰 Palace of Holyroodhouse [397 E3]

Largely a 17th century building, the north-west tower was built in 1501 for James IV. Holyroodhouse is the Queen's official residence in Scotland and it is used for state ceremonies. The Great Gallery occupies the whole of the first floor of the north wing, and in it hang 89 portraits of real and legendary kings of Scotland. The state apartments reflect the changing tastes of successive monarchs and are renowned for their fine stucco ceilings. Mary, Queen of Scots' chambers can be viewed in the west corner tower. The Queen's Gallery, for which there is a separate charge, hosts a programme of changing exhibitions from the Royal Collection, focusing primarily on works from the Royal Library at Windsor Castle.

☎ 0131 556 5100   www.royal.gov.uk

Our Dynamic Earth

🏰 Paxton House [287 G4]

Superb 18th century Palladian mansion, designed by John and James Adam and further embellished by brother Robert, providing an interesting contrast in styles. As well as the notable interior decoration, this is essential viewing for furniture enthusiasts, with one of the greatest Chippendale collections in Scotland and fine Regency furniture by William Trotter of Edinburgh. The large art gallery, an out-station for the National Galleries for Scotland, has a programme of temporary exhibitions.

The 80 acres (32ha) of parkland surrounding the house offer walks along the banks of the River Tweed and an adventure playground.

☎ 01289 386291   www.paxtonhouse.com

🏛 People's Story Museum [397 E3]

A lively museum, in the picturesque Canongate Tolbooth which was built in 1591. It uses oral history, reminiscence and written sources to tell the story of the lives, work and leisure of the ordinary people of Edinburgh, from the late 18th century to the present day.

☎ 0131 529 4057   www.cac.org.uk

❈ Pitmedden Garden (NTS) [313 D2]

A 17th century walled garden, notable for the Great Garden which is made up of four parterres of elaborate designs in boxwood hedging. These are filled with colourful annual bedding in summer. Interest is also provided by large herbaceous borders, roses, espalier fruit trees, roses and an herb garden. On the surrounding 100 acre (40ha) estate there is the Museum of Farming Life.

☎ 01651 842352   www.nts.org.uk

🏰 Pollok House (NTS) [374 B3]

The Pollok Estate has been the home of the Maxwell family since the 13th century and the current house, an impressive Edwardian country mansion, was built in 1740. Sir William Stirling Maxwell (1818 – 1878) was an authority on the art and history of Spain and his collection of works by Goya and El Greco is superb. There is also a fine collection of the work of English poet and artist William Blake, as well as silverware and furnishings from the Edwardian period. The gardens are also worth a look with a collection of over 1000 species of rhododendron. Entrance is free from November to March.

☎ 0141 616 6410   www.nts.org.uk

🏰 Preston Mill & Phantassie Dovecot (NTS) [286 C2]

A picturesque 18th century grain mill that was used commercially up until 1959. Today the mill no longer produces grain but visitors can see and hear the machinery and water wheel in action. There is an exhibition on milling and a display on the history of Preston Mill. It is a short scenic walk to the Phantassie Dovecot which once held 500 birds.

☎ 01620 860426   www.nts.org.uk

❈ Priorwood (NTS) [277 G2]

A specialist garden with varied and colourful herbaceous borders, plants being especially selected for drying qualities. This takes place on the premises where visitors can learn about the art of dried flower arranging. The garden also has an organic orchard growing historic apple varieties.

☎ 01896 822493   www.nts.org.uk

Queensferry Museum 285 F2

Traces the history of the people of Queensferry, the historic ferry crossing to Fife, the building of the Forth road and rail bridges, and the wildlife in the Forth estuary.

☎ 0131 331 5545 www.cac.org.uk

Rannoch Moor 299 F4

A wild, remote and fairly level area of around 50 sq miles (130 sq km), at an altitude of 1000ft (305m) surrounded by mountains. It is predominantly covered in a mixture of heather, peat bogs, rocks, and numerous lochs and streams. From the moor, enjoy fine views of Black Mount, Glencoe and the Grampians.

Rannoch Station can be found at the end of the B846, from where the only way to cross east to west is by foot. The main roads travel along its outer edges, while the West Highland Railway crosses it from south to north. Both the north and the south shores of the 10 mile (16km) long Loch Rannoch can be travelled along, with the south being the more scenic. The Blackwood of Rannoch, situated on the southern shore, is one of the last remaining examples of ancient Caledonian Forest and an important source of Scots Pine seed. An ancient burial ground of St Michael's can also be found. Loch Ericht lies to the north, accessed via a tunnel aqueduct.

There are plenty of scenic walks to enjoy on the moor. The lochs are also popular for trout fishing, while their sandy shores and islands attract many birds such as black-throated divers and goosander.

Ring of Brogar 340 A5

The Ring of Brodgar (also known as the Ring of Brogar) is a magnificent circle of upright stones, dating back to the Neolithic period. A ditch encloses the stones and is spanned by entrance causeways.

☎ 01855 841815 www.historic-scotland.gov.uk

Rosslyn Chapel 285 G3

A mysterious 15th century chapel that is thought to be just part of a much larger once-planned collegiate church whose foundations have been excavated. The carvings on the exterior and inside are outstanding; there are botanically accurate plants and leaves as well as biblical, pagan and masonic symbology.

☎ 0131 440 2159 www.rosslynchapel.org.uk

Royal Botanic Garden

Rannoch Moor

Royal Botanic Garden 373 B1

The Botanics are acknowledged to be some of the finest gardens in the world and the beautifully landscaped gardens cover an area of over 70 acres (28ha). The amazing Glasshouse Experience, a series of ten themed glasshouses with five different climatic zones to suit plants from all over the world, is home to giant water lilies and amazing orchids. There is an elegant 1850s glass topped Palm House, which is Britain's tallest and houses a 200 year old palm tree. Other spectacular areas are the Chinese Hillside, the renowned Rock Garden, the Scottish Heath Garden and an arboretum with over 200 species of tree. Guided tours are available between April and September for a fee.

☎ 0131 552 7171 www.rbge.org.uk

Royal Museum of Scotland 397 E2

Thirty-six galleries of varying sizes present artefacts from around the globe, natural history specimens, and engines and other industrial machinery. The Main Hall, with its elegant Victorian bird-cage design, is flooded with natural light and provides a great sense of space and tranquility with fountains and fish ponds.

☎ 0131 247 4219 www.nms.ac.uk

Royal Scots Regimental Museum, The 397 E1

Housed in a 1900 Drill Hall, this museum contains paintings, artefacts, silver and medals illustrating the Regiment's illustrious history from its formation in 1633.

☎ 0131 310 5016 www.theroyalscots.co.uk/museum

St Abb's Head (NTS) 287 G3

A 200 acre (80ha) National Nature Reserve on a dramatic, isolated promontory of black volcanic rock. Between April and August sheer 300ft (91m) cliffs provide nest sites for seabird colonies including kittiwakes, guillemots, razorbills and fulmars, while puffins tunnel into the clifftop. The visitor centre's remote camera link allows observation of the birds during the nesting season (entry fee). The headland provides splendid coastal views while the offshore waters are part of Scotland's first voluntary marine nature reserve.

☎ 01890 771443 www.nts.org.uk

St Andrews Cathedral 294 D3

The remains of one of the largest cathedrals in Scotland and the associated domestic ranges of the priory. The museum houses an outstanding collection of early Christian and medieval monuments, and other objets trouvés. St Rules Tower, in the precinct, is part of the first church of the Augustinian canons at St Andrews, built early in the 12th century. A climb up 150 steps is rewarded with fabulous views at the top. Combine a visit with St Andrews Castle.

☎ 01334 472563 www.historic-scotland.gov.uk

St Bride's Church 275 G2

The oldest structure in the village of Douglas, this church was built during the late 14th century. Originally the parish church of Douglas, it later became the mausoleum of the Black Douglas family. The restored choir, which contains three canopied monuments to the Douglas family, and the south side of the nave remain. Access to the church can be arranged by contacting the key keeper, details of which are on the church gate.

☎ 01555 851657 www.historic-scotland.gov.uk

St Giles Cathedral 397 E2

Not strictly a cathedral, as it was only the seat of a bishop on two brief occasions in the 17th century, but the historical title seems to have stuck. The basic structure of the church is late 15th century, although parts of the early 12th century Norman chapel still remain. The cathedral is renowned for its Victorian and 20th century stained glass, Reiger organ and beautiful Thistle Chapel.

☎ 0131 225 9442 www.stgiles.net

St Magnus Cathedral 338 D2

The cathedral was founded by Jarl Rognvald and dedicated to his uncle, St Magnus. The remains of both men are in the massive east choir piers. The original building dates from 1137 – 1200, but sporadic additional work went on until the late 14th century. It contains some of the finest examples of Norman architecture in Scotland, with small additions in transitional styles and some early Gothic work. A charge applies to tour the tower and upper areas, and should be booked in advance.

☎ 01856 874894

Scone Palace `293 G2`

A castellated palace, enlarged and embellished in 1803, incorporating the 16th century and earlier palaces. Notable for its grounds and pinetum, and its magnificent collection of porcelain, furniture, ivories, 18th century clocks and 16th century needlework. From the 9th century, Moot Hill at Scone was the site of the famous Coronation Stone of Scone (the Stone of Destiny), and crowning place of Scottish Kings. In 1296 the English seized the Stone and took it to Westminster Abbey. Returned to Scotland's Edinburgh Castle in 1997, a replica now stands on Moot Hill.

☎ 01738 552300　　　www.scone-palace.co.uk

★ **Scottish Crannog Centre** `300 C5`

A unique re-creation of an Iron Age loch dwelling, or crannog, this timbered and thatched house, standing on stilts within Loch Tay, has been authentically built using evidence obtained from underwater archaeological excavations of crannogs preserved in the loch.

☎ 01887 830583　　　www.crannog.co.uk

🏛 **Scottish Fisheries Museum** ♿ `295 D4`

Housed in 16th to 19th century buildings, the museum describes the history of fishing in Scotland up to the present day.

☎ 01333 310628　　www.scottish-fisheries-museum.org

🏛 **Scottish Maritime Museum** `274 B2`

An informative museum on the harbourside at Irvine, with sailing and working boats, lifeboats and a collection of documents, photographs and artefacts interpreting Scotland's maritime history.

Indoor exhibits are based in the huge Linthouse Engine Shop which was dismantled and relocated from the Linthouse Shipyard in Govan in 1992. Nearby is a restored tenement flat, typical home to a 1920s shipyard worker. The floating exhibits are moored by the quay. In addition, there is ongoing restoration work on a variety of vessels.

☎ 01294 278283　　www.scottishmaritimemuseum.org

🏛 **Scottish National Gallery of Modern Art** ♿ `373 B1`

Set in beautiful parkland, the gallery has a superb collection of 20th century paintings, graphic art and sculpture amounting to almost 4000 pieces. There are fine examples of work by Lichtenstein, Matisse and Picasso and an unrivalled collection of Scottish art including works by Charles Rennie Mackintosh. The sculpture garden in the grounds has work by Barbara Hepworth, Eduardo Paolozzi and Henry Moore.

☎ 0131 624 6200　　　www.natgalscot.ac.uk

🏛 **Scottish National Portrait Gallery** ♿ `397 D2`

Provides a unique visual history of Scotland, told through portraits of the figures who shaped it: royals and rebels, poets and philosophers, heroes and villains. The portraits are all of Scots although not all are by Scots; there is work by Rodin, Van Dyck and Gainsborough. The gallery is also home to the Scottish National Photographic Collection.

☎ 0131 624 6200　　　www.natgalscot.ac.uk

🐾 **Scottish Seabird Centre** `286 C1`

Visitors can watch live pictures, via remote cameras, of the sea birds that make the islands in the Firth of Forth their home. Amongst the estimated 150,000 sea birds are gannets, thought to be the largest colony in the world, terns, guillemots and puffins, as well as seals and dolphins. There is also a cinema showing films on the wildlife, interactive displays and boat trips out to the islands themselves. There are superb views of Bass Rock and the other islands in the Firth of Forth from the roof terrace.

☎ 01620 890202　　　www.seabird.org

✝ **Seton Collegiate Church** `286 B2`

The chancel and apse of a lovely 15th century church with a transept and steeple added in 1513. Much of the church is in good condition and is full of interesting detail. The grounds of the church have the remains of a number of buildings thought to be priests' houses and there is a display of stonework from Seton Palace, destroyed in 1715.

☎ 01875 813334　　www.historic-scotland.gov.uk

 Skara Brae `340 A5`

This site contains the best preserved group of Stone Age houses in Western Europe. A storm in 1850 lifted the sand covering the area to reveal the remains of this former fishing village. Ten one-roomed houses can be found, joined by covered passages, and contain their original stone furniture, hearths and drains. They provide a remarkable illustration of life in Neolithic times.

☎ 01856 841815　　www.historic-scotland.gov.uk

🏛 **Smith Art Gallery & Museum** ♿ `292 C5`

Displays and exhibitions encapsulate the history of Stirling through a wonderful collection of fine art and natural history. Some unusual pieces on view include the world's oldest dated curling stone, ancient tartans, prehistoric whalebones and the world's oldest football.

☎ 01786 471917　　www.smithartgallery.demon.co.uk

Stirling Castle – Robert the Bruce statue

★ **Smoo Cave** `334 D2`

This impressive limestone cave has formed at the head of a narrow coastal inlet. An easy and safe access path leads into the cave from the road above. At 100ft (30m) wide and 50ft (15m) high, this is arguably one of the largest cave entrances in Britain. A wooden pathway extends into the second inner chamber, where Allt Smoo falls from an opening in the roof. A small boat provides access to the third chamber. The outer cave contains an ancient midden, indicating that Stone Age man once lived there. The cave is free to enter on foot, whilst a charge applies to enter by boat.

☎ 01971 511259　　　www.smoocave.org

 Souter Johnnie's Cottage (NTS) `274 A5`

A thatched cottage, home to souter (cobbler) John Davidson, a drinking companion of Robert Burns, and inspiration for Souter Johnnie in Burns' poem 'Tam O' Shanter'. The cottage contains Burns memorabilia and a reconstructed cobbler's workshop.

☎ 01655 760603　　　www.nts.org.uk

★ **Staffa (Fingal's Cave) (NTS)** `288 C1`

This romantic, uninhabited island is famed for its extraordinary basaltic column formations. The best known of these is Fingal's Cave, 227ft (69m) deep and 66ft (20m) high. This cathedral-like structure, constantly pounded by the sea, was the inspiration for Mendelssohn's Hebrides overture. The cave can be viewed from a boat, which lands on the island if weather conditions permit. A colony of puffins can also be found nesting during spring and summer.

☎ 01631 570000　　　www.nts.org.uk

🏛 **Stewartry Museum** ♿ `266 A5`

A purpose-built Victorian building opened in 1893 providing a home for a fascinating and quirky range of exhibits depicting the social and natural history of the Solway coast. There are also works by local artists, temporary exhibitions and a family and local history information service.

☎ 01557 331643

🏰 **Stirling Castle** ♿ `292 C5`

Considered by many as Scotland's grandest castle, it is certainly one of the most important. Most of the building dates from the 15th and 16th centuries, when it became a popular Royal residence. The castle architecture is outstanding. The Great Hall and the Gatehouse, built by James IV, the magnificent Renaissance palace, built by James V, and the Chapel Royal, rebuilt by James VI, are amongst the key highlights. Mary, Queen of Scots was crowned here in 1543 and narrowly escaped death by fire in 1561. The medieval kitchens have been re-created, complete with models of cooks preparing a banquet in the 16th century.

Stirling Castle is set high on a volcanic outcrop, and commands stunning views, including the battlefields of Stirling Bridge and Bannockburn, Ben Lomond and the Trossachs.

☎ 01786 450000　　　www.historic-scotland.gov.uk

★ **Storybook Glen** `313 D5`

A delight for children of all ages, this 20 acre (8ha) unusual theme park has over 100 models of fairytale and nursery rhyme characters set in beautiful landscaped gardens.

☎ 01224 732941　　www.storybookglenaberdeen.co.uk

🌲 **Strathclyde Country Park** `375 F4`

1000 acres (404ha) of woodland, rough wetlands, wildlife refuges and neat open parkland surround the 200 acre (80ha) man-made Strathclyde Loch. The park offers a huge variety of recreational activities (many of which have a fee) including watersports, horse riding, fishing, orienteering and cycling as well as numerous way-marked trails, sports pitches, sandy beaches and picnic areas. The visitor centre has information on the natural history and wildlife of the park. Within the park are the remains of Bothwellhaugh Roman Fort and Bathhouse. The park is also home to Scotland's largest theme park, M & D's, which has more than 40 rides and a large indoor entertainment complex.

☎ 01698 266155　www.northlan.gov.uk/leisure+and+tourism

★ Strathisla Distillery `323 G4`

The oldest working distillery in the Highlands, established in 1786, and home to Chivas Regal blended Scotch whisky in which Strathisla single malt is predominant. The distillery takes water from the Broomhill Spring which Dominican monks used to make beer in the 13th century. There is a comprehensive self-guided tour of the distillery and whisky tasting.

☎ 01542 783044   www.chivas.com

🏛 Strathnaver Museum `335 G2`

The former parish church of Farr was converted into this local museum and shows the story of the Strathnaver Clearances and the Clan Mackay.

☎ 01641 521418

🚂 Strathspey Railway `310 B3`

A trip on this steam railway, reopened in 1978, runs 5 miles (8km) from Aviemore to Boat of Garten. The line now extends to Broomhill, also known as Glenbogle in the BBC TV series 'Monarch of the Glen'.

It operates mainly throughout the summer, but also on other occasions, so it is advisable to check the timetable.

☎ 01479 810725   www.strathspeyrailway.co.uk
☎ 01479 812220 (talking timetable)

🏛 Summerlee Heritage Park `375 F2`

Said to be Scotland's noisiest museum, Summerlee Heritage Park preserves and interprets the history of the steel and engineering industries that were once dominant in the surrounding area. Spread over 25 acres (10ha), there is plenty to see including a reconstructed Miners Row where the living conditions of the miners from the 1840s to the 1960s can be experienced, and a re-created mine where their working conditions can be examined.

☎ 01236 431261   www.northlan.gov.uk/leisure+ and+tourism

✝ Sweetheart Abbey `267 D4`

Splendid late 13th/early 14th century ruin founded by Devorgilla, Lady of Galloway, in memory of her husband John Balliol, and named because she was buried with her husband's embalmed heart which she carried with her in a casket after his death.

The 30 acre (12ha) site is dominated by the shell of the abbey church with its substantial central tower and lofty arched nave, but the most interesting feature is the great precinct wall. While not perhaps a professional defensive work, it was sufficiently formidable to deter raiding gangs.

☎ 01387 850397   www.historic-scotland.gov.uk

Strathclyde Country Park

🏰 Tantallon Castle `286 C1`

This formidable castle has a majestic setting on cliffs overlooking the Firth of Forth and Bass Rock. A stronghold of the Douglas family, it was built at the end of the 14th century but after a number of sieges it was finally destroyed by Cromwell in 1651. The massive 50ft (15m) high curtain wall is all that remains intact.

☎ 01620 892727   www.historic-scotland.gov.uk

🏰 Thirlestane Castle `286 C5`

Originally a 14th century fortress converted to a home by William Maitland, Secretary of State to Mary, Queen of Scots. Further restyling in the 17th century by Sir William Bruce created state rooms with arguably some of the finest plasterwork ceilings in Britain. Paintings include works by Gainsborough, Romney and Hopper, whilst the nursery wing contains a large collection of historic toys. The Border Country Life Museum is located here, and there are woodland walks and an adventure playground in the grounds.

☎ 01578 722430   www.thirlestanecastle.co.uk

🏰 Threave Castle `266 B4`

Set on an island in the River Dee, access is by ferry following a 0.5 mile (1km) walk across fields.

Though probably settled here as far back as AD500, the present structure, a massive 5-storey keep, was built by Archibald the Grim in the 1370s. The castle had a turbulent history as home of the 'Black' Douglas clan, and was extended in the 15th century with substantial artillery fortification during a significant disagreement with James II. Besieged by the Covenanters, it was slighted and abandoned in 1640, but was briefly used to house Napoleonic prisoners of war.

☎ 0131 668 8800   www.historic-scotland.gov.uk

✴ Threave Gardens (NTS) `266 B4`

Gardens of around 60 acres (24ha), developed as a horticultural training centre by the National Trust for Scotland and maintained by students. Well worth visiting at almost any time, with spectacular springtime displays of nearly 200 varieties of daffodil, complemented by rhododendrons and other early flowering shrubs, extensive herbaceous colour in summer, striking trees and heathers in autumn, and rock, peat, walled and formal gardens.

☎ 01556 502575   www.nts.org.uk

🏰 ✴ Torosay Castle `289 G1`

This Victorian family home contains furniture, pictures, china, family albums and scrapbooks dating from Edwardian times. The surrounding 12 acres (5ha) of gardens include formal terraces and a statue walk set amidst fuchsia hedges. There are also woodland and water gardens, a eucalyptus walk, oriental garden and rockery. Extensive views past Duart Castle and the Sound of Mull to the mountains of Arran and Lorne.

☎ 01680 812421   www.holidaymull.org/ members/torosay.html

★ Torridon (NTS) `319 F4`

Around 16,000 acres (6475ha) of some of Scotland's finest mountain scenery whose peaks rise over 3000ft (914m). Of major geological interest, Liathach and Beinn Alligin are formed of red sandstone, some 750 million years old, and their summits of white quartzite, some 600 million years old. The visitor centre, at the junction of the A896 and Diabaig road, has an audiovisual presentation on the local wildlife. There is also a deer museum and deer park, and ranger-led walks in season.

☎ 01445 791221   www.nts.org.uk

🏰 Traquair House `277 E2`

Dating from the 12th century, and originally a royal hunting lodge, this is considered the oldest continuously inhabited house in Scotland, visited by 27 Scottish and English monarchs. Presenting a striking, whitewashed façade, internally many original features remain, including vaulted cellars, a medieval staircase and priest's hole. Furniture, fittings and memorabilia bear a fascinating testimony to the vagaries of Scottish political and domestic life over the centuries. There is also an 18th century working brewery with tastings in summer, maze, trails and adventure playground.

☎ 01896 830323   www.traquair.co.uk

🏰 Urquhart Castle `309 E2`

The ruins of one of the largest castles in Scotland are found on the shores of Loch Ness. First built in the 1230s on the site of a vitrified fort, the castle fell into decay after 1689 and was blown up in 1692 to prevent it being occupied by Jacobites. Many of the remains are 14th century and the Grant Tower is 16th century.

☎ 01456 450551   www.historic-scotland.gov.uk

★ Vikingar! Experience, The `282 D3`

A multimedia display on local Viking history, from the earliest raids to their defeat at the Battle of Largs in 1263. The adjacent leisure complex houses a swimming pool, cinema and play area.

☎ 01475 689777   www.vikingar.co.uk

🏰 Weaver's Cottage (NTS) `283 F3`

The village of Kilbarchan was, in 1830, home to over 800 weavers' looms. Today, the last remaining hand loom can be seen in this typical 18th century weaver's cottage. There are displays of local and historical weaving interest, an attractive cottage garden where plants are grown to make natural dyes and a presentation explaining the village's links with the famous Paisley patterned shawls.

☎ 01505 705588   www.nts.org.uk

★ West Highland Line `298 D2`

Travel from Fort William to Mallaig on the West Highland Line, either on Scotrail or on the Jacobite Steam Train, which leaves in the morning and returns late afternoon. The round trip covers 84 miles (135km) and tours through magnificent Highland scenery.

Cross the 100ft (30m) high Glenfinnan Viaduct, and go past Loch Shiel and the monument commemorating where Bonnie Prince Charlie raised his standard. Travel through Arisaig, the UK's most westerly main line railway station, then via Loch Morar, which, at 1077ft (328m), is Britain's deepest loch. Enjoy great views en route of the Isles of Rum, Eigg, Muck and Canna, and the southern tip of Skye.

The journey stops at Glenfinnan and there is plenty of time to explore Mallaig and its harbour before returning.

☎ 01463 239026   www.steamtrain.info
www.scotrail.co.uk

✝ Whithorn Priory `257 E2`

St Ninian founded a church here around AD400, and this site is considered the cradle of Christianity in Scotland. The ruined priory, once the cathedral church of Galloway, was built in the 12th century as his tomb had become a place of pilgrimage. The ecclesiastical history of the site is complex, and finds from the ongoing archaeological work, including some fine Celtic crosses, are on display in the museum.

☎ 01988 500508   www.historic-scotland.gov.uk

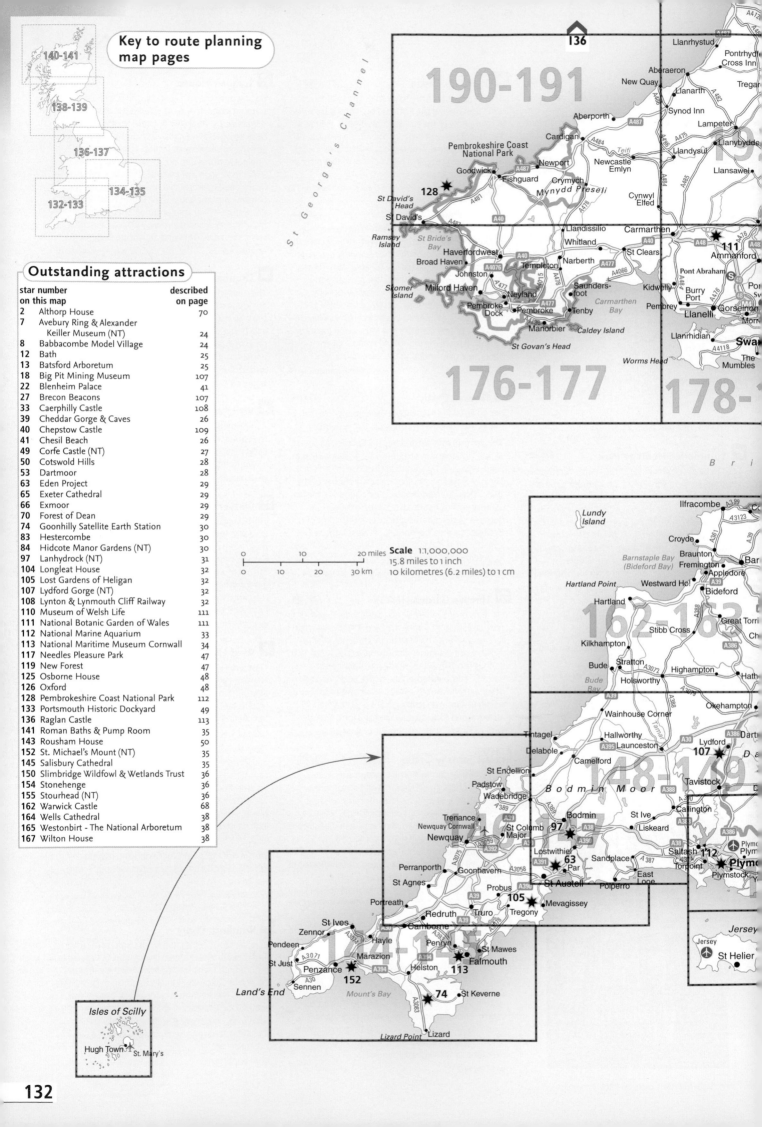

140-141

138-139

136-137

134-135

132-133

Scale 1:1,000,000
15.8 miles to 1 inch
10 kilometres (6.2 miles) to 1 cm

0   10   20 miles
0   10   20   30 km

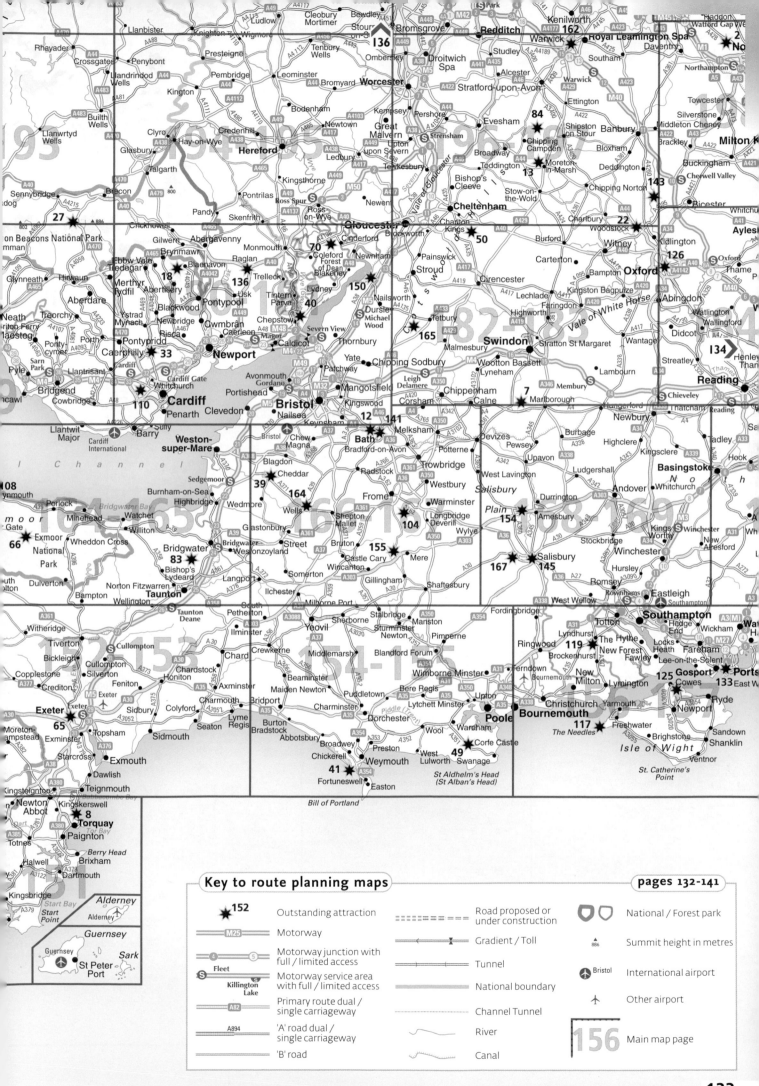

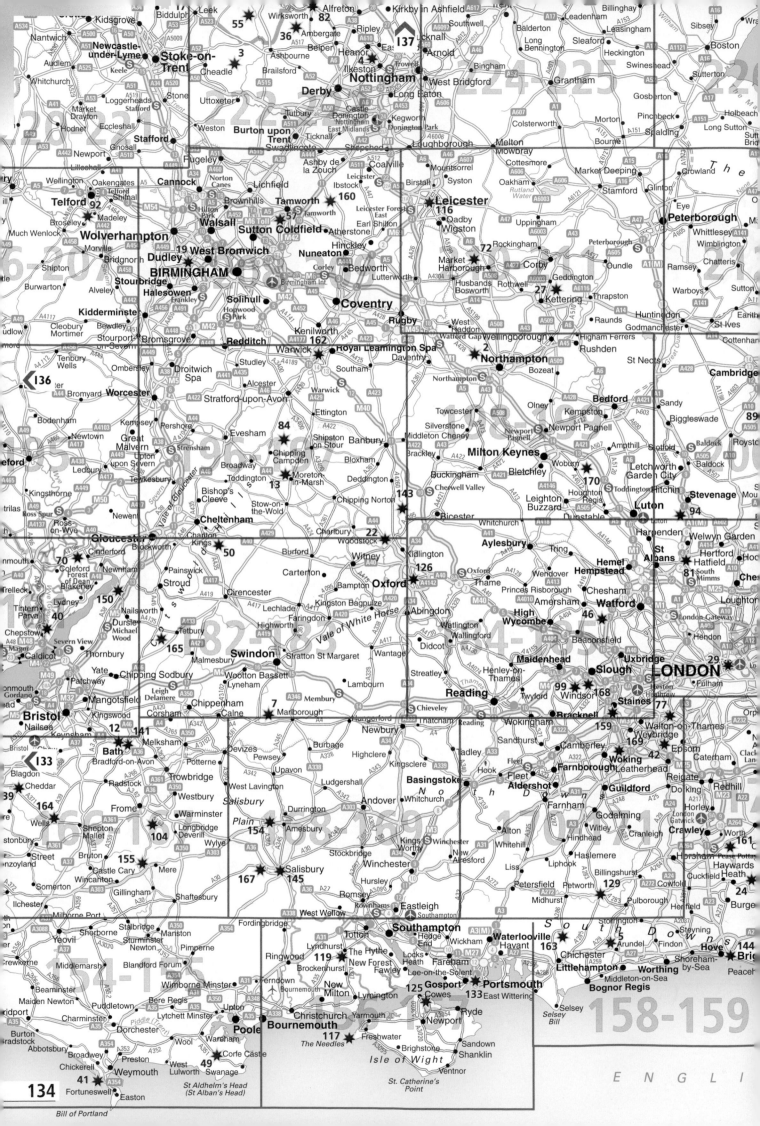

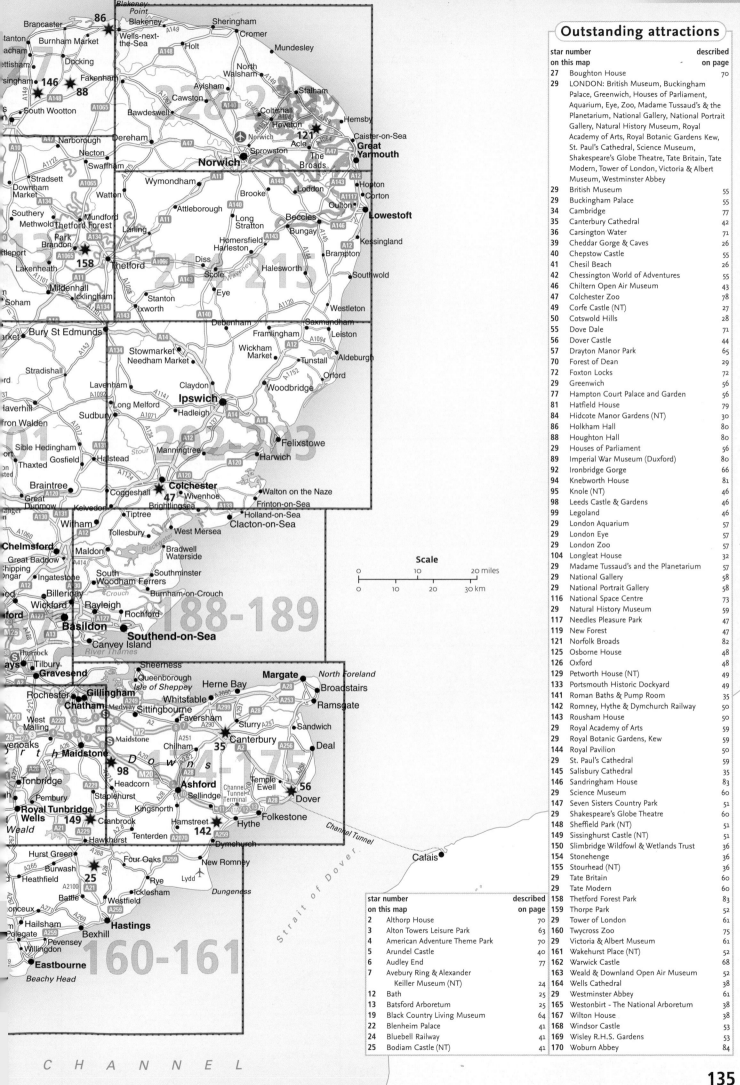

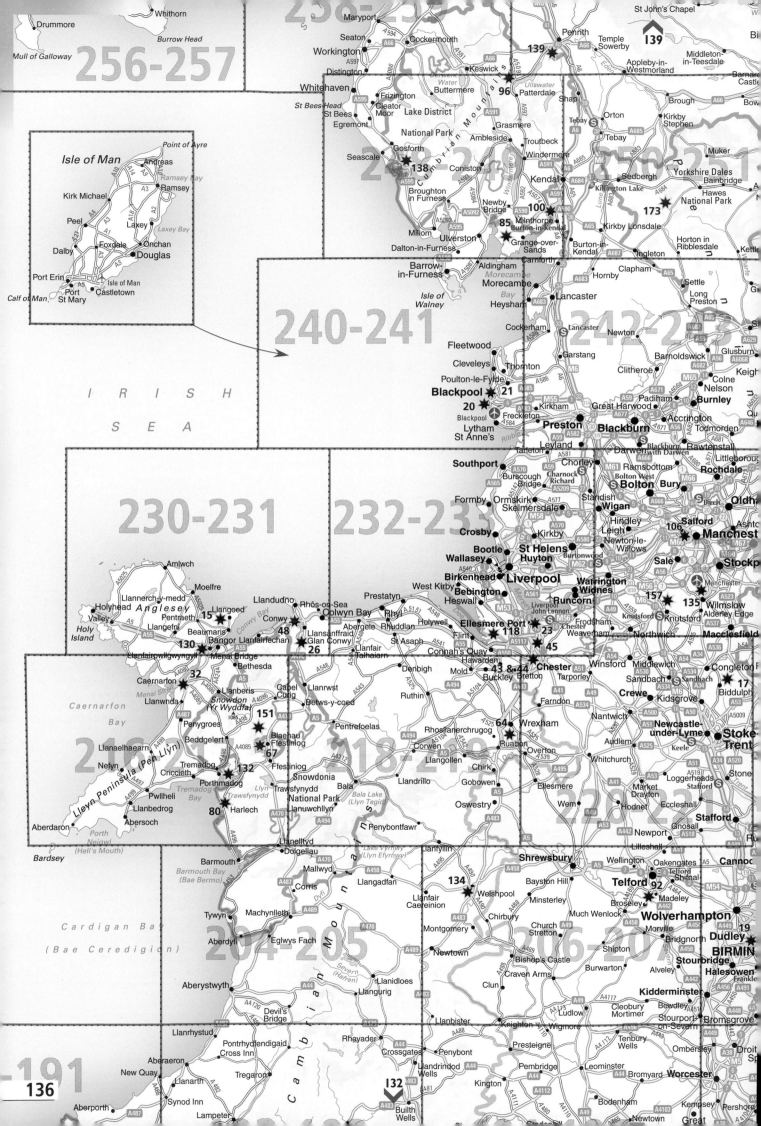

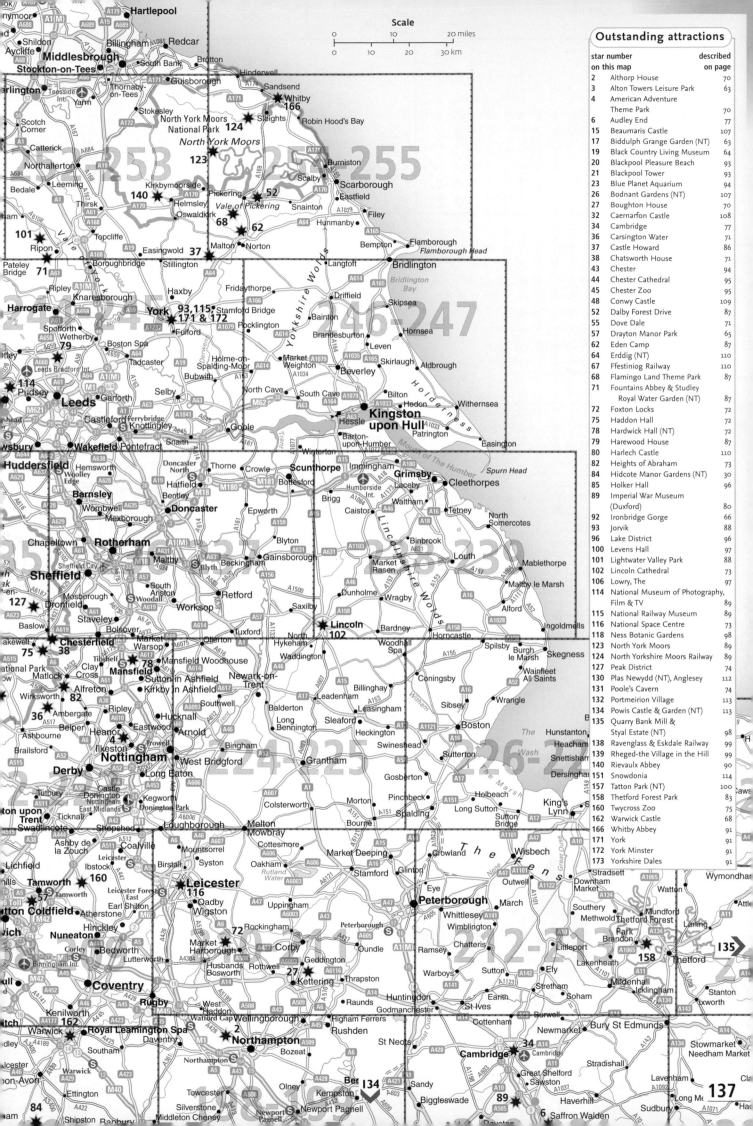

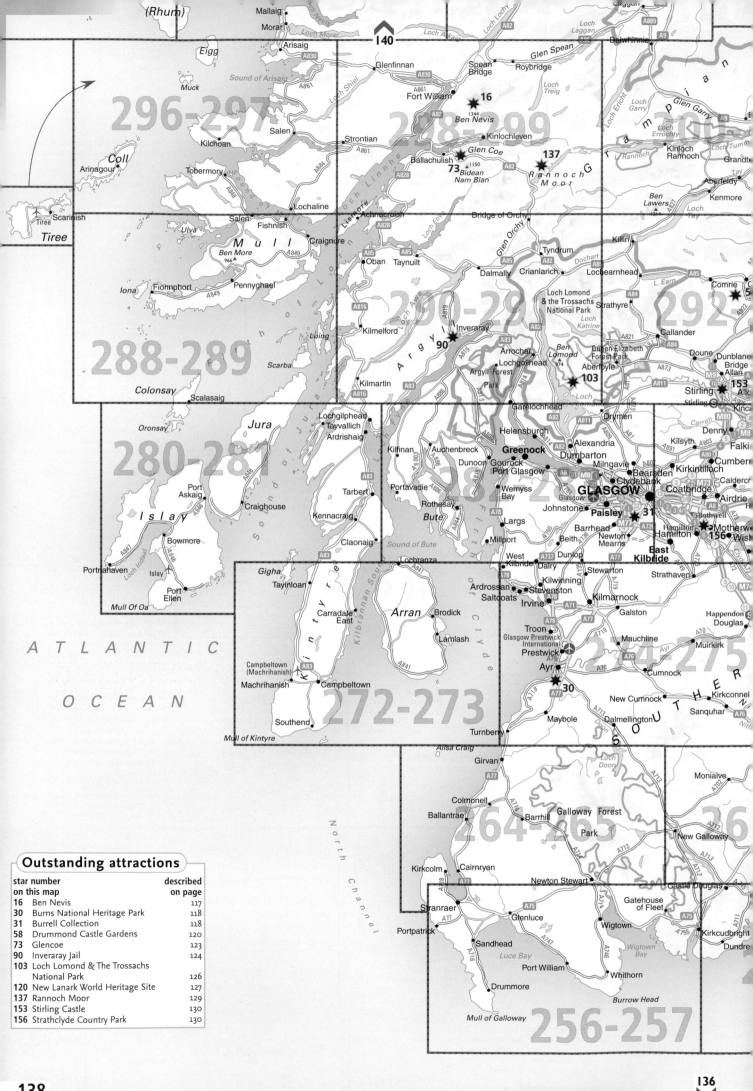

140

136

Outstanding attractions

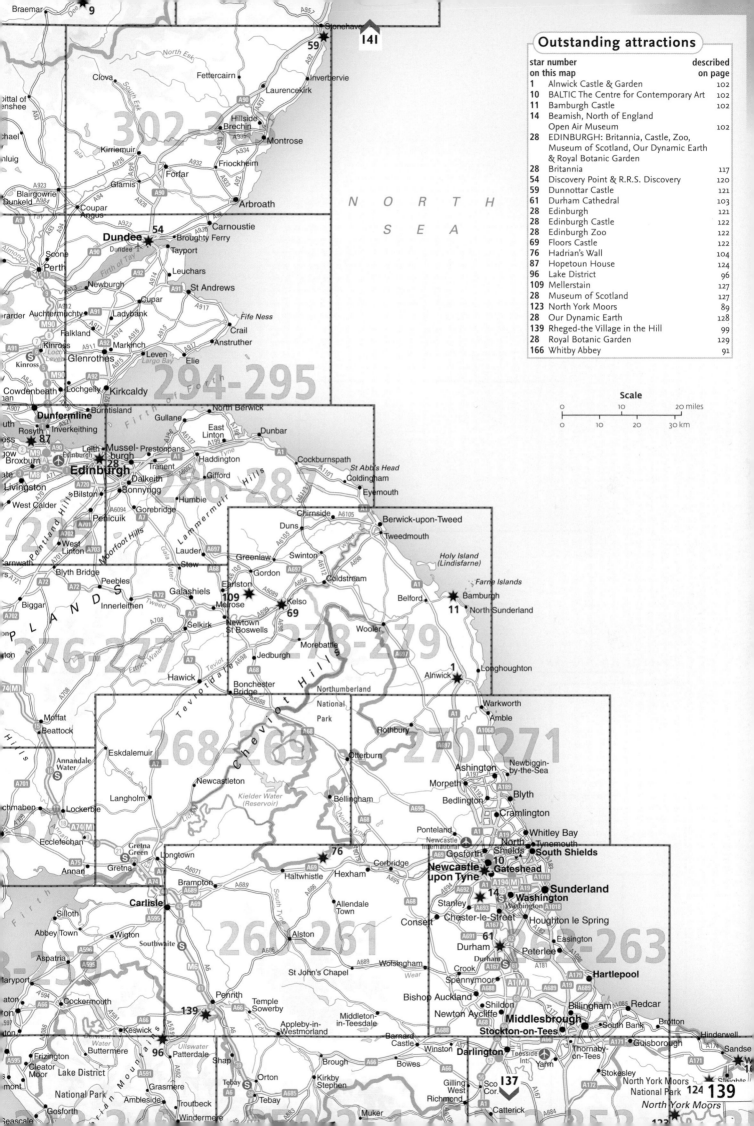

Outstanding attractions

star number on this map		described on page
1	Alnwick Castle & Garden	102
10	BALTIC The Centre for Contemporary Art	102
11	Bamburgh Castle	102
14	Beamish, North of England Open Air Museum	102
28	EDINBURGH: Britannia, Castle, Zoo, Museum of Scotland, Our Dynamic Earth & Royal Botanic Garden	
28	Britannia	117
54	Discovery Point & R.R.S. Discovery	120
59	Dunnottar Castle	121
61	Durham Cathedral	103
28	Edinburgh	121
28	Edinburgh Castle	122
28	Edinburgh Zoo	122
69	Floors Castle	122
76	Hadrian's Wall	104
87	Hopetoun House	124
96	Lake District	96
109	Mellerstain	127
28	Museum of Scotland	127
123	North York Moors	89
28	Our Dynamic Earth	128
139	Rheged-the Village in the Hill	99
28	Royal Botanic Garden	129
166	Whitby Abbey	91

Scale
0   10   20 miles
0   10   20   30 km

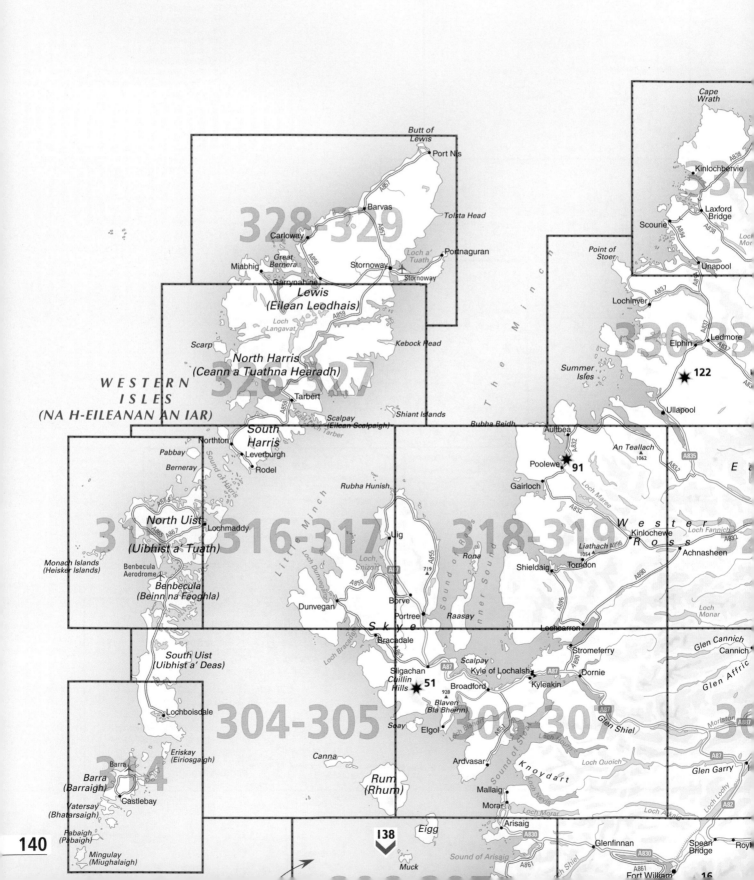

Outstanding attractions

star number on this map		described on page
9	Balmoral Castle	116
51	Cuillin Hills	119
59	Dunnottar Castle	121
60	Dunrobin Castle	121
91	Inverewe Gardens (NTS)	125
122	North West Highlands	128

Scale

0   10   20 miles

0   10   20   30 km

Cape Wrath

Kinlochbervie

Laxford Bridge

Scourie

Unapool

Loch Mor

Point of Stoer

Butt of Lewis

Port Nis

Barvas

Tolsta Head

328-329

Carloway

Loch a' Tuath

Portnaguran

Lochinver

Miabhig

Great Bernera

Stornoway

Stornoway

A837

A837

Elphin

Ledmore

A838

A894

A838

A894

A837

A835

330-33

Garrynahine

Lewis (Eilean Leodhais)

A859

A858

Loch Langavat

Scarp

Kebock Head

North Harris (Ceann a Tuathna Hearadh)

326-327

Summer Isles

★ 122

Ullapool

*W E S T E R N
I S L E S*
(NA H-EILEANAN AN IAR)

Tarbert

A859

Scalpay (Eilean Scalpaigh)

Shiant Islands

Rubha Reidh

Aultbea

A832

The Minch

An Teallach
1062

A835

Northton

Pabbay

South Harris

Leverburgh

Rodel

Berneray

Sound of Harris

Rubha Hunish

Poolewe

★ 91

Loch Maree

A832

A832

E

Gairloch

A832

W e s t e r

Monach Islands (Heiser Islands)

A865

A865

A867

North Uist

Lochmaddy

(Uibhist a' Tuath)

316-317

Little Minch

Uig

Loch Snizort

Rona

Sound of Raasay

318-319

Kinlochewe

Loch Fannich

Liathach
1054

A896

**W e s t e r
R o s s**

A832

Achnasheen

A890

Benbecula Aerodrome

Benbecula (Beinn na Faoghla)

A850

Dunvegan

Loch Dunvegan

A87

719

Borve

Loch Bracadale

Shieldaig

Torridon

A896

Loch Monar

South Uist (Uibhist a' Deas)

Portree

Raasay

Inner Sound

Lochcarron

S k y e

Bracadale

Stromeferry

Glen Cannich

Cannich

Sligachan

Cuillin Hills

★ 51

A87

Scalpay

Kyle of Lochalsh

A87

A87

Dornie

Kyleakin

Glen Affric

Broadford

928

Blaven (Bla Bheinn)

304-305

Lochboisdale

A863

Soay

Elgol

Loch Bishop

305-307

Glen Shiel

Loriston

A87

Glen Garry

Eriskay (Eiriosgaigh)

Canna

Rum (Rhum)

Ardvasar

Sound of Sleat

Knoydart

Loch Quoich

3

A855

A865

A850

A855

Mallaig

Loch Nevis

Loch Morar

Barra (Barraigh)

Barra

Castlebay

Vatersay (Bhatarsaigh)

Morar

Arisaig

A830

A830

A861

Glenfinnan

Spean Bridge

Loch Lochy

A82

Roy

Pabaigh (Pabbay)

Mingulay (Miughalaigh)

140

138

Eigg

Muck

Sound of Arisaig

A861

A830

A861

Fort William

16

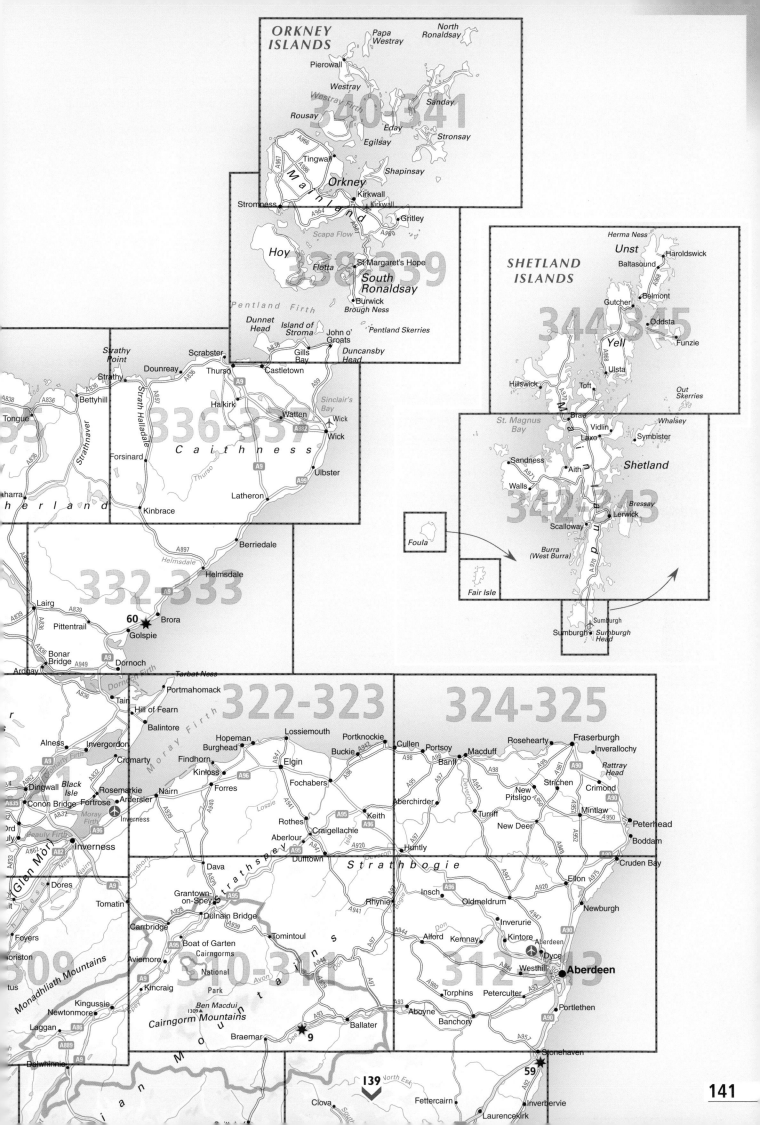

ORKNEY ISLANDS

340-341

North Ronaldsay

Papa Westray

Pierowall

Westray

Westray Firth

Rousay

Sanday

Eday

Egilsay

Stronsay

A966

A967

A986

Tingwall

Shapinsay

Mainland

Orkney

Kirkwall

A965

Stromness

Kirkwall

Gritley

A964

A960

Scapa Flow

338-339

Hoy

Flotta

St Margaret's Hope

South Ronaldsay

Burwick

Brough Ness

Pentland Firth

Dunnet Head

Island of Stroma

Pentland Skerries

John o' Groats

A836

Gills Bay

Duncansby Head

SHETLAND ISLANDS

344-345

Herma Ness

Unst

Haroldswick

Baltasound

A968

Gutcher

Belmont

Oddsta

Yell

Funzie

A968

Ulsta

Hillswick

Toft

Out Skerries

Brae

Whalsey

St. Magnus Bay

Vidlin

A970

Laxo

Symbister

342-343

Sandness

Aith

Shetland

Walls

A971

Mainland

Foula

Lerwick

A970

Scalloway

Bressay

Burra (West Burra)

Fair Isle

A970

Sumburgh

Sumburgh Head

Sumburgh

Strathy Point

Strathy

Scrabster

Thurso

Castletown

Dounreay

A9

A836

A836

A838

Bettyhill

A897

Strath Halladale

Halkirk

Watten

Sinclair's Bay

A836

Tongue

Strathnaver

Forsinard

336-337

Caithness

Wick

A882

Wick

A99

Thurso

A9

Ulbster

A99

Latheron

Kinbrace

herland

Berriedale

Helmsdale

A897

Helmsdale

Lairg

332-333

A9

Pittentrail

A839

60 ★ Brora

A839

Golspie

A836

Bonar Bridge

A949

Dornoch

Ardgay

Dornoch Firth

Tarbat Ness

Portmahomack

Tain

Hill of Fearn

322-323

Balintore

Hopeman

Lossiemouth

Portknockie

324-325

Alness

Invergordon

Moray Firth

Burghead

Findhorn

Elgin

Buckie

A942

Cullen

Portsoy

Macduff

Rosehearty

Fraserburgh

Inverallochy

Cromarty

A941

Banff

A98

A941

A832

Black Isle

Rosemarkie

Nairn

Forres

Fochabers

A98

Aberchirder

New Pitsligo

Strichen

Crimond

Rattray Head

Dingwall

A835

A862

Conon Bridge

Ardersier

A96

A939

A95

Lossie

A941

Rothes

Keith

A96

Turriff

New Deer

Mintlaw

A952

Peterhead

A832

Moray Firth

Inverness

A95

Aberlour

Craigellachie

A920

Huntly

A97

Boddam

A96

Beauly Firth

A862

A82

A833

Glen Mor

Ness

Dava

Dufftown

Strathbogie

Cruden Bay

Dores

A9

Grantown-on-Spey

A95

Rhynie

Insch

A96

Oldmeldrum

Ellon

A920

A975

Newburgh

Foyers

Tomatin

Carrbridge

A939

Dulnain Bridge

Tomintoul

Rhynie

A944

Inverurie

A947

A90

309

Boat of Garten

Cairngorms

Alford

Kemnay

Kintore

Aberdeen

Dyce

312-313

Monadhliath Mountains

Aviemore

National

A9

Kincraig

Park

Ben Macdui
1309

310-311

Avon

Don

Westhill

Aberdeen

Kingussie

Newtonmore

Cairngorm Mountains

A93

Ballater

Torphins

Peterculter

Portlethen

Laggan

A86

Braemar

Dee

9 ★

Aboyne

Banchory

A957

A90

A889

Balwhinnie

A9

Stonehaven

59 ★

139 ⌄ North Esk

Clova

Fettercairn

Inverbervie

Laurencekirk

KEY TO MAP SYMBOLS

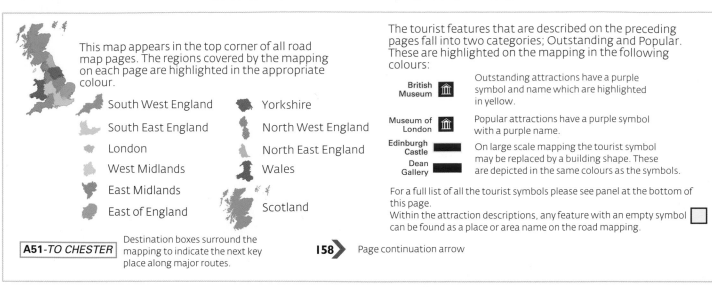

This map appears in the top corner of all road map pages. The regions covered by the mapping on each page are highlighted in the appropriate colour.

South West England

South East England

London

West Midlands

East Midlands

East of England

Yorkshire

North West England

North East England

Wales

Scotland

A51-TO CHESTER — Destination boxes surround the mapping to indicate the next key place along major routes.

158 ▶ Page continuation arrow

The tourist features that are described on the preceding pages fall into two categories; Outstanding and Popular. These are highlighted on the mapping in the following colours:

British Museum — Outstanding attractions have a purple symbol and name which are highlighted in yellow.

Museum of London — Popular attractions have a purple symbol with a purple name.

Edinburgh Castle

Dean Gallery — On large scale mapping the tourist symbol may be replaced by a building shape. These are depicted in the same colours as the symbols.

For a full list of all the tourist symbols please see panel at the bottom of this page.

Within the attraction descriptions, any feature with an empty symbol can be found as a place or area name on the road mapping.

Road mapping · pages 144-345

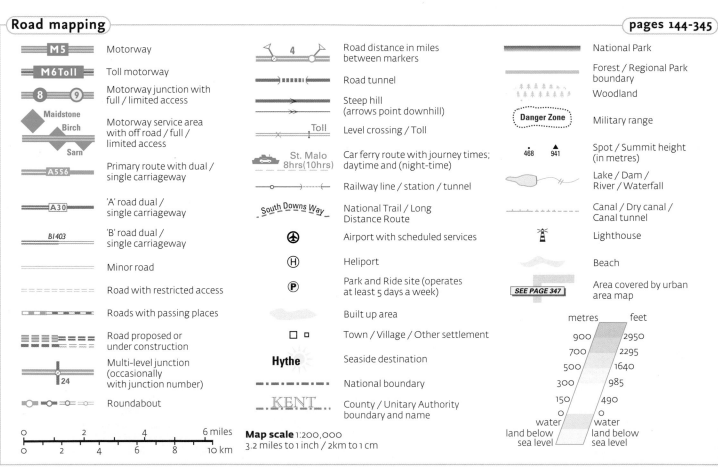

M5	Motorway
M6Toll	Toll motorway
8 9	Motorway junction with full / limited access
Maidstone / Birch / Sarn	Motorway service area with off road / full / limited access
A556	Primary route with dual / single carriageway
A30	'A' road dual / single carriageway
B1403	'B' road dual / single carriageway
	Minor road
	Road with restricted access
	Roads with passing places
	Road proposed or under construction
24	Multi-level junction (occasionally with junction number)
	Roundabout

Scale: 0 to 6 miles / 0 to 10 km

4	Road distance in miles between markers
	Road tunnel
	Steep hill (arrows point downhill)
Toll	Level crossing / Toll
St. Malo 8hrs(10hrs)	Car ferry route with journey times; daytime and (night-time)
	Railway line / station / tunnel
South Downs Way	National Trail / Long Distance Route
✈	Airport with scheduled services
(H)	Heliport
(P)	Park and Ride site (operates at least 5 days a week)
	Built up area
□ □ ▫	Town / Village / Other settlement
Hythe	Seaside destination
	National boundary
KENT	County / Unitary Authority boundary and name

Map scale 1:200,000
3.2 miles to 1 inch / 2km to 1 cm

	National Park
	Forest / Regional Park boundary
	Woodland
Danger Zone	Military range
468 ▲ 941	Spot / Summit height (in metres)
	Lake / Dam / River / Waterfall
	Canal / Dry canal / Canal tunnel
⚓	Lighthouse
	Beach
SEE PAGE 347	Area covered by urban area map

metres	feet
900	2950
700	2295
500	1640
300	985
150	490
water land below sea level	water land below sea level

Tourist information · pages 144-375

A selection of tourist detail is shown on the mapping. It is advisable to check with the attraction or local tourist information centre regarding opening times and facilities available. Where a symbol appears purple on the map, its description can be found within pages 23–131.

ℹ	Tourist information centre (open all year)
ℹ	Tourist information centre (open seasonally)
m	Ancient monument
✕ 1643	Battlefield
▲ ⚏	Camp site / Caravan site
Castle
Country park
✝	Ecclesiastical building

⚽	Football club (Major British club)
❀	Garden
⚑	Golf course
Historic house
£	Major shopping centre / Outlet village
Major sports venue
Motor racing circuit
🏛	Museum / Art gallery

| Nature reserve |
| Preserved railway |
| Racecourse |
| Theme park |
| University |
| Wildlife park or Zoo |
| ★ | Other interesting feature |
| (NT) (NTS) | National Trust / National Trust for Scotland property |

142

Urban area maps

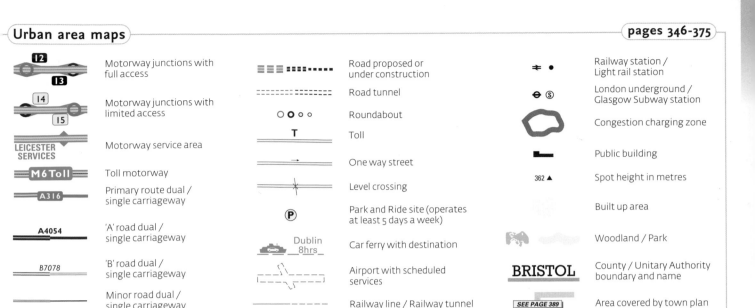

Motorway junctions with full access	Road proposed or under construction	Railway station / Light rail station
Motorway junctions with limited access	Road tunnel	London underground / Glasgow Subway station
Motorway service area	Roundabout	Congestion charging zone
Toll motorway	Toll	Public building
Primary route dual / single carriageway	One way street	Spot height in metres
'A' road dual / single carriageway	Level crossing	Built up area
'B' road dual / single carriageway	Park and Ride site (operates at least 5 days a week)	Woodland / Park
Minor road dual / single carriageway	Car ferry with destination	County / Unitary Authority boundary and name
	Airport with scheduled services	Area covered by town plan
	Railway line / Railway tunnel	

Central city maps

pages 376-387

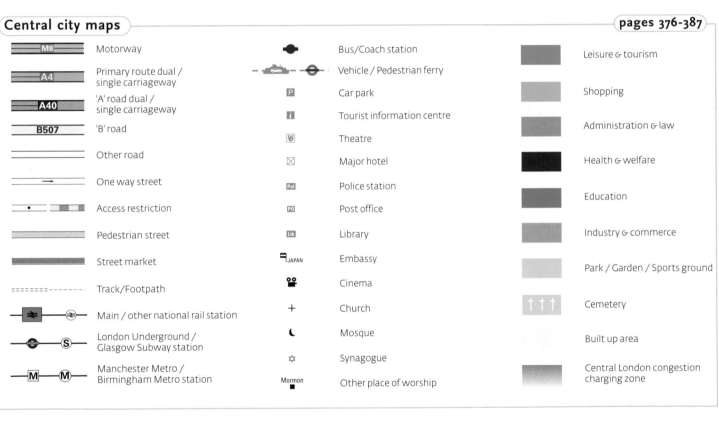

Motorway	Bus/Coach station	Leisure & tourism
Primary route dual / single carriageway	Vehicle / Pedestrian ferry	Shopping
'A' road dual / single carriageway	Car park	Administration & law
'B' road	Tourist information centre	Health & welfare
Other road	Theatre	Education
One way street	Major hotel	Industry & commerce
Access restriction	Police station	Park / Garden / Sports ground
Pedestrian street	Post office	Cemetery
Street market	Library	Built up area
Track/Footpath	Embassy	Central London congestion charging zone
Main / other national rail station	Cinema	
London Underground / Glasgow Subway station	Church	
Manchester Metro / Birmingham Metro station	Mosque	
	Synagogue	
	Other place of worship	

Town plans

pages 388-415

Motorway	Path / Footbridge	Ecclesiastical building
Primary route dual / single carriageway	One way street	Tourist information centre (open all year / seasonally)
'A' road dual / single carriageway	Car park	Tourist building
'B' road dual / single carriageway	Park and Ride site (operates at least 5 days a week)	Important building
Through route dual / single carriageway	Railway line / station	Higher Education building
Other road dual / single carriageway	Underground station	Hospital
Restricted access street	Metro station	Cemetery
Pedestrian street	Light rail station	Recreational area / Open space

143

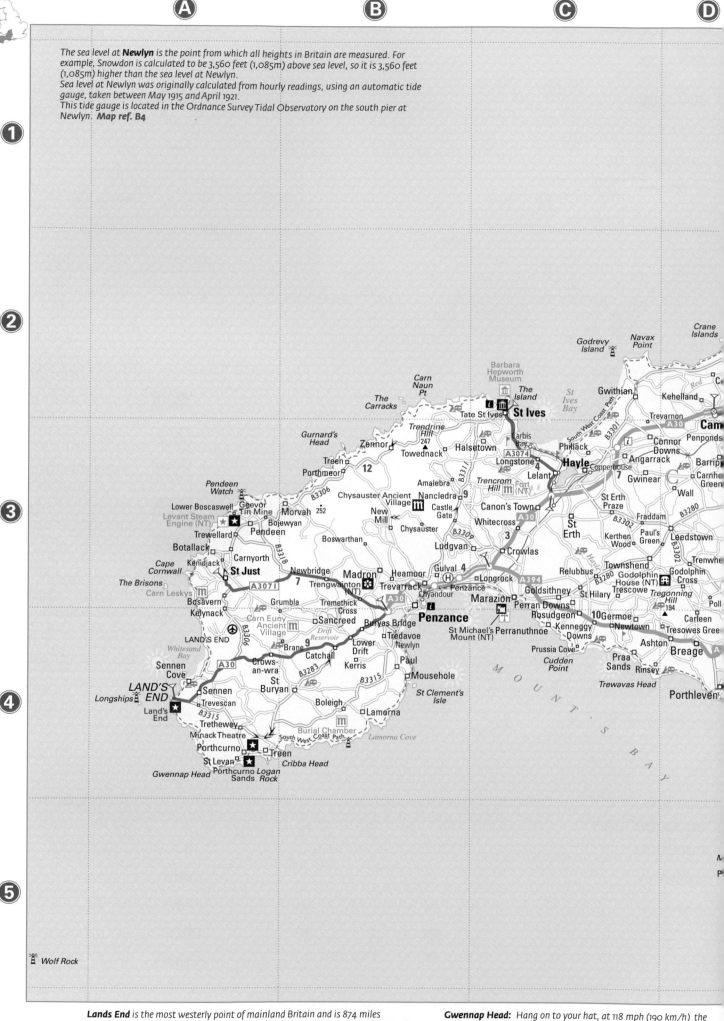

The sea level at **Newlyn** is the point from which all heights in Britain are measured. For example, Snowdon is calculated to be 3,560 feet (1,085m) above sea level, so it is 3,560 feet (1,085m) higher than the sea level at Newlyn.

Sea level at Newlyn was originally calculated from hourly readings, using an automatic tide gauge, taken between May 1915 and April 1921.

This tide gauge is located in the Ordnance Survey Tidal Observatory on the south pier at Newlyn. **Map ref. B4**

Lands End is the most westerly point of mainland Britain and is 874 miles (1,407km) by road from John O' Groats. It is the closest point to North America, if you travel due west, for 2,500 miles (4,000km), from here, you will arrive in Newfoundland. **Map ref. A4 Also on page 31**

Gwennap Head: Hang on to your hat, at 118 mph (190 km/h) the highest ever gust of wind, on a low level site in Britain, was recorded h on the 15th December 1979. **Map ref. A4**

A392–TO NEWQUAY A39–TO WADEBRIDGE A30–TO BODMIN A391–TO BODMIN

West Pentire
Holywell
Bay
Crantock
Carines Roselisston
Downs Mou
Kestle Mill
White
Cross
St Columb Road
Enniscaven
Trezaise
Coldvreath
Bugle
Penhale Point
Holywell
Ligger Pt
Holywell Bay Fun Park
Newquay
Pearl
Tresean
Retyn
Indian Queens
St Dennis
Gothers
Hensbarrow
Downs
Roseve
Penwith
Cubert
Trerice
(NT)
St Enoder
Fraddon
Blue Anchor
Whitemoor
Nanpean
Carthew
Penhale
Sands
Mount
Newlyn
East
A3058
A3076
Summercourt
Meledor
Treviscoe
Foxhole
Ruddimoor
B3274
Stenale
Ligger Bay
(Perran Bay)
Rose
Rejerrah
Lappa
Valley Rly
Chapel
Town
Scarcewater
High
Street
Tregre
Ed
Perranporth
Goonhavern
Newlyn
Downs
Mitchell
Brighton
St Stephen
A3058
ST AUSTELL
Wheal
Martyn
Coast Path
B3285
Carland
Cross
Trelassick
New
Mills
Coombe
Trewoon
St Mewan
A390–TO LISKEARD
147
Bawden Rocks
(Man and his Man)
Trevellas
Bolingey
Zelah
St
Allen
Truthan
Trispen
Tregear
Ladock
Grampound Road
Hewas Water
Sticker
Polgooth
London
St
Agnes
Head
St Agnes Leisure Park
St Agnes
Mithian
Penhallow
Perranzabuloe
The Cornish
Cyder Farm
8
St Erme
Probus
Trewithen
Creed
Grampound
Lost Gardens
of Heligan
Goonbell
A30
Truro
Tresillian
Coombe
8
Pente
Tregiske
Goonvrea
Towan
Cross
Allet Common
Shortlanesend
Idless
St Ewe
Kestle
Pen
Northtowan
Mawla
Mount
Hawke
B3277
Tregavethan
6
Kenwyn
Tresillian
5
A390
St Michael
Caerhays
Mevag
Portme
Cornish
Goldsmiths
Blackwater
A30
2
Gloweth
Royal
Cornwall
Museum
Kenwyn
2
Cathedral
Merther
Polmassick
2
Chacewater
Threemilestone
Hugus
Baldhu
Truro
St Clement
Trewarthenick
Ruan
Lanihorne
Portholland
Boswinger
Gorran Churchto
Redruth
St Day
Twelveheads
Cross Lanes
Kea
Malpas
Lamorran
Tregony
Trevarrick
Gorran
A3047
Carn
Brea
Carn Brea Village
Pennance
Gwennap
Bissoe
Carnon
Downs
Playing
Place
Penelewey
Old
Kea
St Michael
Penkevil
Veryan
Green
Gorran Chur
Maenea
Carnkie
Cornish
engines
(NT)
Lanner
A393
Carharrack
Cusgarne
Perranwell Sta
Coombe
Trelissick
B3289
Treworga
Veryan
Portloe
Veryan Bay
Penare
Four Lanes
Perranarworthal
Devoran
B3289
Trelissick
(NT)
Philleigh
12
Treworlas
South West Coast Path
Dodman
Point
Bolenowe
Penhalvean
Angarrick
Penpol
Treworthal
Trewithian
Nare
Head
Stithians
Ponsanooth
Stockdale
Feock
A3078
Portscatho
Gerrans Bay
Burras
Long
Downs
1
Mylor
Bridge
St Just
in Roseland
Gerrans
Greeb
Point
Carnkie
Rame
Penryn
Mylor
St Just
in Roseland
Porkellis
8
Mabe
Burnthouse
Flushing
P
A39
Falmouth
St Mawes
Castle Pt
St Mawes
Crelly
Lezerea
Edgcumbe
Budock
Water
St Mawes
Bohortha
St Anthony
A394
Trenear
Seworgan
Treverva
Pendennis
Trevenen
Brill
Penjerrick
Pendennis
Point
Zone
Point
Wendron
Trebarvah
Maenporth
National Maritime
Mus Cornwall
FALMOUTH
BAY
Constantine
Mawnan Smith
Porth
Navas
Glendurgan
(NT)
Durgan
Rosemullion Head
Helston
Gweek
Cornish
Seal
Sanctuary
Trebah
Garden
Mawnan
Trelowarren
Helford
Helford
St Anthony-in-Meneage
Mawgan
Garras
Manaccan
Flushing
Nare Point
Halliggye
Fogou
St Martin
Roskorwell
Porthallow
Winwaloe
Goonhilly
Satellite
Earth Station
Newtown-in-
St-Martin
Tregidden
Tregarne
Porthoustock
Manacle Point
Cury
Cross Lanes
Tumuli
Traboe
Lanarth
8
St
Keverne
Rosenithon
The Manacles
A3083
LIZARD PENINSULA
Goonhilly Downs
Trelan
Lowland
Pt
llion
B3296
Penhale
8
Erisey
Barton
Gwenter
Coverack
Gwendreath
Ponsongath
South West Coast Path
Black Head
Ruan
Major
Kuggar
Kennack Sands
St
Ruan
Ruan Minor
Cadgwith
Toll
Grade
Kynance
Cove
Landewednack
Lizard
Hot
Point

LIZARD
POINT

At 49° 57' 30" N **Lizard Point** is the most southerly point
of mainland Britain. **Map ref. D5**

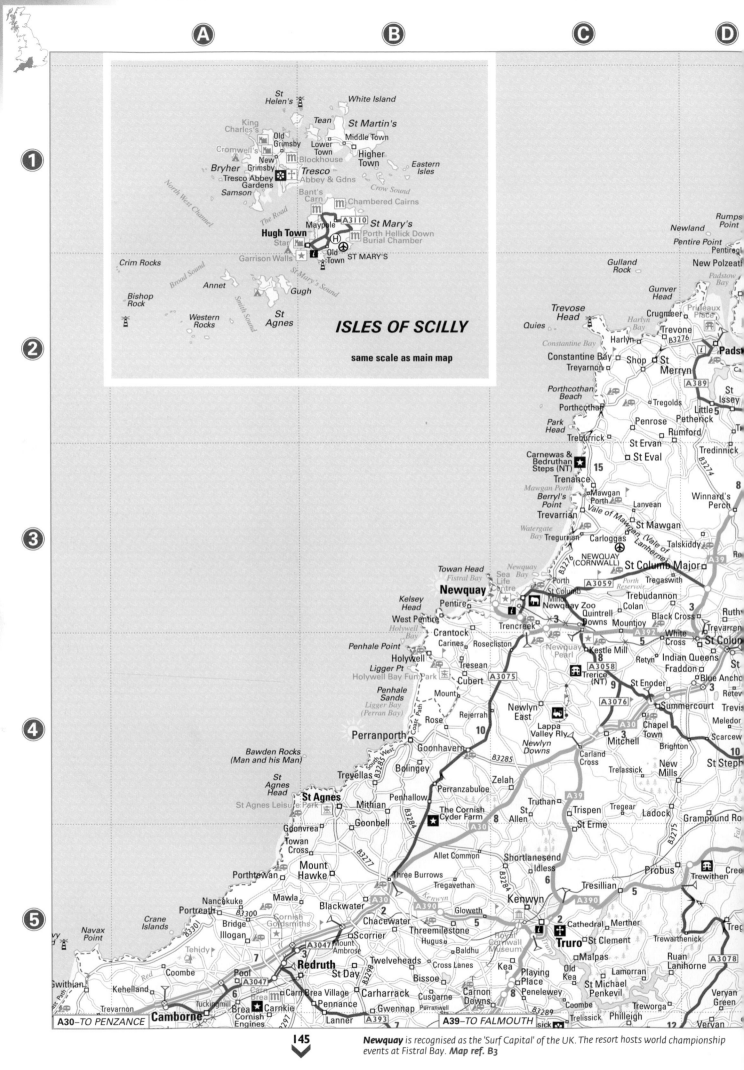

ISLES OF SCILLY

same scale as main map

A **B** **C** **D**

1 **2** **3** **4** **5**

St Helen's
White Island
Tean
St Martin's
King Charles's
Old Grimsby
Middle Town
Cromwell's
New Grimsby
Higher Town
Blockhouse
Bryher
Tresco Abbey Gardens
Tresco
Abbey & Gdns
Eastern Isles
Samson
Crow Sound
Bant's Carn
Chambered Cairns
The Road
A3110
Maypole
St Mary's
Porth Hellick Down Burial Chamber
Hugh Town
Star
Old Town
ST MARY'S
Garrison Walls
North West Channel
Crim Rocks
Broad Sound
Annet
Gugh
St Mary's Sound
Bishop Rock
Western Rocks
St Agnes
Smith Sound

Newland
Rumps Point
Pentire Point
Pentireglaze
New Polzeath
Gulland Rock
Padstow Bay
Gunver Head
Trevose Head
Crugmeer
Prideaux Place
Quies
Harlyn Bay
Trevone
B3276
Constantine Bay
Harlyn
Shop
St Merryn
Pads
Treyarnon
St Issey
A389
Porthcothan Beach
Tregolds
Little Petherick 5
Porthcothan
Penrose
St Ervan
Rumford
Tredinnick
Park Head
Treburrick
St Eval
B3274
Carnewas & Bedruthan Steps (NT)
15
Trenance
Winnard's Perch 8
Mawgan Porth
St Mawgan
Berryl's Point
Mawgan Porth
Lanvean
Trevarrian
Vale of Mawgan (Vale of Lanherne)
Talskiddy
Watergate Bay
Tregurrian
Carloggas
A39
Towan Head
Fistral Bay
NEWQUAY (CORNWALL)
St Columb Major
Tregaswith
Trebudannon
Newquay Sea Life Centre
Porth
Porth Reservoir
Newquay Bay
B3276
St Columb Minor
A3059
3
Newquay
Kelsey Head
Pentire
Newquay Zoo
Colan
Black Cross
Ruth
West Pentire
Trencreek
3
Quintrell Downs
Mountjoy
Trevarren
Crantock
Newquay Pearl
White Cross
St Colu
Holywell Bay
Carines
Rosecliston
5
A392
St
Penhale Point
Kestle Mill
Retyn
Indian Queens
Holywell
Tresean
A3075
8
Fraddon
Blue Anch
Ligger Pt
Cubert
Trerice (NT)
St Enoder
Retev
Holywell Bay Fun Park
Mount
9
Summercourt
Trevi
Penhale Sands
A3058
3
Meledor
Ligger Bay (Perran Bay)
Newlyn East
A3076
Chapel Town
Scarcew
Rose
Rejerrah
Lappa Valley Rly
Mitchell
Brighton
10
Coast Path
10
Newlyn Downs
Carland Cross
New Mills
St Steph
Perranporth
Goonhavern
B3285
Trelassick
Bawden Rocks (Man and his Man)
Bolingey
Zelah
A30
Truthan
Tregear
Ladock
South West Coast Path
Trevellas
Perranzabuloe
A39
Trispen
Grampound Ro
St Agnes Head
Penhallow
The Cornish Cyder Farm
St Allen
St Erme
B3275
St Agnes Leisure Park
Mithian
B3284
8
St Agnes
Allet Common
Goonvrea
Goonbell
Shortlanesend
Idless
Probus
Trewithen
Cree
Towan Cross
B3277
Three Burrows
Tresillian
6
5
Porthtowan
Tregavethan
Kenwyn
A390
Mount Hawke
Kenwyn
Truro
2
Cathedral
Merther
Nancekuke
Mawla
Blackwater
A30
2
Gloweth
Royal Cornwall Museum
Trewarthenick
Crane Islands
Bridge
Chacewater
Threemilestone
5
Truro
St Clement
A3078
Navax Point
B3301
Illogan
Scorrier
Hugus
Baldhu
Malpas
Tehidy
Mount Ambrose
Kea
Lamorran
Treworga
Playing Place
Old Kea
Coombe
Twelveheads
Cross Lanes
Penelewey
St Michael Penkevil
Gwithian
A3047
Pool
Redruth
St Day
Bissoe
Veryan Green
Kehelland
6
Carn
Brea Village
Cusgarne
Carnon Downs
8
Coombe
Trevarnon
Tuckingmill
Brea
Carnkie
Pennance
Gwennap
Perranwell
B3289
Trelissick
Phillei
Vervan
Camborne
Cornish Engines
Lanner
A393
7
A30-TO PENZANCE
A39-TO FALMOUTH

Newquay is recognised as the 'Surf Capital' of the UK. The resort hosts world championship events at Fistral Bay. **Map ref. B3**

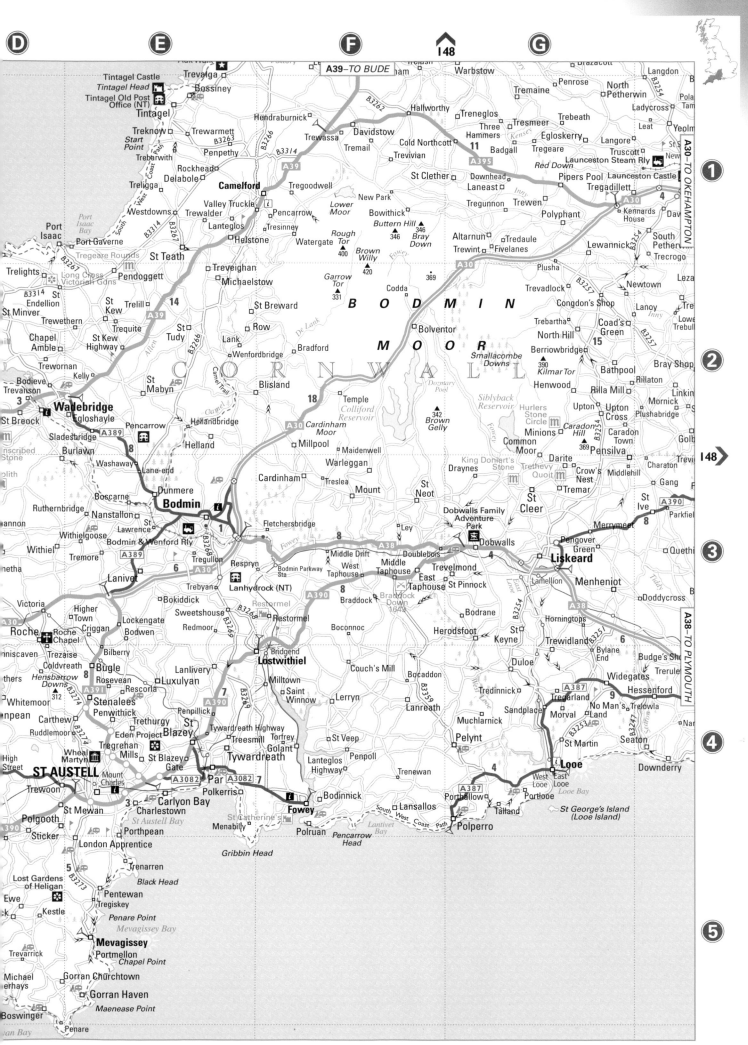

In 1584 Sir Francis Drake was voted into the House of Commons as MP for **Bossiney**. **Map ref. E**1

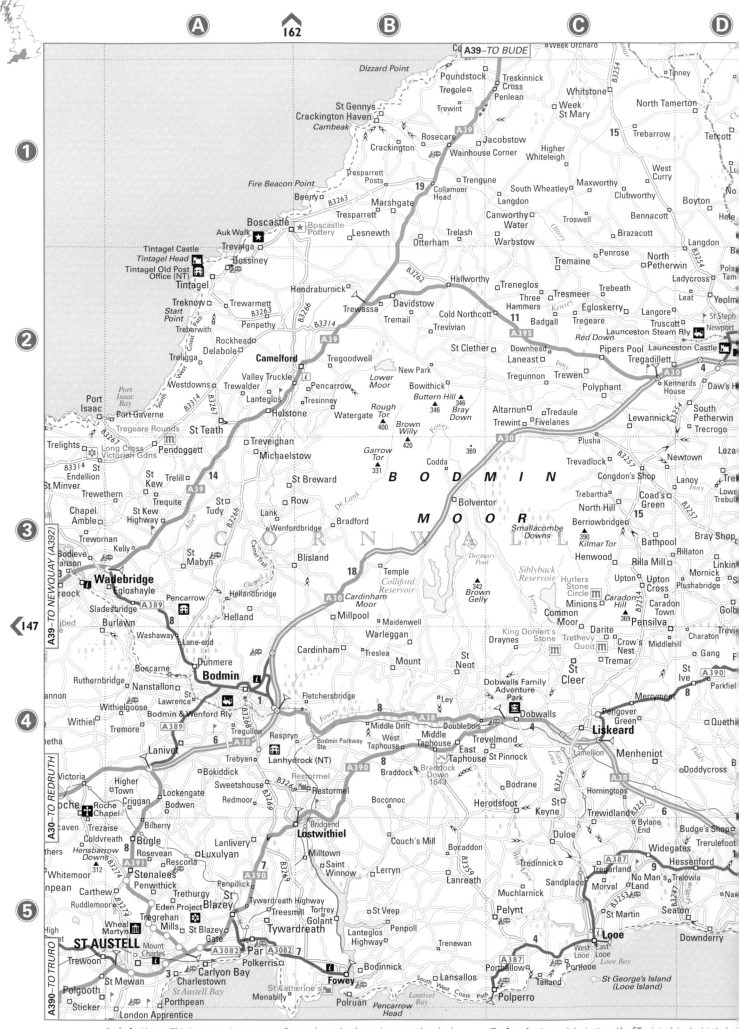

Bodmin Moor: This is a sweeping expanse of rugged moorland covering over a hundred square miles of central Cornwall. The area is seeped in myth and legend, not least the tales of the 'Beast of Bodmin Moor'. Over the last twenty years there have been more than sixty recorded sighting of the 'Beast', generally thought to be a big cat, like a panther, which preys on other wild animals and farm livestock. **Map ref. B3 Also on page 25**

Tavistock: Crowndale, just south of Tavistock is the birthplac[e] [of] Sir Francis Drake. Drake is one of Britain's most famous sea[-] captains. He was the first Englishman to sail around the Worl[d] 1580 and later became famous for routing the Spanish Armada[.] **Map ref. E3**

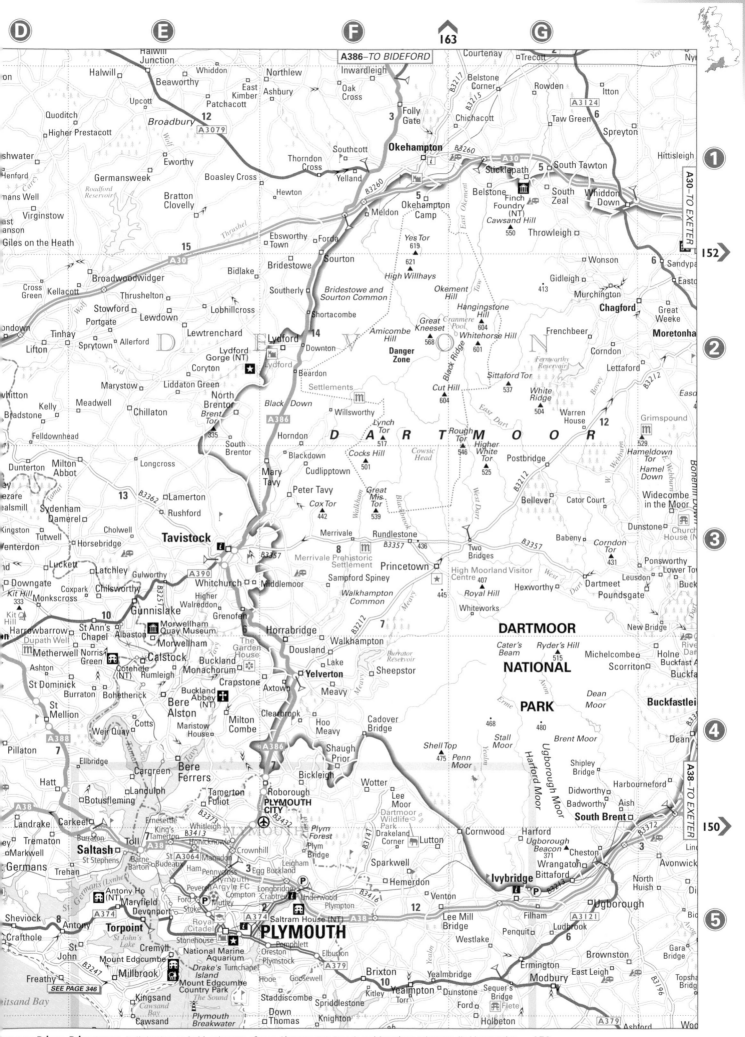

Dartmoor Prison, Princetown: Built in 1809 to hold prisoners of war. Almost 1,500 French and American prisoners died here under a very brutal regime and were all buried just outside the prison walls. Dartmoor closed as a prisoner of war establishment in 1815 but was reopened in 1850 for civilian prisoners serving long sentences and those subject to hard labour. It was always regarded as 'the end of the line' for inmates and there have been numerous calls for it to close. However, as a listed building it cannot be demolished, and since 1980 it has been revamped and modernised and continues to be part of the prison system. **Map ref. F3**

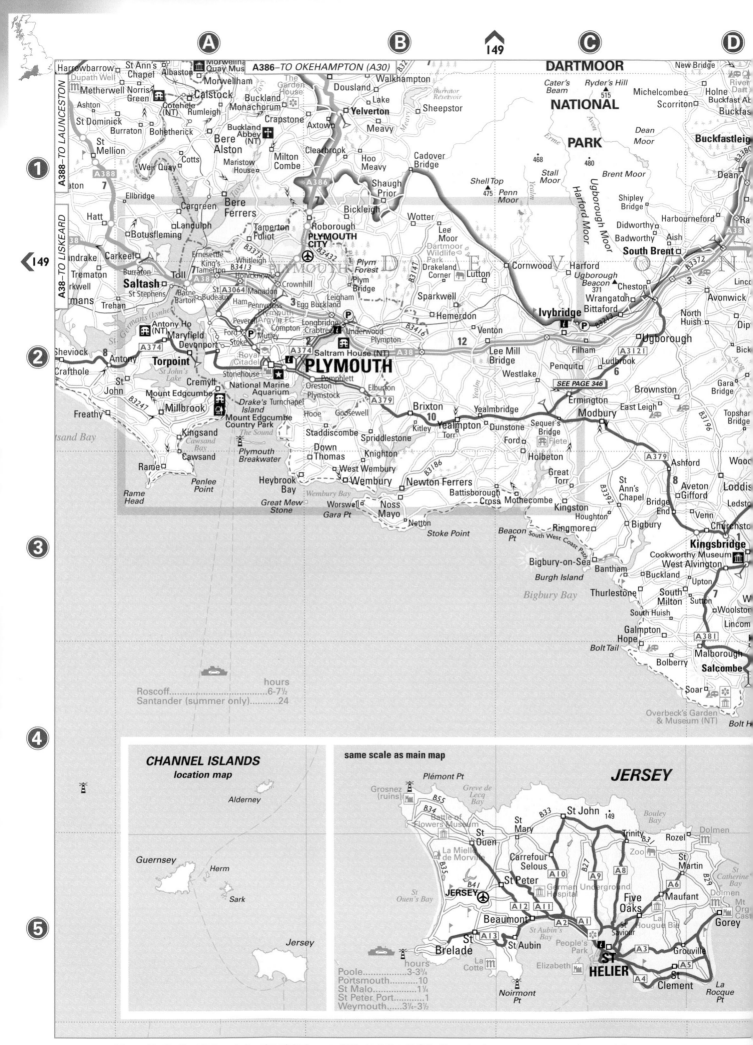

Plymouth: On the 15th August 1620 the original group of 'Pilgrim Fathers' left Southampton in two ships, the Speedwell and the Mayflower. But the Speedwell became un-seaworthy before they reached Land's End and both ships returned to Plymouth. There, many of the Speedwell's passengers transferred to the Mayflower and on the 6th September 1620 they set off again in search of their new life in the New World. The Mayflower took 66 days to reach Cape Cod where eventually the settlers created a new settlement which they called Plymouth. **Map ref. A2**

Devonport: Infamous double agent Guy Burge was born here in 1910. He became a Soviet spy a fled to Russia in 1951. Burgess died in Moscow i 1963. **Map ref. A2**

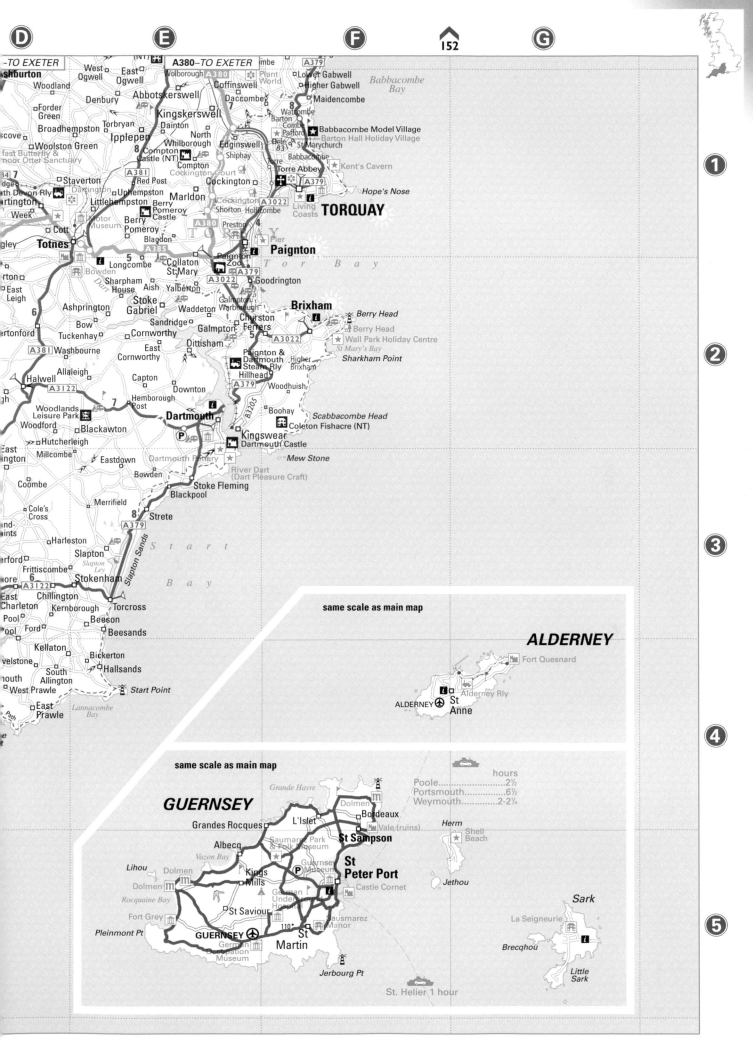

Slapton Sands: During Exercise Tiger, a training exercise for D Day, German E-Boats intercepted and sank some of the small landing craft, killing over 700 American soldiers. A recovered Sherman Tank, on the beach, is a permanent memorial to this action. **Map ref. E3**

Torquay: The Gleneagles Hotel in Asheldon Road, Wellswood was the original setting for Fawlty Towers the 1970s comedy series which starred John Cleese. **Map ref. F1**

Torquay: Agatha Christie, Britain's greatest 'whodunnit' novelist, was born here in 1896. In all she wrote 78 crime stories and died aged 80 in 1976. **Map ref. F1**

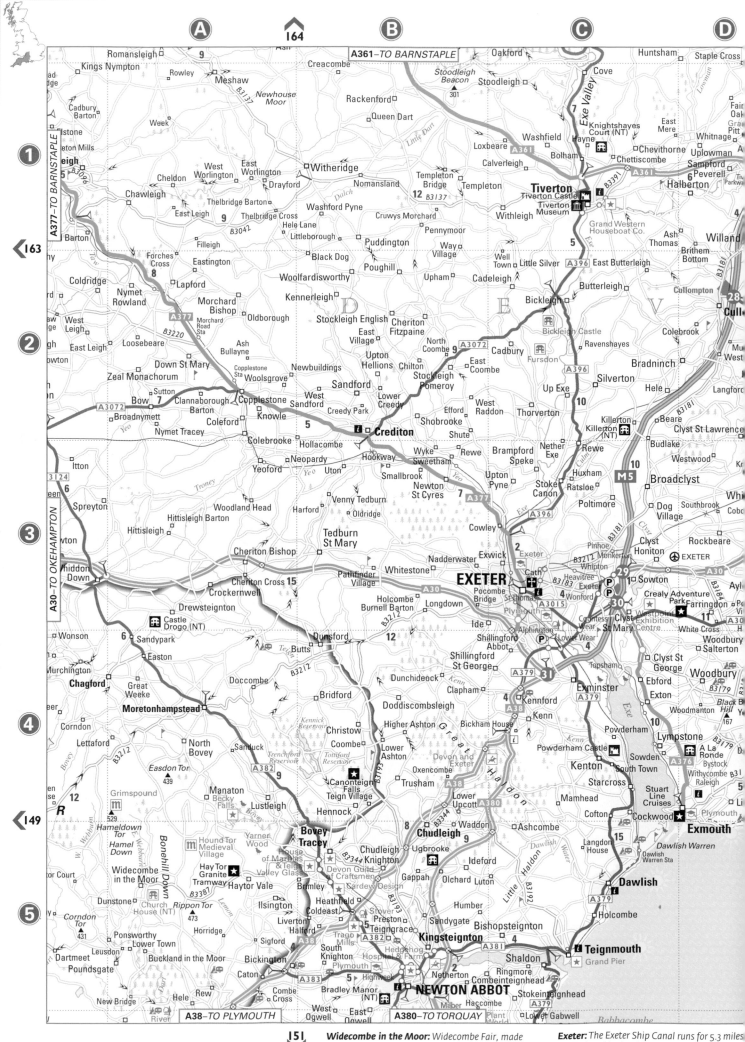

163

149

151

Widecombe in the Moor: Widecombe Fair, made famous in the song concerning the adventures of Old Uncle Tom Cobley and all, is held here. The fair dates back to around the 1850s. **Map ref. A5**

Exeter: The Exeter Ship Canal runs for 5.3 miles (8.5km) and is the oldest post-Roman canal in Britain, dating back to 1563. **Map ref. C3**

M5–TO BRIDGWATER   A358–TO TAUNTON

A303–TO YEOVIL (A3088)

M5 26

SOMERSET

Wellington Monument (NT)

Hackpen Hill 258

Down Hills

Staple Hill

Black Down Hills

Culm Valley

Luxhay Reservoir

Bollham Water

Ilminster

South Pet

Chard

The Wildlife Park at Cricket St Thomas

Cricket St Thomas

Forde Abbey

Pilsdon Pen 277

A303

A30

A358

A30

B3162

A30

B3165

B3164

A35–TO DORCHESTER

154

Honiton

Ottery St Mary

Axminster

Axminster Museum

Lyme Regis

Charmouth

Golden Cap 191

Seaton

Beer

Beer Head

Seaton Bay

Sidmouth

Donkey Sanctuary

Fairlynch Arts Centre & Museum

Budleigh Salterton

South West Coast Path

1

2

3

4

5

...minster carpets were first produced here in ...s and the company is still located here today. *...p ref. F3*

Lyme Regis, and the beach along to Charmouth, is a haven for fossil hunters. Along with the more common ammonites, belemnites and gryphaea, finds also include dinosaur fossils, such as ichthyosaur, plesiosaur and pterosaur, in the Jurassic rocks. **Map ref. G3**

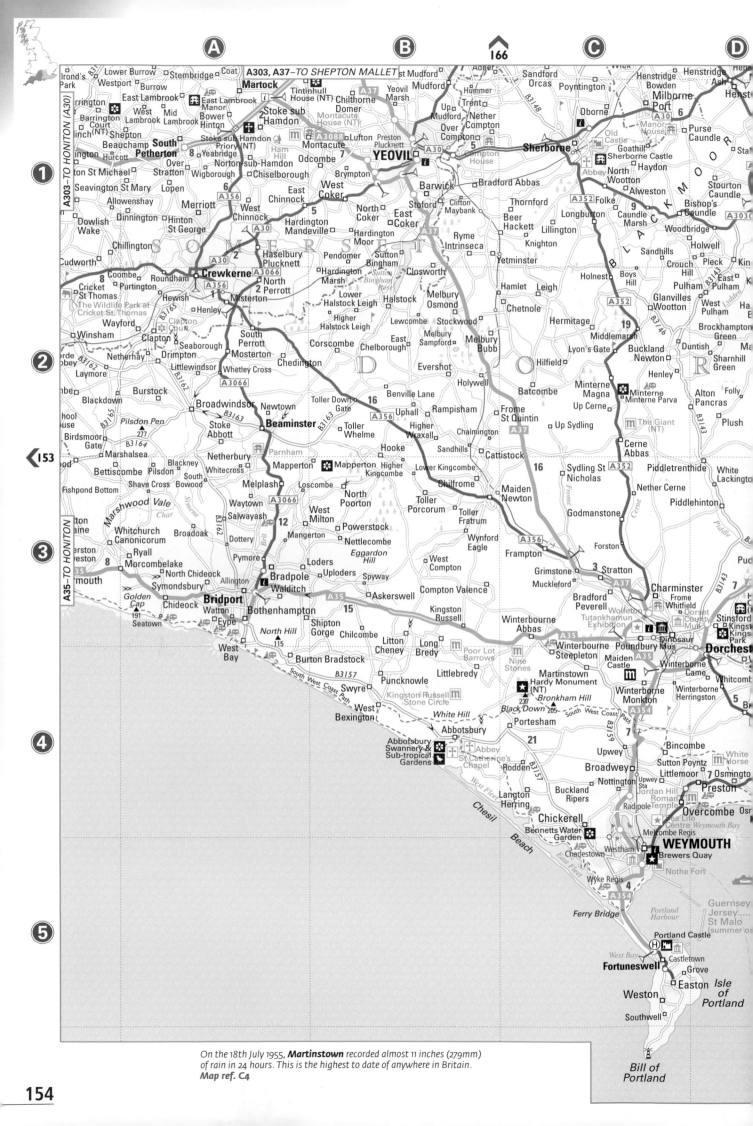

On the 18th July 1955, **Martinstown** recorded almost 11 inches (279mm) of rain in 24 hours. This is the highest to date of anywhere in Britain.
Map ref. C4

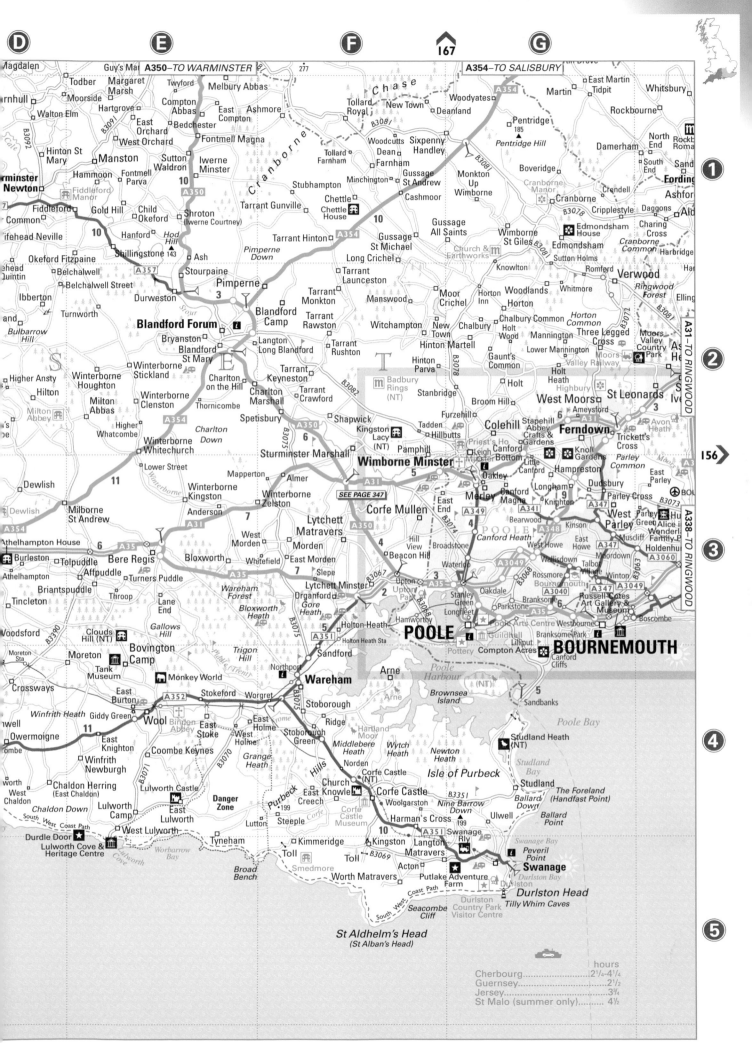

A350–TO WARMINSTER   A354–TO SALISBURY

1

2

156 ▶

3

4

5

A31–TO RINGWOOD

A338–TO RINGWOOD

uddle: Six farm labourers were arrested here in 1834 for trade union activity and *nced* to be transported to Australia. They became known as the Tolpuddle Martyrs. *owing* this a great working class struggle was organised demanding the freedom of *six* and they were eventually returned to England. **Map ref. D3**

Clouds Hill: This is the former home of T E Lawrence, commonly known as Lawrence of Arabia. He died in the nearby Bovington Camp Military Hospital on the 19th May 1935 following an accident on his Brough Superior Motorcycle. **Map ref. E3 Also on page 27**

Cowes has a sailing history that is second to none and is generally renowned as the home of World Yachting. Throughout the year it hosts some of the greatest international sailing events especially during 'Cowes Week' in August and is home to The Royal Yacht Squadron which was founded in 1815. The world's first hovercraft - the Saunders-Roe SRN1 – flew here in 1959. *Map ref. D3*

The **New Forest** was created by William the Conqueror in 1079 mainly for the purpose of hunting deer and wild boars. 21 years later, his son, William II, was killed while hunting in the forest by a misdirected arrow near the spot now marked by the Rufus Stone. It is now an important recreational area which retains many original rural practices such as the pasturing of ponies and the rights of local inhabitants known as commoners. It is soon to become Britain's smallest National Park. *Map ref. B2 Also on page 47*

Parkhurst: Nearby is Parkhurst Prison which has held some of most dangerous and notorious prisoners in Britain, including th Great Train Robbers, the Kray twins and the Yorkshire Ripper. T prison was opened in 1838 and the location was chosen because was close to a deep water anchorage that could be used by ship transporting the convicts to Australia. *Map ref. D3*

1

2

3

4

5

A3 – TO GUILDFORD

A3(M)

A27 – TO CHICHESTER

158 ▸

SEE PAGES 348-49

HAMPSHIRE

Crowdhill
Fisher's Pond
Lower Upham
Corhampton
Meonstoke
Exton
Corhampton
Droxford
11
South Harting
Elsted
Treyfo
Didl

Fair Oak
Wintershill
Ashton
Newtown
Dundridge
Brockbridge
Chidden
Clanfield
Chidden Holt
Clanfield
Chalton
Queen Elizabeth
270
244
North
Marden
West
Marden
East
Harting

UTHAMPTON
Durley
Street
Bishop's Waltham Swanmore
Bishop's Palace
Upper Swanmore
Soberton
Hambledon
Catherington
Uppark (NT)
North
Marden
Compton
East Marden
Chilgro

HAMPSHIRE
Moorgreen
Long Common
Curdridge
Waltham Chase
Hillpound
Soberton Heath
Hoe Gate
Horndean
Blendworth
Finchdean
Forestside
Stoughton
King
Vale

Botley
Shedfield
Shirrell Heath
Newtown
Worlds End
Anthill Common
Lovedean
Cowplain
Deanlane End
Rowland's Castle
Aldsworth
Lordington
Walderton

Burridge
Swanwick
Whiteley
Crockerhill
Funtley
North Boarhunt
Furzeley Corner
Denmead
Anmore
Country Park
Staunton
Leigh Park
Durrants
New Brighton
Funtington
Woodmancote
Woodend

Bursledon
Lower Swanwick
Park Gate
M27
Titchfield Abbey
Boarhunt
Forest of Bere
WATERLOOVILLE
Stakes
HAVANT
Denvilles
Westbourne
Emsworth
Hambrook
Broad

Locks Heath
Warsash
Catisfield
Wallington
Ports Down
Purbrook
Bedhampton
Warblington
Southbourne
Nutbourne
Fishb

Hamble-le-Rice
Hook
Titchfield
Little Posbrook
Meon
Catisfield
Port Solent
Wymering
Cosham
Drayton
Langstone
Hermitage
Holy Trinity
Chidham
Bosham

Stubbington
Bridgeman
Fort Brockhurst
Portchester Castle
Horsea Island
Northney
North Hayling
West Thorney
Bosham Hoe
Dell Qu

FAREHAM
Portchester
Whale Island
Hardway
Portsea Island
Stoke
Hayling Island
Thorney Island

Lee-on-the-Solent
Rowner
Brockhurst
Portsmouth Historic Dockyard
Fratton
North End
Langstone Harbour
Fleet
West Town
South Hayling
West Itchenor
Shipton Green

GOSPORT
Browndown
Alverstoke
Portsea
Portsmouth FC
Milton
Eastoke
East Wittering
Earnley
Bracklesha

Southsea Castle & Museum
Stokes Bay
Gilkicker Point
Southsea
Cathedral
Hayling Bay
West Wittering
Windmill

PORTSMOUTH

M275
A3
A288
A2030
A288

SOLENT

Cowes
Cowes Roads
East Cowes
Osborne Bay
½ hr
Bracklesham Bay

Northwood
Whippingham
Osborne
Osborne House
St Mildred
Ryde Roads
Fishbourne
Quarr Hill
Ryde
Spring Vale
Nettlestone Point

Parkhurst
Parkhurst Forest
Forest Side
Wootton Common
Littletown
Cross Lane
Wootton
Wootton Bridge
Binstead
Swanmore
Brickfields Horse Country
Oakfield
Seaview
Nettlestone
Flamingo Park

NEWPORT

Hunny Hill
Staplers
Isle of Wight Steam Rly
Havenstreet
St Helens
Bembridge Point

Carisbrooke Castle & Mus
Robin Hill
Downend
East Ashey
Nunwell
Roman Villa
Bembridge
Foreland

Blackwater
Arreton
Alverstone
Brading
Bembridge Windmill (NT)
Whitecliff Bay

Merstone
Newchurch
Queen's Bower
Isle of Wight Zoo
Yaverland
Culver Cliff

Rookley
Winford
Geology Museum
Sandown
Hillway

ISLE OF WIGHT

Chillerton
Rookley Green
Apse Heath
ISLE OF WIGHT (SANDOWN)
Lake
Sandown Bay

Kingston
Godshill
All Saints
Whiteley Bank
Sandford
Shanklin Chine

Chale Green
Sandford
Shanklin

Rookley
A3020

Pyle
Chale
21
236
Bierley
Whitwell
Appuldurcombe
Stenbury Down
Nettlecombe
235
235
Wroxall
Luccombe Village
Dunnose

Blackgang
Chine
Niton
St Lawrence
Bonchurch
Ventnor
Ventnor Botanic Gardens
The Undercliff

Rocken End
St Catherine's Point

	hours
Bilbao	35
Caen	6-(7¼)
Caen (summer only)	3¾
Cherbourg	2¾-(7)
Guernsey	6½
Jersey	10
Le Havre	2¾-5
St. Malo	8¾(10½)

Ryde: *The seaside pier is a typical English invention. Ryde Pier, on the Isle of Wight, opened on 26th July 1814 and was the first of the numerous promenade piers which are still major features of English seaside resorts.* **Map ref. E3**

e **Needles:** *These are a series of chalk stacks on the western most point of the Isle of Wight. The around The Needles is treacherous and the first lighthouse was built here in 1785. The current thouse, at the western edge of The Needles was built in 1850.* **Map ref. B4 Also on page 47** all the Isle of Wight has 60 miles (97km) of coastline and there are over 4000 shipwrecks recorded he Admiralty Charts of the area.* **Map ref. D4 Also on page 47**

Lee-on-the-Solent: *Location of the former Fleet Air Arm base H.M.S. Daedalus. From here in 1931 a Supermarine S6b designed by RJ Mitchell, creator of the Spitfire, set a new world air speed record of 407.5 mph (656km/h)* **Map ref. E2**

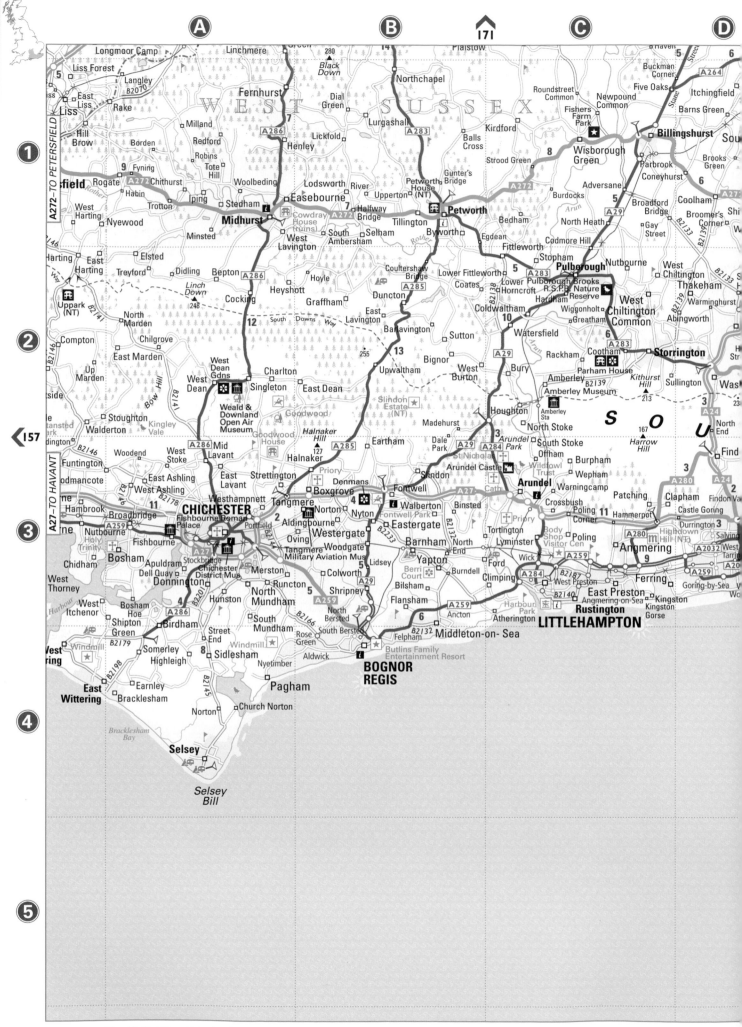

The airfield at **Tangmere** played a crucial role in the 1940 Battle of Britain. One of its most famous fighter pilots was Douglas Bader who was stationed there, first as CO of 242 Squadron, flying Hurricanes and later as leader of three Spitfire Squadrons.
On 9th August 1941 Bader shot down two German ME109s before colliding with a third. He was forced to bale out and was taken POW by the Germans. In all he was credited with destroying 23 enemy aircraft. His exciting association with Tangmere is marked by the nearby Bader Arms Public House. **Map ref. B3**

Brighton: The Aquarium roundabout near Brigh Pier is claimed to be Britain's oldest traffic roundabout, dating from 1925. **Map ref. F3**

TO DORKING   **A23**–TO LONDON GATWICK AIRPORT (M23)   **A22**–TO EAST GRINSTEAD   **A26**–TO ROYAL TUNBRIDGE WELLS

Bluebell Railway: Following the swingeing cuts of the 1960s the Bluebell Railway became the first preserved standard gauge passenger railway in the world. It has now been in service for over 40 years. Today, whenever you see an old railway or railway station on a film or TV programme, chances are it is this one. *Map ref. F1 Also on page 41*

Battle of Lewes 1264: Following the rebel barons' victory over King Henry III, Simon de Montfort established England's first parliament before he was killed in battle at Evesham in 1265. *Map ref. F2*

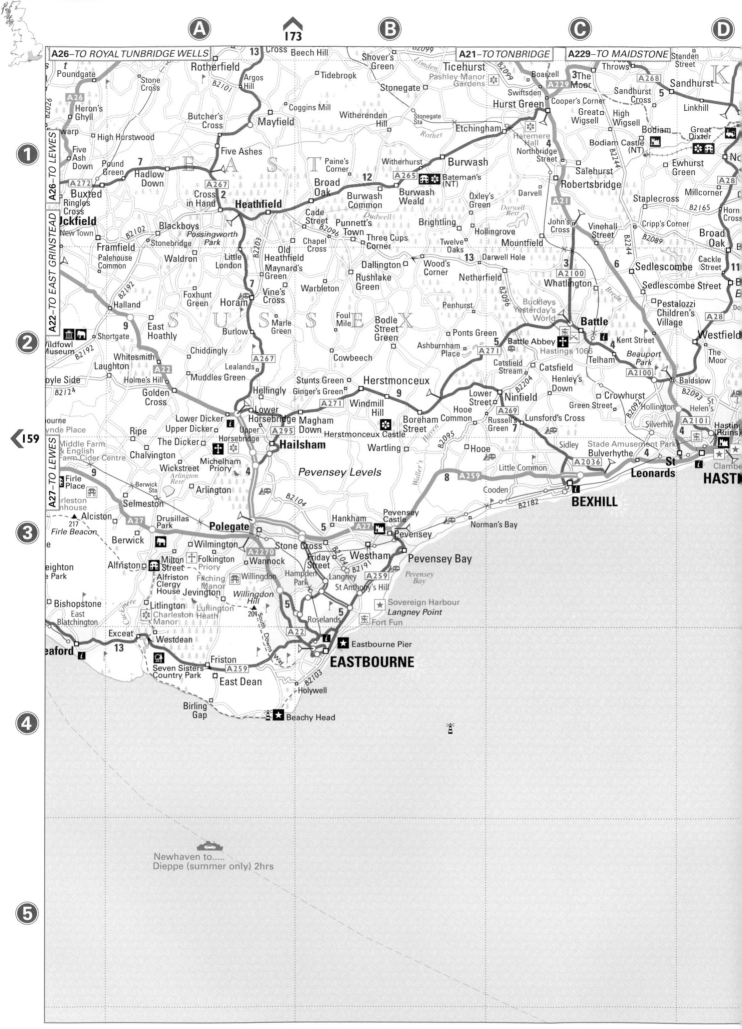

John 'Mad Jack' Fuller was born in **Brightling** in 1757 and inherited a thriving iron forge which made weapons for the British Navy. Mad Jack later became Squire of Brightling and an MP but is best remembered as a great English eccentric who was obsessed with building follies. The Sussex countryside is dotted with his creations which include towers, a temple, a needle and a pyramid. He gifted a lifeboat station and the first wooden lighthouse at Beachy Head. Mad Jack also bought Bodiam Castle in order to save it from a firm of builders who intended to demolish it. He died in 1834. **Map ref. B1**

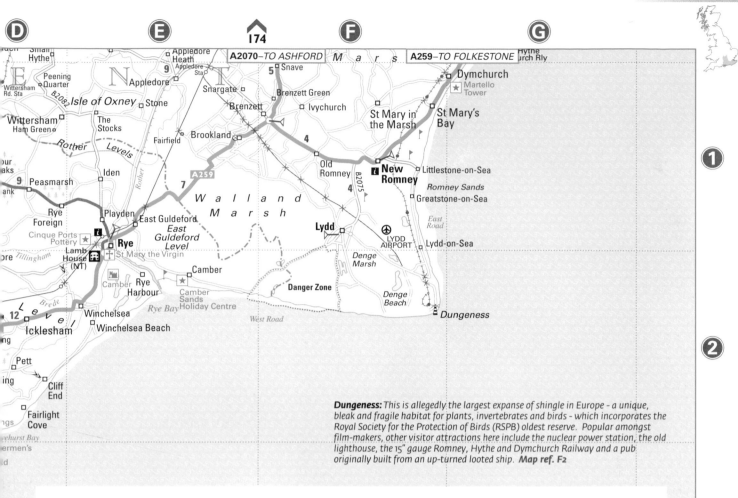

A2070–TO ASHFORD   M a r s   **A259**–TO FOLKESTONE   Hythe urch Rly

D
Small
Hythe
Peening
Quarter
Wittersham
Rd. Sta
Appledore
Heath
Appledore
Snave
Dymchurch
Martello
Tower
E N T
Isle of Oxney   Stone
Appledore
Appledore
Sta
Snargate
Brenzett Green
Brenzett
Ivychurch
St Mary in
the Marsh
St Mary's
Bay
Wittersham
Ham Green
The
Stocks
Fairfield
Brookland
Old
Romney
**New
Romney**
Littlestone-on-Sea
Rother   Levels
9   Peasmarsh
A259
W a l l a n d
M a r s h
Romney Sands
Greatstone-on-Sea
Rye
Foreign
Playden
East Guldeford
East
Guldeford
Level
Lydd
East
Road
Cinque Ports
Pottery
Rye
St Mary the Virgin
LYDD
AIRPORT
Lydd-on-Sea
Lamb
House
(NT)
Camber
Denge
Marsh
Tillingham
Camber
Rye
Harbour
Camber
Sands
Holiday Centre
Danger Zone
Denge
Beach
Brede
Level
Winchelsea
Icklesham   Winchelsea Beach
Rye Bay   West Road
Dungeness
Pett
Cliff
End
Fairlight
Cove

Dungeness: *This is allegedly the largest expanse of shingle in Europe - a unique, bleak and fragile habitat for plants, invertebrates and birds - which incorporates the Royal Society for the Protection of Birds (RSPB) oldest reserve. Popular amongst film-makers, other visitor attractions here include the nuclear power station, the old lighthouse, the 15" gauge Romney, Hythe and Dymchurch Railway and a pub originally built from an up-turned looted ship.* **Map ref. F2**

CHANNEL TUNNEL TERMINAL MAPS

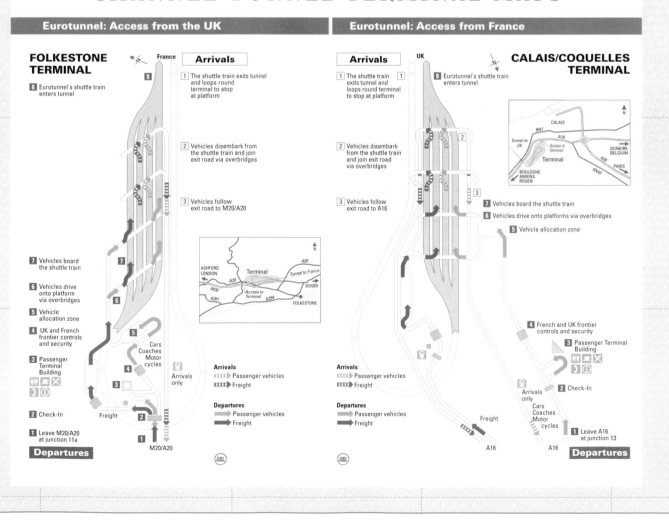

Eurotunnel: Access from the UK

FOLKESTONE TERMINAL

France

8 Eurotunnel's shuttle train enters tunnel

Arrivals

1 The shuttle train exits tunnel and loops round terminal to stop at platform

2 Vehicles disembark from the shuttle train and join exit road via overbridges

3 Vehicles follow exit road to M20/A20

7 Vehicles board the shuttle train

6 Vehicles drive onto platform via overbridges

5 Vehicle allocation zone

4 UK and French frontier controls and security

3 Passenger Terminal Building

2 Check-In

1 Leave M20/A20 at junction 11a

Cars
Coaches
Motor
cycles

Arrivals
only

Freight

M20/A20

Departures

Arrivals
Passenger vehicles
Freight

Departures
Passenger vehicles
Freight

Eurotunnel: Access from France

Arrivals

1 The shuttle train exits tunnel and loops round terminal to stop at platform

2 Vehicles disembark from the shuttle train and join exit road via overbridges

3 Vehicles follow exit road to A16

UK

8 Eurotunnel's shuttle train enters tunnel

CALAIS/COQUELLES TERMINAL

CALAIS
RN1
A16
Tunnel to
UK
Access to
Terminal
Terminal
DUNKIRK
BELGIUM
A26
PARIS
BOULOGNE
AMIENS
ROUEN
RN43

7 Vehicles board the shuttle train

6 Vehicles drive onto platforms via overbridges

5 Vehicle allocation zone

4 French and UK frontier controls and security

3 Passenger Terminal Building

2 Check-In

Arrivals
only

Cars
Coaches
Motor
cycles

1 Leave A16 at junction 13

Freight

A16   A16

Departures

Arrivals
Passenger vehicles
Freight

Departures
Passenger vehicles
Freight

(inset map) N   ASHFORD LONDON   A20   Terminal   Tunnel to France   A20   DOVER   A261   Access to Terminal   A259   FOLKESTONE

Norman's Bay: *The Norman Army sailed from St. Valery across the English Channel on the evening of the 27th September 1066 and landed in England, on the morning of 28th September, at what has since been called Norman's Bay. From there they proceeded inland and two weeks later defeated King Harold at the Battle of Hastings.* **Map ref. B3**

Rye: *This picturesque Sussex town was one of the entry points for the 'Black Death' which plagued Britain from 1348 to 1353. The Cinque Ports of the south east, which traded with the rest of the world, and the smugglers who haunted the marshes, brought in the fleas which carried the deadly Tersina Pestis bacteria which eventually killed a third of Europe's people. Deadman's Lane, in Rye, is thought to be where they buried their plague victims.* **Map ref. E1**

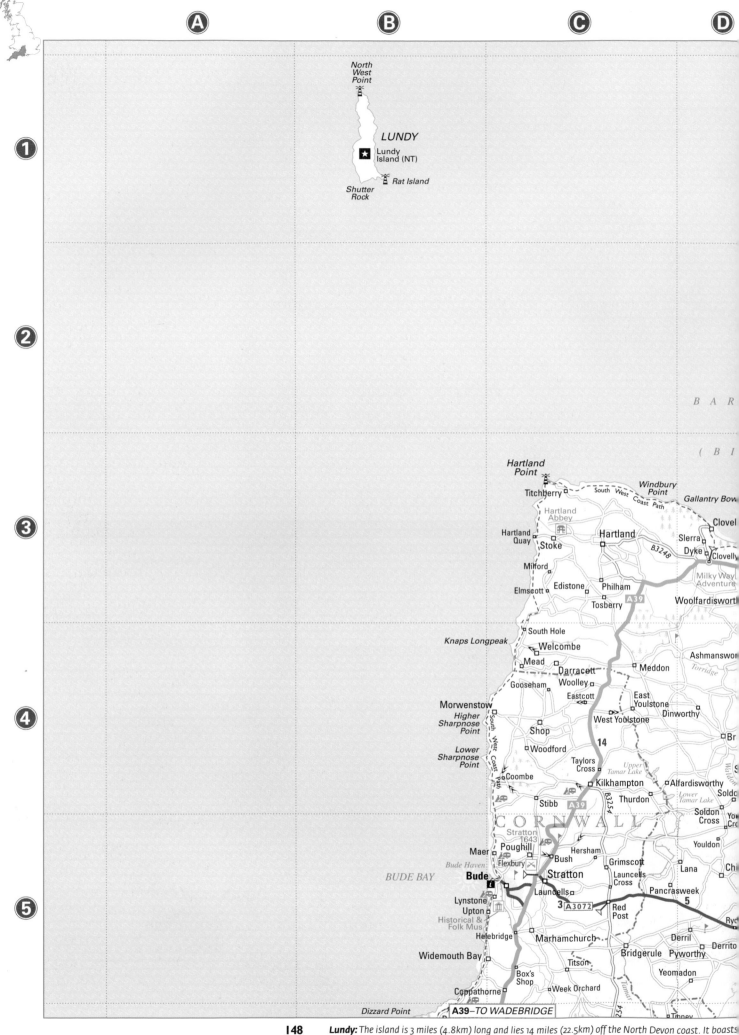

① ② ③ ④ ⑤

North
West
Point

LUNDY

★ Lundy
Island (NT)

Rat Island

Shutter
Rock

B A R

(B I

Hartland
Point

Windbury
Point

Titchberry

South West Coast Path

Gallantry Bow

Hartland
Abbey

Clovel

Hartland
Quay

Stoke

Hartland

Slerra

Dyke

B3248

Clovelly

Milford

Milky Way
Adventure

Elmscott

Edistone

Philham

A39

Tosberry

Woolfardisworth

South Hole

Knaps Longpeak

Welcombe

Ashmanswo

Mead

Darracott

Meddon

Torridge

Gooseham

Woolley

Eastcott

East
Youlstone

Dinworthy

Morwenstow

West Youlstone

Higher
Sharpnose
Point

South West Coast Path

Shop

14

Lower
Sharpnose
Point

Woodford

Taylors
Cross

*Upper
Tamar Lake*

Wald

Coombe

Kilkhampton

Alfardisworthy

*Lower
Tamar Lake*

Soldo

Stibb

A39

Thurdon

B3254

Soldon
Cross

Yo
Cro

C O R N W A L L

Stratton
1643

Youldon

Maer

Poughill

Bush

Hersham

Grimscott

Lana

Ch

Flexbury

Bude Haven

Bude

Stratton

Launcells
Cross

BUDE BAY

Launcells

Pancrasweek

5

Lynstone

3 A3072

Red
Post

Ryd

Upton

Historical &
Folk Mus

Helebridge

Marhamchurch

Derril

Widemouth Bay

Titson

Bridgerule Pyworthy

Yeomadon

Box's
Shop

Week Orchard

Tamai

Coppathorne

Dizzard Point

A39–TO WADEBRIDGE

254

Tinney

148

Lundy: *The island is 3 miles (4.8km) long and lies 14 miles (22.5km) off the North Devon coast. It boasts*
castle, three lighthouses, an inn and a church and is the first designated Marine Nature Reserve in Brit
Lundy's rugged shores have proved to be a graveyard for over 130 ships which lie wrecked off its coast.
Map ref. B1 Also on page 32

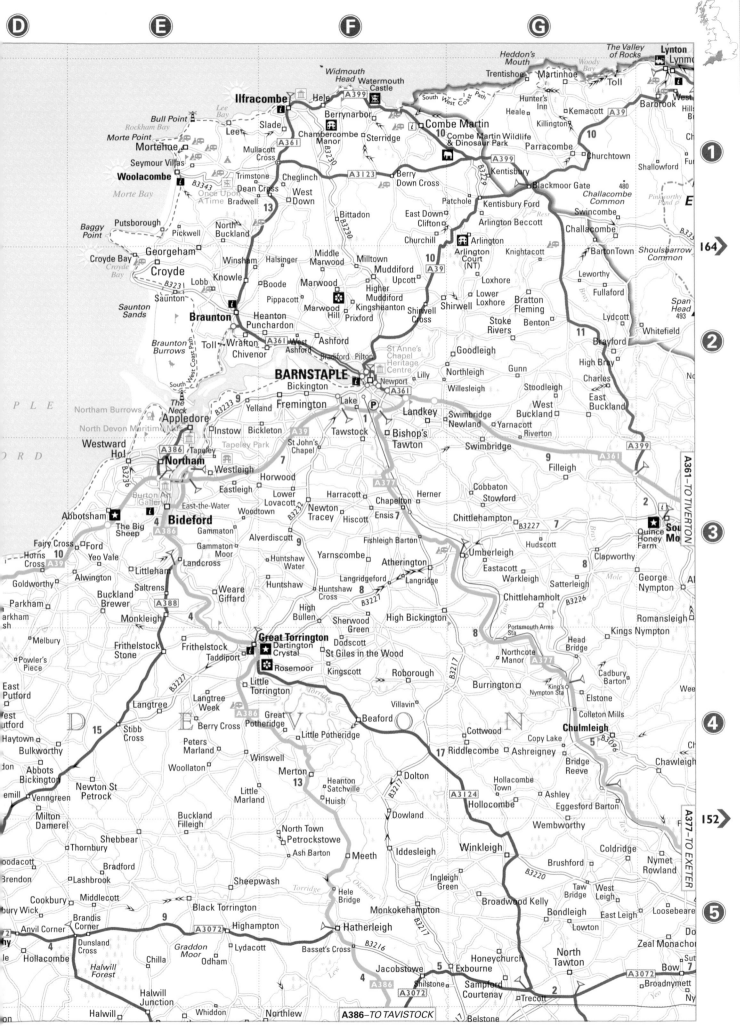

The Valley of Rocks
Lynton
Lynmouth
Heddon's Mouth
Woody Bay
Trentishoe
Martinhoe
Toll
West
Hills
Barbrook
Widmouth Head
Watermouth Castle
Hele
South West Coast Path
Hunter's Inn
Heale
Kemacott
Killington
A39
Ilfracombe
Berrynarbor
Combe Martin
Parracombe
Churchtown
Shallowford
Bull Point
Rockham Bay
Lee Bay
Slade
Lee
Chambercombe Manor
Sterridge
Combe Martin Wildlife & Dinosaur Park
A399
Kentisbury
Blackmoor Gate
Morte Point
Mortehoe
Mullacott Cross
A361
West Down
Berry Down Cross
A39
Kentisbury Ford
Challacombe Common
480
Swincombe
Seymour Villas
Trimstone
Cheglinch
A3123
Patchole
Arlington Beccott
Challacombe
Woolacombe
B3343
Dean Cross
Bradwell
Bittadon
B3230
East Down
Clifton
Churchill
Arlington
Arlington Court (NT)
Knightacott
BartonTown
Shoulsbarrow Common
Morte Bay
Once Upon A Time
North Buckland
Middle Marwood
Milltown
Muddiford
Loxhore
Leworthy
Fullaford
Span Head 493
Putsborough
Pickwell
Winsham
Halsinger
Marwood
Higher Muddiford
Upcott
Lower Loxhore
Shirwell
Bratton Fleming
Lydcott
Whitefield
Baggy Point
Georgeham
Croyde
Knowle
Boode
Pippacott
Marwood Hill
Kingsheanton
Prixford
Shirwell Cross
Benton
Stoke Rivers
High Bray
Croyde Bay
B3231
Lobb
Heanton Punchardon
Prixford
Goodleigh
Brayford
Saunton Sands
Braunton
Toll
Wrafton
Chivenor
West Ashford
Ashford
Bradiford
Pilton
St Anne's Chapel Heritage Centre
Northleigh
Gunn
Stoodleigh
Charles
East Buckland
Braunton Burrows
South West Coast Path
BARNSTAPLE
Bickington
Newport
A361
Willesleigh
West Buckland
The Neck
Appledore
North Devon Maritime Mus
Yelland
Fremington
Lake
P
Landkey
Swimbridge Newland
Yarnacott
Riverton
Swimbridge
A361
A399
Northam Burrows
Bickleton
A39
Tawstock
Bishop's Tawton
Filleigh
Westward Ho!
A386
Tapeley
Westleigh
Horwood
St John's Chapel
Tapeley Park
A377
Herner
Cobbaton
Stowford
Northam
Burton Art Gallery
Eastleigh
Lower Lovacott
Harracott
Newton Tracey
Chapelton
Ensis
Chittlehampton
B3227
Quince Honey Farm
Sou Mo
Abbotsham
The Big Sheep
Bideford
Gammaton
Woodtown
Hiscott
Fishleigh Barton
Umberleigh
Hudscott
Clapworthy
George Nympton
Fairy Cross
Ford
Yeo Vale
A386
Gammaton Moor
Landcross
Alverdiscott
Yarnscombe
Atherington
Eastacott
Warkleigh
Satterleigh
Romansleigh
Horns Cross
A39
Alwington
Littleham
Saltrens
Weare Giffard
Huntshaw Water
Langridgeford
Langridge
Chittlehamholt
B3226
Kings Nympton
Goldworthy
Buckland Brewer
Huntshaw
Huntshaw Cross
B3227
Portsmouth Arms Sta
Northcote Manor
A377
Parkham
Monkleigh
High Bullen
Sherwood Green
High Bickington
Head Bridge
Cadbury Barton
Melbury
Frithelstock
Frithelstock Stone
Taddiport
Great Torrington
Dartington Crystal
St Giles in the Wood
Dodscott
Kingscott
Roborough
Burrington
King's Nympton Sta
Elstone
Powler's Piece
B3227
Rosemoor
Little Torrington
Villavin
Colleton Mills
Chulmleigh
East Putford
Langtree
Langtree Week
A386
Great Potheridge
Beaford
Little Potheridge
Cottwood
Copy Lake
Bridge Reeve
B3096
Chawleigh
West Putford
Stibb Cross
Berry Cross
Riddlecombe
Ashreigney
Haytown
Bulkworthy
Peters Marland
Winswell
Merton
Dolton
Hollacombe Town
Ashley
Eggesford Barton
Abbots Bickington
Woollaton
Heanton Satchville
A3124
Hollocombe
Wembworthy
Coldridge
Nymet Rowland
Newton St Petrock
Little Marland
Huish
Dowland
Winkleigh
Brushford
Venngreen
Meeth
Iddesleigh
Ingleigh Green
Broadwood Kelly
Taw Bridge
West Leigh
Loosebeare
Milton Damerel
North Town
Petrockstowe
Ash Barton
Dowland
Bondleigh
East Leigh
Shebbear
Buckland Filleigh
Monkokehampton
Lowton
Thornbury
Bradford
Sheepwash
Hele Bridge
North Tawton
Zeal Monachor
Bow
Cookbury
Middlecott
Black Torrington
Honeychurch
A3072
Lashbrook
Highampton
Basset's Cross
B3216
B3217
A3072
Broadnymett
Brandis Corner
A3072
Hatherleigh
Jacobstowe
Exbourne
Sampford Courtenay
Trecott
Anvil Corner
Dunsland Cross
Chilla
Lydacott
Odham
Graddon Moor
A386
Shilstone
A3072
Hollacombe
Halwill Forest
Whiddon
Northlew
A386—TO TAVISTOCK
Belstone
Halwill Junction
Halwill

149
Braunton Burrows: Almost 2450 acres (1000ha) of shifting sand dunes make this area so unusual that it has been designated by UNESCO as a 'Biosphere Reserve'. This recognises its status and affords it international protection. *Map ref. E2.*

163

A361—TO TIVERTON

A377—TO EXETER

1

2

Lynmouth: *Scene of the disastrous floods of the East and West Lyn rivers during the night of 15 August 1952 which resulted in the destruction of much of the village. 34 people were killed and 165 buildings wholly or partially destroyed.* **Map ref. A3.**

B R I S T O L   C H A

Monknash   Monkton
Marcross   Llanmaes
St   Llantwit   Eglwys-Brewis   St Athan
Nash Point   Donats   Major   Boverton   B4265
       Gileston
       West Aberthaw
       Breaksea Pt

Foreland Point
Lynton & Lynmouth Cliff Rly
Lynmouth Bay
Countisbury Cove
The Valley of Rocks
Lynton
Woody Bay
Lynmouth
Countisbury
Watersmeet House (NT)
Culbone   Porlock Weir   Porlock Bay   Selworthy Beacon
Toll   South   West   Coast Path   308   South   West   Coast Path
East Lyn   Wilsham   387   *Culbone Hill*   Toll   Lynch   Holnicote Estate (NT)
West Lyn   Malmsmead   A39   413   11   West   Bossington   North Hill   Woodcombe   **Minehead**
Barbrook   Brendon   Oare   Porlock   **Porlock**   Allerford   Hindon   8   Bratton   Periton   Butlins Family
emacott   A39   Hillsford Bridge   Tippacott   Toll   Holnicote   Selworthy   A39   Alcombe   Entertainment Resort
10   Cheriton   *Brendon Common*   *South Common*   Horner   Tivington   Dunster Sta   Blue Anchor Bay
Churchtown   Shallowford   Furzehill   9   B3223   Luccombe   Huntscott   Wootton Courtenay   Knowle   **Dunster**   Marsh Street   Blue An
3
Gate   480   *Hoaroak Hill*   Stoke Pero   *Dunkery Hill*   Ranscombe   Cowbridge   Dunster Castle   Carhampt
Challacombe Common   473   E X M O O R   Dry Hill   *Dunkery Beacon*   Burrow   7   & Gardens(NT)   Dunster Old
Swincombe   *Pinkworthy Pond*   444   *Codsend Moors*   519   Timberscombe   Watermill (NT)   A39
hallacombe   B3358   9   *Dure Down*   *Exe*   **EXMOOR**   *Quarme*   Bickham   *Croydon Hill*   Withycombe   Bi
193   BartonTown   *Shoulsbarrow Common*   10   B3223   Edgcott   B3224   Cutcombe   365   Rodhuish   Cleev
Leworthy   Simonsbath   Exford   Luckwell Bridge   Wheddon Cross   Luxborough   Lower Roadwat
Fullaford   *Barle*   409   Triscombe   *Lype Hill*   Roadwater
Lydcott   *Span Head*   Long Holcombe   Blacklands   Great Nurcot   423   B R E N D O N   Kingsbridge   Treborough
11   Brayford   493   Whitefield   436   *Withypool Common*   Withypool   *Winsford Hill*   North Quarme   H I L L S   Withiel Florey   Leig
High Bray   North Radworthy   *Kinsford Water*   *Worth Hill*   426   Winsford   West Howetown   Gupworthy   B3224   Ch
4
Charles   North Heasley   S O M E R   Exton   Woolcotts
East Buckland   Heasley Mill   South Radworthy   *Dane's Brook*   Knaplock   Liscombe   Week   A396   Brompton Regis   Clutter Rese
     Twitchen   *Molland Common*   Tarr Steps   Higher Combe   15   317   B3190
A399   North Molton   Molland   Hawkridge   Hartford   *Wimbleball Lake*   Upton   Huish Cha
A361   D E V O N   *Yeo*   *Barle*   Skilgate
2   4   Bish Mill   West Anstey   **Dulverton**   B3222   Battleton   Bury   *Haddon Hill*   Chip
Quince Honey Farm   **South Molton**   B3227   Newtown   Yeo Mill   East Anstey   Nightcott   Brushford   B3223   Timewell   Rad
5
Bishops Nympton   *Yeo*   Oldways End   Sowerhill   Upcott   Morebath   B3227   12
8   Clapworthy   Ash Mill   12   East Knowstone   B3227   Highleigh   Exebridge   Petton
George Nympton   Alswear   *Crooked Oak*   Knowstone   A396   Oakfordbridge   **Bampton**   Shillingford   Clayhanger
226   Mariansleigh   Rose Ash   14   *Rackenford Moor*   Oakford   Huntsham   Staple Cros
Romansleigh   *Mole*   9   Creacombe   A361–TO TIVERTON   dleigh   Cove
Kings Nympton   Rowley

A361–TO BARNSTAPLE

Porlock Hill: *Over the years this notorious stretch of road, with its 25% (1 in 4) incline and tight curves, has caused travellers countless problems. The main coast road was first negotiated by a motor car in 1900 as a bet. If required, the nearby scenic toll road avoids the need to travel along this road.* **Map ref. B3**

152 **Quantock Hills:** *Covering an area of 48 square miles and reaching a height of 1260 fee (384m) the Quantock countryside is one of the most delightful areas of Britain. It was first in England to get AONB (Area of Outstanding Natural Beauty) status back in 1950 and is also designated as a SSSI (Site of Special Scientific Interest) because it contains almost 10% of the world's maritime heathland.* **Map ref. E3**

M5–TO BRISTOL

1

A368,A38–TO BRISTOL

2

166

3

A39–TO GLASTONBURY

4

5

BARRY

WESTON-SUPER-MARE

Steep Holm

Brean Down (NT)

Berrow

Burnham-on-Sea

Stert Island

Stert Flats

Highbridge

Watchfield

BRIDGWATER

TAUNTON

Wellington

VALE OF TAUNTON DEANE

Williton

QUANTOCK HILLS

Quantock Forest

M5–TO EXETER

A358–TO ILMINSTER

Langport

tch Beauchamp: *The nearby church is the final resting
ce of Col. John Rouse Merriot Chard VC Royal Engineers.
Lt. Chard be commanded a small garrison of 140 soldiers
ch heroically defended Rorke's Drift during the Zulu Wars.
p ref. G5*

Weston-super-Mare: *Traditional seaside resort with two piers. The Grand Pier built in
1904 is still open and is listed by the Department of the Environment as a monument
of historic importance. The other, Birnbeck Pier, which opened in 1867, is now closed,
but is unusual because it is the only pier in the country that links the mainland to an
island. This pier is a Grade II listed structure. Map ref. G1*

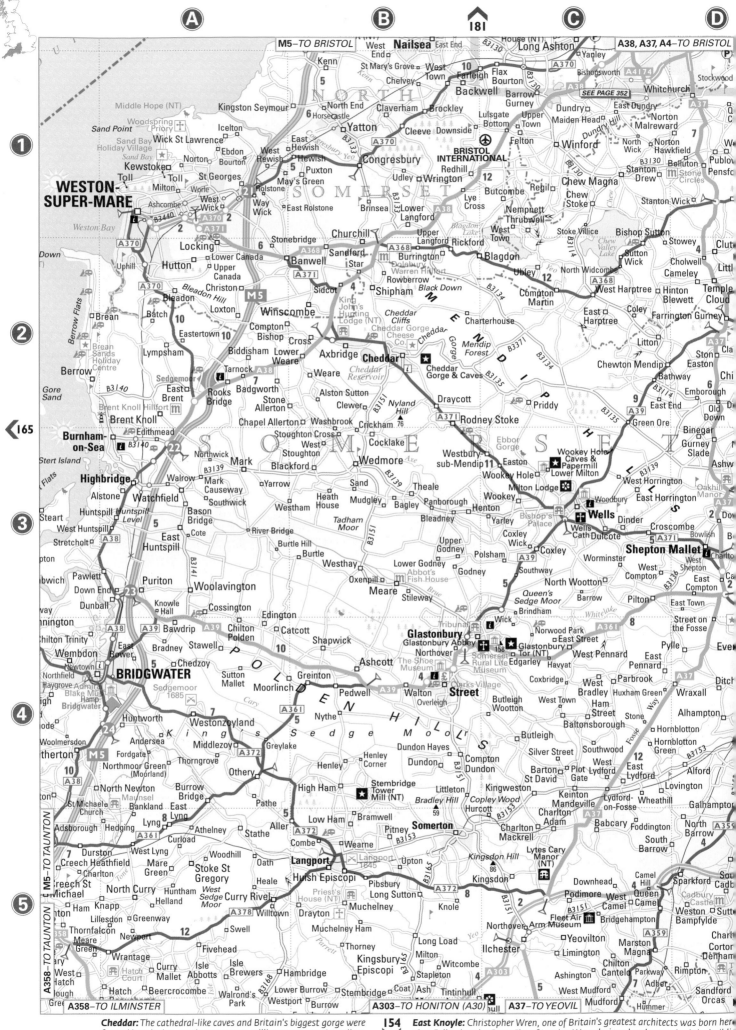

181

165

154

Cheddar: The cathedral-like caves and Britain's biggest gorge were formed here by ice-age rivers over one million years ago. As well as being a major UK tourist attraction for over 200 years the area is also an SSSI (Site of Special Scientific Interest). **Map ref. B2**

East Knoyle: Christopher Wren, one of Britain's greatest architects was born here 1632. Following the Great Fire of London Wren designed and supervised the building of 51 London Churches including St Paul's Cathedral. **Map ref. F4**

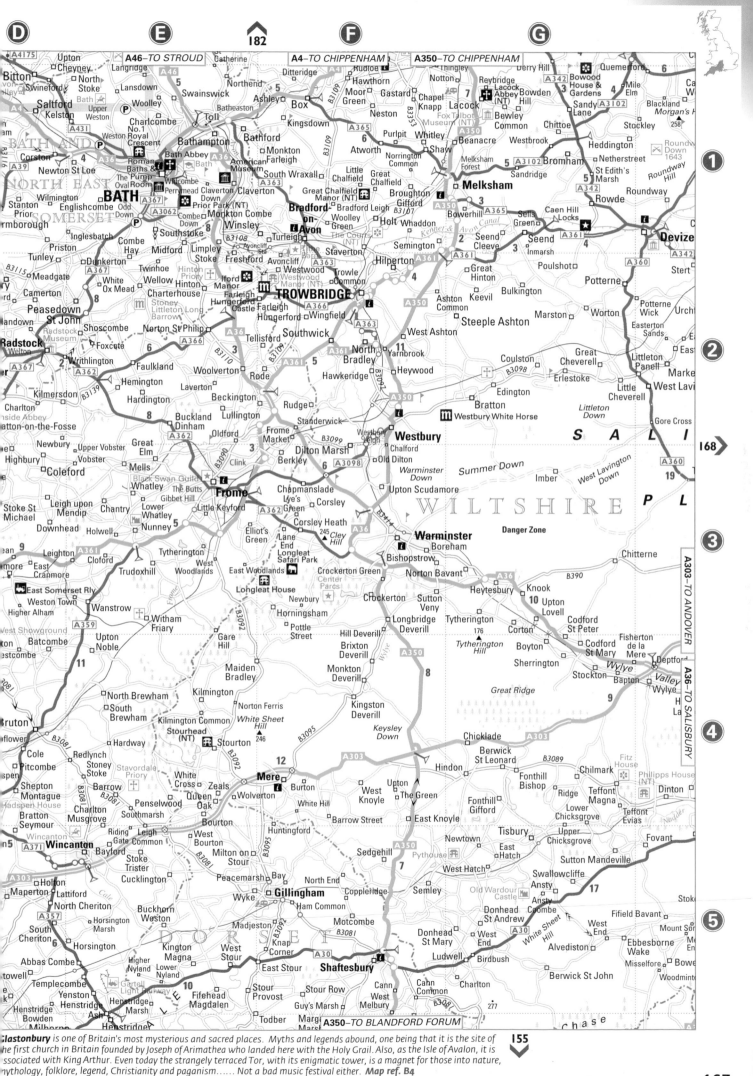

Glastonbury is one of Britain's most mysterious and sacred places. Myths and legends abound, one being that it is the site of the first church in Britain founded by Joseph of Arimathea who landed here with the Holy Grail. Also, as the Isle of Avalon, it is associated with King Arthur. Even today the strangely terraced Tor, with its enigmatic tower, is a magnet for those into nature, mythology, folklore, legend, Christianity and paganism...... Not a bad music festival either. Map ref. B4

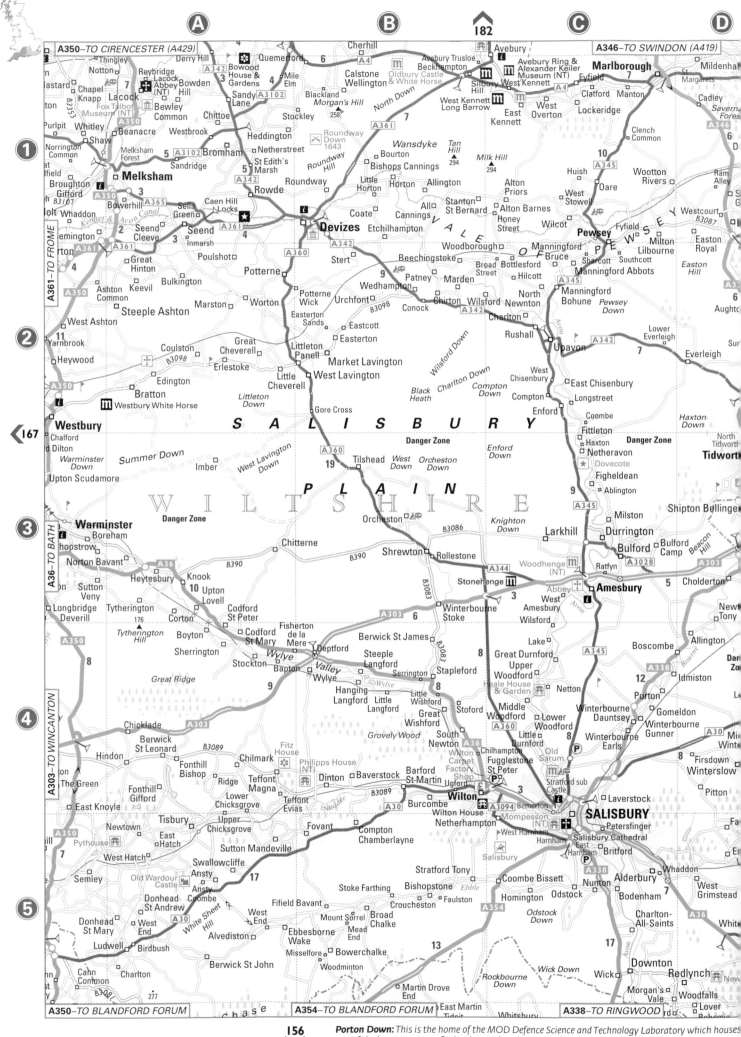

Ⓐ Ⓑ Ⓒ Ⓓ

A350–TO CIRENCESTER (A429)

A346–TO SWINDON (A419)

Marlborough

Melksham

Devizes

Pewsey

Westbury

V A L E   O F   P E W S E Y

S A L I S B U R Y

167

Danger Zone

Tidworth

W I L T S H I R E   P L A I N

Danger Zone

Warminster

Stonehenge

Amesbury

Larkhill

Durrington

Bulford

Salisbury Plain

Wilton

SALISBURY

Salisbury Cathedral

A350–TO BLANDFORD FORUM

A354–TO BLANDFORD FORUM

A338–TO RINGWOOD

156

Porton Down: This is the home of the MOD Defence Science and Technology Laboratory which houses one of the largest groups of scientists and engineers employed within Britain's public service. From 1939 up to the 1960s it is alleged that almost 20,000 so called human 'guinea pigs' volunteered to assist in tests carried out here which were supposedly aimed at finding a cure for the common cold. Map ref. C4/D4

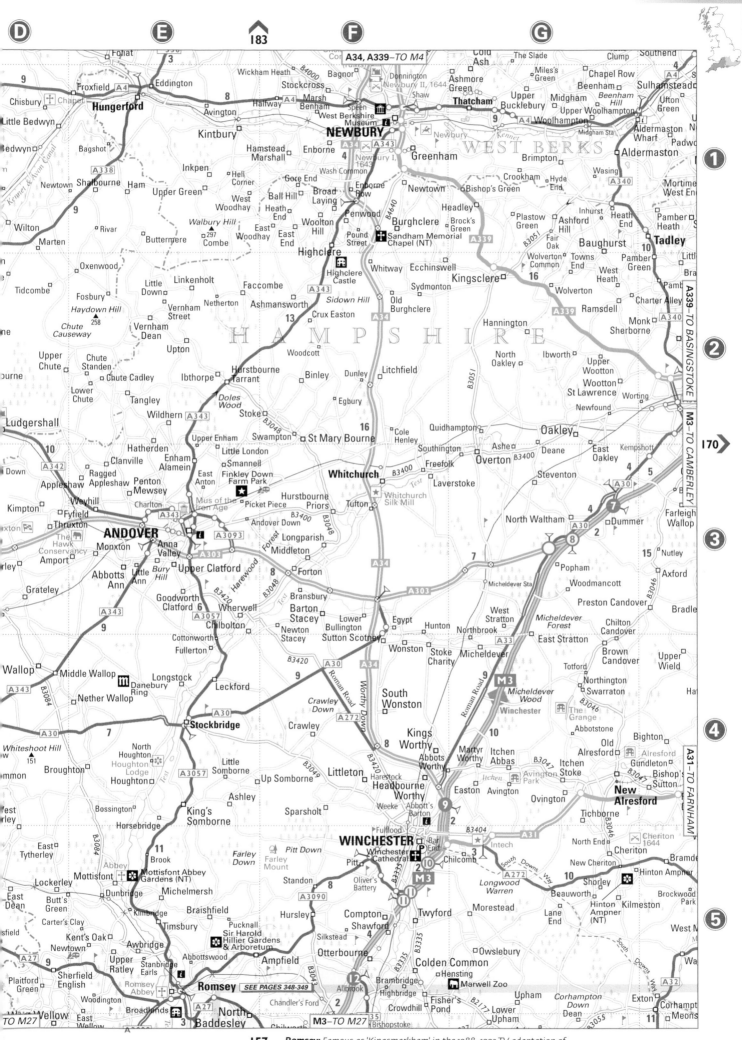

A34, A339–TO M4

NEWBURY

West Berkshire Museum

WEST BERKS

Newbury I, 1643

Newbury II, 1644

Donnington

Thatcham

Sandham Memorial Chapel (NT)

Highclere Castle

HAMPSHIRE

Haydown Hill ▲ 258

Chute Causeway

Walbury Hill ▲ 297 Combe

Hungerford

Kennet & Avon Canal

A338

A343

A34

A339–TO BASINGSTOKE

A340

Tadley

M3–TO CAMBERLEY

170 ▶

Mus of the Iron Age

Finkley Down Farm Park

ANDOVER

The Hawk Conservancy

A3093

A303

A343

Harewood Forest

A3057

A30

Whitchurch

Whitchurch

Whitchurch Silk Mill

Oakley

Overton

Dummer

7

8

15 Nutley

A30

Micheldever Forest

A33

M3

Micheldever Wood

Winchester

The Grange

A31–TO FARNHAM

A342

Ludgershall

Danebury Ring

Whiteshoot Hill ▲ 151

Stockbridge

A30

A3057

A272

Worthy Down

Roman Road

South Wonston

Kings Worthy

New Alresford

Old Alresford

Alresford

Cheriton

Cheriton 1644

A272

South Downs Way

A32

Mottisfont Abbey Gardens (NT)

Sir Harold Hillier Gardens & Arboretum

A3090

WINCHESTER

Winchester Cathedral

Oliver's Battery

M3

Intech

Marwell Zoo

Romsey   Romsey Abbey

SEE PAGES 348–349

A27

M3–TO M27

M3–TO M27

169

Romsey: Famous as 'Kingsmarkham' in the 1988–1993 TV adaptation of the Ruth Rendell Mysteries starring George Baker. **Map ref. E5**

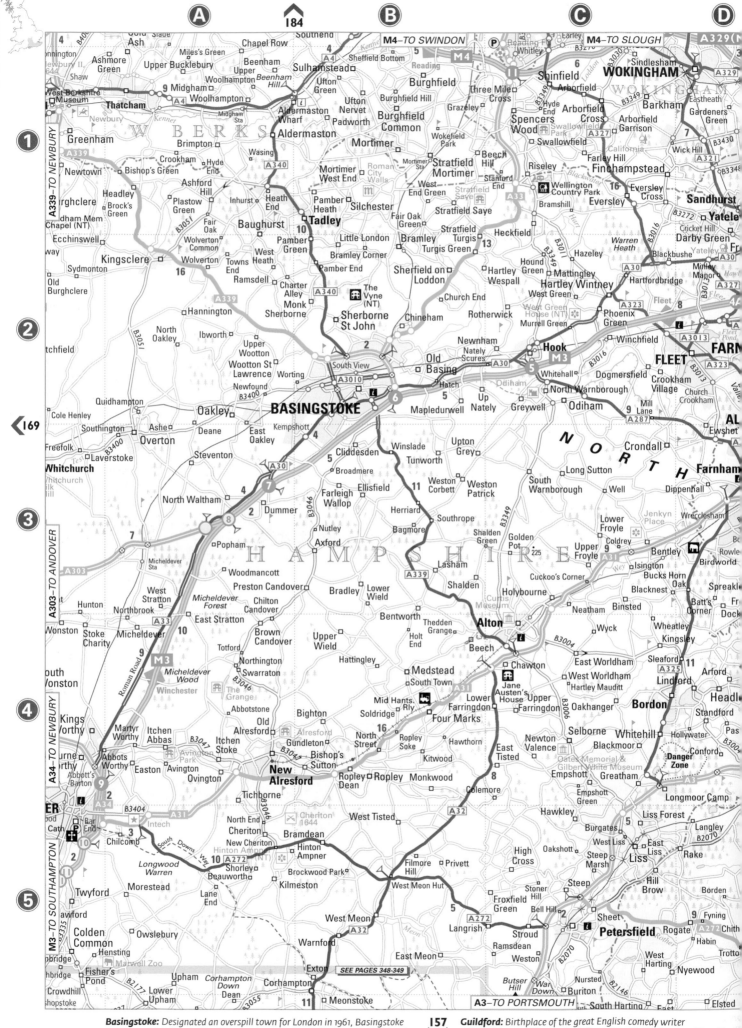

169

157

Basingstoke: Designated an overspill town for London in 1961, Basingstoke was almost totally rebuilt with a new town centre, pedestrian precincts and multi-storey car parks. The population increased from 26,000 in 1960 to 60,000 in 1973 and is today over 100,000. **Map ref. B2**

Guildford: Birthplace of the great English comedy writer P G Wodehouse (1881–1975). Pelham Grenville Wodehouse, 'Plum' to his friends, is best remembered for the creation of Bertie Wooster and his faithful and resourceful manservant Jeeves. **Map ref. E3**

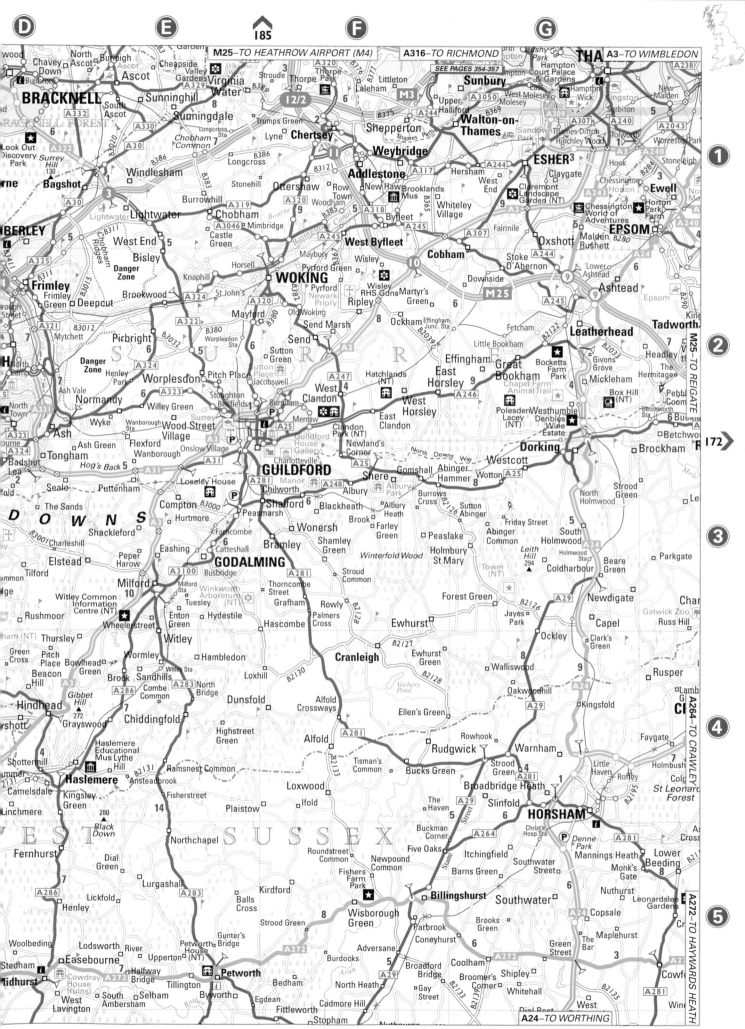

orsham: *During a violent hailstorm on 5th*
otember 1958 hailstones of 2–3 inches
(50–80mm) diameter were measured. One
single hailstone weighed in at 6.7 oz (190
gms) and is the largest recorded hailstone
in Britain. **Map ref. G4**

Brookwood: *From the mid nineteenth century, the amount of bodies in London requiring burial was causing*
great concern, so 2,000 acres (800ha) of Woking's common land was purchased from Lord Onslow in 1852
in order to establish a single great metropolitan cemetery. By 1854 Brookwood was the largest cemetery in
the world and even today it remains the largest in the UK. Since 1854 almost a quarter of a million bodies
have been interred here. Since 1917 separate military cemeteries, administered by the Commonwealth War
Graves Commission have also been located here. **Map ref. E2**

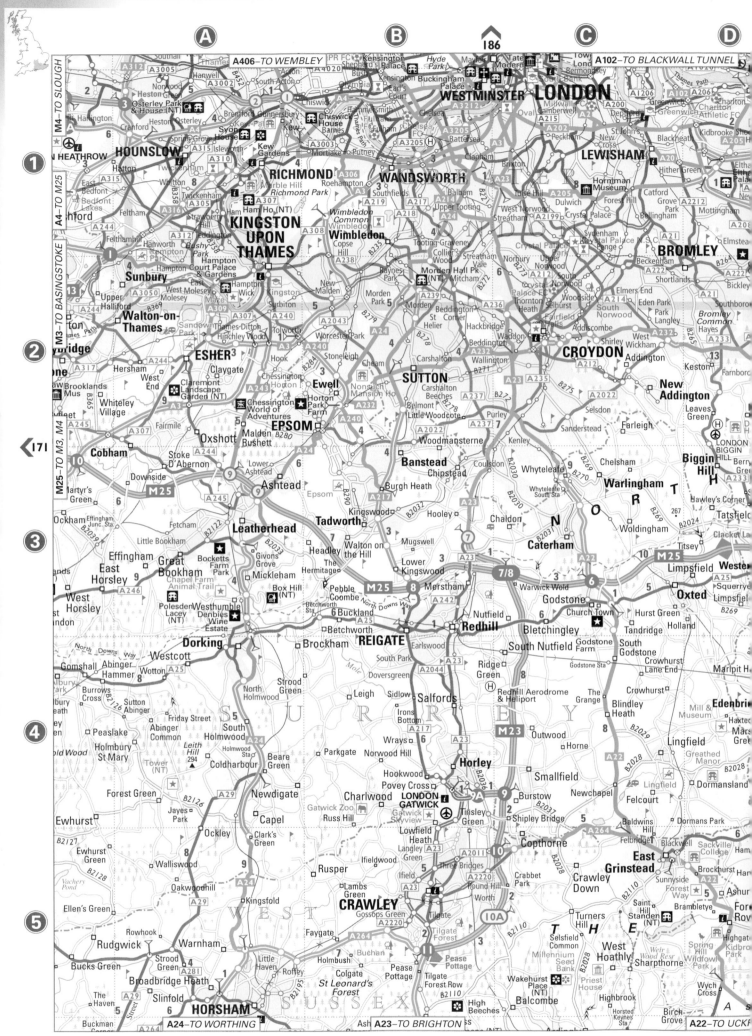

171
159

Purley: In February 1898 Henry Lindfield became the first person ever to die in a car crash. He died from injuries he sustained when his car left the road at Purley Corner whilst driving to Brighton. **Map ref. C2**

Biggin Hill Airport was first established as a Royal Flying Corps station in 1917, but it is best known as a World War II 'fighter station' from which the RAF fought the crucial 'Battle of Britain' in the summer of 1940. **Map ref. D2**

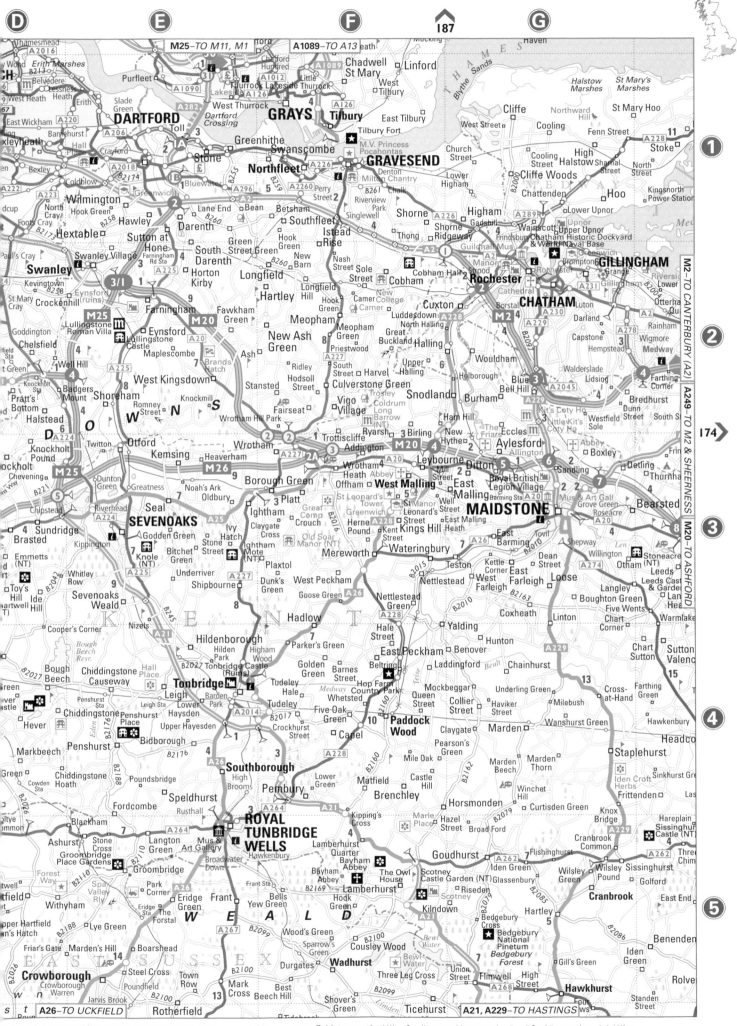

Thamesmead
A2016
Wood
B2137
Erith Marshes
Belvedere
West Heath
Heath
Erith
East Wickham
A220
Barnehurst
Bexleyheath
Crayford
Hall
A223
Wilmington
Hook Green
Sutton at Hone
Hextable
Foots Cray
B2173
Swanley
Kevingtown
B258
St Mary Cray
Crockenhill
Chelsfield
Goddington
Well Hill
Knockholt Sta
Badgers Mount
Pratt's Bottom
Halstead
Knockholt
Knockholt Pound
Chevening
Dunton Green
Greatness
Chipstead
Riverhead
Sundridge
Brasted
Kippington
Emmetts (NT)
Toy's Hill
Ide Hill
Whitley Row
Sevenoaks Weald
Cooper's Corner
Bough Beech Resr.
Bough Beech
Chiddingstone Causeway
Penshurst Sta
Hever
Chiddingstone
Markbeech
Penshurst
Chiddingstone Hoath
Cowden Sta
Hartfield
Withyham
Friar's Gate
Marden's Hill
Crowborough
Crowborough Warren
Jarvis Brook

M25–TO M11, M1
A1089–TO A13
Purfleet
Thurrock Lakeside Thurrock
West Thurrock
A126
DARTFORD
Toll
Stone
Greenhithe
Swanscombe
Northfleet
GRAYS
Tilbury
Tilbury Fort
M.V. Princess Pocahontas
GRAVESEND
Chadwell St Mary
Linford
West Tilbury
East Tilbury
Cliffe
West Street
Cooling
Blythe Sands
Halstow Marshes
St Mary's Marshes
St Mary Hoo
Northward Hill
High Halstow
Fenn Street
Stoke
A228
Cooling Street
Sharnal Street
North Street
Kingsnorth Power Station
Hoo
Lower Upnor
Upper Upnor
Chattenden
Cliffe Woods
Higham
Shorne
Chatham Historic Dockyard & World Naval Base
Frindsbury
Strood
Rochester
GILLINGHAM
Grange
Rainham
Wigmore
Medway
CHATHAM
Luton
Darland
Capstone
Hempstead
Walderslade
Lidsing
Farthing Corner
Bredhurst
Dunn Street
Detling
Thurnham

orking: Sir Laurence Olivier (1907–1989) was born here.
won an Academy Award for his role as Hamlet in 1948
d went on to become one of Britain's best known actors.
p ref. A4

Hartfield: In 1925 the Milne family moved into nearby Cotchford Farm where A A Milne
wrote his Winnie the Pooh books, including his son Christopher Robin in the stories.
Some of the locations from the stories are identifiable in the area, including the
recently restored bridge where the Poohsticks game was invented. *Map ref. D5*

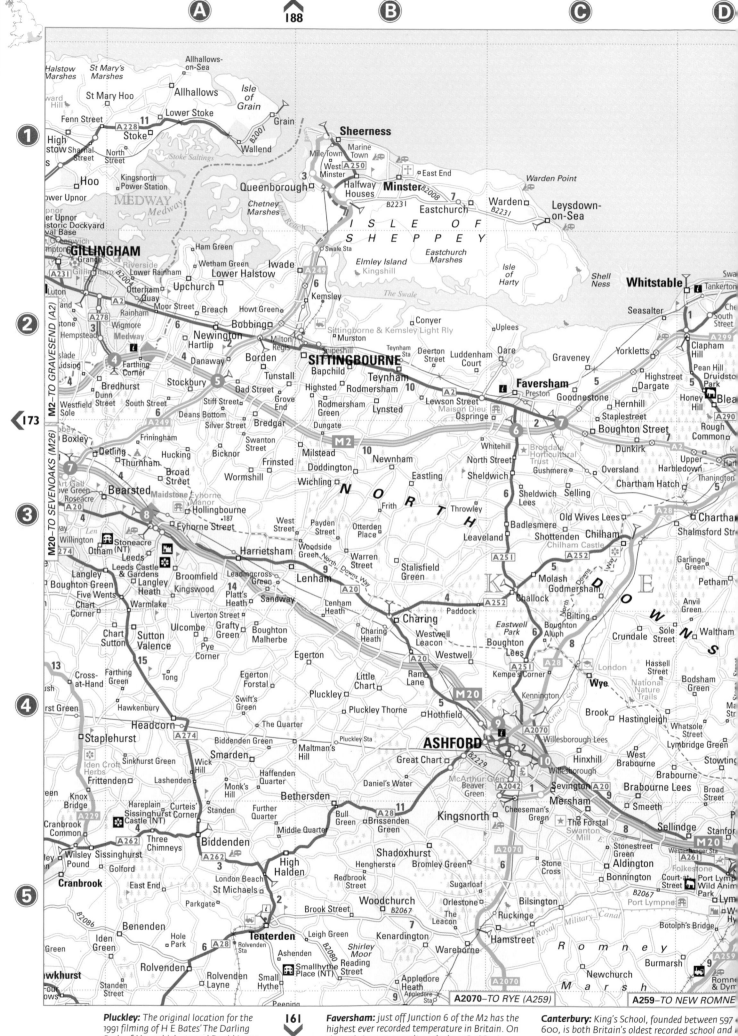

1

High
stow

173

2

M2–TO GRAVESEND (A2)

M20–TO SEVENOAKS (M26)

3

4

5

174

161

**Halstow
Marshes**   St Mary's
Marshes   Allhallows-
on-Sea   Isle
of
Grain
St Mary Hoo   Allhallows
ward
Hill
Fenn Street   Lower Stoke   Grain
A228   11   Stoke   B2001   Wallend
North Street   Shanal
Street   Stoke Saltings

Hoo
ower Upnor
er Upnor
istoric Dockyard
val Base   Kingsnorth
Power Station
MEDWAY   Medway

Chetney
Marshes
Queenborough   Halfway
Houses   Minster

GILLINGHAM
Grange   Riverside
Gillingham   Iwade
A231   B200   Lower Rainham
Otterham
Quay   Upchurch   Lower Halstow
A2   Moor Street   Breach   Howt Green   Kemsley
A278   Rainham   Bobbing
Wigmore   Newington   Milton
Regis   Murston
2   3   Hartlip   Bapchild
Hempstead   Borden   **SITTINGBOURNE**
slade   Medway   Danaway   Tunstall   Teynham
idsing   4   Farthing
Corner   Stockbury   Highsted   Rodmersham
Bredhurst   5   Oad Street   Rodmersham
Green   Lynsted
4   Dunn   South Street   Stiff Street   Grove
End   Dungate
Street   Deans Bottom   Silver Street   Bredgar
Westfield
Sole   A249   Frininghm   Swanton
Street   Milstead
bey   Boxley   Hucking   Bicknor   Frinsted   Doddington
Detling   Thurnham   Broad
Street   Wormshill   Wichling
Art Gall   Bearsted   Maidstone   Eyhorne
rove Green   Roseacre   187   West
Street   Payden
Street
A20   Otham   Hollingbourne   Eyhorne Street   Woodside
Green
Stoneacre   Leeds
(NT)

7

8

Sheerness
Mile Town   Marine
Town
West
Minster   A250   East End
Warden Point
Minster   B2008   Warden
B2231   Eastchurch   B2231   Leysdown-
on-Sea
ISLE OF
SHEPPEY
Elmley Island
Kingshill   Eastchurch
Marshes   Isle
of
Harty
The Swale   Shell
Ness   **Whitstable**
Tankerton
Swale Sta
Conyer   Uplees   Seasalter   South
Street   Clapham
Hill
A299
Sittingbourne & Kemsley Light Rly
Teynham
Sta   Deerton
Street   Luddenham
Court   Oare   Graveney   Yorkletts   Highstreet   Pean Hill   Druidsto
Dargate   Honey   Park
Lewson Street   Ospringe   **Faversham**   Goodnestone   Hill   Blea
Preston   Maison Dieu   Hernhill   A290
10   A2   6   7   Staplestreet   Boughton Street   Rough
Common
2   Brogdale
Horticultural
Trust   Dunkirk   A2
Whitehill   Gushmere   Upper
Harbledown
North Street   Overland   Harbledown   Thanington   Har
NORTH   Sheldwich   Selling   Chartham Hatch
Sheldwich   Chartham
Lees   Old Wives Lees   Chartha
Throwley   Badlesmere   Shalmsford Str
Frith   Leaveland   Shottenden   Chilham
Otterden
Place   Stalisfield
Green   Chilham Castle
Warren
Street   5   Molash   A252   Garlinge
Green

D

Tankerton   Sw
South
Street   1
A299
Pean Hill   Druidsto
Honey   Park
Hill   Blea
A290   Rough
Common
A2
Upper
Harbledown
Thanington   Har
Chartham Hatch
Chartham
Old Wives Lees   Chartha
Shalmsford Str
Chilham
Garlinge
Green
Anvil
Green   Petham
Sole   Waltham
Street
DOWNS
Crundale
Hassell   Bodsham
Street   Green
London   Wye   National
Nature
Trails
Hastingleigh
Brook   Whatsole   Ma
Street   Str
Willesborough Lees   West
Brabourne   Lymbridge Green   Stowting
Hinxhill
Willesborough   Brabourne
Sevington   A20   Brabourne Lees   Broad
Mersham   9   Smeeth   Street
Cheeseman's
Green   The Forstal   8   Sellindge   Stanfor
Swanton   Stonestreet
Mill   Green
Stone   Aldington   A261
Cross   Westenhanger Sta   A20
Bonnington   Court-at
Sugarloaf   Street   Port Lym
Orlestone   Stone   Wild Anim
Cross   Park   Lym
Bilsington   B2067   Port Lympne
The   Port Lympne
Leacon   Ruckinge
Romney
Hamstreet   Royal Military   Canal   Marsh
Wareborne   Botolph's Bridge
Newchurch   Burmarsh   Romn
& Dyr
A2070   A259

KA   Godmersham   Bilting   Boughton
Aluph   8   Bilting
Challock   Boughton
Lees   Kempe's Corner
4   Eastwell
Park   Boughton
A251   A28
Westwell
Leacon   Westwell   Ram
Lane   Kennington
Charing   A20   M20
Charing
Heath
A20   Little
Chart   9
Egerton   Hothfield   **ASHFORD**   10
Pluckley   B2229
Egerton
Forstal   Swift's
Green   Pluckley Thorne   Hothfield   Great Chart
Pluckley Sta   5
Maltman's
Hill   B229
Smarden   Biddenden Green   Haffenden   Daniel's Water   McArthur Glen
Quarter   Beaver   A2042
Wick   Monk's   Green   1
Hill   Hill   Bethersden   Kingsnorth
Lashenden   Further
Quarter   11   A28   Brissenden   Shadoxhurst
Standen   Middle Quarter   Bull   Green
Green   Hengherst   Bromley Green   6
Biddenden   A262   High
Halden   Redbrook
Street
A262   3   London Beach   Woodchurch   A2070
Sissinghurst   St Michaels   B2067
East End   Shirley   The
Moor   Leacon
Parkgate   2   Brook Street   Orlestone
Benenden   Leigh Green   Reading
Street   Kenardington   Ruckinge
Hole   i   Kenardington   Wareborne
Park   **Tenterden**   B2080   Appledore
Iden   Rolvenden
Green   Sta   Smallhythe   Shirley Moor   Heath
Place (NT)   Appledore
Small   Sta
Cranbrook   Rolvenden   Hythe   A2070

Langley   Broomfield
Boughton Green   Langley   Kingswood
Five Wents   Heath   Platt's   14
Chart   Warmlake   Heath   Sandway
Corner   Liverton Street   Lenham
Heath
Langley   Ulcombe   Grafty   Boughton
13   Green   Malherbe
Cross-   15   Farthing   Pye   Egerton
at-Hand   Green   Corner
sh   Sutton   Tong
Valence   Hawkenbury   The Quarter
urst Green   Headcorn
Staplehurst   A274   Biddenden Green
Smarden
Iden Croft   Sinkhurst Green   Wick
Herbs   Frittenden   Hill
Knox   Lashenden   Monk's
Bridge   Hareplain   Curteis'   Hill
Cranbrook   Sissinghurst Corner   Standen
Common   A229   Castle (NT)   4
ey   Wilsley   Sissinghurst   Three   Biddenden
Pound   Golford   Chimneys   3
Cranbrook   East End   High
Halden
B2086   Iden   Hole   St Michaels
Green   Park   Parkgate
Green   Benenden
wkhurst   Rolvenden
ot   Standen   Rolvenden   Small
ws   Street   Layne   Hythe   Peening

North Downs Way

North Downs Way

Len   Willington
A274
way
Leeds Castle
& Gardens

Harrietsham   Leadingcross
Green   Lenham   Lenham Heath
9
Sandway   A20
Charing

Otterden
Place   Payden
Street
West
Street   Warren
Street   Stalisfield
Green

Leaveland   Challock   A252
Shottenden
A251
Molash

Throwley   Badlesmere
Frith

NORTH

Sheldwich
Lees   Selling
6   Sheldwich

Chart
Sutton   Grafty
Green   Boughton
Malherbe   Egerton
Pye   Egerton
Corner   Forstal   Little
Chart   Ram
Lane
Egerton   Swift's   Pluckley   Westwell
Green   Leacon
Pluckley   A20
Pluckley Thorne   Westwell
Hothfield   Boughton
Lees   Kempe's Corner   A28
A2070
5   London
Kennington   Wye
M20
Great Chart   9   Brook
ASHFORD   i   Hastingleigh
A2070   10   Willesborough Lees   West
B2229   Willesborough   Brabourne
Great Chart   McArthur Glen   Hinxhill   Lymbridge Green
Beaver   A2042   1   Sevington   A20   Brabourne
Green   Mersham   9   Brabourne Lees
Cheeseman's   Smeeth
Kingsnorth   Green   The Forstal   Sellindge   8
Swanton   Stonestreet
A2070   Mill   Green
Shadoxhurst   Stone   Aldington
6   Cross   Bonnington   Court-at
Bromley Green   Sugarloaf   Orlestone   Street
Woodchurch   Bilsington   B2067   Port Lympne
B2067   The   Port Lympne
Leacon   Ruckinge
Hamstreet   Royal Military   Canal
A2070   Wareborne   Botolph's Bridge
Newchurch   Burmarsh
A259–TO NEW ROMNE

Pluckley: The original location for the
1991 filming of H E Bates' The Darling
Buds of May which starred David Jason,
Pam Ferris, Catherine Zeta Jones and
Philip Franks. **Map ref. B4**

Faversham: just off Junction 6 of the M2 has the
highest ever recorded temperature in Britain. On
the 10th August 2003 it peaked at 38.5°C
(101.3°F). **Map ref. C2**

Canterbury: King's School, founded between 597
600, is both Britain's oldest recorded school and
oldest recorded charity. **Map ref. D3**

Channel Tunnel: *The idea of a cross channel tunnel had been around for years before one eventually opened in 1994. An early scheme was discussed between Britain and France in 1802 but never got off the ground because of the Napoleonic Wars. Between 1880 and 1883 trial tunnels were dug on both sides of the channel but were abandoned in 1883 amidst fears of a French invasion. In 1973, after Britain joined the Common Market, it was agreed to build a traditional rail tunnel, but construction was abandoned by Harold Wilson's government due to a financial crisis. Work on the current tunnel started in 1987 and it was eventually opened in 1994, two years late and millions of pounds over budget. The tunnel is 31 miles (50km) long and an average of 150 feet (45.5m) below the seabed. It was constructed by 13,000 engineers and workers. Interestingly the size of Britain increased by 90 acres (36.5ha) when spoil from the tunnel was deposited and landscaped at an area now known as Samphire Hoe.* **Map ref. F4**

Folkestone: *William Harvey (1578–1657) was born here. Harvey studied medicine at Cambridge and is credited with discovering the circulation of the blood.* **Map ref. E5**

Sandwich, Dover, Hythe, New Romney and Hastings: *Collectively these towns are the original 'Cinque Ports'. In medieval times, Royal Charters granted them special privileges such as freedom from tolls and customs duties, freedom of trade and their own judicial courts. This was in return for the use of their fishing and cargo vessels and crews for military service. This service, which lasted over three hundred years eventually formed into the first British Navy.*

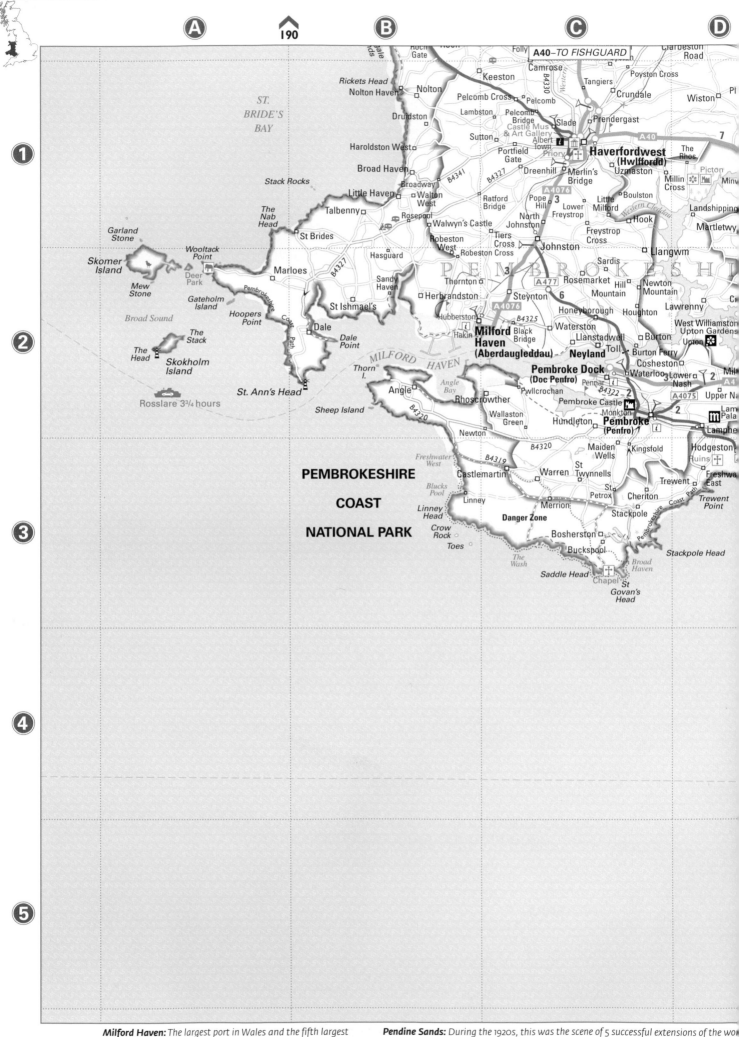

ST. BRIDE'S BAY

Rickets Head
Nolton Haven
Nolton

A40—TO FISHGUARD

Folly
Roch
Gate

Keeston

Camrose
B4330

Tangiers

Poyston Cross

Clarbeston
Road

Pl

Wiston

7

Pelcomb Cross
Pelcomb

Druidston

Lambston
Castle Mus
& Art Gallery

Pelcomb
Bridge
Sutton

Slade
Albert
Town

Prendergast

A40

Crundale

Haroldston West

Portfield
Gate
Priory

Dreenhill

Merlin's
Bridge

Haverfordwest
(Hwlffordd)

Uzmaston

The
Rhos

Picton

Millin
Cross

Minw

Broad Haven

Broadway
B4341

B4327

Pope
Hill

Lower
Freystrop

Little
Milford

Boulston

Landshipping

Little Haven

Walton
West

A4076

North
Johnston

Hook

Martletwy

Stack Rocks

Talbenny

Rosepool

Ratford
Bridge

Tiers
Cross

Freystrop
Cross

Llangwm

The Nab
Head

St Brides

Walwyn's Castle

B4327

Robeston
West

Robeston Cross

Johnston

P E M B R O K E S H I

Garland
Stone

Wooltack
Point

Marloes

Hasguard

Thornton

A477

Rosemarket

Sardis

Hill

Newton
Mountain

Deer
Park

Sandy
Haven

Herbrandston

Steynton

Mountain

Honeyborough

Houghton

Lawrenny

Skomer
Island

Pembrokeshire

St Ishmael's

Hubberston

A4076

B4325

Waterston

Llanstadwell

West Williamston
Upton Gardens

Mew
Stone

Gateholm
Island

Hoopers
Point

Coast

Hakin

Milford
Haven
(Aberdaugleddau)

Black
Bridge

Neyland

Burton

Upton

Broad Sound

Dale

Dale
Point

Thorn
I.

Toll

Burton Ferry

Lower
Nash

2

A4

The
Stack

Path

Pembroke Dock
(Doc Penfro)

Cosheston
Waterloo

Mil

The
Head

Skokholm
Island

St. Ann's Head

Angle

Angle
Bay

Rhoscrowther

Pennar

Pwllcrochan

B4322

Pembroke Castle

Monkton

2

A4075

Upper N

Lam
Pala

Rosslare 3¾ hours

Sheep Island

Newton

B4320

Wallaston
Green

Hundleton

Pembroke
(Penfro)

Lamphe

PEMBROKESHIRE

COAST

NATIONAL PARK

Freshwater
West

B4319

Castlemartin

Blucks
Pool

Linney

B4320

Warren

Maiden
Wells

St
Twynnells

Kingsfold

St
Petrox

Cheriton

Trewent

Hodgeston

Ruins

Freshwa
East

Linney
Head

Merrion

Danger Zone

Stackpole

Coast
Path

Trewent
Point

Crow
Rock
Toes

Bosherston

Buckspool

Stackpole Head

The
Wash

Saddle Head

Chapel

Broad
Haven

St
Govan's
Head

Milford Haven: The largest port in Wales and the fifth largest port in the UK. **Map ref. B2**

Pendine Sands: During the 1920s, this was the scene of 5 successful extensions of the wo land speed record by the drivers Malcolm Campbell and J G Parry-Thomas. Parry-Thomas was tragically killed here trying to take the record back off Campbell in 1927 – the last attempt at the land speed record made on British 'soil'. **Map ref. F2**

Laugharne: *This ancient town is best known for its association with poet and writer Dylan Thomas who lived in the Georgian Boathouse overlooking the River Taf for sixteen years. Dylan Marlais Thomas was born in Swansea on the 27th October 1914 and died in New York on the 9th November 1953. He is buried in Laugharne churchyard.* **Map ref. G1**

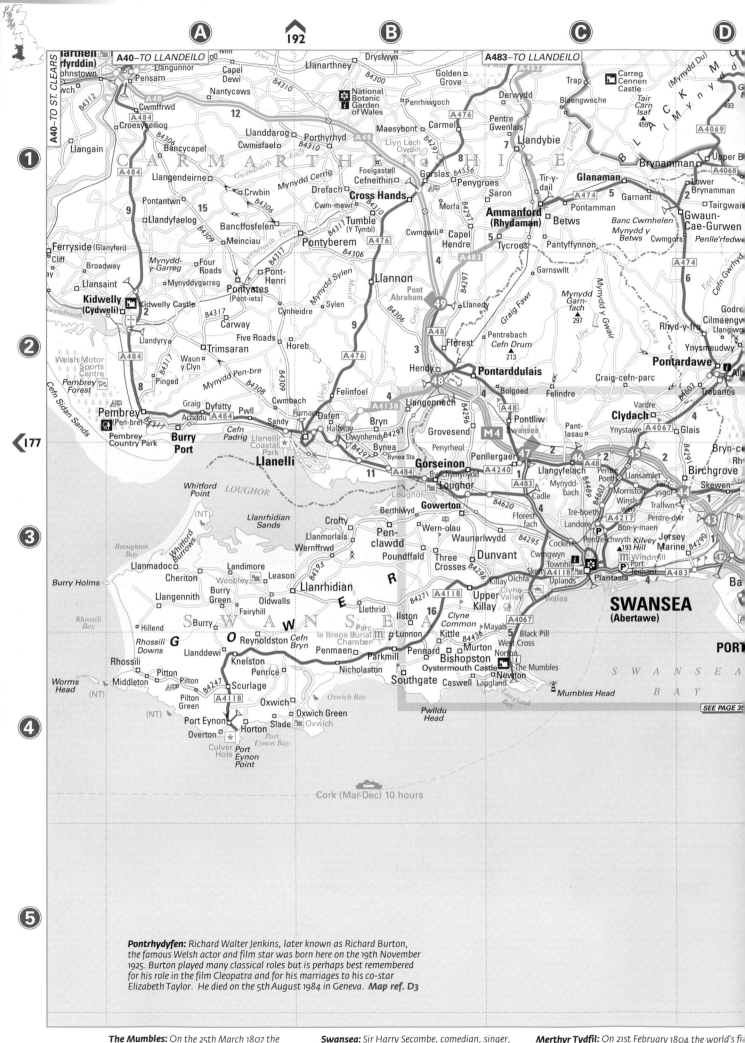

The Mumbles: On the 25th March 1807 the first ever passenger railway service in the world was opened between here and Swansea. Prior to the opening of The Swansea and Mumbles Railway, the only route between the two places was along the beach. **Map ref. C4**

Swansea: Sir Harry Secombe, comedian, singer, film star and writer was born in the St Thomas area of Swansea on the 8th September 1921. Sir Harry is best remembered as Neddy Seagoon, a member of the 'Goon Show'. He died aged 79 on the 12th April 2001. **Map ref. C3**

Merthyr Tydfil: On 21st February 1804 the world's fi[rst] steam railway engine, built by Richard Trevithick, successfully hauled 70 passengers and 10 tons of iro[n] on the 9 mile (14km) route from Merthyr to Abercyno[n]. **Map ref. G2**

Pontrhydyfen: Richard Walter Jenkins, later known as Richard Burton, the famous Welsh actor and film star was born here on the 19th November 1925. Burton played many classical roles but is perhaps best remembered for his role in the film Cleopatra and for his marriages to his co-star Elizabeth Taylor. He died on the 5th August 1984 in Geneva. **Map ref. D3**

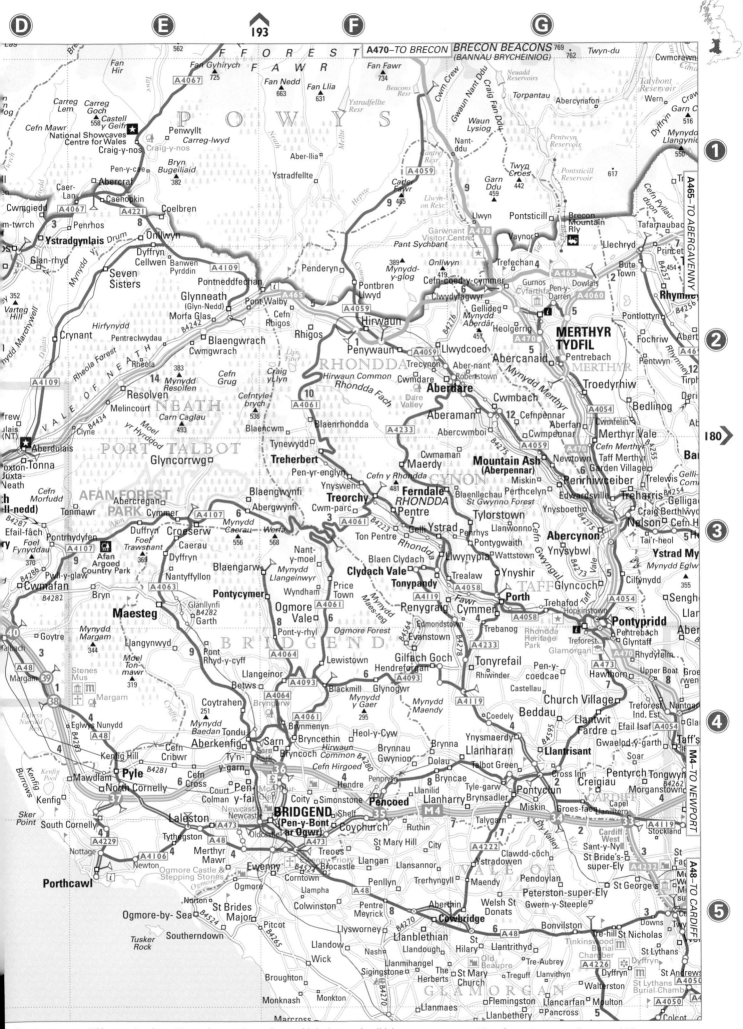

Aberfan: At 9.15 am on Friday 21st October 1966 a coal waste tip, made unstable by heavy rain, slid down a ...elsh mountainside engulfing the Pantglas Junior School and almost twenty houses in the small village of ...erfan. The disaster happened so quickly that nobody was rescued after 11am on hat day and 116 school ...ildren, half of the entire school, and 5 of their teachers were amongst the dead. After a week of round the clock ...gging, the final death toll was confirmed as 144. **Map ref. G2**

Llantrisant: Famous as the town which houses The Royal Mint. Here they produce all the currency for the UK. The Royal Mint is Britain's oldest surviving business, having been founded in London in 886. **Map ref. G4**

164

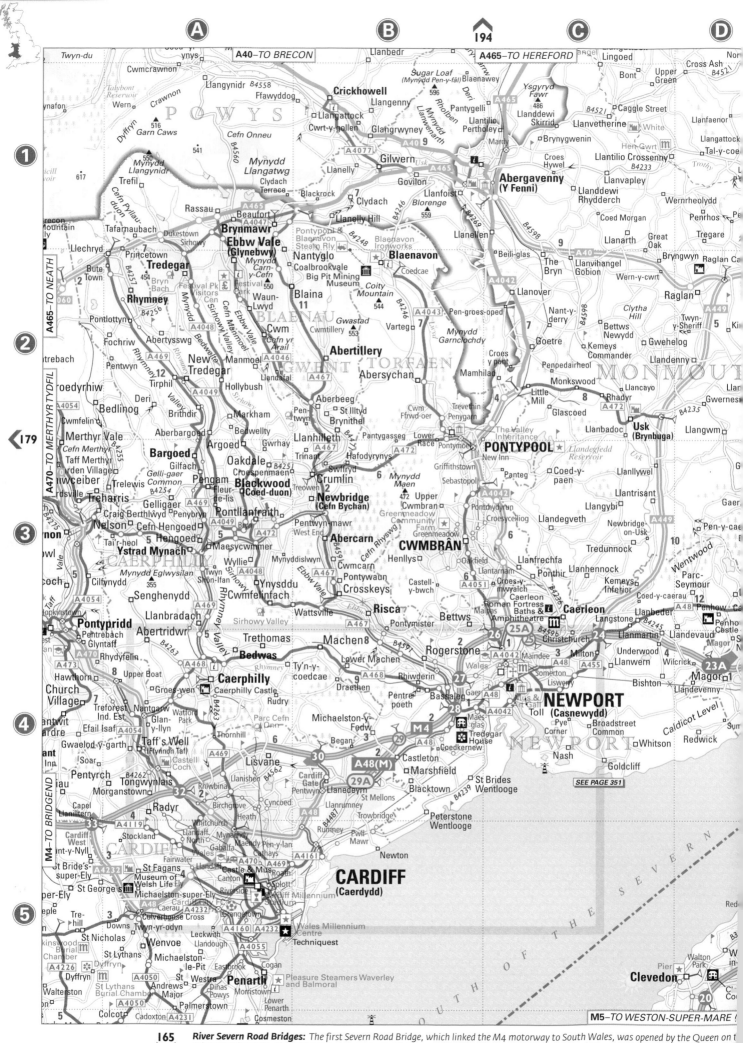

River Severn Road Bridges: The first Severn Road Bridge, which linked the M4 motorway to South Wales, was opened by the Queen on the 8th September 1966. The bridge is in two parts, the first crosses the River Severn and replaced the old Beachley to Aust ferry. The second part spans the River Wye near Chepstow. The main span is 3,240 feet (987m), the tops of the towers reach 445 feet (135.5m) and the structure is built to withstand 100 mph (160km/h) winds. The second Severn Bridge joining England and Wales was opened on the 5th June 1996. It is almost 3.2 miles (5km) long and the pylon heights reach 449 feet (137m). This bridge is reputed to have cost over £300m. **Map ref. E4**

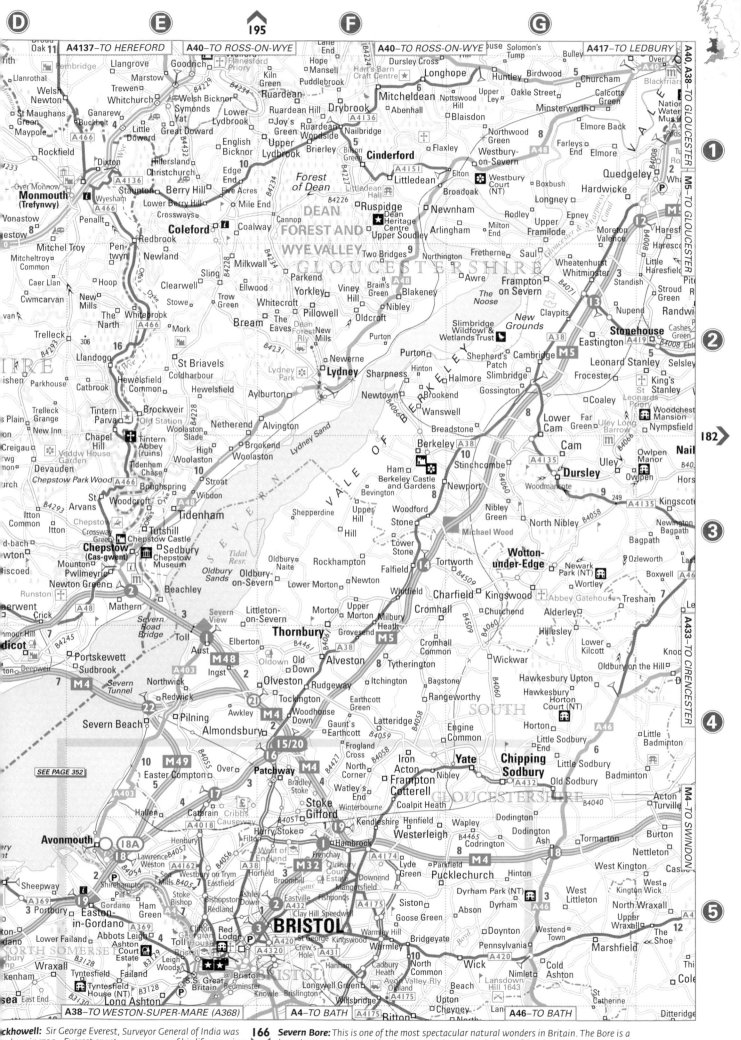

A4137–TO HEREFORD   A40–TO ROSS-ON-WYE   A40–TO ROSS-ON-WYE   A417–TO LEDBURY   M5–TO GLOUCESTER

Broad Oak 11
Llanrothal
Pembridge
Llangrove
Goodrich
Marstow
Welford
Flanesford Priory
Lane End
Hope
Mansell
Puddlebrook
Dursley Cross
Longhope
Solomon's Tump
Bulley
Over
Blackfriars

St Maughans Green
Maypole
Welsh Newton
Trewen
Whitchurch
Welsh Bicknor
Symonds Yat
Kiln Green
Ruardean
Hart's Barn Craft Centre
Longhope
Huntley
Birdwood
Churcham
Calcotts Green

Rockfield
Ganarew
Buckholt
Little Doward
Great Doward
Hillersland
English Bicknor
Lower Lydbrook
Ruardean Hill
Joy's Green
Ruardean Woodside
Nailbridge
Abenhall
Nottswood Hill
Upper Ley
Oakle Street
Minsterworth

Dixton
Staunton
Berry Hill
Edge End
Upper Lydbrook
Brierley
Bilson Green
Flaxley
Northwood Green
Westbury-on-Severn
Elmore Back
Elmore
Quedgeley
Hardwicke

Monmouth (Trefynwy)
Wyesham
Lower Berry Hill
Five Acres
Mile End
Cinderford
Littledean
Littledean Hall
Broadoak
Westbury Court (NT)
Boxbush
Longney
Rodley
Upper Framilode
Moreton Valence
Haresfield

Vonastow
Penallt
Crossways
Coleford
Coalway
Cannop
Forest of Dean
Ruspidge
Dean Heritage Centre
Upper Soudley
Newnham
Arlingham
Milton End
Epney
Hardwicke

Mitchel Troy
Pentwyn
Redbrook
Newland
Milkwall
Two Bridges
Northington
Awre
Fretherne
Saul
Wheatenhurst
Whitminster
Little Haresfield
Standish

Caer Llan
Hoop
Clearwell
Sling
Parkend
Yorkley
Brain's Green
Blakeney
The Noose
Frampton on Severn
Claypits
Nupend
Randwick

New Mills
The Narth
Whitebrook
Stowe
Ellwood
Whitecroft
Viney Hill
Nibley
Oldcroft
Shepherd's Patch
Cambridge
Stonehouse
Eastington
Cashes Green

Trelleck
Mork
Bream
The Eaves
Dean Forest Rly
New Mills
Purton
Slimbridge & Wetlands Trust
Slimbridge
Leonard Stanley
Selsley

Llandogo
St Briavels
Coldharbour
Hewelsfield
Lydney Park
Lydney
Sharpness
Halmore
Gossington
Frocester
King's Stanley

Trelleck Grange
Catbrook
Hewelsfield Common
Aylburton
Newtown
Brookend
Wanswell
Coaley
St Leonards Priory
Woodchester Mansion
Nympsfield

New Inn
Brockweir
Old Station
Netherend
Alvington
Breadstone
Lower Cam
Far Green
Uley Long Barrow

Chapel Hill
Tintern Parva
Tintern Abbey (ruins)
Woolaston Slade
High Woolaston
Brookend
Lydney Sand
Berkeley
Stinchcombe
Cam
Uley
Owlpen Manor
Nail

Devauden
Veddw House Garden
Tidenham Chase
Woolaston
Ham
Berkeley Castle and Gardens
Newport
Nibley Green
Dursley
Owlpen
Hors

Chepstow Park Wood
Boughspring
Stroat
Wibdon
Shepperdine
Upper Hill
Woodford
Stone
North Nibley
Woodmancote
Kingscote

St Arvans
Woodcroft
Tidenham
Hill
Lower Stone
Michael Wood
Newington Bagpath

Itton Common
Crossway Green
Tutshill
Chepstow Castle
Oldbury Naite
Rockhampton
Falfield
Tortworth
Wotton-under-Edge
Newark Park (NT)
Ozleworth
Boxwell

Itton
Chepstow Museum
Sedbury
Chepstow Museum
Oldbury Sands
Oldbury-on-Severn
Lower Morton
Newton
Whitfield
Charfield
Kingswood
Abbey Gatehouse
Wortley
Tresham

Chepstow (Cas-gwent)
Mounton
Beachley
Tidal Resr.
Hill
Churchend
Alderley
Hillesley

Pwllmeyric
Newton Green
Severn View
Littleton-on-Severn
Upper Morton
Milbury Heath
Cromhall
Lower Kilcott

Mathern
Severn Road Bridge
Toll
Aust
Elberton
Thornbury
Grovesend
Cromhall Common
Wickwar
Hawkesbury Upton

Crick
Portskewett
Sudbrook
Severn Tunnel
Northwick
Ingst
Oldown
Old Down
Alveston
Tytherington
Hawkesbury Horton Court (NT)
Oldbury on the Hill

Deepweir
Redwick
Pilning
Olveston
Rudgeway
Itchington
Bagstone
Rangeworthy
Engine Common
Horton
Little Badminton

Severn Beach
Awkley
Tockington
Woodhouse Down
Earthcott Green
Latteridge
Little Sodbury End
Badminton

Almondsbury
Gaunt's Earthcott
Frogland Cross
North Corner
Iron Acton
Yate
Chipping Sodbury
Little Sodbury
Acton Turville

SEE PAGE 352
Easter Compton
Over
Patchway
Bradley Stoke
Watley's End
Frampton Cotterell
Nibley
Old Sodbury
Dodington

Hallen
Catbrain
Cribbs Causeway
Stoke Gifford
Winterbourne
Coalpit Heath
Dodington
Burton

Avonmouth
Henbury
Harry Stoke
Filton
Hambrook
Kendleshire
Henfield
Wapley
Codrington
Tormarton
Nettleton

Lawrence Weston
Westbury on Trym
West of England
Oldbury Court Estate
Frenchay
Lyde Green
Parkfield
Pucklechurch
Hinton
West Kington

Shirehampton
Pill
Sea Mills
Horfield
Broomhill
Downend
Mangotsfield
Dyrham Park (NT)
Dyrham
North Wraxall
West Littleton

Sheepway
Portbury
Easton-in-Gordano
Stoke Bishop
Bishopston
Redland
Eastville
Fishponds
Clay Hill
Speedwell
Abson
Doynton
Pennsylvania
Upper Wraxall

Lower Failand
Abbots Leigh
Clifton
Red Lodge
BRISTOL
Kingswood
Warmley Hill
Bridgeyate
Westend Town
Marshfield
The Shoe

North Somerset
Tyntesfield
Failand
Leigh Woods
S.S. Great Britain
Bedminster
Knowle
Brislington
Longwell Green
Willsbridge
Warmley
Wick
Cold Ashton
St Catherine

Wraxall
Tyntesfield House (NT)
Long Ashton
Toll
Bristol
Bishopsworth
Hartcliffe
Whitchurch
Keynsham
Saltford
Marshfield

A38–TO WESTON-SUPER-MARE (A368)   A4–TO BATH   A46–TO BATH

M48   M4   M49   M5   M32

kholl: Sir George Everest, Surveyor General of India was n here in 1790. Everest spent over 25 years of his life mapping ia and was the first person to survey the Himalayas. He was ghted in 1861 and the highest peak in the Himalayas was cially named after him in 1865. **Map ref. B1**

Severn Bore: This is one of the most spectacular natural wonders in Britain. The Bore is a large 'surge wave' caused by the huge tidal range and shape of the river estuary. It can reach up to 10 feet (3m) in height and travel at up to 13 mph (21km/h). The best Bores usually occur ahead of the spring tide and travel up the river for over 20 miles (32km) between Awre and Gloucester. The Severn is also Britain's longest river at 220 miles (354km). **Map ref. G2**

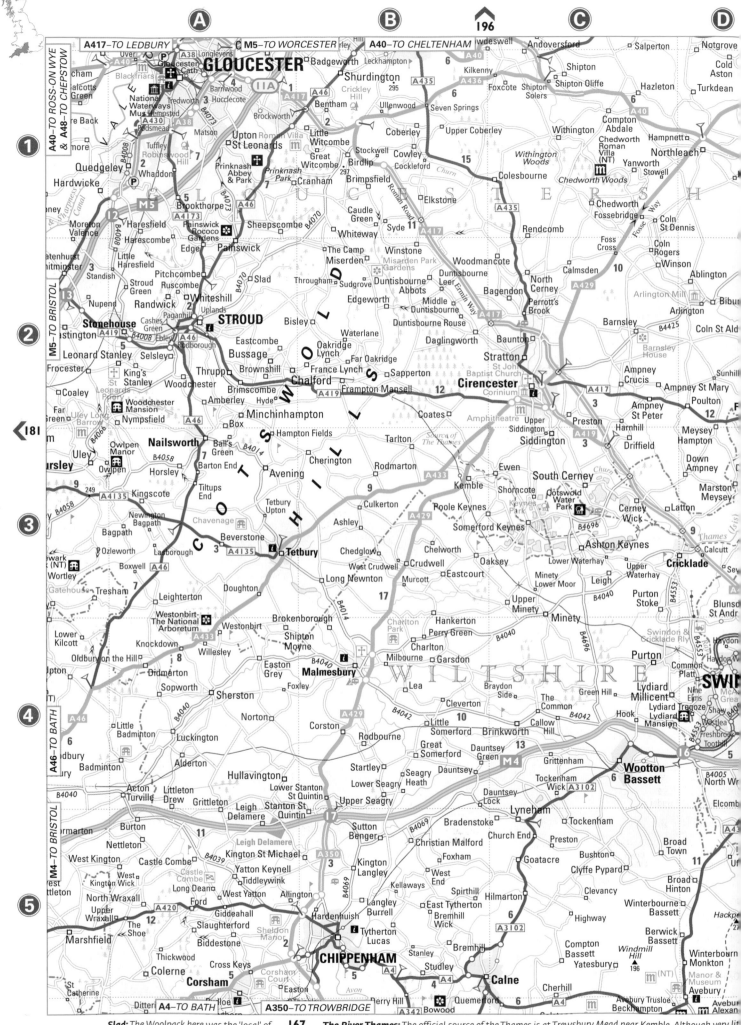

A417–TO LEDBURY   **C M5**–TO WORCESTER   rley   Hill   **A40**–TO CHELTENHAM   wdeswell   Andoversford   Salperton   Notgrove

GLOUCESTER   Badgeworth   Leckhampton   Kilkenny   Shipton   Cold Aston

Shurdington   Crickley Hill   295   Foxcote   Shipton Oliffe   Hazleton   Turkdean

(Map of Gloucestershire & Wiltshire region)

181   **167**

Slad: *The Woolpack here was the 'local' of the writer Laurie Lee. The pub features in his most famous book 'Cider with Rosie'. Laurie Lee died in 1997 and is buried in the churchyard just across the road.* **Map ref. A2**

The River Thames: *The official source of the Thames is at Trewsbury Mead near Kemble. Although very lit water is visible at this point, a stone marks the exact spot. From its source the River Thames journeys som 215 miles (346km) to the North Sea, making it England's longest river, with 191 miles (307km), from Lechla being navigable waterway. Below Teddington Lock the river is tidal although it remains as fresh water de as far as Battersea.* **Map ref. B3**

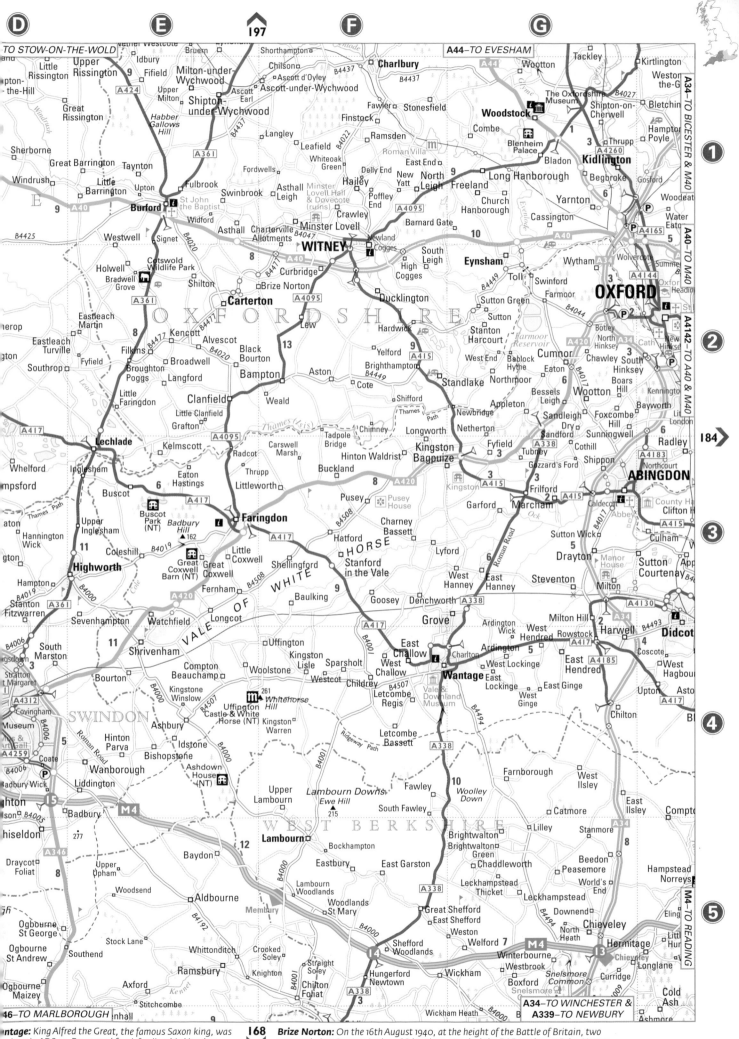

TO STOW-ON-THE-WOLD

A44–TO EVESHAM

1

Nether Westcote · Bruern · Shorthampton

Upper Rissington 9 · Idbury · Fifield · Milton-under-Wychwood · Chilson · Charlbury · Wootton · Tackley · Kirtlington · Weston-the-G

Little Rissington · Ascott d'Oyley · B4437 · The Oxfordshire Museum · Shipton-on-Cherwell · Bletchin

pton-the-Hill · Upper Milton · Shipton-under-Wychwood · Ascott Earl · Ascott-under-Wychwood · Stonesfield · Woodstock · Hampton Poyle · Thrupp

Great Rissington · Habber Gallows Hill · Langley · Leafield · Ramsden · Combe · Blenheim Palace · Bladon · Kidlington · A4260

Sherborne · Taynton · Fordwells · Whiteoak Green · Delly End · New Yatt · North Leigh · Long Hanborough · Begbroke · Gosford · Woodeat

Great Barrington · Fulbrook · Hailey · Poffley End · Freeland · Church Hanborough · Yarnton · Wolvercote · Water Eato

Windrush · Little Barrington · Upton · Swinbrook · Asthall Leigh · Crawley · Barnard Gate · Cassington · Wytham · OXFORD

TO MARLBOROUGH

▲ 197   184 ▶   168 ▼

Vantage: King Alfred the Great, the famous Saxon king, was ... n here in AD849. Renowned for defending his kingdom ... inst the Vikings, and for burning the cakes, Alfred died in ... 899 at the age of 50 and is buried in Winchester Cathedral. ... p ref. F4

Brize Norton: On the 16th August 1940, at the height of the Battle of Britain, two marauding German Junkers 88 bombers attacked the RAF station at Brize Norton destroying 46 British aircraft which were still in the hangers of the maintenance unit and training school. **Map ref. E2**

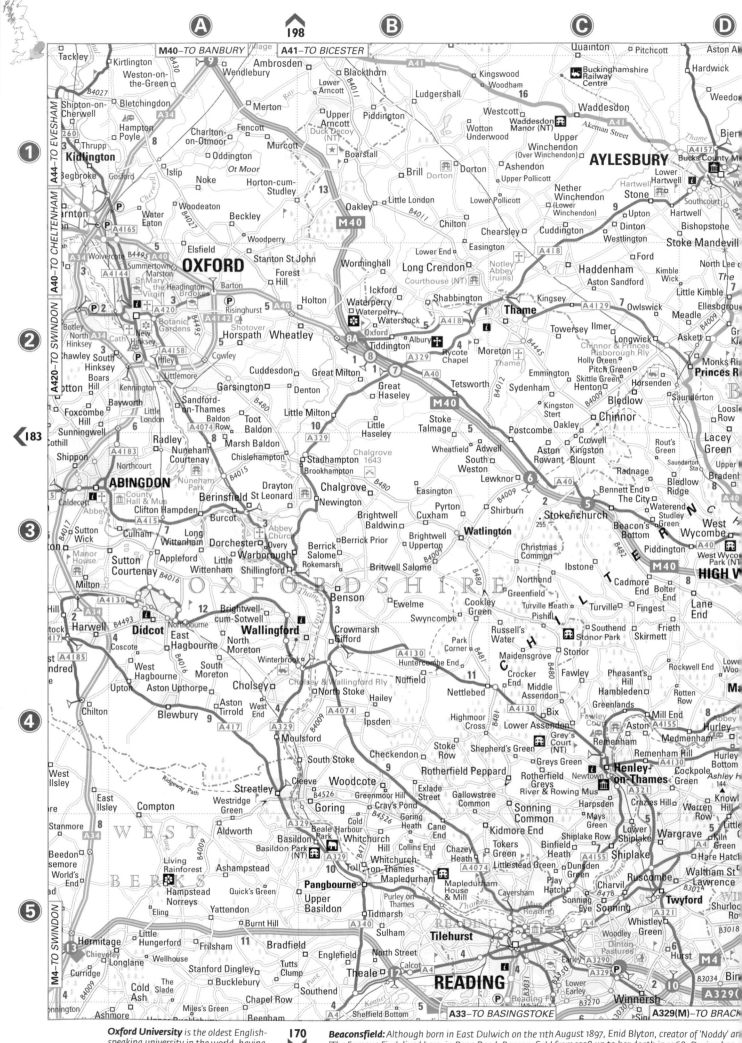

M40–TO BANBURY   **A41**–TO BICESTER

1

2

183

3

4

5

Oxford University is the oldest English-speaking university in the world, having been founded over 900 years ago. During this time it has provided the world with 40 Nobel prize-winners and the country with 25 Prime Ministers. **Map ref. A2**

170

Beaconsfield: Although born in East Dulwich on the 11th August 1897, Enid Blyton, creator of 'Noddy' and 'The Famous Five', lived here, in Penn Road, Beaconsfield from 1938 up to her death in 1968. During her lifetime she wrote over 700 books which were translated into 40 different languages and sold over 400 million copies worldwide. **Map ref. E3**

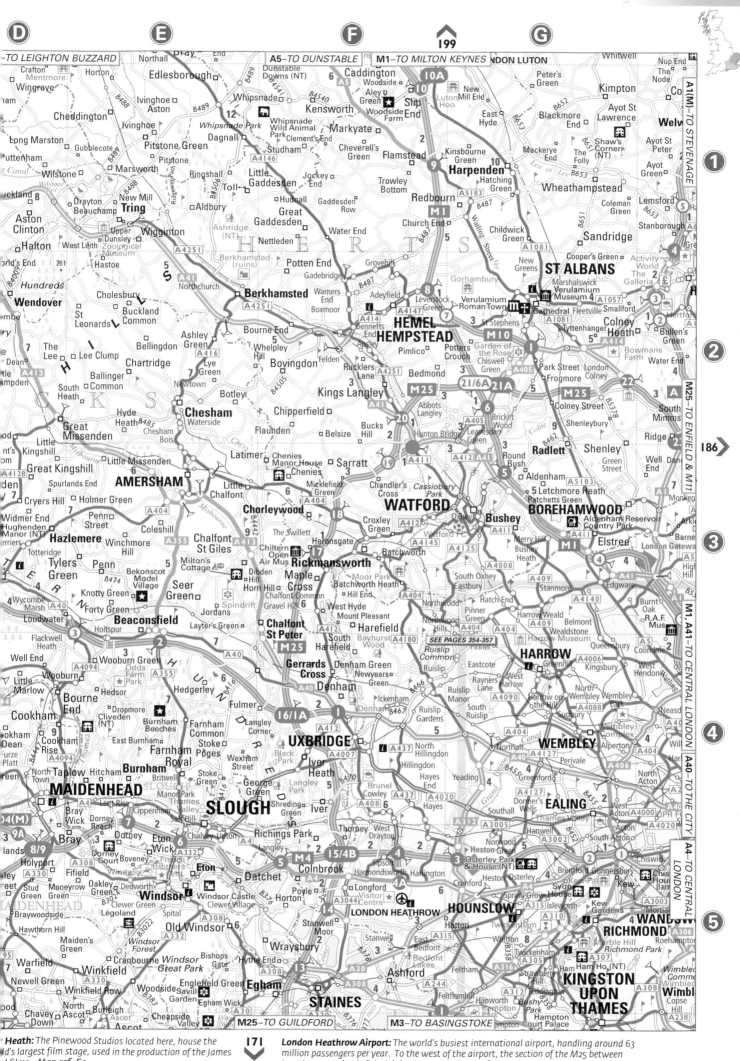

TO LEIGHTON BUZZARD

A5–TO DUNSTABLE M1–TO MILTON KEYNES NDON LUTON

Crafton Mentmore Northall Bray End
Wingrave Horton Edlesborough Dunstable Downs (NT) Caddington Whitwell Nup End The Node
Long Marston Ivinghoe Aston Whipsnade Kensworth Woodside Aley Green New Mill End Peter's Green Kimpton Co
Cheddington Ivinghoe 12 Whipsnade Park Markyate Woodside Farm Luton Hoo East Hyde Blackmore End Ayot St Lawrence Welw
Puttenham Gubblecote Pitstone Green Whipsnade Wild Animal Park Clement's End Studham Flamstead Kinsbourne Green Mackerye End The Folly Ayot St Peter Welv
Wilstone Marsworth Pitstone Ringshall Little Gaddesden Jockey End Trowley Bottom Harpenden Hatching Green Shaw's Corner (NT) Ayot Green

1

Buckland Drayton Beauchamp New Mill Aldbury Great Gaddesden Gaddesden Row Redbourn Wheathampstead Coleman Green Lemsford
Aston Clinton West Leith Tring Upper Dunsley Wigginton Ashridge (NT) Water End Church End Childwick Green Sandridge Stanborough
Halton Hastoe Berkhamsted (ruins) Nettleden Cooper's Green St Stephens Activity World The Galleria Hertf

2

Wendover Cholesbury St Leonards Buckland Common Northchurch Berkhamsted Warners End Adeyfield Gorhambury ST ALBANS Marshalswick Colney Heath Bullen's Green
The Lee Lee Clump Ashley Green Bourne End Whelpley Hill Bovingdon Felden Pimlico Potters Crouch Garden of the Rose Park Street Frogmore Bowmans Farm Water End
Ballinger Chartridge Lye Green Newtown Kings Langley Abbots Langley Chiswell Green Park Street London Colney South Mimms

HEMEL HEMPSTEAD

Great Missenden Hyde Heath Chesham Waterside Chipperfield Bucks Hill Hunton Bridge Leavesden Green Colney Street Shenleybury Ridge
Little Kingshill Chesham Bois Flaunden Belsize Abbots Langley Bricket Wood Shenley Well End Radlett

3

Amersham Latimer Chenies Manor House Sarratt Round Bush Radlett Green Street
Great Kingshill Little Missenden Chenies Micklefield Green Chandler's Cross Cassiobury Park WATFORD Aldenham Letchmore Heath Patchetts Green
Spurlands End Little Chalfont Croxley Green BOREHAMWOOD
Cryers Hill Holmer Green Chorleywood Heronsgate Batchworth Oxhey Bushey Aldenham Reservoir Country Park Elstree
Hazlemere Winchmore Hill Chalfont St Giles Chiltern Open Air Mus Rickmansworth Merry Hill Bushey Heath London Gatewa
Penn Street Coleshill Milton's Cottage Dibden Purlieus Maple Cross Moor Park South Oxhey Eastbury Stanmore Edgware Barne
Tylers Green Penn Bekonscot Model Village Seer Green Horn Hill Chalfont Common Gravel Hill West Hyde Mount Pleasant Northwood Hatch End Pinner Green Harrow Weald Wealdstone Burnt Oak R.A.F. Mus
Beaconsfield Holtspur Jordans Layter's Green South Harefield Harefield Bayhurst Wood Northwood Hills Pinner Belmont Colindale

Forty Green Knotty Green Spindrift Chalfont St Peter Denham Green SEE PAGES 354–357 Ruislip Common Eastcote Harrow on the Hill Harrow Museum Queensbury Neasd

4

Wooburn Green Gerrards Cross Newyears Green Ruislip Rayners Lane South Harrow Kingsbury West Hendon
Wooburn Hedgerley Fulmer Denham Ickenham Denham Ruislip Manor South Ruislip North Wembley WEMBLEY North Acton
Bourne End Hedsor Burnham Beeches Farnham Common Stoke Poges Langley Corner UXBRIDGE North Hillingdon Yeading Northolt Perivale Alperton Acton
Cookham Cliveden (NT) East Burnham Farnham Royal Wexham Street Black Park Iver Heath Hillingdon Hayes End Greenford EALING West Acton
Cookham Rise Taplow Hitcham Burnham Stoke Green Langley Park Iver Hayes Southall Dormer's Wells South Acton
Maidenhead North Town Cippenham Manor Park George Green SLOUGH Shreding Green Iver Thames Valley Thorney West Drayton Hanwell Thames Valley Hounslow

MAIDENHEAD SLOUGH

Bray Wick Dorney Reach Salt Hill Richings Park Langley Brunel Cowley Hayes Heston Green Osterley Park & House (NT) Brentford Gunnersbury Chiswick Kew
Bray Dorney Chalvey Upton Colnbrook Sipson Harmondsworth Harlington Cranford Heston Osterley Spring Grove House Syon Pak Kew Gardens
Holyport Dorney Court Eton Wick Datchet Longford Visitor Centre Poyle Horton LONDON HEATHROW Cranford HOUNSLOW Isleworth Richmond
Fifield Oakley Green Dedworth Eton Windsor Stanwell Moor Stanwell East Bedfont Hatton Twickenham Marble Hill

5

Moneyrow Green Windsor Castle Clewer Village Legoland Old Windsor Wraysbury Bedfont Lakes Feltham Whitton Twickenham Richmond Park WANDSW
Stud Green Clewer Green Spital Windsor Englefield Green Egham Ashford Feltham KINGSTON UPON THAMES Wimbl
Warfield Winkfield Cranbourne Windsor Great Park Bishops Gate Savill Garden STAINES Hythe End Hanworth Bushy Park Teddington Copse Hill
Newell Green Winkfield Row Woodside Egham Wick M25–TO GUILDFORD M3–TO BASINGSTOKE mpton Court Palace A238
North Chavey Down Ascot Cheapside Valley Burleigh

186
171

Heath: The Pinewood Studios located here, house the ld's largest film stage, used in the production of the James d films. **Map ref. F4**

London Heathrow Airport: The world's busiest international airport, handling around 63 million passengers per year. To the west of the airport, the section of the M25 between junctions 13 and 14 is Britain's busiest road. **Map ref. F5**

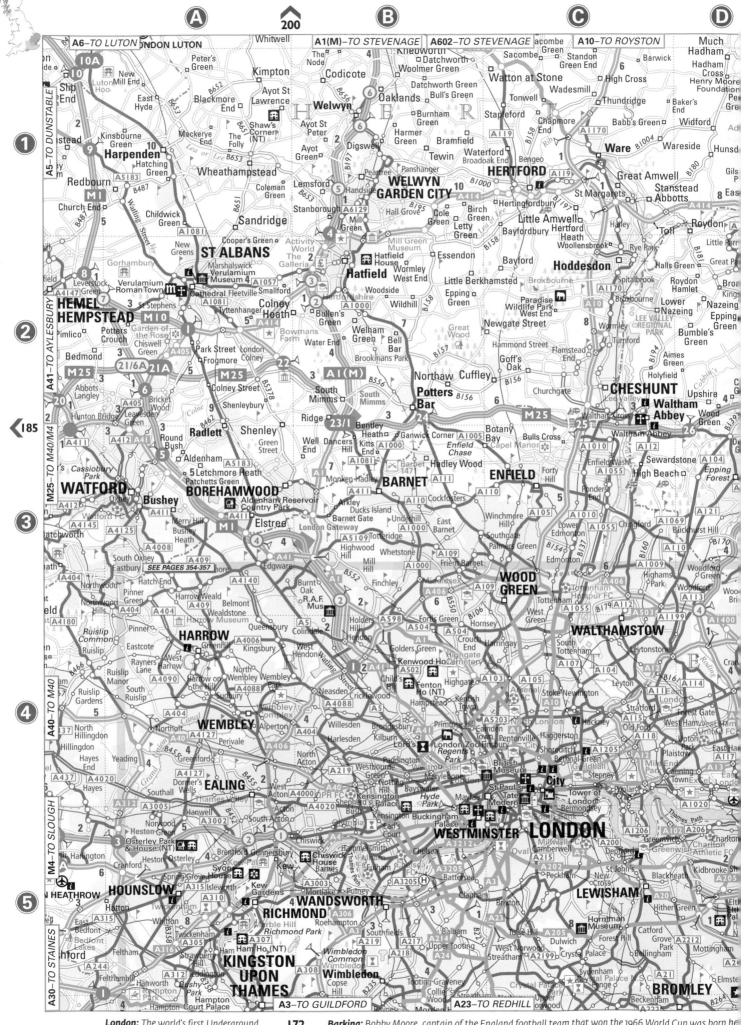

A6-TO LUTON LONDON LUTON   A1(M)-TO STEVENAGE   A602-TO STEVENAGE   A10-TO ROYSTON

1

Whitwell · The Node · Kneeworth · Datchworth · Woolmer Green · Watton at Stone · Sacombe · Much Hadham · Barwick · Hadham Cross · Henry Moore Foundation

Peter's Green · Kimpton · Codicote · Datchworth Green · Bull's Green · High Cross · Wadesmill · Thundridge · Baker's End · Widford · Great

New Mill End · Luton Hoo · East Hyde · Blackmore End · Mackerye End · Ayot St Lawrence · Oaklands · Burnham Green · Stapleford · Chapmore End · Ware · Wareside

Slip End · Kinsbourne Green · Hatching Green · The Folly · Ayot St Peter · Welwyn · Harmer Green · Tewin · Waterford · Broadoak End · Bengeo · Great Amwell · Wareside

Harpenden · Wheathampstead · Ayot Green · Digswell · Bramfield · HERTFORD · St Margarets · Stanstead Abbotts

Redbourn · Coleman Green · Lemsford · Handside · **WELWYN GARDEN CITY** · Hall Grove · Cole Green · Letty Green · Hertingfordbury · Little Amwell · Bayfordbury · Hertford Heath · Woollensbrook · Harley · Toll · Roydon · Little Park

Church End · Childwick Green · Sandridge · Stanborough · Mill Green · Birch Green · Hatfield House · Bayford · Hoddesdon · Broxbourne · Spitalbrook · Roydon Hamlet · Nazeing

HEMEL HEMPSTEAD · **ST ALBANS** · Cooper's Green · **Hatfield** · Woodside · Essendon · Little Berkhamsted · Epping Green · Paradise Wildlife Park · West End · Newgate Street · Lower Nazeing · Epping Green

2

Pimlico · Potters Crouch · Chiswell Green · Park Street · Frogmore · London Colney · Water End · Welham Green · Bell Bar · Brookmans Park · Goff's Oak · Hammond Street · Flamstead End · Turnford · Bumble's Green · Holyfield

Bedmond · Garden of the Rose · Tyttenhanger · Colney Heath · Bullen's Green · Great Wood · Northaw · Cuffley · **CHESHUNT** · Upshire

Abbots Langley · Bricket Wood · Colney Street · South Mimms · South Mimms · Ridge · Bentley Heath · Potters Bar · Ganwick Corner · Enfield Chase · Botany Bay · Bulls Cross · Waltham Cross · **Waltham Abbey** · Wood Green

Hunton Bridge · Leavesden Green · Shenleybury · Dancers Hill · Kitts End · A1000 · Capel Manor · Enfield Wash · Sewardstone · Epping Forest

WATFORD · Round Bush · **Radlett** · Shenley · Green Street · Well End · Monken Hadley · Hadley Wood · **ENFIELD** · Forty Hill · High Beach

3

Bushey · Aldenham · Letchmore Heath · Patchetts Green · Aldenham Reservoir Country Park · Arkley · Ducks Island · **BARNET** · Cockfosters · Winchmore Hill · Ponders End · Buckhurst Hill

Oxhey · Merry Hill · Bushey Heath · **Elstree** · London Gateway · Barnet Gate · Underhill · East Barnet · Southgate · Palmers Green · Lower Edmonton · Chingford

South Oxhey · Eastbury · Edgware · Highwood Hill · Totteridge · Whetstone · Friern Barnet · Edmonton · Woodford

SEE PAGES 354-357 · Burnt Oak · Mill Hill · Finchley · Middlesex · **WOOD GREEN** · Tottenham · Highams Park · Woodford

Northwood · Hatch End · Pinner Green · Belmont · Wealdstone · R.A.F. Mus. · Holders Hill · Hendon · Forts Green · Hornsey · West Green · South Tottenham · **WALTHAMSTOW** · Leytonstone

4

Ruislip Common · Pinner · Harrow Weald · Harrow Museum · Queensbury · Colindale · Golders Green · Highgate Cemetery · Crouch End · Harringay · Stoke Newington · Leyton

Ruislip · Eastcote · Greenhill · **HARROW** · Kingsbury · West Hendon · Kenwood Ho · Highgate · Arsenal FC · North London

Rayners Lane · Wembley · North Wembley · Neasden · Cricklewood · Fenton Ho (NT) · Kentish Town · Child's Hill · Hampstead

Ruislip Manor · West Harrow · Harrow on the Hill · Sudbury · **WEMBLEY** · Wembley Complex · Alperton · Willesden · Brondesbury · Kilburn · Camden Town · Finsbury · North London · Hackney · West Ham Utd FC · Stratford · Forest Gate · Upton

North Hillingdon · Northolt · Perivale · Greenford · North Acton · Harlesden · Lord's · London Zoo · Regents Park · Primrose Hill · Pentonville · Haggerston · Old Ford · Plaistow · Canning Town

Hayes End · Yeading · **EALING** · West Acton · Westbourne Green · Paddington · British Museum · City · Stepney · Mile End · Poplar · East Ham

5

Hayes · Southall · Hanwell · South Acton · **A4000** QPR FC · Notting Hill · Bayswater · Marylebone · St Paul's · Tate Modern · Bermondsey · Tower of London

Heston · Osterley Park & House (NT) · Brentford · Gunnersbury · Kew · Chiswick House · Barnes · Kensington Palace · Shepherd's Bush · Hyde Park · Mayfair · Buckingham Palace · **WESTMINSTER** · **LONDON** · Southwark · Greenwich · Charlton · Charlton Athletic FC

Cranford · Heston · Osterley · Spring Grove House · Syon Ho · Kew Gardens · Earl's Court · Chelsea · Oval · Camberwell · Peckham · New Cross · Deptford · Blackheath · Kidbrooke

HOUNSLOW · Isleworth · Mortlake · Putney · Fulham FC · Battersea · Clapham · Brixton · **LEWISHAM** · Hornman Museum

HEATHROW · Hatton · Twickenham · **RICHMOND** · **WANDSWORTH** · Roehampton · Southfields · Balham · Tulse Hill · Catford

Hanworth · Whitton · Marble Hill · Richmond Park · Wimbledon Common · **Wimbledon** · Upper Tooting · West Norwood · Streatham · Forest Hill · Bromley

KINGSTON UPON THAMES · Ham Ho (NT) · Wimbledon Copse Hill · Tooting Graveney · Collier's Wood · Crystal Palace · Sydenham · **BROMLEY**

Hampton · Bushy Park · Hampton Court Palace · A3-TO GUILDFORD · A23-TO REDHILL

London: The world's first Underground railway was opened by the Metropolitan Railway Company in 1863 between Paddington and Farringdon. **Map ref. B4**

 172

Barking: Bobby Moore, captain of the England football team that won the 1966 World Cup was born here on the 12th April 1941. He began his career at West Ham in 1956 and is acknowledged to be one of the best defenders ever to play in the English league. Bobby died of cancer on the 24th February 1993 at the age of Map ref. D4

D **E** **F** **G**

A130–TO LONDON STANSTED AIRPORT (A120) A131–TO BRAINTREE

A12–TO COLCHESTER

1

188

2

3

A127–TO SOUTHEND-ON-SEA

4

5

Greensted: The Saxon church here is known as the
oldest wooden church in the world. **Map ref. E2**

173

187

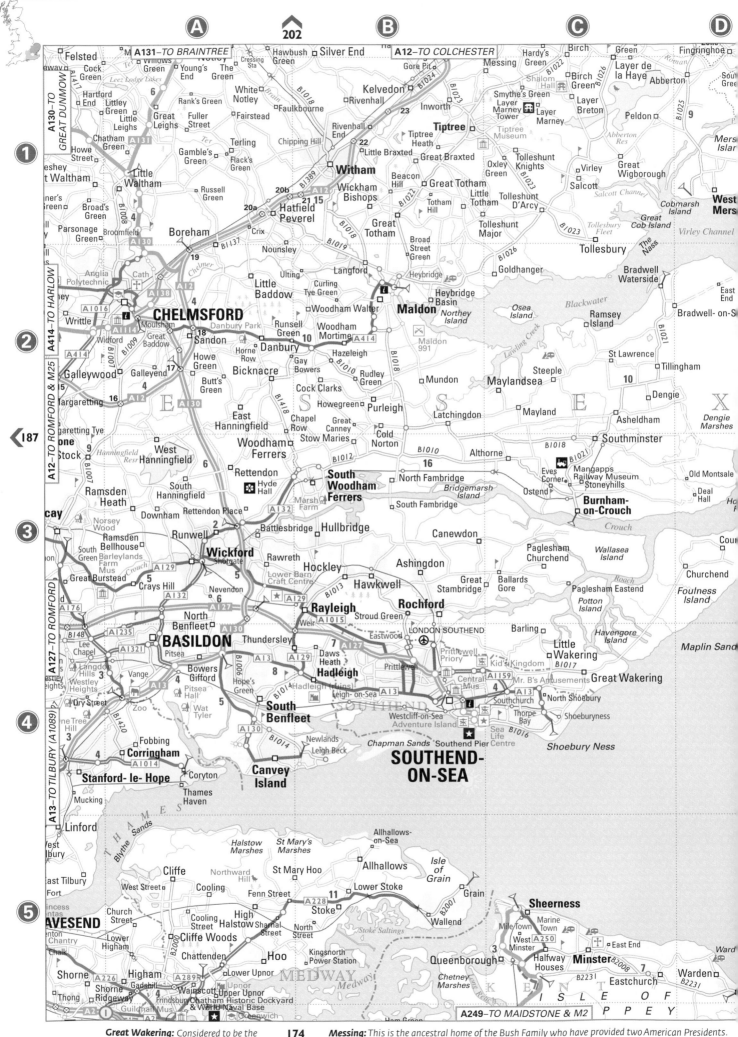

A131–TO BRAINTREE   **A12**–TO COLCHESTER

A130–TO GREAT DUNMOW

A414–TO HARLOW   **A12**–TO ROMFORD & M25

A12–TO ROMFORD

A127–TO ROMFORD

A13–TO TILBURY (A1089)

A13–TO TILBURY

Felsted, Cock Green, Hartford End, Littley Green, Little Leighs, Great Leighs, Chatham Green, Howe Street, Little Waltham, Broad's Green, Parsonage Green, Broomfield, Writtle, Widford, Galleywood, Margaretting, Margaretting Tye, Stock, Ramsden Heath, Downham, Ramsden Bellhouse, Runwell, Great Burstead, Crays Hill, Nevendon, **BASILDON**, North Benfleet, Lee Chapel, Pitsea, Vange, Langdon Hills, Westley Heights, Bowers Gifford, Hope's Green, Fobbing, **Corringham**, **Stanford-le-Hope**, Coryton, Mucking, Linford, **CHELMSFORD**, Moulsham, Great Baddow, Sandon, Howe Green, Galleyend, Butt's Green, East Hanningfield, West Hanningfield, South Hanningfield, Rettendon, Rettendon Place, Battlesbridge, **Wickford**, Shotgate, Rawreth, **Rayleigh**, Weir, Thundersley, Daws Heath, **Hadleigh**, **South Benfleet**, **Canvey Island**, Newlands, Leigh Beck, Chapman Sands, Leigh-on-Sea

Willows Green, Young's End, The Green, Rank's Green, Fairstead, Terling, Gamble's Green, Flack's Green, Faulkbourne, Chipping Hill, **Witham**, Hatfield Peveral, Crix, Nounsley, Little Baddow, Curling Tye Green, Woodham Walter, Runsell Green, **Danbury**, Horne Row, Bicknacre, Gay Bowers, Cock Clarks, Howegreen, Chapel Row, Stow Maries, Great Canney, **Woodham Ferrers**, **South Woodham Ferrers**, Hyde Hall, Marsh Farm, Hullbridge, Hockley, Hawkwell, **Rochford**, Stroud Green, Eastwood, Prittlewell, **SOUTHEND-ON-SEA**, Westcliff-on-Sea, Southchurch, Thorpe Bay, Shoeburyness, Shoebury Ness, Southend Pier

Hawbush Green, Silver End, Cressing Sta, Gore Pit, Kelvedon, Rivenhall, Inworth, **Tiptree**, Tiptree Heath, Tiptree Museum, Little Braxted, Great Braxted, Wickham Bishops, Beacon Hill, Great Totham, Little Totham, Totham Hill, Broad Street Green, Heybridge, Langford, Ulting, Woodham Mortimer, Hazeleigh, Rudley Green, Purleigh, Mundon, Cold Norton, Althorne, North Fambridge, Bridgemarsh Island, South Fambridge, Canewdon, Ashingdon, Great Stambridge, Ballards Gore, Paglesham Churchend, Paglesham Eastend, Barling, **Great Wakering**, North Shoebury, Little Wakering, **Maldon**, Heybridge Basin, Northey Island, Goldhanger, Steeple, Mayland, Maylandsea, Latchingdon, St Lawrence, Tillingham, Asheldham, Dengie, **Southminster**, **Burnham-on-Crouch**, Eves Corner, Ostend, Mangapps Railway Museum, Stoneyhills, Old Montsale, Deal Hall

Hardy's Green, Messing, Birch Green, Layer de la Haye, Abberton, Peldon, Great Wigborough, Salcott, Tolleshunt Knights, Tolleshunt D'Arcy, Tolleshunt Major, Tollesbury, Bradwell Waterside, Bradwell-on-Sea, West Mersea, Cobmarsh Island, Great Cob Island, Osea Island, Ramsey Island, Smythe's Green, Shalom Hall, Layer Marney Tower, Layer Marney, Layer Breton, Virley, Oxley

A132, **A130**, **A127**, **A129**, **A13**, **A1015**, **A1159**, **A1016**, **A1114**, **A414**, **A12**, **A138**, **A131**, **A130**, **A176**, **A1235**, **A1321**, **A13**, **A1420**, **A1014**, **A130**, **A228**, **A250**, **A249**, **A289**, **A226**, **A2**

Halstow Marshes, St Mary's Marshes, Allhallows-on-Sea, Allhallows, Isle of Grain, Cliffe, West Street, Cooling, Northward Hill, St Mary Hoo, Fenn Street, Lower Stoke, Grain, Cooling Street, High Halstow, Sharnal Street, Stoke, North Street, **Sheerness**, Marine Town, Mile Town, West Minster, **A250**, Church Street, Lower Higham, Cliffe Woods, Chattenden, Hoo, Kingsnorth Power Station, Queenborough, Halfway Houses, **Minster**, Eastchurch, **ISLE OF SHEPPEY**, **MEDWAY**, Shorne, Higham, Shorne Ridgeway, Thong, Chalk, Gadshill, Wainscott, Frindsbury, Upper Upnor, Lower Upnor, Chatham Historic Dockyard & World Naval Base, Guildhall Mus, **GRAVESEND**, **A2**

A249–TO MAIDSTONE & M2

Great Wakering: Considered to be the driest place in Britain with an average rainfall of less than 20 inches (500mm) per year. **Map ref. C4**

Messing: This is the ancestral home of the Bush Family who have provided two American Presidents. The Bush family left Essex to settle in America during the 17th Century. **Map ref. C1**

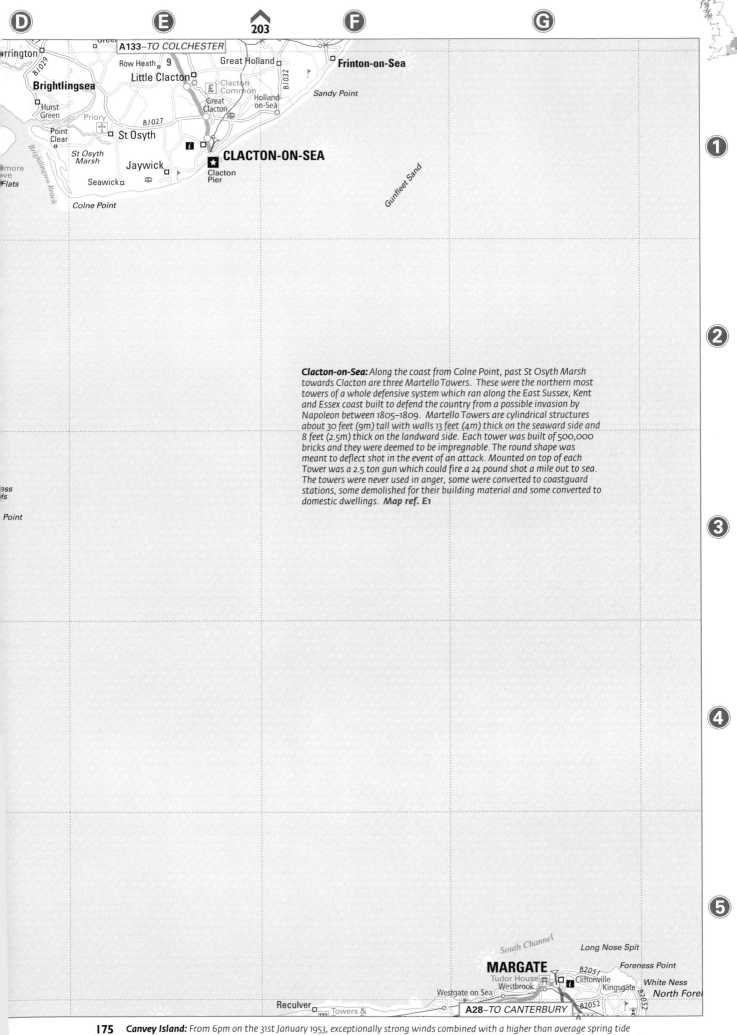

A133–TO COLCHESTER
Green
Row Heath 9
Great Holland
Frinton-on-Sea
Brightlingsea
Little Clacton
Clacton
Common
B1032
B1029
Sandy Point
Great
Clacton
Holland-
on-Sea
Hurst
Green
Priory
B1027
St Osyth
Point
Clear
Clacton
Pier
St Osyth
Marsh
Jaywick
CLACTON-ON-SEA
Seawick
Colne Point
more
ve
Flats
Gunfleet Sand

ess
ds

Point

2

Clacton-on-Sea: *Along the coast from Colne Point, past St Osyth Marsh towards Clacton are three Martello Towers. These were the northern most towers of a whole defensive system which ran along the East Sussex, Kent and Essex coast built to defend the country from a possible invasion by Napoleon between 1805–1809. Martello Towers are cylindrical structures about 30 feet (9m) tall with walls 13 feet (4m) thick on the seaward side and 8 feet (2.5m) thick on the landward side. Each tower was built of 500,000 bricks and they were deemed to be impregnable. The round shape was meant to deflect shot in the event of an attack. Mounted on top of each Tower was a 2.5 ton gun which could fire a 24 pound shot a mile out to sea. The towers were never used in anger, some were converted to coastguard stations, some demolished for their building material and some converted to domestic dwellings.* **Map ref. E1**

South Channel
Long Nose Spit
Foreness Point
MARGATE
B2051
Tudor House
Cliftonville
White Ness
Westbrook
Kingsgate
North Fore
Westgate on Sea
Reculver
Towers &
A28–TO CANTERBURY
B2052

Canvey Island: *From 6pm on the 31st January 1953, exceptionally strong winds combined with a higher than average spring tide caused a 'storm surge' which led to devastating flooding all along the east coast of England. Hurricane force winds were recorded at 10pm at Felixstowe and the surge reached Canvey Island just after midnight on the 1st February causing absolute devastation. In all 307 people lost their lives in the flood, over 250,000 acres (100,000ha) of land were immersed and the cost in today's figures would be over five billion pounds. These floods are generally regarded as Britain's worst ever peacetime disaster.* **Map ref. A4**

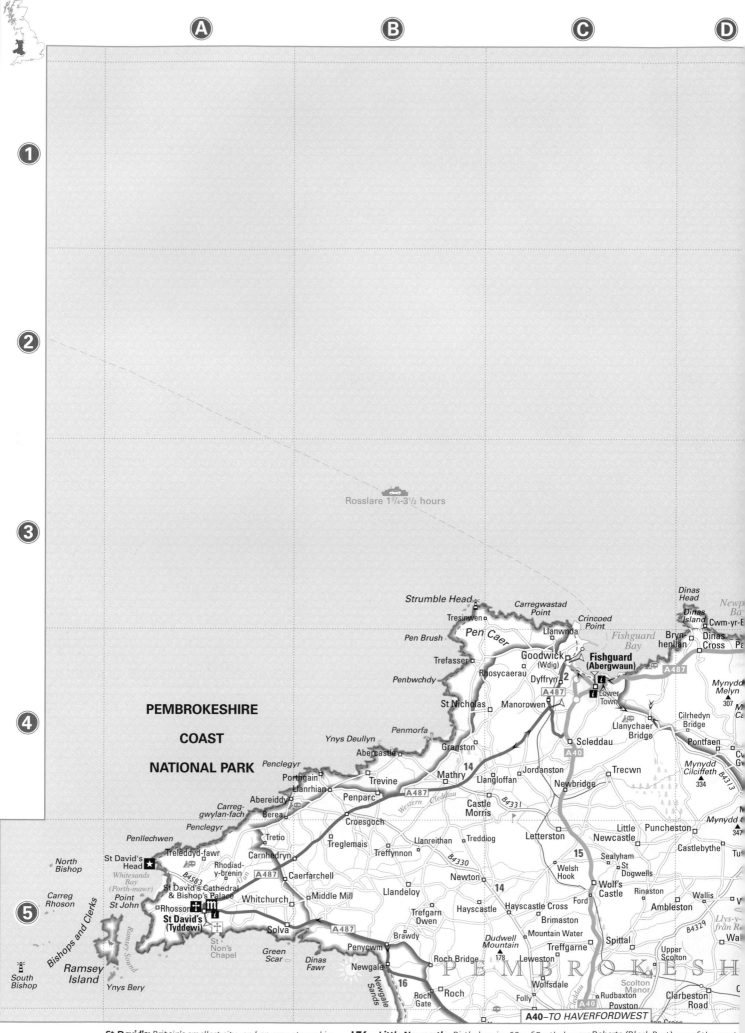

St Davids: Britain's smallest city, and an area steeped in ancient religion, both Christian and pagan. St David's Cathedral, built in AD1180 has been a place of pilgrimage for over 1200 years. It is a Celtic Cathedral and a focal point of Celtic heritage. **Map ref. A5**

176

Little Newcastle: Birthplace in 1682 of Bartholomew Roberts (Black Bart) one of the most notorious Pirates ever. Roberts was the first sea captain to fly the 'Jolly Roger' (the skull and crossbones flag). He was killed by grapeshot aboard his flagship Royal Fortune, during a battle with HMS Swallow, off the coast of Gabon in 1722. **Map ref. C5**

New Quay Head   New Quay Bay   Ffos

New Quay (Ceinewydd)   Llwyn-on   Llain
Maen-y-groes   Gilfachrheda
Cwmtudu   4   Cross Inn   Llanarth
Nanternis   Pe
Caerwedros   Synod Inn (Post-mawr)
Ynys-Lochtyn   Llwyndafydd
Llangrannog   Blaencelyn
Pontgarreg   Wervil Grange   Plwmp
Morfa   Pentregat   Talgarreg
Pencribach   Penbryn
Cardigan Island   Parcllyn   Aberporth   Tresaith   Sarnau   Brynhoffnant   Wstrws   Bwlchyfadf
Cemaes Head   15   8   Capel Cynon   Cas
Gwbert   Ferwig   Blaenannerch   Tan-y-groes   Rhydlewis   Ffostrasol   Ho
Pen-yr-afr   Cippyn   Tremain   Blaenporth   Glynarthen   Ceri   Penrhiw-pâl   Tre-groes
Pwllygranant   Blaenporth   Betws Ifan   Falin-Wnda   B4571   Maesllyn   Pr
Ceibwr Bay   Tre-Rhys   St Dogmaels (Llandudoch)   Cardigan (Aberteifi)   New Town   Penparc   Noyadd Trefawr   Beulah   Troedyraur   Coed y-bryn   Croes- lan
Moylgrove   Abbey   Llangoedmor   Pantgwyn   Ponthirwaun   Brongest   Llangynllo   Penrhiw-llan   Horeb
Monington   Cardigan Cilgerran (NT)   Llechryd   Llandygwydd   Capel Tygwydd   Aber banc   7
Glanrhyd   Pen-y-bryn   Cwm Plysgog   Manordeifi   Carreg-wen   10   Cwm-cou   Llandyfriog   Teifi Valley   Penrhiw-llan   2
Tredrissi   Bridell   Cilgerran   Newcastle Emlyn (Castell   Henllan   Llanfair-Orllwyn   Lland
Berry Hill   Llantood   Trewilym   Rhos-hill   Pentre Mansion   Abercych   Penrhiw   Newydd Emlyn)   Pentrecagal   6   Llangeler   Pontwe
Nevern   Velindre   Newchapel   Clynfyw   Penrherber   Aber-Arad National Woollen Museum   Drefach   Saron   Pentre-cwrt
ort   Eglwyswrw   Llanfair-Nant-Gwyn   B4332   Cilwendeg   Felindre   Drefelin   3   Bancyffor
Burial Chamber   Crosswell   Blaenffos   Boncath   Cwmhiraeth   Cwmpengraig   Bwlch-clawdd   257
Cilgwyn   Whitechurch   Brynberian   Glaspant   Bwlch-y-groes   Capel Iwan   Moelfre 335   Penboyr   Rhos   Dolgra
Foel Eryr 468   Tafarn-y-bwlch   Llanfair-Nant-Gwyn   Star   Clydey   Cilrhedyn   Cwm-Morgan   326   Gorllwyn   6
Foel Cwmcerwyn 536   Mynachlog-ddu   Crymych   Taf   Tegryn   Hermon
Greenway   Foel Drych 368   Pentre Galar   Hermon   Trelech   Cwmduad
Rosebush   262   Llanfyrnach   Dinas   B4299   Hermon
21   Glandwr   Blaen-y-coed   Llanpumsaint
Maenclochog   Llangolman   Hebron   Blaenwaun   14   Cynwyl Elfed   Llwyn-croes
New Moat   Llanglydwen   Post House   Llanwinio   Pen-y-bont   Esgair   B430
Efailwen   Cwmbach   Talog   6   Bwlchnewydd   Newchurch
Llanycefn   Login   Cefn-y-pant   Cwmfelin Mynach   Gellywen   Abernant   Bronwydd Arms   A
Llandre   Maesgwynne   Llanboidy   Nant Cynnen   Tre-vaughan
Llandissilio   Cwm-miles   CARMARTHENSHIRE   Carmarthen (Caerfyrddin)   Li
Clynderwen   Rhydywrach   Henllan Amgoed   Meidrim   Merthyr   Johnstown
Llangynin   Castell Gorfod   Sarnau

CEREDIGION

A487-TO ABERYSTWYTH

A486

A484

A478

MYNYDD PRESELI (PRESCELLY MTS)

Eastern Cleddau

nydd Preseli (Prescelly Mountains) : Up to 80 4-ton 'blue stones' used in the building of Stonehenge in
tshire were quarried here. They were probably transported overland from the mountains down to
ford Haven and then taken by raft and finally overland again to their destination, a distance of 135 miles.
p ref. D4

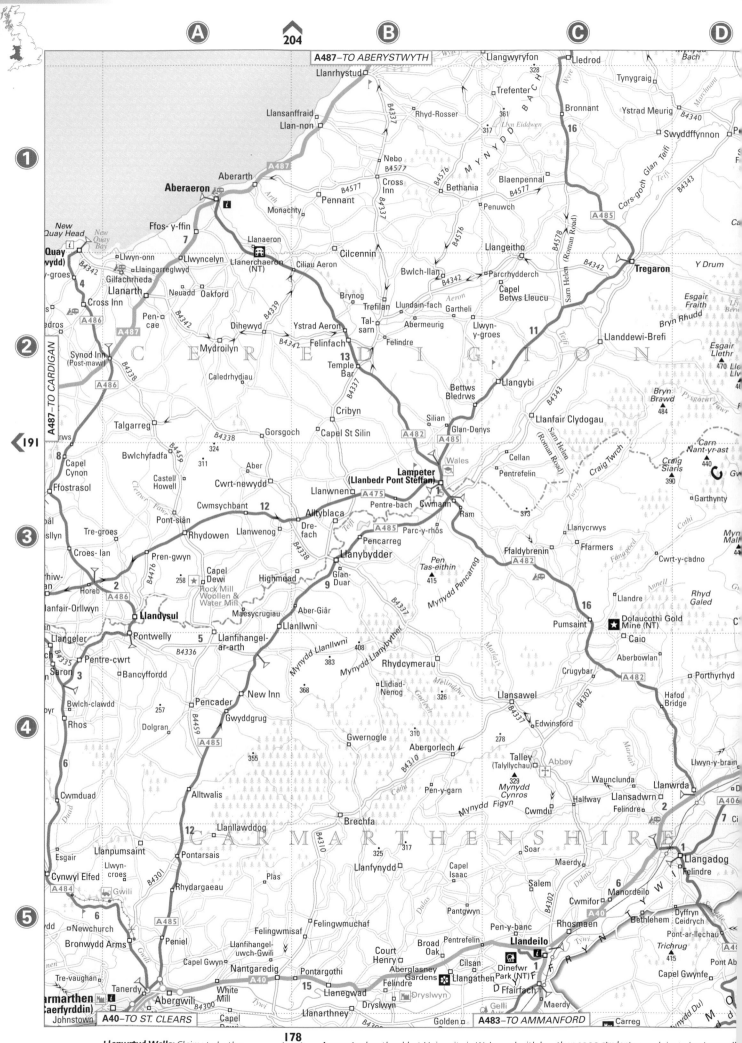

A487–TO ABERYSTWYTH

Llangwyryfon
Llanrhystud
Lledrod
Tynygraig
Trefenter
Bronnant
Ystrad Meurig
Swyddffynnon

Llansanffraid
Llan-non
Rhyd-Rosser
361
317
Llyn Eiddwen
328
16

A487
Aberarth
Nebo
B4577
Cross Inn
Bethania
Blaenpennal
Penuwch
A485

Aberaeron
Pennant
Monachty
B4576
B4578

New Quay Head
Ffos-y-ffin
Llanaeron
Cilcennin
Llangeitho
Tregaron
Y Drum

New Quay Bay
Llwyn-onn
Llwyncelyn
Llanerchaeron (NT)
Ciliau Aeron
Bwlch-llan
Parcrhydderch
Capel Betws Lleucu
Esgair Fraith
Bryn Rhudd

Quay (wydd)
y-groes
Llaingarreglwyd
Gilfachrheda
Brynog
Trefilan
Llundain-fach
Gartheli
Llwyn-y-groes
11
Llanddewi-Brefi
Esgair Llethr
470

4
Llanarth
Pen-cae
Oakford
Neuadd
Dihewyd
Ystrad Aeron
Talsarn
Abermeurig
CEREDIGION
Cross Inn
pedros
Mydroilyn
Felinfach
Felindre
Llangybi
Bryn Brawd 484

Synod Inn (Post-mawr)
Caledrhydiau
13
Temple Bar
Bettws Bledrws
Llanfair Clydogau
Craig Siarls 390

rws
191
Talgarreg
Gorsgoch
Cribyn
Silian
Glan-Denys
Cellan
Pentrefelin
Carn Nant-yr-ast 440

8
Bwlchyfadfa
324
311
Aber
Capel St Silin
A485
Wales
Garthynty

Capel Cynon
Castell Howell
Cwrt-newydd
Lampeter (Llanbedr Pont Steffan)
373

Ffostrasol
Cwmsychbant
12
Alltyblaca
Llanwnen
A475
Cwmann
Ram
Llanycrwys

Tre-groes
Pont-siân
Llanwenog
Drefach
Pentre-bach
Parc-y-rhôs
Ffaldybrenin
Ffarmers
Cwrt-y-cadno

Croes-lan
Rhydowen
Pencarreg
Pen Tas-eithin 415
A482
Llandre
Rhyd Galed

Pren-gwyn
Capel Dewi
Highmead
Llanybydder
Glan-Duar
9
Mynydd Pencarreg
16
Dolaucothi Gold Mine (NT)

Horeb
258
Rock Mill Woollen & Water Mill
Maesycrugiau
Aber-Giâr
Pumsaint
Caio
Aberbowlan

Llandysul
Pontwelly
Llanllwni
Mynydd Llanllwni 408
Rhydcymerau
Crugybar
A482
Porthyrhyd

Llangeler
5
Llanfihangel-ar-arth
383
Mynydd Llanybyther
326
Llansawel
Hafod Bridge

Pentre-cwrt
Bancyffordd
New Inn
368
Llidiad-Nenog
Edwinsford

Saron
3
Pencader
Gwyddgrug
Gwernogle
310
Abergorlech
278
Talley (Talyllychau)
Abbey
Waunclunda
Llanwrda

Rhos
Bwlch-clawdd
257
Dolgran
355
329 Mynydd Cynros
Pen-y-garn
Cwmdu
Llansadwrn
A406

Cwmduad
Alltwalis
Brechfa
Mynydd Figyn
Soar
Halfway
Felindre

Esgair
Llanllawddog
CARMARTHENSHIRE
325
317
Maerdy
Llangadog
Felindre

Llanpumsaint
Pontarsais
Llanfynydd
Capel Isaac
Salem
Manordeilo

Cynwyl Elfed
Llwyn-croes
Rhydargaeau
Plas
Pantgwyn
Cwmifor
Rhosmaen
Bethlehem

Newchurch
Peniel
Felingwmuchaf
Pen-y-banc
Pentrefelin
Llandeilo
Dyffryn Ceidrych

Bronwydd Arms
Capel Gwyn
Llanfihangel-uwch-Gwili
Broad Oak
Dinefwr Park (NT)
Trichrug 415

Tre-vaughan
Tanerdy
Nantgaredig
Pontargothi
15
Llanegwad
Aberglasney Gardens
Llangathen
Ffairfach
Pont-ar-llechau

Carmarthen (Caerfyrddin)
Abergwili
White Mill
Dryslwyn
Cilsan
Gelli
Maerdy
Capel Gwynfe

Johnstown
A40–TO ST. CLEARS
Capel Dewi
Golden
A483–TO AMMANFORD
Carreg

Llanwrtyd Wells: *Claims to be the smallest town in Wales and is the home of the annual World Bog Snorkelling Championships.* **Map ref. E3**

Lampeter *has the oldest University in Wales and with less than 2000 students can claim to be the smallest university in Europe. It was founded by Bishop Thomas Burgess in 1822 and admitted its first students on David's Day 1827.* **Map ref. B3**

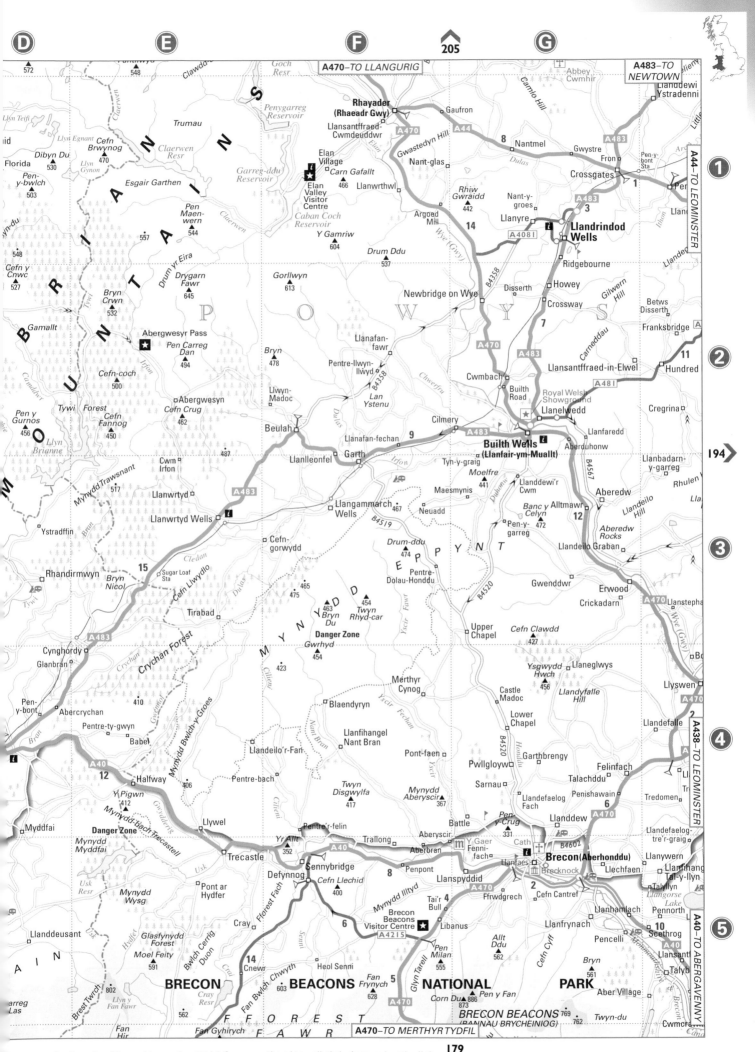

A470–TO LLANGURIG
A483–TO NEWTOWN

A44–TO LEOMINSTER

1

Rhayader
(Rhaeadr Gwy)

Llanddewi
Ystradenni

Gaufron

572

548

Trumau

Penygarreg
Reservoir

Llansantffraed-
Cwmdeuddwr

A44

8

Nantmel

Gwystre

Fron

Pen-y-
bont
Sta

Florida

Dibyn Du

Cefn
Brwynog

470
530

Llyn
Egnant

Claerwen

Claerwen
Resr

Elan
Village

Carn Gafallt
466

Llanwrthwl

Gwastedyn Hill

Nant-glas

Rhiw
Gwraidd
442

Nant-y-
groes

A483

Crossgates

1

Pen

Pen-
y-bwlch
503

Esgair Garthen

Garreg-ddu
Reservoir

Elan
Valley
Visitor
Centre

Argoed
Mill

14

Llanyre

A483

3

548

Cefn
Cnwc
527

Pen
Maen-
wern
544

557

Caban Coch
Reservoir

Y Gamriw
604

Drum Ddu
537

Wye (Gwy)

A4081

Llandrindod
Wells

Ridgebourne

Betws
Disserth

2

Drum yr Eira

Drygarn
Fawr
645

Gorllwyn
613

Newbridge on Wye

Disserth

Howey

Gilwern
Hill

194

Bryn
Crwn
532

P

W   Y   S

Crossway

Franksbridge

Bamallt

Abergwesyr Pass

Pen Carreg
Dan
494

Bryn
478

Llanafan-
fawr

Carneddau

Llansantffraed-in-Elwel

A481

Hundred

11

Cefn-coch
500

Pen y
Gurnos
456

Tywi
Forest

Cefn
Fannog
450

Abergwesyn

Cefn Crug
462

Pentre-llwyn-
llwyd

Lan
Ystenu

B4358

Cwmbach

Builth
Road

Royal Welsh
Showground

Llanelwedd

Cregrina

Llyn
Brianne

Beulah

Llwyn-
Madoc

487

Garth

Cilmery

A483

Builth Wells
(Llanfair-ym-Muallt)

Llanfaredd

Aberduhonw

Llanbadarn-
y-garreg

3

Mynydd Trawsnant
517

Llanwrtyd

Llanafan-fechan

9

Tyn-y-graig

Moelfre
441

Llanddewi'r
Cwm

B4567

Aberedw

Llandeilo
Hill

Rhulen

Ystradffin

Bran

Llanwrtyd Wells

Llangammarch
Wells
467

B4519

Neuadd

Maesmynis

Banc y
Celyn

Pen-y-
garreg

Alltmawr

472

12

Aberedw
Rocks

Llandeilo Graban

194

Rhandirmwyn

Bryn
Nicol

15

Sugar Loaf
Sta

Cefn
Llwydlo

Cefn-
gorwydd

Dulas

465

475

Drum-ddu
474

Pentre-
Dolau-Honddu

B4520

Gwenddwr

Erwood

Llanstepha

A470

Wye (Gwy)

3

Tirabad

Bryn
Du
463

Twyn
Rhyd-car
454

Mynydd

E   P   P   Y   N   T

Crickadarn

Cynghordy

Crychan Forest

Danger Zone

Gwrhyd
454

Upper
Chapel

Cefn Clawdd
427

Llyswen

A470

Bo

Glanbran

410

423

Cilieni

Merthyr
Cynog

Castle
Madoc

Ysgwydd
Hwch
456

Llaneglwys

Llandyfalle
Hill

Llandefalle

A438–TO LEOMINSTER

4

Pen-
y-bont

Abercrychan

Pentre-ty-gwyn

Babel

Mynydd Bwlch-y-Groes

Llandeilo'r-Fan

Blaendyryn

Llanfihangel
Nant Bran

Lower
Chapel

Llandefaelog
Fach

Tredomen

A40

12

Halfway

406

Pentre-bach

Twyn
Disgwylfa
417

Mynydd
Aberyscir
367

Pwllgloyw

Garthbrengy

Felinfach

Penishawain

6

Myddfai

Y Pigwn
412

Mynydd bach Trecastell

Llywel

352

Pentre'r-felin

Yr Allt

Twyn

Battle

Pen
y-Crug
331

Llanddew

A470

Llandefaelog-
tre'r-graig

Mynydd
Myddfai

Danger Zone

Trecastle

Cefn Llechid
400

Aberyscir

Y Gaer
Fenni-
fach

Cath

B4602

Brecon (Aberhonddu)

Llanywern

Llanfihang
Tal-y-llyn

A40–TO ABERGAVENNY

Trallong

Aberbran

Talachddu

Sarnau

5

Llanddeusant

Mynydd
Wysg

Pont ar
Hydfer

Sennybridge

Defynnog

8

Penpont

Llanspyddid

A470

Tai'r
Bull

4

Ffrwdgrech

2

Brecknock

Llechfaen

Cefn Cantref

Llanhamlach

Talyllyn

Langorse
Lake

Pennorth

10

Scethrog

5

Usk
Resr

Cray

6

Glasfynydd
Forest

Moel Feity
591

Cnewr

Bwlch Cerrig
Duon

Heol Senni

Brecon
Beacons
Visitor Centre

Mynydd Illtyd

Libanus

Allt
Ddu
562

Cefn Cyff

Bryn
561

Llanfrynach

Pencelli

Llansant

Aber Village

BrestTwrch
802

Llyn y
Fan Fawr

14

Cray
Resr
562

BRECON

BEACONS

Fan Bwlch
Chwyth
603

5

Fan
Frynych
628

Glyn Tarell

NATIONAL

Pen
Milan
555

PARK

Corn Du
873

886

Pen y Fan

BRECON BEACONS
(BANNAU BRYCHEINIOG)

769

Twyn-du
762

Cwmcr

Fan
Hir

Fan Gyhirych

F F O R E S T   F A W R

A470–TO MERTHYR TYDFIL

Tregaron: *A 19th century 'Drovers' town where Welsh farmers gathered to walk their sheep and cattle all the way to London to sell at the markets. Famous as the birthplace of Twm Sion Cati, an outlaw described as the Welsh Robin Hood on whom the popular TV series Hawkmoor was based. To the north of the town, Tregaron Bog (Cors Caron) is the best remaining example of an active raised bog in Wales.* **Map ref. C2**

193

A483–TO NEWTOWN

◄ 193

180 ▼

A44–TO RHAYADER

A483–TO BUILTH WELLS

A470–TO BUILTH WELLS

A470–TO MERTHYR TYDFIL

A40–TO LLANDOVERY

A40–TO ABERGAVENNY

A465–TO ABERGAVENNY

Hay-on-Wye: *Small market town on the banks of the River Wye famous for its large concentration of bookshops. With over 30 of these to choose from Hay-on-Wye is the most popular centre in Britain for booklovers.* **Map ref. B3**

Hereford Cathedral houses the famous Mappa Mundi. This is one of the first maps of the world create on a single sheet of vellum (calf skin) around AD1300. As well as being a map it also depicts the histor of mankind and illustrates the marvels of the natural world, biblical events and mythology. **Map ref.**

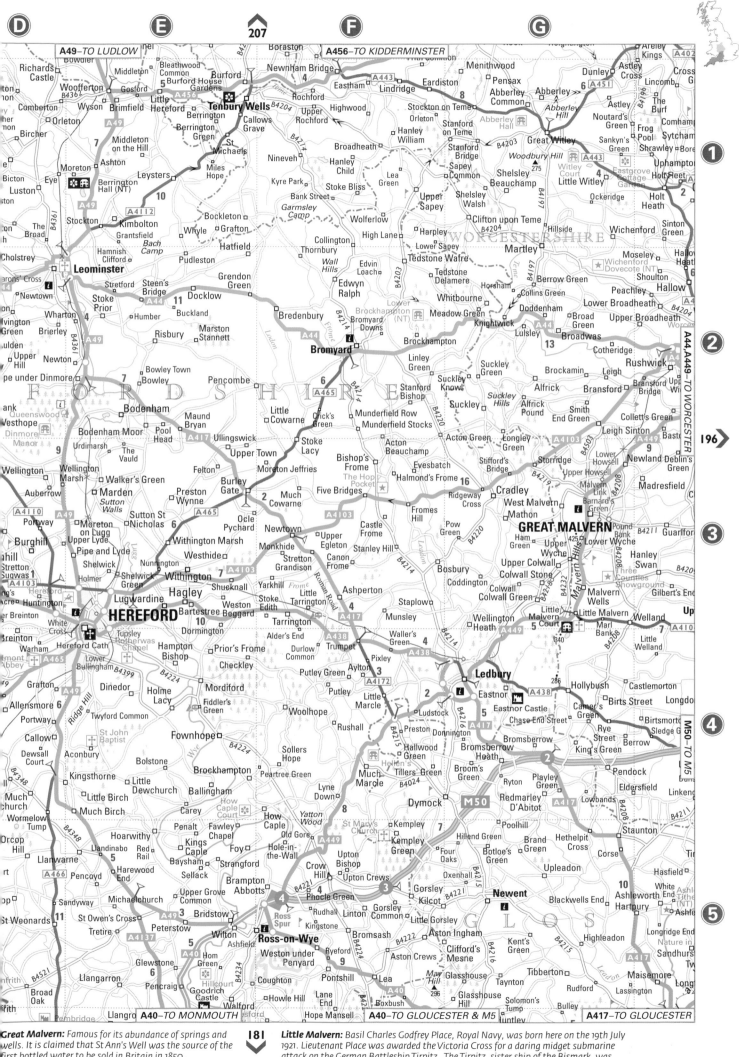

A49–TO LUDLOW   A456–TO KIDDERMINSTER

1

Richards Castle
Bowdler
Woofferton
Comberton
Orleton
Bircher
Moreton
Eye
Luston
The Broad
Cholstrey
Leominster
Newtown
Stoke Prior
Wharton
Brierley
Upper Hill
Newton
Queenswood
Westhope
Dinmore Manor
Wellington
Wellington Marsh
Auberrow
A4110
Marden
Sutton Walls
Sutton St Nicholas
Burghill
Portway
Moreton on Lugg
Upper Lyde
Pipe and Lyde
Shelwick
Shelwick Green
Holmer
Stretton Sugwas
Hereford
Huntington
White Cross
Breinton
Warham
Hereford Cath
Lower Bullingham
Grafton
Allensmore
Portway
Callow
Dewsall Court
Aconbury
Kingsthorne
Little Birch
Much Birch
Wormelow Tump
Orcop Hill
Llanwarne
Pencoyd
Sandyway
Michaelchurch
St Owen's Cross
St Weonards
Tretire
Glewstone
Llangarron
Pencraig
Broad Oak

Middleton
Gosford
Brimfield
Wyson
Ashton
Middleton on the Hill
Leysters
Kimbolton
Grantsfield
Bach Camp
Whyle
Hamnish Clifford
Pudleston
Docklow
Humber
Buckland
Risbury
Marston Stannett
Bowley Town
Bowley
Pencombe
Bodenham
Maund Bryan
Bodenham Moor
Pool Head
Urdimarsh
The Vauld
Ullingswick
Upper Town
Felton
Walker's Green
Preston Wynne
Burley Gate
Ocle Pychard
Withington Marsh
Westhide
Withington
Nunnington
Shucknall
Hagley
Lugwardine
Bartestree
Weston Beggard
Stoke Edith
Tarrington
Dormington
Hampton Bishop
Prior's Frome
Checkley
Mordiford
Holme Lacy
Fiddler's Green
Dinedor
Woolhope
Sollers Hope
Fownhope
Brockhampton
Ballingham
Carey
How Caple
Penalt
Kings Caple
Fawley Chapel
Foy
Baysham
Sellack
Strangford
Upper Grove Common
Harewood End
Red Rail
Llandinabo
Bridstow
Peterstow
Wilton
Ross-on-Wye
Ashfield
Weston under Penyard
Hom Green
Goodrich Castle
Walford
Hillcourt Gardens
Coughton
Howle Hill

Burford
Burford House Gardens
Little Hereford
Berrington
Berrington Green
St Michaels
Miles Hope
Nineveh
Kyre Park
Bank Street
Garmsley Camp
Bockleton
Grafton
Hatfield
Grendon Green
Edwyn Ralph
Bredenbury
Bromyard Downs
Bromyard
Linley Green
Stanford Bishop
Little Cowarne
Crick's Green
Stoke Lacy
Much Cowarne
Moreton Jeffries
Bishop's Frome
Five Bridges
Castle Frome
Newtown
Monkhide
Stretton Grandison
Canon Frome
Yarkhill
Little Tarrington
Ashperton
Staplow
Munsley
Waller's Green
Trumpet
Aylton
Pixley
Putley Green
Putley
Little Marcle
Ludstock
Rushall
Preston
Donnington
Much Marcle
Hallwood Green
Tillers' Green
Broom's Green
Dymock
Ryton
Lyne Down
Kempley
Kempley Green
Upton Bishop
Upton Crews
Crow Hill
Phocle Green
Rudhall
Linton
Gorsley Common
Kingstone
Bromsash
Aston Ingham
Ryeford
Aston Crews
Pontshill
Lea
May Hill
Glasshouse
Lane End
Boxbush
Hope Mansell

Boraston
Newnham Bridge
Eastham
Lindridge
Eardiston
Highwood
Upper Rochford
Rochford
Stockton on Teme
Orleton
Stanford on Teme
Stanford Bridge
Sapey Common
Hanley William
Hanley Child
Broadheath
Lea Green
Upper Sapey
Shelsley Beauchamp
Shelsley Walsh
Clifton upon Teme
Harpley
Lower Sapey
Tedstone Wafre
Collington
Thornbury
Wall Hills
Edvin Loach
Tedstone Delamere
Horsham
Whitbourne
Meadow Green
Knightwick
Lulsley
Broadwas
Cotheridge
Brockamin
Leigh
Suckley Green
Suckley Knowl
Suckley
Alfrick
Bransford
Suckley Hills
Alfrick Pound
Smith End Green
Leigh Sinton
Collett's Green
Longley Green
Acton Green
Stifford's Bridge
Storridge
Upper Howsell
Lower Howsell
Newland
Cradley
West Malvern
Mathon
Ridgeway Cross
Fromes Hill
Pow Green
Bosbury
Coddington
Upper Colwall
Colwall Stone
Colwall
Colwall Green
Wellington Heath
Little Malvern
Eastnor
Eastnor Castle
Chase End Street
Bromsberrow
Bromsberrow Heath
Playley Green
Redmarley D'Abitot
Poolhill
Hillend Green
Four Oaks
Oxenhall
Newent
Gorsley
Kilcot
Little Gorsley
Clifford's Mesne
Kent's Green
Glasshouse
Taynton
Solomon's Tump

Menithwood
Pensax
Abberley
Abberley Common
Stockton on Teme
Great Witley
Shelsley Beauchamp
Little Witley
Ockeridge
Holt Heath
Wichenford
Martley
Moseley
Shoulton
Berrow Green
Peachley
Lower Broadheath
Upper Broadheath
Broad Green
Broadwas
Cotheridge
Rushwick
Bransford Bridge
Collett's Green
Leigh Sinton
Newland
Madresfield
Upper Howsell
Lower Howsell
Malvern Link
Barnard's Green
Great Malvern
Upper Wyche
Lower Wyche
Malvern Wells
Little Malvern
Malvern Court
Marl Bank
Welland
Little Welland
Hollybush
Castlemorton
Birts Street
Camer's Green
Rye Street
Birtsmorton
Sledge Green
Berrow
Pendock
Eldersfield
King's Green
Lowbands
Staunton
Brand Green
Botloe's Green
Hethelpit Cross
Corse
Upleadon
Hasfield
Blackwells End
Hartpury
Ashleworth
Longridge End
Highleadon
Tibberton
Rudford
Maisemore

Dunley
Astley Cross
Areley Kings
Lincomb
Noutard's Green
Shrawley
Frog Pool
Sankyn's Green
The Burf
Sytcham
Uphampton
Holt Fleet
Holt
Sinton Green
Moseley
Hallow
Worcester
Guarlford
Hanley Swan
Gilbert's End
Upton

WORCESTERSHIRE

HEREFORDSHIRE

GLOS

2

196 ▶

3

4

M50–TO M5

5

A44,A449–TO WORCESTER

A40–TO MONMOUTH   A40–TO GLOUCESTER & M5   A417–TO GLOUCESTER

Great Malvern: Famous for its abundance of springs and wells. It is claimed that St Ann's Well was the source of the first bottled water to be sold in Britain in 1850.
Map ref. G3

181

Little Malvern: Basil Charles Godfrey Place, Royal Navy, was born here on the 19th July 1921. Lieutenant Place was awarded the Victoria Cross for a daring midget submarine attack on the German Battleship Tirpitz. The Tirpitz, sister ship of the Bismark, was 50,000 tons and had a crew of 2,340. The attack at Kaa Fjord, Norway on the 22nd September 1943 involved attaching magnetic mines to the hull which put the battleship out of action for several weeks. Lt. Place VC died in December 1994. **Map ref. G3**

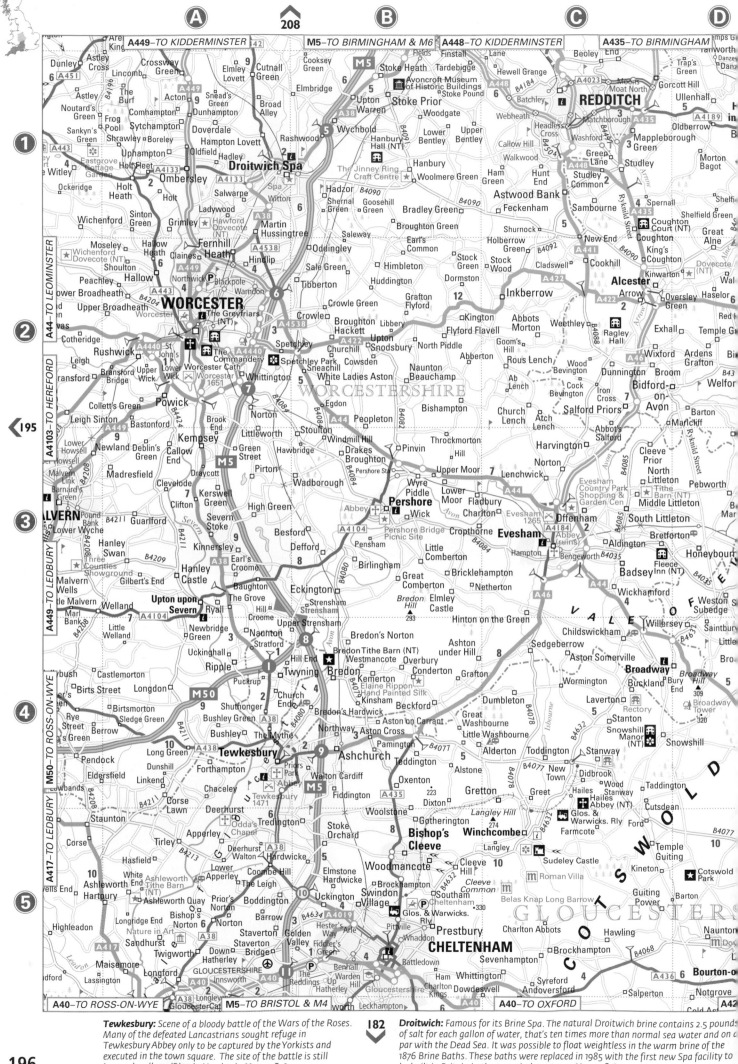

A449–TO KIDDERMINSTER M5–TO BIRMINGHAM & M6 A448–TO KIDDERMINSTER A435–TO BIRMINGHAM

REDDITCH

WORCESTER

WORCESTERSHIRE

Droitwich Spa

MALVERN

Pershore

Evesham

Broadway

Upton upon Severn

VALE OF EVESHAM

Tewkesbury

Ashchurch

COTSWOLD

Bishop's Cleeve

CHELTENHAM

Alcester

Bidford-on-Avon

GLOUCESTER

A40–TO ROSS-ON-WYE M5–TO BRISTOL & M4 A40–TO OXFORD

A44–TO LEOMINSTER
A4103–TO HEREFORD
A449–TO LEDBURY
M50–TO ROSS-ON-WYE
A417–TO LEDBURY

195

Tewkesbury: Scene of a bloody battle of the Wars of the Roses.
Many of the defeated Lancastrians sought refuge in
Tewkesbury Abbey only to be captured by the Yorkists and
executed in the town square. The site of the battle is still
known locally as 'Bloody Meadow'. **Map ref. A4.**

182

Droitwich: Famous for its Brine Spa. The natural Droitwich brine contains 2.5 pounds
of salt for each gallon of water, that's ten times more than normal sea water and on a
par with the Dead Sea. It was possible to float weightlessly in the warm brine of the
1876 Brine Baths. These baths were replaced in 1985 with the first new Spa facility to
be built in Britain in the twentieth century. **Map ref. A1.**

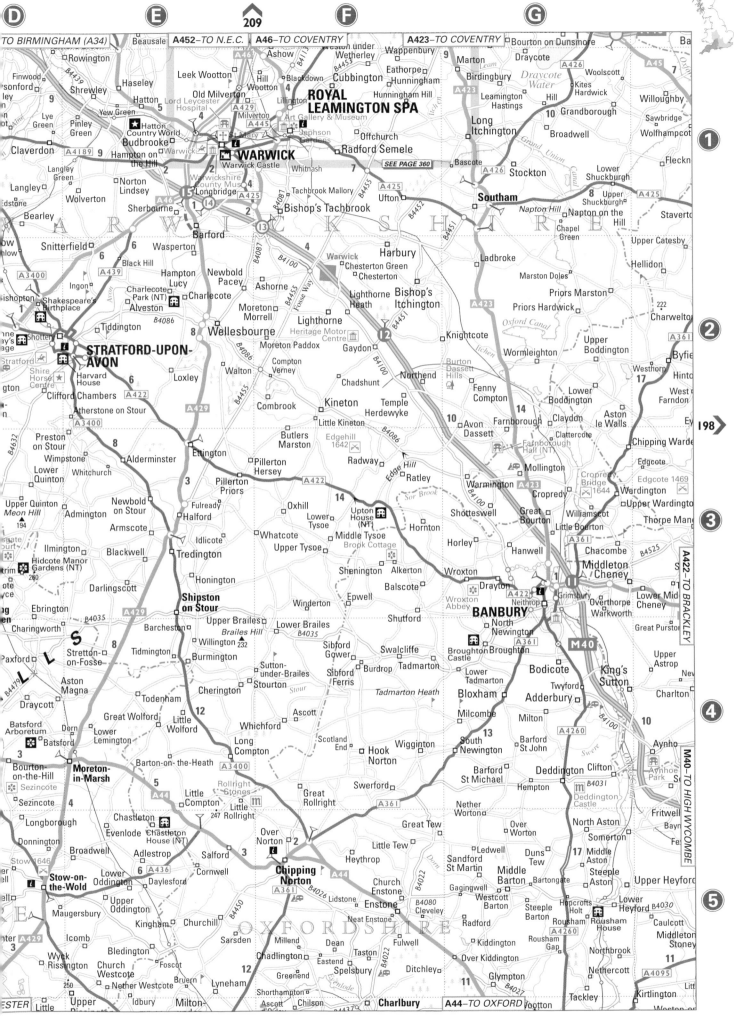

Rowington
Finwood
sford
Haseley
Shrewley
Leek Wootton
Ashow
Weston under Wetherley
Wappenbury
Marton
Draycote
Bourton on Dunsmore
Ba
A45

Lye Green
Pinley Green
Hatton
Old Milverton
Hill Wootton
Blackdown
Cubbington
Eathorpe
Hunningham
Birdingbury
Leamington Hastings
Woolscott
Kites Hardwick
Sawbridge
Willoughby
Fleckn

Claverdon
A4189
Hampton on the Hill
Budbrooke
Lord Leycester Hospital
Milverton
Lillington
ROYAL LEAMINGTON SPA
Hunningham Hill
Long Itchington
Grandborough
Broadwell
Wolfhampcot

Langley Green
Yew Green
St Mary
Art Gallery & Museum
Offchurch
Hill
Lower Shuckburgh

Langley
dstone
Norton Lindsey
A429
A445
WARWICK
Jephson Gardens
Radford Semele
Bascote
Stockton
Upper Shuckburgh
Staverto
A425

Bearley
Wolverton
Warwick Castle
Whitnash
SEE PAGE 360
7
A426
Southam
Napton Hill
Napton on the Hill
Upper Catesby
A425

Snitterfield
Sherbourne
Longbridge
Barford
Bishop's Tachbrook
Ufton
Chapel Green
Hellidon

Wasperton
A4087
A425
A4452

ishopton
A3400
A439
Black Hill
Ingon
Hampton Lucy
Newbold Pacey
Ashorne
Harbury
Chesterton Green
Chesterton
Ladbroke
Marston Doles
Priors Marston
Charwelto
222

Shakespeare's Birthplace
Charlecote Park (NT)
Charlecote
Alveston
Moreton Morrell
Warwick
Lighthorne Heath
Bishop's Itchington
A423
Priors Hardwick
A361

Tiddington
B4086
Wellesbourne
Lighthorne
Heritage Motor Centre
Knightcote
Wormleighton
Upper Boddington
Byfie

STRATFORD-UPON-AVON
Moreton Paddox
Gaydon
Westhorp
Hinto

Shottery
Harvard House
Loxley
Walton
Compton Verney
Northend
Burton Dassett Hills
Fenny Compton
Lower Boddington
17
West Farndon

Clifford Chambers
A422
Chadshunt
Avon Dassett
14
Aston le Walls
Chipping Warde

Atherstone on Stour
A429
Kineton
Temple Herdewyke
10
Farnborough
Claydon
Clattercote
Edgcote

Preston on Stour
Wimpstone
Aldermister
Ettington
Butlers Marston
Little Kineton
Edgehill 1642
Farnborough Hall (NT)
Mollington
Cropredy Bridge
1644
Edgcote 1469
Wardington

Lower Quinton
Whitchurch
Pillerton Hersey
Radway
Warmington
A423
Cropredy
Williamscot
Upper Wardingto

Upper Quinton
Meon Hill
194
Admington
Newbold on Stour
Pillerton Priors
3
Oxhill
Edge Hill
Ratley
A4100
Great Bourton
Little Bourton
Thorpe Man

Ilmington
Halford
Fulready
14
Upton House (NT)
Hornton
Shotteswell
Hanwell
Chacombe
B4525

Hidcote Manor Gardens (NT)
260
Blackwell
Idlicote
Whatcote
Middle Tysoe
Brook Cottage
Horley
Wroxton
Middleton Cheney

Darlingscott
Tredington
Honington
Lower Tysoe
Upper Tysoe
Shenington
Alkerton
Balscote
Wroxton Abbey
Drayton
A422
1
A422–TO BRACKLEY

Ebrington
Shipston on Stour
Winderton
Epwell
Shutford
BANBURY
Neithrop
Grimsbury
Lower Mid Cheney

Charingworth
A429
Upper Brailes
Lower Brailes
Sibford Gower
North Newington
A361
Overthorpe
Warkworth
Great Purstor

axford
Stretton-on-Fosse
Tidmington
Barcheston
Willington
Brailes Hill 232
B4035
Swalcliffe
Broughton Castle
Broughton
M40
Upper Astrop

Aston Magna
Burmington
Sutton-under-Brailes
Sibford Ferris
Burdrop
Tadmarton
Lower Tadmarton
Bodicote
King's Sutton
Charlton

Draycott
Todenham
Cherington
Stourton
Stour
Tadmarton Heath
Bloxham
Twyford
Adderbury
New

Batsford Arboretum
Great Wolford
Little Wolford
Whichford
Ascott
Milcombe
Milton
A4260
Aynho

Batsford
Lower Lemington
Scotland End
Wigginton
South Newington
13
Barford St John
Swere
Aynhoe Park

Bourton-on-the-Hill
Moreton-in-Marsh
12
Long Compton
Hook Norton
Barford St Michael
Deddington
Clifton
A4260
10
Fritwell

Sezincote
A44
Barton-on-the-Heath
A3400
Swerford
Hempton
A4031
Fes

Longborough
Little Compton
Rollright Stones
Great Rollright
Great Tew
Nether Worton
Deddington Castle
North Aston
Baynt

Donnington
Chastleton
Evenlode
Chastleton House (NT)
Salford
247
Little Rollright
Great Tew
Over Worton
Somerton
17
Middle Aston

Broadwell
Adlestrop
Cornwell
Over Norton
2
Little Tew
Heythrop
Ledwell
Duns Tew
Steeple Aston
Upper Heyfor

Stow 1646
Lower Oddington
A436
Daylesford
Chipping Norton
A44
Church Enstone
Sandford St Martin
Middle Barton
Bartongate
Lower Heyford

Stow-on-the-Wold
Upper Oddington
A361
A4026
Lidstone
Enstone
Gagingwell
Westcott Barton
Steeple Barton
B4030

Maugersbury
Kingham
Churchill
Neat Enstone
B4080 Cleveley
Radford
Hopcrofts Holt
Rousham
Rousham House
Caulcott
Middleto
Stoney

Icomb
Bledington
Foscot
Sarsden
Millend
Dean
Taston
Fulwell
Over Kiddington
Kiddington
Rousham Gap
Northbrook
11
A4095

Wyck Rissington
Church Westcote
Bruern
Lyneham
Greenend
Eastend
Spelsbury
Ditchley
Glympton
Nethercott
Kirtlington
Litt

nter A429
250
Nether Westcote
Idbury
Milton-
Shorthampton
Chilson
Ascott
Charlbury
A44–TO OXFORD
Wootton
Tackley
Weston-on-

Stow-on-the-Wold: *The Royalist in Digbeth Street is probably the oldest pub building in Britain, containing beams carbon-dated to 947AD.* **Map ref. D5.**

Banbury: *The place in the nursery rhyme 'Ride a Cock Horse to Banbury Cross'. In fact there have been several Banbury Crosses over the years but the surviving one stands at the junction of four major roads and was built in 1859 to commemorate the marriage of the then Princess Royal to Prince Frederick of Prussia.* **Map ref. G3.**

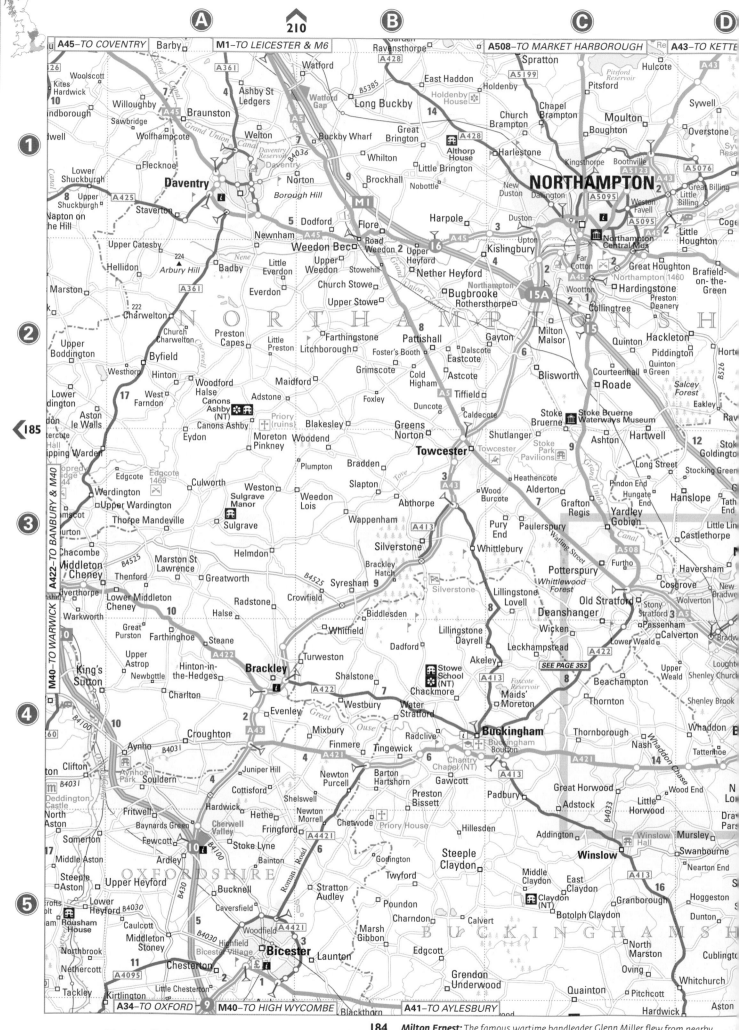

Stony Stratford: The Cock and The Bull Inns sit side by side on the main street which was the old coach route from London. Coach drivers would stop over here and exchange gossip; this gave rise to the term Cock and Bull Story. **Map ref. C3**

184

Milton Ernest: The famous wartime bandleader Glenn Miller flew from nearby Twinwood Airfield, in a single-engine Norseman aircraft on Friday 15th December 194_ and was never seen again. His band were due to play a concert to allied troops station_ in Paris and Miller was flying out ahead of the main band. At 6pm on Christmas Eve 1944 a Press Release announced that Glenn Miller was dead. **Map ref. F2**

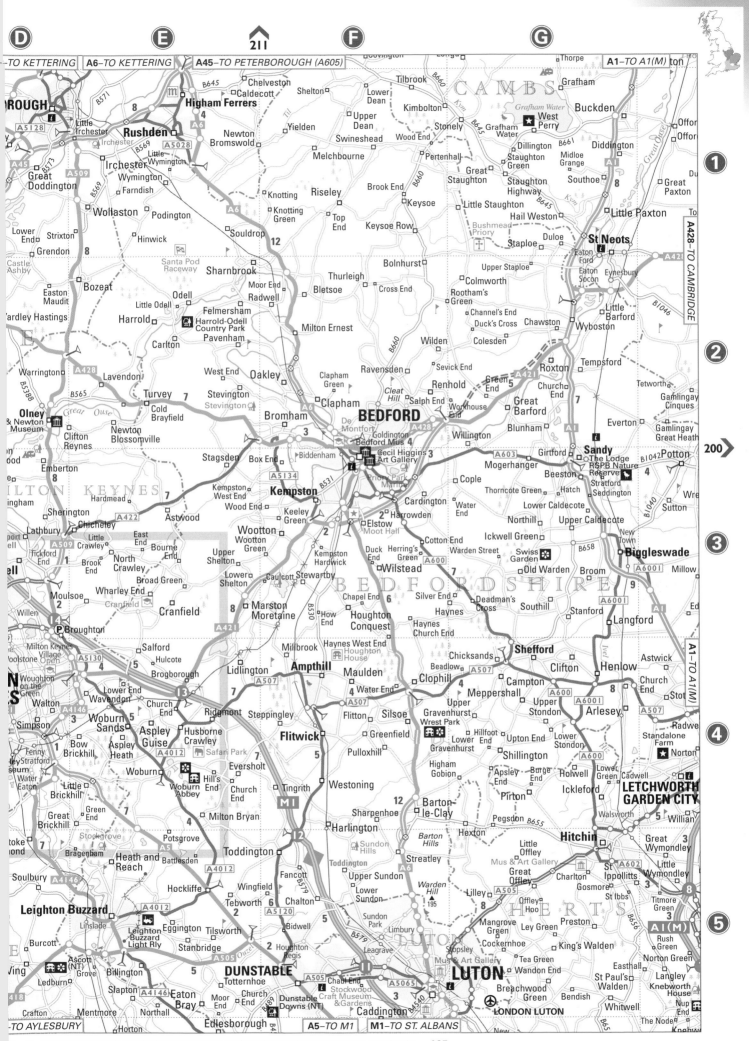

C A M B S

1

A428—TO CAMBRIDGE

2

200

3

A1—TO A1(M)

B E D F O R D S H I R E

4

5

The M1 Motorway: towards Birmingham was opened on the 2nd November 1959 by Ernest Marples the Minister of Transport. When it was first opened there was no speed limit. The first 72 miles was built in 9 months, employing a 5,000 labour force, at a cost of £17,000,000. One mile was constructed every 3 days. The motorway currently carries 88,000 vehicles per day compared to 13,000 when it was first opened. Traffic is heaviest between junctions 7 and 10, St Albans to Luton.

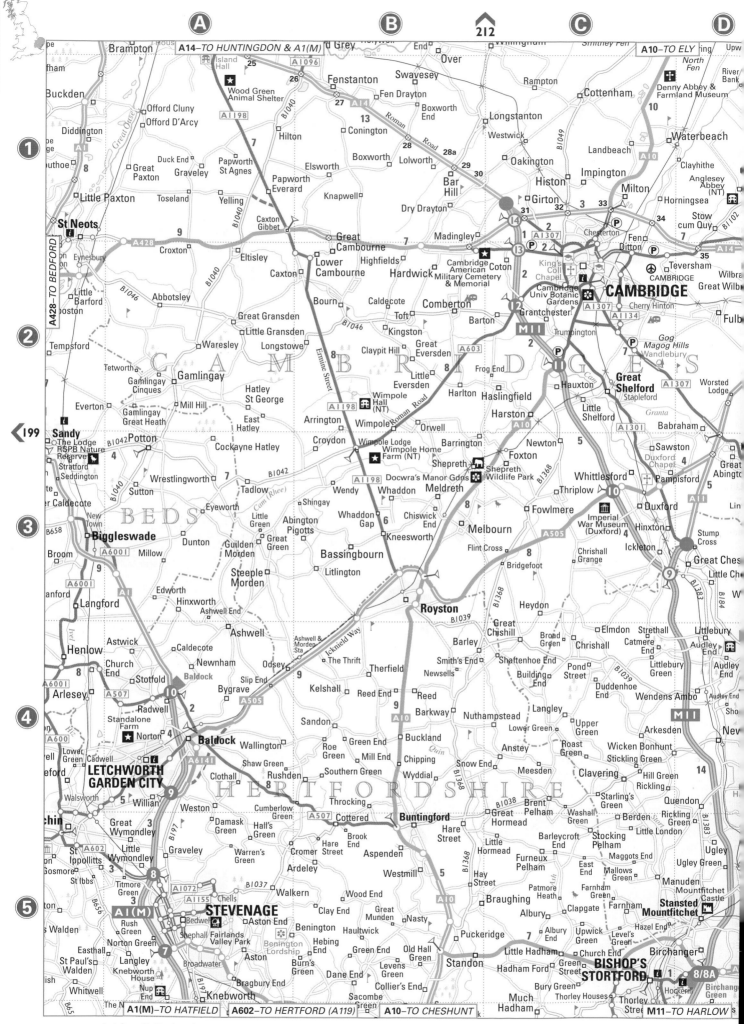

Ⓐ   Ⓑ   Ⓒ   Ⓓ

A14—TO HUNTINGDON & A1(M)

A10—TO ELY

Brampton
d Grey
Smithey Fen
Upw

Buckden
Island Hall
25
A1096
26
Over
Willingham
North Fen
River Bank

ofham
Wood Green Animal Shelter
Swavesey
Rampton
Cottenham
Denny Abbey & Farmland Museum

Diddington
Offord Cluny
Offord D'Arcy
Fenstanton
Fen Drayton
Longstanton
Westwick
Landbeach
Waterbeach

1
Duck End
Graveley
Papworth St Agnes
27
A14
Boxworth End
Oakington
Impington
Clayhithe
Anglesey Abbey (NT)

Great Paxton
Hilton
13
Elsworth
Boxworth
28
28a
Histon
Milton
Horningsea

Little Paxton
Toseland
Yelling
Papworth Everard
Knapwell
29
30
Bar Hill
Girton
31
32
33
34
Stow cum Quy

St Neots
Eynesbury
Caxton Gibbet
Great Cambourne
Dry Drayton
Madingley
14
13
A1307
2
Chesterton
Fen Ditton
35
A14

A428—TO BEDFORD
A428
9
Croxton
Eltisley
Lower Cambourne
Highfields
Cambridge American Military Cemetery & Memorial
Coton
King's Coll Chapel
Teversham

Little Barford
Boston
Abbotsley
Caxton
Hardwick
Comberton
Barton
Cambridge Univ Botanic Gardens
CAMBRIDGE
Cherry Hinton
Great Wilb

2
Tempsford
Great Gransden
Bourn
Caldecote
Toft
Grantchester
A1307
A1134
Fulb

Tetworth
Little Gransden
Longstowe
Kingston
Great Eversden
A603
12
Trumpington
Gog Magog Hills
Wandlebury
Worsted Lodge

Gamlingay Cinques
Gamlingay
Hatley St George
Claypit Hill
Little Eversden
Harlton
Haslingfield
Frog End
Hauxton
Great Shelford
Stapleford
A1307

199
Everton
Mill Hill
East Hatley
Arrington
Wimpole Hall (NT)
Wimpole
Harston
Little Shelford
A10
Babraham

Sandy
The Lodge RSPB Nature Reserve
Stratford
Seddington
Cockayne Hatley
Croydon
Wimpole Lodge
Wimpole Home Farm (NT)
Orwell
Barrington
Newton
Foxton
Shepreth
Shepreth Wildlife Park
Whittlesford
Pampisford
Sawston
Duxford Chapel
Great Abingto

3
Potton
Wrestlingworth
Tadlow
Whaddon
Docwra's Manor Gdns
Meldreth
B1368
Thriplow
Fowlmere
Imperial War Museum (Duxford)
Duxford
Lin

Biggleswade
Sutton
Eyeworth
Wendy
Shingay
Whaddon Gap
Chiswick End
Melbourn
A505
Hinxton
Ickleton
Stump Cross

Broom
Dunton
Guilden Morden
Great Green
Kneesworth
Flint Cross
Bridgefoot
Chrishall Grange
Great Ches

Langford
Edworth
Hinxworth
Steeple Morden
Bassingbourn
Litlington
9
Heydon
Elmdon
Strethall
Littlebury

4
Henlow
Astwick
Caldecote
Ashwell
Ashwell & Morden Sta
Therfield
Barley
Great Chishill
Chrishall
Catmere End
Littlebury Green
Audley End

Church End
Stotfold
Newnham
Odsey
The Thrift
Smith's End
Shaftenhoe End
Building End
Duddenhoe End
Wendens Ambo

Arlesey
Baldock
Bygrave
A505
Kelshall
Reed End
Reed
Barkway
Langley
Upper Green
Arkesden

Radwell
Standalone Farm
Norton
Wallington
Sandon
Green End
Buckland
Nuthampstead
Lower Green
Roast Green
Wicken Bonhunt
Stickling Green

LETCHWORTH GARDEN CITY
Baldock
Clothall
Rushden
Roe Green
Mill End
Chipping
Wyddial
Anstey
Clavering
Hill Green
Rickling

Walsworth
Willian
Weston
Shaw Green
Throcking
Snow End
Meesden
Brent Pelham
Washall Green
Quendon
Rickling Green

5
Great Wymondley
Little Wymondley
Damask Green
Hall's Green
Cumberlow Green
A507
Cottered
Buntingford
Hare Street
Great Hormead
Barleycroft End
Stocking Pelham
Berden
Little London

St Ippollitts
Graveley
Warren's Green
Cromer Street
Aspenden
Westmill
Little Hormead
Furneux Pelham
East End
Maggots End
Ugley

St Ibbs
Titmore Green
Walkern
Ardeley
Braughing
Farnham Green
Mallows Green
Ugley Green

STEVENAGE
A1155
Chells
Clay End
Great Munden
Nasty
Albury
Clapgate
Farnham
Manuden
Mountfitchet Castle

A1(M)
Bedwell
Fairlands Valley Park
Benington Lordship
Benington
Haultwick
Puckeridge
Albury End
Upwick Green
Church End
Stansted Mountfitchet

Shephall
Aston End
Hebing End
Green End
Old Hall Green
Standon
Little Hadham
Level's Green
Hazel End

Norton Green
Aston
Burn's Green
Levens Green
Hadham Ford
Street
Upwick Green
Bury Green
Birchanger

Knebworth House
Broadwater
Bragbury End
Dane End
Collier's End
Much Hadham
Thorley Houses
Hockerill
BISHOP'S STORTFORD
8/8A

A1(M)—TO HATFIELD   **A602**—TO HERTFORD (A119)   **A10**—TO CHESHUNT   **M11**—TO HARLOW

Letchworth Garden City: This was the first Garden City to be built in Britain. Ebenezer Howard (1850–1928) was the driving force behind its development. He and others formed Garden City Ltd. in 1903 and issued shares to raise the capital needed. They purchased Letchworth Manor and the surrounding land and building work started in 1903. **Map ref. A4**

186

Newmarket: Horse Racing started here with the first recorded race taking place in 1622. A horse belonging to Lord Salisbury bea one owned by the Marquess of Buckingham for a prize of £100. **Map ref. E1**

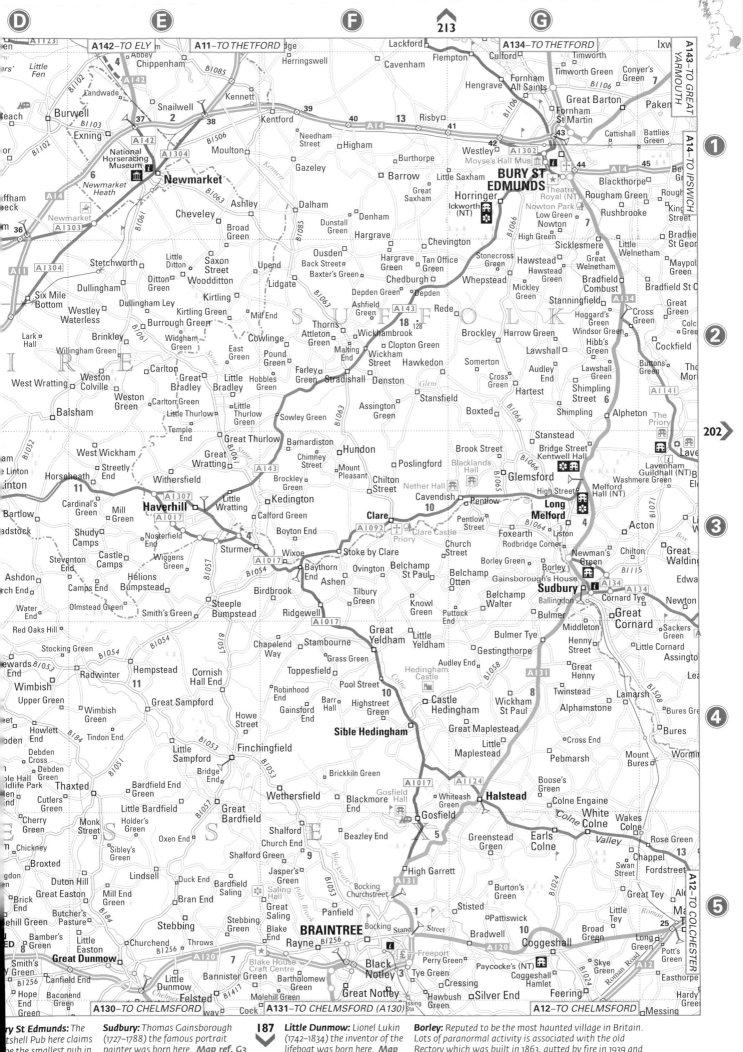

D · A1123 · *Little Fen* · A142–TO ELY · A11–TO THETFORD · A134–TO THETFORD · A143–TO GREAT YARMOUTH · A14–TO IPSWICH

Lackford
Flempton
Culford
Timworth
Ixw
Abbey Chippenham
Herringswell
Cavenham
Hengrave
Timworth Green
Conyer's Green
B1085
7
Landwade
Kennett
Fornham All Saints
B1106
Paken

A142
Snailwell
39
Kentford
40
A14
13
Risby
41
Great Barton
Fornham St Martin
43
Cattishall
Battlies Green

Burwell
37
2
38
Needham Street
Higham
42
Westley
A1302
44
45
Be
Exning
Moulton
Gazeley
Barrow
Burthorpe
Moyse's Hall Mus
BURY ST EDMUNDS
Blackthorpe
Gr

National Horseracing Museum
A1304
Newmarket
Great Saxham
Little Saxham
Horringer
Theatre Royal (NT)
Rougham Green
Rough

Newmarket Heath
Cheveley
Ashley
Dalham
Denham
Ickworth (NT)
Nowton Park
Low Green
Nowton
7
Rushbrooke
King Street
Bradfie St Geor

36
Stetchworth
Broad Green
Little Ditton
Saxon Street
Woodditton
Upend
Ousden
Back Street
Hargrave
Chevington
Tan Office Green
Depden
Stonecross Green
Hawstead
Great Welnetham
Little Welnetham
Maypol Green

Six Mile Bottom
Dullingham
Ditton Green
Kirtling
Mill End
Depden Green
Ashfield Green
Rede
A143
Whepstead
Hawstead Green
Mickley Green
Bradfield Combust
Bradfield St C

Westley Waterless
Dullingham Ley
Kirtling Green
Lidgate
Thorns
Attleton Green
Wickhambrook
18
128
Brockley
Harrow Green
Lawshall
Hoggard's Green
Windsor Green
Cross Green
Colc Gree

Lark Hall
Brinkley
Burrough Green
Widgham Green
East Green
Malting End
Wickham Street
Hawkedon
Somerton
Cross Green
Audley End
Hibb's Green
Lawshall Green
Buttons' Green
Cockfield

West Wratting
Weston Colville
Great Bradley
Little Bradley
Hobbles Green
Pound Green
Farley Green
Stradishall
Denston
Stansfield
Hartest
Shimpling Street
6
The Mor

Weston Green
Carlton
Sowley Green
Assington Green
Boxted
Shimpling
Alpheton
The Priory

Balsham
Carlton Green
Little Thurlow Green
Temple End
Great Thurlow
Barnardiston
Hundon
Chimney Street
Mount Pleasant
Stanstead
Bridge Street
Kentwell Hall
202

West Wickham
Streetly End
Withersfield
Great Wratting
Brockley Green
Poslingford
Brook Street
Blacklands Hall
Glemsford
Lavenham Guildhall (NT)
Washmere Green
El
Lave

Horseheath
Cardinal's Green
Haverhill
A143
Chilton Street
Nether Hall
High Street
Melford Hall (NT)

Bartlow
Mill Green
A1307
Little Wratting
Kedington
Cavendish
Pentlow
Long Melford
4
Acton
Great Waldin

Linton
Nosterfield End
A1017
Calford Green
Boyton End
Pentlow Street
Foxearth
B1064
Liston
Newman's Green
Chilton

Shudy Camps
Steventon End
Castle Camps
Wiggens Green
Sturmer
4
Wixoe
Stoke by Clare
A1092
Clare
10
Church Street
Rodbridge Corner
B1115
Great Waldin

Water End
Camps End
Helions Bumpstead
Birdbrook
Ashen
Baythorn End
Ovington
Tilbury Green
Clare Castle Priory
Borley Green
Borley
Sudbury
A134
A134
Edwa

Red Oaks Hill
Olmstead Green
Smith's Green
Steeple Bumpstead
Ridgewell
Knowl Green
Belchamp St Paul
Belchamp Otten
Belchamp Walter
Bulmer
Ballingdon
Cornard Tye
Newton

Stocking Green
B1053
Radwinter
Hempstead
11
Cornish Hall End
A1017
Great Yeldham
Little Yeldham
Puttock End
Bulmer Tye
Middleton
Great Cornard
Sackers Green
Little Cornard
Assingto

Upper Green
Wimbish
Wimbish Green
Great Sampford
Chapelend Way
Stambourne
Grass Green
Toppesfield
Pool Street
Hedingham Castle
Audley End
Henny Street
Great Henny
Twinstead
Lamarsh
Bures Gre

Howlett End
Tindon End
B1184
Little Sampford
Robinhood End
Barr Hall
Highstreet Green
Castle Hedingham
Wickham St Paul
Alphamstone
Bures
Lea

Debden Cross
Debden
Finchingfield
Gainsford End
Howe Street
Sible Hedingham
Great Maplestead
Little Maplestead
Cross End
Mount Bures
Wormi

Thaxted
Cutlers Green
Bardfield End Green
Bridge End
Wethersfield
Brickkiln Green
A1017
A1124
Boose's Green
Colne Engaine

Cherry Green
Monk Street
Holder's Green
Little Bardfield
Great Bardfield
Blackmore End
Gosfield Hall
Whiteash Green
Halstead
White Colne
Wakes Colne
Rose Green
13

Chickney
Broxted
Sibley's Green
Oxen End
Shalford
Shalford Green
9
Beazley End
Gosfield
5
Greenstead Green
Earls Colne
Colne Valley
Swan Street
Chappel
Fordstreet
A12–TO COLCHESTER

Duton Hill
Great Easton
Lindsell
Duck End
Bardfield Saling
Jasper's Green
High Garrett
Burton's Green
Great Tey
Little Tey
Al
Ma

Brick End
Great Dunmow
Mill End Green
Bran End
Saling Hall
Great Saling
B1053
Bocking Churchstreet
A131
Stisted
Pattiswick
Bradwell
Broad Green
Long Green
Pott's Green
25

Bamber's Green
Little Easton
Stebbing
Stebbing Green
Blake End
Panfield
Great Notley
BRAINTREE
Bocking
Street
10
Coggeshall
Skye Green
A12

Smith's Green
8
Churchend
Throws
Rayne
B1256
A120
Bocking
Black Notley
3
Tye Green
Perry Green
Cressing
Hawbush Green
Silver End
Paycocke's (NT)
Coggeshall Hamlet
Feering
Easthorpe

Great Dunmow
7
Blake House Craft Centre
Bannister Green
Bartholomew Green
Freeport
Great Notley
Molehill Green
Felsted
B1417
Little Dunmow
Canfield End
Hope End Green
Baconend Green
A130–TO CHELMSFORD
A131–TO CHELMSFORD (A130)
A12–TO CHELMSFORD
Messing
Hardy Gree

Bury St Edmunds: The Nutshell Pub here claims to be the smallest pub in Britain. **Map ref. G1**

Sudbury: Thomas Gainsborough (1727–1788) the famous portrait painter was born here. **Map ref. G3**

187 ▽ **Little Dunmow:** Lionel Lukin (1742–1834) the inventor of the lifeboat was born here. **Map ref. E5**

Borley: Reputed to be the most haunted village in Britain. Lots of paranormal activity is associated with the old Rectory which was built in 1863, gutted by fire in 1939 and demolished in 1944. **Map ref. G3**

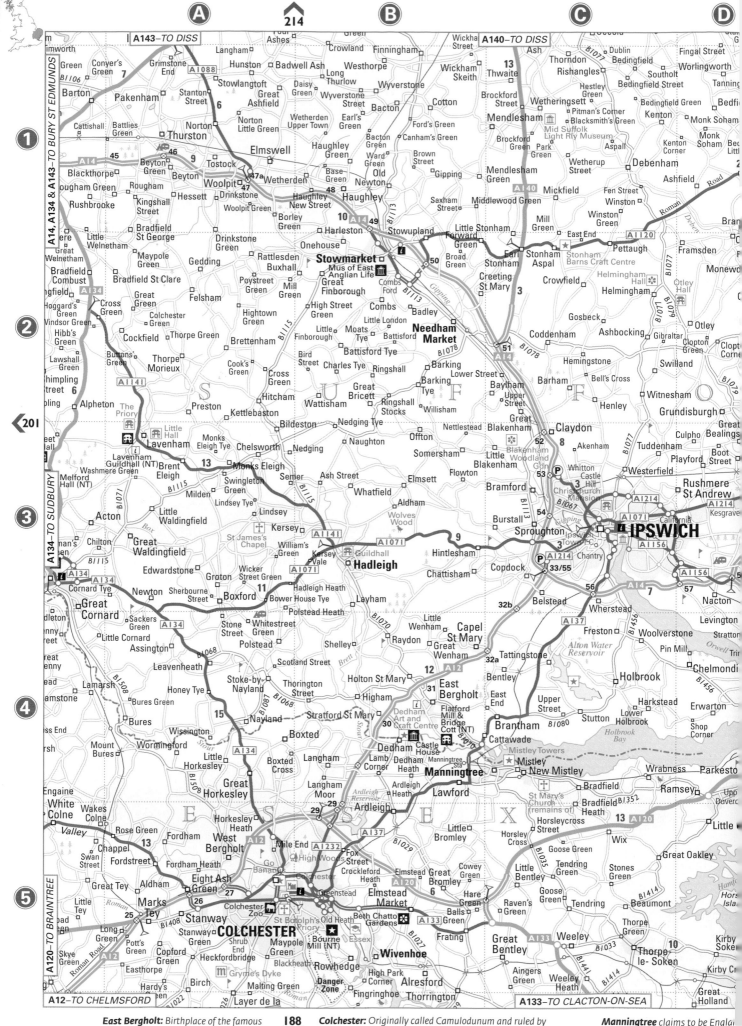

Stowmarket

Mus of East Anglian Life

Needham Market

IPSWICH

Hadleigh

Dedham Art and Craft Centre

Manningtree

New Mistley

Mistley Towers

COLCHESTER

Wivenhoe

East Bergholt: Birthplace of the famous painter John Constable (1776–1837) who went to school at nearby Dedham. So famous are his works that the surrounding area is known as Constable Country. *Map ref. B4*

188

Colchester: Originally called Camulodunum and ruled by King Cunobelin, who was Old King Cole in the nursery rhyme. Colchester claims to be the oldest recorded town in Britain. It was a main centre of Roman Britain and its Norman Castle is the biggest in Europe. *Map ref. A5 Also on page 78*

Manningtree claims to be Engla smallest market town. *Map ref.*

A12–TO LOWESTOFT

A12

Owl's Green

undish

tead

Dennington

Badingham

Goddard's Corner

Capon's Green

A1120

Peasenhall

Sibton

Yoxford

Darsham

Westleton Heath

Westleton

Dunwich Heath (NT)

Vineyard & Winery

Bruisyard

Bruisyard Street

Dorley's Corner

Curlew Green

Middleton

Middleton Moor

North Green

East Green

Theberton

East Bridge

Framlingham Castle

Brabling Green

Cransford

Rendham

Carlton

Kelsale

Leiston Abbey

Apsey Green

Cole's Green

Swefling

Saxmundham

Knodishall Green

Leiston

Sizewell

North Green

Great Glemham

Benhall Street

Sternfield

Knodishall

Coldfair Green

Aldringham

Parham

Mill Green

Silverlace Green

Stratford St Andrew

Benhall Green

Snape Watering

Friston

Knodishall Common

Thorpe Ness

Kettleburgh

Easton

Hacheston

Marlesford

Farnham

Gromford

Church Common

Moot Hall

Thorpeness

Easton Farm Park

Little Glemham

Glemham Hall

Snape

Wickham Market

Campsea Ashe

Blaxhall

Iken

High Street

Aldeburgh

Pettistree

Wickham Market Sta

Slaughden

A12

Ufford

Rendlesham

Tunstall

Sudbourne

Aldeburgh Bay

Melton

Bromeswell

Eyke

Friday Street

Butley

Tunstall Forest

Chillesford

Butley Mills

B1078

Sutton Hoo Tumuli

Rendlesham Forest

Butley Abbey

Butley Low Corner

Orford Castle

Orford

Orford Ness

Woodbridge Tide Mill

Capel St Andrew

Gedgrave Hall

Orford Ness (NT)

Sutton

Boyton

Orford Beach

Waldringfield

Shottisham

Hollesley

Newbourne

Ramsholt

Shingle Street

Hollesley Bay

Hemley

Alderton

Bawdsey

Kirton

Falkenham

Felixstowe Ferry

Bawdsey Manor

Mary

Walton

Old Felixstowe

Felixstowe

Manning's Amusement Park

Gate

Landguard Fort

Landguard Point

The Naze

ferry hours

Esbjerg.............................19
Cuxhaven (Hamburg)............20
Hoek van Holland.............3¾

on the Naze

Pier

Sea

...nwich Heath: *Set within an Area of Outstanding Natural ...uty (AONB), this is a remnant of the original Sandlings Heaths. ...an important conservation area and very popular with ...watchers as it is home to some rare species such as the Nightjar ...Dartford Warbler.*
... p ref. F1 *Also on page 78*

189 **Felixstowe:** *This is the largest container port in the UK and one of the largest in Europe. Almost 50% of all British deep sea container trade now passes through Felixstowe. The port was first developed as 'The Felixstowe Railway and Pier Company', by Colonel George Tomline in 1875.*
Map ref. E4

A470—TO BETWS-Y-CO

Uwch-mynydd
Taicynhaeaf
Pen-y-bryn
A470
Cym
Abb
2

Bontddu
Caerdeon
Toll
Abergwynant
Penmaenpool
Dolgella

Llanaber
461
Cutiau
10
Abergwynant

Barmouth
(Abermaw)

Morfa
Mawddach Sta
Arthog
Islawr-dref

Barmouth Bay
(Bae Bermo)

SNOWDONIA
661

GWYN
IDRIS
Mynydd
Moel
855

Fairbourne & Barmouth Rly
Fairbourne
The Bar

CADAIR
Penygadair
893

18
Friog

Pen y Garn
459

Mynydd Pennant
463

Mynydd
Pencoed
622

Tal-y-llyn Lake

Llwyngwril

Gwril

Llanfihangel-y-pennant

Tal-y-llyn

B4405

Graig Goch

PARK

Co
Uc

Castell y Bere (Ruin)

Llangelynin

Esgair Berfa

Rhoslefain
Llanegryn
Peniarth
Foel Wyllt
Dolgoch
313

390

Mynydd Tan-y-coed

Abergynolwyn

Tarren-y-Ge
666

Llanfendigaid
Tonfanau

Bryncrug
492

Pen Trum-gwr
511

Tarrenhendre
633

Foel-y-Geifr
Pantpe

Aber Dysynni

Pandy

Trum Gelli
535

Pennal-isaf

Rhyd-yr-onnen

Tywyn
Talyllyn Rly
Pennal
Cwrt

A493

DYFI

A487
Derwer
Glaspwll

Caethle Farm

279

Aberdovey
17
Penhelig

Eglwys Fach
Ysgubor-y-coed

Aberdyfi Bar
Furnace

Dyfi Furnace

Pen Carreg Gopa
447

Twyni Bâch

Traeth Maelgwyn
Dyfi (Dovey)

18

Cwm Einion

Ynys Tachwedd

Fochno

B4353

Foel Goch
475

Angler's Re
Moel-y-Llyn
521

Ynyslas

Tre'r-ddol

Llancynfelyn

Taliesin

Cwm
Cletwr
Ceulan

Cors

Leri

Borth
Glanwern

Talybont

Nant-y-moc
Reservoir

Upper Borth

Dôl-y-bont

CEREDIGI

Llandre

B4353

Bont-goch
(Elerch)

Sarn Cynfelyn

Leri

Disg
Fa

A487

Llangorwen

Bow Street
Pen-y-garn

Garth
Salem

Llyn
Syfydrin

Great Aberystwyth
Camera Obscura
Cliff Rly

Clarach
Penrhyn-coch

Cwmsymlog

Cefn Llwyd

Ceredigion Museum

Comins Coch

Capel Dewi
Pen-bont
Rhydybeddau
Cwmerfyn

National Library of Wales

Waun Fawr

Old Goginan
Goginan

13
A44
Pont

Aberystwyth

A4159

Blaengeufforddd

The Bar
Aberystwyth Arts Centre
Llanbadarn
Fawr

Capel Bangor

Cwmbrwyno

Penparcau

Vale of Rheidol Rly

(Summer only) P
Southgate

13

Rhydyfelin

Capel Seion

A4120

Aberffrwd

Ystumtuen
Rheidol Falls

1
Allt Wen

Gors

Llanfarian

B4340

New Cross

Llanfihangel-y-Creuddyn

Devil's Bridge
(Pontarfynach)

Chancery

Abermad

Llanilar

Cnwch Coch

Trisant

Blaenplwyf

Pentre-llyn

B4575

Rhos-y-garth

Ne
Ro

Rhodmad

A487

A485

Crosswood

Llanafan

Wenallt

Mynydd
Bach

Carreg Ti-pw

B4576

Llanddeiniol

Wyre

14

Llangwyryfon
328

Lledrod

Tynygraig

A487—TO ABERAERON

Aberystwyth: *Home of the National Library of Wales the University of Wales, Aberystwyth. The river Rheidol, which feeds into the old harbour is the steepest river in Britain and the Electric Cliff Railway, which climbs Constitution Hill, is the longest cliff railway in the country.* **Map ref. B4**

 192

Trannon: *The moor here is home to the Carno Wind Farm, which at time of completion in 1996 was the largest in Europe. There are 56 turbines with a combined maximum generating capacity of 33.6MW. Map ref. F3*

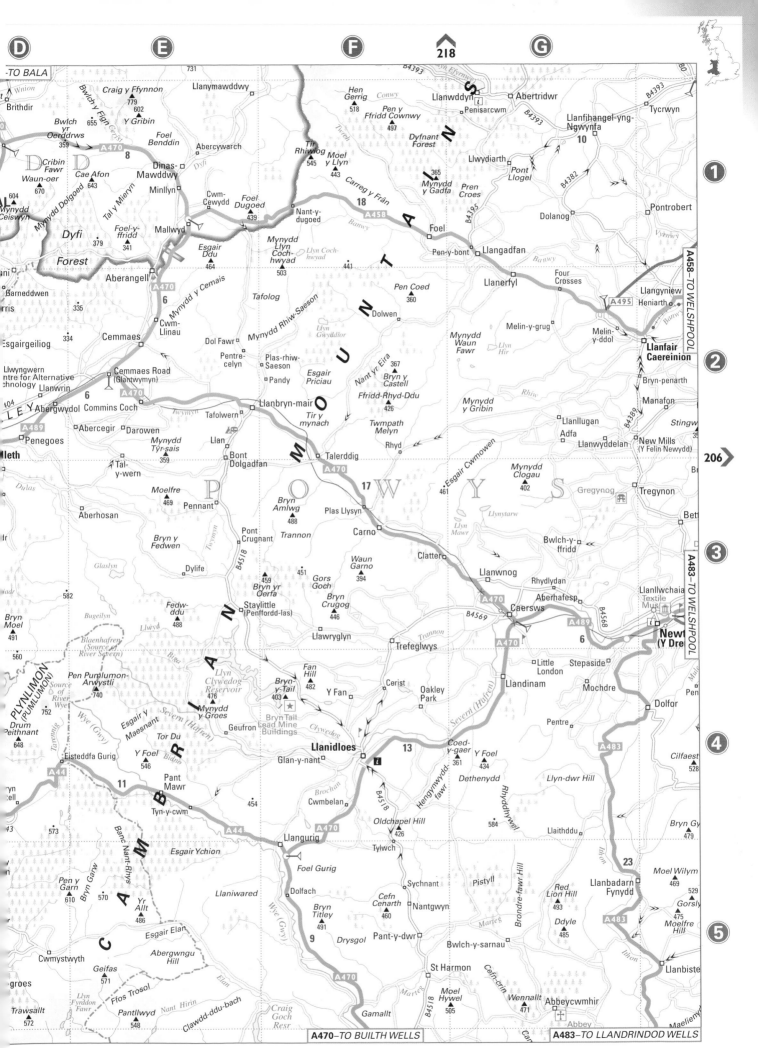

fihangel yng Ngwynfa: Anne Griffiths, the famous sh Methodist hymn writer was born here in 1776. Anne te 70 hymns in her short life. She died, aged 29 on the 12th ust 1805 and is buried in the village. **Map ref. G1**

193

Llyn Clywedog: The Dam, at the southern end of Llyn Clywedog Reservoir is the highest dam in Britain. It was constructed 1965–67 to regulate the flow of water into the River Severn. The dam is 236 feet (72m) high, 750 feet (229m) long and holds back 11,000,000 gallons (50,000 cubic metres) of water. The lake has a surface area of 615 acres (249ha), is 216 feet (66m) deep and 6 miles (9.5km) long. **Map ref. F4**

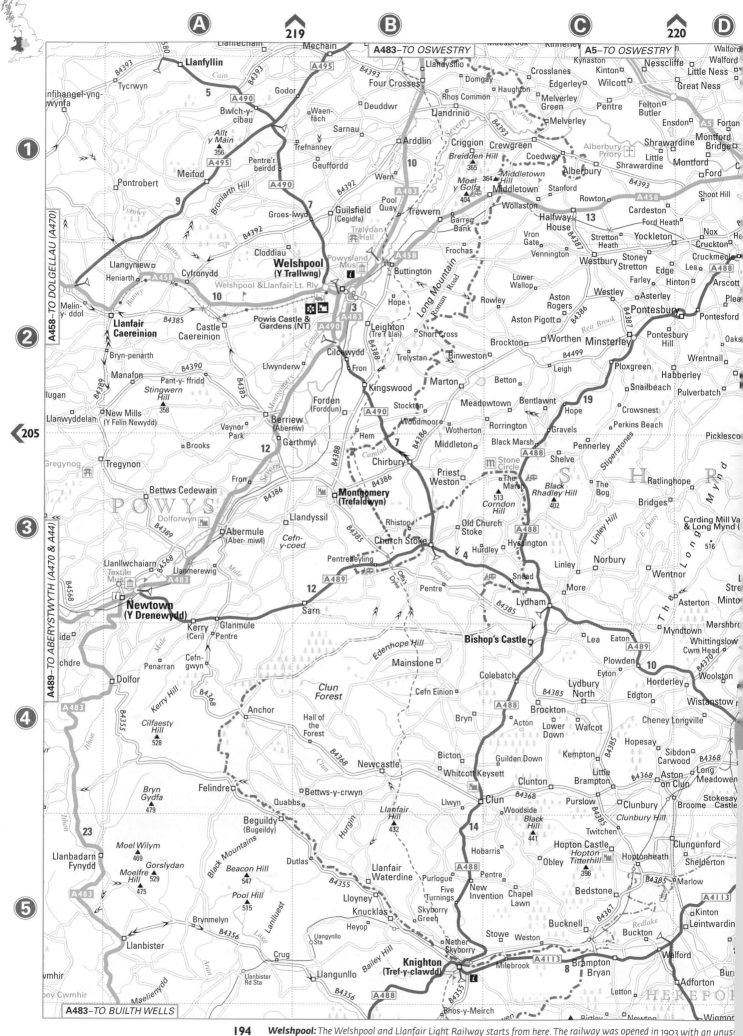

A483–TO OSWESTRY   **A5**–TO OSWESTRY

① ② ③ ④ ⑤

◄ 205

◄ 23

A458–TO DOLGELLAU (A470)

A489–TO ABERYSTWYTH (A470 & A44)

A483–TO BUILTH WELLS

Welshpool
(Y Trallwng)

Llanfair
Caereinion

Newtown
(Y Drenewydd)

Montgomery
(Trefaldwyn)

Bishop's Castle

Knighton
(Tref-y-clawdd)

Llanfyllin

Minsterley

Pontesbury

⬆ 194

⬇ 194

Welshpool: The Welshpool and Llanfair Light Railway starts from here. The railway was opened in 1903 with an unusu
gauge of 2 feet 6 inches to allow it to negotiate the tight curves and steep gradients. It officially closed in 1956 but wa
re-opened by a group of enthusiasts in 1963. It is remarkable for the miscellany of rolling stock which they have source
from different countries around the world. These include a Taiwan Sugar Corporation Locomotive, Romanian ballast
hopper wagons and other locomotives that have seen service in Antigua, Sierra Leone, Austria and Finland. *Map ref.*

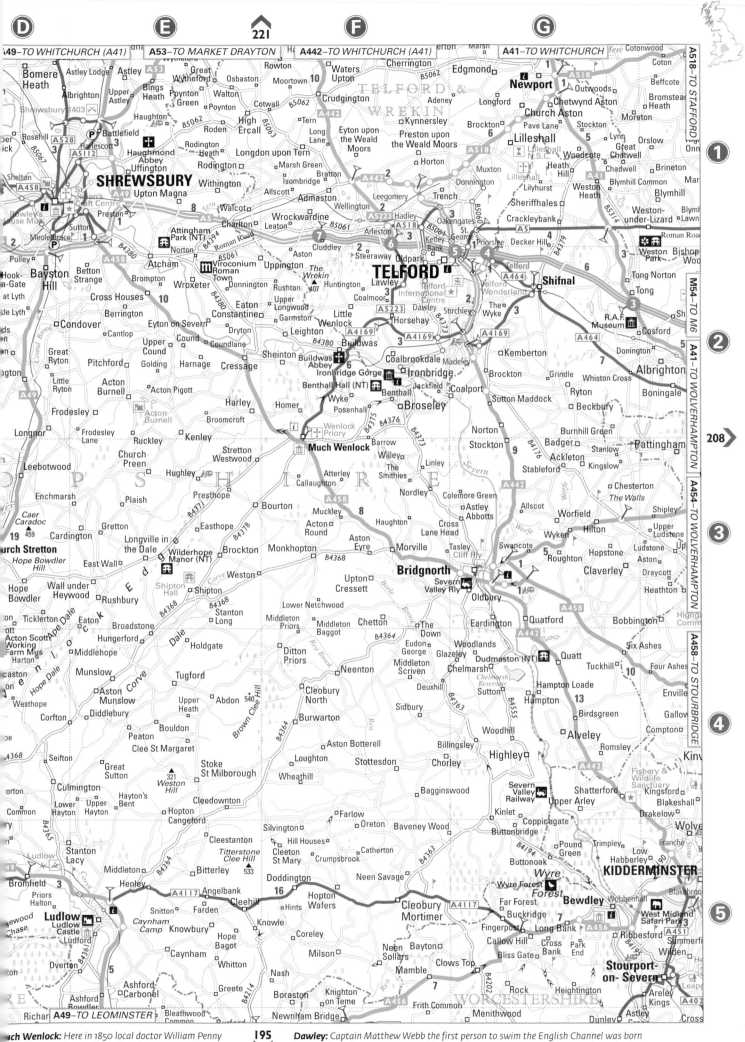

A49–TO WHITCHURCH (A41)   A53–TO MARKET DRAYTON   A442–TO WHITCHURCH (A41)   A41–TO WHITCHURCH

SHREWSBURY

TELFORD

Shifnal

Much Wenlock

Bridgnorth

Ludlow

KIDDERMINSTER

Bewdley

Stourport-on-Severn

A49–TO LEOMINSTER

Much Wenlock: Here in 1850 local doctor William Penny Brookes started the Wenlock Olympian Games, which inspired the modern revival of the Olympic Games. The games are still held annually. **Map ref. F2**

195

Dawley: Captain Matthew Webb the first person to swim the English Channel was born here on the 19th January 1848. Webb swam from Dover to Cap Gris Nez on the 24/25th August 1875 in 21 hours 45 minutes. In total he swam 38 miles (61km) to cover the 20 mile (32km) straight line distance. Webb died on the 24th July 1883 in an attempt to swim across the bottom of Niagara Falls. **Map ref. F2**

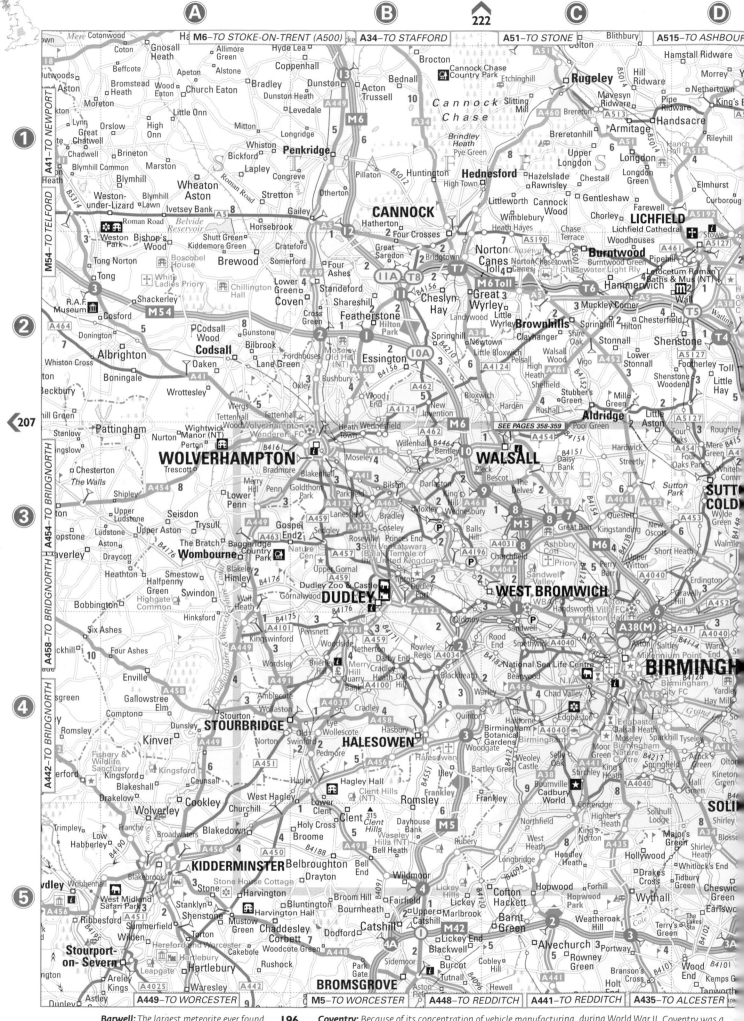

207

196

Barwell: The largest meteorite ever found in Britain, weighing almost 7 stone (44Kg), landed here on the 24th December 1965. **Map ref. G3**

Coventry: Because of its concentration of vehicle manufacturing, during World War II, Coventry was a major target for German air raids. On the night of the 14th November 1940 500 German bombers dropped 500 tons of explosives and 900 incendiary bombs on the city in less than 10 hours. The city, including the Cathedral was almost totally destroyed and many people were killed. In 1948 during major rebuilding work Coventry opened Europe's first ever traffic-free shopping precinct and in 1962 a new Cathedral was consecrated alongside the ruins of the old one. **Map ref. F5 Also on page 64**

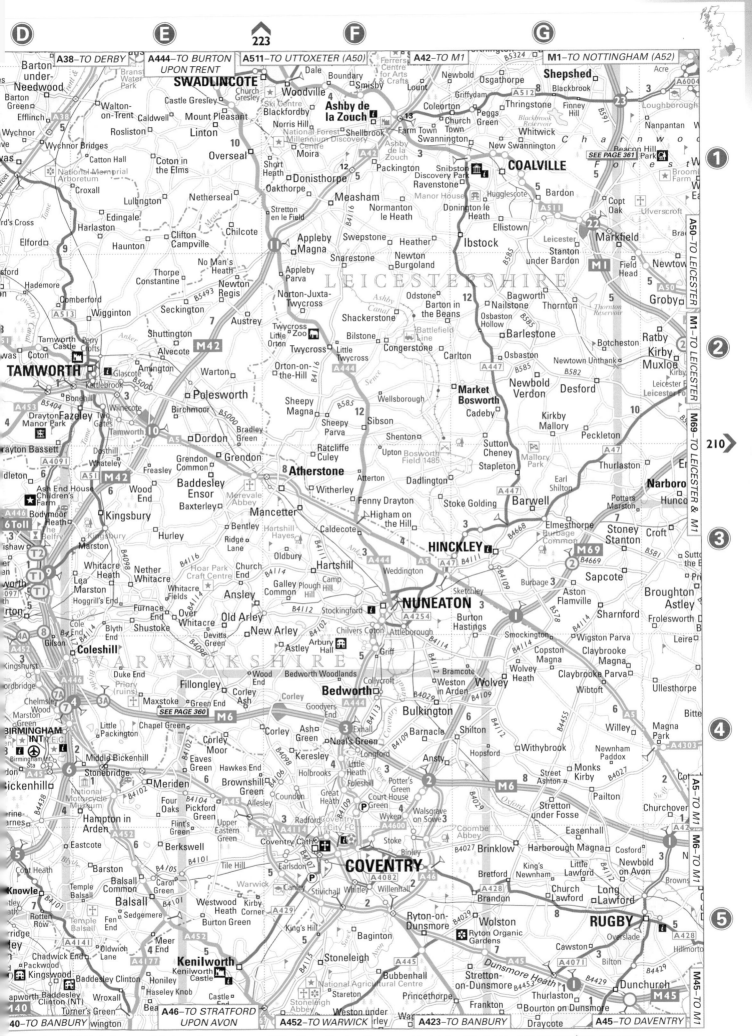

A38–TO DERBY   A444–TO BURTON UPON TRENT   A511–TO UTTOXETER (A50)   A42–TO M1   M1–TO NOTTINGHAM (A52)

SEE PAGE 361

A50–TO LEICESTER
M1–TO LEICESTER
M69–TO LEICESTER & M1
A5–TO M1
M6–TO M1
M45–TO M1

SWADLINCOTE

SHEPSHED

Ashby de la Zouch

COALVILLE

Markfield

LEICESTERSHIRE

TAMWORTH

Market Bosworth

Narboro

Atherstone

HINCKLEY

NUNEATON

WARWICKSHIRE

Coleshill

Bedworth

Wolvey

BIRMINGHAM INT

COVENTRY

RUGBY

Kenilworth

A46–TO STRATFORD UPON AVON   A452–TO WARWICK   A423–TO BANBURY   A45–TO DAVENTRY

A40–TO BANBURY

rlsdon: *Sir Frank Whittle, inventor of the jet engine was born here in 1907. The first jet aircraft to fly in Britain, a ster E28/39, made its maiden flight on the 15th May 1941 ed by Gerry Sayer the Gloster test pilot. Frank Whittle ved to the USA in 1976 and died at his home in Maryland the 8th August 1996. Map ref. F5*

197

Fenny Drayton: *The geographical centre of England is at Lindley Hall Farm, just 1.5km east of Fenny Drayton, OS Grid Reference SP 36373.66 96143.05. Traditionally however, the village of Meriden near Coventry (square E4) has always been considered the centre and an historic monument there marks the spot. The point furthest from the sea in the whole of Britain is actually near Coton in the Elms (square E1). Map ref. F3*

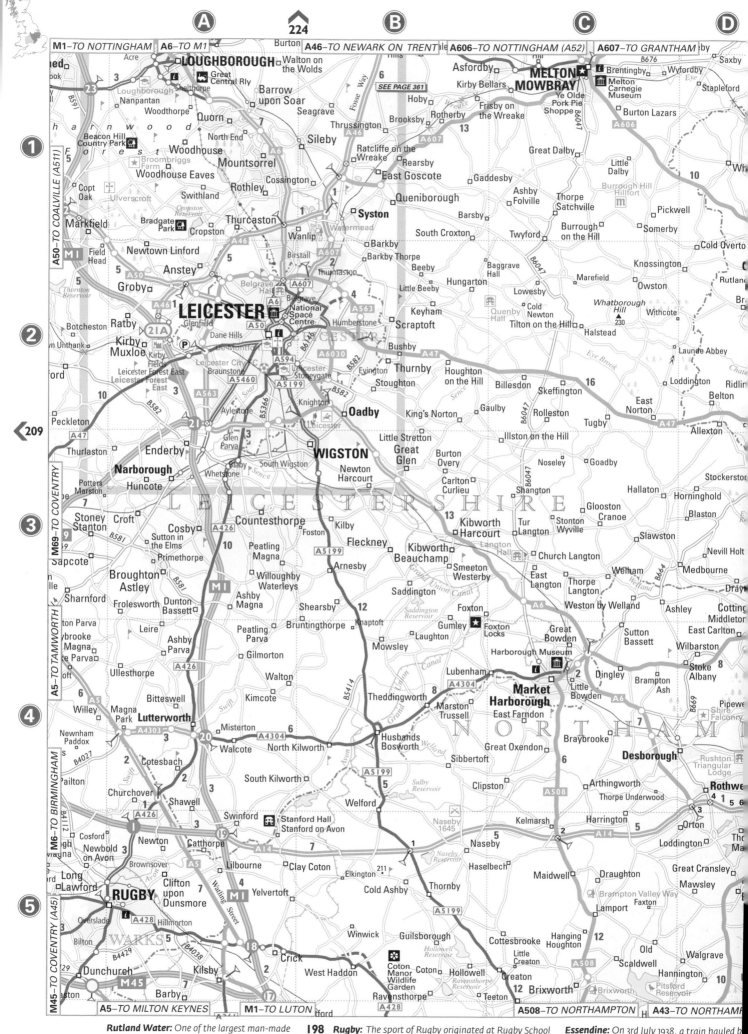

LOUGHBOROUGH

Burton on the Wolds

SEE PAGE 361

Asfordby   Brentingby   Wyfordby   Saxby

MELTON MOWBRAY

Kirby Bellars   Melton Carnegie Museum

Ye Olde Pork Pie Shoppe

Great Central Rly

Barrow upon Soar   Seagrave   Hoby   Rotherby   Frisby on the Wreake   Burton Lazars

Nanpantan   Woodthorpe   Quorn   Thrussington   Brooksby

Beacon Hill Country Park

Broombriggs Farm

Ratcliffe on the Wreake   Rearsby   Great Dalby

Woodhouse   North End   Gaddesby   Little Dalby

Copt Oak   Woodhouse Eaves   Cossington   **East Goscote**   Ashby Folville   Thorpe Satchville   Pickwell   Somerby

Ulverscroft   Rothley   Queniborough   Barsby   Burrough on the Hill

Markfield   Bradgate Park   Cropston Reservoir   Thurcaston   Wanlip   **Syston**   South Croxton   Twyford   Knossington   Owston

Cropston   Birstall   Baggrave Hall   Marefield

Field Head   Newtown Linford   Barkby   Hungarton   Cold Overton

Groby   Anstey   Belgrave Hall   Thurmaston   Barkby Thorpe   Beeby   Little Beeby   Lowesby

Botcheston   Ratby   Glenfield   **National Space Centre**   Keyham   Whatborough Hill 230   Withcote

LEICESTER   Dane Hills   Humberstone   **Scraptoft**   Quenby Hall   Cold Newton   Tilton on the Hill

Kirby Muxloe   De Montfort   Leicester Stoneygate   Bushby   Halstead   Launde Abbey

Leicester Fields   Braunstone   Evington   Thurnby   Houghton on the Hill   Billesdon   Skeffington

Leicester Forest East   Knighton   Stoughton   Gaulby   Rolleston   Tugby   East Norton   Loddington   Ridlington

Peckleton   Aylestone   **Oadby**   King's Norton   Illston on the Hill   Allexton   Belton

Thurlaston   Enderby   Glen Parva   Little Stretton   Burton Overy   Noseley   Goadby   Stockerston

Narborough   Whetstone   **WIGSTON**   Great Glen   Carlton Curlieu   Shangton   Hallaton   Horninghold

Huncote   South Wigston   Newton Harcourt   Glooston   Cranoe   Blaston

Potters Marston   Kibworth Harcourt   Tur Langton   Stonton Wyville   Slawston   Nevill Holt

Stoney Stanton   Croft   Countesthorpe   Kilby   Kibworth Beauchamp   Medbourne

Sapcote   Cosby   Foston   Fleckney   Church Langton   Welham   Drayton

Sutton in the Elms   Peatling Magna   Smeeton Westerby   East Langton   Ashley   Cotting Middleton

Broughton Astley   Primethorpe   Arnesby   Saddington   Thorpe Langton   East Carlton

Willoughby Waterleys   Saddington Reservoir   Weston by Welland   Wilbarston

Sharnford   Frolesworth   Dunton Bassett   Ashby Magna   Shearsby   Foxton   Sutton Bassett   Stoke Albany

Leire   Bruntingthorpe   Gumley   Foxton Locks   Great Bowden   Brampton Ash   Pipewell

Ashby Parva   Peatling Parva   Mowsley   Laughton   Harborough Museum   Dingley   Shire Falconry

Ullesthorpe   Gilmorton   Lubenham   Little Bowden

Bitteswell   Kimcote   Walton   Theddingworth   **Market Harborough**   Braybrooke

Magna Park   **Lutterworth**   Misterton   North Kilworth   Husbands Bosworth   Marston Trussell   East Farndon   Great Oxendon   **Desborough**

Newnham Paddox   Walcote   Sibbertoft   Rushton Triangular Lodge   **Rothwell**

Cotesbach   South Kilworth   Arthingworth   Thorpe Underwood

Churchover   Shawell   Welford   Clipston   Orton   Loddington

Swinford   Sulby Reservoir   Kelmarsh   Harrington

Newton   Catthorpe   Stanford Hall   Stanford on Avon   Naseby 1645   Naseby   Maidwell   Draughton   Great Cransley   Mawsley

Newbold on Avon   Lilbourne   Clay Coton   Elkington   Naseby Reservoir   Haselbech   Lamport   Brampton Valley Way

Long Lawford   Clifton upon Dunsmore   Yelvertoft   Cold Ashby   Thornby   Faxton

RUGBY   Hillmorton   Winwick   Guilsborough   Cottesbrooke   Hanging Houghton   Old   Walgrave

Overslade   Crick   Hollowell Reservoir   Little Creaton   Scaldwell   Hannington

Bilton   Dunchurch   Kilsby   West Haddon   Coton Manor Wildlife Garden   Hollowell   Creaton   Brixworth   Pitsford Reservoir

Barby   Ravensthorpe   Teeton   **Brixworth**

Rutland Water: One of the largest man-made reservoirs in Europe covering 3,100 acre (1,225ha). Completed in 1977 to supply 65 million gallons (300,000 cubic metres) of water per day to cities in the east Midlands. **Map ref. D2**

198

Rugby: The sport of Rugby originated at Rugby School in the 19th Century. It is reputed that during a football game in 1823, William Webb Ellis picked up the ball and ran with it. His name lives on through the Webb Ellis Trophy, that is presented to the winners of the Rugby World Cup. **Map ref. A5**

Essendine: On 3rd July 1938, a train hauled by Class A4 locomotive 'Mallard' here achieved the world rail record speed for steam traction of 126 mph (201km/h). **Map ref. F1**

A1–TO GRANTHAM (A52)   A15–TO LINCOLN   A16–TO BOSTON

LINCOLNSHIRE

Witham
Creeton
Red Hall
Eastgate
Twenty
Cuckoo Bridge
Deeping St Nich
mondham
Thistleton
Castle Bytham
Little Bytham
Lound
Northorpe
North Drove Drain
Deeping Fen
Market Overton
Clipsham
Careby
Toft
Thurlby
Deeping Common
Barrow
Stretton
Aunby
Witham on the Hill
Carlby
Manthorpe
Obthorpe
Thetford
Baston
Hop Pole
Ashwell
Greetham
Pickworth
Wilsthorpe
Braceborough
Langtoft
Crowland Common
Cottesmore
Essendine
Greatford
A16
Exton
RUTLAND
Ryhall
Barholm
Market Deeping
Crowla
Burley
Barnsdale Gardens
Great Casterton
Little Casterton
Belmesthorpe
Tallington Lakes Leisure Centre
Deeping Gate
Deeping St James
thorpe
Oakham Castle
Whitwell
Tickencote
Uffington
Northfields
West Deeping
Northborough
Borough Fen
Egleton
Empingham
Tinwell
Stamford
Tallington
Maxey
Peakirk Wildfowl Refuge
Upper Hambleton
Rutland Water
Burghley House
Bainton
Etton
Glinton
Peakirk
Newborou
Manton
Edith Weston
Ketton
Easton on the Hill
Pilsgate
Barnack
Ashton
Ufford
Helpston
Marholm
Werrington
Walton
Dogsthorpe
Lyndon
North Luffenham
Southorpe
Upton
Wing
Collyweston
Wittering
Thornhaugh
PETERBOROUGH
New England
Newark
Glaston
South Luffenham
Morcott
Tixover
Duddington
Wansford
Ailsworth
Peterborough Cathedral
Peterborough Museum & Art Gall
Barrowden
Wakerley
King's Cliffe
Stibbington
Sutton
Castor
Longthorpe
Flag Ag
Bisbrooke
Shotley
Yarwell
Nene Valley Rly
Peterbor Green
Seaton
Harringworth
Laxton
Water Newton
Ferry Meadows
Orton Longueville
Old Fletton
Lyddington Bede House
Thorpe by Water
Blatherwycke
Apethorpe
Nassington
Chesterton
Orton Waterville
Stanground
Farcet
Caldecott
Gretton
Bulwick
Woodnewton
Fotheringhay
Alwalton
Hampton
Rockingham
Deene
Deenethorpe
Southwick
Elton
Elton Hall
Haddon
Big Sky Adventure Play
Farcet Fen
Rockingham Motor Speedway
Kirby Hall
Deene Hall
Glapthorn
Tansor
Eaglethorpe
Warmington
Morborne
Yaxley
Whittlesey Mere
CORBY
Weldon
Upper Benefield
Lower Benefield
Oundle
Cotterstock
Ashton
Folksworth
Stilton
Holme
Stanion
Brigstock
Lyveden New Bield (NT)
Barnwell
Polebrook
Lutton
Caldecote
Denton
Great Oakley
Little Oakley
Brigstock
Pilton
Stoke Doyle
Armston
Glatton
Conington
Geddington
Cross
Sudborough
Lilford Park
Wadenhoe
Hemington
Barnwell St Andrew
Barnwell All Saints
Luddington in the Brook
Sawtry
Church End
Woodwalton
Boughton House
Aldwincle
Achurch
Wigsthorpe
Thurning
Great Gidding
Little Gidding
Weekley
Warkton
Grafton Underwood
Lowick
Thorpe Waterville
Clopton
Winwick
Steeple Gidding
Coppingford
KETTERING
Slipton
Islip
Titchmarsh
Hamerton
Hamerton Zoo Park
Upton
Alconbury Hill
Abbots Ripton
Barton Seagrave
Twywell
Thrapston
CAMBS
Alconbury Weston
Cranford St Andrew
Cranford St John
Denford
Old Weston
Buckworth
Alconbury
Little Stukeley
Wicksteed Park
Woodford
Molesworth
Brington
Great Stukeley
Burton Latimer
Great Addington
Ringstead
Keyston
Bythorn
Barham
Leighton Bromswold
Woolley
Isham
Little Addington
Catworth
Wenni
Finedon
Raunds
Little Catworth
Spaldwick
Easton
Ellington
Great
Irthlingborough
Stanwick
Hargrave
Covington
Stow Longa
Ellington Thorpe
Brampton

INGBOROUGH   A45–TO NORTHAMPTON   A6–TO BEDFORD   A1–TO STEVENAGE (A1(M))

Stamford: *The film of George Eliot's classic novel Middlemarch, released in 1994, was made on location around Stamford.* **Map ref. F2**

199

Seaton and Harringworth: *The largest brick-built railway viaduct in Britain crosses the River Welland between these two villages. Built in 1875, of 20 million bricks, it stands 69 feet (21m) high, is 3,750 feet (1,143m) long and has 82 arches. The viaduct is no longer used by mainline passenger trains.* **Map ref. E3**

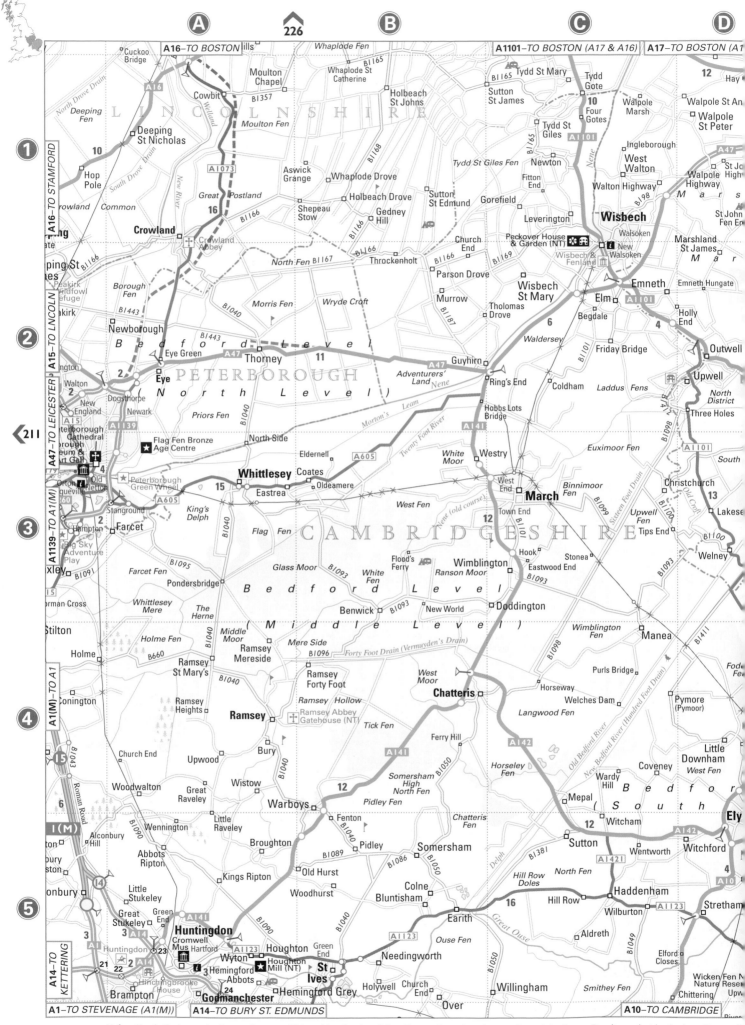

A16–TO BOSTON   A1101–TO BOSTON (A17 & A16)   A17–TO BOSTON (A1

1

Cuckoo Bridge
North Drove Drain
Deeping Fen
L I N C O L N S H I R E
Deeping St Nicholas
Hop Pole
Great Postland
Crowland Common
South Drove Drain
New River
A16
A1073
Cowbit
B1357
Moulton Fen
Moulton Chapel
Whaplode Fen
Whaplode St Catherine
B1165
Holbeach St Johns
B1165
Tydd St Mary
Tydd Gote
Sutton St James
A1101
Ingleborough
Walpole Marsh
Four Gotes
10
Walpole St An
Walpole St Peter
A47
Aswick Grange
Whaplode Drove
Holbeach Drove
Shepeau Stow
Gedney Hill
B1166
Sutton St Edmund
B1168
Tydd St Giles Fen
Tydd St Giles
Newton
West Walton
Walton Highway
B198
Walpole Highway
16
10
12

Crowland
Crowland Abbey
B1166
Throckenholt
North Fen B1167
B1166
Church End
Gorefield
Leverington
B1169
Parson Drove
Murrow
B1166
Wisbech
Peckover House & Garden (NT)
Wisbech & Fenland
Walsoken
New Walsoken
Emneth
Emneth Hungate
St John
Fen End
M a r s
Marshland St James
M a r

2

A15–TO LINCOLN
A47–TO LEICESTER
Peakirk Wildfowl Refuge
Newborough
B1443
Borough Fen
B1443
Eye Green
Thorney
A47
Morris Fen
Wryde Croft
B1040
Wisbech St Mary
Walderley
Tholomas Drove
B1187
6
Begdale
Elm
Friday Bridge
B1101
Holly End
4
Outwell
Upwell

Walton
New England
Dogsthorpe
Newark
A1139
Eye
P E T E R B O R O U G H
(N o r t h L e v e l)
Priors Fen
North Side
Guyhirn
Adventurers' Land
Nene
Ring's End
Coldham
Laddus Fens
A1101
North District
Three Holes
Euximoor Fen
B1098
South
B1101
2

211

A47–TO LEICESTER
Peterborough Cathedral
Museum & Art Gall
Old Fletton
Orton gueville
A15
A1139
Flag Fen Bronze Age Centre
Peterborough Green Wheel
A605
Whittlesey
Eastrea
Coates
Oldeamere
Eldernell
A605
Morton's Leam
Twenty Foot River
White Moor
Westry
West End
March
Binnimoor Fen
Upwell Fen
A1101
Tips End
Christchurch
Lakese
13

3

A1139–TO A1(M)
Stanground
Farcet
Hampton
Big Sky Adventure Play
King's Delph
Flag Fen
C A M B R I D G E S H I R E
West Fen
Nene (old course)
Town End
Hook
12
Stonea
Eastwood End
B1099
B1093
Welney
B1100
B1100

xley
B1091
Farcet Fen
B1095
Pondersbridge
Glass Moor
B1093
White Fen
Flood's Ferry
Wimblington
Ranson Moor
B1093
Doddington
Wimblington Fen
Manea
B1411
Fod
Fe

Norman Cross
Whittlesey Mere
The Herne
B1040
Middle Moor
Ramsey Mereside
Mere Side
Benwick
B1093
New World
B e d f o r d L e v e l
(M i d d l e L e v e l)
B1098
Purls Bridge
Horseway
Welches Dam
Langwood Fen
Pymore (Pymoor)

4

A1(M)–TO A1
Stilton
Holme
Holme Fen
B660
Ramsey St Mary's
B1040
Ramsey Forty Foot
Ramsey Hollow
Forty Foot Drain (Vermuyden's Drain)
B1096
West Moor
Chatteris
Ferry Hill
A141
A142
Horseley Fen
Old Bedford River (Hundred Foot Drain)
New Bedford River (Hundred Foot Drain)
Wardy Hill
Coveney
West Fen
B e d f o r
(S o u t h
Little Downham

Conington
15
B1043
Roman Road
Ramsey Heights
Ramsey
Bury
Upwood
Wistow
Ramsey Abbey Gatehouse (NT)
Tick Fen
B1040
A141
Somersham High North Fen
B1050
Chatteris Fen
Pidley Fen
Mepal
12
Witcham
Ely
Little Downham

1(M)

6
14
Alconbury Hill
B1090
Woodwalton
Great Raveley
Warboys
12
Fenton
Pidley
Somersham
B1050
Witcham
A142
Witchford
4
A10

5

A1(M)–TO KETTERING
A14–TO KETTERING
onbury
Little Stukeley
Wennington
Little Raveley
Broughton
Old Hurst
Woodhurst
B1089
Pidley
B1086
Colne
Bluntisham
Somersham
Hill Row Doles
North Fen
Hill Row
A1421
Sutton
Wentworth
Haddenham
Wilburton
A1123
Stretha

Great Stukeley
Green End
A141
Huntingdon
Cromwell Mus
Hartford
Wyton
Houghton Mill (NT)
Houghton
Green End
St Ives
Needingworth
Ouse Fen
A1123
Earith
Great Ouse
B1050
Aldreth
Elford Closes
A1049

A1–TO STEVENAGE (A1(M))
21 22 24 23
Hemingford Abbots
Hinchingbrooke House
Brampton
Godmanchester
Hemingford Grey
Holywell
Church End
Over
A14–TO BURY ST EDMUNDS
Willingham
Smithey Fen
Chittering
Wicken Fen Nature Rese
Upw
A10–TO CAMBRIDGE

Holme Fen is the lowest land area of Britain. It is 9 feet (2.75m) below sea level. *Map ref. A4*

 200

Huntingdon: Oliver Cromwell was born here on the 25th April 1599. Despite modest beginnings, Cromwell became Lord Protector when Great Britain became a Commonwealth following the execution of Charles I in 1649. In 1657 he was offered the crown of England but refused it. He died on the 3rd September 1658 and was granted a state funeral. With the restoration of Charles II to the throne in 1660 Cromwell was discredited and on the 30th January 1661 his body was exhumed and he was symbolically executed and reburied at Tyburn. *Map ref. A5*   **See page 78 for Cromwell Museum**

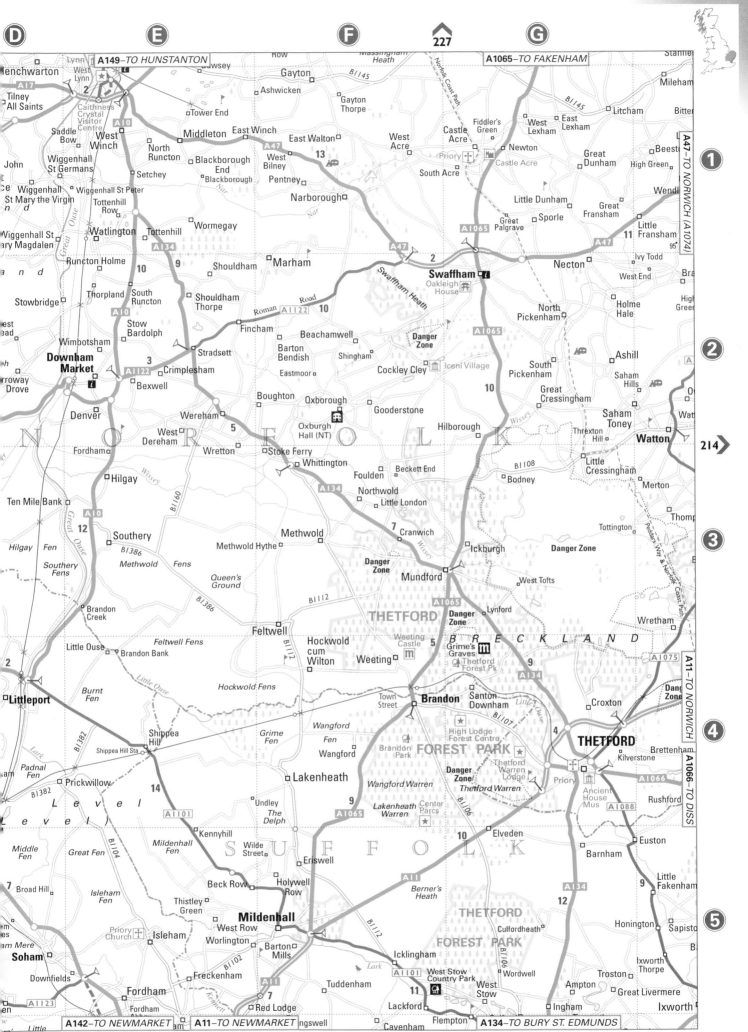

Mildenhall : RAF Mildenhall officially opened in 1934 and just days later became the starting point for what is still known as the 'greatest air race in the world'. 20 aircraft from 7 different countries competed in the Royal Aero Club race to Melbourne, Australia. The winners, Charles Scott and Thomas Black, flying a De Havilland DH88 Comet, completed the flight in 2 days 23 hours. **Map ref. F5**

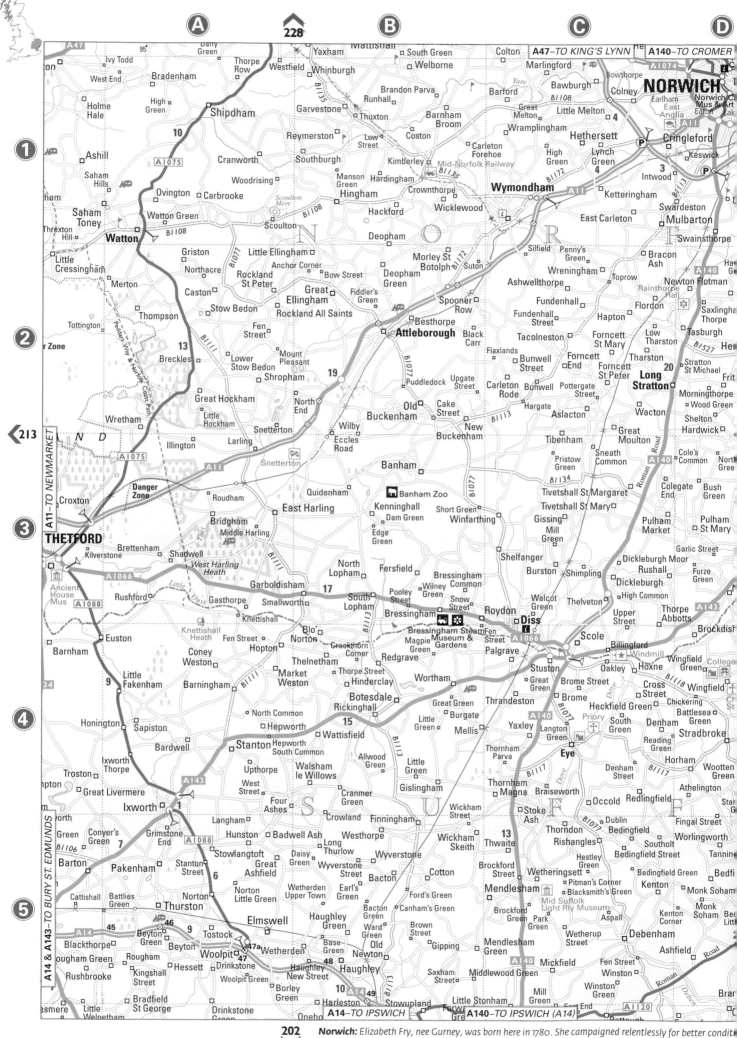

A47—TO KING'S LYNN   A140—TO CROMER

NORWICH

1

◄ 213

2

3

THETFORD

4

5

A14—TO IPSWICH   A140—TO IPSWICH (A14)

Norwich: Elizabeth Fry, nee Gurney, was born here in 1780. She campaigned relentlessly for better conditions for prisoners, particularly women prisoners. In 1840 she founded the Institute of Nursing Sisters to train nurses to care for poor people in their own homes. Elizabeth Fry died in 1845. **Map ref. D1**

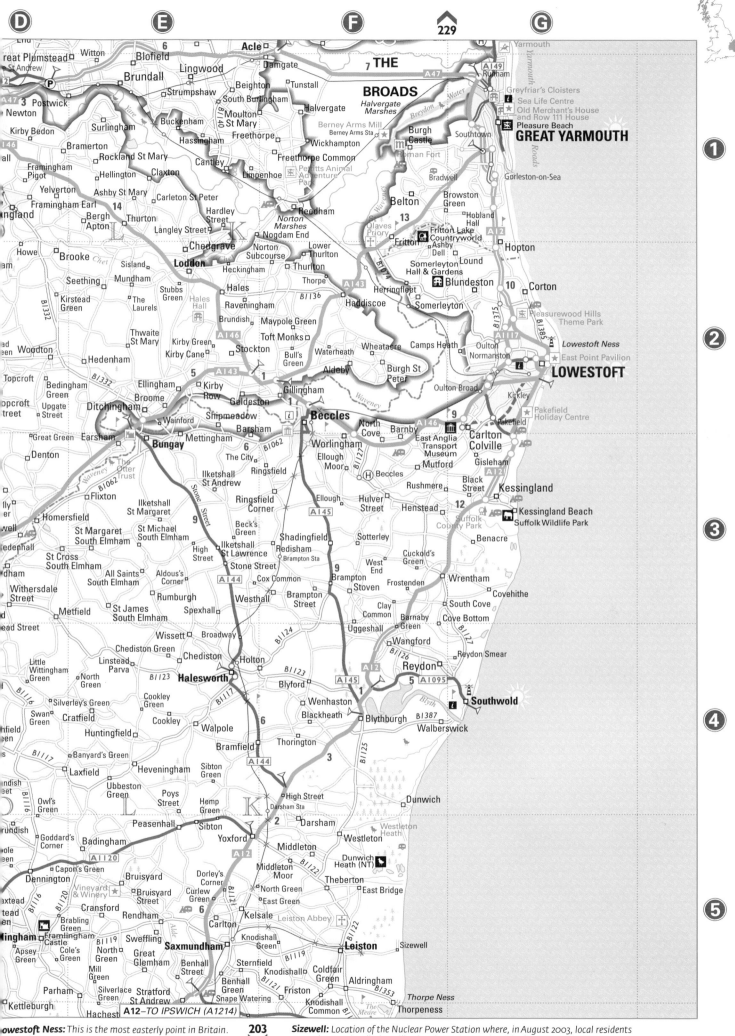

1

7 THE

BROADS

Yarmouth
Rollham

Greyfriar's Cloisters
Sea Life Centre
Old Merchant's House
and Row 111 House
Pleasure Beach

GREAT YARMOUTH

Witton
Blofield
Acle
Damgate
Lingwood
reat Plumstead
St Andrew
Brundall
Beighton
Tunstall
Strumpshaw
South Burlingham
Halvergate
Halvergate Marshes
Moulton St Mary
Freethorpe
Berney Arms Mill
Berney Arms Sta
Burgh Castle
Southtown
Gorleston-on-Sea
Bradwell

Postwick
Newton
Surlingham
Buckenham
Hassingham
Freethorpe Common
Roman Fort
Kirby Bedon
Bramerton
Rockland St Mary
Cantley
Wickhampton
Belton
Browston Green
Framingham Pigot
Hellington
Claxton
Limpenhoe
Pettitts Animal Adventure Park
Hobland Hall
Yelverton
Ashby St Mary
Carleton St Peter
Reedham
Olaves Priory
Fritton Lake Countryworld
Hopton
Framingham Earl
Bergh Apton
Thurton
Hardley Street
Norton Marshes
Fritton
Ashby Dell
Somerleyton Hall & Gardens
Lound
Corton
Brooke
Langley Street
Nogdam End
Lower Thurlton
Blundeston
Somerleyton
Pleasurewood Hills Theme Park
Chedgrave
Norton Subcourse
Thurlton
Herringfleet
Seething
Mundham
Heckingham
Thorpe
Haddiscoe
Lowestoft Ness
East Point Pavilion
Kirstead Green
Stubbs Green
Hales
Camps Heath
Oulton
Normanston
LOWESTOFT
The Laurels
Raveningham
Herringfleet
Burgh St Peter
Kirkley
Hedenham
Brundish
Maypole Green
Aldeby
Oulton Broad
Pakefield Holiday Centre
Topcroft
Bedingham Green
Thwaite St Mary
Toft Monks
Waterheath
Wheatacre
Pakefield
Woodton
Kirby Green
Stockton
Bull's Green
Gillingham
North Cove
Barnby
East Anglia Transport Museum
Carlton Colville
Ellingham
Kirby Cane
Geldeston
Beccles
Worlingham
Gisleham
Broome
Shipmeadow
Ellough Moor
Mutford
Ditchingham
Wainford
Barsham
Beccles
Rushmere
Black Street
Kessingland
Great Green
Mettingham
The City
Ringsfield
Ellough
Henstead
Suffolk County Park
Kessingland Beach
Suffolk Wildlife Park
Denton
Bungay
Ilketshall St Andrew
Ringsfield Corner
Hulver Street
Earsham
The Otter Trust
Flixton
Ilketshall St Margaret
Beck's Green
Shadingfield
Sotterley
Cuckold's Green
Benacre
Homersfield
St Michael South Elmham
High Street
Ilketshall St Lawrence
Redisham
Brampton Sta
West End
Frostenden
St Margaret South Elmham
Stone Street
Brampton
Stoven
Wrentham
Covehithe
St Cross South Elmham
All Saints South Elmham
Aldous's Corner
Cox Common
Clay Common
South Cove
Withersdale Street
Rumburgh
Westhall
Brampton Street
Barnaby Green
Cove Bottom
Metfield
St James South Elmham
Spexhall
Uggeshall
Wangford
Reydon Smear
Wissett
Broadway
Reydon
Little Wittingham Green
Linstead Parva
Chediston Green
Chediston
Holton
Blyth
Southwold
North Green
Halesworth
Blyford
Wenhaston
Blythburgh
Walberswick
Silverley's Green
Cookley Green
Blackheath
Swan Green
Cratfield
Cookley
Walpole
Thorington
Dunwich
Huntingfield
Bramfield
Banyard's Green
Laxfield
Heveningham
Sibton Green
Owl's Green
Ubbeston Green
Poys Street
High Street
Darsham Sta
Peasenhall
Sibton
Darsham
Westleton Heath
Westleton
Dunwich Heath (NT)
Goddard's Corner
Badingham
Yoxford
Middleton
Capon's Green
Bruisyard
Dorley's Corner
Middleton Moor
Theberton
East Bridge
Dennington
Bruisyard Street
Curlew Green
North Green
Cransford
Rendham
East Green
Leiston Abbey
Brabling Green
Kelsale
ingham
Framlingham Castle
Carlton
Sizewell
Apsey Green
Cole's Green
Sweffling
Saxmundham
Knodishall Green
Leiston
Sizewell
Mill Green
North Green
Great Glemham
Benhall Green
Knodishall
Coldfair Green
Aldringham
Parham
Silverlace Green
Stratford St Andrew
Benhall Street
Snape Watering
Friston
Thorpe Ness
Kettleburgh
Hachest
A12–TO IPSWICH (A1214)
Knodishall Common
The Meare
Thorpeness

Lowestoft Ness: This is the most easterly point in Britain.
Map ref. G2

Sizewell: Location of the Nuclear Power Station where, in August 2003, local residents were given anti-radiation pills aimed at reducing the risk of cancer in the thyroid.
Map ref. F5

Map labels

A **B** **230** **C** **D**

1 **2** **3** **4** **5**

Bethel
Trefdraeth
Aberffraw
Llangadwaladr
Hermon
Malltraeth
A4080
Aberffraw Bay
Bodorgan
Malltraeth Sands
ANG
Newborough
(Niwbwrch)
Malltraeth
Bay
Newborough
Warren
Llanddwyn
Island
Llanddwyn
Bay
Abermenai Po
The Bar

C A E R N A R F O N

B A Y

Dinas Dinll
Lla

Pontllyfni
Trwyn Maen Dylan
Aberdesach
Tai'n
Clynnog- fawr
Cap
10
Gyrn Goch
Bwlch
Mawr
Gyrn Ddu
509
G
Trefor
522
Trwyn y
Gorlech
Yr Eifl
llanaelhaearn
564
A499
Cefn-caer-
B4417
6
Llithfaen
Ferch
Carreg Ddu
7
Cy
Porth
Pistyll
Pencaenewydd
Dinllaen
Llwyndyrys
Llangybi
Morfa Nefyn
Nefyn
B4354
Fron
B4354
Lla
Groesffordd
Edern
Garn
PENINSULA
Y Ffôr
Boduan
Rhos-
Porth Ysgaden
Tan-y-graig
fawr
Pena
Rhos-y-llan
Ceidio
Hendre
Bodfuan
Medi
Fawr
Llannor
Tudweiliog
Dinas
LLEYN PEN
Efailnewydd
Denio
Abererch
Carn Fadryn
371
Penllech
Garnfadryn
B4415
A497
Porth Colmon
Bryn-
Rhyd-y-clafdy
Pen-y-Graig
Llaniestyn
Pwllheli
mawr
Porth Colmon
Carreg yr Imbill
Llangwnnadl
Penrhos
Sarn Meyllteyrn
7
Penrhyn
Rhedyn
Y Gamlas
Mawr
Bryncroes
Ty-
Nanhoron
B4413
hen
Botwnnog
Llanbedrog
Methlem
Llandegwning
B4413
Mynytho
Trwyn Llanbedrog
Porth
Rhydlios
A499
Oer
Mynydd Rhiw
Llangian
Capel Carmel
Rhoshirwaun
305
Plas-yn-
Abersoch
Braich Anelog
Rhiw
Rhiw (NT)
St
Llawr-y-dref
Tudwal's
Anelog
Road
Mynydd Anelog
Rhydolion
Llanengan
191
Llanfaelrhys
Sarn Bach
Bwlchtocyn
Pwlldefaid
Aberdaron
St Tudwal's
Braich y Pwll
Aberdaron
Islands
Bay
Ynys Gwylan-fawr
Porth Neigwl
Trwyn yr Wylfa
Uwchmynydd
(Hell's Mouth)
Porth
Pen y Cil
Cilan Uchaf
Ceiriad
Bardsey Sound (Swnt Enlli)
Trwyn Cilan
St Mary's Abbey
Bardsey Island
(Ynys Enlli)

Bardsey Island (Ynys Enlli): *A place of pilgrimage and centre of the Celtic church from the 6th century where according to legend 20,000 saints are buried. Particularly noted for its wildlife, it is home to a large breeding colony of up to 16,000 Manx Shearwater.* **Map ref. A5**

Llanystumdwy: *Although born in Manchester where his father was a schoolteacher, David Lloyd George was brought up here in Llanystumdwy. served as Prime Minister from 1916–22 and has been credited with the introduction of the Welfare State.* **Map ref.D4**

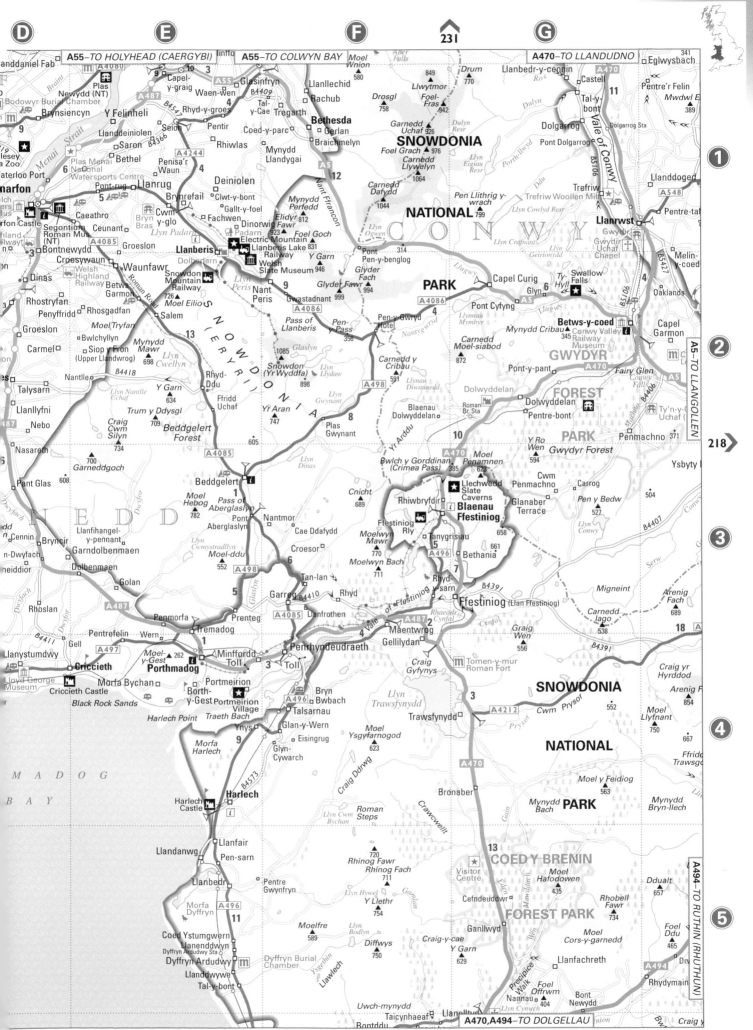

A55–TO HOLYHEAD (CAERGYBI)

A55–TO COLWYN BAY

A470–TO LLANDUDNO

A5–TO LLANGOLLEN

A494–TO RUTHIN (RHUTHUN)

A470,A494–TO DOLGELLAU

Plas Newydd (NT)

Bodowyr Burial Chamber

Brynsiencyn

Y Felinheli

Anglesey Sea Zoo

Waterloo Port

Caernarfon

Segontium Roman Mus

Bontnewydd

Croesywaun

Dinas

Rhostryfan

Penyffridd

Groeslon

Carmel

Talysarn

Llanllyfni

Nebo

Nasareth

Pant Glas

Bryncir

Garndolbenmaen

Dolbenmaen

Golan

Rhoslan

Llanystumdwy

Lloyd George Museum

Criccieth

Criccieth Castle

Morfa Bychan

Black Rock Sands

Porthmadog

Moel-y-Gest 262

Borth-y-Gest

Portmeirion

Portmeirion Village

Harlech Point

Tremadog

Wern

Penmorfa

Prenteg

Minffordd Toll

Toll

Bryn Bwbach

Talsarnau

Glan-y-Wern

Traeth Bach

Ynys

Morfa Harlech

Glyn-Cywarch

Eisingrug

Harlech

Harlech Castle

Llanfair

Pen-sarn

Llandanwg

Llanbedr

Pentre Gwynfryn

Morfa Dyffryn

Coed Ystumgwern

Llanenddwyn

Dyffryn Ardudwy

Llanddwywe

Tal-y-bont

Dyffryn Burial Chamber

Capel-y-graig

Waen-wen

Rhyd-y-groes

Pentir

Rhiwlas

Seion

Llanddeiniolen

Saron

Bethel

Penisa'r Waun

Llanrug

Brynrefail

Clwt-y-bont

Gallt-y-foel

Fachwen

Cwm-y-glo

Llanberis

Dolbadarn

Snowdon Mountain Railway

Moel Eilio 726

Salem

Waunfawr

Betws Garmon

Rhosgadfan

Moel Tryfan

Bwlchyllyn

Siop y Fron (Upper Llandwrog)

Y Garn 634

Mynydd Mawr 698

Trum y Ddysgl 709

Craig Cwm Silyn 734

Garneddgoch 700

Moel Hebog 782

Beddgelert

Pass of Aberglaslyn

Pont Aberglaslyn

Nantmor

Cae Ddafydd

Moel-ddu 552

Croesor

Tan-lan

Garreg

Rhyd

Llanfrothen

Llyn Cwmystradllyn

Pen-y-Cae Tregarth

Rachub

Gerlan

Braichmelyn

Bethesda

Coed-y-parc

Mynydd Llandygai

Deiniolen

Dinorwig

Padarn

Electric Mountain

Llanberis Lake Railway

Welsh Slate Museum

Nant Peris

Gwastadnant

Pass of Llanberis

Pen-y-Pass

Mynydd Perfedd

Elidyr Fawr 923

Foel Goch 831

Y Garn 946

Glyder Fawr 999

Glyder Fach

Snowdon (Yr Wyddfa) 898

Glaslyn

Llyn Llydaw

Yr Aran 747

Plas Gwynant

Yr Arddu

Llyn Dinas

Cnicht 689

Rhiwbryfdir

Ffestiniog Rly

Moelwyn Mawr 770

Moelwyn Bach 711

Llechwedd Slate Caverns

Blaenau Ffestiniog

Tanygrisiau

Bethania

Rhyd-y-sarn

Maentwrog

Gellilydan

Penrhyndeudraeth

Vale of Ffestiniog

Ffestiniog (Llan Ffestiniog)

Rhaeadr Cynfal

Craig Gyfynys

Tomen-y-mur Roman Fort

Trawsfynydd

Llyn Trawsfynydd

Bronaber

Moel Ysgyfarnogod 623

Craig Ddrwg

Roman Steps

Llyn Cwm Bychan

Rhinog Fawr 720

Rhinog Fach 711

Y Llethr 754

Llyn Hywel

Moelfre 589

Llyn Bodlyn

Diffwys 750

Craig-y-cae

Y Garn 629

Ysgethin

Llawlech

Moel Cors-y-garnedd

Llanfachreth

Precipice Walk

Foel Offrwm 404

Nannau

Bont Newydd

Uwch-mynydd

Taicynhaeaf

Bontddu

SNOWDONIA

Foel Grach 976

Carnedd Llywelyn 1064

Carnedd Dafydd 1044

Pen Llithrig y-wrach 799

NATIONAL

Llyn Ogwen

Pont Pen-y-benglog 314

Pen-y-Gwryd 356

Pen-y-Gwryd Hotel

Carnedd y Cribau 591

Carnedd Moel-siabod 872

Llynnau Mymbyr

Capel Curig

Pont Cyfyng

Glyn

Swallow Falls

Ty-Hyll

Betws-y-coed

Mynydd Cribau 345

Conwy Valley Railway Museum

Pont-y-pant

Dolwyddelan

Pentre-bont

Roman Br Sta

Y Ro Wen

Moel Penamnen 594

Bwlch y Gorddinan (Crimea Pass) 385

Moel 623

Cwm Penmachno

Glanaber Terrace

Carrog

Pen y Bedw 527

Penmachno 371

Gwydyr Forest

Migneint

Arenig Fach 689

Carnedd Iago 538

Graig Wen 556

Arenig Fawr 854

Craig yr Hyrddod

Moel Llyfnant 750

Cwm Prysor

Prysor

Moel y Feidiog 563

Mynydd Bach

Mynydd Bryn-llech

Moel Hafodowen 435

Rhobell Fawr 734

Dduallt 657

Foel Ddu 465

Cefndeuddwr

Ganllwyd

PARK

GWYDYR

FOREST

PARK

SNOWDONIA

NATIONAL

PARK

COED Y BRENIN

Visitor Centre 13

FOREST PARK

CONWY

Aber Falls

Drosgl 758

Llwytmor

Foel-Fras 942

Garnedd Uchaf 926

Drum 770

Dolgarrog

Pont Dolgarrog

Dolgarrog Sta

Llyn Eigiau Resr

Llyn Cowlyd Resr

Llyn Crafnant

Llyn Geirionydd

Gwydyr Uchaf Chapel

Trefriw

Trefriw Woollen Mill

Llanrwst

Pentre-taf

Llanddoged

Oaklands

Capel Garmon

Melin-y-coed

Fairy Glen

Conwy Falls

Ty'n-y-groes Uchaf

Penmachno

Ysbyty

Moel Wnion 580

Llanllechid

Glasinfryn

Llanfairfechan

Llandaniel Fab

National Watersports Centre

Vale of Conwy

Castell

Tal-y-bont

Mwdwl E 389

Pentre'r Felin

Eglwysbach

204
↓

Snowdon: At 3,560 feet (1085 metres) Snowdon is the highest mountain in England and Wales.
It is possible to ascend the north-western side of Snowdon on the Snowdon Mountain Railway.
This passenger railway opened on the 6th April 1896 but an accident on the first day led to its
closure for the next year. The service reopened in April 1897 and has operated safely ever since.
Map ref. F2 Also on page 14

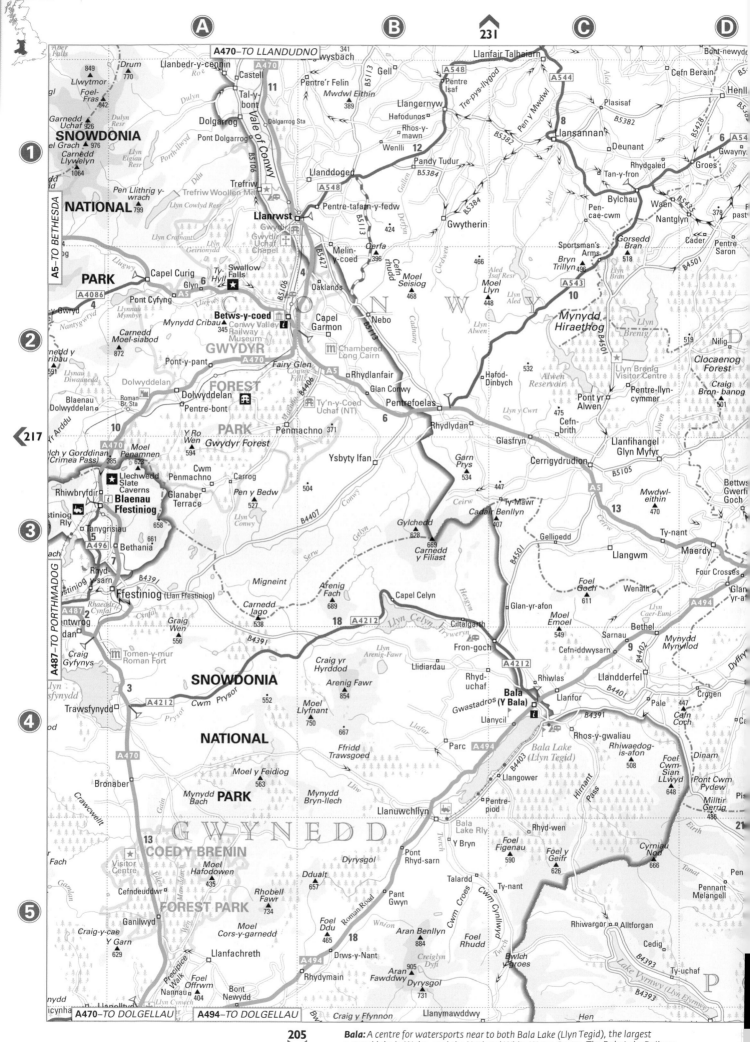

Bala: A centre for watersports near to both Bala Lake (Llyn Tegid), the largest natural lake in Wales, and the National White Water Centre. The Bala Lake Railway runs along the south-eastern shoreline of the lake. **Map ref. C4**

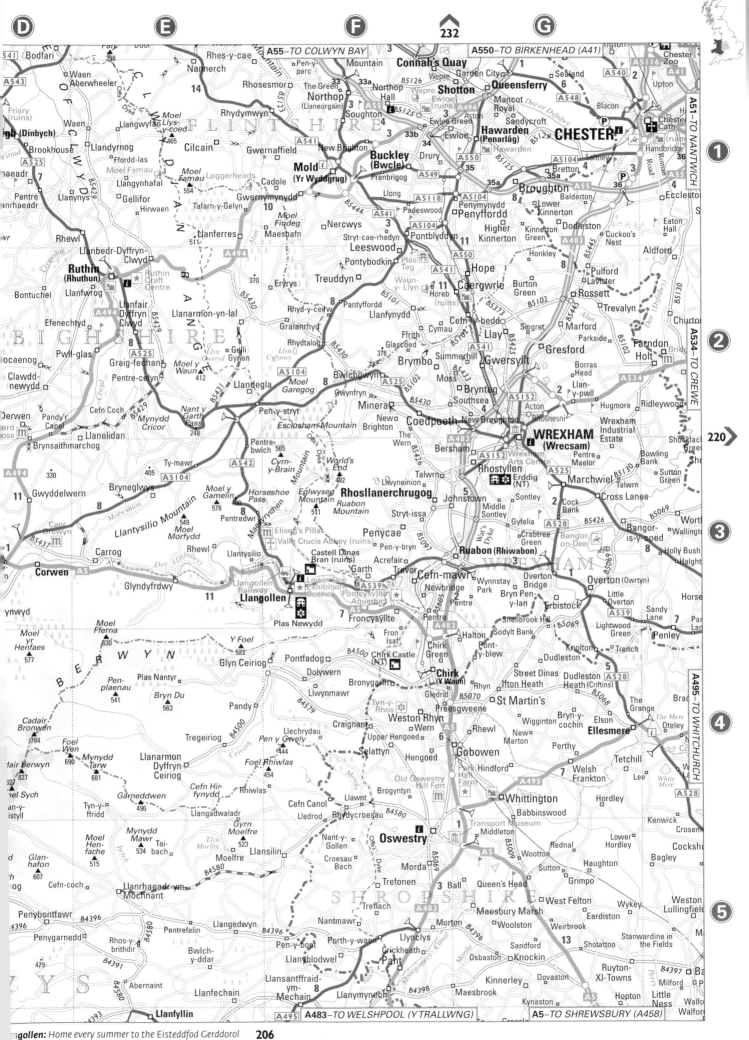

A55–TO COLWYN BAY   A550–TO BIRKENHEAD (A41)

A51–TO NANTWICH

1

Bodfari
Waen Aberwheeler
Nannerch
Rhes-y-cae
Pen-y-parc
Mountain
Connah's Quay
Garden City
Wepre
Sealand
Chester Zoo
Upton
Chester Cath

Friary (ruins)
Brookhouse
Llandyrnog
Ffordd-las
Cilcain
Rhydymwyn
Gwernaffield
New Brighton
Northop
(Llaneurgain)
Soughton
Ewloe Green
Mancot Royal
Sandycroft
Aston
Blacon
CHESTER
Handbridge
Roman (ruins)

FLINTSHIRE

Pentre
Llanynys
Gellifor
Hirwaen
Tafarn-y-Gelyn
Gwernymynydd
Cadole
Loggerheads
Moel Findeg
Maeshafn
Nercwys
Mold
(Yr Wyddgrug)
Prenbrigog
Llong
Padeswood
Penymynydd
Penyffordd
Higher Kinnerton
Lower Kinnerton
Dodleston
Eaton Hall
Ecclest...

Rhewl
Llanbedr-Dyffryn-Clwyd
Llanfair Dyffryn Clwyd
Llanferres
Graianrhyd
Rhyd-y-ceirw
Pantyffordd
Llanfynydd
Cefn-y-bedd
Llay
Gresford
Farndon
Holt

Ruthin
(Rhuthun)
Ruthin Craft Centre
Bontuchel
Llanfwrog
Efenechtyd
Pwll-glas
Eryrys
Treuddyn
Ffrith
Cymau
Llan-y-pwll
Hope
Caergwrle
Burton Green
Rossett
Trevalyn
Marford
Pulford
Lavister

2

DENBIGHSHIRE

Pentre-celyn
Graig-fechan
Moel y Waun
Llandegla
Moel Garegog
Bwlchgwyn
Gwynfryn
Minera
New Brighton
Brymbo
Summerhill
Moss
Gwersyllt
Southsea
Acton
New Broughton
Rhosnesni
Hugmore
Ridleywood

Derwen
Pandy'r Capel
Cefn Coch
Mynydd Cricor
Nant y Garth Pass
Pen-y-stryt
Esclusham Mountain
Coedpoeth
WREXHAM
(Wrecsam)
Wrexham Industrial Estate

220

Brynsaithmarchog
Llanelidan
Ty-mawr
Bryneglwys
Moel y Gamelin
Horseshoe Pass
Pentredwr
World's End
Eglwyseg Mountain
Ruabon Mountain
Rhosllanerchrugog
Johnstown
Bersham
The Wern
Talwrn
Rhostyllen
Erddig (NT)
Marchwiel
Cross Lanes

3

Gwyddelwern
Caer Drewyn
Llantysilio Mountain
Moel Morfydd
Carrog
Rhewl
Llantysilio
Castell Dinas Bran (ruins)
Garth
Trevor
Penycae
Stryt-issa
Sontley
Middle Sontley
Gyfelia
Crabtree Green
Bangor-on-Dee
Bangor-is-y-coed

Corwen
Glyndyfrdwy
Llangollen Railway
Lower Dee Exhibition Centre
Llangollen
Valle Crucis Abbey (ruins)
Eliseg's Pillar
Pen-y-bryn
Ruabon (Rhiwabon)
Acrefair
Cefn-mawr
Wynnstay Park
Overton Bridge
Overton (Owrtyn)

4

Moel Fferna
Moel yr Henfaes
Y Foel
Plas Newydd
Froncysyllte
Pontcysyllte Aqueduct
Newbridge
Pentre
Fron Isaf
Bryn Pen-y-lan
Erbistock
Little Overton
Penley

Moel Pen-plaenau
Bryn Du
Pandy
Glyn Ceiriog
Pontfadog
Dolywern
Bronygarth
Chirk Castle (NT)
Chirk
(Y Waun)
Chirk Green
Pont-y-blew
Halton
Sodylt Bank
Shellbrook Hill
Lightwood Green
Sandy Lane
Penley

Cadair Bronwen
Foel Wen
Mynydd Tarw
Llanarmon Dyffryn Ceiriog
Tregeiriog
Llwynmawr
Tyn-y-Rhos
Craignant
Weston Rhyn
Wern
Gledrid
Preesgweene
St Martin's
Bryn-y-cochin
Elson
Ellesmere
Tetchill

Cadair Berwyn
Moel Sych
Garneddwen
Cefn Hirfynydd
Rhiwlas
Pen y Gwely
Foel Rhiwlas
Llechrydau
Upper Hengoed
Selattyn
Hengoed
Gobowen
Park Hall
Hindford
Perthy
Welsh Frankton
Lee
White Mere

Glanhafon
Moel Henfache
Tai-bach
Gyrn Moelfre
Llansilin
Moelfre
Cefn Canol
Croesau Bach
Llawnt
Brogyntyn
Old Oswestry Hill Fort
Whittington
Babbinswood
Kenwick

Cefn-coch
Llanrhaeadr-ym-Mochnant
Moelfre
Llwyn Moelfre
Llansantffraid
Nant-y-Gollen
Rhydycroesau
Lledrod
Oswestry
Transport Museum
Middleton
Woolston
Maesbury Marsh
West Felton
Rednal
Lower Hordley
Bagley

5

Penybontfawr
Pentrefelin
Llangedwyn
Llanfechain
Pen-y-bont
Porth-y-waen
Treflach
Nantmawr
Llynclys
Crickheath
Morda
Trefonen
Ball
Queen's Head
Sutton
Grimpo
Maesbrook
Haughton
Ruyton-XI-Towns
Milford
Little Ness
Walfo...

Penygarnedd
Abernaint
Pentrefelin
Llanymynech
Sandford
Osbaston
Knockin
Dovaston
Kynaston
Hopton

Llanfyllin

A483–TO WELSHPOOL (Y TRALLWNG)   A5–TO SHREWSBURY (A458)

Llangollen: Home every summer to the Eisteddfod Gerddorol Gydwladol Llangollen (International Musical Eisteddfod) a colourful festival of music, costume and dance famous the world over. The 14th century bridge here is one of the "Seven Wonders of Wales". **Map ref. F3**

A550—TO BIRKENHEAD (A41) | M53—TO BIRKENHEAD | A556—TO M56 | A49—TO WARRING

A | B | C | D

FOREST PARK

CHESTER

219

WREXHAM (Wrecsam)

Ruabon (Rhiwabon)

Chirk (Y Waun)

Ellesmere

Whitchurch

Malpas

Tarporley

Wem

Hodnet

A5—TO SHREWSBURY (A458) | A49, A53—TO SHREWSBURY | A442—TO T

Wem: Home of the Sweet Pea, created by Henry Eckford and now famous throughout the world. Each July there is a Sweet Pea Festival in the town. **Map ref. C5**

206

Ruyton XI Towns: A village created from eleven small hamlets under a charter of 1310. Believed to be the o village in Britain with Roman Numerals in its name. **Map ref. A5**

207 ***Stoke-on-Trent:*** *The city of Stoke-on-Trent is unique in that it is made up of six separate towns;*
Tunstall, Burslem, Hanley, Stoke, Fenton and Longton. Together they are affectionately known as
'The Potteries' and are the home of Britain's ceramics industry. Some of the world's leading pottery
manufacturers such as Wedgwood, Royal Doulton and Spode are based here. **Map ref. F3**

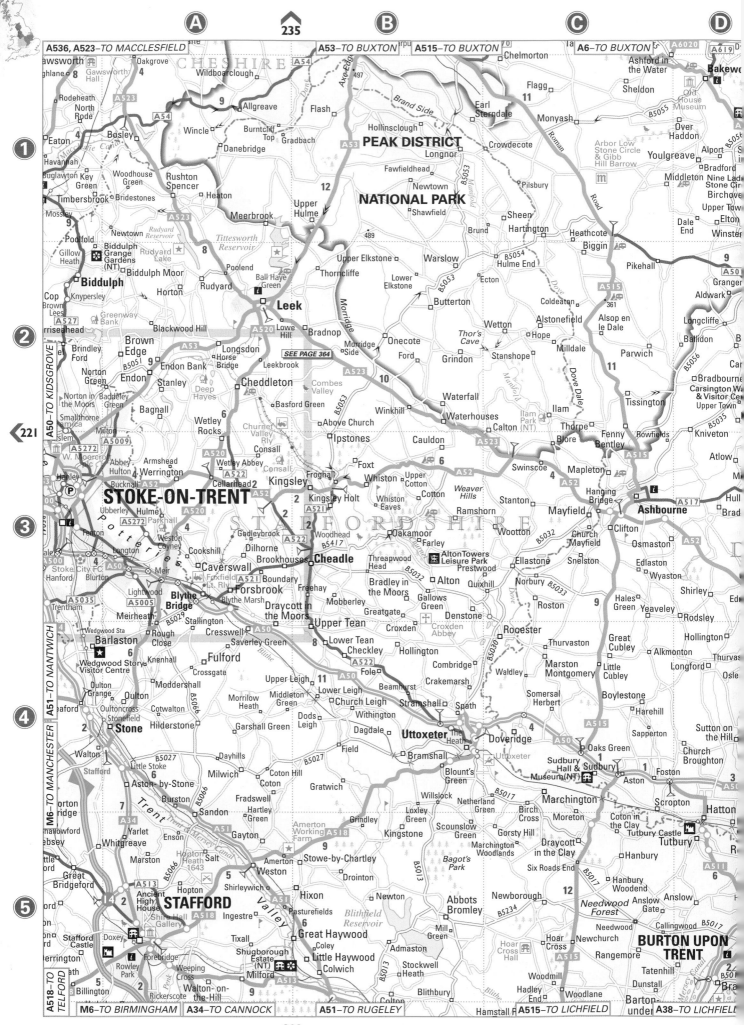

A536, A523-TO MACCLESFIELD | A53-TO BUXTON | A515-TO BUXTON | A6-TO BUXTON

A **B** **C** **D**

CHESHIRE

1

Gawsworth
Oakgrove
Wildboarclough
Allgreave
Wincle
Burntcliff Top
Danebridge
Gradbach
Flash
Hollinsclough
PEAK DISTRICT
Longnor
Fawfieldhead
Newtown
Shawfield
NATIONAL PARK

Chelmorton
Ashford in the Water
Flagg
Sheldon
Monyash
Earl Sterndale
Crowdecote
Pilsbury
Over Haddon
Arbor Low Stone Circle & Gibb Hill Barrow
Youlgreave
Alport
Middleton
Bradford
Nine Lad Stone Cir
Birchove
Upper Tow
Elton
Winster

Eaton
Rodeheath
North Rode
Havannah
Buglawton
Key Green
Timbersbrook
Mossley
Poolfold
Gillow Heath
Biddulph
Grange Gardens (NT)
Biddulph Moor
Horton
Rudyard
Biddulph
Knypersley
Cop Brown Lees

Bosley
Woodhouse Green
Bridestones
Newtown
Rudyard Reservoir
Rudyard Lake
Meerbrook
Upper Hulme
Blackwood Hill
Ball Haye Green
Tittesworth Reservoir
Heaton
Rushton Spencer

489
Upper Elkstone
Lower Elkstone
Thorncliffe
Brund
Sheen
Hartington
Warslow
Hulme End
Ecton
Heathcote
Biggin
Pikehall
Dale End
Longcliffe
Ballidon
Granger
Aldwark
Winster

2

Brown Edge
Brindley Ford
Norton Green
Endon
Norton in the Moors
Baddeley Green
Smallthorne
Milton
Endon Bank
Horse Bridge
Leekbrook
Longsdon
Leek
Lowe Hill
Bradnop

Morridge
Bagnall
Stanley
Deep Hayes
Cheddleton
Combes Valley
Basford Green
Churnet Valley Rly
Consall

SEE PAGE 364
Morridge Side
Onecote
Ford
Grindon
Waterfall
Above Church
Winkhill
Waterhouses
Thor's Cave
Wetton
Hope
Milldale
Stanshope
Calton
Ilam Park (NT)
Ilam
Blore
Thorpe
Fenny Bentley
Rowfields
Parwich
Bradbourne
Carsington Wa & Visitor Ce
Upper Town
Tissington
Kniveton
Atlow

3

Slem
W. Moorcroft
Hanley
Abbey Hulton
Bucknall
STOKE-ON-TRENT
Ubberley
Fenton
Longton
Weston Coyney
Parkhall
Armshead
Werrington
Cellarhead
Wetley Rocks
Wetley Abbey
Consall
Kingsley
Froghall
Foxt
Whiston
Kingsley Holt
Upper Cotton
Whiston Eaves
Cotton
Godleybrook
Dilhorne
Woodhead
Cheadle
Oakamoor
Farley
Alton Towers Leisure Park
Prestwood
STAFFORDSHIRE
Mapleton
Swinscoe
Church Mayfield
Mayfield
Clifton
Snelston
Ellastone
Norbury
Wootton
Hanging Bridge
Ashbourne
Osmaston
Edlaston
Wyaston
Shirley

Potteries
Stoke City FC
Hanford
Blurton
Meir
Cookshill
Brookhouses
Threapwood Head
Bradley in the Moors
Gallows Green
Denstone
Quixhill
Roston
Hales Green
Yeaveley
Rodsley

Caverswall
Forsbrook
Blythe Bridge
Blythe Marsh
Freehay
Mobberley
Greatgate
Croxden
Croxden Abbey
Rocester
Thurvaston
Great Cubley
Hollington
Alkmonton
Thurvas
Osle

4

Lightwood
Meirheath
Rough Close
Stallington
Cresswell
Saverley Green
Lower Tean
Checkley
Hollington
Combridge
Waldley
Marston Montgomery
Little Cubley
Boylestone
Harehill
Sapperton
Church Broughton

Wedgwood Sta
Barlaston
Wedgwood Story Visitor Centre
Knenhall
Fulford
Crossgate
Moddershall
Upper Leigh
Lower Leigh
Fole
Beamhurst
Crakemarsh
Spath
Stramshall
Uttoxeter
The Heath
Doveridge
Oaks Green
Sudbury
Aston
Foston
Scropton
Hatton

Oulton Grange
Oultoncross
Stonefield
Hilderstone
Cotwalton
Morrilow Heath
Middleton Green
Church Leigh
Withington
Dagdale
Bramshall
Blount's Green
Sudbury Hall & Museum (NT)
Marchington
Tutbury Castle
Tutbury

5

Walton
Little Stoke
Stone
Aston-by-Stone
Dayhills
Milwich
Field
Coton Hill
Coton
Gratwich
Willslock
Netherland Green
Loxley Green
Marchington Woodlands
Moreton
Coton in the Clay
Hanbury
Hanbury Woodend
Anslow
Anslow Gate

Burston
Sandon
Fradswell
Hartley Green
Grindley
Kingstone
Scounslow Green
Gorsty Hill
Draycott in the Clay
Six Roads End
Newborough
Needwood Forest
Newchurch
BURTON UPON TRENT
Rangemore

Whitgreave
Yarlet
Marston
Enson
Salt
Gayton
Weston
Stowe-by-Chartley
Amerton Working Farm
Bagot's Park
Abbots Bromley
Admaston
Woodmill
Dunstall

Great Bridgeford
Ancient High House
Hopton
Shirleywich
Hixon
Droitwich
Newton
Mill Green
Hanbury
Hadley End
Woodlane

STAFFORD
Stafford Castle
Doxey
Shire Hall Gallery
Forebridge
Rowley Park
Tixall
Ingestre
Pasturefields
Shugborough Estate (NT)
Milford
Great Haywood
Coley
Little Haywood
Colwich
Blithfield Reservoir
Stockwell Heath
Hoar Cross
Hoar Cross Hall
Needwood
Callingwood
Tatenhill
Barton-under

Billington
Rickerscote
Walton-on-the-Hill
Weeping Cross
Blithbury

A518-TO TELFORD | M6-TO BIRMINGHAM | A34-TO CANNOCK | A51-TO RUGELEY | A515-TO LICHFIELD | A38-TO LICHFIELD

Flash: The highest village in Britain at 1,514 feet (461m) above sea level. It used to be known as a centre outlawed activities, such as the production of counterfeit money, which became known as 'flash' because of its origin. Its position near the junction of three counties helped the locals to evade police forces by moving out of their jurisdiction into the next county. **Map ref. B1**

Melbourne: *Thomas Cook (1820–1892) was born here. Cook pioneered packaged holiday travel through the rail excursions he organised in 1841.* **Map ref.** *E5*

Eastwood: *D H Lawrence, famous as the writer of risqué novels detailing relationships between men and women, was born here on the 11th September 1885. Lawrence left England in 1918 and settled in Italy. He eventually moved to France where he died on the 2nd March 1930. He is buried at Venice overlooking the Adriatic.* **Map ref.** *F3*

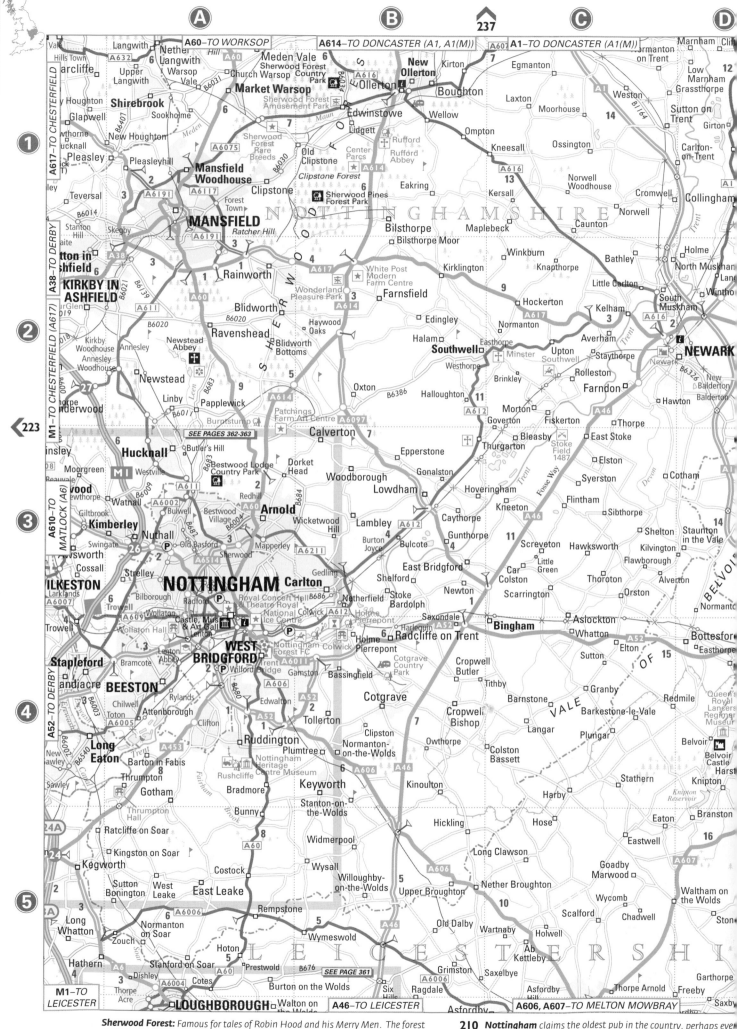

Sherwood Forest: Famous for tales of Robin Hood and his Merry Men. The forest contains the 'Major Oak', a tree reputed to be well over 800 years old. Its vital statistics are: spread over 90 feet (27.5m), girth 33 feet (10m) and weight estimated to be 23 tons (23.4 tonnes). It is so big that Robin is reputed to have hidden from his enemies inside its hollow trunk. In 1972 it was fenced off from the public after the 200,000 plus visitors it attracts every year were judged to be causing it damage. *Map ref. B1 Also on page 75*

210 Nottingham claims the oldest pub in the country, perhaps even the World. Ye Olde Trip to Jerusalem claims to date back to 1189 which was when King Richard I ascended the throne. It is said that the pub was a favourite resting place for soldiers on their way to the Crusades and in old English the word trip actually means rest or stop rather than journey as it does now. *Map ref. A3*

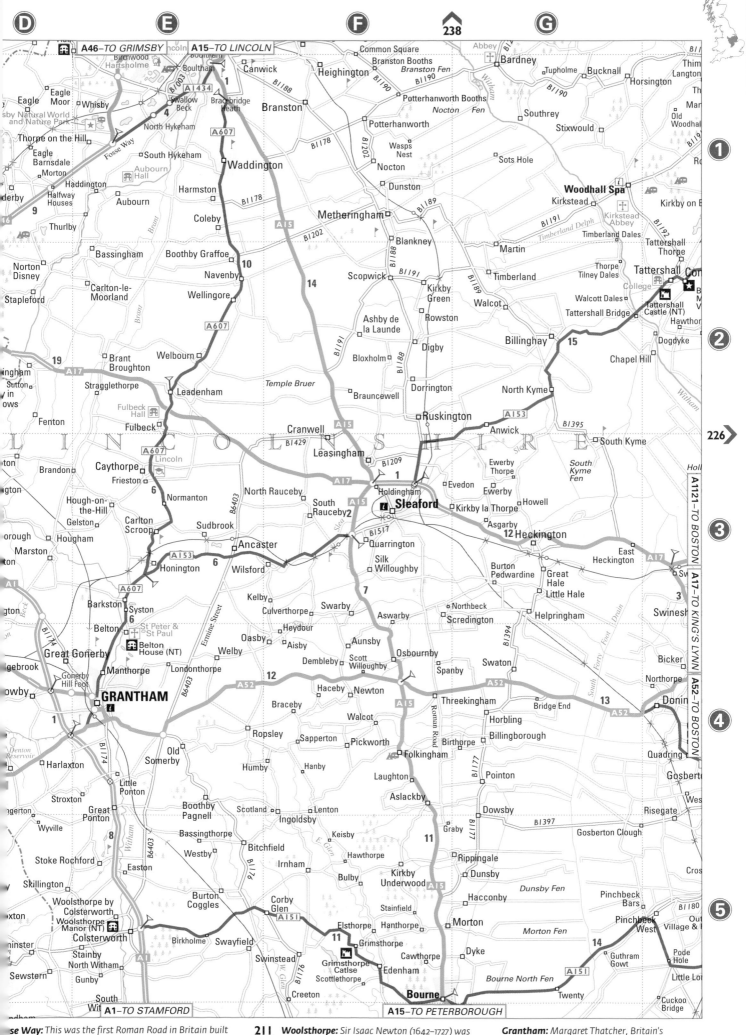

A46-TO GRIMSBY   A15-TO LINCOLN

Lincoln
Birchwood
Hartsholme
Boultham
Canwick
Common Square
Branston Booths
Branston Fen
Abbey
Bardney
Tupholme Bucknall
Horsington
Thim
Langton

Eagle Eagle Moor Whisby Swallow Beck Bracebridge Heath Heighington Potterhanworth Booths Nocton Fen Southrey Stixwould Old Woodhall

North Hykeham Branston Potterhanworth Wasps Nest Sots Hole
Thorpe on the Hill South Hykeham Auborn Hall Waddington Nocton Dunston Woodhall Spa Kirkstead Kirkby on E
Eagle Barnsdale Morton Harmston Metheringham Kirkstead Abbey
Haddington Coleby Blankney Martin Timberland Delph Timberland Dales Tattershall Thorpe
Halfway Houses Aubourn Bassingham Boothby Graffoe Scopwick Timberland Thorpe Tilney Dales Tattershall Col

Norton Disney Navenby Kirkby Green Walcott Dales College
Carlton-le-Moorland Wellingore Ashby de la Launde Rowston Walcot Tattershall Bridge Tattershall Castle (NT) Hawthor
Stapleford Welbourn Bloxholm Digby Billinghay 15 Dogdyke
Brant Broughton Temple Bruer Brauncewell North Kyme Chapel Hill
Stragglethorpe Leadenham Dorrington A153 Anwick B1395 South Kyme
Fenton Fulbeck Hall Cranwell Ruskington Ewerby Thorpe South Kyme Fen Holl

LINCOLNSHIRE

Caythorpe Fulbeck Leasingham Evedon Ewerby Howell
Brandon Frieston Lincoln North Rauceby Holdingham Kirkby la Thorpe
Hough-on-the-Hill Normanton South Rauceby Sleaford Asgarby Heckington
Gelston Carlton Scroop Sudbrook Quarrington Burton Pedwardine Great Hale East Heckington
Hougham Ancaster Wilsford Silk Willoughby Little Hale Swines
Marston Honington Kelby Swarby Aswarby Northbeck Helpringham Swinesh
Barkston Syston Heydour Culverthorpe Scredington Bicker
Belton St Peter & St Paul Oasby Aisby Scott Willoughby Osbournby Spanby Swaton Northorpe
Great Gonerby Belton House (NT) Welby Dembleby Newton Threekingham Bridge End 13 Donin
Manthorpe Londonthorpe Haceby Walcot Horbling Swaton
GRANTHAM Braceby Billingborough Quadring
Gonerby Hill Foot Ropsley Sapperton Pickworth Birthorpe Gosbert
Harlaxton Old Somerby Humby Hanby Folkingham Pointon
Stroxton Little Ponton Laughton Dowsby Risegate
Wyville Great Ponton Scotland Lenton Aslackby Graby Gosberton Clough
Stoke Rochford Boothby Pagnell Ingoldsby Keisby Rippingale Dunsby Pinchbeck Bars
Skillington Bassingthorpe Hawthorpe Kirkby Underwood Hacconby Pinchbeck West Village &
Woolsthorpe by Colsterworth Westby Bitchfield Bulby Stainfield Morton Dunsby Fen Pinchbeck
Woolsthorpe Manor (NT) Burton Coggles Irnham Corby Glen Elsthorpe Hanthorpe Dyke Pode Hole
Colsterworth Birkholme Swayfield Grimsthorpe Cawthorpe Morton Fen 14 Guthram Gowt
Stainby North Witham Swinstead Grimsthorpe Catsle Scottlethorpe Edenham Bourne North Fen Little Lo
Gunby Creeton Bourne Twenty Cuckoo Bridge
South Wit A1-TO STAMFORD A15-TO PETERBOROUGH

211 ∨

se Way: This was the first Roman Road in Britain built und AD47. It extended from Exeter to Lincoln, running ugh Bath, Cirencester and Leicester. Much of its nment is followed by present-day roads such as the A46. p ref. C3

Woolsthorpe: Sir Isaac Newton (1642–1727) was born at nearby Woolsthorpe Manor. Newton devoted his life to science, researching and developing theories on colour, light and the laws of motion, but is best remembered for his theory of universal gravitation. **Map ref. A4 Also on page 75**

Grantham: Margaret Thatcher, Britain's first female Prime Minister, was born here on the 13th October 1925. She was elected as MP for Finchley in 1959 and went on to serve as PM from 1979 until her resignation in 1990. **Map ref. E4**

225

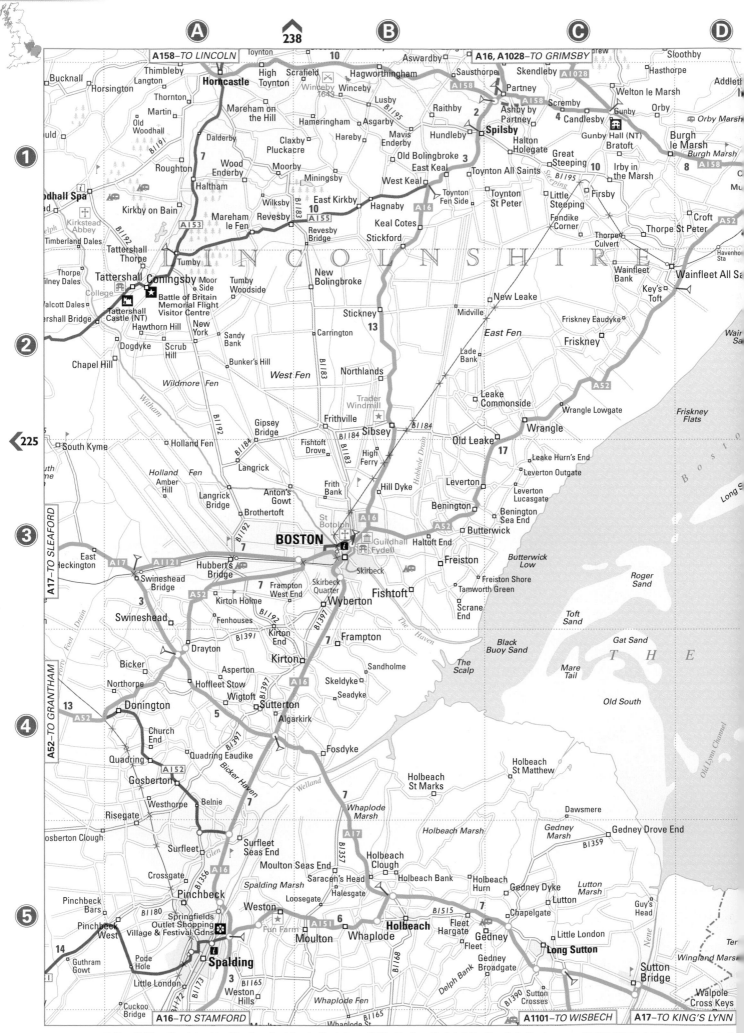

A158–TO LINCOLN

A16, A1028–TO GRIMSBY

Bucknall
Horsington
Thimbleby
Langton
Horncastle
High Toynton
Toynton
Scrafield
Hagworthingham
Aswardby
Skendleby
Sloothby
Hasthorpe
Addlett
Sausthorpe
Welton le Marsh

Thornton
Martin
Old Woodhall
Mareham on the Hill
Winceby 1643
Winceby
Lusby
Hameringham
Asgarby
Raithby
Mavis Enderby
Partney
Scremby
Gunby
Orby
Orby Marsh

Dalderby
Claxby Pluckacre
Moorby
Hareby
Old Bolingbroke
East Keal
Ashby by Partney
Spilsby
Halton Holegate
Candlesby
Gunby Hall (NT)
Bratoft
Burgh le Marsh
Burgh Marsh

Roughton
Haltham
Wood Enderby
Miningsby
West Keal
Toynton All Saints
Toynton St Peter
Great Steeping
Irby in the Marsh
Firsby
Croft
Thorpe St Peter

Kirkby on Bain
Mareham le Fen
Wilksby
East Kirkby
Hagnaby
Keal Cotes
Toynton Fen Side
Little Steeping
Fendike Corner
Thorpe Culvert
Wainfleet All Sa

Woodhall Spa
Kirkstead Abbey
Timberland Dales
Revesby
Stickford
New Leake
Wainfleet Bank
Key's Toft

Thorpe Tilney Dales
Walcott Dales
Tattershall Thorpe
Tumby
Coningsby
Moor Side
New Bolingbroke
Midville
Friskney Eaudyke
Friskney

Tattershall Bridge
College
Tattershall Castle (NT)
Battle of Britain Memorial Flight Visitor Centre
Tumby Woodside
Stickney
East Fen
Wainfleet All Sa

Dogdyke
Hawthorn Hill
New York
Scrub Hill
Sandy Bank
Carrington
Lade Bank
Northlands

Chapel Hill
Bunker's Hill
Stickney
East Fen
Leake Commonside
Wrangle Lowgate

South Kyme
Holland Fen
Wildmore Fen
West Fen
Trader Windmill
Frithville
Sibsey
Old Leake
Wrangle
Leake Hurn's End

LINCOLNSHIRE

Gipsey Bridge
Fishtoft Drove
High Ferry
Hobhole Drain
Leverton Outgate
Leverton Lucasgate

Langrick
Holland Amber Hill
Langrick Bridge
Anton's Gowt
Brothertoft
Frith Bank
Hill Dyke
Leverton
Benington

BOSTON
St Botolph
Guildhall
Fydell
Haltoft End
Freiston
Butterwick
Butterwick Low

East Heckington
Hubbert's Bridge
Swineshead Bridge
Frampton West End
Skirbeck Quarter
Skirbeck
Fishtoft
Freiston Shore
Tamworth Green

Swineshead
Kirton Holme
Fenhouses
Kirton End
Wyberton
Scrane End

Bicker
Northorpe
Drayton
Asperton
Kirton
Frampton
Sandholme
The Scalp
Black Buoy Sand

Donington
Hoffleet Stow
Wigtoft
Sutterton
Algarkirk
Skeldyke
Seadyke
Fosdyke

Church End
Quadring Eaudike
Quadring
Gosberton
Westhorpe
Belnie
Risegate

Holbeach St Matthew
Holbeach St Marks
Holbeach Marsh
Gedney Marsh
Dawsmere
Gedney Drove End

Gosberton Clough
Surfleet
Surfleet Seas End
Whaplode Marsh
Holbeach Clough
Holbeach Bank
Holbeach Hurn
Gedney Dyke
Lutton Marsh
Lutton

Pinchbeck Bars
Pinchbeck West
Crossgate
Pinchbeck
Weston
Moulton Seas End
Saracen's Head
Halesgate
Holbeach
Fleet Hargate
Gedney
Chapelgate
Little London
Guy's Head

Guthram Gowt
Springfields Outlet Shopping Village & Festival Gdns
Pode Hole
Spalding
Moulton
Whaplode
Long Sutton
Sutton Bridge
Walpole Cross Keys

Little London
Weston Hills
Whaplode Fen
Delph Bank
Gedney Broadgate
Sutton Crosses
Wingland Marsh

A16–TO STAMFORD
A1101–TO WISBECH
A17–TO KING'S LYNN

Sutton Bridge: King John, travelling from Spalding to King's Lynn is reputed to have lost his crown jewels here in the 12th Century. The coastal track running by The Wash was swamped by the incoming tide and the King's baggage train was swept away, never to be seen again. **Map ref. C5**

212

Boston: St. Botolph's Church, better known as Boston Stump, is the largest parish ch in England. It measures 282 feet (86m) long stands 272 feet (83m) high and covers 20,0 square feet (1865 sq m) in area. The main church was begun in 1309 and the tower wa completed in 1520. From the tower, on a clear day, it is possible to see Lincoln Cathed 32 miles (50km) away. **Map ref. B3**

Ingoldmells
Point
Fantasy Island
Butlins Family
Entertainment Resort
Skegness Water
Leisure Park

Skegness

Skegness Natureland Seal
Sanctuary

Gibraltar
Point
braltar
tar Pt

S   H

I Sand

Peter Black
Sand

Bulldog
Sand

Ongar Hill

North Wootton

KING'S LYNN

St George's
Guildhall (NT)
Lynn

lenchwarton

Holkham
Bay

Brancaster Bay   Norton   Creek

Holme next the Sea   Titchwell   Brancaster   Burnham   Burnham   Wells
Marsh   Staithe   Deepdale   Overy Staithe
Thornham   A149   17   Burnham Norton   Holkham
Titchwell   Brancaster   Burnham   Holkham
Burnham Market   Overy Town   Hall
Sea Life Centre   Burnham Thorpe

Ringstead   Wig   **228** ▶

Hunstanton

Creake
Abbey   Shirehall Museum

Heacham   Norfolk
Lavender   North   Egmere
Creake   Shri
Summerfield   B1155   of W

Eaton   B1454   Docking   B1155   South   North
Sedgeford   Stanhoe   Creake   Barsham
East Barsham
Snettisham   Fring   Bircham   Barmer   West Bars
A149   Newton
Southgate   Sculthorpe

Shernborne   Bircham   Bagthorpe   Syderstone
Ingoldisthorpe   Great Bircham   Tofts
13   B1155   A148   Dunton   i
Sheredon   Fak
Dersingham   Anmer   Houghton Hall   Tattersett   Fake
Sandringham   East Rudham   Hempton
Wolferton   House   Coxford   Tatterford   Toftrees
Sandringham   Colkirk
West Newton   New Houghton   West Rudham   Oxwick
St Mary   B1153   Helhoughton   A1065
Magdalene Chapel   **17**   Harpley   East
Flitcham   A148   West Raynham   Raynham
Trinity   Whisso
Hospital   Hillington   Little Massingham   South Raynham
Castle Rising   Great
A148   Massingham   Wellingham   Hornington
Castle Rising   Congham   Godwick
South   A148   Roydon   Weasenham St Peter   Tittleshall
A1078   Wootton   Grimston   Weasenham All Saints   **16**
A149   Pott   Massingham   Rougham   Stanfie
Row   Heath
Gaywood   B1145   Bawsey
A149–TO DOWNHAM MARKET (A10)   Gayton   B1145   **A1065–TO SWAFFHAM**

N   O   R   F   O   L   K

Peddars Way & Norfolk Coast Path

A148–TO CROMER

gness: Billy Butlin opened his first ever holiday camp here
935. The camp was taken over by the Royal Navy for the
ation of World War II and named HMS Royal Arthur. It was
n returned to Butlins in 1946 and continued as Butlin's
day Camp until it was bought by the Rank Organisation in
. **Map ref. D1**

213 ⌄

Burnham Thorpe: Lord Nelson was born here in 1758. As Horatio Nelson he joined the Navy
at the age of twelve and from then on spent almost his entire life at sea. He was dogged by
ill health but from 1793 was almost always involved in a battle. He lost an eye at Calvi in
Corsica, an arm at Santa Cruz in Tenerife and finally his life at the Battle of Trafalgar.
As a monument to this inspirational leader Nelson's column was built in Trafalgar Square
in London in 1840 and stands 170 feet (52m) high. **Map ref. G3**

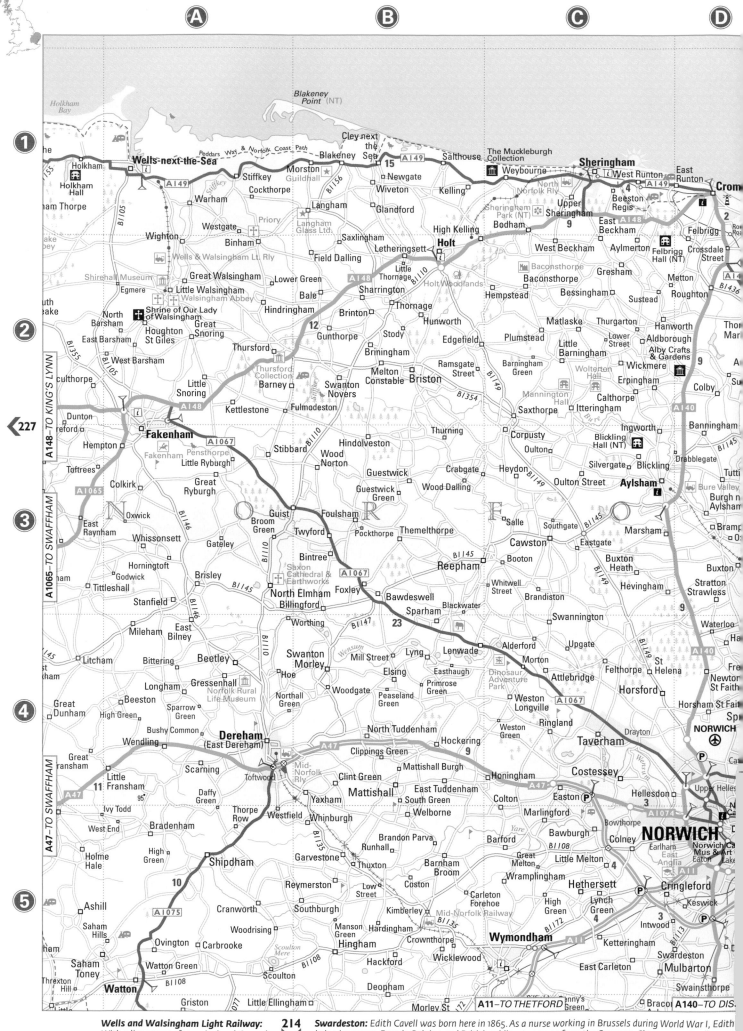

1

Holkham Bay

Blakeney Point (NT)

Holkham

Holkham Hall

Wells-next-the-Sea

Peddars Way & Norfolk Coast Path

Stiffkey

Cockthorpe

Warham

Morston Guildhall

Blakeney

Cley next the Sea

Newgate

Wiveton

Kelling

Salthouse

The Muckleburgh Collection

Weybourne

North Norfolk Rly

Sheringham

West Runton

East Runton

Crom

A148

Beeston Regis

Upper Sheringham

East Beckham

Felbrigg

Langham

Glandford

High Kelling

Bodham

West Beckham

Aylmerton

Felbrigg Hall (NT)

Crossdale Street

Metton

Roughton

Westgate

Binham

Saxlingham

Letheringsett

Holt

Little Thornage

Sharrington

Holt Woodlands

Baconsthorpe

Baconsthorpe

Gresham

Bessingham

Sustead

Wighton

Priory

Langham Glass Ltd.

Field Dalling

Wells & Walsingham Lt. Rly

Lower Green

Great Walsingham

Little Walsingham

Walsingham Abbey

Shrine of Our Lady of Walsingham

Great Snoring

Thursford

Bale

Hindringham

Brinton

Thornage

Hunworth

Stody

Edgefield

Hempstead

Matlaske

Plumstead

Little Barningham

Barningham Green

Lower Street

Hanworth

Aldborough

Wickmere

Wolterton Hall

Erpingham

Colby

2

Egmere

North Barsham

Houghton St Giles

East Barsham

West Barsham

Thursford Collection

Barney

Swanton Novers

Melton Constable

Briston

Ramsgate Street

Mannington Hall

Saxthorpe

Itteringham

Calthorpe

Ingworth

Banningham

culthorpe

Sculthorpe

Kettlestone

Fulmodeston

Thurning

Corpusty

Oulton

Heydon

Blickling Hall (NT)

Silvergate

Blickling

Drabblegate

A1067

Dunton

Hempton

Fakenham

Penshurst

Stibbard

Hindolveston

Guestwick

Crabgate

Wood Dalling

Oulton Street

Aylsham

Bure Valley

227

A148

A1065—TO SWAFFHAM

reford

Toftrees

Little Ryburgh

Wood Norton

Guestwick Green

Salle

Southgate

Eastgate

Marsham

Buxton

Brampton

Colkirk

Great Ryburgh

Foulsham

Themelthorpe

Buxton Heath

Hevingham

Stratton Strawless

3

East Raynham

Oxwick

Guist

Broom Green

Twyford

Pockthorpe

Booton

B1145

Cawston

Reepham

Whissonsett

Gateley

Bintree

Saxon Cathedral & Earthworks

Whitwell Street

Brandiston

Swannington

Upgate

Waterloo

Horningtoft

Godwick

Brisley

Foxley

North Elmham

Bawdeswell

Sparham

Blackwater

Alderford

Felthorpe

St Helena

Newtor

Tittleshall

Billingford

Morton

St Faith

Stanfield

Worthing

B1147

Lyng

Lenwade

Dinosaur Adventure Park

Attlebridge

Horsford

Horsham St Fait

Mileham

East Bilney

Swanton Morley

Mill Street

Elsing

Easthaugh

Primrose Green

Weston Longville

Ringland

Drayton

NORWICH

Litcham

Bittering

Beetley

Hoe

Woodgate

Northall Green

Peaseland Green

Weston Green

Longham

Gressenhall

Norfolk Rural Life Museum

Taverham

Horsham St Fait

4

Great Dunham

High Green

Beeston

Sparrow Green

Bushy Common

Dereham (East Dereham)

Mid-Norfolk Rly

North Tuddenham

Clippings Green

Hockering

Weston

Honingham

Costessey

Hellesdon

Upper Helles

Wendling

Scarning

Toftwood

Clint Green

Mattishall Burgh

Easton

A47

A1074

Great Fransham

Little Fransham

Daffy Green

Thorpe Row

Yaxham

Mattishall

East Tuddenham

South Green

Colton

Marlingford

Bowthorpe

NORWICH

Ivy Todd

West End

Bradenham

High Green

Westfield

Whinburgh

Welborne

Brandon Parva

Barford

Great Melton

Bawburgh

Colney

Earlham East Anglia

Norwich Cat Mus & Art

Eaton

Holme Hale

Shipdham

Garvestone

Runhall

Thuxton

Barnham Broom

Little Melton

Wramplingham

Hethersett

Cringleford

Keswick

5

Ashill

Saham Hills

Cranworth

Reymerston

Woodrising

Southburgh

Low Street

Coston

Kimberley

Carleton Forehoe

High Green

Lynch Green

Intwood

Mid-Norfolk Railway

Saham Toney

Ovington

Carbrooke

Scoulton Mere

Hardingham

Manson Green

Hingham

Crownthorpe

Wicklewood

Wymondham

Ketteringham

Swardeston

Mulbarton

Threxton Hill

Watton

Watton Green

Scoulton

Hackford

Deopham

East Carleton

Swainsthorpe

Griston

Little Ellingham

Morley St

Brace

A11—TO THETFORD

A140—TO DIS

214

Wells and Walsingham Light Railway: With a line gauge of 10.25 inches (260mm), this is the narrowest public railway in the world. **Map ref. A2**

Swardeston: Edith Cavell was born here in 1865. As a nurse working in Brussels during World War I, Edith helped over 200 French, Belgian and British soldiers to escape from the Germans. She was eventually arrested, convicted of treason and executed by firing squad on the 12th October 1915. After the war her body was exhumed and reburied in Norwich Cathedral. **Map ref. D5**

ingham: Norfolk is best known for its flat fenland and
ds. The highest point in the entire county is Roman Camp
Sheringham at just 336 feet (103 metres) above sea level.
ref. C1

215
∨

Great Yarmouth: Anna Sewell, writer of the children's classic Black Beauty was born here
on the 30th March 1820. Anna was crippled at an early age but constantly championed
the better treatment and understanding of horses through her writing. She died on the
25th April 1878 and is buried at Lammas, near Buxton. **Map ref. G5**

The Skerries

West Mouse

Middle Mouse

Porth Wen Bay

Bull Bay (Porth Llechog)

Point Lynas

Carmel Head

Cemlyn Bay

Cemaes Bay

Llanbadrig

Amlwch

Llaneilian

(NT)

Cemaes

Neuadd

Burwen

Amlwch Port

Pengorffwysfa

Tregele

Llanfairynghornwy

Llanfechell

Bodewryd

Pen-y-sarn

Nebo

Ynys Dulas

Mynyddmechell

Rhos-goch

B5111

Parys Mountain

A5025

Dulas

HOLYHEAD BAY

Rhyd-wyn

Llanrhyddlad

Carreglefn

Rhos-y-bol

8

Dulas Bay

Church Bay

Llanfflewyn

Llaneuddog

Lligwy Bay

Llanfaethlu

17

Llanbabo

City Dulas

Brynrefail

Capel Lligwy

A5025

Llyn Alaw

Capel Parc

Rhoslligwy

ISLE OF

Gwredog

Llandyfrydog

Din

Lligwy Burial

Moelfre

hours

Dublin Port..............2¾
Dún Laoghaire..........1¾

Windmill

Llanddeusant

Elim

Ceidio

Llannerch-y-medd

Maenaddwyn

Llanallgo

North Stack

Llanfwrog

Marian-glas

Tyn-y-gongl

South Stack Cliffs

220

Holyhead Mountain

Holyhead (Caergybi)

Roman Fort

Salt Island

Stryd y Facsen

Tregwehelydd Standing Stone

Llantrisant

B5112

Bachau

Bryn-teg

Benll

South Stack

Llaingoch

Kingsland

Llanfachraeth

Llanfigael

Pen-llyn

ANGLESEY

Carmel

Capel Coch

B5108

Hut Circles

Standing Stones

Burial Chamber

Penrhos

Llanynghenedl

A5

B5109

Llyn Llywenan

Llechcynfarwy

ANGLESEY

Llanbedrgoch

B5110

Penrhyn Mawr

Treaddur

Ty Felin Valley

3

Bodedern

Burial Chambers

Trefor

(YNYS MÔN)

Llanddyfnan

Re

Caergeiliog

9

B5112

Llangwyllog

Tregaian

10

Four Mile Bridge

Bryngwran

Llynfaes

Llyn Frogwy

Cefni Resr

Rhosmeirch

B5109

Pe

HOLY ISLAND

Bodior

Llanfihangel-yn-Nhywyn

A5

Gwalchmai

Bodffordd

Talwrn

Rhoscolyn

Llanfair-yn-neubwll

Capel Gwyn

5

Heneglwys

A55

A5

Llangefni

Cymyran Bay

Tywyn Trewan

A4080

3

Ty Newydd Burial Chamber

Cerrigceinwen

6

Rhostrehwfa

Ceint

Penmyny

Rhosneigr

Pencarnisiog

Burial Chamber

Llangristiolus

6

7

7

Llanfairpwllgwy

Llanfaelog

A4080

Capel Mawr

Pentre Berw

Gaerwen

A5

7A

Ty Croes Sta

B4422

Cefni

Maltraeth Marsh

B5420

M

Barclodiad y Gawres Chambered Cairn

Bethel

B4419

Llanddaniel Fab

Pe

Llyn Coron

Trefdraeth

Bryn Celli Ddu Burial Chamber

Pl

Llangadwaladr

Llandudno: *Wales' largest seaside resort. The town has numerous attractions and is the only place in Britain to feature a redundant lighthouse as a B&B.* **Map ref: F4**

216 ∨

Llanfairpwllgwyngyllgogerychwyrndrobwllllantysiliogogogoch: *This is the village with the longest n in Britain. The final 38 characters of the name were added on in the 19th Century to attract tourists. The name actually means 'The Church of St Mary in a hollow of white hazel near a rapid whirlpool and near Tysilio's Church by the red cave….but now it's generally called Llanfair PG. Add the .com, and since 199 also been the world's longest single-word internet domain name.* **Map ref: D5**

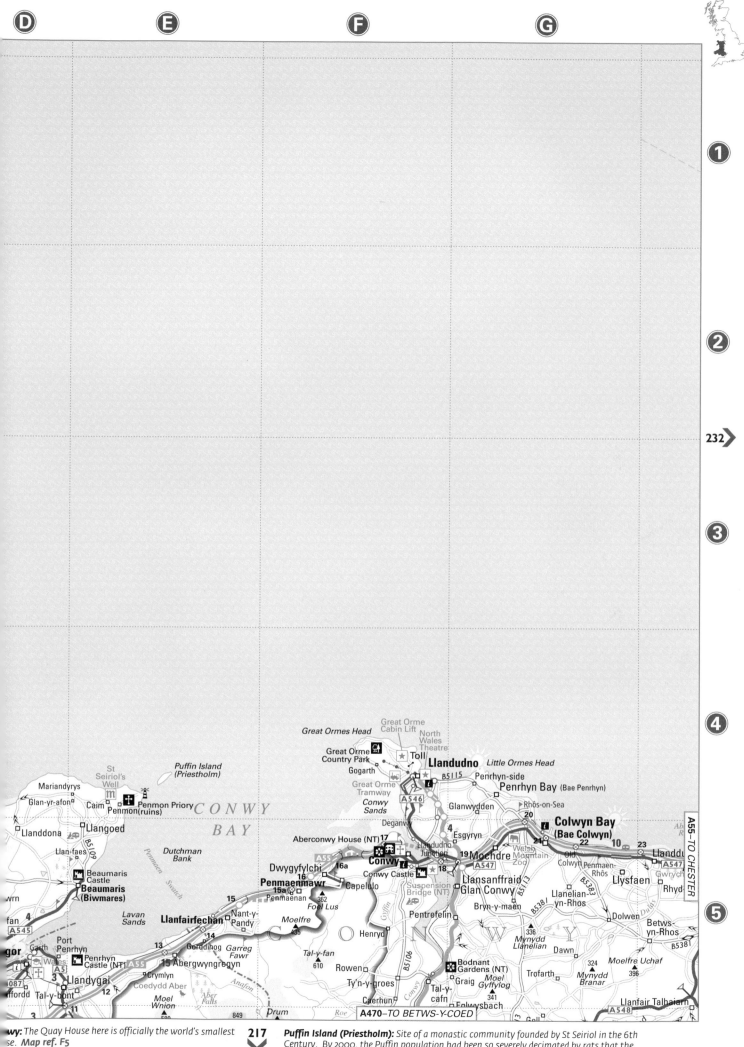

1

2

232

3

4

5

Mariandyrys
Glan-yr-afon
St Seiriol's Well
Puffin Island (Priestholm)
Caim
Penmon Priory
Penmon (ruins)
C O N W Y   B A Y
Great Ormes Head
Great Orme Cabin Lift
North Wales Theatre
Great Orme Country Park
Gogarth
Toll
Llandudno
Little Ormes Head
Penrhyn-side
Penrhyn Bay (Bae Penrhyn)
Llanddona
Llangoed
Dutchman Bank
Great Orme Tramway
Conwy Sands
B5115
A546
Glanwydden
Rhôs-on-Sea
Llan-faes
B5109
Penmaen Swatch
Deganwy
Aberconwy House (NT)
17
20
Colwyn Bay (Bae Colwyn)
A55–TO CHESTER
Beaumaris Castle
Llandudno Junction
Esgyryn
21
22
10
23
A547
Llanddu
Beaumaris (Biwmares)
4
Dwygyfylchi
16
16a
Conwy
4
19
Mochdre
Welsh Mountain Zoo
Old Colwyn
Penmaen-Rhôs
B5383
Llysfaen
Lavan Sands
A545
fan
15
Penmaenmawr
Penmaenan
Foel Lus
362
Capelulo
Conwy Castle
18
Suspension Bridge (NT)
Llansanffraid Glan Conwy
Bryn-y-maen
B5113
Llanelian-yn-Rhos
B538
Rhyd
Port Penrhyn
13
14
Gorddinog
Garreg Fawr
Nant-y-Pandy
Moelfre
435
Henryd
Pentrefelin
336
Mynydd Llanelian
Dawn
Betws-yn-Rhos
B538
gor
A5
Penrhyn Castle (NT)
A55
15
Abergwyngregyn
Tal-y-fan
610
Rowen
Ty'n-y-groes
Bodnant Gardens (NT)
Graig
Moel Gyffylog
341
Trofarth
324
Mynydd Branar
Moelfre Uchaf
396
Llandygai
Crymlyn
Coedydd Aber
12
Moel Wnion
Aber Falls
Anafon
Caerhun
Tal-y-cafn
Eglwysbach
Llanfair Talhaiarn
Tal-y-bont
11
Drum
849
Roe
A470–TO BETWS-Y-COED
A548
Goll

wy: The Quay House here is officially the world's smallest se. **Map ref. F5**

217

Puffin Island (Priestholm): *Site of a monastic community founded by St Seiriol in the 6th Century. By 2000, the Puffin population had been so severely decimated by rats that the Royal Air Force were called in to airlift in 2.5 tons of poisoned wheat onto the island in an attempt to wipe out the rat population.* **Map ref. E4**

Port Sunlight: Village created by William Hesketh Lever who owned a soap factory making Sunlight Soap. This later became Lever Bros. The village was built to house his workforce. Work started on the 3rd March 1888 and by 1909 the village had 700 dwellings with all the facilities: school, theatre, library etc. **Map ref. E4**

Prestatyn: Offa's Dyke was built by Offa, King of Mercia AD 757–796, to mark the boundary between England and Wales. It runs from Prestatyn in the north, to Sedbury, near Chepstow in the south, a distance of 182 miles (293km). **Map ref. B4**

Rhyl: Ruth Ellis was born here in 1926. She was hanged on the 13th July 1955 at Holloway Prison for the murder of her lover. The execution so enraged the population that it opened the whole debate on capital punishment and she became the last woman in Britain to be hanged for murder. All executions were subsequently suspended from 1965 and capital punishment was abolished altogether in 1970. **Map ref.**

A59-TO PRESTON   M6-NORTH   M61-TO PRESTON

SOUTHPORT

Horse Bank
Angry Brow
Southport Pier
Pleasureland Amusement Park
Trans Pennine Trail
Royal Birkdale
Ainsdale-on-Sea
Holiday Centre
Dunes

Marshside
Crossens
Churchtown
Blowick
Birkdale
Brown Edge
Snape Green
Scarisbrick
Bescar
Shirdley Hill
Woodvale
Ainsdale
Pinfold
Hurlston Green
Halsall

LANCASHIRE

Mere Brow
Holmes
Sollom
Martin Mere
Holmeswood
Rufford Old Hall (NT)
Rufford
Tarlscough
New Lane Sta
Causeway End
New Lane
Burscough Bridge
Hoscar
Ring o' Bells
Newburgh

Croston
Breteston
Barber's Moor
Eccleston
Camelot Theme Park
Heskin Green
Mawdesley
Wrightington Bar
Bispham Green
Robin Hood
Parbold
Appley Bridge
Dalton

Euxton
Astley Hall Museum & Gardens
Runshaw Moor
White Copp
CHORLEY
Charnock Richard
Cowling
Coppull
Adlington
Coppull Moor
Mossy Lea
Shevington Moor
Standish
Shevington
Red Rock
Haigh
Blackrod
Aspu

1

Formby
Freshfield
Little Altcar
Cabin Hills (NT)
Hightown
Lady Green

Barton
Bangor's Green
Haskayne
Downholland Cross
Great Altcar
Ince Blundell
Carr Houses

ORMSKIRK
Aughton Park
Town Green
Stanley Gate
Bickerstaffe
Aughton
Bowker's Green

Westhead
Scarth Hill
Skelmersdale
Blaguegate
Elmer's Green
Digmoor
Up Holland
Longshaw

Bank Top
Gathurst
Roby Mill
Beacon Park
Orrell
Pemberton
Marylebone
Marsh Green
Goose Green

Wigan Athletic FC
WIGAN
Wheelley
Newtown
Ince-in-Makerfield
Platt Bridge

2

Maghull
Lydiate
Little Crosby
Thornton

Moss Side
Melling Mount
Royal Oak
Barrow Nook

Crawford
King's Moss
Rainford
Crank
Billinge
Garswood
Bryn
Abram
Bryn Gates
Stubshaw Cross
Ashton-in-Make
Golbor

234

CROSBY
Blundellsands
Great Crosby
Waterloo
Seaforth
Netherton
Ford
Aintree
Fazakerley
Melling
Waddicar
Westvale
Northwood
Kirkby
Southdene

Moss Bank
Haydock
Blackbrook
Newton-le-Willows
Earlestown
Town of Lowton
Lowton
Wargrave
3

SEE PAGES 366-367

BOOTLE
Orrell
Walton
Anfield
Everton
LIVERPOOL

Croxteth Hall
Knowsley
Knowsley Safari Park
ST HELENS
West Park
World of Glass
Peasley Cross
Thatto Heath
Collins Green
Burtonwood
Hermitage Green
Winwick

Prescot
Whiston
Rainhill
Sutton Leach
Abbotsfield
Clock Face
22
9

New Palace & Adventureland
WALLASEY
Liscard
New Brighton
Seacombe
Bidston

HUYTON
Broad Green
Roby
Childwall
National Wildflower Centre
Gateacre

Rainhill Stoops
Cronton
Bold Heath
Town End
Penketh
Great Sankey
Stockton Heath
WA
Latchford

BIRKENHEAD
Oxton
Tranmere
Prenton
Woodhey
Rock Ferry
New Ferry
Lady Lever Art Gallery & Mus
Port Sunlight

H.M. Customs & Excise National Museum
Sudley Art Gallery & Mus
Mossley Hill
Aigburth
Grassendale
Allerton
Woolton

Farnworth
Cronton
Hough Green
Appleton
Cuerdley Cross
Higher Walton
Moore
Lower Walton
4

BEBINGTON
Woodchurch
Landican
Storeton
Bromborough
Eastham Woods
Garston
Speke
Ditton
WIDNES
RUNCORN
Keckwick
Hatton
Daresbury
Norcott Brook
Walton Hall (

Barnston
Brimstage
Fairfield
Thornton Hough
Raby
Hinderton
Speke Hall (NT)
Oglet
Hale
Hale Bank
Weston Point
Norton Priory
Halton
Weston
Preston on the Hill
Preston Brook
Dutton

LIVERPOOL JOHN LENNON
Eastham Sands
MERSEY
Dungeon Banks

Neston
Little Neston
Parkgate
Ness Botanic Gardens
Burton
Puddington
White Sands
Shotwick
Saughall
Connah's

Willaston
Hooton
Childer Thornton
Overpool
Little Sutton
Ledsham
Capenhurst
Dunkirk
Two Mills
Mollington

Mount Manisty
Stanlow Banks
Ince Banks
Ellesmere Port Boat Museum
ELLESMERE PORT
McArthurGlen Cheshire Oaks
Great Blue Planet Sutton Aquarium
Whitby
Whitbyheath
Little Stanney
Stoak
Backford
Wervin
Picton
Chester Zoo
Mickle
Trafford
Flemstall

Manchester Ship Canal
Stanlow Elton
Ince
Chester
Elton
Thornton-le-Moors
Helsby
Newton
Alvanley
Dunham-on-the-Hill
Bridge Trafford
Little Barrow

Frodsham
Netherton
Overton
Bradley
Aston
Weaver
Sutton Weaver
Sutton Heath
Acton Bridge
Crowton
Kingsley
Norley
Bryn
Cuddington
Sandiw
Weaver

CHESHIRE
DELAMERE FOREST
Hatchmere
Delamere Sta
Blakemere Craft Centre
Manley
Mouldsworth
Ashton
Stonehouse

5

A550-TO QUEENSFERRY   A41, M53-TO CHESTER   A49-TO WHITCHURCH

Southport: The sands here were the scene of Henry Segrave's successful attempt on the world land speed record. On 16th March 1926, he took his Sunbeam to 152.3 mph (245km/h) to beat Malcolm Campbell's record. **Map ref. E1**

Eastham: The Manchester Ship Canal starts here and runs for 35 miles (56km) to Salford. Construction on the canal started in 1887 and it was opened to the first ships on the 1st January 1894. **Map ref. E4**

St. Asaph (Llanelwy): This tiny city boasts the smallest cathedral in Britain. **Map ref. B5**

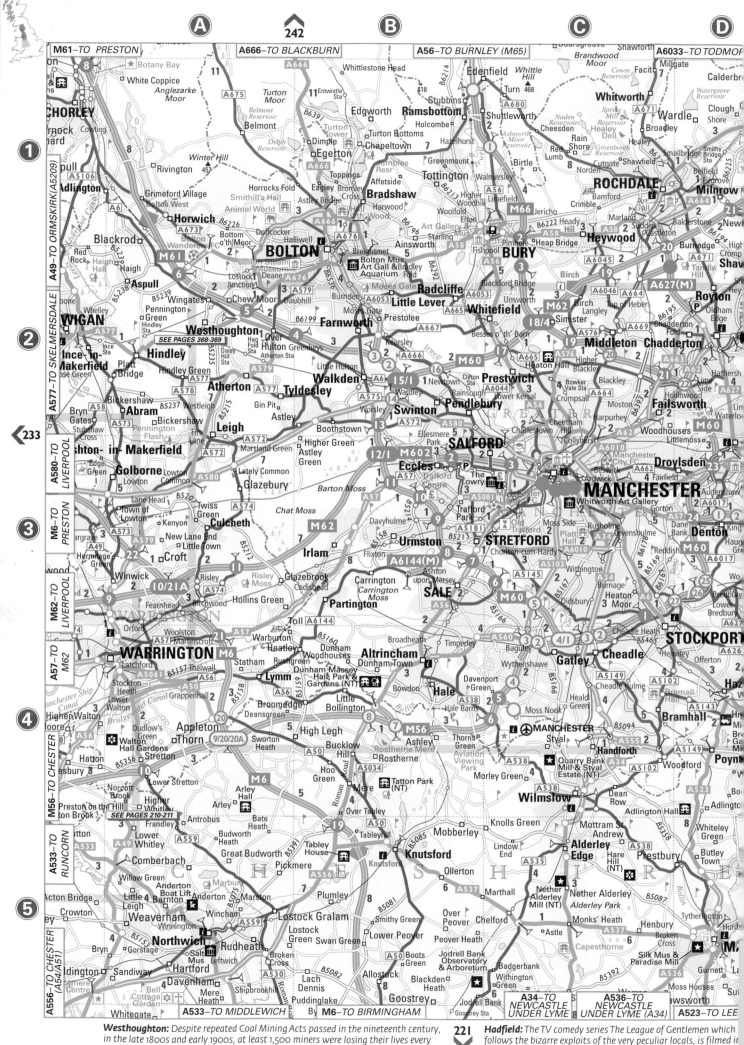

M61-TO PRESTON   A666-TO BLACKBURN   A56-TO BURNLEY (M65)   A6033-TO TODMOR

A49-TO ORMSKIRK (A5209)

A577-TO SKELMERSDALE

A580-TO LIVERPOOL

M6-TO PRESTON

M62-TO LIVERPOOL

A57-TO M62

A56-TO CHESTER

A533-TO RUNCORN

A556-TO CHESTER (A54/A51)

CHORLEY   Adlington   Horwich   Blackrod   Aspull   WIGAN   Ince-in-Makerfield   Hindley   Abram   Golborne   Culcheth   Croft   Winwick   WARRINGTON   Appleton Thorn   Stretton   Northwich   Hartford   Weaverham

BOLTON   Westhoughton   Atherton   Tyldesley   Leigh   Walkden   Farnworth   Radcliffe   Little Lever   Swinton   Pendlebury   Eccles   Irlam   Partington   Altrincham   Lymm   Knutsford

BURY   Whitefield   Middleton   Prestwich   SALFORD   MANCHESTER   Stretford   Urmston   SALE   Hale   Wilmslow   Alderley Edge   Jodrell Bank Observatory & Arboretum

ROCHDALE   Milnrow   Heywood   Chadderton   Royton   Failsworth   Droylsden   Denton   STOCKPORT   Gatley   Cheadle   Bramhall   Handforth   Woodford   Prestbury

Whitworth   Wardle

A533-TO MIDDLEWICH   M6-TO BIRMINGHAM   A34-TO NEWCASTLE UNDER LYME   A536-TO NEWCASTLE UNDER LYME (A34)   A523-TO LEE

Westhoughton: Despite repeated Coal Mining Acts passed in the nineteenth century, in the late 1800s and early 1900s, at least 1,500 miners were losing their lives every year down the pits. England's worst pit disaster occurred here, between Atherton and Westhoughton, on the 21st December 1910. An underground explosion at Hulton Colliery's Pretoria Pit, Number 3 Bank, killed 344 mine workers. It was later proved that over 300 of these had died from Carbon Monoxide poisoning. **Map ref. A2**

221

Hadfield: The TV comedy series The League of Gentlemen which follows the bizarre exploits of the very peculiar locals, is filmed in Hadfield. In the programme the village is known as Royston Vas. **Map ref. E3**

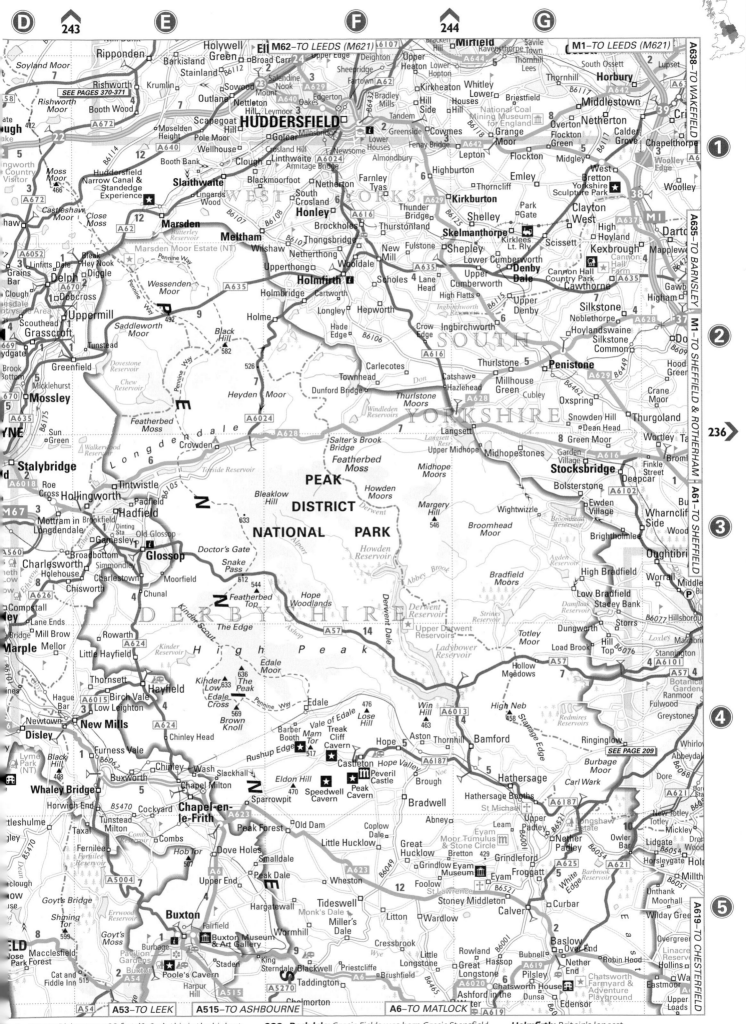

1

2

236

3

4

5

Kinder Scout: Rising to 2,088 feet (636m), this is the highest point in the Peak District National Park. On the 24th April 1932 over 450 Ramblers set off from Bowden Bridge near Hayfield on an organised 'mass trespass' in order to gain access to Kinder Scout members of the public. They eventually succeeded when, in 1951, it was designated as Britain's first National Park. **Map ref. E4**

222

Rochdale: Gracie Fields was born Gracie Stansfield here in 1898. She went on to become a famous music hall star and recording artist. She eventually retired to the Isle of Capri and was created Dame of the British Empire in 1979. She died later the same year. **Map ref. C1**

Holmfirth: Britain's longest running comedy series, Last of the Summer Wine has been filmed on location here since 1973. **Map ref. F2**

M1–TO LEEDS (M621)   A638–TO WAKEFIELD   A628–TO PONTEFRACT   A1–TO WETHERBY   A19–TO SELBY

NORTH YORKS

Horbury
Netherton
Crigglestone
39
SEE PAGES 370-371
Chapelthorpe
Woolley Edge

Sharlston
Crofton
Sandal Magna
Walton
Newmillerdam
Wintersett
Woolgreaves

Heath
West Hardwick
Ackworth School
Ackworth Moor Top
Fitzwilliam
Kinsley
Hemsworth Water Park

Purston Jaglin
Darrington
East Hardwick
Low Ackworth
Thorpe Audlin
Badsworth

Womersley
Little Smeaton
Kirk Smeaton
Norton
Campsall
Askern

Walden Stubbs
Fenwick
Moss

1

Horbury

Hemsworth
North Elmsall
Upton
Hampole
Skelbrooke
Barnsdale Bar
Sutton
Burghwallis
Skellow
Carcroft

Braithwaite
Kirk Bramwith

Royston
Shafton
Brierley
South Kirkby
South Elmsall

Darton
Staincross
Mapplewell
New Lodge
Grimethorpe
Clayton
Howell Wood
Hooton Pagnell
Brodsworth
Adwick le Street
Toll Bar
New Village
Arksey

Cudworth
Great Houghton
Marr

2

BARNSLEY
Dodworth
Worsbrough
Wombwell

Monk Bretton
Ardsley
Darfield
Middlecliff
Billingley
Thurnscoe
Goldthorpe
Bolton upon Dearne
Barnburgh
Hickleton
Cusworth Hall and Museum

DONCASTER
Sprotbrough
Wheatley Park
Bentley
Bentley Rise
Cusworth

235

Birdwell
Hood Green
Crane Moor
Thurgoland
Wortley
Tankersley
Bromley

Hemingfield
Brampton
Elsecar
West Melton
Wentworth
Elsecar Discovery Centre

Wath upon Dearne
Adwick upon Dearne
Swinton
Mexborough
Warmsworth
High Melton
Denaby Main
Denaby
Cadeby
Conisbrough
Hooton Roberts

Loversall
Rossington
New Rossington

3

Hoyland
Harley
Hood Hill
Burncross
Chapeltown
Wood Seats
Bracken Hill

Nether Haugh
Rawmarsh
Kilnhurst
Parkgate
Greasbrough
Dalton
Thrybergh
Ravenfield
Clifton
Old Edlington
Wadworth

New Edlington
Micklebring
Braithwell
Stainton
Tickhill

Wharncliffe Side
Oughtibridge
High Bradfield
Worrall
Ecclesfield
Grenoside
Kimberworth

ROTHERHAM
Eastwood
Dalton Magna
Sunnyside
Bramley
Hellaby
Carr

Maltby
Harworth
Styrup
Langold
Blyth

3

Middlewood
Hillsborough
Stannington
Malinbridge
Wadsley Bridge
Shirecliffe
Grimesthorpe
Wincobank
Meadowhall
Tinsley
Magna Centre
Brinsworth
Whiston

Herringthorpe
Wickersley
Hooton Levitt
Slade Hooton
Brookhouse
Firbeck
Oldcotes

SHEFFIELD
Darnall
Handsworth
Catcliffe
Treeton
Guilthwaite
Morthen
Upper Whiston
Thurcroft
Laughton en le Morthen
Throapham
Letwell

4

Fulwood
Ranmoor
Greystones
Nether Edge
Heeley
Gleadless
Woodhouse
Aughton
Aston
North Anston
Dinnington
South Anston
Carlton in Lindrick

Ringinglow
Whirlow
Norton Woodseats
Abbeydale
Beauchief
Greenhill
Highlane
Ridgeway
Beighton
Mosborough
Waterthorpe
Rother Valley
Waleswood
Todwick
Kiveton Park
Wales
Thorpe Salvin
Shireoaks
Gateford

WORKSOP

Dore
Totley
Coal Aston
Marsh Lane
Eckington
Renishaw Hall & Gardens
Spinkhill
High Woodall Moor
Harthill
Nethertorpe
Rhodesia
Kilton
Manton

Holmesfield
Dronfield
Apperknowle
West Handley
Middle Handley
Renishaw
Barlborough
Whitwell
Hodthorpe
Clumber Country Park

5

Owler Bar
Lidgate
Horsleygate
Millthorpe
Unstone
Unstone Green
Nether Handley
Barrow Hill
Mastin Moor
Barlborough

Common Side
Wilday Green
Barlow
Whittington
Staveley
Woodthorpe
Poolsbrook
Brimington
Clowne
Creswell
Welbeck Abbey
The Dukeries
Clumber Chapel
Norton

DERBYSHIRE

Overgreen
Linacre Reservoirs
Upper Newbold
Newbold
Tapton Grove
Inkersall
Inkersall Green
Duckmanton
Long Duckmanton
Shuttlewood
Elmton
Holbeck
Holbeck Woodhouse

CHESTERFIELD
Old Brampton
Brampton
Calow
Arkwright
Bolsover
Whaley
Whaley Thorns
Cuckney
Meden Vale

A61–TO DERBY (A38)   A617–TO MANSFIELD   M1–TO NOTTINGHAM   A60–TO MANSFIELD

Doncaster: *The legendary Flying Scotsman was built here in 1923 for just under £8000. As a passenger express train on the East Coast main line between London and Edinburgh it regularly reached a speed of 100 mph (160km/h). During its working life, up to 1963, it covered 2.4 million miles (3.86 million km). The Flying Scotsman is now in the National Railway Museum, York.* **Map ref. C2**

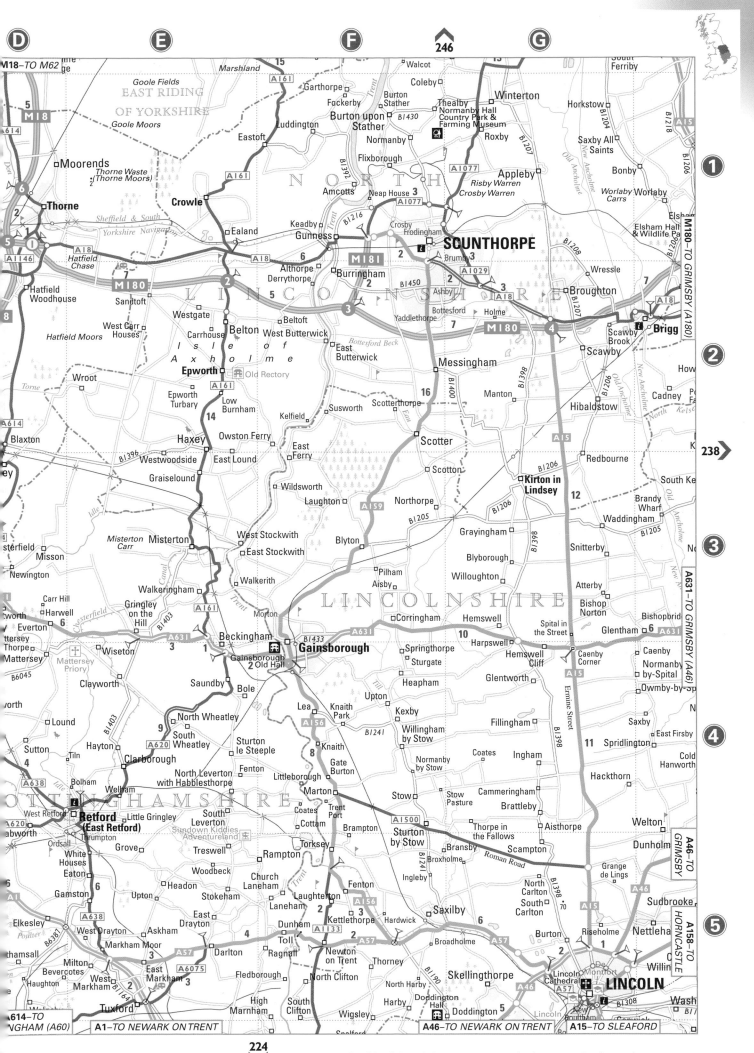

D   **E**   **F**   **G**

1
2
238
3
4
5

M18-TO M62

EAST RIDING
OF YORKSHIRE
Goole Moors
Goole Fields
Marshland

Moorends
Thorne Waste
(Thorne Moors)

Thorne

Crowle

Eastoft
Luddington

Garthorpe
Fockerby
Burton upon
Stather
Normanby
Flixborough
Amcotts

Walcot
Coleby
Burton
Stather

Thealby
Normanby Hall
Country Park &
Farming Museum
Roxby

Winterton
Horkstow

South
Ferriby

Saxby All
Saints
Bonby

Worlaby
Worlaby
Carrs

Elsham
Elsham Hall
& Wildlife Park

Appleby

Risby Warren
Crosby Warren

Hatfield
Chase

Hatfield
Woodhouse

Sandtoft

Westgate

Belton

Carrhouse

West Carr
Houses

Hatfield Moors

Isle of
Axholme

Epworth

Old Rectory

Ealand

Gunness

Althorpe
Derrythorpe

Beltoft
West Butterwick

East
Butterwick

Keadby
Crosby
Frodingham

Burringham

SCUNTHORPE

Brumby

Ashby

Bottesford

Holme

Yaddlethorpe

Broughton

Scawby
Brook

Scawby

Brigg

Messingham

Manton

Hibaldstow

Cadney

Wressle

How

Wroot

Epworth
Turbary

Low
Burnham

Haxey

Owston Ferry

East Lound

Westwoodside

Graiselound

Kelfield

Susworth

Scotterthorpe

Scotter

Scotton

Redbourne

South Ke

Blaxton

Misson

Newington

Wildsworth

Laughton

Northorpe

Kirton in
Lindsey

Brandy
Wharf

Waddingham

Grayingham

Snitterby

Misterton
Carr

Misterton

West Stockwith

East Stockwith

Blyton

Pilham
Aisby

Blyborough

Willoughton

Atterby

Bishop
Norton

Bishopbrid

terfield

Walkeringham

Walkerith

LINCOLNSHIRE

Glentham

Carr Hill
Harwell

Everton

Gringley
on the
Hill

Beckingham

Morton

Corringham

Hemswell

Spital in
the Street

Glentham

Caenby

Mattersey
Thorpe

Wiseton

Gainsborough
Old Hall

Gainsborough

Springthorpe
Sturgate

Harpswell

Hemswell
Cliff

Caenby
Corner

Normanby
by-Spital

Owmby-by-Sp

Mattersey
Priory

Clayworth

Saundby

Bole

Lea

Upton

Heapham

Glentworth

Saxby

Lound

Sutton

Hayton

Clarborough

North Wheatley

South
Wheatley

Sturton
le Steeple

Knaith
Park

Knaith

Kexby

Willingham
by Stow

Normanby
by Stow

Fillingham

East Firsby

Spridlington

Cold
Hanworth

West Retford

Retford
(East Retford)

Little Gringley

North Leverton
with Habblesthorpe

Fenton

Littleborough

Gate
Burton

Coates

Ingham

Hackthorn

Welton

Dunholm

Sutton

Tiln

Bolham
Welham

Marton

Stow

Stow
Pasture

Cammeringham

Brattleby

Aisthorpe

Ordsall

Grove

Treswell

Woodbeck

Coates
Cottam

Trent
Port

Brampton

Sturton
by Stow

Thorpe in
the Fallows

Scampton

Grange
de Lings

White
Houses
Eaton

Gamston

Headon

Upton

Stokeham

Church Laneham

Laneham

Fenton

Ingleby

Broxholme

North
Carlton
South
Carlton

Burton

Riseholme

Sudbrooke

Elkesley

West Drayton

Askham

East
Drayton

Dunham

Kettlethorpe

Hardwick

Saxilby

Broadholme

Nettleha

Willin

Milton
Bevercotes

Haughton

West
Markham

Markham Moor

East
Markham

Darlton

Ragnall

Toll

Newton
on Trent

Thorney

Skellingthorpe

Lincoln
Cathedral

LINCOLN

Wash

Tuxford

Fledborough

High
Marnham

South
Clifton

North Clifton

North Harby

Harby

Doddington
Hall

Doddington

De
Montfort

Wigsley

New
Brimford

A1-TO NEWARK ON TRENT

A46-TO NEWARK ON TRENT

A15-TO SLEAFORD

NGHAM (A60)

224

coln: The world's first military tank was built here in 1915.
tank was built by Fosters and, to protect its secrecy, it
designated as a water carrier, hence it became shortened
ank'. **Map ref. G5**

Scampton: On the night of the 16/17th May 1943, 65 Squadron's Lancaster Bombers took
off from their base at RAF Scampton to attack dams in the Ruhr area of Germany. This
was the famous Dam Busters raid. Although the operation was hailed as a great
success, it cost the lives of 53 airmen and over 1300 mainly Ukrainian prisoners of war
who were being held at a camp close to one of the dams. **Map ref. G5**

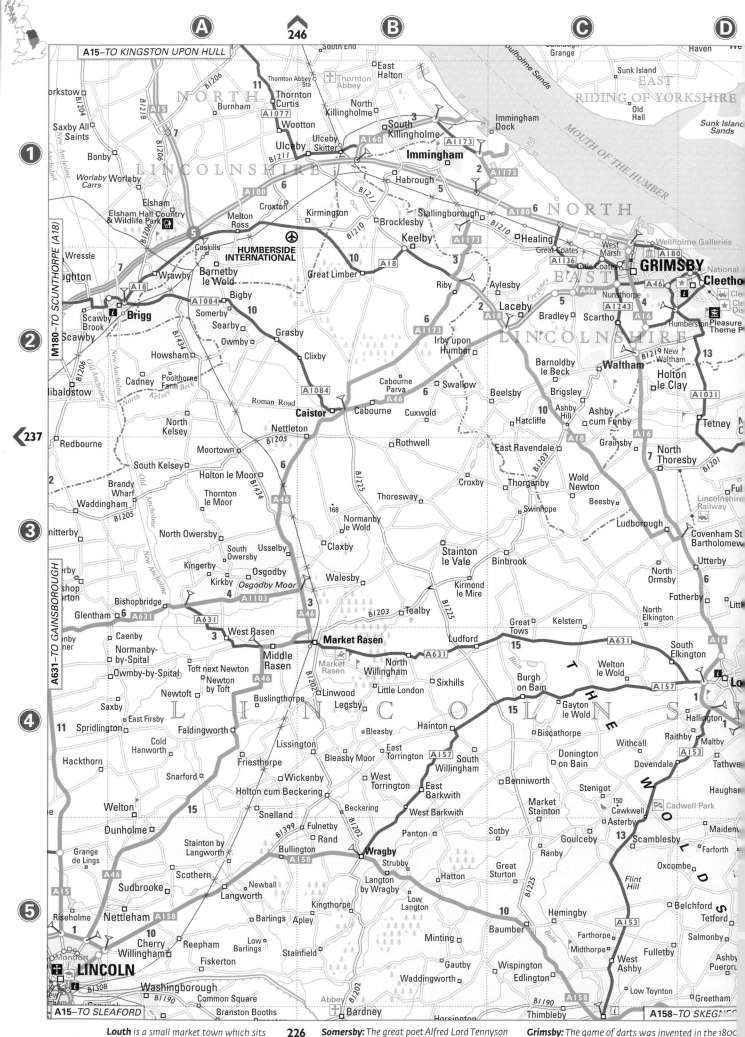

A15—TO KINGSTON UPON HULL

NORTH LINCOLNSHIRE

South End
East Halton
Thornton Abbey Sta
Thornton Abbey
Thornton Curtis
Burnham
North Killingholme
Wootton
Immingham Dock
South Killingholme
Ulceby
Ulceby Skitter
Habrough
Immingham

orkstow
B1206
B1218
Saxby All Saints
Bonby
Worlaby Carrs
Worlaby
ighton
Elsham
Elsham Hall Country & Wildlife Park
Wressle
Wrawby
Barnetby le Wold
Bigby
Somerby
Searby
Howsham
Owmby
Grasby
Clixby

Croxton
Kirmington
Brocklesby
Keelby
Great Limber
Riby
Aylesby
Laceby
Irby upon Humber
Cabourne Parva
Swallow
Cabourne
Cuxwold

Stallingborough
Healing
Great Coates
West Marsh
GRIMSBY
Little Coates
Nunsthorpe
Bradley
Scartho

MOUTH OF THE HUMBER

EAST RIDING OF YORKSHIRE
Salthouse Grange
Sunk Island
Old Hall
Haven
Sunk Island Sands

Wellholme Galleries
Cleetho
Cle
Cle
Dis
Humberston
Pleasure Theme P

M180—TO SCUNTHORPE (A18)

Scawby
Scawby Brook
Brigg
Scawby
ilibaldstow
Cadney
Poolthorne Farm
Redbourne
North Kelsey
Moortown
South Kelsey
Brandy Wharf
Waddingham
Holton le Moor
Thornton le Moor
North Owersby
Usselby
Claxby
Normanby le Wold
Kingerby
Kirkby
Osgodby
Osgodby Moor
Walesby
Bishopbridge
Glentham
West Rasen
Caenby
Normanby-by-Spital
Owmby-by-Spital
Middle Rasen
Toft next Newton
Newton by Toft
Newtoft
Saxby
East Firsby
Spridlington
Cold Hanworth
Faldingworth
Buslingthorpe
Linwood
Legsby
Hackthorn
Welton
Dunholme
Snelland
Friesthorpe
Lissington
Bleasby
Bleasby Moor
Holton cum Beckering
Snarford
Wickenby
Stainton by Langworth
Langworth
Sudbrooke
Scothern
Newball
Nettleham
Riseholme
Cherry Willingham
Reepham
Fiskerton
LINCOLN
De Montfort
Washingborough
Common Square
Branston Booths

Nettleton
Caistor
Roman Road
Thoresway
168
Claxby
Tealby
Market Rasen
North Willingham
Sixhills
Ludford
Hainton
Little London
Bleasby
East Torrington
South Willingham
West Torrington
East Barkwith
West Barkwith
Beckering
Panton
Fulnetby
Rand
Bullington
Wragby
Strubby
Hatton
Langton by Wragby
Low Langton
Kingthorpe
Barlings
Apley
Low Barlings
Stainfield
Minting
Gautby
Waddingworth
Bardney

Rothwell
Croxby
Thorganby
Wold Newton
Beesby
Swinhope
Stainton le Vale
Binbrook
Kirmond le Mire
Great Tows
Kelstern
Welton le Wold
Burgh on Bain
Gayton le Wold
Biscathorpe
Donington on Bain
Benniworth
Market Stainton
Sotby
Goulceby
Ranby
Great Sturton
Baumber
Hemingby
Wispington
Edlington
Hatcliffe
East Ravendale
Ashby Hill
Ashby cum Fenby
Grainsby
Ludborough
Covenham St Bartholomew
Utterby
North Ormsby
Fotherby
North Elkington
South Elkington
Withcall
Dovendale
Stenigot
Cawkwell
Asterby
Scamblesby
Farforth
Oxcombe
Flint Hill
Belchford
West Ashby
Farthorpe
Midthorpe
Low Toynton
Tetford
Salmonby
Fulletby
Greetham

Barnoldby le Beck
Brigsley
Waltham
Holton le Clay
Tetney
North Thoresby
New Waltham
Beelsby
Lincolnshire Railway
Covenham St Bartholomew
Cadwell Park
150
Maltby
Raithby
Haughar
Maiden
Tathwe
Litt

A631—TO GAINSBOROUGH
A631—TO GAINSBORO
A15—TO SLEAFORD
A158—TO SKEGNE

Louth is a small market town which sits astride the Greenwich Meridian and is famous for its magnificent 15th Century church. The spire of St James at 295 feet (91 metres) high is the tallest parish church spire in England. **Map ref. D4**

Somersby: The great poet Alfred Lord Tennyson was born here on the 5th August 1809. He was the fourth son of the Rev. George Tennyson, Rector of Somersby and Bag Enderby. **Map ref. D5**

Grimsby: The game of darts was invented in the 180c by the landlord of the Docker Arms Pub which stood i Freeman Street. The Spider's Web Pub, in Carr Lane, i called because of the design of a dartboard **Map ref.**

1

Skeffling

Easington

Kilnsea

Kilnsea Clays

Spurn Head · ★ Spurn Head

Centre

Light Rly

2

🚢 Kingston upon Hull to... hours
Rotterdam.................12
Zeebrugge.................14

3

arshchapel
Eskham
Wragholme · Donna Nook
Meals
thorpe
North Somercotes
Ludney · Church End
Conisholme · Skidbrooke North End
t Mary · South Somercotes · A1031 · Saltfleet
h · Skidbrooke
South Somercotes Fen Houses · 12
ivingham · Saltfleetby St Clements · *Great Eau*
Saltfleetby All Saints
rth · South Cockerington · Saltfleetby St Peter · Theddlethorpe St Helen
ngton
er · Grimoldby
B1200 · Manby · Theddlethorpe All Saints · A1031

4

IRE
Little Carlton · Great Carlton · E · *Great Eau*
Legbourne · North Reston · South Reston · Gayton le Marsh
thorpe · 11 · Strubby · A1104 · 3 · ℹ️ Mablethorpe
Authorpe · Withern · A157 · Thorpe · 4 · Trusthorpe
Tothill · Woodthorpe · B1373 · H · Maltby le Marsh · A52 · ▲ Sutton on Sea
Sutton le Marsh · Sandilands
Claythorpe · Beesby · Hagnaby · 6 · 5
on · Saleby · Hannah
ell · Aby · Greenfield · Markby · A52
8 · Belleau · A1104 · A1111
White Pit · Thoresthorpe · Asserby · The Grange · Anderby Creek
Swaby · Ailby · Bilsby · Thurlby · Huttoft
Ketsby · South Thoresby · ℹ️ · Alford · B1449 · Anderby
Rigsby · Bilsby Field
Calceby · Haugh · 3 · Farlesthorpe · 5
Driby · A1104 · Well · B1196 · Mumby
Ulceby Cross · Mawthorpe · Cumberworth · Authorpe Row
Sutterby · Ulceby · Helsey · Hogsthorpe
rton · A16 · Skendleby Psalter · Bonthorpe · Chapel St Leonards
🏛️ Harrington Hall · Willoughby
rdby · Langton · Claxby St Andrew · 10
nghar · 4 · Dalby · 5 · Slooth由 · A52
A16–TO BOSTON · A1028–TO SKEGNESS (A158)

5

urn Head: *Because of the rapid coastal erosion in this ea, the road to the head is frequently eroded away and s to be relaid.* **Map ref. E1**

Donna Nook: *An RAF Bombing Range which on the 18th July 2002 became the first national nature reserve to be established on MOD land. The reserve, which stretches for over 6 miles (10km) along the coast, is home to a range of flora and fauna including a colony of grey seals.* **Map ref. E3**

ISLE OF MAN

Point of Ayre

The Ayres
Rue Point
Ayres Visitor Centre
Glentruan
Cranstal
The Lhen
Dhowin
Bride
13
Sartfield
Andreas
Shellag Point
Jurby Head
Jurby East
Jurby West
Ballasalla
Sandygate
Regaby
Jurby
Crawyn
Ballachurry Fort
The Cronk
St Judes
Dhoor
Ramsey Bay
Orrisdale
Kella
Orrisdale Head
Ballaugh
Sulby
Churchtown
Ramsey
The Curraghs
Curraghs Wildlife Park
Port e Vullen
Maughold Head & Broogs
Ravensdale
Glen Auldyn
Dreemskerry
Maughold Head
Kirk Michael
Slieau Curn 351
Slieau Managh 383
North Barrule 565
Maughold
Ballajora
Slieau Dhoo 424
Port Mooar
Ballacarnane Beg
Slieau Freoaghane 488
Corrany
Glen Mona
Barregarrow
Sartfell 454
Clagh Ouyr 551
Gob y Deigan
Sulby Reservoir
Snaefell 621
Slieau Lhean 469
Dhoon
Manx Electric Rly
Knocksharry
Port Cornaa
St German's Cath
Cronk-y-Voddy
Little London
Laxey Wheel
Peel
Injebreck
Beinn-y-Phott 546
Snaefell Mountain Rly
Bulgham Bay
St Patrick's Isle Peel Castle & Round Tower
Ballagyr
Lambfell Moar
Colden 487
Laxey Glen
Laxey
House of Manannan
Neb
Injebreck Reservoir
Ballaheannagh
Contrary Head
Ballig
Slieau Ruy 478
Laxey Head
Knockaloe Moar
Patrick
Baldwin
Ballacannell
Heysham 3½
St John's
Greeba Mountain 422
Sulby
Baldrine
Glenmaye
333
Lower Foxdale
Crosby
Hillberry
Garwick Bay
Dalby Point
Dalby Mountain 280
Fairy
Garth
Glen Vine
Onchan
Clay Head
Dalby
Foxdale
Union Mills
Strang
Port Groudle
Niarbyl Island
Stuggadhoo
Braaid
Cooil
Onchan Head
Niarbyl Bay
South Barrule 483
Close Clark
Newtown
Quine's Hill
DOUGLAS
Douglas Bay
Stroin Vuigh
341
Ballamodha
St Mark's
Douglas Head
Ronague
Lingague
Grenaby
Ballaveare
Little Ness
Liverpool 2½-4hrs
Ballakilpheric
Rushen
Isle of Man Steam Rly
Bradda Head
Colby
Ballabeg
Ballasalla
Bradda
Ballafesson
Santon Head
Port Erin
Croit e Caley
Balladoole
Port Grenaugh
Calf of Man
ISLE OF MAN Nautical Mus
Derbyhaven
Meayl Circle
Cregneash
The Howe
Port St Mary
Castle Rushen
Castletown
Derby Fort
Bay ny Carrickey
St Michael's Island
Spanish Head
Castletown Bay
Langness
Chicken Rock
Dreswick Point

hours
Belfast (summer only).......2¾
Dublin (summer only)..2¾-4¾

Laxey: *The Lady Isabella water wheel, built in 1854 to pump water from local mine workings, is allegedly the world's largest water wheel, with a diameter of over 72 feet (22 metres). It still turns, but no longer pumps.* **Map ref. C3**

Isle of Man: The Isle of Man is a self-governing Island. Although a Crown Dependency it doesn't belong to either the UK or the European Union. The Island is 33 miles (53km) long, 13 miles (21km) wide and covers square miles (588 sq km). Over 40% of the island is uninhabited. Its strange three legged symbol means 'Quocunque Jeceris Stabit' (whichever way you throw me I stand). **Map ref. B3**

A590–TO KENDAL (A591)
Uendron　A5087
Scale
Dock Museum
Vickerstown　　Roose　Leece
Tummer　A590　Roosecote　Newbiggin
Hill Scar　　BARROW-IN-FURNESS
CUMBRIA　　　4
Biggar　　Roosebeck
Roa Island　Rampside　Mort Bank
Isle of　Sheep Island
Walney　South End　Foulney Island
Piel　Piel Island
Piel Bar

1

MORECAMBE　BAY

Cartmel Wharf

Lancaster Sound

Morecambe **1**
West
Sandylands
A5105
Heysham　A683–TO LANCASTER
Middleton
Ov

Hilpsford Point

Douglas, Isle of Man 3½ hrs

Yeoman Wharf

Heysham Lake

Larne 8hrs

Sunderland Bank
Sunderland
Sunderland Point **2**
Lune
Cockersand Abbey

Bernard Wharf

242 **⟩**

North Wharf
Pilling Lane　Ladies Hill
Rossall Point　Knott End-on-Sea　Fisher's
Fleetwood　　Pilling
Freeport　22　Stake Poo
Preesall　Scronkey
A588　Stalmine
Wyre　LANCS　Moor End
A585　　Eaglan Hill **3**
A587　Staynall　Cold　Sower Carr
Burn Naze　Row　Hale Nook
Cleveleys　7　Trunnah Stanah　Hambleton
Thornton　Little　Out Rawcliffe
Little Bispham　Thornton　Whin Lane End
Norbreck　Carleton　Skippool　Larbreck　Toll
Bispham　　A586　Little　Little
North Shore　Warbreck　Singleton　Eccleston　Co
BLACKPOOL　Poulton-　Singleton
BLACKPOOL　A584　Normoss　le-Fylde　Els
Hardhorn　B5266
Newton　Thistleton
Layton　Staining　Greenhalgh　A585
Blackpool Tower　A587　Blackpool Zoo　Esprick
Sea　A583　Mythop　Weeton　M
Life　Great　Mereside　3 **4**
South Shore　Centre　Marton　A583　1　M55–TO M6
South Pier　A5073　Great　Wes
Blackpool　Common Edge　Plumpton
Pleasure Beach　Squires Gate　Little　A583–TO PRESTON
A5230　Peel　Plumpton　Westby
4　Lower Ballam　Wrea Green
Blackpool Holiday Centre　BLACKPOOL　Higher　Bryning
Ballam　Moss　Hall Cross
St Anne's　Hey Houses　Side
LYTHAM ST ANNE'S　Ansdell　Warton **4**
Fairhaven　Saltcotes　Warton
Royal Lytham　Lytham　10　Bank
& St. Anne's　A584
Salter's　Ribble
Bank
Banks Sands　Ribble Estuary　**5**
Hesl

Hundred End
Banks
Horse Bank　9
Marshside　Crossens　Holmes

233 ⌄

nx Electric Railway: Cars 1 and 2, dating from 1893, are
oldest trams still in service in the world, regularly
ning the 18 miles (29km) between Douglas and Ramsey.
p ref. C3

Barrow in Furness: Famous for its steel and shipbuilding. In 1876
Barrow in Furness had the largest steelworks in the world. Today, it
is England's busiest shipyard with the largest covered ship building
hall in Europe. **Map ref. F1**

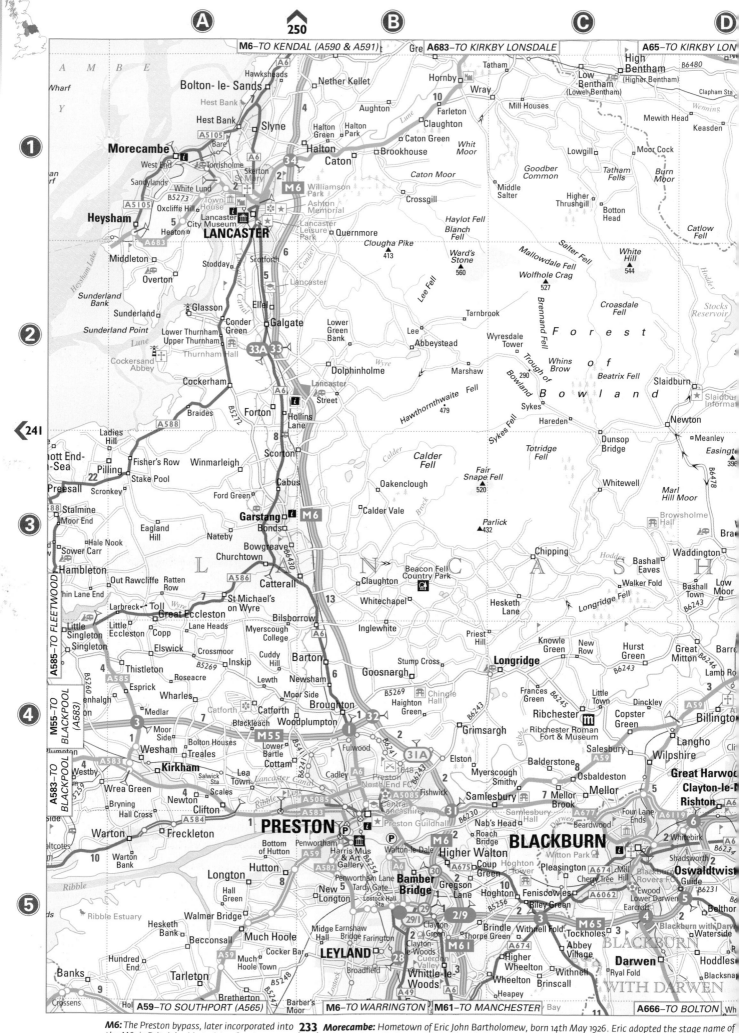

M6–TO KENDAL (A590 & A591)   Gre A683–TO KIRKBY LONSDALE   A65–TO KIRKBY LON

① Morecambe
Heysham
LANCASTER
Garstang
Kirkham
PRESTON
LEYLAND
Bamber Bridge
BLACKBURN
Darwen
Great Harwood
Clayton-le-
Rishton
Oswaldtwist

A59–TO SOUTHPORT (A565)   M6–TO WARRINGTON   M61–TO MANCHESTER   A666–TO BOLTON   Wh

M6: The Preston bypass, later incorporated into the M6, is Britain's oldest piece of motorway and was opened on 5th December 1958. **Map ref. B4**

233 Morecambe: Hometown of Eric John Bartholomew, born 14th May 1926. Eric adopted the stage name of Morecambe and, along with Ernie Wise, formed 'Morecambe and Wise'. They became one of Britain's mos successful comedy double-acts. Eric died on the 28th May 1984. **Map ref. A1**

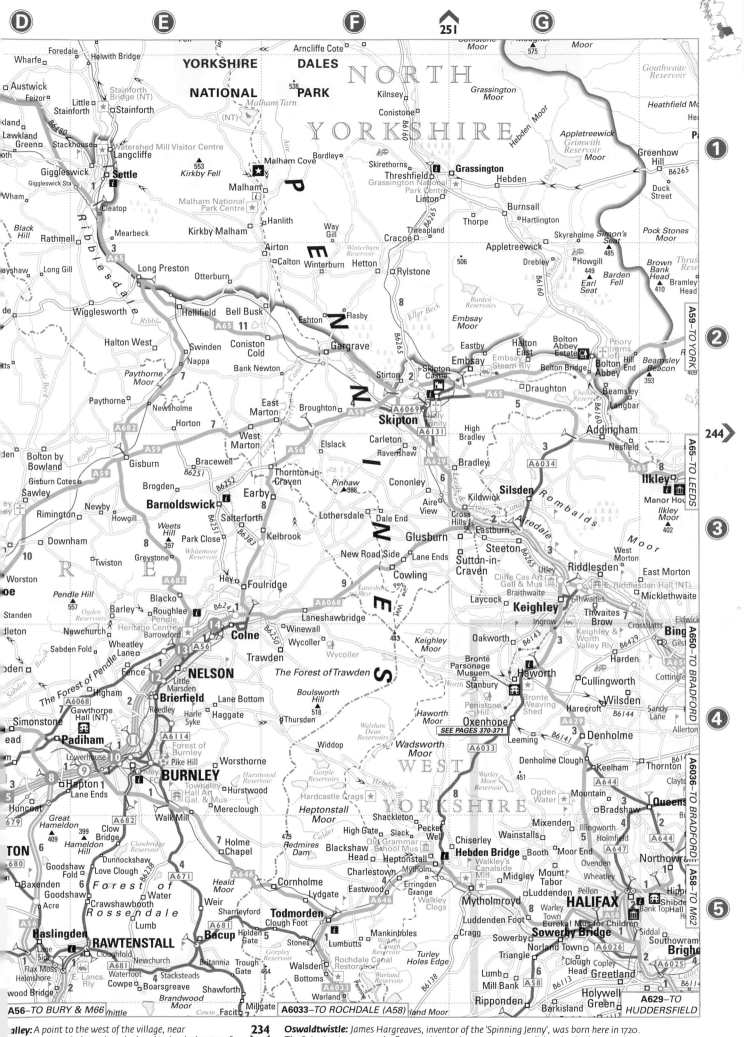

...lley:** A point to the west of the village, near ...derstones Hospital, can be calculated to be the 'centre of ...vity' of mainland Britain. **Map ref. D4**

Oswaldtwistle: James Hargreaves, inventor of the 'Spinning Jenny', was born here in 1720. The Spinning Jenny was the first machine to improve on the traditional spinning wheel and was capable of doing the work of 8 traditional spinners. The invention put Britain at the forefront of the textile industry. **Map ref. D5**

244 ›

234

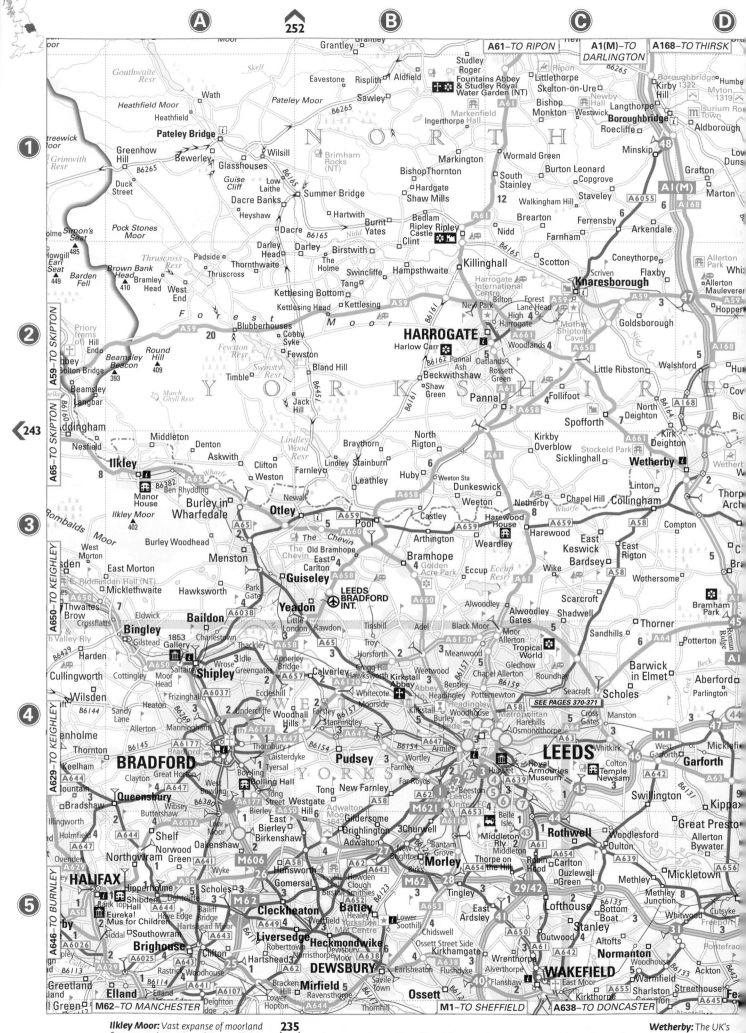

Ilkley Moor: Vast expanse of moorland famous as the setting of the unofficial Yorkshire anthem recognised throughout the world 'On Ilkley Moor Bah t 'at'. *Map ref. A3*

235

York: Guy Fawkes was born in York in 1570. Along with a group of conspirators he tried to blow up the Houses of Parliament on the 5th November 1605 but was arrested in the cellars before he could ignite the explosives. He is remembered every 5th November when we celebrate Bonfire Night. *Map ref. F2*

Wetherby: The UK's longest lasting rainbow (6 hours) was recorded here on 14th March 199... *Map ref. D3*

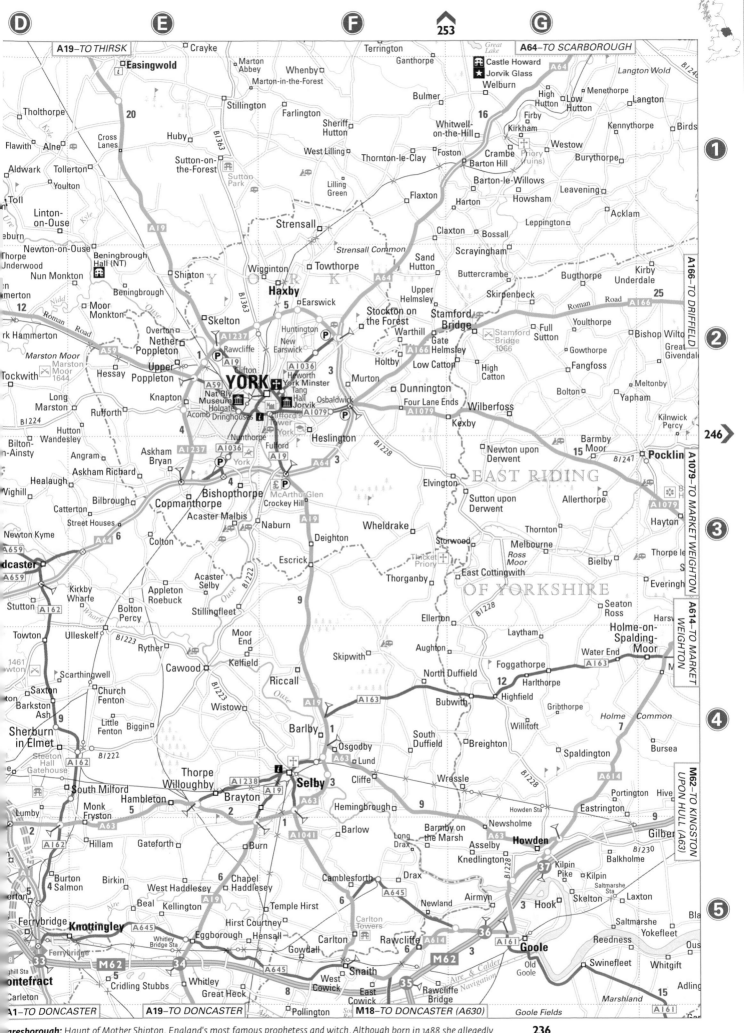

...resborough: Haunt of Mother Shipton, England's most famous prophetess and witch. Although born in 1488 she allegedly *...told of the Civil War, the Black Death and the Great Fire of London and one of her best known rhymes is uncannily accurate: ...riages without horses shall go, and accidents fill the world with woe. Around the world thoughts shall fly, in the twinkling of an eye. ...der water men shall walk, shall ride, shall sleep, shall talk. In the air men shall be seen, in white, in black and in green. ...n the water shall float, as easy as a wooden boat.* **Map ref. C2**

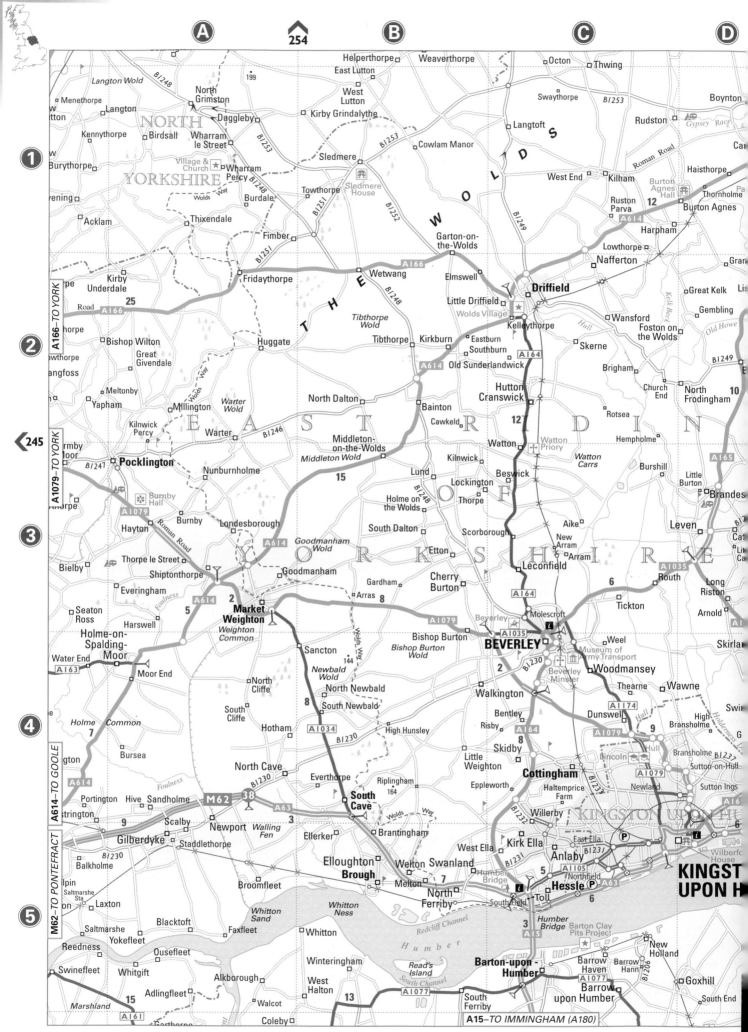

237 **Humber Bridge:** *Despite plans for a tunnel scheme in 1872 and numerous plans for a bridge, the first traffic did finally cross the river until the 24th June 1981. Work on the present suspension bridge began in 1973 with, at times, over 1000 workers being employed on the construction. The bridge was finally opened by HM The Queen on the 17th July 1981. At this time it had the longest bridge span in the world of 4626 feet (1410m). **Map ref. C5***

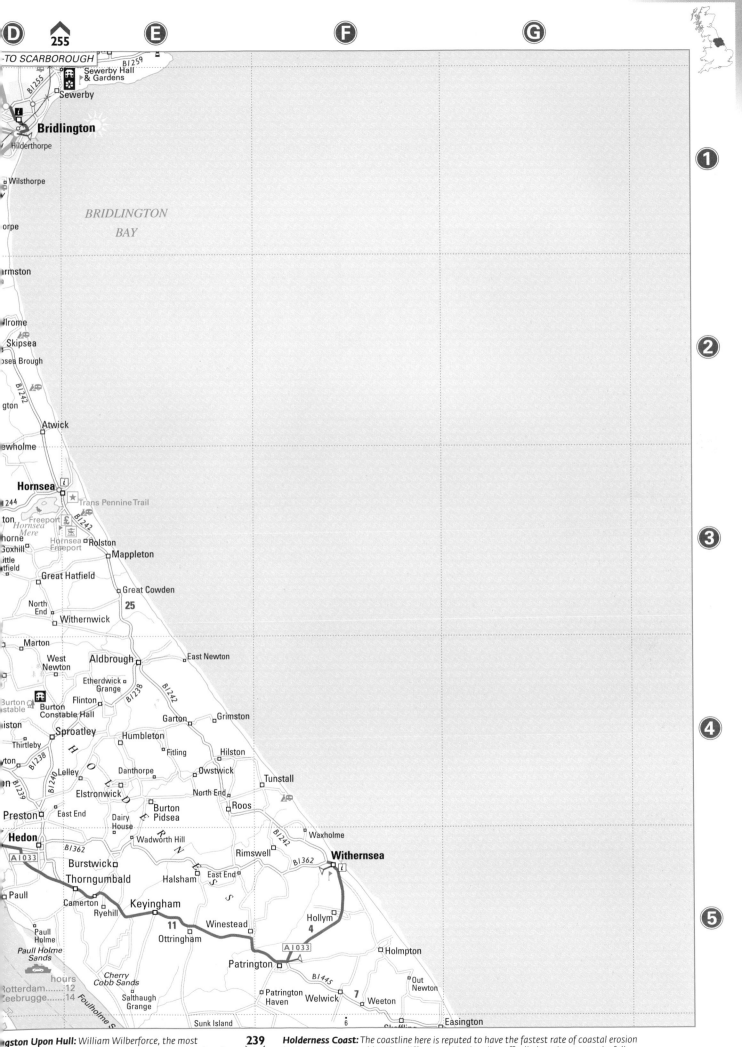

-TO SCARBOROUGH

Sewerby Hall & Gardens
Sewerby
B1259
B1255

Bridlington
Hilderthorpe

Wilsthorpe

BRIDLINGTON BAY

orpe

armston

Irome
Skipsea
sea Brough
B1242
gton

Atwick
ewholme

Hornsea
244
Trans Pennine Trail
ton
Freeport
Hornsea Mere
horne
Hornsea Freeport
Rolston
Goxhill
Mappleton
ittle
atfield
Great Hatfield
Great Cowden
North End
25
Withernwick
Marton
West Newton
Aldbrough
East Newton
Etherdwick Grange
B1238
B1242
Burton onstable
Burton Constable Hall
Flinton
Garton
Grimston
iston
Sproatley
Humbleton
Thirtleby
Fitling
Hilston
yton
B1238
Lelley
Danthorpe
Owstwick
B1240
Elstronwick
North End
Tunstall
B1239
Preston
East End
Dairy House
Burton Pidsea
Roos
Hedon
Wadworth Hill
Waxholme
A1033
B1362
Rimswell
B1242
Withernsea
Burstwick
B1362
Thorngumbald
Halsham
East End
Paull
Camerton
Ryehill
Keyingham
Hollym
11
Winestead
4
Paull Holme
Ottringham
A1033
Paull Holme Sands
Holmpton
hours
Rotterdam......12
Zeebrugge......14
Cherry Cobb Sands
Patrington
Out Newton
B1445
Sunk Island
Salthaugh Grange
Patrington Haven
Welwick
Weeton
7
Foulholme S
6
Easington

gston Upon Hull: William Wilberforce, the most
portant figure in the abolition of slavery, was born here in
9. After years of campaigning, Wilberforce died on the 29th
1833 and just one month later Parliament passed the
very Abolition Act which gave all slaves in the British
pire their freedom. **Map ref. D5**

Holderness Coast: The coastline here is reputed to have the fastest rate of coastal erosion
in the world. The Boulder Clay cliffs along this shoreline offer little resistance to the full
force of the sea and are constantly 'slumping' (sliding slowly into the sea). This part of the
coast from Spurn Head to Bridlington has lost a mile of shore in the last hundred years
and is currently losing a further 6.5 feet (2m) every year. **Map ref. E4**

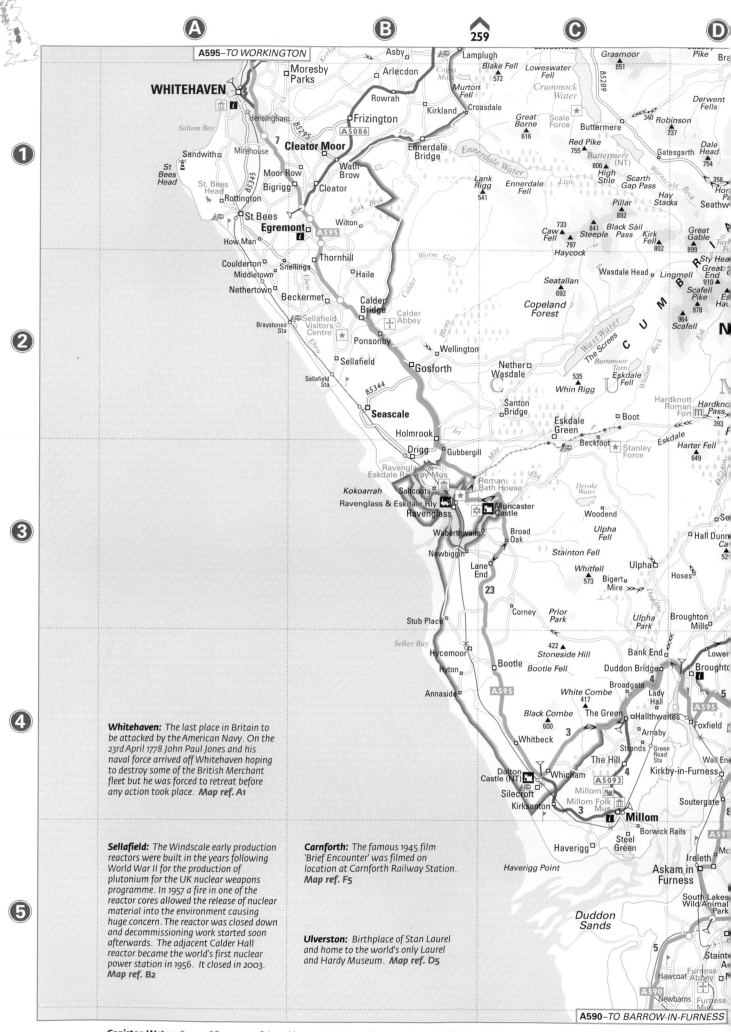

A595–TO WORKINGTON

1

WHITEHAVEN

Moresby
Parks

Asby

Lamplugh

Blake Fell
572

Lowswater
Fell

Grasmoor
851

Lowswater

Arlecdon

Loweswater
Fell

Murton
Fell

Crummock
Water

Derwent
Fells

Rowrah

Kirkland

Croasdale

Great
Borne
616

Scale
Force

340

Robinson
737

Frizington

Buttermere

A5086

Ennerdale
Bridge

Ehen

Red Pike
755

Buttermere
(NT)

Gatesgarth

Dale
Head
754

Hensingham

Cleator Moor

7

Saltom Bay

Sandwith
Mirehouse

Wath
Brow

Ennerdale
Water

Lank
Rigg
541

Ennerdale
Fell

Liza

High
Stile
806

Scarth
Gap Pass

358

Seathw

St
Bees
Head

Moor Row

Bigrigg

Cleator

Pillar
892

Hay
Stacks

St. Bees
Head

Kirk Beck

Wilton

733

Caw
Fell

841
Steeple
797

Black Sàil
Pass

Kirk
Fell
802

Great
Gable
899

Rottington

Egremont

A595

Copeland
Forest

Haycock

Scafell
Pike
978

Est
Hau

How Man

Thornhill

Worm
Gill

Seatallan
692

Wasdale Head

Lingmell
910

Great
End

964
Scafell

Coulderton
Middletown

Snellings

Haile

Calder

Wasdale Head

C
U
M

Nethertown

Beckermet

Calder
Bridge

Calder
Abbey

Wast Water

The Screes

Burnmoor
Tarn
535

Eskdale
Fell

Hardknott
Roman
Fort

Scafell

N

Braystones
Sta

Ehen

Sellafield
Visitors
Centre

Ponsonby

Bleng

Wellington

Nether
Wasdale

Whin Rigg

Will

Hardkn
Pass
393

2

Sellafield

Santon
Bridge

Gosforth

B5344

Eskdale
Green

Boot

Sellafield
Sta

Seascale

Stanley
Force

Eskdale

Harter Fell
649

Duddo

Holmrook

Irt

Beckfoot

Gubbergill

Drigg

Mire

Esk

Ravenglass &
Eskdale Railway Mus

Roman
Bath House

Devoke
Water

Woodend

Kokoarrah

Saltcoats

Ravenglass & Eskdale Rly
Ravenglass

Muncaster
Castle

Ulpha
Fell

Hall Dunn
Ca
52

3

Waberthwaite

Broad
Oak

Stainton Fell

Ulpha

Hoses

Newbiggin

Lane
End

Whitfell
573

Bigert
Mire

23

Corney

Prior
Park

Ulpha
Park

Broughton
Mills

Stub Place

422
Stoneside Hill

Bank End

Broughton

Selker Bay

Hycemoor

Duddon Bridge

Lower

Hyton

Bootle

Bootle Fell

Broadgate

4

A595

Annaside

A595

White Combe
417

Lady
Hall

5

4

Whitbeck

Black Combe
600

The Green

Arnaby

Foxfield

Hallthwaites

Strands

Green
Road
Sta

Wall En

3

The Hill

Kirkby-in-Furness

Dalton
Castle (NT)

Whicham

A5093

4

Silecroft

Millom

Soutergate

Kirksanton

Millom Folk
Mus

3

Millom

Borwick Rails

Haverigg

Steel
Green

A590

Ireleth

Haverigg Point

Askam in
Furness

South Lakes
Wild Animal
Park

Duddon
Sands

5

5

Staint
A

Hawcoat

Furness
Abbey

Newbarns

Furness
Mu

A590–TO BARROW-IN-FURNESS

Whitehaven: *The last place in Britain to be attacked by the American Navy. On the 23rd April 1778 John Paul Jones and his naval force arrived off Whitehaven hoping to destroy some of the British Merchant fleet but he was forced to retreat before any action took place.* **Map ref. A1**

Sellafield: *The Windscale early production reactors were built in the years following World War II for the production of plutonium for the UK nuclear weapons programme. In 1957 a fire in one of the reactor cores allowed the release of nuclear material into the environment causing huge concern. The reactor was closed down and decommissioning work started soon afterwards. The adjacent Calder Hall reactor became the world's first nuclear power station in 1956. It closed in 2003.* **Map ref. B2**

Carnforth: *The famous 1945 film 'Brief Encounter' was filmed on location at Carnforth Railway Station.* **Map ref. F5**

Ulverston: *Birthplace of Stan Laurel and home to the world's only Laurel and Hardy Museum.* **Map ref. D5**

Coniston Water: *Scene of five successful world water speed record attempts by Malcolm Campbell and Donald Campbell between 1939 and 1959. Donald Campbell was killed here on the 4th January 1967 whilst trying to break his own record, when his boat Bluebird K7 bounced off the surface of the lake at about 300 mph (483 km/h), somersaulted several times and then sank. The wreck of Bluebird and Campbell's remains were eventually recovered from the lake in March 2001.* **Map ref. E3**

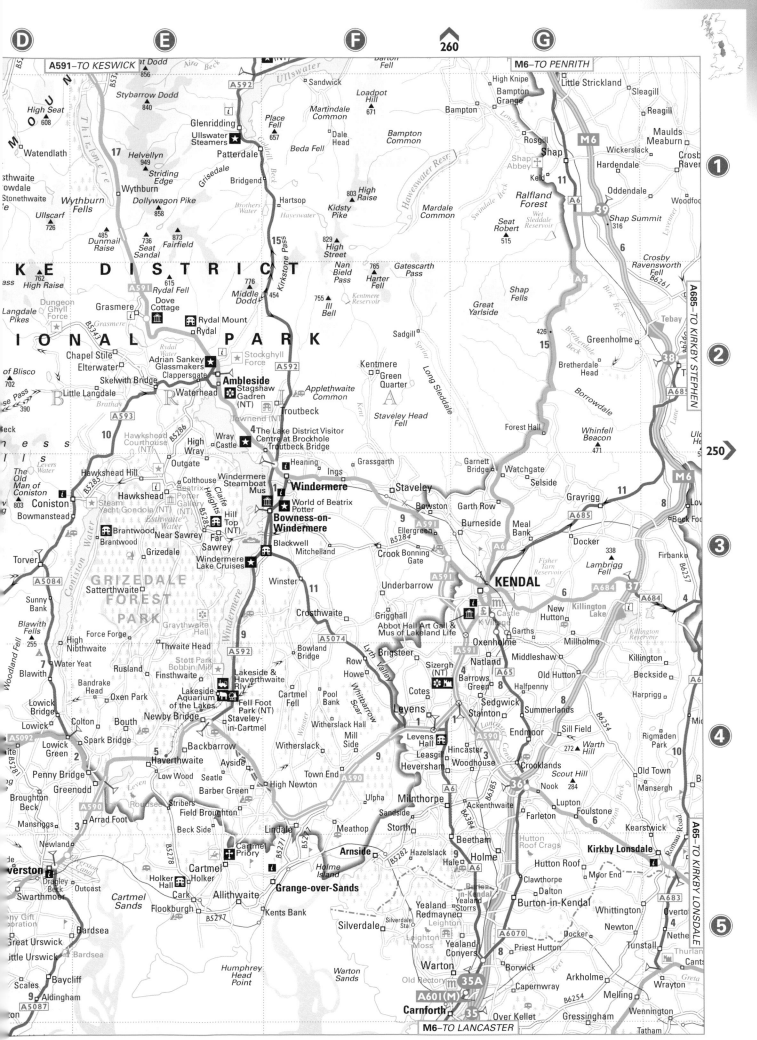

Grasmere: William Wordsworth lived for a number of years at nearby Dove Cottage. He died in 1850 and is buried in the churchyard of St Oswald's Church. His simple tombstone has since become one of the most visited literary shrines in the world. **Map ref. E2**

242

Windermere: Lake Windermere is the largest natural lake in England. It is 12 miles (19.3km) long, 1 mile (1.6km) wide and 220 feet (67m) deep. The lake is a major centre for water sports and there are over 10,000 boats registered on the lake. Henry Segrave was killed here in breaking the world water speed record in 1930. **Map ref. E3**

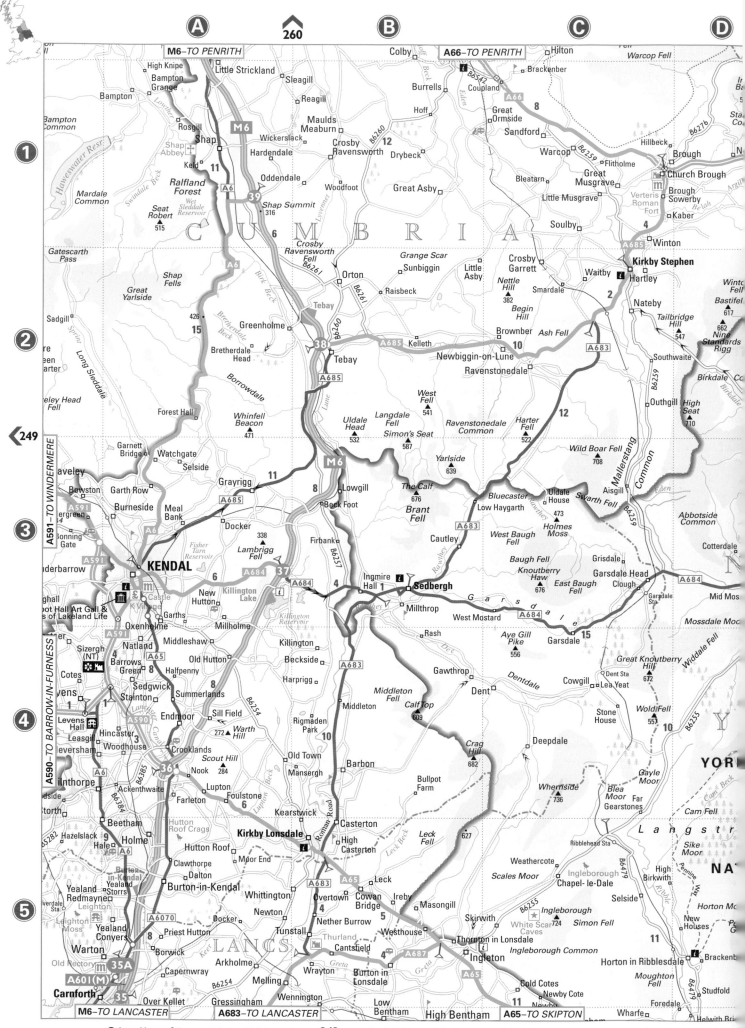

A6—TO PENRITH
A66—TO PENRITH

CUMBRIA

M6—TO PENRITH

Kirkby Stephen

KENDAL

Sedbergh

Kirkby Lonsdale

Ingleton

M6—TO LANCASTER
A683—TO LANCASTER
A65—TO SKIPTON

Orton: *Home of George Whitehead (1636–1723) one of the founders of the Quaker Movement. Like many Quakers at the time Whitehead was imprisoned for his beliefs.* **Map ref. B2**

Kendal: *Home of the famous Kendal Mint Cake, popular as an energy boosting food and eaten by Shackleton on his 1914–1917 Transarctic Expedition and by the 1953 Everest Expedition. Reputedly made by accident when a local confectioner Joseph Wiper, at his tiny Ferney Green factory, was intending to make glacier mints. It is now famous the world over.* **Map ref. A3**

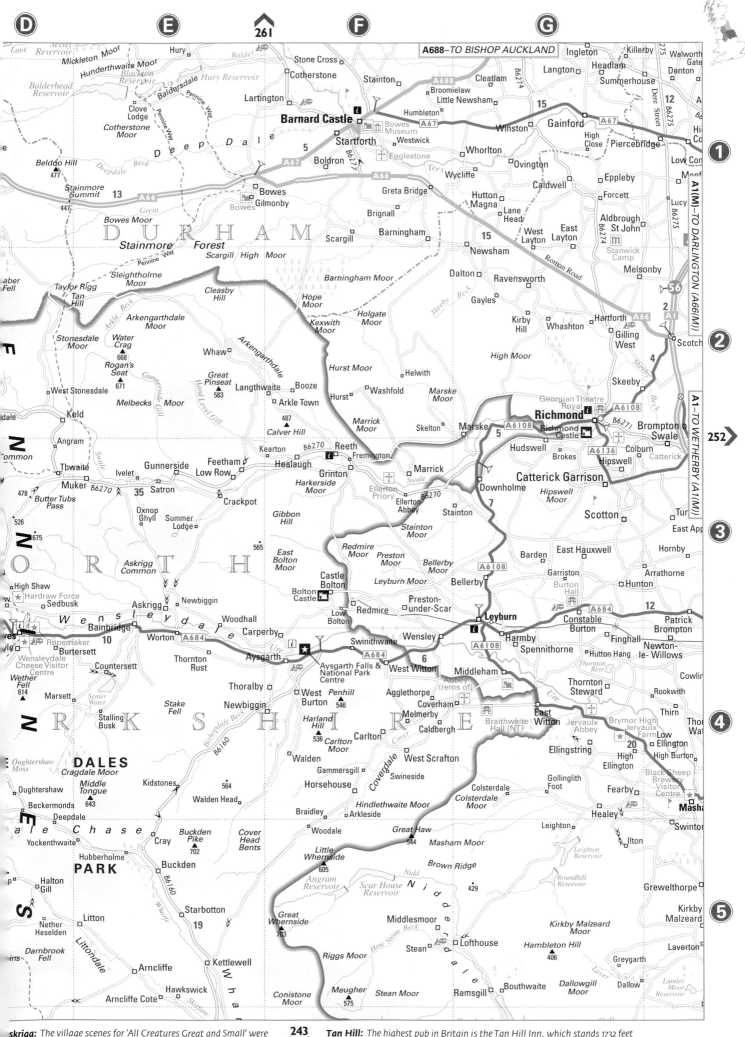

261

skrigg: *The village scenes for 'All Creatures Great and Small' were* *lmed here. The TV series, based on books by James Herriot was* *bout country vets located in the Yorkshire Dales. The series ran* *om 1978 to 1990.* **Map ref. E3**

243

Tan Hill: *The highest pub in Britain is the Tan Hill Inn, which stands 1732 feet* *(528m) above sea level.* **Map ref. E2**

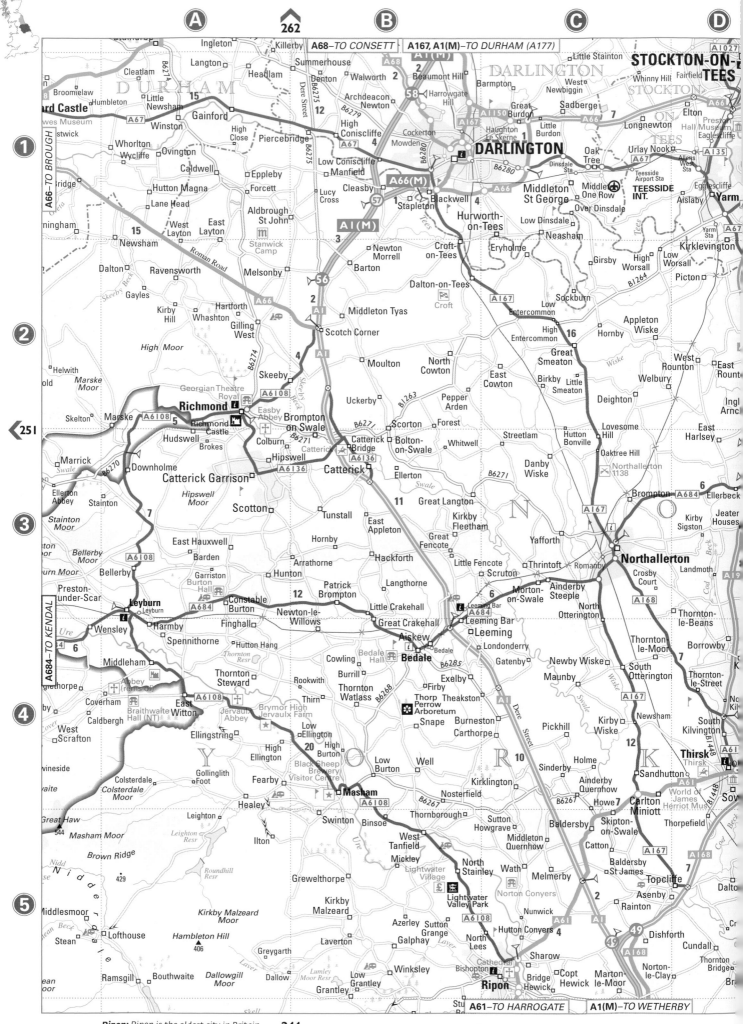

STOCKTON-ON-TEES

DARLINGTON

DURHAM

rd Castle

Richmond

Catterick Garrison

Catterick

Northallerton

Leyburn

A684–TO KENDAL

Bedale

Masham

Thirsk

A66–TO BROUGH

251

Ripon

Ripon: Ripon is the oldest city in Britain
with a charter dating back to AD886.
Map ref. C5

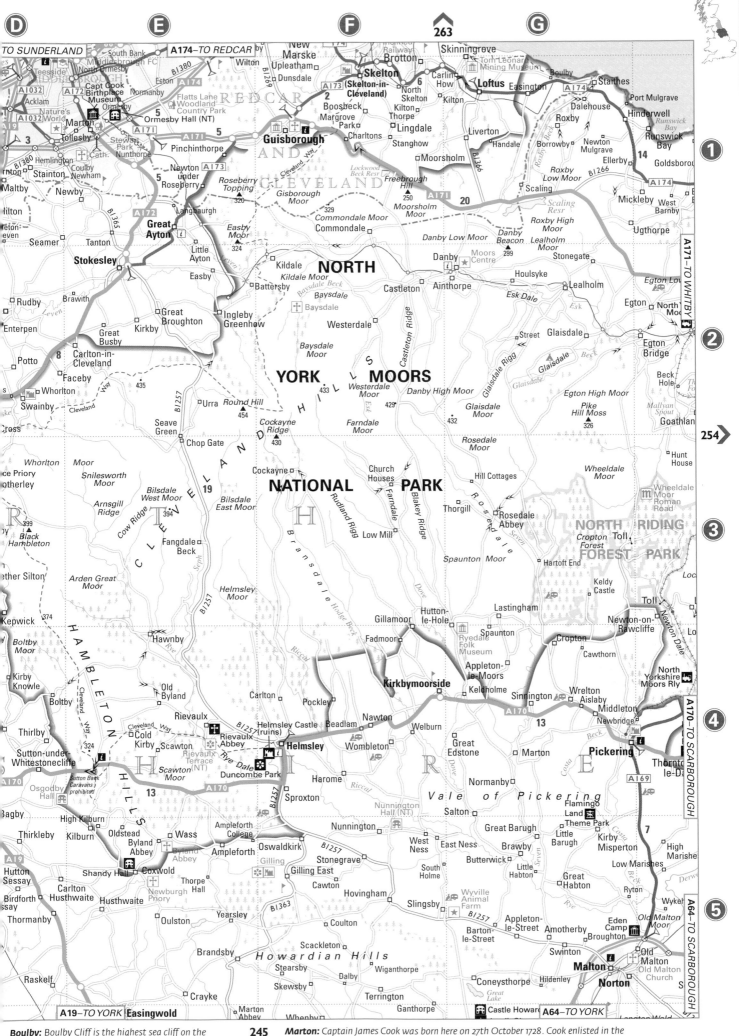

Boulby: Boulby Cliff is the highest sea cliff on the east coast of Britain at 666 feet (203m). **Map ref. G1**

245

Marton: Captain James Cook was born here on 27th October 1728. Cook enlisted in the Royal Navy and in 1768 began the first of three voyages to the Pacific where he spent over eight years charting previously unknown islands. He was stabbed to death by natives on the island of Hawaii in February 1779. **Map ref. G4**

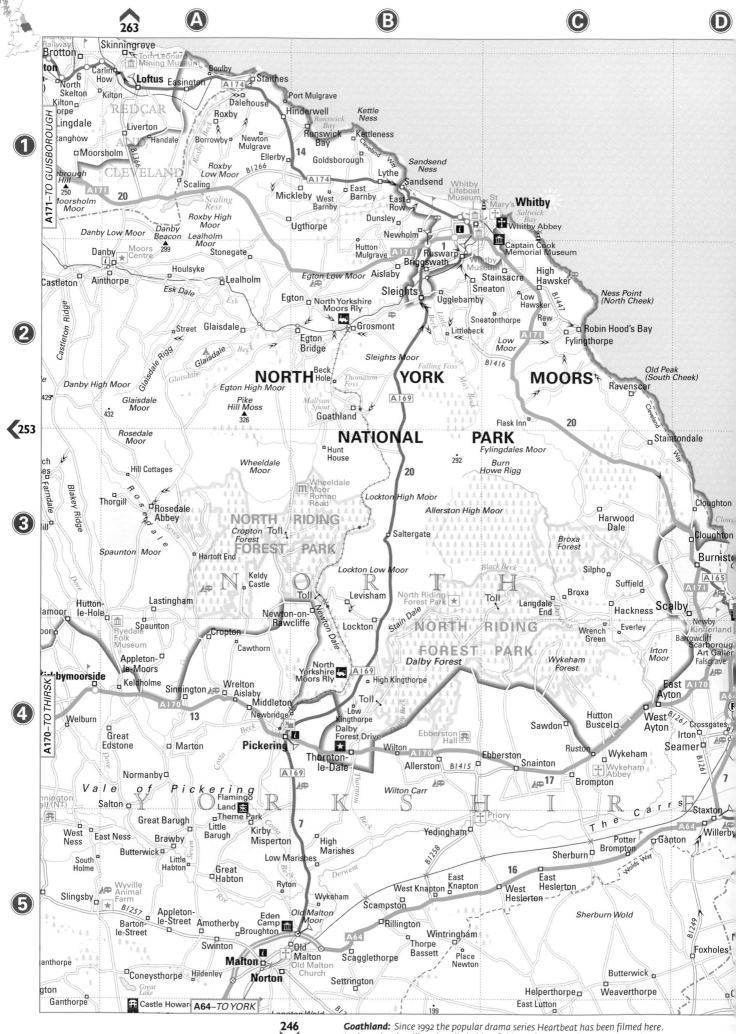

A B C D

1 2 3 4 5

253

Goathland: Since 1992 the popular drama series Heartbeat has been filmed here. In the series the village is called Aidensfield and frequent references are made to nearby Whitby **Map ref. B2.**
The spin-off hospital series 'The Royal' is located in Scarborough. **Map ref. D4**

cks

Bay
ture Railway
orough Castle

BOROUGH

Complex

Rocks

odby
Cayton Bay

ron 7

ston

Gristhorpe

rtford A165

A1039

West Muston
Flotmanby

Hunmanby

The Wyke

Filey Brigg

Filey

Filey Bay

Reighton Sands

Reighton

Speeton

Crab Rocks

B1229

Buckton

Bempton Bempton Cliffs

B1255

Flamborough B1255

Flamborough Head

Burton
Fleming

10

Grindale A165

T RIDING OF YORKSHIRE

ng

Marton B1259

Sewerby Hall
& Gardens

A165–TO BRIDLINGTON

ey: *The Royal Crescent, built by John Wilkes Unett*
850, was for 100 years the most fashionable address
he whole of the north of England. **Map ref. E4**

247

Flamborough Head: *This rocky chalk headland juts out 6 miles into the*
North Sea and features picturesque coves and sea caves. Because of its
chalk-loving flora it is designated a Special Area of Conservation (SAC).
Map ref. F5

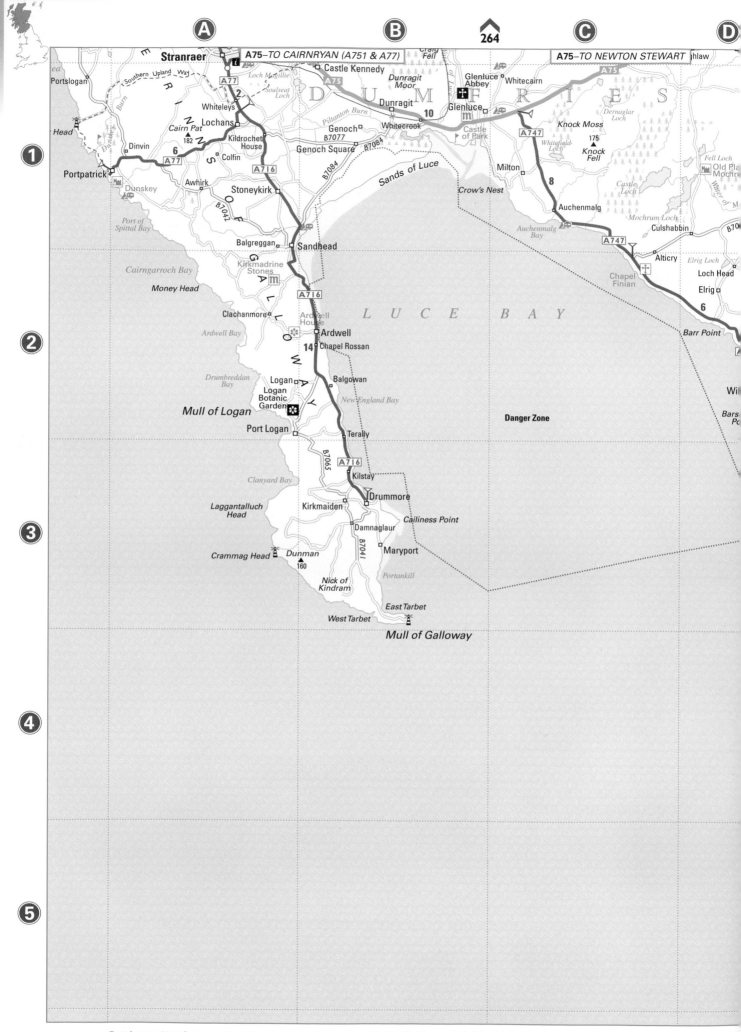

Portslogan

Stranraer

A75–TO CAIRNRYAN (A751 & A77)

Castle Kennedy

DRUMFRIES

Dunragit Moor

Glenluce Abbey

Whitecairn

A75–TO NEWTON STEWART

hlaw

Loch Magillie

Soulseat Loch

Southern Upland Way

Head

A77

Whiteleys

Lochans

Cairn Pat
182

Kildrochet House

Dunragit

Whitecrook

Genoch
B7077

Glenluce

10

Castle of Park

Knock Moss

Dernaglar Loch

Glenluce

A747

Whitefield Loch

175

Knock Fell

Fell Loch

Castle Loch

Old Pla Mochru

Dinvin

6

A77

Colfin

Awhirk

Genoch Square

B7084

B7084

Milton

8

Portpatrick

Dunskey

Stoneykirk

A716

Sands of Luce

Crow's Nest

Auchenmalg

Auchenmalg Bay

A747

Culshabbin

B70

Port of Spittal Bay

B7042

Balgreggan

Sandhead

Alticry

Loch Head

Cairngarroch Bay

Kirkmadrine Stones

Chapel Finian

Elrig Loch

Money Head

A716

L U C E   B A Y

Elrig

6

Clachanmore

Ardwell House

Ardwell

Barr Point

Ardwell Bay

14

Chapel Rossan

Drumbreddan Bay

Logan

Balgowan

New England Bay

Danger Zone

Wi

Logan Botanic Garden

Bars Po

Mull of Logan

Port Logan

Terally

B7065

A716

Clanyard Bay

Kilstay

Laggantalluch Head

Kirkmaiden

Drummore

Cailiness Point

Crammag Head

Dunman
160

Damnaglaur

B7041

Maryport

Portankill

Nick of Kindram

East Tarbet

West Tarbet

Mull of Galloway

1

2

3

4

5

Port Logan: Now famous as the setting for the BBC Television Series '2000 Acres of Sky', which starred Michelle Collins.
Map ref. A2

Mull of Galloway: A Mull is a high point of land on a rocky coast that juts out into the sea. Here, the Mull of Galloway is the most southerly point in Scotland.
Map ref. B3

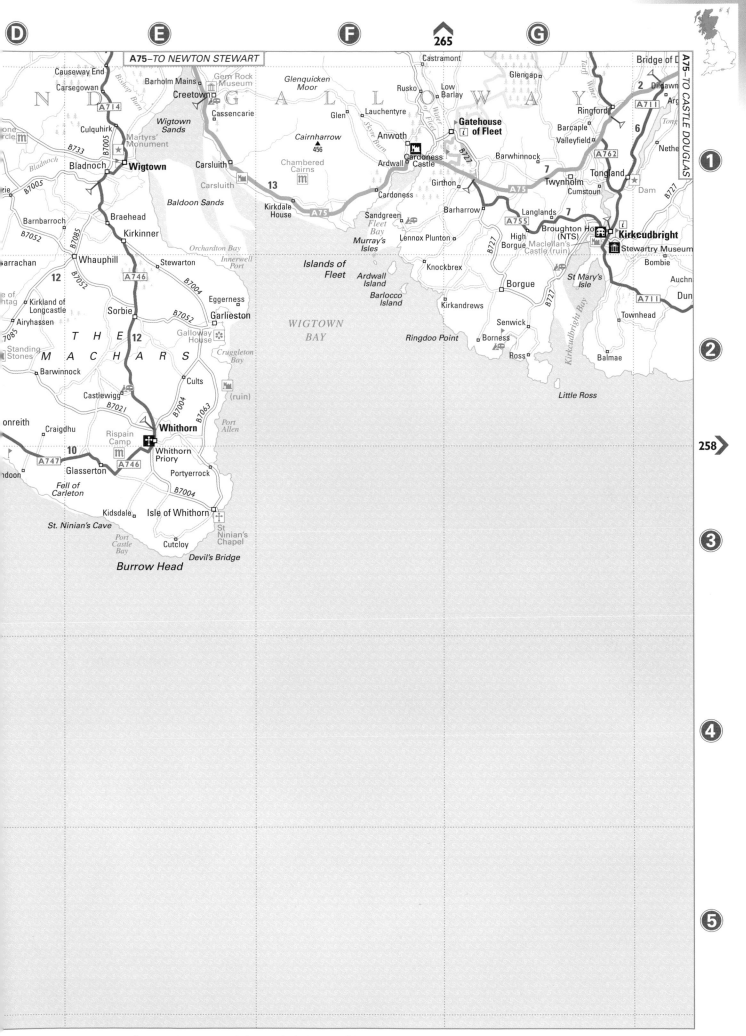

A75–TO NEWTON STEWART

A75–TO CASTLE DOUGLAS

Castramont

Bridge of D

N D   GALLOWAY

Glenquicken
Moor

Causeway End

Carsegowan

Barholm Mains

Creetown

Gem Rock
Museum

Glengap

2   Dildawn

A714

Culquhirk

Wigtown
Sands

Cassencarie

Rusko

Low
Barlay

Ringford

A711

6   Arg

Martyrs'
Monument

Glen

Lauchentyre

**Gatehouse
of Fleet**

Barcaple

Valleyfield

Nethe

Bladnoch

Wigtown

Carsluith

Cairnharrow

456

Anwoth
Ardwall

Cardoness
Castle

Barwhinnock

A762

Tongland

Tong

1

B733

B7005

Chambered
Cairns

13

Cardoness

Girthon

Twynholm
Cumstoun

Dam

B727

Braehead

Carsluith

Baldoon Sands

Kirkdale
House

A75

Sandgreen

Barharrow

Langlands

7

Broughton Ho
(NTS)

i

Kirkcudbright

Barnbarroch

Kirkinner

Orchardton Bay
Innerwell
Port

*Fleet
Bay*

Murray's
Isles

Lennox Plunton

High
Borgue

Maclellan's
Castle (ruin)

Stewartry Museum

B7052

B7085

Whauphill

Stewarton

B7004

*Islands of
Fleet*

Ardwall
Island

Knockbrex

Borgue

St Mary's
Isle

Bombie

Auchn

arrachan

12

A746

Eggerness

Barlocco
Island

B727

Dun

e of
htag

Kirkland of
Longcastle

B7052

Sorbie

Garlieston

*WIGTOWN
BAY*

Kirkandrews

A711

Airyhassen

B7052

Galloway
House

Ringdoo Point

Senwick

Townhead

7085

T H E

12

*Cruggleton
Bay*

Borness

Ross

Balmae

Standing
Stones

M A C H A R S

Barwinnock

Cults

Little Ross

Castlewigg

B7004

B7021

Whithorn

*Port
Allen*

(ruin)

onreith

Craigdhu

Rispain
Camp

Whithorn
Priory

258

A747

10

A746

Glasserton

Portyerrock

ndoon

Fell of
Carleton

B7004

Kidsdale

Isle of Whithorn

St. Ninian's Cave

*Port
Castle
Bay*

Cutcloy

St
Ninian's
Chapel

Devil's Bridge

Burrow Head

Wigtown: *The Martyrs Stake here marks the location of the execution
by drowning of the 'Covenanters' Margaret Wilson and Margaret
McLachlane in 1685. Their gravestones are in Wigtown churchyard.*
Map ref. E1

A75–TO DUMFRIES

Br

Rhonehouse
(Kelton Hill)

Dildawn

Breoch

Gelston

B736

B727

Palnackie

Dalbeattie
Forest

B793

Kirkbean

Carsethorn

Cavens

Borron Point

Argrennan House

Airieland

Barnbarroch

Fairgirth

Caulkerbush

Southwick

A710

Arbigland

⌂

2

A711

6

Tongland Loch

Netherthird

Screel
Hill
▲ 343

391
▲

Bengairn

Kippford
(Scaur)

Orchardton
Tower

Mote of
Mark
(NTS)

Rough
Firth

White
Loch

A710

Sandyhills

Mainsriddle

Preston Merse

Gillfoot
Bay

✿

A762

Tongland

Dam

Rockcliffe

Colvend

Port o' Warren

Mersehead Sands

Southerness

Southerness
Point

stoun

DUMFRIES
&
GALLOWAY

Castlehill Point

Almorness Point

Barnhourie
Sands

A75–TO STRANRAER

Kirkcudbright

Auchencairn

Stewartry Museum

Bombie

Bankhead

Auchencairn
Bay

Hestan
Island

Hazlefield

Balcary Point

Mary's
Isle

Auchnabony

Rascarrel

Dundrennan

A711

Orroland

Rascarrel
Bay

Townhead

Abbey

Barlocco Bay

Balmae

Port Mary

S O L W A Y   F I R T H

Abbey Head

Ross

Maryport

A596

Seaton

WORKINGTON

Stainburn

Schoose

A597

A596

Westfield
Salterbeck

3

High Harrington

Harrington

Distington

A595

Pica

Howgate

5

Low Moresby

Parton

Moresby
Parks

WHITEHAVEN

Hensingham

B5295

Saltom Bay

Cleator Moor

Sandwith

Mirehouse

7

Moor Row

St
Bees
Head

St. Bees
Head

B5345

Bigrigg

Cleator

Rottington

St Bees

Egremont

How Man

A595

Wilto

Cockermouth: *Fletcher Christian, ringleader of the Mutiny on the Bounty was born here in 1789. Following the mutiny Christian and eight other mutineers took refuge on Pitcairn Island where they founded a settlement.* **Map ref. E3**

St Bees: *The nearby RSPB Nature Reserve is home to England's only colony of Black Guillemots.* **Map ref. C5**

A74–TO GRETNA

National Nature Reserve

Glasson Burgh Marsh Beaumont Cargo

Cardurnock Bowness Common Drumburgh Hadrian's Wall (Course of) Monkhill Grinsdale Houghton

Anthorn Easton Boustead Hill Longburgh Burgh by Sands Kingstown Brun

Whitrigg Fingland Kirkandrews-upon-Eden Stanwix B6264

Grune Point Moricambe Angerton B5307 Kirkbampton Moorhouse CARLISLE

Skinburness Newton Arlosh Studholme Oughterby Great Orton Carlisle Castle

Silloth Calvo Seaville Wedholme Flow Aikton Wiggonby Little Orton Newby West Longsowerby Tullie House

Blitterlees Causewayhead Abbey Town Kelsick Oulton Lessonhall Micklethwaite Moorend Thursby Dalston

Wolsty Highlaws Dundraw Waverbridge Dockray A595 Cardew Buckabank Durdar Brisco

Beckfoot Pelutho Southerfield 11 Blencogo Waverton Wigton West Curthwaite Nether Welton Gaitsgill Burthwaite

Mawbray 13 Holme St Cuthbert Aikshaw Bromfield Red Dial B5304 Warblebank Rosley Welton Thethwaite High Bridge Ivegill

Edderside Langrigg 12 Westward B5305 Raughton Head Stockdalewath Southwa

Westnewton 17 Fletchertown Bolton Wood Lane Brocklebank Cheik Beck Sebergham Low Braithwaite

Hayton Baggrow Mealsgate Bolton Low Houses Faulds Brow 344 Whelpo Caldbeck Sowerby Row Thoma Clos 260

Aspatria Harriston Blennerhasset Boltongate B5299 Whitrigg Parkend Newlands Hesket Newmarket Middlescer Hutt

Oughterside Ellen Torpenhow Ireby Branthwaite Millhouse Lamonby

Allerby Arkleby Plumbland Snittlegarth High Ireby Uldale Caldbeck Fells Calebreck Ellonby

Crosby Villa Parsonby Bothel Ruthwaite Longlands High Pike 658 Hutton Roof

Crosby Gilcrux 251 Moota Hill Binsey 447 Bewaldeth Uldale Fells Knott 710 Carrock Fell Greystoke Forest Johnb

Greengill Tallentire 7 Sunderland A595 Over Water Great Calva 690 Mosedale Berrier Hill 357 Greyst

Dearham Blindcrake Bassenthwaite Bowscale Mungrisedale

6 Bridekirk C U M B R I A

Dovenby Papcastle Bassenthwaite Lake LAKE DISTRICT Skiddaw Forest

Brigham Cockermouth Embleton 12 Skiddaw 931 Blencathra (Saddleback) Penruddo A66–TO PENRITH

Greysouthen Wordsworth House (NT) A66 Little Crosthwaite Mirehouse 658 Scales Troutbeck

Eaglesfield Whinlatter Forest 15 Thornthwaite Forest A591 Millbeck Threlkeld 7 Great Mell Fell 536

Deanscales WHINLATTER FOREST PARK Lord's Seat 552 Cumberland Pencil Mus A66 Little Me Fell 505

Dean Low Lorton Thornthwaite Applethwaite Great Crosthwaite Latrigg 367 Clough Head 726 Matterdale End Watern

Pardshaw High Lorton Whinlatter Pass 300 Portinscale Keswick Castlerigg Stone Circle Matterdale Common Dockray

16 Mockerkin Whinlatter Forest Grisedale Pike 790 Braithwaite Castlerigg A591 Dowthwaitehead Ulcat Row

Hopegill Head Borrowdale (NT) Great Dodd 856 Aira Force (NT)

Loweswater Brackenthwaite Fell Stair Stybarrow Dodd 840 Ullswater

Lamplugh Loweswater Grasmoor 851 Causey Pike Brandelhow Great Dodd

Murton Fell Blake Fell 572 Loweswater Fell Little Town High Seat 608 Glenridding Place Fell 657

Kirkland Crummock Water 340 Robinson 737 Derwent Fells Grange Ullswater Steamers Patterdale Beda Fe

Croasdale Great Borne 616 Scale Force Buttermere Dale Head 754 Watendlath Helvellyn 949 Striding Edge Bridgend

Cogra Moss Red Pike 755 Gatesgarth Seatoller Rosthwaite Grisedale

nerdale Bridge Ennerdale Water Buttermere (NT) Borrowdale Stonethwaite 17 Wythburn Dollywagon Pike 858 Hartsop

Lank Rigg 541 Ennerdale Fell High Stile 806 Scarth Gap Pass Hay Stacks Honister Pass 358 Seathwaite Borrowdale Fells Wythburn Fells Brothers Water Hayeswater

Pillar 892 Ullscarf 726

Caw Fell 733 841 Black Sàil Pass Great Gable 781 Dunmail Raise 485 736 Seat Sandal 873 Fairfield 15

797 Haycock Steeple Kirk Fell 802 899 Glaramara Sty Head Stone Pass

Worm Gill Taylorgill Force Allen A591–TO WINDERMERE

Seathwaite: *The small village of Seathwaite is northeast of Scafell Pike, at 3,210 feet (978m) the highest mountain in England. Seathwaite is thought to be the wettest settlement in Britain with about 130 inches (330 cm) average rainfall per year.* **Map ref. F5**

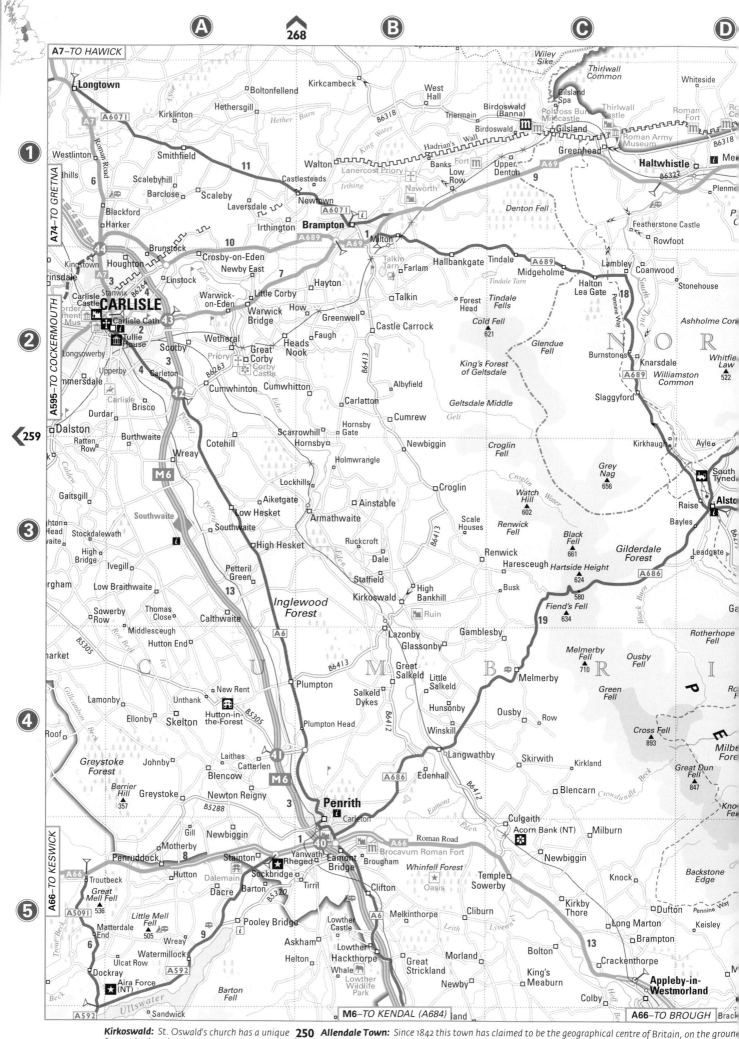

A7–TO HAWICK

A74–TO GRETNA

A595–TO COCKERMOUTH

A66–TO KESWICK

259

1
Longtown
Westlinton
Ihills
Smithfield
Kirklinton
Scalebyhill
Barclose
Scaleby
Blackford
Harker
Laversdale
Boltonfellend
Hethersgill
Kirkcambeck
West Hall
Triermain
Birdoswald (Banna)
Birdoswald
Wiley Sike
Thirlwall Common
Gilsland Spa
Thirlwall Castle
Poltross Burn Milecastle
Gilsland
Roman Army Museum
Greenhead
Whiteside
Roman Fort
Haltwhistle
Me
Hadrian's Wall
Banks
Low Row
Upper Denton
Denton Fell
Featherstone Castle
Rowfoot
Plenme
Walton
Lanercost Priory
Naworth
Brampton
Newtown
Irthington
Milton
Hallbankgate
Farlam
Tindale
Midgeholme
Halton Lea Gate
Lambley
Coanwood
Stonehouse
Ashholme Com
18

2
CARLISLE
Carlisle Castle
Border Regiment Mus
Carlisle Cath
Tullie House
Longsowerby
Upperby
Kingstown
Houghton
Brunstock
Crosby-on-Eden
Newby East
Stanwix
Linstock
Warwick-on-Eden
Little Corby
Warwick Bridge
How
Greenwell
Heads Nook
Faugh
Castle Carrock
Talkin
Talkin Tarn
Tindale Tarn
Forest Head
Tindale Fells
Cold Fell 621
Glendue Fell
Burnstones
Knarsdale
Williamston Common
Slaggyford
Whitfield Law 522
N O R
Wetheral
Great Corby
Corby Castle
Priory
Scotby
Carleton
Cumwhinton
Cumwhitton
Albyfield
Carlatton
King's Forest of Geltsdale
Geltsdale Middle
Gelt
44
43
42
2
3
4
3
Kirkhaugh
Ayle

3
Dalston
Ratten Row
Gaitsgill
High Bridge
Ivegill
Low Braithwaite
Stockdalewath
Southwaite
Low Hesket
Southwaite
High Hesket
Aiketgate
Petteril Green
Calthwaite
Thomas Close
Middlesceugh
Hutton End
Sowerby Row
Lamonby
Durdar
Brisco
Burthwaite
Wreay
Cotehill
Scarrowhill
Hornsby Gate
Hornsby
Holmwrangle
Lockhills
Armathwaite
Ruckcroft
Dale
Staffield
Kirkoswald
High Bankhill
Ruin
Newbiggin
Croglin
Ainstable
Scale Houses
Renwick
Haresceugh
Hartside Height 624
Busk
Renwick Fell
Croglin Fell
Watch Hill 602
Black Fell 661
Grey Nag 656
Gilderdale Forest
Raise
Bayles
Leadgate
Alston
South Tyned
Fiend's Fell 634
19
580
Inglewood Forest
13
A6
M6
C U M B E R L A N D

4
Roof
Lamonby
Ellonby
Skelton
New Rent
Unthank
Hutton-in-the-Forest
Laithes
Catterlen
Blencow
Newton Reigny
Plumpton
Salkeld Dykes
Great Salkeld
Little Salkeld
Hunsonby
Winskill
Langwathby
Edenhall
Skirwith
Kirkland
Blencarn
Plumpton Head
Johnby
Greystoke Forest
Berrier Hill 357
Greystoke
Ousby
Row
Melmerby
Melmerby Fell 710
Green Fell
Ousby Fell
Rotherhope Fell
Cross Fell 893
Great Dun Fell 847
Milbe Fore
Kirk
Fe
P
Ro
H
E
M6
41
3
Penrith
Carleton
40

5
Dockray
Aira Force (NT)
Matterdale End
Little Mell Fell 505
Ulcat Row
Wreay
Watermillock
Great Mell Fell 536
Troutbeck
Great Strickland
Penruddock
Hutton
Motherby
Newbiggin
Gill
Stainton
Dalemain
Sockbridge
Barton
Dacre
Tirril
Pooley Bridge
Askham
Helton
Yanwath
Rheged
Eamont Bridge
Brougham
Clifton
Lowther Castle
Lowther
Hackthorpe
Whale
Lowther Wildlife Park
Melkinthorpe
Whinfell Forest
Oasis
Temple Sowerby
Cliburn
Morland
King's Meaburn
Newby
Colby
Bolton
Kirkby Thore
Knock
Long Marton
Brampton
Dufton
Keisley
Backstone Edge
Appleby-in-Westmorland
Crackenthorpe
Culgaith
Acorn Bank (NT)
Milburn
Newbiggin
Brocavum Roman Fort
Roman Road
A66
13
8
9
6
Barton Fell
Sandwick
Ullswater
A592
A5091
A5320
B5288
B5320
B5305
B5305

M6–TO KENDAL (A684)

A66–TO BROUGH

Kirkoswald: St. Oswald's church has a unique feature in that the church bell tower is perched on a hill top 200 yards (180m) away from the actual church building. **Map ref. B3**

250

Allendale Town: Since 1842 this town has claimed to be the geographical centre of Britain, on the ground that it is halfway between Cape Wrath and Beachy Head. Latitude and longitude figures are displayed on sundial on the church tower. However, nearby Haltwhistle (Map ref. D1) also makes this claim, as the m point of Britain's longest line of longitude which stretches from the Orkney Islands to Dorset. **Map ref. E**

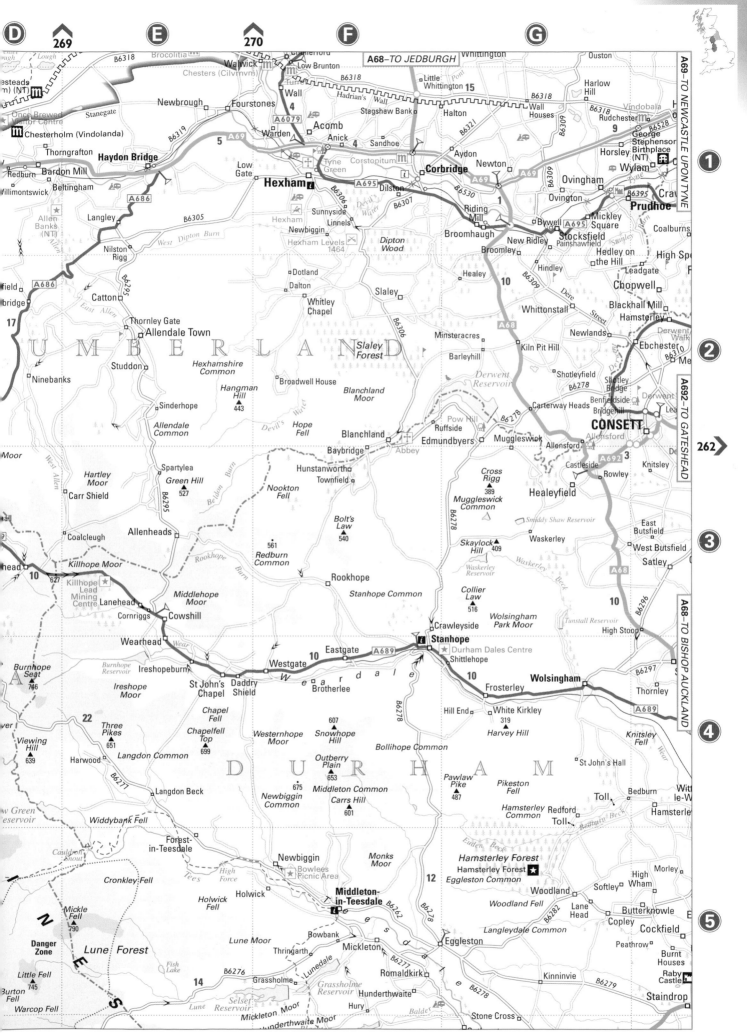

xham: This is the administrative centre for Tynedale, largest local authority district in England. With a land of 856 square miles (2217 sq km) and only 57,400 dents, the authority has a population density of just eople per square mile (26 per sq km). **Map ref. F1**

251

Cauldron Snout: This is now commonly cited as England's highest waterfall at 200 feet (61m), although it is more a cascade than a single unbroken fall. **Map ref. E5**

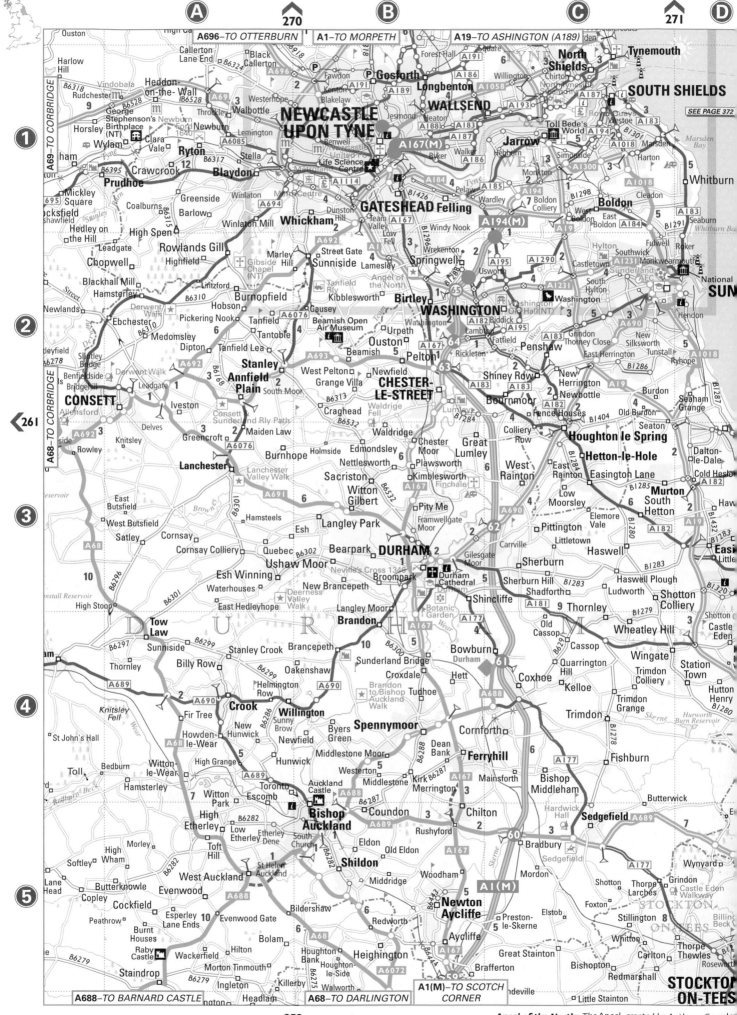

A696-TO OTTERBURN   A1-TO MORPETH   A19-TO ASHINGTON (A189)

NEWCASTLE UPON TYNE

WALLSEND

North Shields

Tynemouth

SOUTH SHIELDS

SEE PAGE 372

Jarrow

Whitburn

GATESHEAD Felling

Boldon

WASHINGTON

CONSETT

CHESTER-LE-STREET

Houghton le Spring

Hetton-le-Hole

Murton

Lanchester

DURHAM

Durham Cathedral

Brandon

Tow Law

Crook

Willington

Spennymoor

Ferryhill

Sedgefield

Bishop Auckland

Shildon

Newton Aycliffe

STOCKTON ON-TEES

A68-TO CORRIDGE

261

A688-TO BARNARD CASTLE   A68-TO DARLINGTON   A1(M)-TO SCOTCH CORNER

Angel of the North: The Angel, created by Anthony Gormley, was Britain's largest sculpture when opened in 1998, standing 65 feet (20m) high, a wingspan of 175 feet (54m) and weighing 197 tons (200 tonnes). The sculpture is made of weather resistant steel, can withstand 100 mph (160km/h) winds and has an estimated lifespan of 100 years. **Map ref. B2**

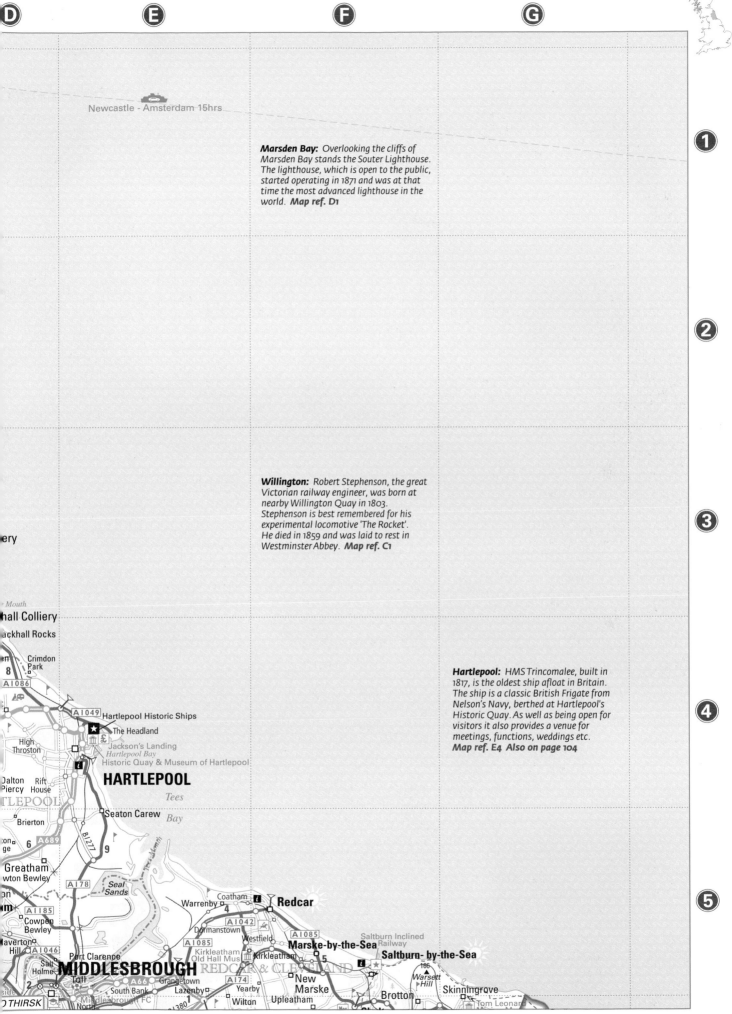

Newcastle - Amsterdam 15hrs

Marsden Bay: *Overlooking the cliffs of Marsden Bay stands the Souter Lighthouse. The lighthouse, which is open to the public, started operating in 1871 and was at that time the most advanced lighthouse in the world.* **Map ref. D1**

Willington: *Robert Stephenson, the great Victorian railway engineer, was born at nearby Willington Quay in 1803. Stephenson is best remembered for his experimental locomotive 'The Rocket'. He died in 1859 and was laid to rest in Westminster Abbey.* **Map ref. C1**

Hartlepool: *HMS Trincomalee, built in 1817, is the oldest ship afloat in Britain. The ship is a classic British Frigate from Nelson's Navy, berthed at Hartlepool's Historic Quay. As well as being open for visitors it also provides a venue for meetings, functions, weddings etc.* **Map ref. E4 Also on page 104**

ery

Mouth

hall Colliery

ackhall Rocks

Crimdon
Park

8

A1086

A1049 Hartlepool Historic Ships

The Headland

High
Throston

Jackson's Landing
Hartlepool Bay
Historic Quay & Museum of Hartlepool

HARTLEPOOL

Dalton
Piercy

Rift
House

Tees

TLEPOOL

Seaton Carew *Bay*

Brierton

6 A689

B1277

9

Greatham

wton Bewley

A178

*Seal
Sands*

Coatham

Warrenby 4 **Redcar**

A1042

m A1185

Cowpen
Bewley

Dormanstown

A1085

Westfield

A1085

Saltburn Inclined
Railway

Marske-by-the-Sea

averton
Hill A1046

Port Clarence

Salt
Holme

MIDDLESBROUGH

Kirkleatham
Old Hall Mus Kirkleatham

REDCAR & CLEVELAND

5

Saltburn- by-the-Sea

Grangetown Lazenby

South Bank

Middlesbrough FC
North

THIRSK

Yearby

A174

Wilton Upleatham

**New
Marske**

Brotton

Warsett
Hill

Tom Leonard

Skinningrove

253 **Middlesbrough:** *The Middlesbrough Transporter Bridge, which featured prominently in a series of TV's 'Auf Wiedersehen Pet', is the only Transporter Bridge in Britain still running a daily service. It was built in 1911 and is over 850 feet (260m) long, 220 feet (67m) high and crosses the River Tees.* **Map ref. D5**

A77–TO AYR

1

Ailsa Craig

Ailsa Craig: *Unpopulated Island but features a lighthouse on Foreland Point built by Thomas and David Stevenson in 1886. Until 1935 all contact between the lighthouse and the mainland was by carrier pigeon. It is now unmanned and powered by solar panels.* **Map ref.B1**

Girvan

Houdston
Saugh Hill
296

Glendoune

Black Neuk

Glendrissaig

A714

Ardwell

Pinminnoch

Kennedy's
Pass

Grey Hill
297

7

12

Pinmore

Water of Lendal

Lendalfoot

Motte

Aldons

A77

Carleton
Fishery

Daljarrock

Poundland

Pinwherry

2

Bennane
Head

Colmonell

B734

Dalreoch

B734

9

Glenduis

Knockdolian
265

Stinchar

Craigneil

A714

Balloch

Ballantrae Bay

B7044

Mains of Tig

Water of Tig

Shiel Hill
230

Bar

Ballantrae

Auchairne

Balkissock

Glenapp Castle

Downan Point

Smyrton

Cross Water

Kilantringan
Loch

Craigie
Fell

Beneraird
439

Chirmorrie

3

Finnarts
Point

Carlock
Hill
323

Milljoan
Hill
403

Altimeg
Hill

Glen App

Main Water of Luce

Markdhu

Stand
Ston

Cairnryan-Larne.... 1-1¾
Stranraer-Belfast.... 1½-3¾

hours

Milleur Point

A77

17

Dalnigap

Glenwhilly

Cross Water of Luce

D U M F R I

Corsewall
Point

LOCH

Barnhills

North Cairn

Cairnryan

South Cairn

B738

Kirkcolm

Corsewall

Cairn
Point

A77

Beoch
Burn

Braid
Fell
235

4

Dounan Bay

Airies

Ervie

Loch
Connell

St Mary's
Croft

7

A718

Innermessan

New
Luce

Portobello

B798

B738

Sole
Burn

Soleburn

A77

Auchmantle

Knocknain

Leswalt

B7043

A751

Lochinch Castle

Galdenoch

Lochnaw

B738

Piltanton
Burn

B737

Black
Loch

Castle Kennedy

Craig
Fell
164

THE

Stranraer

White Loch

Dunragit
Moor

Glenluce
Abbey

Whitecairn

Broadsea
Bay

Portslogan

Southern Upland Way

A77

Loch Maberlie

A75

Castle Kennedy

Dunragit

Castle
of Park

A747

5

Dunkery
Burn

Whiteleys

2

Soulseat
Loch

Piltanton Burn

Whitecrook

10

Glenluce

Milton

Black Head

Cairn Pat
182

Lochans

Kildrochet
House

Genoch
B7077

Genoch Square

B7084

Sands of Luce

Crow's Nest

Portpatrick

Dunskey

Divin

6

A77

Awhirk

Colfin

A716

Stoneykirk

B7084

Auchenma
Bay

Port of
Spittal Bay

B7042

Balgreggan

Sandhead

Kirkmadrine

Stranraer: *The world's first high-speed ferry operates from Stranraer to Belfast and is known as Stena HSS. This is one of the largest ferries in the world, capable of carrying 1500 passengers plus their cars and coaches. It is powered by four jet engines which provide the same thrust as that required for a jumbo jet and give it a cruising speed of 40 knots.* **Map ref. B4**

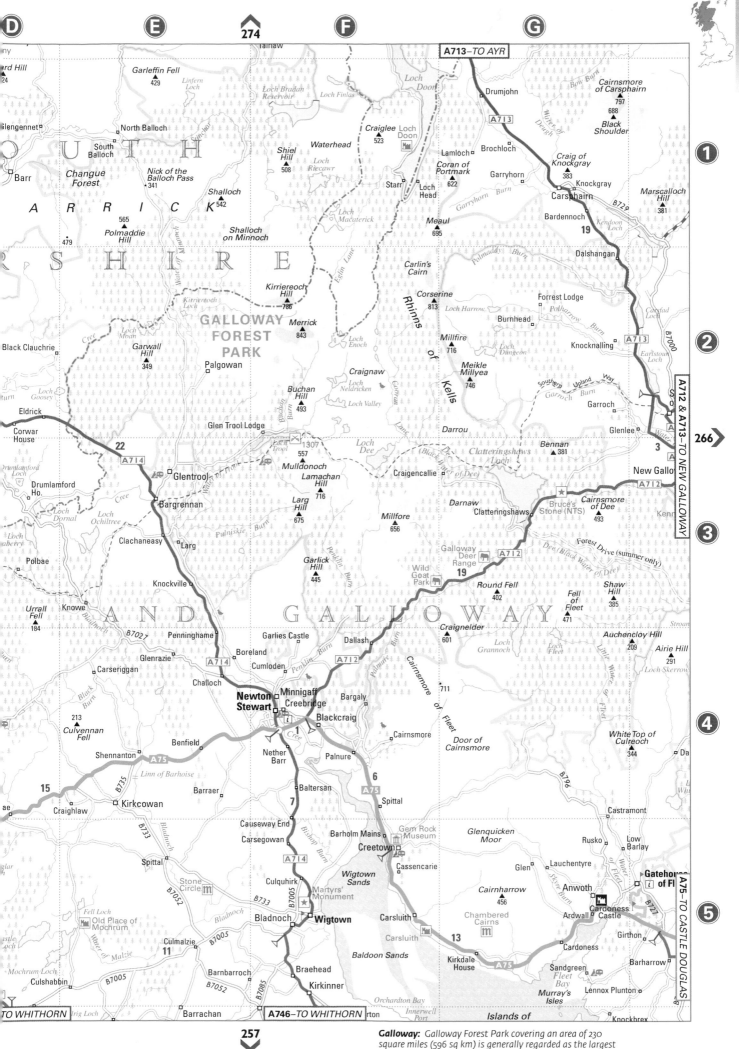

A713–TO AYR

rd Hill
24

Garleffin Fell
429

Linfern
Loch

Tainaw

Loch Bradan
Reservoir

Loch Finlas

Loch Doon

Bow Burn

Cairnsmore
of Carsphairn
797

Drumjohn

Water of Deugh

688

Black
Shoulder

O U T H

North Balloch

South
Balloch

Changue
Forest

Shiel
Hill
508

Waterhead

Craiglee
523

Loch
Doon

Lamloch

Brochloch

A713

Craig of
Knockgray
383

Knockgray

Marscalloch
Hill
381

Barr

Nick of the
Balloch Pass
341

Shalloch
542

Loch
Riecawr

Starr

Loch
Head

Coran of
Portmark
622

Garryhorn

Carsphairn

B729

A R R I C K

565

Polmaddie
Hill

K

Shalloch
on Minnoch

Loch
Macaterick

Meaul
695

Garryhorn Burn

Bardennoch

Kendoon
Loch

19

Dalshangan

479

R S H I R E

Kirriereoch
Loch

Kirriereoch
Hill
786

Merrick
843

Eglin Lane

Carlin's
Cairn

Corserine
813

Loch Harrow

Polmaddy Burn

Forrest Lodge

Caesfad
Loch

B7000

Black Clauchrie

Cree

GALLOWAY
FOREST
PARK

Garwall
Hill
349

Loch
Moan

Palgowan

Loch
Enoch

Craignaw

Loch
Neldricken

Rhinns

Millfire
716

Loch
Dungeon

Meikle
Millyea
746

Loch
Valley

of
Kells

Southern

Upland

Way

Polharrow Burn

Knocknalling

A713

Earlstoun
Loch

2

266

Eldrick

Loch
Goosey

Corwar
House

22

A714

Drumlamford
Loch

Eldrick

Drumlamford
Ho.

Loch
Dornal

Glen Trool Lodge

Buchan
Hill
493

Loch
Trool

1307

Mulldonoch
557

Garroch
Burn

Southern

Garroch

Glenlee

Garroch

Bennan
381

Clatteringshaws
Loch

Glenlee

3

New Gallo

A712

Glentrool

Water of Trool

Lamachan
Hill
716

Loch
Dee

(Black Water of Dee)

Craigencallie

Darnaw

Clatteringshaws

Bruce's
Stone (NTS)

Cairnsmore
of Dee
493

Ken

Bargrennan

Cree

Loch
Ochiltree

Larg
Hill
675

Pulniskie Burn

Millfore
656

Forest Drive (summer only)

Dee (Black Water of Dee)

Clachaneasy

Larg

Garlick
Hill
445

Penkiln Burn

Galloway
Deer
Range

A712

Wild
Goat
Park

19

Round Fell
402

Fell
of
Fleet
471

Shaw
Hill
385

Polbae

Knowe

Urrall
Fell
184

Bladnoch

A N D

Penninghame

B7027

Craignelder
601

Loch
Grannoch

Loch
Fleet

Craigenelder

Auchencloy Hill
209

Airie Hill
291

Loch-Skerrow

Glenrazie

Carseriggan

Boreland

A714

Garlies Castle

Cumloden

Dallash

A712

Palnure Burn

711

Cairnsmore of Fleet

Door of
Cairnsmore

White Top of
Culreoch
344

Da

Challoch

Newton
Stewart

Minnigaff

Creebridge

Bargaly

G A L L O W A Y

Cairnsmore

Castramont

213

Culvennan
Fell

Benfield

Blackcraig

Cree

1

Nether
Barr

Palnure

6

A75

B796

Shennanton

A75

Barraer

Baltersan

Spittal

15

Kirkcowan

B735

Linn of Barhoise

Black Burn

B733

7

A714

Causeway End

Gem Rock
Museum

Glenquicken
Moor

Rusko

Low
Barlay

Craighlaw

Carsegowan

Barholm Mains

Creetown

Cassencarie

Glen

Lauchentyre

Castramont

Spittal

B7052

Stone
Circle

Culquhirk

Bishop Burn

Wigtown
Sands

Cairnharrow
456

Skyre Burn

Anwoth

Gatehous
of Fl

A75–TO CASTLE DOUGLAS

Fell Loch

Old Place of
Mochrum

B7005

B733

Bladnoch

B7005

Martyrs'
Monument

Bladnoch

Wigtown

Carsluith

Chambered
Cairns

Water of Fleet

Ardwall

Cardoness
Castle

Girthon

Cardoness

Barharrow

Mochrum Loch

Culshabbin

B7005

Culmalzie

B7005

Barnbarroch

11

B7052

Braehead

B7085

Kirkinner

Carsluith

13

Baldoon Sands

A75

Kirkdale
House

Sandgreen

Fleet
Bay

Lennox Plunton

castle
och

TO WHITHORN

Irig Loch

Barrachan

A746–TO WHITHORN

rton

Murray's
Isles

Orchardton Bay

Innerwell
Port

Islands of

Knockbrex

Galloway: *Galloway Forest Park covering an area of 230
square miles (596 sq km) is generally regarded as the largest
forest in Britain. The park contains over 200 miles (320km) of
cycle routes.* **Map ref. E2**

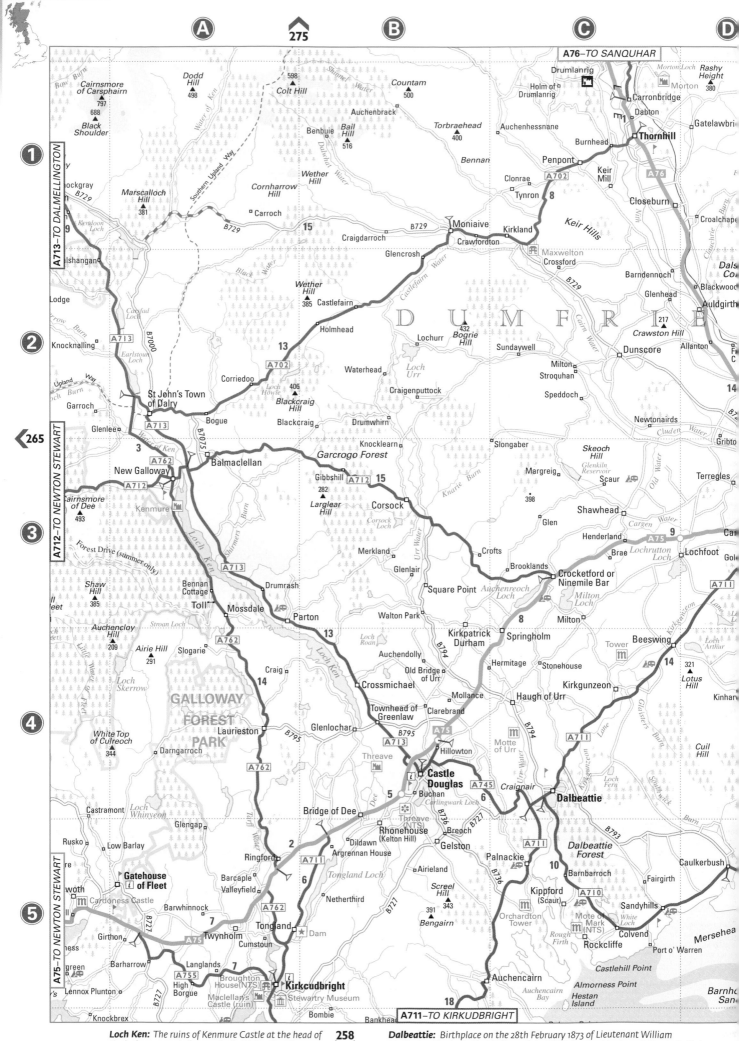

A76–TO SANQUHAR

1

A713–TO DALMELLINGTON

A712–TO NEWTON STEWART

265

2

3

A75–TO NEWTON STEWART

4

5

A711–TO KIRKUDBRIGHT

Loch Ken: The ruins of Kenmure Castle at the head of the loch were made famous in Sir Walter Scott's ballad 'Young Lochinvar' and also in Robert Burns Jacobite song 'Kenmure's up and awa', Willie' **Map ref. A3**

258

Dalbeattie: Birthplace on the 28th February 1873 of Lieutenant William McMaster Murdoch, First Officer of the RMS Titanic. Lieutenant Murdoch died aboard ship when the Titanic struck an iceberg and sank on the 15th April 1912. **Map ref. C4**

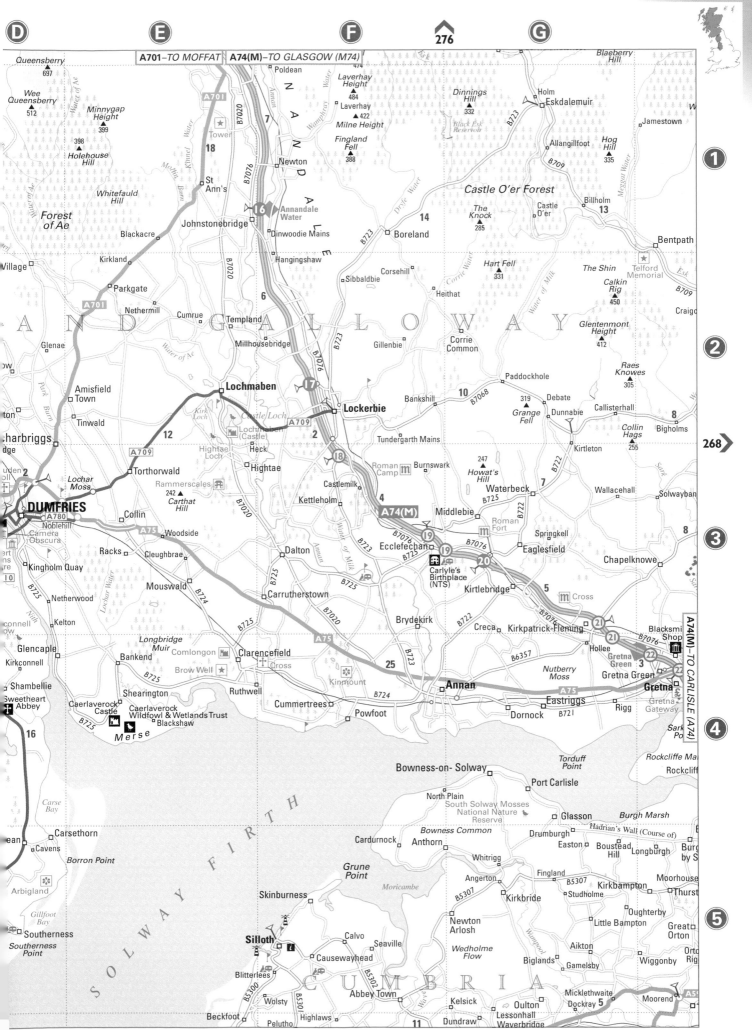

Queensberry
697

Wee
Queensberry
512

Minnygap
Height
399

398

Holehouse
Hill

Whitefauld
Hill

Forest
of Ae

Poldean

Laverhay
Height
484

Laverhay
422

Milne Height

Fingland
Fell
388

Dinnings
Hill
332

Black Esk
Reservoir

Holm

Eskdalemuir

Blaeberry
Hill

Jamestown

Allangillfoot

Hog
Hill
335

B709

1

Kinnel Water

Tower

18

St
Ann's

Newton

Annandale
Water

Johnstonebridge

Dinwoodie Mains

Hangingshaw

Blackacre

Kirkland

Castle O'er Forest

The
Knock
285

Castle
O'er

Billholm

Bentpath

13

Village

Parkgate

Nethermill

Cumrue

Templand

Millhousebridge

Boreland

14

Sibbaldie

Corsehill

Gillenbie

Heithat

Hart Fell
331

The Shin

Telford
Memorial

B709

Glenae

A N D   G A L L O W A Y

Corrie
Common

Glentenmont
Height
412

Craigo

2

Amisfield
Town

Tinwald

Lochmaben

Lockerbie

Bankshill

B7068

Paddockhole

Debate

Dunnabie

Grange
Fell
319

Callisterhall

Raes
Knowes
305

Collin
Hags
255

Bigholms

8

268

harbriggs

12

A709

Torthorwald

Kirk
Loch

Castle Loch

Lochmaben
(Castle)

Heck

Hightae
Loch

Hightae

A709

Rammerscales

Carthat
Hill
242

Kettleholm

Castlemilk

Tundergarth Mains

Roman
Camp

Burnswark

Howat's
Hill
247

Waterbeck

B725

Roman
Fort

B722

Springkell

Wallacehall

Solwayban

8

3

DUMFRIES
A780

Noblehill

Camera
Obscura

Collin

Woodside

A75

Dalton

4

A74(M)

Middlebie

Ecclefechan

19

Eaglesfield

Chapelknowe

Racks

Cleughbrae

Mouswald

Carrutherstown

Carlyle's
Birthplace
(NTS)

20

Kirtlebridge

5

Cross

Kingholm Quay

Kinghorn

Netherwood

Kelton

Longbridge
Muir

Bankend

Comlongon

Clarencefield

Cross

Brydekirk

Creca

Kirkpatrick-Fleming

21

Blacksmith
Shop

A74(M)–TO CARLISLE (A74)

Glencaple

Kirkconnell

Shearington

Ruthwell

Kinmount

25

B724

Annan

Nutberry
Moss

Gretna
Green

21

Hollee

Gretna Green

22

Gretna

Shambellie

Sweetheart
Abbey

Caerlaverock
Castle

Caerlaverock
Wildfowl & Wetlands Trust

Blackshaw

Cummertrees

Powfoot

Eastriggs

Dornock

Rigg

Gretna
Gateway

Sark
Po

16

Merse

Bowness-on- Solway

Port Carlisle

Torduff
Point

Rockcliffe Ma

Rockcliff

4

Carse
Bay

North Plain

South Solway Mosses
National Nature
Reserve

Glasson

Burgh Marsh

Carsethorn

Cavens

Borron Point

Cardurnock

Anthorn

Bowness Common

Drumburgh

Easton

Whitrigg

Hadrian's Wall (Course of)

Boustead
Hill

Longburgh

Burg
by S

Arbigland

Gillfoot
Bay

Grune
Point

Moricambe

Angerton

Fingland

B5307

Kirkbride

Studholme

Moorhouse

Thurst

5

Southerness
Southerness
Point

Skinburness

Calvo

Seaville

Wedholme
Flow

Newton
Arlosh

Aikton

Biglands

Gamelsby

Little Bampton

Oughterby

Wiggonby

Great
Orton

Orto
Rig

Silloth

Causewayhead

Blitterlees

Wolsty

C U M B R I A

Abbey Town

Kelsick

Oulton

Dundraw

Micklethwaite

Dockray

A5

Beckfoot

Highlaws

Pelutho

11

Lessonhall

Waverbridge

Moorend

hwell: Dr Henry Duncan (1774–1846) opened the worlds first bank when he was the minister of this parish. He is regarded as the der of savings banks and is remembered in Henry Duncan House, the burgh headquarters of a national banking group. **Map ref. E4**

Lockerbie: On the evening of the 21st December 1988 terrorists placed a bomb on board Pan Am flight 103. The plane exploded 6 miles (9.65km) above this small Scottish town. All 259 people on board, plus 11 people on the ground lost their lives in what proved to be the biggest mass murder in British history. **Map ref. F2**

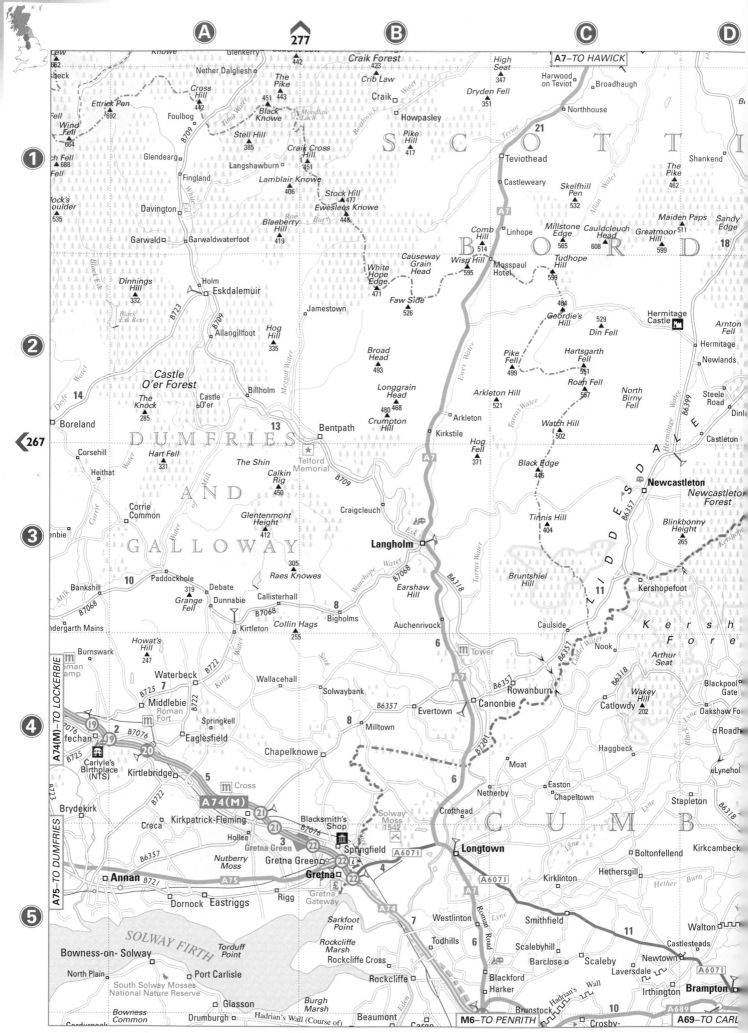

Newcastleton: This village was planned and built specifically as a handloom weaving centre, in 1793, by the Duke of Buccleuch for his employees. *Map ref.* C3

259

Gretna: Britain's worst ever rail disaster happened at Quintinshill, just north-east of Gretna on the 22nd May 1915. A troop train, towing wooden carriages, collided with a stationary passenger train and was then itself hit by an oncoming express train. 227 people, most of them soldiers, were killed in the crashes and subsequent fire. *Map ref.* B5

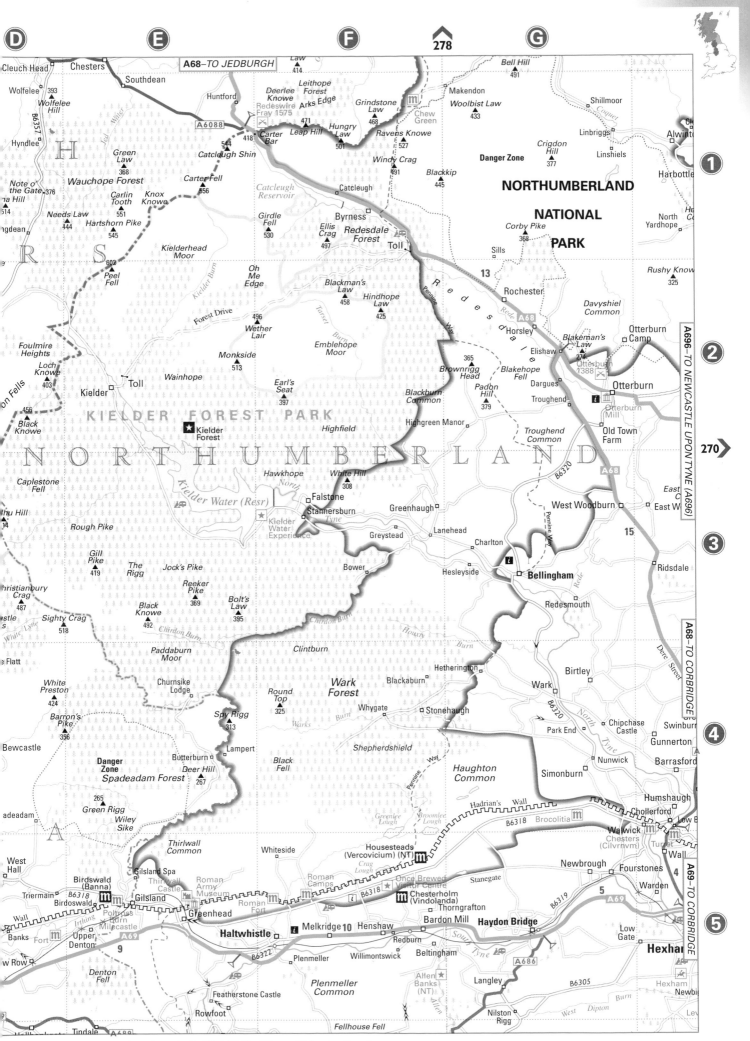

Cleuch Head
Chesters
Southdean
Wolfelee 393
Wolfelee Hill
Hyndlee
Green Law 368
Wauchope Forest
Note o' the Gate 376
Carlin Tooth 551
Knox Knowe
Needs Law 444
Hartshorn Pike 545
Kielderhead Moor
Peel Fell 602
Foulmire Heights
Loch Knowe 403
Black Knowe 456
Toll
Kielder
Wainhope
KIELDER FOREST PARK
Kielder Forest ★
Caplestone Fell
Rough Pike
Gill Pike 419
The Rigg
Jock's Pike
Reeker Pike 369
Black Knowe 492
Bolt's Law 395
Christianbury Crag 487
Sighty Crag 518
Paddaburn Moor
Clintburn
Churnsike Lodge
Round Top 325
White Preston 424
Barron's Pike 356
Spy Rigg 313
Lampert
Green Rigg 265
Wiley Sike
Danger Zone
Spadeadam Forest
Butterburn
Deer Hill 267
Thirlwall Common
Bewcastle
West Hall
Birdswald (Banna)
Triermain
Gilsland Spa
Thirlwall Castle
Roman Army Museum
Gilsland
Birdoswald
Banks
Poltross Burn Milecastle
Upper Denton
Denton Fell
Tindale
Rowfoot
Featherstone Castle
Fellhouse Fell

A68–TO JEDBURGH
Huntford
A6088
Deerlee Knowe
Redeswire Fray 1575
Carter Bar 418
544
Catcleugh Shin
Carter Fell 556
Girdle Fell 530
Catcleugh Reservoir
Byrness
Ellis Crag 497
Redesdale Forest
Toll
Oh Me Edge
Blackman's Law 458
Hindhope Law 425
Forest Drive 496
Wether Lair
Monkside 513
Emblehope Moor
Earl's Seat 397
Highfield
Hawkhope
White Hill 308
North
Falstone
Kielder Water (Resr)
Kielder Water Experience ★
Stannersburn
Tyne
Greenhaugh
Greystead
Bower
Wark Forest
Clirdon Burn
Blackaburn
Hetherington
Whygate
Stonehaugh
Shepherdshield
Black Fell
Haughton Common
Greenlee Lough
Broomlee Lough
Housesteads (Vercovicium) (NT)
Crag Lough
Roman Camps
Whiteside
Once Brewed Visitor Centre
Chesterholm (Vindolanda)
Stanegate
Thorngrafton
Bardon Mill
Roman Fort
Greenhead
Haltwhistle
Melkridge 10
Henshaw
Redburn
Plenmeller
Willimontswick
Beltingham
Langley
Nilston Rigg
Allen Banks (NT)
B6322
B6318
B6319

Law 414
Leithope Forest
Arks Edge
Grindstone Law 468
Chew Green
Leap Hill 471
Hungry Law 501
Ravens Knowe 527
Windy Crag 491
Catcleugh
Blackman's Law
Blackmam's Law
Pennine Way
Redesdale
Blackburn Common
Highgreen Manor
Brownrigg Head
Padon Hill 379
Troughend Common
Bellingham
Hesleyside
Charlton
Lanehead
Wark
Park End
Simonburn
Nunwick
Hadrian's Wall
Brocolitia
B6318
Newbrough

Bell Hill 491
Makendon
Woolbist Law 433
Shillmoor
Linbriggs
Alwint
Crigdon Hill 377
Danger Zone
Linshiels
NORTHUMBERLAND
NATIONAL
Corby Pike 368
Sills
PARK
Rushy Know 325
13
Rochester
Davyshiel Common
Horsley
Blakeman's Law 274
Otterburn Camp
Elishaw
Otterburn 1388
Blakehope Fell
Dargues
Troughend
Otterburn Mill
Old Town Farm
West Woodburn
East W
Ridsdale
15
Birtley
Chipchase Castle
Swinbur
Gunnerton
Barrasford
Humshaugh
Chollerford
Walwick
Chesters (Cilvrnvm)
Wall
Fourstones
Warden
Newbrough
Low Gate
Hexhar
Hexham
Newbi

A696–TO NEWCASTLE UPON TYNE (A696)
A68
A68–TO CORBRIDGE
A69–TO CORBRIDGE
270
365
B6320
North Tyne
Dere Street
B6305
A69
A686
West Dipton

1
2
3
4
5

NORTHUMBERLAND

der Forest: This is the largest forest in England ering an area of 200 square miles (518 sq km) and nted with over 150 million trees. The forest is n-made and the first tree was planted at Smales m in 1926. **Map ref. E2**

260 **Kielder Water:** With a shoreline of over 27 miles (44km), Kielder Water is the largest artificial lake in Northern Europe. **Map ref. E3**

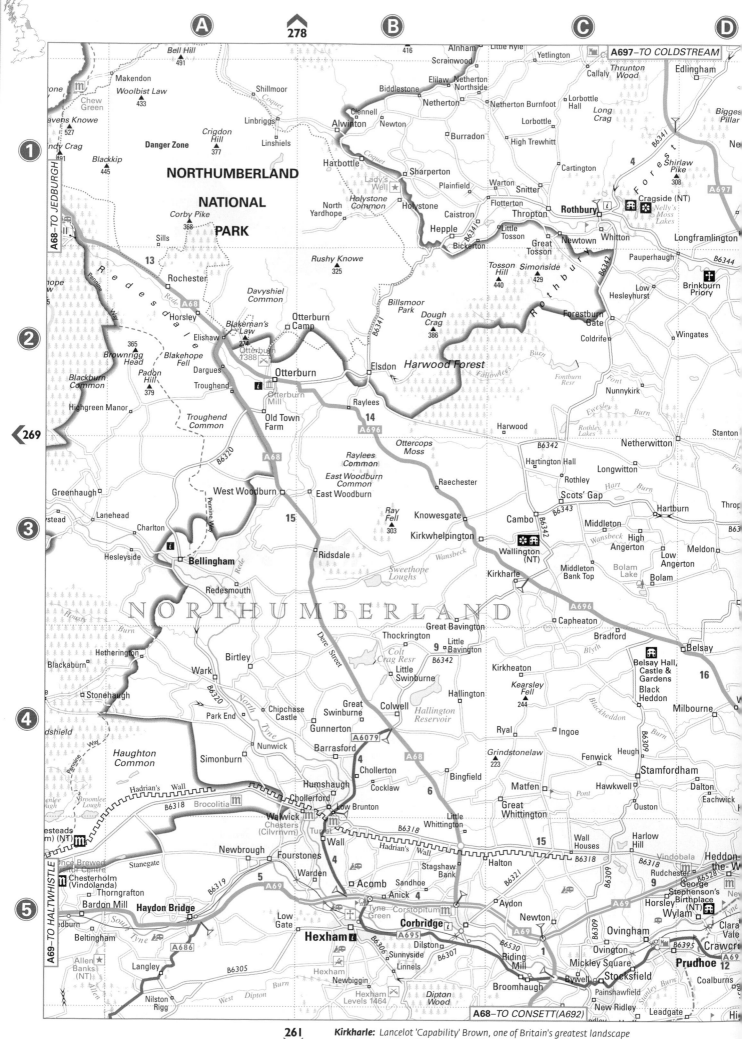

A697-TO COLDSTREAM

Alnham
Little Ryle
Yetlington
Thrunton Wood
Edlingham
Scrainwood
Eliaw
Netherton
Callaly
Lorbottle Hall
Biddlestone
Northside
Long Crag
Clennell
Netherton
Netherton Burnfoot
Lorbottle
Alwinton
Newton
Burradon
High Trewhitt
Cartington
Bigges Pillar
Shilmoor

NORTHUMBERLAND

Bell Hill 491

Makendon

Woolbist Law 433

Chew Green

Ⓜ

Ravens Knowe 527

Danger Zone

NATIONAL

PARK

Corby Pike 368

Sills

Crigdon Hill 377

Linbriggs

Linshiels

Harbottle

Sharperton

Warton
Snitter
Flotterton
Shirlaw Pike 308
A697

Lady's Well ★

Holystone Common

Plainfield

Caistron
Thropton
Rothbury
Ⓜ ✿ Cragside (NT)
Nelly's Moss Lakes

North Yardhope

Holystone

Hepple

Little Tosson
Great Tosson
Newtown
Whitton
Longframlington

Rushy Knowe 325

Bickerton

Tosson Hill 440
Simonside 429

Rothbury

Pauperhaugh
B6344

Blackkip 445

Blakeman's Law 274

Otterburn Camp

Billsmoor Park
Dough Crag 386

Harwood Forest

Low Hesleyhurst
Forestburn Gate
Coldrife
Brinkburn Priory
Wingates

Brownrigg Head 365

Padon Hill 379

Blakehope Fell

Dargues
Troughend

Otterburn 1388 ✕

Elsdon

Raylees

Wingates

Nunnykirk

Rochester

Davyshiel Common

Horsley

Elishaw

Otterburn Mill Ⓜ

Old Town Farm

Raylees

14 A696

Harwood

Netherwitton

Stanton

Highgreen Manor

Blackburn Common

Troughend Common

Raylees Common

Ottercops Moss

B6342

Hartington Hall

Longwitton

Rothley

Esweley

Greenhaugh

Lanehead

Charlton

West Woodburn

East Woodburn Common

East Woodburn

Raechester

Scots' Gap

Hartburn

stead

Hesleyside

Ⓜ

Bellingham

15

Ridsdale

Ray Fell 303

Knowesgate
Kirkwhelpington

Cambo
Wallington (NT) Ⓜ✿

Middleton

High Angerton
Low Angerton

Meldon

Redesmouth

Sweethope Loughs

Kirkharle

Middleton Bank Top
Bolam Lake

Bolam

NORTHUMBERLAND

Hetherington

Great Bavington

Thockrington

Capheaton

Bradford

Belsay

Blackaburn

Birtley

Wark

Colt Crag Resr

9 Little Bavington
B6342

Blyth

Belsay Hall, Castle & Gardens
Black Heddon

Stonehaugh

Little Swinburne

Kirkheaton

16

North Tyne

Park End

Chipchase Castle

Great Swinburne

Colwell

Kearsley Fell 244

Hallington Reservoir

Milbourne

shield

Haughton Common

Nunwick

Gunnerton

4

A6079

Barrasford

A68

Ryal

Ingoe

Heugh

Stamfordham

Simonburn

Chollerton

Bingfield

Grindstonelaw 223

Fenwick

Dalton
Eachwick

Hadrian's Wall

Brocolitia Ⓜ

B6318

Walwick

Chollerford

Humshaugh

Cocklaw

6

Matfen

Hawkwell

Ouston

Broomlee Lough

Chesters (Cilvrnvm)

Low Brunton

Great Whittington

Harlow Hill

Wall

Little Whittington

B6318

Wall Houses

15

Vindobala

steads (m) (NT) Ⓜ

Newbrough

Fourstones

Turret

Hadrian's Wall

Halton

B6321

Rudchester

Heddon-the-W

Once Brewed
Centre

Stanegate

4

Warden

Stagshaw Bank

B6318

B6309

9

George Stephenson's Birthplace Ⓜ

Chesterholm (Vindolanda) Ⓝ

B6319

5

Acomb

Sandhoe

Ⓜ

Halton

Wylam

Bardon Mill

Thorngrafton

A69

Anick

4

Aydon

Newton

A69

Horsley (NT)

Haydon Bridge

Low Gate

Tyne Green

Corstopitum Ⓜ

A69

Ovingham

Clara Vale

Beltingham

Hexham Ⓘ

A695

Corbridge Ⓘ

Dilston

Riding Mill

Mickley Square

Stocksfield

Prudhoe
12

Langley

A686

Sunnyside

B6307

1

Ovington

B6395

Crawcro

Allen Banks ★ (NT)

Hexham Newbiggin

Linnels

B6306

Broomhaugh

Bywell

Painshawfield

New Ridley

Coalburns

Nilston Rigg

West Dipton

Hexham Levels 1464

Dipton Wood

B6530

Stanley Burn

Leadgate

A68-TO CONSETT (A692)

Kirkharle: Lancelot 'Capability' Brown, one of Britain's greatest landscape gardeners, was born here in 1715. He designed gardens for many stately homes and became head gardener at Hampton Court Palace in 1761. 'Capability' Brown died on the 6th February 1783. **Map ref. C3**

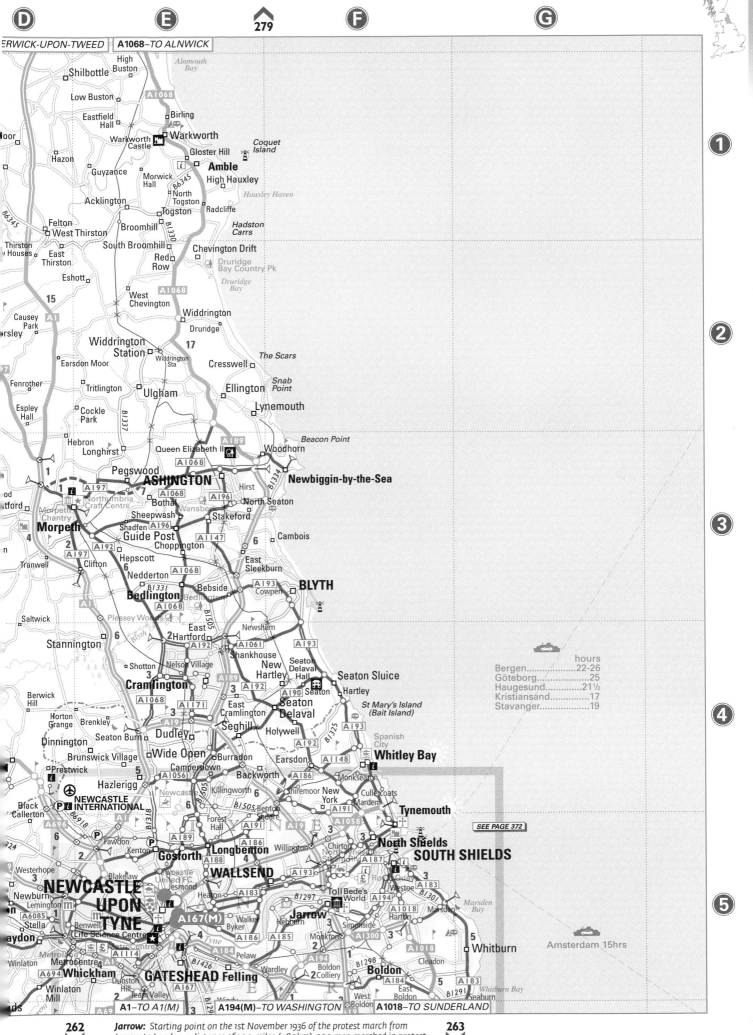

Shilbottle
High Buston
Low Buston
Eastfield Hall
Birling
Warkworth Castle
Warkworth
Alnmouth Bay
Gloster Hill
Coquet Island
Amble
Hazon
Guyzance
Morwick Hall
High Hauxley
Acklington
North Togston
Togston
Radcliffe
Hadston Carrs
Hauxley Haven
Felton
West Thirston
Broomhill
South Broomhill
Chevington Drift
Thirston Houses
East Thirston
Red Row
Druridge Bay Country Pk
Eshott
Druridge Bay
West Chevington
Widdrington
Causey Park
Druridge
Widdrington Station
Widdrington Sta
The Scars
Earsdon Moor
Cresswell
Fenrother
Tritlington
Ulgham
Ellington
Snab Point
Espley Hall
Cockle Park
Lynemouth
Hebron
Longhirst
Beacon Point
Queen Elizabeth II
Woodhorn
Pegswood
ASHINGTON
Newbiggin-by-the-Sea
Morpeth Chantry
Northumbria Craft Centre
Bothal
Hirst
North Seaton
Morpeth
Sheepwash
Wansbeck
Stakeford
Guide Post
Shadfen
Choppington
Cambois
Hepscott
Clifton
Nedderton
East Sleekburn
Tranwell
Bedlington
Bedlington Sta
Cowpen
BLYTH
Saltwick
Plessey Woods
Bebside
Stannington
Newsham
Berwick Hill
East Hartford
Shotton
Nelson Village
Shankhouse
New Hartley
Seaton Delaval Hall
Seaton Sluice
Cramlington
Horton Grange
East Cramlington
Seaton
Hartley
Brenkley
Seghill
Seaton Delaval
St Mary's Island (Bait Island)
Dinnington
Dudley
Holywell
Brunswick Village
Wide Open
Burradon
Earsdon
Whitley Bay
Prestwick
Camperdown
Spanish City
Hazlerigg
Backworth
Monkseaton
NEWCASTLE INTERNATIONAL
Killingworth
Shiremoor
New York
Cullercoats
Marden
Tynemouth
Black Callerton
Forest Hall
Benton Square
SEE PAGE 372
Fawdon
Kenton
Willington
Chirton
North Shields
Westerhope
Gosforth
Longbenton
SOUTH SHIELDS
Newburn
Blakelaw
Jesmond
WALLSEND
Westoe
Lemington
Heaton
Toll Bede's World
NEWCASTLE UPON TYNE
Walker
Byker
Jarrow
Hebburn
Marsden Bay
Stella
Life Science Centre
Pelaw
Monkton
Hartton
Whitburn
MetroCentre
Wardley
Boldon Colliery
Cleadon
Whickham
Felling
Boldon
Winlaton Mill
GATESHEAD
West Boldon
East Boldon
Whitburn Bay
Team Valley
Winlaton

hours
Bergen...............22-26
Göteborg................25
Haugesund...........21½
Kristiansand...........17
Stavanger...............19

Amsterdam 15hrs

Jarrow: Starting point on the 1st November 1936 of the protest march from Jarrow to London a distance of 300 miles (480km). 200 men marched in protest at the miseries of unemployment and the injustice of 'means testing'. The last surviving marcher Cornelius Whalen died in September 2003 aged 93. **Map ref. F5**

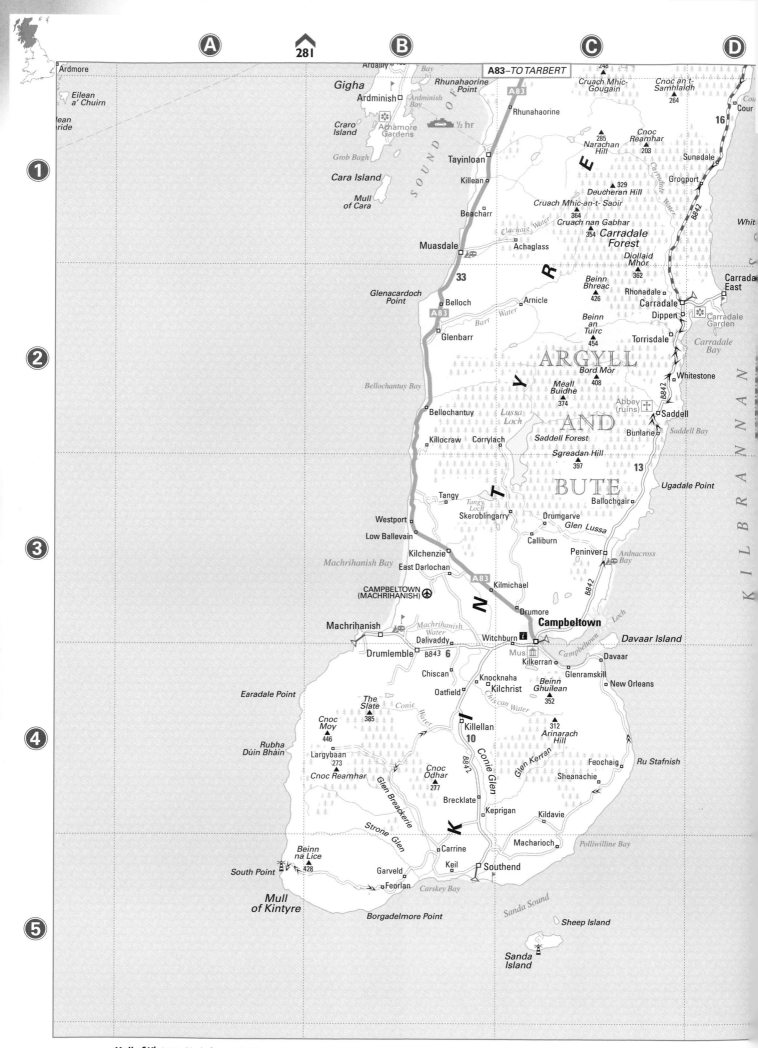

A83–TO TARBERT

Ardmore

Eilean a' Chuirn

lean ride

Gigha

Ardally Bay

Rhunahaorine Point

Ardminish

Ardminish Bay

Craro Island

Achamore Gardens

½ hr

Grob Bagh

Cara Island

Mull of Cara

Tayinloan

Killean

Beacharr

Muasdale

Achaglass

Glenacardoch Point

Belloch

Arnicle

Glenbarr

Barr Water

Bellochantuy Bay

Bellochantuy

Lussa Loch

Killocraw

Corrylach

Tangy

Tangy Loch

Skeroblingarry

Westport

Low Ballevain

Kilchenzie

Machrihanish Bay

East Darlochan

CAMPBELTOWN (MACHRIHANISH)

Machrihanish

Machrihanish Water

Dalivaddy

Drumlemble

B843

Chiscan

Earadale Point

Oatfield

The Slate 385

Conie

Cnoc Moy 446

Rubha Dùin Bhàin

Largybaan 273

Cnoc Reamhar

Glen Breackerie

Cnoc Odhar 277

Water

Brecklate

Strone Glen

Carrine

Beinn na Lice 428

Keil

Garveld

South Point

Feorlan

Carskey Bay

Mull of Kintyre

Borgadelmore Point

Sanda Sound

Cruach Mhic-Gougain

Cnoc an t-Samhlaidh 264

Narachan Hill 285

Cnoc Reamhar 203

Sunadale

329 Deucheran Hill

Cruach Mhic-an-t- Saoir 364

Grogport

16

Cour

Whit

Clachaig Water

Cruach nan Gabhar 354

Carradale Forest

Diollaid Mhòr 362

Carrada East

Beinn Bhreac 426

Rhonadale

Carradale

Dippen

Carradale Garden

ARGYLL

Beinn an Tuirc 454

Torrisdale

Carradale Bay

Bord Mòr 408

Meall Buidhe 374

AND

Abbey (ruins)

Saddell

Bunlarie

Saddell Bay

Saddell Forest

Sgreadan Hill 397

BUTE

13

Ugadale Point

Ballochgair

Drumgarve

Glen Lussa

Calliburn

Peninver

Ardnacross Bay

Kilmichael

Drumore

Campbeltown

Davaar Island

Witchburn

Mus

Kilkerran

Davaar

Glenramskill

New Orleans

Chiscan

Knocknaha

Kilchrist

Beinn Ghuilean 352

Killellan

B842

10

Arinarach Hill 312

Feochaig

Ru Stafnish

Sheanachie

Glen Kerran

Conie Glen

Keprigan

Kildavie

Macharioch

Polliwilline Bay

Southend

Sheep Island

Sanda Island

Mull of Kintyre: *Made famous in the song 'Mull of Kintyre' by Paul McCartney and Wings in 1977.* **Map ref. A5**

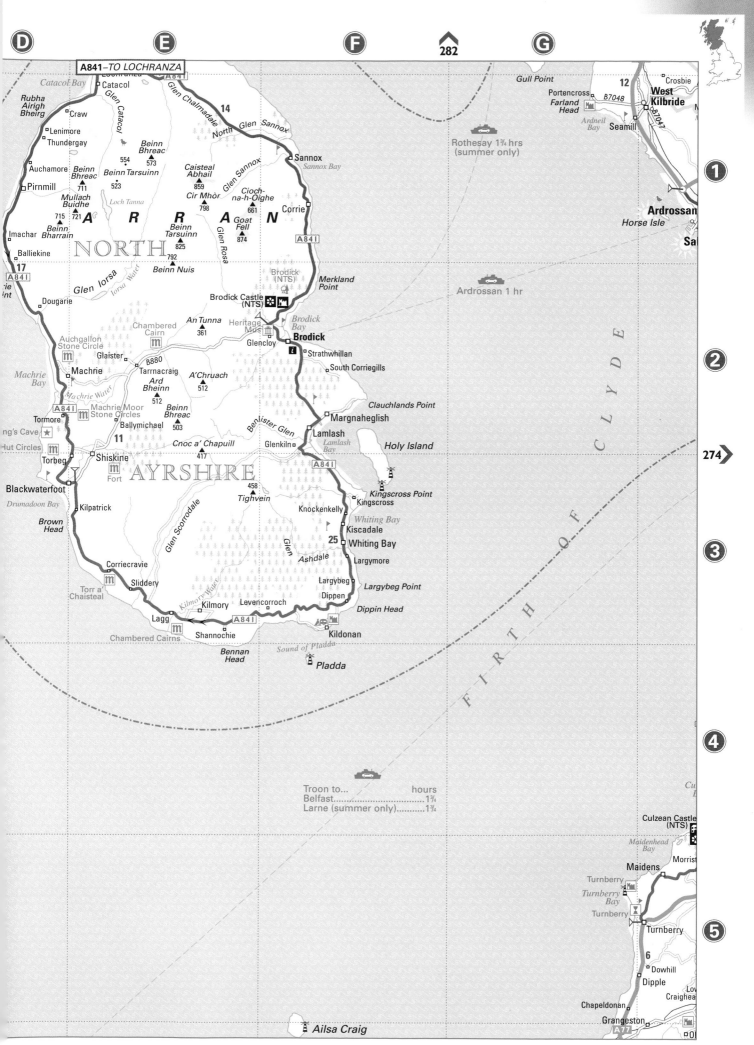

A841–TO LOCHRANZA

Catacol Bay
Catacol
Lochranza
Rubha Airigh Bheirg
Craw
Lenimore
Thundergay
Auchamore
Beinn Bhreac
Pirnmill
Beinn Bhreac 573
Beinn Tarsuinn
554
523
Mullach Buidhe 711
715 721
Beinn Bharrain
Imachar
Balliekine
A841
17

Glen Catacol
Glen Chalmadale
14
North Glen Sannox
Sannox
Sannox Bay
Caisteal Abhail 859
Cir Mhòr 798
Cioch-na-h-Oighe 661
Corrie
Glen Sannox
Goat Fell 874
A841

A R R A N
NORTH
Loch Tanna
Beinn Tarsuinn 825 792
Beinn Nuis
Glen Rosa
Glen Iorsa
Iorsa Water

Gull Point
Portencross
Farland Head
B7048
12
Crosbie
WEST KILBRIDE
B7047
Ardneil Bay
Seamill

Rothesay 1¾ hrs (summer only)

Ardrossan 1 hr

Ardrossan
Horse Isle
Sa

Dougarie
An Tunna 361
Brodick (NTS)
Merkland Point
Brodick Castle (NTS)
Heritage Mus
Brodick Bay
Glencloy
Brodick
Strathwhillan
South Corriegills

Auchgallon Stone Circle
Glaister
B880
Tarrnacraig
Ard Bheinn 512
A'Chruach 512
Chambered Cairn
Machrie Bay
Machrie
Machrie Water
Machrie Moor Stone Circles
Beinn Bhreac 503
Tormore
Ballymichael
Cnoc a' Chapuill 417
Benlister Glen
Margnaheglish
Lamlash
Glenkiln
Lamlash Bay
A841
Clauchlands Point
Holy Island

King's Cave
Hut Circles
Torbeg
Shiskine
Fort
AYRSHIRE
458
Tighvein
Glenkiln
274

Blackwaterfoot
Drumadoon Bay
Kilpatrick
Brown Head
Corriecravie
Sliddery
Torr a' Chaisteal
Glen Scorrodale
Kilmory Water
Lagg
Kilmory
Shannochie
Levencorroch
A841
Chambered Cairns
Bennan Head
Sound of Pladda
Pladda

Glen Ashdale
Knockenkelly
Whiting Bay
Kiscadale
25 Whiting Bay
Largymore
Largybeg
Dippen
Largybeg Point
Dippin Head
Kildonan

Kingscross Point
Kingscross

F I R T H   O F   C L Y D E
F I R T H   O F

Troon to...   hours
Belfast.....................1¾
Larne (summer only)...........1¾

Culzean Castle (NTS)
Maidenhead Bay
Morris
Maidens
Turnberry
Turnberry Bay
Turnberry
Turnberry
5
6
Dowhill
Dipple
Craighea
Low
Chapeldonan
Grangeston
A77

Ailsa Craig
264

Lamlash Bay is where King Haakon of Norway sheltered his fleet on the way to the Battle of Largs in 1263. A cave on nearby Holy Island contains Viking inscriptions thought to have been made by his fighters.
Map ref. F2

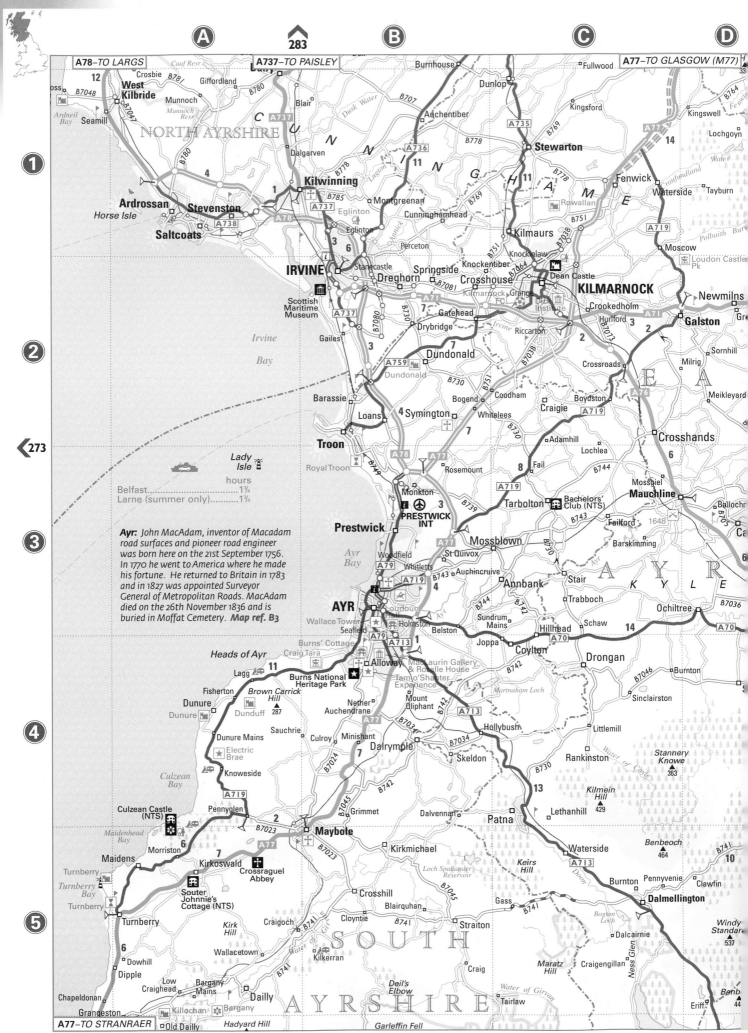

A78–TO LARGS   A737–TO PAISLEY   A77–TO GLASGOW (M77)

12

West Kilbride
Crosbie
Giffordland
B781
B780
Blair
Munnoch
Caaf Resr
Munnoch Resr
Dalry
Burnhouse
Dunlop
Fullwood
Auchentiber
B707
Kingsford
Kingswell
Lochgoyn
Tayburn

NORTH AYRSHIRE
Seamill
Ardneil Bay
B7048
B7047
Dalgarven
C U N N I N G H A M E
Stewarton
Fenwick
Waterside
Moscow

1

Ardrossan
Stevenston
Saltcoats
Horse Isle
A738
A78
Kilwinning
A737
Eglinton
Montgreenan
Cunninghamhead
Rowallan
Kilmaurs
Knocklaw
Dean Castle
KILMARNOCK
Newmilns
Loudon Castle Pk

Stanecastle
Dreghorn
Springside
Knockentiber
Crosshouse
Grange
Kilmarnock FC
Dick Institute
Crookedholm
Galston
Moscow

IRVINE
Scottish Maritime Museum
Gailes
Gatehead
Drybridge
Riccarton
Hurlford
Crossroads
Milrig
Sornhill

2

Irvine Bay
Barassie
Loans
Dundonald
A759
Dundonald
Bogend
Coodham
Whitelees
Craigie
Boydston
Meikleyard

273

Troon
Royal Troon
Symington
Adamhill
Lochlea
Crosshands
6

Lady Isle
hours
Belfast..........1¾
Larne (summer only)..........1¾

Monkton
Rosemount
Fail
Mossgiel
Mauchline
Ballochr
Failford

Ayr: John MacAdam, inventor of Macadam road surfaces and pioneer road engineer was born here on the 21st September 1756. In 1770 he went to America where he made his fortune. He returned to Britain in 1783 and in 1827 was appointed Surveyor General of Metropolitan Roads. MacAdam died on the 26th November 1836 and is buried in Moffat Cemetery. **Map ref. B3**

PRESTWICK INT
Tarbolton
Bachelors' Club (NTS)
1648
Barskimming

Prestwick
Woodfield
St Quivox
Mossblown
Ayr Bay

3

Whitletts
Auchincruive
Annbank
Stair
K Y L E
Ochiltree

AYR
Wallace Tower
Seafield
Holmston
Belston
Joppa
Sundrum Mains
Hillhead
Schaw
14

Heads of Ayr
Burns' Cottage
Craig Tara
Alloway
MacLaurin Gallery & Rozelle House
Tam o'Shanter Experience
Coylton
Drongan
Burnton

Lagg
11
Burns National Heritage Park
Nether Auchendrane
Mount Oliphant
Martnaham Loch
Hollybush
Rankinston
Sinclairston

4

Fisherton
Brown Carrick Hill
Dunduff
287
Minishant
Dalrymple
Skeldon
Littlemill
Stannery Knowe
363

Dunure
Dunure Mains
Sauchrie
Culroy
Electric Brae
Knoweside
Culzean Bay
Kilmein Hill
429
Lethanhill

Culzean Castle (NTS)
Pennyglen
Grimmet
Dalvennan
Patna
Benbeoch
464
Waterside
10

Maidenhead Bay
Morriston
Maybole
Kirkmichael
Keirs Hill
Burnton
Pennyvenie
Clawfin
Dalmellington

Maidens
Turnberry
Turnberry Bay
Kirkoswald
Crossraguel Abbey
Loch Spallander Reservoir
Windy Standard
537

5

Turnberry
Souter Johnnie's Cottage (NTS)
Kirk Hill
Craigoch
Blairquhan
Crosshill
Cloyntie
Straiton
Maratz Hill
Craigengillan
Benb
44

Dowhill
Dipple
Chapeldonan
Grangeston
A77–TO STRANRAER
Low Craighead
Bargany Mains
Dailly
Wallacetown
Kilkerran
Deil's Elbow
Craig
Ness Glen
Dalcairnie
Eriff

SOUTH AYRSHIRE
Killochan
Old Dailly
Hadyard Hill
Garleffin Fell
Tairlaw

274

265

Turnberry: Robert Bruce (1274–1329) was born here. Bruce was proclaimed King of Scotland following the execution of William Wallace in 1306 and went on to defeat the English in several battles culminating at the Battle of Bannockburn on the 23–24th June 1314. **Map ref. A5**

Alloway: Scotland's most famous poet, Robert Burns, was born here on the 25th January 1 He died on the 21st July 1796 of heart disease at the age of 37, on the same day as his wife Je gave birth to his last son. It is said that 10,000 people turned out for his funeral and, in h honour, Burns Nights are celebrated all around the world on his birthday. See Burns Natio Heritage Park. **Map ref. B4 Also on page 118**

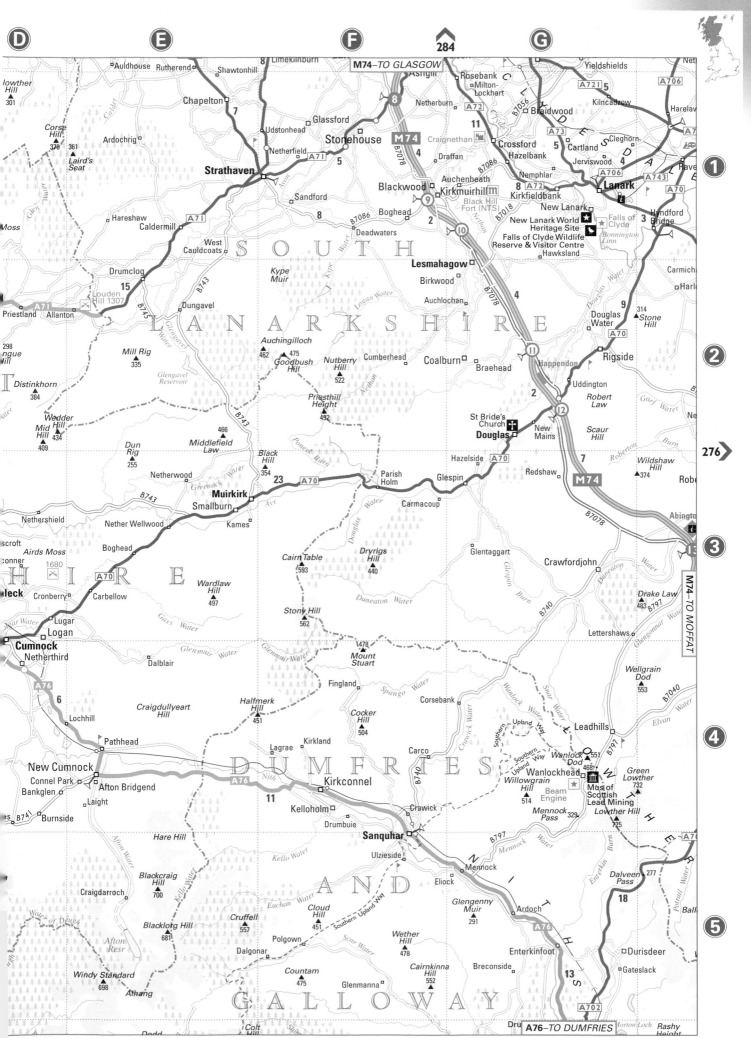

284

M74-TO GLASGOW

8

Auldhouse
Rutherend
Shawtonhill
Limekilnburn
Ashgill
Rosebank
Milton-Lockhart
Yieldshields
A721
A706

Chapelton
7
Glassford
Netherburn
A72
B7056
Braidwood
Kilncadzow
Harelaw
A706

Corse Hill
376
361
Ardochrig
Udstonhead
Stonehouse
M74
Craignethan
Crossford
Hazelbank
Cartland
Jerviswood
Cleghorn
Rave

Laird's Seat
Netherfield
A71
Draffan
B7086
Nemphlar
A706
A743
A70

Strathaven
5
Blackwood
Kirkmuirhill
8
A72
Kirkfieldbank
Lanark

Hareshaw
Caldermill
A71
Sandford
Boghead
Black Hill Fort (NTS)
New Lanark
Hyndford Bridge

West Cauldcoats
8
B7086
Deadwaters
B7018
New Lanark World Heritage Site
Falls of Clyde
3

Drumclog
15
Kype Muir
Birkwood
Falls of Clyde Wildlife Reserve & Visitor Centre
Bonnington Linn

Louden Hill 1307
Lesmahagow
Hawksland

Priestland
Allanton
A71
B743
Dungavel
Auchlochan
4
Douglas Water
9
Stone Hill 314
Carmicha

298
Distinkhorn 384
Mill Rig 335
Auchingilloch 462
Goodbush Hill 475
Nutberry Hill 522
Cumberhead
Coalburn
Braehead
11
Happendon
Uddington
A70
Rigside
Harl

Wedder Hill 434
Mid Hill 409
Dun Rig 255
Middlefield Law
Priesthill Height 492
St Bride's Church
2
Robert Law
Scaur Hill
Robertor
Wildshaw Hill 374
Rob

Netherwood
Black Hill 354
Ponesk Burn
Parish Holm
Douglas
New Mains
Hazelside
A70
Redshaw
M74

Muirkirk
23
A70
Glespin
7

Nethershield
Smallburn
Kames
Carmacoup
Glentaggart
Crawfordjohn

Airds Moss
Boghead
Cairn Table 593
Dryrigs Hill 440
Duneaton Water
B740
Drake Law 483
A797

1680
Wardlaw Hill 497
Lettershaws

Cronberry
Carbellow
Stony Hill 562
Glespin Burn

Cumnock
Netherthird
Lugar
Logan
Glenmuir Water
478
Mount Stuart
Wellgrain Dod 553
B7040

A76
6
Dalblair
Fingland
Corsebank
Leadhills
A797
Elvan Water

Lochhill
Craigdullyeart Hill
Halfmerk Hill 451
Cocker Hill 504
Carco
Wanlock Dod
551
Green Lowther 732

Pathhead
Lagrae
Kirkland
B740
Wanlockhead 468
Mus of Scottish Lead Mining
Lowther Hill 725

New Cumnock
Afton Bridgend
Kirkconnel
Crawick
Willowgrain Hill 514
Beam Engine
Mennock Pass 329

Connel Park
Bankglen
Laight
A76
11
Kelloholm
Drumbuie
Crawick
Dalveen Pass 277

Burnside
Hare Hill
Sanquhar
Ulzieside
Mennock
Eliock
Ardoch
A76
18

Blackcraig Hill 700
Kello Water
Cruffell 557
Cloud Hill 451
Wether Hill 478
Glengenny Muir 291
Ent);
Enterkinfoot

Craigdarroch
Blacklorg Hill 681
Polgown
Dalgonar
Southern Upland Way
Cairnkinna Hill 552
Breconside
Durisdeer
13
Gateslack

Windy Standard 698
Athang
Countam 475
Glenmanna
A702

SOUTH LANARKSHIRE

DUMFRIES AND GALLOWAY

266

A76-TO DUMFRIES

Map ref: D2
Map ref: F5

vel: Sir Alexander Fleming, medical scientist and discoverer of the world's first
biotic drug Penicillin was born at nearby Lochfield Farm in 1881. He made his
very in 1928 and was widely honoured with a knighthood in 1944 and the Nobel
for Medicine in 1945. Fleming died in 1955 and is buried in St Paul's Cathedral,
on. **Map ref: D2**

Sanquhar Home to the oldest post office in the world, established in 1712.
Map ref: F5

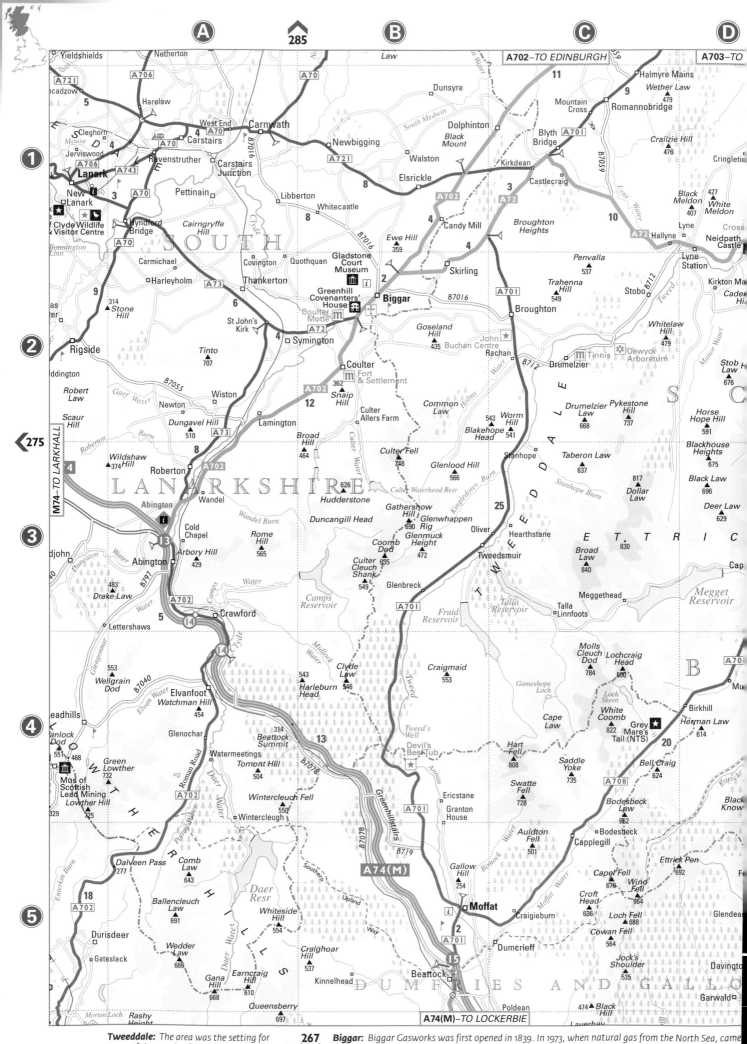

A702–TO EDINBURGH   **A703**–TO

11

9

5

1

3

2

9

275

4

3

5

4

5

M74–TO LARKHALL

A74(M)–TO LOCKERBIE

S O U T H

L A N A R K S H I R E

T W E E D D A L E

E T T R I C

D U M F R I E S   A N D   G A L L O

Yieldshields, Netherton, cadzow, Harelaw, West End, Carnwath, Carstairs, Carstairs Junction, Pettinain, Cleghorn, Mouse, Jerviswood, Lanark, New Lanark, f Clyde Wildlife & Visitor Centre, Hyndford Bridge, Ravenstruther, Newbigging, Walston, Elsrickle, Libberton, Whitecastle, Dunsyre, Black Mount, Dolphinton, Kirkdean, Blyth Bridge, Castlecraig, Mountain Cross, Romannobridge, Halmyre Mains, Wether Law, Crailzie Hill, Black Meldon, White Meldon, Cringletie, Lyne, Neidpath Castle, Hallyne, Lyne Station, Kirkton Ma, Cader, Stobo, Whitelaw Hill, Kirton

Carmichael, Harleyholm, Carngryffe Hill, Clyde, Thankerton, Covington, Quothquan, Gladstone Court Museum, Greenhill Covenanters' House, Biggar, Candy Mill, Skirling, Ewe Hill 359, Broughton Heights, Penvalla 537, Trahenna Hill 549, Broughton

Stone Hill 314, St John's Kirk, Goulter Motte, Symington, Coulter, Goseland Hill 435, John Buchan Centre, Rachan, Tinnis, Drumelzier, Dawyck Arboretum, Stob Law 676

Rigside, Tinto 707, Wiston, Newton, Lamington, Snaip Hill, Culter Fort & Settlement 362, Culter Allers Farm, Common Law, Worm Hill 543, Blakehope Head 541, Drumelzier Law 668, Pykestone Hill 737, Horse Hope Hill 591

Robert Law, Scaur Hill, Wildshaw Hill 374, Dungavel Hill 510, Roberton, Wandel, Broad Hill 464, Hudderstone 626, Culter Fell 748, Glenlood Hill 566, Culter Waterhead Resr, Stanhope, Taberon Law 637, Dollar Law 817, Blackhouse Heights 675, Black Law 696, Deer Law 629

Abington, Cold Chapel, Rome Hill 565, Arbory Hill 429, Duncangill Head, Gathershow Hill 690, Glenwhappen Rig, Glenmuck Height 472, Coomb Dod 635, Oliver, Hearthstane, Tweedsmuir, Broad Law 840, Meggethead, Megget Reservoir, Cap

Drake Law 483, Letlershaws, Wellgrain Dod 553, Crawford, Camps Reservoir, Clyde Law 546, Harleburn Head 543, Craigmaid 553, Gameshope Loch, Loch Skeen, Molls Cleuch Dod 784, Lochcraig Head 800, Talla Reservoir, Talla Linnfoots, Fruid Reservoir

Elvanfoot, Watchman Hill 454, Glenochar, Watermeetings, Beattock Summit 314, Tomont Hill 504, Devil's Beef Tub, Tweed's Well, Cape Law, Hart Fell 808, White Coomb 822, Grey Mare's Tail (NTS), Herman Law 614, Bell Craig 624, Birkhill, Mu

Green Lowther 732, Wintercleuch Fell 550, Wintercleugh, Ericstane, Granton House, Saddle Yoke 735, Swatte Fell 728, Bodesbeck Law 662, Black Know

Mus of Scottish Lead Mining, Lowther Hill 725, Roman Road, Comb Law 643, Dalveen Pass 277, Ballencleuch Law 691, Whiteside Hill 554, Daer Resr, Gallow Hill 254, Auldton Fell 501, Bodesbeck, Capplegill, Croft Head 636, Capel Fell 678, Wind Fell 664, Ettrick Pen 692

Durisdeer, Gateslack, Wedder Law 666, Craighoar Hill 537, Gana Hill 668, Earncraig Hill 610, Queensberry 697, Kinnelhead, Beattock, Moffat, Craigieburn, Dumcrieff, Loch Fell 688, Cowan Fell 564, Jock's Shoulder 535, Croft Head, Black Hill 474, Poldean, Garwald, Davingto, Glendea

Poldean, Laverhay

Tweeddale: The area was the setting for some of the novels of John Buchan (1875-1940) – most famously The Thirty-Nine Steps. **Map ref. C3**

267

Biggar: Biggar Gasworks was first opened in 1839. In 1973, when natural gas from the North Sea, came the town, the gasworks closed. However, unlike most other towns, Biggar didn't demolish its gasworks instead it made it into a Gasworks Museum. It is now preserved for future generations by Historic Buil and Monuments and the Museums of Scotland. **Map ref. B2**

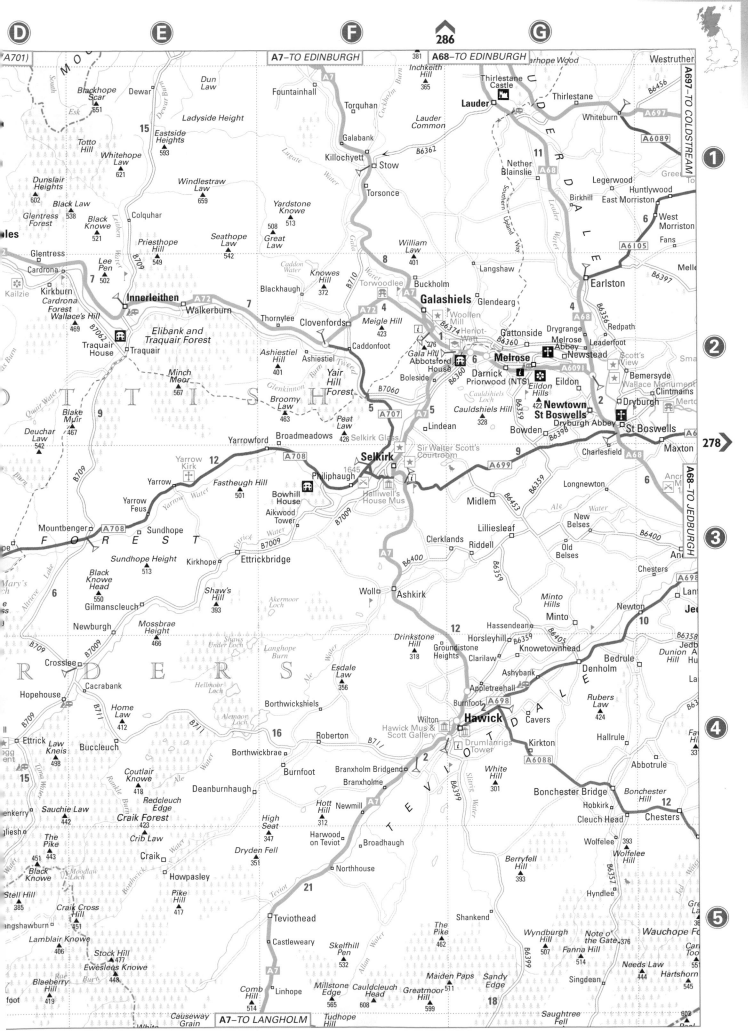

A7–TO EDINBURGH A68–TO EDINBURGH

A701

A697–TO COLDSTREAM

1

MOORFOOT

Blackhope
Scar
651

Dewar

Dun
Law

Fountainhall

Inchkeith
Hill
365

Cockholm Burn

Yarhope Wood

Westruther

B6456

Thirlestane
Castle

Thirlestane

Lauder

Whiteburn

A697

A6089

Totto
Hill

Whitehope
Law
621

Ladyside Height

Eastside
Heights
593

15

Dun
Law

Torquhan

Galabank

B6362

Lauder
Common

Nether
Blainslie

A68

Legerwood

Birkhill

Huntlywood

East Morriston

Greenlaw To

Fans

Melle

6

West
Morriston

Dunslair
Heights
602

Black Law
538

Windlestraw
Law
659

Killochyett

Stow

Torsonce

Southern Upland Way

11

Leader Water

A6105

Glentress
Forest

Black
Knowe
521

Colquhar

Yardstone
Knowe
513

Langshaw

A6105

Earlston

B6397

les

Glentress

Cardrona

Priesthope
Hill
549

Seathope
Law
542

Great
Law

508

William
Law
401

8

Buckholm

Glendearg

4

Redpath

B6356

Kailzie

Kirkburn

Lee
Pen
502

B709

Leithen Water

Caddon Water

Knowes
Hill
372

Torwoodlee

A72

Galashiels

Woollen
Mill

B6374

Heriot-
Watt

Drygrange

A68

Leaderfoot

Gattonside

Melrose
Abbey

Newstead

Scott's
View

4

2

7

Innerleithen

Walkerburn

7

Thornylee

Clovenfords

Meigle Hill
423

Caddonfoot

Abbotsford
House

276

Gala Hill

6

Melrose

Darnick

A6091

Eildon

Bemersyde

Wallace Monument

Clintmains

Sma

Cardrona
Forest

Wallace's Hill
469

B7062

Traquair
House

Traquair

Elibank and
Traquair Forest

Ashiestiel
Hill
401

Ashiestiel

Yair
Hill
Forest

Tweed

Boleside

B6360

Priorwood (NTS)

Eildon
Hills
422

**Newtown
St Boswells**

Dryburgh

Mert

B7060

Cauldshiels
Loch

2

St Boswells

SCOTTISH

Quair Water

Blake
Muir
467

9

Minch
Moor
567

Broomy
Law
463

Glenkinnon Burn

Peat
Law
426

A707

A7

Lindean

Cauldshiels Hill
328

Bowden

B6359

Dryburgh Abbey

B6398

Maxton

A6

Deuchar
Law
542

Yarrowford

Broadmeadows

Selkirk Glass

Sir Walter Scott's
Courtroom

Charlesfield

A68

278

Yarrow
Kirk

12

A708

Selkirk

1645

A699

9

Longnewton

6

Ancr

M

A68–TO JEDBURGH

Mary's
ch

Yarrow

Fastheugh Hill
501

Philiphaugh

Halliwell's
House Mus

Midlem

B6453

New
Belses

B6400

3

ss

6

Yarrow
Feus

Bowhill
House

B7009

Lilliesleaf

Old
Belses

Chesters

A698

Lan

Mountbenger

A708

Sundhope

Aikwood
Tower

B7009

Clerklands

Riddell

Minto
Hills

Newton

10

B6358

Je

FOREST

Sundhope Height
513

Kirkhope

Ettrickbridge

Woll

Ashkirk

Minto

B6405

Bedrule

Dunion
Hill

Hu

pe

Black
Knowe
Head
550

Shaw's
Hill
393

Akermoor
Loch

A7

Hassendean

Horsleyhill

B6359

Knowetownhead

Denholm

La

R   D   E   R   S

Gilmanscleuch

Newburgh

Mossbrae
Height
466

Shaws
Under Loch

Langhope
Burn

Drinkstone
Hill
318

Groundistone
Heights

Clarilaw

Ashybank

Rubers
Law
424

B6

Crosslee

B7009

Esdale
Law
356

Appletreehall

Ashkirk

A698

4

Hopehouse

Cacrabank

Home
Law
412

Hellmoor
Loch

Borthwickshiels

Burnfoot

Wilton

Hawick Mus &
Scott Gallery

2

Hawick

Cavers

Hallrule

Fa
Hi
33

ll

Ettrick

Law
Kneis
498

Buccleuch

Alemoor
Loch

B711

16

Roberton

Drumlanrigs
Tower

Kirkton

A6088

Abbotrule

15

Sauchie Law
442

Coutlair
Knowe
418

Deanburnhaugh

Borthwickbrae

Burnfoot

Branxholm Bridgend

Branxholme

2

A7

White
Hill
301

B6399

Bonchester Bridge

Bonchester
Hill

12

Chesters

enkerry

The
Pike
451

Craik Forest

443

Crib Law

Redcleuch
Edge
423

High
Seat
347

Newmill

Hott
Hill
312

Hobkirk

Cleuch Head

Wolfelee
393

gliesh

Black
Knowe

Crib Law

Craik

Harwood
on Teviot

Broadhaugh

Wolfelee
Hill

Stell Hill
385

Craik Cross
Hill
451

Moodlaw
Loch

Howpasley

Pike
Hill
417

Dryden Fell
351

Northhouse

Teviot

21

Berryfell
Hill
393

Wolfelee

Hyndlee

Gre
La

B6357

5

angshawburn

Lamblair Knowe
406

Stock Hill
477

Eweslees Knowe
448

The
Pike
462

Shankend

Wyndburgh
Hill
507

Note o'
the Gate
376

Fanna Hill
514

Wauchope Fo

Car
Too

foot

Blaeberry
Hill
419

Rae
Burn

A7

Comb
Hill
514

Linhope

Millstone
Edge
565

Cauldcleuch
Head
608

Greatmoor
Hill
599

Maiden Paps

Sandy
Edge

511

Singdean

Needs Law
444

Hartshorn

55

Singdean

602

Causeway
Grain

Teviothead

Castleweary

Skelfhill
Pen
532

Tudhope
Hill

18

Saughtree
Fell

A7–TO LANGHOLM

268

*Selkirk: Stomping ground of William Wallace 'Braveheart' who was declared
'Guardian of Scotland' here in the 13th Century. For much of his life Wallace
lived like an outlaw attacking anything English. He was finally caught and
executed in 1305.* **Map ref. F3**

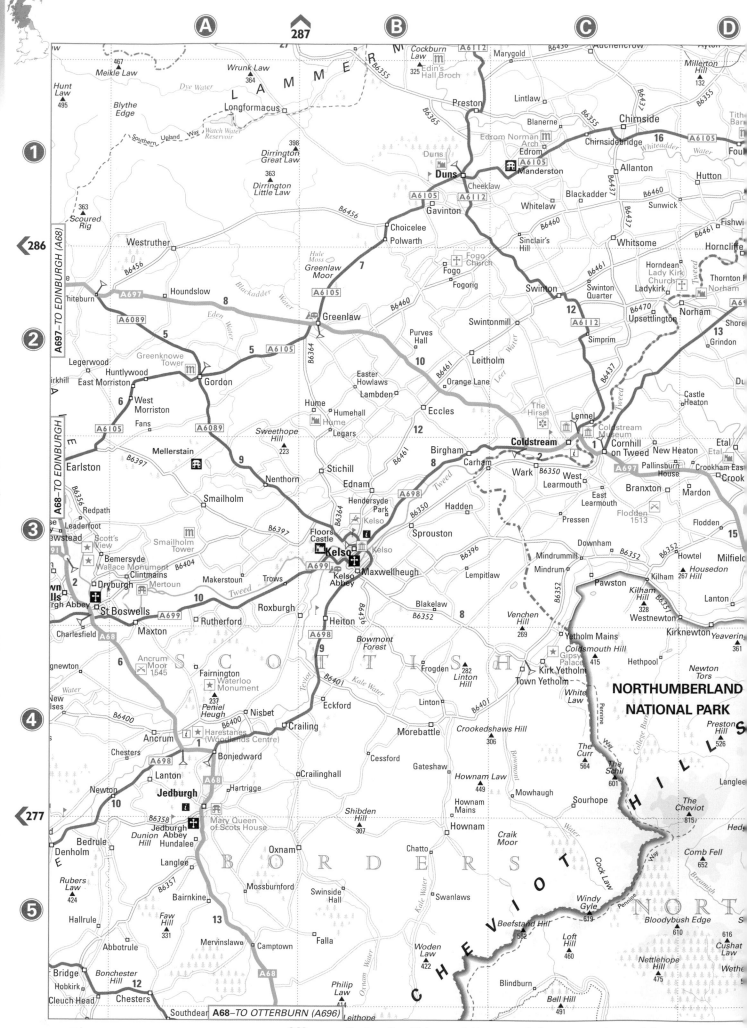

NORTHUMBERLAND NATIONAL PARK

Chesters: Steve Hislop regarded by many as the fastest motorcycle racer of all time, was born here on the 11th January 1962. 'Hizzy' won 11 TT races on the Isle of Man and was British Superbike Champion in 1995 and 2002. He was tragically killed in a helicopter crash near Teviothead on the 30th July 2003. *Map ref. A4*

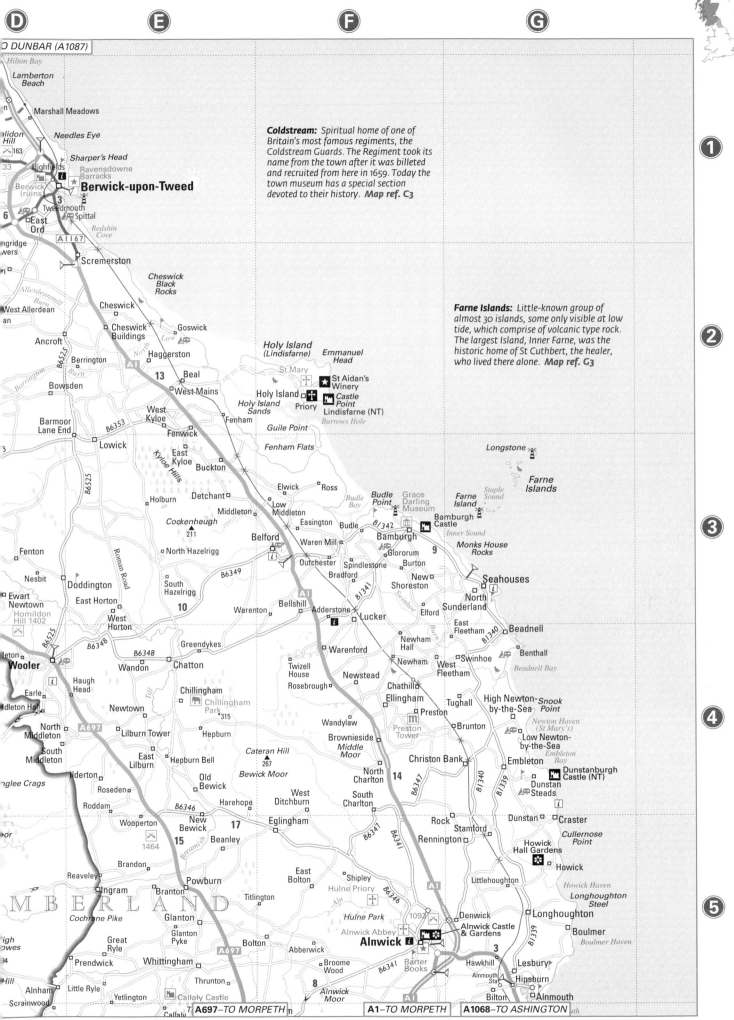

Coldstream: *Spiritual home of one of Britain's most famous regiments, the Coldstream Guards. The Regiment took its name from the town after it was billeted and recruited from here in 1659. Today the town museum has a special section devoted to their history.* **Map ref. C3**

Farne Islands: *Little-known group of almost 30 islands, some only visible at low tide, which comprise of volcanic type rock. The largest Island, Inner Farne, was the historic home of St Cuthbert, the healer, who lived there alone.* **Map ref. G3**

TO DUNBAR (A1087)

Berwick-upon-Tweed

Wooler

Alnwick

Holy Island (Lindisfarne)

Farne Islands

Bamburgh

Seahouses

A697–TO MORPETH   A1–TO MORPETH   A1068–TO ASHINGTON

mburgh: *The great sandstone castle here was the first stle in Britain to be attacked by cannon fire when it was sieged by the artillery of Edward IV in 1464.* **ap ref. F3 Also on page 102**

270

Bamburgh: *Grace Darling lived here with her father, a lighthouse keeper. She is famous for spotting a shipwreck during a dreadful storm and then assisting her father in the rescue of 5 survivors she had seen clinging to Big Harcar Rock. Grace died of flu in October 1842.* **Map ref. F3**

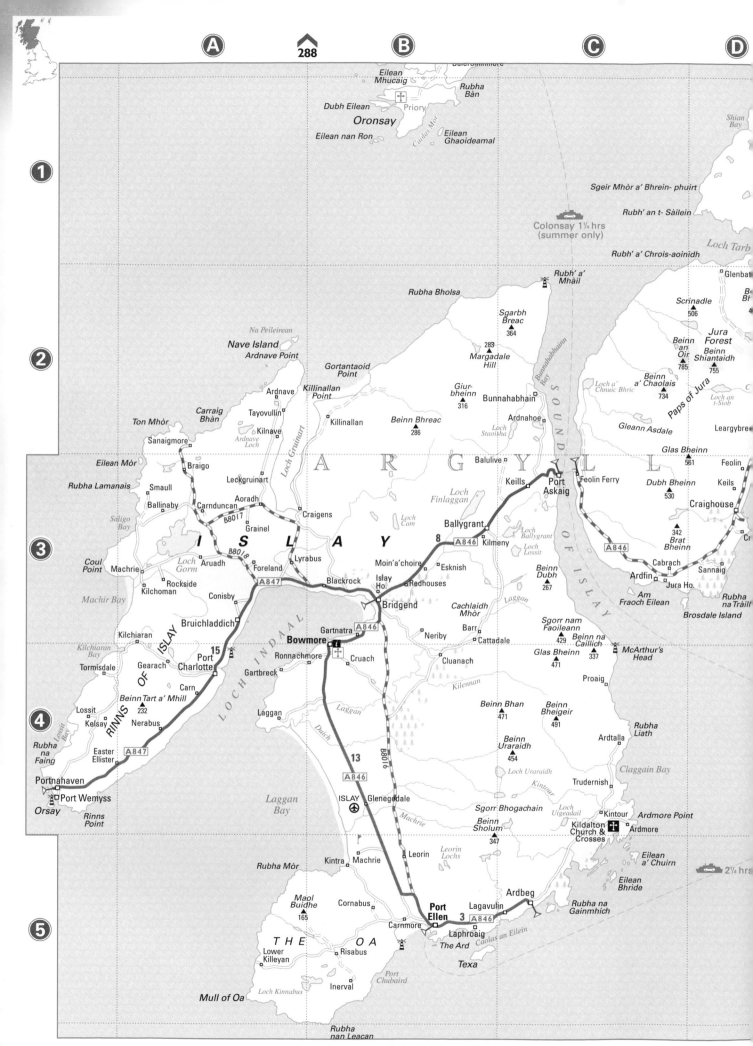

Eilean Mhucaig
Rubha Bàn
Dubh Eilean
Priory
Oronsay
Eilean nan Ron
Eilean Ghaoideamal
Caolas Mòr
Shian Bay

Ⓘ①

Sgeir Mhòr a' Bhrein- phuirt

Rubh' an t- Sàilein

Colonsay 1¼ hrs
(summer only)

Rubh' a' Chrois-aoinidh

Loch Tarb

Rubha Bholsa

Rubh' a' Mhàil

Glenbat

Scrinadle
506

Jura Forest

Na Peileirean

Nave Island
Ardnave Point

Gortantaoid Point

Sgarbh Breac
364

283

Margadale Hill

Beinn an Oir
785

Beinn Shiantaidh
755

Ⓘ②

Ardnave

Killinallan Point

Giur-bheinn
316

Bunnahabhain

Loch a' Chnuic Bhric

Beinn a' Chaolais
734

Paps of Jura

Loch an t-Siob

Carraig Bhàn

Tayovullin

Killinallan

Beinn Bhreac
286

Ardnahoe

Gleann Asdale

Leargybre

Ton Mhòr

Kilnave

Ardnave Loch

Loch Staoisha

Glas Bheinn
561

Feolin

Sanaigmore

Braigo

A R G Y L L

Balulive

Keills

Port Askaig

Feolin Ferry

Dubh Bheinn
530

Keils

Eilean Mòr

Leckgruinart

Aoradh

Loch Gruinart

Loch Finlaggan

Craighouse

Rubha Lamanais

Smaull

Carnduncan

B8017

Craigens

Ballygrant

8 A846 Kilmeny

Loch Ballygrant

342

Cabrach

Sannaig

Ⓘ③

Ballinaby

Grainel

Moin'a'choire

Esknish

Loch Lossit

Brat Bheinn

Ardfin

Jura Ho.

Saligo Bay

Aruadh

B8018

Lyrabus

Blackrock

Islay Ho.

Redhouses

Beinn Dubh
267

Am Fraoch Eilean

Coul Point

Machrie

Loch Gorm

Foreland

A847

Laggan

Rubha na Traill

Rockside

Kilchoman

Conisby

Bridgend

Cachlaidh Mhòr

Brosdale Island

Machir Bay

Bruichladdich

Gartnatra

A846

Barr

Sgorr nam Faoileann
429

Beinn na Caillich

McArthur's Head

Kilchiaran

Port Charlotte

15

Bowmore

Ronnachmore

Neriby

Cattadale

Glas Bheinn
471

337

Kilchiaran Bay

Gearach

Carn

Gartbreck

Cruach

Cluanach

Proaig

Tormisdale

R I N N S

Beinn Tart a' Mhill
232

Laggan

Kilennan

Ardtalla

Ⓘ④

Lossit

Kelsay

Nerabus

O F

Laggan

Beinn Bhan
471

Beinn Bheigeir
491

Rubha Liath

Rubha na Faing

Easter Ellister

I S L A Y

A847

Duich

Beinn Uraraidh
454

Loch Uraraidh

Claggain Bay

Portnahaven

13

Kintour

Trudernish

Port Wemyss

A846

Machrie

B8016

Loch Uigeadail

Kintour

Ardmore Point

Orsay

Rinns Point

Laggan Bay

ISLAY
Glenegedale

Leorin

Sgorr Bhogachain

Beinn Sholum
347

Kildalton Church & Crosses

Ardmore

Rubha Mòr

Kintra

Machrie

Leorin Lochs

Eilean a' Chuirn

Eilean Bhride

2¼ hrs

Maol Buidhe
165

Cornabus

Risabus

Ardbeg

Lagavulin

Rubha na Gainmhich

Ⓘ⑤

Port Ellen

3 A846

T H E   O A

Lower Killeyan

Carnmore

Laphroaig

The Ard

Caolas an Eilein

Texa

Inerval

Port Chubaird

Mull of Oa

Loch Kinnabus

Rubha nan Leacan

Islay: Known as the 'Jewel of the Hebrides' this beautiful island is a major bird watching destination and is home to 8 different whisky distilleries. Islay enjoys a sort of micro-climate, warmed by the Gulf Stream: it has more hours of sunshine than most of mainland Britain and relatively mild winters as well. **Map ref. A3**

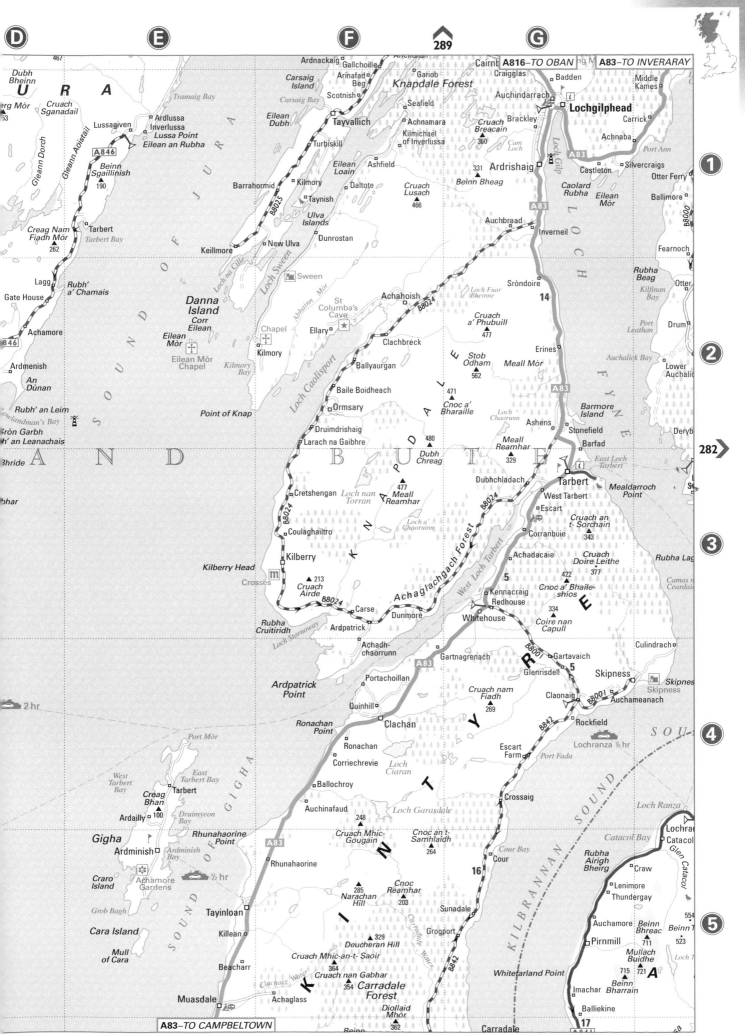

282 ▶

272 ▼

Ardrishaig: The 9 mile (14.5km) long Crinan Canal was started here in 1794 by John Rennie. The canal links Loch Fyne with the Atlantic Ocean and cuts out a 120 mile (193km) voyage around the Mull of Kintyre. *Map ref. G1*

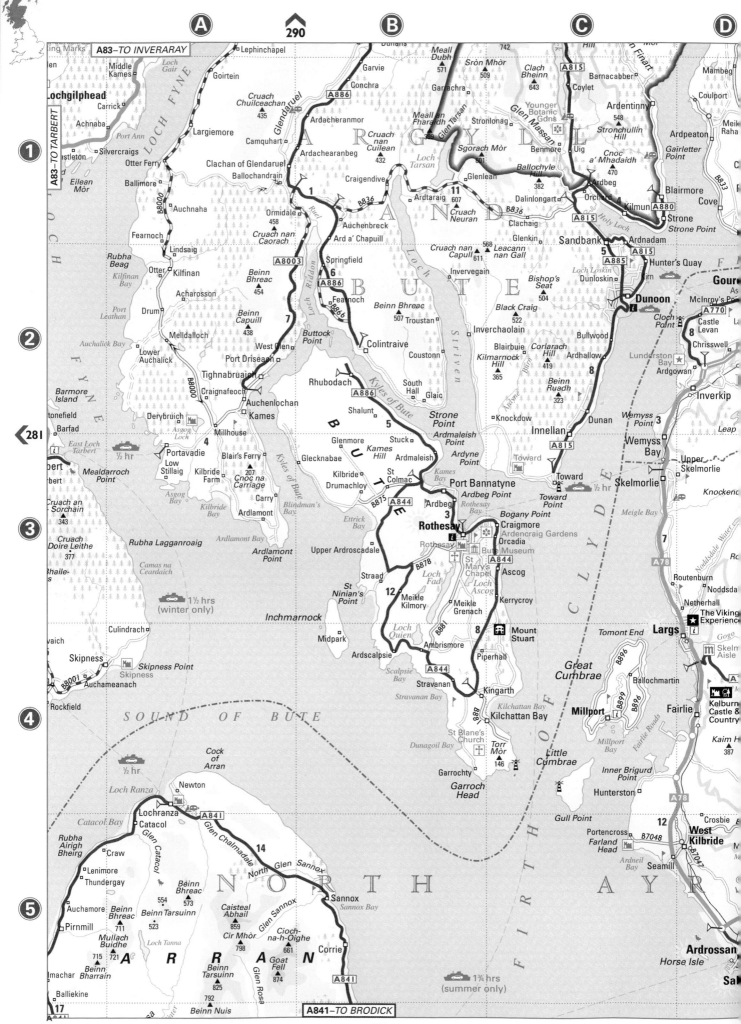

Holy Loch: During the Cold War of the 1960s this was a controversial US Navy nuclear submarine base housing Polaris Missiles. Over 700 Americans lived in the area and when it closed in 1992 many feared that the local economy would collapse. However the Government allocated £12 million to recreate employment in the area and a crisis was averted. **Map ref. C1**

273 Largs: Scene of a great Scottish victory over the Vikings in 1263. The Viking fleet, under Haakon left their base in the Western Isles to sail down the Clyde to subdue the Scottish resistance to Viking rule. But the Scots army, under Alexander III, helped by bad weather managed to repulse the assault and end the Viking threat to mainland Scotland. The b... is commemorated by a monument just south of the town. **Map ref. D4**

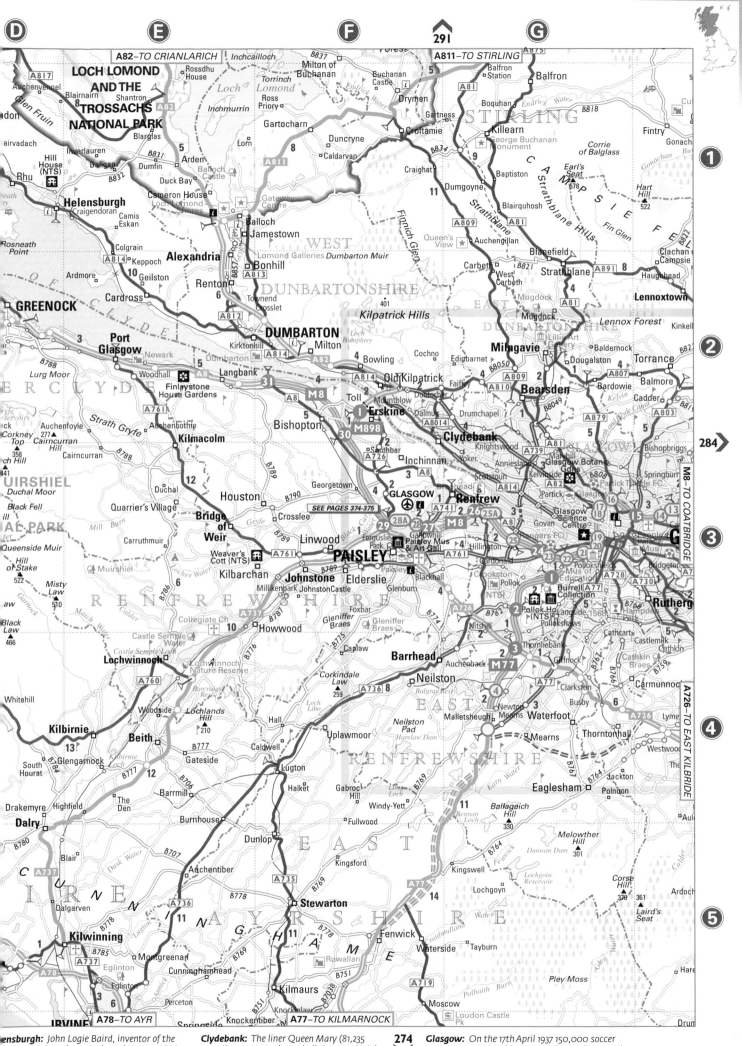

D **E** **F** **G**

A82–TO CRIANLARICH
A811–TO STIRLING

LOCH LOMOND AND THE TROSSACHS NATIONAL PARK

284 ▶

M8–TO COATBRIDGE

A726–TO EAST KILBRIDE

ensburgh: John Logie Baird, inventor of the vision was born here on the 13th August 1888. reated the first televised pictures of an object in ion in 1925. He died on the 14th June 1946 at hill, East Sussex. **Map ref. D1**

Clydebank: The liner Queen Mary (81,235 tons/82,539 tonnes) was built here at the John Brown Shipyard. It is said that over one million people turned out to watch her leaving the Clyde on the 24th March 1936. **Map ref. F3**

274
▼

Glasgow: On the 17th April 1937 150,000 soccer supporters crammed into Hampden Park to watch Scotland play England. This is the European attendance record and stood as a world record until 1950. **Map ref. G3**

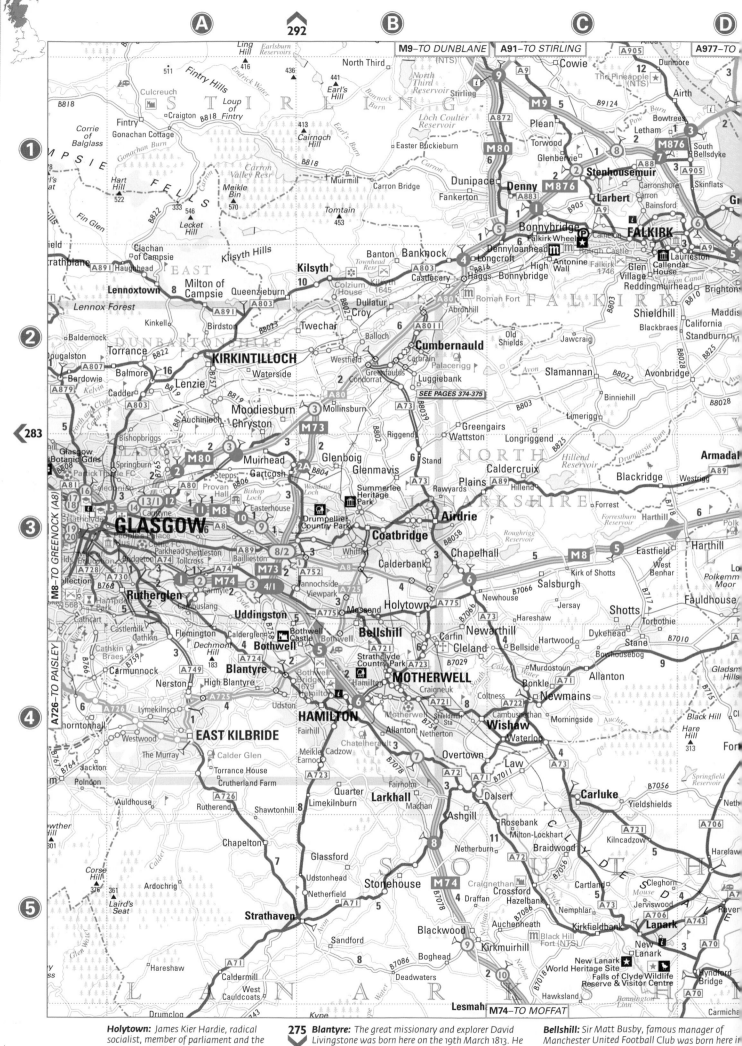

M9-TO DUNBLANE   A91-TO STIRLING   A977-TO

SEE PAGES 374-375

283

1

2

3

4

5

M74-TO MOFFAT

Holytown: James Kier Hardie, radical socialist, member of parliament and the person central to the formation of the British Independent Labour Party was born at nearby Legbranock in 1856. Hardie died in Glasgow in 1915. **Map ref. B3**

275 **Blantyre:** The great missionary and explorer David Livingstone was born here on the 19th March 1813. He first went to Africa in 1841 and whilst mapping the Zambezi River discovered and named the Victoria Falls. Livingstone died of fever in Africa in 1873 and his embalmed body was brought back to England and buried in Westminster Abbey. **Map ref. A4**

Bellshill: Sir Matt Busby, famous manager of Manchester United Football Club was born here in He is credited with re-building the team following Munich Air Disaster of 1958. He was knighted for services to football in 1967, retired as manager in and died in 1994. **Map ref. B4**

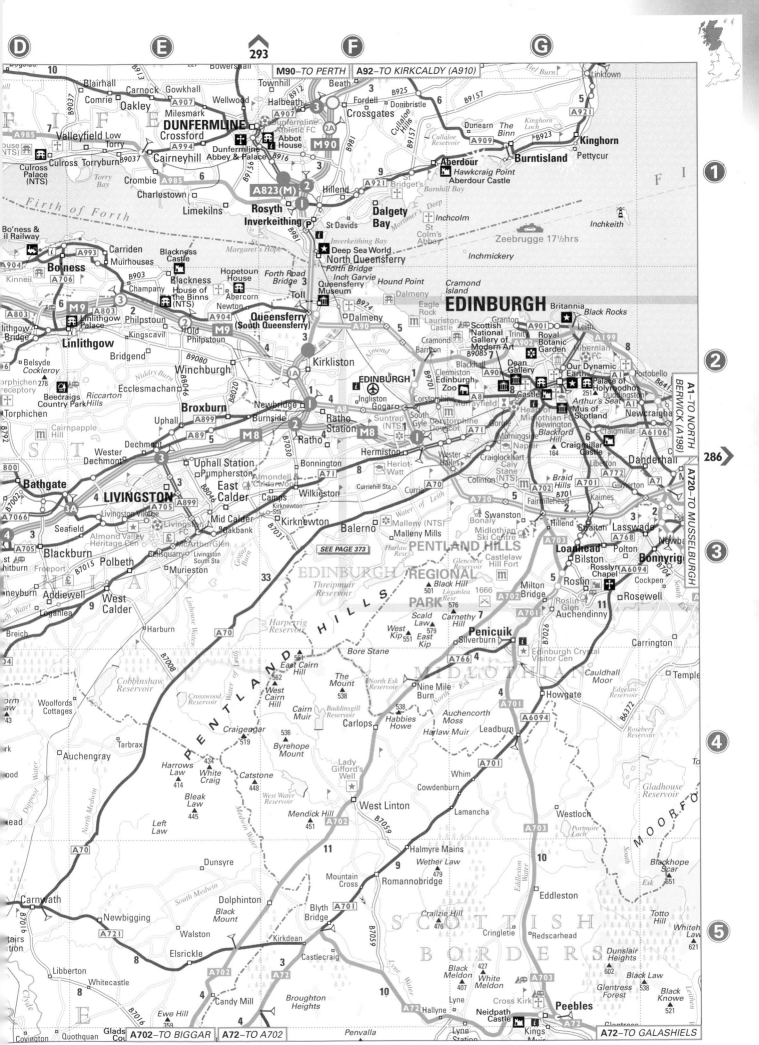

M90-TO PERTH A92-TO KIRKCALDY (A910)

10
Bowershall
Blairhall   Gowkhall   Townhill   Beath
Comrie   Carnock   Wellwood   Halbeath   Fordell   B925   Donibristle
Oakley   Milesmark   B912   Crossgates   Cullaloe Hills   Dunearn   The Binn   Linktown
A907   DUNFERMLINE   Dunfermline   M90   Cullaloe Reservoir   B9157   A909   Kinghorn Loch
Valleyfield Low   Crossford   Athletic FC   2A   A921   Kinghorn
Torry   Dunfermline   Abbot   B981   9   B923   Pettycur
Culross   Torryburn   Abbey & Palace   House   A921   Aberdour   Burntisland
Palace (NTS)   Cairneyhill   A994   M90   St Bridget's   Hawkcraig Point
Crombie   A985   Hillend   Aberdour Castle
Charlestown   A823(M)   2   Dalgety   Inchcolm
Firth of Forth   Rosyth   Bay   St Colm's Abbey   Inchkeith
Limekilns   Inverkeithing   St Davids   Zeebrugge 17½hrs   Inchmickery

Bo'ness & Railway
Carriden   Deep Sea World   Hound Point   Cramond Island   EDINBURGH   Britannia   Black Rocks
Bo'ness   Muirhouses   Blackness Castle   North Queensferry   Dalmeny   Eagle Rock   Granton   Royal Botanic Garden   Leith
A904   Champany   Hopetoun House   Forth Bridge   Queensferry   Lauriston   Scottish National Gallery of Modern Art   Trinity   A199
M9   A803   House of the Binns (NTS)   Abercorn   Museum   Cramond   Castle   Dean Gallery   Hibernian FC
Linlithgow Palace   Newton   Toll   B924   Barnton   Clermiston   A90   Our Dynamic Earth   Portobello
Linlithgow   Old Philpstoun   Queensferry   Dalmeny   Blackhall   Castle   Palace of Holyroodhouse   A1   Newcraighall
Bridgend   M9   A90   Kirkliston   Edinburgh Zoo   Corstorphine   Murrayfield   Arthur's Seat   Mus of Scotland
Belsyde   Winchburgh   EDINBURGH   Ingliston   Gogar   South   Morningside   Blackford Hill   Craigmillar
Ecclesmachan   Newbridge   Gyle   Napier   164   Craigmillar Castle   Danderhall
Broxburn   Burnside   Ratho Station   Suntrap (NTS)   Hermiston   A71   Craiglockhart   Braid Hills   A701   A7
Uphall   A899   Ratho   M8   Wester Hailes   Colinton   A702   Fairmilehead   Gilmerton   Kaimes
Dechmont   A89   M8   Bonnington   Currie   Water of Leith   A720   5   Hillend   Lasswade
Wester Dechmont   Uphall Station   Pumpherston   Almondell & Calderwood   A71   Heriot-Watt   Swanston   Straiton   A768   Newbattle
BATHGATE   East Calder   Camps   Wilkieston   Currie   Bonaly   Midlothian Ski Centre   Loanhead   Polton   Bonnyrigg
LIVINGSTON   A899   Mid Calder   Kirknewton   Balerno   Malleny (NTS)   PENTLAND HILLS   Roslin Glen   Rosslyn Chapel   Cockpen
Livingston Village   A705   Oakbank   B7031   Malleny Mills   SEE PAGE 373   Castlelaw Hill Fort   Milton Bridge   Roslin   Rosewell
Blackburn   Livingston South Sta   EDINBURGH REGIONAL   Black Hill   A702   Auchendinny

Forth Rail Bridge: At 1.5 miles (2.4km) long and 150 feet (46m) high, this remarkable cantilever structure is universally recognised as an engineering marvel. Its span of 1,710 feet (521m) is the largest of any railway bridge in Britain. Construction began under Sir William Arrol in 1883 and it was opened by the Prince of Wales in 1890. In all it cost £3.2 million and used 54,000 tons (54,900 tonnes) of steel, 640,000 cubic feet (18,123 cubic metres) of granite and 6.5 million rivets. It also cost the lives of 57 construction workers. And, yes, for over 100 years it was continuously being painted. Map ref. F2

FIRTH OF FORTH

Rosyth to Zeebrugge 17½hrs

Kinghorn
Pettycur
Linktown
5
921
Inchkeith
Black Rocks

A1–TO EDINBURGH
A199
8
A1
Portobello
Musselburgh
Palace of
Holyroodhouse
Duddingston
r's Seat
of
land
Craigmillar
Castle
iberton
A6106
Danderhall
Newcraighall
Millerhill
Gilmerton
A7
Craigmillar Castle
285
A772
A768
2
Eskbank
A6064
Lasswade
A720–TO M8 & M9
Caimes
3
Gilberton
Dalkeith
A6124
A68
Whitehill
Newbattle
B6482
Easthouses
Bonnyrigg
B701
Cockpen
Mayfield
Newtongrange
Rosewell
A6094
Arniston
Engine
Newlandrig
Bilston
Rosslyn Chapel
A7
Polton
Gilston

SEE PAGE 373

Cockenzie
and Port Seton
Preston Tower &
Hamilton House (NTS)
Prestonpans
Prestonpans 1745
Cross
Levenhall
Inveresk
Pinkie
1547
Inveresk
Wallyford
Tranent
A199
Penston
Macmerry
New
Winton
Elphinstone
Whitecraig
Carberry Tower
Crossgatehall
Ormiston
Cousland
A6093
Pencaitland
West Saltoun
Market
Cross
Winton
House
New Town
East
Saltoun
Peastonbank
Peaston
Gilchriston
Oxenfoord
Edgehead
Ford
Pathhead
Crichton
Vogrie
Humbie
Fala
Dam
Fala
Crichton
Castle
Borthwick
Tynehead
Fala
Moor
Gilston
Soutra
Hill
368
Dun Law
394 *363
Turf
Law

SEE PAGE 373

Seton
Collegiate Church
B1348
Longniddry
7
Elvingston
B6363
Gladsmuir
A1
Samuelston
Bolton
B6368
Gifford
Church
Gifford
Longyester
Danskine
B6355
B6457
Dean
Burn

Yellowcraig
Fidra
Lamb
Muirfield
Gullane
Bents
Gullane Bay
Gullane Point
Gullane
A198
Dirleton
Dirleton
Castle & Gardens
Fenton
Barns
Luffness
Aberlady
Craigielaw
Craigielaw Point
Luffness
Friary
Drem
Mungoswells
5
Gosford
House
Ballencrieff
B1377
Spittal
A6137
Garleton Hills
B1343
A198
Longniddry
Bents
Aberlady
Bay
Gosford
Bay

North
Berwick
Craigleith
Scottish
Seabird Centre
Tantallon
Castle
St
Baldred's
Boat
Auldhame
Scoughall
North
Berwick
Law
187
Kingston
Whitekirk
Pinkerton
A198
8
Peffer Burn
Tyninghame
House
East Fortune
B1377
Museum of
Flight
Church
of Plaque
Athelstaneford
Preston
Preston Mill
& Phantassie
Dovecot (NTS)
B407
Tyningham
East
Linton
A199
Hailes
Traprain
Traprain
Law Fort
Luggate
Luggate
Burn
Papple
B6370
Whitelaw
Hill
Garvald
Carfrae
Nunraw
Abbey
Clints Do
White
398
400
Rangely
Kip
Newlands
Hill
423

Bass
Rock
St
Baldred's
Boat

Haddington
A6093
St Mary's
Church
Lennoxlove
Colstoun
Water
Gifford
Water
Faseny

Lammer
Law
528
Crib
Law
509
West
Hill
451
Hopes
Resr
Meikle Says
Law
535
Seenes Law
513
467
Meikle Law
Hunt
Law
495
Hogs
Law
448
Blythe
Edge
Penshie
Hill
Southern
Upland

MIDLOTHIAN
Carrington
Cauldhall
Moor
Edgelaw
Reservoir
B6372
Temple
Middleton
Roseberry
Reservoir
Gorebridge
Borthwick
North Middleton
B6367
B6458
13
6
A7
Torfichen
Hill
460
B7007
Heriot
Gladhouse
Reservoir
MOORFOOT HILLS
Falahill
Heriot
Water
B709
Heriot Water

Dewar
Burn
Dun
Law
Fountainhall
Torquhan
Gala
Water
A7
9
M
Cockholm
Burn
Oxton
Carfraemill
A68
Edgarhope Wood
8
A697
Scoured
Rig
363
Westruther
B6456

LAMMERMUIR
Earnscleugh Water
Collie
Law
381
Inchkeith
Hill
365
Thirlestane
Castle
Thirlestane
Lauder
Lauder
Common
A697
Whitburn
Legerwood
Greenkno
To
Huntlywood
East Morriston
A6089
West
Morriston
Fans
6
A6105

Dunslair
Heights
602
Black Law
538
Glentress
Forest
Black
Knowe
521
Glentress
Leithen
Whitehope
Law
621
15
Eastside
Heights
593
Ladyside Height
Windlestraw
Law
659
Colquhar
Priesthope
Hill
549
Seathope
Law
542
Yardstone
Knowe
513
508
Great
Law
Lugate
Water
Blackhope
Scar
651
Dewar
Galabank
Killochyett
Stow
Torsonce
B6362
Nether
Blainslie
A68
Birkhill
Caddon
William
Law
Southern Upland Way
Leader
Water
11

A7–TO GALASHIELS

A68–TO NEWTOWN
ST BOSWELLS

Portobello: The great singer and music hall entertainer Sir Harry Lauder was born here in 1870. Lauder died in 1950 and is buried in Bent Cemetery, Hamilton. *Map ref. A2*

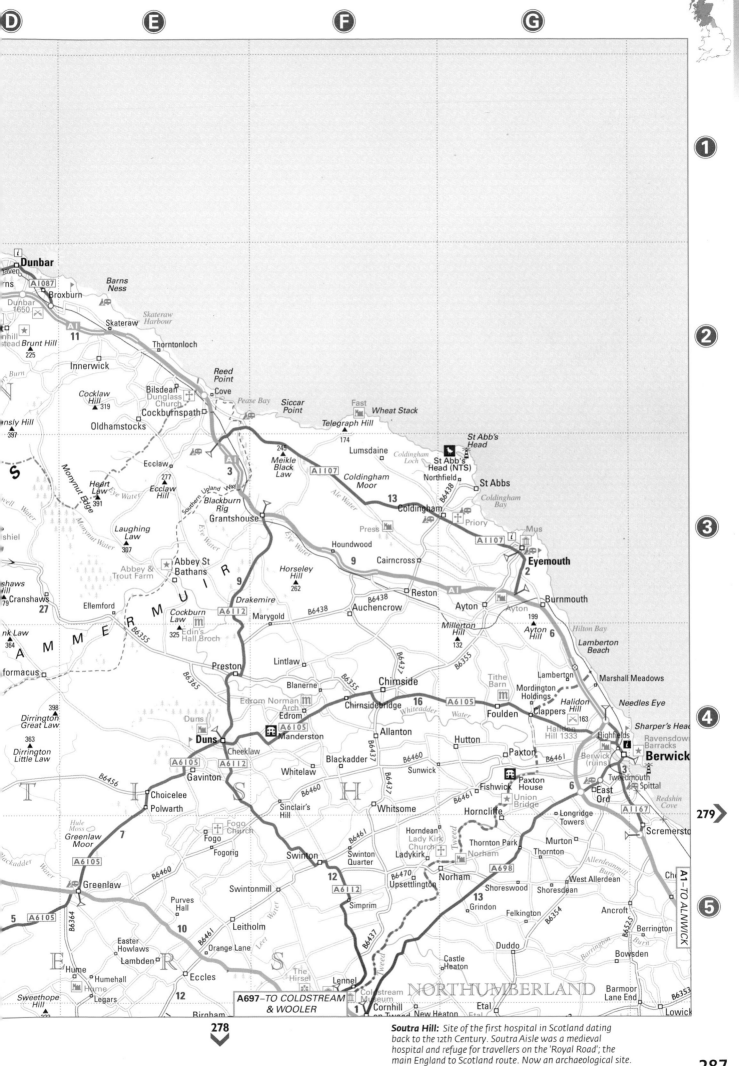

Dunbar
A1087
Broxburn
Dunbar 1650
A1
11
Skateraw
Barns Ness
Thorntonloch
Skateraw Harbour
Innerwick
Reed Point
Cove
Pease Bay
Siccar Point
Wheat Stack
Bilsdean
Dunglass Church
Cockburnspath
Fast
Telegraph Hill
174
St Abb's Head
Oldhamstocks
Cocklaw Hill 319
Ecclaw
245
Meikle Black Law
A1107
Lumsdaine
Coldingham Loch
St Abb's Head (NTS)
Northfield
St Abbs
Coldingham Bay
Heart Law 391
Ecclaw Hill 277
A1
3
Southern Upland Way
Blackburn Rig
Grantshouse
Coldingham Moor
13
Coldingham
Priory
Laughing Law 307
Eye Water
Abbey & Trout Farm
Abbey St Bathans
9
Horseley Hill 262
Press
Houndwood
9
Cairncross
A1107
Mus
i
Eyemouth
2
Cranshaws 27
Ellemford
Drakemire
A6112
Marygold
B6438
Auchencrow
B6438
Reston
Ayton
A1
Burnmouth
Cockburn Law
Edin's Hall Broch 325
Lintlaw
Millerton Hill 132
Ayton Hill 199
6
Hilton Bay
Lamberton Beach
Preston
Blanerne
B6355
Chirnside
B6437
Tithe Barn
Lamberton
Marshall Meadows
Needles Eye
Dirrington Great Law 398
Edrom Norman Arch
Edrom
Chirnsidebridge
16
A6105
Whiteadder Water
Foulden
Mordington Holdings
Clappers
Halidon Hill 163
Sharper's Head
Dirrington Little Law 363
Duns
Manderston
A6105
Allanton
Hutton
Halidon Hill 1333
Highfields
Ravensdowne Barracks
Berwick
Cheeklaw
A6105
A6112
Blackadder
Paxton
B6461
Berwick (ruins)
3
Tweedmouth
Spittal
B6456
Gavinton
Whitelaw
B6460
Sunwick
Fishwick
Paxton House
6
East Ord
Redshin Cove
Choicelee
Polwarth
Sinclair's Hill
Whitsome
Union Bridge
Horncliffe
Longridge Towers
A1167
Scremersto
Hule Moss
Greenlaw Moor
7
Fogo Church
Fogo
Fogorig
Horndean
Lady Kirk Church
Thornton Park
Murton
Thornton
A697–TO COLDSTREAM & WOOLER
A6105
Greenlaw
Swinton
12
Swinton Quarter
Ladykirk
B6470
Upsettlington
Norham
A698
Shoreswood
West Allerdean
Shoresdean
A1–TO ALNWICK
5
A6105
B6364
10
Purves Hall
Swintonmill
Leitholm
Simprim
B6112
B6437
13
Grindon
Felkington
B6354
Ancroft
Berrington
Hume
Humehall
Easter Howlaws
Lambden
Orange Lane
Eccles
Leer Water
The Hirsel
Lennel
Duddo
Castle Heaton
Bowsden
Sweethope Hill
Legars
12
Birgham
Coldstream Museum
Cornhill on Tweed
New Heaton
Etal
Barmoor Lane End
Lowick
NORTHUMBERLAND
B6353

Soutra Hill: *Site of the first hospital in Scotland dating back to the 12th Century. Soutra Aisle was a medieval hospital and refuge for travellers on the 'Royal Road'; the main England to Scotland route. Now an archaeological site.*
Map ref. B4

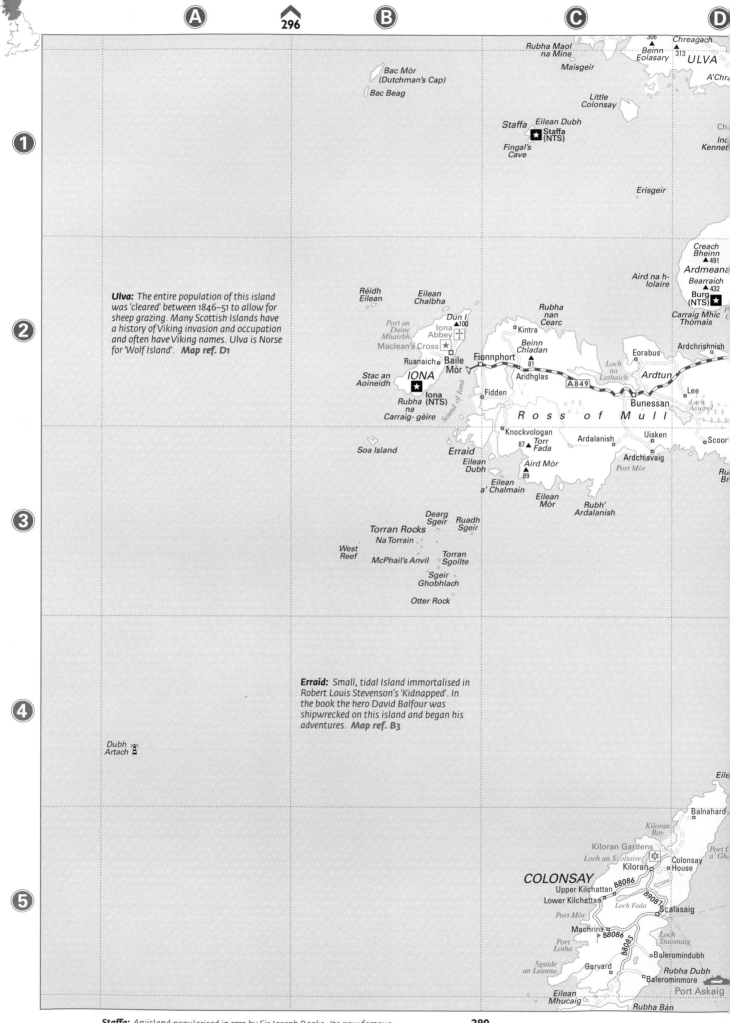

1

Rubha Maol na Mine
Chreagach
Beinn Eolasary 306
313
ULVA
A'Chra
Maisgeir

Bac Mòr (Dutchman's Cap)
Bac Beag

Little Colonsay

Staffa
Eilean Dubh
Staffa (NTS)
Inc Kennet

Fingal's Cave

Erisgeir

2

Ulva: The entire population of this island was 'cleared' between 1846–51 to allow for sheep grazing. Many Scottish Islands have a history of Viking invasion and occupation and often have Viking names. Ulva is Norse for 'Wolf Island'. **Map ref. D1**

Réidh Eilean
Eilean Chalbha

Creach Bheinn ▲491
Ardmeana

Port an Duine Mhairbh
Dun I ▲100
Iona Abbey ✝
Kintra
Rubha nan Cearc
Aird na h-Iolaire
Bearraich ▲432
Burg (NTS) ★

Maclean's Cross ★
Beinn Chladan ▲81
Carraig Mhic Thòmais

Ruanaich
Baile Mòr
Fionnphort
Aridhglas
A849
Loch na Lathaich
Eorabus
Ardchrishnish

Stac an Aoineidh
IONA ★
Fidden
Ardtun
Lee

Rubha na Carraig-gèire
Iona (NTS)
Bunessan
Loch Assapol

Soa Island
Ross of Mull

Knockvologan
Torr Fada 87▲
Ardalanish
Uisken
Scoor

Erraid
Eilean Dubh
Aird Mòr 89▲
Ardchiavaig
Port Mòr
Ru Br

Eilean a' Chalmain
Eilean Mòr
Rubh' Ardalanish

3

Dearg Sgeir
Ruadh Sgeir

Torran Rocks
Na Torrain

West Reef
McPhail's Anvil
Torran Sgoilte

Sgeir Ghobhlach

Otter Rock

4

Erraid: Small, tidal Island immortalised in Robert Louis Stevenson's 'Kidnapped'. In the book the hero David Balfour was shipwrecked on this island and began his adventures. **Map ref. B3**

Dubh Artach

Eile

5

Balnahard

Kiloran Bay

Kiloran Gardens
Loch an Sgoltaire
Kiloran
Colonsay House
Port C a'Gh

COLONSAY
Upper Kilchattan
Lower Kilchattan
B8086
B9087
Loch Fada
Scalasaig

Port Mòr

Machrins
B8086
Loch Staosnaig

Port Lotha
B8085
Baleromindubh

Sguide an Leanna
Garvard
Rubha Dubh
Balerominmore

Eilean Mhucaig
Port Askaig
Rubha Bàn

Staffa: An island popularised in 1772 by Sir Joseph Banks. Its now famous Fingals Cave is said to have been the inspiration behind Mendelssohn's 'Hebrides Overture'. This natural phenomenon has been visited by many famous people including Queen Victoria, David Livingstone and Jules Verne. **Map ref. C1 Also on page 130**

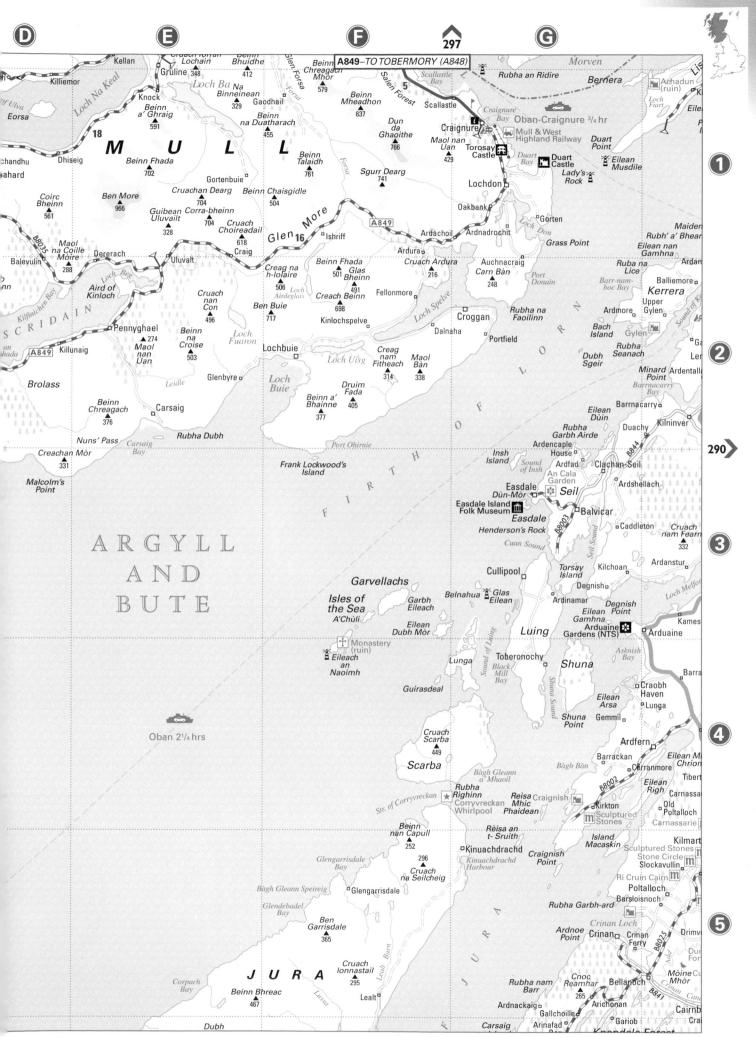

1

Kellan
Gruline 348
Beinn Bhuidhe 412
Beinn Chreagach Mhòr 579
Beinn Mheadhon 637
Salen Forest
Scallastle Bay
Rubha an Ridire
Morven
Bernera
Achadun (ruin)
Loch Fiart
Killiemor
Loch Ba
Glen Forsa
Scallastle
Craignure
Oban-Craignure ¾ hr
Loch Na Keal
Eorsa
Knock
Beinn a' Ghraig 591
Na Binneinean
Gaodhail
329
Beinn na Duatharach 455
Dun da Ghaoithe 766
Craignure
Mull & West Highland Railway
Duart Point
Dhiseig
Torosay Castle
Eilean Musdile
chandhu
vahard
Beinn Fhada 702
Gortenbuie
Maol nan Uan 429
Duart Bay
Duart Castle
Lady's Rock
M   U   L   L
Cruachan Dearg 704
Beinn Chaisgidle 504
Sgurr Dearg 741
Lochdon
Coirc Bheinn 561
Ben More 966
Guibean Uluvailt 328
Corra-bheinn 704
Cruach Choireadail 618
Glen More 16
A849
Ishriff
Ardachoil
Oakbank
Gorten
Maiden
Rubh' a' Bhear
Eilean nan Gamhna
Ardnadrochit
Ardura
Ruba na Lice
Maol na Coille Moire 288
Uluvalt
Craig
Creag na h-Iolaire 506
Beinn Fhada 501
Glas Bheinn 491
Cruach Ardura 216
Auchnacraig
Carn Bàn 248
Grass Point
Loch Don
Balliemore
Kerrera
B8035
Dererach
Loch Beg
Loch Airdeglais
Creach Beinn 698
Fellonmore
Ruba na Faoilinn
Barr-nam-boc Bay
Ardmore
Upper Gylen
Aird of Kinloch
Cruach nan Con 496
Ben Buie 717
Kinlochspelve
Croggan
Rubha na Faoilinn
Bach Island
Gylen
2
Kilfinichen Bay
SCRIDAIN
an hada
A849
Killunaig
Pennyghael
Beinn na Croise 503
274
Maol nan Uan
Loch Fuaron
Lochbuie
Loch Uisg
Dalnaha
Portfield
Creag nam Fitheach 314
Maol Bàn 338
Dubh Sgeir
Rubha Seanach
Minard Point
Ardentalla
Brolass
Leidle
Glenbyre
Loch Buie
Beinn a' Bhainne 377
Druim Fada 405
Barnacarry
Barnacarry Bay
Beinn Chreagach 376
Carsaig
Eilean Dùin
Duachy
Kilninver
Nuns' Pass
Carsaig Bay
Rubha Dubh
Port Ohirnie
Rubha Garbh Airde
Ardencaple House
B844
290 ▶
Creachan Mòr 331
Frank Lockwood's Island
Ardfad
Clachan-Seil
Malcolm's Point
Insh Island
Sound of Insh
An Cala Garden
Easdale
Dùn-Mòr
Seil
Ardshellach
Easdale Island Folk Museum
Easdale
Balvicar
3
A R G Y L L
A N D
B U T E
Henderson's Rock
Cuan Sound
Caddleton
Cruach nam Fearn 332
Garvellachs
Isles of the Sea
A'Chùli
Garbh Eileach
Belnahua
Glas Eilean
Cullipool
Torsay Island
Kilchoan
Ardinamar
Degnish
Ardanstur
Eilean Dubh Mòr
Sound of Luing
Eilean Gamhna
Degnish Point
Monastery (ruin)
Eileach an Naoimh
Luing
Arduaine Gardens (NTS)
Arduaine
Kames
Guirasdeal
Lunga
Toberonochy
Shuna
Asknish Bay
Barra
Black Mill Bay
Eilean Arsa
Craobh Haven
Oban 2¼ hrs
Shuna Sound
Gemmil
Lunga
4
Cruach Scarba 449
Shuna Point
Ardfern
Barrackan
Eilean M Chrion
Scarba
Bàgh Gleann a' Mhaoil
Bàgh Bàn
B8002
Corranmore
Eilean Righ
Tibert
Rubha Righinn
Corryvreckan Whirlpool
Reisa Mhic Phaidean
Craignish
Kirkton
Sculptured Stones
Carnassa
Old Poltalloch
Carnassarie
Str. of Corryvreckan
Beinn nan Capull 252
Rèisa an t- Sruith
Island Macaskin
Kilmart
Sculptured Stones
296
Kinuachdrachd
Craignish Point
Stone Circle
Slockavullin
Glengarrisdale Bay
Cruach na Seilcheig
Kinuachdrachd Harbour
Ri Cruin Cairn
Poltalloch
Bàgh Gleann Speireig
Glengarrisdale
Barsloisnoch
Rubha Garbh-ard
5
Glendebadel Bay
Crinan Loch
Ben Garrisdale 365
Ardnoe Point
Crinan
Crinan Ferry
Drimv
B8025
J   U   R   A
Corpach Bay
Cruach Ionnastail 295
Cnoc Reamhar 265
Bellanoch
Mòine Mhòr
Dun For
Beinn Bhreac 467
Lealt
Rubha nam Barr
Arichonan
B841
Cairnb
Dubh
Luasa
Ardnackaig
Gallchoille
Gariob
Cra
Carsaig
Arinafad
Knapdale Forest

Clachan-Seil: A hump-backed stone bridge here links Seil Island to the mainland. It is known as 'The Bridge over the Atlantic' and was designed by Thomas Telford in 1792. **Map ref. G3**

Corryvreckan: The swirling whirlpool here is one of the largest in the world and makes the Straits of Corryvreckan the most dangerous stretch of water around the British Isles. The sound of the raging water can often be heard 10 miles (16km) away. **Map ref. F4**

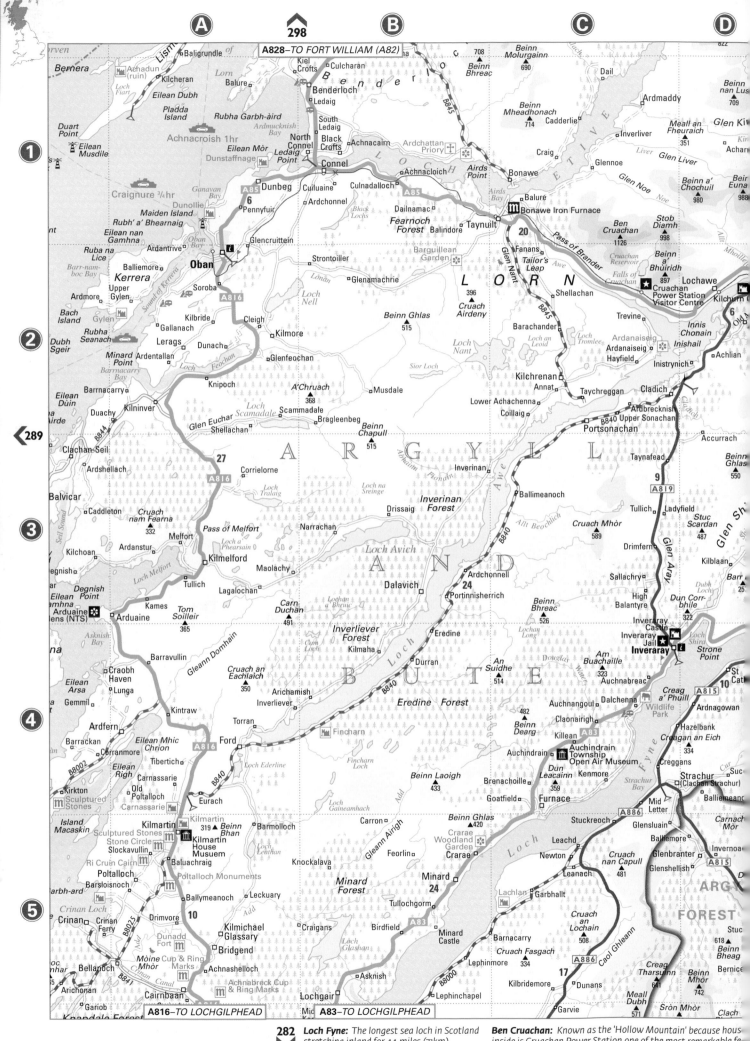

A828–*TO FORT WILLIAM (A82)*

B
C
D

1

2

3

4

5

289

Oban

Kerrera

LORN

ARGYLL

AND

BUTE

Inveraray

FOREST

ARG X

A816–*TO LOCHGILPHEAD*
A83–*TO LOCHGILPHEAD*

282

Loch Fyne: The longest sea loch in Scotland stretching inland for 44 miles (71km). **Map ref. B5**

Ben Cruachan: Known as the 'Hollow Mountain' because hous inside is Cruachan Power Station one of the most remarkable fe engineering in Scotland. Deep in the mountain a huge man-mac cavern houses the world's first 'high head reversible pumped sto hydro scheme'. **Map ref. C2 Also on page 119**

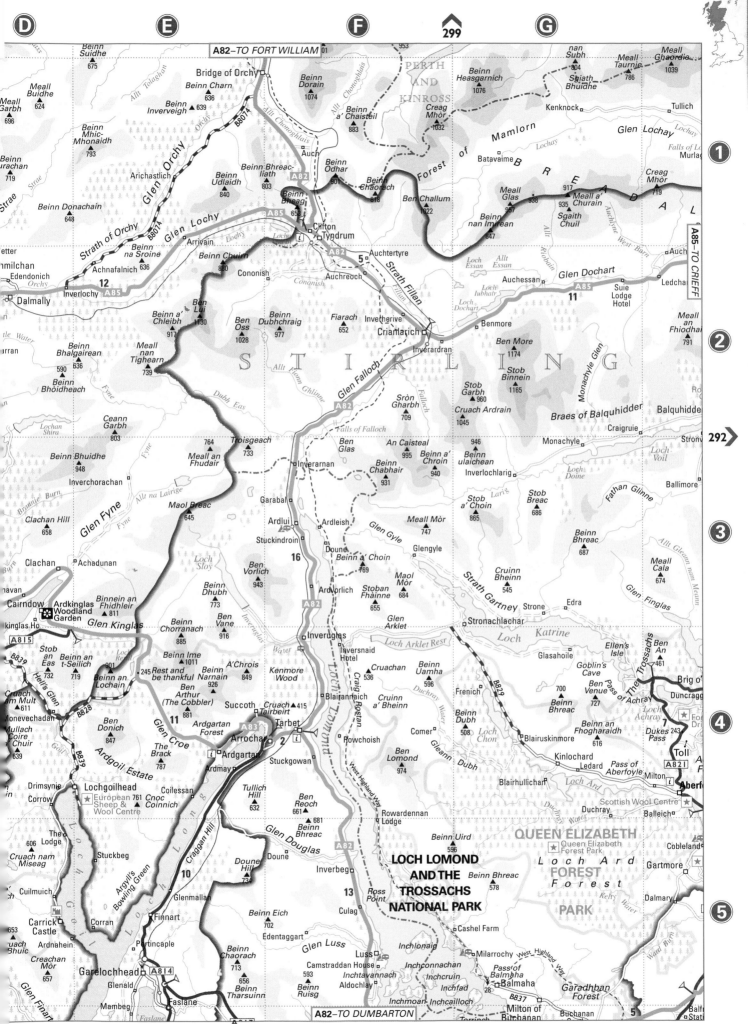

A82—TO FORT WILLIAM

PERTH AND KINROSS

Beinn Suidhe 675

Meall Buidhe 624

Meall Garbh 696

Beinn Dorain 1074

Beinn a' Chaisteil 883

Beinn Heasgarnich 1076

nan Subh 804

Meall Taurnie 786

Meall Ghaordie 1039

Bridge of Orchy

Beinn Charn 636

Beinn Inverveigh 639

Beinn Mhic-Mhonaidh 793

Arichastlich

Beinn Udlaidh 840

Beinn Bhreac-liath 803

Auch

Beinn Odhar 901

Beinn Chaorach 818

Creag Mhòr 1032

Forest of Mamlorn

Ben Challum 1022

Batavaime

Meall Glas 957

Sgiath Bhuidhe

Kenknock

Glen Lochay

Meall a' Churain 935

Sgaith Chuil 917

Creag Mhòr 719

Murlag

Glen Orchy

Beinn Donachain 648

Beinn Bhreag

A82

A85 653

Beinn nan Imirean 847

Tullich

Falls of L

Strath of Orchy

Beinn na Sroine 636

Glen Lochy

Clifton

Tyndrum

Achnafalnich

Arrivain

Lochy

A82

Auchtertyre

Strath Fillan

Loch Essan

Allt Essan

Glen Dochart

Auch

A85—TO CRIEFF

imilchan

Edendonich Orchy

Dalmally

12

Inverlochy

A85

Beinn Chuirn 880

Cononish

Cononish

Auchreoch

5

Strath Fillan

Loch Iubhair

Auchessan

11

Suie Lodge Hotel

Ledcha

Meall an Fhiodhat 791

le Water

arran

Beinn a' Chleibh 917

Ben Lui 1130

Ben Oss 1028

Beinn Dubhchraig 977

Fiarach 652

Invetherive

Crianlarich

Inverardran

Benmore

Ben More 1174

Meall an Fhiodha 791

Beinn Bhalgairean 636

Beinn Bhòidheach

590

Meall nan Tighearn 739

STIRLING

Allt Fionn Ghlinne

Glen Falloch

A82

Stob Binnein 1165

Ceann Garbh 803

Lochan Shira

Beinn Bhuidhe 948

Inverchorachan

Troisgeach 733

764

Meall an Fhudair 733

Dubh Eas

Falls of Falloch

Sròn Gharbh 709

Falloch

Ben Glas

An Caisteal 995

Beinn a' Chroin 940

Stob Garbh 960

Cruach Ardrain 1045

Monachyle Glen

Braes of Balquhidder

Monachyle

Craigruie

Balquhidde

Stron

292

Glen Fyne

Fyne

Allt na Lairige

Maol Breac 645

Inverarnan

Beinn Chabhair 931

Beinn ulaichean 946

Inverlochlarig

Loch Doine

Ballimore

Clachan Hill 658

Garabal

Stob a' Choin 865

Larig

Stob Breac 686

Fathan Glinne

Beinn Bhreac 687

Meall Cala 674

3

Clachan

Achadunan

Loch Sloy

16

Ardlui

Ardleish

Doune

Beinn a' Choin 769

Glen Gyle

Glengyle

Meall Mòr 747

Cruinn Bheinn 545

Strath Gartney

Glen Finglas

navan

Cairndow

Ardkinglas Woodland Garden

Glen Kinglas

Stuckindroin

Ben Vorlich 943

Ardvorlich

Stoban Fhàinne 655

Maol Mòr 684

Strone

Edra

Ben An 461

The Trossachs

Binnein an Fhidhleir 811

Beinn Dhubh 773

Ben Vane 916

Glen Arklet

Stronachlachar

Loch Katrine

Ellen's Isle

Goblin's Cave

Brig o'

Duncragg

A815

inglas Ho

kinglas

Stob an Eas 732

Beinn an t-Seilich 719

901

Beinn an Lochain

245

Rest and be thankful

Beinn Chorranach 885

Beinn Ime 1011

A'Chrois 849

Kenmore Wood

Inveruglas

Inversnaid Hotel

Loch Arklet Resr

Cruachan 536

Beinn Uamha

Frenich

Ben Venue 727

700

Beinn Breac

The Trossachs

Pass of Achray

Loch Achray

Fo Dr

Cruach am Mult 611

Monevechadan

Mullach Coire Chuir 639

B828

Ben Donich 847

B839

Glen Croe

A'Chrois

Beinn Narnain 926

Ben Arthur (The Cobbler) 881

Succoth

Cruach Tairbeirt 415

Tarbet

Blairannaich

Craig Rostan

Cruinn a' Bheinn

Beinn Dubh 508

Loch Chon

Beinn an Fhoghairaidh 616

Blairuskinmore

Kinlochard

1

Dukes Pass 243

Toll

Aberf

The Brack 787

Ardgartan Forest

Arrochar

A83

2

Ardgartan

Stuckgowan

Rowchoish

Comer

Ledard

Pass of Aberfoyle

Milton

A821

i

Drimsynie

Lochgoilhead

Corrow

European Sheep & Wool Centre

Coilessan

Cnoc Coinnich 761

Ardmay

Tullich Hill 632

West Highland Way

Ben Lomond 974

Blairhullichan

Loch Ard

Duchray

Scottish Wool Centre

Balleich

The Lodge 606

Cruach nam Miseag

Stuckbeg

Argyll's Bowling Green

Craggan Hill

Ben Reoch 661

Beinn Bhreac 681

Glen Douglas

A82

Doune

Inverbeg

Beinn Uird 596

QUEEN ELIZABETH

Queen Elizabeth Forest Park

Loch Ard FOREST Forest

Cobleland

Gartmore

10

Doune Hill 734

Rowardennan Lodge

LOCH LOMOND AND THE TROSSACHS NATIONAL PARK

Beinn Bhreac 578

PARK

Kelty Water

Dalmary

5

Cuilmuich

Glenmallan

13

Ross Point

Culag

Garadhban Forest

Balf

Carrick Castle

653

Corran

Finnart

Beinn Eich 702

Edentaggart

Loch Lomond

Cashel Farm

Glen Finart

Creachan Mòr 657

Ardnahein

Cruach Bhuic

Portincaple

Beinn Chaorach 713

Beinn Tharsuinn 656

Glen Luss

Beinn Ruisg 593

Luss

Camstraddan House

Inchtavannach

Aldochlay

Inchlonaig

Inchconnachan

Inchcruin

Inchmoan Inchcailloch

Inchfad

Milarrochy

West Highland Way

Pass of Balmaha

Balmaha

28

B837

Garelochhead

A814

Glenald

Mambeg

Faslane

Glen Finart

A

Inchmurrin

Torrinch

Milton of Buchanan

Buchanan

Balf Stati

A82—TO DUMBARTON

ch Lomond: In Scotland the word 'loch' refers to an inland body of water. ch Lomond is the largest such feature in Scotland. It has an area of 27.5 square les (71 sq km) and is 617 feet (190m) deep. Here on 16th July 1932 Kaye Don in Miss gland 3 raised the world water speed record to 119.81 mph (193km/h). **Map ref. F4** Loch Lomond & The Trossachs National Park **on page 126**

283 An area known as **The Trossachs** which was immortalised in Sir Walter Scott's ballads 'The Lady of the Lake' (1810) and 'Rob Roy' (1817). *So wondrous wild the whole might seem* *The scenery of a fairy dream.* **Map ref. G4** See Loch Lomond & The Trossachs National Park **on page 126**

291

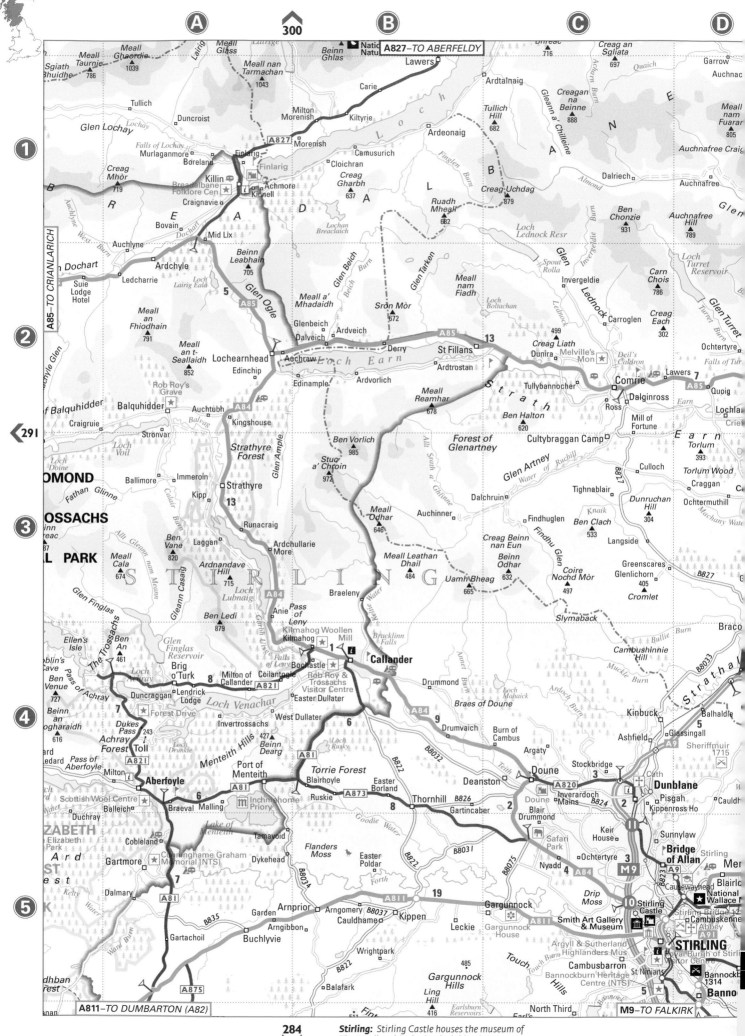

A827–TO ABERFELDY

A85–TO CRIANLARICH

1

Meall Taurnie 786
Sgiath Bhuidhe
Meall Ghaordie 1039
Meall Glass
Lairig
Meall Laraige
Beinn Ghlas
Natio
Natu
Lawers
Creag an Sgliata 697
Garrow
Auchnac

Tullich
Glen Lochay
Lochay
Duncroist
Milton Morenish
Carie
Kiltyrie
Ardtalnaig
Breac 716
Creag an
Creagan na Beinne 888
Meall nam Fuaran 805

Murlaganmore
Boreland
Finlarig
A827
Morenish
Camusurich
Ardeonaig
Tullich Hill 682
Dalriech
Auchnafree

Killin
Finlarig
Achmore
Cloichran
Creag Gharbh 637
Ruadh Mheal 682
Creag Uchdag 879
Ben Chonzie 931
Auchnafree Craig

Breadalbane Folklore Cen
Kinnell
Craignavie
Creag Mhòr 719
Bovain

Loch Tay

2

Auchlyne
Mid Lix
Beinn Leabhain 705
Lochan Breaclaich
Glen Beich Burn
Loch Lednock Resr
Glen Rolla
Invergeldie
Ben Chonzie 931
Loch Turret Reservoir

Glen Lochay
Dochart
Ardchyle
Ledcharrie
Loch Lairig Eala
Meall a' Mhadaidh
Sròn Mòr 672
Spout of Rolla
Invergeldie
Lednock
Carn Chois 786
Glen Turret

Dochart
Suie Lodge Hotel
Meall an Fhiodhain 791
Glen Ogle
A85
Glenbeich
Dalveich
Ardveich
Meall nam Fiadh
Loch Boltachan
Creag Liath
Creag Each 302

291

Balquhidder Glen
Meall an t-Seallaidh 852
Lochearnhead
Edinchip
Auchraw
Derry
St Fillans
A85
13
Creag 499
Dunira
Melville's Mon
Comrie
Lawers 7
A85
Quoig
Lochla

Rob Roy's Grave
Balquhidder
Auchtubh
A84
Edinample
Ardvorlich
Ardtrostan
Tullybannocher
Dalginross
Ross
Falls of Tur

3

OMOND
OSSACHS
PARK
Craigruie
Stronvar
Kingshouse
A84
Ardvorlich
Meall Reamhar 678
Ben Halton 620
Ben Halton
Mill of Fortune
Earn
Crie

Fathan Glinne
Loch Voil
Ballimore
Immeroin
Strathyre Forest
Glen Ample
Ben Vorlich 985
Forest of Glenartney
Cultybraggan Camp
Torlum 393
Torlum Wood
Ochtermuthill

Loch Doine
Meall Cala 674
Ben Vane 820
Laggan
Kipp
Strathyre
13
Stuc a' Chroin 972
Glen Artney
Water of Ruchill
Dalchruin
Tighnablair
Ben Clach 533
Dunruchan Hill 304
Craggan

L PARK
Glen Finglas
Ardnandave Hill 715
Runacraig
Ardchullarie More
Meall Odhar 646
Auchinner
Findhuglen
Langside
Greenscares
Glenlichorn 405
Cromlet
B827

4

Glen Finglas
Ben Ledi 879
Loch Lubnaig
A84
Meall Leathan Dhail 484
Meall Odhar 632
Creag Beinn nan Eun
Beinn Odhar
Uamh Bheag 665
Coire Nochd Mòr 497
Slymaback
Braco

Ellen's Isle
Ben An 461
Anie
Pass of Leny
Braeleny
Cambushinnie Hill
B8033
Stratha

oblin's Cave
The Trossachs
Brig o'Turk
Kilmahog Woollen Mill
Kilmahog
Bracklinn Falls
Muckle Burn

Ben Venue 727
Pass of Achray
Loch Achray
Milton of Callander
Coilantogle
Bochastle
Callander
Drummond
Braes of Doune
Ardoch Burn
Kinbuck
Balhaldie

Beinn an Fhogharaidh 616
Duncraggan
Lendrick Lodge
Forest Drive
8
A821
Loch Venachar
Easter Dullater
Rob Roy & Trossachs Visitor Centre
Drumvaich
Burn of Cambus
Argaty
Ashfield
A9
Sheriffmuir 1715
Glassingall

Dukes Pass 243
Achray Forest Toll
Invertrossachs
West Dullater
6
A84
9
Drumvaich
Argaty
Stockbridge
3

5

Pass of Aberfoyle
Milton
Aberfoyle
Scottish Wool Centre
Balleich
Braeval
Malling
Menteith Hills
Port of Menteith
Blairhoyle
Torrie Forest
B822
Easter Borland
Thornhill
B826
Gartincaber
Doune
A820
Deanston
Blair Drummond
Inverardoch Mains
B824
Doune
Keir House
Dunblane
Pisgah
Kippenross Ho
M9
Bridge of Allan
A9
Mer

Duchray
Gartmore
Cuninghame Graham Memorial (NTS)
Cobleland
Beinn Dearg 427
Inchmahome Priory
Ruskie
A873
Blair Drummond
Safari Park
Nyadd
Ochtertyre
B8075
A84
3
Keir House
Sunnylaw
Stirling
Causewayhead
Blairlc
National Wallace

Elizabeth
ard
St Forest
Dalmary
A81
Gartachoil
Buchlyvie
Cobleland
Dykehead
Flanders Moss
Easter Poldar
Goodie Water
Forth
B8031
Drip Moss
Gargunnock
A811
19
Stirling Castle
Smith Art Gallery & Museum
A811
Stirling Bridge
Cambuskenneth Abbey

Kelty
B835
Garden
Arnprior
Arngomery
Kippen
Leckie
Gargunnock House
Argyll & Sutherland Highlanders Mus
STIRLING
yal Burgh of Stir or Centre
Cambusbarron
Bannockburn Heritage Centre (NTS)
St Ninians
Banno

Arngibbon
Cauldhame
Wrightpark
B822
Gargunnock Hills
Touch
Ling Hill 416
North Third
Bannockburn 1314
Banno

A811–TO DUMBARTON (A82)   **M9–TO FALKIRK**

Stirling: Stirling Castle houses the museum of The Argyll and Sutherland Highlanders. This famous regiment won 6 Victoria Crosses in a single day's action at the Battle of Lucknow (India) in 1857. **Map ref. C5 Also on page 130**

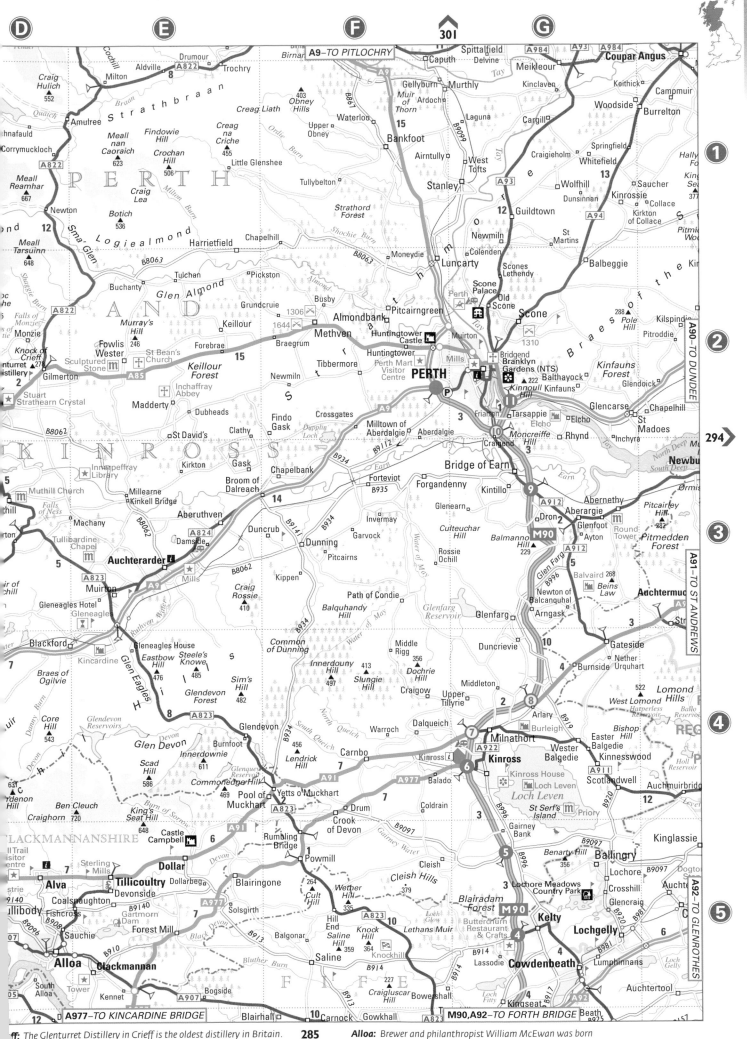

Crieff: The Glenturret Distillery in Crieff is the oldest distillery in Britain. ...he 18th century illegal stills were rife in this area and one operated ...e from 1717. It was legalised in 1775 and was a working still up to 1921 ...n it ceased production. It was re-born in 1957 and today is one of the ...hland's established malts. **Map ref. D2**

Alloa: Brewer and philanthropist William McEwan was born here in 1827. He went on to establish the Fountain Brewery in Edinburgh and to brew McEwans Export. He died in 1913 but both the brewery and beer survive. **Map ref. D5**

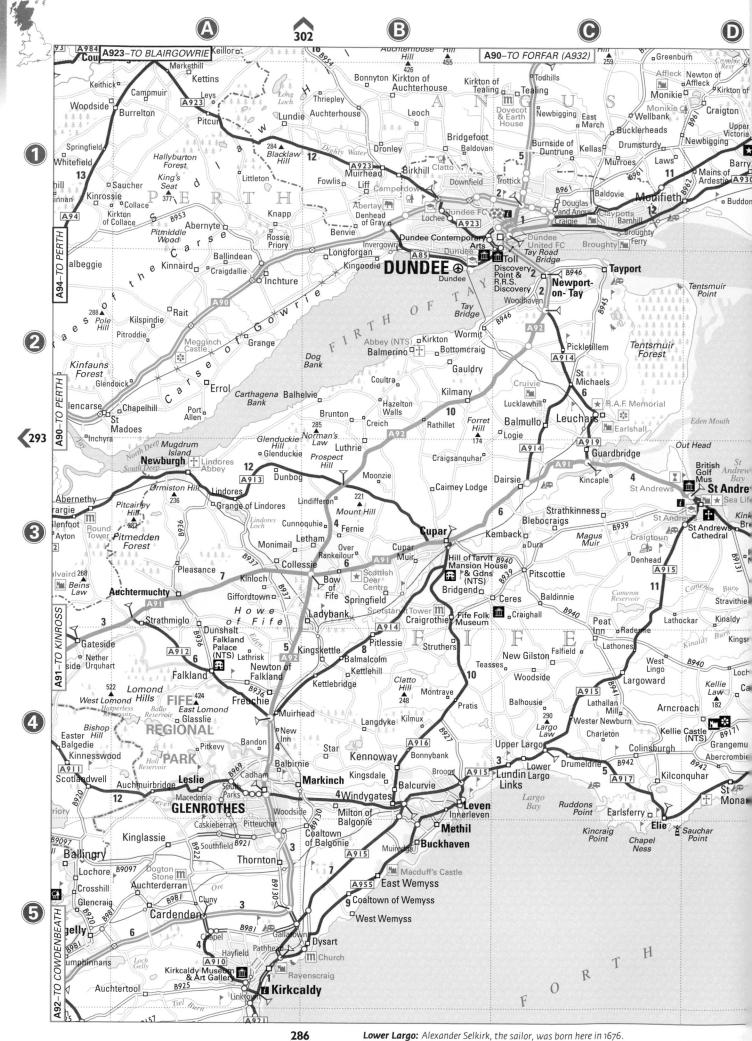

A923–TO BLAIRGOWRIE · **A90**–TO FORFAR (A932)

A   **B**   **C**   **D**

A984

Cou

Keillor
Markethill
Kettins
Campmuir
Leys
Keithick
Woodside
Burrelton
Pitcur
A923
Keithick
Springfield
Whitefield
13
Hallyburton Forest
Blacklaw Hill
284
12
Saucher
King's Seat
377
Littleton
Kinrossie
Collace
Kirkton of Collace
A94
Abernyte
Knapp
Benvie
Rossie Priory
Pitmiddle Wood
Denhead of Gray
Longforgan
Invergowrie
Kingoodie

PERTH

Bonnyton
Kirkton of Auchterhouse
Auchterhouse Hill
426
Auchterhouse Hill
455
Thrieple
Auchterhouse
Leoch
Bridgefoot
Baldovan
Dronley
Dighty Water
Birkhill
Downfield
Clatto
A923
Camperdown
Muirhead
Liff
Fowlis
Abertay
Lochee
ANGUS

Tealing
Kirkton of Tealing
Todhills
Newbigging
Dovecot & Earth House
East March
Burnside of Duntrune
Kellas
Murroes
Douglas and Angus
Craigie
Craigton
Monikie
Monifieth
Wellbank
Drumsturdy
Laws
Baldovie
B96
B961
Newbigging
Upper Victoria
Barry
Buckleheads
Mains of Ardestie
Buddon

DUNDEE

Dundee Contemporary Arts
Dundee
Toll
Dundee United FC
Tay Road Bridge
Discovery Point & R.R.S. Discovery
Broughty Ferry
Broughty
Claypotts
Barnhill

FIRTH OF TAY

Tay Bridge
Woodhaven
Newport-on-Tay
Tayport
B946
B946
Newton
Greenburn
Crombie Rest
Affleck
Newton of Affleck
Kirkton of

302
286
294

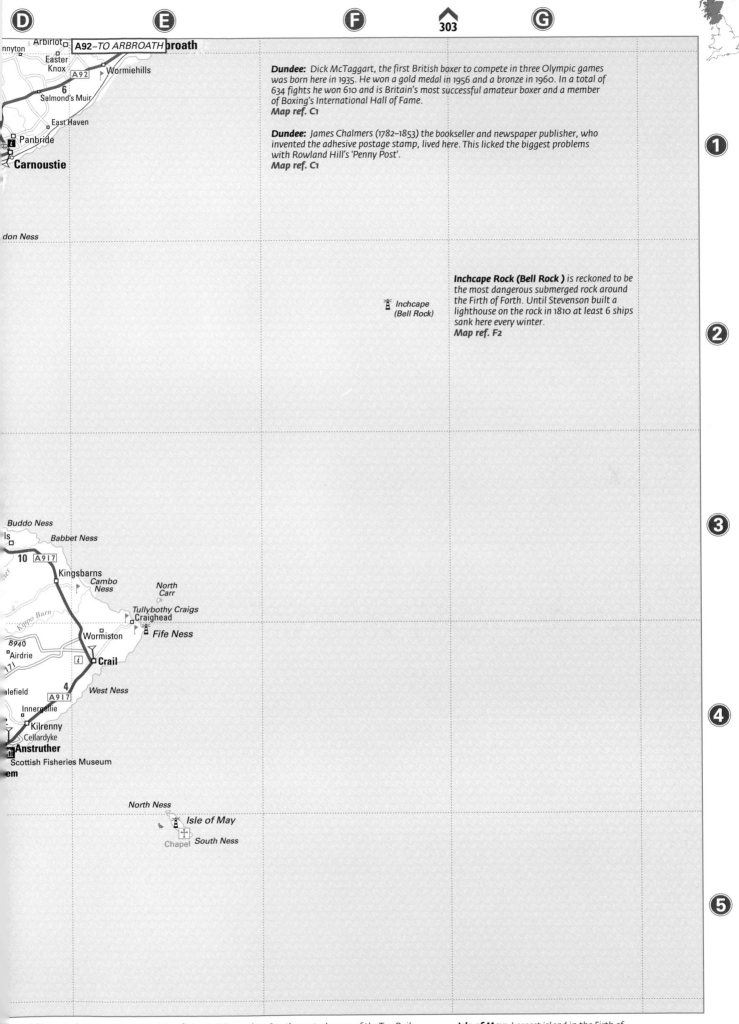

A92–TO ARBROATH broath

Arbirlot
nnyton
Easter
Knox A92
Wormiehills
6
Salmond's Muir
East Haven
Panbride
Carnoustie

don Ness

Dundee: Dick McTaggart, the first British boxer to compete in three Olympic games was born here in 1935. He won a gold medal in 1956 and a bronze in 1960. In a total of 634 fights he won 610 and is Britain's most successful amateur boxer and a member of Boxing's International Hall of Fame.
Map ref. C1

Dundee: James Chalmers (1782–1853) the bookseller and newspaper publisher, who invented the adhesive postage stamp, lived here. This licked the biggest problems with Rowland Hill's 'Penny Post'.
Map ref. C1

Inchcape
(Bell Rock)

Inchcape Rock (Bell Rock) is reckoned to be the most dangerous submerged rock around the Firth of Forth. Until Stevenson built a lighthouse on the rock in 1810 at least 6 ships sank here every winter.
Map ref. F2

Buddo Ness
Babbet Ness
ls
10 A917
Kingsbarns
Cambo
Ness
North
Carr
Tullybothy Craigs
Craighead
Wormiston
Fife Ness
B940
Airdrie
i Crail
Airlie
4
lefield A917
West Ness
Innergellie
Kilrenny
Cellardyke
Anstruther
Scottish Fisheries Museum
em

North Ness
Isle of May
Chapel South Ness

ail Bridge: At about 7.15pm on the night of the 28th December 1879 the central spans of the Tay Rail e collapsed during gale force winds. The bridge had only been open for 19 months. A passenger train from urgh, which was crossing the bridge at the time, plunged into the water below. In all 75 people lost their n the disaster, there were no survivors and only 46 bodies were ever found. The engine itself, however, was ered from the river bed and put back into service where it continued to haul carriages until 1908.
today the supporting masonry piers of the old bridge in the river are still visible. **Map ref. B2**

Isle of May: Largest island in the Firth of Forth and site of the first permanently manned lighthouse beacon in Scotland built by Alexander Cunningham in 1636.
Map ref. E5

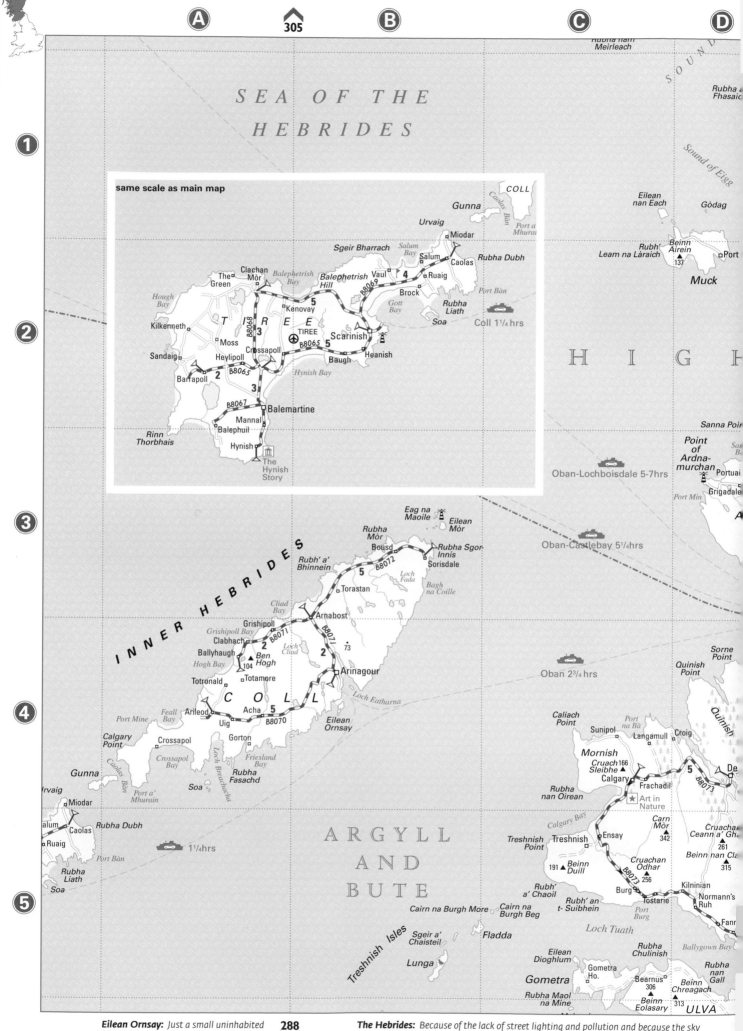

SEA OF THE HEBRIDES

same scale as main map

COLL

Gunna

Urvaig

Miodar

Sgeir Bharrach

Salum Bay

Salum

Caolas

Rubha Dubh

Caolas Bàn

Port a'
Mhurain

Eilean
nan Each

Gòdag

Rubh'
Leam na Làraich

Beinn
Airein
137

Port

Muck

The Green

Clachan Mòr

Balephetrish Bay

Balephetrish Hill

Vaul

B8069

Brock

4

Ruaig

Rubha
Liath

HIGH

Hough Bay

TIREE

B8068

3

Kilkenneth

Moss

Kenovay

5

Scarinish

Gott
Bay

Soa

Rubha
Liath

Port Bàn

Coll 1¼ hrs

Sandaig

Heylipoll

Crossapoll

B8065

5

Baugh

Heanish

Barrapoll

2

B8065

3

Hynish Bay

B8067

Balemartine

Mannal

Balephuil

Hynish

The Hynish Story

Rinn Thorbhais

Rubha nam
Meirleach

Sound of Eigg

Rubha
Fhasaic

SOUND

D

INNER HEBRIDES

Eag na
Maoile

Eilean
Mòr

Rubha
Mòr

Bousd

Rubha Sgor-
Innis

Sorisdale

Rubh' a'
Bhinnein

5

B8072

Loch
Fada

Bagh
na Coille

Oban-Lochboisdale 5-7hrs

Oban-Castlebay 5¼hrs

Torastan

Cliad
Bay

Arnabost

B8071

Grishipoll

Grishipoll Bay

Clabhach

2

B8071

Loch
Cliad

2

·73

Oban 2¾ hrs

Sorne
Point

Quinish
Point

Ballyhaugh

Ben
Hogh

104

Arinagour

Hogh Bay

Totronald

Totamore

COLL

Loch Eatharna

Caliach
Point

Port
na Bà

Quinish

Port Mine

Feall
Bay

Arileod

Acha

5

Uig

B8070

Gorton

Eilean
Ornsay

Mornish

Cruach 166
Sleibhe

Calgary

Frachadil

5

B8073

De

Langamull

Croig

Calgary
Point

Crossapol

Crossapol
Bay

Friesland
Bay

Rubha
Fasachd

Rubha
nan Oirean

Art in
Nature

Calgary Bay

Carn
Mòr
342

Cruacha
Ceann a' Gh

Gunna

Caolas Bàn

Soa

Port a'
Mhurain

Beinn nan Cla
315

Treshnish
Point

Treshnish

Ensay

Beinn
Duill
191

Cruachan
Odhar
256

261

Irvaig

Miodar

Salum

Caolas

Ruaig

Rubha Dubh

Port Bàn

1¼hrs

ARGYLL

AND

BUTE

Rubh'
a' Chaoil

Rubh' an
t- Suibhein

Burg

B8073

Kilninian

Normann's
Ruh

Fan

Rubha
Liath

Soa

Cairn na Burgh More

Cairn na
Burgh Beg

Port
Burg

Loch Tuath

Rubha
Chulinish

Rubha
nan Gall

Treshnish Isles

Sgeir a'
Chaisteil

Fladda

Eilean
Dioghlum

Ballygown Bay

Lunga

Gometra
Ho.

Bearnus
306

Beinn
Chreagach

Gometra

Rubha Maol
na Mine

Beinn
Eolasary
313

ULVA

288 ⌄

Eilean Ornsay: *Just a small uninhabited island. There are dozens like it called Eilean something or other. In this case Eilean simply means Island.* **Map ref. B4**

The Hebrides: *Because of the lack of street lighting and pollution and because the sky is unusually clear, the Hebridean Islands are the best place in the UK for seeing the Aurora Borealis (The Northern Lights). This fantastic lightshow occurs naturally every autumn in the Arctic regions.*

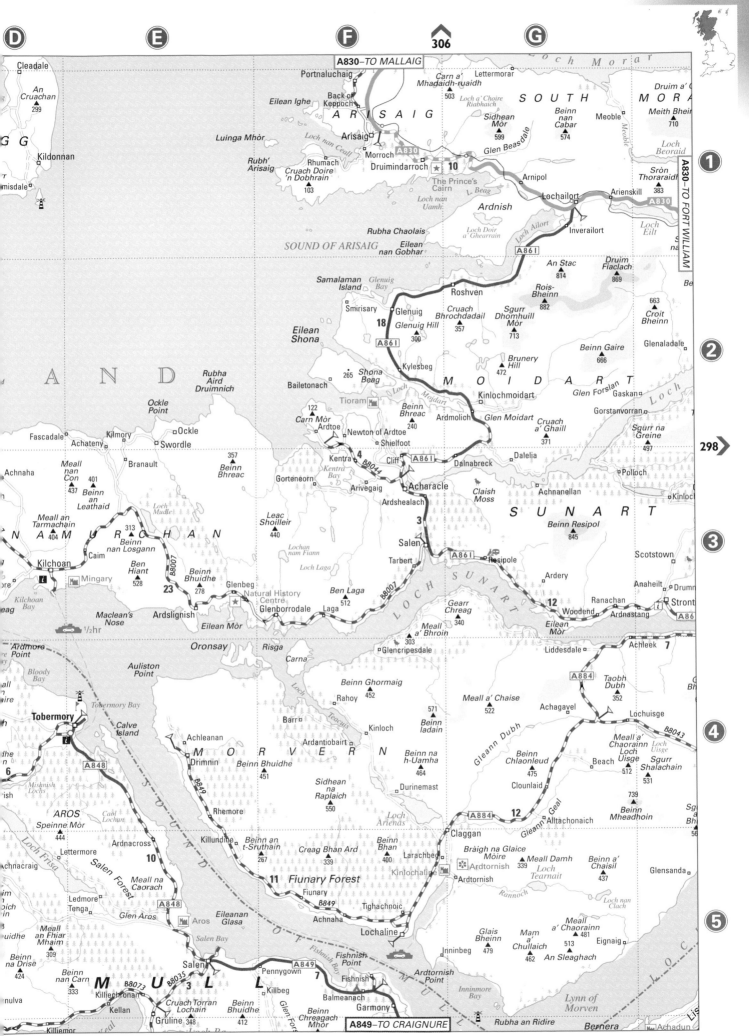

Cleadale

An
Cruachan
299

Kildonnan

misdale

A830–TO MALLAIG

Portnaluchaig

Back of
Keppoch

Carn a'
Mhadaidh-ruaidh

Lettermorar

503

Loch a' Choire
Riabhaich

SOUTH

MORA

Druim a'

Meith Bhei
710

Eilean Ighe

ARISAIG

Rhumach

Sidhean
Mòr
599

Beinn
nan
Cabar
574

Meoble

Luinga Mhòr

Arisaig

Morroch

A830

Meoble

Loch
Beoraid

Rubh'
Arisaig

Cruach Doire
'n Dobhrain
103

Druimindarroch

The Prince's
Cairn

★ **10**

Glen Beasdale

Arnipol

Lochailort

Arienskill

A830

Sròn
Thoraraid
383

Loch
Eilt

A830–TO FORT WILLIAM

Ardnish

Inverailort

L. Beag

Loch
Doir
a' Ghearrain

Loch Ailort

Loch nan
Uamh

Rubha Chaolais

Eilean
nan Gobhar

SOUND OF ARISAIG

Samalaman
Island

Glenuig
Bay

Roshven

An Stac
814

Druim
Fiaclach
869

Be

Smirisary

Glenuig

18

Glenuig Hill
300

Cruach
Bhrochdadail
357

Rois-
Bheinn
882

Sgurr
Dhomhuill
Mòr
713

663

Croit
Bheinn

Glenaladale

Eilean
Shona

A861

Kylesbeg

265

Shona
Beag

Brunery
Hill
472

MOIDART

Beinn Gaire
666

2

AND

Rubha
Aird
Druimnich

Bailetonach

Tioram

Loch
Moidart

Beinn
Bhreac
240

Ardmolich

Kinlochmoidart

Glen Forslan

Gaskan

Gorstanvorran

Loch

Ockle
Point

Carn Mòr
122

Ardtoe

Glen Moidart

Cruach
a' Ghaill
371

Sgurr na
Greine
497

Fascadale

Achateny

Kilmory

Ockle

Swordle

357

Newton of Ardtoe

Shielfoot

A861

Dalnabreck

Dalelia

Polloch

Kinloch

Achnaha

Meall
nan
Con
437

401

Beinn
Bhreac

Kentra

4

B8044

Cliff

A861

Achnanellan

298 ▸

Beinn
an Leathaid

Branault

Gortenorn

Kentra
Bay

Arivegaig

Acharacle

Claish
Moss

SUNART

Meall an
Tarmachain
404

NA

313

Loch
Mudle

Leac
Shoilleir
440

Ardshealach

3

Beinn Resipol
845

MURCHAN

Beinn
nan Losgann

B8007

Lochan
nam Fiann

Salen

A861

Resipole

Scotstown

Kilchoan

Caim

Ben
Hiant
528

Beinn
Bhuidhe
278

Loch Laga

Tarbert

Ardery

Anaheilt

Drumm

3

i

Mingary

23

Glenbeg

Natural History
Centre

★

Laga

B8007

Ben Laga
512

LOCH

SUNART

12

Woodend

Ranachan

Ardnastang

i

Stron

A86

Kilchoan
Bay

Maclean's
Nose

Ardslignish

Glenborrodale

Eilean Mòr

Gearr
Chreag
340

Eilean
Mòr

½hr

Oronsay

Risga

Meall
a' Bhroin
303

Glencripesdale

Liddesdale

Achleek

7

Ardmore
Point

Bloody
Bay

Auliston
Point

Carna

Beinn Ghormaig
452

A884

Taobh
Dubh
352

C
Bh

all
ire

Tobermory

Tobermory Bay

Calve
Island

Achleanan

Rahoy

Kinloch

Beinn
Iadain
571

Meall a' Chaise
522

Achagavel

Lochuisge

B8043

4

Mishnish
Lochs

6

A848

Drimnin

Beinn Bhuidhe
451

Ardtiobairt

Beinn na
h-Uamha
464

Gleann Dubh

Beinn
Chlaonleud
475

Meall a'
Chaorainn
512

Loch
Uisge

Beach

Sgurr
Shalachain
531

rish

MORVERN

Barr

Durinemast

Clounlaid

739

Beinn
Mheadhoin

Sg
Bh

AROS

Speinne Mòr
444

Caol
Lochan

Rhemore

Sidhean
na
Raplaich
550

Loch
Arienas

A884

12

Gleann Geal

Alltachonaich

Loch Frisa

Lettermore

Ardnacross

Killundine

Beinn an
t-Sruthain
267

Creag Bhan Ard
339

Beinn
Bhan
400

Larachbeg

Claggan

Bràigh na Glaice
Mòire
339

Meall Damh
437

Beinn a'
Chaisil
437

Glensanda

10

Ledmore

Tenga

Meall na
Caorach

11

Fiunary Forest

Kinlochaline

Ardtornish

Loch
Tearnait

chnacraig

im
ich
in

A848

Glen Aros

Aros

Eileanan
Glasa

Fiunary

B849

Achnaha

Tighachnoic

Ardtornish

Rannoch

Loch nan
Clach

5

Meall
an Fhiar
Mhaim
309

Salen Bay

Salen

Lochaline

Inninbeg

Glais
Bheinn
479

Mam
a' Chullaich
462

Meall
a' Chaorainn
481

Beinn
Mheadhoin
513

Eignaig

Beinn
na Drise
424

MULL

Beinn
nan Carn
333

B8073

Killiechronan

Kellan

Gruline

Cruach Torran
Lochain
348

Pennygown

Killbeg

Fishnish
Point

Fishnish

7

Balmeanach

Garmony

Ardtornish
Point

An Sleaghach

Inninmore
Bay

Lynn of
Morven

Bernera

Achadun

nulva

Gruline

Beinn
Bhuidhe
412

Glen
Forsa

Beinn
Chreagach
Mhòr

A849–TO CRAIGNURE

Rubha an Ridire

Lis

Killiemor

B8035

289 ⌄

Eigg: Feuding and fighting amongst the Scottish clans is legendary. Massacre Cave on the south side of Eigg is where 395 MacDonalds died in 1577. They were hiding in the cave when the MacLeods caught up with them. The MacLeods blocked the cave entrance and started a fire which suffocated the MacDonalds. After being owned by a succession of absentee landlords, the 60 islanders set up a trust which succeeded in buying Eigg for £1.5 million in 1997 and is dedicated to conserving the island and developing a sustainable economy.
Map ref. D1

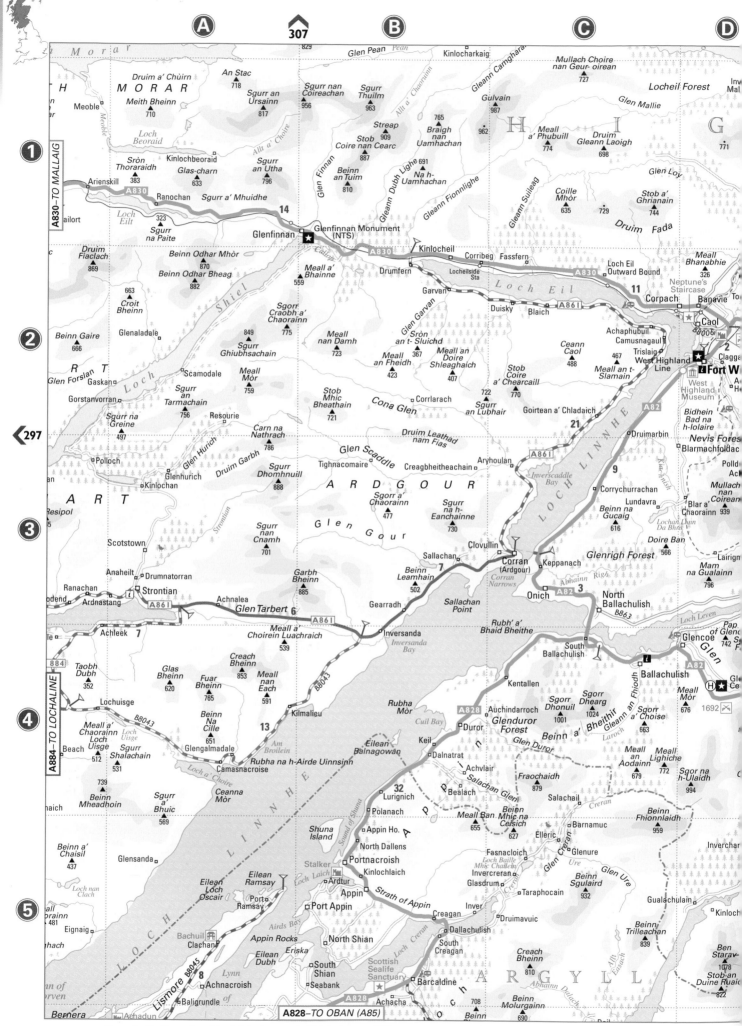

1

Glen Pean   Pean   Kinlocharkaig

Mullach Choire
nan Geur- oirean
727

Locheil Forest

Inv
Mal

M O R A R

Druim a' Chùirn
718

An Stac
718

Sgurr nan
Coireachan
956

Sgurr
Thuilm
963

Gulvain
987

H I

Druim
Gleann Laoigh
698

Meith Bheinn
710

Sgurr an
Ursainn
817

Streap
909

Braigh
nan
Uamhachan

962

Meall
a' Phubuill
774

Meoble

Stob
Coire nan Cearc
887

765

Loch
Beoraid

Sròn
Thoraraidh
383

Kinlochbeoraid

Glas-charn

Beinn
an Tuim
810

Na h-
Uamhachan
691

Coille
Mhòr
635

729

Stob a'
Ghrianain
744

771

Sgurr
an Utha
796

633

Glen Loy

14

Arienskill

Ranochan

Sgurr a' Mhuidhe

Druim Fada

ailort

323

Glenfinnan

Glenfinnan Monument
(NTS)

Kinlocheil

Corribeg   Fassfern

Meall
Bhanabhie
326

Loch
Eilt

Druim
Fiaclach
869

Beinn Odhar Mhòr
870

Meall a'
Bhainne
559

Drumfern

Garvan

Locheilside
Sta

Duisky   Blaich

Loch Eil

Loch Eil
Outward Bound

Neptune's
Staircase

11   Corpach   Banavie

Beinn Odhar Bheag
882

Achaphubuil
Camusnagaul

467

Trislaig
West Highland
Line

Caol

Clagga

663

Croit
Bheinn

2

Beinn Gaire
666

Glenaladale

Scamodale

Sgorr
Craobh a'
Chaorainn
775

849

Sgurr
Ghiubhsachain

Meall
nan Damh
723

Glen Garvan

Sròn
an t-
Sluichd
367

Ceann
Caol

Meall an t-
Slamain

2

Fort W

West Highland
Museum

Meall
an Doire
Shleaghaich

Stob
Coire
a' Chearcaill
770

722

Bidhein
Bad na
h-Iolaire

Glen Forslan

Gaskan

Sgurr
an
Tarmachain
756

Meall
Mòr
759

Meall
an Fheidh
423

Corrlarach

Sgurr
an Lubhair

Goirtean a' Chladaich

Druimarbin

Nevis Fores

Gorstanvorran

Resourie

Cona Glen

Blarmachfoldac

297

Sgurr na
Greine
497

Carn na
Nathrach
786

Stob
Mhic
Bheathain
721

Druim Leathad
nam Fias

21

Polld
Ac

Polloch

Glen Hurich

Druim Garbh

Glen Scaddle

Glen
Tighnacomaire

Creagbheitheachain

Aryhoulan

Inverscaddle
Bay

9

Mullach
nan
Coirean
939

Glenhurich

Kinlochan

Sgurr
Dhomhnuill
888

A R D G O U R

Sgorr a'
Chaorainn
477

Glen Gour

Sgurr
na h-
Eanchainne
730

Corrychurrachan

Lundavra

Beinn na
Gucaig
616

Blar a'
Chaorainn

Lochan Dubh
Da Bhra

Doire Ban
566

Lairigan

3

Scotstown

Sgurr
nan
Cnamh
701

Sallachan

Beinn
Leamhain
502

7

Clovullin

Corran
(Ardgour)

Keppanach

Glenrigh Forest

Mam
na Gualainn
796

Anaheilt   Drumnatorran

Garbh
Bheinn
885

Corran
Narrows

Abhainn
Righ

North
Ballachulish

Ranachan

Strontian

Achnalea

Gearradh

Onich

3

B863

Pap
of Glen
742

Ardnastang

A861

Glen Tarbert   **6**

Sallachan
Point

Rubh' a'
Bhaid Bheithe

South
Ballachulish

Glencoe

Glen

odend

Achleek   **7**

Meall a'
Choirein Luachraich
539

Inversanda

Inversanda
Bay

Ballachulish

Meall
Mòr
676

884

Taobh
Dubh
352

Glas
Bheinn
620

Creach
Bheinn
853

Meall nan
Each
591

Rubha
Mòr

B8043

Kentallen

Auchindarroch

Sgorr
Dhonuill
1001

Sgorr
Dhearg
1024

Sgorr
a' Choise
663

1692

Gle
Ce

4

Lochuisge

Fuar
Bheinn
765

Kilmalieu

Cuil Bay

A828

Duror

Glenduror
Forest

Beinn a'

Bheithir

Gleann an Fhiodh

Laroch

4

Meall a'
Chaorainn Loch
Uisge
512

Sgurr
Shalachain
531

B8043

Glengalmadale

13

Camasnacroise

Rubha na h-Airde Uinnsinn

Dalnatrat

Achvlair

Glen Duror

Salachan Glen

Bealach

Fraochaidh
879

Salachail

Meall
an
Aodainn
679

Meall
Lighiche
772

Sgor na
h-Ulaidh
994

Beinn
Mheadhoin
739

Sgurr
a'
Bhuic
569

Ceanna
Mòr

Lurignich

32

Polanach

Meall Ban Mhic na
Ceilsich
655

Beinn
Mhic na
Ceilsich

Elleric

Barnamuc

Beinn
Fhionnlaidh
959

Inverchar

5

Beinn a'
Chaisil
437

Glensanda

Shuna
Island

Appin Ho.

North Dallens

Portnacroish

Fasnacloich

Invercreran

Glenure

Glen Ure

Beinn
Sgulaird
932

Kinloch

Eilean
Loch
Oscair

Eilean
Ramsay

Stalker

Ardtur

Kinlochlaich

Glasdrum

Taraphocain

Gualachulain

Port
Ramsay

Port Appin

Appin

Strath of Appin

Inver

Druimavuic

5

all
rainn
481

Eignaig

Bachuil
Clachan

Appin Rocks

Eilean
Dubh

North Shian

Creagan

Dallachulish

South
Creagan

Creach
Bheinn
810

Beinn
Trilleachan
839

Ben
Stara
1078

haich

Eriska

Scottish
Sealife
Sanctuary

Barcaldine

Stob a'
Duine Ruaid
822

Bernera

Achadun

Baligrundle

8

Lynn

South
Shian

Seabank

A828

Achacha

Beinn
708

Beinn
Molurgainn
690

A R G Y L L

Corpach: Starting point of the Caledonian Canal which is the longest canal in Scotland and connects Corpach, near Fort William to Clachnacarry, near Inverness, a distance of 60 miles (96.5km). Much of its length is made up of the lochs it passes through. *Map ref. D2*

290

Ballachulish: James Stewart was hanged here in 1752 for the 'Appin' murder of the King's Factor, Colin Campbell of Glenure, as he rode through the woods of Lettermoor. Stewart's body was left on the gibbet for years afterwards with his bones wired. *Map ref. C4*

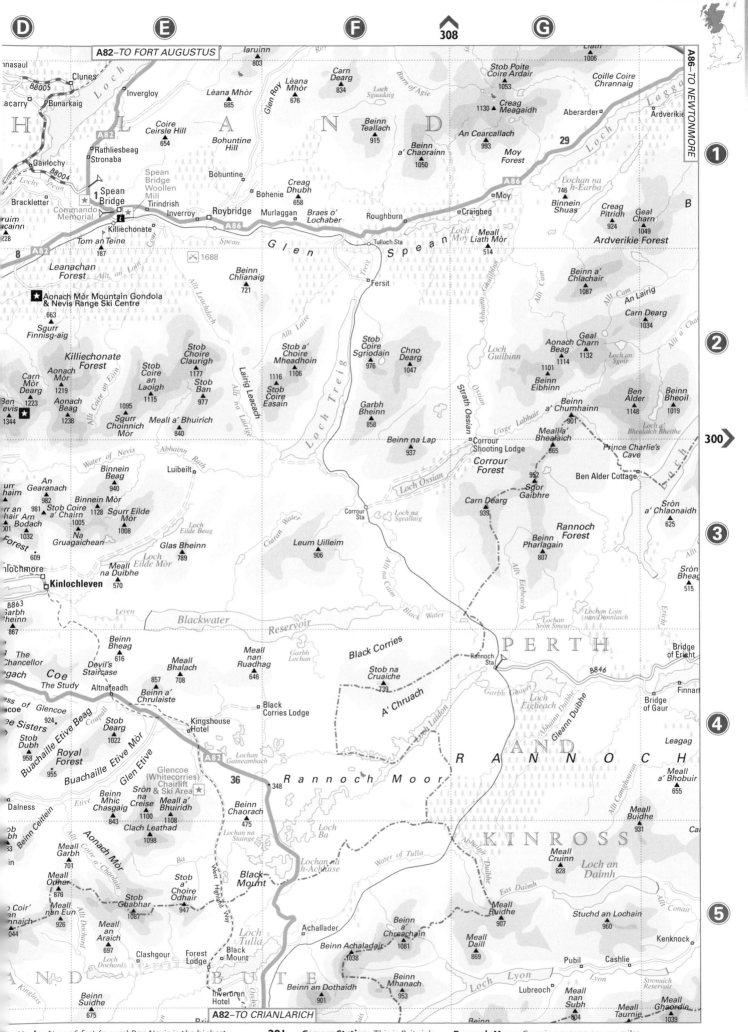

A82–TO FORT AUGUSTUS

A86–TO NEWTONMORE

Iaruinn
803

Glen Roy

Lèana Mhòr
676

Carn Dearg
834

Loch Sguadaig

Burn of Agie

Liath
1006

Stob Poite Coire Ardair
1053

Coille Coire Chrannaig

Clunes
B8005

Invergloy

Lèana Mhòr
685

1130 ▲ Creag Meagaidh

Aberarder

Ardverikie

Bunarkaig

H I G H L A N D

An Cearcallach
993

Moy Forest

29

Loch Laggan

Coire Ceirsle Hill
654

Bohuntine Hill

Beinn Teallach
915

Beinn a' Chaorainn
1050

A86

Lochan na h-Earba

Rathliesbeag

Stronaba

Bohuntine

746 ▲ Binnein Shuas

Creag Pitridh
924

Geal Charn
1049

B

Gairlochy
B8004

Spean Bridge Woollen Mill

Creag Dhubh
658

Bohenie

Moy

Craigbeg

Ardverikie Forest

Brackletter

Spean Bridge

Tirindrish

Inverroy

Roybridge

Murlaggan

Braes o' Lochaber

Roughburn

Killiechonate

A86

Tulloch Sta

Loch Moy

Meall Liath Mòr
514

Commando Memorial

Tom an Teine
187

Glen

Spean

8 A82

Leanachan Forest

Allt an Loin

Beinn Chlianaig
721

Treig

Fersit

Beinn a' Chlachair
1087

An Lairig

Aonach Mòr Mountain Gondola & Nevis Range Ski Centre

663

Allt Leachdaich

1688

Allt Laire

Carn Dearg
1034

Sgurr Finnisg-aig

Killiechonate Forest

Stob Choire Claurigh
1177

Stob a' Choire Mheadhoin
1106

Stob Coire Sgriodain
976

Chno Dearg
1047

Loch Guilbinn

Aonach Beag
1114

Geal Charn
1132

2

Carn Mòr Dearg
1223

Aonach Mòr
1219

Stob Coire an Laoigh
1115

Stob Ban
977

1116

Stob Coire Easain

Aonach Beag
1101

Beinn Eibhinn
1102

Loch an Sgoir

Ben Nevis
1344

Aonach Beag
1238

1095

Meall a' Bhuirich
840

Garbh Bheinn
858

Beinn a' Chumhainn
901

Ben Alder
1148

Beinn Bheoil
1019

Sgurr Choinnich Mòr

Abhainn Rath

Beinn na Lap
937

Corrour Shooting Lodge

Mealla' Bhealaich
665

Prince Charlie's Cave

Loch a' Bhealaich Bheithe

300

Water of Nevis

Binnein Beag
940

Luibeilt

Corrour Forest

952

Sgor Gaibhre

Ben Alder Cottage

An Gearanach
982

Binnein Mòr
1128

Sgurr Eilde Mòr
1008

Loch Eilde Beag

Corrour Sta

Loch na Sgeallaig

Carn Dearg
939

Rannoch Forest

Sròn a' Chlaonaidh
625

Stob Coire a' Chairn
1005

Na Gruagaichean

Glas Bheinn
789

Leum Uilleim
906

Beinn Pharlagain
807

Sròn Bheag
515

Am Bodach
1032

609

Meall Eilde Mòr

Loch Ossian

3

Kinlochmore

Meall na Duibhe
570

Kinlochleven

Blackwater

Reservoir

Black Water

Lochan Loin nan Donnlaich

B863

Garbh Bheinn
867

Leven

Lochan Sròn Smeur

PERTH

Beinn Bheag
616

Meall Bhalach
708

Meall nan Ruadhag
646

Garbh Lochan

Black Corries

Stob na Cruaiche
739

Rannoch Sta

Bridge of Ericht

The Chancellor

Devil's Staircase

857

A' Chruach

B846

Finnart

Coe

The Study

Altnafeadh

Beinn a' Chrulaiste

Black Corries Lodge

Loch Laidon

Loch Eigheach

Bridge of Gaur

4

Pass of Glencoe

Three Sisters
924

Stob Dearg
1022

Kingshouse Hotel

A82

Leagag

Stob Dubh
958

Royal Forest

Buachaille Etive Beag

Coupall

Buachaille Etive Mòr

Glen Etive

A82

36

348

Rannoch Moor

Meall a' Bhobuir
655

955

Glencoe (Whitecorries) Chairlift & Ski Area

Lochan Gaineamhach

Meall Buidhe
931

Dalness

Beinn Mhic Chasgaig
843

Sròn na Creise
1100

Meall a' Bhuiridh
1108

Beinn Chaorach
475

Etive

Clach Leathad
1098

Lochan na Stainge

Loch Ba

K I N R O S S

Beinn Ceitlein

Meall Garbh
701

Aonach Mòr

Ba

Lochan na h-Achlaise

Meall Cruinn
828

Loch an Daimh

Coire a' Chaolain

Stob a' Choire Odhair

Black Mount

Water of Tulla

Stuchd an Lochain
960

Meall Odhar
876

Stob Ghabhar
1087

947

Meall Buidhe
907

Kenknock

Coir' nan Eun
926

Meall nan Eun

Meall an Araich
697

Clashgour

Forest Lodge

Loch Dochard

Black Mount

Loch Tulla

Achallader

Beinn a' Chreachain
1081

Meall Daill
869

Eas Daimh

Pubil

Meall nan Subh

Meall Taurnie

Meall Ghaordie
1039

Beinn Suidhe
675

Inveroran Hotel

Beinn an Dothaidh
901

Beinn Achaladair
1038

Beinn Mhanach
953

Loch Lyon

Lubreoch

Cashlie

Stronuich Reservoir

A82–TO CRIANLARICH

291 ⌄

Ben Nevis: At 4406 feet (1344m) Ben Nevis is the highest mountain in Britain. Scotland has 284 distinct mountains over 3000 feet (914.4m) which are collectively known as Munros, after Sir Hugh Munro who was the first man to catalogue them.
Map ref. D2

Corrour Station: This is Britain's most isolated railway station – there isn't even a road to it.
Map ref. F3

Rannoch Moor: Covering over 50 square miles and stretching from Bridge of Orchy to Loch Rannoch, this area is thought to be the largest uninhabited wilderness in Britain.
Map ref. F4 Also on page 129

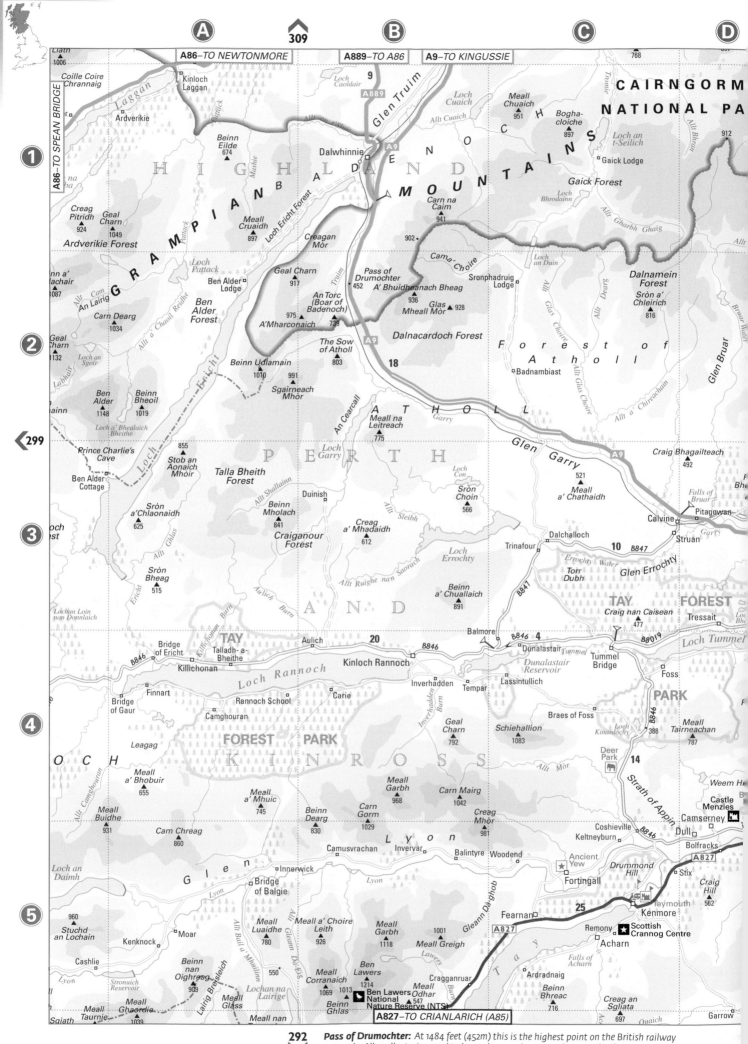

A   **309**   **B**   **C**   **D**

Liath
1006

Coille Coire
Chrannaig

A86–TO SPEAN BRIDGE

Laggan

Kinloch
Laggan

Ardverikie

Beinn
Eilde
674

Loch
Caoldair

9

Glen Truim

Loch
Cuaich

Meall
Chuaich
951

CAIRNGORM

NATIONAL PA

768

A889

1

Dalwhinnie

A9

Gaick Lodge

Bogha-
cloiche
897

Loch an
t-Seilich

912

na
ha

Creag
Pitridh
924

Geal
Charn
1049

Meall
Cruaidh
897

Loch Ericht Forest

Gaick Forest

Loch
Bhrodainn

Ardverikie Forest

Creagan
Mòr

Carn na
Caim
941

Allt Gharbh Ghaig

Allt

nn a'
achair
1087

An Lairig

Loch
Pattack

Ben Alder
Lodge

Geal Charn
917

Pass of
Drumochter
452

Cama-
Choire

902•

A' Bhuidheanach Bheag
936

Loch
an Duin

Dalnamein
Forest

Sròn a'
Chleirich
816

2

Geal
Charn
1132

Carn Dearg
1034

Ben
Alder
Forest

An Torc
(Boar of
Badenoch)
739

A'Mharconaich
975

Glas
Mheall Mòr
928

Dalnacardoch Forest

F o r e s t o f

A t h o l l

Glen Bruar

Bruar Water

ainn

Allt a' Chaoil Reidhe

Beinn Udlamain
1010

The Sow
of Atholl
803

A9

Badnambiast

Geal
Charn

Ben
Alder
1148

Beinn
Bheoil
1019

Sgairneach
Mhòr
991

18

A T H O L L

Allt a' Chireachain

299

Loch a' Bhealaich
Bheithe

Labhair

Ericht

An Cearcall

Meall na
Leitreach
775

Garry

Glen Garry

A9

Craig Bhagailteach
492

Prince Charlie's
Cave

Ben Alder
Cottage

Stob an
Aonaich
Mhòir
855

P E R T H

Loch
Garry

Loch
Con

Sròn
Choin
566

Meall
a' Chathaidh
521

Falls of
Bruar

Bh

3

och
est

Sròn
a'Chlaonaidh
625

Talla Bheith
Forest

Allt Shallainn

Duinish

Allt Sleibh

Creag
a' Mhadaidh
612

521

Dalchalloch

Trinafour

Calvine

Pitagowan

Struan

Garry

Allt Glas

Beinn
Mholach
841

Craiganour
Forest

10

B847

Glen Errochty

Errochty Water

Sròn
Bheag
515

Allt Ruighe nan Saorach

Loch
Errochty

Beinn
a' Chuallaich
891

B847

Torr
Dubh

TAY

FOREST

Tressait

Lochan Loin
nan Donnlaich

Aulich Burn

Balmore

B846

4

B8019

Loch
Bho

Loch Tummel

Craig nan Caisean
477

4

Bridge
of Ericht

B846

Talladh-a-
Bheithe

Killichonan

Aulich

20

B846

Dunalastair

Tummel

Dunalastair
Reservoir

Tummel
Bridge

Foss

PARK

Killiecrankie Burn

Loch Rannoch

Kinloch Rannoch

Inverhadden

Tempar

Lassintullich

B846

Braes of Foss

Meall
Tairneachan
787

Finnart

Bridge
of Gaur

Rannoch School

Carie

Inverhadden Burn

Geal
Charn
792

Schiehallion
1083

388

Loch
Kinardochy

Strath of Appin

Camghouran

FOREST

K I N R O S S

Allt Mòr

Deer
Park

14

Weem H

Castle
Menzies

OCH

Meall
a' Bhobuir
655

Meall
a' Mhuic
745

Meall
Garbh
968

Carn Mairg
1042

Camserney

5

Meall
Buidhe
931

Cam Chreag
860

Beinn
Dearg
830

Carn
Gorm
1029

Creag
Mhòr
981

Coshieville

Keltneyburn

B846

Dull

Bolfracks

A827

Loch an
Daimh

Glen

Camusvrachan

Invervar

Balintyre

Woodend

L y o n

Ancient
Yew

Drummond
Hill

Stix

Craig
Hill
562

Bridge
of Balgie

Lyon

Fortingall

25

A827

Kenmore

Stuchd
an Lochain
960

Moar

Meall
Luaidhe
780

Meall a' Choire
Leith
926

Meall
Garbh
1118

1001

Fearnan

Remony

Scottish
Crannog Centre

Kenknock

Beinn
nan Oighreag
909

Allt Gleann Dà-Eig

Meall
Greigh
697

Lawers

Acharn

Falls of
Acharn

Craig an
Sgliata
697

Cashlie

Stronuich
Reservoir

Meall
Glass

Lochan na
Lairige

Meall
Corranaich
1069

1013

Ben
Lawers
1214

Meall
Odhar
547

Cragganruar

Ardradnaig

Beinn
Bhreac
716

Garrow

Meall
Tauirnie

Meall
Ghaordie
1039

Lairig Breisleich

Meall nan

Beinn
Ghlas

Ben Lawers
National
Nature Reserve (NTS)

A827–TO CRIANLARICH (A85)

Tay

Quaich

292

Pass of Drumochter: At 1484 feet (452m) this is the highest point on the British railway network. Allegedly, trains used to be so slow coming up to the summit, that passengers used to get off and walk instead. Nearby Dalwhinnie (**Map ref. B1**) claims to be the highest village in the Scottish Highlands at 1160 feet (358 metres). **Map ref. B2**

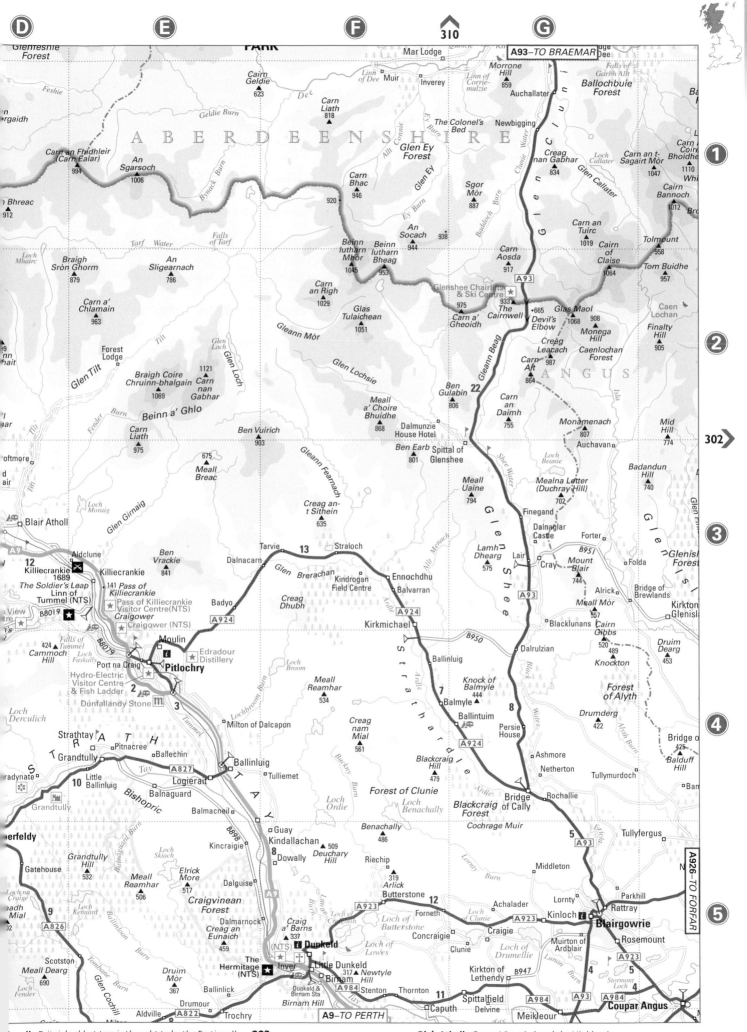

PARK

A93-TO BRAEMAR

Glensfeshie Forest

Glenfeshie Forest

Mar Lodge

Morrone Hill 859

Auchallater

Ballochbuie Forest

Linn of Dee   Muir

Inverey

Linn of Corrie-mulzie

Falls of Garbh Allt

Falls of Dee

Dee

A B E R D E E N S H I R E

Cairn Geldie 623

Carn Liath 818

The Colonel's Bed

Newbigging

Creag nan Gabhar 834

Loch Callater

Glen Callater

Carn an t-Sagairt Mòr 1047

Carn a' Coire Bhoidhe 1110

Carn an Fhidhleir (Carn Ealar) 994

An Sgarsoch 1006

Geldie Burn

Carn Bhac 946

Glen Ey

Glen Ey Forest

Sgor Mòr 887

Carn Aosda 917

Cairn Bannoch 1012

Bhreac 912

Tarf Water

Falls of Tarf

Beinn Iutharn Mhòr 1045

Beinn Iutharn Bheag 953

An Socach 944

Carn an Tuirc 1019

Cairn of Claise 1064

Tolmount 958

Braigh Sròn Ghorm 879

An Sligearnach 786

Carn an Righ 1029

A93

Glen Clunie

Glen Beag

Tom Buidhe 957

Loch Mhairc

Carn a' Chlamain 963

Glas Tulaichean 1051

Carn a' Gheoidh 975

Glenshee Chairlifts & Ski Centre 933

The Cairnwell 665

Glas Maol 1068

Monega Hill 908

Caen Lochan

Finalty Hill 905

Forest Lodge

Gleann Mòr

Glen Lochsie

Devil's Elbow

Creag Leacach 987

Caenlochan Forest

Glen Tilt

Glen Loch

Gleann Mòr

Carn Aft 864

A N G U S

Braigh Coire Chruinn-bhalgain 1069

1121

Carn nan Gabhar

Meall a' Choire Bhuidhe 868

Ben Gulabin 806

Carn an Daimh 755

Monamenach 807

Mid Hill 774

Beinn a' Ghlo

Carn Liath 975

Ben Vuirich 903

675

Dalmunzie House Hotel

Auchavan

Badandun Hill 740

Fender Burn

Meall Breac

Ben Earb 801

Spittal of Glenshee

Loch Beanie

Glen Isla

Carn Liath 975

Creag an-t Sithein 635

Meall Uaine 794

Mealna Letter (Duchray Hill) 702

Glen Fernate

Blair Atholl

A9

Ben Vrackie 841

Tarvie

13

Straloch

Dalnacarn

Glen Brerachan

Kindrogan Field Centre

Ennochdhu

Balvarran

Finegand

Dalnaglar Castle

Lamh Dhearg 575

Lair

Cray

Forter

B951

Mount Blair 744

Folda

Glenisla Forest

12 Killiecrankie 1689

Aldclune

Killiecrankie

141 Pass of Killiecrankie

Badyo

Creag Dhubh

Kirkmichael

Ardle

A924

Ballinluig

A93

Dalrulzian

Blacklunans

Meall Mòr 557

Alrick

Cairn Gibbs

Bridge of Brewlands

Kirkton of Glenisla

The Soldier's Leap Linn of Tummel (NTS)

Pass of Killiecrankie Visitor Centre(NTS)

Craigower

Craigower (NTS)

Moulin

Edradour Distillery

Meall Reamhar 534

Knock of Balmyle 444

7

Balmyle

Knock of Balmyle

520 489

Druim Dearg 453

Knockton

B8019

Falls of Tummel

Cammoch Hill 424

Pitlochry

Loch Broom

Creag nam Mial 561

Ballintuim

Persie House

8

Drumderg 422

Forest of Alyth

Hydro-Electric Visitor Centre & Fish Ladder

Port na Craig

2

3

Dunfallandy Stone

Milton of Dalcapon

A924

Blackcraig Hill 479

Ashmore

Netherton

Bridge of 425

Balduff Hill

Loch Derculich

Strathtay

Pitnacree

Ballechin

Ballinluig

Tulliemet

Forest of Clunie

Bridge of Cally

Rochallie

Tullymurdoch

Grandtully

A827

Logierait

Balnaguard

Loch Ordie

Cochrage Muir

5

Tullyfergus

Little Ballinluig

10

Tay

Balmacneil

Loch Benachally

A93

Grandtully

Bishopric

Guay

Kindallachan

8

Dowally

Benachally 486

Riechip

Middleton

A926-TO FORFAR

erfeldy

Gatehouse

Grandtully Hill 532

Loch Skiach

Kincraigie

Deuchary Hill 509

Lornty Burn

Lornty

Parkhill

Meall Reamhar 506

Elrick More 517

Dalguise

Arlick 319

Butterstone

A923

Forneth

Achalader

Kinloch

Rattray

Loch na Craige

9

adh Mial

A826

Craigvinean Forest

Dalmarnock

Craig a' Barns

Loch of Craiglush

12

Loch of Butterstone

Craigie

Concraigie

Loch of Clunie

Clunie

Muirton of Ardblair

Blairgowrie

Rosemount

Scotston

Meall Dearg 690

Druim Mòr 367

Creag an Eunaich 459

Dunkeld

The Hermitage (NTS)

Inver

Little Dunkeld

Birnam

337

Newtyle Hill

317

Stenton

Loch of Lowes

Forneth

Kirkton of Lethendy

B947

A923

A984

4

5

Stormont Loch

Loch Fender

Ballinlick

Drumour

Birnam Hill

Caputh

Thornton

11

Spittalfield

Delvine

Meikleour

A984

A93

A984

Coupar Angus

Aldville

A822

Trochry

A9-TO PERTH

ingall: Britain's oldest tree is thought to be the Fortingall (Taxus baccata) in the churchyard, which is estimated to 00 years old and consequently the oldest living thing in e. There is a long oral tradition that Pontius Pilate was in the village. **Map ref. C5**

Blair Atholl: Queen Victoria loved the Highlands and was a keen 'rambler'. A cairn, close to here, marks the spot where she had a picnic in October 1861. **Map ref. D3**

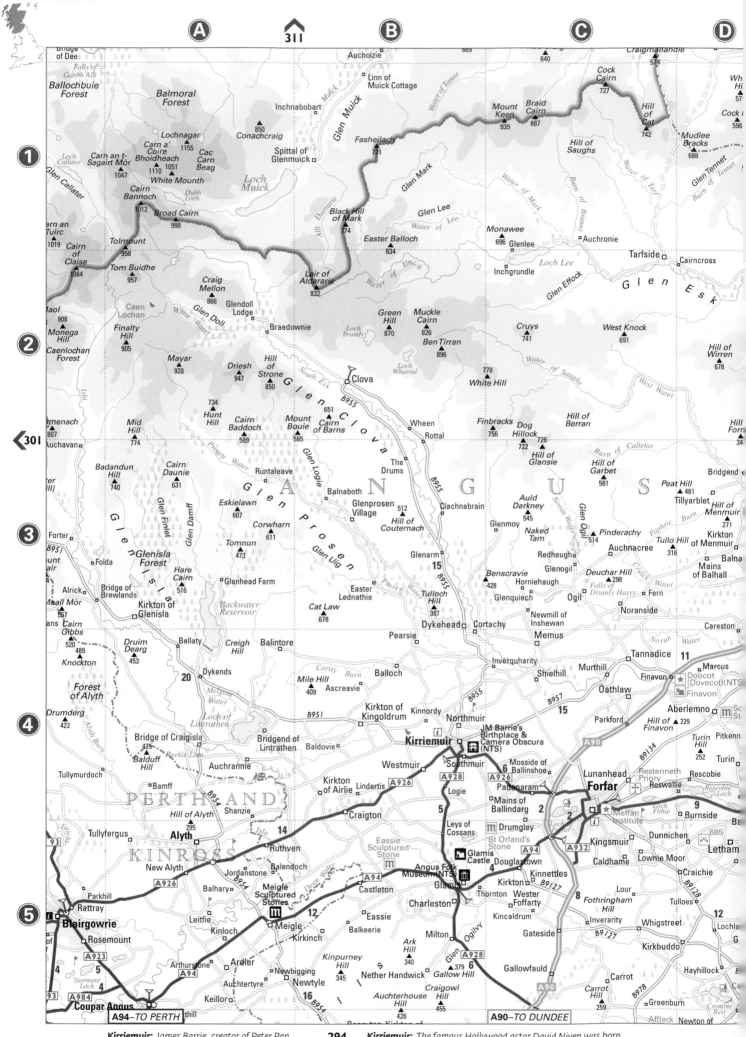

A   B   C   D

301

Bridge
of Dee
Falls of
Garbh Allt
Ballochbuie
Forest
Balmoral
Forest
Inchnabobart
Linn of
Muick Cottage
Aucholzie
640
Craigmahandle
574
Cock Cairn
727
Mount
Keen
939
Braid
Cairn
887
Hill of
Cat
742
Cock
598
Wh
Hi
57

Conachcraig
850
Fasheilach
721
Hill of
Saughs
Mudlee
Bracks
688
Glen Tennet

Lochnagar
Carn a'
Coire
Bhoidheach
1110
Cac
Carn
Beag
1051
Carn an t-
Sagairt Mòr
1047
White Mounth
1155
Glen Muick
Loch
Muick
Glen Mark
Water of Mark

Loch
Callater
Cairn
Bannoch
1012
Broad Cairn
998
Black Hill
of Mark
774
Glen Lee
Water of Lee
Monawee
696
Glenlee
Tarfside
Cairncross

arn an
Tuirc
1019
Cairn
of
Claise
1064
Tolmount
958
Lair of
Aldararie
832
Easter Balloch
834
Water of Unich
Inchgrundle
Loch Lee
Glen Effock
Glen Esk

Maol
908
Monega
Hill
Tom Buidhe
957
Craig
Mellon
866
Glendoll
Lodge
Green
Hill
870
Muckle
Cairn
826
Cruys
741
West Knock
691
Hill of
Wirren
678

Caenlochan
Forest
Finalty
Hill
905
Caen
Lochan
Glen Doll
Braedownie
Loch
Brandy
Ben Tirran
896
Water of Saughs
Hill of
Forn
34

menach
807
Auchavan
Mayar
928
Driesh
947
Hill
of
Strone
850
South Esk
Loch
Wharral
Clova
White Hill
778
West Water

Mid
Hill
774
Hunt
Hill
734
Cairn
Baddoch
589
Mount
Bouie
585
Cairn
of Barns
651
Wheen
Rottal
Finbracks
756
Dog
Hillock
726
Hill of
Berran
Hill of
Garbet
581
Peat Hill
481
Bridgend
Tillyarblet

A N G U S

Badandun
Hill
740
Cairn
Daunie
631
Runtaleave
Balnaboth
The
Drums
Auld
Darkney
545
Glenogil
722
Hill of
Glansie
Hill of
Menmuir
271

Forter
Glen Finlet
Eskielawn
607
Glenprosen
Village
512
Clachnabrain
Glenmoy
Naked
Tam
Pinderachy
514
Tullo Hill
316
Kirkton
of Menmuir
Balna

B951
Glenisla
Forest
Corwharn
611
Hill of
Couternach
Glenarm
15
Benscravie
428
Horniehaugh
Redheugh
Glenogil
Deuchar Hill
298
Falls of
Drumly Harry
Fern
Mains
of Balhall

Folda
Hare
Cairn
516
Tomnun
473
Easter
Lednathie
Tulloch
Hill
387
Glenquiech
Ogil
Newmill of
Inshewan
Noranside

Alrick
Bridge of
Brewlands
Glenhead Farm
Backwater
Reservoir
Cat Law
678
B955
Dykehead
Cortachy
Memus
Careston

Meall Mòr
557
Cairn
Gibbs
Kirkton of
Glenisla
Bellaty
Balintore
Pearsie
Balloch
Inverquharity
Shielhill
Murthill
Tannadice
11
Marcus
Finavon

Druim
Dearg
453
520
489
Knockton
Creigh
Hill
Dykends
Carity
Burn
Mile Hill
409
Ascreavie
Kirkton of
Kingoldrum
Kinnordy
Northmuir
B957
15
Parkford
Oathlaw
Aberlemno
Doocot
(Dovecot)(NTS)
Hill of
Finavon
229
So
St

Drumderg
422
20
Forest
of Alyth
Bridge of Craigisla
425
Balduff
Hill
Bridgend of
Lintrathen
Baldovie
Kirkton of
Airlie
Lindertis
Logie
A926
JM Barrie's
Birthplace &
Camera Obscura
(NTS)
Mosside of
Ballinshoe
6
Lunanhead
Turin
Hill
252
Pitkenn
Turin

Tullymurdoch
Bamff
Auchrannie
A928
Westmuir
Southmuir
Kirriemuir
Padanaram
A926
Forfar
Restenneth
Priory
Rescobie
Loch
Fithie
Rescobie
Loch
9
Burnside

Hill of Alyth
295
Shanzie
Kirkton
of Airlie
Craigton
5
Mains of
Ballindarg
2
A932
Meffan
Institute
Dunnichen
685
Letham

Tullyfergus
Alyth
Ruthven
14
Isla
Leys of
Cossans
Drumgley
St Orland's
Stone
A94
Kingsmuir
Caldhame
Lownie Moor
Craichie

New Alyth
Jordanstone
Balendoch
Glamis
Castle
Douglastown
Kinnettles
B9127
Lour
Tulloes

Parkhill
A926
Balhary
Meigle
Sculptured
Stones
A94
Angus Folk
Museum (NTS)
Glamis
Kirkton
Thornton
Wester
Foffarty
Fothringham
Hill
8
Inverarity
B9128
12

Blairgowrie
Rosemount
Leitfie
Kinloch
Meigle
12
Castleton
Eassie
Balkeerie
Charleston
Kincaldrum
Gateside
Whigstreet
Lochla

A923
Arthurstone
Ardler
A94
Newbigging
Newtyle
Kinpurney
Hill
345
Ark
Hill
340
Milton
Glen Ogilvy
Gallow Hill
379
A928
6
Gallowfauld
A90
Carrot
Hayhillock

4
5
93
A984
Coupar
Angus
Keillor
16
B954
Nether Handwick
Auchterhouse
Hill
426
Craigowl
Hill
455
Carrot
Hill
259
B978
Greenburn
Crombie
Resr

A94–TO PERTH   A90–TO DUNDEE

294

Kirriemuir: James Barrie, creator of Peter Pan, 'the boy who wouldn't grow up', was born here in 1860. The book was published in 1904. Barrie died on the 19th June 1937 and is buried next to his mother in Kirriemuir. **Map ref. B4**

Kirriemuir: The famous Hollywood actor David Niven was born here in 1909. He starred in over 100 films including 'Separate Tables', for which he won an Academy Award in 1958. Although Scottish, David Niven was invariably cast as the archetypal Englishman. **Map ref. B4**

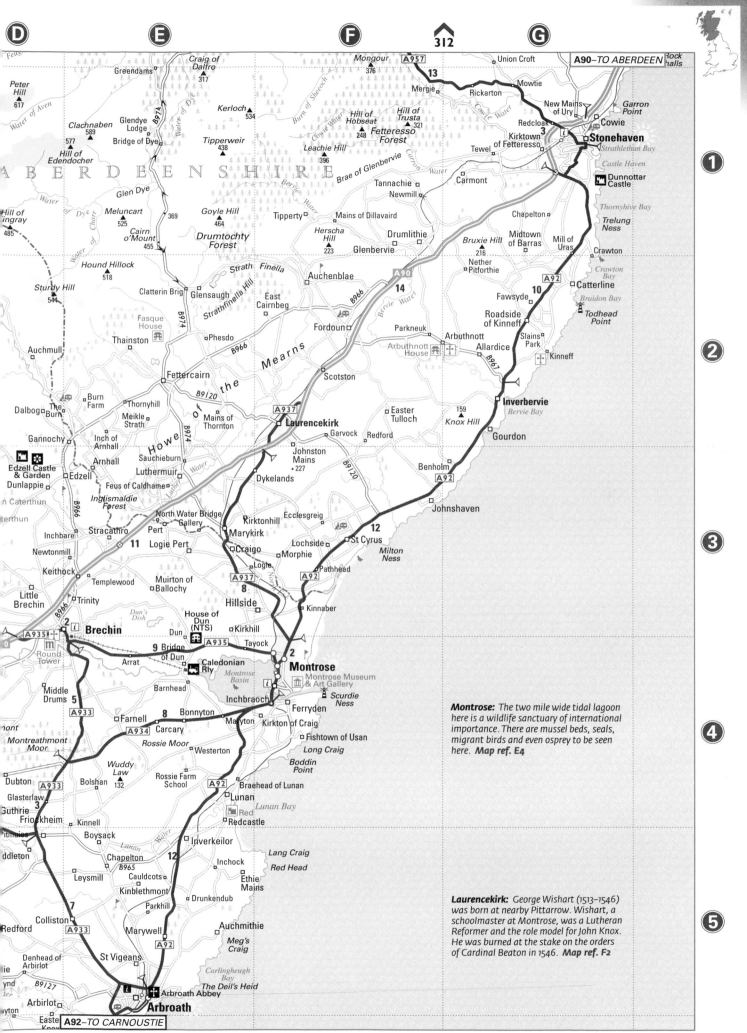

Montrose: The two mile wide tidal lagoon here is a wildlife sanctuary of international importance. There are mussel beds, seals, migrant birds and even osprey to be seen here. **Map ref. E4**

Laurencekirk: George Wishart (1513–1546) was born at nearby Pittarrow. Wishart, a schoolmaster at Montrose, was a Lutheran Reformer and the role model for John Knox. He was burned at the stake on the orders of Cardinal Beaton in 1546. **Map ref. F2**

Arbroath: Home of the legendary Arbroath Smokie, pairs of haddock tied by their tails and smoked over hardwood chips. Arbroath Smokies are afforded the same protection under EU law as Champagne and Parma Ham if they don't come from Arbroath then they cannot be called Arbroath Smokies. **Map ref. E5**

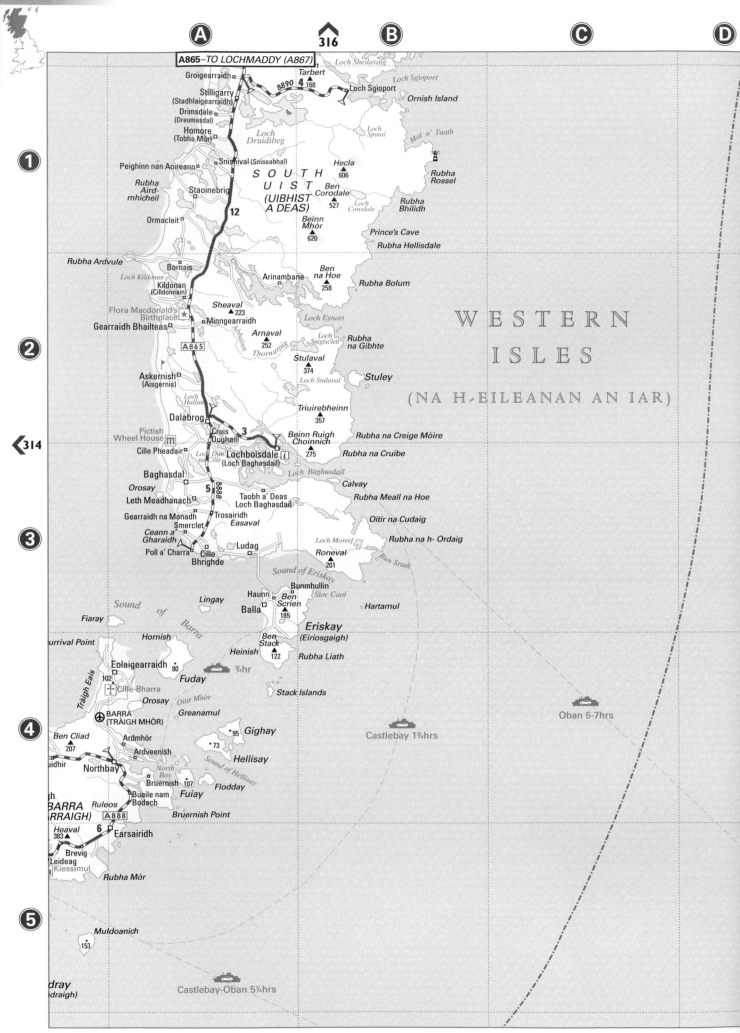

A865—TO LOCHMADDY (A867)

Loch Sheilavaig

Groigearraidh

Loch Sgioport

Tarbert
B890   4   168

Loch Sgioport

Ornish Island

Stilligarry
(Stadhlaigearraidh)

Drimsdale
(Dreumasdal)

Homore
(Tobha Mòr)

Loch
Druidibeg

Loch
Spotal

Mol a' Tuath

1

Peighinn nan Aoireann

Snishival (Sniseabhal)

Hecla
606

Rubha
Rossel

Rubha
Aird-
mhicheil

S O U T H
U I S T
(UIBHIST
A DEAS)

Ben
Corodale
527

Loch
Corodale

Rubha
Bhilidh

Staoinebrig

Ormacleit

12

Beinn
Mhòr
620

Prince's Cave

Rubha Hellisdale

Rubha Ardvule

Bornais

Loch Kildonan

Kildonan
(Cilldonnain)

Arinambane

Ben
na Hoe
258

Rubha Bolum

Flora Macdonald's
Birthplace ★

Gearraidh Bhailteas

Sheaval
▲ 223

Minngearraidh

Arnaval
▲
252

Loch Eynort

Rubha
na Gibhte

W E S T E R N

I S L E S

2

A865

Askernish
(Aisgernis)

Abhainn Thornaraig

Stulaval
▲
374

Loch Stulaval

Loch
Snigisclett

Stuley

(NA H-EILEANAN AN IAR)

Loch
Hallan

Triuirebheinn
▲
357

314

Dalabrog

Pictish
Wheel House 🏛

Crois
Dughaill

3

Cille Pheadair

Loch Dun na Cille

Lochboisdale
(Loch Baghasdail) ℹ

Beinn Ruigh
Choinnich
275

Rubha na Creige Mòire

Rubha na Cruibe

Loch Baghasdail

Baghasdal

Orosay

Leth Meadhanach

5

B888

Taobh a' Deas
Loch Baghasdail

Calvay

Rubha Meall na Hoe

Oitir na Cudaig

3

Gearraidh na Monadh
Smerclet

Trosairidh

Easaval

Ludag

Loch Moreef

Rubha na h- Ordaig

Ceann a'
Gharaidh

Poll a' Charra △ Cille
Bhrighde

Roneval
▲
201

Bun Sruth

Bunmhullin

Lingay

Haunn

Ben
Scrien
▲
185

Sloc Caol

Sound of Eriskay

Hartamul

Sound

of

Fiaray

Hornish

Barra

Balla

Eriskay
(Eiriosgaigh)

Ben
Stack
▲
122

Rubha Liath

urrival Point

Heinish

🚗 ¾ hr

Eolaigearraidh
▲
102

80

Fuday

Cille-Bharra ✝

Orosay

Oitir Mhòr

Stack Islands

Oban 5-7hrs 🚢

4

BARRA (TRÀIGH MHÒR) ✈

Greanamul

Gighay

95

Castlebay 1¾hrs 🚗

Ben Cliad
▲ 207

Ardmhòr

Ardveenish

73

Hellisay

uidhir

Northbay

North
Bay

Sound of Hellisay

Bruernish

107

Floddday

Fuiay

~~h~~
BARRA
~~RRAIGH)~~

Ruleos

Buaile nam
Bodach

Bruernish Point

A888

Heaval
383 ▲

6

Earsairidh

Brevig

Leideag
Kiessimul

Rubha Mòr

5

Muldoanich
▲
153

Castlebay-Oban 5¼hrs 🚢

dray
draigh)

304

Flora Macdonald's Birthplace: *South Uist was the home of Flora MacDonald who helped Bonnie Prince Charlie escape from the English army after the defeat of his army at the battle of Culloden in April 1746. After narrowly evading the enemy several times she eventually got him to the Isle of Skye and then on to safety. Her home is now a ruin but a nearby memorial marks the site.* **Map ref. A2**

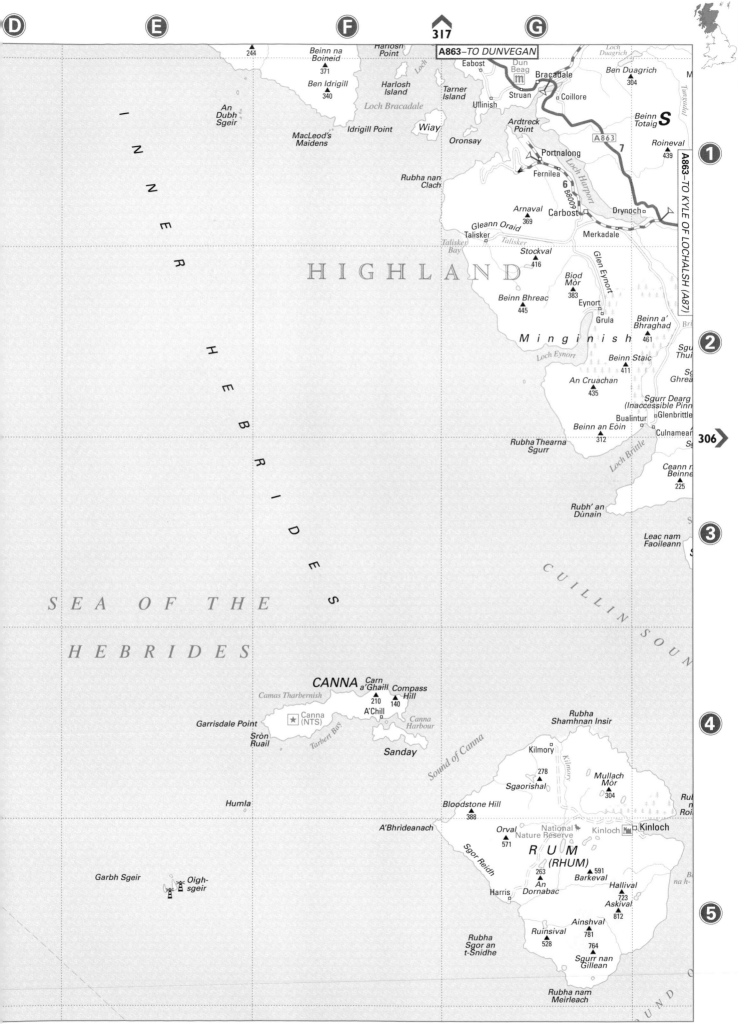

A863–TO DUNVEGAN

A863–TO KYLE OF LOCHALSH (A87)

244
Beinn na
Boineid
371

Ben Idrigill
340

Harlosh
Point

Harlosh
Island

Tarner
Island

Ullinish

Eabost

Dun
Beag

Bracadale

Ben Duagrich
304

Struan

Coillore

Beinn
Totaig **S**

An
Dubh
Sgeir

MacLeod's
Maidens

Idrigill Point

Loch Bracadale

Wiay

Oronsay

Ardtreck
Point

Portnalong

Fernilea

A863

7

Roineval
439

Rubha nan
Clach

Arnaval
369

Carbost

Drynoch

B8009

6

Talisker

Gleann Oraid

Merkadale

Talisker

Talisker
Bay

Stockval
416

H I G H L A N D

Biod
Mòr
383

Glen Eynort

Beinn Bhreac
445

Eynort

Grula

Beinn a'
Bhraghad
461

Bri

M i n g i n i s h

Loch Eynort

Beinn Staic
411

Sgu
Thui

Sg
Ghrea

An Cruachan
435

Sgurr Dearg
(Inaccessible Pinn
Glenbrittle

Bualintur

Beinn an Eòin
312

Culnamear

Rubha Thearna
Sgurr

Loch Brittle

Ceann r
Beinne
225

Rubh' an
Dùnain

**I
N
N
E
R**

**H
E
B
R
I
D
E
S**

Leac nam
Faoileann

S

C U I L L I N   S O U N

S E A   O F   T H E

H E B R I D E S

Camas Tharbernish

CANNA

Carn
a'Ghaill
210

Compass
Hill
140

A'Chill

Garrisdale Point

★ Canna
(NTS)

Sròn
Ruail

Tarbert Bay

Canna
Harbour

Sanday

Humla

A'Bhrideanach

Garbh Sgeir

Oigh-
sgeir

Sound of Canna

Rubha
Shamhnan Insir

Kilmory

278
Sgaorishal

Mullach
Mòr
304

Bloodstone Hill
388

Orval
571

National
Nature Reserve

Kinloch

Kilmory

Ru
n
Roi

Kinloch

R U M
(RHUM)

Sgor Reidh

263
An
Dornabac

Barkeval
591

Hallival
723

Askival
812

Harris

Ainshval
781

Ruinsival
528

764
Sgurr nan
Gillean

Rubha
Sgor an
t-Snidhe

Ba
na h–

Rubha nam
Meirleach

SOUND O

Rum: *Semi precious stones and rocks on this island are similar to those found on the moon. In the 19th Century the island was 'cleared' for sheep farming and the residents shipped off to Nova Scotia. It is now owned by the Nature Conservancy Council.* **Map ref. G5**

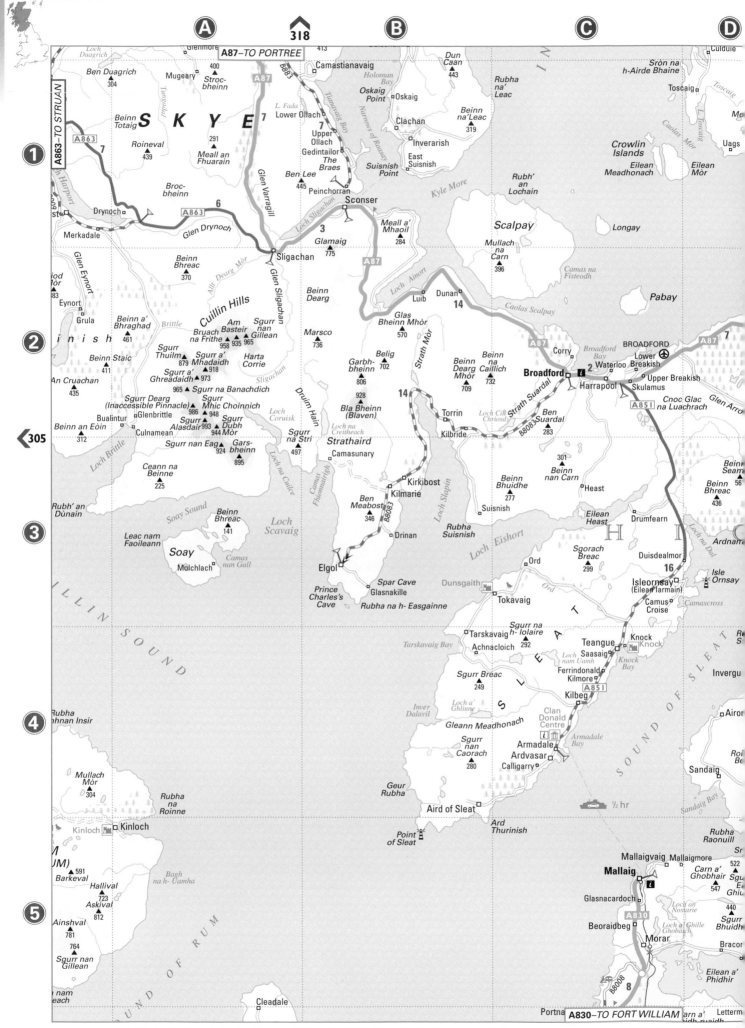

Loch Morar: Known as the 'Loch without a bottom'. Loch Morar covers an area of over 10 square miles (28.6 sq km) and at 1077 feet (328m) is the deepest lake in Britain. **Map ref. D5**

297

The Cuillin Hills Considered by many to be the most dramatic mountain range in Britain. Comprises the tall, jagged peaks of the main Cuillin Ridge, known as the Black Cuillin and the more rounded hills of the Red Cuillin. There are over 20 Munros in the Cuillin Hills which have a fascinating geological composition dating back 500 million years. **Map ref. A2 Also on page 119**

Elgol: Just south of the villa a cave called Suidhe Biorach where Bonnie Prince Charlie said to have hidden before m his escape to Europe in 1746 **Map ref. B3**

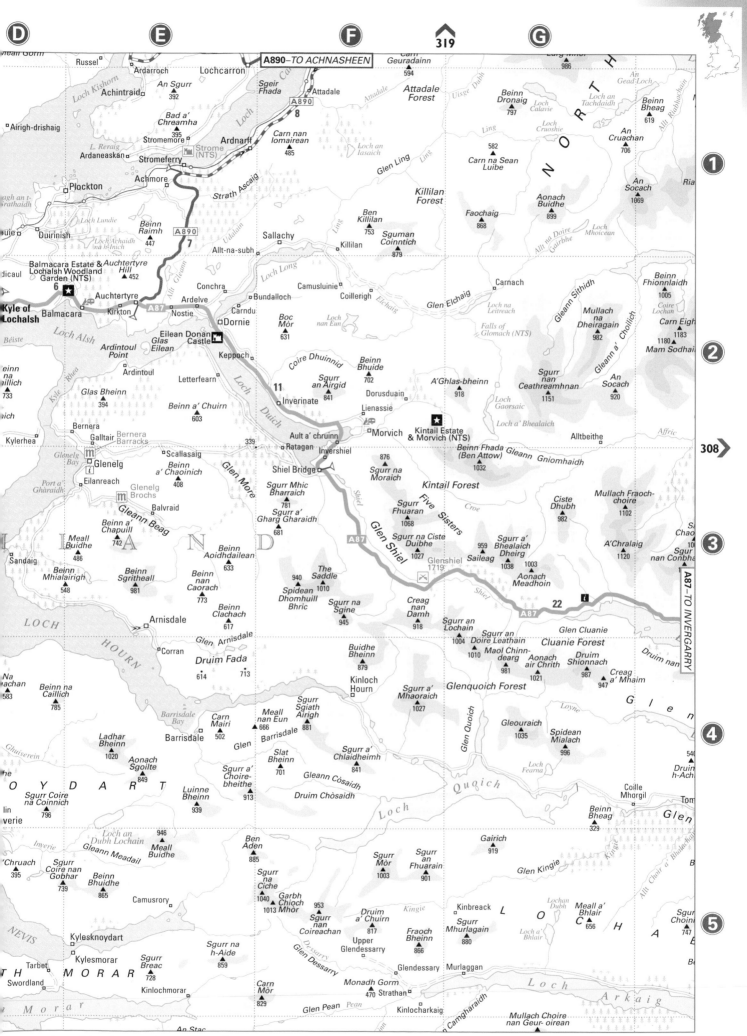

A890–TO ACHNASHEEN

Meall Gorm

Russel

Ardarroch   Lochcarron

An Sgurr   392

Achintraid

Sgeir Fhada

Attadale

A890

8

Carn Geuradainn   594

Larg Mhor   986

NORTH

Attadale Forest

Beinn Dronaig   797

Loch an Tachdaidh

Beinn Bheag   619

An Gead Loch

Airigh-drishaig

Bad a' Chreamha   395

Stromemore

Ardaneaskan

Ardnarff

Carn nan Iomairean   485

Loch an Iasaich

Uisge Dubh

Loch Calavie

Loch Cruoshie

An Cruachan   706

Ardneaskan

Stromeferry

Strome (NTS)

582

Carn na Sean Luibe

Glen Ling

Aonach Buidhe   899

Loch Mhoicean

Ria

Plockton

Achmore

A890

7

Strath Ascaig

Killilan Forest

Faochaig   868

Allt na Doire Gairbhe

agh an t-srathaidh

uje

Duirinish

L. Reraig

Loch Lundie

Beinn Raimh   447

A890

Loch Achaidh na h-Inich

Udalan

Sallachy

Allt-na-subh

Killilan

Ben Killilan   753

Sguman Coinntich   879

Balmacara Estate & Lochalsh Woodland Garden (NTS)

dicaul

6

Kyle of Lochalsh

Balmacara

Auchtertyre Hill   ▲ 452

Auchtertyre

Kirkton

Nostie

A87

Ardelve

Conchra

Bundalloch

Ardintoul Point

Glas Eilean

Eilean Donan Castle

Dornie

Carndu

Keppoch

Camusluinie

Coillerigh

Boc Mòr   631

Loch nan Eun

Glen Elchaig

Loch na Leitreach

Carnach

Falls of Glomach (NTS)

Gleann Sithidh

Beinn Fhionnlaidh   1005

Mullach na Dheiragain   982

Coire Lochan

Carn Eigh   1183

1180

Mam Sodhail

2

einn na aillich   733

Loch Alsh

Balmacara

Letterfearn

Glas Bheinn   394

Beinn a' Chuirn   603

Coire Dhuinnid

Sgurr an Airgid   841

Inverinate

11

Beinn Bhuide   702

Dorusduain

Lienassie

A'Ghlas-bheinn   918

Loch Gaorsaic

Loch a' Bhealaich

Sgurr nan Ceathreamhnan   1151

An Socach   920

Gleann a' Choilich

Affric

ich

Kylerhea

Bernera

Galltair

Bernera Barracks

Scallasaig

339

Ault a' chruinn

Ratagan

Morvich

Invershiel

Kintail Estate & Morvich (NTS)

Alltbeithe

Glenelg Bay

Glenelg

Eilanreach

Beinn a' Chaoinich   408

Shiel Bridge

Sgurr Mhic Bharraich   781

Sgurr na Moraich

Beinn Fhada (Ben Attow)   1032

Gleann Gniomhaidh

308

Glenelg Brochs

Balvraid

Sgurr a' Gharg Gharaidh   681

Sgurr Fhuaran   1068

Kintail Forest

Croe

Five Sisters

Gleann Beag

Beinn a' Chapuill   742

Beinn Aoidhdailean   633

The Saddle   1010

940

Sgurr na Ciste Duibhe   1027

Sgurr a' Bhealaich Dheirg   1038

959

Saileag   1003

Ciste Dhubh   982

Mullach Fraoch-choire   1102

A'Chralaig   1120

Sgurr nan Conbha

S Chao

10

3

Meall Buidhe   486

ISLAND

Beinn Mhialairigh   548

Beinn Sgritheall   981

Beinn nan Caorach   773

Spidean Dhomhuill Bhric

Sgurr na Sgine   945

Glenshiel 1719

Aonach Meadhoin

22

A87–TO INVERGARRY

Sandaig

Beinn Clachach   617

Arnisdale

Corran

Glen Arnisdale

Creag nan Damh   918

Sgurr an Lochain   1004

Sgurr an Doire Leathain   1010

Glen Cluanie

Druim nan

LOCH HOURN

Druim Fada   614   713

Buidhe Bheinn   879

Kinloch Hourn

Maol Chinn-dearg   981

Aonach air Chrith   1021

Cluanie Forest

Druim Shionnach   987

Creag a' Mhaim   947

Glen

4

Na achan   583

Beinn na Caillich   785

Barrisdale Bay

Carn Mairi   502

Meall nan Eun   666

Sgurr Sgiath Airigh   881

Sgurr a' Mhaoraich   1027

Glenquoich Forest

Gleouraich   1035

Loyne

Spidean Mialach   996

540

Druim h-Ach

Ladhar Bheinn   1020

Aonach Sgoilte   849

Barrisdale

Glen

Barrisdale

Slat Bheinn   701

Sgurr a' Chlaidheimh   841

Gleann Còsaidh

Loch Quoich

Loch Fearna

Coille Mhorgil

Tom

Glen

OYDART

Sgurr Coire na Coinnich   796

Luinne Bheinn   939

Sgurr a' Choire-bheithe   913

Druim Chòsaidh

Beinn Bheag   329

'Chruach   395

Sgurr Coire nan Gobhar   739

Beinn Bhuidhe   865

Loch an Dubh Lochain   946

Gleann Meadail

Meall Buidhe

Ben Aden   885

Sgurr na Ciche   1040

Sgurr Mòr   1003

Sgurr an Fhuarain   901

Gairich   919

Glen Kingie

Kinbreack

Lochan Dubh

Meall a' Bhlair   656

Sgurr Choinn   747

5

NEVIS

Kyleknoydart

Kylesmorar

Camusrory

Sgurr Breac   728

Sgurr na h-Aide   859

Garbh Chioch Mhor   1013

953

Sgurr nan Coireachan

Druim a' Chuirn   817

Upper Glendessarry

Kingie

Fraoch Bheinn   866

Sgurr Mhurlagain   880

Loch a' Bhlair

L O C H A

Tarbet

Swordland

MORAR

Kinlochmorar

Carn Mòr   829

Glen Dessarry

Glendessary

Murlaggan

Loch Arkaig

MORAR

An Stac

Glen Pean

Pean

Monadh Gorm   470

Strathan

Kinlocharkaig

Mullach Choire nan Geur-oirean

aig: Former home of the enigmatic writer Gavin Maxwell 1969) which he described as Camusfearna in his iographical 'Ring of Bright Water'. His grave is on the site of use which burned down in 1968. **Map ref. D3**

Eilean Donan Castle is used as a location for several famous films, including 'Highlander', 'Entrapment' and 'The World is not Enough'. It was originally built in the 13th century as a defence against the Vikings and was destroyed by three English warships during the 1715 Jacobite uprising. It was rebuilt in the 1930s and is today one of Scotland's most picturesque castles. **Map ref. E2 Also on page 122**

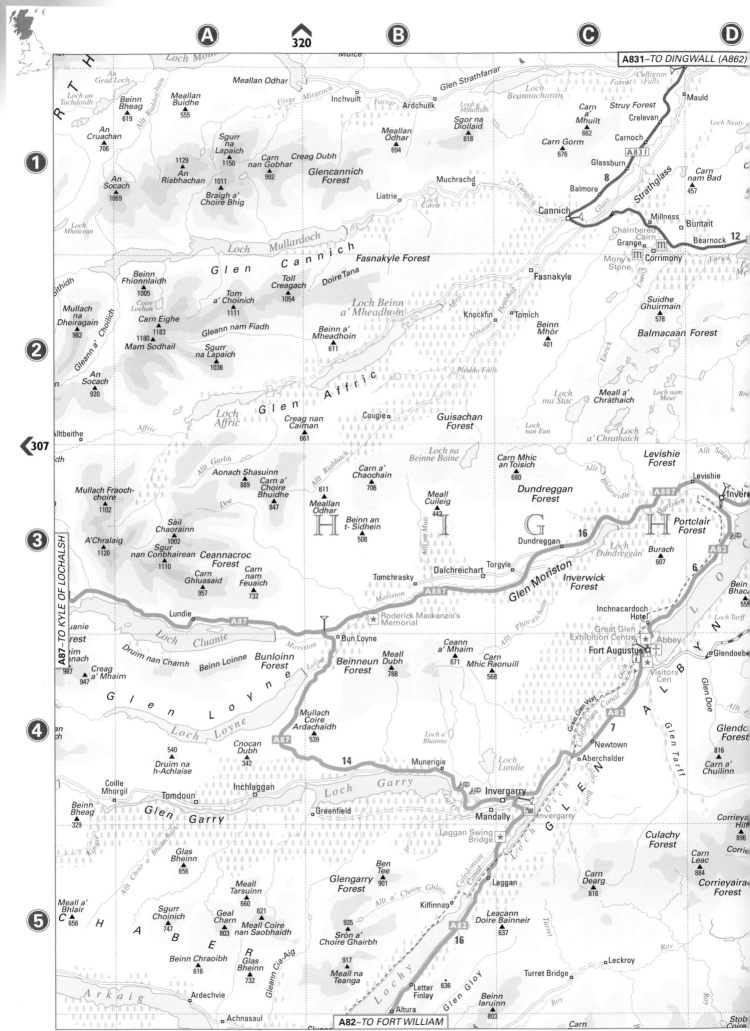

A831–TO DINGWALL (A862)

1

Loch Mone

An Gead-Loch

Loch an Tachdaidh

Beinn Bheag 619

Meallan Buidhe 555

Meallan Odhar

Muile

Glen Strathfarrar

Farrar

Culligran Falls

Mauld

An Cruachan 706

Allt Riabhachain

Uisge Misgeach

Inchvuilt

Farrar

Ardchuilk

Loch Beannacharan

Carn a' Mhuilt 662

Struy Forest

Crelevan

An Socach 1069

Sgurr na Lapaich 1129

Meallan Odhar 694

Sgor na Diollaid 818

Carn Gorm 676

Carnoch

Loch Neaty

Carn nam Bad 457

An Riabhachan 1011

Sgurr na Lapaich 1150

Carn nan Gobhar 992

Creag Dubh

Glencannich Forest

Muchrachd

Glassburn

Carnoch

A831

8

Balmore

Millness

Buntait

Braigh a' Choire Bhig

Liatrie

Loch Carrie

Cannich

Bearnock

12

Loch Mhoicean

Loch Mullardoch

Chambered Cairn

Grange

Corrimony

Mony's Stone

2

Bithidh

Beinn Fhionnlaidh 1005

Glen Cannich

Toll Creagach 1054

Doire Tana

Fasnakyle Forest

Fasnakyle

Suidhe Ghuirmain 578

Mullach na Dheiragain 982

Coire Lochan

Tom a' Choinich 1111

Loch Beinn a' Mheadhoin

Affric

Knockfin

Tomich

Beinn Mhòr 401

Balmacaan Forest

Carn Eighe 1183

Gleann nam Fiadh

Beinn a' Mheadhoin 611

Abhainn Deabhag

1180

Mam Sodhail

Sgurr na Lapaich 1036

Plodda Falls

Loch ma Stac

Meall a' Chràthaich

Loch nam Meur

Gleann a' Choilich

An Socach 920

Loch Affric

Glen Affric

Loch na Beinne Baine

Loch nan Eun

Loch a' Chrathaich

307

Alltbeithe

Affric

Allt Garbh

Creag nan Caiman 661

Cougie

Guisachan Forest

Levishie Forest

dh

Aonach Shasuinn 889

Allt Riabhach

Carn a' Chaochain 611

Carn Mhic an Toisich 680

Levishie

Mullach Fraoch-choire 1102

Carn a' Choire Bhuidhe 847

Meallan Odhar

Meall Cuileig 443

Dundreggan Forest

A887

Inver

Moriston

Portclair Forest

A'Chralaig 1120

Sàil Chaorainn 1002

Beinn an t-Sidhein 508

H

I

G

Dundreggan

16

Loch Dundreggan

Burach 607

A82

6

3

A87–TO KYLE OF LOCHALSH

Sgur nan Conbhairean 1110

Ceannacroc Forest

Carn Ghluasaid 957

Carn nam Feuaich 732

Allt na Muic

Tomchrasky

Dalchreichart

Torgyle

Glen Moriston

Inverwick Forest

Inchnacardoch Hotel

Beinn Bhac 55

Loch Tarff

987

Lundie

Creag a' Mhaim 947

A87

Loch Cluanie

Druim nan Cnamh

Moriston

Bun Loyne

Roderick Mackenzie's Memorial

Moriston

Allt Phocachain

Great Glen Exhibition Centre

Abbey

Glendoeb

uanie

Beinn Loinne

Bunloinn Forest

Loyne

Beinneun Forest

Meall Dubh 788

Ceann a' Mhaim

Carn Mhic Raonuill 568

Fort Augustus

Visitors Cen

Glendoeb

4

an

Glen Loyne

Loch Loyne

Mullach Coire Ardachaidh 539

Loch a' Bhainne

Great Glen Way

Caledonian Canal

Glendo Forest

Carn a' Chuilinn 816

ch

Creag a' Mhaim

Cnocan Dubh 342

A87

14

Munerigie

Loch Lundie

Newtown

A82

7

Oich

Coille Mhorgil

Druim na h-Achlaise 540

Inchlaggan

Loch Garry

Aberchalder

Carn Dearg 816

Corrieya Hill 896

Tomdoun

Greenfield

Carn

Invergarry

Glen Garry

Beinn Bheag 329

Glen Garry

Mandally

Invergarry

Culachy Forest

Corrie

Kingie

Allt Choir a' Bhlachaich

Laggan Swing Bridge

Caledonian Canal

Carn Leac 884

Corrieyaira Forest

5

Meall a' Bhlair 656

Glas Bheinn 656

Meall Tarsuinn 660

821

Glengarry Forest

Ben Tee 901

Laggan

Carn Dearg 816

C

Sgurr Choinich 747

Geal Charn 803

Meall Coire nan Saobhaidh

Allt a' Choire Ghlais

Kilfinnan

Leacann Doire Bainneir 637

Leckroy

Beinn Chraoibh 616

Glas Bheinn 732

935

Sròn a' Choire Ghairbh

A82

16

Roy

Ardechvie

Gleann Cia-Aig

917

Meall na Teanga

Glen Gloy

Turret Bridge

Achnasaul

Letter Finlay

636

Beinn Iaruinn 803

Arkaig

Altura

A82–TO FORT WILLIAM

Carn

Stob

A **B** **E** **R** **T** **H** **A** **B** **E** **R**

Invergarry: Historic home of the MacDonells of Glen Garry whose nearby castle was repeatedly attacked and finally razed in 1746 by the Duke of Cumberland. It remains today as a ruin. **Map ref. C4**

299

Loch Ness: John Cobb, the 'record breakers' record breaker', died here whilst attempting to beat the world speed record on 29th September 1952. Cobb had dedicated his life to speed records as a racing driver at Brooklands, then as holder of the world land speed record. He was recovered from the water following the accident and carried up the hill to Achnahannet where he died. Fifty years later his speedboat Crusader was located in 650 feet (200m) of water on the bed of Loch Ness. **Map ref. E2**

308

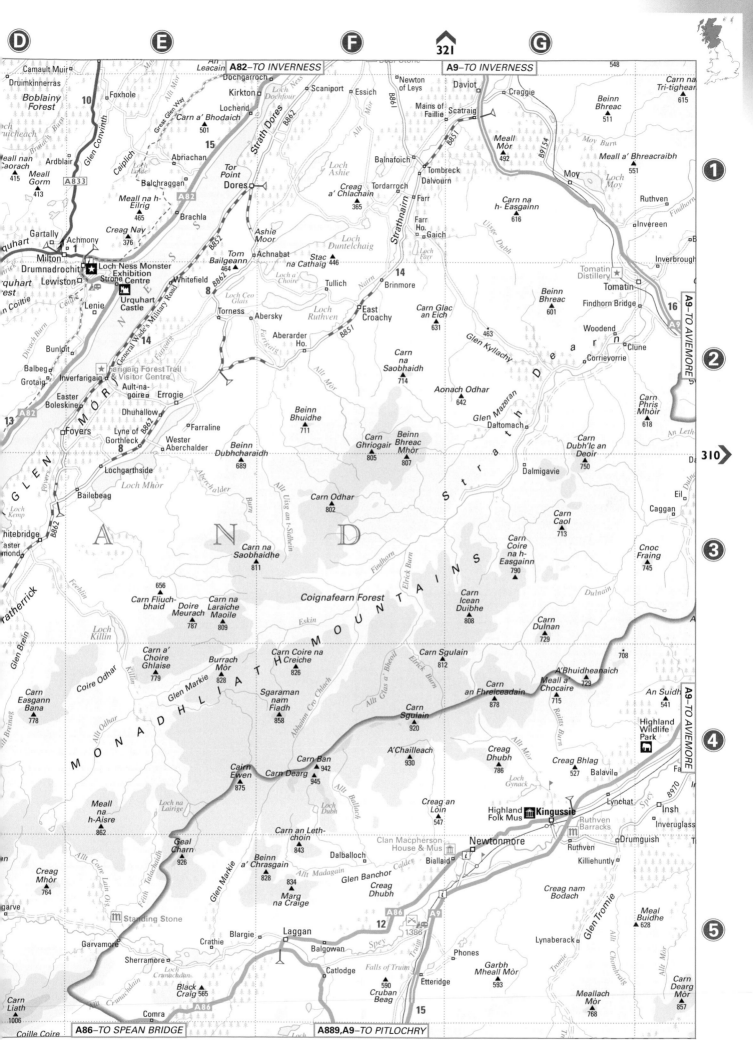

D **E** **F** **G**

A82-TO INVERNESS

A9-TO INVERNESS

1

2

310 ▶

3

A9-TO AVIEMORE

4

5

A86-TO SPEAN BRIDGE

A889,A9-TO PITLOCHRY

300 **Newtonmore:** The Spey valley is the heartland of the sport of Shinty. The advantages of being double-handed in the sport have led to the area having allegedly the highest proportion of left-handed golfers in the country: about half of the members of Newtonmore Golf Club play left-handed, and it regularly hosts the Scottish left-handed golf championships. **Map ref. G5**

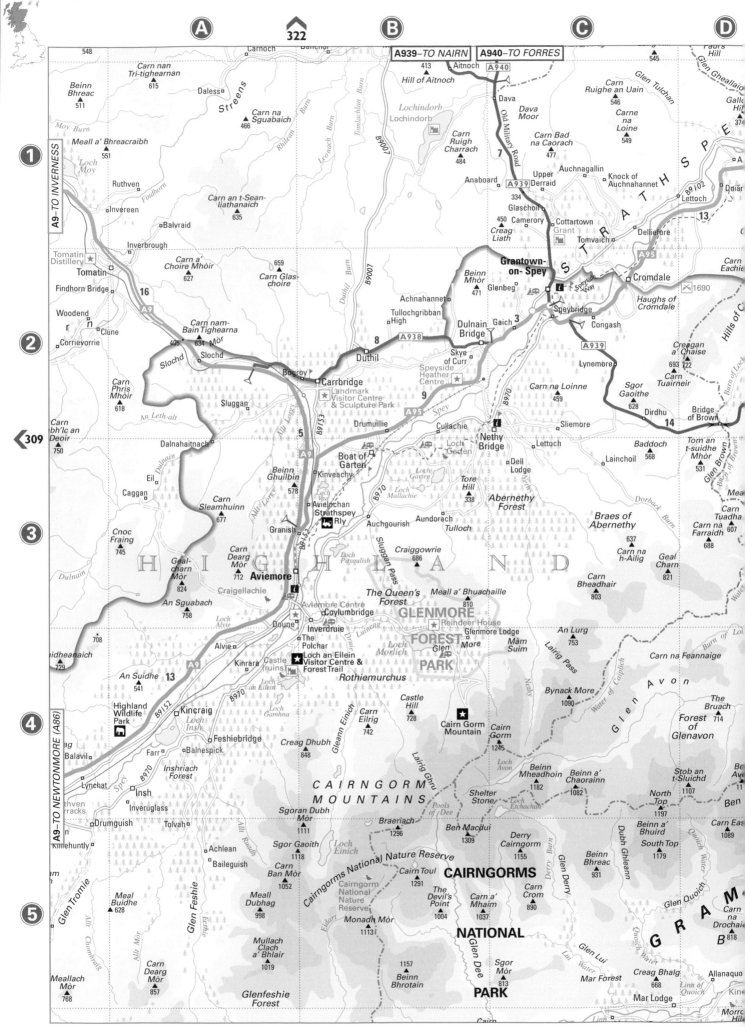

309

Findhorn: One of the best fishing rivers in Scotland, famous for its salmon and trout. It is said that 360 salmon were caught here in one day from a single pool. **Map ref. A1**

Cairngorms: Home of Brita... biggest Ski Centre with 28 r... and over 22 miles (35km) of ... **Map ref. B4**

301

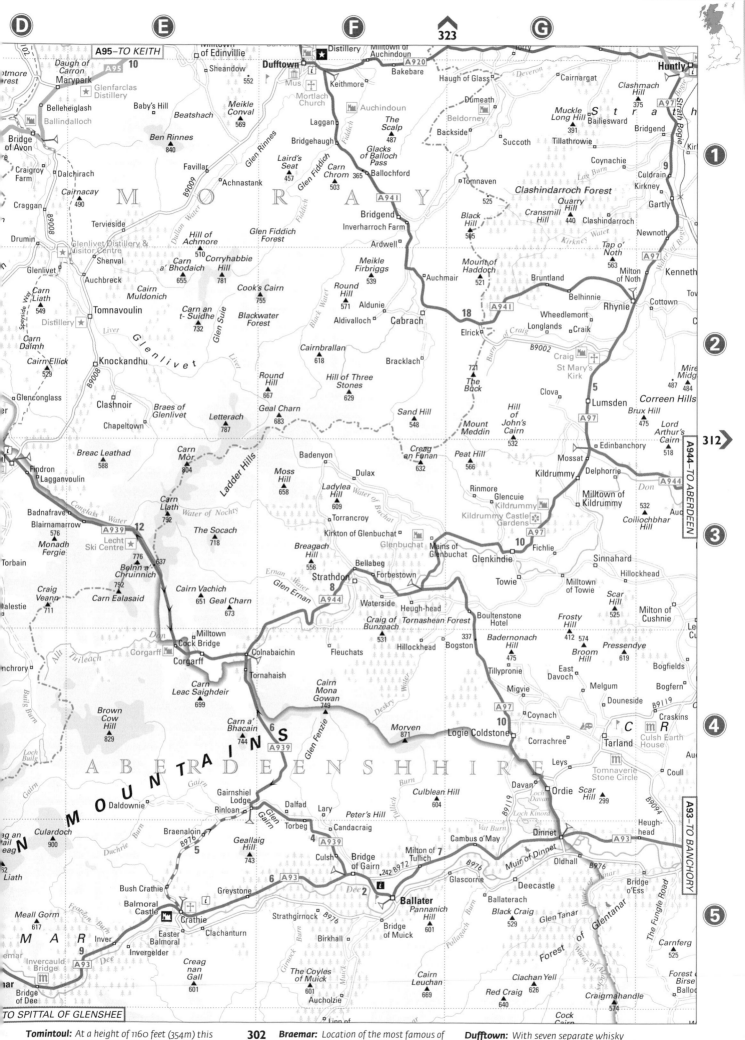

A95–TO KEITH

Daugh of Carron

Marypark

Glenfarclas Distillery

Belleheiglash

Ballindalloch

Bridge of Avon

Craigroy Farm

Dalchirach

Cairnacay 490

Craggan

Drumin

Glenlivet Distillery & Visitor Centre

Glenlivet

Auchbreck

Carn Liath 549

Tomnavoulin

Distillery

Carn Daimh

Cairn Ellick 529

Glenconglass

Clashnoir

Chapeltown

Findron

Lagganvoulin

Breac Leathad 588

Badnafrave

Blairnamarrow 576

Monadh Fergie

Torbain

Craig Veann 711

Balestie

Lecht Ski Centre

Beinn a' Chruinnich 792

Carn Ealasaid

Brown Cow Hill 829

Culardoch 900

Liath

Meall Gorm 617

MAR

Invercauld Bridge

Bridge of Dee

TO SPITTAL OF GLENSHEE

Mintown of Edinvillie

Sheandow

Dufftown

Mus

Mortlach Church

552

Baby's Hill

Beatshach

Meikle Conval 569

Ben Rinnes 840

Favillar

Achnastank

Hill of Achmore

Corryhabbie Hill 781

Carn a' Bhodaich 655

Cairn Muldonich

Carn an t- Suidhe 732

Blackwater Forest

Knockandhu

Braes of Glenlivet

Letterach 787

Carn Mòr 904

Ladder Hills

Carn Llath 792

The Socach 718

Carn Leac Saighdeir 699

Daldownie

Gairnshiel Lodge

Rinloan

Braenaloin

Geallaig Hill 743

Bush Crathie

Balmoral Castle

Easter Balmoral

Inver

Invergelder

Crathie

Clachanturn

Creag nan Gall 601

Laird's Seat 457

Glen Fiddich

Carn Chrom 503

Bridgehaugh

Ballochford

Glen Fiddich Forest

Hill of Achmore 510

Round Hill 571

Aldunie

Aldivalloch

Cairnbrallan 618

Round Hill 667

Hill of Three Stones 629

Geal Charn 683

Badenyon

Moss Hill 658

Ladylea Hill 609

Torrancroy

Kirkton of Glenbuchat

Breagach Hill 556

Bellabeg

Strathdon

Glen Ernan

Geal Charn 673

Cairn Vachich 651

Milltown

Cock Bridge

Corgarff

Tornahaish

Cairn Mona Gowan 749

Carn a' Bhacain 744

Glen Fenzie

Dalfad

Lary

Torbeg

Candacraig

Culsh

Bridge of Gairn

Greystone

Strathgirnock

Birkhall

Bridge of Muick

The Coyles of Muick 601

Aucholzie

Distillery

Milltown of Auchindoun

Keithmore

Auchindoun

Laggan

Glen Rinnes

Bridgend

Inverharroch Farm

Ardwell

Meikle Firbriggs 539

Auchmair

Cabrach

Bracklach

The Buck 721

Sand Hill 548

Mount Meddin

Creag an Fhuaran 632

Dulax

Water of Buchan

Glenbuchat

Mains of Glenbuchat

Forbestown

Waterside

Heugh-head

Craig of Bunzeach 531

Fleuchats

Hillockhead

Bogston 337

Deskry Water

Morven 871

Peter's Hill

Milton of Tullich

Cambus o'May

Glascorrie

A95

A941

A941

Glacks of Balloch Pass

487 The Scalp

Bakebare

Haugh of Glass

Dumeath

Beldorney

Backside

Succoth

Tomnaven 525

Black Hill 505

Mount of Haddoch 521

Elrick

Clova

Hill of John's Cairn 532

Peat Hill 566

Rinmore

Glencuie

Kildrummy

Kildrummy Castle Gardens

Glenkindie

Towie

Tornashean Forest

Boultenstone Hotel

Badernonach Hill 475

Tillypronie

Migvie

Logie Coldstone

Corrachree

Leys

Davan

Culblean Hill 604

Ordie

Dinnet

Milton of Tullich

Ballater

Pannanich Hill 601

Ballaterach

Black Craig 529

Clachan Yell

Red Craig 640

Cairn Leuchan 669

Huntly

Clashmach Hill 375

Cairnargat

Bridgend

Coynachie

Culdrain

Kirkney

Gartly

Newnoth

Clashindarroch Forest

Quarry Hill

Cransmill Hill 440

Clashindarroch

Kirkney Water

Bruntland

Belhinnie

Wheedlemont

Longlands

Craik

Craig

St Mary's Kirk

Lumsden

Brux Hill 475

Lord Arthur's Cairn 518

Correen Hills

Mire Midg 487 484

Edinbanchory

Mossat

Delphorrie

Milltown of Kildrummy

532

Coiliochbhar Hill

Fichlie

Sinnahard

Hillockhead

Milltown of Towie

Scar Hill 525

Milton of Cushnie

Frosty Hill 412 574

Broom Hill 619

Pressendye

East Davoch

Coynach

Melgum

Douneside

Tarland

Culsh Earth House

Tomnaverie Stone Circle

Coull

Craskins

Bogfern

Bogfields

Scar Hill 299

Heugh-head

Deecastle

Oldhall

Bridge o'Ess

The Fungle Road

Glen Tanar

Forest of Glentanar

Carnferg 525

Craigmahandle 574

Cock Cairn

Strath Bogie

Bailiesward

Milton of Noth

Kenneth

Cottown

Tap o' Noth 563

Rhynie

A97

A944–TO ABERDEEN

312

A93–TO BANCHORY

Tomintoul: At a height of 1160 feet (354m) this claims to be the highest village in the Scottish Highlands. The A939 from here across the Lecht pass to Cock Bridge (**Map ref. E4**) is frequently closed in winter. **Map ref. D3**

302

Braemar: Location of the most famous of the Highland Games. The Braemar Gathering has a history going back almost 1,000 years and is always held on the first Saturday in September. **Map ref. D5**

Dufftown: With seven separate whisky distilleries, the earliest of which dates back to 1823, Dufftown is described as the Malt Whisky Capital of Scotland. **Map ref. F1**

311

A96-TO ELGIN

A947-TO BANFF

Ⓐ   Ⓑ   Ⓒ   Ⓓ

Huntly

Drumblade   Corse   B9001   Kirktown of Auchterless   Backhill

Fyvie Castle (NTS)   Woodhead

Mosshead   Brideswell   Badenscoth   Gordonstown   Fyvie

Clashmach Hill 375   Slioch   Ythanwells   Logie Newton   Rothiebrisbane   Greenmyre

Bargat   Bailiesward   Denend   Millburn   Redhill   Blackford   Rothienorman   Petty   Cromblet   Bartho Chapel

S t r a t h b o g i e   Thomastown   Hill of Tillymorgan 381   Fisherford   St Katherines   17   South Flobbets   Silverm

Bridgend   Kirkstile   Winds Eye 314   Bainshole   Skares   Cairnhill   Springleys   Core Hill 245   The Banking   Balgove

1   Coynachie   9   Culdrain   Backburn   Glens of Foudland   Kirkton of Culsalmond   Colpy   Tocher   Newseat   Folla Rule   Cross of Jackston   South Blackbog   Tulloch

Kirkney   Gartly   Wishach Hill 419   Hill of Foudland 467   Meikle Wartle   11   Jackstown   F o r m a

Clashindarroch   Cults   Knockandy Hill 434   Slack   Largie   Wrangham   Bonnyton   Kirkton of Rayne   Pitinnan   Mounie Castle   Glengarioch Distillery

Tap o' Noth 563   Newnoth   Leith Hall (NTS)   Wardhouse   Aulton   Upper Boddam   Greenhall   Old Rayne   Durno   Daviot   Whitefield   Fingask   1308   Oldmeldrum

Milton of Noth   Kennethmont   Glanderston   Picardy Stone   The Shevock   Mains of Glack   Hill of Barra 193   Mill of Kingoodie

Rhynie   Cottown   Towie   Ardlair   Rothney   Insch   Ardoyne   Westhall   13   Whiteford   Milton of Inveramsay   1411   Kirkton of Bourtie   Hatton

Craik   Clatt   Duncanston   Hill of Christ's Kirk   Christkirk   Ryehill   Oyne   Pitcaple   Balhalgardy   Hillbrae   Whit

2   Mary's   5   Lumsden   New Leslie   Old Leslie   Kirkton   G a r i o c h   Archaeolink Prehistory Park   Maiden Stone   Newmill   Neth

Mire of Midgates 484   Whitehaugh Forest   Leslie   Auchleven   Pittodrie Ho.   Chapel of Garioch   Inverurie   Port Elphinstone   Balbithan

311   Brux Hill 475   Suie Hill 415   Knock Saul 412   Black Hill 430   Bennachie   Mither Tap 518   Easter Aquhorthies Stone Circle   Kinkell Church

Lord Arthur's Cairn 518   Correen Hills   Millburn   Muckletown   A B E R D E E N S H   Balbithan

Edinbanchory   Tepersie Castle   Redhouse   Glenton   Millstone Hill 408   Bograxie   Burnhervie   Thainstone   Tavelty   Wester Fintray

Delphorrie   Tullynessle   Keig   Woodend   Kemnay Forest   Overton   Dalmadilly   Clovenstone   Balbithan

6   Milltown of Kildrummy   Grampian Transport Mus   Montgarrie   Bankhead   Rorandle   Grantlodge   Fetternear Ho.   Kintore

Auchintoul   532   Bridge of Alford   Haughton House   Gateside   Cairn William 448   Pitfichie   Kemnay   Cottown   Denhead

Coiliochbhar Hill   Alford   Pitfichie Forest   Monymusk   Leschangie   Kinellar

3   Sinnahard   Aslou   Dorsell   Kingsford   Howe of Alford   Whitehouse   Pitmunie   Craigearn   Lauchintilly   Leylodge   12   Blackburn

Hillockhead   Ley   Bridgeton   Kirkton   Todlachie   Black Hill   Castle Fraser (NTS)   Burnside   Blackchambers

Towie   Scar Hill 525   Muir of Fowlis   Tillyfourie   Tillycairn Castle 185   Sauchen   Lyne of Skene   Clinterty

Milton of Cushnie   Muirhead   Ardgowse   Little Ley   Ordhead   24   Achath   Old Kinnernie   Dunecht   East Auchronie

574   Pressendye 619   Leochel-Cushnie   Craigievar Castle (NTS)   Tillyfour   Corrennie Forest   Shiels   Mains of Linton   Lyne   Barmekin Hill 274   Loch of Skene

Broom Hill   Bogfields   Kintocher   Corrennie Moor   Benaquhallie 494   Corsindae   Comers   Kirkton of Skene   Elrick

Melgum   Bogfern   Oldmill   Tullochvenus   Bankhead   Echt   Garlogie   Cairnie   We

4   Douneside   Collmuir   Craiglich 476   Glenshalg   Perkhill   Tillybirloch   Lapidary Workshops   Redhill   Wester Ord

C R O M A R   Craskins   Tornaveen   Drumlasie   Auchorrie   South Kirkton   Landerberry   Cullerlie Stone Circle   Benthoul

Tarland   Culsh Earth House   Wartle   Lumphanan   East Learney   Midmar Forest   The Birks   Milton of Cullerlie   Hardgate   Craigton

Tomnaverie Stone Circle   Milton of Auchinhove   Cairnbeathie   Peel Ring   Hill of Fare 471   1562   Drum Castle (NTS)   Petercult

Coull   Cill 299   Mortlich 380   Kincardine O'Neil   Craigmyle Ho.   Milton of Campfield   Raemoir Ho.   Hirna   Glashmore   Mains of Drum   Craiglug

5   A93-TO BALLATER   Heughhead   Rosehill   16   Torphins   14   Mid Beltie   Glassel   Kennerty   Brathens   Drumoak   Upper Muirskie   Denside

Aboyne   Birsemore   Cordach   Tillydrine   Backhill of Trustach   Bridge of Canny   East Mains   Upper Lochton   Crathes Castle (NTS)   West Park   Crathes   Kirkton of Durris

Bridge o'Ess   Birse   Potarch   Allancreich   Inchmarlo   The Neuk   3   Myrebird

Balfour   Marywell   Tom's Cairn 310   Blackhall Forest   Hill of Goauch 337   Auchattie   Bridge of Feugh   Crossroads   Durris Forest   Borrowfield

Glentanar   The Fungle Road   Ballogie   Finzean   Baulds   Drumhead   Whitestone   Blackness   Scolty 299   Invery Ho.   Blairydryne   Darnford   Cairn-mon-earn 378   266   Meikle Carewe H

Carnferg 525   Glencat   Lamahip 404   Percie   Strachan   Westerton   Mongour   A957

Craigmahandle 574   Forest of Birse   Ballochan   Bridge of Bogendreip   Greendams   Craig of Dalfro 317   A957-TO STONEHAVEN

Banchory

Huntly: George MacDonald, novelist, poet and preacher was born here in 1824. His works of fantasy and fairy tales are said to have influenced the work of J R R Tolkien and C S Lewis. He died in Italy in 1905. **Map ref. A1**

Tillyfour: In the 1820s William McCombie an others in this area perfected the breeding of th 'Aberdeen Angus' which is acknowledged as o the best cattle breeds in the world. **Map ref.**

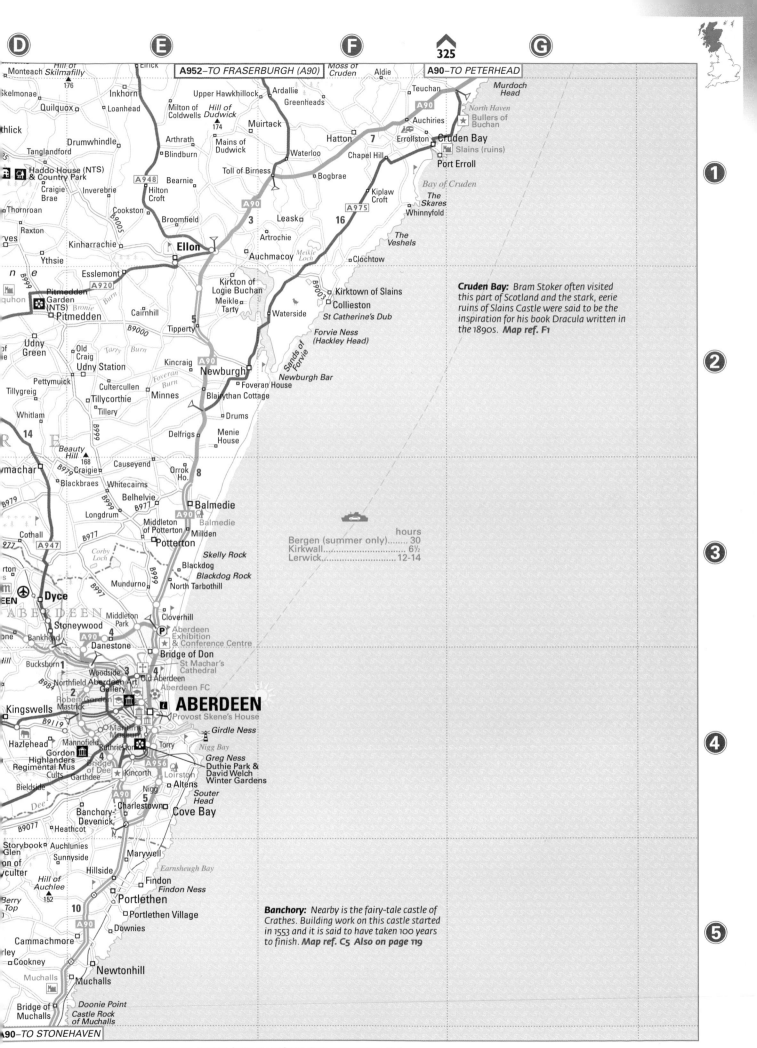

A952–TO FRASERBURGH (A90)   Moss of Cruden

A90–TO PETERHEAD

Einick
Monteach *Hill of Skilmafilly*
176
Skelmonae
Quilquox Inkhorn
Loanhead
thlick
Drumwhindle
Tanglandford
Haddo House (NTS) & Country Park
Craigie Brae
Thornroan
Inverebrie
Raxton
Kinharrachie
ves
Ythsie

Upper Hawkhillock
Milton of Coldwells *Hill of Dudwick*
174
Arthrath
Blindburn
Bearnie
Hilton Croft
Cookston
Broomfield

Ardallie
Greenheads
Muirtack
Mains of Dudwick
Waterloo
Toll of Birness
Bogbrae

Teuchan
Aldie
Auchiries
Hatton 7
Errollston
Chapel Hill
Kiplaw Croft

Murdoch Head
North Haven ★ Bullers of Buchan
Cruden Bay
🏛 Slains (ruins)
Port Erroll

Ellon
A90 3
Leask
Artrochie
16
A975
Bay of Cruden
The Skares
Whinnyfold
The Veshels

Esslemont
Pitmedden Garden (NTS)
quhon *Bronie*
Pitmedden
Cairnhill

Kirkton of Logie Buchan
Meikle Tarty
Waterside
B9003

Kirktown of Slains
Collieston
St Catherine's Dub

Udny Green
Old Craig
Udny Station
Kincraig
Newburgh
Foveran House
Foveran Burn
Tipperty 5
Minnes

Forvie Ness (Hackley Head)
Sands of Forvie
Newburgh Bar

Cruden Bay: Bram Stoker often visited this part of Scotland and the stark, eerie ruins of Slains Castle were said to be the inspiration for his book Dracula written in the 1890s. **Map ref. F1**

Pettymuick
Tillygreig
Cultercullen
Tillycorthie
Tillery
Whitlam

Blairythan Cottage
Drums
Delfrigs
Menie House

Beauty Hill
168
Craigie
Causeyend
Orrok Ho. 8
Blackbraes Whitecairns
Belhelvie
Longdrum
Balmedie
A90 Balmedie
Middleton of Potterton Millden
Potterton

vmachar
14
Cothall
A947
Corby Loch
Mundurno
Skelly Rock
Blackdog
Blackdog Rock
North Tarbothill

Bergen (summer only)........ 30
Kirkwall............................. 6½
Lerwick......................... 12-14
hours

rton
Dyce
Stoneywood
Bankhead
ABERDEEN
Middleton Park
Cloverhill
Aberdeen Exhibition & Conference Centre

Bucksburn 1
Woodside 3
Northfield Aberdeen Art Gallery
Robert Gord
2
Kingswells
Mastrick
B9119

Bridge of Don
St Machar's Cathedral
Old Aberdeen
Aberdeen FC
ABERDEEN
Provost Skene's House

Hazlehead
Mannofield
Gordon Highlanders Regimental Mus
Cults Garthdee
Bieldside
Mastrick
Ruthrieston
Torry
Bridge of Dee
Kincorth
Loirston
Altens
Nigg
Charlestown

Girdle Ness
Nigg Bay
Greg Ness
Duthie Park & David Welch Winter Gardens
Souter Head
Cove Bay

Banchory Devenick
Heathcot
B9077

Storybook Glen
on of yculter
Auchlunies
Sunnyside
Hillside
Hill of Auchlee
152
Findon
Findon Ness
Portlethen
Earnsheugh Bay
Marywell

Banchory: Nearby is the fairy-tale castle of Crathes. Building work on this castle started in 1553 and it is said to have taken 100 years to finish. **Map ref. C5 Also on page 119**

Berry Top
10
Portlethen Village
Downies
Cammachmore
rley
Cookney
Muchalls
Newtonhill
Muchalls
Bridge of Muchalls
Doonie Point
Castle Rock of Muchalls

A90–TO STONEHAVEN

Kemnay: Famous for its magnificent silver-grey granite which was quarried here for generations before the main quarry closed in 1960. Kemnay granite was used in building many of the bridges over the River Thames. **Map ref. C3**

1 2 3 4 5

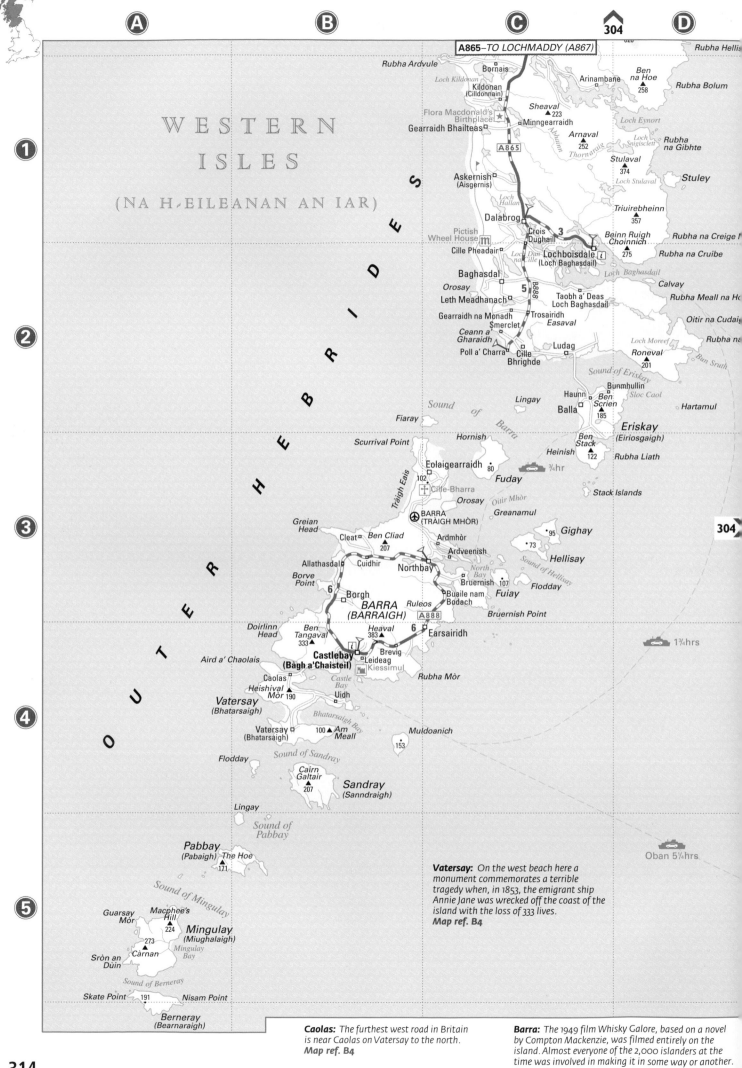

WESTERN
ISLES

(NA H-EILEANAN AN IAR)

OUTER HEBRIDES

A865—TO LOCHMADDY (A867)

Rubha Ardvule

Bornais

Loch Kildonan

Kildonan
(Cilldonnain)

Arinambane

Ben
na Hoe
258

Rubha Bolum

Rubha Hellis

Flora Macdonald's
Birthplace

Gearraidh Bhailteas

Sheaval
223

Minngearraidh

Loch Eynort

A865

Arnaval
252

Loch
Thornaraig

Rubha
na Gibhte

Askernish
(Aisgernis)

Stulaval
374

Triuirebheinn
357

Stuley

Dalabrog

Crois
Dughaill

Loch
Hallan

3

Beinn Ruigh
Choinnich
275

Rubha na Creige M

Pictish
Wheel House

Cille Pheadair

Lochboisdale
(Loch Baghasdail)

Rubha na Cruibe

Baghasdal

Loch
na Cille

Loch Baghasdail

Calvay

Orosay

Leth Meadhanach

5

Taobh a' Deas
Loch Baghasdail

Rubha Meall na Ho

Oitir na Cudaig

Gearraidh na Monadh

Trosairidh

Easaval

Ceann a'
Gharaidh

Smerclet

Ludag

Loch Moreef

Rubha na

Poll a' Charra

Cille
Bhrighde

Roneval
201

Bun Sruth

Sound of Eriskay

Bunmhullin

Lingay

Haunn

Ben
Scrien
185

Sloc Caol

Rubha na

Fiaray

Sound

of

Balla

Eriskay
(Eiriosgaigh)

Hartamul

Barra

Hornish

Ben
Stack
122

Heinish

Rubha Liath

Scurrival Point

Eolaigearraidh

80

Fuday

¾hr

Traigh Eais

102

Cille-Bharra

Orosay

Stack Islands

Greian
Head

BARRA
(TRÀIGH MHÒR)

Oitir Mhòr

Greanamul

Gighay
95

Cleat

Ben Cliad
207

Ardmhòr

73

Allathasdal

Cuidhir

Northbay

Ardveenish

Hellisay

Sound of Hellisay

Borve
Point

6

Borgh

North
Bay

Bruernish
107

Fuiay

Flodday

BARRA
(BARRAIGH)

Ruleos

Buaile nam
Bodach

Doirlinn
Head

Ben
Tangaval
333

Heaval
383

6

Earsairidh

A888

Bruernish Point

1¾hrs

Aird a' Chaolais

Castlebay
(Bàgh a'Chaisteil)

Leideag

Brevig

Kiessimul

Rubha Mòr

Caolas

Heishival
Mòr 190

Uidh

Castle
Bay

Vatersay
(Bhatarsaigh)

Bhatarsaigh Bay

Muldoanich

Vatersay
(Bhatarsaigh)

100 Am
Meall

153

Flodday

Sound of Sandray

Lingay

Sound of
Pabbay

Cairn
Galtair
207

Sandray
(Sanndraigh)

Oban 5¾hrs

Pabbay
(Pabaigh)

The Hoe
171

Sound of Mingulay

Vatersay: On the west beach here a
monument commemorates a terrible
tragedy when, in 1853, the emigrant ship
Annie Jane was wrecked off the coast of the
island with the loss of 333 lives.
Map ref. B4

Guarsay
Mòr

Macphee's
Hill
224

Mingulay
(Miughalaigh)

Sròn an
Dùin

273

Càrnan

Mingulay
Bay

Skate Point

191

Nisam Point

Sound of Berneray

Berneray
(Bearnaraigh)

Caolas: The furthest west road in Britain
is near Caolas on Vatersay to the north.
Map ref. B4

Barra: The 1949 film Whisky Galore, based on a novel
by Compton Mackenzie, was filmed entirely on the
island. Almost everyone of the 2,000 islanders at the
time was involved in making it in some way or another.
Map ref. B3

304

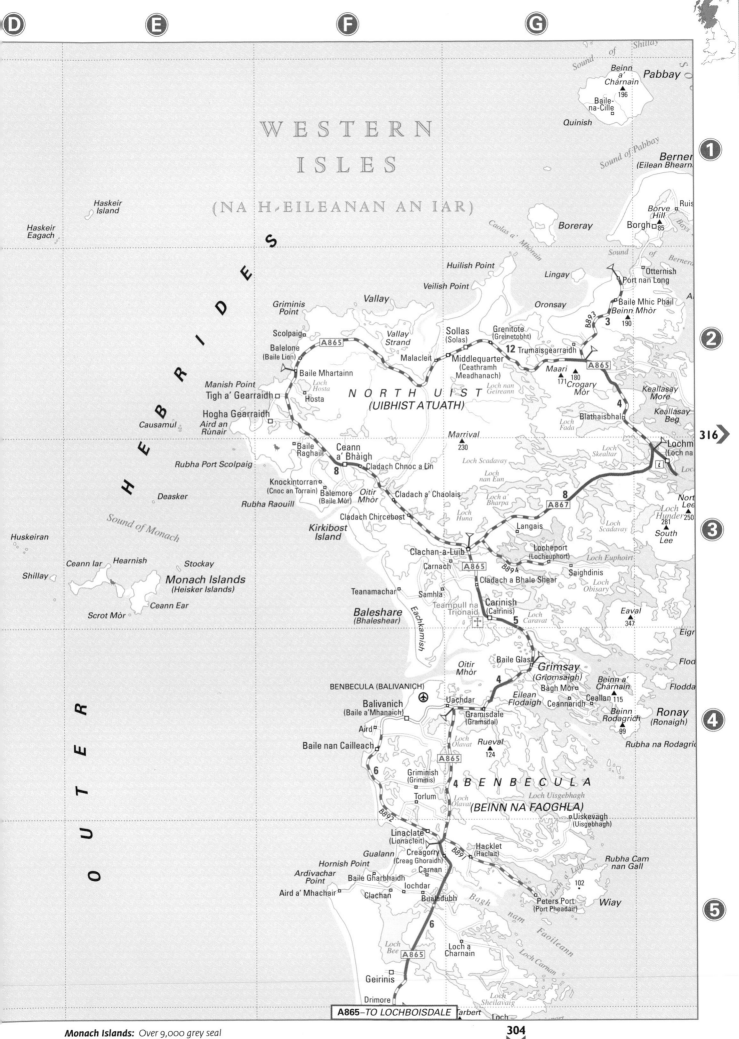

**WESTERN
ISLES**

(NA H-EILEANAN AN IAR)

HEBRIDES

OUTER

Sound of Shillay

Beinn a' Chárnain 196

Baile-na-Cille

Quinish

Pabbay

Sound of Pabbay

Berner (Eilean Bhearn)

Haskeir Island

Haskeir Eagach

Sound *of* *Bernera*

Borve Hill

Ruis

Borgh 85

Boreray

Lingay

Oronsay

Huilish Point

Veilish Point

Otternish
Port nan Long

Baile Mhic Phail
Beinn Mhòr

2

Valley

Griminis Point

Scolpaig

Balelone (Baile Lìon)

A865

Baile Mhartainn

Manish Point
Tigh a' Gearraidh

Valley Strand

Loch Hosta

Hosta

Sollas (Solas)

Malacleit

Grenitote (Greinetobht)

Middlequarter (Ceathramh Meadhanach)

12 Trumaisgearraidh

Maari 171

180

A865

Crogary Mòr

3 190

B893

Blathaisbhal

4

Keallasay More

Keallasay Beg

Lochm (Loch na

Hogha Gearraidh
Aird an Rùnair

NORTH UIST
(UIBHIST A TUATH)

Marrival 230

Loch nan Geireann

Loch Fada

316

Causamul

Baile Raghaill

Ceann a' Bhàigh

Cladach Chnoc a Lin

8

Loch Scadavay

Loch Skealtar

i

Loch

Rubha Port Scolpaig

Deasker

Knockintorran (Cnoc an Torrain)

Balemore (Baile Mòr)

Oitir Mhòr

Cladach a' Chaolais

Loch nan Eun

Loch a' Bharpa

8

A867

Nort Lee

South Lee

Rubha Raouill

Cladach Chircebost

Kirkibost Island

Loch Huna

Langais

Loch Scadavay

Loch Hunder 281

250

Huskeiran

Sound of Monach

Shillay

Ceann Iar

Hearnish

Stockay

Monach Islands (Heisker Islands)

Ceann Ear

Scrot Mòr

Clachan-a-Luib

Carnach

A865

B894

Locheport (Locheuphort)

Loch Euphoirt

Saighdinis

Loch Obisary

Teanamachar

Samhla

Cladach a Bhale Shear

Teampull na Trionaid

Carinish (Cairinis)

Eaval 347

Eigr

Baleshare (Bhaleshear)

Loch Caravat

5

Baile Glas

Grimsay (Griomsaigh)

Flod

Oitir Mhòr

Bàgh Mòr

Beinn a' Chárnain

Ceallan 115

Flodda

4

Eilean Flodaigh

Ceannaridh

Beinn Rodagrich 99

Ronay (Ronaigh)

BENBECULA (BALIVANICH) ✈

Uachdar

Gramisdale (Gramsdal)

Rubha na Rodagric

Balivanich (Baile a'Mhanaich)

Aird

Loch Olavat

Rueval 124

Baile nan Cailleach

A865

6

Griminish (Griminis)

4 **BENBECULA**

Loch Uisgebhagh

Torlum

Loch Olavat

(BEINN NA FAOGHLA)

B892

Uiskevagh (Uisgebhagh)

Linaclate (Lionacleit)

Gualann

Creagorry (Creag Ghoraidh)

Hacklet (Haclait)

Rubha Cam nan Gall

Hornish Point

Ardivachar Point

Baile Gharbhaidh

Carnan

B891

102

Wiay

Aird a' Mhachair

Clachan

Iochdar

Bualadubh

Bagh nam Faoileann

Peters Port (Port Pheadair)

6

Loch Bee

A865

Loch a Charnain

Loch Caman

Geirinis

Drimore

Loch Sheilavaig

A865–*TO LOCHBOISDALE*

Tarbert

Loch

Monach Islands: Over 9,000 grey seal
pups are born on these islands every year.
Map ref. E3

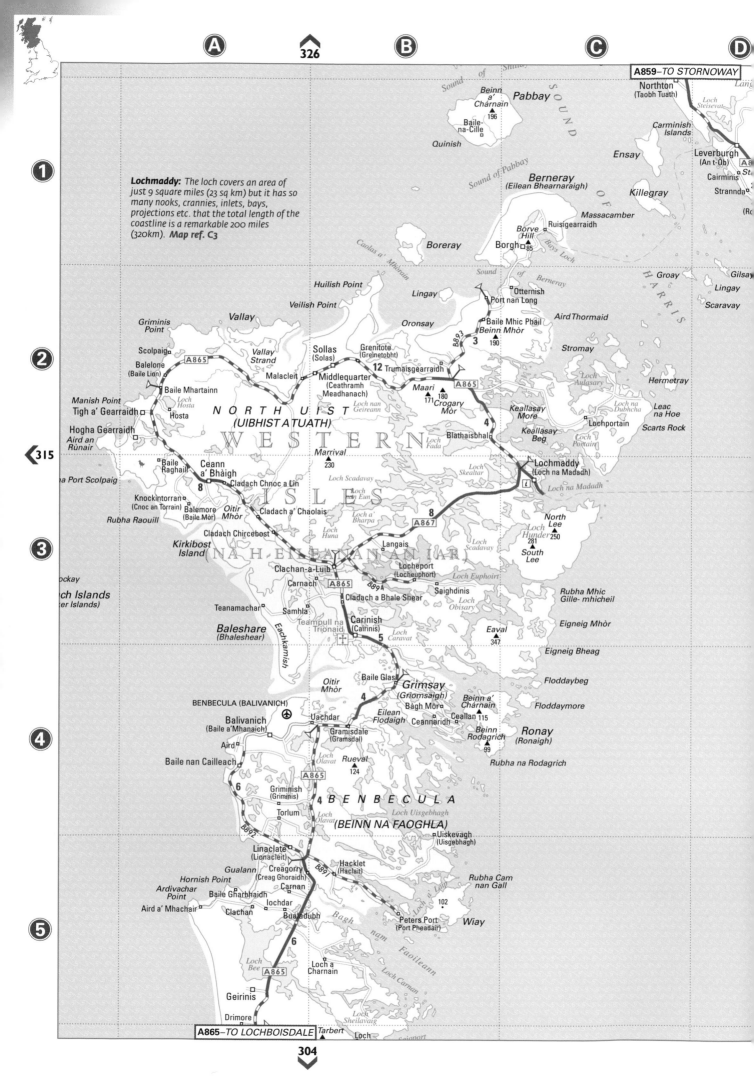

A859–TO STORNOWAY

1

Lochmaddy: The loch covers an area of
just 9 square miles (23 sq km) but it has so
many nooks, crannies, inlets, bays,
projections etc. that the total length of the
coastline is a remarkable 200 miles
(320km). **Map ref. C3**

Pabbay

Beinn a' Chárnain
196

Baile-na-Cille

Quinish

Berneray
(Eilean Bhearnaraigh)

Sound of Pabbay

Northton (Taobh Tuath)

Carminish Islands

Leverburgh (An t-Òb)

Cairminis

Strannda

Ensay

Killegray

HARRIS

Groay

Gilsay

Lingay

Scaravay

2

Huilish Point

Veilish Point

Vallay

Griminis Point

Scolpaig

Balelone (Baile Lion)

Baile Mhartainn

Manish Point

Tigh a' Gearraidh

Hogha Gearraidh

Aird an Rùnair

Valley Strand

Malacleit

Hosta

Loch Hosta

A865

Sollas (Solas)

Middlequarter (Ceathramh Meadhanach)

Grenitote (Greinetobht)

12

Trumaisgearraidh

Oronsay

Lingay

Beinn Mhòr
190

Baile Mhic Phail

B893

3

Massacamber

Ruisigearraidh

Borve Hill

Borgh
85

Otternish

Port nan Long

Aird Thormaid

Stromay

Hermetray

Bay's Loch

Sound of Berneray

Maari
171

Crogary Mòr
180

A865

Keallasay More

Keallasay Beg

Loch Aulasary

Loch na Dubhcha

Scarts Rock

Leac na Hoe

NORTH UIST (UIBHIST A TUATH)

WESTERN ISLES

Marrival
230

Loch Fada

4

Blathaisbhal

Lochportain

Loch Pórtain

315

Baile Raghaill

Ceann a' Bhàigh

Cladach Chnoc a Lin

8

Knockintorran (Cnoc an Torrain)

Balemore (Baile Mòr)

Oitir Mhòr

Cladach a' Chaolais

Rubha Raouill

Cladach Chircebost

Kirkibost Island

(NA H-EILEANAN AN IAR)

Loch Scadavay

Loch nan Eun

Loch a' Bharpa

Loch Huna

Langais

Loch Skealtar

Loch Euphoirt

Lochmaddy (Loch na Madadh)

Loch na Madadh

North Lee

Loch Hunder
281
250

South Lee

8

A867

3

Clachan-a-Luib

Carnach

A865

Samhla

Teanamachar

Baleshare (Bhaleshear)

Teampull na Trionaid

Eachkamish

Lochport (Locheuphort)

Cladach a Bhale Shear

Saighdinis

Loch Obisary

Carinish (Cairinis)

Rubha Mhic Gille- mhicheil

Eigneig Mhòr

Eaval
347

Eigneig Bheag

Loch Caravat

5

ch Islands (er Islands)

Balivanich (Baile a'Mhanaich)

BENBECULA (BALIVANICH)

Uachdar

Aird

Baile nan Cailleach

6

Griminish (Griminis)

Torlum

A865

B892

Oitir Mhòr

Baile Glas

Grimsay (Griomsaigh)

Bàgh Mòr

Eilean Flodaigh

Ceannaridh

Gramisdale (Gramsdal)

Loch Olavat

Rueval
124

Ceallan
115

Beinn a' Chárnain

Beinn Rodagrich
99

Floddaybeg

Floddaymore

Ronay (Ronaigh)

Rubha na Rodagrich

4

4

BENBECULA (BEINN NA FAOGHLA)

Loch Olavat

Loch Uisgebhagh

Uiskevagh (Uisgebhagh)

Linaclate (Lionacleit)

Gualann

Hornish Point

Ardivachar Point

Baile Gharbhaidh

Aird a' Mhachair

Creagorry (Creag Ghoraidh)

Carnan

Iochdar

Clachan

Bualadubh

Hacklet (Haclait)

B891

Rubha Cam nan Gall

Loch a' Laip

102

Peters Port (Port Pheadair)

Wiay

Bagh nam Faoileann

5

6

A865

Loch Bee

Geirinis

Loch a Charnain

Loch Carnan

Drimore

A865–TO LOCHBOISDALE

Tarbert

Loch Sheilavaig

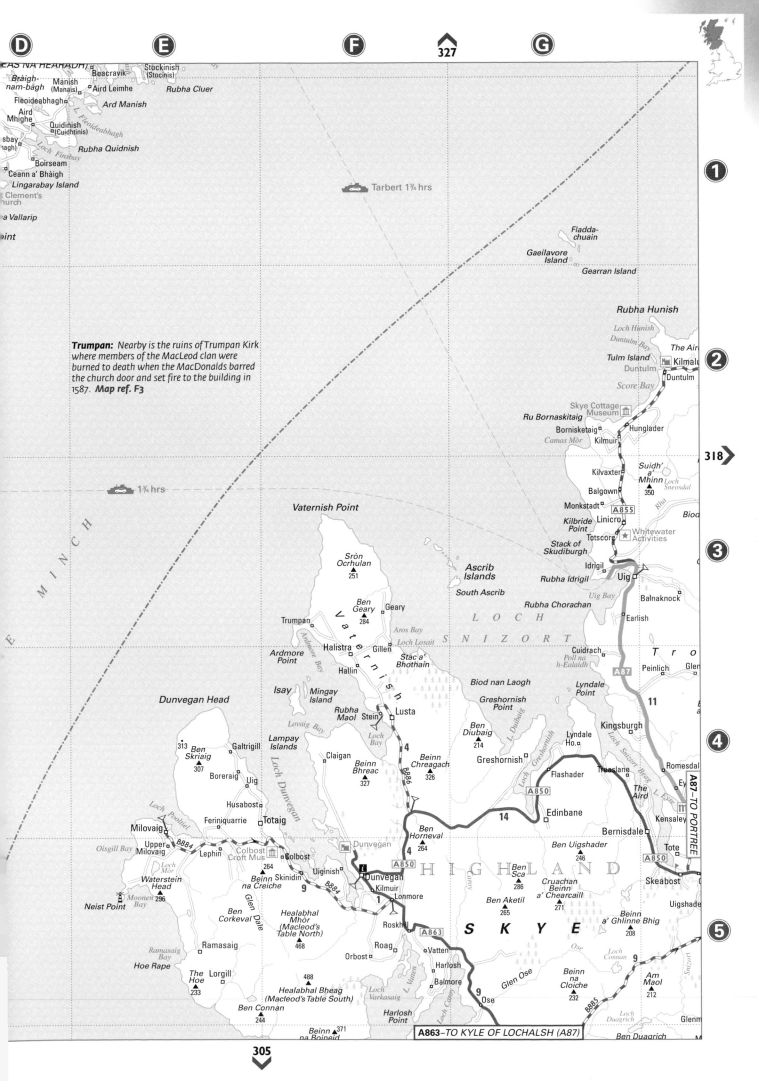

1

Tarbert 1¾ hrs

Trumpan: Nearby is the ruins of Trumpan Kirk where members of the MacLeod clan were burned to death when the MacDonalds barred the church door and set fire to the building in 1587. **Map ref. F3**

Fladda-
chuain

Gaeilavore
Island

Gearran Island

Rubha Hunish

Loch Hunish
Duntulm Bay
The Air

Tulm Island Kilmaluag
Duntulm Duntulm
Score Bay

2

Skye Cottage
Museum

Ru Bornaskitaig
Bornisketaig
Camas Mòr Kilmuir Hunglader

Kilvaxter Suidh'
a'
Mhinn Loch
Balgown 350 Sneosdal

Monkstadt
Kilbride Linicro
Point Totscore Whitewater
Activities

Stack of
Skudiburgh Idrigil

318

1¾ hrs

Vaternish Point

Sròn
Ochrulan
251

Ben
Geary Geary
264

Trumpan

Halistra Gillen
Ardmore Hallin Stac a'
Point Bhothain

Isay Mingay
Island
Rubha
Maol Stein Lusta

Dunvegan Head

Lampay
Islands

313 Ben
Skriaig
307 Galtrigill
Boreraig Uig

Husabost
Feriniquarrie Totaig

Milovaig
Upper B884 Lephin
Milovaig
Oisgill Bay Loch
Mòr
Waterstein 264
Head Colbost
296 Moonen Beinn
Bay Skinidin Uiginish
na Creiche
Neist Point 9
Glen Kilmuir
Ben Dale Roskhill
Corkeval
Ramasaig Healabhal
Ramasaig Mhòr
Bay (Macleod's Roag
Table North) Orbost
Hoe Rape 468
The Lorgill Healabhal Bheag Vatten
Hoe 488 (Macleod's Harlosh
233 Table South)
Ben Connan Balmore
244 Harlosh
Point
Beinn 371
na Boineid Ben Duagrich

Ascrib
Islands
South Ascrib

L O C H
Rubha Chorachan
S N I Z O R T

Aros Bay
Loch Losait Cuidrach
Poll na
Biod nan Laogh h-Ealaidh Peinlich Glen
Greshornish
Point Lyndale A87
Point 11

Ben
Diubaig Lyndale
214 Ho. Kingsburgh

Beinn Greshornish
Chreagach Flashader Treaslane Romesdal
326 A850 Ey
The A87-TO PORTREE
Ben 14 Edinbane Aird Kensaley
Horneval A850
264 Bernisdale Tote
Ben Uigshader
4 246 Skeabost
Ben A850
H I G H L A N D Sca
286 Cruachan Uigshade
Beinn
Ben Aketil a' Chearcaill a' Ghlinne Bhig
S K Y E 265 271 208

Ose Beinn
Glen Ose na 9 Am
A863 Cloiche Maol
9 232 B885 212
Ose Loch
Connan
Loch
Duagrich Glenm

A863-TO KYLE OF LOCHALSH (A87)

3

11

4

5

M I N C H

T r o

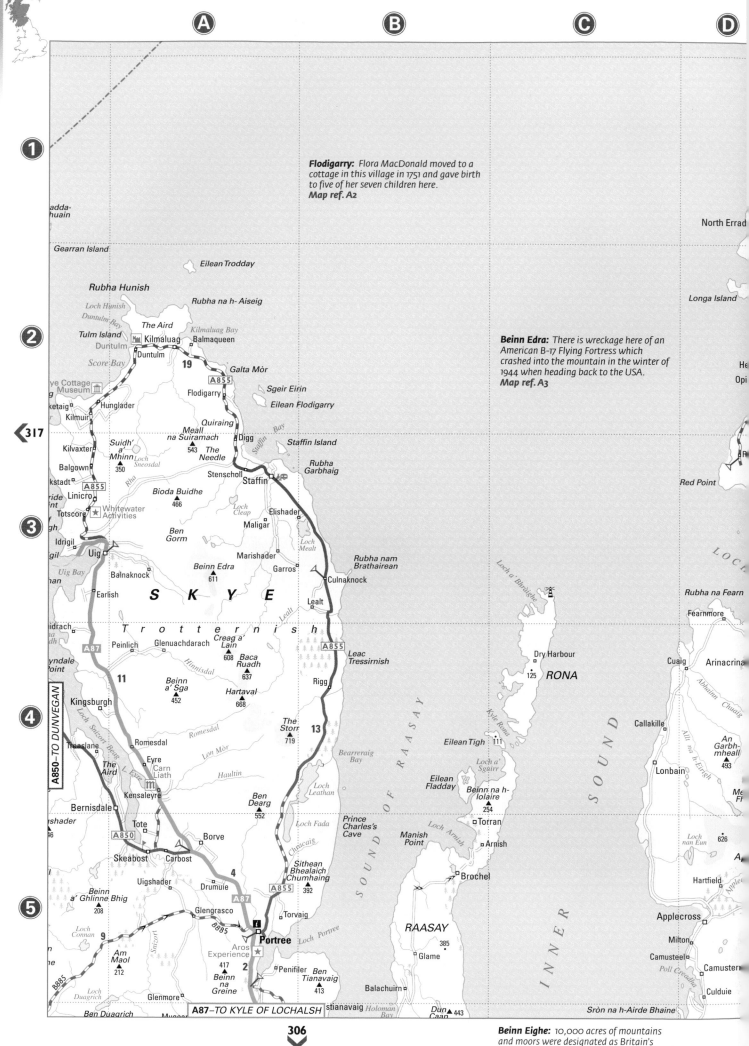

①

Flodigarry: Flora MacDonald moved to a cottage in this village in 1751 and gave birth to five of her seven children here.
Map ref. A2

North Errad

Gearran Island

Eilean Trodday

Longa Island

Rubha Hunish

Rubha na h- Aiseig

②

Loch Hunish

Duntulm Bay

The Aird

Kilmaluag Bay

He

Opi

Tulm Island   Kilmaluag   Balmaqueen

Duntulm

Score Bay   Duntulm

19   Galta Mòr

A855

Beinn Edra: There is wreckage here of an American B-17 Flying Fortress which crashed into the mountain in the winter of 1944 when heading back to the USA.
Map ref. A3

e Cottage   Museum

Flodigarry

Sgeir Eirin

ketaig   Hunglader

Eilean Flodigarry

Kilmuir

317 ◄

Quiraing

Meall   na Suiramach

Digg   Staffin Bay

Staffin Island

Red Point

Kilvaxter

Suidh' a' Mhinn   543   The Needle

kstadt

A855

350   Loch Sneosdal

Stenscholl   Staffin

Rubha Garbhaig

ride   nt   Linicro

③

gh

Totscore   Whitewater Activities

Bioda Buidhe   466

Elishader

Maligar

Idrigil

Ben Gorm

Loch Cleap

Loch Mealt

Uig

Balnaknock

Marishader

Garros

Rubha nam Brathairean

LOCH

Uig Bay

Beinn Edra   611

Culnaknock

Rubha na Fearn

han

Earlish

S   K   Y   E

Lealt

Fearnmore

idrach   a   dh

A87   Peinlich

T   r   o   t   t   e   r   n   i   s   h

Creag a' Lain   608

Glenuachdarach

Leac Tressirnish

A855

Loch a' Bhraighe

Dry Harbour

Cuaig   Arinacrina

yndale   Point

11

Baca Ruadh   637

125   *RONA*

Kingsburgh

Beinn a' Sga   452

Hartaval   668

Rigg

Abhainn Chuaig

Treaslane

④

A850–TO DUNVEGAN

Romesdal

The Aird

Eyre   Carn Liath

Lon Mòr

Haultin

The Storr   719

13

Bearreraig Bay

Eilean Tigh   111

S   O   U   N   D   O   F   R   A   A   S   A   Y

Kyle Rona

Callakille

An Garbh-mheall   493

Lonbain

Me Fl

Kensaleyre

Ben Dearg   552

Loch Leathan

Eilean Fladday

Beinn na h-Iolaire   254

Loch a' Sguirr

I   N   N   E   R

Loch nan Eun   626

Bernisdale

Loch Fada

Prince Charles's Cave

Loch Arnish

Torran

A850   Tote

Borve

Chràcaig

Manish Point

Arnish

Loch nan Eun

A

shader   46

Skeabost   Carbost

4

Sithean Bhealaich Chumhaing   392

Brochel

Hartfield

Appl

Uigshader   Drumuie

A855

Glame

Milton

⑤

Beinn a' Ghlinne Bhig   208

A87

Glengrasco

Torvaig

S   O   U   N   D

385   Glame

RAASAY

Camusteel

Poll Creadha

Camuster

B885   *i*

Portree

Loch Portree

Applecross

9

Am Maol   212

Aros Experience

Balachuirn

Loch Connan

Snizort

417   **2**

Peninfler

Ben Tianavaig   413

Milton

Camusteel

Loch Duagrich

Beinn na Greine

Glenmore

Poll Creadha

Culduie

Ben Duagrich

Mu

A87–TO KYLE OF LOCHALSH   stianavaig   Holoman Bay

Dun Caan   443

Sròn na h-Airde Bhaine

Beinn Eighe: 10,000 acres of mountains and moors were designated as Britain's first national nature reserve in 1951.
Map ref. F3

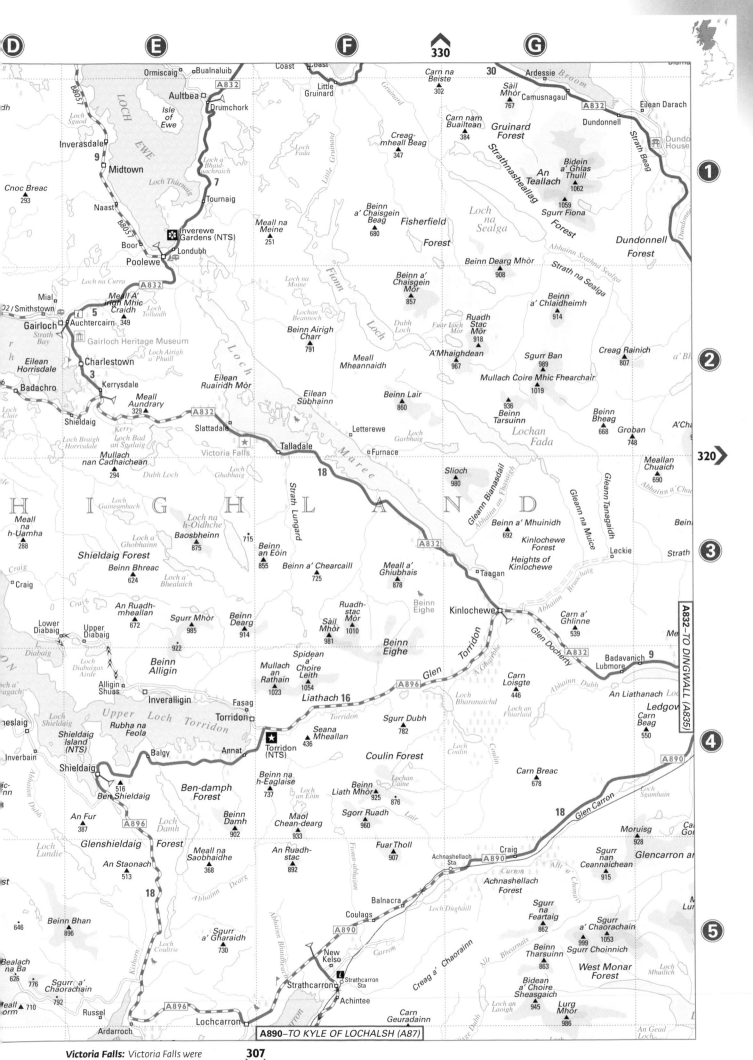

Ormiscaig   Bualnaluib   Coast   Coast   Little   Carn na   Ardessie   Broom   1
B8057   Gruinard   Beiste   Sàil   Camusnagaul   A832   Eilean Darach
Aultbea   A832   302   Mhòr   767   Dundonnell   Strath Beag   Dundo
Drumchork   Carn nam   Gruinard   Sgurr Fiona   House
Isle   Buailtean   Forest   Strathnasheallag   An Teallach   Bidein
of Ewe   384   Loch   1062   a' Ghlas   Thuill
Inverasdale   Creag-   na   1059   Dundonnell
9   mheall Beag   Sealga   Sgurr Fiona   Forest
Midtown   347   Loch   Abhainn Srathnd Sealga
Loch   Bhaid-   Fada   Fisherfield
THE   Thurnaig   luachrach   Beinn   Forest   Beinn Dearg Mhòr   Strath na Sealga
7   Tournaig   a' Chaisgein   908
Naast   Beag   Beinn
Meall na   680   Beinn a'   a' Chlaidheimh
Meine   Chaisgein   914
Inverewe   251   Mòr
Gardens (NTS)   857   Ruadh   Creag Rainich   2
Boor   Londubh   Fionn   Stac   807
Poolewe   A832   Loch na   Dubh   Mòr   Sgurr Ban
Moine   Loch   Ruadh Stac Mòr   989
Loch na Curra   Loch   A'Mhaighdean   918   Mullach Coire Mhic Fhearchair
Mial   Smithstown   Lochan   967   1019
Meall A'   Tollaidh   Beannoch   Meall
irigh Mhic   Beinn Airigh   Mheannaidh   Beinn   Beinn   320
Craidh   Charr   Bheag   A'Cha
Gairloch   5   349   791   668   Groban
Auchtercairn   Beinn Lair   Beinn   748
860   Tarsuinn   Lochan   Meallan
Gairloch Heritage Museum   Loch Airigh   Eilean   936   Fada   Chuaich
Charlestown   a' Phuill   Ruairidh Mòr   Beinn   690
3   Eilean   Tarsuinn
Eilean   Sùbhainn   Letterewe
Horrisdale   Kerrysdale   Loch   Slioch
Badachro   Meall   A832   Garbhaig   980   Gleann   Gleann Tanagaidh
Aundrary   Slattadale   Furnace   Bianasdail
329   Talladale   Abhainn an Fhuaraidh   Leckie   Strath
Kerry   Victoria Falls   18   Beinn   3
Loch Braigh   Loch Bad   a' Mhuinidh
Horrisdale   an Sgalaig   Strath   692   Kinlochewe
Shieldaig   Lungard   H I G H L A N D   Forest   Leckie
Mullach   Dubh Loch   Heights of
nan Cadhaichean   Loch   Kinlochewe
294   Ghabhaig   Beinn   Kinlochewe   A832
Loch   an Eòin   Meall a'   Taagan   Carn a'   Badavanich   9
Meall   Gaineamhach   855   Ghiubhais   Ghlinne   Lubmore
na   Baosbheinn   715   Beinn a' Chearcaill   878   Beinn   539   An Liathanach
h-Uamha   875   725   Eighe   Glen Docherty   Ledgov
288   Shieldaig Forest   Ruadh-   (A835)
Craig   Beinn Bhreac   stac   Carn   Carn
Craig   624   An Ruadh-   Sgurr Mhòr   Beinn   Mòr   Beinn   Loisgte   Beag
mheallan   985   Dearg   Sàil   1010   Eighe   446   550
672   914   Mhòr   Spidean   Torridon   Loch   An Liathanach
Lower   922   981   a'   Bharanaichd   Loch an
Diabaig   Upper   Choire   Fhiarlaid   A890
Diabaig   Mullach   Leith   Glen
Diabaig   Beinn   an Rathain   1054   Sgurr Dubh   Carn Breac
Loch Diabaigas   Alligin   1023   782   678
Airde   Liathach 16   A896   Glen   4
Alligin   Torridon   Glen Carron
Shuas   Fasag   Coulin Forest   Lochan   A890
Inveralligin   Torridon   Uaine   Loch
Upper   Torridon   Seana   Sgamhain
Shieldaig   Rubha na   Mheallan   Beinn   18   Glen Carron
Island   Feola   436   Liath Mhòr   Carn Breac
(NTS)   Balgy   Annat   925   876   678   Moruisg
Inverbain   Shieldaig   Ben-damph   Torridon   Sgorr Ruadh   Carron   928
Shieldaig   516   Forest   (NTS)   960   Craig   A890
Ben Shieldaig   Beinn na   Achnashellach   Sgurr
An Fur   h-Eaglaise   Beinn   Sta   Achnashellach   nan
387   A896   737   Damh   Maol   Forest   Ceannaichean
Glenshieldaig   Loch   902   Chean-dearg   Fuar Tholl   915
Forest   Damh   933   907   Sgurr
Meall na   An Ruadh-   Balnacra   a' Chaorachain
An Staonach   Saobhaidhe   stac   Sgurr   1053
513   368   892   Coulags   na   Sgurr
Beinn Bhan   Feartaig   a' Chaorachain
646   896   Sgurr   A890   862   999   Sgurr Choinnich
Beinn   a' Gharaidh   New   Beinn   West Monar
Bealach   Damh   730   Kelso   Tharsuinn   Forest
na Ba   Loch   863
626   Coultrie   Strathcarron   Bidean
776   Sgurr a'   Russel   Strathcarron   Carn   a' Choire   Lurg
792   Chaorachain   Sta   Geuradainn   Sheasgaich   Mhòr
meall   710   Achintee   945   986
orm   Ardarroch   Lochcarron   A896
A832-TO DINGWALL

A890-TO KYLE OF LOCHALSH (A87)

Victoria Falls: Victoria Falls were
named after a visit to Loch Maree by
Queen Victoria in 1877. **Map ref. E2**

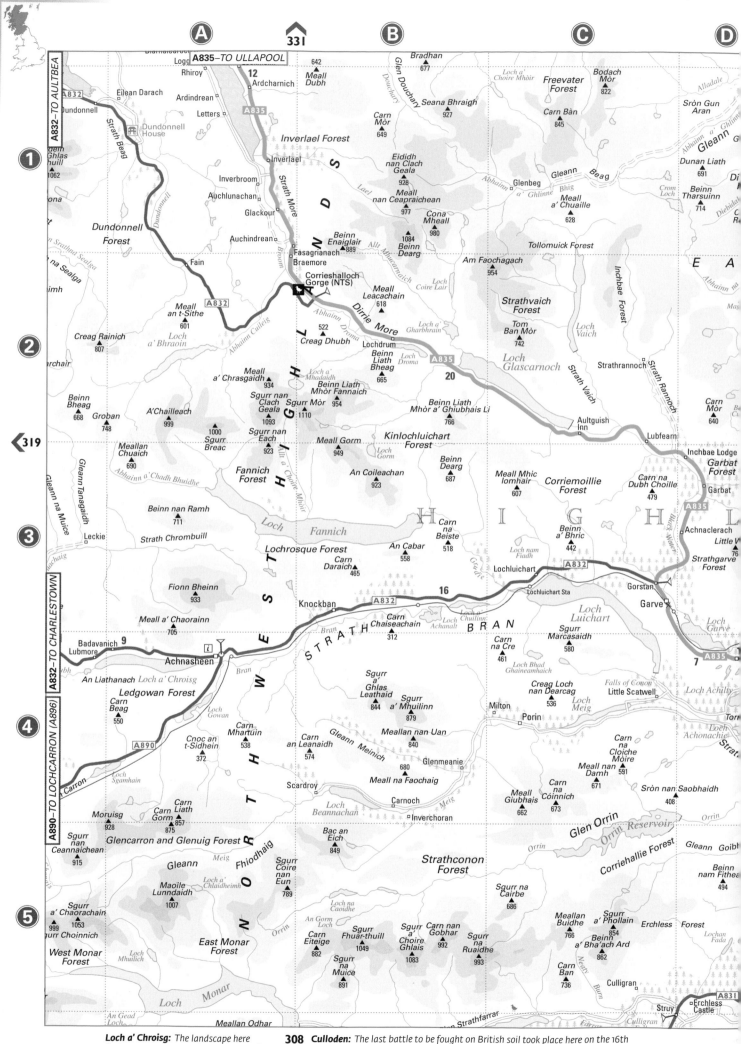

A835–TO ULLAPOOL
A832–TO AULTBEA

Loggi
Rhiroy
Ardcharnich
Diamalacarrach
642
Meall
Dubh

Bradhan
677

Loch a'
Choire Mhòir

Freevater
Forest

Bodach
Mòr
822

Eilean Darach
Ardindrean
Letters
A835

Glen Douchary

Carn Bàn
845

Sròn Gun
Aran

A832
Dundonnell

Dundonnell
House

Inverlael Forest

Carn
Mòr
649

Seana Bhraigh
927

Carn Bàn
845

Gleann
Beag

Dunan Liath
691

Di

Strath Beag

Inverlael

Eididh
nan Clach
Geala
928

Glenbeg

Gleann
a' Ghlinne

Beinn
Tharsuinn
714

Crom
Loch

Diebi
Re

Inverbroom

Auchlunachan

Meall
nan Ceapraichean
977

Cona
Mheall
980

Beag
Bhig

Meall
a' Chuaille
628

E

Dundonnell
Forest

Glackour

Auchindrean

Beinn
Enaiglair
889

Meall
1084

Beinn
Dearg

Tollomuick Forest

Am Faochagach
954

⚠1

Fain

Fasagrianach
Braemore

Allt
Mhucarnaich

Loch
Coire Lair

Strathvaich
Forest

Corrieshalloch
Gorge (NTS)

Meall
Leacachain
618

Tom
Ban Mòr
742

Meall
an t-Sithe
601

A832

Abhainn Cuileig

Abhainn Droma

Dirrie More

Loch a'
Gharbhrain

Loch
Vaich

Creag Rainich
807

Loch
a' Bhraoin

522
Creag Dhubh

Lochdrum

Loch
Droma

A835

20

Loch
Glascarnoch

Strath Vaich

Strathrannoch

Strath Rannoch

Carn
Mòr
640

⚠2

Beinn
Bheag
668

Groban
748

A'Chailleach
999

Meall
a' Chrasgaidh
934

Sgurr nan
Clach
Geala
1093

Beinn Liath
Mhòr Fannaich

Sgurr Mòr
1110

Sgurr Mòr
954

Beinn
Liath
Bheag
665

Beinn Liath
Mhòr a' Ghiubhais Li
766

Aultguish
Inn

Lubfearn

Inchbae Lodge
Garbat
Forest

⚠319

Meallan
Chuaich
690

Sgurr nan
Each
923

Meall Gorm
949

Loch
Gorm

Beinn
Dearg
687

Meall Mhic
Iomhair
607

Corriemoillie
Forest

Carn na
Dubh Choille
479

Garbat

A835

Achnaclerach

Little

Gleann Tanagaidh

Abhainn a' Chadh Bhuidhe

Sgurr nan
Breac

Fannich
Forest

An Coileachan
923

Beinn
a' Bhric
442

Buck Water

⚠3

Gleann na Muice

Beinn nan Ramh
711

Strath Chrombuill

Leckie

Loch

Fannich

An Cabar
558

Carn na
Beiste
518

Loch nam
Fiadh

Lochluichart

A832

H I G H

Strathgarve
Forest

Gorstan

Garve

Loch
Garve

Lochrosque Forest

Carn
Daraich
465

Lochluichart Sta

Loch
Luichart

A835

Fionn Bheinn
933

16

Sgurr
Marcasaidh
580

⚠ 7

Knockban

A832

Carn
Chaiseachain
312

Loch a'
Chuilinn

Loch
Achanalt

Meall a' Chaorainn
705

STRATH

BRAN

Carn
na Cre
461

Loch Bhad
Ghaineamhaich

Creag Loch
nan Dearcag
536

Little Scatwell

Falls of Conon

Loch Achulty

A832–TO CHARLESTOWN

Badavanich
9
Lubmore

Achnasheen

Bran

Sgurr
a'
Ghlas
Leathaid
844

Sgurr
a' Mhuilinn
879

Milton

Porin

Loch
Meig

Loch
Achonachie

An Liathanach

Loch a' Chroisg

i

Ledgowan Forest

Carn
Beag
550

Carn
Mhartuin
538

Meallan nan Uan
840

Gleann Meinich

Glenmeanie
680

Carn
na
Cloiche
Mòire

Meall nan
Damh
591

Tor

Loch

A890–TO LOCHCARRON (A896)

A890

Cnoc an
t-Sidhein
372

Carn
an Leanaidh
574

Meall na Faochaig

Scardroy

Carnoch

Loch
Beannachan

Meig

Inverchoran

Meall
Giubhais
662

Carn
na
Cóinnich
673

Sròn nan Saobhaidh
408

A Carron

Loch
Sgamhain

Moruisg
928

Carn
Gorm
875

Carn
Liath
857

Bac an
Eich
849

Strathconon
Forest

Glen Orrin

Orrin Reservoir

Corriehallie Forest

Gleann Goibh

⚠4

Sgurr
nan
Ceannaichean
915

Glencarron and Glenuig Forest

Gleann

Meig

Fhiodhaig

Sgurr
Coire
nan
Eun
789

Loch a'
Chlaidheimh

Orrin

Sgurr na
Cairbe
686

Meallan
Buidhe
766

Sgurr
a' Phollain
854

Beinn
nam Fithea
494

Erchless
Forest

Sgurr
a' Chaorachain
1053

Maoile
Lunndaidh
1007

Loch na
Caoidhe

An Gorm
Loch

Carn
Eiteige
882

Sgurr
Fhuar-thuill
1049

Sgurr
a'
Choire Ghlais
1083

Carn nan
Gobhar
992

Sgurr
na
Ruaidhe
993

Meallan
Buidhe
766

Beinn
a' Bha'ach Ard
862

Lochan
Fada

⚠5

urr Choinnich

West Monar
Forest

East Monar
Forest

Loch
Mhuilich

Orrin

Sgurr
na
Muice
891

Carn
Ban
736

Culligran

Strathfarrar

Neart
Burn

A831

Loch Monar

An Gead
Loch

Meallan Odhar

Struy
Erchless
Castle

Culligran

Edrin

A831

320

Loch a' Chroisg: The landscape here features some spectacular reminders of the ice-age. Here the moving glaciers have left unusual flat-topped terraces on the south side of the Loch. **Map ref. A4**

308 **Culloden:** The last battle to be fought on British soil took place here on the 16th April 1746 between the supporters of Bonnie Prince Charlie, known as Jacobites and the Government troops, known as Hanoverians. The engagement itself was over in less than an hour and resulted in a resounding defeat for the Jacobites, who lost over 1,200 men on the battlefield. **Map ref. G5 Also on page 119**

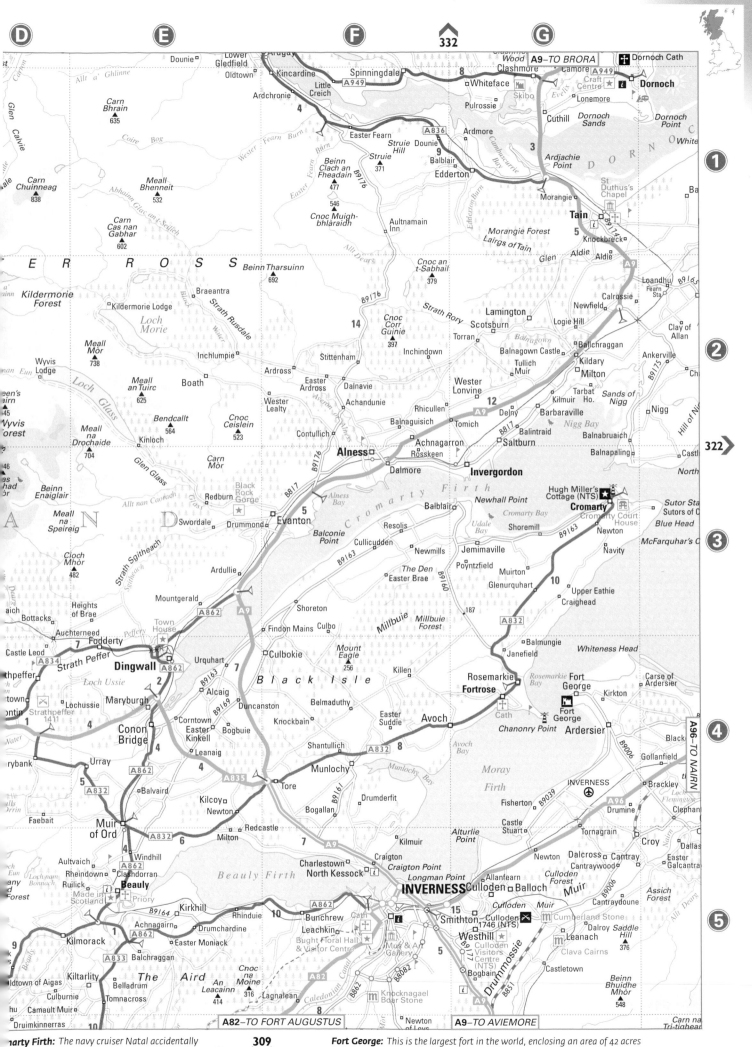

A9–TO BRORA

Dornoch Cath

Lower Gledfield
Dounie
Ardgay
Kincardine
Oldtown
Spinningdale
Clashmore
Camore
A949
Whiteface
Skibo
Lonemore
Dornoch
Craft Centre

Carn Bhrain 635
Little Creich
Ardchronie
A949
Pulrossie
Cuthill
Dornoch Sands
Dornoch Point
White

1

Glen Calvie
Allt a' Ghlinne
Easter Fearn
A836
Ardmore
Ardjachie Point
St Duthus's Chapel
Morangie

Carn Chuinneag 838
Meall Bhenneit 532
Beinn Clach an Fheadain 477
Struie Hill
Struie 371
Dounie
Balblair
Edderton
Morangie

Carn Cas nan Gabhar 602
Cnoc Muigh-bhlàraidh 546
B9176
Aultnamain Inn
Tain
Knockbreck

E R R O S S
Beinn Tharsuinn 692
Braeantra
Strath Rusdale
Cnoc an t-Sabhail 379
Lamington
Scotsburn
Logie Hill
Loandhu
Fearn Sta
B9165
Calrossie
Newfield
Clay of Allan
Ankerville

2

Kildermorie Forest
Kildermorie Lodge
Inchlumpie
Cnoc Corr Guinie 397
Strath Rory
Inchindown
Torran
Balnagown Castle
Ballchraggan
Kildary
Milton

Loch Morie
Meall Mòr 738
Meall an Tuirc 625
Boath
Ardross
Easter Ardross
Dalnavie
Achandunie
Wester Lonvine
A9
Delny
Kilmuir
Tullich Muir
Tarbat Ho.
Sands of Nigg
Nigg

Meall na Drochaide 704
Bendcallt 564
Cnoc Ceislein 523
Wester Lealty
Contullich
Balnaguisich
Tomich
Rhicullen
B817
Barbaraville
Balintraid
Nigg Bay
Balnabruaich
Balnapaling
Hill of N

Carn Mòr
Achnagarron
Rosskeen
Alness
Saltburn
North

322

Beinn Enaiglair
Redburn
Swordale
Evanton
Dalmore
Invergordon
Cromarty Bay
Newhall Point
Balblair
Hugh Miller's Cottage (NTS)
Cromarty
Cromarty Court House
Sutor Sta
Sutors of
Blue Head

3

Meall na Speireig
Black Rock Gorge
Drummond
B817
Alness Bay
Balconie Point
Cullicudden
Shoremill
Newton
B9163
Navity
McFarquhar's C

Cioch Mhòr 482
Ardullie
Mountgerald
A862 A9
Shoreton
Findon Mains
Culbo
Newmills
Jemimaville
The Den
Easter Brae
Poyntzfield
Muirton
Glenurquhart
187
B9160
Upper Eathie
Craighead

Heights of Brae
Bottacks
Auchterneed
Fodderty
Town House
Urquhart
Culbokie
Mount Eagle 256
Killen
Balmungie
Janefield
Whiteness Head
Carse of Ardersier

4

Castle Leod
A834
Strath Peffer
Dingwall
A862
B9163
Alcaig
Duncanston
Belmaduthy
Knockbain
Easter Suddie
Rosemarkie
Rosemarkie Bay
Fortrose
Fort George
Kirkton
Fort George
Ardersier
B9006
Black

A96–TO NAIRN

Strathpeffer 1411
Lochussie
Maryburgh
Corntown
Easter Kinkell
Bogbuie
Leanaig
Shantullich
Avoch
Avoch Bay
Chanonry Point
Gollanfield
Clephan

Conon Bridge
Urray
Balvaird
Kilcoy
Newton
A835
Tore
Munlochy
A832
Moray Firth
Fisherton
B9039
INVERNESS
Castle Stuart
Drumine
Brackley
Tornagrain
Croy
Dalcross
Easter Galcantra

Muir of Ord
Windhill
Milton
Redcastle
Kilmuir
A9
Bogallan
Drumderfit
Munlochy Bay
Longman Point
Alturlie Point
Newton
Dalcross
Cantray
Dallas

5

Aultvaich
Rheindown
Ruilick
Clashdorran
Beauly
Priory
B9164
Kirkhill
Rhinduie
Bunchrew
Charlestown
North Kessock
Craigton
Craigton Point
Beauly Firth
Allanfearn
Culloden
Culloden Forest
Balloch
Muir
Cantraydoune
Assich Forest

Kilmorack
A862
Easter Moniack
Leachkin
Bught Floral Hall & Visitor Centre
Mus & Art Gallery
Caledonian Canal
INVERNESS
Smithton
Westhill
Culloden 1746 (NTS)
Cumberland Stone
Leanach
Dalroy
Saddle Hill 376

A833
Balchraggan
Cnoc na Moine 316
Lagnalean
Knocknagael Boar Stone
Culloden Visitors Centre (NTS)
Bogbain
Castletown
Clava Cairns

Kiltarlity
Belladrum
Drumchardan
An Leacainn 414
B862
Newton of Leys
Drummossie
Beinn Bhuidhe Mhòr 548
Carn na Tri-tighear

Kildown of Aigas
Culburnie
Tomnacross
Camault Muir
Druimkinnerras
The Aird

A82–TO FORT AUGUSTUS

309

A9–TO AVIEMORE

marty Firth: The navy cruiser Natal accidentally ...ded here on the 30th December 1915. Although over 280 ...vors were plucked from the water, over 370 officers and ...ost their lives including many preparing to celebrate ...manay on board ship. **Map ref. F3**

Fort George: This is the largest fort in the world, enclosing an area of 42 acres (17ha) and almost a mile (1.6km) around. The fort was built during the reign of George II as a defence against any further unrest by the Jacobite Army. Despite taking 21 years to build, Fort George never saw any military action. **Map ref. G4 Also on page 123**

Burghead: Site of the biggest 'Iron Age' fort in Britain built on the end of a promontory by the Picts between the 4th and 7th centuries AD. The Picts lived in northern Britain and though very little is known about them they are thought to be the original inhabitants of Scotland. From the 9th century however they seem to have vanished, perhaps swallowed up in battles with the Vikings, Romans and between their own tribes. *Map ref. D3.*

321

A939, A940—TO GRANTOWN-ON-SPEY

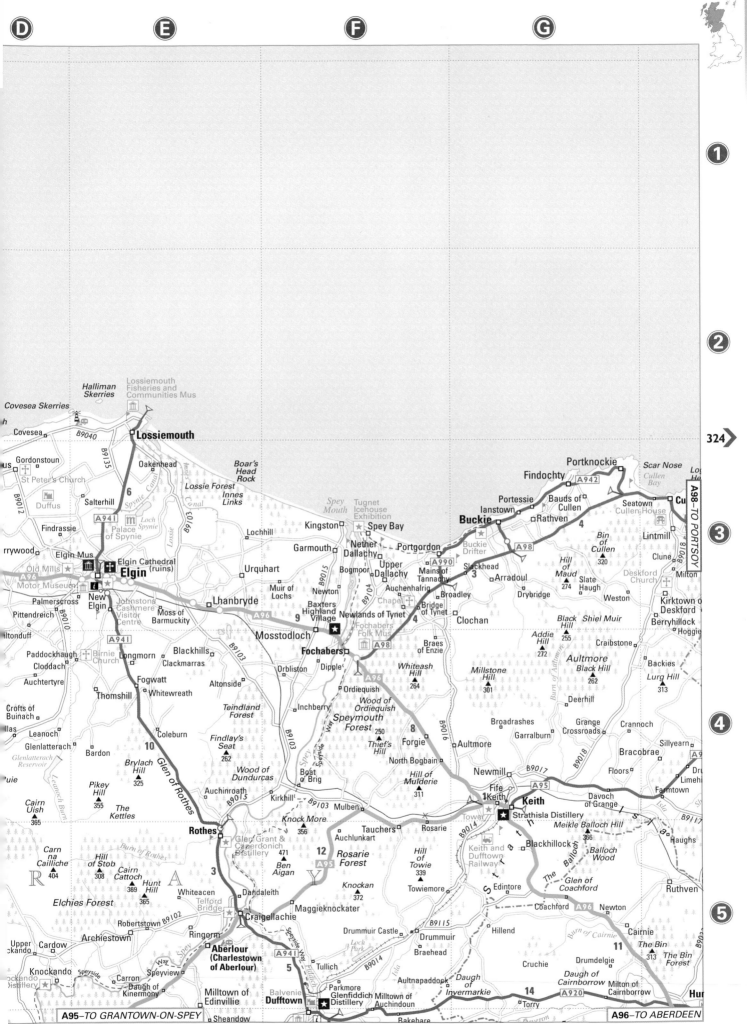

324 ▶

Halliman Skerries
Covesea Skerries
Covesea
Gordonstoun
St Peter's Church
B9012
Duffus
B9040
B9135
Salterhill
Findrassie
A941
Palace of Spynie
Loch Spynie
Spynie Canal
Lossie Forest
Innes Links
Lossie
B9103
Oakenhead
Lossiemouth
Lossiemouth Fisheries and Communities Mus
Boar's Head Rock
Spey Mouth
Tugnet Icehouse Exhibition
Kingston
Spey Bay
Lochhill
Nether Dallachy
Garmouth
Upper Dallachy
Portgordon
Bogmoor
Mains of Tannachy
Slackhead
A990
Buckie Drifter
Buckie
Portessie
Ianstown
Bauds of Cullen
Rathven
Seatown
Cullen House
Cu
Findochty
Portknockie
A942
Scar Nose
Cullen Bay
Los He
A98–TO PORTSOY
B1068
Lintmill
Clune
Bin of Cullen
320
Deskford Church
Milton
rrywood
Elgin Mus
Old Mills
A96
Motor Museum
Elgin
Elgin Cathedral (ruins)
New Elgin
Johnstons Cashmere Visitor Centre
Lhanbryde
A96
9
Mosstodloch
Fochabers
Fochabers Folk Mus
A98
Newlands of Tynet
Bridge of Tynet
Chapel
8
Broadley
Clochan
Braes of Enzie
Auchenhalrig
Whiteash Hill
264
Millstone Hill
301
Broadrashes
Garralburn
Grange Crossroads
Deerhill
Aultmore
Black Hill
262
Addie Hill
255
Black Hill
272
Shiel Muir
Craibstone
Backies
Lurg Hill
313
Berryhillock
Hoggie
Kirktown of Deskford
Weston
Drybridge
Slate Haugh
Arradoul
3
Hill of Maud
274
Palmerscross
Pittendreich
B9010
iltonduff
A941
Paddockhaugh
Birnie Church
Cloddach
Auchtertyre
Crofts of Buinach
llas
Leanoch
Crofts of Buinach
Glenlatterach Reservoir
uie
Leawoch Burn
Cairn Uish
365
Bardon
Thomshill
Fogwatt
Whitewreath
Longmorn
Blackhills
Clackmarras
Altonside
Orbliston
Dipple
Ordiequish
Wood of Ordiequish
Speymouth Forest
250
Thief's Hill
Forgie
North Bogbain
Hill of Mulderie
311
Aultmore
Newmill
B9017
A95
Fife Keith
Keith
Strathisla Distillery
Davoch of Grange
A9
Dru Limehi
Farmtown
Sillyearn
Floors
Bracobrae
Crannoch
Muir of Lochs
Newton
Baxters Highland Village
B9015
B9104
B9016
B9018
Teindland Forest
Findlay's Seat
262
Coleburn
10
Glen of Rothes
Pikey Hill
355
The Kettles
Brylach Hill
325
Wood of Dundurcas
Boat o' Brig
Auchinroath
Kirkhill
B9015
B9103
Mulben
Knock More
356
Tauchers
Auchlunkart
Rosarie
Glen Grant & Caperdonich Distillery
Rothes
Carn na Cailliche
404
Hill of Stob
308
Cairn Cattoch
369
Hunt Hill
365
Whiteacen
Telford Bridge
Dandaleith
12
A95
Rosarie Forest
471
Ben Aigan
Knockan
372
Knock More
Towiemore
Hill of Towie
339
Keith and Dufftown Railway
Tower
Meikle Balloch Hill
366
Blackhillock
Balloch Wood
Glen of Coachford
Ruthven
Edintore
Coachford
A96
Newton
Cairnie
11
The Bin
313
The Bin Forest
R
Elchies Forest
A
Robertstown
B9102
Archiestown
Ringorm
Whiteacen
Maggieknockater
Drummuir Castle
Loch Park
Drummuir
Braehead
Hillend
Cruchie
Drumdelgie
Daugh of Cairnborrow
Milton of Cairnborrow
Upper ckando
Cardow
ckando Distillery
Knockando
Speyside Way
Carron
Speyview
Daugh of Kinermony
Milltown of Edinvillie
Sheandow
Aberlour (Charlestown of Aberlour)
A941
5
Tullich
Parkmore
Glenfiddich Distilery
Balvenie
Dufftown
Milltown of Auchindoun
Aultnapaddock
Daugh of Invermarkie
Bakehare
B9014
B9115
14
A920
Torry
Hu

311
▼

Lossiemouth: *Birthplace in 1866 of James Ramsay MacDonald, Britain's first Labour Prime Minister. After a successful first term in 1924 he was re-elected in 1929 to form a 'National Government' during the Depression. He died at sea, en-route to South America, in 1937 and is buried near Lossiemouth in Old Spynie churchyard. Map ref. E2.*

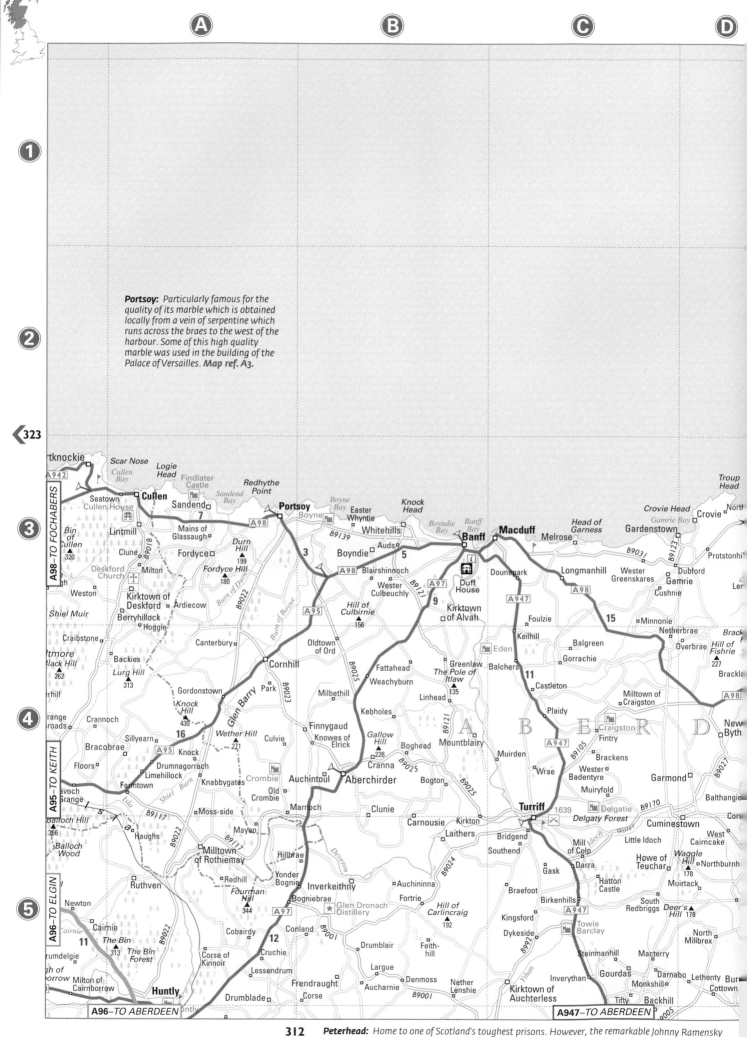

Portsoy: *Particularly famous for the quality of its marble which is obtained locally from a vein of serpentine which runs across the braes to the west of the harbour. Some of this high quality marble was used in the building of the Palace of Versailles.* **Map ref. A3.**

◄ 323

A942

A98–TO FOCHABERS

tknockie

Scar Nose

Cullen Bay

Logie Head

Findlater Castle

Redhythe Point

Seatown

Cullen House

Cullen

Sandend

Sandend Bay

Boyne

Portsoy

Boyne Bay

Easter Whyntie

Knock Head

Boyndie Bay

Banff Bay

Troup Head

Crovie Head

Gamrie Bay

Crovie

North

7

A98

B9139

Whitehills

Boyndie Bay

Macduff

Head of Garness

Crovie Head

Gardenstown

Lintmill

Mains of Glassaugh

Durn Hill

Bin of Cullen

320

Clune

Fordyce

Boyndie

Auds

5

Banff

Melrose

B9031

B9123

Dubford

Protstonhi

Ler

Fordyce Hill

180

Blairshinnoch

A98

Wester Culbeuchly

B9121

A97

9

Kirktown of Alvah

Duff House

Dounepark

A947

Longmanhill

A98

Wester Greenskares

Gamrie

Cushnie

199

Durn Hill

Deskford Church

Milton

Kirktown of Deskford

Ardiecow

B9022

Hill of Culbirnie

156

Foulzie

15

Netherbrae

Minnonie

Overbrae

Brack

Hill of Fishrie

227

Brackla

A98

Weston

Shiel Muir

Berryhillock

Hoggle

Canterbury

Burn of Boyne

Oldtown of Ord

Fattahead

Weachyburn

Eden

Greenlaw The Pole of Itlaw

135

Keilhill

Balgreen

Gorrachie

Craibstone

Backies

Lurg Hill

313

Gordonstown

Cornhill

B9025

Milbethill

Linhead

Balchers

11

Castleton

Milltown of Craigston

A98

tmore

lack Hill

262

rhill

Knock Hill

430

Park

B9023

Glen Barry

Kebholes

B9121

A B E R D

Plaidy

Craigston

Fintry

New Byth

range roads

Crannoch

Sillyearn

16

A95

Wether Hill

271

Culvie

Finnygaud

Knowes of Elrick

Gallow Hill

226

Boghead

Mountblairy

Muirden

Wrae

A947

B9105

Brackens

Wester Badentyre

Muiryfold

Garmond

B9027

Balthangie

Bracobrae

Knock

Drumnagorrach

Crombie

Aberchirder

Cranna

Bogton

B9025

Floors

Limehillock

Farmtown

Shiel Burn

Knabbygates

Old Crombie

Marnoch

Clunie

B9025

Carnousie

Kirkton

Turriff

1639

Delgatie

Delgaty Forest

Cuminestown

avoch range

Balloch Hill

356

Haughs

Isla

B9117

Moss-side

Mayen

Laithers

Bridgend

Southend

Mill of Colp

Little Idoch

West Cairncake

Balloch Wood

Ruthven

Milltown of Rothiemay

Redhill

Hillbrae

Devern

Yonder Bognie

Inverkeithny

Auchininna

Fortrie

B9024

Gask

Darra

Howe of Teuchar

Waggle Hill

178

Northburnh

Muirtack

A96–TO ELGIN

A96–TO KEITH

A95–TO KEITH

Newton

Cairnie

Cairnie

The Bin

313

Fourman Hill

344

Bogniebrae

A97

Conland

Glen Dronach Distillery

Hill of Carlincraig

192

Braefoot

Birkenhills

A947

Kingsford

Dykeside

Towie Barclay

South Redbriggs

Deer's Hill

178

North Millbrex

rumdelgie

gh of orrow

Milton of Cairnborrow

11

The Bin Forest

Huntly

B9022

Cobairdy

12

Cruchie

Corse of Kinnoir

Lessendrum

Drumblade

Conland

B9001

Drumblair

Largue

Feith-hill

Denmoss

Nether Lenshie

Kirktown of Auchterless

Steinmanhill

B9124

Inverythan

Gourdas

Macterry

Darnabo

Lethenty

Cottown

Bur

Frendraught

Corse

Aucharnie

B9001

Tifty

Backhill

D005

A96–TO ABERDEEN

A947–TO ABERDEEN

312 ▼

Peterhead: *Home to one of Scotland's toughest prisons. However, the remarkable Johnny Ramensky escaped from it five times (three times in a single year in 1958). Ramensky was a career burglar who was released from prison in 1942 and joined a crack commando unit which operated behind German lines. Usi his explosives and burglary skills he stole important documents. His wartime exploits became legendary he was awarded the Military Medal and granted a free pardon. Unfortunately he returned to a life of crim and died while serving time in Perth Prison, in 1972 at the age of 67.* **Map ref. G5.**

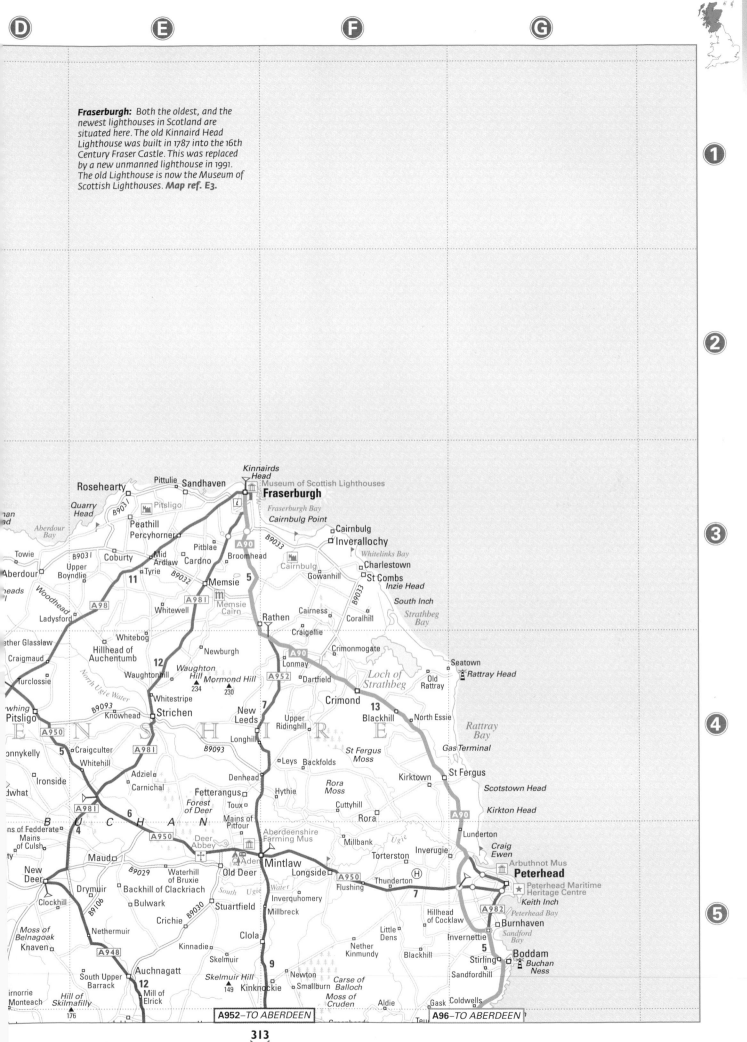

Fraserburgh: *Both the oldest, and the newest lighthouses in Scotland are situated here. The old Kinnaird Head Lighthouse was built in 1787 into the 16th Century Fraser Castle. This was replaced by a new unmanned lighthouse in 1991. The old Lighthouse is now the Museum of Scottish Lighthouses.* **Map ref. E3.**

Kinnairds Head

Museum of Scottish Lighthouses

Fraserburgh

Rosehearty   Pittulie   Sandhaven

Quarry Head   Pitsligo

Fraserburgh Bay

Cairnbulg Point

Aberdour Bay

Peathill   Percyhorner

Cairnbulg

Inverallochy

B9033

Whitelinks Bay

Towie

B9031   Upper Boyndlie

Coburty

Pitblae

Broomhead

Cairnbulg

Charlestown

Gowanhill

St Combs

Aberdour

11

Mid Ardlaw   Cardno

Tyrie   B9032

Memsie

5

Inzie Head

heads

Woodhead

Ladysford

A98

Whitewell

Whitebog

Memsie Cairn

Rathen

Cairness

Craigellie

Coralhill

South Inch

Strathbeg Bay

ether Glasslaw

Craigmaud

Hillhead of Auchentumb

Newburgh

12

Waughton Hill

Waughtonhill

Mormond Hill

Crimonmogate

Seatown

Rattray Head

Turclossie

North Ugie Water

234

230

Lonmay

Dartfield

Loch of Strathbeg

Old Rattray

Whitestripe

Strichen

New Leeds

Crimond

13

Blackhill

North Essie

rwhing

Pitsligo

A950

B9093

Knowhead

7

Longhill

Upper Ridinghill

Rattray Bay

onnykelly

5

Craigculter

Whitehill

A981

B9093

Leys

Backfolds

St Fergus Moss

Gas Terminal

Adziel

Carnichal

Denhead

Hythie

Rora Moss

Kirktown

St Fergus

hwat

Ironside

Fetterangus

Toux

Cuttyhill

Scotstown Head

6

Forest of Deer

Mains of Pitfour

Rora

A90

Kirkton Head

B U C H A N

4

A981

ns of Feddrate

Mains of Culsh

A950

Deer Abbey

Aberdeenshire Farming Mus

Aden

Millbank

Torterston

Inverugie

Lunderton

Craig Ewen

Arbuthnot Mus

Maud

B9029

Waterhill of Bruxie

Old Deer

Mintlaw

Longside

A950

Thunderton

7

Peterhead

New Deer

Drymuir

Backhill of Clackriach

South Ugie Water

Flushing

Peterhead Maritime Heritage Centre

Clockhill

Bulwark

Inverquhomery

Keith Inch

Moss of Belnagoak

Knaven

A948

Nethermuir

Crichie

B9030

Stuartfield

Millbreck

Little Dens

Nether Kinmundy

Blackhill

Hillhead of Cocklaw

A982

Peterhead Bay

Burnhaven

Invernettie

Sandford Bay

South Upper Barrack

12

Mill of Elrick

Clola

Kinnadie

Skelmuir

9

Newton

Smallburn

Carse of Balloch

Stirling

Boddam

Buchan Ness

irnorrie Monteach

Hill of Skilmafilly

176

Skelmuir Hill

149

Kinknockie

Moss of Cruden

Aldie

Sandfordhill

Gask

Coldwells

A952–TO ABERDEEN

313

A96–TO ABERDEEN

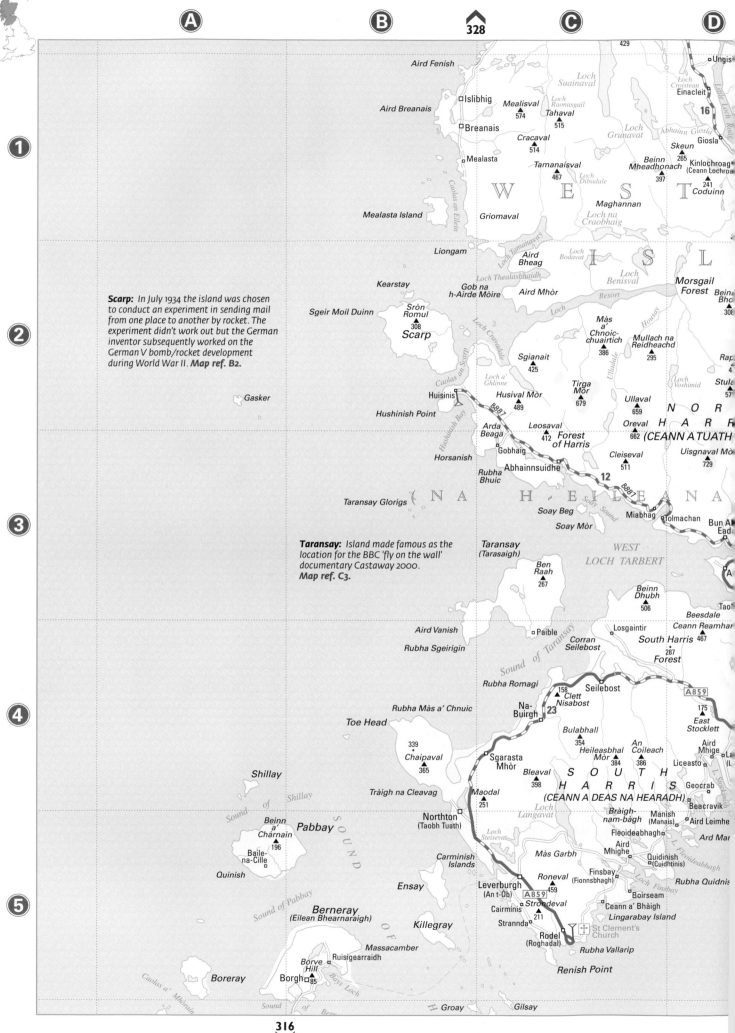

Scarp: In July 1934 the island was chosen to conduct an experiment in sending mail from one place to another by rocket. The experiment didn't work out but the German inventor subsequently worked on the German V bomb/rocket development during World War II. **Map ref. B2.**

Taransay: Island made famous as the location for the BBC 'fly on the wall' documentary Castaway 2000. **Map ref. C3.**

Aird Fenish

Islibhig
Aird Breanais
Breanais

Aird Fenish

Loch Suainaval

429

Loch Croistean
Einacleit

Ungis

Mealisval
574
Tahaval
515

Loch Raonasgail

Loch Grunavat

16

Abhainn Giosla

Little Loch Roag

Cracaval
514

Loch

Skeun
Giosla

Mealasta

Tamanaisval
467

Loch Dibadale

Beinn Mheadhonach
397

Maghannan

Loch na Craobhaig

Beinn
265
Kinlochroag
(Ceann Lochroa

241
Coduinn

W　E　S　T

Mealasta Island

Griomaval

Liongam

Loch Tamanaisva

Aird Bheag

Loch Bodavat

Loch Thealasbhaidh

Loch Benisval

Morsgail Forest

Bein
Bho
308

Kearstay

Gob na h-Airde Mòire

Aird Mhòr

Loch

Resort

Sgeir Moil Duinn

Sròn Romul
308
Scarp

Sgianait
425

Màs a' Chnoic-chuairtich
386

Mullach na Reidheachd
295

Housay

Ulladale

Rap
4

Loch Voshimid

Stula
57

Caolas an Scarp

Huisinis

B887

Husival Mòr
489

Tirga Mòr
679

Ullaval
659

Oreval
662

Loch Cravadale

N O R
H A R R
(CEANN A TUATH

Hushinish Point

Arda Beaga

Leosaval
412

Forest of Harris

Uisgnaval Mò
729

Loch a' Ghlinne

Cleiseval
511

Horsanish

Gobhaig

Abhainnsuidhe

12

B887

Rubha Bhuic

Taransay Glorigs

(N A

H · E I L E A N A

Soay Beg

Soay Mòr

Miabhag

Soby Sound

Tolmachan

Bun A
Ead

Taransay
(Tarasaigh)

Ben Raah
267

WEST LOCH TARBERT

Pa

Beinn Dhubh
506

Tao

Beesdale

Aird Vanish

Paible

Losgaintir

Corran Seilebost

Ceann Reamhar
467

Rubha Sgeirigin

South Harris
287
Forest

Sound of Taransay

Rubha Romagi

Rubha Màs a' Chnuic

Toe Head

Na-Buirgh

158
Clett Nisabost

Seilebost

A859

23

175
East Stocklett

Bulabhall
354

Aird Mhige
Le
(L

339

Heileasbhal Mòr
384

An Coileach
386

Liceasto

Chaipaval
365

Sgarasta Mhòr

S O U T H

Aird Mhige

Shillay

Bleaval
398

H A R R I S

Geocrab

Beinn a' Chàrnain
196

Pabbay

SOUND

Tràigh na Cleavag

Maodal
251

(CEANN A DEAS NA HEARADH)

Bràigh-nam-bàgh

Manish (Manais)

Aird Leimhe

Baile-na-Cille

Fleodeabhagh

Ard Mar

Sound of Shillay

Loch Làngavat

Màs Garbh

Aird Mhighe

Quidinish (Cuidhtinis)

Quinish

Northton
(Taobh Tuath)

Loch Steisevat

Finsbay (Fionnsbhagh)

Rubha Quidnis

Carminish Islands

Roneval
459

Boirsean

Ensay

Leverburgh
(An t-Òb)

A859

Cairminis

Stròndeval
211

Ceann a' Bhàigh

Lingarabay Island

Berneray
(Eilean Bhearnaraigh)

Killegray

Strannda

Rodel
(Roghadal)

St Clement's Church

Boreray

Massacamber

Ruisigearraidh

Borve Hill
85

Borgh

Rubha Vallarip

Renish Point

Caolas a' Mhòrain

Sound of Pabbay

Bays Loch

Groay

Gilsay

ahaval
256
Griomarstaidh
B8011
Loch
ungavat
Loch Cleit
Steirmeis
3
Eitshal
Beinn
Bhuna
Achadh Mòr

A859—TO STORNOWAY

149
A859
Loch Thota
Bridein
Loch Orasay
Arnish Moor
Arnish
Pt
Rubh' a'
Bhàigh Uaine
Ceann na
Circ
Suardail
Lower
Bayble
(Pabail Iarach)

Loch
Fadagoa
Loch
Nisreaval
Leurbost
(Liùrbost)
B897
Grimshader
(Griomsiadar)
Loch Grimsiadar

1

Loch
Trealaval
Loch
nam Falcag
Loch
Fada
Crosbost
Ranish
(Ranais)
Raerinish Point

Loch
na h-Fhir Mhaoil
Beinn Mohal
207
Loch Airigh
na h-Airde
RN
Mhòr
Roineval
281
12
Balallan
(Baile Ailein)
A859
Lacasaigh
Keose
(Ceos)
Loch Erisort
Eilean
Chaluim Chille
Tabhaigh Mhòr
Gleann Ghrabhair
Orasaigh

S
Sleiteachal
Mhòr
248
Kintarvie
Airidh a'
Bhruaich
Sildinis
B8060
Cearsiadar
Tabost
Gearraidh
Bhaird
Cabharstadh
Torraigh
Marbhig

erod
18
A859
Aird an
Troim
Kearnaval
378
Beinn
a'
Mhuil
370
Malasgair
172
Loch
Sgibacleit
13
Calbost
Rubha Iosal

Loch
angavat
Liuthaid
492
Sidhean
an
Airgid
381
Mòr
Mhonadh
401
Ceann Loch
Shiphoirt
Feirihisval
326
Glen Ouirn
Loch
Shanndabhat
Grabhair
Tom an
Fhuadain
Loch Odhairn

2

473
h a' Ruisg
Ath
Linne
Beinn na
h-Uamha
389
Eisgean
Orasaigh
Leumrabhagh
Kebock Head

Aird a'
Mhulaidh
DH)
Seaforth
Island
Muaithabhal
424
Beannan
Mòr
242
Loch
Shell
Gob na Milaid
Srianach

n
Clett Ard
328
Beinn Mhòr
572
Corlabhadh
298
Eilean
Iubhard

P   a   r   k
Uisenis
371
Mulhagery

A859
Maraig
(Maaruig)
Kenmore
Crionaig
470
Mol Truisg

3

gaoth
Aird
559
Straiaval
389
Toddun
528
Caiteshal
449
Loch Seaforth
Tathas
Mhòr
Loch Claidh
Loch Bhrollum
Gob Rubh' Uisenis
Garbh
Eilean
161
Eilean Mhuire

Laxadale
Lochs
Beinn a' Chaolais
Rhenigidale
(Reinigeadal)
Bhalamus
Rubha Bhrollum
Eilean an Tighe

ert
eart)
Urgha
Carragrich
Uieseval
334
Eilean Mòr
a' Bháigh
Sgeir na
h-Eigheach
Rubh' a' Bhaird
Shiant Islands

Sgeotasaigh
Kyles Scalpay
(Caolas Scalpaigh)
Sound of
Scalpay
SOUND OF SHIANT

nn
Scalpay
Ben Scoravick
104
Scalpay☐
(Eilean Scalpaigh)
Kennavay

4

East Loch
Tarbert
Meall Challibost

Shiant Islands: Uninhabited group of
Islands home to 50,000 breeding pairs
of Puffins. **Map ref. G4.**

er
Kennacley
Plocropol
Scadabhagh
Rubha
Bocaig

Cluer

Uig 1¾ hours

5

Fladda-
chuain
Gaeilavore
Island
Gearran Island

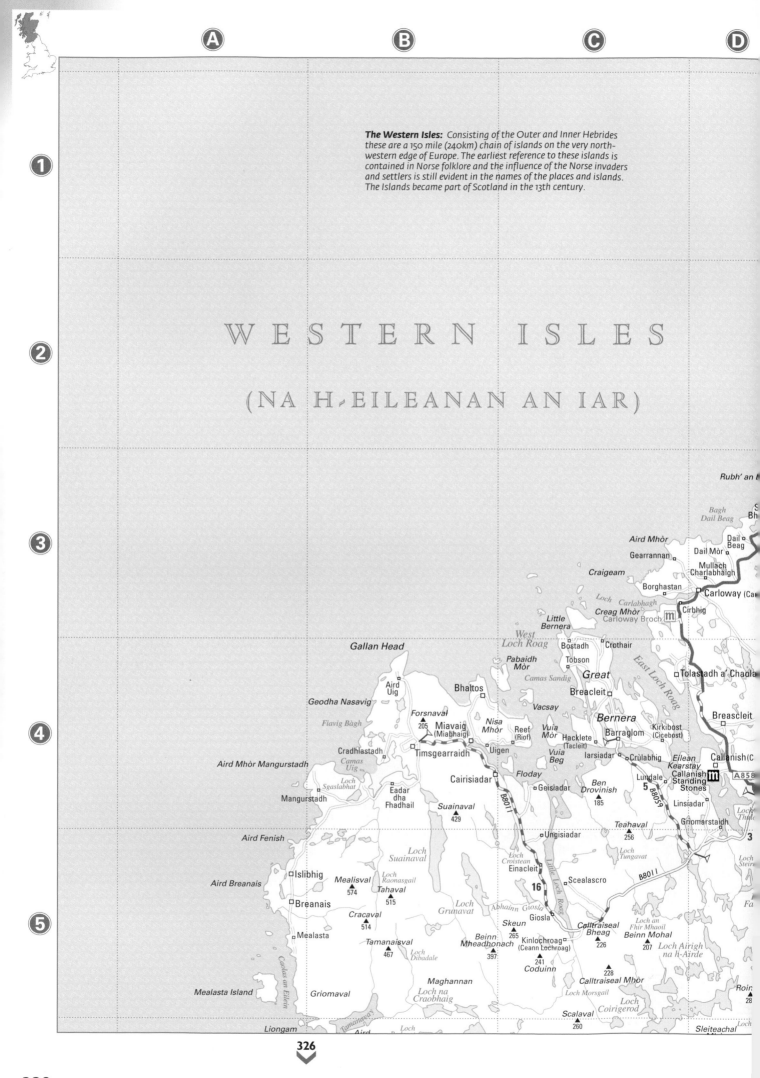

The Western Isles: Consisting of the Outer and Inner Hebrides these are a 150 mile (240km) chain of islands on the very north-western edge of Europe. The earliest reference to these islands is contained in Norse folklore and the influence of the Norse invaders and settlers is still evident in the names of the places and islands. The Islands became part of Scotland in the 13th century.

WESTERN ISLES

(NA H-EILEANAN AN IAR)

Rubh' an

Bagh
Dail Beag

Aird Mhòr
Gearrannan

Dail
Beag

Dail Mòr

Craigeam

Mullach
Charlabhaigh

Borghastan

Carloway (Ca

Loch   Carlabhagh

Creag Mhòr
Carloway Broch

Cirbhig

Little
Bernera

West
Loch Roag

Bostadh

Crothair

Gallan Head

Pabaidh
Mòr

Tobson

East Loch Roag

Tolastadh a' Chaola

Aird
Uig

Great

Camas Sandig

Breacleit

Bhaltos

Geodha Nasavig

Breascleit

Vacsay

Bernera

Fiavig Bàgh

Forsnaval
205

Nisa
Mhòr

Reef
(Riof)

Vuia
Mòr

Hacklete
(Tacleit)

Barraglom

Kirkibost
(Cicebost)

Miavaig
(Miabhaig)

Cradhlastadh

Uigen

Vuia
Beg

Iarsiadar

Crùlabhig

Eilean
Kearstay

Callanish (C

Aird Mhòr Mangurstadh

Timsgearraidh

Camas
Uig

Callanish
Standing
Stones

A858

Cairisiadar

Floday

Lundale
5

Eadar
dha
Fhadhail

Mangurstadh

Loch
Sgaslabhat

Geisiadar

Ben
Drovinish
185

B8059

Linsiadar

Suainaval
429

Loch
Thule

Aird Fenish

Teahaval
256

Griomarstaidh

3

Ungisiadar

Loch
Tungavat

Loch
Steir

Loch
Suainaval

Loch
Croistean
Einacleit

Islibhig

Mealisval
574

Loch
Raonasgail

Tahaval
515

Aird Breanais

Scealascro

B8011

Fa

Breanais

Abhainn Giosla

Giosla

16

Cracaval
514

Loch
Grunavat

Calltraiseal
Bheag
226

Beinn Mohal
207

Loch Airigh
na h-Airde

Mealasta

Skeun
265

Kinlochroag
(Ceann Lochroag)

Tamanaisval
467

Loch
Dibadale

Beinn
Mheadhonach
397

Coduinn
241

Calltraiseal Mhòr
228

Roir

28

Mealasta Island

Caolas an Eilean

Griomaval

Maghannan
Loch na
Craobhaig

Loch Morsgail

Loch
Coirigerod

Scalaval
260

Liongam

Tamallavas
Aird

Loch

Sleiteachal

Loch

Butt of Lewis
(Rubha Robhanais)   Port a' Stoth

Teampull Mholuidh
Cunndal
Eoropaidh   Cóig Peighinnean
Bad an Fhithich   Lionel
(Lional)   Port Ness
(Port Nis)
Swainbost
(Suaineabost)   Harbost (Tabost)
Aird Dhail   Eorodal   Port Skigersta
South Dell (Dail Bho Dheas)   North   Cross (Cros)   Sgiogarstaigh
Dell   Ness
Toa Galson   (Dail Bho   (Niss)
Thuath)   Glen Cross   Meall Geal
A857   Port Alasdair
Airigh   Cuidhaseadair   Laimhrig
na
Gabhsunn Bho Thuath   Glaice
Gabhsunn Bho Dheas   Broch   Ben   Airighean   Cellar Head
Melbost Borve   Dell   Beinn nan
(Mealabost)   m   Caorach
Roinn a' Bhuic   15   Loch
Borve   High Borve   Langavat
(Borgh)   Airighean
Siadar Iarach   Loch
Rubha Leathann   Breihavat
Siadar Uarach   m   Steinacleit Cairn   Loch Mòr
Baile an Truiseil   & Standing Stones   Sandavat
Diaval   Geiraha
A857
Glen Shader
Goile   Loch Gress   Port Geiraha
Rinn   Chroic   Loch   Upper Barvas   Tolastadh
Druim   Mòr   Muirneag   Úr
Tallig   Blackhouse   Brue   Bharabhais   Barvas   248   Tolastadh
Labost   Port   (Bru)   (Barabhas)   Loch Mòr   Tolsta Head
Arnol   A858   Abhainn Thorraigh   Sandavit   B895   Port nam Bothag
Bragar   Arnol   Loch   Gleann Mòr Bharabhais   Loch Mòr   Gleann Tholastaidh
Siabost Bho   Casgro   Tobair   Port Bun a' Ghlinne
Thuath   Loch Urrahag   Gleann Bhruthadail   Loch Breivat   Loch   Sgeireach Mòr   12   Creag Fhraoch
Beinn   Beinn   Roishal   A857   Gress
Bragar   Choinnich   Mòr   174   (Griais)
261   210   248   ISLE OF   LEWIS   11   Bac
einn   Loch na   (EILEAN   LEODHAIS)   Col   Tiumpan
acleit   Scarvat   Col Uarach   Breibhig   Head
Loch Mòr   Rubha Bhataisgeir   (Rubha an Tiumpain)
Beinn Mholach   an Stairr   Col   Portnaguran
292   Sands   (Port nan Giúran)
Stacashal   B895   Portvoller
216   Tunga   Flesherin   Aird   Rubha Deas
Abhainn Lacsddail   Aird Thunga   Siulaisiadar
Loch nam   New   Sròn   10   Eye   Seisiadar
Breac   Loch nan   Valley   Newmarket   Ruadh   LOCH A' TUATH   Peninsula
Stearnag   Laxdale   Melbost Sands   (Broad Bay)   East   Garrabost   (An Rubha)   Rubha na Greine
Loch Airigh   Loch Vatandip   (Lacasdal)   i   Roisnish
nan Sloc   Stornoway (Steornabhagh)   Aiginis   Rubha na Bearnaich
Loch Uraval   Marybank   Stenis   STORNOWAY   Melbost   Cnoc   Upper Bayble (Pabail Uarach)
ibhne)   Beinn   A858   Nan Eilean   A866   St
nan   Lews   Sandwick   Suardail   Lower
Surrag   13   Castle   Stornoway   (Sanndabhaig)   Columba's   Bayble
223   200   149   4   Harbour   Holm   Church   Ceann na   (Pabail Iarach)
Eitshal   Beinn a'   Arnish   (Tolm)   Branahuie   Circ   Bagh Phabail
Bhuna   Pt   Banks
Achadh Mòr   Arnish Moor   Rubh' a'
Loch Thota   A859   Loch   Bhàigh Uaine   Ullapool 2¾hrs
Bridein   Orasay   6   Raerinish Point
Loch   Leurbost   Grimshader
Nisreaval   (Liùrbost)   B897   (Griomsiadar)   Loch Grimsiadar
Loch   Crosbost   Ranish   Tabhaigh Mhòr
nam   (Ranais)
Falcag   12   Keose   Eilean   Gleann Ghrabhair
och   Balallan   A859   Lacasaigh   (Ceos)   Chaluim Chille   Orasaigh
aval   (Baile Ailein)   Cearsiadar   Cabharstadh   Torraigh
9–TO TARBERT   Gearraidh   Tabost   Bhaird

327
∨

Stornoway: One of Stornoway's most famous sons is Sir Alexander Mackenzie who, in 1793, became the first European to cross the North American continent as far as the Arctic Ocean. The river that he followed was subsequently called the Mackenzie River. **Map ref. F4.**

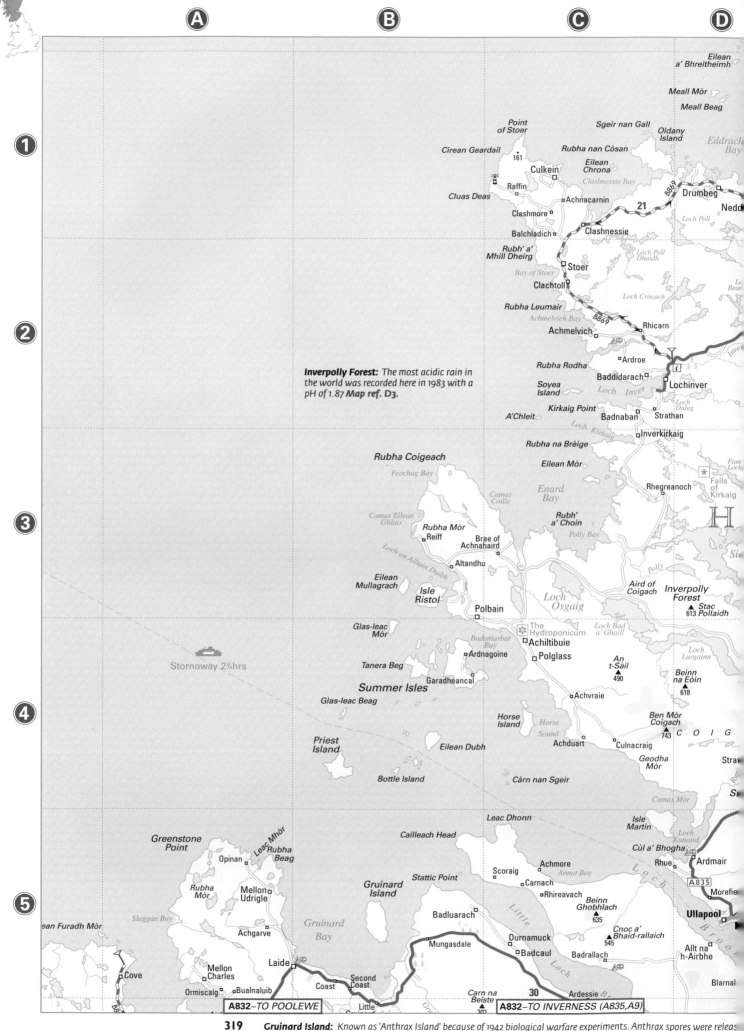

1

Eilean
a' Bhreitheimh

Meall Mòr

Meall Beag

Point
of Stoer

Sgeir nan Gall

Rubha nan Còsan

Oldany
Island

Eddrach
Bay

Cirean Geardail

161

Eilean
Chrona

Clashnessie Bay

B869

Drumbeg

Nedd

Culkein

Raffin

Achnacarnin

21

Loch Poll

Cluas Deas

Clashmore

Clashnessie

Balchladich

Loch Poll
Dhaidh

Rubh' a'
Mhill Dheirg

Stoer

Loch Cròcach

Bay of Stoer

Lo
Bear

2

Clachtoll

Rubha Leumair

Achmelvich Bay

B869

Rhicarn

Achmelvich

Ardroe

Inver

Rubha Rodha

Baddidarach

Lochinver

Inverpolly Forest: *The most acidic rain in
the world was recorded here in 1983 with a
pH of 1.87* **Map ref. D3.**

Soyea
Island

Loch Inver

Loch
Oulag

A'Chleit

Kirkaig Point

Badnaban

Strathan

Inverkirkaig

Rubha na Brèige

Loch Kirkaig

Fion
Loch

Rubha Coigeach

Eilean Mòr

Rhegreanoch

Falls
of
Kirkaig

Feochag Bay

Enard
Bay

★

3

Camas
Coille

Rubh'
a' Choin

Polly
Bay

H

Camas Eilean
Ghlais

Rubha Mòr

Reiff

Brae of
Achnahaird

Polly

Si

Loch an Alltain Duibh

Altandhu

Aird of
Coigach

Inverpolly
Forest

Eilean
Mullagrach

Isle
Ristol

Loch
Osgaig

▲ Stac
613 Pollaidh

Polbain

Glas-leac
Mòr

The
Hydroponicum

Loch Bad
a' Ghaill

Loch
Lurgainn

Badentarbat
Bay

Achiltibuie

An
t-Sàil

Beinn
na Eòin

4

Stornoway 2¾hrs

Tanera Beg

Ardnagoine

Polglass

490

618

Garadheancal

Achvraie

Ben Mòr
Coigach

Glas-leac Beag

Summer Isles

Horse
Island

Horse
Sound

Achduart

743 ▲

C O I G

Priest
Island

Eilean Dubh

Culnacraig

Geodha
Mòr

Stra

Bottle Island

Càrn nan Sgeir

Camas Mòr

S

5

Leac Dhonn

Isle
Martin

Loch
Kanaird

Cùl a' Bhogha

Greenstone
Point

Leac Mhòr

Rubha
Beag

Cailleach Head

Scoraig

Achmore

Annat Bay

Rhue

Ardmair

Opinan

Stattic Point

Carnach

A835

Rubha
Mòr

Mellon
Udrigle

Gruinard
Island

Rhireavach

Beinn
Ghobhlach

Morefie

ean Furadh Mòr

Slaggan Bay

*Gruinard
Bay*

Badluarach

635

Cnoc a'
Bhaid-rallaich

Ullapool

Achgarve

Durnamuck

545 ▲

Allt na
h-Airbhe

Cove

Mellon
Charles

Laide

Badcaul

Badrallach

Loch
Broo

Blarnal

Ormiscaig

Bualnaluib

Coast

Second
Coast

Mungasdale

Carn na
Beiste
302

30

Ardessie

319
⌄

Gruinard Island: *Known as 'Anthrax Island' because of 1942 biological warfare experiments. Anthrax spores were releas
this 520 acre (210ha), uninhabited island to test its killing power on a flock of sheep. The island was so contaminated th
remained out of bounds for 50 years. In 1986 a company was paid £500,000 to decontaminate it by soaking the ground
276 tons (280 tonnes) of formaldehyde diluted in 1,968 tons (2,000 tonnes) of sea water. Also much of the topsoil was re
in sealed containers. A flock of sheep have since grazed there without harm…still not the place to go for a picnic!* **Map**

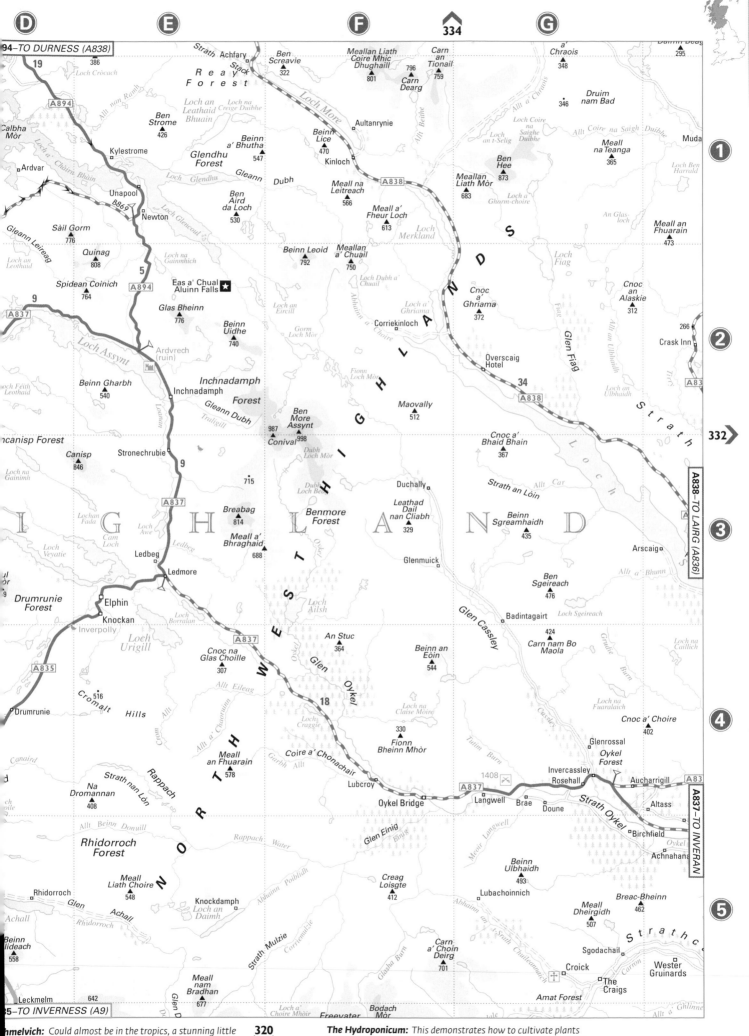

94–TO DURNESS (A838)
A894
Loch Cròcach
Calbha Mòr
Loch a' Chàirn Bhàin
Ardvar
A837
Gleann Leireag
Sàil Gorm 776
Quinag 808
Spidean Coinich 764
Kylestrome
Unapool
B869
Newton
Ben Strome 426
Glendhu Forest
Gleann Glendhu
Loch an Leathaid Bhuain
Loch na Creige Duibhe
Beinn a' Bhutha 547
Ben Aird da Loch 530
Gleann
Loch Glencoul
Loch na Gainmhich
Glas Bheinn 776
Eas a' Chual Aluinn Falls ★
Beinn Uidhe 740
Ardvreck (ruin)
Loch Assynt

Strath Stack
Achfary
Reay Forest
Ben Screavie 322
Meallan Liath Coire Mhic Dhughaill 801
Carn an Tionail 759
Carn Dearg 796
Loch More
Beinn Lice 470
Kinloch
Aultanrynie
Meall na Leitreach 566
A838
Meall a' Fheur Loch 613
Loch Merkland
Beinn Leoid 792
Meallan a' Chuail 750
Loch Dubh a' Chuail
Loch an Eircill
Abhainn a' Choire
Loch a' Ghriama
Corriekinloch

a' Chraois 348
Loch a' Chraois
Druim nam Bad 346
Loch Coire na Saighe Duibhe
Coire na Saigh Duibhe
Ben Hee 873
Meall na Teanga 365
Loch Ben Harrald
Muda
Meallan Liath Mòr 683
Loch a' Ghorm-choire
An Glas-loch
Meall an Fhuarain 473
Loch Fiag
Cnoc a' Ghriama 372
Cnoc an Alaskie 312
266
Crask Inn
A83

H I G H L A N D S

Inchnadamph Forest
Beinn Gharbh 540
Inchnadamph
Gleann Dubh
Traligill
Ben More Assynt 998
Conival 987
Dubh Loch Mòr
Dubh Loch Beag
715
Benmore Forest
Breabag 814
Meall a' Bhraghaid 688
Loch Awe
Ledbeg
Ledmore
Ledbeg
Cam Loch
Loch Veyatie
Lochan Fada
Maovally 512
Overscaig Hotel
34
A838
Cnoc a' Bhaid Bhain 367
Duchally
Strath an Lòin
Allt Car
Leathad Dail nan Cliabh 329
Glenmuick
Glen Cassley
Beinn Sgreamhaidh 435
Arscaig
Ben Sgeireach 476
Loch Sgeireach
Badintagairt
Glen Fiag
Strath
A838–TO LAIRG (A836)

N O R T H W E S T
Drumrunie Forest
Elphin
Knockan
Inverpolly
A835
Loch Urigill
516
Drumrunie
Cromalt Hills
Loch Borralan
A837
Cnoc na Glas Choille 307
An Stuc 364
Oykel
Glen Oykel
18
Loch Craggie
330
Fionn Bheinn Mhòr
Loch na Claise Mòire
Tutim Burn
424
Carn nam Bo Maola
Cassley
Cnoc a' Choire 402
Glenrossal
Oykel Forest
Invercassley
Rosehall
Aucharrigill
A83
Altass
A837–TO INVERAN

Canaird
Na Dromannan 408
Strath nan Lòn
Rappach
Meall an Fhuarain 578
Garbh Allt
Coire a' Chonachair
Lubcroy
Oykel Bridge
A837
1408
Langwell
Brae
Doune
Strath Oykel
Birchfield
Oykel
Achnahana

Beinn Ilideach 558
Rhidorroch Forest
Rhidorroch
Glen Achall
Leckmelm 642
85–TO INVERNESS (A9)
Meall Liath Choire 548
Knockdamph
Loch an Daimh
Achall
Rhidorroch
Glen Einig
Creag Loisgte 412
Strath Mulzie
Corriemulzie
Meall nam Bradhan 677
Glen
Abhainn Poiblidh
Rappach Water
Glasha Burn
Carn a' Choin Deirg 701
Bodach Mòr
Loch a' Choire Mhòir
Freevater
Meur Langwell
Beinn Ulbhaidh 493
Lubachoinnich
Abhainn an t-Srath Chuileannaich
Meall Dheirgidh 507
Sgodachail
Crocroick
Amat Forest
Meall Dheirgidh
Breac-Bheinn 462
Croick
The Craigs
Wester Gruinards
Strathc
Carron
Allt a' Ghlinne

mmelvich: Could almost be in the tropics, a stunning little
y with fantastic white sand and clear turquoise water.
on, check it out. **Map ref. C2.**

The Hydroponicum: This demonstrates how to cultivate plants
by growing them in gravel or similar material and pumping water
containing dissolved nutrient salts through them. **Map ref. C4.**

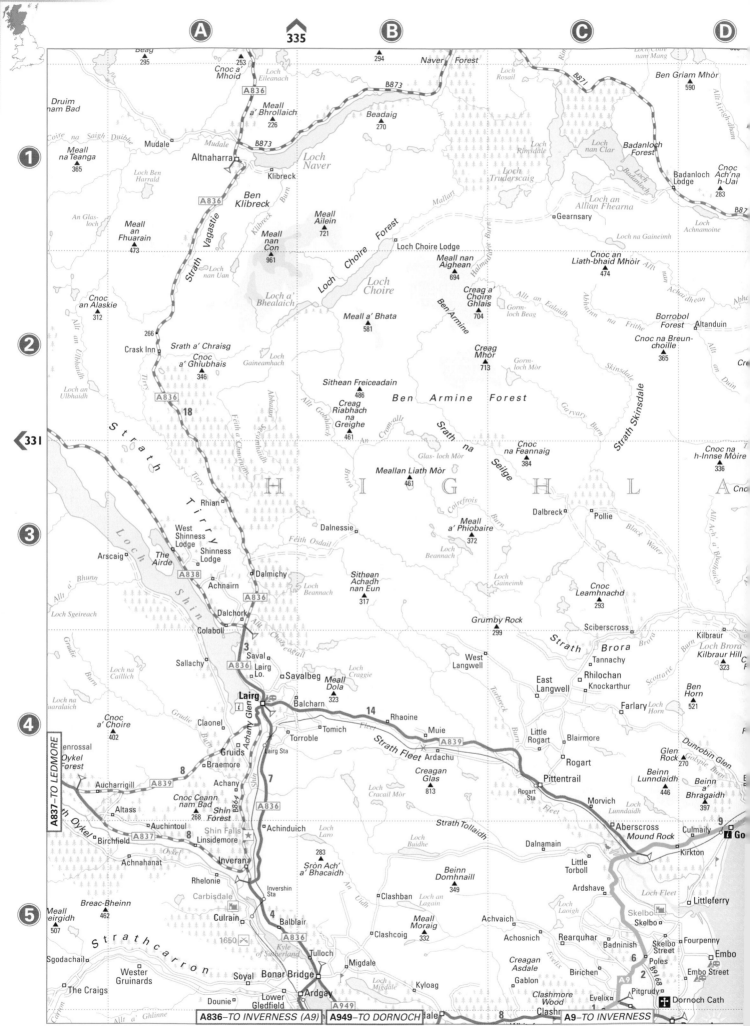

Beag 295

Cnoc a' Mhoid 253

294

Naver Forest

Ben Griam Mhòr 590

Druim nam Bad

Meall a' Bhrollaich 226

Beadaig 270

Loch Rosail

Loch Rimsdale

Loch nan Clar

Badanloch Forest

Badanloch Lodge

Cnoc Ach'na h-Uai 283

1

Coire na Saigh Duible

Meall na Teanga 365

Mudale

Mudale

B873

B873

Altnaharra

Klibreck

Loch Naver

Loch Truderscaig

Loch Badanloch

Loch an Allan Fhearna

Gearnsary

Loch na Gaineimh

Loch Achnamoine

An Glas-loch

Meall an Fhuarain 473

Ben Klibreck

Strath Vagastie

Loch Ben Harrald

Meall nan Con 961

Meall Ailein 721

Loch Choire Forest

Loch Choire Lodge

Meall nan Aighean 694

Creag a' Choire Ghlais 704

Gorm-loch Beag

Cnoc an Liath-bhaid Mhòir 474

Cnoc na Breun-choille 365

Borrobol Forest

Altanduin

2

Cnoc an Alaskie 312

Crask Inn

266

Loch nan Uan

Strath a' Chraisg

Cnoc a' Ghiubhais 346

Loch Gaineamhach

Loch a' Bhealaich

Meall a' Bhata 581

Sithean Freiceadain 486

Creag Riabhach na Greighe 461

Ben Armine

Creag Mhòr 713

Ben Armine Forest

Gorm-loch Mòr

Skinsdale

Strath Skinsdale

An Glas-loch

A836

18

Loch an Ulbhaidh

Allt an Ulbhaidh

Strath Tirry

Loch Shin

Loch Sgeireach

H I G H L A

Meallan Liath Mòr 461

Glas-loch Mòr

Strath na Seilge

Coirefrois

Cnoc na Feannaig 384

Dalbreck

Pollie

Black Water

Cnoc na h-Innse Mòire 336

3

331

Rhian

West Shinness Lodge

Shinness Lodge

The Airde

Arscaig

Dalnessie

Feith Osdail

Sithean Achadh nan Eun 317

Loch Beannach

Meall a' Phiobaire 372

Loch Gaineimh

Cnoc Leamhnachd 293

A838

Achnairn

Dalmichy

A836

Loch Beannach

4

Dalchork

Colaboll

3

Saval

Sallachy

A836

Lairg Lo.

Savalbeg

Meall Dola 323

Grumby Rock 299

Scriberscross

West Langwell

Strath Brora

Tannachy

Rhilochan

Knockarthur

Kilbraur

Kilbraur Hill 323

Loch Brora

A837–TO LEDMORE

enrossal

Oykel Forest

Cnoc a' Choire 402

Claonel

Balcharn

14

Rhaoine

East Langwell

Farlary

Ben Horn 521

Achany Glen

Tomich

Muie

A839

Little Rogart

Blairmore

Loch Horn

Dunrobin Glen

Glen Rock 270

Golspie Burn

Aucharrigill

A839

Braemore

Achany

Gruids

Torroble

Lairg Sta

Strath Fleet

Ardachu

Creagan Glas 813

Rogart

Rogart Sta

Beinn Lunndaidh 446

Beinn a' Bhragaidh 397

Altass

Cnoc Ceann nam Bad 268

8

Shin Forest

7

B864

A836

Strath Tollaidh

Dalnamain

Morvich

Loch Lunndaidh

9

Auchintoul

A837

Birchfield

8

Linsidemore

Shin Falls

Achinduich

Loch Laro

283

Loch Buidhe

Beinn Domhnaill 349

Little Torboll

Aberscross Mound Rock

Culmaily

Go

Achnahanat

Inveran

Rhelonie

Sròn Ach' a' Bhacaidh

An Uidh

Clashban

Loch an Lagain

Meall Moraig 332

Achvaich

Ardshave

Kirkton

Littleferry

Loch Fleet

5

Meall eirgidh 507

Breac-Bheinn 462

Carbisdale

Invershin Sta

Culrain

Balblair

4

Clashcoig

Achosnich

Rearquhar

Badninish

Skelbo

Skelbo Street

Fourpenny

Embo

Sgodachail

Wester Gruinards

1650

A836

Kyle of Sutherland

Tulloch

Migdale

Loch Migdale

Kyloag

Creagan Asdale

Gablon

Birichen

Poles

Skelbo

Evelix

Embo Street

Pitgrudy

The Craigs

Strathcarron

Soyal

Bonar Bridge

Ardgay

Lower Gledfield

Dounie

A949

A836–TO INVERNESS (A9)   A949–TO DORNOCH

Clashmore Wood

Clashm

Evelix

A9–TO INVERNESS

Dornoch Cath

Loch Shin: The largest freshwater lake in Sutherland. The Lairg Dam, at the southern end of the loch is 1,400 feet (427m) long and 40 feet (12m) high. It raised the water level of the loch by 36 feet (11m) and is used to create hydro-electricity. It is the most northern hydro-electric scheme in mainland Britain. **Map ref. A3.**

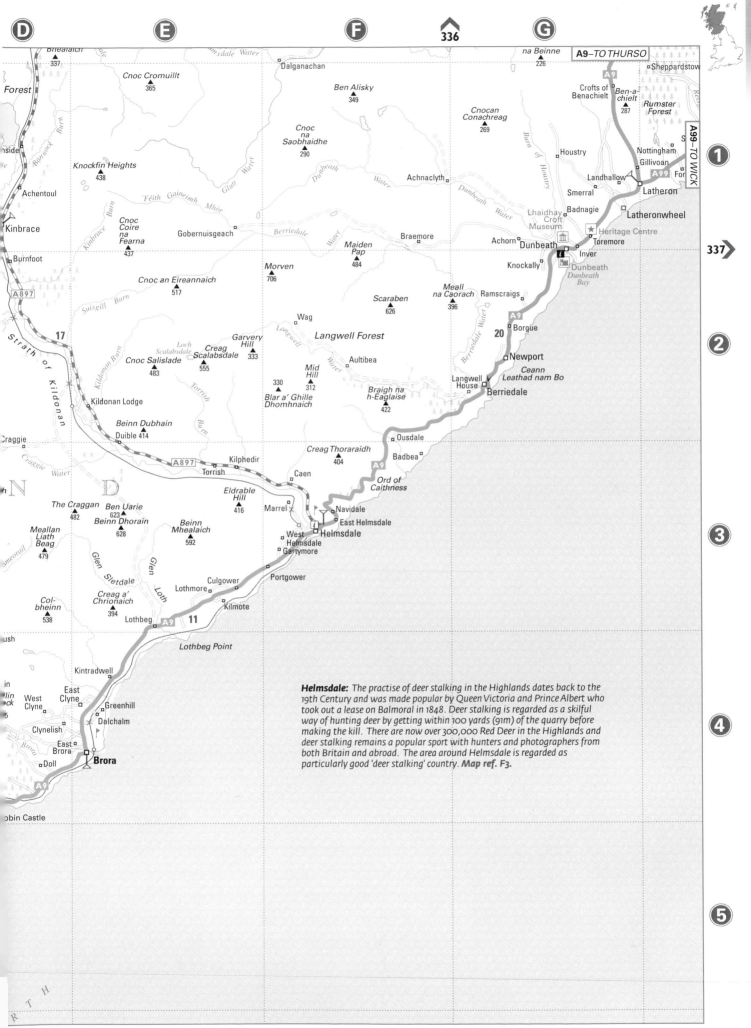

Helmsdale: The practise of deer stalking in the Highlands dates back to the 19th Century and was made popular by Queen Victoria and Prince Albert who took out a lease on Balmoral in 1848. Deer stalking is regarded as a skilful way of hunting deer by getting within 100 yards (91m) of the quarry before making the kill. There are now over 300,000 Red Deer in the Highlands and deer stalking remains a popular sport with hunters and photographers from both Britain and abroad. The area around Helmsdale is regarded as particularly good 'deer stalking' country. **Map ref. F3.**

Dunbeath: Purpose built village created in the early 1800s to take advantage of the Herring boom. Dunbeath is also the birthplace of Neil Miller Gunn the celebrated Scottish novelist (1891–1973). **Map ref. G1.**

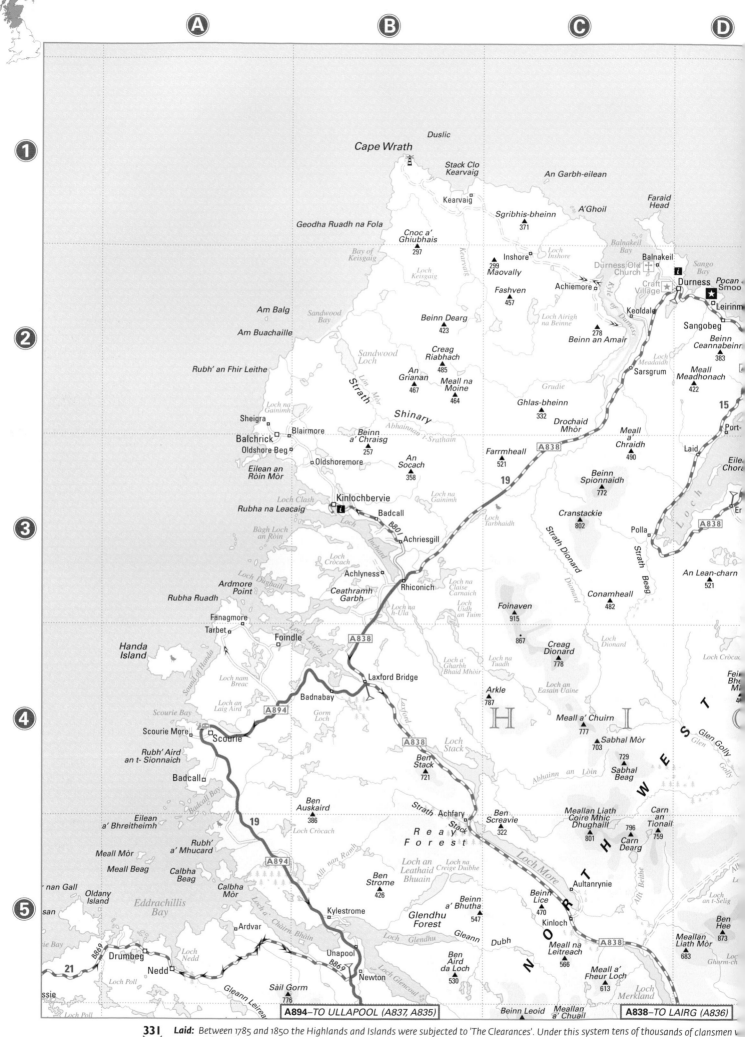

331 **Laid:** *Between 1785 and 1850 the Highlands and Islands were subjected to 'The Clearances'. Under this system tens of thousands of clansmen were removed from their homes and holdings to make way for large-scale sheep farming by the wealthy landowners. Though generally acrimonious, resettlement took place often involving re-location to poorer land along the coast where fishing and kelping were supposed to compensate for their previous existence. Some however were more fortunate and new villages were built to house them. Such a place is Laid which was created in 18 house those cleared from Eriboll on the other side of the loch.* **Map ref. D3.**

A894—TO ULLAPOOL (A837, A835)

A838—TO LAIRG (A836)

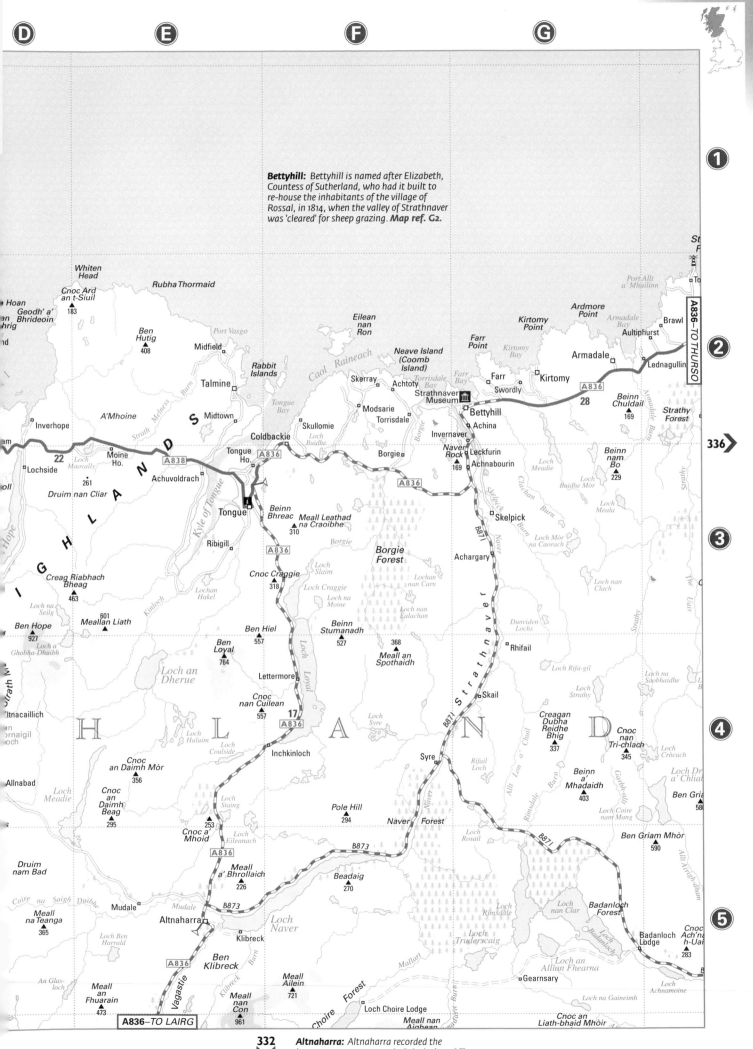

Bettyhill: Bettyhill is named after Elizabeth, Countess of Sutherland, who had it built to re-house the inhabitants of the village of Rossal, in 1814, when the valley of Strathnaver was 'cleared' for sheep grazing. **Map ref. G2.**

St.
F

A836—TO THURSO

Whiten
Head
Cnoc Ard
an t-Siuil
183

Rubha Thormaid

Port.Allt
a' Mhuilinn

To

Ardmore
Point

Armadale
Bay

Brawl

Hoan
Geodh' a'
Bhrideoin
hrig

nd

Ben
Hutig
408

Midfield

Port Vasgo

Rabbit
Islands

Eilean nan
Ron

Neave Island
(Coomb
Island)

Farr
Point

Kirtomy
Point

Kirtomy
Bay

Aultiphurst

Armadale

Lednagullin

2

A'Mhoine

Midtown

Talmine

Tongue
Bay

Skerray

Achtoty

Torrisdale
Bay

Farr
Bay

Farr

Swordly

Kirtomy

A836

Beinn
Chuldail
169

28

Strathy
Forest

Inverhope

Coldbackie

Skullomie

Modsarie
Torrisdale

Strathnaver
Museum

Bettyhill

Achina

336

Lochside

Moine
Ho.

Loch
Maovally

22

A838

Tongue
Ho.

A836

Loch
Buidhe

Borgie

Invernaver

Naver
Rock
169

Leckfurin

Achnabourin

Beinn
nam
Bo
229

Loch
Meadie

Loch
Buidhe Mòr

Loch
Meala

Achuvoldrach

Kyle of Tongue

A836

Druim nan Cliar

261

Ben Hope
927

Loch a'
Ghobha-Dhuibh

Creag Riabhach
Bheag
463

Loch na
Seilg

Meallan Liath
601

Tongue

Beinn
Bhreac
310

Meall Leathad
na Craoibhe

A836

Ribigill

Cnoc Craggie
318

Borgie

Loch
Slaim

Loch
Craggie

Borgie
Forest

Lochan
nan Carn

Loch
Hakel

Kinloch

Lochan
Hakel

Loch na
Moine

Beinn
Stumanadh
527

Loch nan
Ealachan

Achargary

B871

Naver

Strathnaver

Skelpick

Loch Mòr
na Caorach

Loch nan
Clach

Loch
Meadie

Skelpick
Burn

Clachan
Burn

3

Ben Hiel
557

Ben
Loyal
764

Beinn
Stumanadh
527

Meall an
Spothaidh

368

Dunviden
Lochs

Rhifail

Loch Rifa-gil

Loch
Strathy

Loch na
Saobhaidhe

tnacaillich

n
rnaigil
och

Loch an
Dherue

Lettermore

Loch
Loyal

Skail

Creagan
Dubha Reidhe
Bhig
337

Cnoc
nan
Tri-chlach
345

Loch
Cròcach

4

Allnabad

Loch
Meadie

Cnoc
an Daimh Mòr
356

Cnoc nan Cuilean
557

17
A836

Loch
Halium

Loch
Coulside

Inchkinloch

Loch
Syre

Syre

Rifail
Loch

Naver

Allt Loin a' Chuil

Beinn
a'
Mhadaidh
403

Ben Gria
58

Loch Dr
a' Chlia

Cnoc
an
Daimh
Beag
295

253

Cnoc a'
Mhoid

A836

Loch
Staing

Loch
Eileanach

Pole Hill
294

Naver Forest

Loch
Rosail

B871

Ben Griam Mhòr
590

Allt Airigh-dhm

Druim
nam Bad

Meall
a' Bhrollaich
226

B873

Beadaig
270

Loch Coire
nam Mang

Loch
Rimsdale

Badanloch
Forest

Rimsdale Burn

Coire na
Saigh Duibhe

Mudale

Meall
na Teanga
365

Altnaharra

Mudale

B873

Loch Naver

Loch Ben
Harrald

Klibreck

Loch
nan Clar

Loch
Truderscaig

Loch an
Allan Fhearna

Badanloch
Lodge

Loch
Badanloch

Cnoc
Ach'na
h-Uai
283

5

An Glas-
loch

A836

Ben Klibreck

Meall
an
Fhuarain
473

Vagastie

Klibreck Burn

Meall
nan Con
961

Meall
Ailein
721

Choire
Forest

Loch Choire Lodge

Gearnsary

Mallart

Loch na Gaineimh

Loch
Achnamoine

B

A836—TO LAIRG

Meall nan
Aighean

Cnoc na
Liath-bhaid Mhòir

Altnaharra: Altnaharra recorded the lowest ever temperature in Britain (-27.2°C) on the 30th December 1955. **Map ref. E5.**

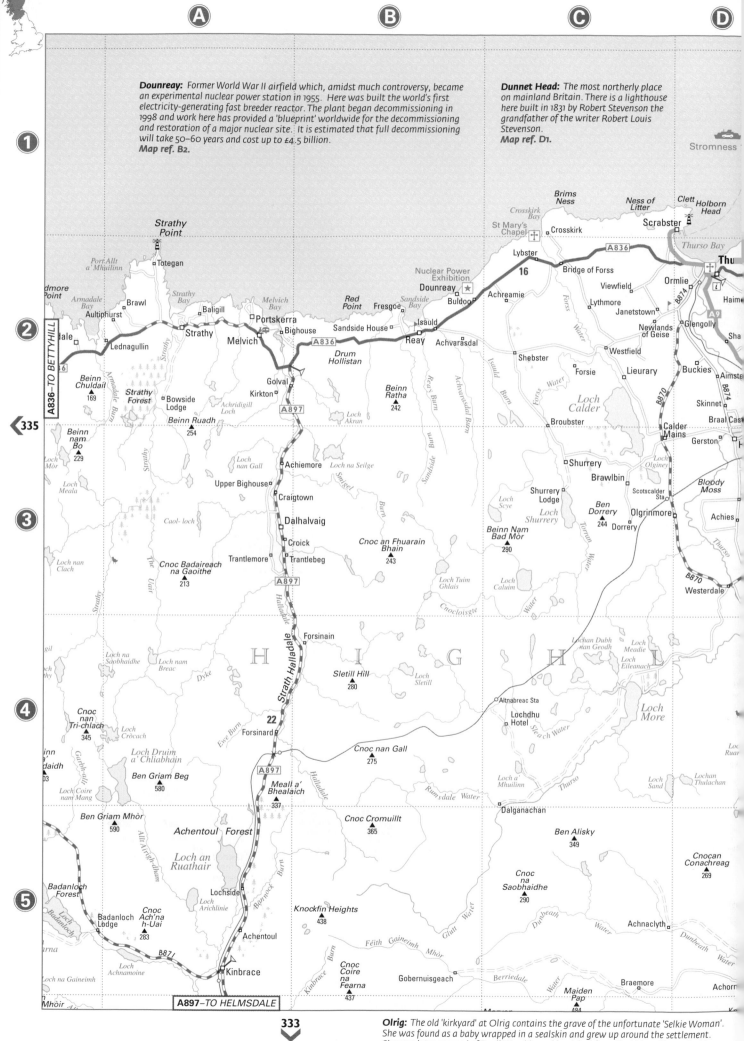

Dounreay: Former World War II airfield which, amidst much controversy, became an experimental nuclear power station in 1955. Here was built the world's first electricity-generating fast breeder reactor. The plant began decommissioning in 1998 and work here has provided a 'blueprint' worldwide for the decommissioning and restoration of a major nuclear site. It is estimated that full decommissioning will take 50–60 years and cost up to £4.5 billion. **Map ref. B2.**

Dunnet Head: The most northerly place on mainland Britain. There is a lighthouse here built in 1831 by Robert Stevenson the grandfather of the writer Robert Louis Stevenson. **Map ref. D1.**

Stromness

① ② ③ ④ ⑤

A836–TO BETTYHILL

335

Strathy Point

Totegan

Port Allt a' Mhuilinn

Armadale Bay

...dmore Point

Brawl

Aultiphurst

...dale

Lednagullin

Beinn Chuldail 169

Strathy Forest

Bowside Lodge

Beinn Ruadh 254

Beinn nam Bo 229

Loch Mòr

Loch Meala

Strathy Bay

Baligill

Strathy

Melvich

Portskerra

Bighouse

Melvich Bay

Golval

Kirkton

Achiemore

Upper Bighouse

Craigtown

Dalhalvaig

Croick

Trantlemore

Trantlebeg

Cnoc Badaireach na Gaoithe 213

Caol- loch

Loch nan Clach

Achridigill Loch

Loch nan Gall

Drum Hollistan

Sandside House

Red Point

Fresgoe

Loch Akran

Loch na Seilge

Smigel Burn

Cnoc an Fhuarain Bhain 243

Beinn Ratha 242

Isauld

Reay

Achvarasdal

Sandside Bay

Nuclear Power Exhibition

Dounreay ★

Buldoo

Achreamie

Shebster

Broubster

Shurrery

Shurrery Lodge

Beinn Nam Bad Mòr 290

Loch Scye

Loch Shurrery

Ben Dorrery 244

Dorrery

Brawlbin

Scotscalder Sta.

Olgrinmore

16

Lybster

Bridge of Forss

Viewfield

Lythmore

Janetstown

Newlands of Geise

Westfield

Forsie

Lieurary

Crosskirk Bay

St Mary's Chapel

Crosskirk

Brims Ness

Ness of Litter

Clett Holborn Head

Scrabster

Thurso Bay

Thu...

Ormlie

Glengolly

Haim...

Sha...

Buckies

Aimste...

Skinnet

Braal Cast...

Calder Mains

Gerston

Loch Calder

Loch Olginey

Bloody Moss

Achies

H I G H L I...

Strath Halladale

Forsinain

Sletill Hill 280

Loch Sletill

Lochan Dubh nan Geodh

Loch Meadie

Loch Eileanach

Loch More

Loch Ruar...

22

Forsinard

Cnoc nan Tri-chlach 345

Loch Cròcach

Ewe Burn

Loch Druim a' Chliabhain

Ben Griam Beg 580

Meall a' Bhealaich 337

Cnoc nan Gall 275

Altnabreac Sta.

Lochdhu Hotel

Sleach Water

Thurso

Dalganachan

Loch a' Mhuilinn

Runsdale Water

Loch Sand

Lochan Thulachan

...inn ...daidh ...03

Garbh-allt

Loch Coire nam Mang

Ben Griam Mhòr 590

Achentoul Forest

Cnoc Cromuillt 365

Ben Alisky 349

Cnocan Conachreag 269

Badanloch Forest

Badanloch Lodge

Loch Badanloch

Cnoc Ach'na h-Uai 283

Loch an Ruathair

Loch Arichlinie

Lochside

Knockfin Heights 438

Cnoc na Saobhaidhe 290

Achnaclyth

...arna

Loch na Gaineimh

Achentoul

B871

Loch Achnamoine

Kinbrace

Cnoc Coire na Fearna 437

Gobernuisgeach

Knockfin ...

Féith Gaineimh Mhòr

Glutt Water

Dunbeath Water

Dunbeath

Braemore

Achorn...

...Mhòr...

Berriedale

Maiden Pap 484

Ke...

Olrig: The old 'kirkyard' at Olrig contains the grave of the unfortunate 'Selkie Woman'. She was found as a baby wrapped in a sealskin and grew up around the settlement. She was later accused of Devil Worship and banished from the kirk and later died in childbirth. It is said that the stone which covers her grave fills with tears and never dries out. **Map ref. D2.**

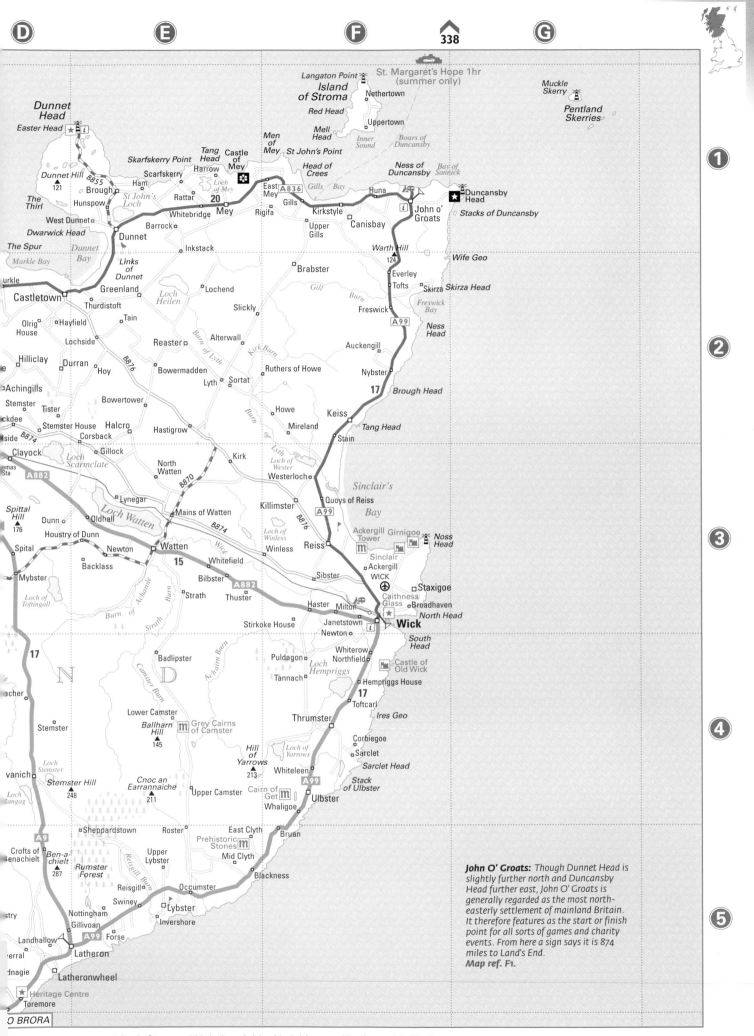

John O' Groats: Though Dunnet Head is slightly further north and Duncansby Head further east, John O' Groats is generally regarded as the most north-easterly settlement of mainland Britain. It therefore features as the start or finish point for all sorts of games and charity events. From here a sign says it is 874 miles to Land's End. **Map ref. F1.**

Island of Stroma: This is the only island in Caithness and has been uninhabited since 1962. Once the home of the notorious Sweyn the Pirate who raided and plundered along the northern coast of Scotland in the 12th Century. **Map ref. F1.**

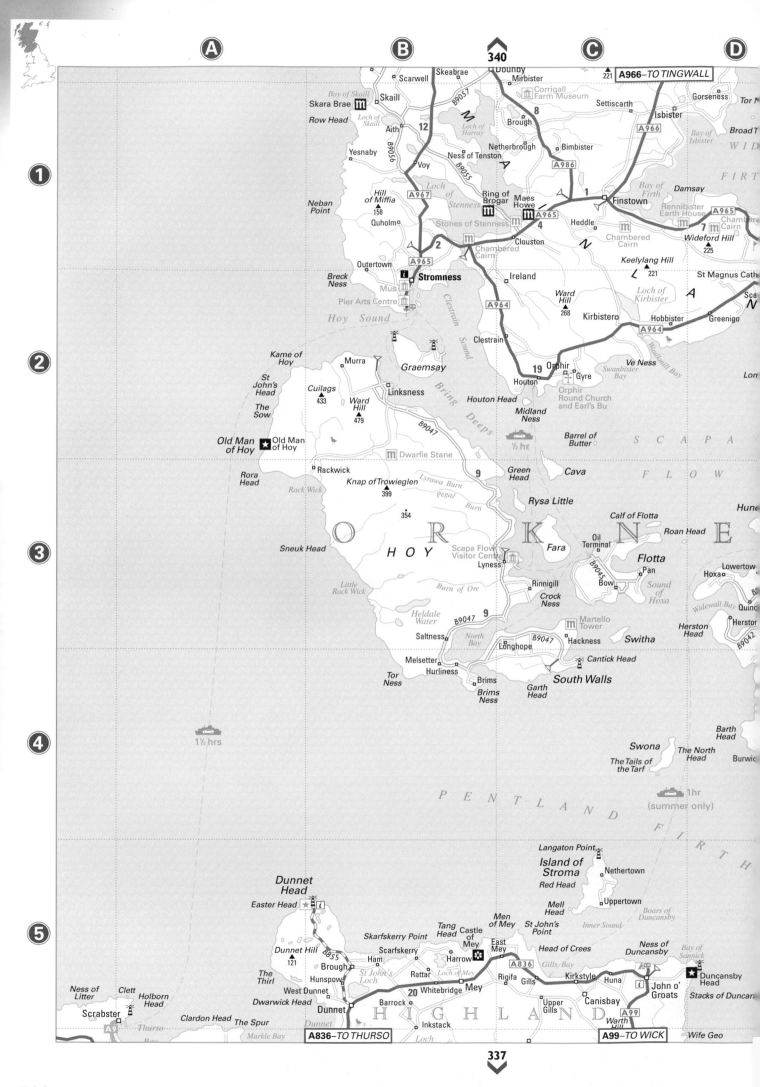

A966 - TO TINGWALL

Gorseness

Tor N

Scarwell
Skeabrae
Dounby
Mirbister
221
Isbister
Broad T

Bay of Skaill
Skaill
B9057
Corrigall Farm Museum
Settiscarth
WID
FIRT

Skara Brae
Row Head
Aith
12
Netherbrough
Brough
8
A966
Isbister
Bay of Isbister

Yesnaby
B9056
Ness of Tenston
Bimbister
A986
Damsay
Chambe
Cairn

Voy
Loch of Harray
A967
Rennibister Earth House
A965
7

Neban Point
Hill of Miffia
158
Ring of Brogar
Maes Howe
1
Finstown
Heddle
Chambered Cairn
Wideford Hill
225

Quholm
Loch of Stenness
Stones of Stenness
A965
4
Clouston
Chambered Cairn
Keelylang Hill
221

Outertown
A965
2
Chambered Cairn
Ireland
Ward Hill
268
St Magnus Cath
Sca
N

Breck Ness
Stromness
Mus
A964
Kirbister
Loch of Kirbister
A

Pier Arts Centre
Hoy Sound
Clestrain
A964
Hobbister
Greenigo

Clestrain Sound
Clestrain
19
Orphir
Gyre
Ve Ness
Lo

Kame of Hoy
Murra
Graemsay
Houton
Houton
Swanbister Bay

St John's Head
Cuilags
433
Linksness
Houton Head
Orphir Round Church and Earl's Bu

The Sow
Ward Hill
479
B9047
Midland Ness
Barrel of Butter
SCAPA

Old Man of Hoy
Old Man of Hoy
Bring Deeps
½ hr

Rora Head
Rackwick
Dwarfie Stane
9
Green Head
Cava
FLOW

Rack Wick
Knap of Trowieglen
399
Lyrawa Burn
Pegal Burn
Rysa Little
Calf of Flotta
Roan Head
Hune

354
ORKNE
E

Sneuk Head
HOY
Scapa Flow Visitor Centre
Lyness
Fara
Oil Terminal
Flotta
Pan
Hoxa
Lowertown
Quinc

Little Rack Wick
Burn of Ore
Rinnigill
Bow
Sound of Hoxa
Herston Head
Herstor

Heldale Water
B9047
9
Crock Ness
Martello Tower
Hackness
Switha
Widewall Bay
B9042

Saltness
North Bay
Longhope
B9047

Melsetter
Hurliness
Brims
Garth Head
Cantick Head
South Walls
Barth Head

Tor Ness
Brims Ness
Swona
The North Head
Burwic

The Tails of the Tarf

1½ hrs
PENTLAND
1hr (summer only)

FIRTH

Langaton Point
Island of Stroma
Nethertown
Red Head

Dunnet Head
Men of Mey
Mell Head
Uppertown
Boars of Duncansby

Easter Head
Tang Head
Castle of Mey
St John's Point
Inner Sound

Dunnet Hill
121
Skarfskerry Point
East Mey
Head of Crees
Ness of Duncansby
Bay of Sannick

The Thirl
B855
Brough
Scarfskerry
Ham
Harrow
A836
Gills Bay
Kirkstyle
Huna
John o' Groats
Duncansby Head

Holborn Head
Hunspow
St John's Loch
Rattar
Rigifa
Gills
Canisbay
Stacks of Duncan

Ness of Litter
Clett
West Dunnet
Mey
Whitebridge
20
Barrock
Upper Gills
Warth Hill

Scrabster
Dwarwick Head
Dunnet
Inkstack
HIGHLAND
A99
Wife Geo

A9
Clardon Head
The Spur
Murkle Bay

A836 - TO THURSO   A99 - TO WICK

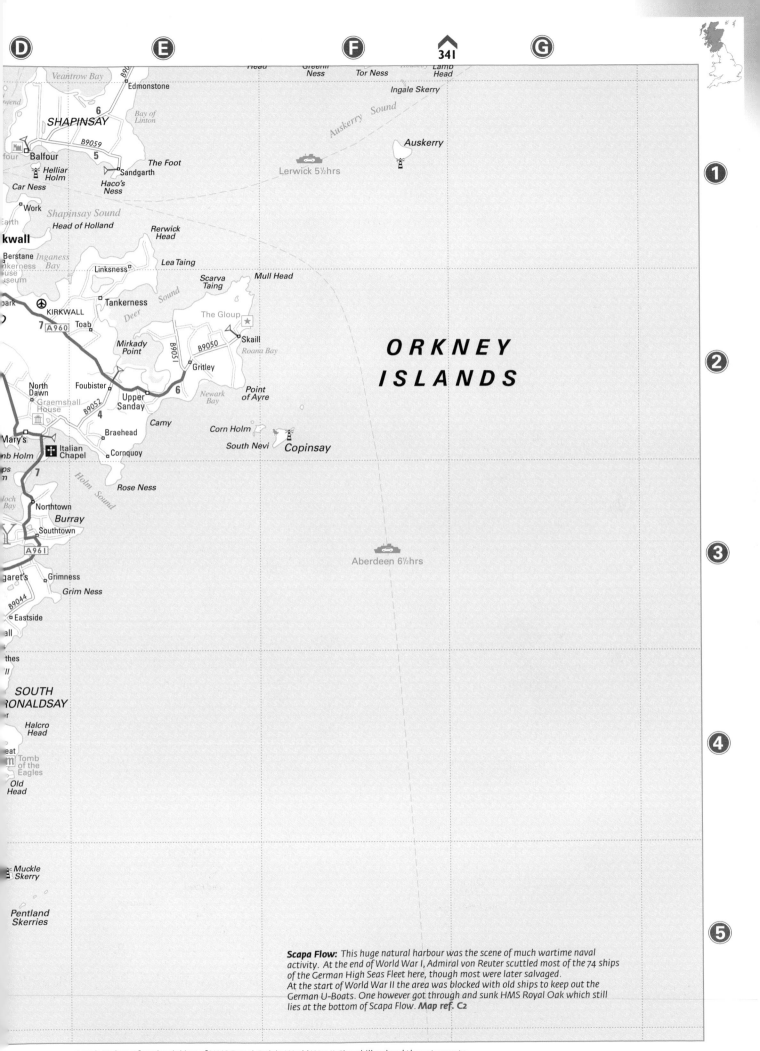

Veantrow Bay

Edmonstone

Head   Greenh   Tor Ness   Lamb
     Ness   Head

Ingale Skerry

SHAPINSAY

6

Bay of
Linton

Auskerry   Sound

Auskerry

B9059

5

Balfour

Helliar
Holm

The Foot

Sandgarth

Lerwick 5½hrs

Car Ness

Haco's
Ness

Work

Shapinsay Sound

Head of Holland

Rerwick
Head

kwall

Berstane
Inganess
nkerness   Bay
use
seum

Linksness

Lea Taing

Scarva
Taing

Mull Head

park

KIRKWALL

Tankerness

Deer   Sound

The Gloup

★

7 A960

Toab

Mirkady
Point

B9051

B9050

Skaill

Roana Bay

ORKNEY ISLANDS

Gritley

North
Dawn

Foubister

B9052

Upper
Sanday

6

Newark
Bay

Point
of Ayre

Graemshall
House

4

Mary's

Braehead

Camy

Corn Holm

mb Holm

Italian
Chapel

Cornquoy

South Nevi

Copinsay

ps
n

7

Holm   Sound

Rose Ness

och
Bay

Northtown

Burray

Southtown

Aberdeen 6½hrs

A961

Grimness

aret's

Grim Ness

B9044

Eastside

all

thes
ll

SOUTH RONALDSAY

Halcro
Head

eat

Tomb
of the
Eagles

Old
Head

Muckle
Skerry

Pentland
Skerries

Scapa Flow: *This huge natural harbour was the scene of much wartime naval activity. At the end of World War I, Admiral von Reuter scuttled most of the 74 ships of the German High Seas Fleet here, though most were later salvaged. At the start of World War II the area was blocked with old ships to keep out the German U-Boats. One however got through and sunk HMS Royal Oak which still lies at the bottom of Scapa Flow.* **Map ref. C2**

Lamb Holm: *After the sinking of HMS Royal Oak in World War II Churchill ordered the entrance to Scapa Flow to be filled in. This work was carried out by Italian Prisoners of War and became known as the Churchill Barrier. During their stay the Italians converted two Nissen huts into a Roman Catholic Chapel which still stands today.* **Also on page 125.** *The barrier now forms part of the A961 road.* **Map ref. D2**

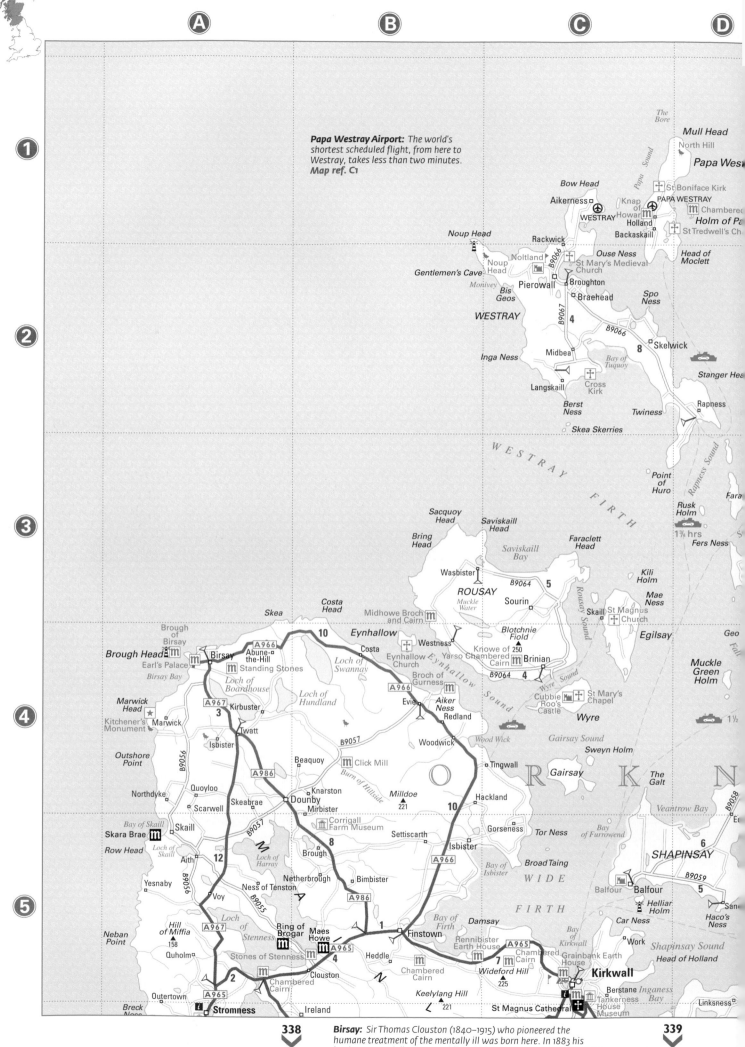

Papa Westray Airport: The world's shortest scheduled flight, from here to Westray, takes less than two minutes. *Map ref. C1*

The Bore

Mull Head

North Hill

Papa West

Bow Head

St Boniface Kirk

Aikerness

Knap of Howar

PAPA WESTRAY

Chambered

WESTRAY

Holland

Holm of Pa

Backaskaill

St Tredwell's Ch.

Noup Head

Rackwick

Ouse Ness

Head of Moclett

Noltland

St Mary's Medieval Church

Noup Head

Broughton

Gentlemen's Cave

Spo Ness

Pierowall

Braehead

Monivey

Bis Geos

WESTRAY

B9067

4

B9066

8

Skelwick

Midbea

Bay of Tuquoy

Inga Ness

Stanger Hea

Langskaill

Cross Kirk

Berst Ness

Rapness

Twiness

Skea Skerries

WESTRAY FIRTH

Point of Huro

Rapness Sound

Sacquoy Head

Saviskaill Head

Rusk Holm

Fara

Bring Head

Saviskaill Bay

Faraclett Head

1¾ hrs

Fers Ness

Wasbister

B9064

5

Kili Holm

ROUSAY

Sourin

Mae Ness

Muckle Water

Rousay Sound

Skaill

St Magnus Church

Egilsay

Costa Head

Skea

Midhowe Broch and Cairn

Eynhallow

Blotchnie Fiold

Geo

Brough of Birsay

Costa

Westness

Knowe of 250

Brinian

Fa

Brough Head

Birsay

Abune-the-Hill

Eynhallow Church

Yarso Chambered Cairn

Muckle Green Holm

Earl's Palace

A966

Standing Stones

Loch of Swannay

Broch of Gurness

B9064

4

Birsay Bay

Wyre Sound

Marwick Head

Kirbuster

A967

3

Loch of Boardhouse

A966

Cubbie Roo's Castle

St Mary's Chapel

Kitchener's Monument

Marwick

Twatt

Loch of Hundland

Evie

Aiker Ness

Wyre

1½

Isbister

Redland

B9057

Woodwick

Wood Wick

Gairsay Sound

Sweyn Holm

Outshore Point

Beaquoy

Click Mill

R

Gairsay

K

N

Burn of Hillside

O

Tingwall

The Galt

Northdyke

Quoyloo

Knarston

Milldoe 221

Hackland

Veantrow Bay

B9058

Ed

Scarwell

Skeabrae

A986

Dounby

Mirbister

10

Isbister

Gorseness

Bay of Furrowend

6

SHAPINSAY

Bay of Skaill

Corrigall Farm Museum

Settiscarth

A966

Tor Ness

Skaill

Skara Brae

B9057

Brough

8

Broad Taing

Bay of Isbister

WIDE

Balfour

Balfour

B9059

5

Row Head

Loch of Skaill

Aith

12

Loch of Harray

Netherbrough

Bimbister

A986

FIRTH

Helliar Holm

Yesnaby

B9056

Ness of Tenston

Bay of Firth

Damsay

Car Ness

Haco's Ness

San

Voy

Ring of Brogar

Maes Howe

1

Finstown

Rennibister Earth House

Bay of Kirkwall

Work

Shapinsay Sound

Neban Point

Hill of Miffia 158

Loch of Stenness

A965

Grainbank Earth House

Head of Holland

Quholm

A967

Stones of Stenness

4

Heddle

7

Chambered Cairn

Kirkwall

Berstane

Inganess Bay

2

Chambered Cairn

Clouston

Chambered Cairn

Wideford Hill 225

Linksness

Stromness

Ireland

Keelylang Hill 221

St Magnus Cathedral

Tankerness House Museum

Breck Ness

Birsay: Sir Thomas Clouston (1840–1915) who pioneered the humane treatment of the mentally ill was born here. In 1883 his book on mental diseases established his international reputation as a leading figure in the diagnosis and treatment of such illnesses. *Map ref. A4*

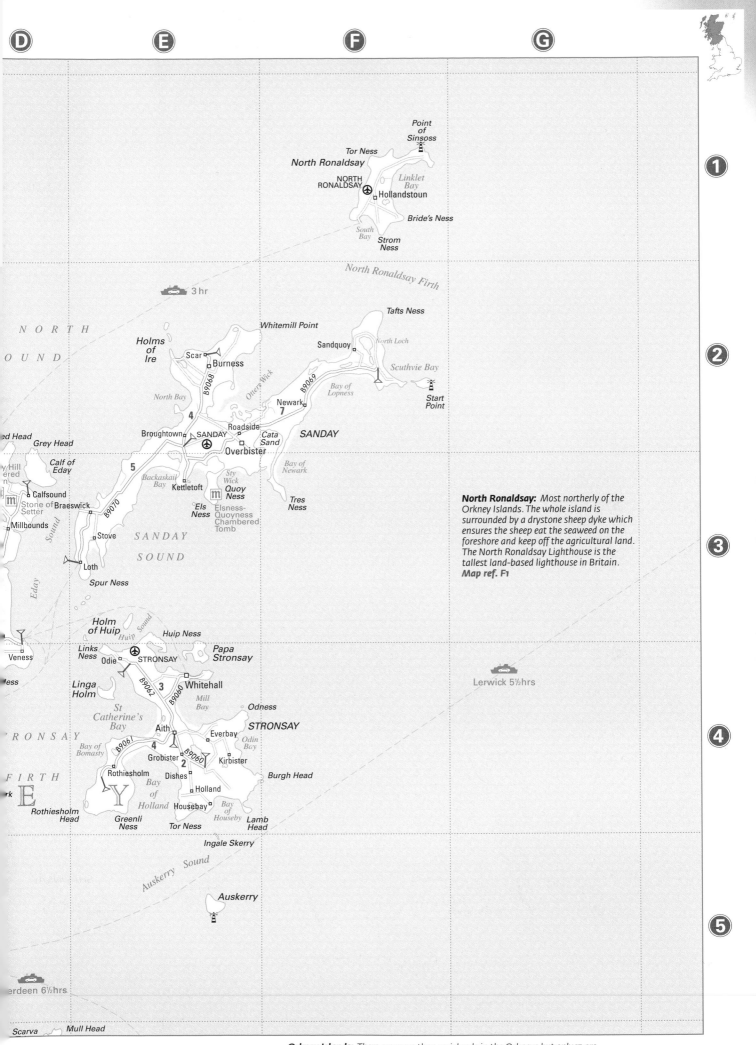

Point
of
Sinsoss

Tor Ness

North Ronaldsay

NORTH
RONALDSAY

Hollandstoun

Linklet
Bay

Bride's Ness

South
Bay

Strom
Ness

North Ronaldsay Firth

3 hr

N O R T H

S O U N D

Whitemill Point

Tafts Ness

Holms
of
Ire

Scar

Burness

Sandquoy

North Loch

Scuthvie Bay

B9068

North Bay

Otters Wick

B9069

*Bay of
Lopness*

Start
Point

Newark

4

7

ed Head

Grey Head

Broughtown

SANDAY

Roadside

*Cata
Sand*

SANDAY

Overbister

Calf of
Eday

y Hill
ered

5

*Backaskail
Bay*

Kettletoft

*Sty
Wick*

Quoy
Ness

*Bay of
Newark*

m

Calfsound

Stone of
Setter

Braeswick

B9070

Els
Ness

Elsness-
Quoyness
Chambered
Tomb

m

Tres
Ness

North Ronaldsay: *Most northerly of the
Orkney Islands. The whole island is
surrounded by a drystone sheep dyke which
ensures the sheep eat the seaweed on the
foreshore and keep off the agricultural land.
The North Ronaldsay Lighthouse is the
tallest land-based lighthouse in Britain.*
Map ref. F1

Millbounds

Stove

S A N D A Y

S O U N D

Loth

Spur Ness

*Eday
Sound*

Holm
of Huip

Huip Sound

Huip Ness

Links
Ness

Papa
Stronsay

Veness

Odie

STRONSAY

ess

Linga
Holm

3

B9060

Whitehall

Lerwick 5½hrs

B9062

*Mill
Bay*

*St
Catherine's
Bay*

Odness

STRONSAY

Aith

Everbay

*Odin
Bay*

RONSAY

*Bay of
Bomasty*

B9061

4

Grobister

B9060

2

Kirbister

Burgh Head

Rothiesholm

FIRTH

rk

E

Dishes

Holland

Housebay

*Bay
of
Housey*

Lamb
Head

Rothiesholm
Head

*Bay
of
Holland*

Y

Greenli
Ness

Tor Ness

Ingale Skerry

Auskerry Sound

Auskerry

Aberdeen 6½hrs

Scarva

Mull Head

Orkney Islands: *There are more than 70 islands in the Orkneys but only 17 are
inhabited. Orkney summers feature almost continual daylight with the sun
above the horizon for over 18 hours a day....by contrast, in winter, the sun rises
after 9am and sets around 3.30pm so there are barely 7 hours of daylight.*

341

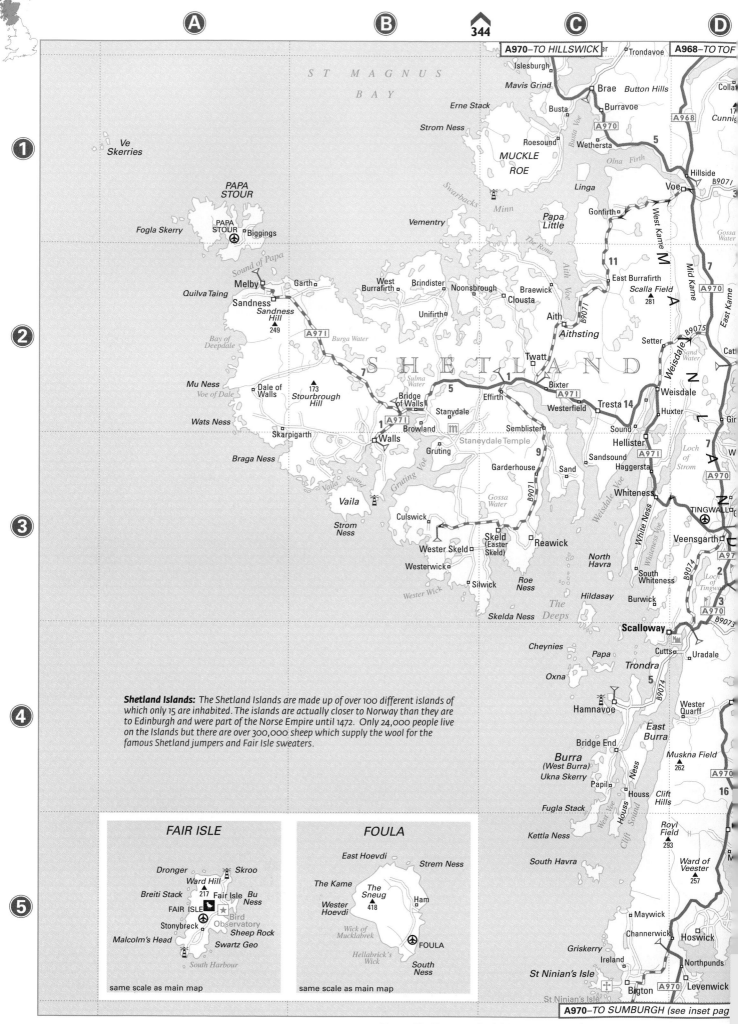

A970–TO HILLSWICK   er   Trondavoe   **A968**–TO TOF

Islesburgh

Mavis Grind   **Brae**   Button Hills   Colla

Busta   Burravoe   **A968**

Erne Stack   17

Strom Ness   Roesound   Wethersta   Cunnig

Ve
Skerries   **MUCKLE
ROE**   Busta Voe   **5**

Linga   Olna Firth   Hillside   B9071

**PAPA
STOUR**   Swarbacks   Papa
Little   Minn   Gonfirth   West Kame   Voe   M

Fogla Skerry   **PAPA
STOUR**   Biggings   Vementry   The Rona   **11**   East Burrafirth   Scalla Field
281   A   Gossa
Water

Sound of Papa   West
Burrafirth   Brindister   Noonsbrough   Braewick
Clousta   **B9071**   Aith Voe   **7**

Melby   Garth   **Aithsting**   Setter   **B9075**   Cat

Quilva Taing   Unifirth   **Twatt**   N   Sand
Water

Sandness   Sandness
Hill
249   **A971**   Burga Water   S H E T L A N D   **1**   Bixter   **A971**   Weisdale   Huxter   L   Gir

Bay of
Deepdale   Sulma
Water   **5**   Effirth   Westerfield   Tresta **14**   Weisdale   A

Mu Ness   Dale of
Walls   173
Stourbrough
Hill   **7**   Bridge
of Walls   Stanydale   Semblister   Sound   Hellister   **A971**   A970   **7**
Voe of Dale   Loch
of
Strom

Wats Ness   **1** A971   Browland   **m**   Sandsound   Haggersta   A970

Skarpigarth   **Walls**   Gruting   Staneydale Temple   **9**   Sand   Whiteness   Z

Braga Ness   Garderhouse   **B9071**   Gossa
Water   Sandsound   White Voe   **TINGWALL**   A

Vaila   Culswick   Weisdale Voe   Whiteness Voe   North
Havra   Veensgarth   A97

Strom
Ness   Vaila Sound   Skeld
(Easter
Skeld)   Reawick   South
Whiteness   **B9074**   **2**
Loch
of
Tingwa

Wester Skeld   Burwick   A970   **3**
B9073

Westerwick   Roe
Ness   Hildasay   **Scalloway**

Skelda Ness   Wester Wick   Silwick   The
Deeps   Cheynies   Papa   Cutts   Uradale

Shetland Islands: The Shetland Islands are made up of over 100 different islands of
which only 15 are inhabited. The islands are actually closer to Norway than they are
to Edinburgh and were part of the Norse Empire until 1472. Only 24,000 people live
on the Islands but there are over 300,000 sheep which supply the wool for the
famous Shetland jumpers and Fair Isle sweaters.   Oxna   **Trondra**   **5**   B9074   Wester
Quarff

Hamnavoe   **East
Burra**

Bridge End   Muskna Field
262   A970

Burra
(West Burra)   Ness   Clift
Hills   **16**

Ukna Skerry   Papil   Houss

Fugla Stack   West Voe   Houss Sound   Royl
Field
293

Kettla Ness   Ward of
Veester
257   M

South Havra   Clift Voe   Maywick

FAIR ISLE   **FOULA**   Channerwick   Hoswick

Dronger   Skroo   East Hoevdi   Strem Ness   Griskerry   Northpunds

Ward Hill   The Kame   The
Sneug
418   Ham   Ireland

Breiti Stack   217   Fair Isle   Bu
Ness   Wester
Hoevdi   **St Ninian's Isle**   Bigton   Levenwick

FAIR ISLE   Bird
Observatory   **FOULA**   St Ninian's Isle   A970

Stonybreck   Sheep Rock   Wick of
Mucklabrek   **A970**–TO SUMBURGH (see inset pag

Malcolm's Head   Swartz Geo   Hellabrick's
Wick   South
Ness

South Harbour

same scale as main map   same scale as main map

Twatt: The Norse meaning is 'clearing in the trees',
proving that at some time there must have been
trees growing here.
Map ref. C2

1

Lunna
Taing of Kelswick
¾ hr
Lunning
West Linga
Challister Ness
Skaw Taing
Filla
1½ hrs
dlin
Lunnasting
Skaw
Skelberry
Challister
Brough
Marrister
Isbister
WHALSAY
Grif Skerry
Huxter
½ hr
Symbister
East Linga
Dury Voe
Stava Ness
Clett Head

2

SHETLAND
ISLANDS

xfirth
Billister
J 10
Neap
89075
Brettabister
The Keen
South Nesting Bay
Skellister
Ling Ness
Benston
Eswick
Moul of Eswick
Gletness
2½ hrs
South Isle of Gletness

3

Hawks Ness

Kebister Ness

hours
Bergen (summer only).............12½
Seydisfjordur (summer only)....31
Torshavn (summer only)..........13

Score Head
Aith Ness
Gunnista
Bressay
Heogan
Loder Head
Shetland Mus
Maryfield
Setter
Isle of Noss
Lerwick
Brough
Fort Charlotte
Grindiscol
Brei Wick
Millburn Geo
Feadda Ness
Kirkabister
226
Ward of Bressay
Bard Head

4

Ireland
A970–TO LERWICK
St Ninian's Isle
A970
Bigton
Levenwick
Mousa Sound
St Ninian's Isle Church
No Ness
Colsay
B9122
Blovid
4
Scousburgh
6
Fora Ness
Skelberry
Troswick Ness
Wick of Shunni
Loch of Spiggie
Boddam
Hillwell
Voe
Quendale
5
Lambhoga Head
283
A970
Fitful Head
Bay of Quendale
Exanboe
Siggar Ness
Toab
SUMBURGH
Lady's Holm
Grutness
Jarlshof Prehistoric & Norse Centre
Sumburgh
Ness of Burgi
Sumburgh Head

5

elli Ness
kerry
hours
Aberdeen....12-14
Kirkwall..........5½
Mousa

same scale as main map

Lerwick: *Arthur Anderson (1792–1868) was born here. Anderson formed the Union Steam Ship Company in 1853 which later became the great Union-Castle Line.*
Map ref. D3

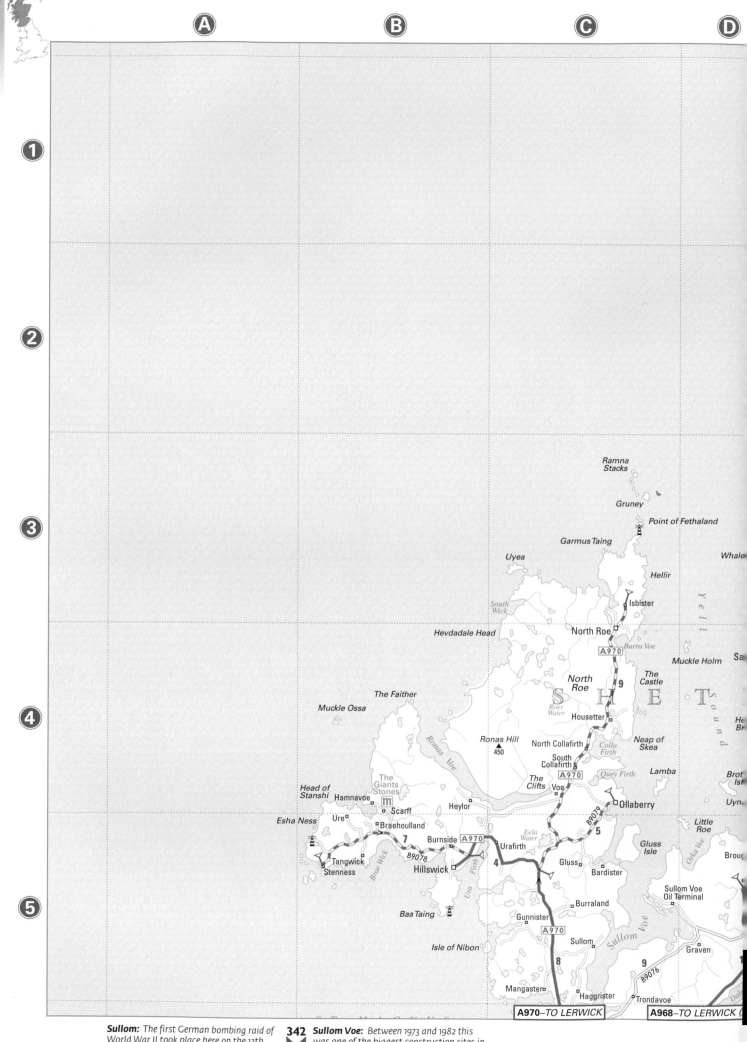

1

2

3

Ramna
Stacks

Gruney

Point of Fethaland

Garmus Taing

Uyea

Whale

South
Wick

Hellir

Isbister

Hevdadale Head

North Roe

Burra Voe

A970

Muckle Holm

Sa

North
Roe

S H E

The
Castle

T

4

The Faither

Muckle Ossa

Ronas Hill
▲
450

Roer
Water

Housetter

North Collafirth

Colla
Firth

Neap of
Skea

So

He
Br

South
Collafirth

The
Clifts

A970

Quey Firth

Lamba

Brot
Isl

Voe

Uyn

The
Giants
Stones

Head of
Stanshi

Hamnavoe

Scarff

Heylor

Ollaberry

Little
Roe

Gluss
Isle

Brough

Esha Ness

Ure

Braehoulland

7

Burnside

A970

Urafirth

Eela
Water

5

Bardister

Gluss

B9079

Tangwick
Stenness

Brae Wick

B9078

Hillswick

Ura Firth

4

Sullom Voe
Oil Terminal

Baa Taing

Gunnister

Burraland

5

Isle of Nibon

A970

Sullom

Sullom Voe

Graven

8

9

B9076

Mangaster

Haggrister

Trondavoe

A970–TO LERWICK   A968–TO LERWICK (

Sullom: The first German bombing raid of World War II took place here on the 13th November 1939 and the first casualty of a German bomb on British soil was a rabbit.
Map ref. C5

342 **Sullom Voe:** Between 1973 and 1982 this was one of the biggest construction sites in Europe with over 6,000 people employed building the oil terminal.
Map ref. C5

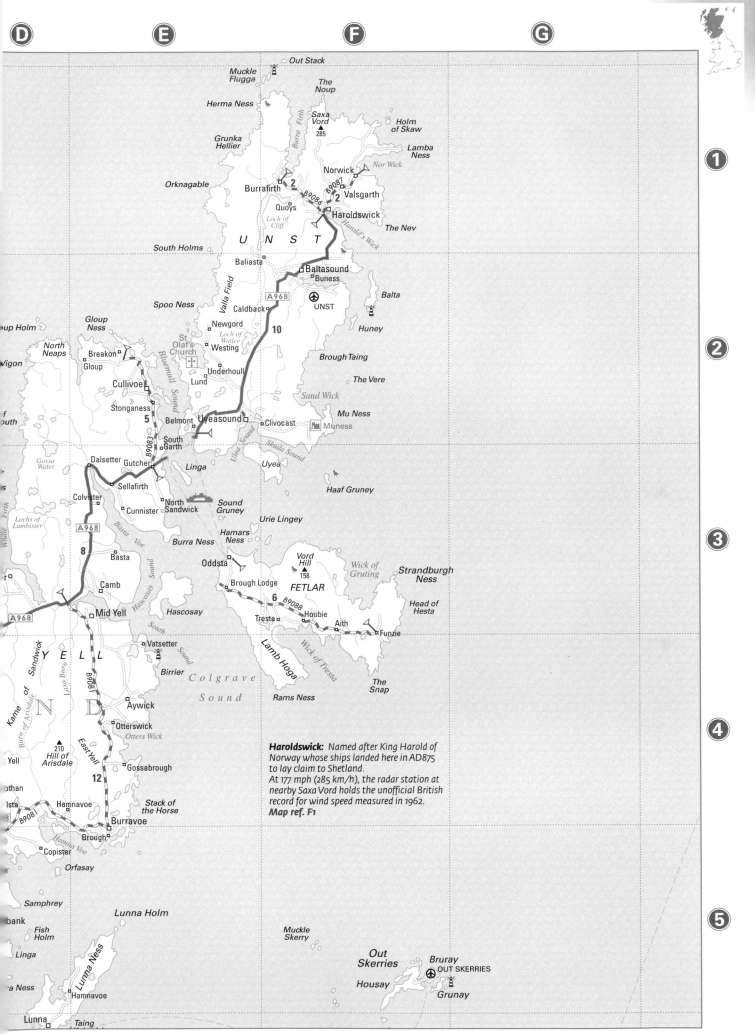

Out Stack

Muckle
Flugga

The
Noup

Herma Ness

Saxa
Vord
▲
285

Holm
of Skaw

Grunka
Hellier

Lamba
Ness

Norwick   Nor Wick

Orknagable

B9087

Burrafirth   **2**   Valsgarth

B9086   **2**

Quoys

Haroldswick

The Nev

Loch of
Cliff

Harold's Wick

U N S T

Baliasta

South Holms

Baltasound

Buness

A968

Valla Field

Caldback

Balta

Spoo Ness

Newgord

Loch of
Watlee

UNST

Gloup
Ness

St
Olaf's
Church

Westing

Huney

North
Neaps

Breakon

Brough Taing

Gloup

Underhoull

Lund

The Vere

Cullivoe

Sand Wick

Stonganess

5

Bluemull Sound

Belmont

Uyeasound

Clivocast

Muness

Mu Ness

South
Garth

B9083

Linga

Uyea

Skuda Sound

Ulsta Sound

Gossa
Water

Dalsetter

Gutcher

Sellafirth

Haaf Gruney

Colvister

Cunnister

North
Sandwick

Sound
Gruney

Lochs of
Lumbister

A968

Burra Ness

Hamars
Ness

Urie Lingey

8

Basta

Oddsta

Vord
Hill
▲
158

Wick of
Gruting

Strandburgh
Ness

Basta Voe

Camb

Brough Lodge

FETLAR

Head of
Hesta

A968

6

B9088

Houbie

Hascosay Sound

Mid Yell

Hascosay

Tresta

Aith

Funzie

Vatsetter

South Sound

N   D

Birrier

Lamb Hoga

Wick of Tresta

The
Snap

Colgrave
Sound

B9081

Y E L L

Aywick

Otterswick

Rams Ness

Karne of Arisdale

Otters Wick

East Yell

Laxa Burn

Hill of
Arisdale
▲
210

12

Gossabrough

Stack of
the Horse

Hamnavoe

Ista

Burravoe

B9081

Brough

Hamna Voe

Copister

Orfasay

Samphrey

Lunna Holm

Linga

Lunna Ness

Fish
Holm

bank

Muckle
Skerry

Out
Skerries

Bruray

OUT SKERRIES

Ness

Hamnavoe

Housay

Grunay

Lunna   Taing

Haroldswick: Named after King Harold of
Norway whose ships landed here in AD875
to lay claim to Shetland.
At 177 mph (285 km/h), the radar station at
nearby Saxa Vord holds the unofficial British
record for wind speed measured in 1962.
Map ref. F1

343
∨

raven: During the war this was an air base from
hich the RAF flying boats patrolled the North
lantic in search of German U Boats. **Map ref. D5**

Muckle Flugga: When the lighthouse keeper was at home this
was once the most northerly inhabited island in Britain. The next
rock along, the uninhabited 'Out Stack' is the most northern bit of
the whole of Britain. **Map ref. F1**

PLYMOUTH

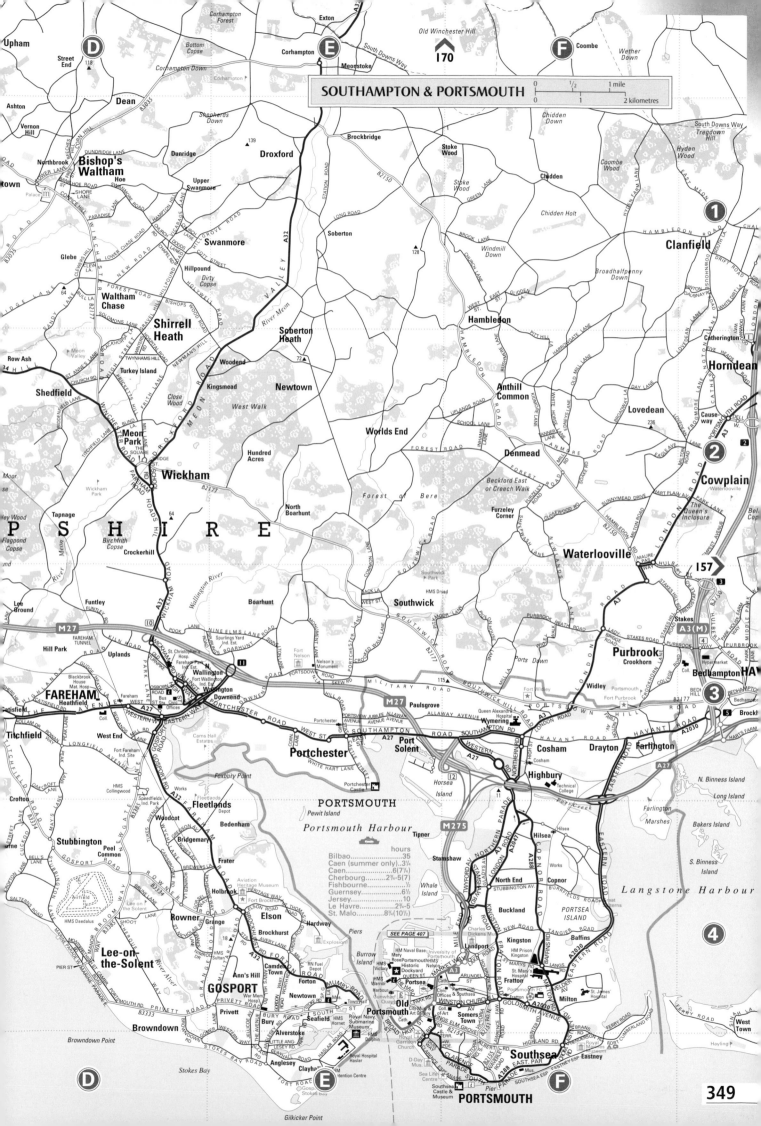

BRISTOL CHANNEL

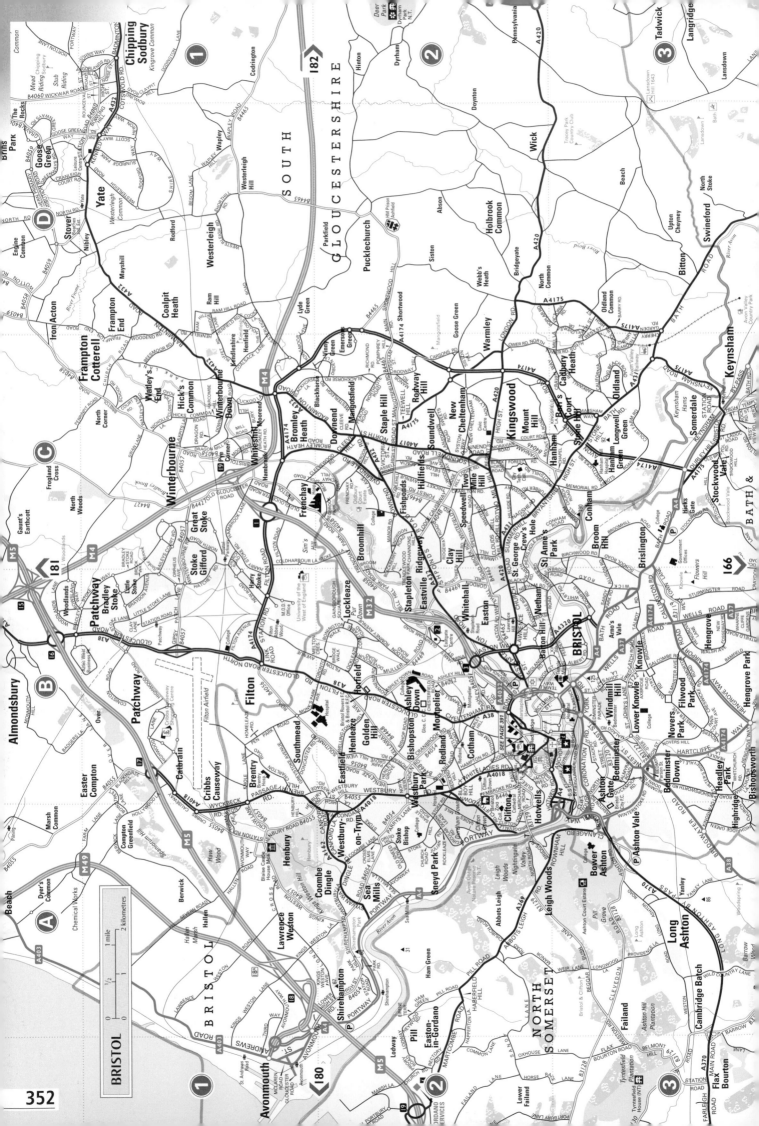

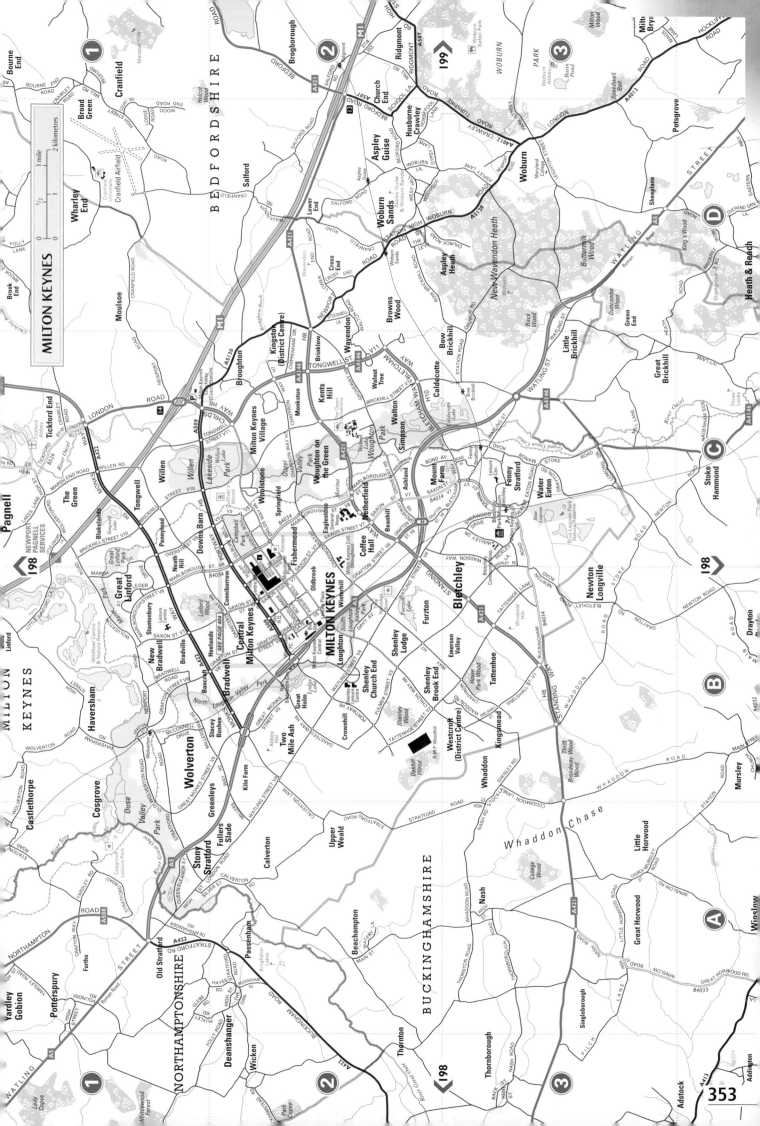

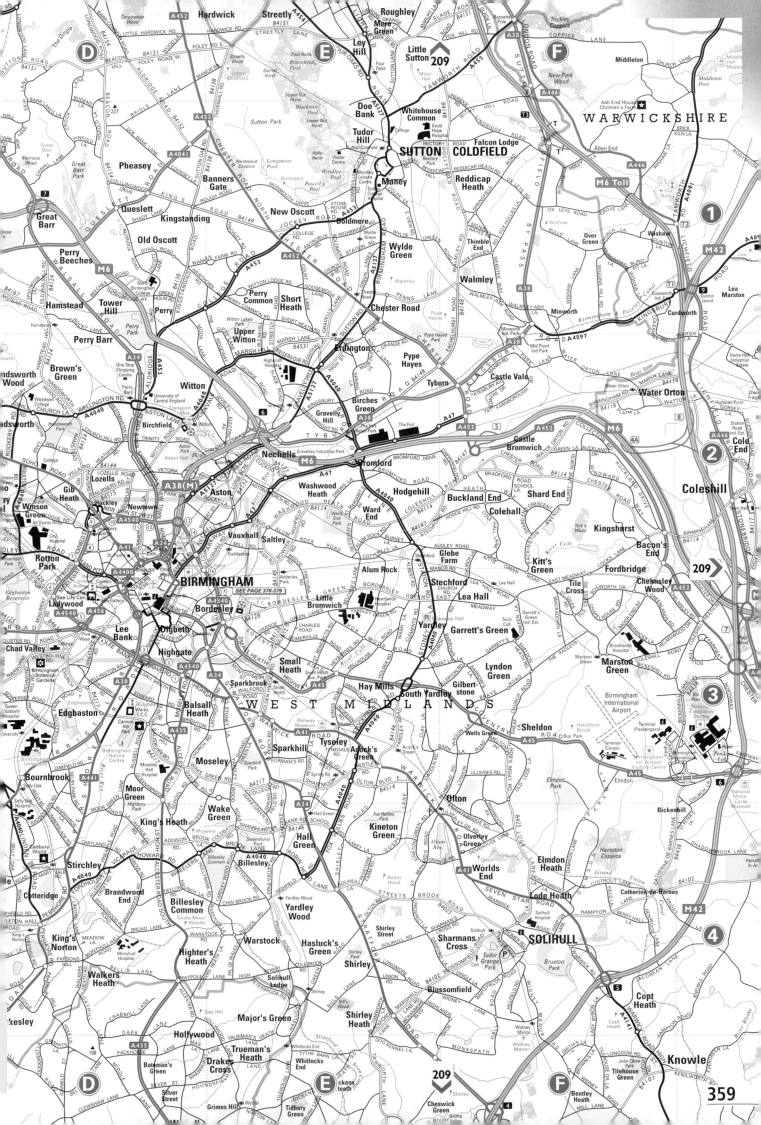

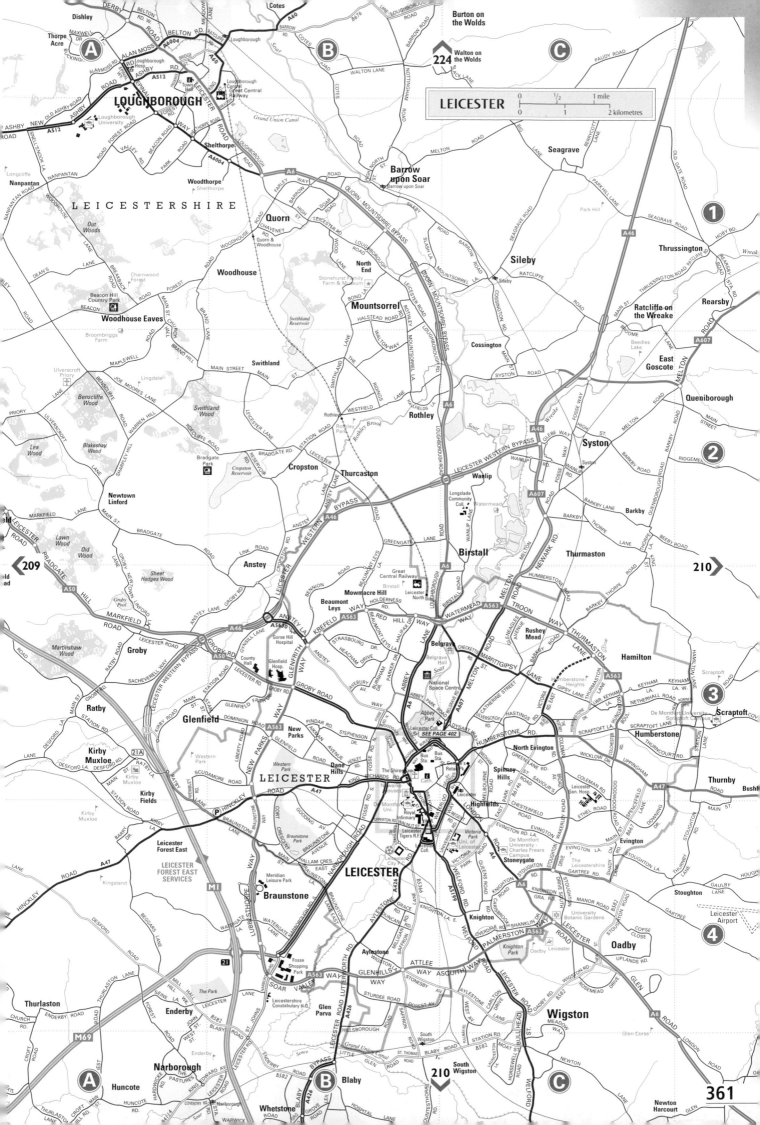

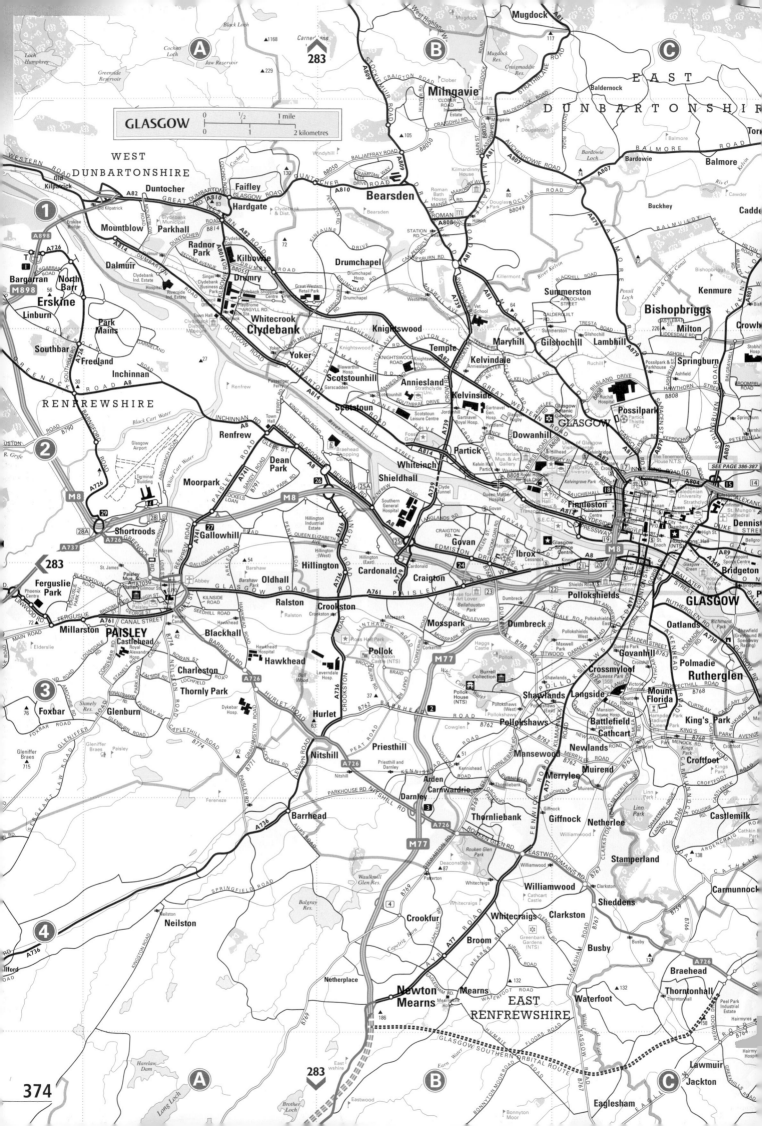

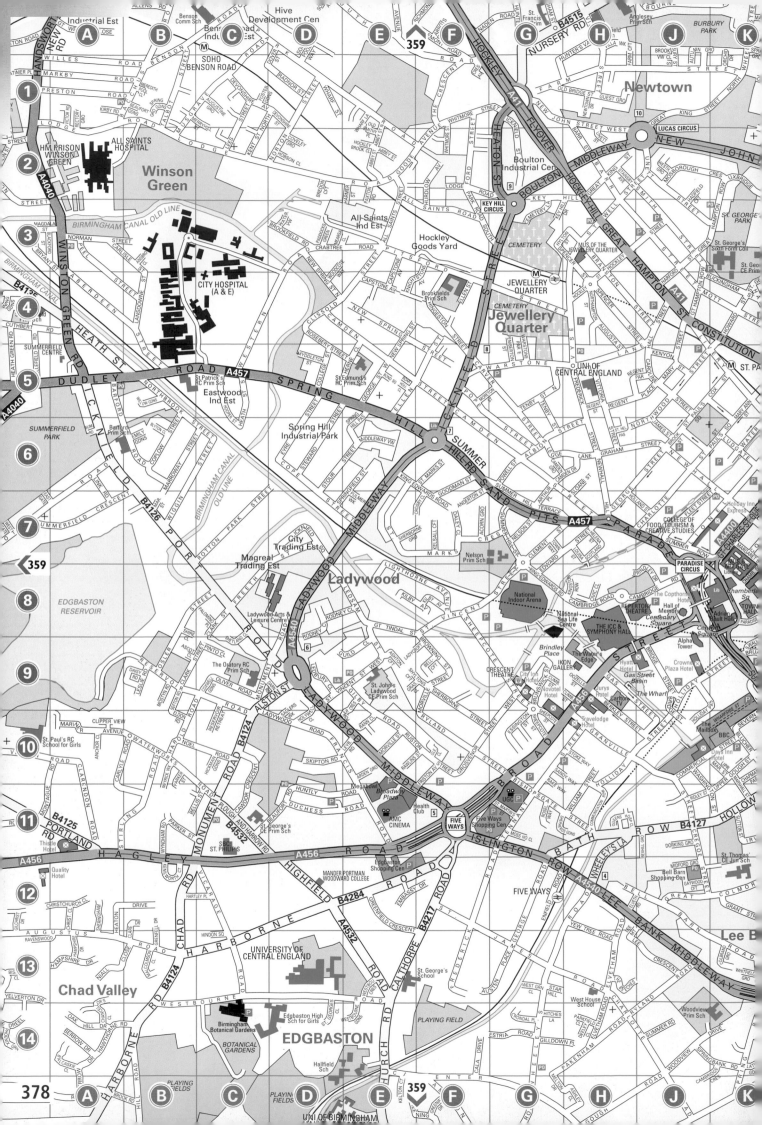

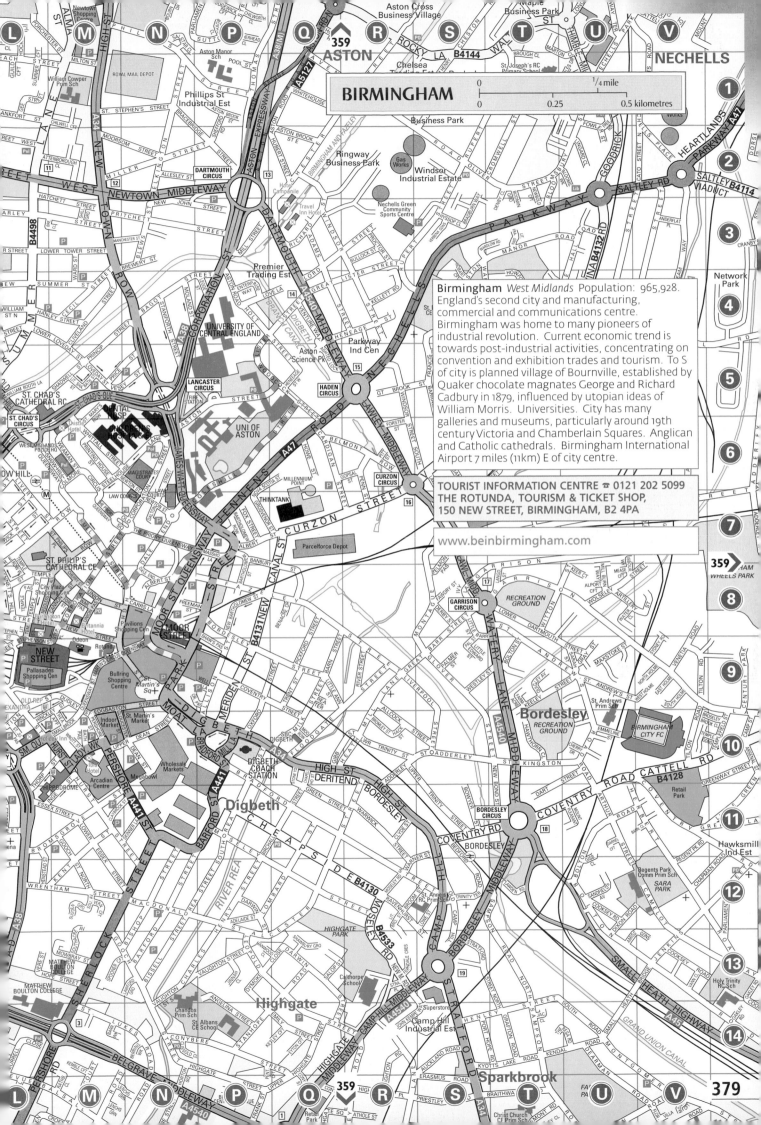

Birmingham *West Midlands* Population: 965,928. England's second city and manufacturing, commercial and communications centre. Birmingham was home to many pioneers of industrial revolution. Current economic trend is towards post-industrial activities, concentrating on convention and exhibition trades and tourism. To S of city is planned village of Bournville, established by Quaker chocolate magnates George and Richard Cadbury in 1879, influenced by utopian ideas of William Morris. Universities. City has many galleries and museums, particularly around 19th century Victoria and Chamberlain Squares. Anglican and Catholic cathedrals. Birmingham International Airport 7 miles (11km) E of city centre.

TOURIST INFORMATION CENTRE ☎ 0121 202 5099
THE ROTUNDA, TOURISM & TICKET SHOP,
150 NEW STREET, BIRMINGHAM, B2 4PA

www.beinbirmingham.com

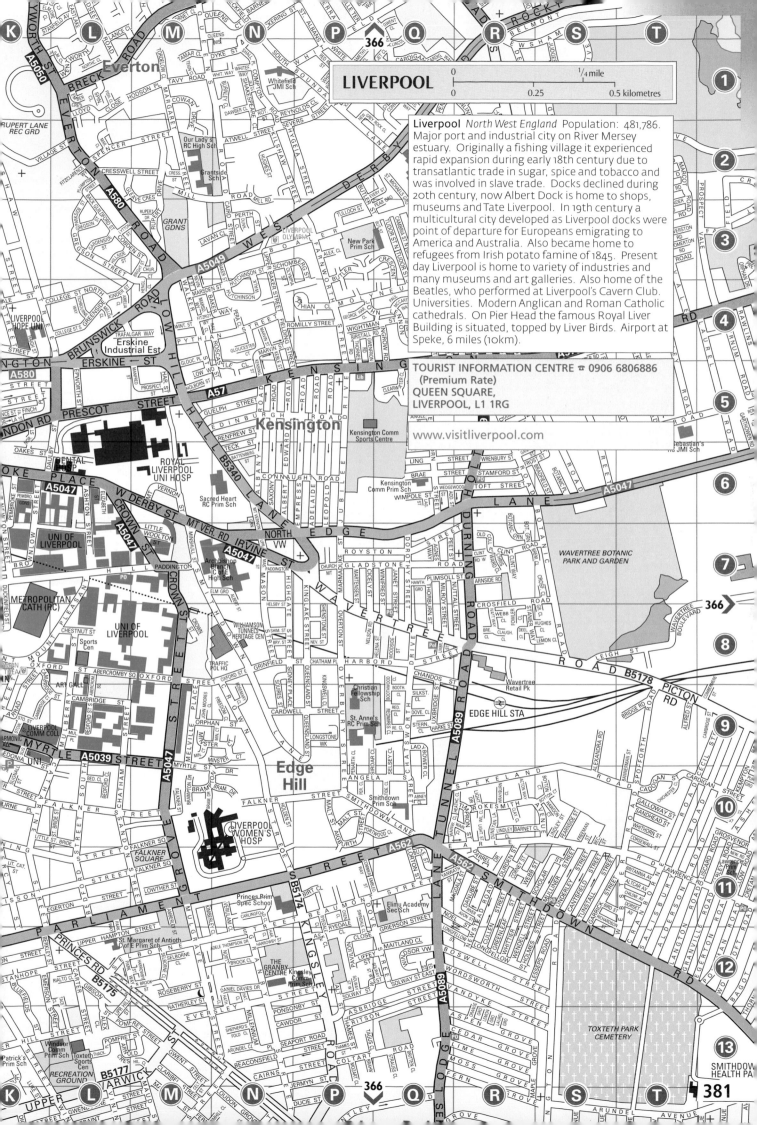

LIVERPOOL

0   1/4 mile

0   0.25   0.5 kilometres

Liverpool *North West England* Population: 481,786. Major port and industrial city on River Mersey estuary. Originally a fishing village it experienced rapid expansion during early 18th century due to transatlantic trade in sugar, spice and tobacco and was involved in slave trade. Docks declined during 20th century, now Albert Dock is home to shops, museums and Tate Liverpool. In 19th century a multicultural city developed as Liverpool docks were point of departure for Europeans emigrating to America and Australia. Also became home to refugees from Irish potato famine of 1845. Present day Liverpool is home to variety of industries and many museums and art galleries. Also home of the Beatles, who performed at Liverpool's Cavern Club. Universities. Modern Anglican and Roman Catholic cathedrals. On Pier Head the famous Royal Liver Building is situated, topped by Liver Birds. Airport at Speke, 6 miles (10km).

TOURIST INFORMATION CENTRE ☎ 0906 6806886
(Premium Rate)
QUEEN SQUARE,
LIVERPOOL, L1 1RG

www.visitliverpool.com

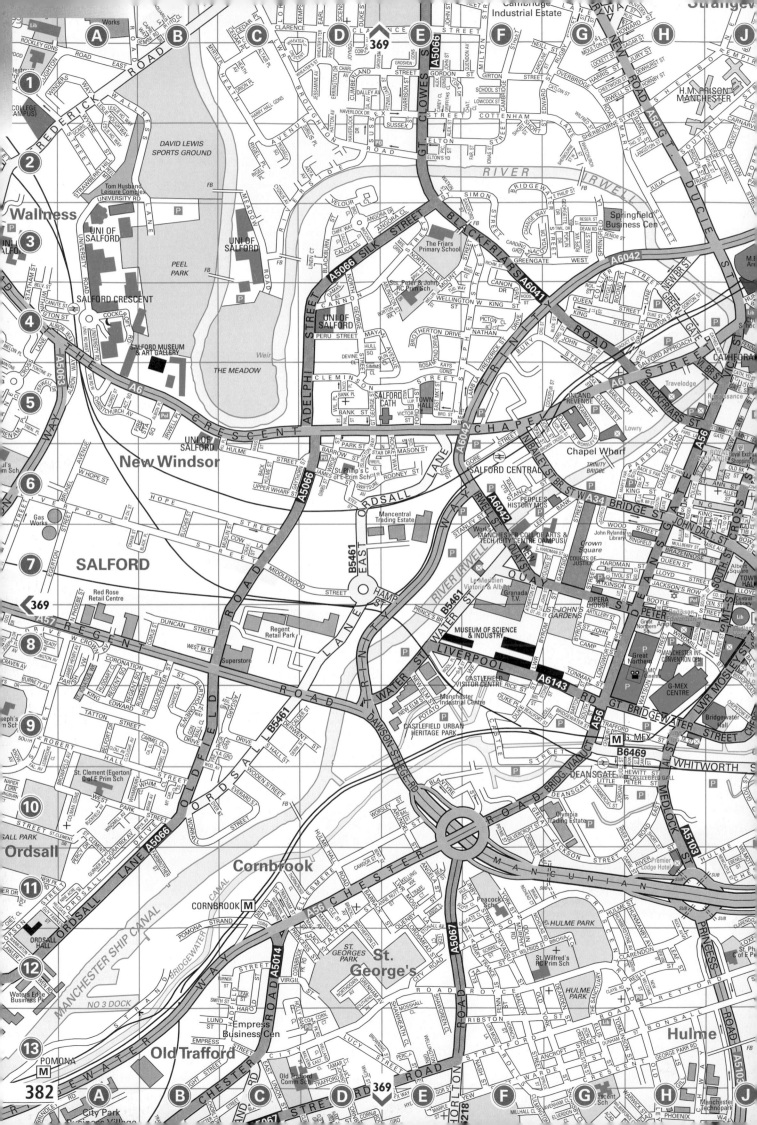

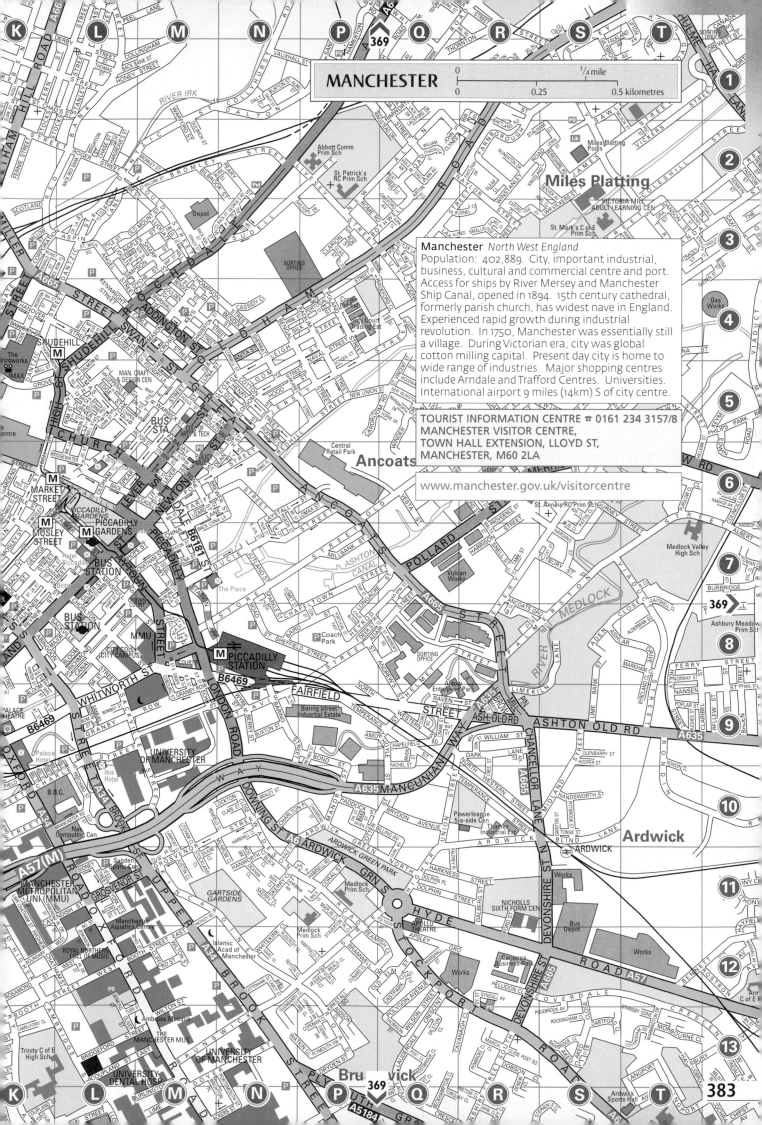

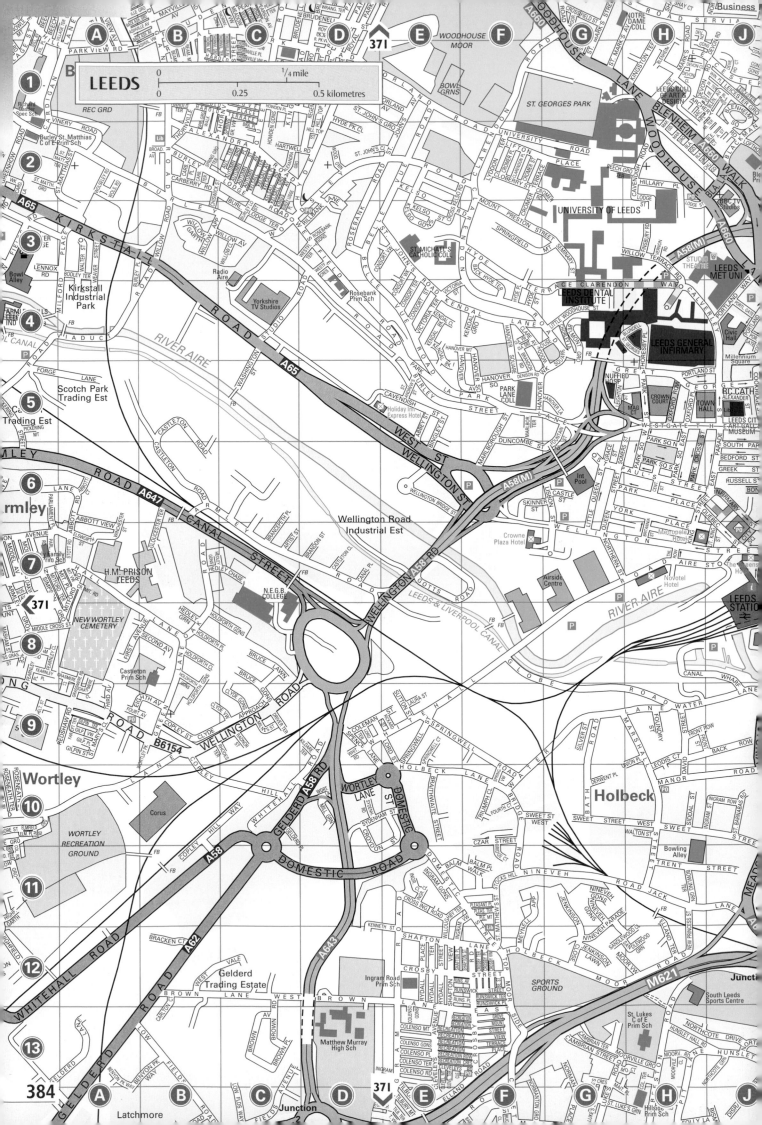

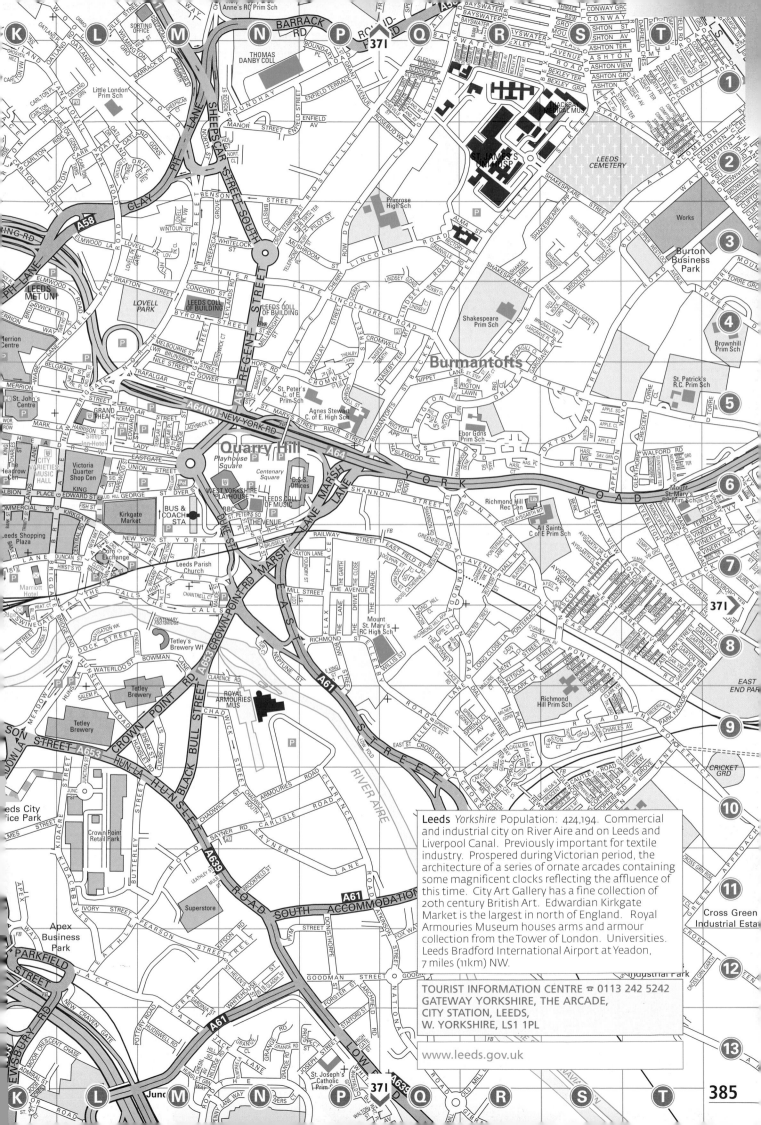

Leeds *Yorkshire* Population: 424,194. Commercial and industrial city on River Aire and on Leeds and Liverpool Canal. Previously important for textile industry. Prospered during Victorian period, the architecture of a series of ornate arcades containing some magnificent clocks reflecting the affluence of this time. City Art Gallery has a fine collection of 20th century British Art. Edwardian Kirkgate Market is the largest in north of England. Royal Armouries Museum houses arms and armour collection from the Tower of London. Universities. Leeds Bradford International Airport at Yeadon, 7 miles (11km) NW.

TOURIST INFORMATION CENTRE ☎ 0113 242 5242
GATEWAY YORKSHIRE, THE ARCADE,
CITY STATION, LEEDS,
W. YORKSHIRE, LS1 1PL

www.leeds.gov.uk

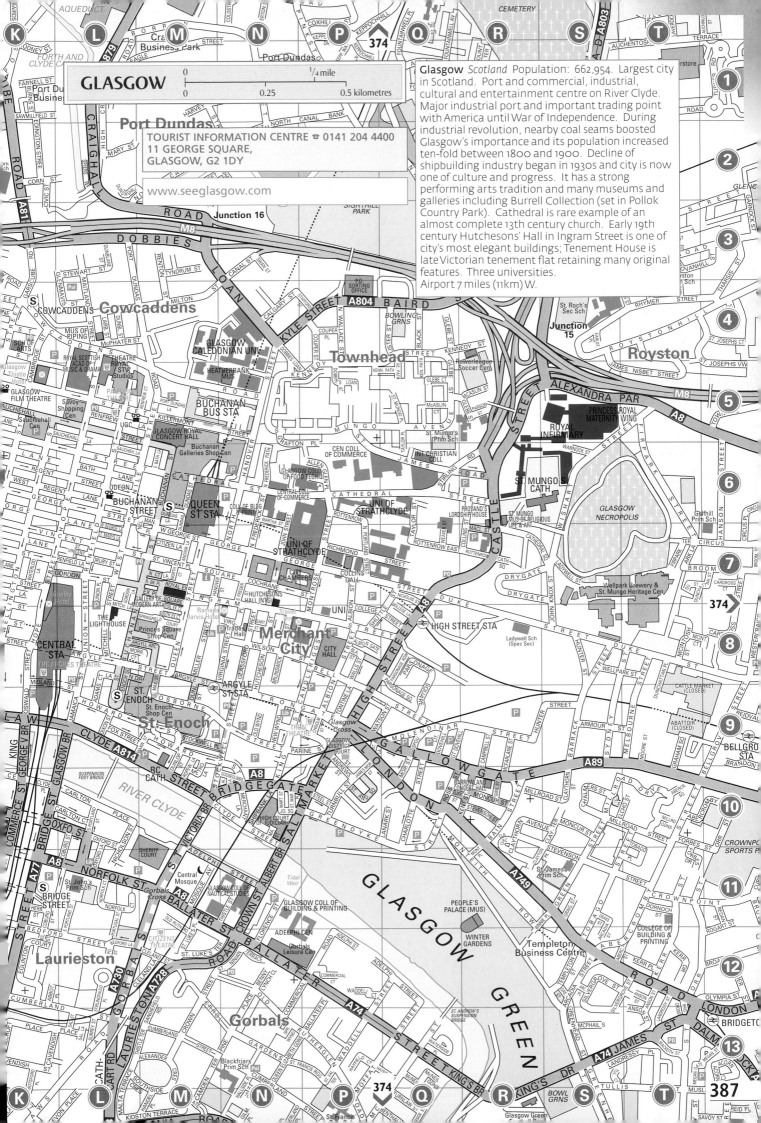

ABERDEEN   BATH

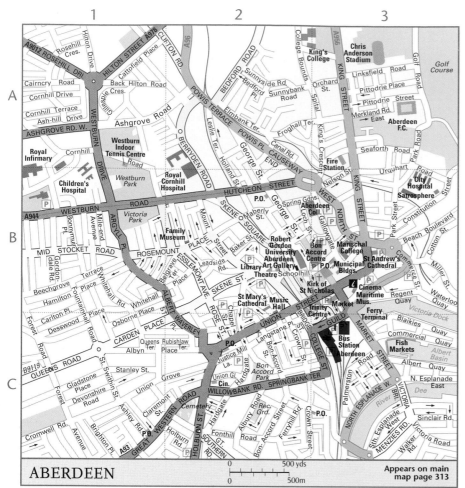

TOURIST INFORMATION CENTRE ☎ 01224 288828
23 UNION STREET,
ABERDEEN, AB11 5BP

HOSPITAL A & E ☎ 01224 681818
ABERDEEN ROYAL INFIRMARY,
FORESTERHILL, ABERDEEN, AB25 2ZN

COUNCIL OFFICE ☎ 01224 522000
ST. NICHOLAS HOUSE, BROAD STREET,
ABERDEEN, AB10 1AR

Aberdeen *Scotland* Population: 189,707. Cathedral and university city and commercial centre on E coast. Known as 'The Granite City', local stone having been used in many of its buildings. By 13th century, Aberdeen had become an important centre for trade and fishing and remains a major port and commercial base. In 19th century shipbuilding brought great prosperity to the city. These industries had receded by mid 20th century but the city's prospects were transformed when North Sea oil was discovered in 1970, turning it into a city of great wealth. St. Machar's Cathedral at Old Aberdeen. Many museums and art galleries. Extensive flower gardens. Airport at Dyce, 6 miles (9km) NW of Aberdeen.

LOCAL RADIO:
BBC RADIO SCOTLAND 585, 810, 990 AM / 92.6-94.7 FM;
NORTHSOUND ONE 96.9, 97.6, 103 FM;
NORTHSOUND TWO 1035 AM

www.agtb.org

TOURIST INFORMATION CENTRE ☎ 0906 7112000
   (Premium Rate)
ABBEY CHAMBERS, ABBEY CHURCHYARD,
BATH, BA1 1LY

HOSPITAL A & E ☎ 01225 428331
ROYAL UNITED HOSPITAL, COMBE PARK,
BATH, BA1 3NG

COUNCIL OFFICE ☎ 01225 477000
THE GUILDHALL, HIGH STREET,
BATH, BA1 5AW

Bath *South West England* Population: 85,202. City, spa on River Avon. Abbey church rebuilt 1501. Natural hot springs unique in Britain drew Romans to Bath, which they named 'Aquae Sulis'. Roman baths and 18th century Pump Room are open to visitors. In 18th century, it was most fashionable resort in country. Many Georgian buildings and elegant crescents remain, including The Circus and Royal Crescent. Museum of Costume in restored Assembly Rooms. Holds annual summer music festival. University 3 miles (4km) SE.

LOCAL RADIO:
BBC RADIO BRISTOL 1548 AM / 104.6 FM; BATH FM 107.9 FM;
CLASSIC GOLD 1260 AM; GWR (BATH) FM 103 FM

www.visitbath.co.uk

BLACKPOOL   BOURNEMOUTH

TOURIST INFORMATION CENTRE ☎ 01253 478222
1 CLIFTON STREET,
BLACKPOOL, FY1 1LY

HOSPITAL A & E ☎ 01253 300000
VICTORIA HOSPITAL, WHINNEY HEYS ROAD,
BLACKPOOL, FY3 8NR

COUNCIL OFFICE ☎ 01253 477477
TOWN HALL, TALBOT SQUARE,
BLACKPOOL, FY1 1AD

Blackpool *North West England* Population: 146,262. Town, large coastal resort and conference centre on Irish Sea. 19th century fashionable resort, still very popular today. 7 miles (11km) long 'Golden Mile' of tram route, beach, piers and amusement arcades. Blackpool Pleasure Beach, 518 ft (158m) high Tower entertainment complex, annual autumn Illuminations along 5 miles (8km) of Promenade, Zoo, Sea Life Centre, The Sandcastle indoor pool complex and Winter Gardens. Airport 3 miles (5km) S.

LOCAL RADIO:
BBC RADIO LANCASHIRE 104.5 FM
MAGIC 999 AM; WAVE 96.5 FM; ROCK FM 97.4 FM

www.visitblackpool.com

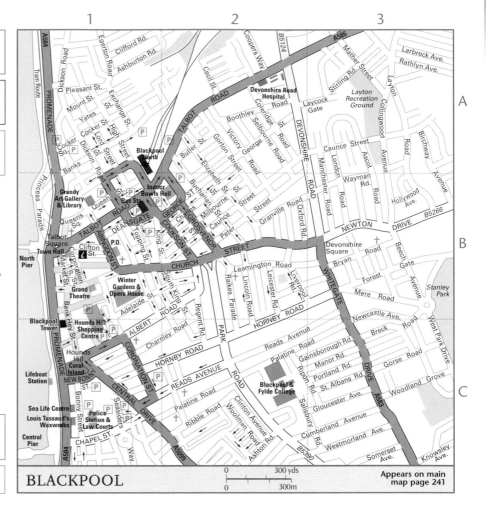

BLACKPOOL

Appears on main map page 241

TOURIST INFORMATION CENTRE ☎ 0906 802 0234
  (Premium Rate)
WESTOVER ROAD, BOURNEMOUTH, BH1 2BU

HOSPITAL A & E ☎ 01202 303626
ROYAL BOURNEMOUTH HOSPITAL,
CASTLE LANE EAST, BOURNEMOUTH, BH7 7DW

COUNCIL OFFICE ☎ 01202 451451
TOWN HALL, BOURNE AVENUE,
BOURNEMOUTH, BH2 6DY

Bournemouth *South West* Population: 155,488. Town, large seaside resort with mild climate. Town developed from a few cottages in 1810 to present conurbation. Sandy beach and pier. Extensive parks and gardens including Compton Acres, a display of international garden styles. Russell-Cotes Art Gallery and Museum houses Victorian and oriental collection. University. Conference, business and shopping centre. Bournemouth International Airport, 5 miles (8km) NE of town centre.

LOCAL RADIO:
BBC RADIO SOLENT (DORSET) 1359 AM / 103.8 FM;
2CR FM 102.3 FM; CLASSIC GOLD 828 AM; FIRE 107.6 FM;
WAVE 105 105.2 FM

www.bournemouth.co.uk

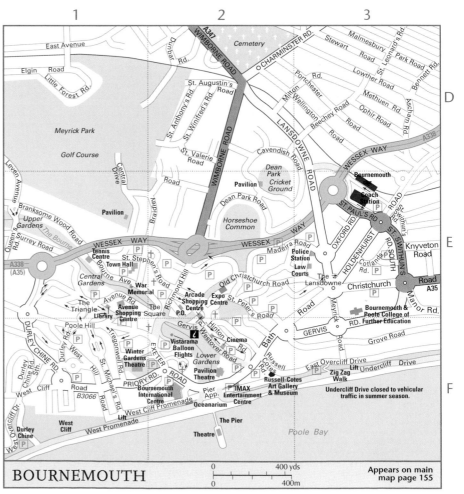

BOURNEMOUTH

Appears on main map page 155

BRADFORD BRIGHTON

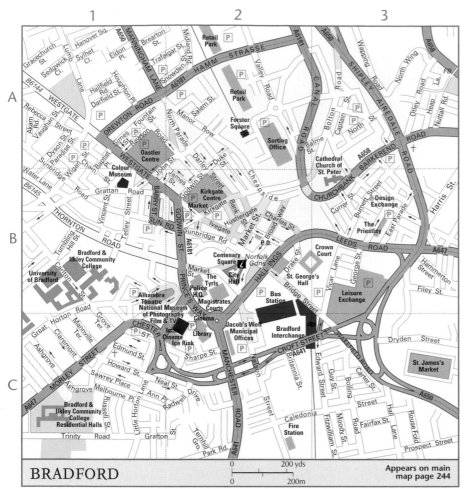

Appears on main map page 244

BRADFORD

0   200 yds
0   200m

TOURIST INFORMATION CENTRE ☎ 01274 753678
CITY HALL, CENTENARY SQUARE,
BRADFORD, BD1 1HY

HOSPITAL A & E ☎ 01274 542200
BRADFORD ROYAL INFIRMARY, DUCKWORTH
LANE, BRADFORD, BD9 6RJ

COUNCIL OFFICE ☎ 01274 752111
CITY HALL, CENTENARY SQUARE,
BRADFORD, BD1 1HY

Bradford *Yorkshire* Population: 289,376. Industrial city. Cathedral is former parish church. Previously known as wool capital of the world, Bradford is now less dependent upon the textile industry. Colour Museum documents history of dyeing and textile printing. University. Home to National Museum of Photography, Film and Television with IMAX cinema screen. Titus Salt built Saltaire 3 miles (5km) N, which is now considered a model industrial village. Salt's Mill, originally for textiles, now houses David Hockney art in the 1853 gallery. Leeds Bradford International Airport at Yeadon, 6 miles (10km) NE.

LOCAL RADIO:
BBC RADIO LEEDS 774 AM / 92.4, 95.3 FM;
WEST YORKS CLASSIC GOLD 1278 AM; THE PULSE 97.5 FM;
SUNRISE RADIO 103.2 FM

www.visitbradford.com

BRIGHTON

0   200 yds
0   200m

Appears on main map page 159

TOURIST INFORMATION CENTRE ☎ 0906 711 2255
 (Premium Rate)
10 BARTHOLOMEW SQUARE, BRIGHTON, BN1 1JS

HOSPITAL A & E ☎ 01273 696955
ROYAL SUSSEX COUNTY HOSPITAL, EASTERN
ROAD, BRIGHTON, BN2 5BE

COUNCIL OFFICE ☎ 01273 290000
TOWN HALL, BARTHOLOMEW SQUARE
BRIGHTON, BN1 1JA

Brighton *South East England* Population: 124,851. Town, seaside resort, sailing and conference centre. Previously a fishing village known as Brighthelmstone, centred on current Lanes area. Brighton became fashionable as a sea-bathing resort in the 18th century. Patronized by the Prince Regent in 1780s who built the Royal Pavilion in Oriental style as a summer palace. Regency squares at Kemp Town Amusement arcades on 1899 Palace Pier. Annual festivals. Language schools. Universities.

LOCAL RADIO:
BBC SOUTHERN COUNTIES RADIO 1485 AM / 95.3 FM;
CAPITAL GOLD 1323 AM; SOUTHERN FM 103.5; JUICE 107.2 FM

www.visitbrighton.com

TOURIST INFORMATION CENTRE ☎ 0906 711 2191
  (Premium Rate)
THE ANNEXE, WILDSCREEN WALK, HARBOURSIDE,
BRISTOL, BS1 5DB

HOSPITAL A & E ☎ 0117 923 0000
BRISTOL ROYAL INFIRMARY,
MARLBOROUGH STREET, BRISTOL, BS2 8HW

COUNCIL OFFICE ☎ 0117 922 2000
THE COUNCIL HOUSE, COLLEGE GREEN,
BRISTOL, BS1 5TR

Bristol *South West England* Population: 407,992. City.
Port on River Avon dates from medieval times. Bristol
grew from transatlantic trade in rum, tobacco and
slaves. In Georgian times, Bristol's population was
second only to London and many Georgian buildings
still stand, including the Theatre Royal, the oldest
working theatre in the country. Bristol is now a
commercial and industrial centre. Cathedral dates
from 12th century and was originally an abbey. 15th
century Temple Church tower and walls (English
Heritage). Restored iron ship SS Great Britain and
Industrial Museum in city docks area. Universities.
245 ft (75m) high Clifton Suspension Bridge completed
in 1864 across the Avon Gorge NW of the city. Bristol
International Airport at Lulsgate 7 miles (11km) SW.

LOCAL RADIO:
BBC RADIO BRISTOL 1548 AM / 94.9 FM; CLASSIC GOLD 1260 AM;
GWR FM 96.3 FM; VIBE 101 97.2 FM; STAR 107.2 FM

www.visitbristol.co.uk

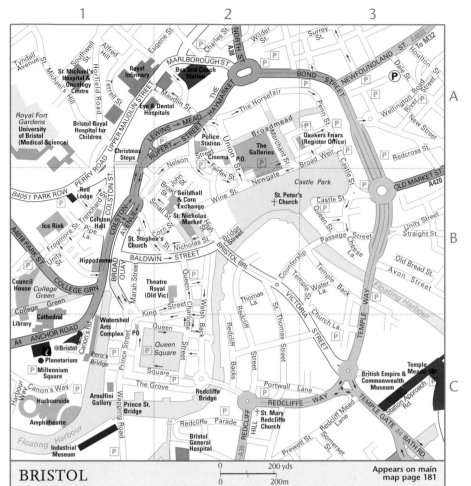

BRISTOL

Appears on main
map page 181

TOURIST INFORMATION CENTRE ☎ 0870 225 4900
WHEELER STREET, CAMBRIDGE,
CAMBRIDGESHIRE, CB2 3QB

HOSPITAL A & E ☎ 01223 245151
ADDENBROOKE'S HOSPITAL, HILLS ROAD,
CAMBRIDGE, CB2 2QQ

COUNCIL OFFICE ☎ 01223 457000
THE GUILDHALL, MARKET SQUARE,
CAMBRIDGE, CB2 3QJ

Cambridge *East of England* Population: 95,682.
University city on River Cam. First college founded
here in 1284. Historic tensions existed between
students and townspeople since 14th century, and
came to a head during Peasants' Revolt of 1381 in
which five townsfolk were hanged. Oliver Cromwell
was a graduate of Sidney Sussex College and local MP
at a time when the University was chiefly Royalist.
1870's saw foundation of first women's colleges, but
women were not awarded degrees until after 1947.
University's notable graduates include prime
ministers, foreign heads of state, literary giants,
philosophers and spies. Cambridge Footlights
regularly provide a platform for future stars of stage,
screen and television. Cambridge boasts many fine
museums, art galleries and buildings of interest,
including King's College Chapel and Fitzwilliam
Museum. Airport at Teversham 3 miles (4km) E.

LOCAL RADIO:
BBC RADIO CAMBRIDGESHIRE 96 FM;
Q 103 FM; STAR 107.9 FM

www.visitcambridge.org

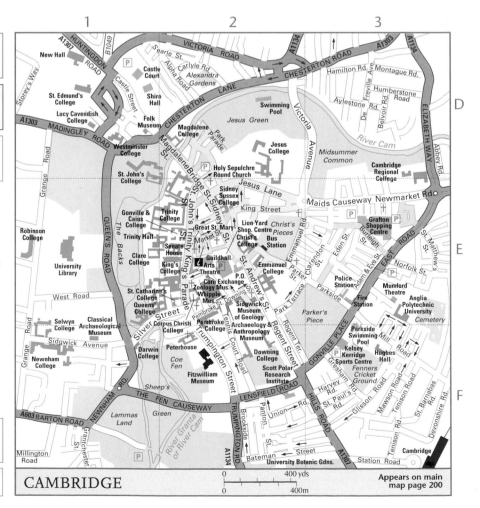

CAMBRIDGE

Appears on main
map page 200

CANTERBURY   CARDIFF

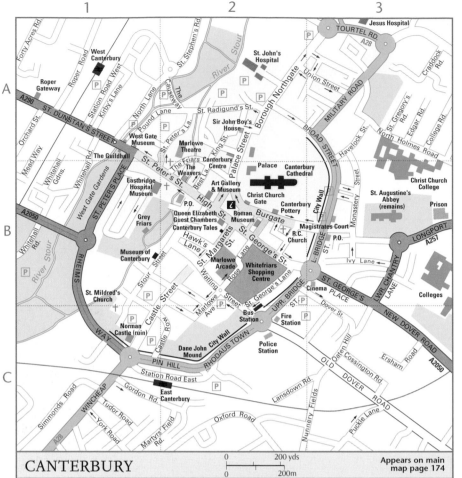

CANTERBURY

0 _____ 200 yds
0 _____ 200m

Appears on main map page 174

CARDIFF

0 _____ 400 yds
0 _____ 400m

Appears on main map page 180

TOURIST INFORMATION CENTRE ☎ 01227 378100
12/13 SUN STREET, THE BUTTERMARKET,
CANTERBURY, CT1 2HX

HOSPITAL A & E ☎ 01227 766877
KENT & CANTERBURY HOSPITAL,
ETHELBERT ROAD, CANTERBURY, CT1 3NG

COUNCIL OFFICE ☎ 01227 862000
COUNCIL OFFICES, MILITARY ROAD,
CANTERBURY, CT1 1YW

Canterbury *South East England* Population: 36,464.
Premier cathedral city and seat of Primate of Church
of England on Great Stour River. Site of Roman
settlement Durovernum. After Romans left, Saxons
renamed town Cantwarabyrig. First cathedral in
England built on site of current Christ Church
Cathedral in AD 602. Thomas à Becket assassinated
in Canterbury in 1170, turning Cathedral into great
Christian shrine and destination of many pilgrimages,
such as those detailed in Geoffrey Chaucer's
Canterbury Tales. Becket's tomb destroyed on orders
of Henry VIII. Cathedral was backdrop for premiere of
T.S. Eliot's play 'Murder in the Cathedral' in 1935. City
suffered extensive damage during World War II. Many
museums and galleries explaining city's rich heritage.
Roman and medieval remains, including city walls.
Modern shopping centre; industrial development on
outskirts. University of Kent on hill to N.

LOCAL RADIO:
BBC RADIO KENT 774 AM / 97.6 FM;
INVICTA FM 103.1 FM; KM-fm 106 FM

www.canterbury.co.uk

TOURIST INFORMATION CENTRE ☎ 029 2022 7281
CARDIFF VISITOR CENTRE, 16 WOOD STREET,
CARDIFF, CF10 1ES

HOSPITAL A & E ☎ 029 2074 7747
UNIVERSITY HOSPITAL OF WALES, HEATH PARK,
CARDIFF, CF14 4XW

COUNCIL OFFICE ☎ 029 2087 2087
THE HELP CENTRE, MARLAND HOUSE,
CENTRAL SQUARE, CARDIFF, CF10 1EP

Cardiff (Caerdydd) *Wales* Population: 272,129. City,
capital of Wales since 1955, since when, many
governmental, administrative and media
organisations have moved to city. Romans founded
military fort and small settlement on site of present
day Cardiff. Uninhabited between departure of
Romans and Norman conquest centuries later.
Fishing village until development of coal mining in
19th century. Population rose from 1000 in 1801 to
170,000 a century later, becoming one of busiest
ports in the world. Dock trade collapsed in 1930's.
Major development programme still under way.
Cardiff Bay area now major tourist centre and
includes Techniquest, a science discovery centre, and
the location of the new Welsh Assembly building.
Millennium Stadium Cardiff Arms Park is the home of
the Welsh Rugby Union and also hosts other sporting
and entertainment events. Many museums including
National Museum of Wales. Universities.

LOCAL RADIO:
BBC RADIO WALES 657, 882 AM / 103.9 FM; CAPITAL GOLD 1305,
1359 AM; RED DRAGON FM 103.2 FM; REAL 105-106 FM

www.visitcardiff.info

TOURIST INFORMATION CENTRE ☎ 01228 625600
CARDIFF VISITOR CENTRE, OLD TOWN HALL,
GREEN MARKET, CARLISLE, CA3 8JH

HOSPITAL A & E ☎ 01228 523444
CUMBERLAND INFIRMARY, NEWTOWN ROAD,
CARLISLE, CA2 7HY

COUNCIL OFFICE ☎ 01228 817000
CARLISLE CITY COUNCIL, THE CIVIC CENTRE,
CARLISLE, CA3 8QG

Carlisle *North West England* Population: 72,439.
Cathedral city at confluence of River Eden and River
Caldew. Once a Roman military base and later fought
over by Scots and English, line of Hadrian's wall runs
through the northern suburbs. Castle above the River
Eden, completed in 12th century, houses a military
museum. Cathedral partially destroyed by fire in 17th
century has two surviving bays of 12th century and a
magnificent East window. Tullie House Museum
imaginatively tells of the city's turbulent past.
University of Northumbria. Racecourse .
Airport 6 miles (9km) NE.

LOCAL RADIO:
BBC RADIO CUMBRIA 95.6, 96.1 & 104.1 FM;
CFM RADIO 96.4 FM

www.historic-carlisle.org.uk

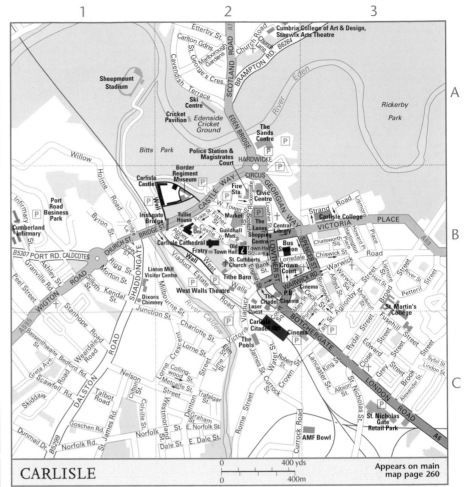

CARLISLE

Appears on main
map page 260

TOURIST INFORMATION CENTRE ☎ 01242 522878
77 THE PROMENADE, CHELTENHAM,
GLOUCESTERSHIRE, GL50 1PJ

HOSPITAL A & E ☎ 08454 222222
CHELTENHAM GENERAL HOSPITAL,
SANDFORD ROAD, CHELTENHAM, GL53 7AN

COUNCIL OFFICE ☎ 01242 262626
MUNICIPAL OFFICES, THE PROMENADE,
CHELTENHAM, GL50 1PP

Cheltenham *South West England* Population: 91,301.
Largest town in The Cotswolds. Shopping and tourist
centre, with some light industry. Mainly residential,
with many Regency and Victorian buildings and
public gardens. Formerly a spa town, Pittville Pump
Room built between 1825 and 1830 overlooks Pittville
Park and is now used for concerts. Art Gallery and
Museum. Ladies' College founded 1853. Racecourse
to the N hosts Cheltenham Gold Cup race meeting,
Cheltenham International Music Festival and Festival
of Literature, among other events. Birthplace of
composer Gustav Holst. University of
Gloucestershire.

LOCAL RADIO:
BBC RADIO GLOUCESTERSHIRE 1413 AM / 104.7 FM;
CLASSIC GOLD 774 AM; SEVERN SOUND FM 102.4 FM;
STAR 107.5 FM

www.visitcheltenham.info

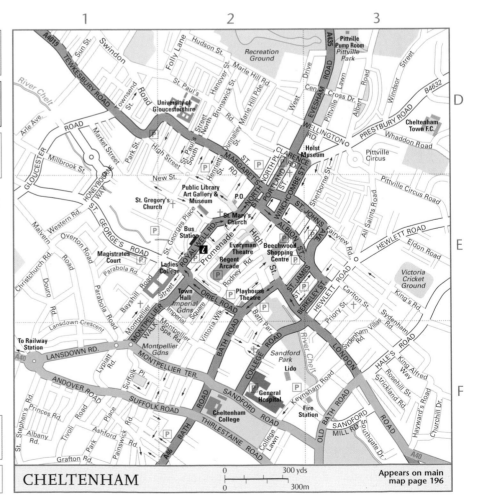

CHELTENHAM

Appears on main
map page 196

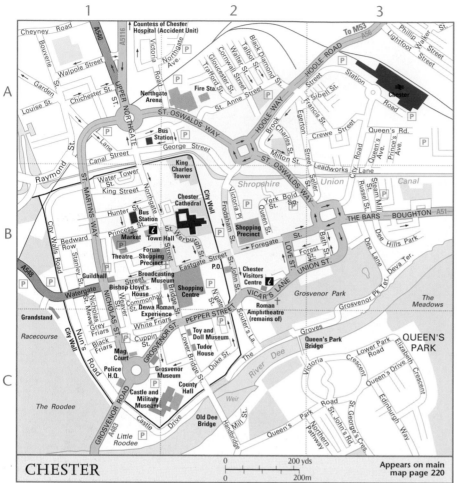

CHESTER

Appears on main map page 220

Chester info

TOURIST INFORMATION CENTRE ☎ 01244 402111
TOWN HALL, NORTHGATE STREET,
CHESTER, CHESHIRE, CH1 2HJ

HOSPITAL A & E ☎ 01244 365000
COUNTESS OF CHESTER HOSPITAL, HEALTH PK,
LIVERPOOL ROAD, CHESTER, CH2 1UL

COUNCIL OFFICE ☎ 01244 324324
THE FORUM,
CHESTER, CH1 2HS

Chester *North West England* Population: 80110. County town and cathedral city on River Dee. Commercial, financial and tourist centre built on Roman town of Deva. Includes biggest Roman amphitheatre in Britain and well preserved medieval walls. Castle, now county hall, includes 12th century Agricola Tower. Cathedral with remains of original Norman abbey. Famed for Tudor timber-framed buildings which include Chester Rows, two-tier galleried shops and Bishop Lloyd's House, with ornate 16th century carved façade. Eastgate clock built to commemorate Queen Victoria's diamond jubilee in 1897. Racecourse and zoo.

LOCAL RADIO:
BBC RADIO MERSEYSIDE 95.8 FM;
MAGIC 1548 AM; MFM 103.4 FM; RADIO CITY 96.7 FM

www.chestercc.gov.uk/tourism

COVENTRY

Appears on main map page 209

Coventry info

TOURIST INFORMATION CENTRE ☎ 024 7622 7264
BAYLEY LANE, COVENTRY,
WEST MIDLANDS, CV1 5RN

HOSPITAL A & E ☎ 024 7622 4055
COVENTRY & WARWICKSHIRE HOSPITAL,
STONEY STANTON ROAD, COVENTRY, CV1 4FH

COUNCIL OFFICE ☎ 024 7683 3333
COUNCIL HOUSE, EARL STREET,
COVENTRY, CV1 5RR

Coventry *West Midlands* Population: 299,316. City. St. Michael's cathedral built 1954-62 beside ruins of medieval cathedral destroyed in air raid in 1940. The centre of the city was rebuilt in the 1950s and 1960s following WW II bombing, but some old buildings remain, including Bonds Hospital and the medieval Guildhall. A town rich from textile industry in middle ages, Coventry is now known for its motor car industry; other important industries are manufacturing and engineering. Coventry Transport Museum. Herbert Art Gallery and Museum. Universities. Civil airport at Baginton to S. Coventry Canal runs N to Trent and Mersey Canal at Fradley Junction near Lichfield.

LOCAL RADIO:
BBC RADIO WM 103.7 FM; CLASSIC GOLD 1359 AM; KIX 96.2 FM; MERCIA FM 97 FM; HEART FM 100.7 FM

www.visitcoventry.co.uk

Appears on main
map page 223

Appears on main
map page 175

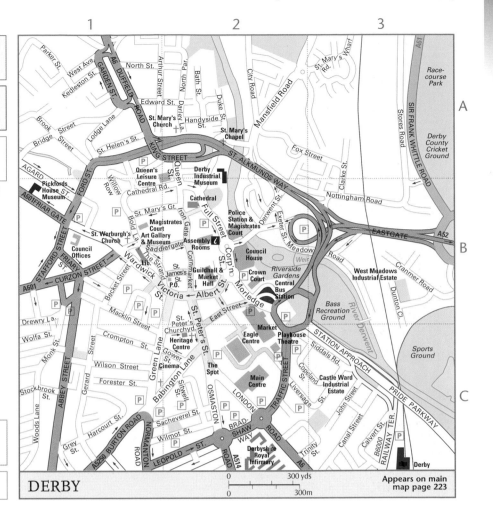

DERBY

1   2   3

A B C

0   300 yds
0   300m

TOURIST INFORMATION CENTRE ☎ 01332 255802
ASSEMBLY ROOMS, MARKET PLACE,
DERBY, DE1 3AH

HOSPITAL A & E ☎ 01332 347141
DERBYSHIRE ROYAL INFIRMARY,
LONDON ROAD, DERBY, DE1 2QY

COUNCIL OFFICE ☎ 01332 293111
THE COUNCIL HOUSE, CORPORATION STREET,
DERBY, DE1 2FS

Derby *East Midlands* Population: 223,836. Industrial city and county town on River Derwent. Shopping and entertainment centre. Cathedral mainly by James Gibbs, 1725. Both manufacturing and engineering are important to local economy. Derby Industrial Museum charts city's industrial history with emphasis on Rolls Royce aircraft engineering. Tours at Royal Crown Derby porcelain factory. University.

LOCAL RADIO:
BBC RADIO DERBY 1116 AM / 104.5 FM;
CLASSIC GOLD GEM 945 AM; RAM FM 102.8 FM;
96 TRENT FM 96.2 FM

www.visitderby.co.uk

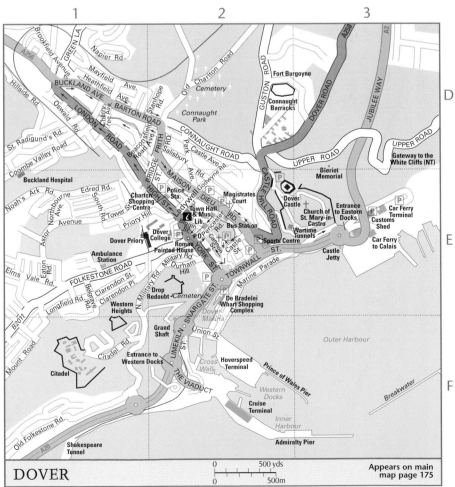

DOVER

1   2   3

D E F

0   500 yds
0   500m

TOURIST INFORMATION CENTRE ☎ 01304 205108
THE OLD TOWN GAOL, BIGGIN STREET,
DOVER, CT16 1DL

HOSPITAL A & E ☎ 01227 766877
KENT & CANTERBURY HOSPITAL,
ETHELBERT ROAD, CANTERBURY, CT1 3NG

COUNCIL OFFICE ☎ 01304 821199
WHITE CLIFFS BUSINESS PARK,
DOVER, CT16 3PJ

Dover *South East England* Population: 34,179. Town, cinque port, resort and Channel port on Strait of Dover, with large modern docks for freight and passengers. Dominated by high white cliffs and medieval castle enclosing the Pharos, AD50 remains of Roman lighthouse. Remains of 12th century Knights Templar Church across valley from castle. Sections of moat of 19th century fort at Western Heights, above town on W side of harbour.

LOCAL RADIO:
BBC RADIO KENT 774 AM / 104.2 FM;
KM-fm 106.8 FM; INVICTA FM 97 FM

www.whitecliffscountry.org.uk

DUNDEE DURHAM

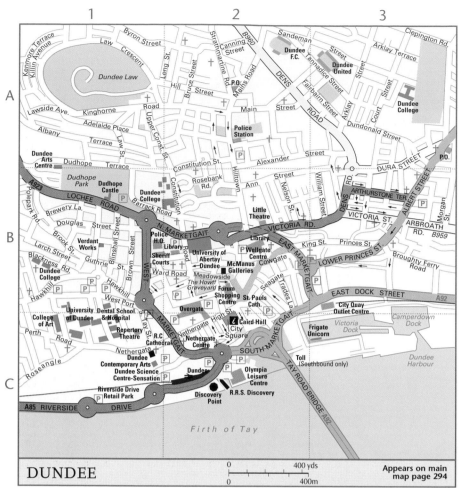

DUNDEE

Scale: 0 400 yds / 0 400m

Appears on main map page 294

TOURIST INFORMATION CENTRE ☎ 01382 527527
21 CASTLE STREET,
DUNDEE, DD1 3AA

HOSPITAL A & E ☎ 01382 660111
NINEWELLS HOSPITAL, NINEWELLS ROAD,
DUNDEE, DD1 9SY

COUNCIL OFFICE ☎ 01382 434000
CITY CHAMBERS, 21 CITY SQUARE,
DUNDEE, DD1 3BY

Dundee *Scotland* Population: 158,981. Scotland's fourth largest city, commercial and industrial centre and port. Robert the Bruce declared King of the Scots in Dundee in 1309. Sustained severe damage during Civil War and again prior to Jacobite uprising. City recovered in early 19th century and became Britain's main processor of jute. One of largest employers in Dundee today is D.C. Thomson, publisher of The Beano and The Dandy. Many museums and art galleries. Cultural centre, occasionally playing host to overflow from Edinburgh Festival. Episcopal cathedral on site of former castle. Universities. Ship 'Discovery' in which Captain Scott travelled to Antarctic has returned to Victoria dock, where she was built.

LOCAL RADIO:
BBC RADIO SCOTLAND 585, 810, 990 AM / 92.6-94.7 FM;
TAY AM 1161 AM; TAY FM 102.8 FM; WAVE 102 FM

www.angusanddundee.co.uk

DURHAM

Scale: 0 400 yds / 0 400m

Appears on main map page 262

TOURIST INFORMATION CENTRE ☎ 0191 384 3720
2 MILLENNIUM PLACE, DURHAM,
COUNTY DURHAM, DH1 1WA

HOSPITAL A & E ☎ 0191 333 2333
UNIVERSITY HOSPITAL OF NORTH DURHAM,
NORTH ROAD, DURHAM, DH1 5TW

COUNCIL OFFICE ☎ 0191 386 4411
COUNTY HALL,
DURHAM, DH1 5UB

Durham *North East England* Population: 36,937. Cathedral city on narrow bend in River Wear. Norman-Romanesque cathedral founded in 1093 on site of shrine of St. Cuthbert is World Heritage Site. England's third oldest University founded in 1832. Motte-and-bailey castle dating from 1072 now part of the University. Collection in Fulling Mill Museum of Archaelogy illustrates history of city. Museum of Oriental Art. Light Infantry Museum. Art Gallery. University Botanic Garden S of city.

LOCAL RADIO:
BBC RADIO NEWCASTLE 95.4 FM;
SUN FM 103.4 FM; GALAXY 105-106 105.3, 105.6, 105.8 & 106.4 FM

www.durhamtourism.co.uk

EASTBOURNE   EDINBURGH

TOURIST INFORMATION CENTRE ☎ 01323 411400
3 CORNFIELD ROAD,
EASTBOURNE, BN21 4QL

HOSPITAL A & E ☎ 01323 417400
EASTBOURNE DISTRICT GENERAL HOSPITAL,
KING'S DRIVE, EASTBOURNE, BN21 2UD

COUNCIL OFFICE ☎ 01323 410000
EASTBOURNE BOROUGH COUNCIL, TOWN HALL,
GROVE ROAD, EASTBOURNE BN21 4UG,

Eastbourne *South East England* Population: 94,793. Town, coastal resort and conference centre. Towner Art Gallery in 18th century manor house shows a contemporary collection of work. South Downs Way begins at Beachy Head, the 536 ft (163m) chalk cliff on the outskirts of the town. Eastbourne hosts an international Folk Festival and international tennis at Devonshire Park.

LOCAL RADIO:
BBC SOUTHERN COUNTIES RADIO 1161 AM / 104.5 FM;
SOVEREIGN RADIO 107.5 FM

www.eastbourne.org

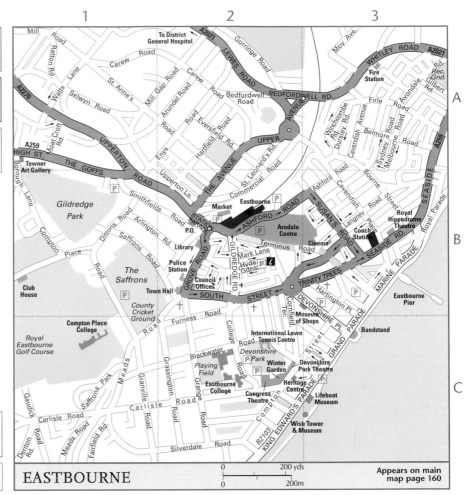

EASTBOURNE

Appears on main map page 160

TOURIST INFORMATION CENTRE ☎ 0131 473 3800
EDINBURGH & SCOTLAND INFORMATION CENTRE,
3 PRINCES STREET, EDINBURGH, EH2 2QP

HOSPITAL A & E ☎ 0131 536 1000
ROYAL INFIRMARY OF EDINBURGH
(LITTLE FRANCE), 51 LITTLE FRANCE CRESCENT,
EDINBURGH, EH16 4SA

COUNCIL OFFICE ☎ 0131 200 2000
COUNCIL HEADQUARTERS, 10 WATERLOO PLACE,
EDINBURGH, EH1 3EG

Edinburgh *Scotland* Population: 401,910. City, capital of Scotland, built on a range of rocky crags and extinct volcanoes, on S side of Firth of Forth. Administrative, financial and legal centre of Scotland. Medieval castle overlooks centre and was one of main seats of Royal court, while Arthur's Seat (largest of the volcanoes) guards eastern approaches. Three universities. Royal Yacht Britannia docked at Leith and is open to public. Important industries include brewing, distilling, food and electronics. Palace of Holyroodhouse is chief royal residence of Scotland. Old Town typified by Gladstone's Land, 17th century six-storey tenement with arcaded front, outside stair and stepped gables. Birthplace of Sir Arthur Conan Doyle. Many galleries and museums including National Gallery of Scotland. Largest arts festival in the world attracting over a million visitors each year.

LOCAL RADIO:
BBC RADIO SCOTLAND 585, 810, 990 AM / 92.6-94.7 FM;
BEAT 106 105.7 FM; FORTH ONE 97.3, 97.6, 102.2 FM;
FORTH 2 1548 AM; REAL RADIO 101.1, 100.3 FM

www.edinburgh.org

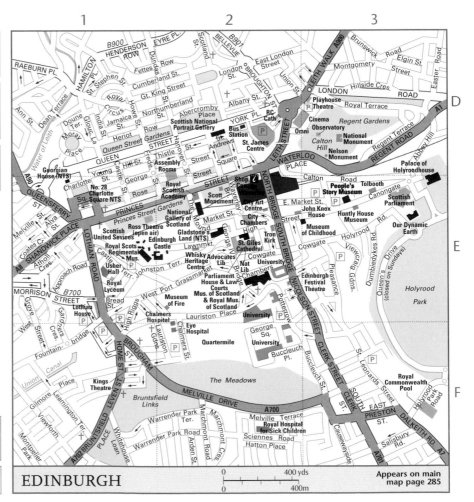

EDINBURGH

Appears on main map page 285

EXETER

Map grid columns: 1, 2, 3   **Rows:** A, B, C

Station Rd., Cowley Bridge Rd., B3183, Streatham Rise, Streatham Drive, New North Road, University of Exeter, Prince of Wales Road, Devon County Cricket Club, West Avenue, Pennsylvania Rd., Devonshire Place, Victoria Street, Prospect Park, Mt. Pleasant Rd., Iddesleigh Rd., Rd., BONHAY, Velwell, Fire Station, Danes Rd., Howell Road, Hooper's Hill, Thornton Hill, Blackall Road, York Road, Oxford Road, St. James' Park, St. James' Rd., Exeter City Football Ground, Elmside, B3212, BLACKBOY ROAD, Desmond, Exeter Tech. College, Bury Meadow Park, Hele Rd., Longbrook Street, Sidwell Street, Belmont Park, Belmont Rd., Clifton Hill, St. David's Hill, St. David's, Loce Rd., Clock Tower, H.M. Prison, NEW NORTH RD., Exeter Central, Rougemont Castle, Royal Albert Museum, Connection Discovery Centre, Sports Centre & Golf Driving Range, Cortland St., Clifton St., Richmond Rd., Iron Bridge, Queen Street, Library, PARIS ST., Bus & Coach Sta., WAY, Magistrates Court & Police Station, Heavitree Hospital (not A & E), Haldon, River Exe, Exwick Playing Fields, BONHAY ROAD, Catacombs, Harlequins Arcade, Paul St., High Street, Guildhall Shopping Centre, Bedford St., Civic Centre, P.O., WESTERN, Pyramids Leisure Centre, HEAVITREE ROAD, Denmark Rd., Spicer Road, College Road, B3183, St. Luke's College, St. Nicholas Priory, Bartholomew, South Street, Exeter Cathedral, City Wall, Barnfield, Theatre, Southernhay, Crown Court, MAGDALEN, Magdalen Road, Tuckers Hall, Spacex Gallery, Picture House, New Rd., WESTERN WAY, Bull Meadow Park, HOLLOWAY ST., Radford Rd., St. Leonard's Rd., East Grove Rd., Wonford Rd., Marlborough Rd., Lyndhurst Road, Wonford Rd., Commercial Rd., Quay House Visitor Centre, Okehampton Rd., Western Rd., Buller Road, Albion St., St. Thomas, COWICK STREET, ALPHINGTON ST., Riverside Leisure Centre, Church Road, Foot Ferry (Summer only), The Quay, Haven Rd., Isca Road, Water Lane, Canal, Matford Lane, St. Leonard's Rd., East Grove Rd., Matford Rd., Matford Avenue, Matford, Belle Isle Park, Weir, Devon County Hall, A3015, B3212, County Ground & Exeter R.F.C., Queen's Rd., A377, Picnic Area

Scale: 0–400 yds / 0–400m

Appears on main map page 152

TOURIST INFORMATION CENTRE ☎ 01392 265700
CIVIC CENTRE, PARIS STREET, EXETER,
DEVON, EX1 1JJ

HOSPITAL A & E ☎ 01392 411611
ROYAL DEVON & EXETER HOSPITAL (WONFORD),
BARRACK ROAD, EXETER, EX2 5DW

COUNCIL OFFICE ☎ 01392 277888
CIVIC CENTRE, PARIS STREET,
EXETER, EX1 1JN

Exeter *South West England* Population: 94,717. City, county capital on River Exe. Major administrative, business and financial centre on site of Roman town Isca Dumnoniorum. Cathedral is decorated, with Norman towers and façade with hundreds of stone statues. 15th century guildhall. Modern buildings in centre built after extensive damage from World War II. Beneath the city lie remains of medieval water-supply system built in 14th century to supply fresh water to city centre. Royal Albert Memorial Museum and Art Gallery. Early 16th century mansion of Bowhill, with preserved Great Hall, 2 miles (3km) SW. University. Airport 5 miles (8km) E at Clyst Honiton.

LOCAL RADIO:
BBC RADIO DEVON 990 AM / 95.8 FM;
CLASSIC GOLD 666 AM; GEMINI FM 97 & 103 FM

www.exeter.gov.uk/visiting

FOLKESTONE

Map grid columns: 1, 2, 3   **Rows:** D, E, F

M20, Junct. 13, A259, A20, CHERRY GARDEN AVENUE, CHURCHILL AVENUE, A260, HILL, DOVER HILL, DOVER ROAD, B2011, Links Way, Lucy Avenue, Park Farm Industrial Estate, Downs Road, Dolphins, Wingate Rd., Beatty Rd., Wood Avenue, Ivy Way, Dover Rd., Wear Bay Road, Sports Ground, CANTERBURY ROAD, Joyes Road, Tyson Rd., Coniston Rd., Park Farm Road, Alder Road, Mead Rd., Sidney St., Marshall St., Archer Road, Davison, Recreation Ground, Sports Ground, Royal Victoria Hospital, Cornwallis, PAVILION RD., RADNOR PARK, Radnor Park Avenue, Grove Rd., Radnor Park Road, Wilton Road, BLACK BULL ROAD, Linden Cres., FOORD ROAD, Radnor Bridge Road, THE TRAM ROAD, Wear Bay Cres., CHERITON ROAD, A2034, Broadfield Rd., South Kent Technical College, Folkestone Central, Broadmead Rd., Guildhall St., Bradstone Rd., DOVER RD., Harbour Way, Bathurst Rd., Shorncliffe Road, Brockman Rd., Coolinge Rd., Cheriton Rd., TONTINE, Museum & Library, Guildhall, High Street, The Stade, East Pier, Godwyn Road, EARLS AVENUE, Palting House, Civic Centre, Castle Hill Avenue, Christchurch Rd., Manor Rd., Bus Sta., Shopping Centre (under construction), Russian Submarine, Harbour, Turketel Rd., Grimston Gdns., Grimston Avenue, Police Station, Law Courts, West, P.O., War Memorial, Harbour Station, Pier, Bouverie Road West, Augusta Gdns., SANDGATE ROAD, Cliff Lifts, Marine Parade, Rotunda Amusement Park, Dixwell Rd., Westbourne Gdns., SANDGATE HILL, Clifton Gdns., The Leas, Toll Road, A259, Metropole Art Gallery, The Leas, Lower Sandgate Road, Leas Cliff Hall, Picnic Area

Scale: 0–200 yds / 0–200m

Appears on main map page 175

TOURIST INFORMATION CENTRE ☎ 01303 258594
HARBOUR STREET, FOLKESTONE,
KENT, CT20 1QN

HOSPITAL A & E ☎ 01233 633331
WILLIAM HARVEY HOSPITAL, KENNINGTON RD,
WILLESBOROUGH, ASHFORD, TN24 0LZ

COUNCIL OFFICE ☎ 01303 850388
CIVIC CENTRE, CASTLE HILL AVENUE,
FOLKESTONE, CT20 2QY

Folkestone *South East England* Population: 45,587. Town, Channel port and resort. Russian submarine docked in harbour is open to the public. The Lear marine promenade accessed by Victorian cliff lift. Ornate Victorian hotels. Martello tower on East Cliff. Kent Battle of Britain Museum at Hawkinge airfield 3 miles (5km) N. Channel Tunnel terminal on N side.

LOCAL RADIO:
BBC RADIO KENT 97.6 FM;
INVICTA FM 97 FM

www.discoverfolkestone.co.uk

TOURIST INFORMATION CENTRE ☎ 01452 421188
28 SOUTHGATE STREET, GLOUCESTER,
GLOUCESTERSHIRE, GL1 2DP

HOSPITAL A & E ☎ 08454 222222
GLOUCESTERSHIRE ROYAL HOSPITAL
GREAT WESTERN RD, GLOUCESTER, GL1 3NN

COUNCIL OFFICE ☎ 01452 522232
COUNCIL OFFICES, NORTH WAREHOUSE,
THE DOCKS, GLOUCESTER, GL1 2EP

Gloucester *South West England* Population: 114,003. Industrial city on River Severn, on site of Roman town of Glevum. Norman era saw Gloucester grow in political importance, from here William the Conqueror ordered survey of his Kingdom which resulted in Domesday Book of 1086. City became a religious centre during middle ages. Cathedral built of mixture of Norman and Perpendicular styles, has cloisters and England's largest stained glass window, dating from 14th century. Remains of 15th century - 13th century Franciscan friary, Greyfriars. Historic docks, now largely redeveloped, on Gloucester and Sharpness Canal. Three Choirs Festival held every third year.

LOCAL RADIO:
BBC RADIO GLOUCESTERSHIRE 1413 AM / 104.7 FM;
CLASSIC GOLD 774 AM, SEVERN SOUND FM 102.4 & 103 FM

www.gloucester.gov.uk/tourism

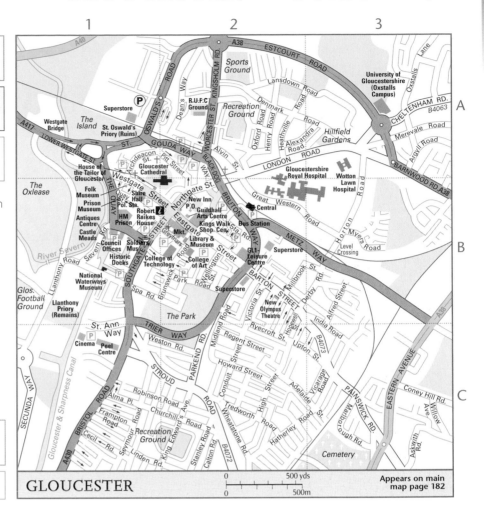

GLOUCESTER

0   500 yds
0   500m

Appears on main
map page 182

TOURIST INFORMATION CENTRE ☎ 01483 444333
14 TUNSGATE,
GUILDFORD, GU1 3QT

HOSPITAL A & E ☎ 01483 571122
ROYAL SURREY COUNTY HOSPITAL,
EGERTON ROAD, GUILDFORD, GU2 5XX

COUNCIL OFFICE ☎ 01483 505050
GUILDFORD BOROUGH COUNCIL,
MILLMEAD HOUSE, MILLMEAD,
GUILDFORD, GU2 4BB

Guildford *South East England* Population: 65,998. County town and former weaving centre on River Wey. High Street lined with Tudor buildings, the Guildhall the most impressive. Remains of Norman castle keep built c.1173, on an 11th century motte, used as county gaol for 400 years. Cathedral consecrated in 1961 and built of red brick, the interior is designed in modern gothic style. University of Surrey. Royal Grammar School noted for its chained library

LOCAL RADIO:
BBC SOUTHERN COUNTIES RADIO 104.6 FM;
THE EAGLE 96.4 FM; COUNTY SOUND 1566 AM

www.guildfordborough.co.uk

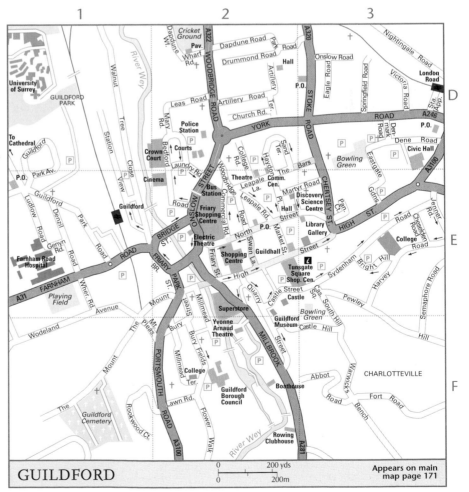

GUILDFORD

0   200 yds
0   200m

Appears on main
map page 171

HARROGATE   HASTINGS

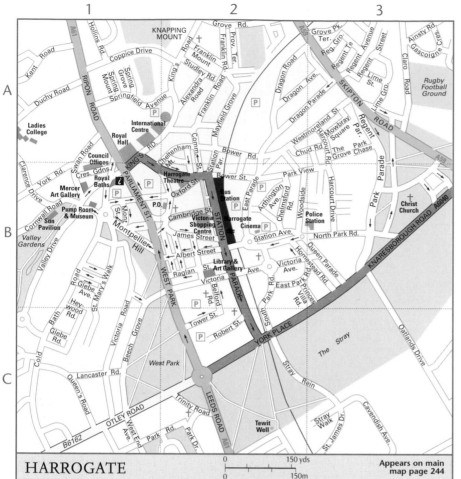

HARROGATE

HARROGATE

| 0 | 150 yds |
| 0 | 150m |

Appears on main
map page 244

Appears on main map page 244

TOURIST INFORMATION CENTRE ☎ 01423 537300
ROYAL BATHS ASSEMBLY ROOMS, CRESCENT RD,
HARROGATE, NORTH YORKSHIRE, HG1 2RR

HOSPITAL A & E ☎ 01423 885959
HARROGATE DISTRICT HOSPITAL,
LANCASTER PARK ROAD, HARROGATE, HG2 7SX

COUNCIL OFFICE ☎ 01423 500600
COUNCIL OFFICES, CRESCENT GARDENS
HARROGATE, HG1 2SG

Harrogate *Yorkshire* Population: 66,178. Spa town and conference centre. Fashionable spa town of 19th century with many distinguished Victorian buildings, extensive gardens and pleasant tree-lined streets. Royal Baths Assembly Rooms (1897) open for Turkish baths. Royal Pump Room (1842) now a museum. Th Stray park and gardens are S of town centre. The Valley Gardens to the SW are the venue for band concerts and flower shows. Harlow Carr Botanical Gardens and Museum of Gardening 2 miles (3km) SW Mother Shipton's cave, reputed home to the 16th century prophetess, near Knaresborough, 4 miles (6km) NW.

LOCAL RADIO:
BBC RADIO YORK 103.7 FM;
STRAY FM 97.2 FM

www.harrogate.gov.uk/tourism

HASTINGS

| 0 | 500 yds |
| 0 | 500m |

Appears on main
map page 160

Appears on main map page 160

TOURIST INFORMATION CENTRE ☎ 01424 781111
QUEENS SQUARE, PRIORY MEADOW,
HASTINGS, TN34 1TL

HOSPITAL A & E ☎ 01424 755255
CONQUEST HOSPITAL, THE RIDGE,
ST. LEONARDS-ON-SEA, TN37 7RD

COUNCIL OFFICE ☎ 01424 781066
HASTINGS BOROUGH COUNCIL, TOWN HALL,
QUEENS ROAD, HASTINGS, TN34 1QR

Hastings *South East England* Population: 84,139. Town, Cinque port and seaside resort. Remains of Norman castle built 1068-1080 on hill in town centre houses the 1066 exhibition which relates the history of castle and Norman invasion. Battle of 1066 fough at Battle, 6 miles (9km) NW. Former smugglers cave have a display on smuggling, once a vital part of the towns economy.

LOCAL RADIO:
BBC SOUTHERN COUNTIES RADIO 1161 AM / 104.5 FM;
ARROW FM 107.8 FM

www.visithastings.com

HEREFORD   INVERNESS

TOURIST INFORMATION CENTRE ☎ 01432 268430
1 KING STREET,
HEREFORD, HR4 9BW

HOSPITAL A & E ☎ 01432 355444
COUNTY HOSPITAL,
STONEBOW ROAD, HEREFORD, HR1 2ER

COUNCIL OFFICE ☎ 01432 260456
COUNCIL OFFICES, THE TOWN HALL,
ST. OWEN STREET, HEREFORD, HR1 2PJ

Hereford *West Midlands* Population: 54,326. County town and cathedral city on River Wye. Many old buildings and museums, including Waterworks Museum and City Museum and Art Gallery. 1621 Old House is a museum of local history. Medieval Wye Bridge. Cathedral includes richly ornamented Early English style Lady chapel. New building houses Chained Library of 1500 volumes and 1289 Mappa Mundi Map of the world. Three Choirs Festival every third year. Cider Museum and King Offa Distillery W of city centre depicts history of cider making.

LOCAL RADIO:
BBC RADIO HEREFORD & WORCESTER 1584 AM / 94.7 FM
WYVERN FM 97.6 FM; CLASSIC HITS 954 AM

www.visitherefordshire.co.uk

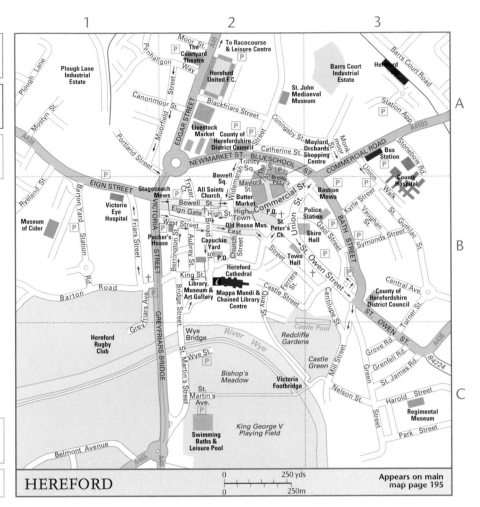

HEREFORD

| 0 | | 250 yds |
| 0 | | 250m |

Appears on main
map page 195

TOURIST INFORMATION CENTRE ☎ 0845 2255121
CASTLE WYND,
INVERNESS, HIGHLAND, IV2 3BJ

HOSPITAL A & E ☎ 01463 704000
RAIGMORE HOSPITAL, OLD PERTH ROAD,
INVERNESS, IV2 3UJ

COUNCIL OFFICE ☎ 01463 702000
COUNCIL OFFICES, GLENURQUHART ROAD,
INVERNESS, IV3 5NX

Inverness *Scotland* Population: 41,234. Town, at mouth of River Ness at entrance to Beauly Firth. Administrative, commercial and tourist centre. Caledonian Canal passes to W of town. Victorian Castle in town centre used as law courts. Inverness Museum and Art Gallery depicts history of Highlands. Balnain House is a museum of Highland music and musical instruments. University of the Highlands and Islands. 1746 Culloden battle site 5 miles (8km) E. Airport at locality of Dalcross, 7 miles (11km) NE of town.

LOCAL RADIO:
BBC RADIO SCOTLAND 585, 810, 990 AM / 92.6-94.7 FM
MORAY FIRTH RADIO (MFR) 1107 AM / 96.6, 96.7, 97.4, 102.5, 102.8 FM

www.visithighlands.com/inverness-loch-ness

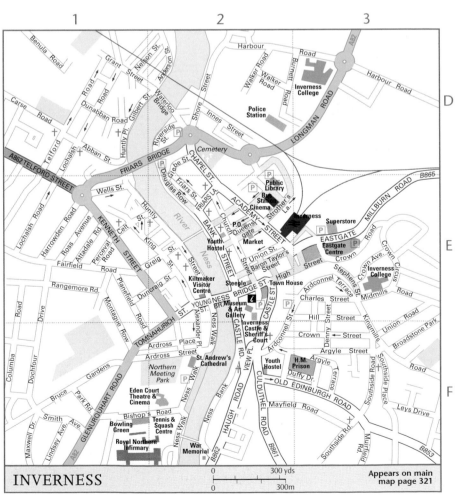

INVERNESS

| 0 | | 300 yds |
| 0 | | 300m |

Appears on main
map page 321

KINGSTON UPON HULL   LEICESTER

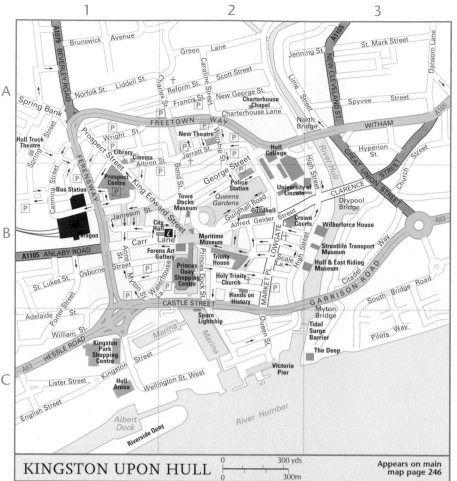

TOURIST INFORMATION CENTRE ☎ 01482 223559
1 PARAGON STREET,
KINGSTON UPON HULL, HU1 3NA

HOSPITAL A & E ☎ 01482 328541
HULL ROYAL INFIRMARY, ANLABY ROAD,
KINGSTON UPON HULL, HU3 2JZ

COUNCIL OFFICE ☎ 01482 300300
GUILDHALL, ALFRED GELDER STREET,
KINGSTON UPON HULL, HU1 2AA

Kingston upon Hull (Commonly known as Hull.) *Yorkshire* Population: 310,636. City, port at confluence of Rivers Humber and Hull. Much of town destroyed during bombing of World War II; town centre has been rebuilt. Formerly had a thriving fishing industry. Major industry nowadays is frozen food processing. Restored docks, cobble streeted Old Town and modern marina. Universities. Birthplace of William Wilberforce, slavery abolitionist, 1759. Wilberforce Museum covers history of slavery. Streetlife Transport Museum. Town Docks Museum explores city's maritime history. Famous for associations with poets Andrew Marvell, Stevie Smith and Philip Larkin.

LOCAL RADIO:
BBC RADIO HUMBERSIDE 1485 AM / 95.9 FM;
MAGIC 1161 AM; VIKING FM 96.9 FM

www.hullcc.gov.uk/visithull

KINGSTON UPON HULL

| 0 | 300 yds |
| 0 | 300m |

Appears on main map page 246

TOURIST INFORMATION CENTRE ☎ 0906 294 1113
  (Premium Rate)
7-9 EVERY STREET, TOWN HALL SQUARE,
LEICESTER, LE1 6AG

HOSPITAL A & E ☎ 0116 254 1414
LEICESTER ROYAL INFIRMARY,
INFIRMARY SQUARE, LEICESTER, LE1 5WW

COUNCIL OFFICE ☎ 0116 252 6480
COUNCIL OFFICES, NEW WALK CENTRE,
WELFORD PLACE, LEICESTER, LE1 6ZG

Leicester *East Midlands* Population: 318,518. City, county town and commercial and industrial centre on River Soar, on site of Roman town of Ratae Coritanorum. Industries include hosiery and footwear, alongside more modern industries. Universities. Many historic remains including Jewry Wall , one of largest surviving sections of Roman wall in the country, Roman baths and a medieval guildhall. Saxon Church of St. Nicholas. 11th century St. Martin's Cathedral. Victorian clock tower. Newarke Houses Museum explores the city's social history. Home to England's second biggest street festival after Notting Hill Carnival. Joseph Merrick, the 'Elephant Man' born and lived here.

LOCAL RADIO:
BBC RADIO LEICESTER 104.9 FM
SABRAS 1260 AM; LEICESTER SOUND 105.4 FM

www.discoverleicester.co.uk

LEICESTER

| 0 | 200 yds |
| 0 | 200m |

Appears on main map page 210

LINCOLN

Lincoln *East Midlands* Population: 80,281. County town and cathedral city on River Witham, on site of Roman town of Lindum. City grew as a result of strategic importance in the wool trade. Many ancient monuments and archaeological features. Castle built by William I. 13th century cathedral, is the third largest in Britain with its three towers on hilltop dominating the skyline. Carvings in the Angel Choir include the stone figure of the Lincoln Imp which is the city's emblem. Lincoln Bishop's Old Palace is medieval building on S side of cathedral. 12th century Jew's House. Museum of Lincolnshire Life. Universities.

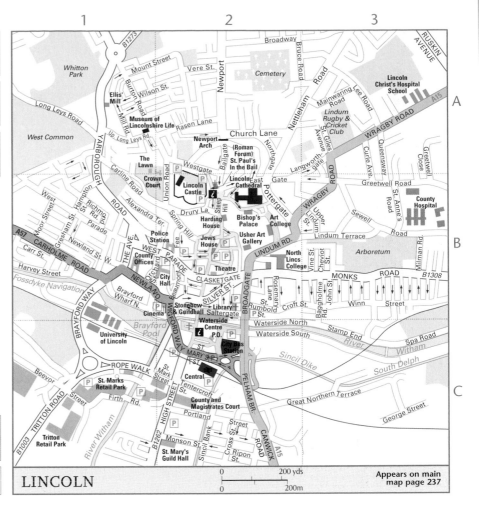

LINCOLN

Appears on main map page 237

MIDDLESBROUGH

Middlesbrough *North East England* Population: 147,430. Town, port, with extensive dock area, on S bank of River Tees, forming part of Teesside urban complex. A former iron and steel town, its chief industries now involve oil and petrochemicals. Unusual 1911 transporter bridge over River Tees. University of Teesside. Captian Cook Birthplace Museum in Stewart Park at Marton.

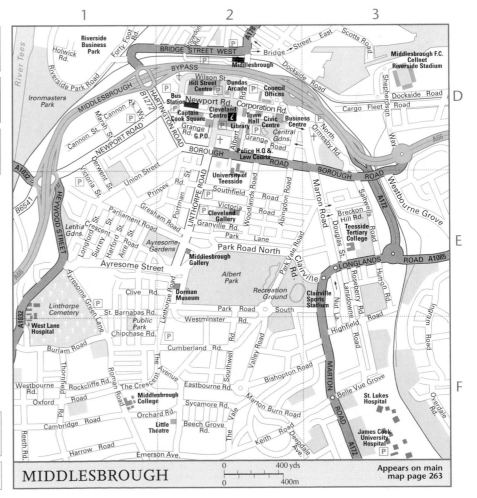

MIDDLESBROUGH

Appears on main map page 263

403

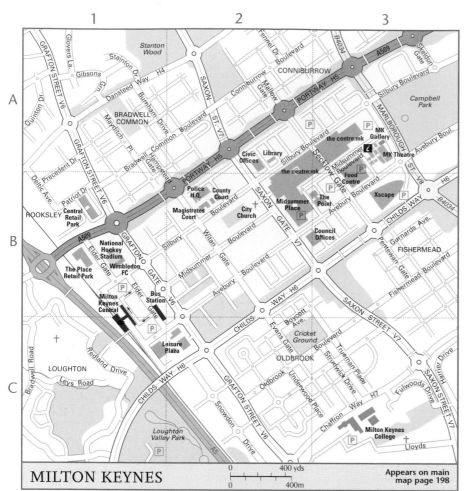

MILTON KEYNES

0 400 yds
0 400m

Appears on main map page 198

TOURIST INFORMATION CENTRE ☎ 01908 558300
MARGARET POWELL SQUARE,
890 MIDSUMMER BOULEVARD,
MILTON KEYNES, MK9 3QA

HOSPITAL A & E ☎ 01908 660033
MILTON KEYNES GENERAL HOSPITAL,
STANDING WAY, EAGLESTONE,
MILTON KEYNES, MK6 5LD

COUNCIL OFFICE ☎ 01908 691691
CIVIC OFFICES, 1 SAXON GATE EAST,
MILTON KEYNES, MK9 3HQ

Milton Keynes *South East England*
Population: 156,148. New town designated in 1967.
Includes Bletchley, Stony Stratford, Wolverton and
original village of Milton Keynes. Regional
commercial centre and location for many
international companies. The centre:mk is one of the
longest under-cover shopping areas in Europe. Major
open-air concert venue at the National Bowl. MK
Theatre and art gallery. Cinema, bowling, climbing
wall and Europe's largest indoor snow ski slope at
Xscape. The Open University at Walton Hall. Woburn
Safari Park 8 miles (13km) SE.

LOCAL RADIO:
BBC THREE COUNTIES RADIO 1161 AM / 104.5 FM;
FM 103 HORIZON 103.3 FM

www.mkweb.co.uk/visitorinfo

NEWCASTLE

0 400 yds
0 400m

Appears on main map page 262

TOURIST INFORMATION CENTRE ☎ 0191 277 8000
132 GRAINGER STREET, NEWCASTLE
UPON TYNE, TYNE & WEAR, NE1 5AF

HOSPITAL A & E ☎ 0191 273 8811
NEWCASTLE GENERAL HOSPITAL, WESTGATE
ROAD, NEWCASTLE UPON TYNE, NE4 6BE

COUNCIL OFFICE ☎ 0191 232 8520
CIVIC CENTRE, BARRAS BRIDGE,
NEWCASTLE UPON TYNE, NE99 1RD

Newcastle upon Tyne *North East England*
Population: 189,150. City, port on River Tyne about
11 miles (17km) upstream from river mouth. The 'new
castle' of city's name started in 1080 by Robert
Curthose, eldest son of William the Conqueror.
13th century castle gatehouse known as 'Black Gate'.
Commercial and industrial centre, previously
dependent upon coalmining and shipbuilding. In its
heyday, 25 percent of world's shipping built here.
Cathedral dates from 14th to 15th century. Bessie
Surtees House comprises 16th and 17th century
merchants' houses. Tyne Bridge, opened in 1928 and
longest of its type at the time. Venerable Bede (AD
672-735) born near Jarrow. Catherine Cookson, writer
also born in Jarrow, Universities. Newcastle
International Airport 5m/8km NW.

LOCAL RADIO:
BBC RADIO NEWCASTLE 95.4 FM;
MAGIC 1152 AM; METRO RADIO 97.1 FM; CENTURY FM 101.8 FM

www.visitnewcastlegateshead.com

TOURIST INFORMATION CENTRE ☎ 0870 225 4830
THE FORUM, MILLENNIUM PLAIN,
NORWICH, NR2 1TF

HOSPITAL A & E ☎ 01603 286286
NORFOLK & NORWICH UNIVERSITY HOSPITAL,
COLNEY LANE, NORWICH, NR4 7UZ

COUNCIL OFFICE ☎ 01603 622233
CITY HALL, ST. PETER'S STREET,
NORWICH, NR2 1NH

Norwich *East of England* Population: 171,304.
County town and cathedral city at confluence of River
Wensum and River Yare. Middle ages saw Norwich
become second richest city in country through
exporting textiles. Medieval streets and buildings are
well preserved. Sections of 14th century flint city wall
defences still exist, including Cow Tower. Current
chief industries are high technology and computer
based. Notable buildings include partly Norman
cathedral with second highest spire in Britain,
Norman castle with keep (now museum and art
gallery), 15th century guildhall, modern city hall,
numerous medieval churches. University of East
Anglia. Airport 3 miles (5km) N.

LOCAL RADIO:
BBC RADIO NORFOLK 95.1, 104.4 FM;
CLASSIC GOLD AMBER 1152 AM; BROADLAND 102 102.4 FM

www.visitnorwich.co.uk

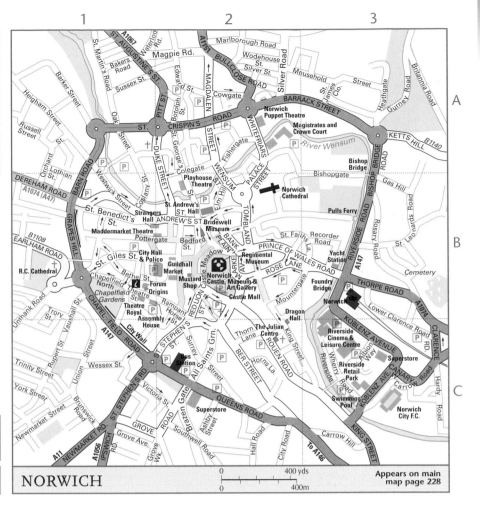

NORWICH

Appears on main
map page 228

TOURIST INFORMATION CENTRE ☎ 0115 915 5330
1-4 SMITHY ROW,
NOTTINGHAM, NG1 2BY

HOSPITAL A & E ☎ 0115 924 9924
QUEENS MEDICAL CENTRE, UNIVERSITY HOSP,
DERBY ROAD, NOTTINGHAM, NG7 2UH

COUNCIL OFFICE ☎ 0115 915 5555
THE GUILDHALL, SOUTH SHERWOOD STREET,
NOTTINGHAM, NG1 4BT

Nottingham *East Midlands* Population: 270,222.
City, on River Trent. Originally Saxon town built on
one of a pair of hills. In 1068, Normans built castle on
other hill and both communities traded in valley
between. Important commercial, industrial,
entertainment and sports centre. Key industries
include manufacture of lace, mechanical products,
tobacco and pharmaceuticals. 17th century castle,
restored 19th century, houses museum and art
gallery. Two universities. Repertory theatre.

LOCAL RADIO:
BBC RADIO NOTTINGHAM 103.8 FM; CENTURY FM 106 FM;
CLASSIC GOLD GEM 999 AM; SAGA 101.4, 106.6 FM;
TRENT FM 96.2 FM

www.nottinghamcity.gov.uk/visitors

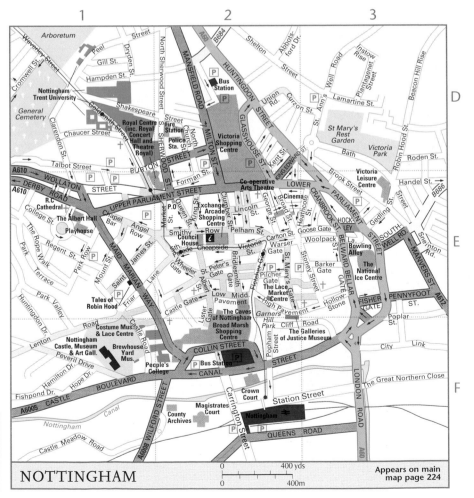

NOTTINGHAM

Appears on main
map page 224

OXFORD   PERTH

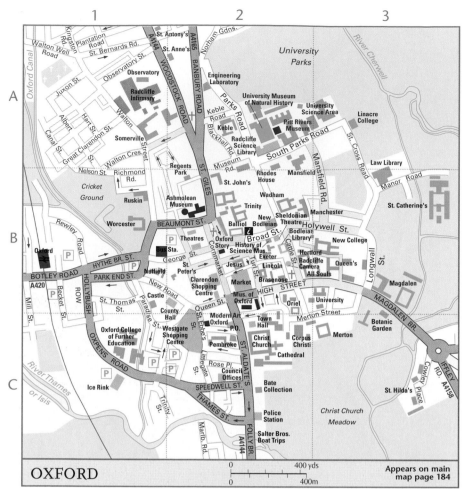

OXFORD

Map grid references 1, 2, 3 / A, B, C

Appears on main map page 184

400 yds / 400m

TOURIST INFORMATION CENTRE ☎ 01865 726871
15-16 BROAD STREET,
OXFORD, OX1 3AS

HOSPITAL A & E ☎ 01865 741166
JOHN RADCLIFFE HOSPITAL, HEADLEY WAY,
HEADINGTON, OXFORD, OX3 9DU

COUNCIL OFFICE ☎ 01865 249811
PO BOX 10,
OXFORD, OX1 1EN

Oxford *South East England* Population: 118,795. City, at confluence of Rivers Thames and Cherwell. Began as Saxon settlement, flourished under Normans when it was chosen as royal residence. University dating from 13th century, recognised as being among best in the world. Many notable buildings create spectacular skyline. Cathedral. Bodleian Library, second largest in UK. Ashmolean museum, oldest public museum in country. Tourist and commercial centre. Ancient St. Giles Fair held every September. Oxford Brookes University at Headington. Airport at Kidlington.

LOCAL RADIO:
BBC RADIO OXFORD 95.2 FM;
FOX FM 102.6 FM; FUSION 107.3 FM

www.visitoxford.org

PERTH

Appears on main map page 293

300 yds / 300m

TOURIST INFORMATION CENTRE ☎ 01738 450600
LOWER CITY MILLS, WEST MILL STREET,
PERTH, PH1 5QP

HOSPITAL A & E ☎ 01738 623311
PERTH ROYAL INFIRMARY,
TAYMOUNT TERRACE, PERTH, PH1 1NX

COUNCIL OFFICE ☎ 01738 475000
PERTH & KINROSS COUNCIL,
2 HIGH STREET, PERTH, PH1 5PH

Perth *Scotland* Population: 41,453. Ancient cathedral city (Royal Charter granted 1210) on River Tay. Once capital of Medieval Scotland. Centre of livestock trade. Previously cotton manufacturing centre; now important industries include whisky distilling. St. John's Kirk founded 1126. 15th century Balhousie Castle houses regimental headquarters and Museum of the Black Watch. Art Gallery and Museum. 16th century Fair Maid's House. Gothic mansion Scone Palace 2 miles (3km) N contains collections of furniture, needlework and porcelain with site of Coronation Stone of Destiny in its grounds. Airfield (Scone) to NE.

LOCAL RADIO:
BBC RADIO SCOTLAND 810 AM / 92.4-94.7 FM;
TAY AM1584, TAY FM 96.4 FM

www.perthshire.co.uk

Plymouth *South West England* Population: 245,295. Largest city in SW England. Port and naval base. Regional shopping centre. City centre rebuilt after bombing in World War II. Has strong commercial and naval tradition. In 1588 Sir Francis Drake sailed from Plymouth to defeat Spanish Armada. Captain Cook's voyages to Australia, South Seas and Antarctica all departed from here. University. Plymouth City Airport to N of city.

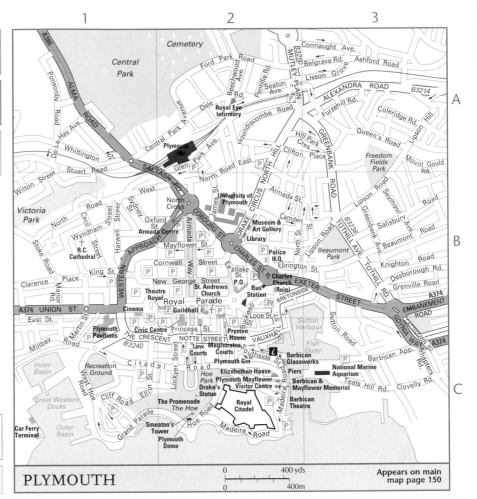

PLYMOUTH

Appears on main map page 150

Portsmouth *South East England* Population: 174,690. City, port and naval base (Portsmouth Harbour, on W side of city), extending from S end of Portsea Island to S slopes of Ports Down. Various industries, including tourism, financial services and manufacturing. Partly bombed in World War II and now rebuilt; however, some 18th century buildings remain. Boat and hovercraft ferries to Isle of Wight. University. Two cathedrals. Nelson's ship, HMS Victory, in harbour, alongside which are remains of Henry VIII's flagship, Mary Rose, which sank in 1545. King James's Gate and Landport Gate were part of 17th century defences, and Fort Cumberland is 18th century coastal defence at Eastney. Royal Garrison Church was 16th century chapel prior to Dissolution. Museums, many with nautical theme.

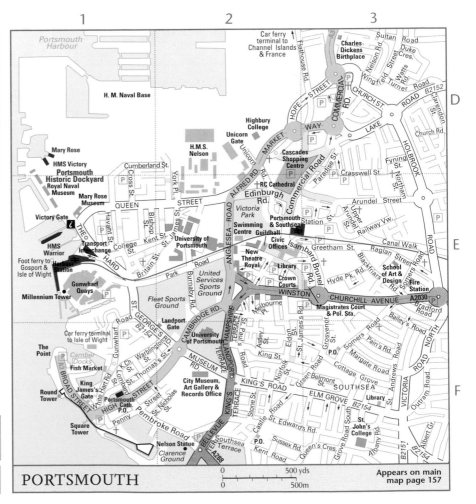

PORTSMOUTH

Appears on main map page 157

READING   SALISBURY

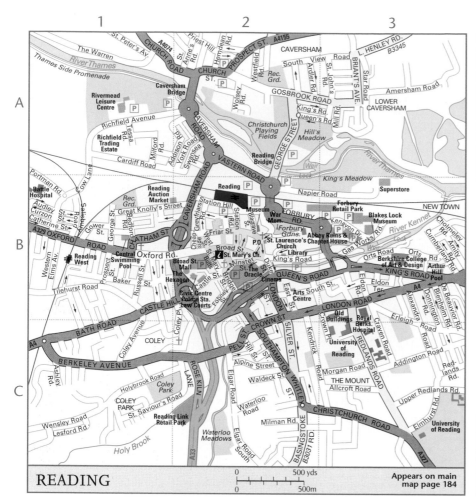

READING

Appears on main map page 184

0   500 yds
0   500m

TOURIST INFORMATION CENTRE ☎ 0118 956 6226
CHURCH HOUSE, CHAIN STREET,
READING, RG1 2HX

HOSPITAL A & E ☎ 0118 987 5111
ROYAL BERKSHIRE HOSPITAL, LONDON ROAD,
READING, RG1 5AN

COUNCIL OFFICE ☎ 0118 939 0900
CIVIC CENTRE,
READING, RG1 7TD

Reading *South East England* Population: 213,474. County and industrial town and railway centre on River Thames. During Victorian times Reading was an important manufacturing town, particularly for biscuit-making and brewing. University. Remains of Norman abbey, founded by Henry I who lies buried there. Currently major centre for information technology.

LOCAL RADIO:
BBC RADIO BERKSHIRE 104.4 FM;
CLASSIC GOLD 1431/1485 AM; 2-TEN FM 97 FM; READING 107 FM

www.readingtourism.org.uk

SALISBURY

Appears on main map page 168

0   200 yds
0   200m

TOURIST INFORMATION CENTRE ☎ 01722 334956
FISH ROW,
SALISBURY, SP1 1EJ

HOSPITAL A & E ☎ 01722 336262
SALISBURY DISTRICT HOSPITAL, ODSTOCK ROAD,
SALISBURY, SP2 8BJ

COUNCIL OFFICE ☎ 01722 336272
THE COUNCIL HOUSE, BOURNE HILL,
SALISBURY, SP1 3UZ

Salisbury (Former and official name New Sarum) *South East England* Population: 39,268. Cathedral city at confluence of Rivers Avon and Nadder. Shopping centre and market town, with buildings ranging from medieval to Victorian; several medieval churches. Cathedral, in Early English style, built between 1220 and 1260, has the tallest spire in England at 123 metres (404ft).

LOCAL RADIO:
BBC WILTSHIRE SOUND 1368 AM / 103.5 FM;
SPIRE FM 102 FM

www.visitsalisbury.com

TOURIST INFORMATION CENTRE ☎ 0114 221 1900
1 TUDOR SQUARE,
SHEFFIELD, S1 2LH

HOSPITAL A & E ☎ 0114 243 4343
NORTHERN GENERAL HOSPITAL, HERRIES ROAD,
SHEFFIELD, S5 7AU

COUNCIL OFFICE ☎ 0114 272 6444
FIRST POINT, 1 UNION STREET,
SHEFFIELD, S1 2SH

Sheffield *Yorkshire* Population: 431,607. City, on
River Don. Former centre of heavy steel industry,
now largely precision steel and cutlery industries.
University of Sheffield and Sheffield Hallam
University. Various museums dedicated to Sheffield's
industrial past. Meadowhall shopping centre and
Sheffield City Airport, 3 miles (5km) NE of city centre.

LOCAL RADIO:
BBC RADIO SHEFFIELD 88.6 FM; GALAXY 105 105.6 FM;
HALLAM FM 97.4 FM; MAGIC AM 1548 AM; REAL RADIO 107.7 FM

www.sheffield.gov.uk/out--about

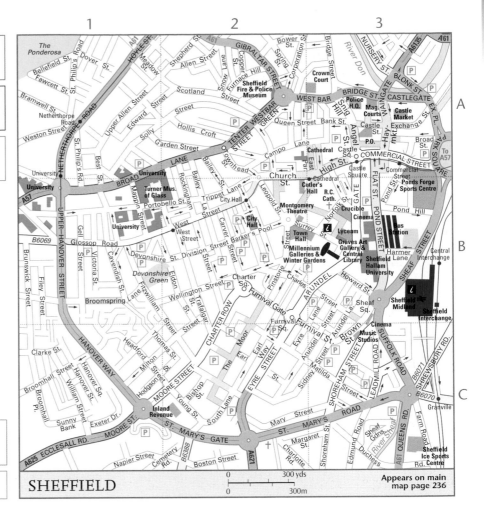

SHEFFIELD

Appears on main
map page 236

TOURIST INFORMATION CENTRE ☎ 023 8083 3333
9 CIVIC CENTRE ROAD,
SOUTHAMPTON, SO14 7FJ

HOSPITAL A & E ☎ 023 8077 7222
SOUTHAMPTON GENERAL HOSP, TREMONA RD,
SHIRLEY, SOUTHAMPTON, SO16 6YD

COUNCIL OFFICE ☎ 023 8083 3333
CIVIC CENTRE, CIVIC CENTRE ROAD,
SOUTHAMPTON, SO14 7LY

Southampton *South East England* Population:
210,138. City, at confluence of Rivers Itchen and Test
at head of Southampton Water. Southern centre for
business, culture and recreation. Container and
transatlantic passenger port, dealing with 7 percent
of UK's seaborne trade. Site of many famous
departures: Henry V's army bound for Agincourt; the
Pilgrim Fathers sailed to America on the Mayflower in
1620; maiden voyage of Queen Mary and only voyage
of Titanic. Remains of medieval town walls.
Medieval Merchant's House has authentically
recreated furnishings. Boat and helicopter ferries to
Isle of Wight. Host to many international boating
events including Southampton International Boat
Show, Whitbread Round the World, and BT Global
Challenge. University. Southampton International
Airport 1 mile (2km) S of Eastleigh.

LOCAL RADIO:
BBC RADIO SOLENT 999 AM / 96.1 FM;
CAPITAL GOLD 1557 AM; POWER FM 103.2 FM;
SOUTHCITY 107.8 FM; WAVE 105.2 FM

www.southampton.co.uk/leisure/tourism

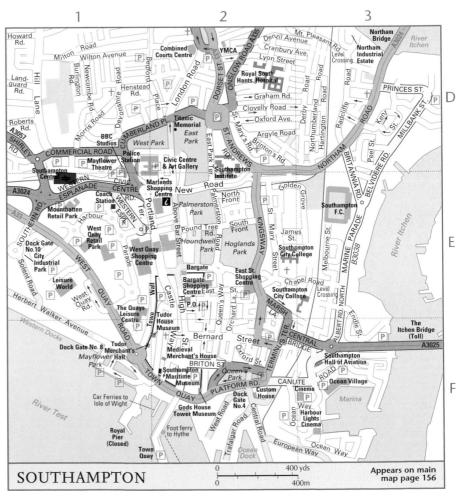

SOUTHAMPTON

Appears on main
map page 156

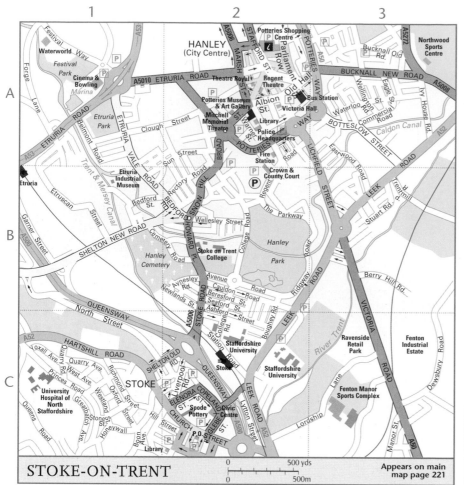

STOKE-ON-TRENT

Scale: 0 — 500 yds; 0 — 500m

Appears on main map page 221

Appears on main map page 221

TOURIST INFORMATION CENTRE ☎ 01782 236000
POTTERIES SHOPPING CENTRE, QUADRANT ROAD,
HANLEY, STOKE-ON-TRENT, ST1 1RZ

HOSPITAL A & E ☎ 01782 715444
UNIVERSITY HOSP. OF NORTH STAFFORDSHIRE,
PRINCE'S ROAD, STOKE-ON-TRENT, ST4 7LN

COUNCIL OFFICE ☎ 01782 234567
TOWN HALL, CIVIC CENTRE, GLEBE STREET,
STOKE-ON-TRENT, ST4 1RN

Stoke-on-Trent *West Midlands* Population: 266,543. City, on River Trent. Centre for employment, shopping and leisure. Created by an amalgamation of former Stoke-upon-Trent and the towns of Burslem, Fenton, Hanley, Longton and Tunstall in 1910. Capital of The Potteries (largest claywear producer in the world), now largely a finishing centre for imported pottery. Many pottery factories open to public including Wedgwood, Royal Doulton and Spode. Potteries Museum in Hanley charts history of the potteries. Gladstone Pottery Museum in Longton is centred around large bottle-kiln and demonstrates traditional skills of pottery production. Staffordshire University.

LOCAL RADIO:
BBC RADIO STOKE 94.6 FM
SIGNAL TWO 1170 AM; SIGNAL 1 102.6 FM

www.visitstoke.co.uk

STRATFORD-UPON-AVON

Scale: 0 — 500 yds; 0 — 500m

Appears on main map page 197

TOURIST INFORMATION CENTRE ☎ 0870 160 7930
BRIDGEFOOT, STRATFORD-UPON-AVON,
WARWICKSHIRE, CV37 6GW

HOSPITAL A & E ☎ 01926 495321
WARWICK HOSPITAL, LAKIN ROAD,
WARWICK, CV34 5BW

COUNCIL OFFICE ☎ 01789 267575
COUNCIL OFFICES, ELIZABETH HOUSE,
CHURCH ST, STRATFORD-UPON-AVON, CV37 6HX

Stratford-upon-Avon (Also called Stratford-on-Avon.) *West Midlands* Population: 22,231. Town, on River Avon. Tourist centre. Many attractive 16th century buildings. Reconstructed Shakespeare's Birthplace. Elizabethan garden at New Place. Hall's Croft Eizabethan town house and doctor's dispensary. Royal Shakespeare Theatre. Shakespeare's grave at Holy Trinity Church. Anne Hathaway's Cottage to W, at Shottery.

LOCAL RADIO:
BBC RADIO COVENTRY & WARWICKSHIRE 94.8 & 103.7 FM
FM 102 - THE BEAR 102 FM

www.shakespeare-country.co.uk

Sunderland *North East England* Population 183,310.
Industrial city and seaport at mouth of River Wear.
Previously largest ship-building town in the world;
coal mining was also important. Several museums
celebrate city's industrial past. Service sector and
manufacturing account for largest contribution to
local economy. National Glass Centre
commemorates importance of stained glass to area.
University.

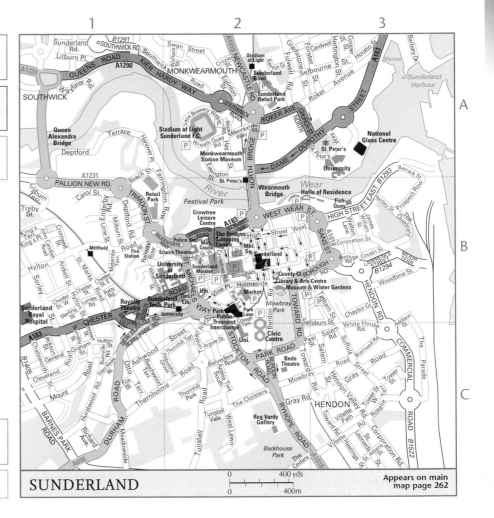

SUNDERLAND

Appears on main map page 262

Swansea (Abertawe) *Wales* Population: 171,038. City,
port on Swansea Bay at mouth of River Tawe, and
Wales' second city. Settlement developed next to
Norman castle built in 1099, but claims made that a
Viking settlement existed before this date. Previously
a port for local metal smelting industries. Bombed in
World War II, and city centre rebuilt. Birthplace of
Dylan Thomas, who described it as 'an ugly, lovely
town'. Remains of 14th century castle or fortified
manor house. University of Wales. Tropical plant and
wildlife leisure centre, Plantasia. Airport 5 miles
(9km) W at Fairwood Common.

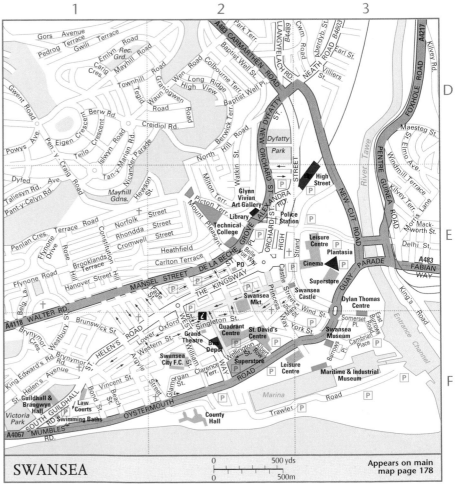

SWANSEA

Appears on main map page 178

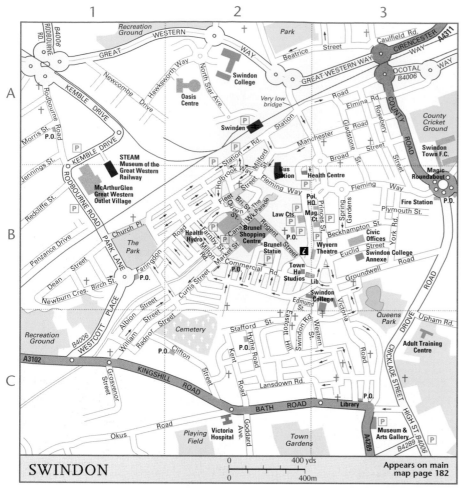

SWINDON

Appears on main map page 182

TOURIST INFORMATION CENTRE ☎ 01793 530328
37 REGENT STREET,
SWINDON, SN1 1JL

HOSPITAL A & E ☎ 01793 604020
GREAT WESTERN HOSPITAL, MARLBOROUGH RD,
SWINDON, SN3 6BB

COUNCIL OFFICE ☎ 01793 463000
CIVIC OFFICES, EUCLID STREET,
SWINDON, SN1 2JH

Swindon *South West England* Population: 145,236. Town, industrial and commercial centre. Large, modern shopping centre. Town expanded considerably in 19th century with arrival of the railway. The Museum of the Great Western Railway exhibits Swindon built locomotives and documents the history of the railway works.

LOCAL RADIO:
BBC WILTSHIRE SOUND 103.6 FM / 1368 MW;
CLASSIC GOLD 1161 AM; GWR FM 97.2 FM

www.swindon.gov.uk/tourism

TORQUAY

Appears on main map page 151

TOURIST INFORMATION CENTRE ☎ 01803 297428
VAUGHAN PARADE,
TORQUAY, TQ2 5JG

HOSPITAL A & E ☎ 01803 614567
TORBAY DISTRICT GENERAL HOSPITAL,
NEWTON ROAD, TORQUAY, TQ2 7AA

COUNCIL OFFICE ☎ 01803 201201
TOWN HALL, CASTLE CIRCUS,
TORQUAY, TQ1 3DR

Torquay *South West England* Population: 59,587. Chief town and resort of Torbay English Riviera district, with harbour and several beaches. Noted for mild climate. Torre Abbey with 15th century gatehouse, is a converted monastery housing a collecion of furniture and glassware. Torquay Museum has display on crimewriter Agatha Christie born in Torquay. Kent's Cavern showcaves are an important prehistoric site. Babbacombe Model village 2 miles (3km) N.

LOCAL RADIO:
BBC RADIO DEVON 104.3 FM;
CLASSIC GOLD 954 AM; GEMINI FM 96.4 FM;
SOUTH HAMS RADIO 100.8 FM

www.theenglishriviera.co.uk

WATFORD   WESTON-SUPER-MARE

TOURIST INFORMATION CENTRE ☎ 01727 864511
TOWN HALL, MARKET PLACE,
ST ALBANS, AL3 5DJ

HOSPITAL A & E ☎ 01923 244366
WATFORD GENERAL HOSPITAL, VICARAGE ROAD,
WATFORD, WD1 8HB

COUNCIL OFFICE ☎ 01923 226400
WATFORD COUNCIL, TOWN HALL,
WATFORD, WD17 3EX

Watford *East of England* Population: 113,080. Old market town on River Colne. Printing and brewing developed as the main industries; now the industrial base is more diverse. Shopping and leisure centre with modern sculptures in redeveloped central area. Parish church of Saint Mary's has 16th century chapel. Local history museum housed in Georgian house. Edwardian Palace Theatre originally opened as a music hall in 1908.

LOCAL RADIO:
BBC THREE COUNTIES RADIO 1161 AM / 103.8 FM;
MERCURY 96.6 FM

www.watford.gov.uk/tourism

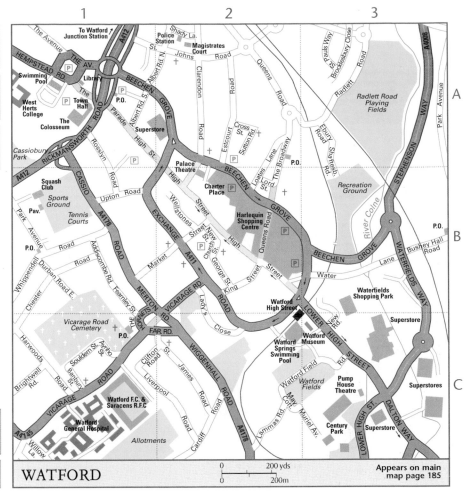

WATFORD

0   200 yds
0   200m

Appears on main
map page 185

TOURIST INFORMATION CENTRE ☎ 01934 888800
BEACH LAWNS,
WESTON-SUPER-MARE, BS23 1AT

HOSPITAL A & E ☎ 01934 636363
WESTON GENERAL HOSPITAL, GRANGE ROAD,
UPHILL, WESTON-SUPER-MARE, BS23 3NT

COUNCIL OFFICE ☎ 01934 888888
NORTH SOMERSET COUNCIL, TOWN HALL,
WESTON-SUPER-MARE, BS23 1UJ

Weston-super-Mare *South West England* Population: 69,372. Town and popular resort on the Bristol Channel, situated on Weston Bay and first developed in the 19th century. Over 1 mile (2km) of sands with traditional beach donkeys; promenade, marine lake, miniature steam railway and Winter Gardens. Amusement park located on the central Grand Pier, built in 1904. The Aquarium houses ocean and coastal waters display tanks. Local history and heritage museums give an insight into the town as a Victorian seaside resort. Annual motorbike beach race, Enduro, is held in October. International Helicopter Museum at Locking 2 miles (3km) E.

LOCAL RADIO:
BBC SOMERSET SOUND 94.9, 104.6 FM
STAR 107.7 FM

www.somersetcoast.com

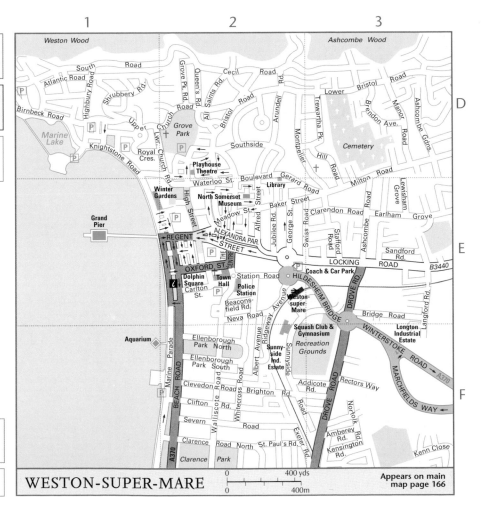

WESTON-SUPER-MARE

0   400 yds
0   400m

Appears on main
map page 166

WINCHESTER WINDSOR

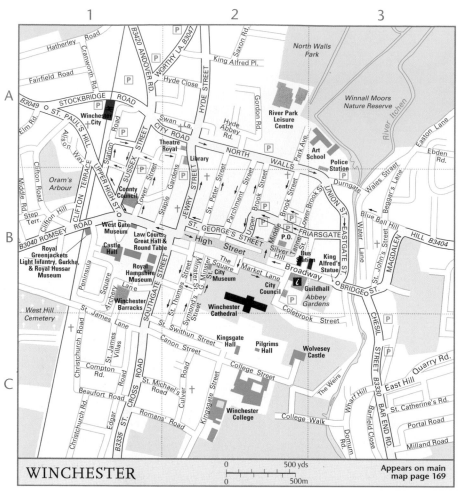

WINCHESTER

Scale: 0 — 500 yds / 0 — 500m

Appears on main map page 169

TOURIST INFORMATION CENTRE ☎ 01962 840500
GUILDHALL, THE BROADWAY, WINCHESTER
HAMPSHIRE, SO23 9LJ

HOSPITAL A & E ☎ 01962 863535
ROYAL HAMPSHIRE COUNTY HOSPITAL,
ROMSEY ROAD, WINCHESTER, SO22 5DG

COUNCIL OFFICE ☎ 01962 840222
CITY OFFICES, COLEBROOK STREET,
WINCHESTER, SO23 9LJ

Winchester *South East England* Population: 36,121.
City, county town on River Itchen on site of Roman
town of Venta Belgarum. Ancient capital of Wessex
and of Anglo-Saxon England. 11th century cathedral,
longest in Europe with carved Norman font and
England's oldest complete choir-stalls. Winchester
College, boys' public school founded 1382. 13th
century Great Hall is only remaining part of
Winchester Castle. Westgate Museum is in 12th
century gatehouse in medieval city wall, once a
debtors' prison. 12th century hospital of St. Cross.
City Mill, built over river in 18th century. To S across
river, St. Catherine's Hill, Iron Age fort. Extensive
ruins of medieval Wolvesey Castle, also known as Old
Bishop's Palace, 1 mile (2km) SE.

LOCAL RADIO:
BBC RADIO SOLENT 999 AM / 96.1 FM;
OCEAN FM 96.7 FM; WIN 107.2 FM

www.visitwinchester.co.uk

WINDSOR

Scale: 0 — 400 yds / 0 — 400m

Appears on main map page 185

TOURIST INFORMATION CENTRE ☎ 01753 743900
24 HIGH STREET,
WINDSOR, SL4 1LH

HOSPITAL A & E ☎ 01753 633000
WEXHAM PARK HOSPITAL, WEXHAM STREET,
SLOUGH, SL2 4HL

COUNCIL OFFICE ☎ 01753 810525
COUNCIL OFFICES, YORK HOUSE, SHEET STREET,
WINDSOR, SL4 1DD

Windsor *South East England* Population: 26,369.
Town, attractive market town on S bank of River
Thames. Castle is royal residence. Great Park to S of
town is open to public; Home Park bordering river is
private. St. George's Chapel is impressive. Many
Georgian houses, and guildhall designed by Sir
Christopher Wren.

LOCAL RADIO:
BBC RADIO BERKSHIRE 95.4 FM;
STAR FM 106.6 FM

www.windsor.gov.uk

TOURIST INFORMATION CENTRE ☎ 01905 726311
THE GUILDHALL, HIGH STREET,
WORCESTER, WR1 2EY

HOSPITAL A & E ☎ 01905 763333
WORCESTERSHIRE ROYAL HOSPITAL,
CHARLES HASTINGS WAY,
WORCESTER, WR5 1DD

COUNCIL OFFICE ☎ 01905 723471
THE GUILDHALL, HIGH STREET,
WORCESTER, WR1 2EY

Worcester *West Midlands* Population: 82,661. City, on River Severn. Shopping, cultural, sports and industrial centre; industries include porcelain and sauces and condiments. 18th century Guildhall. Cathedral mainly Early English includes England's largest Norman crypt, 13th century choir and Lady Chapel and tomb of King John. Three Choirs Festival held here every third year. Civil War Centre at the Commandery, headquarters for Charles II during Battle of Worcester. Factory tours and museum at Royal Worcester Porcelain. Elgar's Birthplace, home of composer Sir Edward Elgar, in Broadheath, 3 miles (5km) W.

LOCAL RADIO:
BBC RADIO HEREFORD & WORCESTER 738 AM / 104 FM;
CLASSIC HITS 1530 AM; WYVERN FM 102.8 FM

www.visitworcester.com

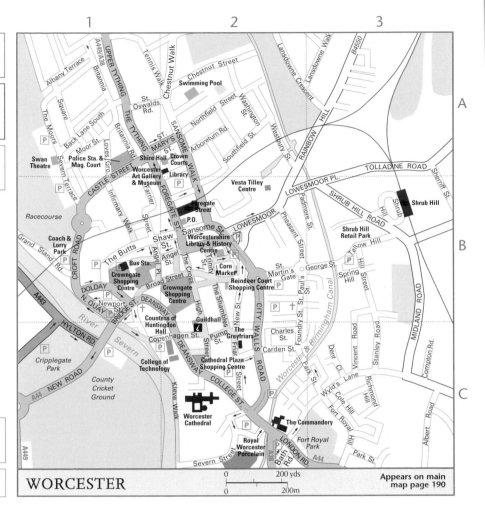

WORCESTER

Appears on main map page 190

TOURIST INFORMATION CENTRE ☎ 01904 621756
DE GREY ROOMS, EXHIBITION SQUARE,
YORK, YO1 2HB

HOSPITAL A & E ☎ 01904 631313
YORK DISTRICT HOSPITAL, WIGGINTON ROAD,
YORK, YO31 8HE

COUNCIL OFFICE ☎ 01904 613161
THE GUILDHALL,
YORK, YO1 9QN

York *Yorkshire* Population: 124,609. Ancient city and archiepiscopal see on River Ouse. On site of Roman Eboracum. Constantine the Great proclaimed Roman Emperor in York in AD 306; only emperor to be enthroned in Britain. City fell to Danes in AD 867 and became known as Jorvik. Medieval wall largely intact, other fortifications including Clifford's Tower. York Minster has largest Medieval stained glass window in country. Previously a wool trading, craft and railway centre. Home to National Railway Museum. Jorvik Viking Centre in Coppergate. Merchant Adventurers' Hall in Fossgate is finest remaining guildhall in Europe. University of York at Heslington. Racecourse at Knavesmire.

LOCAL RADIO:
BBC RADIO YORK 666, 1260 AM / 103.7 FM;
MINSTER FM 104.7 FM; GALAXY 105 105.1 FM

www.visityork.org

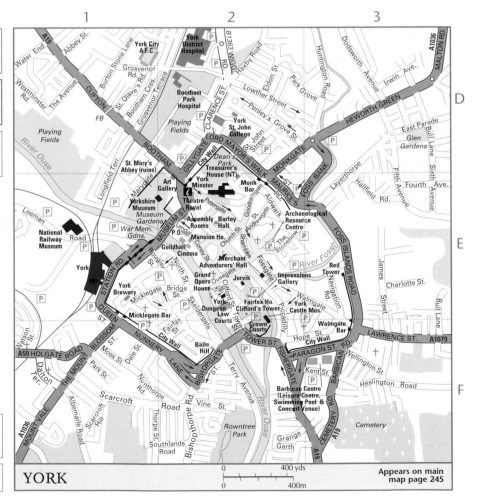

YORK

Appears on main map page 245

INDEX

Places of interest are shown in the index in **purple** type.

416

Buckspool	176	C3
Buckton *E.Riding*	255	E5
Buckton *Here.*	206	C5
Buckton *Northumb.*	279	E3
Buckworth	211	G5
Budbrooke	197	E1
Budby	236	D5
Buddon	294	D1
Bude	162	C5
Budge's Shop	148	D5
Budlake	152	C2
Budle	279	F3
Budleigh Salterton	153	D4
Budock Water	145	E3
Budworth Heath	234	A5
Buerton	221	D3
Bugbrooke	198	B2
Bugeildy (Beguildy)	206	A5
Buglawton	221	F1
Bugle	147	E4
Bugthorpe	245	G2
Building End	200	C4
Buildwas	207	F2
Buildwas Abbey	64	
Builth Road	193	G2
Builth Wells	193	G2
Bulby	225	F5
Bulcote	224	B3
Buldoo	336	B2
Bulford	168	C3
Bulford Camp	168	C3
Bulkeley	220	C2
Bulkington *Warks.*	209	F4
Bulkington *Wilts.*	168	A2
Bulkworthy	163	D4
Bull Bay	230	C5
Bull Green	174	B5
Bullbridge	223	E2
Bullbrook	171	D1
Bullen's Green	186	A2
Bulley	181	G1
Bullington	238	A5
Bullpot Farm	250	B4
Bulls Cross	186	C3
Bull's Green *Herts.*	186	B1
Bull's Green *Norf.*	215	F2
Bullwood	282	C2
Bulmer *Essex*	201	G3
Bulmer *N.Yorks.*	245	F1
Bulmer Tye	201	G4
Bulphan	187	F4
Bulstone	153	E4
Bulverhythe	160	C3
Bulwark	325	E5
Bulwell	223	G4
Bulwick	211	E3
Bumble's Green	186	D2
Bun Abhainn Eadarra	326	D3
Bun Loyne	308	B4
Bunarkaig	299	D1
Bunbury	220	C2
Bunbury Heath	220	C2
Bunchrew	321	F5
Bundalloch	307	E2
Buness	345	E1
Bunessan	288	C2
Bungay	215	E3
Bunker's Hill	226	A4
Bunlarie	272	C2
Bunloit	309	E2
Bunmhullin	314	C2
Bunnahabhain	280	C2
Bunny	223	G5
Buntait	308	C1
Buntingford	200	B5
Bunwell	214	C2
Bunwell Street	214	C2
Burbage *Derbys.*	235	E5
Burbage *Leics.*	209	G4
Burbage *Wilts.*	168	D1
Burchett's Green	184	D4
Burcombe	168	B4
Burcot *Oxon.*	184	A3
Burcot *Worcs.*	208	B5
Burcott	199	D5
Burdale	246	A1
Burdocks	171	F5
Burdon	262	C2
Burdrop	197	F4
Bures	202	A4
Bures Green	202	A4
Burf, The	196	A1
Burfa	194	B1
Burford *Oxon.*	183	E1
Burford *Shrop.*	195	E5
Burford House Gardens	64	
Burg *Arg. & B.*	296	C5
Burg	118	
Burgate	214	B4
Burgates	170	C5
Burge End	199	G4
Burgess Hill	159	F2
Burgh	202	D2
Burgh by Sands	259	G1
Burgh Castle	229	F5
Burgh Heath	172	B3
Burgh le Marsh	226	C1
Burgh next Aylsham	228	D3
Burgh on Bain	238	C4
Burgh St. Margaret (Fleggburgh)	229	F4
Burgh St. Peter	215	F2
Burghclere	169	F1
Burghead	322	D3
Burghfield	170	B1
Burghfield Common	170	B1
Burghfield Hill	170	B1
Burghill	195	D3
Burghley House	77	
Burghwallis	236	C1
Burham	173	G2
Buriton	170	C5
Burland	220	C2
Burlawn	147	D3

Burleigh	171	E1
Burlescombe	153	D1
Burleston	155	D3
Burley *Hants.*	156	B2
Burley *Rut.*	211	D1
Burley *W.Yorks.*	244	B4
Burley Gate	195	E3
Burley in Wharfedale	244	A3
Burley Street	156	B2
Burley Woodhead	244	A3
Burleydam	220	D3
Burlingjobb	194	B2
Burlow	160	A2
Burlton	220	B5
Burmarsh	174	D5
Burmington	197	E4
Burn	245	E5
Burn Farm	303	E2
Burn Naze	241	G3
Burn of Cambus	292	C4
Burn, The	303	D2
Burnage	234	C3
Burnaston	223	D4
Burnby	246	A3
Burncross	236	A3
Burndell	158	B3
Burnden	234	B2
Burnedge	234	D1
Burnend	324	D5
Burneside	249	G3
Burness	341	E2
Burneston	252	C4
Burnett	167	D1
Burnfoot *High.*	333	D2
Burnfoot *P. & K.*	293	E4
Burnfoot *Sc.Bord.*	277	G4
Burnfoot *Sc.Bord.*	277	F4
Burnham Beeches	42	
Burnham Deepdale	227	G3
Burnham Green	186	B1
Burnham Market	227	G3
Burnham Norton	227	G3
Burnham Overy Staithe	227	G3
Burnham Overy Town	227	G3
Burnham Thorpe	227	G3
Burnham-on-Crouch	188	C3
Burnham-on-Sea	166	A3
Burnhaven	325	G5
Burnhead *D. & G.*	265	G2
Burnhead *D. & G.*	266	C1
Burnhervie	312	C3
Burnhill Green	207	G2
Burnhope	262	A3
Burnhouse	283	E4
Burniston	254	D3
Burnley	243	E4
Burnmouth	287	G3
Burnopfield	262	A2
Burn's Green	200	B5
Burns National Heritage Park	118	
Burnsall	243	G1
Burnside *Aber.*	312	C3
Burnside *Angus*	302	D4
Burnside *E.Ayr.*	275	D4
Burnside *Fife*	293	G4
Burnside *Shet.*	344	B5
Burnside *W.Loth.*	285	E2
Burnside of Duntrune	294	C1
Burnstones	260	C2
Burnswark	267	F3
Burnt Hill	184	A5
Burnt Houses	262	A5
Burnt Oak	186	B3
Burnt Yates	244	B1
Burntcliff Top	221	G1
Burntisland	285	G1
Burnton *E.Ayr.*	274	C4
Burnton *E.Ayr.*	274	C5
Burntwood	208	C2
Burntwood Green	208	C2
Burnworthy	153	E1
Burpham *Surr.*	171	F2
Burpham *W.Suss.*	158	C3
Burra	342	C4
Burradon *Northumb.*	270	B1
Burradon *T. & W.*	271	E4
Burrafirth	345	F1
Burraland	344	C5
Burras	145	D3
Burraton *Cornw.*	150	A1
Burraton *Cornw.*	150	A2
Burravoe *Shet.*	345	E5
Burravoe *Shet.*	342	C1
Burray	339	D3
Burrell Collection	118	
Burrells	250	B1
Burrelton	294	A1
Burridge *Devon*	153	G2
Burridge *Hants.*	157	E1
Burrill	252	B4
Burringham	237	F2
Burrington *Devon*	163	G4
Burrington *Here.*	206	D5
Burrington *N.Som.*	166	C4
Burrough Green	201	E2
Burrough on the Hill	210	C1
Burrow *Som.*	164	C3
Burrow *Som.*	154	A1
Burrow Bridge	166	A4
Burrowhill	171	E1
Burrows Cross	171	F3
Burry	178	A3
Burry Green	178	A3
Burry Port	178	A2
Burscough	233	F1
Burscough Bridge	233	F1
Bursea	246	A4
Burshill	246	C3
Bursledon	157	D2
Burslem	221	F3
Burstall	202	C3
Burstock	154	A2

Burston *Norf.*	214	C3
Burston *Staffs.*	221	G4
Burstow	172	C4
Burstwick	247	E5
Burtersett	251	D4
Burthorpe	201	F1
Burthwaite	260	A3
Burtle	166	B3
Burtle Hill	166	A3
Burton *Ches.*	233	E5
Burton *Ches.*	220	C1
Burton *Dorset*	156	A3
Burton *Lincs.*	237	G5
Burton *Northumb.*	279	F3
Burton *Pembs.*	176	C2
Burton *Som.*	165	E3
Burton *Wilts.*	182	A5
Burton *Wilts.*	167	F4
Burton Agnes	246	D1
Burton Bradstock	154	A4
Burton Coggles	225	E5
Burton Constable Hall	86	
Burton End	200	D5
Burton Ferry	176	C2
Burton Fleming	255	D5
Burton Green *Warks.*	209	E5
Burton Green *Wrex.*	220	A2
Burton Hastings	209	G4
Burton in Lonsdale	250	B5
Burton Joyce	224	B3
Burton Latimer	211	E5
Burton Lazars	210	C1
Burton Leonard	244	C1
Burton on the Wolds	223	G5
Burton Overy	210	B3
Burton Pedwardine	225	G3
Burton Pidsea	247	E4
Burton Salmon	245	D5
Burton Stather	237	F1
Burton upon Stather	237	F1
Burton upon Trent	222	D5
Burton-in-Kendal	249	G5
Burton's Green	201	G5
Burtonwood	233	G3
Burwardsley	220	C2
Burwarton	207	F4
Burwash	160	B1
Burwash Common	160	B1
Burwash Weald	160	B1
Burwell *Cambs.*	201	D1
Burwell *Lincs.*	239	D5
Burwen	230	C3
Burwick *Ork.*	338	D4
Burwick *Shet.*	342	C3
Bury *Cambs.*	212	A4
Bury *Gt.Man.*	234	C1
Bury *Som.*	164	C5
Bury *W.Suss.*	158	C2
Bury End	196	C4
Bury Green	200	C5
Bury St. Edmunds	201	G1
Buryas Bridge	144	B4
Burythorpe	245	G1
Busbridge	171	E3
Busby *E.Renf.*	283	G4
Busby *P. & K.*	293	F2
Buscot	183	E3
Buscot Park	42	
Bush	162	C5
Bush Bank	195	D2
Bush Crathie	311	E5
Bush Green	214	D3
Bushbury	208	B2
Bushby	210	B2
Bushey	186	A3
Bushey Heath	186	A3
Bushley	196	A4
Bushley Green	196	A4
Bushton	182	C5
Bushy Common	228	A4
Busk	260	C3
Buslingthorpe	238	A4
Bussage	182	A2
Busta	342	C1
Butcher's Common	229	E3
Butcher's Cross	160	A1
Butcher's Pasture	201	E5
Butcombe	166	C1
Bute	282	B3
Bute Town	180	A2
Buthill	322	D3
Butleigh	166	C4
Butleigh Wootton	166	C4
Butler's Cross	184	D2
Butler's Hill	223	G3
Butlers Marston	197	F3
Butlersbank	220	C5
Butley	203	E2
Butley Abbey	203	E3
Butley Low Corner	203	E3
Butley Mills	203	E2
Butley Town	234	D5
Butt Green	221	D2
Butt Lane	221	F2
Butterburn	269	E4
Buttercrambe	245	G2
Butterknowle	262	A5
Butterleigh	152	C2
Butterley	223	F2
Buttermere *Cumb.*	259	E5
Buttermere *Wilts.*	169	E1
Butters Green	221	F2
Buttershaw	244	A4
Butterstone	301	F5
Butterton *Staffs.*	222	B2
Butterton *Staffs.*	221	F3
Butterwick *Dur.*	262	C5
Butterwick *Lincs.*	226	B3
Butterwick *N.Yorks.*	254	C5
Butterwick *N.Yorks.*	253	E5
Buttington	206	B2
Buttonbridge	207	G5
Buttonoak	207	G5
Buttons' Green	202	A2

Butts	152	B4
Butt's Green *Essex*	187	G2
Butt's Green *Hants.*	169	D5
Butts, The	167	E3
Buttsash	156	D2
Buxhall	202	B2
Buxted	159	G1
Buxton *Derbys.*	235	E5
Buxton *Norf.*	228	D3
Buxton Heath	228	C3
Buxton Museum & Art Gallery	70	
Buxworth	235	E4
Bwcle (Buckley)	219	F1
Bwlch	194	A5
Bwlch-clawdd	191	G4
Bwlch-derwin	217	D3
Bwlchgwyn	219	F2
Bwlch-llan	192	B2
Bwlchnewydd	191	G5
Bwlchtocyn	216	C5
Bwlch-y-cibau	206	A1
Bwlch-y-ddar	219	E5
Bwlchyfadfa	192	A3
Bwlch-y-ffridd	205	G3
Bwlch-y-groes	191	F4
Bwlchyllyn	217	E2
Bwlchymynydd	178	B3
Bwlch-y-sarnau	205	G5
Byers Green	262	B4
Byfield	198	A2
Byfleet	171	F1
Byford	194	C3
Bygrave	200	A4
Byker	262	B1
Byland Abbey	253	E5
Bylane End	147	G4
Bylchau	218	C1
Byley	221	E1
Bynea	178	B3
Byrness	269	F1
Bystock	152	D4
Bythorn	211	F5
Byton	194	C1
Bywell	261	G1
Byworth	171	E5

C

Cabharstadh	329	E5
Cabinet War Rooms	55	
Cabourne	238	B2
Cabourne Parva	238	B2
Cabrach *Arg. & B.*	280	C3
Cabrach *Moray*	311	F2
Cabus	242	A3
Cackle Street *E.Suss.*	160	D2
Cackle Street *E.Suss.*	159	G1
Cacrabank	277	E4
Cadair Idris	108	
Cadboll	322	A2
Cadbury	152	C2
Cadbury Barton	163	G4
Cadbury Heath	181	F5
Cadbury World	64	
Cadder	284	A2
Cadderlie	290	C1
Caddington	185	G2
Caddleton	289	G3
Caddonfoot	277	E2
Cade Street	160	B1
Cadeby *Leics.*	209	G2
Cadeby *S.Yorks.*	236	C2
Cadeleigh	152	C2
Cader	218	D1
Cadgwith	145	E5
Cadham	294	A2
Cadhay	26	
Cadishead	234	B3
Cadle	178	C3
Cadley *Lancs.*	242	B4
Cadley *Wilts.*	168	D1
Cadmore End	184	C3
Cadnam	156	B1
Cadney	238	A2
Cadole	219	F1
Cadover Bridge	150	B1
Cadoxton	165	E1
Cadoxton-Juxta-Neath	179	D3
Cadwell	199	G4
Cadwst	218	D4
Cadzow	284	B4
Cae Ddafydd	217	F3
Cae Llan	181	D2
Caeathro	217	E1
Caehopkin	179	E1
Caen	333	F3
Caen Hill Locks	26	
Caenby	238	A4
Caenby Corner	237	G4
Caerau *Bridgend*	179	E3
Caerau *Cardiff*	180	A5
Caerdeon	204	C1
Caerfarchell	190	A5
Caerfyrddin (Carmarthen)	192	A5
Caergeiliog	230	B5
Caergwrle	220	A2
Caergybi (Holyhead)	230	A4
Caerhun	231	F5
Caer-Lan	179	E1
Caerlaverock Castle	118	
Caerlaverock Wildfowl & Wetlands Trust	118	
Caerleon	180	C3
Caerleon Roman Fortress, Baths & Amphitheatre	108	
Caernarfon	217	D1
Caernarfon Castle	108	
Caerphilly	180	A4
Caerphilly Castle	108	
Caersws	205	G3
Caerwedros	191	G2
Caerwent	181	D3
Caerwys	232	C5

Caethle Farm	204	C3
Caggan	310	A3
Caggle Street	180	C1
Caim *High.*	297	E3
Caim *I.o.A.*	231	E4
Cainscross	182	A2
Cairinis (Carinish)	315	G3
Cairisiadar	328	B4
Cairminis	326	C5
Cairn Gorm Mountain	118	
Cairnargat	311	G1
Cairnbaan	290	A5
Cairnbeathie	312	A4
Cairnbrogie	313	D2
Cairnbulg	325	F3
Cairncross *Angus*	302	D2
Cairncross *Sc.Bord.*	287	F3
Cairncurran	283	E3
Cairndoon	257	D3
Cairndow	291	D3
Cairness	325	F3
Cairney Lodge	294	B3
Cairneyhill	285	E1
Cairngorms National Park	118	
Cairnhill *Aber.*	313	D3
Cairnhill *Aber.*	312	B1
Cairnie *Aber.*	312	D4
Cairnie *Aber.*	323	G5
Cairnorrie	325	D5
Cairnryan	264	B4
Cairnsmore	265	F4
Caister-on-Sea	229	G4
Caistor	238	B2
Caistor St. Edmund	228	D5
Caistron	270	B1
Cake Street	214	B2
Cakebole	208	A5
Calanais (Callanish)	328	D4
Calbost	327	G2
Calbourne	156	D4
Calceby	239	D5
Calcoed	232	C5
Calcot	184	B5
Calcott *Kent*	175	D2
Calcott *Shrop.*	206	D1
Calcotts Green	181	G1
Calcutt	182	D3
Caldarvan	283	F1
Caldback	345	F2
Caldbeck	259	G3
Caldbergh	251	F4
Caldecote *Cambs.*	200	B2
Caldecote *Cambs.*	211	G4
Caldecote *Herts.*	200	A4
Caldecote *Northants.*	198	B2
Caldecote *Warks.*	209	F3
Caldecott *Northants.*	199	E1
Caldecott *Oxon.*	183	G3
Caldecott *Rut.*	211	D3
Calder Bridge	248	B2
Calder Grove	236	A1
Calder Mains	336	C3
Calder Vale	242	B3
Calderbank	284	B3
Calderbrook	234	D1
Caldercruix	284	C3
Calderglen	284	A4
Calderglen Country Park	118	
Caldermill	284	A5
Caldey Island	177	E3
Caldhame	302	C5
Caldicot	181	D4
Caldwell *Derbys.*	209	E1
Caldwell *E.Renf.*	283	F4
Caldwell *N.Yorks.*	252	A1
Caldy	232	D4
Calebreck	259	G3
Caledonian Railway	118	
Caledrhydiau	192	A2
Calford Green	201	E3
Calfsound	341	D3
Calgary	296	C4
Califer	322	C4
California *Falk.*	284	D2
California *Norf.*	229	G4
California *Suff.*	202	D3
Calke	223	E5
Calke Abbey	70	
Callakille	318	C4
Callaly	270	C1
Callander	292	B4
Callanish (Calanais)	328	D4
Callanish Standing Stones	118	
Callaughton	207	F3
Callendar House	118	
Callerton Lane End	262	A1
Calliburn	272	C3
Calligarry	306	C4
Callington	149	D4
Callingwood	222	C5
Callisterhall	268	A3
Callow	195	D4
Callow End	196	A3
Callow Hill *Wilts.*	182	C4
Callow Hill *Worcs.*	207	G5
Callow Hill *Worcs.*	196	C1
Callows Grave	195	E1
Calmore	156	C1
Calmsden	182	C2
Calow	236	B5
Calrossie	321	G2
Calshot	157	D2
Calstock	150	A1
Calstone Wellington	168	B1
Calthorpe	228	C2
Calthwaite	260	A3
Calton *N.Yorks.*	243	F2
Calton *Staffs.*	222	C2
Calveley	220	C2
Calver	235	G5
Calver Hill	194	C3
Calverhall	220	D4
Calverleigh	152	C1

Calverley	244	B4
Calvert	198	B5
Calverton *M.K.*	198	C4
Calverton *Notts.*	224	B3
Calvine	300	C3
Calvo	259	E1
Cam	181	G3
Camasnacroise	298	A4
Camastianavaig	306	B1
Camasunary	306	B3
Camault Muir	321	E5
Camb	345	E3
Camber	161	E2
Camberley	171	D1
Camberwell	186	C5
Camblesforth	245	F5
Cambo	270	C2
Cambois	271	F3
Camborne	145	D3
Cambridge *Cambs.*	77	
Cambridge *Glos.*	181	G2
Cambridge American Military Cemetery & Memorial	78	
Cambridge University Botanic Gardens	78	
Cambus	293	D5
Cambus o'May	311	G5
Cambusbarron	292	D5
Cambuskenneth	292	D5
Cambuslang	284	A3
Cambusnethan	284	C4
Camden Town	186	B4
Camel Hill	166	C5
Cameley	166	D2
Camelford	147	F1
Camelon	284	D1
Camelot Theme Park	94	
Camelsdale	171	D4
Camer	173	F2
Camer's Green	195	G4
Camerton *B. & N.E.Som.*	167	D2
Camerton *Cumb.*	258	D3
Camerton *E.Riding*	247	E5
Camghouran	300	A4
Camis Eskan	283	E1
Cammachmore	313	E5
Cammeringham	237	G4
Camore	332	C5
Camp Hill *Pembs.*	177	E1
Camp Hill *Warks.*	209	F3
Camp, The	182	B2
Campbeltown	272	C3
Campbeltown (Machrihanish) Airport	272	B3
Camperdown	271	E4
Campmuir	294	A1
Camps	285	E2
Camps End	201	E3
Camps Heath	215	G2
Campsall	236	C1
Campsea Ashe	203	E2
Campton	199	G4
Camptown	278	A5
Camquhart	282	A1
Camrose	190	C5
Camserney	300	D5
Camstraddan House	291	F5
Camus Croise	306	C3
Camus-luinie	307	F2
Camusnagaul *High.*	298	D2
Camusnagaul *High.*	319	D2
Camusrory	307	E4
Camusteel	318	D5
Camusterrach	318	D5
Camusurich	292	B1
Camusvrachan	300	B5
Canada	156	B1
Canaston Bridge	177	D1
Candacraig	311	F5
Candlesby	226	C1
Candy Mill	285	E3
Cane End	184	B5
Canewdon	188	B3
Canfield End	201	D5
Canford Bottom	155	G2
Canford Cliffs	155	G4
Canford Magna	155	G3
Canham's Green	202	B1
Canisbay	337	F1
Canley	209	F5
Cann	167	F5
Cann Common	167	F5
Canna	305	D4
Cannard's Grave	166	D3
Cannich	308	C1
Canning Town	186	D4
Cannington	165	F4
Cannock	208	B2
Cannock Chase Country Park	64	
Cannock Wood	208	C1
Cannon Hall Country Park	86	
Cannon Hill Park	64	
Cannop	181	F1
Canon Bridge	194	D3
Canon Frome	195	F3
Canon Pyon	195	D3
Canonbie	268	B4
Canons Ashby *Northants.*	198	A2
Canons Ashby *Northants.*	70	
Canon's Town	144	C3
Canonteign Falls	26	
Canterbury *Aber.*	324	A4
Canterbury *Kent*	174	D3
Canterbury Cathedral	42	
Canterbury Tales, The	42	
Cantley *Norf.*	229	E5
Cantley *S.Yorks.*	236	D2
Cantlop	207	E2

Canton	180	A5
Cantray	321	G5
Cantraydoune	321	G5
Cantraywood	321	G5
Cantsfield	250	B5
Canvey Island	187	G4
Canwell Hall	208	D2
Canwick	225	E1
Canworthy Water	148	C1
Caol	298	D2
Caolas *Arg. & B.*	296	B2
Caolas *W.Isles*	314	B4
Caolas Scalpaigh (Kyles Scalpay)	327	E4
Caolasnacon	298	D3
Capel *Kent*	173	F4
Capel *Surr.*	171	G3
Capel Bangor	204	C4
Capel Betws Lleucu	192	C2
Capel Carmel	216	A5
Capel Celyn	218	A3
Capel Coch	230	C4
Capel Curig	218	A2
Capel Cynon	191	G3
Capel Dewi *Carmar.*	192	A5
Capel Dewi *Cere.*	204	C4
Capel Dewi *Cere.*	192	A3
Capel Garmon	218	B2
Capel Gwyn *Carmar.*	192	A5
Capel Gwyn *I.o.A.*	230	B5
Capel Gwynfe	192	C5
Capel Hendre	178	B1
Capel Isaac	192	B5
Capel Iwan	191	F4
Capel le Ferne	175	E4
Capel Llanilltern	179	G4
Capel Mawr	230	C5
Capel Parc	230	C4
Capel St. Andrew	203	E3
Capel St. Mary	202	B4
Capel St. Silin	192	B2
Capel Seion	204	C5
Capel Tygwydd	191	F3
Capeluchaf	216	D3
Capelulo	231	F5
Capel-y-ffin	194	B4
Capel-y-graig	217	E1
Capenhurst	233	E5
Capernwray	249	G5
Capheaton	270	C3
Caplaw	283	F4
Capon's Green	203	D1
Cappercleuch	276	D3
Capplegill	276	C5
Capstone	173	G2
Captain Cook Birthplace Museum	103	
Captain Cook Memorial Museum	86	
Capton *Devon*	151	E2
Capton *Som.*	165	D4
Car Colston	224	C3
Caradon Town	147	G2
Carbellow	275	E3
Carbeth	283	G2
Carbis Bay	144	C3
Carbost *High.*	318	A5
Carbost *High.*	305	G1
Carbrain	284	B2
Carbrooke	228	A5
Carcary	303	E4
Carco	275	F4
Carcroft	236	C1
Cardenden	294	A5
Cardeston	206	C1
Cardew	259	G2
Cardiff (Caerdydd)	180	A5
Cardiff Castle & Museum	108	
Cardiff International Airport	165	D1
Cardigan (Aberteifi)	191	E3
Cardinal's Green	201	E3
Carding Mill Valley and Long Mynd	64	
Cardington *Beds.*	199	F3
Cardington *Shrop.*	207	E3
Cardinham	147	F3
Cardno	325	E3
Cardonald	283	G3
Cardoness	265	G5
Cardoness Castle	118	
Cardow	323	D5
Cardrona	277	D3
Cardross	283	E2
Cardurnock	259	E1
Careby	211	F1
Careston	302	D4
Carew	176	D2
Carew Castle	109	
Carew Cheriton	176	D2
Carew Newton	176	D2
Carey	195	E4
Carfin	284	B4
Carfrae	286	C3
Carfraemill	286	B3
Cargate Green	229	E4
Cargen	267	D3
Cargenbridge	267	D3
Cargill	293	G1
Cargo	259	G1
Cargreen	150	A1
Carham	278	B3
Carhampton	164	D3
Carharrack	146	A5
Carie *P. & K.*	300	B4
Carie *P. & K.*	292	B1
Carines	146	B4
Carinish (Cairinis)	315	G3
Carisbrooke	157	D4
Carisbrooke Castle & Museum	42	
Cark	249	E5
Carkeel	150	A1
Carlabhagh (Carloway)	328	D3
Carland Cross	146	C4

Carlatton 260 B2
Carlby 211 F1
Carlecotes 235 F2
Carleen 144 D4
Carleton Cumb. 260 A2
Carleton Cumb. 260 B5
Carleton Lancs. 241 G3
Carleton N.Yorks. 243 F3
Carleton W.Yorks. 245 D5
Carleton Fishery 264 C2
Carleton Forehoe 228 B5
Carleton Rode 214 C2
Carleton St. Peter 229 E5
Carlin How 253 G1
Carlisle 260 A2
Carlisle Castle 94
Carlisle Cathedral 94
Carloggas 146 C3
Carlops 285 F4
Carloway (Carlabhagh) 328 D3
Carlton Beds. 199 E2
Carlton Cambs. 201 E2
Carlton Leics. 209 F2
Carlton N.Yorks. 245 F5
Carlton N.Yorks. 251 F4
Carlton N.Yorks. 253 F4
Carlton Notts. 224 B3
Carlton S.Yorks. 236 A1
Carlton Stock. 262 C5
Carlton Suff. 203 E1
Carlton W.Yorks. 244 C5
Carlton Colville 215 G2
Carlton Curlieu 210 B3
Carlton Green 201 E2
Carlton Husthwaite 253 D5
Carlton in Lindrick 236 C4
Carlton Miniott 252 C4
Carlton Scroop 225 E3
Carlton-in-Cleveland 253 E2
Carlton-le-Moorland 225 E2
Carlton-on-Trent 224 D1
Carluke 284 C4
Carlyle's Birthplace 119
Carlyon Bay 147 E4
Carmacoup 275 F3
Carmarthen (Caerfyrddin) 192 A5
Carmel Carmar. 178 B1
Carmel Flints. 232 C5
Carmel Gwyn. 217 D2
Carmel I.o.A. 230 B4
Carmichael 276 A2
Carmont 303 G1
Carmunnock 283 G4
Carmyle 284 A3
Carmyllie 303 D5
Carn 280 A4
Carn Brea Village 146 A5
Carn Dearg 319 D2
Carnaby 246 D1
Carnach High. 307 G2
Carnach High. 330 C5
Carnach W.Isles 315 G3
Carnan 315 F5
Carnassarie 290 A4
Carnbee 294 D4
Carnbo 293 F4
Carndu 307 E2
Carnduncan 280 A3
Carnewas & Bedruthan Steps 26
Carnforth 249 F5
Carnhedryn 190 B5
Carnhell Green 144 D3
Carnichal 325 E4
Carnkie Cornw. 145 D3
Carnkie Cornw. 145 E3
Carnmore 280 B5
Carno 205 F3
Carnoch High. 308 C1
Carnoch High. 320 B4
Carnoch High. 322 A5
Carnock 285 E1
Carnon Downs 146 C5
Carnousie 324 B4
Carnoustie 295 D1
Carntyne 284 A3
Carnwath 285 D5
Carnyorth 144 A3
Carol Green 209 E5
Carperby 251 F4
Carr 236 C3
Carr Hill 237 D3
Carr Houses 233 E2
Carr Shield 261 E3
Carr Vale 236 B5
Carradale 272 C2
Carradale East 272 D2
Carragrich 327 D4
Carrbridge 310 B2
Carrefour Selous 150 C5
Carreg Cennen Castle 109
Carreg-lefn 230 B4
Carreg-wen 191 F3
Carrhouse 237 E2
Carrick 282 A1
Carrick Castle 291 D5
Carriden 285 E1
Carrine 272 B5
Carrington Gt.Man. 234 B3
Carrington Lincs. 226 B2
Carrington Midloth. 286 A3
Carroch 266 A1
Carrog Conwy 218 A3
Carrog Denb. 219 E3
Carroglen 292 C2
Carrol 332 D4
Carron Arg. & B. 290 B5
Carron Falk. 284 C1
Carron Moray 323 E5
Carron Bridge 284 B1
Carronbridge 266 C1
Carronshore 284 C1
Carrot 302 C5
Carrow Hill 180 D3
Carrutherstown 267 F3
Carruthmuir 283 E3
Carrville 262 C3
Carry 282 A3
Carsaig 289 E2
Carscreugh 264 D4
Carse 281 F3
Carse of Ardersier 322 A4
Carsegowan 265 F5
Carseriggan 265 E4
Carsethorn 267 D5
Carsgoe 336 D2
Carshalton 172 B2
Carshalton Beeches 172 B2
Carsington 223 D2
Carsington Water 71
Carsluith 265 F5
Carsphairn 265 G1
Carstairs 284 D5
Carstairs Junction 285 D5
Carswell Marsh 183 F3
Carter's Clay 169 E5
Carterton 183 E2
Carterway Heads 261 G2
Carthew 147 E4
Carthorpe 252 C4
Cartington 270 C1
Cartland 284 C5
Cartmel 249 E5
Cartmel Fell 249 F4
Cartmel Priory 94
Cartworth 235 F2
Carway 178 A2
Cascob 194 B1
Cas-gwent (Chepstow) 181 E3
Cashel Farm 291 G5
Cashes Green 182 A2
Cashlie 299 G5
Cashmoor 155 F1
Caskieberran 294 A4
Casnewydd (Newport) 180 C4
Cassencarie 265 F5
Cassington 183 G1
Cassop 262 C4
Castell 218 A1
Castell Dinas Bran 109
Castell Gorfod 191 F5
Castell Howell 192 A3
Castell Newydd Emlyn (Newcastle Emlyn) 191 G3
Castellau 179 G4
Castell-Nedd (Neath) 179 D3
Castell-y-bwch 180 B3
Casterton 250 B5
Castle Acre 213 G1
Castle Ashby 199 D2
Castle Bolton 251 F3
Castle Bromwich 208 D4
Castle Bytham 211 E1
Castle Caereinion 206 A2
Castle Campbell 119
Castle Camps 201 E3
Castle Carrock 260 B2
Castle Cary 166 D4
Castle Combe 182 A5
Castle Donington 223 F5
Castle Douglas 266 B4
Castle Drogo 26
Castle Eaton 182 D3
Castle Eden 262 D4
Castle End 209 E5
Castle Fraser 119
Castle Frome 195 F3
Castle Gate 144 B3
Castle Goring 158 D3
Castle Green 171 E1
Castle Gresley 209 E1
Castle Heaton 287 G5
Castle Hedingham 201 F4
Castle Hill Kent 173 F4
Castle Hill Suff. 202 C3
Castle House (Sir Alfred Munnings Art Museum) 78
Castle Howard 86
Castle Kennedy 264 C5
Castle Leod 321 D4
Castle Levan 282 D2
Castle Madoc 193 G4
Castle Menzies 119
Castle Morris 190 C4
Castle O'er 268 A2
Castle of Mey 119
Castle Rising 227 E5
Castle Stuart 321 G5
Castlebay (Bàgh a' Chaisteil) 314 B4
Castlebythe 190 D5
Castlecary 284 B2
Castlecraig High. 322 A3
Castlecraig Sc.Bord. 285 F5
Castlefairn 266 B2
Castleford 244 D5
Castlemartin 176 C3
Castlemilk D. & G. 267 F3
Castlemilk Glas. 284 A4
Castlemorton 195 G4
Castlerigg 259 F4
Castlerigg Stone Circle 94
Castleside 261 G3
Castlesteads 260 B1
Castlethorpe 198 D3
Castleton Aber. 324 C4
Castleton Angus 302 B5
Castleton Arg. & B. 281 G1
Castleton Derbys. 235 F4
Castleton Gt.Man. 234 C1
Castleton N.Yorks. 253 F2
Castleton Newport 180 B4
Castleton Sc.Bord. 268 D2
Castletown Dorset 154 C5
Castletown High. 337 D2
Castletown High. 321 G5
Castletown I.o.M. 240 A5
Castletown T. & W. 262 C2
Castleweary 277 F5
Castlewigg 257 E2
Castley 244 B3
Caston 214 A2
Castor 211 G3
Castramont 265 G4
Caswell 178 B4
Cat and Fiddle Inn 235 E5
Catacol 282 A5
Catbrain 181 E4
Catbrook 181 E2
Catchall 144 B4
Catcleugh 269 F1
Catcliffe 236 B4
Catcott 166 A4
Caterham 172 C3
Catfield 229 E3
Catfirth 342 D2
Catford 186 C5
Catforth 242 A4
Cathays 180 A5
Cathcart 283 G3
Cathedine 194 A5
Catherine-de-Barnes 209 D4
Catherington 157 F1
Catherston Leweston 153 G3
Catherton 207 F5
Cathkin 284 A4
Catisfield 157 E2
Catlodge 309 F5
Catlowdy 268 C4
Catmere End 200 C4
Catmore 183 G4
Caton Devon 152 A5
Caton Lancs. 242 B1
Caton Green 242 B1
Cator Court 149 G3
Catrine 274 D3
Catsfield 160 C2
Catsfield Stream 160 C2
Catshaw 235 G2
Catshill 208 B5
Cattadale 280 B3
Cattal 244 D2
Cattawade 202 B4
Catterall 242 B3
Catterick 252 B3
Catterick Bridge 252 B3
Catterick Garrison 252 A3
Catterlen 260 A4
Catterline 303 G2
Catterton 245 E3
Catteshall 171 E3
Catthorpe 210 A5
Cattishall 201 G1
Cattistock 154 B2
Catton N.Yorks. 252 C5
Catton Norf. 228 D4
Catton Northumb. 261 E2
Catton Hall 209 E1
Catwick 246 D3
Catworth 211 F5
Caudle Green 182 B1
Caulcott Beds. 199 F3
Caulcott Oxon. 198 A5
Cauldcots 303 E5
Cauldhame Stir. 292 B5
Cauldhame Stir. 292 D4
Cauldon 222 B3
Caulkerbush 266 D5
Caulside 268 C3
Caundle Marsh 154 C1
Caunsall 208 A4
Caunton 224 C1
Causeway End D. & G. 265 F4
Causeway End Essex 187 F1
Causeway End Lancs. 233 F1
Causewayhead Cumb. 259 E1
Causewayhead Stir. 292 D5
Causey 262 B2
Causey Park 271 D2
Causeyend 313 E3
Cautley 250 B3
Cavendish 201 G3
Cavendish Bridge 223 F5
Cavenham 201 F1
Cavens 267 D5
Cavers 277 G4
Caversfield 198 A5
Caversham 184 C5
Caverswall 221 G3
Cawdor 322 A4
Cawdor Castle 119
Cawkeld 246 B2
Cawkwell 238 C4
Cawood 245 E4
Cawsand 150 A3
Cawston Norf. 228 C3
Cawston Warks. 209 G5
Cawthorn 253 G4
Cawthorne 235 G2
Cawthorpe 225 F5
Cawton 253 F5
Caxton 200 B2
Caxton Gibbet 200 A1
Caynham 207 E5
Caythorpe Lincs. 225 E3
Caythorpe Notts. 224 B3
Cayton 255 D4
Ceallan 315 G4
Ceann a' Bhàigh W.Isles 315 F3
Ceann a' Bhàigh W.Isles 326 C5
Ceann Loch Shiphoirt 327 E2
Ceann Lochroag (Kinlochroag) 328 C5
Ceannaridh 315 G4
Cearsiadar 327 F2
Ceathramh Meadhanach (Middlequarter) 315 G2
Cecil Higgins Art Gallery 78
Cedig 218 C5
Cefn Berain 218 C1
Cefn Bycharn (Newbridge) 180 B3
Cefn Canol 219 F4
Cefn Cantref 193 G5
Cefn Coch 219 E2
Cefn Cribwr 179 E4
Cefn Cross 179 E4
Cefn Einion 206 B4
Cefn Hengoed 180 A3
Cefn Llwyd 204 C4
Cefn Rhigos 179 F2
Cefn-brith 218 C2
Cefn-caer-Ferch 216 D3
Cefn-coch 219 E5
Cefn-coed-y-cymmer 179 G2
Cefn-ddwysarn 218 C4
Cefndeuddwr 218 A5
Cefneithin 178 B1
Cefn-gorwydd 193 F3
Cefn-gwyn 206 A4
Cefn-mawr 219 F3
Cefnpennar 179 G2
Cefn-y-bedd 220 A2
Cefn-y-pant 191 E5
Cegidfa (Guilsfield) 206 B1
Ceidio 230 C4
Ceidio Fawr 216 B4
Ceinewydd (New Quay) 191 G1
Ceint 230 C5
Cellan 192 C3
Cellardyke 295 D4
Cellarhead 221 G3
Celtica 109
Cemaes 230 B3
Cemmaes 205 E2
Cemmaes Road (Glantwymyn) 205 E2
Cenarth 191 F3
Cennin 217 D3
Centre For Alternative Technology 109
Ceos (Keose) 329 E5
Ceredigion Museum 109
Ceres 294 C3
Cerist 205 F4
Cerne Abbas 154 C2
Cerney Wick 182 C3
Cerrigceinwen 230 C5
Cerrigydrudion 218 C3
Cessford 278 B4
Ceunant 217 E1
Chaceley 196 A4
Chacewater 146 B5
Chackmore 198 B4
Chacombe 197 G3
Chad Valley 208 C4
Chadderton 234 D2
Chadderton Fold 234 C2
Chaddesden 223 E4
Chaddesley Corbett 208 A5
Chaddleworth 183 G5
Chadlington 197 F5
Chadshunt 197 F2
Chadstone 199 D2
Chadwell Leics. 224 C5
Chadwell Shrop. 207 G1
Chadwell St. Mary 187 F5
Chadwick End 209 E5
Chaffcombe 153 G1
Chafford Hundred 187 F5
Chagford 152 A4
Chailey 159 F2
Chainhurst 173 G4
Chalbury 155 G2
Chalbury Common 155 G2
Chaldon 172 C3
Chaldon Herring (East Chaldon) 155 D4
Chale 157 D5
Chale Green 157 D4
Chalfont Common 185 F3
Chalfont St. Giles 185 E3
Chalfont St. Peter 185 F3
Chalford Glos. 182 A2
Chalford Wilts. 167 F3
Chalgrove 184 B3
Chalk 187 F5
Chalk End 187 F1
Challacombe 163 G1
Challister 343 E1
Challoch 265 E4
Challock 174 C3
Chalmington 154 B2
Chalton Beds. 199 F5
Chalton Hants. 157 G1
Chalvey 185 E5
Chalvington 160 A3
Chambercombe Manor 26
Champany 285 E2
Chancery 204 B5
Chandler's Cross 185 F3
Chandler's Ford 169 F5
Channel Islands 150 A5
Channel's End 199 G2
Channerwick 342 D5
Chantry Som. 167 E3
Chantry Suff. 202 C3
Chapel 294 A5
Chapel Allerton Som. 166 B2
Chapel Allerton W.Yorks. 244 C4
Chapel Amble 147 D2
Chapel Brampton 198 C1
Chapel Chorlton 221 F4
Chapel Cleeve 164 D3
Chapel Cross 160 B1
Chapel End 199 F3
Chapel Green Warks. 209 E4
Chapel Green Warks. 197 G1
Chapel Haddlesey 245 E5
Chapel Hill Aber. 313 F1
Chapel Hill Lincs. 226 A2
Chapel Hill Mon. 181 E2
Chapel Hill N.Yorks. 244 C3
Chapel Knapp 167 F1
Chapel Lawn 206 C5
Chapel Leigh 165 E5
Chapel Milton 235 E4
Chapel of Garioch 312 C2
Chapel Rossan 256 B2
Chapel Row Essex 187 G2
Chapel Row W.Berks. 169 G1
Chapel St. Leonards 239 F5
Chapel Stile 249 E2
Chapel Town 146 C4
Chapelbank 293 F3
Chapeldonan 273 G5
Chapelend Way 201 F4
Chapel-en-le-Frith 235 E4
Chapelgate 226 C5
Chapelhall 284 B3
Chapelhill High. 322 A2
Chapelhill P. & K. 294 A2
Chapelhill P. & K. 293 F1
Chapelknowe 268 B4
Chapel-le-Dale 250 C5
Chapelthorpe 236 A1
Chapelton Aber. 303 G1
Chapelton Angus 303 E5
Chapelton Devon 163 F3
Chapelton S.Lan. 284 A5
Chapeltown B'burn. 234 B1
Chapeltown Cumb. 268 C4
Chapeltown Moray 311 E2
Chapeltown S.Yorks. 236 A3
Chapmans Well 149 D1
Chapmanslade 167 F3
Chapmore End 186 C1
Chappel 201 G5
Charaton 148 D4
Chard 153 G2
Chard Junction 153 G2
Chardleigh Green 153 G1
Chardstock 153 G2
Charfield 181 G3
Charing 174 B4
Charing Cross 156 A1
Charing Heath 174 B4
Charingworth 197 D4
Charlbury 183 F1
Charlcombe 167 E1
Charlecote 197 E2
Charlecote Park 64
Charles 163 G2
Charles Tye 202 B2
Charlesfield 277 G3
Charleshill 171 D3
Charleston 302 B5
Charlestown Aber. 325 F3
Charlestown Aberdeen 313 E4
Charlestown Cornw. 147 E4
Charlestown Derbys. 235 E3
Charlestown Dorset 154 C5
Charlestown Fife 285 E1
Charlestown Gt.Man. 234 C2
Charlestown High. 319 E2
Charlestown High. 321 F5
Charlestown W.Yorks. 244 A4
Charlestown W.Yorks. 243 F5
Charlestown of Aberlour (Aberlour) 323 E5
Charlesworth 235 E3
Charleton 294 C4
Charlinch 165 F4
Charlotteville 171 F3
Charlton Gt.Lon. 186 D5
Charlton Hants. 169 E3
Charlton Herts. 199 G5
Charlton Northants. 198 A4
Charlton Northumb. 270 A3
Charlton Oxon. 183 G4
Charlton Som. 167 D2
Charlton Som. 166 D3
Charlton Som. 167 E4
Charlton Tel. & W. 207 E1
Charlton W.Suss. 158 A2
Charlton Wilts. 168 A5
Charlton Wilts. 182 B4
Charlton Wilts. 168 C2
Charlton Worcs. 196 C3
Charlton Abbots 196 C5
Charlton Adam 166 C5
Charlton Horethorne 167 D5
Charlton Kings 196 B5
Charlton Mackrell 166 C5
Charlton Marshall 155 E2
Charlton Musgrove 167 E5
Charlton on the Hill 155 E2
Charlton-All-Saints 168 C5
Charlton-on-Otmoor 184 A1
Charltons 253 F1
Charlwood 172 B4
Charminster 154 C3
Charmouth 153 G3
Charndon 198 B5
Charney Bassett 183 F3
Charnock Richard 233 G1
Charsfield 203 D2
Chart Corner 173 G4
Chart Sutton 174 A4
Charter Alley 169 G2
Charterhouse 166 B2
Charterville Allotments 183 F2
Chartham 174 D3
Chartham Hatch 174 D3
Chartridge 185 E2
Chartwell 42
Charvil 184 C5
Charwelton 198 A2
Chase End Street 195 G4
Chase Terrace 208 C2
Chasetown 208 C2
Chastleton 197 E5
Chastleton House 43
Chasty 162 D5
Chatburn 243 D3
Chatcull 221 E4
Chatham 173 G2
Chatham Green 187 G1
Chatham Historic Dockyard & World Naval Base 43
Chathill 279 F4
Chatsworth House 71
Chattenden 187 G5
Chatteris 212 B4
Chattisham 202 B3
Chatto 278 B5
Chatton 279 E4
Chaul End 199 F5
Chavey Down 171 D1
Chawleigh 152 A1
Chawley 183 G2
Chawston 199 G2
Chawton 170 C4
Chazey Heath 184 B5
Cheadle Gt.Man. 234 C4
Cheadle Staffs. 222 B3
Cheadle Heath 234 C4
Cheadle Hulme 234 C4
Cheam 172 B2
Cheapside 171 E1
Chearsley 184 C1
Chebsey 221 F5
Checkendon 184 B4
Checkley Ches. 221 E3
Checkley Here. 195 E4
Checkley Staffs. 222 B4
Checkley Green 221 E3
Chedburgh 201 F2
Cheddar 166 B2
Cheddar Gorge & Caves 26
Cheddington 185 E1
Cheddleton 221 G2
Cheddon Fitzpaine 165 F5
Chedglow 182 B3
Chedgrave 215 E2
Chedington 154 A2
Chediston 215 E4
Chediston Green 215 E4
Chedworth 182 C1
Chedworth Roman Villa 26
Chedzoy 166 A4
Cheeklaw 287 E4
Cheesden 234 C1
Cheeseman's Green 174 C5
Cheetham Hill 234 C2
Cheglinch 163 F1
Cheldon 152 A1
Chelford 234 C5
Chellaston 223 E4
Chells 200 A5
Chelmarsh 207 G4
Chelmondiston 202 D4
Chelmorton 222 C1
Chelmsford 187 G2
Chelmsley Wood 209 D4
Chelsea 186 B5
Chelsfield 173 D2
Chelsham 172 C3
Chelston Heath 165 E5
Chelsworth 202 A3
Cheltenham 196 B5
Chelveston 199 E1
Chelvey 166 B1
Chelwood 166 D1
Chelwood Common 159 G1
Chelwood Gate 159 G1
Chelworth 182 B3
Cheney Longville 206 D4
Chenies 185 F3
Chenies Manor House 43
Chepstow (Cas-gwent) 181 E3
Chepstow Castle 109
Chepstow Museum 109
Chequer, The 220 B3
Cherhill 182 C5
Cherington Glos. 182 B3
Cherington Warks. 197 E4
Cheriton Devon 164 A3
Cheriton Hants. 169 G5
Cheriton Kent 175 D5
Cheriton Pembs. 176 C3
Cheriton Swan. 178 A3
Cheriton Bishop 152 A3
Cheriton Cross 152 A3
Cheriton Fitzpaine 152 B2
Cherrington 221 D5
Cherry Burton 246 B3
Cherry Green 201 D5
Cherry Hinton 200 C2
Cherry Tree 242 C5
Cherry Willingham 238 A5
Chertsey 171 F1
Cheselbourne 155 D3
Chesham 185 E2
Chesham Bois 185 E2
Cheshunt 186 C2
Chesil Beach 26
Cheslyn Hay 208 B2
Chessington 171 G1
Chessington World of Adventures 55
Chestall 208 C1
Chester 94
Chester Cathedral 95
Chester Moor 262 B3
Chester Zoo 95
Chesterblade 167 D3
Chesterfield Derbys. 236 A5
Chesterfield Staffs. 208 D2
Chesterholm Roman Fort (see Vindolanda Roman Fort) 105
Chester-le-Street 262 B2
Chesters Sc.Bord. 278 A5
Chesters Sc.Bord. 278 A4
Chesterton Cambs. 200 C1
Chesterton Cambs. 211 G3
Chesterton Oxon. 198 A5
Chesterton Shrop. 207 G3
Chesterton Staffs. 221 F3
Chesterton Warks. 197 F2
Chesterton Green 197 F2
Chestfield 174 D2
Cheston 150 C2
Cheswardine 221 E5
Cheswick 279 E2
Cheswick Buildings 279 E2
Cheswick Green 208 D5
Chetnole 154 C2
Chettiscombe 152 C1
Chettisham 212 D4
Chettle 155 F1
Chettle House 26
Chetton 207 F3
Chetwode 198 B5
Chetwynd Aston 207 G1
Chetwynd Park 221 E5
Cheveley 201 E1
Chevening 173 D3
Cheverell's Green 185 F1
Chevington 201 F2
Chevington Drift 271 E2
Chevithorne 152 C1
Chew Magna 166 C1
Chew Moor 234 A2
Chew Stoke 166 C1
Chewton Keynsham 166 D1
Chewton Mendip 166 C2
Chichacott 149 G1
Chicheley 199 E3
Chichester 158 A3
Chichester District Museum 43
Chickerell 154 C4
Chickering 214 D4
Chicklade 168 A4
Chickney 201 D5
Chicksands 199 G4
Chidden 157 F1
Chidden Holt 157 F1
Chiddingfold 171 E4
Chiddingly 160 A2
Chiddingstone 173 D4
Chiddingstone Causeway 173 E4
Chiddingstone Hoath 173 D4
Chideock 154 A3
Chidham 157 G2
Chidswell 244 B5
Chieveley 183 G5
Chignall St. James 187 F2
Chignall Smealy 187 F1
Chigwell 186 D3
Chigwell Row 187 D3
Chilbolton 169 E3
Chilcomb 169 G5
Chilcombe 154 B3
Chilcompton 167 D2
Chilcote 209 E1
Child Okeford 155 E1
Childer Thornton 233 E5
Childerditch 187 F4
Childrey 183 F4
Child's Ercall 221 D5
Child's Hill 186 B4
Childswickham 196 C4
Childwall 233 F4
Childwick Green 186 A1
Chilfrome 154 B3
Chilgrove 158 A2
Chilham 174 C3
Chilhampton 168 B4
Chilla 163 E5
Chillaton 149 E2
Chillenden 175 E3
Chillerton 157 D4
Chillesford 203 E2
Chilley 151 D2
Chillingham 279 E4
Chillington Devon 151 D3
Chillington Som. 153 G1
Chilmark 168 A4
Chilson Oxon. 183 F1
Chilson Som. 153 G2
Chilsworthy Cornw. 149 E3
Chilsworthy Devon 162 D5
Chiltern Open Air Museum 43
Chilterns 43
Chilthorne Domer 154 B1
Chilton Bucks. 184 B1
Chilton Devon 152 B2
Chilton Dur. 262 B5
Chilton Oxon. 183 G4
Chilton Suff. 201 G3
Chilton Candover 169 G4
Chilton Cantelo 166 C5
Chilton Foliat 183 F5
Chilton Polden 166 A4
Chilton Street 201 F3
Chilton Trinity 165 F4
Chilvers Coton 209 F3
Chilwell 223 G4
Chilworth Hants. 156 D1
Chilworth Surr. 171 F3
Chimney 183 F2
Chimney Street 201 F3
Chineham 170 B2
Chingford 186 C3
Chinley 235 E4
Chinley Head 235 E4
Chinnor 184 C2
Chipchase Castle 270 A4

Chipley 165 E5
Chipnall 221 E4
Chippenham *Cambs.* 201 E1
Chippenham *Wilts.* 182 B5
Chipperfield 185 F2
Chipping *Herts.* 200 B4
Chipping *Lancs.* 242 C3
Chipping Campden 197 D4
Chipping Hill 188 B1
Chipping Norton 197 F5
Chipping Ongar 187 E2
Chipping Sodbury 181 G4
Chipping Warden 197 G3
Chipstable 164 D5
Chipstead *Kent* 173 D3
Chipstead *Surr.* 172 B3
Chirbury 206 B3
Chirk (Y Waun) 219 F4
Chirk Castle 109
Chirk Green 219 F4
Chirmorrie 264 D3
Chirnside 287 F4
Chirnsidebridge 287 F4
Chirton *T. & W.* 262 C1
Chirton *Wilts.* 168 B2
Chisbury 169 D1
Chiscan 272 B4
Chiselborough 154 A1
Chiseldon 183 D5
Chiserley 243 G5
Chislehampton 184 A3
Chislehurst 186 D5
Chislet 175 E2
Chiswell Green 186 A2
Chiswick 186 B5
Chiswick End 200 B3
Chiswick House 55
Chisworth 235 D3
Chithurst 170 D5
Chittering 212 C5
Chitterne 168 A3
Chittlehamholt 163 G3
Chittlehampton 163 G3
Chittoe 168 A1
Chivelstone 151 D4
Chivenor 163 F2
Chobham 171 E1
Choicelee 287 E4
Cholderton 168 D3
Cholesbury 185 E2
Chollerford 270 B4
Chollerton 270 B4
Cholmondeley Castle Gardens 95
Cholsey 184 A4
Cholstrey 195 D2
Cholwell *B. & N.E.Som.* 166 D2
Cholwell *Devon* 149 E3
Chop Gate 253 E3
Choppington 271 E3
Chopwell 262 A2
Chorley *Ches.* 220 C2
Chorley *Lancs.* 233 G1
Chorley *Shrop.* 207 F4
Chorley *Staffs.* 208 C1
Chorleywood 185 F3
Chorlton 221 E2
Chorlton Lane 220 B3
Chorlton-cum-Hardy 234 C3
Chowley 220 B2
Chrishall 200 C4
Chrishall Grange 200 C3
Chrisswell 282 D2
Christchurch *Cambs.* 212 C3
Christchurch *Dorset* 156 A3
Christchurch *Glos.* 181 E1
Christchurch *Newport* 180 C4
Christchurch Priory 26
Christian Malford 182 B5
Christleton 220 B1
Christmas Common 184 C3
Christon 166 A2
Christon Bank 279 G4
Christow 152 B4
Christskirk 312 B2
Chryston 284 A2
Chudleigh 152 B5
Chudleigh Knighton 152 B5
Chulmleigh 163 G4
Chunal 235 E3
Church 242 D5
Church Aston 207 G1
Church Brampton 198 C1
Church Brough 250 C1
Church Broughton 222 D4
Church Charwelton 198 A2
Church Common 203 E2
Church Crookham 170 D2
Church Eaton 208 A1
Church End *Beds.* 199 G4
Church End *Beds.* 199 E5
Church End *Beds.* 199 G2
Church End *Beds.* 199 E3
Church End *Beds.* 199 E4
Church End *Cambs.* 212 B2
Church End *Cambs.* 212 B5
Church End *Cambs.* 212 A4
Church End *E.Riding* 246 C2
Church End *Essex* 201 D3
Church End *Essex* 201 F5
Church End *Glos.* 196 A4
Church End *Hants.* 170 B2
Church End *Herts.* 186 A1
Church End *Herts.* 200 C5
Church End *Lincs.* 226 A4
Church End *Lincs.* 239 E3
Church End *Warks.* 209 E3
Church End *Wilts.* 182 C5
Church Enstone 197 F5
Church Farm Museum 71
Church Fenton 245 E4
Church Green 153 E3
Church Gresley 209 E1
Church Hanborough 183 G1
Church Hill *Ches.* 220 D1
Church Hill *Derbys.* 223 F1
Church Houses 253 F3
Church Knowle 155 F4
Church Laneham 237 F5
Church Langley 187 D2
Church Langton 210 C3
Church Lawford 209 G5
Church Lawton 221 F2
Church Leigh 222 B4
Church Lench 196 C2
Church Mayfield 222 C3
Church Minshull 221 D1
Church Norton 158 A4
Church Preen 207 E3
Church Pulverbatch 206 D2
Church Stoke 206 B3
Church Stowe 198 B2
Church Street *Essex* 201 F3
Church Street *Kent* 187 G5
Church Stretton 207 D3
Church Town *Leics.* 209 F1
Church Town *Surr.* 172 C3
Church Village 179 G4
Church Warsop 223 G1
Church Westcote 197 E5
Church Wilne 223 F4
Churcham 181 G1
Churchdown 182 A1
Churchend *Essex* 188 D3
Churchend *Essex* 201 E5
Churchend *S.Glos.* 181 G3
Churchfield 208 C3
Churchgate 186 C2
Churchgate Street 187 D1
Churchill *Devon* 163 F1
Churchill *Devon* 153 F2
Churchill *N.Som.* 166 B2
Churchill *Oxon.* 197 E5
Churchill *Worcs.* 196 B2
Churchill *Worcs.* 208 A5
Churchingford 153 F1
Churchover 210 A4
Churchstanton 153 E1
Churchstow 150 D3
Churchtown *Devon* 163 G1
Churchtown *I.o.M.* 240 C2
Churchtown *Lancs.* 242 A3
Churchtown *Mersey.* 233 E1
Churnsike Lodge 269 E4
Churston Ferrers 151 F2
Churt 171 D4
Churton 220 B2
Churwell 244 B5
Chute Cadley 169 E2
Chute Standen 169 E2
Chwilog 216 D4
Chwitffordd (Whitford) 232 C5
Chyandour 144 B3
Chysauster 144 B3
Chysauster Ancient Village 26
Cilan Uchaf 216 B5
Cilcain 219 E1
Cilcennin 192 B1
Cilcewydd 206 B2
Cilfrew 179 D2
Cilfynydd 179 G3
Cilgerran 191 E3
Cilgwyn *Carmar.* 192 D4
Cilgwyn *Pembs.* 191 D4
Ciliau Aeron 192 B2
Cilldonnain (Kildonan) 314 C1
Cille Bhrighde 314 C2
Cille Pheadair 314 C2
Cilmaengwyn 178 D2
Cilmery 193 G2
Cilrhedyn 191 F4
Cilrhedyn Bridge 190 D4
Cilsan 192 B5
Ciltalgarth 218 B3
Cilwendeg 191 F4
Cilybebyll 178 D2
Cilycwm 193 D3
Cimla 179 D3
Cinderford 181 F1
Cippenham 185 E4
Cippyn 191 E3
Cirbhig 328 C3
Cirencester 182 C2
City *Gt.Lon.* 186 C4
City *V. of Glam.* 179 F5
City Airport 186 D4
City Dulas 230 C4
City, The *Bucks.* 184 C3
City, The *Suff.* 215 E3
Clabhach 296 A4
Clachaig 282 C1
Clachan *Arg. & B.* 291 D3
Clachan *Arg. & B.* 298 A5
Clachan *Arg. & B.* 281 F4
Clachan *High.* 306 B1
Clachan *W.Isles* 315 F5
Clachan Mòr 296 A2
Clachan of Campsie 284 A2
Clachan of Glendaruel 282 A1
Clachan Strachur (Strachur) 290 C4
Clachan-a-Luib 315 G3
Clachandhu 289 D1
Clachaneasy 265 E3
Clachanmore 256 A2
Clachan-Seil 289 G3
Clachanturn 311 E5
Clachbreck 281 F2
Clachnabrain 302 B3
Clachnaharry 321 F5
Clachtoll 330 C2
Clackmannan 293 E5
Clackmarras 323 E4
Clacton Pier 78
Clacton-on-Sea 189 E1
Cladach a Bhale Shear 315 G3
Cladach a' Chaolais 315 F3
Cladach Chircebost 315 F3
Cladach Chnoc a Lin 315 F3
Cladich 290 C2
Cladswell 196 C2
Claggan *High.* 298 D2
Claggan *High.* 297 G5
Claigan 317 F4
Claines 196 A2
Clandon Park 43
Clandown 167 D2
Clanfield *Hants.* 157 G1
Clanfield *Oxon.* 183 E2
Clannaborough Barton 152 A2
Clanville 169 E3
Claonaig 281 G4
Claonairigh 290 C4
Claonel 332 A4
Clapgate 200 C5
Clapham *Beds.* 199 F2
Clapham *Devon* 152 B4
Clapham *Gt.Lon.* 186 B5
Clapham *N.Yorks.* 242 D1
Clapham *W.Suss.* 158 C3
Clapham Green 199 F2
Clapham Hill 174 D2
Clappers 287 G4
Clappersgate 249 E2
Clapton *Som.* 154 A2
Clapton *Som.* 166 D2
Clapton-in-Gordano 181 D5
Clapton-on-the-Hill 183 D1
Clapworthy 163 G3
Clara Vale 262 A1
Clarach 204 C4
Clarbeston 191 D5
Clarbeston Road 190 D5
Clarborough 237 E4
Clardon 336 D2
Clare 201 F3
Clarebrand 266 B4
Claremont Landscape Garden 43
Clarencefield 267 E4
Clarilaw 277 G4
Clark's Green 171 G4
Clarkston 283 G4
Clashban 332 B5
Clashcoig 332 B5
Clashdorran 321 E5
Clashgour 299 E5
Clashindarroch 311 G1
Clashmore *High.* 321 G1
Clashmore *High.* 330 C1
Clashnessie 330 C1
Clashnoir 311 E2
Clatford 168 C1
Clathy 293 E2
Clatt 312 A2
Clatter 205 F3
Clattercote 197 G3
Clatterford 157 D4
Clatterford End 187 E2
Clatterin Brig 303 E2
Clatteringshaws 265 G3
Clatworthy 165 D4
Claughton *Lancs.* 242 B1
Claughton *Lancs.* 242 B3
Clavelshay 165 F4
Claverdon 197 D1
Claverham 166 B1
Clavering 200 C4
Claverley 207 G3
Claverton 167 E1
Claverton Down 167 E1
Clawdd-côch 179 G5
Clawdd-newydd 219 D2
Clawfin 274 D5
Clawthorpe 249 G5
Clawton 149 D1
Claxby 238 B3
Claxby Pluckacre 226 B1
Claxby St. Andrew 239 E5
Claxton *N.Yorks.* 245 F1
Claxton *Norf.* 229 E5
Claxton Grange 263 D5
Clay Common 215 F3
Clay Coton 210 A5
Clay Cross 223 E1
Clay End 200 B5
Clay Hill 181 F5
Clay of Allan 322 A2
Claybrooke Magna 209 G4
Claybrooke Parva 209 G4
Claydene 173 D4
Claydon *Bucks.* 43
Claydon *Oxon.* 197 G2
Claydon *Suff.* 202 C3
Claygate *Kent* 173 G4
Claygate *Surr.* 171 G1
Claygate Cross 173 F3
Clayhanger *Devon* 164 D5
Clayhanger *W.Mid.* 208 C2
Clayhidon 153 E1
Clayhill *E.Suss.* 160 D1
Clayhill *Hants.* 156 C2
Clayhithe 200 D1
Clayock 337 D3
Claypit Hill 200 B2
Claypits 181 G2
Claypole 224 D3
Claythorpe 239 E5
Clayton *S.Yorks.* 236 B2
Clayton *Staffs.* 221 F3
Clayton *W.Suss.* 159 E2
Clayton *W.Yorks.* 244 A4
Clayton Green 242 B5
Clayton West 235 G1
Clayton-le-Moors 242 D4
Clayton-le-Woods 242 B5
Clayworth 237 E4
Cleadale 297 D1
Cleadon 262 C1
Clearbrook 150 B1
Clearwell 181 E2
Cleasby 252 B1
Cleat *Ork.* 339 D4
Cleat *W.Isles* 314 B3
Cleatlam 252 A1
Cleatop 243 E1
Cleator 258 D5
Cleator Moor 258 D5
Cleckheaton 244 A5
Clee St. Margaret 207 E4
Cleedownton 207 E4
Cleehill 207 E5
Cleestanton 207 E5
Cleethorpes 238 D2
Cleeton St. Mary 207 F5
Cleeve *N.Som.* 166 B1
Cleeve *Oxon.* 184 B4
Cleeve Abbey 26
Cleeve Common 27
Cleeve Hill 196 B5
Cleeve Prior 196 C3
Cleghorn 284 C5
Clehonger 195 D4
Cleigh 290 A2
Cleish 293 F5
Cleland 284 B4
Clement's End 185 F1
Clench Common 168 C1
Clenchwarton 227 D5
Clennell 270 B1
Clent 208 B5
Cleobury Mortimer 207 F5
Cleobury North 207 F4
Clephanton 322 A4
Clerklands 277 G3
Clermiston 285 F2
Clestrain 338 C2
Cleuch Head 277 G4
Cleughbrae 267 E3
Clevancy 182 C5
Clevedon 180 D5
Clevedon Court 27
Cleveland Tontine Inn 252 D3
Cleveley 197 F5
Cleveleys 241 G3
Clevelode 196 A3
Cleverton 182 B4
Clewer 166 B2
Clewer Green 185 E5
Clewer Village 185 E5
Cley next the Sea 228 B1
Cliburn 260 B5
Cliddesden 170 B3
Cliff *Carmar.* 177 G2
Cliff *High.* 297 F3
Cliff End 161 D2
Cliff Grange 220 D4
Cliffe *Lancs.* 242 D4
Cliffe *Med.* 187 G5
Cliffe *N.Yorks.* 245 F4
Cliffe Woods 187 G5
Clifford *Here.* 194 B3
Clifford *W.Yorks.* 244 D3
Clifford Chambers 197 D2
Clifford's Mesne 195 F5
Cliffs End 175 F2
Clifton *Beds.* 199 G4
Clifton *Bristol* 181 E5
Clifton *Cumb.* 260 B5
Clifton *Derbys.* 222 C3
Clifton *Devon* 163 F1
Clifton *Lancs.* 242 A4
Clifton *N.Yorks.* 244 A3
Clifton *Northumb.* 271 E3
Clifton *Nott.* 223 G4
Clifton *Oxon.* 197 G4
Clifton *S.Yorks.* 236 C3
Clifton *Stir.* 291 F1
Clifton *W.Yorks.* 244 A5
Clifton *Worcs.* 196 A3
Clifton *York* 245 E2
Clifton Campville 209 E1
Clifton Hampden 184 A3
Clifton Maybank 154 B1
Clifton Reynes 199 E2
Clifton upon Dunsmore 210 A5
Clifton upon Teme 195 G1
Cliftonville 175 F1
Climping 158 C3
Climpy 284 D4
Clink 167 E3
Clint 244 B2
Clint Green 228 B4
Clinterty 312 D3
Clintmains 278 A3
Clippesby 229 F4
Clippings Green 228 B4
Clipsham 211 E1
Clipston *Northants.* 210 C4
Clipston *Notts.* 224 B4
Clipstone 223 G1
Clitheroe 242 D3
Clive 220 C5
Cliveden 43
Clivocast 345 F2
Clixby 238 B2
Clocaenog 219 D2
Clochan 323 G3
Clochtow 313 F1
Clock Face 233 G3
Clockhill 325 D5
Cloddach 323 D4
Cloddiau 206 A2
Clodock 194 C5
Cloford 167 E3
Cloichran 292 B1
Clola 325 F5
Clonrae 266 C1
Clophill 199 F4
Clopton 211 F4
Clopton Corner 202 D2
Clopton Green *Suff.* 201 F2
Clopton Green *Suff.* 202 D2
Close Clark 240 A4
Closeburn 266 C1
Closworth 154 B1
Clothall 200 A4
Clothan 345 D4
Clotton 220 C1
Clouds Hill 27
Clough *Cumb.* 250 C3
Clough *Gt.Man.* 234 D1
Clough *Gt.Man.* 234 D2
Clough *W.Yorks.* 235 E1
Clough Foot 243 F5
Clough Head 243 G5
Cloughfold 243 E5
Cloughton 254 D3
Cloughton Newlands 254 D3
Clounlaid 297 G4
Clousta 342 C2
Clouston 340 B5
Clova *Aber.* 311 G2
Clova *Angus* 302 B2
Clove Lodge 251 E1
Clovelly 27
Clovelly Cross 162 D3
Clovenfords 277 F2
Clovenstone 312 C3
Cloverhill 313 E3
Cloves 322 D3
Clovullin 298 C3
Clow Bridge 243 E5
Clowne 236 B5
Clows Top 207 G5
Cloyntie 274 B5
Cluanach 280 B4
Clubworthy 148 C1
Cluddley 207 F1
Cluer 326 D4
Clumber Country Park 71
Clun 206 B4
Clunas 322 A5
Clunbury 206 C4
Clune *High.* 309 G2
Clune *Moray* 324 A3
Clunes 299 E1
Clungunford 206 C5
Clunie *Aber.* 324 B4
Clunie *P. & K.* 301 G5
Clunton 206 C4
Cluny 294 A5
Clutton *B. & N.E.Som.* 166 D2
Clutton *Ches.* 220 B2
Clwt-y-bont 217 E1
Clwydyfagwyr 179 G2
Clydach *Mon.* 180 B1
Clydach *Swan.* 178 C2
Clydach Terrace 180 A1
Clydach Vale 179 F3
Clydebank 283 F3
Clydey 191 F4
Clyffe Pypard 182 C5
Clynder 282 D1
Clynderwen 177 E1
Clyne 179 E2
Clynelish 333 D4
Clynfyw 191 F4
Clynnog-fawr 216 D3
Clyro 194 B3
Clyst Honiton 152 C3
Clyst Hydon 152 D2
Clyst St. George 152 C4
Clyst St. Lawrence 152 D2
Clyst St. Mary 152 C3
Clyst William 153 D2
Cnewr 193 E5
Cnoc 329 F4
Cnoc an Torrain (Knockintorran) 315 F3
Cnwch Coch 204 C5
Coachford 323 G5
Coad's Green 147 G2
Coal Aston 236 A5
Coalbrookdale 207 F2
Coalbrookvale 180 A2
Coalburn 275 G2
Coalburns 262 A1
Coalcleugh 261 E3
Coaley 181 G2
Coalmoor 207 F2
Coalpit Heath 181 F4
Coalpit Hill 221 F2
Coalport 207 G2
Coalsnaughton 293 E5
Coaltown of Balgonie 294 B5
Coaltown of Wemyss 294 B5
Coalville 209 G1
Coalway 181 E1
Coanwood 260 C2
Coast 330 B5
Coat 166 B5
Coatbridge 284 B3
Coate *Swin.* 183 D4
Coate *Wilts.* 168 B1
Coates *Cambs.* 212 B3
Coates *Glos.* 182 B2
Coates *Lincs.* 237 G4
Coates *Notts.* 237 F4
Coates *W.Suss.* 158 B2
Coatham 263 E5
Coatham Mundeville 262 B5
Cobairdy 324 A5
Cobbaton 163 G3
Cobbler's Plain 181 D2
Cobby Syke 244 A2
Cobden 152 D3
Coberley 182 B1
Cobhall Common 195 D4
Cobham *Kent* 173 F2
Cobham *Surr.* 171 G1
Cobham Hall 43
Cobleland 292 A5
Cobley Hill 208 C5
Cobnash 195 D1
Coburty 325 E3
Cochno 283 F2
Cock Alley 223 F1
Cock Bank 220 A3
Cock Bevington 196 C2
Cock Bridge 311 E4
Cock Clarks 188 B2
Cock Green 187 G1
Cockayne 253 F3
Cockayne Hatley 200 A3
Cockburnspath 287 E2
Cockenzie and Port Seton 286 B2
Cocker Bar 242 B5
Cockerham 242 A2
Cockermouth 259 E3
Cockernhoe 199 G5
Cockerton 252 B1
Cockett 178 C3
Cockfield *Dur.* 262 A5
Cockfield *Suff.* 202 A2
Cockfosters 186 B3
Cocking 158 A2
Cockington 151 E1
Cocklake 166 B3
Cocklaw 270 B4
Cockle Park 271 E2
Cockleford 182 B1
Cockley Beck 248 D2
Cockley Cley 213 F2
Cockpen 286 A3
Cockpole Green 184 C4
Cockshutt 220 B5
Cockthorpe 228 A1
Cockwood *Devon* 152 C4
Cockwood *Som.* 165 F3
Cockyard 235 E4
Codda 147 F2
Coddenham 202 C2
Coddington *Ches.* 220 B2
Coddington *Here.* 195 G3
Coddington *Notts.* 224 D2
Codford St. Mary 168 A4
Codford St. Peter 168 A4
Codicote 186 B1
Codmore Hill 158 C2
Codnor 223 F3
Codnor Park 223 F2
Codrington 181 G5
Codsall 208 A2
Codsall Wood 208 A2
Coed Morgan 180 C1
Coed Ystumgwern 217 E5
Coedcae 180 B2
Coed-duon (Blackwood) 180 A3
Coedely 179 G4
Coedkernew 180 B4
Coedpoeth 219 F2
Coedway 206 C1
Coed-y-bryn 191 G3
Coed-y-caerau 180 C3
Coed-y-paen 180 C3
Coed-y-parc 217 F1
Coed-yr-ynys 194 A5
Coelbren 179 E1
Coffinswell 151 E1
Cofton 152 C4
Cofton Hackett 208 C5
Cogan 180 A5
Cogenhoe 198 D1
Cogges 183 F2
Coggeshall 201 G5
Coggeshall Hamlet 201 G5
Coggins Mill 160 A1
Cóig Peighinnean 329 G1
Coilantogle 292 A4
Coileitir 298 D5
Coilessan 291 E4
Coillaig 290 C2
Coille Mhorgil 307 G4
Coille-righ 307 F2
Coillore 305 G1
Coity 179 F4
Col 329 F4
Col Uarach 329 F4
Colaboll 332 A3
Colan 146 C3
Colaton Raleigh 153 D4
Colbost 317 F5
Colburn 252 A3
Colbury 156 C1
Colby *Cumb.* 260 C5
Colby *I.o.M.* 240 A4
Colby *Norf.* 228 D2
Colby Woodland Garden 109
Colchester 202 A5
Colchester Castle Museum 78
Colchester Green 202 A2
Colchester Zoo 78
Colcot 165 E1
Cold Ash 169 G1
Cold Ashby 210 B5
Cold Ashton 181 G5
Cold Aston 182 D1
Cold Blow 177 E1
Cold Brayfield 199 E2
Cold Chapel 276 A3
Cold Cotes 250 C5
Cold Hanworth 238 A4
Cold Harbour 184 B4
Cold Hatton 220 D5
Cold Hatton Heath 220 D5
Cold Hesledon 262 D3
Cold Higham 198 B2
Cold Inn 177 E2
Cold Kirby 253 E4
Cold Newton 210 C2
Cold Northcott 147 G1
Cold Norton 188 B2
Cold Overton 210 D2
Cold Row 241 G3
Coldbackie 335 F2
Coldblow 187 E5
Coldean 159 F3
Coldeast 152 B5
Coldeaton 222 C2
Colden Common 169 F5
Coldfair Green 203 F1
Coldham 212 C2
Coldharbour *Glos.* 181 E2
Coldharbour *Surr.* 171 G3
Coldingham 287 G3
Coldrain 293 F4
Coldred 175 E4
Coldrey 170 C3
Coldridge 163 G5
Coldrife 270 C2
Coldstream 278 C3
Coldvreath 147 D4
Coldwaltham 158 C2
Coldwells 325 G5
Cole 167 D4
Cole End 209 D4
Cole Green 186 B1
Cole Henley 169 F2
Colebatch 206 C4
Colebrook 152 D2
Colebrooke 152 A2
Coleburn 323 E4
Coleby *Lincs.* 225 E1
Coleby *N.Lincs.* 237 F1
Coleford *Devon* 152 A2
Coleford *Glos.* 181 E1
Coleford *Som.* 167 D3
Colegate End 214 C3
Colehill 155 G2
Coleman Green 186 A1
Coleman's Hatch 172 D5
Colemere 220 B4
Colemore 170 C4
Colemore Green 207 G3
Colenden 293 G2
Coleorton 209 G1
Coleridge Cottage 27
Colerne 182 A5
Cole's Common 214 D3
Cole's Cross 151 D3
Cole's Green 203 D1
Colesbourne 182 C1
Colesden 199 G2
Coleshill *Bucks.* 185 E3
Coleshill *Oxon.* 183 E3
Coleshill *Warks.* 209 E4
Colestocks 153 D2
Coleton Fishacre 27
Coley *B. & N.E.Som.* 166 C2
Coley *Staffs.* 222 B5
Colfin 264 B5
Colgate 172 B5
Colgrain 283 E2
Colindale 186 B4
Colinsburgh 294 C4
Colinton 285 G3
Colintraive 282 B2
Colkirk 228 A3
Coll 296 A4
Collace 294 A1
Collafirth 342 D1
Collamoor Head 148 B1
Collaton St. Mary 151 E1
Collessie 294 A3
Colleton Mills 163 G4
Collett's Green 196 A2
Collier Row 187 E3
Collier Street 173 G4
Collier's End 200 B5
Collier's Wood 186 B5
Colliery Row 262 C3
Collieston 313 F2
Collin 267 E3
Collingbourne Ducis 168 D2
Collingbourne Kingston 168 D2
Collingham *Notts.* 224 D1
Collingham *W.Yorks.* 244 C3
Collington 195 F1
Collingtree 198 C2
Collins End 184 B5
Collins Green *Warr.* 233 G3
Collins Green *Worcs.* 195 G2
Colliston 303 E5
Colliton 153 D2
Collmuir 312 A4
Collycroft 209 F4
Collyhurst 234 C2
Collynie 312 D1
Collyweston 211 E2
Colmonell 264 C2
Colmworth 199 G2
Coln Rogers 182 C2
Coln St. Aldwyns 182 D2
Coln St. Dennis 182 C1
Colnabaichin 311 E4
Colnbrook 185 F5
Colne *Cambs.* 212 B5
Colne *Lancs.* 243 E4
Colne Engaine 201 G4
Colney 228 C5
Colney Heath 186 B2
Colney Street 186 A2
Colonsay 288 C5
Colonsay House 288 C5
Colour Museum 87
Colpy 312 B1
Colquhar 286 A5
Colsterdale 252 A4
Colsterworth 225 E5
Colston Bassett 224 C4
Coltfield 322 D3
Colthouse 249 E3
Coltishall 229 D4
Coltness 284 C4
Colton *Cumb.* 249 E4
Colton *N.Yorks.* 245 E3
Colton *Norf.* 228 C5
Colton *Staffs.* 222 B5
Colton *W.Yorks.* 244 C4
Colva 194 B2
Colvend 266 C5
Colvister 345 E3
Colwall 195 G3
Colwall Green 195 G3
Colwall Stone 195 G3
Colwell 270 B4
Colwich 222 B5
Colwick 224 B4
Colwinston 179 F5
Colworth 158 B3
Colwyn Bay (Bae Colwyn) 231 G5
Colyford 153 F3
Colyton 153 F3

Foxcombe Hill 183 G2
Foxcote *Glos.* 182 C1
Foxcote *Som.* 167 E2
Foxdale 240 A4
Foxearth 201 G3
Foxfield 248 D4
Foxham 182 B5
Foxhole *Cornw.* 147 D4
Foxhole *High.* 309 E1
Foxholes 254 D5
Foxhunt Green 160 A2
Foxley *Here.* 194 D3
Foxley *Norf.* 228 B3
Foxley *Northants.* 198 B2
Foxley *Wilts.* 182 A4
Foxt 222 B3
Foxton *Cambs.* 200 C3
Foxton *Dur.* 262 C5
Foxton *Leics.* 210 B3
Foxton Locks 72
Foxup 251 D5
Foxwist Green 220 D1
Foy 195 E5
Foyers 309 D2
Frachadil 296 C4
Fraddam 144 C3
Fraddon 146 D4
Fradley 209 D1
Fradswell 221 G4
Fraisthorpe 247 D1
Framfield 159 G1
Framingham Earl 229 D5
Framingham Pigot 229 D5
Framlingham 203 D1
Framlingham Castle 79
Frampton *Dorset* 154 C3
Frampton *Lincs.* 226 B4
Frampton Cotterell 181 F4
Frampton Mansell 182 B2
Frampton on Severn 181 G2
Frampton West End 226 A3
Framsden 202 D2
Framwellgate Moor 262 B3
France Lynch 182 B2
Frances Green 242 C4
Franche 208 A5
Frandley 234 A5
Frankby 232 D4
Frankfort 229 E3
Frankley 208 C4
Franksbridge 194 A2
Frankton 209 G5
Frant 173 E5
Fraserburgh 325 E3
Frating 202 B5
Fratton 157 F2
Freasley 209 E3
Freathy 149 D5
Freckenham 213 E5
Freckleton 242 A5
Freeby 224 D5
Freefolk 169 F3
Freehay 222 B3
Freeland 183 G1
Freester 343 D2
Freethorpe 229 F5
Freethorpe Common 229 F5
Freiston 226 B3
Freiston Shore 226 B3
Fremington *Devon* 163 F2
Fremington *N.Yorks.* 251 F3
Frenchay 181 F5
Frenchbeer 149 G2
Frendraught 324 B5
Frenich 291 G4
Frensham 170 D3
Fresgoe 336 B2
Freshbrook 182 D4
Freshfield 233 D2
Freshford 167 E2
Freshwater 156 C4
Freshwater Bay 156 C4
Freshwater East 176 D3
Fressingfield 215 D4
Freston 202 C4
Freswick 337 F2
Fretherne 181 G2
Frettenham 228 D4
Freuchie 294 A4
Freystrop Cross 176 C1
Friars Carse 266 D2
Friar's Gate 173 D5
Friarton 293 G2
Friday Bridge 212 C2
Friday Street *E.Suss.* 160 B3
Friday Street *Suff.* 202 D2
Friday Street *Suff.* 203 E2
Friday Street *Surr.* 171 G3
Fridaythorpe 246 A2
Friern Barnet 186 B3
Friesthorpe 238 A4
Frieston 225 E3
Frieth 184 C3
Frilford 183 G3
Frilsham 184 A5
Frimley 171 D2
Frimley Green 171 D2
Frindsbury 173 G2
Fring 227 F4
Fringford 198 B5
Friningham 174 A3
Frinsted 174 A3
Frinton-on-Sea 189 F1
Friockheim 303 D4
Friog 204 C1
Frisby on the Wreake 210 B1
Friskney 226 C2
Friskney Eaudyke 226 C2
Friston *E.Suss.* 160 A4
Friston *Suff.* 203 F1
Fritchley 223 E2
Frith 174 B3
Frith Bank 226 B3
Frith Common 195 F1
Fritham 156 B1
Frithelstock 163 E4
Frithelstock Stone 163 E4
Frithville 226 B2
Frittenden 174 A4
Frittiscombe 151 E3
Fritton *Norf.* 214 D2
Fritton *Norf.* 229 F5
Fritton Lake Countryworld 79
Fritwell 198 A5
Frizinghall 244 A4
Frizington 258 D5
Frocester 181 G2
Frochas 206 B2
Frodesley 207 E2
Frodesley Lane 207 E2
Frodingham 237 F1
Frodsham 233 G5
Frog End 200 C2
Frog Pool 195 G1
Frogden 278 B4
Froggatt 235 G5
Froghall 222 B3
Frogham 156 A1
Frogland Cross 181 F4
Frogmore *Devon* 151 D3
Frogmore *Hants.* 170 D2
Frogmore *Herts.* 186 A2
Frogwell 148 D4
Frolesworth 210 A3
Frome 167 E3
Frome Market 167 F2
Frome St. Quintin 154 B2
Frome Whitfield 154 C3
Fromes Hill 195 F3
Fron *Gwyn.* 216 C4
Fron *Powys* 206 B2
Fron *Powys* 193 G1
Fron *Powys* 206 A3
Fron Isaf 219 F4
Froncysyllte 219 F3
Fron-goch 218 C4
Frostenden 215 F3
Frosterley 261 G4
Froxfield 169 E1
Froxfield Green 170 C5
Fryerning 187 F2
Fugglestone St. Peter 168 C4
Fulbeck 225 E2
Fulbourn 200 D2
Fulbrook 183 E1
Fulflood 169 F5
Fulford *Som.* 165 F5
Fulford *Staffs.* 221 G4
Fulford *York* 245 F3
Fulham 186 B5
Fulking 159 E2
Full Sutton 245 G2
Fullaford 163 G2
Fuller Street 187 G1
Fuller's Moor 220 B2
Fullerton 169 E4
Fulletby 238 C5
Fullwood 283 F4
Fulmer 185 F4
Fulmodeston 228 A2
Fulnetby 238 B5
Fulready 197 E3
Fulstone 235 F2
Fulstow 238 D3
Fulwell *Oxon.* 197 F5
Fulwell *T. & W.* 262 C2
Fulwood *Lancs.* 242 B4
Fulwood *S.Yorks.* 236 A4
Fundenhall 214 C2
Fundenhall Street 214 C2
Funtington 158 A3
Funtley 157 E2
Funzie 345 F3
Furley 153 F2
Furnace *Arg. & B.* 290 C4
Furnace *Carmar.* 178 B2
Furnace *Cere.* 204 C3
Furnace *High.* 319 F2
Furnace End 209 E3
Furner's Green 159 G1
Furness Abbey 95
Furness Vale 235 E4
Furneux Pelham 200 C5
Furnham 153 G2
Further Quarter 174 A5
Furtho 198 C3
Furze Green 214 D3
Furze Platt 185 D4
Furzehill *Devon* 164 A3
Furzehill *Dorset* 155 G2
Furzeley Corner 157 F1
Furzey Lodge 156 C2
Furzley 156 B1
Fyfett 153 F1
Fyfield *Essex* 187 E2
Fyfield *Glos.* 183 E2
Fyfield *Hants.* 169 D3
Fyfield *Oxon.* 183 G3
Fyfield *Wilts.* 168 C1
Fyfield *Wilts.* 168 C1
Fylingthorpe 254 C2
Fyning 170 D5
Fyvie 312 C1
Fyvie Castle 123

G

Gabalfa 180 A5
Gabhsunn Bho Dheas 329 F2
Gabhsunn Bho Thuath 329 F2
Gablon 332 C5
Gabroc Hill 283 F4
Gaddesby 210 B1
Gaddesden Row 185 F1
Gadebridge 185 F2
Gadshill 187 G5
Gaer *Newport* 180 B4
Gaer *Powys* 194 A5
Gaer-fawr 180 D3
Gaerllwyd 180 D3
Gaerwen 230 C5
Gagingwell 197 G5
Gaich *High.* 310 C2
Gaich *High.* 309 F1
Gaick Lodge 300 C1
Gailes 274 B2
Gailey 208 B1
Gainford 252 A1
Gainsborough 237 F3
Gainsborough Old Hall 72
Gainsborough's House 79
Gainsford End 201 F4
Gairloch 319 D2
Gairlochy 299 D1
Gairney Bank 293 G5
Gairnshiel Lodge 311 E4
Gaitsgill 259 G2
Galabank 286 B5
Galashiels 277 F2
Galdenoch 264 C4
Gale 234 D1
Galgate 242 A2
Galhampton 166 D5
Gallanach 290 A2
Gallantry Bank 220 C2
Gallatown 294 A5
Gallchoille 289 G5
Gallery 303 E3
Gallery of Modern Art 123
Galley Common 209 F3
Galleyend 187 G2
Galleywood 187 G2
Gallowfauld 302 C5
Gallowhill 283 F3
Gallows Green 222 B3
Gallowstree Common 184 B4
Gallowstree Elm 208 A4
Gallt Melyd (Meliden) 232 B4
Galltair 307 E2
Gallt-y-foel 217 E1
Gallypot Street 173 D5
Galmington 165 F5
Galmisdale 297 D1
Galmpton *Devon* 150 C3
Galmpton *Torbay* 151 E2
Galmpton Warborough 151 E2
Galphay 252 B5
Galston 274 C2
Galtrigill 317 E4
Gamble's Green 187 G1
Gamblesby 260 C4
Gamelsby 259 F1
Gamesley 235 E3
Gamlingay 200 A2
Gamlingay Cinques 200 A2
Gamlingay Great Heath 200 A2
Gammaton 163 E3
Gammaton Moor 163 E3
Gammersgill 251 F4
Gamrie 324 C3
Gamston *Notts.* 237 E5
Gamston *Notts.* 224 B4
Ganarew 181 E1
Gang 148 D4
Ganllwyd 218 A5
Gannochy 303 E2
Ganstead 247 D4
Ganthorpe 253 F5
Ganton 254 C5
Ganwick Corner 186 B3
Gaodhail 289 F1
Gappah 152 B5
Gara Bridge 150 D2
Garabal 291 F3
Garadheancal 330 B4
Garbat 320 D3
Garbhallt 290 C5
Garboldisham 214 B3
Garden 292 A5
Garden City 220 A1
Garden Village 235 G3
Gardeners Green 170 D1
Gardenstown 324 C3
Garderhouse 342 C3
Gardham 246 B3
Gare Hill 167 E3
Garelochhead 291 E5
Garford 183 G3
Garforth 244 D4
Gargrave 243 F2
Gargunnock 292 C5
Gariob 281 F1
Garlic Street 214 D3
Garlies Castle 265 F4
Garlieston 257 E2
Garlinge Green 174 D3
Garlogie 312 C4
Garmelow 221 F5
Garmond 324 D4
Garmony 297 F5
Garmouth 323 F3
Garmston 207 F2
Garnant 178 C1
Garndolbenmaen 217 D3
Garneddwen 205 D2
Garnett Bridge 249 G3
Garnfadryn 216 B4
Garnswllt 178 C2
Garrabost 329 G4
Garrachra 282 B1
Garralburn 323 G4
Garras 145 E4
Garreg 217 F3
Garreg Bank 206 B1
Garrett's Green 209 D4
Garrick 292 D3
Garrigill 260 D3
Garriston 252 A3
Garroch 265 G2
Garrochty 282 B4
Garros 318 A3
Garrow 292 D1
Garryhorn 265 G1
Garrynahine (Gearraidh na h-Aibhne) 328 D4
Garsdale 250 C4
Garsdale Head 250 C3
Garsdon 182 B4
Garshall Green 221 G4
Garsington 184 A2
Garstang 242 A3
Garston 233 F4
Garswood 233 G3
Gartachoil 292 A5
Gartally 309 D1
Gartavaich 281 G4
Gartbreck 280 A4
Gartcosh 284 A3
Garth *Bridgend* 179 E3
Garth *Cere.* 204 C4
Garth *Gwyn.* 231 D5
Garth *I.o.M.* 240 B4
Garth *Powys* 193 F3
Garth *Shet.* 342 B2
Garth *Wrex.* 219 F3
Garth Row 249 G3
Garthbrengy 193 G4
Garthdee 313 E4
Gartheli 192 B2
Garthmyl 206 A3
Garthorpe *Leics.* 224 D5
Garthorpe *N.Lincs.* 237 F1
Garths 249 G3
Garthynty 192 D3
Gartincaber 292 B4
Gartly 312 A1
Gartmore 292 A5
Gartnagrenach 281 F4
Gartnatra 280 B3
Gartness 283 G1
Gartocharn 283 F1
Garton 247 E4
Garton-on-the-Wolds 246 B1
Gartymore 333 F3
Garvald 286 C2
Garvamore 309 E5
Garvan 298 B2
Garvard 288 C5
Garve 320 C3
Garveld 272 B5
Garvestone 228 B5
Garvie 282 B1
Garvock *Aber.* 303 F2
Garvock *Inclyde* 283 D2
Garvock *P. & K.* 293 F3
Garwald 276 D5
Garwaldwaterfoot 276 D5
Garway 195 D5
Garway Hill 194 D5
Gask *Aber.* 325 F5
Gask *Aber.* 324 C5
Gask *P. & K.* 293 E3
Gaskan 298 A2
Gass 274 C5
Gastard 167 F1
Gasthorpe 214 A3
Gaston Green 187 E1
Gatcombe 157 D4
Gate Burton 237 F4
Gate Helmsley 245 F2
Gate House 281 D2
Gateacre 233 F4
Gateford 236 C4
Gateforth 245 E5
Gatehead 274 B2
Gatehouse 301 D5
Gatehouse of Fleet 266 A5
Gatelawbridge 266 D1
Gateley 228 A3
Gatenby 252 C4
Gatesgarth 259 E5
Gateshaw 278 B4
Gateshead 262 B1
Gatesheath 220 B1
Gateside *Aber.* 312 B3
Gateside *Angus* 302 C5
Gateside *Fife* 293 G4
Gateside *N.Ayr.* 283 E4
Gateslack 275 G5
Gathurst 233 G2
Gatley 234 C4
Gattonside 277 G2
Gatwick Airport (London Gatwick Airport) 172 B4
Gaufron 193 F1
Gaulby 210 B2
Gauldry 294 B2
Gauntons Bank 220 C3
Gaunt's Common 155 G2
Gaunt's Earthcott 181 F4
Gautby 238 B5
Gavinton 287 E4
Gawber 236 A2
Gawcott 198 B4
Gawsworth 234 C5
Gawthorpe Hall 95
Gawthrop 250 B4
Gawthwaite 249 D4
Gay Bowers 187 G2
Gay Street 171 F5
Gaydon 197 F2
Gayhurst 198 D3
Gayle 251 D4
Gayles 252 A2
Gayton *Mersey.* 233 D4
Gayton *Norf.* 213 F1
Gayton *Northants.* 198 C2
Gayton *Staffs.* 221 G5
Gayton le Marsh 239 E4
Gayton le Wold 238 C4
Gayton Thorpe 213 F1
Gaywood 227 E5
Gazeley 201 F1
Geanies House 322 A2
Gearach 280 A4
Gearnsary 335 G5
Gearradh 298 B3
Gearraidh Bhailteas 314 C1
Gearraidh Bhaird 329 E5
Gearraidh na h-Aibhne (Garrynahine) 328 D4
Gearraidh na Monadh 314 C2
Gearrannan 328 C3
Geary 317 F3
Gedding 202 A2
Geddington 211 D4
Gedgrave Hall 203 F3
Gedintailor 306 B1
Gedling 224 B3
Gedney 226 C5
Gedney Broadgate 226 C5
Gedney Drove End 226 C5
Gedney Dyke 226 C5
Gedney Hill 212 B1
Gee Cross 235 D3
Geevor Tin Mine 30
Geffrye Museum 56
Geilston 283 E2
Geirinis 315 F5
Geisiadar 328 C4
Geldeston 215 E2
Gell *Conwy* 218 B1
Gell *Gwyn.* 217 D4
Gelli 179 F3
Gelli Gynan 219 E2
Gellideg 179 G2
Gellifor 219 E1
Gelligaer 180 A3
Gellilydan 217 F4
Gellioedd 218 C3
Gelly 177 D1
Gellyburn 293 F1
Gellywen 191 F5
Gelston *D. & G.* 266 B5
Gelston *Lincs.* 225 E3
Gembling 246 D2
Gemmil 289 G4
Genoch 264 C5
Genoch Square 264 C5
Gentleshaw 208 C1
Geocrab 326 D4
George Green 185 F4
George Nympton 164 A5
George Stephenson's Birthplace 103
Georgeham 163 E2
Georgetown 283 F3
Georgian House 123
Gerlan 217 F1
Germansweek 149 E1
Germoe 144 C4
Gerrans 145 F3
Gerrards Cross 185 F4
Gerston 336 D3
Gestingthorpe 201 G4
Geuffordd 206 B1
Geufron 205 E4
Gibbet Hill 167 E3
Gibbshill 266 B3
Gibraltar *Lincs.* 227 D2
Gibraltar *Suff.* 202 C2
Gibraltar Point 72
Giddeahall 182 A5
Giddy Green 155 E4
Gidea Park 187 E4
Gidleigh 149 G2
Giffnock 283 G4
Gifford 286 C3
Giffordland 283 D5
Giffordtown 294 A3
Giggleswick 243 E1
Gigha 281 E5
Gilberdyke 246 A5
Gilbert's End 196 A3
Gilchriston 286 B3
Gilcrux 259 E3
Gildersome 244 B5
Gildingwells 236 C4
Gilesgate Moor 262 B3
Gileston 164 D1
Gilfach 180 A3
Gilfach Goch 179 F4
Gilfachrheda 192 A2
Gilgarran 258 D4
Gill 260 A5
Gillamoor 253 F4
Gillen 317 F3
Gillenbie 267 F2
Gillfoot 267 D3
Gilling East 253 F5
Gilling West 252 A2
Gillingham *Dorset* 167 F5
Gillingham *Med.* 173 G2
Gillingham *Norf.* 215 F2
Gillivoan 337 D5
Gillock 337 E3
Gillow Heath 221 F2
Gills 337 F1
Gill's Green 173 G5
Gilmanscleuch 277 E3
Gilmerton *Edin.* 285 G3
Gilmerton *P. & K.* 293 D2
Gilmilnscroft 275 D3
Gilmonby 251 E1
Gilmorton 210 A4
Gilsland 260 C1
Gilsland Spa 260 C1
Gilson 209 D4
Gilstead 244 A4
Gilston 286 B4
Gilston Park 186 D1
Giltbrook 223 F3
Gilwern 180 B1
Gimingham 229 D2
Gin Pit 234 A2
Ginclough 235 D5
Ginger's Green 160 B2
Giosla 328 C5
Gipping 202 B1
Gipsey Bridge 226 A3
Girlsta 342 D2
Girsby 252 C2
Girtford 199 G3
Girthon 266 A5
Girton *Cambs.* 200 C1
Girton *Notts.* 224 D1
Girvan 264 C1
Gisburn 243 E3
Gisburn Cotes 243 E3
Gisleham 215 G3
Gislingham 214 B4
Gissing 214 C3
Gittisham 153 E3
Givons Grove 171 G2
Glackour 320 A1
Gladestry 194 B2
Gladsmuir 286 B2
Gladstone Court Museum 123
Gladstones Land 123
Glaic 282 B2
Glais 178 D2
Glaisdale 253 G2
Glaister 273 E2
Glame 318 B5
Glamis 302 B5
Glamis Castle 123
Glan Conwy 218 B2
Glanaber Terrace 218 A3
Glanaman 178 C1
Glanbran 193 E4
Glan-Denys 192 B2
Glanderston 312 A2
Glandford 228 B1
Glan-Duar 192 B3
Glandwr 191 E5
Glan-Dwyfach 217 D3
Glangrwyney 180 B1
Glanllynfi 179 E3
Glanmule 206 A3
Glan-rhyd *N.P.T.* 179 D2
Glanrhyd *Pembs.* 191 E3
Glanton 279 E5
Glanton Pyke 279 E5
Glantwymyn (Cemmaes Road) 205 E2
Glanvilles Wootton 154 C2
Glanwern 204 C4
Glanwydden 231 G4
Glan-y-don 232 C5
Glanyferi (Ferryside) 177 G1
Glan-y-llyn 180 A4
Glan-y-nant 205 F4
Glan-yr-afon *Gwyn.* 218 C3
Glan-yr-afon *Gwyn.* 218 D3
Glan-yr-afon *I.o.A.* 231 E4
Glan-y-Wern 217 F4
Glapthorn 211 F3
Glapwell 223 F1
Glasahoile 291 G4
Glasbury 194 A4
Glaschoil 310 C1
Glascoed *Mon.* 180 C2
Glascoed *Wrex.* 219 F2
Glascorrie 311 G5
Glascote 209 E2
Glascwm 194 A2
Glasdrum 298 C5
Glasfryn 218 C2
Glasgow 283 G3
Glasgow Airport 283 F3
Glasgow Botanic Garden 123
Glasgow Prestwick International Airport (Prestwick International Airport) 274 B3
Glasgow School of Art 123
Glasgow Science Centre 123
Glashmore 312 C4
Glasinfryn 217 E1
Glasnacardoch 306 C5
Glasnakille 306 B3
Glaspant 191 F4
Glaspwll 204 D3
Glassburn 308 C1
Glassel 312 B5
Glassenbury 173 G5
Glasserton 257 E3
Glassford 284 B5
Glasshouse 195 G5
Glasshouse Hill 195 G5
Glasshouses 244 A1
Glassingall 292 C4
Glasslie 294 A4
Glasson *Cumb.* 268 A5
Glasson *Lancs.* 242 A2
Glassonby 260 B4
Glasterlaw 303 D4
Glaston 211 D2
Glastonbury 166 B4
Glastonbury Abbey 30
Glastonbury Tor 30
Glatton 211 G4
Glazebrook 234 A3
Glazebury 234 A3
Glazeley 207 G4
Gleadless 236 A4
Gleadsmoss 221 F1
Gleann Ghrabhair 329 F5
Gleann Tholastaidh 329 G3
Gleaston 249 D5
Glecknabae 282 B3
Gledhow 244 C4
Gledrid 219 F4
Glemsford 201 G3
Glen *D. & G.* 266 C3
Glen *D. & G.* 265 G5
Glen Auldyn 240 C2
Glen Mona 240 C3
Glen Parva 210 A3
Glen Trool Lodge 265 F2
Glen Village 284 C2
Glen Vine 240 B4
Glenae 267 D2
Glenaladale 298 A2
Glenald 291 E5
Glenamachrie 290 B2
Glenapp Castle 264 B2
Glenarm 302 B3
Glenbarr 272 B2
Glenbatrick 280 D2
Glenbeg *High.* 320 C1
Glenbeg *High.* 310 C2
Glenbeg *High.* 297 E3
Glenbeich 292 B2
Glenbervie *Aber.* 303 F1
Glenbervie *Falk.* 284 C1
Glenboig 284 B3
Glenborrodale 297 F3
Glenbranter 290 D5
Glenbreck 276 B3
Glenbrittle 306 A2
Glenbuck 275 F3
Glenburn 283 F3
Glenbyre 289 E2
Glencaple 267 D4
Glencarse 293 G2
Glencat 312 A5
Glenceitlein 298 D5
Glencloy 273 F2
Glencoe *High.* 298 D4
Glencoe *High.* 123
Glencoe Visitor Centre 123
Glenconglass 311 D2
Glencraig 293 G5
Glencripesdale 297 F4
Glencrosh 266 B2
Glencruittein 290 A2
Glencuie 311 G3
Glendearg *D. & G.* 276 D5
Glendearg *Sc.Bord.* 277 G2
Glendessary 307 F5
Glendevon 293 E4
Glendoebeg 308 D4
Glendoick 294 A2
Glendoll Lodge 302 A2
Glendoune 264 C1
Glendrissaig 264 C1
Glenduckie 294 A3
Glenduisk 264 D2
Glendurgan 30
Glendye Lodge 303 E1
Gleneagles Hotel 293 E3
Gleneagles House 293 E4
Glenearn 293 G3
Glenegedale 280 B4
Glenelg 307 E3
Glenfarg 293 G3
Glenfeochan 290 A2
Glenfiddich Distillery 123
Glenfield 210 A2
Glenfinnan 298 B1
Glenfinnan Monument 123
Glenfoot 293 G3
Glengalmadale 298 A4
Glengap 266 A5
Glengarnock 283 E4
Glengarrisdale 289 F5
Glengennet 265 D1
Glengolly 336 D2
Glengrasco 318 A5
Glengyle 291 F3
Glenhead 266 C2
Glenhead Farm 302 A3
Glenhurich 298 A3
Glenkerry 277 D4
Glenkiln 273 F2
Glenkin 282 C1
Glenkindie 311 G3
Glenlair 266 B3
Glenlatterach 323 E4
Glenlean 282 B1
Glenlee *Angus* 302 C2
Glenlee *D. & G.* 266 A2
Glenlichorn 292 C3
Glenlivet 311 D2
Glenlochar 266 B4
Glenluce 264 C5
Glenluce Abbey 123
Glenmallan 291 E5
Glenmanna 275 F5
Glenmavis 284 B3
Glenmaye 240 A4
Glenmeanie 320 B4
Glenmore *Arg. & B.* 282 B3
Glenmore *High.* 318 A5
Glenmore Lodge 310 B4
Glenmoy 302 C3
Glenmuick 331 F3
Glennoe 290 C1
Glenochar 276 A4
Glenogil 302 C3
Glenprosen Village 302 B3
Glenquiech 302 C3
Glenramskill 272 C4
Glenrazie 265 E4
Glenridding 259 G5
Glenrisdell 281 G4
Glenrossal 331 G4
Glenrothes 294 A4
Glensanda 298 A5
Glensaugh 303 E2
Glensgaich 321 D3
Glenshalg 312 A4
Glenshellish 290 D5
Glensluain 290 C5
Glentaggart 275 G3
Glentham 238 A3
Glenton 312 B2
Glentress 277 D2
Glentrool 265 E3
Glentruan 240 C1
Glenturret Distillery 123
Glentworth 237 G4
Glenuachdarach 318 A4
Glenuig 297 F2
Glenure 298 C5
Glenurquhart 321 G3
Glenwhilly 264 C3
Glespin 275 G3
Gletness 343 D2
Glewstone 195 E5
Glinton 211 G2
Globe Theatre (see Shakespeare's Globe Theatre) 60
Glooston 210 C3

431

Gurnard 157 D3
Gurnett 234 D5
Gurney Slade 166 D3
Gurnos *M.Tyd.* 179 G2
Gurnos *Powys* 179 D2
Gushmere 174 C3
Gussage All Saints 155 G1
Gussage St. Andrew 155 F1
Gussage St. Michael 155 F1
Guston 175 F4
Gutcher 345 E3
Guthram Gowt 225 G5
Guthrie 303 D4
Guyhirn 212 B2
Guynd 303 D5
Guy's Head 226 C5
Guy's Marsh 167 F5
Guyzance 271 E1
Gwaelod-y-garth 180 A4
Gwaenysgor 232 B4
Gwaithla 194 B2
Gwalchmai 230 B5
Gwastad 190 D5
Gwastadnant 217 F2
Gwaun-Cae-Gurwen 178 D1
Gwaynynog 218 D1
Gwbert 191 E3
Gweek 145 E4
Gwehelog 180 C2
Gwenddwr 193 G3
Gwendreath 145 E5
Gwennap 146 B5
Gwenter 145 E5
Gwernaffield 219 F1
Gwernesney 180 D2
Gwernogle 192 B4
Gwernymynydd 219 F1
Gwern-y-Steeple 179 G5
Gwersyllt 220 A2
Gwespyr 232 C4
Gwinear 144 C3
Gwithian 144 C2
Gwredog 230 C4
Gwrhay 180 A3
Gwyddelwern 219 D3
Gwyddgrug 192 A4
Gwynfryn 219 F2
Gwystre 193 G1
Gwytherin 218 B1
Gyfelia 220 A3
Gyre 338 C2
Gyrn Goch 216 C3

H

Habberley 206 C2
Habin 170 D5
Habrough 238 B1
Haccombe 152 B5
Hacconby 225 G5
Haceby 225 F4
Hacheston 203 E2
Hackbridge 172 B2
Hackenthorpe 236 B4
Hackford 228 B5
Hackforth 252 B3
Hackland 340 B4
Hacklet (Haclait) 315 G5
Hacklete (Tacleit) 328 C4
Hackleton 198 D2
Hacklinge 175 F3
Hackness *N.Yorks.* 254 C3
Hackness *Ork.* 338 C3
Hackney 186 C4
Hackthorn 237 G4
Hackthorpe 260 B5
Haclait (Hacklet) 315 G5
Hacton 187 E4
Hadden 278 B3
Haddenham *Bucks.* 184 C2
Haddenham *Cambs.* 212 C5
Haddington *E.Loth.* 286 C2
Haddington *Lincs.* 225 E1
Haddiscoe 215 F2
Haddo House & Country Park 124
Haddon 211 G3
Haddon Hall 72
Hade Edge 235 F2
Hademore 209 D2
Hadfield 235 E3
Hadham Cross 186 D1
Hadham Ford 200 C5
Hadleigh *Essex* 188 B4
Hadleigh *Suff.* 202 B3
Hadleigh Heath 202 A3
Hadley *Tel. & W.* 207 F1
Hadley *Worcs.* 196 A1
Hadley End 222 C5
Hadley Wood 186 B3
Hadlow 173 F4
Hadlow Down 160 A1
Hadnall 220 C5
Hadrian's Wall 104
Hadspen 167 D4
Hadstock 201 D3
Hadzor 196 B1
Haffenden Quarter 174 A4
Hafod Bridge 192 C4
Hafod-Dinbych 218 B2
Hafodunos 218 B1
Hafodyrynys 180 B3
Haggate 243 E4
Haggbeck 268 C4
Haggersta 342 C3
Haggerston *Gt.Lon.* 186 C4
Haggerston *Northumb.* 279 E2
Haggrister 344 C5
Haggs 284 B2
Hagley *Here.* 195 E3
Hagley *Worcs.* 208 B4
Hagley Hall 65
Hagnaby *Lincs.* 226 B1
Hagnaby *Lincs.* 239 E5
Hague Bar 235 D4
Hagworthingham 226 B1
Haigh 234 A2
Haighton Green 242 B4
Hail Weston 199 G1
Haile 248 B2
Hailes 196 C4
Hailes Abbey 30
Hailey *Herts.* 186 C1
Hailey *Oxon.* 184 B4
Hailey *Oxon.* 183 F1
Hailsham 160 A3
Haimer 336 D2
Hainault 187 D3
Haine 175 F2
Hainford 228 D4
Hainton 238 B4
Haisthorpe 246 D1
Hakin 176 B2
Halam 224 B2
Halbeath 285 F1
Halberton 152 D1
Halcro 337 E2
Hale *Cumb.* 249 G5
Hale *Gt.Man.* 234 B4
Hale *Halton* 233 F4
Hale *Hants.* 156 A1
Hale *Surr.* 170 D3
Hale Bank 233 F4
Hale Barns 234 B4
Hale Nook 241 G3
Hale Street 173 F4
Hales *Norf.* 215 E2
Hales *Staffs.* 221 E4
Hales Green 222 C3
Hales Place 174 D3
Halesgate 226 B5
Halesowen 208 B4
Halesworth 215 E4
Halewood 233 F4
Half Way Inn 152 D4
Halford *Devon* 152 B5
Halford *Shrop.* 206 D4
Halford *Warks.* 197 E3
Halfpenny 249 G4
Halfpenny Green 208 A3
Halfway *Carmar.* 192 C4
Halfway *Carmar.* 178 B2
Halfway *Powys* 193 E4
Halfway *S.Yorks.* 236 B4
Halfway *W.Berks.* 169 F1
Halfway Bridge 171 E5
Halfway House 206 C1
Halfway Houses *Kent* 174 B1
Halfway Houses *Lincs.* 225 D1
Halghton Mill 220 B3
Halifax 243 G5
Halistra 317 F4
Halket 283 F4
Halkirk 336 D3
Halkyn 232 D5
Hall 283 F4
Hall Cross 242 A5
Hall Dunnerdale 248 D3
Hall Green *Ches.* 221 F2
Hall Green *Lancs.* 242 A5
Hall Green *W.Mid.* 208 D4
Hall Grove 186 B1
Hall of the Forest 206 B4
Halland 160 A2
Hallaton 210 C3
Hallatrow 166 D2
Hallbankgate 260 B2
Hallen 181 E4
Hallfield Gate 223 E2
Hallin 317 F4
Halling 173 G2
Hallington *Lincs.* 238 D4
Hallington *Northumb.* 270 B4
Halliwell 234 A1
Halloughton 224 B2
Hallow 196 A2
Hallow Heath 196 A2
Hallrule 277 G4
Halls 287 D2
Hall's Croft 65
Halls Green *Essex* 186 D2
Hall's Green *Herts.* 200 A5
Hallsands 151 E4
Hallthwaites 248 C4
Hallwood Green 195 F4
Hallworthy 147 F1
Hallyne 285 F5
Halmer End 221 E3
Halmond's Frome 195 F3
Halmore 181 F2
Halmyre Mains 285 F5
Halnaker 158 B3
Halsall 233 E1
Halse *Northants.* 198 A3
Halse *Som.* 165 E5
Halsetown 144 C3
Halsham 247 E5
Halsinger 163 F2
Halstead *Essex* 201 G4
Halstead *Kent* 173 D2
Halstead *Leics.* 210 C2
Halstock 154 B2
Halsway 165 E4
Haltemprice Farm 246 C4
Haltham 226 A1
Haltoft End 226 B3
Halton *Bucks.* 185 D1
Halton *Halton* 233 G4
Halton *Lancs.* 242 B1
Halton *Northumb.* 261 F1
Halton *Wrex.* 220 A4
Halton East 243 G2
Halton Gill 251 D5
Halton Green 242 B1
Halton Holegate 226 C1
Halton Lea Gate 260 C2
Halton Park 242 B1
Halton West 243 E2
Haltwhistle 260 D1
Halvergate 229 F5
Halwell 151 D2
Halwill 149 E1
Halwill Junction 149 E1
Ham *Devon* 153 F2
Ham *Glos.* 181 F3
Ham *Glos.* 196 B5
Ham *Gt.Lon.* 186 A5
Ham *High.* 337 E1
Ham *Kent* 175 F3
Ham *Plym.* 150 A2
Ham *Shet.* 342 B5
Ham *Som.* 165 F5
Ham *Som.* 153 F1
Ham *Wilts.* 169 E1
Ham Common 167 F5
Ham Green *Here.* 195 G3
Ham Green *Kent* 174 A2
Ham Green *Kent* 161 D1
Ham Green *N.Som.* 181 E5
Ham Green *Worcs.* 196 C1
Ham Hill 173 F2
Ham House 56
Ham Street 166 C4
Hambleden 184 C4
Hambledon *Hants.* 157 F1
Hambledon *Surr.* 171 E4
Hamble-le-Rice 157 D2
Hambleton *Lancs.* 241 G3
Hambleton *N.Yorks.* 245 E4
Hambridge 166 A5
Hambrook *S.Glos.* 181 F5
Hambrook *W.Suss.* 157 G2
Hameringham 226 B1
Hamerton 211 G5
Hamerton Zoo Park 79
Hamilton 284 B4
Hamlet *Devon* 153 E3
Hamlet *Dorset* 154 B2
Hammer 171 D4
Hammerpot 158 C3
Hammersmith 186 B5
Hammerwich 208 C2
Hammerwood 172 D5
Hammerwood Park 45
Hammond Street 186 C2
Hammoon 155 E1
Hamnavoe *Shet.* 342 C4
Hamnavoe *Shet.* 345 D4
Hamnavoe *Shet.* 344 B4
Hamnavoe *Shet.* 345 D5
Hamnish Clifford 195 E2
Hamp 165 F4
Hampden Park 160 B3
Hamperden End 201 D4
Hampnett 182 D1
Hampole 236 C2
Hampreston 155 G3
Hampstead 186 B4
Hampstead Norreys 184 A5
Hampsthwaite 244 B2
Hampton *Devon* 153 F3
Hampton *Gt.Lon.* 171 G1
Hampton *Kent* 175 D2
Hampton *Peter.* 211 G3
Hampton *Shrop.* 207 G4
Hampton *Swin.* 183 D3
Hampton *Worcs.* 196 C3
Hampton Bishop 195 E4
Hampton Court Palace and Garden 56
Hampton Fields 182 A3
Hampton Heath 220 B3
Hampton in Arden 209 E4
Hampton Loade 207 G4
Hampton Lovett 196 A1
Hampton Lucy 197 E2
Hampton on the Hill 197 E1
Hampton Poyle 184 A1
Hampton Wick 171 G1
Hamptworth 156 B1
Hamsey 159 G2
Hamstall Ridware 208 D1
Hamstead 156 C3
Hamstead Marshall 169 F1
Hamsteels 262 A3
Hamsterley *Dur.* 262 A4
Hamsterley *Dur.* 262 A2
Hamsterley Forest 104
Hamstreet 174 C5
Hamworthy 155 F3
Hanbury *Staffs.* 222 C5
Hanbury *Worcs.* 196 B1
Hanbury Hall 65
Hanbury Woodend 222 C5
Hanby 225 F4
Hanchurch 221 F3
Hancock Museum 104
Handa Island 334 A4
Handale 253 G1
Handbridge 220 B1
Handcross 172 B5
Handforth 234 C4
Handley *Ches.* 220 B2
Handley *Derbys.* 223 E1
Handley Green 187 F2
Handsacre 208 C1
Handside 186 B1
Handsworth *S.Yorks.* 236 B4
Handsworth *W.Mid.* 208 C3
Handwoodbank 206 D1
Handy Cross 185 D3
Hanford *Dorset* 155 E1
Hanford *Stoke* 221 F3
Hanging Bridge 222 C3
Hanging Houghton 210 C5
Hanging Langford 168 B4
Hangingshaw 267 F2
Hanham 181 F5
Hankelow 221 D3
Hankerton 182 B3
Hankham 160 B3
Hanley 221 F3
Hanley Castle 196 A3
Hanley Child 195 F1
Hanley Swan 196 A3
Hanley William 195 F1
Hanlith 243 F1
Hanmer 220 B4
Hannah 239 E5
Hannington *Hants.* 169 G2
Hannington *Northants.* 210 D5
Hannington *Swin.* 183 D3
Hannington Wick 183 D3
Hanslope 198 D3
Hanthorpe 225 F5
Hanwell *Gt.Lon.* 186 A4
Hanwell *Oxon.* 197 G3
Hanwood 206 D2
Hanworth *Gt.Lon.* 186 A5
Hanworth *Norf.* 228 C2
Happisburgh 229 E2
Happisburgh Common 229 E3
Hapsford 233 F5
Hapton *Lancs.* 243 D4
Hapton *Norf.* 214 C2
Harberton 151 D2
Harbertonford 151 D2
Harbledown 174 D3
Harborne 208 C4
Harborough Magna 209 G5
Harborough Museum 72
Harbost (Tarbost) 329 G1
Harbottle 270 B1
Harbourneford 150 D1
Harbridge 156 A1
Harbridge Green 156 A1
Harburn 285 E3
Harbury 197 F2
Harby *Leics.* 224 C4
Harby *Notts.* 237 F5
Harcombe 153 E3
Harcombe Bottom 153 G3
Harden *W.Mid.* 208 C2
Harden *W.Yorks.* 243 G4
Hardendale 249 G1
Hardenhuish 182 B5
Hardgate *Aber.* 312 C4
Hardgate *N.Yorks.* 244 B1
Hardham 158 C2
Hardhorn 241 G4
Hardingham 228 B5
Hardingstone 198 C2
Hardington 167 E2
Hardington Mandeville 154 B1
Hardington Marsh 154 B2
Hardington Moor 154 B1
Hardley 156 D2
Hardley Street 229 E5
Hardmead 199 E3
Hardraw 251 D3
Hardstoft 223 F1
Hardway *Hants.* 157 F2
Hardway *Som.* 167 E4
Hardwick *Bucks.* 184 D1
Hardwick *Cambs.* 200 B2
Hardwick *Lincs.* 237 F5
Hardwick *Norf.* 214 D2
Hardwick *Northants.* 199 D1
Hardwick *Oxon.* 183 F2
Hardwick *Oxon.* 198 A5
Hardwick *S.Yorks.* 236 B4
Hardwick *W.Mid.* 208 C3
Hardwick Hall 72
Hardwick Village 236 D5
Hardwicke *Glos.* 196 B5
Hardwicke *Glos.* 181 G1
Hardwicke *Here.* 194 B3
Hardy Monument 30
Hardy's Cottage 30
Hardy's Green 202 A5
Hare Green 202 B5
Hare Hatch 184 D5
Hare Hill 96
Hare Street *Herts.* 200 B5
Hare Street *Herts.* 200 B5
Hareby 226 B1
Harecroft 243 G4
Hareden 242 C2
Harefield 185 F3
Harehill 222 C4
Harehills 244 C4
Harehope 279 E4
Harelaw 284 D5
Hareplain 174 A5
Haresceugh 260 C3
Harescombe 182 A1
Haresfield 182 A1
Hareshaw *N.Lan.* 284 C3
Hareshaw *S.Lan.* 284 A5
Harestock 169 F4
Harewood 244 C3
Harewood End 195 E5
Harewood House 87
Harford *Devon* 150 C2
Harford *Devon* 152 B3
Hargate 214 C2
Hargatewall 235 F5
Hargrave *Ches.* 220 B1
Hargrave *Northants.* 211 F5
Hargrave *Suff.* 201 F2
Hargrave Green 201 F2
Harker 268 B5
Harkstead 202 C4
Harlaston 209 E1
Harlaxton 225 D4
Harle Syke 243 E4
Harlech 217 E4
Harlech Castle 110
Harlequin 224 B4
Harlescott 207 E1
Harlesden 186 B4
Harleston *Devon* 151 D3
Harleston *Norf.* 214 D3
Harleston *Suff.* 202 B1
Harlestone 198 C1
Harley *S.Yorks.* 236 A3
Harley *Shrop.* 207 E2
Harleyholm 276 A2
Harlington *Beds.* 199 F4
Harlington *Gt.Lon.* 185 F5
Harlosh 317 F5
Harlow 186 D1
Harlow Carr 87
Harlow Hill 261 G1
Harlthorpe 245 G4
Harlton 200 B2
Harlyn 146 C2
Harman's Cross 155 F4
Harmby 252 A4
Harmer Green 186 B1
Harmer Hill 220 B5
Harmondsworth 185 F5
Harmston 225 E1
Harnage 207 E2
Harnham 168 C5
Harnhill 182 C2
Harold Hill 187 E3
Harold Park 187 E3
Harold Wood 187 E3
Haroldston West 176 B1
Haroldswick 345 F1
Harome 253 F4
Harpenden 186 A1
Harpford 153 D3
Harpham 246 C1
Harpley *Norf.* 227 F5
Harpley *Worcs.* 195 F1
Harpole 198 B1
Harprigg 250 B4
Harpsdale 336 D3
Harpsden 184 C4
Harpswell 237 G4
Harpur Hill 235 E5
Harpurhey 234 C2
Harracott 163 F3
Harrapool 306 C2
Harrietfield 293 E1
Harrietsham 174 A3
Harringay 186 C4
Harrington *Cumb.* 258 C4
Harrington *Lincs.* 239 D5
Harrington *Northants.* 210 C5
Harringworth 211 E3
Harris 305 G5
Harris Green 214 D2
Harris Museum & Art Gallery 96
Harriseahead 221 F2
Harriston 259 E2
Harrogate 244 C2
Harrold 199 E2
Harrold-Odell Country Park 79
Harrop Fold 242 D3
Harrow *Gt.Lon.* 186 A4
Harrow *High.* 337 E1
Harrow Green 201 G2
Harrow on the Hill 186 A4
Harrow Weald 186 A3
Harrowbarrow 149 E3
Harrowden 199 F3
Harrowgate Hill 252 B1
Harry Stoke 181 F5
Harston *Cambs.* 200 C2
Harston *Leics.* 224 D4
Harswell 246 A3
Hart 263 D4
Hartburn 270 C3
Hartest 201 G2
Hartfield *E.Suss.* 173 D5
Hartfield *High.* 318 D5
Hartford *Cambs.* 212 A5
Hartford *Ches.* 234 A5
Hartford *Som.* 164 C5
Hartford End 187 F1
Hartfordbridge 170 C2
Hartforth 252 A2
Hartgrove 155 E1
Harthill *Ches.* 220 C2
Harthill *N.Lan.* 284 D3
Harthill *S.Yorks.* 236 B4
Hartington 222 C1
Hartington Hall 270 C3
Hartland 162 C3
Hartland Quay 30
Hartlebury 208 A5
Hartlepool 263 E4
Hartlepool Historic Ships 104
Hartley *Cumb.* 250 C2
Hartley *Kent* 173 F2
Hartley *Kent* 173 G5
Hartley *Northumb.* 271 F4
Hartley Green 221 G5
Hartley Mauditt 170 C4
Hartley Wespall 170 B2
Hartley Wintney 170 C2
Hartlington 243 G1
Hartlip 174 A2
Hartoft End 253 G3
Harton *N.Yorks.* 245 G1
Harton *Shrop.* 207 D4
Harton *T. & W.* 262 C1
Hartpury 196 A5
Hartrigge 278 A4
Hartshead 244 A5
Hartshill 209 F3
Hartshorne 223 E5
Hartsop 249 F1
Hartwell *Bucks.* 184 C1
Hartwell *E.Suss.* 173 D5
Hartwell *Northants.* 198 C2
Hartwith 244 B1
Hartwood 284 C4
Harvard House 65
Harvel 173 F2
Harvington *Worcs.* 196 C3
Harvington *Worcs.* 208 A5
Harvington Hall 66
Harwell *Notts.* 237 D3
Harwell *Oxon.* 183 G4
Harwich 202 D4
Harwood *Dur.* 261 E4
Harwood *Gt.Man.* 234 B1
Harwood *Northumb.* 270 C2
Harwood Dale 254 C3
Harwood on Teviot 277 F5
Harworth 236 D3
Hasbury 208 B4
Hascombe 171 F3
Haselbech 210 C5
Haselbury Plucknett 154 A1
Haseley 197 E1
Haseley Knob 209 E5
Haselor 196 D2
Hasfield 196 A5
Hasguard 176 B2
Haskayne 233 E2
Hasketon 203 D2
Hasland 223 E1
Hasland Green 223 E1
Haslemere 171 E4
Haslemere Educational Museum 45
Haslingden 243 D5
Haslingden Grane 243 D5
Haslingfield 200 C2
Haslington 221 E2
Hassall 221 E2
Hassall Green 221 E2
Hassell Street 174 C4
Hassendean 277 G3
Hassingham 229 E5
Hassocks 159 F2
Hassop 235 G5
Haster 337 F3
Hasthorpe 226 C1
Hastigrow 337 E2
Hastingleigh 174 C4
Hastings *E.Suss.* 160 D3
Hastings *Som.* 153 G1
Hastings Castle 45
Hastingwood 187 D2
Hastoe 185 E2
Haswell 262 C3
Haswell Plough 262 C3
Hatch *Beds.* 199 G3
Hatch *Hants.* 170 B2
Hatch Beauchamp 166 A5
Hatch End 186 A3
Hatch Green 153 G1
Hatching Green 186 A1
Hatchlands 45
Hatchmere 233 G5
Hatcliffe 238 C2
Hatfield *Here.* 195 E2
Hatfield *Herts.* 186 B2
Hatfield *S.Yorks.* 237 D2
Hatfield Broad Oak 187 E1
Hatfield Forest 79
Hatfield Heath 187 E1
Hatfield House 79
Hatfield Peverel 187 G1
Hatfield Woodhouse 237 D2
Hatford 183 F3
Hatherden 169 E2
Hatherleigh 163 F5
Hathern 223 F5
Hatherop 183 D2
Hathersage 235 G4
Hathersage Booths 235 G4
Hathershaw 234 D2
Hatherton *Ches.* 221 D3
Hatherton *Staffs.* 208 B1
Hatley St. George 200 A2
Hatt 149 D4
Hattingley 170 B4
Hatton *Aber.* 313 F1
Hatton *Derbys.* 222 D5
Hatton *Gt.Lon.* 186 A5
Hatton *Lincs.* 238 B5
Hatton *Shrop.* 207 D3
Hatton *Warks.* 197 E1
Hatton *Warr.* 233 G4
Hatton Castle 324 C5
Hatton Country World 66
Hatton Heath 220 B1
Hatton of Fintray 312 D3
Hattoncrook 312 D2
Haugh 239 E5
Haugh Head 279 E4
Haugh of Glass 311 G1
Haugh of Urr 266 C4
Haugham 238 D4
Haughhead 284 A2
Haughley 202 B1
Haughley Green 202 B1
Haughley New Street 202 B1
Haughmond Abbey 66
Haughs 324 A5
Haughton *Ches.* 220 C2
Haughton *Notts.* 237 D5
Haughton *Powys* 206 C1
Haughton *Shrop.* 207 F3
Haughton *Shrop.* 207 E1
Haughton *Shrop.* 220 A5
Haughton *Staffs.* 221 F5
Haughton Green 234 D3
Haughton Le Skerne 252 C1
Haultwick 200 B5
Haunn 314 C2
Haunton 209 E1
Hauxton 200 C2
Havannah 221 F1
Havant 157 G2
Haven 194 D2
Haven, The 171 F4
Havenstreet 157 E3
Havercroft 236 A1
Haverfordwest (Hwlffordd) 176 C1
Haverhill 201 E3
Haverigg 248 C5
Havering Park 187 D3
Havering-atte-Bower 187 E3
Haversham 198 D3
Haverthwaite 249 E4
Haverton Hill 263 D5
Haviker Street 173 G4
Havyat 166 C4
Hawarden 220 A1
Hawbridge 196 B3
Hawbush Green 201 F5
Hawcoat 248 D5
Hawes 251 D4
Hawe's Green 214 D2
Hawick 277 G4
Hawkchurch 153 G2
Hawkedon 201 F2
Hawkenbury *Kent* 173 E5
Hawkenbury *Kent* 174 A4
Hawkeridge 167 F2
Hawkerland 153 D4
Hawkes End 209 E4
Hawkesbury 181 G4
Hawkesbury Upton 181 G4
Hawkhill 279 G5
Hawkhurst 173 G5
Hawkinge 175 E4
Hawkley 170 C5
Hawkridge 164 B4
Hawkshead 249 E3
Hawkshead Hill 249 E3
Hawksheads 242 A1
Hawksland 284 C5
Hawkstone Park 66
Hawkswick 251 E5
Hawksworth *Notts.* 224 C3
Hawksworth *W.Yorks.* 244 A3
Hawksworth *W.Yorks.* 244 B4
Hawkwell *Essex* 188 B3
Hawkwell *Northumb.* 270 C4
Hawley *Hants.* 171 D2
Hawley *Kent* 187 E5
Hawley's Corner 172 D3
Hawling 196 C5
Hawnby 253 E4
Haworth 243 G4
Hawstead 201 G2
Hawstead Green 201 G2
Hawthorn *Dur.* 262 D3
Hawthorn *Hants.* 170 B4
Hawthorn *R.C.T.* 179 G4
Hawthorn *Wilts.* 167 F1
Hawthorn Hill *Brack.F.* 185 D5
Hawthorn Hill *Lincs.* 226 A2
Hawthorpe 225 F5
Hawton 224 C2
Haxby 245 F2
Haxey 237 E2
Haxted 172 D4
Haxton 168 C3
Hay Green 212 D1
Hay Mills 208 D4
Hay Street 200 B5
Hay Tor Granite Tramway 30
Haydock 233 G3
Haydon *Dorset* 154 C1
Haydon *Swin.* 182 D4
Haydon Bridge 261 E1
Haydon Wick 182 D4
Hayes *Gt.Lon.* 185 F4
Hayes *Gt.Lon.* 172 D2
Hayes End 185 F4
Hayfield *Arg. & B.* 290 C2
Hayfield *Derbys.* 235 E4
Hayfield *Fife* 294 A5
Hayfield *High.* 337 D2
Haygrove 165 F4
Hayhillock 302 D5
Hayle 144 C3
Hayling Island 157 G2
Haymoor Green 221 D2
Hayne 152 C1
Haynes 199 G3
Haynes Church End 199 F3
Haynes West End 199 F3
Hay-on-Wye 194 B3
Hayscastle 190 B5
Hayscastle Cross 190 C5
Hayton *Cumb.* 260 B2
Hayton *Cumb.* 259 E2
Hayton *E.Riding* 246 A3
Hayton *Notts.* 237 E4
Hayton's Bent 207 E4
Haytor Vale 152 A5
Haytown 163 D4
Haywards Heath 159 F1
Haywood Oaks 224 B2
Hazel End 200 C5
Hazel Grove 234 D4
Hazel Street 173 F5
Hazelbank *Arg. & B.* 290 C4
Hazelbank *S.Lan.* 284 C5
Hazelbury Bryan 154 D2
Hazeleigh 188 B2
Hazeley 170 C2
Hazelhurst 234 B1
Hazelside 275 G3
Hazelslack 249 F5
Hazelslade 208 C1
Hazelton Walls 294 B2
Hazelwood *Derbys.* 223 E3
Hazelwood *Gt.Lon.* 172 D2
Hazlefield 258 A2
Hazlehead *Aberdeen* 313 D4
Hazlehead *S.Yorks.* 235 F2
Hazlemere 185 D3
Hazlerigg 271 E4
Hazleton 182 C1
Hazon 271 D1
Heacham 227 E4
Head Bridge 163 G4
Headbourne Worthy 169 F4
Headcorn 174 A4
Headingley 244 B4
Headington 184 A2
Headlam 252 A1
Headland, The 263 E4
Headless Cross 196 C1
Headley *Hants.* 170 D4
Headley *Hants.* 169 G1
Headley *Surr.* 172 B3
Headley Down 170 D4
Headley Heath 208 C5
Headon 237 E5

Hollyhurst 220 C3
Hollym 247 F5
Hollywater 170 D4
Hollywood 208 C5
Holm *D. & G.* 268 A2
Holm (Tolm) *W.Isles* 329 F4
Holm of Drumlanrig 266 C1
Holmbridge 235 F2
Holmbury St. Mary 171 G3
Holmbush 172 B5
Holme *Cambs.* 211 G4
Holme *Cumb.* 249 G5
Holme *N.Lincs.* 237 G2
Holme *N.Yorks.* 252 C4
Holme *Notts.* 224 D2
Holme *W.Yorks.* 235 F2
Holme Chapel 243 E5
Holme Hale 213 G2
Holme Lacy 195 E4
Holme Marsh 194 C2
Holme next the Sea 227 F3
Holme on the Wolds 246 B3
Holme Pierrepont 224 B4
Holme St. Cuthbert 259 E2
Holme, The 244 B2
Holme-on-Spalding-Moor 246 A4
Holmer 195 E3
Holmer Green 185 E3
Holmes 233 F1
Holmes Chapel 221 E1
Holme's Hill 160 A2
Holmesfield 236 A5
Holmeswood 233 F1
Holmewood 223 F1
Holmfield 243 G5
Holmfirth 235 F2
Holmhead *D. & G.* 266 B2
Holmhead *E.Ayr.* 275 D3
Holmpton 247 F5
Holmrook 248 B2
Holmsgarth 343 D3
Holmside 262 B3
Holmsleigh Green 153 F2
Holmston 274 B3
Holmwrangle 260 B3
Holne 150 D1
Holnest 154 C2
Holnicote 164 C3
Holnicote Estate 31
Holsworthy 162 D5
Holsworthy Beacon 163 D5
Holt *Dorset* 155 G2
Holt *Norf.* 228 B2
Holt *Wilts.* 167 F1
Holt *Worcs.* 196 A1
Holt *Wrex.* 220 B2
Holt End *Hants.* 170 B4
Holt End *Worcs.* 196 C1
Holt Fleet 196 A1
Holt Heath *Dorset* 155 G2
Holt Heath *Worcs.* 196 A1
Holt Wood 155 G2
Holtby 245 F2
Holton *Oxon.* 184 B2
Holton *Som.* 167 D5
Holton *Suff.* 215 F4
Holton cum Beckering 238 B4
Holton Heath 155 F3
Holton le Clay 238 C2
Holton le Moor 238 A3
Holton St. Mary 202 B4
Holtspur 185 E4
Holtye 173 D5
Holtye Common 173 D5
Holway 165 F5
Holwell *Dorset* 154 C1
Holwell *Herts.* 199 G4
Holwell *Leics.* 224 C5
Holwell *Oxon.* 183 E2
Holwell *Som.* 167 E3
Holwick 261 F5
Holworth 155 D4
Holy Cross 208 B5
Holy Island *I.o.A.* 230 A5
Holy Island (Lindisfarne) ***Northumb.*** 104
Holybourne 170 C3
Holyfield 186 C2
Holyhead (Caergybi) 230 A4
Holymoorside 223 E1
Holyport 185 D5
Holystone 270 B1
Holytown 284 B3
Holywell *Cambs.* 212 B5
Holywell *Cornw.* 146 B4
Holywell *Dorset* 154 B2
Holywell *E.Suss.* 160 B4
Holywell (Treffynnon) *Flints.* 232 C5
Holywell *Northumb.* 271 F4
Holywell Green 235 E1
Holywell Lake 165 E5
Holywell Row 213 F5
Holywood 266 D2
Hom Green 195 E5
Homer 207 F2
Homersfield 215 D3
Homington 168 C5
Homore (Tobha Mòr) 304 A1
Honey Hill 174 D2
Honey Street 168 C1
Honey Tye 202 A4
Honeyborough 176 C2
Honeybourne 196 D3
Honeychurch 163 G5
Honicknowle 150 A2
Honiley 209 E5
Honing 229 E3
Honingham 228 C4
Honington *Lincs.* 225 E3
Honington *Suff.* 214 A4
Honington *Warks.* 197 E3
Honiton 153 E2
Honkley 220 A2
Honley 235 F1
Hoo *Med.* 187 G5
Hoo *Suff.* 203 D2
Hoo Green 234 B4
Hoo Meavy 150 B1
Hood Green 236 A2
Hood Hill 236 A3
Hooe *E.Suss.* 160 B3
Hooe *Plym.* 150 B2
Hooe Common 160 B2
Hook *Cambs.* 212 C3
Hook *E.Riding* 245 G5
Hook *Gt.Lon.* 171 G1
Hook *Hants.* 170 C2
Hook *Hants.* 157 E2
Hook *Pembs.* 176 C1
Hook *Wilts.* 182 C4
Hook Green *Kent* 173 F5
Hook Green *Kent* 173 F2
Hook Green *Kent* 187 F5
Hook Green *Kent* 187 E5
Hook Norton 197 F4
Hook-a-Gate 207 D2
Hooke 154 B3
Hookgate 221 E4
Hookway 152 B3
Hookwood 172 B4
Hoole 220 B1
Hooley 172 B3
Hoop 181 E2
Hooton 233 E5
Hooton Levitt 236 C3
Hooton Pagnell 236 B2
Hooton Roberts 236 B3
Hop Farm Country Park 45
Hop Pole 211 G1
Hopcrofts Holt 197 G5
Hope *Derbys.* 235 F4
Hope *Devon* 150 C4
Hope *Flints.* 220 A2
Hope *Powys* 206 B2
Hope *Shrop.* 206 C2
Hope *Staffs.* 222 C2
Hope Bagot 207 E5
Hope Bowdler 207 D3
Hope End Green 201 D5
Hope Mansell 181 F1
Hope under Dinmore 195 E2
Hopehouse 277 D4
Hopeman 322 D3
Hope's Green 187 G4
Hopesay 206 C4
Hopetoun House 124
Hopkinstown 179 G3
Hopley's Green 194 C2
Hopperton 244 D2
Hopsford 209 G4
Hopstone 207 G3
Hopton *Derbys.* 223 D2
Hopton *Norf.* 215 G2
Hopton *Shrop.* 220 C5
Hopton *Shrop.* 220 A5
Hopton *Staffs.* 221 G5
Hopton *Suff.* 214 A4
Hopton Cangeford 207 E4
Hopton Castle 206 C5
Hopton Wafers 207 F5
Hoptonheath 206 C5
Hopwas 209 D2
Hopwood 208 C5
Horam 160 A2
Horbling 225 G4
Horbury 235 G1
Horden 262 D3
Horderley 206 D4
Hordle 156 B3
Hordley 220 A4
Horeb *Carmar.* 178 A2
Horeb *Cere.* 191 G3
Horeb *Flints.* 219 F2
Horfield 181 E5
Horham 214 D4
Horkesley Heath 202 A5
Horkstow 237 G1
Horley *Oxon.* 197 G3
Horley *Surr.* 172 B4
Horn Hill 185 F3
Hornblotton 166 C4
Hornblotton Green 166 C4
Hornby *Lancs.* 242 B1
Hornby *N.Yorks.* 252 B3
Hornby *N.Yorks.* 252 C2
Horncastle 226 A1
Hornchurch 187 E4
Horncliffe 287 G5
Horndean *Hants.* 157 G1
Horndean *Sc.Bord.* 287 G5
Horndon 149 F2
Horndon on the Hill 187 F4
Horne 172 C4
Horne Row 187 G2
Horner 164 B3
Horniehaugh 302 C3
Horniman Museum 56
Horning 229 E4
Horninghold 210 D3
Horninglow 222 D5
Horningsea 200 C1
Horningsham 167 F3
Horningtoft 228 A3
Horningtops 147 G3
Horns Cross *Devon* 163 D3
Horns Cross *E.Suss.* 160 D1
Horns Green 173 D3
Hornsbury 153 G1
Hornsby 260 B3
Hornsby Gate 260 B2
Hornsea 247 E3
Hornsey 186 C4
Hornton 197 F3
Horrabridge 150 B1
Horridge 152 A5
Horringer 201 G1
Horrocks Fold 234 B1
Horse Bridge 221 G2
Horsebridge *Devon* 149 E3
Horsebridge *Hants.* 169 E4
Horsebrook 208 A1
Horsecastle 166 B1
Horsehay 207 F2
Horseheath 201 E3
Horsehouse 251 F4
Horsell 171 E2
Horseman's Green 220 B3
Horsenden 184 C2
Horseshoe Green 173 D4
Horseway 212 C4
Horsey 229 F3
Horsey Corner 229 F3
Horsey Windpump 80
Horsford 228 C4
Horsforth 244 B4
Horsham *W.Suss.* 171 G4
Horsham *Worcs.* 195 G2
Horsham St. Faith 228 D4
Horsington *Lincs.* 225 G1
Horsington *Som.* 167 E5
Horsington Marsh 167 E5
Horsley *Derbys.* 223 E3
Horsley *Glos.* 182 A3
Horsley *Northumb.* 261 G1
Horsley *Northumb.* 270 A2
Horsley Cross 202 C5
Horsley Woodhouse 223 E3
Horsleycross Street 202 C5
Horsleygate 236 A5
Horsleyhill 277 G4
Horsmonden 173 F4
Horspath 184 A2
Horstead 229 D4
Horsted Keynes 159 F1
Horton *Bucks.* 185 E1
Horton *Dorset* 155 G2
Horton *Lancs.* 243 E2
Horton *Northants.* 198 D2
Horton *S.Glos.* 181 G4
Horton *Shrop.* 220 B5
Horton *Som.* 153 G1
Horton *Staffs.* 221 G2
Horton *Swan.* 178 A4
Horton *Tel. & W.* 207 F1
Horton *W. & M.* 185 F5
Horton *Wilts.* 168 B1
Horton Court 31
Horton Cross 153 G1
Horton Grange 271 E4
Horton Green 220 B3
Horton Heath 157 D1
Horton in Ribblesdale 250 D5
Horton Inn 155 G2
Horton Kirby 173 E2
Horton Park Farm 45
Horton-cum-Studley 184 B1
Horwich 234 A1
Horwich End 235 E4
Horwood 163 F3
Hoscar 233 F1
Hose 224 C5
Hoses 248 D3
Hosh 293 D2
Hosta 315 F2
Hoswick 342 D5
Hotham 246 A4
Hothfield 174 B4
Hoton 223 G5
Houbie 345 F3
Houdston 264 C1
Hough 221 E2
Hough Green 233 F4
Hougham 225 D3
Hough-on-the-Hill 225 E3
Houghton *Cambs.* 212 A5
Houghton *Cumb.* 260 A2
Houghton *Devon* 150 C3
Houghton *Hants.* 169 E4
Houghton *Pembs.* 176 C2
Houghton *W.Suss.* 158 C2
Houghton Bank 262 B5
Houghton Conquest 199 F3
Houghton Hall 80
Houghton le Spring 262 C3
Houghton Mill 80
Houghton on the Hill 210 B2
Houghton Regis 199 F5
Houghton St. Giles 228 A2
Houghton-le-Side 262 B5
Houlsyke 253 G2
Hound 157 D2
Hound Green 170 C2
Houndslow 286 D5
Houndsmoor 165 E5
Houndwood 287 F3
Hounsdown 156 C1
Hounslow 186 A5
House of Dun 124
House of the Binns 124
Housebay 341 E4
Househill 322 A4
Houses Hill 235 F1
Houses of Parliament 56
Housesteads (Vercovicium) 104
Housetter 344 C4
Housham Tye 187 E1
Houss 342 C4
Houston 283 F3
Houstry 337 D5
Houstry of Dunn 337 E3
Houton 338 C2
Hove 159 E3
Hove Edge 244 A5
Hoveringham 224 B3
Hoveton 229 E4
Hovingham 253 F5
How 260 B2
How Caple 195 F4
How End 199 F3
How Green 173 D4
How Man 258 C5
Howbrook 236 A3
Howden 245 G5
Howden Clough 244 B5
Howden-le-Wear 262 A4
Howe *Cumb.* 249 F4
Howe *High.* 337 F2
Howe *N.Yorks.* 252 C4
Howe *Norf.* 215 D2
Howe Green 187 G2
Howe of Teuchar 324 C5
Howe Street *Essex* 187 F1
Howe Street *Essex* 201 E4
Howe, The 240 A5
Howegreen 188 B2
Howell 225 G3
Howey 193 G2
Howgate *Cumb.* 258 C4
Howgate *Midloth.* 285 G4
Howgill *Lancs.* 243 E3
Howgill *N.Yorks.* 243 G2
Howick 279 G5
Howick Hall Gardens 104
Howle 221 D5
Howle Hill 195 F5
Howlett End 201 D4
Howletts Wild Animal Park 45
Howley 153 F2
Hownam 278 B5
Hownam Mains 278 B4
Howpasley 277 E5
Howsham *N.Lincs.* 238 A2
Howsham *N.Yorks.* 245 G1
Howt Green 174 A2
Howtel 278 C3
Howton 194 D5
Howwood 283 F3
Hoxa 338 D3
Hoxne 214 C4
Hoy *High.* 337 E2
Hoy *Ork.* 338 B3
Hoylake 232 D4
Hoyland 236 A2
Hoylandswaine 235 G2
Hoyle 158 B2
Hubberholme 251 E5
Hubberston 176 B2
Hubbert's Bridge 226 A3
Huby *N.Yorks.* 245 E1
Huby *N.Yorks.* 244 B3
Hucclecote 182 A1
Hucking 174 A3
Hucknall 223 G3
Huddersfield 235 F1
Huddersfield Narrow Canal & Standedge Experience 88
Huddington 196 B2
Huddlesford 208 D2
Hudnall 185 F1
Hudscott 163 G3
Hudswell 252 A3
Huggate 246 A2
Hugglescote 209 G1
Hugh Miller's Cottage 124
Hugh Town 146 B1
Hughenden Manor 45
Hughenden Valley 185 D3
Hughley 207 E3
Hugmore 220 A2
Hugus 146 B5
Huish *Devon* 163 F4
Huish *Wilts.* 168 C1
Huish Champflower 164 D5
Huish Episcopi 166 B5
Huisinis 326 B2
Hulcote 199 E4
Hulcott 185 D1
Hull 246 D5
Hulland 222 D3
Hulland Ward 223 D3
Hullavington 182 A4
Hullbridge 188 B3
Hulme 221 G3
Hulme End 222 C2
Hulme Walfield 221 F1
Hulver Street 215 F3
Hulverstone 156 C4
Humber *Devon* 152 B5
Humber *Here.* 195 E2
Humberside International Airport 238 A1
Humberston 238 D2
Humberstone 210 B2
Humberton 244 D1
Humbie 286 B3
Humbleton *Dur.* 251 F1
Humbleton *E.Riding* 247 E4
Humbleton *Northumb.* 279 D4
Humby 225 F4
Hume 287 E5
Humehall 287 E5
Hummer 154 B1
Humshaugh 270 B4
Huna 337 F1
Huncoat 243 D4
Huncote 210 A3
Hundalee 278 A5
Hundall 236 A5
Hunderthwaite 261 F5
Hundleby 226 B1
Hundleton 176 C2
Hundon 201 F3
Hundred Acres 157 E1
Hundred End 242 A5
Hundred House 194 A2
Hungarton 210 B2
Hungate End 198 C3
Hungerford *Hants.* 156 A1
Hungerford *Shrop.* 207 E4
Hungerford *W.Berks.* 169 E1
Hungerford Newtown 183 F5
Hungerton 225 D5
Hunglader 317 G2
Hunmanby 255 D5
Hunningham 197 F1
Hunningham Hill 197 F1
Hunny Hill 157 D4
Hunsdon 186 D1
Hunsingore 244 D2
Hunslet 244 C4
Hunsonby 260 B4
Hunspow 337 E1
Hunstanton 227 E3
Hunstanworth 261 F3
Hunston *Suff.* 202 A1
Hunston *W.Suss.* 158 A3
Hunsworth 244 A5
Hunt End 196 C1
Hunt House 254 B3
Huntercombe End 184 B4
Hunters Forstal 175 D2
Hunter's Inn 163 G1
Hunter's Quay 282 C2
Hunterston 282 C4
Huntford 269 E1
Huntham 166 A5
Huntingdon 212 A5
Huntingfield 215 E4
Huntingford 167 F4
Huntington *Here.* 194 B2
Huntington *Here.* 195 D3
Huntington *Staffs.* 208 B1
Huntington *Tel. & W.* 207 F2
Huntington *York* 245 F2
Huntingtower 293 F2
Huntingtower Castle 124
Huntley 181 G1
Huntly 312 A1
Huntlywood 286 D5
Hunton *Hants.* 169 F3
Hunton *Kent* 173 G4
Hunton *N.Yorks.* 252 A3
Hunton Bridge 185 F2
Hunt's Cross 233 F4
Huntscott 164 C3
Huntsham 164 D5
Huntshaw 163 F3
Huntshaw Cross 163 F3
Huntshaw Water 163 F3
Huntspill 166 A3
Huntworth 166 A4
Hunwick 262 A4
Hunworth 228 B2
Hurcott *Som.* 166 C5
Hurcott *Som.* 153 G1
Hurdley 206 B3
Hurdsfield 234 D5
Hurley *W. & M.* 184 D4
Hurley *Warks.* 209 E3
Hurley Bottom 184 D4
Hurlford 274 C2
Hurliness 338 B4
Hurlston Green 233 E1
Hurn 156 A3
Hursley 169 F5
Hurst *N.Yorks.* 251 F2
Hurst *W'ham* 184 C5
Hurst Green *E.Suss.* 160 C1
Hurst Green *Essex* 189 D1
Hurst Green *Lancs.* 242 C4
Hurst Green *Surr.* 172 C3
Hurst Wickham 159 E2
Hurstbourne Priors 169 F3
Hurstbourne Tarrant 169 E2
Hurstpierpoint 159 E2
Hurstwood 243 E4
Hurtmore 171 E3
Hurworth-on-Tees 252 C1
Hury 261 F5
Husabost 317 E4
Husbands Bosworth 210 B4
Husborne Crawley 199 E4
Husthwaite 253 E5
Hutcherleigh 151 D2
Hutchesons' Hall 124
Huthwaite 223 F2
Huttoft 239 F5
Hutton *Cumb.* 260 A5
Hutton *Essex* 187 F3
Hutton *Lancs.* 242 A5
Hutton *N.Som.* 166 A2
Hutton *Sc.Bord.* 287 G4
Hutton Bonville 252 C2
Hutton Buscel 254 C4
Hutton Conyers 252 C5
Hutton Cranswick 246 C2
Hutton End 260 A4
Hutton Hang 252 A4
Hutton Henry 262 D4
Hutton Magna 252 A1
Hutton Mount 187 F3
Hutton Mulgrave 254 B2
Hutton Roof *Cumb.* 249 G5
Hutton Roof *Cumb.* 259 G3
Hutton Rudby 253 D2
Hutton Sessay 253 D5
Hutton Wandesley 245 E2
Hutton-in-the-Forest 96
Hutton-le-Hole 253 G3
Huxham 152 C3
Huxham Green 166 C4
Huxley 220 C1
Huxter *Shet.* 342 C2
Huxter *Shet.* 343 E1
Huyton 233 F3
Hwllfordd (Haverfordwest) 176 C1
Hycemoor 248 B4
Hyde *Glos.* 182 A2
Hyde *Gt.Man.* 234 D3
Hyde End *W'ham* 170 C1
Hyde End *W.Berks.* 169 G1
Hyde Hall 80
Hyde Heath 185 E2
Hyde Lea 208 B1
Hydestile 171 E3
Hyndford Bridge 284 D5
Hyndlee 277 G5
Hynish 296 A3
Hyssington 206 C3
Hythe *Hants.* 156 D2
Hythe *Kent* 175 D5
Hythe End 185 F5
Hythie 325 F4
Hyton 248 B4

I

Ianstown 323 G3
Iarsiadar 328 C4
Ibberton 155 D2
Ible 222 D2
Ibsley 156 A2
Ibstock 209 G1
Ibstone 184 C3
Ibthorpe 169 E2
Ibworth 169 G2
Icelton 166 A1
Ickburgh 213 G3
Ickenham 185 F4
Ickford 184 B2
Ickham 175 E3
Ickleford 199 G4
Icklesham 161 D2
Ickleton 200 C3
Icklingham 213 F5
Ickwell Green 199 G3
Ickworth 80
Icomb 197 E5
Idbury 197 E5
Iddesleigh 163 F5
Ide 152 C3
Ide Hill 173 D3
Ideford 152 B5
Iden 161 E1
Iden Green *Kent* 173 G5
Iden Green *Kent* 174 A5
Idle 244 A4
Idless 146 C5
Idlicote 197 E3
Idmiston 168 C4
Idridgehay 223 D3
Idridgehay Green 223 D3
Idrigil 317 G3
Idstone 183 E4
Idvies 302 D5
Iffley 184 A2
Ifield (Singlewell) *Kent* 187 F5
Ifield *W.Suss.* 172 B5
Ifieldwood 172 B5
Ifold 171 F4
Iford *Bourne.* 156 A3
Iford *E.Suss.* 159 G3
Iford Manor 31
Ifton 181 D4
Ifton Heath 220 A4
Ightfield 220 C4
Ightham 173 E3
Ightham Mote 45
Iken 203 F2
Ilam 222 C2
Ilchester 166 C5
Ilderton 279 E4
Ilford 186 D4
Ilfracombe 163 F1
Ilkeston 223 F3
Ilketshall St. Andrew 215 E3
Ilketshall St. Lawrence 215 E3
Ilketshall St. Margaret 215 E3
Ilkley 244 A3
Illey 208 B4
Illidge Green 221 E1
Illington 214 A3
Illingworth 243 G5
Illogan 146 A5
Illston on the Hill 210 C3
Ilmer 184 C2
Ilmington 197 E3
Ilminster 153 G1
Ilsington *Devon* 152 A5
Ilsington *Dorset* 155 D3
Ilston 178 B3
Ilton *N.Yorks.* 252 A5
Ilton *Som.* 153 G1
Imachar 281 G5
Imber 168 A3
Immeroin 292 A3
Immingham 238 B1
Immingham Dock 238 C1
Imperial War Museum 56
Imperial War Museum (Duxford) 80
Impington 200 C1
Ince 233 F5
Ince Blundell 233 E2
Ince-in-Makerfield 233 G2
Inch Kenneth 288 D1
Inch of Arnhall 303 E2
Inchbae Lodge 320 D3
Inchbare 303 E3
Inchberry 323 F4
Inchbraoch 303 F4
Inchgrundle 302 C2
Inchindown 321 F2
Inchinnan 283 F3
Inchkinloch 335 F4
Inchlaggan 308 A4
Inchlumpie 321 E2
Inchmarlo 312 B5
Inchmarnock 282 B4
Inchnabobart 302 B1
Inchnacardoch Hotel 308 C3
Inchnadamph 331 E2
Inchock 303 E5
Inchrory 311 D4
Inchture 294 A2
Inchvuilt 308 B1
Inchyra 293 G2
Indian Queens 146 D4
Inerval 280 B5
Ingatestone 187 F3
Ingbirchworth 235 G2
Ingerthorpe 244 B1
Ingestre 221 G5
Ingham *Lincs.* 237 G4
Ingham *Norf.* 229 E3
Ingham *Suff.* 213 G5
Ingham Corner 229 E3
Ingleborough 212 C1
Ingleby *Derbys.* 223 E5
Ingleby *Lincs.* 237 F5
Ingleby Arncliffe 252 D2
Ingleby Barwick 252 D1
Ingleby Cross 252 D2
Ingleby Greenhow 253 E2
Ingleigh Green 163 G5
Inglesbatch 167 E1
Inglesham 183 E3
Ingleton *Dur.* 262 A5
Ingleton *N.Yorks.* 250 B5
Inglewhite 242 B4
Ingliston 285 F2
Ingmire Hall 250 B3
Ingoe 270 C4
Ingoldisthorpe 227 E4
Ingoldmells 227 D1
Ingoldsby 225 F4
Ingon 197 E2
Ingram 279 E5
Ingrave 187 F3
Ingrow 243 G4
Ings 249 F3
Ingst 181 E4
Ingworth 228 C3
Inhurst 169 G1
Inistrynich 290 D2
Injebreck 240 B3
Inkberrow 196 C2
Inkersall 236 B5
Inkersall Green 236 B5
Inkhorn 313 E1
Inkpen 169 E1
Inkstack 337 E1
Inmarsh 168 A1
Innellan 282 C3
Innergellie 295 D4
Innerleithen 277 E2
Innerleven 294 B4
Innermessan 264 B4
Innerwick *E.Loth.* 287 E2
Innerwick *P. & K.* 300 A5
Inninbeg 297 F5
Innsworth 196 A5
Insch 312 B2
Insh 310 A4
Inshore 334 C2
Inskip 242 A4
Instow 163 E2
Intake 236 C2
Intwood 228 C5
Inver *Aber.* 311 E5
Inver *Arg. & B.* 298 B5
Inver *High.* 322 A1
Inver *High.* 337 D5
Inver *P. & K.* 301 F5
Inver Mallie 298 D1
Inverailort 297 G1
Inveralligin 319 E4
Inverallochy 325 F3
Inveran 332 A5
Inveraray 290 C4
Inveraray Castle 124
Inveraray Jail 124
Inverardoch Mains 292 C4
Inverardran 291 F2
Inverarish 306 B1
Inverarity 302 C5
Inverarnan 291 F3
Inverasdale 319 E1
Inverbain 319 D4
Inverbeg 291 F5
Inverbervie 303 G2
Inverbroom 320 A1
Inverbrough 310 A2
Invercassley 331 G4
Inverchaolain 282 B2
Invercharnan 298 D5
Inverchorachan 291 E3
Inverchoran 320 B4
Invercreran 298 C5
Inverdruie 310 B3
Inverebrie 313 E1
Invereen 309 G1
Invererne 322 C3
Inveresk 286 A2
Inverewe Gardens 125
Inverey 301 F1
Inverfarigaig 309 E2
Invergarry 308 C4
Invergelder 311 E5
Invergeldie 292 C2
Invergloy 299 E1
Invergordon 321 G3
Invergowrie 294 B1
Inverguseran 306 D4
Inverhadden 300 B4
Inverharroch Farm 311 F1
Inverherive 291 F2
Inverhope 335 D2
Inverie 307 D4
Inverinan 290 B3
Inverinate 307 F2
Inverkeilor 303 E5
Inverkeithing 285 F1
Inverkeithny 324 B5
Inverkip 282 D2
Inverkirkaig 330 C3
Inverlael 320 A1
Inverlauren 283 E1
Inverliever 290 A4
Inverliver 290 C1
Inverlochlarig 291 G3
Inverlochy 291 D2
Inverlussa 281 E1
Invermay 293 F3
Invermoriston 308 D3
Invernaver 335 G2
Inverneil 281 G1
Inverness 321 F5
Inverness Airport 321 G4
Invernettie 325 G5
Invernoaden 290 D5
Inveroran Hotel 299 E5
Inverquharity 302 C4
Inverquhomery 325 F5
Inverroy 299 E1

Inversanda 298 B4
Invershiel 307 F3
Invershore 337 E5
Inversnaid Hotel 291 F4
Invertrossachs 292 A4
Inverugie 325 G5
Inveruglas 291 F4
Inveruglass 310 A4
Inverurie 312 C2
Invervar 300 B5
Invervegain 282 B2
Invery House 312 B5
Inverythan 324 C5
Inwardleigh 149 F1
Inworth 188 B1
Iochdar 315 F5
Iona 288 B2
Iping 171 D5
Ipplepen 151 E1
Ipsden 184 B4
Ipstones 222 B3
Ipswich 202 C3
Irby 233 D4
Irby Hill 233 D4
Irby in the Marsh 226 C1
Irby upon Humber 238 B2
Irchester 199 E1
Ireby *Cumb.* 259 F3
Ireby *Lancs.* 250 B5
Ireland *Ork.* 338 C2
Ireland *Shet.* 342 C5
Ireland's Cross 221 E3
Ireleth 248 D5
Ireshopeburn 261 E4
Irlam 234 B3
Irnham 225 F5
Iron Acton 181 F4
Iron Cross 196 C2
Ironbridge 207 F2
Ironbridge Gorge 66
Irons Bottom 172 B4
Ironside 325 D4
Ironville 223 F2
Irstead 229 E3
Irthington 260 A1
Irthlingborough 211 E5
Irton 254 D4
Irvine 274 B2
Isauld 336 B2
Isbister *Ork.* 340 B5
Isbister *Ork.* 340 A4
Isbister *Shet.* 343 E1
Isbister *Shet.* 344 C3
Isfield 159 G2
Isham 211 D5
Ishriff 289 F1
Isington 170 C3
Island of Stroma 337 F1
Islay 280 A3
Islay Airport 280 B4
Islay House 280 B3
Isle Abbotts 166 A5
Isle Brewers 166 A5
Isle of Lewis (Eilean Leodhais) 329 E3
Isle of Man 240 B3
Isle of Man Airport 240 A5
Isle of May 295 E5
Isle of Noss 343 E3
Isle of Sheppey 174 B1
Isle of Walney 241 E1
Isle of Whithorn 257 E3
Isle of Wight 157 D4
Isle of Wight Pearl 45
Isle of Wight Zoo 45
Isle, The 207 D1
Isleham 213 E5
Isleornsay (Eilean Iarmain) 306 C3
Isles of Scilly (Scilly Isles) 146 B1
Islesburgh 342 C1
Isleworth 186 A5
Isley Walton 223 F5
Islibhig 328 A5
Islip *Northants.* 211 E5
Islip *Oxon.* 184 A1
Isombridge 207 F1
Istead Rise 173 F2
Italian Chapel 125
Itchen 156 D1
Itchen Abbas 169 G4
Itchen Stoke 169 G4
Itchingfield 171 G5
Itchington 181 F4
Itteringham 228 C2
Itton *Devon* 149 G1
Itton *Mon.* 181 D3
Itton Common 181 D3
Ivegill 260 A3
Ivelet 251 E3
Iver 185 F4
Iver Heath 185 F4
Iveston 262 A2
Ivetsey Bank 208 A1
Ivinghoe 185 E1
Ivinghoe Aston 185 E1
Ivington 195 D2
Ivington Green 195 D2
Ivy Hatch 173 E3
Ivy Todd 213 G2
Ivybridge 150 C2
Ivychurch 161 F1
Iwade 174 B2
Iwerne Courtney (Shroton) 155 E1
Iwerne Minster 155 E1
Ixworth 214 A4
Ixworth Thorpe 214 A4

J

Jack Hill 244 A2
Jackfield 207 F2
Jacksdale 223 F2
Jackstown 312 C1
Jackton 283 G4
Jacobstow 148 B1
Jacobstowe 163 F5
Jacobswell 171 E2
Jameston 177 D3
Jamestown *D. & G.* 268 B2
Jamestown *High.* 321 D4
Jamestown *W.Dun.* 283 E1
Jane Austen's House 46
Janefield 321 G4
Janetstown *High.* 336 C2
Janetstown *High.* 337 F3
Jarlshof Prehistoric & Norse Settlement 125
Jarrow 262 C1
Jarvis Brook 173 E5
Jasper's Green 201 F5
Jawcraig 284 C2
Jayes Park 171 G3
Jaywick 189 E1
Jealott's Hill 185 D5
Jeater Houses 252 D3
Jedburgh 278 A4
Jedburgh Abbey 125
Jeffreyston 177 D2
Jemimaville 321 G3
Jericho 234 C1
Jersay 284 C3
Jersey 150 C5
Jersey Airport 150 B5
Jersey Marine 178 D3
Jerviswood 284 C5
Jesmond 262 B1
Jevington 160 A3
J.M. Barrie's Birthplace & Camera Obscura 125
Jockey End 185 F1
Jodrell Bank 234 B5
Jodrell Bank Observatory & Arboretum 96
John o' Groats 337 F1
Johnby 260 A4
John's Cross 160 C1
Johnshaven 303 F3
Johnson Street 229 E4
Johnston 176 C1
Johnston Mains 303 F2
Johnstone 283 F3
Johnstone Castle 283 F3
Johnstonebridge 267 E1
Johnstown *Carmar.* 177 G1
Johnstown *Wrex.* 220 A3
Joppa 274 C4
Jordans 185 E3
Jordanston 190 C4
Jordanstone 302 A5
Jorvik 88
Jorvik Glass 88
Joy's Green 181 F1
Jumpers Common 156 A3
Juniper Hill 198 A4
Jura 281 D1
Jura House 280 C3
Jurassic Coast 31
Jurby East 240 B2
Jurby West 240 B2

K

Kaber 250 C1
Kaimes 285 G3
Kames *Arg. & B.* 282 A2
Kames *Arg. & B.* 290 A3
Kames *E.Ayr.* 275 E3
Kea 146 C5
Keadby 237 F1
Keal Cotes 226 B1
Kearsley 234 B2
Kearstwick 250 B5
Kearton 251 F3
Kearvaig 334 B1
Keasden 242 D1
Kebholes 324 B4
Keckwick 233 G4
Keddington 238 D4
Keddington Corner 239 D4
Kedington 201 F3
Kedleston 223 D3
Kedleston Hall 73
Keelby 238 B1
Keele 221 F3
Keeley Green 199 F3
Keelham 243 G4
Keeres Green 187 E1
Keeston 176 B1
Keevil 168 A2
Kegworth 223 F5
Kehelland 146 A5
Keig 312 B3
Keighley 243 G3
Keil *Arg. & B.* 272 B5
Keil *High.* 298 B4
Keilhill 324 C4
Keillmore 281 E1
Keillor 302 A5
Keillour 293 E2
Keills 280 C3
Keils 280 D3
Keinton Mandeville 166 C4
Keir House 292 C5
Keir Mill 266 C1
Keisby 225 F5
Keisley 260 D5
Keiss 337 F2
Keith 323 G4
Keithick 294 A1
Keithmore 311 F1
Keithock 303 E3
Kelbrook 243 F3
Kelburn Castle & Country Centre 125
Kelby 225 F3
Keld *Cumb.* 249 G1
Keld *N.Yorks.* 251 D2
Keldholme 253 G4
Keldy Castle 253 G3
Kelfield *N.Lincs.* 237 F2
Kelfield *N.Yorks.* 245 E4
Kelham 224 C2
Kella 240 B2
Kellacott 149 E2
Kellan 297 E5
Kellas *Angus* 294 C1
Kellas *Moray* 323 D4
Kellaton 151 D4
Kellaways 182 B5
Kelleth 250 B2
Kelleythorpe 246 C2
Kellie Castle 125
Kelling 228 B1
Kellington 245 E5
Kelloe 262 C4
Kelloholm 275 F4
Kelly *Cornw.* 147 E2
Kelly *Devon* 149 D2
Kelly Bray 149 D3
Kelmarsh 210 C5
Kelmscott 183 E3
Kelsale 203 E1
Kelsall 220 C1
Kelsay 280 A4
Kelshall 200 B4
Kelsick 259 F1
Kelso 278 B3
Kelso Abbey 125
Kelstedge 223 E1
Kelstern 238 C3
Kelston 167 E1
Keltneyburn 300 C5
Kelton 267 D3
Kelton Hill (Rhonehouse) 266 B5
Kelty 293 G5
Kelvedon 188 B1
Kelvedon Hatch 187 E3
Kelvinside 283 G3
Kelynack 144 A4
Kemacott 163 G1
Kemback 294 C3
Kemberton 207 G2
Kemble 182 B3
Kemerton 196 B4
Kemeys Commander 180 C2
Kemeys Inferior 180 C3
Kemnay 312 C3
Kemp Town 159 F3
Kempe's Corner 174 C4
Kempley 195 F5
Kempley Green 195 F5
Kemps Green 208 D5
Kempsey 196 A3
Kempsford 183 D3
Kempshott 169 G3
Kempston 199 F3
Kempston Hardwick 199 F3
Kempston West End 199 E3
Kempton 206 C4
Kemsing 173 E3
Kemsley 174 B2
Kenardington 174 B5
Kenchester 194 D3
Kencott 183 E2
Kendal 249 G3
Kenderchurch 194 D5
Kendleshire 181 F5
Kenfig 179 D4
Kenfig Hill 179 E4
Kenidjack 144 A3
Kenilworth 209 E5
Kenilworth Castle 66
Kenknock *P. & K.* 300 A5
Kenknock *Stir.* 291 G1
Kenley *Gt.Lon.* 172 C2
Kenley *Shrop.* 207 E2
Kenmore *Arg. & B.* 290 C4
Kenmore *High.* 319 D4
Kenmore *P. & K.* 300 C5
Kenmore *W.Isles* 327 E3
Kenn *Devon* 152 C4
Kenn *N.Som.* 166 B1
Kennack Sands 31
Kennacley 327 D4
Kennacraig 281 G3
Kennards House 147 G1
Kennavay 327 E4
Kenneggy Downs 144 C4
Kennerleigh 152 B2
Kennerty 312 B5
Kennet 293 E5
Kennethmont 312 A2
Kennett 201 E1
Kennford 152 C4
Kenninghall 214 B3
Kennington *Kent* 174 C4
Kennington *Oxon.* 184 A2
Kennoway 294 B4
Kenny 153 G1
Kennyhill 213 E5
Kennythorpe 245 G1
Kenovay 296 A2
Kensaleyre 318 A4
Kensington 186 B4
Kensington Palace 57
Kenstone 220 C5
Kensworth 185 F1
Kent & East Sussex Railway 46
Kent Street *E.Suss.* 160 C2
Kent Street *Kent* 173 F3
Kentallen 298 C4
Kentchurch 194 D5
Kentford 201 F1
Kentisbeare 153 D2
Kentisbury 163 G1
Kentisbury Ford 163 G1
Kentish Town 186 B4
Kentmere 249 F2
Kenton *Devon* 152 C4
Kenton *Suff.* 202 C1
Kenton *T. & W.* 262 B1
Kenton Corner 202 D1
Kentra 297 F3
Kents Bank 249 E5
Kent's Green 195 G5
Kent's Oak 169 E5
Kentwell Hall 81
Kenwick 220 B4
Kenwood House 57
Kenwyn 146 C5
Kenyon 234 A3
Keoldale 334 C2
Keose (Ceos) 329 E5
Keppanach 298 C3
Keppoch *Arg. & B.* 283 E2
Keppoch *High.* 307 E2
Keprigan 272 B4
Kepwick 253 D3
Keresley 209 F4
Kernborough 151 D3
Kerrera 290 A2
Kerridge 234 D5
Kerris 144 B4
Kerry 206 A3
Kerrycroy 282 C3
Kerry's Gate 194 C4
Kerrysdale 319 E2
Kersall 224 C1
Kersey 202 B3
Kersey Vale 202 B3
Kershopefoot 268 C3
Kerswell 153 D2
Kerswell Green 196 A3
Kerthen Wood 144 C3
Kesgrave 202 D3
Kessingland 215 G3
Kessingland Beach 215 G3
Kestle 147 D5
Kestle Mill 146 C4
Keston 172 D2
Keswick *Cumb.* 259 F4
Keswick *Norf.* 228 D5
Keswick *Norf.* 229 E2
Ketley Bank 207 F1
Ketsby 239 D5
Kettering 211 D5
Ketteringham 228 C5
Kettins 294 A1
Kettle Corner 173 G3
Kettlebaston 202 A2
Kettlebridge 294 B4
Kettlebrook 209 E2
Kettleburgh 203 D1
Kettlehill 294 B4
Kettleholm 267 F3
Kettleness 254 B1
Kettleshulme 235 D5
Kettlesing 244 B2
Kettlesing Bottom 244 B2
Kettlesing Head 244 B2
Kettlestone 228 A2
Kettlethorpe 237 F5
Kettletoft 341 E3
Kettlewell 251 E5
Ketton 211 E2
Kevingtown 173 D2
Kew 186 A5
Kew Gardens (see Royal Botanic Gardens, Kew) 59
Kewstoke 166 A1
Kexbrough 236 A2
Kexby *Lincs.* 237 F4
Kexby *York* 245 G2
Key Green 221 F1
Keyham 210 B2
Keyhaven 156 C3
Keyingham 247 E5
Keymer 159 F2
Keynsham 167 D1
Key's Toft 226 C2
Keysoe 199 F1
Keysoe Row 199 F1
Keyston 211 F5
Keyworth 224 B4
Kibblesworth 262 B2
Kibworth Beauchamp 210 B3
Kibworth Harcourt 210 B3
Kidbrooke 186 D5
Kiddemore Green 208 A2
Kidderminster 208 A5
Kiddington 197 G5
Kidlington 183 G1
Kidmore End 184 B5
Kidnal 220 B3
Kidsdale 257 E3
Kidsgrove 221 F2
Kidstones 251 E4
Kidwelly (Cydweli) 178 A2
Kidwelly Castle 111
Kiel Crofts 290 A1
Kielder 269 E2
Kielder Forest 105
Kilbarchan 283 F3
Kilbeg 306 C4
Kilberry 281 F3
Kilbirnie 283 E4
Kilblaan 290 D3
Kilbraur 332 D3
Kilbrennan 296 D5
Kilbride *Arg. & B.* 290 A2
Kilbride *Arg. & B.* 282 B3
Kilbride *High.* 306 B2
Kilbride Farm 282 A3
Kilbridemore 290 C5
Kilburn *Derbys.* 223 E3
Kilburn *Gt.Lon.* 186 B4
Kilburn *N.Yorks.* 253 E5
Kilby 210 B3
Kilchattan Bay 282 C4
Kilchenzie 272 B3
Kilcheran 290 A1
Kilchiaran 280 A3
Kilchoan *Arg. & B.* 289 G3
Kilchoan *High.* 297 D3
Kilchoman 280 A3
Kilchrenan 290 C2
Kilchrist 272 B4
Kilchurn Castle 125
Kilconquhar 294 C4
Kilcot 195 F5
Kilcoy 321 E4
Kilcreggan 282 D1
Kildale 253 F2
Kildalton Church & Crosses 125
Kildary 321 G2
Kildavie 272 C4
Kildermorie Lodge 321 E2
Kildonan *N.Ayr.* 273 F3
Kildonan (Cilldonnain) *W.Isles* 314 C1
Kildonan Lodge 333 E2
Kildonnan 297 D1
Kildrochet House 264 B5
Kildrummy 311 G3
Kildwick 243 G3
Kilfinan 282 A2
Kilfinnan 308 B5
Kilgetty 177 E2
Kilgwrrwg Common 181 D3
Kilham *E.Riding* 246 C1
Kilham *Northumb.* 278 C3
Kilkenneth 296 A2
Kilkenny 182 C1
Kilkerran *Arg. & B.* 272 C4
Kilkerran *S.Ayr.* 274 B5
Kilkhampton 162 C4
Killamarsh 236 B4
Killay 178 C3
Killbeg 297 F5
Killean *Arg. & B.* 281 E5
Killean *Arg. & B.* 290 C4
Killearn 283 G1
Killellan 272 B4
Killen 321 F4
Killerby 262 A5
Killerton *Devon* 152 C2
Killerton *Devon* 31
Killichonan 300 A4
Killiechonate 299 E1
Killiechronan 297 E5
Killiecrankie 301 E3
Killiecrankie 125
Killiehuntly 309 G5
Killiemor 289 D1
Killilan 307 F1
Killimster 337 F3
Killin *High.* 333 D4
Killin *Stir.* 292 A1
Killinallan 280 B2
Killinghall 244 B2
Killington *Cumb.* 250 B4
Killington *Devon* 163 G1
Killingworth 271 E4
Killochyett 286 B5
Killocraw 272 B2
Killunaig 289 D2
Killundine 297 E5
Kilmacolm 283 E3
Kilmaha 290 B4
Kilmahog 292 B4
Kilmalieu 298 A4
Kilmaluag 318 A2
Kilmany 294 B2
Kilmarie 306 B3
Kilmarnock 274 C2
Kilmartin 290 A5
Kilmartin House Museum 125
Kilmaurs 283 F5
Kilmelford 290 A3
Kilmeny 280 B3
Kilmersdon 167 D2
Kilmeston 169 G5
Kilmichael 272 B3
Kilmichael Glassary 290 A5
Kilmichael of Inverlussa 281 F1
Kilmington *Devon* 153 F3
Kilmington *Wilts.* 167 E4
Kilmington Common 167 E4
Kilmorack 321 D5
Kilmore *Arg. & B.* 290 A2
Kilmore *High.* 306 C4
Kilmory *Arg. & B.* 281 F1
Kilmory *Arg. & B.* 281 F2
Kilmory *High.* 305 G4
Kilmory *High.* 297 E2
Kilmory *N.Ayr.* 273 E3
Kilmote 333 E3
Kilmuir *High.* 317 F5
Kilmuir *High.* 321 F5
Kilmuir *High.* 321 G2
Kilmuir *High.* 317 G2
Kilmun 282 C1
Kilmux 294 B4
Kiln Green *Here.* 181 F1
Kiln Green *W'ham* 184 D5
Kiln Pit Hill 261 G2
Kilnave 280 A2
Kilncadzow 284 C5
Kilndown 173 G5
Kilnhurst 236 B3
Kilninian 296 D5
Kilninver 290 A2
Kilnsea 239 E1
Kilnsey 243 F1
Kilnwick 246 B3
Kilnwick Percy 246 A2
Kiloran 288 C5
Kilpatrick 273 E3
Kilpeck 194 D4
Kilphedir 333 E3
Kilpin 245 G5
Kilpin Pike 245 G5
Kilrenny 295 D4
Kilsby 210 A5
Kilspindie 294 A2
Kilstay 256 B3
Kilsyth 284 B2
Kiltarlity 321 E5
Kilton *Notts.* 236 C5
Kilton *R. & C.* 253 F1
Kilton *Som.* 165 E3
Kilton Thorpe 253 F1
Kiltyrie 292 B1
Kilvaxter 317 G3
Kilve 165 E3
Kilverstone 213 G4
Kilvington 224 D3
Kilwinning 283 E5
Kimberley *Norf.* 228 B5
Kimberley *Notts.* 223 G3
Kimberworth 236 B3
Kimble Wick 184 D2
Kimblesworth 262 B3
Kimbolton *Cambs.* 199 F1
Kimbolton *Here.* 195 E1
Kimbridge 169 E5
Kimcote 210 A4
Kimmeridge 155 F5
Kimmerston 279 D3
Kimpton *Hants.* 169 D3
Kimpton *Herts.* 186 A1
Kinaldy 294 D3
Kinblethmont 303 E5
Kinbrace 336 A5
Kinbreack 307 G5
Kinbuck 292 C4
Kincaldrum 302 C5
Kincaple 294 C3
Kincardine *Fife* 284 D1
Kincardine *High.* 321 F1
Kincardine O'Neil 312 A5
Kinclaven 293 G1
Kincorth 313 E4
Kincraig *Aber.* 313 E2
Kincraig *High.* 310 A4
Kincraigie 301 E5
Kindallachan 301 E4
Kindrogan Field Centre 301 F3
Kinellar 312 D3
Kineton *Glos.* 196 C5
Kineton *Warks.* 197 F2
Kineton Green 208 D4
Kinfauns 293 G2
King Sterndale 235 E5
Kingarth 282 B4
Kingcoed 180 D2
Kingerby 238 A3
Kingham 197 E5
Kingholm Quay 267 D3
Kinghorn 285 G1
Kinglassie 294 A5
Kingoodie 294 B2
King's Acre 195 D3
King's Bank 161 D1
King's Bromley 208 D1
Kings Caple 195 E5
King's Cliffe 211 F3
King's Coughton 196 C2
King's Green 195 G4
King's Heath 208 C4
Kings Hill *Kent* 173 F3
King's Hill *W.Mid.* 208 B3
King's Hill *Warks.* 209 F5
Kings Langley 185 F2
King's Lynn 227 E5
King's Meaburn 260 C5
Kings Mills 151 E5
King's Moss 233 G2
Kings Muir 277 D2
King's Newnham 209 G5
King's Newton 223 E5
King's Norton *Leics.* 210 B2
King's Norton *W.Mid.* 208 C5
Kings Nympton 163 G4
King's Pyon 194 D2
Kings Ripton 212 A5
King's Somborne 169 E4
King's Stag 154 D1
King's Stanley 182 A2
King's Sutton 197 G4
King's Tamerton 150 A2
King's Walden 199 G5
Kings Worthy 169 F4
Kingsand 150 A2
Kingsbarns 295 D3
Kingsbridge *Devon* 150 D3
Kingsbridge *Som.* 164 C4
Kingsburgh 317 G4
Kingsbury *Gt.Lon.* 186 A4
Kingsbury *Warks.* 209 E3
Kingsbury Episcopi 166 B5
Kingscavil 285 E2
Kingsclere 169 G2
Kingscote 182 A3
Kingscott 163 F4
Kingscross 273 F3
Kingsdale 294 B4
Kingsdon 166 C5
Kingsdown *Kent* 175 F4
Kingsdown *Swin.* 183 D4
Kingsdown *Wilts.* 167 F1
Kingseat 293 G5
Kingsey 184 C2
Kingsfold *Pembs.* 176 C3
Kingsfold *W.Suss.* 171 G4
Kingsford *Aber.* 324 C5
Kingsford *Aber.* 312 A3
Kingsford *Aberdeen* 313 D4
Kingsford *E.Ayr.* 283 F5
Kingsford *Worcs.* 208 A4
Kingsgate 175 F1
Kingshall Street 202 A1
Kingsheanton 163 F2
Kingshouse 292 A2
Kingshouse Hotel 299 E4
Kingshurst 209 D4
Kingskerswell 151 E1
Kingskettle 294 B4
Kingsland *Here.* 194 D1
Kingsland *I.o.A.* 230 A4
Kingsley *Ches.* 233 G5
Kingsley *Hants.* 170 C4
Kingsley *Staffs.* 222 B3
Kingsley Green 171 D4
Kingsley Holt 222 B3
Kingslow 207 G3
Kingsmoor 186 D2
Kingsmuir *Angus* 302 C5
Kingsmuir *Fife* 294 D4
Kingsnorth 174 C5
Kingsnorth Power Station 174 A1
Kingstanding 208 C3
Kingsteignton 152 B5
Kingsteps 322 B4
Kingsthorne 195 D4
Kingsthorpe 198 C1
Kingston *Cambs.* 200 B2
Kingston *Cornw.* 149 D3
Kingston *Devon* 150 C3
Kingston *Devon* 153 D4
Kingston *Dorset* 154 D2
Kingston *Dorset* 155 F5
Kingston *E.Loth.* 286 C1
Kingston *Gt.Man.* 234 D3
Kingston *Hants.* 156 A2
Kingston *I.o.W.* 157 D4
Kingston *Kent* 175 D3
Kingston *Moray* 323 F3
Kingston *W.Suss.* 158 C3
Kingston Bagpuize 183 F3
Kingston Blount 184 C3
Kingston by Sea 159 E3
Kingston Deverill 167 F4
Kingston Gorse 158 C3
Kingston Lacy 31
Kingston Lisle 183 F4
Kingston Maurward 154 D3
Kingston Maurward Park 31
Kingston near Lewes 159 F3
Kingston on Soar 223 G5
Kingston Russell 154 B3
Kingston St. Mary 165 F5
Kingston Seymour 166 B1
Kingston Stert 184 C2
Kingston Upon Hull 246 D5
Kingston upon Thames 171 G1
Kingston Warren 183 F4
Kingstone *Here.* 194 D4
Kingstone *Here.* 195 F5
Kingstone *Som.* 153 G1
Kingstone *Staffs.* 222 B5
Kingstone Winslow 183 E4
Kingstown 259 G1
Kingswear 151 E2
Kingswell 283 G5
Kingswells 313 D4
Kingswinford 208 A4
Kingswood *Bucks.* 184 B1
Kingswood *Glos.* 181 G3
Kingswood *Here.* 194 B2
Kingswood *Kent* 174 A3
Kingswood *Powys* 206 B2
Kingswood *S.Glos.* 181 F5
Kingswood *Som.* 165 E4
Kingswood *Surr.* 172 B3
Kingswood *Warks.* 209 D5
Kingthorpe 238 B5
Kington *Here.* 194 B2
Kington *Worcs.* 196 B2
Kington Langley 182 B5
Kington Magna 167 E5
Kington St. Michael 182 B5
Kingussie 309 G4
Kingweston 166 C4
Kinharrachie 313 E1
Kinharvie 266 D4
Kinkell 284 A2
Kinkell Bridge 293 E3
Kinknockie 325 F5
Kinlet 207 G4
Kinloch *Fife* 294 A3
Kinloch *High.* 334 C5
Kinloch *High.* 297 F4
Kinloch *High.* 306 A5
Kinloch *High.* 321 E2
Kinloch *P. & K.* 302 A5
Kinloch *P. & K.* 301 G5
Kinloch Hourn 307 F4
Kinloch Laggan 300 A1
Kinloch Rannoch 300 B4
Kinlochan 298 A3
Kinlochard 291 G4
Kinlocharkaig 307 F5
Kinlochbeoraid 298 A1
Kinlochbervie 334 B3
Kinlocheil 298 B2
Kinlochetive 298 D5
Kinlochewe 319 G3
Kinlochlaich 298 B5
Kinlochleven 299 D3
Kinlochmoidart 297 G2
Kinlochmorar 307 E5
Kinlochmore 299 D3
Kinlochroag (Ceann Lochroag) 328 C5
Kinlochspelve 289 F2
Kinloss 322 C3
Kinmel Bay (Bae Cinmel) 232 A4
Kinmuck 312 D3
Kinnaber 303 F3
Kinnadie 325 E5
Kinnaird 294 A2
Kinneff 303 G2
Kinnelhead 276 B5
Kinnell *Angus* 303 E4
Kinnell *Stir.* 292 A1
Kinnerley 220 A5
Kinnersley *Here.* 194 C3
Kinnersley *Worcs.* 196 A3
Kinnerton 194 B1
Kinnerton Green 220 A1
Kinnesswood 293 G4
Kinnettles 302 C5
Kinninvie 261 G5
Kinnordy 302 B4
Kinoulton 224 B4
Kinrara 310 A4
Kinross 293 G4
Kinrossie 293 G1
Kinsbourne Green 186 A1
Kinsham *Here.* 194 C1
Kinsham *Worcs.* 196 B4
Kinsley 236 B1
Kinson 155 G3
Kintail Estate & Morvich 125
Kintarvie 327 E2
Kintbury 169 E1
Kintessack 322 B3
Kintillo 293 G3
Kintocher 312 A4
Kinton *Here.* 206 D5
Kinton *Shrop.* 206 C1
Kintore 312 C3
Kintour 280 C4
Kintra *Arg. & B.* 280 B5
Kintra *Arg. & B.* 288 C2

Lee - Lla

Lee *Shrop.* 220 B4
Lee Brockhurst 220 C5
Lee Chapel 187 F4
Lee Clump 185 E2
Lee Mill Bridge 150 B2
Lee Moor 150 B1
Lee, The 185 D2
Leebotten 342 D5
Leebotwood 207 D3
Leece 241 F1
Leeds *Kent* 174 A3
Leeds *W.Yorks.* 244 B4
Leeds Bradford International Airport 244 B3
Leeds Castle & Gardens 46
Leeds City Art Gallery & Museum 88
Leedstown 144 D3
Leegomery 207 F1
Leek 221 G2
Leek Wootton 197 E1
Leekbrook 221 G2
Leeming *N.Yorks.* 252 B4
Leeming *W.Yorks.* 243 G4
Leeming Bar 252 B4
Lee-on-the-Solent 157 E2
Lees *Derbys.* 223 D4
Lees *Gt.Man.* 235 D2
Leeswood 219 F2
Leftwich 234 A5
Legars 287 E5
Legbourne 239 D4
Legerwood 286 C5
Legoland 46
Legsby 238 B4
Leicester 210 A2
Leicester Forest East 210 A2
Leideag 314 B4
Leigh *Dorset* 154 C2
Leigh *Dorset* 155 G3
Leigh *Gt.Man.* 234 A2
Leigh *Kent* 173 E4
Leigh *Shrop.* 206 C2
Leigh *Surr.* 172 B4
Leigh *Wilts.* 182 C3
Leigh *Worcs.* 195 G2
Leigh Beck 188 B4
Leigh Common 167 E5
Leigh Delamere 182 A5
Leigh Green 174 B5
Leigh Park 157 G2
Leigh Sinton 195 G2
Leigh, The 196 A5
Leigh upon Mendip 167 D3
Leigh Woods 181 E5
Leigham 150 B2
Leighland Chapel 164 D4
Leigh-on-Sea 188 B4
Leighterton 182 A3
Leighton *N.Yorks.* 252 A5
Leighton *Powys* 206 B2
Leighton *Shrop.* 207 F2
Leighton *Som.* 167 E3
Leighton Bromswold 211 G5
Leighton Buzzard 199 E5
Leighton Buzzard Light Railway 81
Leighton Hall 97
Leinthall Earls 194 D1
Leinthall Starkes 194 D1
Leintwardine 206 D5
Leire 210 A4
Leirinmore 334 D2
Leiston 203 F1
Leitfie 302 A5
Leith 285 G2
Leitholm 287 E5
Lelant 144 C3
Lelley 247 E4
Lemington 262 A1
Lemnas 324 D3
Lempitlaw 278 B3
Lemsford 186 B1
Lenchwick 196 C3
Lendalfoot 264 C1
Lendrick Lodge 292 A4
Lenham 174 A3
Lenham Heath 174 B4
Lenie 309 E2
Lenimore 281 G5
Lennel 287 F5
Lennox Plunton 266 A5
Lennoxlove 126
Lennoxtown 284 A2
Lent Rise 185 E4
Lenton *Lincs.* 225 F4
Lenton *Nott.* 223 G4
Lenton Abbey 223 G4
Lenwade 228 B4
Lenzie 284 A2
Leoch 294 B1
Leochel-Cushnie 312 A3
Leominster 195 D2
Leonard Stanley 182 A2
Leonardslee Gardens 46
Leorin 280 B5
Lepe 156 D3
Lephin 317 E5
Lephinchapel 290 B5
Lephinmore 290 B5
Leppington 245 G1
Lepton 235 G1
Lerags 290 A2
Lerryn 147 F4
Lerwick 343 D3
Lesbury 279 G5
Leschangie 312 C3
Lescrow 147 F4
Leslie *Aber.* 312 A2
Leslie *Fife* 294 A4
Lesmahagow 275 G2
Lesnewth 148 B1
Lessendrum 324 A5
Lessingham 229 E3
Lessness Heath 187 D5
Lessonhall 259 F1
Leswalt 264 B4
Letchmore Heath 186 A3
Letchworth Garden City 200 A4
Letcombe Bassett 183 F4
Letcombe Regis 183 F4
Leth Meadhanach 314 C2
Letham *Angus* 302 D5
Letham *Falk.* 284 C1
Letham *Fife* 294 B3
Lethanhill 274 C4
Lethenty 324 D5
Letheringham 203 D2
Letheringsett 228 B2
Letocetum Roman Baths & Museum 66
Lettaford 152 A4
Letter Finlay 308 B5
Letterewe 319 F2
Letterfearn 307 E2
Lettermorar 297 G1
Lettermore *Arg. & B.* 297 D5
Lettermore *High.* 335 F4
Letters 320 A1
Lettershaws 275 G3
Letterston 190 C5
Lettoch *High.* 310 C3
Lettoch *High.* 310 D1
Letton *Here.* 206 C5
Letton *Here.* 194 C3
Letty Green 186 B1
Letwell 236 C4
Leuchars 294 C2
Leumrabhagh 327 F2
Leurbost (Liurbost) 329 E5
Leusdon 152 A5
Levedale 208 A1
Level's Green 200 C5
Leven *E.Riding* 246 D3
Leven *Fife* 294 B4
Levencorroch 273 F3
Levenhall 286 A2
Levens 249 F4
Levens Green 200 B5
Levens Hall 97
Levenshulme 234 C3
Levenwick 342 D5
Leverburgh (An T-òb) 326 C5
Leverington 212 C1
Leverstock Green 185 F2
Leverton 226 B3
Leverton Lucasgate 226 C3
Leverton Outgate 226 C3
Levington 202 D4
Levisham 254 B3
Levishie 308 D3
Lew 183 F2
Lewannick 147 G1
Lewcombe 154 B2
Lewdown 149 E2
Lewes 159 G2
Lewes Castle 46
Leweston 190 C5
Lewisham 186 C5
Lewiston 309 E2
Lewistown 179 F4
Lewknor 184 C3
Leworthy 163 G2
Lewson Street 174 B2
Lewth 242 A4
Lewtrenchard 149 E2
Ley *Aber.* 312 A3
Ley *Cornw.* 147 F3
Ley Green 199 G5
Leybourne 173 F3
Leyburn 252 A3
Leyland 242 B5
Leylodge 312 C3
Leymoor 235 F1
Leys *Aber.* 325 F4
Leys *Aber.* 311 G4
Leys *P. & K.* 294 A1
Leys of Cossans 302 B5
Leysdown-on-Sea 174 C1
Leysmill 303 E5
Leysters 195 E1
Leyton 186 C4
Leytonstone 186 C4
Lezant 148 D3
Lezerea 145 D3
Lhanbryde 323 E3
Lhen, The 240 B1
Liatrie 308 B1
Libanus 193 F5
Libberton 285 D5
Libbery 196 B2
Liberton 285 G3
Liceasto 326 D4
Lichfield 208 D2
Lichfield Cathedral 66
Lickey 208 B5
Lickey End 208 B5
Lickfold 171 E5
Liddaton Green 149 E2
Liddel 339 D4
Liddesdale 297 G4
Liddington 183 E4
Lidgate *Derbys.* 236 A5
Lidgate *Suff.* 201 F2
Lidgett 224 B1
Lidlington 199 E4
Lidsey 158 B3
Lidsing 173 G2
Lidstone 197 F5
Lienassie 307 F2
Lieurary 336 C2
Life Science Centre 105
Liff 294 B1
Lifton 149 D2
Liftondown 149 D2
Lightcliffe 244 A5
Lighthorne 197 F2
Lighthorne Heath 197 F2
Lighthouse, The 126
Lightwater 171 E1
Lightwater Valley Park 88
Lightwood 221 G3
Lightwood Green *Ches.* 220 D3
Lightwood Green *Wrex.* 220 A3
Lilbourne 210 A5
Lilburn Tower 279 E4
Lillesdon 166 A5
Lilleshall 207 G1
Lilley *Herts.* 199 G5
Lilley *W.Berks.* 183 G5
Lilliesleaf 277 G3
Lilling Green 245 F1
Lillingstone Dayrell 198 C4
Lillingstone Lovell 198 C3
Lillington *Dorset* 154 C1
Lillington *Warks.* 197 F1
Lilliput 155 G4
Lilly 163 F2
Lilstock 165 E3
Lilyhurst 207 G1
Limbury 199 F5
Lime Side 234 D2
Limefield 234 C1
Limehillock 324 A4
Limehurst 234 D2
Limekilnburn 284 B4
Limekilns 285 E1
Limerigg 284 C2
Limerstone 156 D4
Limington 166 C5
Limpenhoe 229 E5
Limpley Stoke 167 E1
Limpsfield 172 D3
Limpsfield Chart 172 D3
Linaclate (Lionacleit) 315 F5
Linbriggs 270 A1
Linby 223 G2
Linchmere 171 D4
Lincluden 267 D3
Lincoln 237 G5
Lincoln Castle 73
Lincoln Cathedral 73
Lincomb 196 A1
Lincombe *Devon* 150 D2
Lincombe *Devon* 150 D3
Lindal in Furness 249 D5
Lindale 249 F4
Lindean 277 F2
Lindertis 302 B4
Lindfield 159 F1
Lindford 170 D4
Lindifferon 294 B3
Lindisfarne (see Holy Island) 104
Lindley 244 B3
Lindores 294 A3
Lindow End 234 C5
Lindridge 195 F1
Lindsaig 282 A2
Lindsell 201 E5
Lindsey 202 A3
Lindsey Tye 202 A3
Linfitts 235 D2
Linford *Hants.* 156 A2
Linford *Thur.* 187 F5
Linford Wood 198 D3
Lingague 240 A4
Lingards Wood 235 E1
Lingdale 253 F1
Lingen 194 C1
Lingfield 172 C4
Lingley Green 233 G4
Lingwood 229 E5
Linhead 324 B4
Linhope 277 F5
Linicro 317 G3
Linkend 196 A4
Linkenholt 169 E2
Linkhill 160 D1
Linkinhorne 148 D3
Linklater 339 D4
Linksness *Ork.* 338 B2
Linksness *Ork.* 340 D5
Linktown 294 A5
Linley *Shrop.* 206 C3
Linley *Shrop.* 207 F3
Linley Green 195 F2
Linlithgow 285 E2
Linlithgow Bridge 285 D2
Linlithgow Palace 126
Linn of Muick Cottage 302 B1
Linn of Tummel 126
Linnels 261 F1
Linney 176 B3
Linshiels 270 A1
Linsiadar 328 D4
Linsidemore 332 A5
Linslade 199 E5
Linstead Parva 215 E4
Linstock 260 A2
Linthwaite 235 F1
Lintlaw 287 F4
Lintmill 324 A3
Linton *Cambs.* 201 D3
Linton *Derbys.* 209 E1
Linton *Here.* 195 F5
Linton *Kent* 173 G3
Linton *N.Yorks.* 243 F1
Linton *Sc.Bord.* 278 B4
Linton *W.Yorks.* 244 C3
Linton Zoo 81
Linton-on-Ouse 245 D1
Lintzford 262 A2
Linwood *Hants.* 156 A2
Linwood *Lincs.* 238 B4
Linwood *Renf.* 283 F3
Lionacleit (Linaclate) 315 F5
Lional (Lionel) 329 G1
Lionel (Lional) 329 G1
Liphook 170 D4
Lipley 221 E4
Liscard 233 E3
Liscombe 164 B4
Liskeard 147 G3
L'Islet 151 F4
Lismore 290 A1
Liss 170 C5
Liss Forest 170 C5
Lissett 246 D2
Lissington 238 B4
Liston 201 G3
Lisvane 180 A4
Liswerry 180 C4
Litcham 213 G1
Litchborough 198 B2
Litchfield 169 F2
Litherland 233 E3
Litlington *Cambs.* 200 B3
Litlington *E.Suss.* 160 A3
Little Abington 200 D3
Little Addington 211 E5
Little Alne 196 D1
Little Altcar 233 E2
Little Amwell 186 C1
Little Ann 169 E3
Little Asby 250 B2
Little Assynt 330 D2
Little Aston 208 C3
Little Atherfield 157 D5
Little Ayton 253 E1
Little Baddow 187 G2
Little Badminton 182 A4
Little Ballinluig 301 E4
Little Bampton 259 F1
Little Bardfield 201 E4
Little Barford 199 G2
Little Barningham 228 C2
Little Barrington 183 E1
Little Barrow 220 B1
Little Barugh 253 G5
Little Bavington 270 B4
Little Bealings 202 D3
Little Bedwyn 169 D1
Little Beeby 210 B2
Little Bentley 202 C5
Little Berkhamsted 186 B2
Little Billing 198 D1
Little Birch 195 E4
Little Bispham 241 G3
Little Blakenham 202 C3
Little Bloxwich 208 C2
Little Bollington 234 B4
Little Bookham 171 G2
Little Bourton 197 G3
Little Bowden 210 C4
Little Bradley 201 E2
Little Brampton 206 C4
Little Braxted 188 B1
Little Brechin 303 D3
Little Brickhill 199 E4
Little Bridgeford 221 F5
Little Brington 198 B1
Little Bromley 202 B5
Little Broughton 259 D3
Little Budworth 220 C1
Little Burdon 252 C1
Little Burstead 187 F3
Little Burton 246 D3
Little Bytham 211 F1
Little Canford 155 G3
Little Carlton *Lincs.* 239 D4
Little Carlton *Notts.* 224 C2
Little Casterton 211 F1
Little Catwick 246 D3
Little Catworth 211 F5
Little Cawthorpe 239 D4
Little Chalfield 167 F1
Little Chalfont 185 E3
Little Chart 174 B4
Little Chesterford 200 D3
Little Chesterton 198 A5
Little Cheverell 168 A2
Little Clacton 189 E1
Little Clanfield 183 E2
Little Clifton 259 D4
Little Coates 238 C2
Little Comberton 196 B3
Little Common 160 C3
Little Compton 197 E4
Little Corby 260 A2
Little Cornard 201 G4
Little Cowarne 195 F2
Little Coxwell 183 E3
Little Crakehall 252 B3
Little Cransley 210 D5
Little Crawley 199 E3
Little Creaton 210 C5
Little Creich 321 F1
Little Cressingham 213 G3
Little Crosby 233 E2
Little Crosthwaite 259 F4
Little Cubley 222 C4
Little Dalby 210 C1
Little Dens 325 F5
Little Dewchurch 195 E4
Little Ditton 201 E2
Little Doward 181 E1
Little Down 169 E2
Little Downham 212 D4
Little Drayton 221 D4
Little Driffield 246 C2
Little Dunham 213 G1
Little Dunkeld 301 F5
Little Dunmow 201 E5
Little Durnford 168 C4
Little Easton 201 E5
Little Eaton 223 E3
Little Eccleston 242 A4
Little Ellingham 214 B2
Little End 187 E2
Little Everdon 198 A2
Little Eversden 200 B2
Little Fakenham 214 A4
Little Faringdon 183 E2
Little Fencote 252 B3
Little Fenton 245 E4
Little Finborough 202 B2
Little Fransham 228 A4
Little Gaddesden 185 E1
Little Garway 194 D5
Little Gidding 211 G4
Little Glemham 203 E2
Little Glenshee 293 E1
Little Gorsley 195 F5
Little Gransden 200 A2
Little Green *Cambs.* 200 A3
Little Green *Notts.* 224 C3
Little Green *Suff.* 214 B4
Little Green *Suff.* 214 B4
Little Green *Wrex.* 220 B3
Little Grimsby 238 D3
Little Gringley 237 E4
Little Gruinard 319 F1
Little Habton 253 G5
Little Hadham 200 C5
Little Hale 225 G3
Little Hallingbury 187 D1
Little Hampden 185 D2
Little Haresfield 182 A2
Little Harrowden 211 D5
Little Haseley 184 B2
Little Hatfield 247 D3
Little Hautbois 229 D3
Little Haven *Pembs.* 176 B1
Little Haven *W.Suss.* 171 G4
Little Hay 208 D2
Little Hayfield 235 E4
Little Haywood 222 B5
Little Heath 209 F4
Little Hereford 195 E1
Little Hockham 214 A2
Little Horkesley 202 A4
Little Hormead 200 C5
Little Horsted 159 G2
Little Horton 168 B1
Little Horwood 198 C4
Little Houghton 198 D2
Little Hucklow 235 F5
Little Hulton 234 B2
Little Hungerford 184 A5
Little Hutton 253 D5
Little Idoch 324 C5
Little Irchester 199 E1
Little Keyford 167 E3
Little Kimble 184 D2
Little Kineton 197 F2
Little Kingshill 185 D3
Little Langdale 249 E2
Little Langford 168 B4
Little Laver 187 E2
Little Lawford 209 G5
Little Leigh 234 A5
Little Leighs 187 G1
Little Lever 234 B2
Little Ley 312 B3
Little Linford 198 D3
Little Linton 201 D3
Little London *Bucks.* 184 B1
Little London *E.Suss.* 160 A2
Little London *Essex* 200 C5
Little London *Hants.* 169 E3
Little London *Hants.* 170 B2
Little London *I.o.M.* 240 B3
Little London *Lincs.* 226 C5
Little London *Lincs.* 226 A5
Little London *Lincs.* 238 D5
Little London *Lincs.* 238 B4
Little London *Norf.* 227 D5
Little London *Norf.* 213 F3
Little London *Oxon.* 184 A2
Little London *Powys* 205 G4
Little London *Suff.* 202 B2
Little London *W.Yorks.* 244 B4
Little Longstone 235 F5
Little Lyth 207 D2
Little Malvern 195 G3
Little Malvern Court 66
Little Maplestead 201 G4
Little Marcle 195 F4
Little Marland 163 F4
Little Marlow 185 D4
Little Marsden 243 E4
Little Massingham 227 F5
Little Melton 228 C5
Little Milford 176 C1
Little Mill 180 C2
Little Milton 184 B2
Little Missenden 185 E3
Little Moreton Hall 97
Little Musgrave 250 C1
Little Ness 206 D1
Little Neston 233 D5
Little Newcastle 190 C5
Little Newsham 252 A1
Little Oakley *Essex* 202 D5
Little Oakley *Northants.* 211 D4
Little Odell 199 E2
Little Offley 199 G5
Little Onn 208 A1
Little Orton *Cumb.* 259 G1
Little Orton *Leics.* 209 F2
Little Ouse 213 E4
Little Ouseburn 244 D1
Little Overton 220 A3
Little Packington 209 E4
Little Parndon 186 D1
Little Paxton 199 G1
Little Petherick 146 D2
Little Plumpton 241 G4
Little Plumstead 229 E4
Little Ponton 225 E4
Little Posbrook 157 E2
Little Potheridge 163 F4
Little Preston 198 A2
Little Raveley 212 A4
Little Ribston 244 C2
Little Rissington 183 D1
Little Rogart 332 C4
Little Rollright 197 E4
Little Ryburgh 228 A3
Little Ryle 279 E5
Little Ryton 207 D2
Little Salkeld 260 B4
Little Sampford 201 E4
Little Saxham 201 G1
Little Scatwell 320 C4
Little Shelford 200 C2
Little Shrawardine 206 C1
Little Silver 152 C2
Little Singleton 241 G4
Little Smeaton *N.Yorks.* 236 C1
Little Smeaton *N.Yorks.* 252 C2
Little Snoring 228 A2
Little Sodbury 181 G4
Little Sodbury End 181 G4
Little Somborne 169 E4
Little Somerford 182 B4
Little Soudley 221 E5
Little Stainforth 243 E1
Little Stainton 252 C1
Little Stanney 233 F5
Little Staughton 199 G1
Little Steeping 226 C1
Little Stoke 221 G4
Little Stonham 202 C2
Little Street 212 D4
Little Stretton *Leics.* 210 B3
Little Stretton *Shrop.* 206 D3
Little Strickland 249 G1
Little Stukeley 212 A5
Little Sugnall 221 F4
Little Sutton 233 E5
Little Swinburne 270 B4
Little Tarrington 195 F3
Little Tew 197 F5
Little Tey 201 G5
Little Thetford 212 D5
Little Thornage 228 B2
Little Thornton 241 G3
Little Thorpe 262 D3
Little Thurlow 201 E2
Little Thurlow Green 201 E2
Little Thurrock 187 F5
Little Torboll 332 C5
Little Torrington 163 E4
Little Tosson 270 C1
Little Totham 188 B1
Little Town *Cumb.* 259 F5
Little Town *Lancs.* 242 C4
Little Town *Warr.* 234 A3
Little Twycross 209 F2
Little Urswick 249 D5
Little Wakering 188 C4
Little Walden 200 D3
Little Waldingfield 202 A3
Little Walsingham 228 A2
Little Waltham 187 G1
Little Warley 187 F3
Little Washbourne 196 B4
Little Weighton 246 B4
Little Welland 196 A4
Little Welnetham 201 G1
Little Wenham 202 B4
Little Wenlock 207 F2
Little Whittington 261 F1
Little Wilbraham 200 D2
Little Wishford 168 B4
Little Witcombe 182 B1
Little Witley 195 G1
Little Wittenham 184 A3
Little Wittingham Green 215 D4
Little Wolford 197 E4
Little Woodcote 172 B2
Little Wratting 201 E3
Little Wymington 199 E1
Little Wymondley 200 A5
Little Wyrley 208 C2
Little Wytheford 207 E1
Little Yeldham 201 F4
Littlebeck 254 B2
Littleborough *Devon* 152 B1
Littleborough *Gt.Man.* 234 D1
Littleborough *Notts.* 237 F4
Littlebourne 175 E3
Littlebredy 154 B4
Littlebury 200 D4
Littlebury Green 200 C4
Littledean 181 F1
Littleferry 332 D5
Littleham *Devon* 163 E3
Littleham *Devon* 152 D4
Littlehampton 158 C3
Littlehempston 151 E1
Littlehoughton 279 G5
Littlemill *E.Ayr.* 274 C4
Littlemill *High.* 322 B4
Littlemoor *Derbys.* 223 E1
Littlemoor *Dorset* 154 C4
Littlemore 184 A2
Littlemoss 234 D3
Littleover 223 E4
Littleport 213 D4
Littlestead Green 184 C5
Littlestone-on-Sea 161 F1
Littlethorpe 244 C1
Littleton *Ches.* 220 B1
Littleton *Hants.* 169 F4
Littleton *P. & K.* 294 A1
Littleton *Som.* 166 B4
Littleton *Surr.* 171 F1
Littleton Drew 182 A4
Littleton Panell 168 B2
Littleton-on-Severn 181 E3
Littletown *Dur.* 262 C3
Littletown *I.o.W.* 157 E3
Littlewick Green 184 D5
Littlewindsor 154 A2
Littleworth *Glos.* 196 D4
Littleworth *Oxon.* 183 F3
Littleworth *S.Yorks.* 236 D3
Littleworth *Staffs.* 208 C1
Littleworth *Worcs.* 196 A3
Littley Green 187 F1
Litton *Derbys.* 235 F5
Litton *N.Yorks.* 251 E5
Litton *Som.* 166 C2
Litton Cheney 154 B3
Liurbost (Leurbost) 329 E5
Liverpool 233 E3
Liverpool Cathedral 97
Liverpool John Lennon Airport 233 F4
Liverpool Museum 97
Liversedge 244 B5
Liverton *Devon* 152 B5
Liverton *R. & C.* 253 G1
Liverton Street 174 A4
Living Rainforest 46
Livingston 285 E3
Livingston Village 285 E3
Lixwm 232 C5
Lizard 145 E5
Lizard Peninsula 31
Llaingarreglwyd 192 A2
Llaingoch 230 A4
Llaithddu 205 G4
Llampha 179 F5
Llan 205 E2
Llan Ffestiniog (Ffestiniog) 218 A3
Llanaber 204 C1
Llanaelhaearn 216 C3
Llanaeron 192 A1
Llanafan 204 C5
Llanafan-fawr 193 F2
Llanafan-fechan 193 F2
Llanallgo 230 D4
Llanarmon 216 D4
Llanarmon Dyffryn Ceiriog 219 E4
Llanarmon-yn-Ial 219 E2
Llanarth *Cere.* 192 A2
Llanarth *Mon.* 180 C1
Llanarthney 192 B5
Llanasa 232 C4
Llanbabo 230 B4
Llanbadarn Fawr 204 B4
Llanbadarn Fynydd 205 G5
Llanbadarn-y-garreg 194 A3
Llanbadoc 180 C2
Llanbadrig 230 B3
Llanbeder 180 C3
Llanbedr *Gwyn.* 217 E5
Llanbedr *Powys* 194 B5
Llanbedr *Powys* 194 A3
Llanbedr-Dyffryn-Clwyd 219 E2
Llanbedrgoch 230 D4
Llanbedrog 216 C4
Llanbedr-y-cennin 218 A1
Llanberis 217 E2
Llanberis Lake Railway 111
Llanbethery 164 D1
Llanbister 206 A5
Llanblethian 179 F5
Llanboidy 191 F5
Llanbradach 180 A3
Llanbryn-mair 205 E2
Llancadle 164 D1
Llancarfan 179 G5
Llancayo 180 C2
Llancynfelyn 204 C3
Llandafal 180 A2
Llandaff 180 A5
Llandaff North 180 A5
Llandanwg 217 E5
Llandawke 177 F1
Llanddaniel Fab 230 C5
Llanddarog 178 A1
Llanddeiniol 204 B5
Llanddeiniolen 217 E1
Llandderfel 218 C4
Llanddeusant *Carmar.* 193 D5
Llanddeusant *I.o.A.* 230 B4
Llanddew 193 G4
Llanddewi 178 A4
Llanddewi Rhydderch 180 C1
Llanddewi Skirrid 180 C1
Llanddewi Velfrey 177 E1
Llanddewi Ystradenni 194 A1
Llanddewi-Brefi 192 C2
Llanddewi'r Cwm 193 G3
Llanddoged 218 B1
Llanddona 231 D5
Llanddowror 177 F1
Llanddulas 232 A5
Llanddwywe 217 E5
Llanddyfnan 230 D5
Llandefaelog Fach 193 G4
Llandefaelog-tre'r-graig 194 A5
Llandefalle 194 A4
Llandegfan 231 D5
Llandegla 219 E2
Llandegley 194 A1
Llandegveth 180 C3
Llandegwning 216 B4
Llandeilo 192 C5
Llandeilo Abercywyn 177 G1
Llandeilo Graban 193 G3
Llandeilo'r-Fan 193 E4
Llandeloy 190 B5
Llandenny 180 D2
Llandevaud 180 D3
Llandevenny 180 D4
Llandinabo 195 E5
Llandinam 205 G4
Llandissilio 191 E5
Llandogo 181 E2
Llandough *V. of Glam.* 180 A5
Llandough *V. of Glam.* 179 F5

Lower Machen 180 B4
Lower Maes-coed 194 C4
Lower Mannington 155 G2
Lower Middleton Cheney 198 A3
Lower Milton 166 C3
Lower Moor 196 B3
Lower Morton 181 F3
Lower Nash 176 D2
Lower Nazeing 186 C2
Lower Netchwood 207 F3
Lower Nyland 167 E5
Lower Oddington 197 E5
Lower Ollach 306 B1
Lower Penarth 180 A5
Lower Penn 208 A3
Lower Pennington 156 C3
Lower Peover 234 B5
Lower Pollicott 184 C1
Lower Quinton 197 D3
Lower Race 180 B2
Lower Rainham 174 A2
Lower Roadwater 164 D4
Lower Sapey 195 F1
Lower Seagry 182 B4
Lower Shelton 199 E3
Lower Shiplake 184 C5
Lower Shuckburgh 197 G1
Lower Slaughter 197 D5
Lower Soothill 244 B5
Lower Stanton St. Quintin 182 B4
Lower Stoke 174 A1
Lower Stondon 199 G4
Lower Stone 181 F3
Lower Stonnall 208 C2
Lower Stow Bedon 214 A2
Lower Street *Dorset* 155 E3
Lower Street *E.Suss.* 160 C2
Lower Street *Norf.* 229 D2
Lower Street *Norf.* 228 C2
Lower Street *Suff.* 202 C2
Lower Stretton 234 A4
Lower Sundon 199 F5
Lower Swanwick 157 D2
Lower Swell 197 D5
Lower Tadmarton 197 G4
Lower Tale 153 D2
Lower Tean 222 B4
Lower Thurlton 215 F2
Lower Thurnham 242 A2
Lower Town *Cornw.* 145 D4
Lower Town *Devon* 152 A5
Lower Town *I.o.S.* 146 B1
Lower Town *Pembs.* 190 C4
Lower Trebullett 148 D3
Lower Tysoe 197 F3
Lower Upcott 152 B4
Lower Upham 157 E1
Lower Upnor 187 G5
Lower Vexford 165 E4
Lower Wallop 206 C2
Lower Walton 234 A4
Lower Waterhay 182 C3
Lower Weald 198 C4
Lower Wear 152 C4
Lower Weare 166 B2
Lower Welson 194 B2
Lower Whatley 167 E3
Lower Whitley 234 A5
Lower Wick 196 A2
Lower Wield 170 B3
Lower Winchendon (Nether Winchendon) 184 C1
Lower Withington 221 F1
Lower Woodend 184 D4
Lower Woodford 168 C4
Lower Wyche 195 G3
Lowerhouse 243 E4
Lowertown 338 D3
Lowesby 210 C2
Lowestoft 215 G2
Loweswater 259 E4
Lowfield Heath 172 B4
Lowgill *Cumb.* 250 B3
Lowgill *Lancs.* 242 C1
Lowick *Cumb.* 249 D4
Lowick *Northants.* 211 E4
Lowick *Northumb.* 279 E3
Lowick Bridge 249 D4
Lowick Green 249 D4
Lownie Moor 302 C5
Lowry, The 97
Lowsonford 197 D1
Lowther 260 B5
Lowther Castle 260 B5
Lowthorpe 246 C1
Lowton *Devon* 163 G5
Lowton *Gt.Man.* 234 A3
Lowton *Som.* 153 E1
Lowton Common 234 A3
Loxbeare 152 C1
Loxhill 171 F4
Loxhore 163 G2
Loxley 197 E2
Loxley Green 222 B4
Loxton 166 A2
Loxwood 171 F4
Lubachoinnich 331 G5
Lubcroy 331 F4
Lubenham 210 C4
Lubfearn 320 C2
Lubmore 319 G4
Lubreoch 299 G5
Luccombe 164 C3
Luccombe Village 157 E4
Lucker 279 F3
Luckett 149 D3
Luckington 182 A4
Lucklawhill 294 C2
Luckwell Bridge 164 C4
Lucton 194 D1
Lucy Cross 252 B1
Ludag 314 C2
Ludborough 238 C3
Ludbrook 150 C2
Ludchurch 177 E1
Luddenden 243 G5
Luddenden Foot 243 G5
Luddenham Court 174 B2
Luddesdown 173 F2
Luddington *N.Lincs.* 237 F1
Luddington *Warks.* 197 D2
Luddington in the Brook 211 G4
Ludford *Lincs.* 238 B4
Ludford *Shrop.* 207 E5
Ludgershall *Bucks.* 184 B1
Ludgershall *Wilts.* 169 D2
Ludgvan 144 C3
Ludham 229 E4
Ludlow 66
Ludlow Castle 66
Ludney 239 D3
Ludstock 195 F4
Ludstone 208 A3
Ludwell 168 A5
Ludworth 262 C3
Luffincott 148 D1
Luffness 286 B1
Lufton 154 B1
Lugar 275 D3
Luggate 286 C2
Luggate Burn 286 D2
Luggiebank 284 B2
Lugton 283 F4
Lugwardine 195 E3
Luib 306 B2
Luibeilt 299 E3
Luing 289 G3
Lulham 194 D3
Lullingstone Castle 46
Lullingstone Roman Villa 47
Lullington *Derbys.* 209 E1
Lullington *Som.* 167 E2
Lulsgate Bottom 166 C1
Lulsley 195 G2
Lulworth Camp 155 E4
Lulworth Castle 32
Lulworth Cove & Heritage Centre 32
Lumb *Lancs.* 243 E5
Lumb *W.Yorks.* 243 G5
Lumbutts 243 F5
Lumby 245 D4
Lumphanan 312 A4
Lumphinnans 293 G5
Lumsdaine 287 F3
Lumsdale 223 E1
Lumsden 311 G2
Lunan 303 E4
Lunanhead 302 C4
Luncarty 293 F2
Lund *E.Riding* 246 B3
Lund *N.Yorks.* 245 F4
Lund *Shet.* 345 E2
Lundale 328 C4
Lundavra 298 C3
Lunderton 325 G5
Lundie *Angus* 294 A1
Lundie *High.* 308 A3
Lundin Links 294 C4
Lundwood 236 A2
Lundy 162 B1
Lundy Island 32
Lunga 290 A4
Lunna 343 D1
Lunning 343 E1
Lunnon 178 B4
Lunsford's Cross 160 C2
Lunt 233 E2
Luntley 194 C2
Luppitt 153 E2
Lupset 236 A1
Lupton 249 G4
Lurgashall 171 E5
Lurignich 298 B4
Lusby 226 B1
Luss 291 F5
Lussagiven 281 E1
Lusta 317 F4
Lustleigh 152 A4
Luston 195 D1
Luthermuir 303 E3
Luthrie 294 B3
Luton *Devon* 153 D2
Luton *Devon* 152 B5
Luton *Luton* 199 F5
Luton *Med.* 173 G2
Luton Airport (London Luton Airport) 199 G5
Lutterworth 210 A4
Lutton *Devon* 150 B2
Lutton *Dorset* 155 F4
Lutton *Lincs.* 226 C5
Lutton *Northants.* 211 G4
Luxborough 164 C4
Luxulyan 147 E4
Lybster *High.* 336 C2
Lybster *High.* 337 E5
Lydacott 163 E5
Lydbury North 206 C4
Lydcott 163 G2
Lydd 161 F1
Lydd Airport 161 F1
Lydden 175 E4
Lyddington 211 D3
Lyddington Bede House 73
Lydd-on-Sea 161 F1
Lyde Green 181 F5
Lydeard St. Lawrence 165 E4
Lydford 149 F2
Lydford Gorge 32
Lydford-on-Fosse 166 C4
Lydgate *Gt.Man.* 235 D1
Lydgate *Gt.Man.* 235 D2
Lydgate *W.Yorks.* 243 F5
Lydham 206 C3
Lydiard Mansion 32
Lydiard Millicent 182 C4
Lydiard Tregoze 182 D4
Lydiate 233 E2
Lydlinch 154 D1
Lydney 181 F2
Lydstep 177 D3
Lye 208 B4
Lye Cross 166 B1
Lye Green *Bucks.* 185 E2
Lye Green *E.Suss.* 173 E5
Lye Green *Warks.* 197 D1
Lye's Green 167 F3
Lyford 183 F3
Lymbridge Green 174 D4
Lyme Park 97
Lyme Regis 153 G3
Lymekilns 284 A4
Lyminge 175 D4
Lymington 156 C3
Lyminster 158 C3
Lymm 234 A4
Lymore 156 B3
Lympne 174 D5
Lympsham 166 A2
Lympstone 152 C4
Lynaberack 309 G5
Lynch 164 B3
Lynch Green 228 C5
Lynchat 309 G4
Lyndhurst 156 B2
Lyndon 211 E2
Lyne *Aber.* 312 C4
Lyne *Sc.Bord.* 285 G5
Lyne *Surr.* 171 F1
Lyne Down 195 F4
Lyne of Gorthleck 309 E2
Lyne of Skene 312 C3
Lyne Station 285 G5
Lyneal 220 B4
Lynedale House 317 G4
Lynegar 337 E3
Lyneham *Oxon.* 197 E5
Lyneham *Wilts.* 182 C5
Lyneholmeford 268 D4
Lynemore *High.* 310 C2
Lynemore *Moray* 310 D1
Lynemouth 271 E2
Lyness 338 C3
Lynford 213 G3
Lyng *Norf.* 228 B4
Lyng *Som.* 166 A5
Lyngate 229 E3
Lynmouth 164 A3
Lynn 207 G1
Lynsted 174 B2
Lynstone 162 C5
Lynton 164 A3
Lynton & Lynmouth Cliff Railway 32
Lyon's Gate 154 C2
Lyonshall 194 C2
Lyrabus 280 A3
Lytchett Matravers 155 F3
Lytchett Minster 155 F3
Lytes Cary Manor 32
Lyth 337 E2
Lytham 241 G5
Lytham St. Anne's 241 G5
Lythe 254 B1
Lythe Hill 171 E4
Lythes 339 D4
Lythmore 336 C2
Lyveden New Bield 73

M

Maaruig (Maraig) 327 E3
Mabe Burnthouse 145 E3
Mabie 267 D3
Mablethorpe 239 F4
Macclesfield 234 D5
Macclesfield Forest 235 D5
Macduff 324 C3
Macedonia 294 A4
Machan 284 B4
Machany 293 D3
Macharioch 272 C5
Machen 180 B4
Machrie *Arg. & B.* 280 A3
Machrie *Arg. & B.* 280 B5
Machrie *N.Ayr.* 273 D2
Machrihanish 272 B3
Machrins 288 C5
Machynlleth 204 D2
McInroy's Point 282 D2
Mackerye End 186 A1
Mackworth 223 E4
McManus Galleries 126
Macmerry 286 B2
Macterry 324 C5
Madame Tussaud's & The Planetarium 57
Madderty 293 E2
Maddiston 284 D2
Madehurst 158 B2
Madeley *Staffs.* 221 E3
Madeley *Tel. & W.* 207 G2
Madeley Heath 221 E3
Maders 148 D3
Madford 153 E1
Madingley 200 B1
Madjeston 167 F5
Madley 194 D4
Madresfield 196 A3
Madron 144 B3
Maenaddwyn 230 C4
Maenclochog 191 D5
Maendy *Cardiff* 180 A5
Maendy *V. of Glam.* 179 G5
Maenporth 145 E4
Maentwrog 217 F3
Maen-y-groes 191 G2
Maer *Cornw.* 162 C5
Maer *Staffs.* 221 E4
Maerdy *Carmar.* 192 C5
Maerdy *Carmar.* 192 C5
Maerdy *Conwy* 218 D3
Maerdy *R.C.T.* 179 F3
Maes Howe 126
Maesbrook 219 F5
Maesbury Marsh 220 A5
Maes-Glas (Greenfield) *Flints.* 232 C5
Maes-glas *Newport* 180 C4
Maesgwynne 191 F5
Maeshafn 219 F1
Maesllyn 191 G3
Maesmynis 193 G3
Maesteg 179 E3
Maes-Treylow 194 B1
Maesybont 178 B1
Maesycrugiau 192 A3
Maesycwmmer 180 A3
Maesyfed (New Radnor) 194 B1
Magdalen Laver 187 E2
Maggieknockater 323 F5
Maggots End 200 C5
Magham Down 160 B2
Maghull 233 E2
Magna Centre 88
Magna Park 210 A4
Magor 180 D4
Magpie Green 214 B4
Maiden Bradley 167 E4
Maiden Castle 33
Maiden Head 166 C1
Maiden Law 262 A3
Maiden Newton 154 B3
Maiden Wells 176 C3
Maidencombe 151 F1
Maidenhayne 153 F3
Maidenhead 185 D4
Maidens 274 A5
Maiden's Green 185 D5
Maidensgrove 184 C4
Maidenwell *Cornw.* 147 F2
Maidenwell *Lincs.* 238 D5
Maidford 198 B2
Maids' Moreton 198 C4
Maidstone 173 G3
Maidwell 210 C5
Mail 342 D5
Maindee 180 C4
Mainland *Ork.* 340 A5
Mainland *Shet.* 342 C2
Mains of Ardestie 294 D1
Mains of Balgavies 302 D4
Mains of Balhall 302 D3
Mains of Ballindarg 302 C4
Mains of Burgie 322 C4
Mains of Culsh 325 D5
Mains of Dillavaird 303 F1
Mains of Drum 312 D4
Mains of Dudwick 313 E1
Mains of Faillie 309 G1
Mains of Fedderate 325 D5
Mains of Glack 312 C2
Mains of Glassaugh 324 A3
Mains of Glenbuchat 311 F3
Mains of Linton 312 C3
Mains of Melgund 302 D4
Mains of Pitfour 325 E5
Mains of Pittrichie 313 D2
Mains of Sluie 322 C4
Mains of Tannachy 323 F3
Mains of Thornton 303 E2
Mains of Tig 264 C2
Mains of Watten 337 E3
Mainsforth 262 C4
Mainsriddle 266 D5
Mainstone 206 B4
Maisemore 196 A5
Major's Green 208 D5
Makendon 270 A1
Makeney 223 E3
Makerstoun 278 A3
Malacleit 315 F2
Malborough 150 D4
Malden Rushett 171 G1
Maldon 188 B2
Malham 243 F1
Malham Cove 88
Maligar 318 A3
Malinbridge 236 A4
Mallaig 306 C5
Mallaigmore 306 C5
Mallaigvaig 306 C5
Malleny Mills 285 F3
Malletsheugh 283 G4
Malling 292 A4
Mallows Green 200 C5
Malltraeth 216 D1
Mallwyd 205 E1
Malmesbury 182 B4
Malmsmead 164 A3
Malpas *Ches.* 220 B3
Malpas *Cornw.* 146 C5
Malpas *Newport* 180 C3
Maltby *Lincs.* 238 D4
Maltby *S.Yorks.* 236 C3
Maltby *Stock.* 253 D1
Maltby le Marsh 239 E4
Malting End 201 F2
Malting Green 188 C1
Maltman's Hill 174 A4
Malton 253 G5
Malvern Hills 67
Malvern Link 195 G3
Malvern Wells 195 G3
Mam Tor 73
Mambeg 282 D1
Mamble 207 F5
Mamhead 152 C4
Mamhilad 180 C2
Manaccan 145 E4
Manadon 150 A2
Manafon 206 A2
Manais (Manish) 326 D5
Manaton 152 A4
Manby 239 D4
Mancetter 209 F3
Manchester 234 C3
Manchester Airport 234 C4
Manchester Art Gallery 97
Mancot Royal 220 A1
Mandally 308 B4
Manderston 126
Manea 212 C4
Maneight 274 D5
Manfield 252 B1
Mangapps Railway Museum 81
Mangaster 344 C5
Mangerton 154 A3
Mangotsfield 181 F5
Mangrove Green 199 G5
Mangurstadh 328 B4
Manish (Manais) 326 D5
Mankinholes 243 F5
Manley 233 G5
Manmoel 180 A2
Mannal 296 A2
Manningford Abbots 168 C2
Manningford Bohune 168 C2
Manningford Bruce 168 C2
Manningham 244 A4
Mannings Heath 159 E1
Mannington 155 G2
Manningtree 202 C4
Mannofield 313 E4
Manor House 88
Manor Park 185 E4
Manorbier 177 D3
Manorbier Castle 111
Manorbier Newton 176 D2
Manordeifi 191 F3
Manordeilo 192 C5
Manorowen 190 C4
Mansell Gamage 194 C3
Mansell Lacy 194 D3
Mansergh 250 B4
Mansfield 223 G1
Mansfield Woodhouse 223 G1
Manson Green 228 B5
Mansriggs 249 D4
Manston *Dorset* 155 E1
Manston *Kent* 175 F2
Manston *W.Yorks.* 244 C4
Manswood 155 F2
Manthorpe *Lincs.* 211 F1
Manthorpe *Lincs.* 225 E4
Manton *N.Lincs.* 237 G2
Manton *Notts.* 236 C5
Manton *Rut.* 211 D2
Manton *Wilts.* 168 C1
Manuden 200 C5
Manwood Green 187 E1
Maolachy 290 A3
Maperton 167 D5
Maple Cross 185 F3
Maplebeck 224 C1
Mapledurham 184 B5
Mapledurham House & Mill 47
Mapledurwell 170 B2
Maplehurst 171 G5
Maplescombe 173 E2
Mapleton 222 C3
Mapperley *Derbys.* 223 F3
Mapperley *Notts.* 223 G3
Mapperton *Dorset* 154 B3
Mapperton *Dorset* 155 F3
Mapperton *Dorset* 33
Mappleborough Green 196 C1
Mappleton 247 E3
Mapplewell 236 A2
Mappowder 154 D2
Mar Lodge 310 C5
Maraig (Maaruig) 327 E3
Marazion 144 C3
Marbhig 327 G2
Marbury 220 C3
March 212 C3
Marcham 183 G3
Marchamley 220 C5
Marchamley Wood 220 C4
Marchington 222 C4
Marchington Woodlands 222 C5
Marchwiel 220 A3
Marchwood 156 C1
Marcross 164 C1
Marcus 302 D4
Marden *Here.* 195 E3
Marden *Kent* 173 G4
Marden *T. & W.* 271 F4
Marden *Wilts.* 168 B2
Marden Ash 187 E2
Marden Beech 173 G4
Marden Thorn 173 G4
Marden's Hill 173 D5
Mardon 278 D3
Mardy 180 C1
Mare Green 166 A5
Marefield 210 C2
Mareham le Fen 226 A1
Mareham on the Hill 226 A1
Maresfield 159 G1
Marfleet 246 D4
Marford 220 A2
Margam 179 D4
Margaret Marsh 155 E1
Margaret Roding 187 E1
Margaretting 187 F2
Margaretting Tye 187 F2
Margate 175 F1
Margnaheglish 273 F2
Margreig 266 C3
Margrove Park 253 F1
Marham 213 F2
Marhamchurch 162 C5
Marholm 211 G2
Marian Cwm 232 B5
Mariandyrys 231 E4
Marian-Glas 230 D4
Mariansleigh 164 A5
Marine Town 174 B1
Marishader 318 A3
Maristow House 150 A1
Mark 166 A3
Mark Causeway 166 A3
Mark Cross 173 E5
Markbeech 173 D4
Markby 239 E5
Markdhu 264 C3
Markeaton 223 E4
Market Bosworth 209 G2
Market Deeping 211 G1
Market Drayton 221 D4
Market Harborough 210 C4
Market Lavington 168 B2
Market Overton 211 D1
Market Rasen 238 B4
Market Stainton 238 C5
Market Street 229 D3
Market Warsop 223 G1
Market Weighton 246 A3
Market Weston 214 A4
Markethill 294 A1
Markfield 209 G1
Markham 180 A2
Markham Moor 237 E5
Markinch 294 A4
Markington 244 B1
Marks Gate 187 D3
Marks Tey 202 A5
Marksbury 167 D1
Markwell 149 D5
Markyate 185 F1
Marl Bank 195 G3
Marland 234 C1
Marlborough 168 C1
Marlbrook 208 B5
Marlcliff 196 C2
Marldon 151 E1
Marle Green 160 A2
Marlesford 203 E2
Marley Green 220 C3
Marley Hill 262 B2
Marlingford 228 C5
Marloes 176 A2
Marlow *Bucks.* 185 D4
Marlow *Here.* 206 D5
Marlpit Hill 172 D4
Marlpool 223 F3
Marnhull 155 D1
Marnoch 324 A4
Marple 235 D4
Marple Bridge 235 D4
Marr 236 C2
Marrel 333 F3
Marrick 251 F3
Marrister 343 E1
Marros 177 F2
Marsden *T. & W.* 262 C1
Marsden *W.Yorks.* 235 E1
Marsett 251 E4
Marsh 153 F1
Marsh Baldon 184 A3
Marsh Benham 169 F1
Marsh Gibbon 198 B5
Marsh Green *Devon* 152 D3
Marsh Green *Gt.Man.* 233 G2
Marsh Green *Kent* 172 D4
Marsh Green *Tel. & W.* 207 F1
Marsh Lane 236 B5
Marsh Street 164 C3
Marsh, The 206 C3
Marshall Meadows 287 G4
Marshalsea 153 G2
Marshalswick 186 A2
Marsham 228 C3
Marshaw 242 B2
Marshborough 175 F3
Marshbrook 206 D4
Marshchapel 239 D3
Marshfield *Newport* 180 B4
Marshfield *S.Glos.* 181 G5
Marshgate 148 B1
Marshland St. James 212 D2
Marshside 233 E1
Marshwood 153 G3
Marske 252 A2
Marske-by-the-Sea 263 F5
Marsland Green 234 A3
Marston *Ches.* 234 A5
Marston *Here.* 194 C2
Marston *Lincs.* 225 D3
Marston *Oxon.* 184 A2
Marston *Staffs.* 221 G5
Marston *Staffs.* 208 A1
Marston *Warks.* 209 E3
Marston *Wilts.* 168 A2
Marston Doles 197 G2
Marston Green 209 D4
Marston Magna 166 C5
Marston Meysey 182 D3
Marston Montgomery 222 C4
Marston Moretaine 199 E3
Marston on Dove 222 D5
Marston St. Lawrence 198 A3
Marston Stannett 195 E2
Marston Trussell 210 B4
Marstow 181 E1
Marsworth 185 E1
Marten 169 D1
Marthall 234 B5
Martham 229 F4
Martin *Hants.* 155 G1
Martin *Lincs.* 225 G2
Martin *Lincs.* 226 A1
Martin Drove End 168 B5
Martin Hussingtree 196 A1
Martin Mere 98
Martinhoe 163 G1
Martinscroft 234 A4
Martinstown 154 C4
Martlesham 202 D3
Martlesham Heath 202 D3
Martletwy 176 D1
Martley 195 G1
Martock 154 A1
Marton *Ches.* 221 F1
Marton *Cumb.* 248 D5
Marton *E.Riding* 247 D4
Marton *E.Riding* 247 E1
Marton *Lincs.* 237 F4
Marton *Middbro.* 253 E1
Marton *N.Yorks.* 244 D1
Marton *N.Yorks.* 253 G4
Marton *Shrop.* 206 B2
Marton *Shrop.* 220 B5
Marton *Warks.* 197 G1
Marton Abbey 245 E1
Marton-in-the-Forest 245 E1
Marton-le-Moor 252 C5
Martyr Worthy 169 G4
Martyr's Green 171 F2
Marwell Zoo 47
Marwick 340 A4
Marwood 163 F2
Marwood Hill 33
Mary Arden's House 67
Mary Rose 47
Mary Tavy 149 F3
Marybank *High.* 321 D4
Marybank *W.Isles* 329 F4
Maryburgh 321 E4
Maryfield *Cornw.* 150 A2
Maryfield *Shet.* 343 D3
Marygold 287 F4
Maryhill *Aber.* 324 D5
Maryhill *Glas.* 283 G3
Marykirk 303 E3
Marylebone *Gt.Lon.* 186 B4
Marylebone *Gt.Man.* 233 G2
Marypark 311 D1
Maryport *Cumb.* 258 D3
Maryport *D. & G.* 256 B3
Marystow 149 E2
Maryton 303 E4
Marywell *Aber.* 313 E5
Marywell *Aber.* 312 A5
Marywell *Angus* 303 E5
Masham 252 B4
Mashbury 187 F1
Masongill 250 B5
Mastin Moor 236 B5
Mastrick 313 E4
Matchborough 196 C1
Matching 187 E1
Matching Green 187 E1
Matching Tye 187 E1
Matfen 270 C4
Matfield 173 F4
Mathern 181 E3
Mathon 195 G3
Mathry 190 B4
Matlaske 228 C2
Matlock 223 E1
Matlock Bank 223 E1
Matlock Bath 223 D2
Matson 182 A1
Matterdale End 259 G4
Mattersey 237 D4
Mattersey Thorpe 237 D4
Mattingley 170 C2
Mattishall 228 B4
Mattishall Burgh 228 B4
Mauchline 274 C3
Maud 325 E5
Maufant 150 C5
Maugersbury 197 D5
Maughold 240 C2
Mauld 308 C1
Maulden 199 F4
Maulds Meaburn 250 B1
Maunby 252 C4
Maund Bryan 195 E2
Maundown 165 D5
Mautby 229 F4
Mavesyn Ridware 208 C1
Mavis Enderby 226 B1
Maw Green 221 E2
Mawbray 259 D2
Mawdesley 233 F1
Mawdlam 179 E4
Mawgan 145 E4
Mawgan Porth 146 C3
Mawla 146 A5
Mawnan 145 E4
Mawnan Smith 145 E4
Mawsley 210 D5
Mawthorpe 239 E5
Maxey 211 G2
Maxstoke 209 E4
Maxted Street 174 D4
Maxton *Kent* 175 F4
Maxton *Sc.Bord.* 278 A3
Maxwellheugh 278 B3
Maxwelltown 267 D3
Maxworthy 148 C1
Mayals 178 C3
Maybole 274 B5
Maybury 171 F2
Mayen 324 A5
Mayfair 186 B4
Mayfield *E.Suss.* 160 A1
Mayfield *Midloth.* 286 A3
Mayfield *Staffs.* 222 C3
Mayford 171 E2
Mayland 188 C2
Maylandsea 188 C2
Maynard's Green 160 A2
Maypole *I.o.S.* 146 B1
Maypole *Kent* 175 D2
Maypole *Mon.* 181 D1
Maypole Green *Essex* 202 A5
Maypole Green *Norf.* 215 F2
Maypole Green *Suff.* 203 D1
Maypole Green *Suff.* 202 A2
May's Green *N.Som.* 166 A1
Mays Green *Oxon.* 184 C4
Maywick 342 C5
Mead 162 C4
Mead End 168 B5
Meadgate 167 D2
Meadle 184 D2
Meadow Green 195 G2

Meadowhall 236 A3
Meadowmill 286 B2
Meadowtown 206 C2
Meadwell 149 E2
Meaford 221 F4
Meal Bank 249 G3
Mealabost (Melbost Borve) 329 F2
Mealasta 328 A5
Meals 239 E3
Mealsgate 259 F2
Meanley 242 D3
Meanwood 244 B4
Mearbeck 243 E1
Meare 166 B3
Meare Green 165 F5
Mearns 283 G4
Mears Ashby 198 D1
Measham 209 F1
Meathop 249 F4
Meavy 150 B1
Medbourne 210 D3
Meddon 162 C4
Meden Vale 223 G1
Medlar 242 A4
Medmenham 184 D4
Medomsley 262 A2
Medstead 170 B4
Meer Common 194 C2
Meer End 209 E5
Meerbrook 221 G1
Meesden 200 C4
Meeson 221 D5
Meeth 163 F5
Meeting House Hill 229 E3
Meggethead 276 C3
Meidrim 191 F5
Meifod *Denb.* 218 D2
Meifod *Powys* 206 A1
Meigle 302 A5
Meigle Sculptured Stones 126
Meikle Earnock 284 B4
Meikle Grenach 282 B3
Meikle Kilmory 282 B3
Meikle Rahane 282 D1
Meikle Strath 303 E2
Meikle Tarty 313 E2
Meikle Wartle 312 C1
Meikleour 293 G1
Meikleyard 274 D2
Meinciau 178 A1
Meir 221 G3
Meirheath 221 G4
Melbost 329 F4
Melbost Borve (Mealabost) 329 F2
Melbourn 200 B3
Melbourne *Derbys.* 223 E5
Melbourne *E.Riding* 245 G3
Melbourne Hall & Gardens 73
Melbury 163 D4
Melbury Abbas 155 E1
Melbury Bubb 154 B2
Melbury Osmond 154 B2
Melbury Sampford 154 B2
Melby 342 A2
Melchbourne 199 F1
Melcombe Bingham 155 D2
Melcombe Regis 154 C4
Meldon *Devon* 149 F1
Meldon *Northumb.* 270 D3
Meldreth 200 B3
Meledor 146 D4
Melford Hall 81
Melfort 290 A3
Melgarve 309 D5
Melgum 311 G4
Meliden (Gallt Melyd) 232 B4
Melincourt 179 E2
Melin-y-coed 218 B1
Melin-y-ddol 205 G2
Melin-y-grug 205 G2
Melin-y-Wig 218 D3
Melkinthorpe 260 B5
Melkridge 260 D1
Melksham 168 A1
Melksham Forest 168 A1
Melldalloch 282 A2
Mellerstain 127
Melling *Lancs.* 249 G5
Melling *Mersey.* 233 E2
Melling Mount 233 F2
Mellis 214 B4
Mellon Charles 330 A5
Mellon Udrigle 330 A5
Mellor *Gt.Man.* 235 D4
Mellor *Lancs.* 242 C4
Mellor Brook 242 C4
Mells 167 E3
Melmerby *Cumb.* 260 C4
Melmerby *N.Yorks.* 251 F4
Melmerby *N.Yorks.* 252 C5
Melplash 154 A3
Melrose *Aber.* 324 C3
Melrose *Sc.Bord.* 277 G2
Melrose Abbey 127
Melsetter 338 B4
Melsonby 252 A2
Meltham 235 E1
Melton *E.Riding* 246 B5
Melton *Suff.* 203 D2
Melton Carnegie Museum 73
Melton Constable 228 B2
Melton Mowbray 210 C1
Melton Ross 238 A1
Meltonby 245 G2
Melvaig 318 D1
Melverley 206 C1
Melverley Green 206 C1
Melvich 336 A2
Membury 153 F2
Memsie 325 E3
Memus 302 C4
Menabilly 147 E4
Menai Bridge (Porthaethwy) 231 D5
Mendham 215 D3
Mendips 33
Mendlesham 202 C1
Mendlesham Green 202 B1
Menethorpe 245 G1
Menheniot 147 G3
Menie House 313 E2
Menithwood 195 G1
Mennock 275 G5
Menston 244 A3
Menstrie 292 D5
Mentmore 185 E1
Meoble 297 G1
Meole Brace 207 D1
Meon 157 E2
Meonstoke 157 F1
Meopham 173 F2
Meopham Green 173 F2
Mepal 212 C4
Meppershall 199 G4
Merbach 194 C3
Mercaston 223 D3
Merchant Adventurers Hall 88
Mere *Ches.* 234 B4
Mere *Wilts.* 167 F4
Mere Brow 233 F1
Mere Green 208 D3
Mere Heath 234 A5
Mereclough 243 E4
Mereside 241 G4
Meretown 221 E5
Mereworth 173 F3
Mergie 303 F1
Meriden 209 E4
Merkadale 305 G1
Merkinch 321 F5
Merkland 266 B3
Merley 155 G3
Merlin's Bridge 176 C1
Merridge 165 F4
Merrifield 151 E3
Merrington 220 B5
Merrion 176 C3
Merriott 154 A1
Merrivale 149 F3
Merrow 171 F2
Merry Hill *Herts.* 186 A3
Merry Hill *W.Mid.* 208 B4
Merry Hill *W.Mid.* 208 A3
Merrymeet 147 G3
Mersea Island 188 D1
Mersey Ferries 98
Merseyside Maritime Museum 98
Mersham 174 C5
Merstham 172 B3
Merston 158 A3
Merstone 157 E4
Merther 146 C5
Merthyr 191 G5
Merthyr Cynog 193 F4
Merthyr Dyfan 165 E1
Merthyr Mawr 179 E5
Merthyr Tydfil 179 G2
Merthyr Vale 179 G3
Merton *Devon* 163 F4
Merton *Norf.* 214 A2
Merton *Oxon.* 184 A1
Mervinslaw 278 A5
Meshaw 152 A1
Messing 188 C1
Messingham 237 F2
Metcombe 153 D3
Metfield 215 D3
Metheringham 225 F1
Metherwell 150 A1
Methil 294 B5
Methlem 216 A4
Methley 244 C5
Methley Junction 244 C5
Methlick 313 D1
Methven 293 F2
Methwold 213 F3
Methwold Hythe 213 F3
MetroCentre 262 B1
Mettingham 215 E3
Metton 228 C2
Mevagissey 147 E5
Mewith Head 242 D1
Mexborough 236 B3
Mey 337 E1
Meysey Hampton 182 D2
Miabhag *W.Isles* 327 D4
Miabhag *W.Isles* 326 C3
Miabhaig (Miavaig) 328 B4
Mial 319 D2
Miavaig (Miabhaig) 328 B4
Michaelchurch 195 E5
Michaelchurch Escley 194 C4
Michaelchurch-on-Arrow 194 B2
Michaelston-le-Pit 180 A5
Michaelston-super-Ely 180 A5
Michaelston-y-Fedw 180 B4
Michaelstow 147 E2
Michelcombe 150 C1
Micheldever 169 G4
Michelham Priory 47
Michelmersh 169 E5
Mickfield 202 C1
Mickle Trafford 220 B1
Micklebring 236 C3
Mickleby 254 B1
Micklefield 244 D4
Micklefield Green 185 F3
Mickleham 171 G2
Micklehurst 235 D2
Mickleover 223 E4
Micklethwaite *Cumb.* 259 F1
Micklethwaite *W.Yorks.* 243 G3
Mickleton *Dur.* 261 F5
Mickleton *Glos.* 197 D3
Mickletown 244 C5
Mickley *Derbys.* 236 A5
Mickley *N.Yorks.* 252 B5
Mickley Green 201 G2
Mickley Square 261 G1
Mid Ardlaw 325 E3
Mid Beltie 312 B4
Mid Calder 285 E3
Mid Clyth 337 E5
Mid Hants Railway 47
Mid Lambrook 154 A1
Mid Lavant 158 A3
Mid Letter 290 C4
Mid Lix 292 A1
Mid Mossdale 250 D3
Mid Yell 345 E3
Midbea 340 C2
Middle Assendon 184 C4
Middle Aston 197 G5
Middle Barton 197 G5
Middle Bickenhill 209 E4
Middle Bockhampton 156 A3
Middle Claydon 198 C5
Middle Drift 147 F3
Middle Drums 303 D4
Middle Duntisbourne 182 B2
Middle Handley 236 B5
Middle Harling 214 A3
Middle Kames 282 A1
Middle Littleton 196 C3
Middle Maes-coed 194 C4
Middle Marwood 163 F2
Middle Mill 190 B5
Middle Quarter 174 A5
Middle Rasen 238 A4
Middle Rigg 293 F4
Middle Salter 242 C1
Middle Sontley 220 A3
Middle Stoford 165 E5
Middle Taphouse 147 F3
Middle Town 146 B1
Middle Tysoe 197 F3
Middle Wallop 169 D4
Middle Winterslow 168 D4
Middle Woodford 168 C4
Middlebie 268 A4
Middlecliff 236 B2
Middlecott 163 E5
Middleham 252 A4
Middlehill *Aber.* 324 D5
Middlehill *Cornw.* 147 G3
Middlehope 207 E4
Middlemarsh 154 C2
Middlemoor 149 E3
Middlequarter (Ceathramh Meadhanach) 315 G2
Middlesbrough 263 D5
Middlesceugh 260 A3
Middleshaw 249 G4
Middlesmoor 251 F5
Middlestone 262 B4
Middlestone Moor 262 B4
Middlestown 235 G1
Middleton *Aber.* 312 D3
Middleton *Angus* 303 D5
Middleton *Cumb.* 250 B4
Middleton *Derbys.* 223 D2
Middleton *Derbys.* 222 C1
Middleton *Essex* 201 G3
Middleton *Gt.Man.* 234 C2
Middleton *Hants.* 169 F3
Middleton *Here.* 195 E1
Middleton *Lancs.* 242 A2
Middleton *Midloth.* 286 A4
Middleton *N.Yorks.* 253 G4
Middleton *Norf.* 213 E1
Middleton *Northants.* 210 D4
Middleton *Northumb.* 270 C3
Middleton *Northumb.* 279 E3
Middleton *P. & K.* 293 G4
Middleton *P. & K.* 301 G5
Middleton *Shrop.* 206 B3
Middleton *Shrop.* 207 E5
Middleton *Shrop.* 220 A5
Middleton *Suff.* 203 F1
Middleton *Swan.* 178 A4
Middleton *W.Yorks.* 244 A3
Middleton *W.Yorks.* 244 C5
Middleton *Warks.* 209 D3
Middleton Baggot 207 F3
Middleton Bank Top 270 C3
Middleton Cheney 197 G3
Middleton Green 221 G4
Middleton Hall 279 D4
Middleton Moor 203 F1
Middleton of Potterton 313 E3
Middleton on the Hill 195 E1
Middleton One Row 252 C1
Middleton Park 313 E3
Middleton Priors 207 F4
Middleton Quernhow 252 C5
Middleton Railway 88
Middleton St. George 252 C1
Middleton Scriven 207 F4
Middleton Stoney 198 A5
Middleton Tyas 252 B2
Middleton-in-Teesdale 261 F5
Middleton-on-Leven 253 D1
Middleton-on-Sea 158 B3
Middleton-on-the-Wolds 246 B3
Middletown *Cumb.* 248 A2
Middletown *Powys* 206 C1
Middlewich 221 E1
Middlewood *Ches.* 234 D4
Middlewood *S.Yorks.* 236 A3
Middlewood Green 202 B1
Middlezoy 166 A4
Middridge 262 B5
Midfield 335 E2
Midford 167 E1
Midge Hall 242 B5
Midgeholme 260 C2
Midgham 169 G1
Midgley *W.Yorks.* 235 G1
Midgley *W.Yorks.* 243 G5
Midhopestones 235 G3
Midhurst 171 D5
Midlem 277 G3
Midloe Grange 199 G1
Midpark 282 B4
Midsomer Norton 167 D2
Midthorpe 238 C5
Midtown *High.* 335 E2
Midtown *High.* 319 E1
Midtown of Barras 303 G1
Midville 226 B2
Midway 223 E5
Migdale 332 B5
Migvie 311 G4
Milarrochy 291 G5
Milber 152 B5
Milbethill 324 B4
Milborne Port 154 C1
Milborne St. Andrew 155 D3
Milborne Wick 167 D5
Milbourne *Northumb.* 270 D4
Milbourne *Wilts.* 182 B4
Milburn 260 C5
Milbury Heath 181 F3
Milcombe 197 G4
Milden 202 A3
Mildenhall *Suff.* 213 F5
Mildenhall *Wilts.* 168 D1
Mile Elm 168 A1
Mile End *Essex* 202 A5
Mile End *Glos.* 181 E1
Mile Oak 173 F4
Mile Town 174 B1
Milebrook 206 C5
Milebush 173 G4
Mileham 228 A4
Miles Green 221 F3
Miles Hope 195 E1
Milesmark 285 E1
Miles's Green 169 G1
Milfield 278 D3
Milford *Derbys.* 223 E3
Milford *Devon* 162 C3
Milford *Shrop.* 220 B5
Milford *Staffs.* 221 G5
Milford *Surr.* 171 E3
Milford Haven (Aberdaugleddau) 176 B2
Milford on Sea 156 B3
Milkwall 181 E2
Mill Bank 243 G5
Mill Brow 235 D4
Mill End *Bucks.* 184 C4
Mill End *Cambs.* 201 E2
Mill End *Herts.* 200 B4
Mill End Green 201 E5
Mill Green *Cambs.* 201 E3
Mill Green *Essex* 187 F2
Mill Green *Herts.* 186 B2
Mill Green *Norf.* 214 C3
Mill Green *Shrop.* 221 D5
Mill Green *Staffs.* 222 B5
Mill Green *Suff.* 203 E1
Mill Green *Suff.* 202 C2
Mill Green *Suff.* 202 A2
Mill Green *W.Mid.* 208 C2
Mill Hill *B'burn.* 242 C5
Mill Hill *Cambs.* 200 A2
Mill Hill *Gt.Lon.* 186 B3
Mill Houses 242 C1
Mill Lane 170 C2
Mill of Camsail 283 D1
Mill of Colp 324 C5
Mill of Elrick 325 E5
Mill of Fortune 292 C2
Mill of Kingoodie 312 D2
Mill of Monquich 313 D5
Mill of Uras 303 G1
Mill Side 249 F4
Mill Street *Kent* 173 F3
Mill Street *Norf.* 228 B4
Milland 170 D5
Millbank 325 F5
Millbeck 259 F4
Millbounds 341 D3
Millbreck 325 F5
Millbridge 170 D3
Millbrook *Beds.* 199 F4
Millbrook *Cornw.* 150 A2
Millbrook *Devon* 153 G3
Millbrook *S'ham.* 156 C1
Millburn *Aber.* 312 A2
Millburn *Aber.* 312 B1
Millcombe 151 E3
Millcorner 160 D1
Milldale 222 C2
Millden 313 E3
Milldens 302 D4
Millearne 293 E3
Millend 197 F5
Millenheath 220 C4
Millennium Galleries & Winter Gardens 89
Millerhill 286 A3
Miller's Dale 235 F5
Millers Green *Derbys.* 223 D2
Miller's Green *Essex* 187 E2
Millgate 243 E5
Millhalf 194 B3
Millhayes *Devon* 153 E1
Millhayes *Devon* 153 F2
Millholme 249 G3
Millhouse *Arg. & B.* 282 A2
Millhouse *Cumb.* 259 G3
Millhouse Green 235 G2
Millhousebridge 267 F2
Millikenpark 283 F3
Millin Cross 176 C1
Millington 246 A2
Millington Green 223 D3
Millmeece 221 F4
Millness 308 C1
Millom 248 C4
Millow 200 A3
Millpool 147 F2
Millport 282 C4
Millthorpe 236 A5
Millthrop 250 B3
Milltimber 313 D4
Milltown *Aber.* 311 E4
Milltown *Cornw.* 147 F4
Milltown *D. & G.* 268 B4
Milltown *Devon* 163 F2
Milltown *High.* 322 B5
Milltown of Aberdalgie 293 F2
Milltown of Auchindoun 311 F1
Milltown of Craigston 324 C4
Milltown of Edinvillie 323 E5
Milltown of Kildrummy 311 G3
Milltown of Rothiemay 324 A5
Milltown of Towie 311 G3
Milnathort 293 G4
Milners Heath 220 B1
Milngavie 283 G2
Milnrow 234 D1
Milnsbridge 235 F1
Milnthorpe 249 F4
Milovaig 317 E4
Milrig 274 D2
Milson 207 F5
Milstead 174 B3
Milston 168 C3
Milton *Angus* 302 B5
Milton *Cambs.* 200 C1
Milton *Cumb.* 260 B1
Milton *D. & G.* 266 C2
Milton *D. & G.* 266 C3
Milton *D. & G.* 264 D5
Milton *Derbys.* 223 E5
Milton *High.* 320 C4
Milton *High.* 321 G2
Milton *High.* 322 B4
Milton *High.* 318 D5
Milton *High.* 321 E5
Milton *High.* 337 F3
Milton *High.* 309 D1
Milton *Moray* 324 A3
Milton *N.Som.* 166 A1
Milton *Newport* 180 C4
Milton *Notts.* 237 E5
Milton *Oxon.* 197 G4
Milton *Oxon.* 183 G3
Milton *P. & K.* 293 E1
Milton *Pembs.* 176 D2
Milton *Ports.* 157 F3
Milton *Som.* 166 B5
Milton *Stir.* 292 A4
Milton *Stoke* 221 G2
Milton *W.Dun.* 283 F2
Milton Abbas 155 E2
Milton Abbot 149 E3
Milton Bridge 285 G3
Milton Bryan 199 E4
Milton Clevedon 167 D4
Milton Combe 150 A1
Milton Damerel 163 D4
Milton End 181 G1
Milton Ernest 199 F2
Milton Green 220 B2
Milton Hill 183 G3
Milton Keynes 199 D4
Milton Keynes Village 199 D4
Milton Lilbourne 168 C1
Milton Lodge 33
Milton Malsor 198 C2
Milton Morenish 292 B1
Milton of Auchinhove 312 A4
Milton of Balgonie 294 B4
Milton of Buchanan 291 G5
Milton of Cairnborrow 323 G5
Milton of Callander 292 A4
Milton of Campfield 312 B4
Milton of Campsie 284 A2
Milton of Coldwells 313 E1
Milton of Cullerlie 312 C4
Milton of Cushnie 312 A3
Milton of Dalcapon 301 E4
Milton of Inveramsay 312 C2
Milton of Noth 312 A2
Milton of Tullich 311 F5
Milton on Stour 167 E5
Milton Regis 174 A2
Milton Street 160 A3
Miltonduff 323 D3
Miltonhill 322 C3
Miltonise 264 C3
Milton-Lockhart 284 C5
Milton's Cottage 47
Milton-under-Wychwood 183 E1
Milverton *Som.* 165 E5
Milverton *Warks.* 197 F1
Milwich 221 G4
Mimbridge 171 E1
Minack Theatre 33
Minard 290 B5
Minard Castle 290 B5
Minchington 155 F1
Minchinhampton 182 A2
Mindrum 278 C3
Mindrummill 278 C3
Minehead 164 C3
Minera 219 F2
Minety 182 C3
Minety Lower Moor 182 C3
Minffordd *Gwyn.* 204 D1
Minffordd *Gwyn.* 217 E4
Minffordd *Gwyn.* 231 D5
Miningsby 226 B1
Minions 147 G2
Minishant 274 B4
Minley Manor 170 D2
Minllyn 205 E1
Minnes 313 E2
Minngearraidh 314 C1
Minnigaff 265 F4
Minnonie 324 C3
Minskip 244 C1
Minstead 156 B1
Minsted 171 D5
Minster *Kent* 174 B1
Minster *Kent* 175 F2
Minster Lovell 183 F1
Minsteracres 261 G2
Minsterley 206 C2
Minsterworth 181 G1
Minterne 33
Minterne Magna 154 C2
Minterne Parva 154 C2
Minting 238 B5
Mintlaw 325 F5
Minto 277 G3
Minton 206 D3
Minwear 176 D1
Minworth 209 D3
Miodar 296 B1
Mirbister 340 B5
Mirehouse *Cumb.* 258 C5
Mirehouse *Cumb.* 98
Mireland 337 F2
Mirfield 244 B5
Miserden 182 B2
Miskin *R.C.T.* 179 G4
Miskin *R.C.T.* 179 G3
Misselfore 168 B5
Misson 237 D3
Misterton *Leics.* 210 A4
Misterton *Notts.* 237 E3
Misterton *Som.* 154 A2
Mistley 202 C4
Mitcham 172 B2
Mitchel Troy 181 D1
Mitcheldean 181 F1
Mitchell 146 C4
Mitchelland 249 F3
Mitcheltroy Common 181 D2
Mitford 271 D3
Mithian 146 B4
Mitton 208 A1
Mixbury 198 B4
Mixenden 243 G5
Moar 300 A5
Moat 268 C4
Moats Tye 202 B2
Mobberley *Ches.* 234 B5
Mobberley *Staffs.* 222 B3
Moccas 194 C3
Mochdre *Conwy* 231 G5
Mochdre *Powys* 205 G4
Mochrum 256 D2
Mockbeggar *Hants.* 156 A2
Mockbeggar *Kent* 173 G4
Mockerkin 259 D4
Modbury 150 C2
Moddershall 221 G4
Modern Art Oxford 47
Modsarie 335 F2
Moelfre *I.o.A.* 230 D4
Moelfre *Powys* 219 E5
Moffat 276 B5
Mogerhanger 199 G3
Moin'a'choire 280 B3
Moine House 335 E3
Moira 209 F1
Molash 174 C3
Mol-chlach 306 A3
Mold (Yr Wyddgrug) 219 F1
Mole Hall Wildlife Park 81
Molehill Green *Essex* 201 D5
Molehill Green *Essex* 201 F5
Molescroft 246 C3
Molesden 270 D3
Molesworth 211 F5
Mollance 266 B4
Molland 164 B5
Mollington *Ches.* 233 E5
Mollington *Oxon.* 197 G3
Mollinsburn 284 B2
Monach Islands (Heisker Islands) 315 E3
Monachty 192 B1
Monachyle 291 G3
Monevechadan 291 D4
Monewden 202 D2
Moneydie 293 F2
Moneyrow Green 185 D5
Moniaive 266 B1
Monifieth 294 D1
Monikie 294 D1
Monimail 294 A3
Monington 191 E3
Monk Bretton 236 A2
Monk Fryston 245 E5
Monk Hesleden 263 D4
Monk Sherborne 170 B2
Monk Soham 202 D1
Monk Soham Green 202 D1
Monk Street 201 E5
Monken Hadley 186 B3
Monkerton 152 C3
Monkey World 33
Monkhide 195 F3
Monkhill 259 G1
Monkhopton 207 F3
Monkland 195 D2
Monkleigh 163 E3
Monknash 179 F5
Monkokehampton 163 F5
Monks Eleigh 202 A3
Monks Eleigh Tye 202 A3
Monk's Gate 159 E1
Monks' Heath 234 C5
Monk's Hill 174 A4
Monk's House 47
Monks Kirby 209 G4
Monks Risborough 184 D2
Monkscross 149 D3
Monkseaton 271 F4
Monkshill 324 C5
Monksilver 165 D4
Monkstadt 317 G3
Monkswood 180 C2
Monkton *Devon* 153 E2
Monkton *Kent* 175 E2
Monkton *Pembs.* 176 C2
Monkton *S.Ayr.* 274 B3
Monkton *T. & W.* 262 C1
Monkton *V. of Glam.* 179 F5
Monkton Combe 167 E1
Monkton Deverill 167 F4
Monkton Farleigh 167 F1
Monkton Heathfield 165 F5
Monkton Up Wimborne 155 G1
Monkton Wyld 153 G3
Monkwearmouth 262 C2
Monkwood 170 B4
Monmouth (Trefynwy) 181 E1
Monnington Court 194 C4
Monnington on Wye 194 C3
Monreith 257 D2
Montacute 154 B1
Monteach 325 D5
Montford 206 D1
Montford Bridge 206 D1
Montgarrie 312 A3
Montgomery (Trefaldwyn) 206 B3
Montgreenan 283 E5
Montrave 294 B4
Montrose 303 F4
Monument, The 58
Monxton 169 E3
Monyash 222 C1
Monymusk 312 B3
Monzie 293 D2
Moodiesburn 284 A2
Moons Moat North 196 C1
Moonzie 294 B3
Moor Allerton 244 C4
Moor Cock 242 C1
Moor Crichel 155 F2
Moor End *Beds.* 199 F2
Moor End *Beds.* 199 E5
Moor End *Cumb.* 249 G5
Moor End *E.Riding* 246 A4
Moor End *Lancs.* 241 G3
Moor End *N.Yorks.* 245 E4
Moor End *W.Yorks.* 243 G5
Moor Green *W.Mid.* 208 C4
Moor Green *Wilts.* 167 F1
Moor Head 244 A4
Moor Monkton 245 E2
Moor Row 258 D5
Moor Side *Cumb.* 248 D5
Moor Side *Lancs.* 242 A4
Moor Side *Lancs.* 242 A4
Moor Side *Lincs.* 226 A2
Moor Street 174 A2
Moor, The *E.Suss.* 160 D2
Moor, The *Kent* 160 C1
Moorby 226 A1
Moorcot 194 C2
Moordown 155 G3
Moore 233 G4
Moorend 259 G1
Moorends 237 D1
Moorfield 235 E3
Moorgreen *Hants.* 157 D1
Moorgreen *Notts.* 223 F3
Moorhall 236 A5
Moorhampton 194 C3
Moorhouse *Cumb.* 259 G1
Moorhouse *Notts.* 224 C1
Moorland (Northmoor Green) 166 A4
Moorlinch 166 A4
Moors Valley Country Park 33
Moorsholm 253 F1
Moorside *Dorset* 155 D1
Moorside *Gt.Man.* 235 D2
Moorside *W.Yorks.* 244 B4
Moorthorpe 236 B1
Moortown *I.o.W.* 156 D4
Moortown *Lincs.* 238 A3
Moortown *Tel. & W.* 207 F1
Morangie 321 G1
Morar 306 C5
Morborne 211 G3
Morchard Bishop 152 A2
Morcombelake 154 A3
Morcott 211 E2
Morda 219 F5
Morden *Dorset* 155 F3
Morden *Gt.Lon.* 172 B2
Morden Hall Park 58
Morden Park 172 B2
Mordiford 195 E4
Mordington Holdings 287 G4
Mordon 262 C5
More 206 C3
Morebath 164 C5
Morebattle 278 B4
Morecambe 242 A1

441

Portchester 157 F2
Portchester Castle 49
Portencross 282 C5
Portesham 154 C4
Portessie 323 G3
Portfield *Arg. & B.* 289 G2
Portfield *W.Suss.* 158 A3
Portfield Gate 176 C1
Portgate 149 E2
Portgordon 323 F3
Portgower 333 F3
Porth *Cornw.* 146 C3
Porth *R.C.T.* 179 G3
Porth Colmon 216 A4
Porth Mellin 145 D5
Porth Navas 145 E4
Porthaethwy (Menai Bridge) 231 D5
Porthallow *Cornw.* 145 E4
Porthallow *Cornw.* 147 G4
Porthcawl 179 E5
Porthcothan 146 C2
Porthcurno 144 A4
Porthcurno Sands 34
Porthgain 190 B4
Porthill 221 F3
Porthkerry 165 D1
Porthleven 144 D4
Porthmadog 217 E4
Porthmeor 144 B3
Portholland 147 D5
Porthoustock 145 F4
Porthpean 147 E4
Porthtowan 146 A5
Porthyrhyd *Carmar.* 192 D4
Porthyrhyd *Carmar.* 178 B1
Porth-y-waen 219 F5
Portincaple 291 E5
Portington 245 G4
Portinnisherrich 290 B3
Portinscale 259 F4
Portishead 181 D5
Portknockie 323 G3
Portland Castle 34
Portlethen 313 E5
Portlethen Village 313 E5
Portloe 145 G3
Portlooe 147 G4
Portmahomack 322 B1
Portmeirion 217 E4
Portmeirion Village 113
Portmellon 147 E5
Portmore 156 C3
Port-na-Con 334 D2
Portnacroish 298 B5
Portnaguran (Port nan Giùran) 329 G4
Portnahaven 280 A4
Portnalong 305 G1
Portnaluchaig 297 F1
Portobello 286 A2
Porton 168 C4
Portpatrick 264 B5
Portreath 146 A5
Portree 318 A5
Portscatho 145 F3
Portsea 157 F2
Portskerra 336 A2
Portskewett 181 E4
Portslade 159 E3
Portslade-by-Sea 159 E3
Portslogan 264 A5
Portsmouth 157 F3
Portsmouth Cathedral 49
Portsmouth Historic Dockyard 49
Portsonachan 290 C2
Portsoy 324 A3
Portuairk 296 D3
Portvoller 329 G4
Portway *Here.* 194 C3
Portway *Here.* 195 D3
Portway *Here.* 195 D4
Portway *Worcs.* 208 C5
Portwrinkle 149 D5
Portyerrock 257 E3
Posenhall 207 F2
Poslingford 197 F3
Postbridge 149 G3
Postcombe 184 C3
Postling 174 D5
Post-mawr (Synod Inn) 192 A2
Postwick 229 D5
Potarch 312 B5
Potsgrove 199 E5
Pott Row 227 F5
Pott Shrigley 234 D5
Potten End 185 F2
Potter Brompton 254 C5
Potter Heigham 229 F4
Potter Street 187 D2
Pottergate Street 214 C2
Potterhanworth 225 F1
Potterhanworth Booths 225 F1
Potteries Museum & Art Gallery 67
Potterne 168 A2
Potterne Wick 168 B2
Potternewton 244 C4
Potters Bar 186 B2
Potters Crouch 186 A2
Potter's Green 209 F4
Potters Marston 209 G3
Potterspury 198 C3
Potterton *Aber.* 313 E3
Potterton *W.Yorks.* 244 D4
Pottle Street 167 F3
Potto 253 D2
Potton 200 A3
Pott's Green 202 A5
Poughill *Cornw.* 162 C5
Poughill *Devon* 152 B2
Poulshot 168 A2
Poulton 182 D2
Poulton-le-Fylde 241 G4
Pound Bank 195 G3
Pound Green *E.Suss.* 160 A1
Pound Green *Suff.* 201 F2
Pound Green *Worcs.* 207 G5
Pound Hill 172 B5
Pound Street 169 F1
Poundbury 154 C3
Poundffald 178 B3
Poundfield 173 E5
Poundgate 159 G1
Poundland 264 C2
Poundon 198 B5
Poundsbridge 173 E4
Poundsgate 152 A5
Poundstock 148 C1
Povey Cross 172 B4
Pow Green 195 G3
Powburn 279 E5
Powderham 152 C4
Powderham Castle 34
Powerstock 154 B3
Powfoot 267 F4
Powick 196 A2
Powis Castle & Garden 113
Powler's Piece 163 D4
Powmill 293 F5
Poxwell 154 D4
Poyle 185 F5
Poynings 159 E2
Poyntington 167 D5
Poynton *Ches.* 234 D4
Poynton *Tel. & W.* 207 E1
Poynton Green 207 E1
Poyntzfield 321 G3
Poys Street 215 E4
Poyston 176 C1
Poyston Cross 176 C1
Poystreet Green 202 A2
Praa Sands 144 C4
Pratis 294 B4
Pratt's Bottom 173 D2
Praze-an-Beeble 144 D3
Predannack Wollas 145 D5
Prees 220 C4
Prees Green 220 C4
Prees Heath 220 C4
Prees Higher Heath 220 C4
Prees Lower Heath 220 C4
Preesall 241 G3
Preesgweene 219 F4
Prenbrigog 219 F1
Prendergast 176 C1
Prendwick 279 E5
Pren-gwyn 192 A3
Prenteg 217 E3
Prenton 233 E4
Prescot 233 F3
Prescott *Devon* 153 D1
Prescott *Shrop.* 220 B5
Presley 322 C4
Pressen 278 C3
Prestatyn 232 B4
Prestbury *Ches.* 234 D5
Prestbury *Glos.* 196 B5
Presteigne 194 C1
Presthope 207 E3
Prestleigh 166 D3
Prestolee 234 B2
Preston *B. & H.* 159 F3
Preston *Devon* 152 B5
Preston *Dorset* 154 D4
Preston *E.Loth.* 286 C2
Preston *E.Riding* 247 D4
Preston *Glos.* 195 F4
Preston *Glos.* 182 C2
Preston *Herts.* 199 G5
Preston *Kent* 174 C2
Preston *Kent* 175 E2
Preston *Lancs.* 242 B5
Preston *Northumb.* 279 F4
Preston *Rut.* 211 D2
Preston *Sc.Bord.* 287 E4
Preston *Shrop.* 207 E1
Preston *Som.* 165 D4
Preston *Suff.* 202 A2
Preston *Torbay* 151 E1
Preston *Wilts.* 182 C5
Preston Bagot 197 D1
Preston Bissett 198 B4
Preston Bowyer 165 E5
Preston Brockhurst 220 C5
Preston Brook 233 G4
Preston Candover 170 B3
Preston Capes 198 A2
Preston Deanery 198 C2
Preston Gubbals 207 D1
Preston Mill & Phantassie Dovecot 128
Preston on Stour 197 E3
Preston on the Hill 233 G4
Preston on Wye 194 C3
Preston Plucknett 154 B1
Preston upon the Weald Moors 207 F1
Preston Wynne 195 E3
Preston-le-Skerne 262 C5
Prestonpans 286 A2
Preston-under-Scar 251 F3
Prestwich 234 C2
Prestwick *Northumb.* 271 D4
Prestwick *S.Ayr.* 274 B3
Prestwick International Airport (Glasgow Prestwick International Airport) 274 B3
Prestwold 223 G5
Prestwood *Bucks.* 185 D2
Prestwood *Staffs.* 222 C3
Price Town 179 F3
Prickwillow 213 D4
Priddy 166 C2
Priest Hill 242 C4
Priest Hutton 249 G5
Priest Weston 206 B3
Priestcliffe 235 F5
Priestland 275 D2
Priestwood 173 F2
Primethorpe 210 A3
Primrose Green 228 B4
Primrose Hill 186 B4
Princes End 208 B3
Princes Gate 177 E1
Princes Risborough 184 D2
Princethorpe 209 G5
Princetown *Caerp.* 180 A1
Princetown *Devon* 149 F3
Prinknash Abbey & Park 34
Prior Muir 294 D3
Prior Park 34
Prior's Frome 195 E4
Priors Halton 207 D5
Priors Hardwick 197 G2
Priors Marston 197 G2
Prior's Norton 196 A5
Priors Park 196 A4
Priorslee 207 G1
Priorwood 128
Priory Wood 194 B3
Priston 167 D1
Pristow Green 214 C3
Prittlewell 188 B4
Privett 170 B5
Prixford 163 F2
Proaig 280 C4
Probus 146 C5
Protstonhill 324 D3
Prudhoe 261 G1
Prussia Cove 144 C4
Pubil 299 G5
Publow 166 D1
Puckeridge 200 B5
Puckington 153 G1
Pucklechurch 181 F5
Pucknall 169 E5
Puckrup 196 A4
Puddinglake 221 E1
Puddington *Ches.* 233 E5
Puddington *Devon* 152 B1
Puddlebrook 181 F1
Puddledock 214 B2
Puddletown 155 D3
Pudleston 195 E2
Pudsey 244 B4
Pugneys Country Park 90
Pulborough 158 C2
Pulborough Brooks R.S.P.B. Nature Reserve 49
Puldagon 337 F4
Puleston 221 E5
Pulford 220 A2
Pulham 154 D2
Pulham Market 214 C3
Pulham St. Mary 214 D3
Pulley 207 D2
Pulloxhill 199 F4
Pulrossie 321 G1
Pulverbatch 206 D2
Pumpherston 285 E3
Pumsaint 192 C3
Puncheston 190 D5
Puncknowle 154 B4
Punnett's Town 160 B1
Purbrook 157 F2
Purewell 156 A3
Purfleet 187 E5
Puriton 166 A3
Purleigh 188 B2
Purley 172 C2
Purley on Thames 184 B5
Purlogue 206 B5
Purlpit 167 F1
Purls Bridge 212 C4
Purse Caundle 154 C1
Purslow 206 C4
Purston Jaglin 236 B1
Purtington 153 G2
Purton *Glos.* 181 F2
Purton *Glos.* 181 F2
Purton *Wilts.* 182 C4
Purton Stoke 182 C3
Purves Hall 287 E5
Pury End 198 C3
Pusey 183 F3
Putlake Adventure Farm 34
Putley 195 F4
Putley Green 195 F4
Putney 186 B5
Putsborough 163 E1
Puttenham *Herts.* 185 D1
Puttenham *Surr.* 171 E3
Puttock End 201 G3
Putts Corner 153 E3
Puxton 166 B1
Pwll 178 A2
Pwllcrochan 176 C2
Pwlldefaid 216 A5
Pwll-glas 219 E2
Pwllgloyw 193 G4
Pwllheli 216 C4
Pwll-Mawr 180 B5
Pwllmeyric 181 E3
Pwll-trap 177 F1
Pwll-y-glaw 179 D3
Pye Corner *Herts.* 187 D1
Pye Corner *Kent* 174 A4
Pye Corner *Newport* 180 C4
Pye Green 208 B1
Pyecombe 159 E2
Pyle *Bridgend* 179 E4
Pyle *I.o.W.* 157 D5
Pyleigh 165 E4
Pylle 166 D4
Pymore *Cambs.* 212 C4
Pymore *Dorset* 154 A3
Pyrford 171 F2
Pyrford Green 171 F2
Pyrton 184 B3
Pytchley 211 D5
Pyworthy 162 D5

Q

Quabbs 206 B4
Quadring 226 A4
Quadring Eaudike 226 A4
Quainton 198 C5
Quarff 342 D4
Quarley 169 D3
Quarndon 223 E3
Quarr Hill 157 E3
Quarrier's Village 283 E3
Quarrington 225 F3
Quarrington Hill 262 C4
Quarry Bank 208 B4
Quarry Bank Mill & Styal Estate 98
Quarrybank 220 C1
Quarrywood 323 D3
Quarter 284 B4
Quarter, The 174 A4
Quatford 207 G3
Quatt 207 G4
Quebec 262 A3
Quebec House 49
Quedgeley 182 A1
Queen Adelaide 213 D4
Queen Camel 166 C5
Queen Charlton 166 D1
Queen Dart 152 B1
Queen Elizabeth II Country Park 105
Queen Oak 167 E4
Queen Street 173 F4
Queenborough 174 B1
Queen's Bower 157 E4
Queen's Head 220 A5
Queensbury *Gt.Lon.* 186 A4
Queensbury *W.Yorks.* 244 A4
Queensferry (South Queensferry) *Edin.* 285 F2
Queensferry *Flints.* 220 A1
Queensferry Museum 129
Queenzieburn 284 A2
Quemerford 168 B1
Quendale 343 F4
Quendon 200 D4
Queniborough 210 B1
Quenington 182 D2
Quernmore 242 B1
Queslett 208 C3
Quethiock 148 D4
Quholm 340 A5
Quick's Green 184 A5
Quidenham 214 B3
Quidhampton 169 G2
Quidinish (Cuidhtinis) 326 C5
Quilquox 313 E1
Quina Brook 220 C4
Quince Honey Farm 34
Quindry 338 D3
Quine's Hill 240 B4
Quinhill 281 F4
Quinton *Northants.* 198 C2
Quinton *W.Mid.* 208 B4
Quinton Green 198 C2
Quintrell Downs 146 C3
Quixhill 222 C3
Quoditch 149 E1
Quoig 292 D2
Quoiggs House 292 D4
Quoisley 220 C3
Quorn 210 A1
Quothquan 276 A2
Quoyloo 340 A4
Quoys 345 F1
Quoys of Reiss 337 F3

R

Raasay 318 B5
Raby 233 E5
Raby Castle 105
Rachan 276 C2
Rachub 217 F1
Rackenford 152 B1
Rackham 158 C2
Rackheath 229 D4
Racks 267 E3
Rackwick *Ork.* 338 B3
Rackwick *Ork.* 340 C2
Radbourne 223 D4
Radcliffe *Gt.Man.* 234 B2
Radcliffe *Northumb.* 271 E1
Radcliffe on Trent 224 B4
Radclive 198 B4
Radcot 183 E3
Raddington 164 D5
Radernie 294 C4
Radford *B. & N.E.Som.* 167 D2
Radford *Nott.* 223 G3
Radford *Oxon.* 197 G5
Radford *W.Mid.* 209 F4
Radford Semele 197 F1
Radipole 154 C4
Radlett 186 A2
Radley 184 A3
Radley Green 187 F2
Radmore Green 220 C2
Radnage 184 C3
Radstock 167 D2
Radstone 198 A3
Radway 197 F3
Radway Green 221 E2
Radwell *Beds.* 199 F2
Radwell *Herts.* 200 A4
Radwinter 201 E4
Radyr 180 A4
Raechester 270 B3
Raemoir House 312 B5
RAF Museum 67
Raffin 330 C1
Rafford 322 C4
Ragdale 224 B5
Ragged Appleshaw 169 E3
Raglan 180 D2
Raglan Castle 113
Ragley Hall 67
Ragnall 237 F5
Rahoy 297 F4
Railway Age, The 99
Rain Shore 234 C1
Rainford 233 F2
Rainham *Gt.Lon.* 187 E4
Rainham *Med.* 174 A2
Rainhill 233 F3
Rainhill Stoops 233 G3
Rainow 235 D5
Rainsough 234 B2
Rainton 252 C5
Rainworth 223 G2
Raisbeck 250 B2
Raise 260 D3
Rait 294 A2
Raithby *Lincs.* 226 B1
Raithby *Lincs.* 238 D4
Rake 170 D5
Raleigh's Cross 164 D4
Ram 192 B3
Ram Alley 168 D1
Ram Lane 174 B4
Ramasaig 317 E5
Rame *Cornw.* 145 E3
Rame *Cornw.* 150 A3
Rampisham 154 B2
Rampside 241 F1
Rampton *Cambs.* 200 C1
Rampton *Notts.* 237 F5
Ramsbottom 234 B1
Ramsbury 183 E5
Ramscraigs 333 G2
Ramsdean 170 C5
Ramsdell 169 G2
Ramsden 183 F1
Ramsden Bellhouse 187 G3
Ramsden Heath 187 G3
Ramsey *Cambs.* 212 A4
Ramsey *Essex* 202 D4
Ramsey *I.o.M.* 240 C2
Ramsey Forty Foot 212 B4
Ramsey Heights 212 A4
Ramsey Island *Essex* 188 C2
Ramsey Island *Pembs.* 190 A5
Ramsey Mereside 212 A4
Ramsey St. Mary's 212 A4
Ramsgate 175 F2
Ramsgate Street 228 B2
Ramsgill 252 A5
Ramsholt 203 E3
Ramshorn 222 B3
Ramsnest Common 171 E4
Ranachan 297 G3
Ranais (Ranish) 329 F5
Ranby *Lincs.* 238 C5
Ranby *Notts.* 237 D4
Rand 238 B5
Randwick 182 A2
Rangemore 222 C5
Rangeworthy 181 F4
Ranish (Ranais) 329 F5
Rankinston 274 C4
Rank's Green 187 G1
Ranmoor 236 A4
Rannoch Moor 129
Rannoch School 300 A4
Ranochan 298 A1
Ranscombe 164 C3
Ranskill 237 D4
Ranton 221 F5
Ranton Green 221 F5
Ranworth 229 E4
Rapness 340 D2
Rapps 153 G1
Rascarrel 258 A2
Rash 250 B4
Rashwood 196 B1
Raskelf 253 D5
Rassau 180 A1
Rastrick 244 A5
Ratagan 307 F3
Ratby 210 A2
Ratcliffe Culey 209 F3
Ratcliffe on Soar 223 F5
Ratcliffe on the Wreake 210 B1
Ratford Bridge 176 B1
Ratfyn 168 C3
Rathen 325 E3
Rathillet 294 B2
Rathliesbeag 299 E1
Rathmell 243 E1
Ratho 285 F2
Ratho Station 285 F2
Rathven 323 G3
Ratley 197 F3
Ratling 175 E3
Ratlinghope 206 D3
Ratsloe 152 C3
Rattar 337 E1
Ratten Row *Cumb.* 259 G2
Ratten Row *Lancs.* 242 A3
Rattery 150 D1
Rattlesden 202 A2
Rattray 301 G5
Raughton Head 259 G2
Raunds 211 E5
Ravenfield 236 B3
Ravenglass 248 B3
Ravenglass & Eskdale Railway 99
Raveningham 215 E2
Raven's Green 202 C5
Ravenscar 254 C2
Ravensdale 240 B2
Ravensden 199 F2
Ravenshaw 243 F3
Ravenshayes 152 C2
Ravenshead 223 G2
Ravensmoor 220 D2
Ravensthorpe *Northants.* 210 B5
Ravensthorpe *W.Yorks.* 244 B5
Ravenstone *Leics.* 209 G1
Ravenstone *M.K.* 199 D2
Ravenstonedale 250 C2
Ravenstruther 284 D5
Ravensworth 252 A2
Raw 254 C2
Rawcliffe *E.Riding* 245 F5
Rawcliffe *York* 245 E2
Rawcliffe Bridge 245 F5
Rawdon 244 B4
Rawmarsh 236 B3
Rawnsley 208 C1
Rawreth 187 G3
Rawridge 153 F2
Rawson Green 223 E3
Rawtenstall 243 E5
Rawyards 284 B3
Raxton 313 D1
Raydon 202 B4
Raylees 270 B2
Rayleigh 188 B3
Raymond's Hill 153 G3
Rayne 201 F5
Rayners Lane 186 A4
Raynes Park 172 B2
Reach 201 D1
Read 243 D4
Reading 184 C5
Reading Green 214 C4
Reading Street 174 B5
Reagill 250 B1
Rearquhar 332 C5
Rearsby 210 B1
Rease Heath 220 D2
Reaster 337 E2
Reaveley 279 E5
Reawick 342 C3
Reay 336 B2
Reculver 175 E2
Red Ball 153 D1
Red Bull 221 F2
Red Dial 259 F2
Red Hill *Hants.* 157 G1
Red Hill *Warks.* 196 D2
Red Lodge *Bristol* 34
Red Lodge *Suff.* 213 E5
Red Lumb 234 C1
Red Oaks Hill 201 D4
Red Point 318 D3
Red Post *Cornw.* 162 C5
Red Post *Devon* 151 E1
Red Rail 195 E5
Red Rock 233 G2
Red Roses 177 F1
Red Row 271 E2
Red Street 221 F2
Red Wharf Bay (Traeth Coch) 230 D4
Redberth 177 D2
Redbourn 186 A1
Redbourne 237 G3
Redbrook *Glos.* 181 E1
Redbrook *Wrex.* 220 C3
Redbrook Street 174 B5
Redburn *High.* 321 E3
Redburn *High.* 322 B5
Redburn *Northumb.* 261 D1
Redcar 263 F5
Redcastle *Angus* 303 E4
Redcastle *High.* 321 E5
Redcliff Bay 180 D5
Redcloak 303 G1
Reddingmuirhead 284 D2
Reddings, The 196 B5
Reddish 234 C3
Redditch 196 C1
Rede 201 G2
Redenhall 215 D3
Redesmouth 270 A3
Redford *Aber.* 303 F2
Redford *Angus* 303 D5
Redford *Dur.* 261 G4
Redford *W.Suss.* 171 D5
Redgrave 214 B4
Redheugh 302 C3
Redhill *Aber.* 312 B1
Redhill *Aber.* 312 C4
Redhill *Moray* 324 A5
Redhill *N.Som.* 166 B1
Redhill *Notts.* 223 G3
Redhill *Surr.* 172 B3
Redhill Aerodrome & Heliport 172 B4
Redhouse *Aber.* 312 A2
Redhouse *Arg. & B.* 281 G3
Redhouses 280 B3
Redisham 215 F3
Redland *Bristol* 181 E5
Redland *Ork.* 340 B4
Redlingfield 214 C4
Redlynch *Som.* 167 E4
Redlynch *Wilts.* 168 D5
Redmarley D'Abitot 195 G4
Redmarshall 262 C5
Redmile 224 C4
Redmire 251 F3
Redmoor 147 E3
Rednal 220 A5
Redpath 277 G2
Redruth 146 A5
Redscarhead 285 G5
Redshaw 275 G3
Redstone Bank 177 E1
Redwick *Newport* 180 D4
Redwick *S.Glos.* 181 E4
Redworth 262 B5
Reed 200 B4
Reed End 200 B4
Reedham 229 F5
Reedley 243 E4
Reedness 245 G5
Reef (Riof) 328 C4
Reepham *Lincs.* 238 A5
Reepham *Norf.* 228 B3
Reeth 251 F3
Regaby 240 C2
Regil 166 C1
Regoul 322 A4
Reiff 330 B3
Reigate 172 B3
Reighton 255 E5
Reinigeadal (Rhenigidale) 327 E3
Reisgill 337 E5
Reiss 337 F3
Rejerrah 146 B4
Releath 145 D3
Relubbus 144 C3
Relugas 322 B5
Remenham 184 C4
Remenham Hill 184 C4
Remony 300 C5
Rempstone 223 G5
Rendcomb 182 C1
Rendham 203 E1
Rendlesham 203 E2
Renfrew 283 G3
Renhold 199 F2
Renishaw 236 B5
Renishaw Hall & Gardens 74
Rennington 279 G5
Renton 283 E2
Renwick 260 B3
Repps 229 F4
Repton 223 E5
Rescobie 302 D4
Rescorla 147 E4
Resipole 297 G3
Resolis 321 F3
Resolven 179 E2
Resourie 298 A2
Respryn 147 F3
Reston 287 F3
Restormel 147 F3
Reswallie 302 D4
Reterth 146 D3
Retew 146 D4
Retford 237 E4
Rettendon 187 G3
Rettendon Place 187 G3
Retyn 146 C4
Revesby 226 A1
Revesby Bridge 226 B1
Rew 152 A5
Rew Street 157 D3
Rewe *Devon* 152 C3
Rewe *Devon* 152 B3
Reybridge 168 A1
Reydon 215 F4
Reydon Smear 215 G4
Reymerston 228 B5
Reynalton 177 D2
Reynoldston 178 A4
Rezare 149 D3
Rhadyr 180 C2
Rhandirmwyn 193 D3
Rhaoine 332 B4
Rhayader 193 F1
Rhedyn 216 B4
Rheged-the Village in the Hill 99
Rhegreanoch 330 C3
Rheindown 321 E5
Rhelonie 332 A5
Rhemore 297 E4
Rhenigidale (Reinigeadal) 327 E3
Rheola 179 E2
Rhes-y-cae 219 E1
Rhewl *Denb.* 219 E3
Rhewl *Denb.* 219 E1
Rhewl *Shrop.* 220 A4
Rhian 332 A3
Rhicarn 330 C2
Rhiconich 334 B3
Rhicullen 321 F2
Rhidorroch 331 D5
Rhifail 335 G4
Rhigos 179 F2
Rhilochan 332 C4
Rhinduie 321 E5
Rhireavach 330 C5
Rhiroy 320 A1
Rhiston 206 B3
Rhiw 216 B5
Rhiwargor 218 C5
Rhiwbina 180 A4
Rhiwbryfdir 217 F3
Rhiwderin 180 B4
Rhiwinder 179 G4
Rhiwlas *Gwyn.* 217 E1
Rhiwlas *Gwyn.* 218 C4
Rhiwlas *Powys* 219 F4
Rhode 165 F4
Rhodes Minnis 174 D4
Rhodesia 236 C5
Rhodiad-y-brenin 190 A5
Rhodmad 204 B5
Rhonadale 272 C2
Rhonehouse (Kelton Hill) 266 B5
Rhoose 165 D1
Rhos *Carmar.* 191 G4
Rhos *N.P.T.* 178 D2
Rhos Common 206 B1
Rhôs Lligwy 230 C4
Rhos, The 176 D1
Rhosaman 178 D1
Rhoscolyn 230 A5
Rhoscrowther 176 C2
Rhosesmor 219 F1
Rhos-fawr 216 C4
Rhosgadfan 217 E2
Rhos-goch *I.o.A.* 230 C4
Rhosgoch *Powys* 194 A3
Rhos-hill 191 E3
Rhoshirwaun 216 A5
Rhoslan 217 D3
Rhoslefain 204 B2
Rhosllanerchrugog 219 F3
Rhosmaen 192 C5
Rhosmeirch 230 C5
Rhosneigr 230 B5
Rhosnesni 220 A2
Rhôs-on-Sea 231 G4
Rhossili 178 A4
Rhosson 190 A5
Rhostrehwfa 230 C5
Rhostryfan 217 D2
Rhostyllen 220 A3

Place	Page	Grid
Shennanton	265	E4
Shenstone *Staffs.*	208	D2
Shenstone *Worcs.*	208	A5
Shenstone Woodend	208	D2
Shenton	209	F2
Shenval	311	E2
Shepeau Stow	212	B1
Shephall	200	A5
Shepherd's Bush	186	B5
Shepherd's Green	184	C4
Shepherd's Patch	181	G2
Shepherdswell (Sibertswold)	175	E4
Shepley	235	F2
Sheppardstown	337	E5
Shepperdine	181	F3
Shepperton	171	F1
Shepreth	200	B3
Shepreth Wildlife Park	83	
Shepshed	209	G1
Shepton Beauchamp	154	A1
Shepton Mallet	166	D3
Shepton Montague	167	D4
Shepway	173	G3
Sheraton	262	D4
Sherborne *Dorset*	154	C1
Sherborne *Glos.*	183	D1
Sherborne Castle	35	
Sherborne St. John	170	B2
Sherbourne	197	E1
Sherbourne Street	202	A3
Sherburn *Dur.*	262	C3
Sherburn *N.Yorks.*	254	C5
Sherburn Hill	262	C3
Sherburn in Elmet	245	D4
Shere	171	F3
Shereford	227	G5
Sherfield English	169	D5
Sherfield on Loddon	170	B2
Sherford *Devon*	151	D3
Sherford *Som.*	165	F5
Sheriff Hutton	245	F1
Sheriffhales	207	G1
Sheringham	228	C1
Sherington	199	D3
Shernal Green	196	B1
Shernborne	227	F4
Sherramore	309	E5
Sherrington	168	A4
Sherston	182	A4
Sherwood	223	G3
Sherwood Forest Country Park	75	
Sherwood Green	163	F3
Sherwood Pines Forest Park	75	
Shettleston	284	A3
Shevington	233	G2
Shevington Moor	233	G1
Sheviock	149	D5
Shibden Hall	90	
Shide	157	E4
Shiel Bridge	307	F3
Shieldaig *High.*	319	E4
Shieldaig *High.*	319	E2
Shieldhill	284	C2
Shielfoot	297	F2
Shielhill	302	C4
Shiels	312	B4
Shifford	183	F2
Shifnal	207	G2
Shilbottle	271	D1
Shildon	262	B5
Shillingford *Devon*	164	C5
Shillingford *Oxon.*	184	A3
Shillingford Abbot	152	C4
Shillingford St. George	152	C4
Shillingstone	155	E1
Shillington	199	G4
Shillmoor	270	A1
Shilstone	163	F5
Shilton *Oxon.*	183	E2
Shilton *Warks.*	209	G4
Shimpling *Norf.*	214	C3
Shimpling *Suff.*	201	G2
Shimpling Street	201	G2
Shincliffe	262	B3
Shiney Row	262	C2
Shinfield	170	C1
Shingay	200	B3
Shingham	213	F2
Shingle Street	203	E3
Shinness Lodge	332	A3
Shipbourne	173	E3
Shipbrookhill	234	A5
Shipdham	228	A5
Shipham	166	B2
Shiphay	151	E1
Shiplake	184	C5
Shiplake Row	184	C5
Shipley *Northumb.*	279	F5
Shipley *Shrop.*	208	A3
Shipley *W.Suss.*	171	G5
Shipley *W.Yorks.*	244	A4
Shipley Art Gallery	105	
Shipley Bridge *Devon*	150	C1
Shipley Bridge *Surr.*	172	C4
Shipley Common	223	F3
Shipley Country Park	75	
Shipmeadow	215	E2
Shippea Hill	213	E4
Shippon	183	G3
Shipston on Stour	197	E3
Shipton *Glos.*	182	C1
Shipton *N.Yorks.*	245	E2
Shipton *Shrop.*	207	E3
Shipton Bellinger	168	D3
Shipton Gorge	154	A3
Shipton Green	158	A3
Shipton Moyne	182	A4
Shipton Oliffe	182	C1
Shipton Solers	182	C1
Shipton-on-Cherwell	183	G1
Shiptonthorpe	246	A3
Shipton-under-Wychwood	183	E1
Shira	291	D3
Shirburn	184	B3
Shirdley Hill	233	E1
Shire Oak	208	C2
Shirebrook	223	G1
Shirecliffe	236	A3
Shiregreen	236	A3
Shirehampton	181	E5
Shiremoor	271	F4
Shirenewton	181	D3
Shireoaks	236	C4
Shirl Heath	194	D2
Shirland	223	E2
Shirley *Derbys.*	222	D3
Shirley *Gt.Lon.*	172	C2
Shirley *Hants.*	156	A3
Shirley *S'ham.*	156	D1
Shirley *W.Mid.*	208	D5
Shirley Heath	208	D5
Shirley Warren	156	C1
Shirleywich	221	G5
Shirrell Heath	157	E1
Shirwell	163	F2
Shirwell Cross	163	F2
Shiskine	273	E3
Shittlehope	261	G4
Shobdon	194	C1
Shobley	156	A2
Shobrooke	152	B2
Shocklach	220	B3
Shocklach Green	220	B3
Shoe, The	182	A5
Shoeburyness	188	C4
Sholden	175	F3
Sholing	157	D1
Shoot Hill	206	D1
Shooter's Hill	186	D5
Shop *Cornw.*	146	C2
Shop *Cornw.*	162	C4
Shop Corner	202	D4
Shopnoller	165	E4
Shore	234	D1
Shoreditch	186	C4
Shoreham	173	E2
Shoreham-by-Sea	159	E3
Shoremill	321	G3
Shoresdean	287	G5
Shoreswood	287	G5
Shoreton	321	F3
Shorley	169	G5
Shorncote	182	C3
Shorne	187	F5
Shorne Ridgeway	187	F5
Short Cross	206	B2
Short Green	214	B3
Short Heath *Derbys.*	209	F1
Short Heath *W.Mid.*	208	C3
Shortacombe	149	F2
Shortbridge	159	G1
Shortfield Common	170	D3
Shortgate	159	G2
Shortgrove	200	D4
Shorthampton	197	F5
Shortlands	172	C2
Shortlanesend	146	C5
Shorton	151	E1
Shorwell	157	D4
Shoscombe	167	E2
Shotatton	220	A5
Shotesham	214	D2
Shotgate	187	G3
Shotley *Northants.*	211	E3
Shotley *Suff.*	202	D4
Shotley Bridge	261	G2
Shotley Gate	202	D4
Shotleyfield	261	G2
Shottenden	174	C3
Shottermill	171	D4
Shottery	197	D2
Shotteswell	197	G3
Shottisham	203	E3
Shottle	223	E3
Shottlegate	223	E3
Shotton *Dur.*	262	D4
Shotton *Dur.*	262	C5
Shotton *Flints.*	220	A1
Shotton *Northumb.*	271	E4
Shotton Colliery	262	C3
Shotts	284	C3
Shotwick	233	E5
Shouldham	213	E2
Shouldham Thorpe	213	E2
Shoulton	196	A2
Shover's Green	173	F5
Shrawardine	206	C1
Shrawley	196	A1
Shreding Green	185	F4
Shrewley	197	E1
Shrewsbury	207	D1
Shrewton	168	B3
Shrine of Our Lady of Walsingham	83	
Shripney	158	B3
Shrivenham	183	E4
Shropham	214	A2
Shroton (Iwerne Courtney)	155	E1
Shrub End	202	A5
Shucknall	195	E3
Shudy Camps	201	E3
Shugborough Estate	67	
Shurdington	182	B1
Shurlock Row	184	D5
Shurnock	196	C1
Shurrery	336	C3
Shurrery Lodge	336	C3
Shurton	165	F3
Shustoke	209	E3
Shut Heath	221	F5
Shute *Devon*	153	F3
Shute *Devon*	152	B2
Shutford	197	F3
Shuthonger	196	A4
Shutlanger	198	C3
Shutt Green	208	A2
Shuttington	209	E2
Shuttlewood	236	B5
Shuttleworth	234	B1
Siabost (Shawbost)	329	D3
Siabost Bho Dheas	329	D3
Siabost Bho Thuath	329	D3
Siadar Iarach	329	E2
Siadar Uarach	329	E2
Sibbaldbie	267	F2
Sibbertoft	210	B4
Sibdon Carwood	206	D4
Sibertswold (Shepherdswell)	175	E4
Sibford Ferris	197	F4
Sibford Gower	197	F4
Sible Hedingham	201	F4
Sibley's Green	201	E5
Sibsey	226	B2
Sibson *Cambs.*	211	F3
Sibson *Leics.*	209	F2
Sibster	337	F3
Sibthorpe	224	C3
Sibton	203	E1
Sibton Green	215	E4
Sicklesmere	201	G1
Sicklinghall	244	C3
Sidbury *Devon*	153	E3
Sidbury *Shrop.*	207	F4
Sidcot	166	B2
Sidcup	187	D5
Siddal	244	A5
Siddington *Ches.*	234	C5
Siddington *Glos.*	182	C3
Sidemoor	208	B5
Sidestrand	229	D2
Sidford	153	E3
Sidlesham	158	A4
Sidley	160	C3
Sidlow	172	B4
Sidmouth	153	E4
Sigford	152	A5
Sigglesthorne	247	D3
Sigingstone	179	F5
Signet	183	E1
Silbury Hill	36	
Silchester	170	B1
Sildinis	327	E2
Sileby	210	B1
Silecroft	248	C4
Silfield	214	C2
Silian	192	B2
Silk Museum & Paradise Mill	99	
Silk Willoughby	225	F3
Silkstead	169	F5
Silkstone	235	G2
Silkstone Common	235	G2
Sill Field	249	G4
Silloth	259	E1
Sills	270	A1
Sillyearn	324	A4
Silpho	254	C3
Silsden	243	G3
Silsoe	199	F4
Silver End *Beds.*	199	G3
Silver End *Essex*	201	G5
Silver Green	215	D2
Silver Street *Kent*	174	A2
Silver Street *Som.*	166	C4
Silverburn	285	G3
Silvercraigs	281	G1
Silverdale *Lancs.*	249	F5
Silverdale *Staffs.*	221	F3
Silvergate	228	C3
Silverhill	160	C2
Silverlace Green	203	E2
Silverley's Green	215	D4
Silvermoss	312	D1
Silverstone	198	B3
Silverton	152	C2
Silvington	207	F5
Silwick	342	B3
Simister	234	C2
Simmondley	235	E3
Simonburn	270	A4
Simonsbath	164	A4
Simonside	262	C1
Simonstone *Bridgend*	179	F4
Simonstone *Lancs.*	243	D4
Simprim	287	F5
Simpson	199	D4
Sinclair's Hill	287	F4
Sinclairston	274	C4
Sinderby	252	C4
Sinderhope	261	E2
Sindlesham	170	C1
Sinfin	223	E4
Singdean	277	G5
Singleton *Lancs.*	241	G4
Singleton *W.Suss.*	158	A2
Singlewell (Ifield)	187	F5
Singret	220	A2
Sinkhurst Green	174	A4
Sinnahard	311	G3
Sinnington	253	G4
Sinton Green	196	A1
Siop y Fron (Upper Llandwrog)	217	E2
Sipson	185	F5
Sir Alfred Munnings Art Museum (see Castle House)	78	
Sir Harold Hillier Gardens & Arboretum	51	
Sirhowy	180	A1
Sisland	215	E2
Sissinghurst	173	G5
Sissinghurst Castle	51	
Siston	181	F5
Sithney	144	D4
Sittingbourne	174	B2
Siulaisiadar	329	G4
Six Ashes	207	G4
Six Hills	224	B5
Six Mile Bottom	201	D2
Six Roads End	222	C5
Sixhills	238	B4
Sixmile	174	D4
Sixpenny Handley	155	G1
Sizergh Castle & Gardens	99	
Sizewell	203	F1
Skail	335	G4
Skaill *Ork.*	340	A5
Skaill *Ork.*	339	E2
Skaill *Ork.*	340	C3
Skara Brae	130	
Skares *Aber.*	312	B1
Skares *E.Ayr.*	274	D4
Skarpigarth	342	A2
Skateraw	287	E2
Skaw	343	E1
Skeabost	318	A5
Skeabrae	340	A4
Skeeby	252	B2
Skeffington	210	C2
Skeffling	239	D1
Skegby	223	G1
Skegness	227	D1
Skelberry *Shet.*	343	G4
Skelberry *Shet.*	343	D1
Skelbo	332	C5
Skelbo Street	332	C5
Skelbrooke	236	C1
Skeld (Easter Skeld)	342	C3
Skeldon	274	B4
Skeldyke	226	B4
Skellingthorpe	237	G5
Skellister	343	D2
Skellow	236	C1
Skelmanthorpe	235	G1
Skelmersdale	233	F2
Skelmonae	313	D1
Skelmorlie	282	C3
Skelmuir	325	E5
Skelpick	335	G3
Skelton *Cumb.*	260	A4
Skelton *E.Riding*	245	G5
Skelton *N.Yorks.*	251	F2
Skelton *R. & C.*	253	F1
Skelton *York*	245	E2
Skelton-on-Ure	244	C1
Skelwick	340	C2
Skelwith Bridge	249	E2
Skendleby	226	C1
Skendleby Psalter	239	E5
Skenfrith	195	D5
Skerne	246	C2
Skeroblingarry	272	C3
Skerray	335	F2
Skerton	242	A1
Sketchley	209	G3
Sketty	178	C3
Skewen	178	D3
Skewsby	253	F5
Skeyton	228	D3
Skeyton Corner	229	D3
Skidbrooke	239	E3
Skidbrooke North End	239	E3
Skidby	246	C4
Skilgate	164	C5
Skillington	225	D5
Skinburness	259	E1
Skinflats	284	D1
Skinidin	317	F5
Skinnet	336	D2
Skinningrove	253	G1
Skipness	281	G4
Skippool	241	G3
Skipsea	247	D2
Skipsea Brough	247	D2
Skipton	243	F2
Skipton Castle	90	
Skipton-on-Swale	252	C5
Skipwith	245	F4
Skirbeck	226	B3
Skirbeck Quarter	226	B3
Skirethorns	243	F1
Skirlaugh	246	D4
Skirling	276	B2
Skirmett	184	C4
Skirpenbeck	245	G2
Skirwith *Cumb.*	260	C4
Skirwith *N.Yorks.*	250	C5
Skirza	337	F2
Skittle Green	184	C2
Skomer Island	176	A2
Skulamus	306	C2
Skullomie	335	F2
Skyborry Green	206	B5
Skye	306	A1
Skye Green	201	G5
Skye of Curr	310	B2
Skyreholme	243	G1
Slack *Aber.*	312	A1
Slack *Derbys.*	223	E1
Slack *W.Yorks.*	243	F5
Slackhall	235	E4
Slackhead	323	G3
Slad	182	A2
Slade *Devon*	163	F1
Slade *Devon*	153	E2
Slade *Pembs.*	176	C1
Slade *Swan.*	178	A4
Slade Green	187	E5
Slade Hooton	236	C4
Slade, The	184	A5
Sladesbridge	147	E2
Slaggyford	260	C2
Slaidburn	242	D2
Slains Park	303	G2
Slaithwaite	235	E1
Slaley	261	F2
Slamannan	284	C2
Slapton *Bucks.*	199	E5
Slapton *Devon*	151	E3
Slapton *Northants.*	198	B3
Slate Haugh	323	G3
Slatepit Dale	223	E1
Slattadale	319	E2
Slaugham	159	E1
Slaughden	203	F2
Slaughterford	182	A5
Slawston	210	C3
Sleaford *Hants.*	170	D4
Sleaford *Lincs.*	225	F3
Sleagill	249	G1
Sleap	220	B5
Sledge Green	196	A4
Sledmere	246	B1
Sleights	254	B2
Slepe	155	F3
Slerra	162	D3
Slickly	337	E2
Sliddery	273	E3
Sliemore	310	C2
Sligachan	306	A2
Slimbridge	181	G2
Slimbridge Wildfowl & Wetlands Trust	36	
Slindon *Staffs.*	221	F4
Slindon *W.Suss.*	158	B3
Slinfold	171	G4
Sling	181	E2
Slingsby	253	F5
Slioch	312	A1
Slip End *Beds.*	185	F1
Slip End *Herts.*	200	A4
Slipton	211	E5
Slitting Mill	208	C1
Slochd	310	A2
Slockavullin	290	A5
Slogarie	266	A4
Sloley	229	D3
Slongaber	266	C3
Sloothby	239	E5
Slough	185	E4
Slough Green *Som.*	165	F5
Slough Green *W.Suss.*	159	E1
Sluggan	310	A2
Slyne	242	A1
Smailholm	278	A3
Small Dole	159	E2
Small Hythe	174	A5
Smallbridge	234	D1
Smallbrook	152	B3
Smallburgh	229	E3
Smallburn *Aber.*	325	F5
Smallburn *E.Ayr.*	275	E3
Smalldale	235	E5
Smalley	223	F3
Smallfield	172	C4
Smallford	186	A2
Smallhythe Place	51	
Smallridge	153	F2
Smallthorne	221	F2
Smallworth	214	B3
Smannell	169	E3
Smardale	250	C2
Smarden	174	A4
Smaull	280	A3
Smeatharpe	153	E1
Smeeth	174	C5
Smeeton Westerby	210	B3
Smerclet	314	C2
Smerral	337	D5
Smestow	208	A3
Smethwick	208	C4
Smethwick Green	221	F1
Smirisary	297	F2
Smisby	209	F1
Smith Art Gallery & Museum	130	
Smith End Green	195	G2
Smithfield	260	A1
Smithies	236	A2
Smithies, The	207	F3
Smithincott	153	D1
Smith's End	200	B4
Smith's Green *Essex*	201	D5
Smith's Green *Essex*	201	E3
Smithstown	319	D2
Smithton	321	G5
Smithy Green	234	B5
Smockington	209	G4
Smoo Cave	130	
Smyrton	264	C2
Smythe's Green	188	C1
Snailbeach	206	C2
Snailwell	201	E1
Snainton	254	C4
Snaith	245	F5
Snape *N.Yorks.*	252	B4
Snape *Suff.*	203	E2
Snape Green	233	E1
Snape Watering	203	E2
Snarestone	209	F2
Snarford	238	A4
Snargate	161	E1
Snave	161	F1
Sneachill	196	B2
Snead	206	C3
Snead's Green	196	A1
Sneath Common	214	C3
Sneaton	254	B2
Sneatonthorpe	254	C2
Snelland	238	A4
Snellings	248	A2
Snelston	222	C3
Snetterton	214	A2
Snettisham	227	E4
Snibston Discovery Park	75	
Snipeshill	174	B2
Snishival	304	A1
Snitter	270	C1
Snitterby	237	G3
Snitterfield	197	E2
Snitterton	223	D1
Snittlegarth	259	F3
Snitton	207	E5
Snodhill	194	C3
Snodland	173	G2
Snow End	200	C4
Snow Street	214	B3
Snowden Hill	235	G2
Snowdon Mountain Railway	114	
Snowdonia National Park	114	
Snowshill	196	C4
Snowshill Manor	36	
Soar *Cardiff*	179	G4
Soar *Carmar.*	192	C5
Soar *Devon*	150	D4
Soay	306	A3
Soberton	157	F1
Soberton Heath	157	F1
Sockbridge	260	B5
Sockburn	252	C2
Sodom	232	B5
Sodylt Bank	220	A4
Softley	261	G5
Soham	213	D5
Soham Cotes	213	D5
Solas (Sollas)	315	G2
Soldon	162	D4
Soldon Cross	162	D4
Soldridge	170	B4
Sole Street *Kent*	174	C4
Sole Street *Kent*	173	F2
Soleburn	264	B4
Solihull	209	D5
Solihull Lodge	208	C5
Sollas (Solas)	315	G2
Sollers Dilwyn	194	D2
Sollers Hope	195	F4
Sollom	233	F1
Solomon's Tump	181	G1
Solsgirth	293	E5
Solva	190	A5
Solwaybank	268	B4
Somerby *Leics.*	210	C1
Somerby *Lincs.*	238	A2
Somercotes	223	F2
Somerford	208	B2
Somerford Keynes	182	C3
Somerley	158	A4
Somerleyton	215	F2
Somerleyton Hall & Gardens	83	
Somersal Herbert	222	C4
Somersby	238	D5
Somerset House	60	
Somersham *Cambs.*	212	B5
Somersham *Suff.*	202	B3
Somerton *Newport*	180	C4
Somerton *Oxon.*	197	G5
Somerton *Som.*	166	B5
Somerton *Suff.*	201	G2
Sompting	159	D3
Sompting Abbotts	159	D3
Sonning	184	C5
Sonning Common	184	C4
Sonning Eye	184	C5
Sontley	220	A3
Sookholme	223	G1
Sopley	156	A3
Sopworth	182	A4
Sorbie	257	E2
Sordale	336	D2
Sorisdale	296	B3
Sorn	275	D3
Sornhill	274	D2
Soroba	290	A2
Sortat	337	E2
Sotby	238	C5
Sots Hole	225	G1
Sotterley	215	F3
Soudley	221	E5
Soughton	219	F1
Soulbury	199	D5
Soulby	250	C1
Souldern	198	A4
Souldrop	199	E1
Sound *Ches.*	220	D3
Sound *Shet.*	343	D3
Sound *Shet.*	342	C2
Sourhope	278	C4
Sourin	340	C3
Sourton	149	F1
Souter Johnnie's Cottage	130	
Soutergate	248	D4
South Acre	213	G1
South Acton	186	A5
South Alkham	175	E4
South Allington	151	D4
South Alloa	293	D5
South Ambersham	171	E5
South Anston	236	C4
South Ascot	171	E1
South Baddesley	156	C3
South Ballachulish	298	C4
South Balloch	265	E1
South Bank	263	E5
South Barrow	166	D5
South Bellsdyke	284	D1
South Benfleet	187	G4
South Bersted	158	B3
South Blackbog	312	C1
South Bockhampton	156	A3
South Bowood	154	A3
South Brent	150	C1
South Brentor	149	E2
South Brewham	167	E4
South Broomhill	271	E2
South Burlingham	229	E5
South Cadbury	166	D5
South Cairn	264	A4
South Carlton	237	G5
South Cave	246	B4
South Cerney	182	C3
South Chard	153	G2
South Charlton	279	F4
South Cheriton	167	D5
South Church	262	B5
South Cliffe	246	A4
South Clifton	237	F5
South Cockerington	239	D4
South Collafirth	344	C4
South Common	159	F2
South Cornelly	179	E4
South Corriegills	273	F2
South Cove	215	F3
South Creagan	298	B5
South Creake	227	G4
South Crosland	235	F1
South Croxton	210	B1
South Dalton	246	B3
South Darenth	187	E5
South Dell (Dail Bho Dheas)	329	F1
South Devon Railway	36	
South Duffield	245	F4
South Elkington	238	C4
South Elmsall	236	B1
South End *Bucks.*	199	D5
South End *Cumb.*	241	F1
South End *Hants.*	156	A1
South End *N.Lincs.*	246	D5
South Erradale	318	D2
South Fambridge	188	B3
South Fawley	183	F4
South Ferriby	246	B5
South Field	246	C5
South Flobbets	312	C1
South Garth	345	E3
South Godstone	172	C4
South Gorley	156	A1
South Green *Essex*	187	F3
South Green *Essex*	188	D1
South Green *Norf.*	228	B4
South Green *Suff.*	214	C4
South Gyle	285	F2
South Hall	282	B2
South Hanningfield	187	G3
South Harefield	185	F4
South Harting	157	G1
South Hayling	157	G3
South Hazelrigg	279	E3
South Heath	185	E2
South Heighton	159	G3
South Hetton	262	C3
South Hiendley	236	A1
South Hill	148	D3
South Hinksey	184	A2
South Hole	162	C4
South Holme	253	F5
South Holmwood	171	G3
South Hornchurch	187	E4
South Hourat	283	D4
South Huish	150	C3
South Hykeham	225	E1
South Hylton	262	C2
South Kelsey	238	A3
South Kessock	321	F5
South Killingholme	238	B1
South Kilvington	252	D4
South Kilworth	210	B4
South Kirkby	236	B1
South Kirkton	312	C4
South Knighton	152	B5
South Kyme	225	G3
South Lakes Wild Animal Park	99	
South Lancing	159	D3
South Ledaig	290	B1
South Leigh	183	F2
South Leverton	237	E4
South Littleton	196	C3
South Lopham	214	B3
South Luffenham	211	E2
South Malling	159	G2
South Marston	183	D4
South Middleton	279	D4
South Milford	245	D4
South Milton	150	C3
South Mimms	186	B2
South Molton	164	A5
South Moor	262	A2
South Moreton	184	A4
South Mundham	158	A3
South Muskham	224	C2
South Newbald	246	B4
South Newington	197	G4
South Newton	168	B4
South Normanton	223	F2
South Norwood	172	C2
South Nutfield	172	C4
South Ockendon	187	E4
South Ormsby	239	D5
South Ossett	235	G1
South Otterington	252	C4
South Owersby	238	A3
South Oxhey	186	A3
South Park	172	B4
South Parks	294	A4
South Perrott	154	A2
South Petherton	154	A1
South Petherwin	148	D2
South Pickenham	213	G2
South Pool	151	D3
South Queensferry (Queensferry)	285	F2
South Radworthy	164	A4
South Rauceby	225	F3
South Raynham	227	G5
South Redbriggs	324	C5
South Reston	239	E4
South Ronaldsay	339	D4
South Ruislip	186	A4
South Runcton	213	E2
South Scarle	224	D1
South Shian	298	B5
South Shields	262	C1
South Shields Museum & Art Gallery	105	
South Somercotes	239	E3
South Somercotes Fen Houses	239	E3
South Stack Cliffs	114	
South Stainley	244	C1
South Stoke *Oxon.*	184	B4
South Stoke *W.Suss.*	158	C3
South Street *E.Suss.*	159	F2
South Street *Gt.Lon.*	172	D3
South Street *Kent*	173	F2
South Street *Kent*	174	D2
South Street *Kent*	174	A2
South Tawton	149	G1
South Thoresby	239	E5
South Tidworth	168	D3
South Tottenham	186	C4
South Town *Devon*	152	C4
South Town *Hants.*	170	B4
South Tynedale Railway	99	

451

Wyck 170 C4
Wyck Rissington 197 D5
Wycliffe 252 A1
Wycoller 243 F4
Wycomb 224 C5
Wycombe Marsh 185 D3
Wyddial 200 B4
Wye 174 C4
Wyesham 181 E1
Wyfordby 210 C1
Wyke *Devon* 152 B3
Wyke *Dorset* 167 E5
Wyke *Shrop.* 207 F2
Wyke *Surr.* 171 E2
Wyke *W.Yorks.* 244 A5
Wyke Champflower 167 D4
Wyke Regis 154 C5
Wyke, The 207 G2
Wykeham *N.Yorks.* 254 C4
Wykeham *N.Yorks.* 254 B5
Wyken *Shrop.* 207 G3
Wyken *W.Mid.* 209 F4
Wykey 220 A5
Wylam 262 A1
Wylde Green 208 D3
Wyllie 180 A3
Wylye 168 B4
Wymering 157 F2
Wymeswold 224 B5
Wymington 199 E1

Wymondham *Leics.* 211 D1
Wymondham *Norf.* 228 C5
Wyndham 179 F3
Wynford Eagle 154 B3
Wynnstay Park 220 A3
Wynyard 262 D5
Wyre Forest 68
Wyre Piddle 196 B3
Wyresdale Tower 242 C2
Wysall 224 B5
Wyson 195 E1
Wythall 208 C5
Wytham 183 G2
Wythburn 259 G5
Wythenshawe 234 C4
Wyton *Cambs.* 212 A5
Wyton *E.Riding* 247 D4
Wyverstone 202 B1
Wyverstone Street 202 B1
Wyville 225 D5
Wyvis Lodge 321 D2

Y

Y Bryn 218 B5
Y Drenewydd (Newtown) 206 A3
Y Fan 205 F4
Y Felinheli 217 E1
Y Fenni (Abergavenny) 180 B1
Y Fflint (Flint) 232 D5

Y Ffôr 216 C4
Y Trallwng (Welshpool) 206 B2
Y Tymbl (Tumble) 178 B1
Y Waun (Chirk) 219 F4
Yaddlethorpe 237 F2
Yafford 156 D4
Yafforth 252 C3
Yalberton 151 E2
Yalding 173 F4
Yanley 166 C1
Yanwath 260 B5
Yanworth 182 C1
Yapham 245 G2
Yapton 158 B3
Yarburgh 238 D3
Yarcombe 153 F2
Yardley 208 D4
Yardley Gobion 198 C3
Yardley Hastings 199 D2
Yardro 194 B2
Yarford 165 F5
Yarkhill 195 F3
Yarlet 221 G5
Yarley 166 C3
Yarlington 167 D5
Yarm 252 D1
Yarmouth 156 C4
Yarmouth Castle 53
Yarnacott 163 G2
Yarnbrook 167 F2
Yarnfield 221 F4
Yarnscombe 163 F3
Yarnton 183 G1

Yarpole 195 D1
Yarrow *Sc.Bord.* 277 E3
Yarrow *Som.* 166 A3
Yarrow Feus 277 E3
Yarrowford 277 F3
Yarsop 194 D3
Yarwell 211 F3
Yate 181 G4
Yatehouse Green 221 E1
Yateley 170 D1
Yatesbury 182 C5
Yattendon 184 A5
Yatton *Here.* 194 D1
Yatton *N.Som.* 166 B1
Yatton Keynell 182 A5
Yaverland 157 F4
Yawl 153 G3
Yaxham 228 B4
Yaxley *Cambs.* 211 G3
Yaxley *Suff.* 214 C4
Yazor 194 D3
Ye Olde Pork Pie Shoppe 75
Yeabridge 154 A1
Yeading 186 A4
Yeadon 244 B3
Yealand Conyers 249 G5
Yealand Redmayne 249 G5
Yealand Storrs 249 G5
Yealmbridge 150 B2
Yealmpton 150 B2
Yearby 263 F5
Yearsley 253 E5
Yeaton 206 D1

Yeaveley 222 C3
Yeavering 278 D3
Yeavering Bell 105
Yedingham 254 B5
Yelford 183 F2
Yell 345 D4
Yelland *Devon* 163 E2
Yelland *Devon* 149 F1
Yelling 200 A1
Yelvertoft 210 A5
Yelverton *Devon* 150 B1
Yelverton *Norf.* 229 D5
Yenston 167 E5
Yeo Mill 164 B5
Yeo Vale 163 E3
Yeoford 152 A3
Yeolmbridge 148 D2
Yeomadon 162 D5
Yeovil 154 B1
Yeovil Marsh 154 B1
Yeovilton 166 C5
Yerbeston 177 D2
Yesnaby 340 A5
Yetholm Mains 278 C4
Yetlington 279 E5
Yetminster 154 B1
Yettington 153 D4
Yetts o'Muckhart 293 F4
Yew Green 197 E1
Yielden 199 F1
Yieldshields 284 C4
Ynys 217 E4
Ynys Enlli (Bardsey Island) 216 A5

Ynys Môn (Anglesey) 230 B4
Ynysboeth 179 G3
Ynysddu 180 A3
Ynyshir 179 G3
Ynyslas 204 C3
Ynysmaerdy 179 G4
Ynysmeudwy 178 D2
Ynystawe 178 C2
Ynyswen 179 F3
Ynysybwl 179 G3
Yockenthwaite 251 E5
Yockleton 206 C1
Yokefleet 246 A5
Yoker 283 G3
Yonder Bognie 324 B5
York 91
York Castle Museum 91
York Dungeon 91
York Minster 91
Yorkletts 174 C2
Yorkley 181 F2
Yorkshire Dales 91
Yorkshire Museum 91
Yorkshire Sculpture Park 91
Yorton 220 C5
Yorton Heath 220 C5
Youldon 162 D5
Youldonmoor Cross 162 D5
Youlgreave 222 D1
Youlthorpe 245 G2
Youlton 245 D1

Young's End 187 G1
Yoxall 208 D1
Yoxford 203 E1
Yr Wyddgrug (Mold) 219 F1
Ysbyty Cynfyn 205 D5
Ysbyty Ifan 218 B3
Ysbyty Ystwyth 204 D5
Ysceifiog 232 C5
Ysgubor-y-coed 204 C3
Ystalyfera 179 D2
Ystrad 179 F3
Ystrad Aeron 192 B2
Ystrad Meurig 192 D1
Ystrad Mynach 180 A3
Ystradfellte 179 F1
Ystradffin 193 D3
Ystradgynlais 179 D1
Ystradowen *N.P.T.* 178 D1
Ystradowen *V. of Glam.* 179 G5
Ystumtuen 204 D5
Ythanwells 312 B1
Ythsie 313 D1

Z

Zeal Monachorum 152 A2
Zeals 167 E4
Zelah 146 C4
Zennor 144 B3
Zouch 223 G5

Published by Collins
An imprint of HarperCollins*Publishers*
77-85 Fulham Palace Road, Hammersmith, London W6 8JB

www.collins.co.uk

Printed and bound in Slovenia

SG12037 BDB

e-mail: roadcheck@harpercollins.co.uk

CREDITS

Contributors

Published by Mike Cottingham. Pages 5 to 22 researched and written by Karen Lloyd. Consultant geologist Duncan Friend Ph.D. Regional introductions written by Ellen Webster and Mike Cottingham. Attraction descriptions written by Amanda Berry, Andy Slater, Ellen Webster, Gill Coombs, Karen Lloyd, Rebekah Hart, Richard Knight and Rosemary MacLeod. All regional descriptions were edited by Juliet Lawler and Graham Gill. Infosnips compiled by Graham Gill and Mike Cottingham.